PUBLIC PAPERS OF THE PRESIDENTS
OF THE
UNITED STATES

PUBLIC PAPERS OF THE PRESIDENTS
OF THE
UNITED STATES

William J. Clinton

1994

(IN TWO BOOKS)

BOOK II—AUGUST 1 TO DECEMBER 31, 1994

UNITED STATES GOVERNMENT PRINTING OFFICE
WASHINGTON : 1995

Published by the
Office of the Federal Register
National Archives and Records Administration

Contents

OCT – 1997

Foreword

During the second half of 1994, America continued to move forward to help strengthen the American Dream of prosperity here at home and help spread peace and democracy around the world.

The American people saw the rewards that grew out of our efforts in the first 18 months of my Administration. Economic growth increased in strength, and the number of new jobs created during my Administration rose to 4.7 million. After 6 years of delay, the American people had a Crime Bill, which will put 100,000 police officers on our streets and take 19 deadly assault weapons off the street. We saw our National Service initiative become a reality as I swore in the first 20,000 AmeriCorps members, giving them the opportunity to serve their country and to earn money for their education. I signed the Community Development Banking and Financial Institutions Act of 1994, which will make capital available to Americans who have been denied access to basic banking services for far too long.

As we gave our citizens the means to make America stronger at home, we also continued our efforts to assert American leadership in the world. The Congress passed and I signed the implementing legislation for the Uruguay Round Agreement of the GATT, the most comprehensive international trade agreement in history. It helped to put in place expanded export oppportunities for American products that will create more jobs and produce higher incomes for our people for years to come. I travelled to Indonesia for a meeting of the Asian Pacific Economic Cooperation forum in order to expand free trade with the world's most dynamic economies. In December, at the Summit of the Americas in Miami, the leaders of the 34 democratically elected countries in this hemisphere agreed to negotiate on a free trade area for the Americas by 2005, to work together to preserve our natural resources, and to advance democracy and social justice, holding out promise of greater prosperity throughout the hemisphere.

The United States also continued to help bring an end to ancient disputes around the world. We actively supported the efforts of the people of Northern Ireland to work toward a peaceful resolution after many years of conflict. Building on our work to bring peace to the Middle East, I had the great privilege to witness the signing of an historic peace treaty between Israel and Jordan. And closer to home, in our own hemisphere, America took active steps to promote democracy. Our Armed Forces again proved their strength, flexibility, and devotion to freedom as they helped give a second chance to the long-suffering people of Haiti, and renewed hope to freedom-loving people throughout the world.

WITHDRAWN

Preface

This book contains the papers and speeches of the 42d President of the United States that were issued by the Office of the Press Secretary during the period August 1–December 31, 1994. The material has been compiled and published by the Office of the Federal Register, National Archives and Records Administration.

The material is presented in chronological order, and the dates shown in the headings are the dates of the documents or events. In instances when the release date differs from the date of the document itself, that fact is shown in the textnote. Every effort has been made to ensure accuracy: Remarks are checked against a tape recording, and signed documents are checked against the original. Textnotes and cross references have been provided by the editors for purposes of identification or clarity. Speeches were delivered in Washington, DC, unless indicated. The times noted are local times. All materials that are printed full-text in the book have been indexed in the subject and name indexes, and listed in the document categories list.

The Public Papers of the Presidents series was begun in 1957 in response to a recommendation of the National Historical Publications Commission. An extensive compilation of messages and papers of the Presidents covering the period 1789 to 1897 was assembled by James D. Richardson and published under congressional authority between 1896 and 1899. Since then, various private compilations have been issued, but there was no uniform publication comparable to the Congressional Record or the United States Supreme Court Reports. Many Presidential papers could be found only in the form of mimeographed White House releases or as reported in the press. The Commission therefore recommended the establishment of an official series in which Presidential writings, addresses, and remarks of a public nature could be made available.

The Commission's recommendation was incorporated in regulations of the Administrative Committee of the Federal Register, issued under section 6 of the Federal Register Act (44 U.S.C. 1506), which may be found in title 1, part 10, of the Code of Federal Regulations.

A companion publication to the Public Papers series, the Weekly Compilation of Presidential Documents, was begun in 1965 to provide a broader range of Presidential materials on a more timely basis to meet the needs of the contemporary reader. Beginning with the administration of Jimmy Carter, the Public Papers series expanded its coverage to include additional material as printed in the Weekly Compilation. That coverage provides a listing of the President's daily schedule and meetings, when announced, and other items of general interest issued by the Office of the Press Secretary. Also included are lists of the President's nominations submitted to the Senate, materials released by the Office of the Press Secretary that are not printed full-text in the book, and proclamations, Executive orders, and other Presidential documents released by the Office of the Press Secretary and published in the *Federal Register*. This information appears in the appendixes at the end of the book.

Volumes covering the administrations of Presidents Hoover, Truman, Eisenhower, Kennedy, Johnson, Nixon, Ford, Carter, Reagan, and Bush are also available.

The Public Papers of the Presidents publication program is under the direction of Frances D. McDonald, Director of the Presidential Documents and Legislative Division. The series is produced by the Presidential Documents Unit, Gwen H. Estep, Chief. The Chief Editor of this book was Karen Howard Ashlin, assisted by Kent Giles, Margaret A. Hemmig, Carolyn W. Hill, Rachel Rondell, Cheryl E. Sirofchuck, and Michael J. Sullivan.

The frontispiece and photographs used in the portfolio were supplied by the White House Photo Office. The typography and design of the book were developed by the Government Printing Office under the direction of Michael F. DiMario, Public Printer.

Richard L. Claypoole
Director of the Federal Register

John W. Carlin
Archivist of the United States

Cabinet

Secretary of State .... Warren M. Christopher

Secretary of the Treasury .... Lloyd Bentsen
Frank N. Newman
(acting, effective December 22)

Secretary of Defense .... William J. Perry

Attorney General .... Janet Reno

Secretary of the Interior .... Bruce Babbitt

Secretary of Agriculture .... Mike Espy

Secretary of Commerce .... Ronald H. Brown

Secretary of Labor .... Robert B. Reich

Secretary of Health and Human Services .... Donna E. Shalala

Secretary of Housing and Urban
Development .... Henry G. Cisneros

Secretary of Transportation .... Federico Peña

Secretary of Energy .... Hazel Rollins O'Leary

Secretary of Education .... Richard W. Riley

Secretary of Veterans Affairs .... Jesse Brown

United States Representative to the
United Nations .... Madeleine Korbel Albright

Administrator of the Environmental
Protection Agency .... Carol M. Browner

United States Trade Representative .... Michael Kantor

Director of the Office of Management
and Budget .... Alice M. Rivlin

Chief of Staff .... Leon E. Panetta

Counselor to the President .... Thomas F. McLarty III

Chair of the Council of Economic
Advisers .... Laura D'Andrea Tyson

Director of National Drug
Control Policy .... Lee Patrick Brown

Administrator of the Small Business
Administration .... Philip Lader

Administration of William J. Clinton

1994

Remarks at a Health Care Rally in Jersey City, New Jersey
August 1, 1994

Thank you. Mr. McEntee, Mr. Sombrotto, Mr. Rivera, Congressman Torricelli, Congressman Klein, Congressman Menendez, to all those who entertained us and all those who have come here, even those who have come here who disagree with us—I have a few questions I want to ask them in a minute.

You know, I hear a lot of talk today about what constitutes real patriotism, what constitutes being a real American, characterizations of what we're trying to do with health care. I think Carolyn is a real American, and what is their answer to her? Just before I came over here I met the Agneses. He's a barber. He told me how much his health care had gone up and that his business might go down. What is the chanters' answer to him? Just before I came over here I met a woman named Jean McCabe, whose health insurance premiums got almost up to $10,000. And she wrote us a letter and said, "Am I going to have to move to Canada or Germany or someplace where I can find somebody who will treat me like a decent citizen?" What is their answer to her? I met Michael and Joanne Britt. He's a truck driver; she's been sick. Their insurance cost them so much, they were living in a house trailer, and they thought they would never be able to buy a home, never set aside any money for retirement because they couldn't afford their health care, in this, a country that's supposed to be a middle class country that rewards work and family and faith and playing by the rules. What is their answer to her?

I ran for President, my fellow Americans, for some pretty basic reasons. I thought this country was going in the wrong direction. I thought we were in danger of losing the American dream as we went to the 21st century. And I thought we could do something about it. And all the yellers and shouters in the world will not change the basic facts. When I became President, the deficit was going up; now it's going down. The economy was going down, and now it's going up.

Years and years and years, politicians in Washington just talked about things, and now we are doing things. It took 7 years and two vetoes to pass the family leave law to give hard-working middle class people the guarantee that if they had to take a little time off, they wouldn't lose their jobs if it was for their children or their parents. It took 7 years to pass the Brady bill, but now it's keeping people alive by checking the backgrounds of people before they get guns.

I heard all that talk about our economic program. Many of the same people last year were saying, "You pass the President's economic program, it's nothing but a big tax increase; it will collapse the economy." Well, here's what it did.

It had $255 billion in spending cuts. It had tax cuts for 15 million working Americans to keep them at work and off of welfare, including 350,000 New Jersey families. It asked the wealthiest 1½ percent to pay a tax increase, and it reduced the Federal Government—I hear all the time the other side saying we hate big Government. Well, we Democrats passed a budget that will give you the smallest Federal Government since John Kennedy was President, three years of deficit reduction for the first time since Harry Truman was President, and produced 3.8 million new jobs and a 1½ percent unemployment rate drop and the largest number of new businesses formed in any year since World War II. That is what we say to the naysayers, a Government that works for ordinary Americans again.

For 6 years I heard them talking about crime in Washington and how tough they were on crime, except nothing ever happened. But last week, after 6 years and this problem plaguing American families, what happened? The Congress decided to send for a final vote the toughest, smartest crime bill in the history of the country: a 20-percent increase in the number of police officers, 100,000 more in the United States; "three strikes and you're out"; an assault weapons ban like you had here in New Jersey that you had to fight like crazy to keep; a bill that makes it illegal for young people to have handguns unless they're under the supervision of adults; money to keep our schools safer, so our kids don't have to duck under their desks to dodge bullets; and more money to give our young people something to say yes to, summer jobs, midnight basketball, drug treatment programs, the chance to build a better life. That is what we are producing for middle class America to build a better country.

And now, now we come to health care. I don't know if you saw this, but Saturday, Hillary and I went down to Independence, Missouri, to President Truman's hometown, with the Vice President and Mrs. Gore. And the Governor of Missouri got up, and he read all these things. He said, "Just listen to what they're saying about our President. They're saying he wants socialized medicine. They're saying he's going to take health care away from the American people. They're saying he's going to mess it up." He went through all these quotes, and then he said, "This is not what they said about President Clinton; this is what they said 50 years ago about President Truman." The lines are still the same, and the objective is still the same. I am trying to get health care for ordinary American people.

Let me tell you something, folks. When I presented our plan, I went all around the country and I listened to what people said. They said, "We want you to change it some, make it less bureaucratic, provide more flexibility, give bigger breaks to small business, take some more time to phase it in." And we said we would do that. Those changes have been made. But one thing we shouldn't change is whether America at long last will join the ranks of all the other advanced countries in the world and provide health care for all the middle class working people in the United States.

If you're on welfare, you have health care. If you're in jail, you have health care. If you're rich, you have health care. If you're a politician, you've got it. The only people who can lose it are working people. Over 80 percent of the people in the United States without health insurance work for a living every day. And it is not right.

And let me tell you this. I say this to all the people who come here to disagree with us in good faith. How do you explain the fact that all of our competitors cover their people? How do you explain the fact that, while that is happening, in the last 5 years in America, there are now 5 million people in this country today who don't have health insurance who had it 5 years ago, that New Jersey has had almost a 50-percent increase in the number of people without health insurance in the last 5 years? Almost one million people in New Jersey alone don't have it. What is their answer? I have given you my answer. Let's ask the American people to give health insurance to everybody.

Let me say one other thing. I'm a big one on getting beyond all this slogan and name-calling and just asking what works. In the State of Hawaii, for the last 20 years in Hawaii, employers and employees have had the responsibility to make sure that everybody had health insurance. Now, if you've ever been to Hawaii, you know that everything in the entire State of Hawaii is more expensive than it is here because it's way out there in the ocean. That is, everything except one thing: health insurance. It is 30 percent cheaper in Hawaii than it is in the United States, on the average. The healthy population is greater. The infant mortality rate is down. And small business is booming because they can all afford health care. And that's what I want to do for the United States, what we know will work.

What is the answer of those who say, "We don't like what they did in Hawaii; we don't want cheaper health insurance; we don't want healthier people. We want people to be able to get a free ride and stick the taxpayer with what happens. It's all right with us if these country hospitals close down in places like my State and if Dennis Rivera's workers can't afford to take care of all the people without health insurance." What is their answer? It is time for the shoe to be on the other foot. I have been out here for one year saying, let's give health care to the American people.

Now this time who advocates shared responsibility? Who in America says everybody ought to have health insurance? Well, the American Association of Retired People, all these folks in the unions who already have health care, they're doing it for the rest of Americans, spending your money. And I thank you for that. But for the first time, for the first time ever, we have the nurses association, the medical association, the pediatricians, the children's doctors association, the family doctors association, 600,000 small businesses who provide health care for their workers, all of them say, "If everybody did it we could make this a healthier, better, stronger country, and we would lower health care costs for tens of millions of Americans." That's what we're here for. That's what I want you to fight for. That's what I want Congress to vote for.

My fellow Americans, this decision rests no longer in my hands alone. The Congress has been under enormous pressure. There has been enormous disinformation out there. You've got people here holding up signs saying "No Socialized Medicine." What does our plan require? Everybody to buy private insurance. Most of them have parents on Medicare. You want to repeal Medicare, ma'am? Do you think that's socialized medicine? I don't. Medicare, however, is paid for by all of us and by our employers. And they take care of the elderly people of this country; nobody wants to repeal it.

Our plan gives you your choice of doctors. You keep your doctor. You make your decision. It's private insurance. It's just what Hawaii has done. And there are people who say, "Don't ration health care." You talk to anybody who's had their insurance cut back or their premiums up or their deductibles increased. You talk to any doctor who's had to hire somebody just to call the insurance companies to get them to pay the bill. We are rationing health care today; 39 million Americans don't have it. We are losing ground.

There are millions and millions of people who are holding on by their fingernails with worse and worse policies. What I want to do is stop rationing health care, avoid socialized medicine, give good, old-fashioned private American health care to every American working family. That's what we're trying to do. And all the disinformation in the world won't change it.

So I ask you this: Don't let the fear-mongers, don't let the dividers, don't let the people who disseminate false information frighten the United States Congress into walking away from the opportunity of a lifetime. Tell the Members of Congress you will support them. This is not partisan politics.

I met with three families before I came up here with these problems. I don't have any earthly idea whether they are Republicans or Democrats. I couldn't tell you to save my life who they voted for for President. But I can tell you one thing: If they get up and go to work and obey the law and do their best to raise their children, they deserve health insurance. And with your help, we're going to give it to them.

Thank you, and God bless you all.

NOTE: The President spoke at 2:10 p.m. at Liberty State Park. In his remarks, he referred to Gerald W. McEntee, international president, American Federation of State, County and Municipal Employees (AFSCME); Vince Sombrotto, president, National Association of Letter Carriers; Dennis Rivera, president, 1199 National Health and Human Service Employees Union; Health Security Express rider Carolyn Vilas; and Louis and Maria Agnes, of New Jersey, who had written to the President concerning their problems obtaining health insurance.

Statement on Anticrime Legislation
August 1, 1994

Every major law enforcement organization in America supports this crime bill. Republican mayors have written members of their party in Congress to urge swift passage of the bill and Democratic mayors have done the same.

Today, the Nation's prosecutors have come to Washington to add their voices to this mighty chorus with its simple message: Pass the crime bill now.

Police officers want it because it bans the deadly assault weapons that outgun them every day. Mayors want it because it will put 100,000 more police officers on the streets. Prosecutors want it because it's full of tough punishments that will allow them to seek the penalties violent criminals deserve.

The American people want action against the crime and violence that has become a familiar threat in almost every neighborhood.

It's time for the lawmakers to do what the law enforcers have asked: Pass the crime bill now.

Letter to Congressional Leaders on Humanitarian Assistance for Rwandan Refugees
August 1, 1994

Dear Mr. Speaker: (Dear Mr. President:)

Since August 1993, when a fragile peace was signed between Rwandan Government Forces (RGF) and the Rwandan Patriotic Front (RPF), the United Nations has been actively addressing the humanitarian crisis in Rwanda. On April 6, 1994, President Habyarimana of Rwanda, President Ntaryamira of Burundi and a number of government officials were killed when their plane crashed while approaching the airport in Kigali, Rwanda's capital. This incident ruptured the peace and led to a resumption of the civil war that has now resulted in the deaths of hundreds of thousands of Rwandans, many of them Tutsi civilians who were the victims of genocide on the part of radical Hutu elements aligned with the former government.

In early July 1994, the government fell and the RPF assumed power in Kigali, establishing a multi-party government. Since that time they have cooperated fully with us and have even requested human rights monitors to better assure the safety of returning refugees. As a result of the Civil War, the nation's infrastructure has been virtually destroyed. An estimated 2.1 million Rwandan refugees have fled to neighboring Zaire, Burundi, Uganda, and Tanzania, and the United Nations High Commissioner for Refugees (UNHCR) estimates that a further 2.6 million persons are internally displaced.

The need to respond to disease, starvation, and dehydration in the refugee camps, especially in Zaire and Burundi, led me on July 29, 1994, to direct the expansion of capabilities at the Kigali airport to support the UNHCR relief operation more effectively. By providing a support infrastructure for the relief of refugees and displaced persons out of this capital city, I believe we will be better able to draw Rwandans back to their homes, away from the unsanitary conditions of the refugee camps, and closer to a more centralized distribution point for humanitarian aid. We have engaged in negotiations with the new government in order to promote these objectives. We have urged this new government to broaden its political base, refrain from retribution, respect the rule of law, and otherwise create the conditions of safety and security that would permit the refugees to return home.

In the afternoon of July 29, 1994, I directed General Joulwan, Commander in Chief, United States European Command, in addition to the relief operations he is already conducting through Goma, Zaire and Entebbe, Uganda, immediately deploy a contingent of U.S. forces, numbering approximately 200, to the airport at Kigali. These forces began to arrive on July 30, 1994. Other forces from Australia and the United Kingdom are committed to this effort in Kigali as well. During this initial phase of "Operation Support Hope," the United States and other committed nations will establish and operate a logistics base to support UNHCR humanitarian relief operations. In this effort, they will open a logistic coordination center for receiving and distributing relief supplies, provide airfield services and cargo handling, and provide security for the airport at Kigali. These efforts are directed at achieving the objectives of U.N. Security Council Resolutions 929, 925 and 918. No organized resistance has been encountered to our efforts to date and none is expected.

United States Armed Forces will remain in Rwanda only as long as necessary to assist the UNHCR in establishing an effective distribution mechanism for humanitarian relief support to the Rwandan people. While it is not possible to estimate precisely how long it will take to satisfy this requirement, we believe that prolonged operations will not be necessary.

We do not intend that U.S. Armed Forces deployed to Rwanda become involved in hostilities. Nonetheless, a majority of the approximately 200 personnel deployed will be assigned to provide force protection and assure security of the Kigali airport. These security forces are equipped and ready to take such measures as may be needed to accomplish their humanitarian mission and defend themselves if necessary.

I have taken these actions pursuant to my constitutional authority to conduct our foreign relations and as Commander in Chief and Chief Executive. I am providing this report consistent with the War Powers Resolution in accordance with my desire that the Congress be fully informed. I look forward to cooperating with the Congress in this effort to relieve human suffering.

Sincerely,

WILLIAM J. CLINTON

NOTE: Identical letters were sent to Thomas S. Foley, Speaker of the House of Representatives, and Robert C. Byrd, President pro tempore of the Senate. This letter was released by the Office of the Press Secretary on August 2.

Remarks Announcing United States Shipbuilding Industry Initiatives
August 2, 1994

Thank you. Secretary Peña, Secretary Brown, Ambassador Kantor, Admiral Herberger, John Dane, and Doug Ballis. Thanks for saving the sign.

I'd like to introduce the Members of the House who are here who supported this initiative and who have made a major contribution to what we're doing and obviously will be needed in the months and years ahead and whose districts will be affected by the announcements we make today: Congressman Gene Taylor from Mississippi, Congressman Billy Tauzin from Louisiana, Congressman Bobby Scott from Virginia, and Congresswoman Lynn Schenk and Congressman Bob Filner from California. Thank you for your help. Would you stand? [*Applause*]

I'd like to begin by thanking Doug and Richard Vortman, NASSCO's CEO, who is also here, because they gave me one of those seminal experiences you have once in a while in life that takes an idea from your head to your heart. When you know something and you know you ought to do it, that's one thing. But when you feel it, it's another thing altogether.

They stopped work one day in May of 1992, before I was even the nominee of my party for President, so that I could speak to nearly 4,000 of their people and so that I could listen to them. I could see them working together, struggling together, trying to compete in the global economy, building the only commercial ship then being built anywhere in the United States of America. They made me feel welcome, but they also made sure I was aware of what the stakes were and what the issue was and how this was yet one more example of how we could compete and win in an area critical to our future if only we had the policies, the tools, and the drive to do it.

I wish all the people that I met that day could be in this room today. I'm afraid the fire

marshal would evict us all if I had tried to achieve that. But they are the people who really taught me about this issue, and they are the people, they and the millions like them, for whom I fought both before I got here and for whom I try to fight every day in this office.

This is a great day for our American jobs, for our economy, for our shipbuilding industry. It's a great day for the idea that if we all work together we can figure out how to solve our problems even in difficult budgetary times.

Two years ago, every ship in America under construction except one was destined for defense, every one. And now we know that while our United States naval power is still unsurpassed in the world and must remain so, we cannot allow that one commercial vessel I saw under construction in San Diego become a symbol of the past.

We know that one of the things that we needed most in 1992 and one of the things we're trying most to do today is to have a strategy for restructuring our defense industries so that they can fulfill a dual purpose, let me say, not so they can get out of defense work, because we will continue to need major investments in defense technologies for the foreseeable future, but so that with defense being scaled back, those kinds of folks can stay in business by being successful commercially as well.

When I ran for this job, when the economy was going down and the deficit was going up, it was obvious to me that there were many reasons for that, but one of them was that the Government had no strategy. What was our strategy to preserve aerospace, our biggest export? What was our strategy when it came to the shipbuilding industry? What was our strategy to help support our automakers when they had made radical changes all through the 1980's so

1407

that they could be more competitive again? What was our strategy?

And the truth is, we didn't have one. Well, now we do have one. We have strategies for those industries and for others and for our economy. We've concluded trade agreements that expanded the barriers of world trade and enabled us to do more: NAFTA, the GATT we're trying to pass in Congress now, all designed to help hard-working middle class Americans get ahead because they'll have the economic opportunities to do it.

I've said this many times, but I want to repeat it again: The mission of the United States at the close of the 20th century must be to keep the American dream alive in the 21st century. And to do it, we have to restore the economy, rebuild our communities at home, empower individuals to take responsibilities for themselves, put Government back on the side of ordinary people, create a world of greater peace and prosperity. That is what we must do.

And that is exactly what we are celebrating here today, not just four projects for four worthy companies with several thousand worthy American workers. In the last 19 months, we have dramatically reduced the deficit. We're on the verge of getting 3 years of deficit reduction in a row for the first time since Truman was President. We have seen 3.8 million new jobs come into this economy, even as we are scaling back the Federal work force so that by the end of this budget cycle it will be the smallest it's been since President Kennedy was here in the White House. The unemployment rate has gone down by 1½ percent, and we are making real progress in bringing manufacturing back. Between 1989 and 1992, we lost 1.4 million manufacturing jobs. Now we have 104,000 more than we had on the day I was inaugurated.

I am proud of these accomplishments of the American people, getting the American economy in order by getting our economic house in order, by instituting lifetime education and training programs that will have to embrace all of our people from the first day of preschool to the last day they work.

Two years ago, Doug and a lot of other people in NASSCO said, "This has been a great day, but don't forget us if you're elected." And we haven't forgotten them, but we've got to keep following through. And we have to think of this as a permanent partnership. I believe that if you look at the America that we're mov-

ing toward, the Government will adopt a less regulatory role, the Government will become a smaller percentage of our gross national product in the amount of money we spend. But the Government will have to be there in the competition in the global economy of the 21st century in partnership with the private sector to make sure that our people, when they're doing the right things, have a chance to compete and win and have a chance to seize the technologies of the 21st century.

Let me just make a couple of other remarks about that. Secretary Perry could not be here today with our other Cabinet members. But I do want to say that the Defense Department, I think, has done an exemplary job in promoting defense conversion. Secretary Perry has recently awarded the first $30 million in matching grants out of a total of $220 million we'll invest over the next 5 years to apply advanced technologies to make our shipbuilding industry even more competitive. We're spending hundreds of millions of dollars more in other areas to promote defense conversion as well.

I also want to join Secretary Peña in complimenting our Trade Representative, our Ambassador, Mickey Kantor, for the work he did in the OECD negotiations with the European countries on shipbuilding subsidies. They dragged on for 5 years, and his work will bring an end to unfair foreign shipbuilding subsidies that has kept us out of world markets too long. He did a good job with that; he did a good job with the GATT; he did a superb job with NAFTA. And we're selling rice to Japan for the first time—[*laughter*]—which makes my people happy back home in Arkansas. And I thank you, sir.

I also want to say a special word of thanks to the Secretary of Commerce. He was here not very long ago when we announced $6 billion in aircraft exports. We had an announcement the other day of $4 billion in telecommunications exports, and there are more in other high-wage manufacturing industries.

The next step, as Secretary Peña said, in our comprehensive maritime reform is to sustain the U.S. flag merchant fleet. And this week, as the House considers that maritime and security and trade act, I hope that you all will help us see that the Congress passes a bill similar to the one the administration has proposed.

Let me say again, this is a partnership, and this is a good beginning. And we're going in the right direction with the economy as a whole and with shipbuilding in particular, with Government and business and workers walking hand in hand into the 21st century. But we have to make this a part of the permanent process of doing business for America. I ask all of you to support that, to rededicate yourself to these objectives. This is a good day. As my daughter says, this is a big deal. [*Laughter*] But it is just a beginning. Let's keep it going.

Thank you very much.

NOTE: The President spoke at 11:36 a.m. in the Roosevelt Room at the White House. In his remarks, he referred to Adm. Albert Herberger, Administrator, Maritime Administration; John Dane III, president, Trinity Shipyards; and Doug Ballis, National Steel and Shipbuilding Co. (NASSCO) employee.

Teleconference Remarks Announcing Additional California Earthquake Assistance
August 2, 1994

Mayor Richard Riordan. Mr. President, we'd like to thank you for the very quick response you've given to our letter of last Thursday and the extraordinary effort that your A-plus team is still doing for our great city.

Mayor Judy Abdo. We also want to say how grateful we are for the people who have worked so hard together to find these solutions. And Santa Monica is particularly grateful for the quick and decisive response that you've made.

The President. Well, I just want to say that it's been a privilege for all of us here in Washington to work with you to help get southern California back on its feet again.

I visited Los Angeles a couple of days after the earthquake and saw that destruction, and I was terribly moved by it. And now, in some ways, it's more moving to hear about all the progress that's been made in just 6 months. I think the people of southern California have certainly showed a great deal of courage and resilience, and you have all shown strong leadership. And I very much appreciate that.

[*Mayor Riordan and Mayor Abdo discussed the extensive damage to housing and stated that Federal assistance was critical to the recovery effort in that area.*]

The President. What about the ghost towns in the areas, both in Los Angeles and Santa Monica? That's still a problem, isn't it?

Senator Dianne Feinstein. Well, Mr. President, may I say something here?

The President. Sure.

Senator Feinstein. Oh, I think it was—James Lee, was it a month ago we went to them, the ghost towns, with Richard Alarcon?

The President. I don't think he's on the phone.

Senator Feinstein. Oh, he's not on the line. Richard, do you remember when it was?

The President. I know you toured the areas.

[*Senator Feinstein discussed damaged and abandoned apartment buildings and expressed appreciation for increased HUD funding to alleviate the problem.*]

The President. Well, one of the things that we found out and that Henry Cisneros talked to me a lot about was that years after the natural disasters that struck the Bay Area in northern California and in southern Florida, there are still these ghost towns, and communities are still suffering. Now it's more expensive to fix it than if we'd done it right away.

And so, I thought maybe what I would do is let Secretary Cisneros just talk a little bit about what he's working with you, Senator Feinstein, Senator Boxer, and the mayors and the other members of your delegation on.

[*Secretary of Housing and Urban Development Henry Cisneros explained that $225 million will be made available through the Community Development Block Grant Program to help rebuild abandoned neighborhoods.*]

The President. Thank you, Henry. I am really pleased with the idea that you came up with, and I identify with the solution a lot because it's a source of funds I'm familiar with and something I've used myself in my former life when I was a Governor.

Today I sent the formal request to Congress to provide $225 million in additional disaster assistance for the Los Angeles area, $200 million to Los Angeles, $25 million to Santa Monica, as a downpayment on our partnerships with the cities to solve this ghost town problem. This goes beyond the typical Federal disaster response, and it's possible frankly because we've been able to reallocate some other disaster funds. It doesn't meet the total need, and I know we'll have to have full cooperation and participation from local governments in the States as we go through this. But it is a very good beginning, and it gives you a chance to begin to get rid of this problem.

Mayor?

[*Mayor Riordan thanked the President for the extra funds and the flexibility to direct the money where it is most needed. Mayor Abdo then stated that while Santa Monica does not have ghost neighborhoods, the money will be used to repair abandoned buildings.*]

The President. Senator Feinstein?

Senator Feinstein. Mr. President, I want to just ask Judy one question. Judy, do you know how many units that $25 million will cover?

[*Mayor Abdo explained that they will not know how many units the money will cover until they find out how much money will be needed after the SBA loans have been distributed. Senator Feinstein then thanked Secretary Cisneros for his efforts.*]

Secretary Cisneros. Thank you very much, Senator.

Senator Feinstein. And I'm going to miss a vote, so I'm going to have to sign off.

The President. Thank you, Senator.

Senator Feinstein. Thank you, Mr. President.

The President. Well, I just wanted to make one final comment before we all sign off. Today we are marking the 6-month milestone in your recovery effort by releasing a report prepared by our Office of Management and Budget that describes what's been done so far. And I really want to thank again our FEMA Director, James Lee Witt, Secretary Peña, Erskine Bowles, our

SBA Administrator, and of course, Henry Cisneros for all their hard work.

So far we have identified $11.9 billion in Federal assistance to meet California's need after the earthquake. That's the largest amount ever provided to an individual disaster. And with the assistance, obviously, of both of you, Mayor Riordan, Mayor Abdo, and the hard work of your Senators and the California congressional delegation, Congress enacted that emergency relief package in record time.

Our report shows now that record numbers of applications for assistance have been received. FEMA has accepted over 600,000 registrations, which is twice the previous all-time high for Hurricane Hugo. The SBA has accepted over 200,000 disaster loan applications to repair homes and businesses, which is more than for the Midwest floods, Hurricane Andrew, the Loma Prieta earthquake, and Hurricane Hugo combined. And I know that Henry has signed over 12,600 leases providing homes to families who were displaced by the earthquake. So we've tried to be creative and flexible in our response.

Secretary Peña's now-famous cost-plus-time contracting proposal led to the opening of damaged freeways in record time, faster than even I believed it could be done, and I'm an incurable optimist. And the SBA Administrator, Erskine Bowles, exercised his discretionary authority so that disaster loans went to larger numbers of major employers to retain communities. The Commerce Secretary developed new and innovative programs to help rebuild infrastructure and assist small businesses that don't otherwise qualify for Federal assistance. So we've tried to be quick and flexible and helpful.

And I just want to say again, looking back on the last 6 months, I feel good about what all of us have done together. But I know the job is not finished. And I hope this announcement today will give you, the leaders, as well as the citizens of southern California assurances that—my personal pledge and our entire administration—we're still committed over the long haul to make sure that we get over the Northridge earthquake and we make it, over the long run, a net plus for the people of southern California because of the rebound.

[*The mayors expressed their appreciation to the President. Secretary Cisneros then discussed his plans to visit Los Angeles, and the mayors thanked him also.*]

   The President. Thank you very much. Goodbye.

NOTE: The teleconference began at 4:46 p.m. The President spoke from the Oval Office at the White House. During the teleconference, Senator Feinstein referred to Richard Alarcon, member, Los Angeles City Council.

Statement on Additional California Earthquake Assistance
August 2, 1994

Years after natural disasters struck the Bay area and south Florida, ghost towns remain and local communities continue to suffer. We are working today to overcome those problems, when they have become far more difficult and expensive to address. In Los Angeles and Santa Monica, we are proposing to begin the restoration of these ghost towns now, before it is too late.

NOTE: This statement was included in a White House statement announcing that the President requested additional fiscal year 1994 funds for the Department of Housing and Urban Development for the repair and reconstruction of housing damaged by the southern California earthquake earlier this year.

Message to the Congress Reporting on the National Emergency With Respect to Iraq
August 2, 1994

To the Congress of the United States:
   I hereby report to the Congress on the developments since my last report of March 3, 1994, concerning the national emergency with respect to Iraq that was declared in Executive Order No. 12722 of August 2, 1990. This report is submitted pursuant to section 401(c) of the National Emergencies Act, 50 U.S.C. 1641(c), and section 204(c) of the International Emergency Economic Powers Act, 50 U.S.C. 1703(c).
   Executive Order No. 12722 ordered the immediate blocking of all property and interests in property of the Government of Iraq (including the Central Bank of Iraq), then or thereafter located in the United States or within the possession or control of a United States person. That order also prohibited the importation into the United States of goods and services of Iraqi origin, as well as the exportation of goods, services, and technology from the United States to Iraq. The order prohibited travel-related transactions to or from Iraq and the performance of any contract in support of any industrial, commercial, or governmental project in Iraq. United

States persons were also prohibited from granting or extending credit or loans to the Government of Iraq.
   The foregoing prohibitions (as well as the blocking of Government of Iraq property) were continued and augmented on August 9, 1990, by Executive Order No. 12724, which was issued in order to align the sanctions imposed by the United States with United Nations Security Council Resolution 661 of August 6, 1990.
   Executive Order No. 12817 was issued on October 21, 1992, to implement in the United States measures adopted in United Nations Security Council Resolution 778 of October 2, 1992. Resolution 778 requires U.N. Member States temporarily to transfer to a U.N. escrow account up to $200 million apiece in Iraqi oil sale proceeds paid by purchasers after the imposition of U.N. sanctions on Iraq, to finance Iraq's obligations for U.N. activities with respect to Iraq, such as expenses to verify Iraqi weapons destruction, and to provide humanitarian assistance in Iraq on a nonpartisan basis. A portion of the escrowed funds will also fund the activi-

ties of the U.N. Compensation Commission in Geneva, which will handle claims from victims of the Iraqi invasion of Kuwait. Member States also may make voluntary contributions to the account. The funds placed in the escrow account are to be returned, with interest, to the Member States that transferred them to the United Nations, as funds are received from future sales of Iraqi oil authorized by the U.N. Security Council. No Member State is required to fund more than half of the total transfers or contributions to the escrow account.

This report discusses only matters concerning the national emergency with respect to Iraq that was declared in Executive Order No. 12722 and matters relating to Executive Orders Nos. 12724 and 12817 (the "Executive orders"). The report covers events from February 2, 1994, through August 1, 1994.

1. During the reporting period, there were no amendments to the Iraqi Sanctions Regulations.

2. Investigations of possible violations of the Iraqi sanctions continue to be pursued and appropriate enforcement actions taken. There are currently 30 enforcement actions pending. These are intended to deter future activities in violation of the sanctions. Additional civil penalty notices were prepared during the reporting period for violations of the International Emergency Economic Powers Act and Iraqi Sanctions Regulations with respect to transactions involving Iraq. Three penalties totaling $38,450 were collected from three banks for violation of the prohibitions against Iraq, and noncompliance with reporting requirements and an Office of Foreign Assets Control directive license.

3. Investigation also continues into the roles played by various individuals and firms outside Iraq in the Iraqi government procurement network. These investigations may lead to additions to the Office of Foreign Assets Control's listing of individuals and organizations determined to be Specially Designated Nationals ("SDNs") of the Government of Iraq. One Jordanian-Iraqi joint venture company prominently involved in shipments to Iraq was identified as an SDN of Iraq on May 4, 1994. A copy of the notice is attached.

4. Pursuant to Executive Order No. 12817 implementing United Nations Security Council Resolution 778, on October 26, 1992, the Office of Foreign Assets Control directed the Federal Reserve Bank of New York to establish a blocked account for receipt of certain post-August 6, 1990, Iraqi oil sales proceeds, and to hold, invest, and transfer these funds as required by the order. On March 1, 1994, following payments by the Governments of the United Kingdom ($447,761.19), the Netherlands ($1,566,994.55), Australia ($476,110.00), and the European Community ($3,758,310.31), respectively, to the special United Nations-controlled account, entitled United Nations Security Council Resolution 778 Escrow Account, the Federal Reserve Bank of New York was directed to transfer a corresponding amount of $6,240,176.05 from the blocked account it holds to the United Nations-controlled account. Similarly, on March 22, 1994, following the payment of $525,182.50 by the Government of the Netherlands, $2,478,089.89 by the European Community, $2,352,800.00 by the Government of the United Kingdom, $444,444.44 by the Government of Denmark, $1,204,899.30 by the Government of Sweden, and $3,100,000.00 by the Government of Japan, the Federal Reserve Bank of New York was directed to transfer a corresponding amount of $10,105,416.13 to the United Nations-controlled account. Again on June 30, 1994, the Federal Reserve Bank of New York was directed to transfer $6,969,862.89 to the United Nations-controlled account, an amount corresponding to the aggregate total of recent payments by the governments of other Member States: European Community ($1,042,774.31), United Kingdom ($1,570,804.48), the Netherlands ($1,062,219.51), Kuwait ($2,000,000.00), and Sweden ($1,294,064.59). Cumulative transfers from the blocked Federal Reserve Bank of New York account since issuance of Executive Order No. 12817 have amounted to $130,928,726.04 of the up to $200 million that the United States is obligated to match from blocked Iraqi oil payments, pursuant to United Nations Security Council Resolution 778.

5. The Office of Foreign Assets Control has issued a total of 496 specific licenses regarding transactions pertaining to Iraq or Iraqi assets since August 1990. Since my last report, 52 specific licenses have been issued. Licenses were issued for transactions such as the filing of legal actions against Iraqi governmental entities, legal representation of Iraq, and the exportation to Iraq of donated medicine, medical supplies, food intended for humanitarian relief purposes, the execution of powers of attorney relating to the

administration of personal assets and decedents' estates in Iraq, and the protection of preexistent intellectual property rights in Iraq.

6. The expenses incurred by the Federal Government in the 6-month period from February 2, 1994, through August 1, 1994, that are directly attributable to the exercise of powers and authorities conferred by the declaration of a national emergency with respect to Iraq are reported to be about $2.3 million, most of which represents wage and salary costs for Federal personnel. Personnel costs were largely centered in the Department of the Treasury (particularly in the Office of Foreign Assets Control, the U.S. Customs Service, the Office of the Assistant Secretary for Enforcement, and the Office of the General Counsel), the Department of State (particularly the Bureau of Economic and Business Affairs, the Bureau of Near East and South Asian Affairs, the Bureau of International Organizations, and the Office of the Legal Adviser), and the Department of Transportation (particularly the U.S. Coast Guard).

7. The United States imposed economic sanctions on Iraq in response to Iraq's illegal invasion and occupation of Kuwait, a clear act of brutal aggression. The United States, together with the international community, is maintaining economic sanctions against Iraq because the Iraqi regime has failed to comply fully with United Nations Security Council resolutions. Security Council resolutions on Iraq call for the elimination of Iraqi weapons of mass destruction, the inviolability of the Iraq-Kuwait boundary, the release of Kuwaiti and other third-country nationals, compensation for victims of Iraqi aggression, long-term monitoring of weapons of mass destruction capabilities, the return of Kuwaiti assets stolen during Iraq's illegal occupation of Kuwait, renunciation of terrorism, an end to internal Iraqi repression of its own civilian population, and the facilitation of access of international relief organizations to all those in need in all parts of Iraq. Four years after the invasion, a pattern of defiance persists: a refusal to recognize the international boundary with Kuwait or to account for missing Kuwaiti detainees, sponsorship of assassinations in Lebanon and in northern Iraq; incomplete declarations to weapons inspectors, and ongoing widespread human rights violations, among other things. As a result, the U.N. sanctions remain in place; the United States will continue to enforce those sanctions under domestic authority.

The Baghdad government continued to violate basic human rights of its own citizens through systematic repression of minorities and denial of humanitarian assistance. The Government of Iraq has repeatedly said it will not be bound by United Nations Security Council Resolution 688. For more than 3 years, Baghdad has maintained a complete blockade of food, fuel, and medicine on northern Iraq. The Iraqi military routinely harasses residents of the north, and has attempted to "Arabize" Kurdish, Turcomen, and Assyrian areas in the north. Iraq has not relented in its artillery attacks against civilian population centers in the south, or in its burning and draining operations in the southern marshes, which have forced thousands to flee to neighboring States.

In 1991, the United Nations Security Council adopted Resolutions 706 and 712, which would permit Iraq to sell up to $1.6 billion of oil under U.N. auspices to fund the provision of food, medicine, and other humanitarian supplies to the people of Iraq. The resolutions also provide for the payment of compensation to victims of Iraqi aggression and other U.N. activities with respect to Iraq. The equitable distribution within Iraq of this humanitarian assistance would be supervised and monitored by the United Nations. The Iraqi regime so far has refused to accept these resolutions and has thereby chosen to perpetuate the suffering of its civilian population. Nearly a year ago, the Iraqi government informed the United Nations that it would not implement Resolutions 706 and 712.

The policies and actions of the Saddam Hussein regime continue to pose an unusual and extraordinary threat to the national security and foreign policy of the United States, as well as to regional peace and security. The U.N. resolutions require that the Security Council be assured of Iraq's peaceful intentions in judging its compliance with sanctions. Because of Iraq's failure to comply fully with these resolutions, the United States will continue to apply economic sanctions to deter it from threatening peace and stability in the region.

WILLIAM J. CLINTON

The White House,
August 2, 1994.

Statement on Senate Action on Health Care Reform Legislation
August 2, 1994

The bill unveiled by Senator Mitchell achieves what the American people want, health coverage that can never be taken away. The bill provides health security for hard-working middle class Americans who deserve nothing less. And it places a high priority on covering the Nation's precious resource, our children. I applaud the majority leader and the Members of the Senate who have been working diligently to bring a bill to the floor that works for ordinary Americans.

The Senate bill provides for universal coverage, enables Americans to keep their current insurance and their doctor, maintains quality health care, and provides greater opportunity to keep health coverage affordable. It builds on the current system of shared responsibility which we already know works.

We have made tremendous progress. The Senate and House are poised to vote for legislation that covers every American for the first time in our Nation's history. We have come this far, and we must not turn back now. If Congress fails to achieve universal coverage, if hard-working middle class Americans are left out in the cold, and if costs are not controlled, that's simply unacceptable.

The House and Senate will soon begin this debate, a debate that will engage every American family concerned about their health security. While differences in the House and Senate bills will be worked out as the legislative process moves forward, achieving universal coverage remains the critical goal. During the course of this historic floor debate, there will be those who say that reaching universal coverage is not necessary. To those people I say: Let the debate begin. Those of us who are fighting for universal coverage are fighting for middle class Americans. This is a debate that we must win and that we will win.

Statement on the Resignation of Deputy Assistant to the President and Director of Media Affairs Jeff Eller
August 2, 1994

From the earliest days of my campaign for President through our first year and a half in the White House, Jeff has served with dedication and uncompromising loyalty. He played a vital role in redefining the technological means used to communicate my policies and programs, and I will miss his service and counsel.

NOTE: This statement was included in a statement by the Press Secretary announcing that Mr. Eller would be leaving the administration in September.

Appointment of Interim National AIDS Policy Coordinator
August 2, 1994

The President today appointed Patricia S. Fleming to serve as interim National AIDS Policy Coordinator.

Ms. Fleming, currently special assistant to Health and Human Services Secretary Donna E. Shalala, will serve until a permanent coordinator takes office.

"This administration has made significant strides in the fight against this terrible epidemic. We've increased our budgets for AIDS research, treatment, and prevention and have fought hard to provide health insurance for all Americans, regardless of preexisting conditions. Patsy

Fleming will make sure we don't lose our momentum," said the President.

NOTE: This item was part of a statement by the Press Secretary announcing the appointment.

Remarks to Health Security Express Participants
August 3, 1994

The President. My fellow Americans, Congress has to decide whether it's going to listen to the insurance companies or to Jan Cox's last wish.

We all know what the problem is here. You've just ridden a bus across the country, seeing real people who are just working hard, making the best they can of their lives, wanting a decent break. Those of you who have had these kinds of personal experiences that Daniel and Carolyn and John talked about can't figure out why we spend more than anybody else on health care, cover fewer people than any other country, and get poorer health results. It is because organized, intense, discrete minority interests are doing very well on a system that costs more than any other country's and covers fewer people. And every time you try to change it, they say, well, the world will come to an end.

Well, like Hillary said, we ran for this job, along with Vice President and Mrs. Gore, because maybe we could be the home office of the "American association of ordinary citizens." That's what we wanted to do. And every time we try to make a change, that's what they said.

We showed up here; the deficit was going up, and the economy was going down. And I put together a plan, and I urged the people on the other side to work with me. And they said, "No, if we vote for this, the sky will fall, the economy will collapse. And so we'll all vote against it and call it a big tax increase."

But the truth is the plan cut spending, raised taxes on the richest 1½ percent of Americans, gave 15 million working people a tax cut; thanks to the Secretary of Education, gave 20 million Americans an opportunity to refinance their college loans at a lower interest rate. And, lo and behold, it produced a drop in unemployment and 3.8 million new jobs, and the sky didn't fall. Now the deficit's going down, and the economy's coming up. But it's hard to overcome these organized, intense interests.

We had a different sort of fight over the big trade battle last year over on NAFTA. They said, "If you do this, the economy will collapse." But lo and behold, the Congress, this time with a bipartisan effort, passed NAFTA, and we're exporting 5 times as many cars to Mexico as we were last year. They're our biggest, most growing market.

Change is hard up here, because even though most Members of Congress were once just like you, when they get up here they're a long way from home, and they know that you and the President are presented to the folks back home partly through the rhetoric and the money spent by organized, intense minority interests.

And somehow, some way, this fight has got to be about Daniel Lumley and Carolyn Mosley and John and Jan Cox. That's what it's got to be about. It's got to be about my friend Justin Dart, sitting back there, and all the Americans with disabilities who could be in the work force, making money, paying taxes, contributing to our future, if they could just get health insurance while they're in the work force; all the nurses who hired on to help people get well and instead spend all their time calling insurance companies to try to figure out if this or that procedure can be done by the doctor in the first place. Goodness only knows how many people we employ in this country that would be working more productively in any other country. We have to put hundreds of thousands of people to work every day to figure out who's not covered or what's not covered in an insurance policy. There's not anybody else in the world spending their time and spinning their wheels, putting people to work asking them to spend their entire working life reading the fine print of insurance policies to see what is not covered. Can you imagine a more unsatisfying thing to do with your life?

Lee Brown, our drug policy leader, do you know why he's here today? Because if we could pass health insurance for all Americans, it would include drug treatment for all Americans. Now, he's a policeman; he spent all of his life trying to lower crime and fight criminals, be tough on law and order. But he learned as a police officer that there are a lot of people in trouble with drug and alcohol abuse, and they need treatment. And we'd save billions and billions of dollars.

And it's not like we don't know what to do. Twenty years ago, Hawaii said, everybody here is going to get insurance; we're going to have employers and employees cover their health insurance. And if you've never been to Hawaii—I hope you get to go someday; it's a wonderful place—but everything there is more expensive than any place else because it's way out on an island somewhere, everything except health care, where the premiums for small business are 30 percent below the national average because everybody pays and no one runs away and everybody is covered.

And you ought to be taken care of, whether you're a young man riding a motorcycle in the prime of your life or a young woman giving yourself to nursing or a man following a religious mission to work at a Christian radio station or any other thing. It just ought to be that way.

We have a consensus in this country on universal health care. What we do not have is a consensus among people elected to represent the American people on making the tough decisions necessary to get universal health care.

There are lots of things like that in life. A bunch of us, including me, would like to be thinner, but we don't diet. [*Laughter*] A lot of people would like to be stronger, but they don't lift weights.

In the end, it comes down, when you've got something everybody wants to do but is not easy to do, the people that hired on have to make the decisions. And the Members of the United States Congress hired on, just like I did. We didn't say, "Vote for me in a representative form of government, and I will make all the necessary decisions to solve the problems of the country except those that are difficult, controversial, and make people mad." That was not the deal.

And you need to hang around this town, and you need to tell your stories. Because the questions that I get asked are, "Well, what about this detail or that bill, or who is up, or who is down?" I say I have answered my question. My question is, am I for you or not? Answer:

Yes. And secondly, second question, did I offer a plan to solve your problem? The answer: Yes. Third question, was I willing to meet people who had different ideas or better ideas more than halfway? The answer is yes.

These bills provide for longer phase-in. They give less orders, fewer orders. And they give more options to smaller business; they give a better financial break to small business. They are less bureaucratic. We have listened to the American people, and Congress has presented bills to do that. They've bent over backwards to recognize that the American people want options, and they don't like to be told to do anything. I don't blame them. Nobody likes that. But the conservative thing to do is to ask everybody to carry as much of their own load as they can and then for the rest of us to help.

Those who are opposed to universal coverage say, "We've got a whole class of people we're not going to ask to carry any load at all, and we'll ask everybody who's already doing their part to do even more." I think we have the conservative position, my fellow Americans, the responsible position. Everybody should do what they can, and then we'll help those who need more.

I just want to ask you to remember this: Make this debate about John and Jan Cox, about the story Carolyn Mosley told, about the dreams of the future—teaching our children—that Daniel Lumley has, and about the personal stories that are here in this audience and all across America. Don't let it become part of some rhetoric, hot air, process, conflict, interest group deal. And say a simple word: We have moved; we have reached out to people of different views and different parties. This is not a partisan issue. I don't have any earthly idea what political party these three people are in or who they voted for for President, and I do not care. I want them to have health care.

You make the debate about them, and remind the Congress that, just like the President, they signed on to represent ordinary Americans, to make the tough decisions and not to walk away. And this is a decision America has walked away from for 60 years. President Truman, three times, asked the American people to get the Congress to solve this problem, and the Congress said no. President Nixon, 23 years ago, asked the Congress to require employers and employees to split the difference and cover, with private health insurance, all Americans. Now, it's been long enough, folks. I know we're supposed to deliberate up here, but we have now deliberated through three generations. [*Laughter*]

Audience members. Pass it now! Pass it now! Pass it now!

The President. Pass it now, for them and for you.

God bless you all.

NOTE: The President spoke at 11:10 a.m. on the South Lawn at the White House. In his remarks, he referred to Health Security Express riders Daniel Lumley, Carolyn Mosley, John Cox, and Mr. Cox's late wife, Jan.

The President's News Conference
August 3, 1994

The President. Good evening, ladies and gentlemen. Tonight I want to speak with you about crime, health care, and the progress of our national economic strategy. As I have said so many times, the central mission of this administration, renewing the American dream, requires us to restore economic growth, rebuild American communities, empower individual citizens to take personal responsibility for their own futures, and make Government work for ordinary citizens again. We are making progress.

Remember, we are about, now, a year from the time when Congress passed our economic recovery plan. I remember then that our opponents said if that plan passed the sky would fall, unemployment would go up, the deficit would explode. Well, they were wrong. Look at the facts. We cut $255 billion in spending; raised tax rates on only 1.2 percent of the wealthiest Americans; cut taxes for 15 million working families of modest incomes; made 90 percent of our small businesses eligible for a tax cut and 20 million Americans available or eligible to refinance their college loans at lower interest rates. Now the deficit is going down 3 years in a row for the first time since Harry Truman was President. We've got almost 4 million new jobs, very low inflation, a 1½ percent drop in unemployment.

There were other skeptics later who said the sky would fall if we passed the North American Free Trade Agreement. They, too, were wrong. We can see this year that automobile sales, for example, to Mexico are growing at five times the rate of last year, and our trade with Mexico is growing more rapidly than that with any other country. And while I know an awful lot of people are still hurting, the road ahead looks good.

According to Fortune Magazine, for the first time in a decade, all 50 States will expand their private economies next year. Let me say that again. For the first time in a decade, all 50 States will experience economic growth next year.

None of this came without a fight. And now we're involved in two more historic fights. The first is on crime. We have a chance to pass the toughest, smartest crime bill in the history of the United States after 6 years of bickering over it. Let me remind you of what that bill will do. It will put 100,000 police officers on the streets of our communities, a 20 percent increase. It will make "three strikes and you're out" the law of the land. It will ban deadly assault weapons and handgun ownership by minors. It will provide tougher sentences for violent criminals and more prisons to put them in. And we've listened to police, prosecutors, and community leaders who tell us that they need much more for prevention programs, to give our young people something to say yes to as well as something to say no to.

Believe it or not, there are still special interests here in Washington trying to derail this crime bill. But we are fighting them and the American people will win this fight, too.

Still, the recovery we are building, the communities we are trying to make safer, the individual citizens we're trying to empower to compete and win in the global economy, all of these people are at risk unless and until we reform health care.

Our system still costs too much and covers too few. It is actually going in the wrong direction. In the past 5 years, 5 million more Americans have lost their health insurance, almost all of them working people and their children. We're fighting for health care reform not just for those who don't have health insurance, but for those who do have it and who could lose it because they have to change jobs, because someone in their family gets sick, because they simply have to pay too much for it. They deserve better, and we're fighting to see that they get it.

We want to guarantee private, not Government, insurance for every American. The plan I originally proposed has been changed, and much of it for the better. The proposals before Congress are less bureaucratic. They're more flexible. They provide more protection and support for small business. They contain a reasonable phase-in time, over a period of years, to make sure we get it right. No bureaucrat will pick your doctor. You can keep your own plan or pick a better one. This approach controls Government spending but relies on competitive forces in the free market to restrain the growth of private health insurance premiums. Much of it has changed for the better. But one rock-solid principle remains: private insurance guaranteed for everyone.

We know it will work. For 20 years Hawaii has required employers and employees to split the cost of insuring all employees. People still pick their doctors there. Health care is getting better there. The economy is doing well there. And almost everything in Hawaii is more expensive than it is here on the mainland, except for health insurance, where small businesses pay health insurance costs that are, on average, 30 percent lower than they are in the rest of America.

Now, after 60 years of trying and 18 months of sometimes trying debate, the question of guaranteeing coverage for all Americans has come to the floor of the Congress and will be decided in the next few weeks in a few critical votes. The votes will be soon and they will be close. I want to urge the American people to tell their Senators and Congressmen to put aside partisanship and think of the American people and their fundamental interests and needs. We have an historic opportunity. We dare not pass it up. This is a fight for the American people we also have to win.

Health Care Legislation

Q. Mr. President, in January, you waved a pen and said you would veto legislation that didn't guarantee every American private health insurance that could never be taken away. Now you've indicated you will support a Senate bill that does not guarantee coverage and sets a goal of 95 percent, leaving millions of Americans uninsured. Are you now revising your veto threat? And doesn't the fact that you indicated you'd support this less ambitious Senate plan make it harder for House Members to go along with a bill that's more like your original proposal?

The President. Well, first of all, I disagree with your characterization of the Mitchell bill. I believe it will achieve universal coverage for all Americans, and that is the one criteria I have set out. What the Mitchell bill says is, is that if you make a dramatic amount of progress in a short time—that is, if you move from where we are now, at about 83 percent of coverage, up to 95 percent in a few years— that is evidence that we can achieve full coverage in the near future without requiring insurance to be bought. That is what that bill says.

If it is deficit neutral, and if it is passed in the way that it is, I believe it will achieve full coverage, because what the bill also says is, if we don't make that amount of progress in a few years, there will be a requirement on the Congress to provide for full coverage, and if the Congress doesn't act, then automatically employers and employees will be required to purchase insurance. I believe it does meet the objective I set out in the State of the Union Address, and I would sign it.

Q. What about the second part of the question, Mr. President? Doesn't it make the fact that you've now indicated support for a less ambitious Senate bill—won't that make it harder to persuade House people to go along with a stronger bill?

The President. Well, what the Mitchell bill does is to put the employer requirement at the end of the process, rather than at the beginning. And Senator Mitchell is convinced that that is the most ambitious bill he can pass, but that it meets the requirement; and it says to the people who have not been supportive of our approach, "Look, we'll try it in a competitive way first, and if that doesn't work, then we'll have a requirement." I think the same debate is going on in the House.

My own view is that the questions now should shift to the members of the other party, to the congressional Republicans. At one time, when we started this debate and I said I wanted universal coverage, many Members in Congress stood up and clapped, of both parties. At one time there were 2 dozen Republican Senators on a bill to give universal coverage to all Americans. They have all abandoned that bill. We have reached out to them, as was our responsibility to try to work together in a bipartisan fashion, and every time we have done it, they have moved away.

So the questions now should shift to them: Are we going to cover all Americans or not? Are we going to have a bill that provides health care security or not? If you don't like our approaches in the Senate and the House, what is your alternative? That's what I hope we'll see.

Haiti

Q. Mr. President, on Haiti, you sought and received the approval of the United Nations to launch an invasion if necessary. Why do you need a green light from the international community and not from the American Congress? Will you ask lawmakers to take it up?

The President. Well first, let me say that I agree with the resolution adopted by the Senate today that the action of the United Nations should not be interpreted as an approval by Congress. It has no impact on what Congress would do.

Second, let me say I think all Americans should be pleased that the United Nations has stated with a strong, firm voice—that includes many voices from our own area—that we should keep on the table the option of forcibly removing the dictators who had usurped power in Haiti and who have trampled human rights and murdered innocent people.

Now, let me remind you all of what our interests are there. We have Americans living and working there, several thousands of them. We have a million Haitian Americans in this country who have family and friends there. We have an interest in promoting democracy in our hemisphere. We have an interest in stabilizing those democracies that are in our hemisphere. For the first time ever, 33 of the 35 nations in the Caribbean and Central and South America are governed by popularly elected leaders, but many of those democracies are fragile. As we look ahead to the next century, we need a strong and democratic Latin America and Central

America and Caribbean with which to trade and grow.

So those are our fundamental interests. I would welcome the support of the Congress, and I hope that I will have that. Like my predecessors of both parties, I have not agreed that I was constitutionally mandated to get it. But at this moment I think we have done all we need to do because I don't want to cross that bridge until we come to it. We have kept force on the table. We have continued to move it up as an option as the dictators there have been more obstinate. But it is premature, in my judgment, to go beyond that now.

Whitewater Hearings

Q. President Clinton, a number of political analysts, including some who are quite friendly to you, have said that the focus on the Whitewater affair has both undercut public confidence in you and also in your ability to get your programs through Congress. Do you agree with that? And what impact do you think Whitewater has had, particularly with the hearings this week?

The President. Well, I would think, first of all, in the last couple of weeks it should have been very helpful to the administration because we have seen three reports: one from the Special Counsel, Mr. Fiske, who has said there was absolutely no violation of the law in any of these contracts; and then two, one by the Office of Government Ethics and one by Mr. Cutler, the White House Counsel, saying that no ethical rule was violated. Secondly, we have been fully cooperative as we always said we would be. So from my point of view, we've done all we could.

Now, I can't say what the impact has been. All I can tell you is that I said we would cooperate fully, and we have. I have said repeatedly that I did nothing wrong, and I didn't. And I have continued to work for the welfare and the interest of the American people.

Almost all—I've watched none of these hearings. I've not kept up with them. I've been working on jobs and health care and the crime bill and peace in the Middle East and doing the things I was hired to do by the American people. They will have to make up their mind when all the dust clears what they think the impact of it is. But I'm convinced we're having a very productive time. I think we'll get this crime bill. We have health care bills providing universal coverage on the floor of both Houses of Congress for the first time in the history of the Republic. No President since Harry Truman has been able to do that, and many have tried, including President Nixon. So I feel good about the progress we're making, and that's all I can worry about. I've got to get up there every day and go to work and try to help the American people.

Q. Mr. President, Roger Altman ran into a real buzz saw in the Whitewater hearings, and even some Democrats are questioning his truthfulness. Does he have the credibility to continue as number two at Treasury? Are you going to ask for his resignation?

The President. Well, let me say, first of all, he spoke with the Senate committee for more than 10 hours yesterday—that's a very long time—and he answered all of their questions. He then spoke for several hours with the House committee today. In that, he admitted that he had not given all the information to them in a timely fashion that he should have. But he said repeatedly that he had not willfully misled them.

I would like to emphasize, first of all, I do not countenance anybody being less than forthright with the Congress. There have been many people, including people that are not particularly friends of our administration, who have talked about how we have been much more cooperative with these investigations than previous administrations have been. That's what I told the American people I would do, and that is what I have done.

But if you look at the facts, let's go back to the fundamental facts: There was no violation of the law; there was no violation of any ethics rule. The Secretary of the Treasury has pointed out that Mr. Altman has done a superb job in his position. He was critical to the passage of our economic program that produced almost 4 million jobs in 18 months. He was important in the passage of our trade initiatives; he has done a good job there. The Secretary of the Treasury has confidence in him, and so do I. And I think he has now answered all the questions that the Senate could possibly have about an incident that involved no violation of the law and no violation of ethics.

Haiti

Q. Mr. President, to come back to Haiti for a moment, you mentioned a number of American interests that we have in Haiti. But what involves national security, if it's at stake? Is there anything in Haiti that involves our security that would require us to go in and invade the country?

The President. Well first of all, I think our security is caught up in whether people in this hemisphere are moving toward democracy and open markets and observation of the rule of law. And when one country in our hemisphere, on our back door, has an election, votes for a leader, then that leader is deposed by people who murder, who kill, who rape, who maim, who throw the human rights monitors out, who now won't even let people leave who have been approved for leaving, it seems to me that if you look at the possible ramifications of that on other countries in the Caribbean and in Central and South America, that is where our security interest is.

I can tell you that as I was calling other nations to get them to help in the Safe Haven project, to be willing to take some Haitians who leave, that is the thing that other leaders mentioned to me over and over again, "We know that many of our democracies are fragile, but we're moving in the right direction. We don't want to see Latin America take one more wrong turn. We're moving right; we want to stay right." And I think that is profoundly important to us.

North Korea

Q. Mr. President, in just another few weeks we will know whether North Korea has transformed more fuel rods into weapons-grade plutonium. What are the consequences if North Korea does make more weapons-grade plutonium, and are you prepared to carry out that threat?

The President. I think I can do no better than to reiterate what I have always said, that North Korea's fate is still in its own hands; it must decide what it own future should be. I think at this time when North Korea has shown a willingness to stop reprocessing and to stop refueling, and when our talks are about to begin again next Friday, we should take the facts as we have them and keep working for progress.

This is an issue which is very important to the long-term security of the United States. The question of a country that belongs to the nonproliferation regime deciding to become a nuclear power, the prospect that nuclear capacity could be transferred either by design or by accident to other countries or to rogue groups, this is a very serious thing for our long-term security. And we have spent a lot of time to make sure we are firm and deliberate; but that firmness, that deliberateness has led to these talks, which were interrupted when Kim Il-song passed away. We start the talks again on Friday. The agreement the North Koreans made is still holding about refueling and reprocessing. I think we should focus on that now and keep working for a satisfactory conclusion.

Q. Are you confident that we will know whether they violate these agreements?

The President. Yes, I am. I believe that. I have no reason to believe that we will not know if that agreement is violated.

President's Approval Rating

Q. Mr. President, as you pointed out in your opening statement, the economy has been growing. Last week we saw the peace agreement, or the framework for a peace agreement between Israel and Jordan. Yet your approval rating continues to slide in the polls. To what do you attribute that? Is it the message? Is it the messengers? And a related part of that question: Has Leon Panetta made any recommendations to you for changes in the White House to improve things here?

The President. Well, first of all, I'm not the best judge of that. Maybe I'm just not as good a talker as you folks thought I was when I got elected President. Maybe there's so much going on it's hard for anything specific to get through. Maybe it's partly a function of the times in which we live.

Whenever we move from one historic era into another—at the end of World War I, at the end of World War II, moving into the cold war; now at the end of the cold war, moving toward the 21st century—our people are filled with a mixture of hope and concern. Almost every American is genuinely concerned about something now, whether it's their economic circumstances, their health care, insecurity over crime, concern about what's happening to the fabric of our society with so many children being born out of wedlock and so many families breaking down. There's something gripping the concern of most Americans. And when people have these balances going on, hope or fear, it is sometimes difficult to get through with the hope and the progress.

I can't worry about that. All I can do is to show up for work here every day and, as I

said today to the folks who rode the buses for health care, try to make this the home office of the "American association for ordinary citizens." And if I keep doing that, I think that the future will take care of itself. My only concern is to continue to be able to be effective, and that's what I will work for.

Brit [Brit Hume, ABC News].

Health Care Legislation

Q. Mr. President, on health care, there were indications on Capitol Hill today that time is now becoming an important factor; that there's a need to get legislative language, there's a need to get various budgetary estimates, and that it may be very difficult to get a vote before the end of this month. Are you prepared now to insist that Congress remain in session and not take its recess until there is action in both Houses?

The President. Well, my belief is that Senator Mitchell has done enough work on his bill, and that the House bill has been out there in its basic framework, so that the recess will probably have to be delayed, but could still occur. I do believe that they should and will stay here until they can take action on those bills, each House on its own bill. I believe that will happen, and I think that's a good thing, because that's a way of their putting the American people first, which is something I think should be done.

Dan [Dan Balz, Washington Post].

Q. A two-part question on health care: When you put your own health care plan forward, you said you wanted to build on the private insurance industry. The House bill that Congressman Gephardt has put forward could turn control of almost half the health care system over to the Federal Government. Why do you support that approach, as opposed to your original idea? And secondly, is Senator Mitchell's bill now your new bottom line, your new minimum? If there's anything less than that coming out of the Senate, would that draw a veto?

The President. Let me answer the second question. My goal has been what it has always been. I want a system that will take us to universal coverage. If it takes a few years to get there, that's fine with me. We don't want to mess it up; we want to have the chance to continue to work and strengthen the program along the way.

In the case of the House bill, as you know, I have always thought that we ought to allow every American to buy into the Federal Employees Health Insurance bill, which is essentially a private plan. The House bill offers a Medicare program, if you will, like the senior citizens buy into now, but only if people decide not to buy private health insurance. So it still has a preference for private health insurance, and I think that is consistent with what I think we should do. I still believe the best thing to do is to build more on the system that most of us have now.

Q. Which approach do you favor, the Mitchell approach or the Gephardt approach?

The President. Well, I'm not going to get into being a legislator. My job is to try to keep the American people's eye on the ball and to try to keep the Members of Congress working together. What I favor is now for our friends on the other side of the aisle and all the Democrats to get together, think about the interests of the American people and come up with a program that solves the problem.

Let me just say, if I might just stop for a moment and say I think it is terribly important in this debate when these issues tend to be complex and detailed to keep our eye on the central reality here, which is how do we solve the problem? I asked two of the people that rode those buses to come here tonight. I want them to just stand up, Daniel Lumley and John Cox.

And let me answer your question this way. Daniel Lumley was a young man who lost his arm riding a motorcycle. He wants to be a schoolteacher, he wants to be a public servant; he wants to know that he'll always be able to get health insurance when he works, even though he has a very apparent preexisting condition. Like millions and millions of Americans with disabilities, he can work and do fine and pay taxes—which releases the burden on the rest of us—if he can get insurance.

John Cox left his job with health insurance and went to work for a Christian radio station because he thought it was his mission in life to do that. He thought he was covered by health insurance and he thought his employer was paying it, and he wasn't. When his wife came down sick, because they didn't have health insurance even though he was working, they didn't go to the doctor. They just talked to a doctor over the phone for months and months. Finally, she became so ill they had to see a doctor at an emergency room. By that time she had cancer

that had progressed to the point when it could not be fully treated. He took this bus ride across the country when his wife was dying, because she wanted him to. She died during the bus ride. He buried her 2 days ago, and he came up here today to be with us. My answer to you is if the program works for John Cox and for Daniel Lumley, I'll be for it.

Whitewater Hearings

Q. Mr. President, if I could ask you a specific question on these Whitewater hearings, which I know you're not watching, but many of us were watching until 2 a.m. in the morning last night. One of the problems that Roger Altman, the Deputy Treasury Secretary, seems to have is that he didn't recuse himself or step down as chairman of the Resolution Trust Corporation because he feared that there could be some sort of appearance of a conflict. He had decided to step down, but was talked out of it by Bernard Nussbaum, your former Counsel, and other White House aides. That seems to be the source of a lot of problems that he has. And Josh Steiner, the Treasury Chief of Staff, says that you and the First Lady were furious that Roger Altman told the New York Times editorial writer about this decision before you learned about it. What was so bad about his decision to recuse himself if there was nothing that he could have done to interfere in the RTC investigation of Madison Guaranty Savings and Loan?

The President. First of all, I never would promote anybody interfering in any investigation. I welcome this investigation, and it will vindicate what I have been saying all along. I had no problem with Mr. Altman deciding of his own independent judgment and consultation with his superior, the Secretary of the Treasury, that he ought to recuse himself. The only thing that upset me was I did not want to see him stampeded into it if it wasn't the right thing to do. I just wanted the decision to be made on the merits. I think it's a pretty simple, straightforward position I had, and I think it was the right one.

Baseball Strike

Q. Mr. President, Atlanta Braves owner Ted Turner last week called on you to intervene with Government arbitration to head off a baseball strike. Now that your Labor Secretary has met with both sides of the talks, do you see any Government role in this matter? Do you see anything that you personally can do to head off a strike?

The President. Let me say first of all, just as a lifelong baseball fan, I suppose I have a greater interest in this than maybe a President even should. I mean, the prospect of seeing records that are 30 and 40 years old broken, for those of us who like the offensive as well as the defensive side of baseball, this is an exhilarating thing. I think it would be heart-breaking for the American people if our national pastime didn't get through this whole season. And it's a great opportunity for these young players and what they can become.

Secondly, the Secretary of Labor, as you pointed out, did meet with the representatives of the players and the owners. And we discussed what could be done and tried to facilitate a better communications between them. There may be some other things which can be done, but at this time the situation is sufficiently delicate that I think we need to leave it at that. If we can play a constructive role, we will. We do not want to play a destructive role. We all hope that somehow the strike can be averted.

Health Care Legislation

Q. Mr. President, there are many Democratic Members of the House, your allies, who disagree with you, they don't believe that Senator Mitchell's bill is a universal coverage bill. Are you ready to tell them that you think that Senator Mitchell's bill is the best that can possibly come out of Congress this year?

The President. Well, first of all, let's remember how a bill becomes law. [*Laughter*] It's very important. Senator Mitchell has to find a majority for a bill that can pass the Senate. Then there must be a majority of people supporting a bill that passes the House. The Senate task is very hard because, except on the budget, a tiny minority—41 percent of the Senate—can keep any other bill from even coming to a vote. He has a difficult task. Then the bill goes to a conference and a final bill will come back and will be voted on in both Houses. We have seen many times how a bill passes the House, a bill passes the Senate, a final one comes out that's different from either one. We don't know what will happen.

Let me tell you what I hope will happen. What I hope will happen is that the debates on the floor of the Senate and the House will be widely publicized, heavily watched, and that

the debate will grip the imagination of ordinary American citizens who themselves may not be part of any discrete interest group; and that there will be a climate in the country welling up—as I believe it is now—for action that works, that solves the human problem.

I believe George Mitchell, as many of the Senators pointed out, in a situation in which every time he tried to do something, the members of the other party moved away from a position they had previously had—normally when a bill becomes law, if you take one position and the people in the other party take another, you move toward them, they move toward you, you work out an agreement. Here's a case where we had 24 Senators of the other party committed to universal coverage and they have all abandoned the plan they were originally for. And as he has moved toward them, they have moved away. In that environment, I think he has done a fine job with a bill that I personally believe will achieve universal coverage. And that's all I can say. It is my opinion that it will work.

Whitewater Hearings

Q. Mr. President, strictly from a management standpoint, given the conflicting recollections of the various members of the Treasury Department team, do you believe they can continue to work together effectively?

The President. Well, the management of the Treasury Department is under the jurisdiction of the Secretary of the Treasury. All I can tell you is, the important thing for the American people is the Treasury Department has worked very well. Nearly every American, nearly every expert in this town believes that it has worked very well across a whole broad range of issues, and that the Secretary of the Treasury has done an absolutely superb job in both domestic and international economic arenas with the support of his team. The management questions are things that he will have to resolve. But I will say again, there was no violation of the law, there was no violation of the ethics rules. The errors which were made have been acknowledged and questions have been answered at extreme length. I think that is a very good thing.

Health Care Reform

Q. You've worked hard to open new markets for American businesses. Are you upset or disappointed that businesses have worked so hard against health care reform?

The President. No, because not all businesses have. It is true we have worked hard to open markets for business with NAFTA, with the new worldwide GATT agreement, selling our airplanes, selling our high-tech equipment, reviving our shipbuilding industry—all the things we've done. But frankly, I think the amazing story of this health care debate is not that there are still some business interests against it, but that we have more business interests for it than ever before. Let me just say that many of the Fortune 500 companies support the idea that every business should do what it can to cover the employee and the employee should pay something. We now have 600,000 small businesses who cover their employees and are paying too much, who have come out for our position that all of their colleagues should do the same.

I think that is very impressive. When you look at that plus all the other medical groups that have come out for our approach, it is a truly astonishing thing. And what I hope is, again, when this debate starts that all the people who are doing for something, instead of just against something, I hope that they will prevail.

Press Conferences

Q. Mr. President, will you tell us why you hold so few solo press conferences? This is only your third, and you have been heard to complain that the lords of the right-wing radio have uninterrupted communication with the American people. And you have the same chance but don't take it. Could you tell us why?

The President. I think it's a mistake, and I intend to do more on a more regular basis. Besides that, I actually enjoy these, and I think we should do more and do them on a more regular basis, and I intend to. It's one of the changes that I intend to make.

Health Care Legislation

Q. Mr. President—all right, sir. I wanted to just tell you——

The President. I could hear you in the distance. [*Laughter*]

Q. I've just been informed by a volunteer who knows what she's talking about, Mrs. B.A. Bentsen, wife of the Secretary of the Treasury—she works to get prenatal care for millions of mothers. And she says that the money, the Government money has run out completely for pre-

natal care, which means that we will have deformed babies that we will have to pay for the rest of their lives in institutions. Can't you do something about this?

The President. Well, of course we can. One of the things that this health care bill will do, either one of them, would be to cover more prenatal care. One of the biggest problems we have in the United States, with about one in six of our people without health insurance, is that a lot of people don't get preventive care when they should. It is true that when women see the doctor several times before their babies are born, the babies are far more likely to be born healthy and at normal birth weight. And that is a focus of both bills. Senator Mitchell's bill, because of the phase-in time, went out of its way to try to take care of that issue.

Syria

Q. Mr. President, if I could go back to a foreign policy issue. Syria appears to be the big missing piece of the puzzle in the Middle East now. Following the meeting between the Israeli Prime Minister and King Hussein of Jordan, do you see any indication that Syria wants to make peace at this point? Do you see any reason for optimism that they're willing to talk directly to Israel?

The President. I think there are difficult issues still between Israel and Syria, but I believe both leaders do want to make peace. As you know, before I announced that King Hussein and Prime Minister Rabin would come here to end their state of war and to commit to establishing full peace, I had a long talk with President Asad on the telephone. I then spoke with him again. I am convinced that he is still very much interested in a comprehensive peace. And we have one piece of public evidence of that, which is that the whole ceremony between Israel and Jordan signing the Washington Declaration was shown on television in Syria without comment. We have other indications that they are. And you may be sure that the Secretary of State and Dennis Ross and all of our team, as well as I, are doing everything we can to keep pushing that.

Q. What are those other indications, sir?

The President. I don't think I should say more than that. We've been pretty successful in the Middle East by letting the parties make their own decisions and letting them percolate up.

Health Care Legislation

Q. You may not be a legislator, but you are the titular head of the Democratic Party. Why should you ask Democrats in the House for marginal constituencies to vote for the Gephardt bill when, in fact, the Mitchell bill may be more politically palatable?

The President. Well, let me say, again, the Senate and the House are going to debate both these bills, and they will work through the process and decide where to come out. But let me say, if you just take Mr. Cox there, he's from Athens, Texas. Now, Athens, Texas, is no different from New York City or San Francisco, California, or my home in Arkansas when it comes to the existence of people who have these problems. And I think the House and the Senate should each pass a bill which they can best explain to their folks back home as something that solves the problem.

I would remind you that we know that universal coverage is popular with the American people. What we also know is that they're concerned about having something that changes something so fundamental in their lives. They want to make sure we fix what is wrong, keep what is right. So in both bills we have reassured the rank-and-file voters. Both bills in different ways may offend various organized interest groups who may be able to advertise and affect the attitudes of rank-and-file voters, but we know that both these bills, by having a longer phase-in time, less bureaucracy, more flexibility and more support for small business, clear choice of plans, that those things have answered the concerns of American voters in every congressional district in the country.

Haiti

Q. Congressman Bill Richardson went recently to Haiti and met for, I think, 5 hours with General Cédras, and he came back and he said Cédras was not an intransigent man. He has been invited to return to Haiti. Has he talked to you about it, and would you consider it a good idea for him to go back to Haiti now that the U.N. has passed this resolution?

The President. I have talked to Congressman Richardson. I have no comment about any further trips. It is difficult to conclude that Mr. Cédras is not intransigent. After all, he promised to leave Haiti on October 30th at the implementation of the Governors Island accord, and he broke his promise. And he has continued to visit untold misery on his people. He knows what to do to end the problems of the people of Haiti, and he can do it.

Economic Plan

Q. Mr. President, earlier this year, last year, rather, in your economic program, you sacrificed a lot of your investment program to get deficit reduction, as we've learned, over the objections of many of those on your staff. The deficit reduction part has worked out even better than you expected, as you said. But since that time the stock market has drifted lower, long-term interest rates are higher than when you took office, and there are some signs of a slow-down on the horizon. Housing starts and new home sales, for example, are down. At this point, do you think perhaps you make a mistake that you went too far into deficit reduction and that, from your point of view, the country might have been better off had you put more money into infrastructure and into investment?

The President. Absolutely not. Given the options that we had, the right decision was made. Let me take you back in time. We had had the slowest job growth rate for the previous 4 years that we'd had since the Great Depression. The economy was going down; the deficit was going up. Our position in the global economy depended on our ability to get the deficit down. Our ability to generate private economic activity depended on our ability to drive interest rates down.

If someone had told any economist a year and a half ago that we could create almost 4 million jobs, take the unemployment rate down over a point and a half, have no inflation and still have long-term rates almost exactly where they were on the date I took office, no one would have believed that. They'd say if you're going to improve the economy that much, long-term interest rates will go way up.

Because we were committed to bringing the deficit down without inflation, interest rates went way down, and then when we had a lot of economic growth, came back up some. The stock market is higher than it was when I took office, and the long-term expectations are very good.

Most businesses expect to grow next year, both large and small. Every survey shows that. Consumer confidence and business confidence and long-term economic growth are high. The rate of growth may vary from time to time. My job is to keep the growth going and keep jobs coming into the economy and that is what we are doing.

Q. [*Inaudible*]—betrayed your Democratic heritage or your campaign promises?

The President. No.

Q. Do you feel that you're an Eisenhower Republican, as a recent book put it?

The President. No. I think we did the right thing. In the 21st century most job growth is going to come from the private sector. We will have to do more public work in two areas: in infrastructure, just like all of our competitors do, our roads, our bridges, our airports, the things that make you a rich and powerful country; our telecommunications infrastructure that the Vice President's always talking about will have to have various supports. The second thing we'll have to do is we'll have to give more direct or indirect support to create jobs in high unemployment areas. That's what our empowerment zones are all about: enticing people through tax incentives to invest in areas where unemployment is high.

But I would remind you we have increased programs for education and training. We have dramatically increased the availability of low-interest college loans. We have increased the number of people who can apply for national service loans. We have increased Head Start. We have increased immunization eligibility for little kids by millions. We have increased spending on the things which are critical to our future.

Will we have to invest more there? We will. But first we had to get our economic house in order. You cannot keep spending money you don't have and expect to get ahead of the game. We have now done that, and we can focus on investment.

Defense Executive Salaries

Q. Thank you, sir.

The President. You're persistent. I owe it to you just for effort. You'd develop arthritis getting up and down so many times if I didn't— [*laughter*].

Q. Thank you, sir. If I may shift to a fresh subject, the Senate Appropriations Committee is hopping mad about what it calls outrageously high salaries that are being paid to defense and aerospace company executives in this country,

compensation that is frequently paid by the taxpayers under Defense Department regulations, and sometimes to the tune of as much as $7 million or more. The committee is offering language which would rule out payments any higher than the salary that the Defense Secretary makes. Do you agree with the committee's finding? And would you support that kind of limit?

The President. I'm not familiar enough with the issue to give you an intelligent answer. I will look into it, and I'll be glad to give you an answer. But I don't know enough about the issue to answer the question in an appropriate way.

Corporate Megamergers

Q. Mr. President, okay—[*laughter*].

The President. I can't believe a member of the press is pushing a microphone away. This is a historic moment in itself. [*Laughter*]

Q. Mr. President, what is the administration doing to stop the megamergers, particularly in the telecommunications industry, in the pharmaceutical industry, and in retailing? We have seen Viacom-Paramount. We now have—Macy's is trying, and we're reading today about American Cyanamid merging with American Home Products, mergers which are not in the interest of the public and the stockholders. And in the case of Macy's, Macy's Federated has a stockholder meeting on the same day as major competitors. They don't want stockholders to come and ask questions. They're in collusion with the competitors, and the administration is not lifting one finger.

The President. Well, you've drawn a lot of conclusions there in a short time. I don't know if I can answer them all. Let me say this: There are two ways in which mergers can be not in the interest of the people of the United States. First is if they violate our antitrust laws; that is, if they do significant damage to the competitive environment. And our administration has tried to reinvigorate the antitrust division of the Justice Department to a significantly higher level than in the last two administrations.

Secondly is, as you suggest, is if there is some illegal erosion of the rights and interests of the stockholders of these companies, or there are workers or others that have legal rights that are being undermined. That is within the jurisdiction of the Securities and Exchange Commission. I think we have a very able person chairing that Commission.

I would be glad to ask them to look into these things more than I'm sure they already are, but I am not in a position to draw the conclusions you have drawn, because I think they are trying to protect the public interest.

Health Care Legislation

Q. There are 37 million uninsured Americans. If you can't get a bill that will cover all of them, and you get one that will cover, say, 20 million, would you really refuse to sign it? And if you do, and don't get a bill at all, how would you explain that to those 20 million?

The President. First of all, keep in mind that most of our problem is with working Americans. And the problem with the so-called "half a loaf" here is that it won't work. That is, we have evidence now in the States—about 40 States have tried to just change the rules on insurance and put a little more money into covering very poor people to increase health care coverage. No one could say that is not good on its own, but the problem is if that is all you do, what has happened in the States is that putting people into a health insurance pool who cost more to insure without expanding the size of the pools leads to higher rates. Once the rates get higher, small businesses on the margin and individuals who are young and healthy get out. That makes the pool even smaller; and rates go up more.

So what would happen, I am convinced, if we did what you suggest is what has happened in the States. Coverage would go up a little bit for a while; then it would go right back down, as it has in the United States for the last 5 years as States have tried to do this.

So, again, I say we have no evidence that unless we are moving toward full coverage that we can control cost and maintain coverage for the working families of the country.

Yes, one more. We're almost out of time.

Haiti

Q. You spoke with some thoroughness tonight about why you think it is in the United States interest to not have a military dictatorship in Haiti. My question is, if an invasion force is dispatched and overthrows that military regime, what are the United States obligations at that point to nurture, to create an environment in that troubled country where democracy would have a chance? And how long would this last?

The President. I think the United States have significant obligations. But if you look at the United Nations resolution and what we have said all along, over the long run what we need is a United Nations mission in Haiti that the United States would be a part of, but that other countries would participate in also, that would do the following things: Number one, it would have to retrain and reorient the military to engaged in the rebuilding of the country. Number two, it would have to reorient and retrain the police to be a genuine police force, not an instrument of terror for one political group. Number three, we would have to, in addition to that, have a real dedicated effort led by a lot of our Haitian-Americans and others to rebuild the troubled economy of Haiti, which is in terrible, terrible shape. All those things we would have to do. But it would not necessarily be the United States doing it. In fact, it could not be; it would be a United Nations mission as envisaged by the United Nations and the resolution that they adopted.

Thank you very much.

Q. Mr. President, can I follow up here—one last question on health care?

The President. One last question on health care? [*Laughter*] Did I recognize you earlier?

Q. You did, but it's a——

The President. Oh, no—I've got to go. [*Laughter*]

NOTE: The President's 68th news conference began at 8 p.m. in the East Room at the White House. In his remarks, he referred to Leon E. Panetta, Chief of Staff to the President, and Dennis B. Ross, Director, Policy Planning Staff, Department of State.

Statement on National Science Policy
August 3, 1994

The return from our public investment in fundamental science has been enormous. The principal sponsors and beneficiaries are the American people. Our scientific investments are an important national resource which we must sustain and build on for the future.

NOTE: This statement was included in a White House statement announcing the release of the national science policy report, "Science in the National Interest."

Appointment for the President's Committee of Advisors on Science and Technology
August 3, 1994

The President today announced the membership of a private-sector committee to advise him on major science and technology issues and to help guide Federal investments in science and technology toward national goals. The 18-member President's Committee of Advisors on Science and Technology (PCAST) is composed of top-level representatives from industry, education and research institutions, and nongovernmental organizations.

"I am very pleased to name these eminent scientists, engineers, business leaders, and educators as some of my key advisers," the President said. "Drawn from a cross-section of America, they will help ensure that our science and technology policies reflect our Nation's needs: health, prosperity based on long-term economic growth and technological investment, national security, environmental responsibility, and improved quality of life."

The appointment of private-sector advisers to the President highlights the administration's goal of fostering public/private partnerships to achieve national science and education goals. "To achieve our goals, we must strengthen partnerships with industry, with State and local governments, and with schools, colleges, and universities across the country," said the President.

"My goal for this committee is to help encourage those partnerships."

NOTE: The following persons were appointed to PCAST:

John H. Gibbons, Assistant to the President for Science and Technology (Cochair)
John A. Young (Cochair)
Norman R. Augustine
Francisco J. Ayala
Murray Gell-Mann
David A. Hamburg
John P. Holdren
Diana MacArthur
Shirley M. Malcom
Mario J. Molina
Peter H. Raven
Sally K. Ride
Judith Rodin
Charles A. Sanders
Phillip A. Sharp
David E. Shaw
Charles M. Vest
Virginia V. Weldon
Lilian Shiao-Yen Wu

Biographies of the appointees were made available by the Office of the Press Secretary.

Remarks Honoring Recipients of the Young American Medals for Bravery and Service
August 4, 1994

Thank you. Thank you so much, General Reno. And thank you, ladies and gentlemen, for being here. I would like to thank Janet Reno for the superb job she has done as the Attorney General of the United States and for the human face she has put on law enforcement in this country and the understanding she has brought as a career prosecutor to this work, the understanding that really is embodied in these awards today, which is that we have a job to do here in Washington but what really makes America great and what really makes America work is what happens on the streets, in the schools, in the neighborhoods, in the workplaces of America every day.

I want to thank the Director of our Office of Drug Policy, Lee Brown, for being here; two Congressmen from the areas of two of the honorees today, Congressman Jerry Costello of Illinois and Congressman Steve Schiff of New Mexico, thank you for being here. I understand the Mayor of Belleville, Illinois, Roger Cook, is here. I thank the members of the Young American Medals Committee; the Administrator of the DEA, Tom Constantine; and Eduardo Gonzalez, the Director of the Marshals Service, who are also here.

Last year was my first opportunity to engage in this ceremony. I just loved it. And the Attorney General was right. This job of mine is an interesting and diverse job, and on most days it's quite a wonderful job. But it rarely is so filled with joy as when you can recognize the wonder of the work of our young people.

I think of our mission here in our administration at this time as the timeless one of trying to secure a future for our young people, so that every person in this country, without regard to their region or race or income or background, can live up to the fullest of their God-given abilities. In this time, at the end of the cold war and at the beginning of a new era that is not yet fully clear to Americans, moving into a global economy with new opportunities and, to be sure, new troubles as well, that means as a minimum that here we have to restore economic growth and opportunity. We have to help people to rebuild the strength of our com-

munities and our families. We have to empower individuals to do more for themselves. In short, we've got to make this Government work for ordinary citizens in a world we're working to make more peaceful and prosperous.

Now, in the last few weeks, we've had some pretty good news on that. Our economy is clearly coming back. For the first time in 10 years it's predicted that all 50 States will have economic growth next year. We had a peace agreement signed here between Jordan and Israel last week, which must have brought joy to the hearts of every American that has seen that troubled region torn for so long. There are many good things happening. The largest, toughest, smartest crime bill in the history of the United States is in final debating stages and about to be voted on in the Congress. For the first time in the history of our country, both Houses of Congress are considering a bill to provide health care coverage to all Americans.

But still, we have to recognize that in the end it is still true that the strength of this country is what happens on Main Street, what happens in the schools, what happens where ordinary Americans live and work.

Today we celebrate the best of our young people for their courage and their commitment. We know that life requires both to be fully successful. And we know that our country is still around now after 218 years because we've been blessed with an abundance of both.

I must tell you that when I got up this morning and, as is my custom early in the morning, I wandered around, I did some of my routine, and then I sat and read the schedule for the day and I read the stories of these young people, I was reminded of a line that I used in my Inaugural Address but sometimes here in the heat of battle I forget: "There is nothing wrong with this country that cannot be fixed by what is right with this country." Today we honor in dramatic and breathtaking fashion what is right with this country.

The first recipient of the Young American Medal for Bravery is Carlo Montez Clark of Belleville, Illinois. He was on his way to a convenience store when he noticed smoke coming from a nearby building. He tried twice to get into the building, but was overcome by smoke. Finally, on the third try he got into the building, risking his own life, and saved the life of an elderly woman who suffered from emphysema. Let's give him a big hand. [*Applause*] Thank you.

Now I would like to recognize, for service, Robyn Mae Davis of Albuquerque, New Mexico. She's worked hard to spread the important message of the dangers of alcohol abuse among young people. She tried to get the New Mexico State Fair to refrain from serving alcohol for a day or so; they declined. So she organized a human chain around the New Mexico State Fair in protest of their policy. As a result, for 4 days the fair was completely alcohol-free. I wonder if she would like to join my congressional lobbying staff. [*Laughter*] Good for you, Robyn, and congratulations.

Our second winner of the Young American Medal for Bravery is Brandon Sisco of Texarkana, Texas. When Brandon's school bus made a routine stop, a young girl got off the bus and was attacked by two ferocious dogs. She was bitten many times. Brandon jumped off the bus and bravely fought off the dogs, guided the 6-year-old to safety inside the bus where he comforted her until paramedics arrived. At considerable risk to himself, he saved the young girl's life. Let's give him a round of applause. [*Applause*]

Our final recipient is Amanda Stewart of Keyes, Oklahoma. In 1990 Amanda was para-lyzed in a car accident. She began a three-State campaign to raise consciousness regarding the dangers of drinking and driving. She told her peers they should think first about getting into a car with someone who had been drinking. She asked them to think before driving off first without fastening a seat belt. After an experience which would have crushed the spirits and broken the will of many people, even people 2 or 3 times her age, this brave and beautiful young woman has doubtless inspired countless young people to change their behavior, to secure a better future for themselves. And in the process, she has exercised influence, power, and goodness far beyond anything that anyone might have imagined. Thank you, Amanda, for your commitment and your courage.

Ladies and gentlemen, let me close with what I always think of at moments like this. These young people have reminded us, as the Attorney General has said, of the power of one person to make a difference. Each of us in our own way have that power. And I think we would all admit, starting with the President, that every day at the end of the day we have done less than we might have done to exercise that power that is within us all, divinely inspired and given to us for whatever time we're on this Earth. Let's look at them and remember our obligations to make the most of every day.

Thank you, and bless you all.

NOTE: The President spoke at 4:32 p.m. in the East Room at the White House.

Memorandum on the Civil Rights Working Group
August 4, 1994

Memorandum for the Heads of Executive Departments and Agencies

Subject: Civil Rights Working Group

I am writing to you about our responsibility to promote equal opportunity for all Americans. We have accomplished much in our pursuit of a society in which all our people can achieve their God-given potential. But we still have a long way to go.

Americans believe that in spite of our differences, there is in all of us a common core of humanity that obliges us to respect one another and to live in harmony and peace. We must build on this belief and give real meaning to civil rights by tearing down all remaining barriers to equal opportunity—in education, employment, housing, and every area of American life.

Throughout the Nation, each of us must bring new energy to our efforts to promote an open and inclusive society. Those of us who are public servants have a special obligation. At the Federal level, we will do this by re-evaluating the civil rights missions, policies, and resources of every agency, so that they carry out their missions in a manner consistent with the Administration's commitment to equal opportunity. In reviewing our activities, we must seek not only to eliminate barriers to equal access and opportunity, but also to identify opportunities for innovation. No Federal office should be exempt from the obligation to further the struggle for civil rights. And every State and local government should be encouraged to do the same.

On January 17, 1994, I issued an Executive order establishing a President's Fair Housing Council to be chaired by the Secretary of Housing and Urban Development. Working across agencies and programs, this Council will bring new focus and leadership to the administration of the Federal Government's fair housing programs. On February 11, 1994, I issued an Executive order directing agencies to develop strategies to identify, analyze, and address environmental inequities that are the result of Federal policies. That order will increase public participation in the environmental decision-making process.

In addition to these efforts, I believe more can be done to exercise leadership for civil rights enforcement. That is why I hereby establish a Civil Rights Working Group, under the auspices of the Domestic Policy Council, to evaluate and improve the effectiveness of Federal civil rights enforcement missions and policies. The Civil Rights Working Group will identify barriers to equal access, impediments to effective enforcement of the law, and effective strategies to promote tolerance and understanding in our communities and workplaces. More important, I expect the Working Group to develop new approaches to address these issues.

The principal focus of the Working Group will be our civil rights enforcement efforts. We must recognize, however, that public and private enforcement resources will never be fully adequate to the task, and all of the remaining obstacles to opportunity cannot be removed through litigation alone. Therefore, I direct the Working Group to identify innovative strategies that can leverage our limited resources to provide new avenues for equal opportunity and equal rights. Among those potential strategies are new measures relying on civic education and voluntary efforts to engage citizens in overcoming the effects of past discrimination. These new strategies

should be designed to complement our improved and reinvigorated enforcement efforts.

The Attorney General and the Director of the Office of Management and Budget will co-chair the Working Group. The following Administration officials will serve as members: the Secretary of the Treasury, the Secretary of Commerce, the Secretary of Agriculture, the Secretary of the Interior, the Secretary of Education, the Secretary of Health and Human Services, the Secretary of Housing and Urban Development, the Secretary of Labor, the Secretary of Transportation, the Secretary of Veterans Affairs, the Administrator of the Environmental Protection Agency, the Chair of the Equal Employment Opportunity Commission, the Assistant to the President for Economic Policy, the Assistant to the President for Domestic Policy, and the Assistant to the President and Director of Public Liaison. I also have invited the Chairperson of the Commission on Civil Rights to participate in this crucial endeavor on an informal basis, respecting the independent and critical voice we expect of that Commission. Finally, this membership list is not exclusive. I invite and encourage all Cabinet officers and agency heads to participate in the Working Group.

The Working Group will advise appropriate Administration officials and me on how we might modify Federal laws and policies to strengthen protection under the laws and on how to improve coordination of the vast array of Federal programs that directly or indirectly affect civil rights. I direct the Working Group to provide the Cabinet and me with a brief progress report no less than every 6 months, and specifically to:

(a) examine each Federal agency with a significant civil rights mission and provide me with an evaluation of how well that mission is being implemented. These analyses should examine whether each agency uses the experience gained from enforcement activities of other agencies and other levels of government. Counterproductive and inconsistent practices should be identified and proposals for change recommended;

(b) examine cross-cutting civil rights law enforcement challenges such as voting rights and equal access to government benefit programs and identify innovative means of coordinating and leveraging resources;

(c) develop better measures of performance for Federal civil rights enforcement programs, taking into account the real impact of programs on the daily lives of all Americans; and

(d) support and advise all agencies as we reinvent our strategies for the promotion of an open and inclusive society.

With this interagency effort, I underscore the commitment of this Administration to bring new energy and imagination to the opportunity agenda. In departments and agencies throughout the Federal Government, this work is already well underway. The Working Group will provide a mechanism to expand and accelerate that vital work. Its work will be among our greatest contributions to the people we serve.

WILLIAM J. CLINTON

Statement by the Press Secretary on Support From Economists for Prompt Ratification of the GATT Agreement
August 4, 1994

The President received a letter today from 446 economists urging Congress to approve the Uruguay Round agreement immediately. The President welcomed their support, saying, "Economists know that the GATT agreement will help ensure long-term economic growth for America. GATT will add as much as $100 to $200 billion to the United States economy every year when fully implemented. That means hundreds of thousands of new jobs for American workers. Congress should pass GATT now so that the American people can begin to reap the benefits of expanded world trade as soon as possible."

Three of the economists signing the letter had also signed the famous 1930 letter to President Hoover that warned against passage of the Smoot-Hawley Tariff Act. The President expressed his appreciation for their counsel: "In his NAFTA debate last year, Vice President Gore made clear that the Smoot-Hawley Act sharply increased U.S. tariffs and helped touch off the Great Depression. More than 60 years ago, these three men were wise enough to champion free trade and economic growth in the face of tremendous public opposition. We should heed their advice today and pass the GATT now."

NOTE: The letter from the economists was also made available by the Office of the Press Secretary.

Remarks on the Anniversary of the Passage of the Economic Program
August 5, 1994

Well, thank you all. We've established one thing beyond doubt. We all have enough sense to come in out of the rain. [*Laughter*]

Thank you, Mr. Quimby, and thank all of you. We've had representatives of four fine companies speak here today: the head of one of our largest corporations; the head of a medium-sized high-tech company, growing and growing into the world economy; the head of a small company that's doubled the number of—or now a man that's moved from a small job to a large job in a small company that's growing very rap-idly; and a new employee. The Vice President and I wanted these folks here for this announcement today because they represent what our efforts are all about.

I said the other night in my press conference that there are a lot of lobby groups in Washington, but I wanted the White House to be known as the "home office of the 'American association of ordinary citizens.'" And what I mean by that is that in this time of profound change, what we need to be doing is figuring out how we can make the changes necessary together to enable all of our people to live up to their potential, to fulfill their dreams, to move into the next century with the American dream alive in every family and with American leadership secure. And when I sought this job, I was convinced that would require some changes in my political party, some change in the other political party, and some changes in the way we do our work here in Washington.

If you listen to the four stories here, that's really what's behind all these arcane arguments and all the political rhetoric over economic policy: the simple question of whether people will be able to pursue their destinies and their dreams and live up to the fullest of their abilities. I could never hope to say it any better than these four people did, and I think we should give them all another round of applause. [*Applause*]

Today, we celebrate because this morning, as the chart to my left shows, the Labor Department reported that since our administration came into office, our economy has produced more than 4 million new jobs, almost all of them in the private sector. Now, as we know, when I ran for office, I said I thought we could produce 8 million new jobs in 4 years and that we would do 4 by the end of '94. So we're 6 months ahead of schedule.

I do want to correct one thing. You know, I get criticized sometimes for my attention to detail, but I want to show you this. Where is it? I asked for this pen this morning when I looked at this chart because when I looked at the numbers, there are actually not 4 million new jobs but 4.1 million new jobs. And now that we're out of the rain, I'm going to make a correction on it.

Manufacturing jobs have been increasing in this country for 7 months in a row now for the first time in 10 years. All the jobs created last month, 100 percent of them, were in the private sector, not in government. Companies like Kenlee Precision have added those second and third shifts, jobs that made it possible for people like Charles Quimby to get ahead. Companies like Ellicott Machine have been able to hire new workers like Frankie McLaurin. Executives like Bob Eaton and Carol Bartz are making a good beginning in this remarkable partnership we have to renew America. And they described to you, perhaps better than I could, what the role of the National Government is in their

agenda for the future, what we should be doing and what we should not be doing.

None of this has been easy. Indeed, I have been mystified since I got here about why some of these things are as hard as they are and why they take as long as they do. One of the problems is that in this town, sometimes words replace reality. In the computer business and in high technology, virtual reality is a very good thing. It enables you to replicate situations and to avoid future problems. In Washington, I'm not sure we have virtual reality; I think what we have up here is virtual unreality, which is a bad thing because it enables you to almost dehumanize problems and turn them into words and rhetoric and labels. And we have all these word battles up here that don't seem to make any sense to ordinary people.

Once in a while I watch the evening news and—I'm usually working when it's on—once in a while I watch it, and I see the way we're presented, and I look at that and I say, well, heck, if I was still back home I wouldn't be for that guy either. [*Laughter*] Just because of the way it all plays out. You know, it's so—it's kind of unreal. And what we've got to do is find ways to bring reality, your reality, the way you look at the world, the way you live with the world every day, into the decisionmaking of this town.

And that's what we did when we passed that economic plan. Bob Eaton had it right. He said, well, he wouldn't have done it in the same way we did, but he was glad we got the job done. Well, that's the way I feel about his cars. I don't have any idea if I'd make the same decisions he makes on everything, but they make awful good cars and I'm glad they got the job done. In the end, that's the way we should judge ourselves.

And we did the best we could with that economic program, considering the fact that at the moment of voting we had no help from the other side. They said the sky would fall. One of them, and I quote, said, "Taxes will go up. The economy will sputter along. The deficit will reach another record high. It's a recipe for disaster." That was wrong. That was wrong.

What did we do? We did have a tax increase on the wealthiest Americans, but it's still—the rates are well below where they were in 1980. And all the money went to pay down the deficit and to finance a tax break for 15 million working families who were just above the poverty line, and we didn't want them to go back to welfare. We wanted to encourage people with low wages to keep working and to keep raising their kids and to stick by the American dream. There were too many people who were giving up work for welfare, and we wanted it to be the reverse. So I plead guilty to that.

We also cut $255 billion in spending, and we passed a tough budget that helped to drive those interest rates down, get this economy going again. This year, we're about to pass another tough budget that eliminates 100 Government programs outright, contains the first reduction in domestic discretionary spending in 25 years—outright reduction—and continues to drive that deficit down while increasing the money we're spending to empower people to succeed in the global economy: more for education and training, more for Head Start for little kids, the establishment of a lifetime learning system, for world-class standards in our public schools, more apprenticeships for young people who get out of high school and don't want to go to college. And our economic program made it possible for 20 million Americans to refinance their college loans at lower interest rates and better repayment terms. That is the direction in which we ought to be going.

And finally, as you heard Carol and Bob talking about, we're trying to expand the barriers of trade, or tear down the barriers and expand the frontiers. Frankie said that Ellicott was doing well largely because of NAFTA. They also said—a different group said that the sky would fall if we did that. But there we had a bipartisan majority fighting for change. We passed it. Our car sales in Mexico are growing 5 times as fast as they did before NAFTA was passed. Mexico is now our fastest growing trading partner. Even though their economy is in a down period, we're still having explosive growth. Think what it will be like when they start to grow again. This is very important.

We're trying to sell airplanes all around the world. We just announced a new shipbuilding initiative. The Trade Ambassador, Mr. Kantor, has resolved agricultural disputes with Canada. We're selling rice to Japan for the first time. We are moving in to the global economy, and we are working on these things. And I don't know that these things fall very neatly into the kind of words people throw at each other here in this town. Is it liberal or conservative, Republican or Democrat? I don't know, and I don't

care. I just want people to be able to work and to do well and to have this economy grow.

And I know to do that—when we have the deficit coming down for 3 years in a row for the first time since Truman was President, when we're moving toward the smallest Federal Government that we've had since Kennedy was President, and when the economy is growing this rapidly—last year we had more businesses formed than in any year since World War II—we're not doing bad. We've got to get rid of the rhetoric and go back to reality.

And I would say this: The future looks good. Fortune Magazine predicts for the first time in 10 years, the economy in every State in America will grow next year. And that is very good. Most businesses expect to grow next year and to expand. And consumer confidence is high.

But we have to continue to face the tough problems up here. And one of the things that I hope very much will happen is that the experience we had working through these economic problems and the results that have been achieved—when you take on a problem, risk some unpopularity in the short run, even if you win by the narrowest of margins, if you actually address a problem, you get results. That is very good because that proves that Washington is not all that unreal after all, that there really is some connection to our lives up here and the way you live where you are. Because if you ignore the problems in these four companies, 10 years from now there won't be anybody from your companies to show up here and talk at the White House.

In the end, you have to face the challenges before you. We are now seeing that again. We have some challenges ahead of us. The Congress must, must approve the worldwide GATT trade agreement that we negotiated, that we got agreement on, but the Congress has to enact it. It will mean a tax cut in the form of lower tariffs and lower costs for Americans and people all across the world of—listen to this—$744 billion over the next 10 years. It will create hundreds of thousands of high-paying American jobs. We have got to finish the job on the trade issue. The next step is GATT.

Before I close, I want to mention two other issues, but it's the same point, problems you can't run away from. We must address the health care situation this year, not just for the people who don't have health insurance but for the people who do but who pay too much for it and who could lose it, not just for the companies who don't provide health care but for the companies who do and pay too much for it.

Why have the Big Three automakers supported us in health reform all along? Because one of the reasons we lost jobs and market share in the automobile industry is that they were paying too much for health care. And one of the reasons they were paying too much for health care is they were paying for all the people in this country who don't cover themselves and who don't do their own part.

Now, here are some basic facts that nobody can ignore. We can all disagree on the solution; nobody can ignore these facts. Of all the countries in the world, we spend more than anybody else on health care by a long ways, but we're the only major country that doesn't cover everybody with health insurance. Of all the countries in the world with which we compete, we are the only one going in the wrong direction. Today there are 5 million Americans, 85 percent of them working people and their kids, who are in this country today who do not have health insurance, who had it 5 years ago. So we're going in the wrong direction.

We have problems here with people who have health insurance but could lose it if they change jobs, somebody in their family gets sick, they have a preexisting condition, or the cost of the policy goes through the roof.

Yesterday I gave awards to four young Americans who have done heroic things and important community service. The United States has been doing this through the Justice Department for the last 44 years. One of these young Americans was the daughter of a farmer, who happens to be a Republican, in the panhandle of Oklahoma. She was injured and paralyzed from here down in a car wreck in 1990. This girl, a beautiful girl, could have given up on life, but instead she decided she would devote herself to try and encourage other young people not to drink and drive and not to ride with people who drink and drive and always put their seatbelts on in a car. She was going to try to help other people avoid what had happened to her. And her daddy is just a hard-working farmer. She's got a sister who is a lovely girl; she's got a wonderful mother. They were paying over $3,000 a year for a limited health insurance policy with very high deductibles. All of her costs were a couple of years ago, attendant on her wreck. This is 4

years later; they were just notified that their insurance premiums were going from $3,100 a year to $9,300 a year. And this farmer is going to have to drop his insurance.

Now, with these two wonderful kids, he's got to figure out how they're going to college, what they're going to do, living out there in a little town in western Oklahoma. And like he told me, he said, "You know, this is not a political deal." He said, "I'm a Republican; I'm a conservative. I don't want the Government to do anything for me, but we need some help here. There's something wrong if I can't take care of my family, hard as I'm working."

So again, I say to the Members of Congress on this, let's just do something about this. Most small businesses in America are struggling to provide health care, and they're paying too much for it, because they can't get the same rates that big business and Government gets. Some big businesses, like Chrysler, are paying too much for it because when people who don't have health insurance get sick, they still get care. They go to the emergency room, and then their costs are passed along to everybody else in higher hospital bills and higher insurance premiums.

We know that something works. We know what they do in Hawaii works. It's the only State where employers and employees are required to split the difference and cover health insurance. And we know that even though most everything else in Hawaii is more expensive than it is on the mainland because it's way out there in the Pacific, health insurance costs for small business are 30 percent lower there than the national average. Why? Because everybody has to pay something, but you're only paying for yourself, you're not paying for anybody else, number one, and number two, because small and medium-sized companies get to band together in big buying groups so they can buy insurance with the same competitive power as Chrysler and the Federal Government. So we know that works.

So I just think I would say again, all I ask of any of you is to ask the Members of Congress to put aside partisanship, rhetoric, and this sort of word-throwing, and let's just think about the people of America, just like we do here, 4.1 Americans who have jobs, all different races, all different religions, all different political groups. All I know is, we're better off that they're in that line. And we'd be better off if we solved the health care problem, and we're going to pay a terrible price if we don't.

One last issue I want to mention: I went to the Justice Department last week for what was a great celebration. We had hundreds of police officers there to celebrate the fact that after 6 years of bickering, the House and the Senate had both passed crime bills and had agreed on a common bill through their conference committees to send back so that each one of them could pass identical bills, so that I could sign a crime bill into law that would give us 100,000 police officers on the street—that's a 20 percent increase; that would ban 19 kinds of assault weapons and protect 650 hunting and sporting weapons, to make sure that this was not a gun control issue, this was an assault weapons issue; that would ban handgun ownership by minors; provide for safe schools; provide for "three strikes and you're out," tough penalties, more prison cells, and billions of dollars for prevention programs to give children something to say yes to as well as something to say no to, the biggest, toughest, smartest crime bill this country's every passed.

Unbelievably, after 8 days nothing has happened. The bills are there. We need it. The American people know how bad we need it. The Democratic mayors and the Republican mayors have endorsed it. The Democratic Governors and the Republican Governors have endorsed it. Every police organization in the country, the attorney generals, the local prosecutors out there in the country where people know that crime strikes people without regard to race or political party, everybody is for this crime bill. But here the crime bill is, stuck in a web spun by a powerful special interest.

You see, before a bill can come to vote in the House of Representatives, it has to be voted out of the Rules Committee. And then the House has to vote first on whether the bill's going to actually be brought to a vote, not on the bill but whether it's going to be brought to a vote. It's a procedure.

The National Rifle Association is trying to block the vote on the rule because they are against the assault weapons ban, because they know that a majority of the House and the Senate will vote for this bill if it gets to a vote. So they are trying to block the vote on the rule, hoping that people can hide and say, "Well, I didn't really vote against the bill, but there was something about the way it was coming up I didn't like."

I got a letter from a kid from New Orleans last spring who asked me to do something about the crime problem. He said, "I'm 9 years old, and I'm really scared that something's going to happen to me." And 9 days later that kid was shot dead. Now, we've been waiting for 8 days for a vote on this crime bill. We have debated this. We fought the assault weapons ban. I thought the NRA was going to win, but we won fair and square. We only won by two votes, but we won, the police officers and those of us who don't want the cops to be outgunned. It was a fair and square deal. We won. And we won in the Senate. And it's in the bill. And I didn't think we could beat them, but we did. We worked like crazy, and we did.

It is wrong to let the NRA, and other interest groups, too, to be fair, who have some other bone to pick with this bill but who know it cannot be defeated on the merits, to use a procedural vote to keep the American people from getting the police, from the kids from getting this prevention money, from the people from getting the "three strikes and you're out law," from the police from getting the help they need with the prisons, and all the rest of this. This is a good deal, and we're not paying for it with a tax increase. We're paying for it by reducing the size of the Federal bureaucracy by more than a quarter of a million between now and 1999.

And I want to plead with you to ask the Congress over the weekend not to let procedure get in the way of saving the lives and the future of the United States. We showed up here to make decisions. If anybody wants to vote against the crime bill, let them vote against it. There are people who are going to vote against it because they're honestly opposed to capital punishment or because they're honestly opposed to the assault weapons ban or because they're honestly opposed to the prevention funds. Let them vote against it. That's fine.

But do not let us pull another Washington, DC, game here and let this crime bill go down on some procedural hide-and-seek. If we're going to have a shoot out, let's do it in high noon, broad daylight, where everybody knows what the deal is.

Thank you very much.

NOTE: The President spoke at 10:55 a.m. in Room 450 of the Old Executive Office Building. In his remarks, he referred to Charles Quimby, manufacturing manager, Kenlee Precision Corp.; Frankie McLaurin, steelworker, Ellicott Machine Corp.; Robert Eaton, chairman and CEO, Chrysler Corp.; and Carol Bartz, chairman, CEO, and president, Autodesk, Inc.

Letter to Congressional Leaders Reporting on Iraq's Compliance With United Nations Security Council Resolutions
August 5, 1994

Dear Mr. Speaker: (*Dear Mr. President:*)

Consistent with the Authorization for Use of Military Force Against Iraq Resolution (Public Law 102–1), and as part of my effort to keep the Congress fully informed, I am reporting on the status of efforts to obtain Iraq's compliance with the resolutions adopted by the U.N. Security Council.

The International Atomic Energy Agency (IAEA) has effectively disbanded the Iraqi nuclear weapons program at least for the near term. The United Nations has destroyed Iraqi missile launchers, support facilities, and a good deal of Iraq's indigenous capability to manufacture prohibited missiles. U.N. Special Commission on Iraq (UNSCOM) teams have reduced Iraq's ability to produce chemical weapons.

Notably, UNSCOM's Chemical Destruction Group (CDG) concluded its activities on June 14 after establishing an excellent record of destroying Iraq's stocks of chemical munitions, agents, precursor chemicals, and equipment procured for chemical weapons production. With as many as 12 nations participating at any one time, the CDG destroyed over 480,000 liters of chemical warfare agents, over 28,000 chemical munitions, and over 1,040,000 kilograms and 648 barrels of some 45 different precursor chemicals for the production of chemical warfare agents.

Significant gaps in accounting for Iraq's weapons of mass destruction (WMD) programs remain, however. This is particularly true in the biological weapons area. Due to Iraq's insistence that the relevant documentation on its past programs has been destroyed, UNSCOM has had to resort to other, more time-consuming procedures to fill in the gaps.

The United Nations is now preparing a long-term monitoring regime for Iraq as required by U.N. Security Council Resolution (UNSCR) 715. This program must be carefully designed if it is to be so thorough that Iraq cannot rebuild a covert program, as it did before the Gulf War, when it claimed to be in compliance with the Nonproliferation Treaty. Continued vigilance is necessary because we believe that Saddam Hussein is committed to rebuilding his WMD capability once sanctions are lifted.

It is, therefore, extremely important that this monitoring regime be effective, comprehensive, and sustainable. A program of this magnitude is unprecedented and will require continued, substantial assistance for UNSCOM from supporting nations. Rigorous and extensive trial and field testing will be required before UNSCOM can judge the program's effectiveness. The Secretary General's report of June 24 has detailed those areas where work remains to be done.

Rolf Ekeus, the Chairman of UNSCOM, has told Iraq that it must establish a clear track record of compliance before he can report favorably to the Security Council. Chairman Ekeus has said he expects to be able to report by September on the start-up of the long-term monitoring program. We strongly endorse Chairman Ekeus' approach and reject any attempt to limit UNSCOM's flexibility by the establishment of a timetable for determining whether Iraq has complied with UNSCR 715. We insist on a sustained period of complete and unquestionable compliance with the monitoring and verification plans.

The "no-fly zones" over northern and southern Iraq permit the monitoring of Iraq's compliance with UNSCRs 687 and 688. Over the last 3 years, the northern no-fly zone has deterred Iraq from a major military offensive in the region. Tragically, on April 14, 1994, two American helicopters in the no-fly zone were shot down by U.S. fighter aircraft causing 26 casualties. The Department of Defense has completed and made public the unclassified portions of the investigation into the circumstances surrounding this incident.

In southern Iraq, the no-fly zone has stopped Iraq's use of aircraft against its population. However, Iraqi forces still wage a land-based campaign in the marshes, and the shelling of marsh villages continues.

In the spring of 1994, the Iraqi military intensified its campaign to destroy the southern marshes, launching a large search-and-destroy operation. The operation has included the razing of villages concentrated in the triangle bounded by An Nasiriya, Al Qurnah, and Basrah. Iraqi government engineers are draining the marshes of the region while the Iraqi Army is systematically burning thousands of dwellings to ensure that the marsh inhabitants are unable to return to their ancestral homes. The population of the region, whose marsh culture has remained essentially unchanged since 3500 B.C., has in the last few years been reduced by an estimated three-quarters.

As a result of the "browning" of the marshes, civilian inhabitants continue to flee toward Iran, as well as deeper into the remaining marshes. This campaign is a clear violation of UNSCR 688. In northern Iraq, in the vicinity of Mosul, we continue to watch Iraqi troop movements carefully. Iraq's intentions remain unclear.

Iraq still refuses to recognize Kuwait's sovereignty and the inviolability of the U.N. demarcated border, which was reaffirmed by the Security Council in UNSCRs 773 and 833. Iraq has not met its obligations concerning Kuwaitis and third-country nationals it detained during the war and has taken no substantive steps to cooperate fully with the International Committee of the Red Cross (ICRC), as required by UNSCR 687. Indeed, Iraq refused even to attend the ICRC meetings held in July and November 1993 to discuss these issues. While Iraq did attend such a meeting in July 1994, it provided no substantive information on missing individuals. Iraq also has not responded to more than 600 files on missing individuals. We continue to press for Iraqi compliance and regard Iraq's actions on these issues as essential to the resolution of conflict in the region.

The Special Rapporteur of the U.N. Commission on Human Rights (UNHRC), Max van der Stoel, continues to report on the human rights situation in Iraq, particularly the Iraqi military's repression against its civilian populations in the marshes. The Special Rapporteur asserted in this February 1994 report that the Government of Iraq has engaged in war crimes and crimes against humanity, and may have committed violations of the 1948 Genocide Convention. Regarding the Kurds, the Special Rapporteur has judged that the extent and gravity of reported violations place the survival of the Kurds in jeopardy.

The Special Rapporteur has noted that there are essentially no freedoms of opinion, expression, or association in Iraq. Torture is widespread in Iraq and results from a system of state-terror successfully directed at subduing the population. The Special Rapporteur repeated his recommendation for the establishment of human rights monitors strategically located to improve the flow of information and to provide independent verification of reports.

We are pressing for the deployment of human rights monitors and we strongly support their placement. We are gratified that the United Nations recently hired a part-time staffer for the Special Rapporteur. This is an important step, though not the full program of monitors we seek. Van der Stoel's mandate has been extended through February 1995. We will file additional reports to the U.N. General Assembly in the fall and to the UNHRC in early 1995. We are also pursuing efforts to investigate and publicize Iraqi crimes against humanity, war crimes, and other violations of international humanitarian law.

Examples of Iraqi noncooperation and noncompliance continue in other areas. For instance, reliable reports have indicated that the Government of Iraq is offering reward money for terrorist acts against U.N. and humanitarian relief workers in Iraq. And for 3 years there has been a clear pattern of criminal acts linking the Government of Iraq to a series of assassinations and attacks in northern Iraq on relief workers, U.N. guards, and foreign journalists. Ten persons have been injured and two have been killed in such attacks this year. The offering of bounty for such acts, as well as the commission of such acts, in our view constitute violations of UNSCRs 687 and 688.

The Security Council maintained sanctions at its July 18th regular 60-day review of Iraq's compliance with its obligations under relevant resolutions. Despite ongoing efforts by the Iraqi government to convince Security Council members to lift sanctions, member countries were in agreement that Iraq is not in compliance with resolutions of the Council, and that existing sanctions should remain in force unchanged.

The sanctions regime exempts medicine and, in the case of foodstuffs, requires only that the U.N. Sanctions Committee be notified of food shipments. The Sanctions Committee also continues to consider and, when appropriate, approve requests to send to Iraq materials and supplies for essential civilian needs. The Iraqi government, in contrast, has continued to maintain a full embargo against its northern provinces and has acted to distribute humanitarian supplies throughout the country only to its supporters and to the military.

The Iraqi government has refused to sell $1.6 billion in oil, as previously authorized by the Security Council in UNSCRs 706 and 712, to pay for humanitarian goods. Talks between Iraq and the United Nations on implementing these resolutions ended unsuccessfully in October 1993. Iraq could use proceeds from such sales to purchase foodstuffs, medicines, and materials and supplies for essential civilian needs of its population, subject to U.N. monitoring of sales and the equitable distribution of humanitarian supplies (including to its northern provinces). Iraq's refusal to implement UNSCRs 706 and 712 continues to cause needless suffering.

Proceeds from oil sales also would be used to compensate persons injured by Iraq's unlawful invasion and occupation of Kuwait. Of note regarding oil sales, discussions are underway with Turkish officials concerning the possible flushing of Iraqi oil now in the Turkish pipeline that extends from Iraq through Turkey. The flushing is necessary to preserve the pipeline that would then be resealed. The proceeds would be deposited in a U.N. escrow account and used by Turkey to purchase humanitarian goods for Iraq.

The U.N. Compensation Commission (UNCC) has received about 2.4 million claims so far, with another 100,000 expected. The United States Government has now filed a total of 8 sets of individual claims with the Commission, bringing U.S. claims filed to about 3,200 with a total asserted value of over $205 million. One panel of UNCC Commissioners recently submitted its report on the first installment of individual claims for serious personal injury or death. The UNCC Commissioners' report recommended awards for a group of about 670 claimants, of which 11 were U.S. claimants. The Governing Council of the UNCC approved the panel's recommendations at its session in later May. This summer the first U.S. claimants are expected to receive compensation for their losses. The UNCC Commissioners are expected to finish reviewing by the end of the year all claims filed involving death and serious personal injury.

In the fall, the UNCC Commissioners are also expected to issue reports on two other groups of claims. The first group involves persons who were forced to depart suddenly from Kuwait or Iraq during the invasion and occupation. The second group involves claimants who sustained itemized individual losses; e.g., lost salary or personal property. Panels of Commissioners have been meeting this summer to prepare their recommendations on those claims.

With respect to corporate claims, the United States filed two more groups of claims with the UNCC in June. Along with our initial filing in early May, the United States Government has filed a total of approximately $1.4 billion in corporate claims against the Government of Iraq, representing almost 140 business entities. Those claims represented a multitude of enterprises ranging from small family-owned businesses to large multinational corporations.

The United States Government also expects to file five Government claims with the UNCC this August. The five claims are for non-military losses, such as damage to Government property (e.g., the U.S. Embassy compound in Kuwait) and the costs of evacuating U.S. nationals and their families from Kuwait and Iraq. These Government claims have an asserted value of about $17 million. In the future, the United States Government also intends to file one or more additional Government claim(s) involving the costs of monitoring health risks associated with oil well fires and other environmental damage in the Persian Gulf region.

It is clear that Iraq can rejoin the community of civilized nations only through democratic processes, respect for human rights, equal treatment of its people, and adherence to basic norms of international behavior. The Government of Iraq should represent all of Iraq's people and be committed to the territorial integrity and unity of Iraq. The Iraqi National Congress (INC) espouses these goals, the fulfillment of which would make Iraq a stabilizing force in the Gulf region.

We will continue to press to achieve Iraq's full compliance with all relevant U.N. Security Council resolutions. Until that time, the United States will maintain all the sanctions and other measures designed to achieve full compliance.

The continuing support by the Congress of our efforts is especially gratifying.

Sincerely,

WILLIAM J. CLINTON

NOTE: Identical letters were sent to Thomas S. Foley, Speaker of the House of Representatives, and Robert C. Byrd, President pro tempore of the Senate.

Nomination for United States District Court Judges
August 5, 1994

The President today nominated two individuals to serve on the U.S. District Court: Robert N. Chatigny for the District of Connecticut and Judith D. McConnell for the Southern District of California.

"Each of these nominees has an exceptional record of legal achievement," the President said.

"I know they will serve on the Federal bench with distinction."

NOTE: Biographies of the nominees were made available by the Office of the Press Secretary.

Nomination for an Under Secretary of Veterans Affairs
August 5, 1994

The President has formally submitted to the Senate the nomination of Dr. Kenneth W. Kizer as Under Secretary for Health in the Department of Veterans Affairs.

"Dr. Kizer brings a wide range of clinical and administrative expertise to the VA at a time

when tested leadership will be crucial to the Department's success in the framework of national health care reform," the President said.

NOTE: A biography of the nominee was made available by the Office of the Press Secretary.

The President's Radio Address
August 6, 1994

Good morning. This week we celebrated the creation of 4 million new jobs in America since I became President on a platform to renew the American dream by restoring our economy, empowering individual Americans to compete and win in it, making Government work for ordinary citizens, and rebuilding our communities. Since we started our national economic strategy, our

private sector is creating jobs nearly 8 times faster than it was 4 years ago.

It hasn't been easy to make these changes. We had to make some tough decisions to put our economic house in order. We had to break the bad habits that led to mismanagement of our economy and the explosion of our deficit for more than a decade. And we had to break through all of the partisan barriers and political rhetoric that too often keeps us from doing the right thing for the American people here in Washington, DC.

Today I want to talk with you about two other historic decisions that call on us to break through partisan barriers and political rhetoric again. For very soon, Congress will vote on both health care reform and the crime bill, two issues crucial to our mission of renewing the American dream.

I want to talk to you about two young Americans whose stories are the best arguments I've heard for why we have to fix what's wrong with our health care system and make our country safer again for all Americans.

One of those young people is Amanda Stewart from Keyes, Oklahoma. This week, I gave awards to four young people who have done heroic deeds or performed remarkable public service. Amanda was one of them. She was injured in a car wreck in 1990 and paralyzed from the chest down. This wonderful young lady could have given up on life. Instead of becoming bitter or defeated, she's devoted herself to educating other young people not to drink and drive, not to ride with people who do, and to always use seat belts. She's helping others to avoid what happened to her.

I met Amanda's family. Her father is a hard-working farmer in western Oklahoma. She has a lovely mother and a wonderful younger sister. She hasn't had any significant medical costs since just after her accident 4 years ago. The Stewarts have been paying $3,400 a year for a limited health insurance policy with a high deductible. But recently they were told that this month their insurance premiums were going to be raised to $9,600 a year.

Now, Amanda's father happens to be not only a farmer but a Republican. He's in a different party from me, and he made it clear to me that he doesn't want the National Government to give him anything. But he's got a family to raise, and he has no idea how he's going to keep paying for their health insurance. He said to me that if he couldn't take care of his family, as hard as he was working, something was wrong in this country.

People like Amanda and her family are the reason we have to guarantee private, not Government, health insurance for every American, insurance that's always there. It's time to do what's right by those people. We're going in the wrong direction now. There are 5 million

Americans just like Amanda's family who had insurance 5 years ago who don't have it today. Almost every one of them are working people and their children. We can do better, and we must.

It's also time we do what's right for young people like James Darby, the 9-year-old boy from New Orleans who wrote me last April. He asked me to do something about the crime rate. He asked me to stop the killing, because he was afraid that someone might kill him. And just 9 days later, walking home from a Mother's Day picnic, little James Darby was shot in the head and killed.

Well, 9 days ago, after 6 years of delay, a bipartisan committee of the Senate and the House of Representatives reconciled their differences on the smartest, toughest crime bill in the history of this country and sent the bill back to be voted on for final passage in both Houses of Congress. It took a lot of work. It's a bipartisan effort and has been every step of the way. Both Democrats and Republicans have voted for every part of it: "three strikes and you're out" and tougher punishments for other tough criminals; 100,000 new police officers on our streets—that's a 20 percent increase all across America; a ban on deadly assault weapons; a law that makes it illegal for minors to own and possess handguns; new prisons to keep hardened criminals in; and billions for new, effective prevention programs to give our young people something to say yes to, not just something to say no to.

Nine days ago when the bill was sent to both Houses for final passage, I thought it would pass quickly and be sent to my desk for signing. But it still hasn't happened. Here's the one last hurdle: You see, before the House of Representatives can vote on a bill, it must agree on the rules for debate about the bill. There are 435 Members of the House, and they have to have some rules to limit debate. In shorthand, this is called "the rule." The rule is purely a procedural matter, but it must be voted on before the final bill can pass.

Unfortunately, the National Rifle Association, which is opposed to the assault weapons ban in the bill, and some other interests are trying to keep the crime bill from passing by defeating the rule. They're putting pressure on Members of Congress to kill the crime bill in a trick maneuver, because they know that once the bill itself gets to a vote, it will surely pass.

You know, we had a tough fight with the NRA over the ban on assault weapons. And those of us who think they should be banned won by only two votes. But we won fair and square. No parliamentary trick should reverse that result and put the rest of that important crime bill in peril.

Now, some Members of Congress honestly oppose the crime bill. They're against the assault weapons ban or they're against the capital punishment provisions of the bill or they're against spending money on prevention programs to give our kids a better future. Well, let them vote against the bill. Let them vote their conscience. But the NRA and the others should come out of the shadows. They ought to fight this bill on the merits. If they really want a shootout, we really ought to have it at broad daylight and high noon, not in the shadows of parliamentary maneuvering. No one should play any more political games with our Nation's safety.

Nine days after 9-year-old James Darby wrote me saying he was worrying about his safety and pleading with his President to help, he was shot dead. Nine days ago, the House and the Senate got the crime bill. There are lots of other little James Darbys out there, and they've waited long enough.

For Amanda Stewart and her fine family, for James Darby, for every American child and for all of their families and their futures, let's stop playing games with these two important issues. Let's get the job done.

Thanks for listening.

NOTE: The address was recorded at 4:05 p.m. on August 5 in the Roosevelt Room at the White House for broadcast at 10:06 a.m. on August 6.

Remarks Upon Arrival in Detroit, Michigan
August 6, 1994

Hello. Thank you for waiting while I visited with one of your fellow citizens over there and her two children. I want to just get out and shake hands, so I won't make a long speech. But I would like to say, first, be supportive of the new candidate for the United States Senate, Congressman Bob Carr, and our new candidate for Governor, former Congressman Howard Wolpe. I'm glad to be here with Congressman Dingell and Congressman Conyers and Senator Levin and with your State officials and a lot of my friends in Michigan.

I just want to make a comment or two. The lady to my left is Linda Clark. You may have read about her in the Michigan press, she and her two children. In 1993, her husband was killed in his business by five young people with previous criminal records. After he died, she received a $24,000 bill from the hospital for his medical care, even though she didn't have health insurance. Since then, she has become a crusader for health care for all Americans and for a sensible policy on crime and, specifically, a supporter of our crime and health care initiatives. I read her letter again coming in today, and I asked her and her children to come here and be with me today because in Washington, very often what we do gets all caught up in partisan political rhetoric and name-calling and stuff that is very hard for ordinary citizens to understand. And I just want to make two or three points here today.

When I went to Washington as your President, I understood well that there would be forces there who would do anything, anything to fight change, to keep the established order of things, to stop us in our determination to give the American people their Government back again, to make it work for ordinary citizens, and to reawaken the American dream. But I want to ask you to look at the record, not the hype.

When I became President, the deficit was going up, and the economy was going down. By the narrowest of margins, we passed our national economic strategy. It cut $255 billion worth of spending. It raised taxes on the wealthiest 1.2 percent of Americans, and all their money went to pay down the deficit. It gave a tax break to 15 million American working families. In Michigan that means 392,000 families got a tax cut; 41,000 got a tax increase. Ninety-one percent of the American small businesses were made eligible for a tax cut. We shrunk the Federal Government to its smallest size since Kennedy was President, produced 3 years of deficit reduction in a row for the first time since Harry Truman was President, and you've got 4.1 million new jobs in the United States since our administration took office.

And since our administration took office, job growth in Michigan has been 3½ times what it was before. It is no wonder that the other party would rather not talk about economics or crime or health care and instead are interested in other things and division and always saying no. We did not have a single, solitary vote, not one, for that economic strategy from the opposition party. And I have done everything I could to reach out to people without regard to their party and ask for a bipartisan consensus to govern America.

You just remember that, folks, when Bob Carr is up here asking for your vote for the United States Senate. If it hadn't been for him, there would have been no deficit reduction, there would have been no economic recovery fueled by the first sensible economic plan we've had in more than 12 years. They want to go back; we're trying to go forward. And I appreciate your coming out here today saying you don't want to go back, you'd rather go forward, you'd rather create jobs, you'd rather grow the economy, you'd rather keep the American dream alive.

Now, let me just make two other points. There's hardly a family in America that has not been affected by crime. And the Congress has passed the toughest, smartest crime bill in history in each House, but they haven't passed the same bill. There are things in that bill that are controversial. There are people who don't support the capital punishment provisions of the bill. There are people who don't support the fact that the bill bans 19 assault weapons, which are so often used by criminal gangs, even though it protects 650 hunting and sporting weapons from being banned. There are people who think we should not spend a lot of money on prevention programs to give our young people something to say yes to, instead of something to say no to. There are people who don't think it's important, but that crime bill gives 100,000 police to the streets of this country, a 20 percent increase. It makes our streets safer; it bans handgun ownership by minors; it has programs for safe schools; it has programs that will build more prisons and have "three strikes and you're

out" for serious offenders and do more to help kids stay out of trouble. It is a good bill, and it should pass the United States Congress next week. We should stop fooling around with it. There are other families like Linda's family who deserve to have their streets safer and their futures better and brighter, and we ought to quit fooling around with it.

And finally, let me say something about health care. You know, I get tickled at all these people who say that this health care bill is some big Government socialist scheme, that it's some horrible idea to take over a big part of our economy.

Let me ask you something, folks. Here's a few questions, and I'd say the folks that aren't with us owe us some answers. Which country spends the most on health care? The United States. Which advanced country is the only one that doesn't provide health care coverage for everybody? The United States. Which is the only advanced country in the world where we're going in reverse, we're losing ground in health care coverage? The United States. Ten years ago, we had 88 percent of the people with insurance; now it's 83 percent. Today in America, there are 5 million, 5 million Americans, almost all of them working people and their children, who don't have insurance today who had it 5 years ago. Now, until we provide affordable private health insurance for all Americans, we are not going to be able to have a secure, stable family environment, work environment, offer people the chance to grow.

What do they say about this health care plan? They say it's bad for small business. Well, let me ask you this—this is an interesting thing— why, if it's bad for small business, have 600,000 small businesses signed up to support our plan to require everybody to cover their employees and split the difference on the insurance premium? I'll tell you why, because most small businesses do provide health insurance to their employees, and they're getting ripped off today, they're paying too much for it.

I met a farm family from western Oklahoma a couple of days ago when I gave their daughter an award. She's a young teenager who had a car wreck in 1990, paralyzed her from the chest down. She's spent the last 4 years trying to encourage people not to drink and drive, not to ride with drunk drivers, and always to put their seatbelts on—a marvelous girl. But the story this family told me was interesting: a Republican farmer from western Oklahoma, his wife, and their two beautiful daughters, one confined to a wheelchair. They've had almost no medical bills in the last 2 years. But they just got notice that in August, their health insurance premiums are going from $3,400 a year to $9,600 a year. And they are going to have to drop their health insurance.

Now, this is not a partisan political issue. Anybody working that hard with two kids to educate, one of them with a serious illness—injury in the past, deserves affordable health insurance.

The only State that has ever provided health care to all its citizens is Hawaii. For 20 years, employers and employees have had to provide health care. And you know what? Insurance premiums in Hawaii are 30 percent lower than they are in the rest of the country.

We can do this. I am tired of people saying, we cannot do this, we cannot do that, we cannot do the other thing. The violent, extremist interests in this country that are trying to keep health care out of the reach of ordinary American working people are a disgrace to the American dream. Most of them have health care, and most of them have parents on Medicare. Why do they not want you to have the same thing that they have? Why? Why don't they want you to

have what they can? Let them give up their health care and see how they like it.

Now, folks, we're going to have to make some tough decisions here. I don't mind being a controversial figure. You didn't invite me to go to Washington to sit in the White House and warm the chair. We are changing this country. We are rebuilding the economy, we're taking on crime, we're taking on welfare reform, we're taking on health care, we're taking on the tough issues. But I cannot do it alone; you have to help. Support the Members of Congress. Tell them you want them to move on the crime bill. Tell them you want them to move on health care. Tell them a simple message: We are coming to the end of this century; we have got to keep the American dream alive. The only way to do it is to restore the economy, empower individuals to take advantage of it, and rebuild our communities and families.

Let's make Government work for ordinary citizens again. That's what I'm fighting for. Thank you for being here to help me make the fight.

God bless you.

NOTE: The President spoke at 5 p.m. at Selfridge Air National Guard Base.

Remarks at a Democratic Party Reception in Detroit
August 6, 1994

Thank you very much. I'm glad to be back in Michigan and glad to be back in Detroit. I'm glad to be on this stage with all these wonderful Democrats, and I thank them for the work they have done for your State and for your country. I also would like to say a special word of thanks to all the people of Michigan who have been so kind to me and to Hillary and to our administration, for the victory we won here in the primary in 1992 and in the general election, and since then, for all the work that has been done, including the wonderful host we had in Detroit in Mayor Archer, when we had the jobs conference here a few months ago. I thank you for that.

Ladies and gentlemen, I ran for this job because I wanted to change this country. I was worried about the direction in which we were

going. I thought the economy was going down, the deficit was going up, the country was coming apart, we were in danger of losing the American dream, and our Government wasn't working for ordinary people. I wanted to change all that. And after a year and a half, I can tell you that the change is well underway.

A lot of people don't like it, and they've fought it every step of the way. When I try to unite people in Washington, there are always people there trying to divide us. When I try to talk in ordinary terms to ordinary people, there are always people there throwing around political hot air and divisive rhetoric. But I can tell you that we are moving forward.

Since this administration took office, we have implemented a national economic strategy. We have launched a full-scale assault on crime. We have made a sweeping proposal on welfare reform. We have got bills to the floor of both Houses of Congress for the first time in the history of the United States to provide affordable health care to all Americans.

And I want to point out, when I came to Michigan in 1992, people told me they wanted something done about this economy. When I offered our national economic plan to the Congress, I was told in a meeting by the congressional leaders of the other party that there would be no votes from the other party for the budget, no votes for the economic plan, that they would not help us to reverse 12 years of exploding deficits, declining investment, and a declining economy. And so, by the narrowest of margins, we passed that economic plan. And they said the sky would fall, the economy would collapse, the deficit would go up, jobs would be lost, the end of the world had come. Chicken Little was on the floor of the Senate and the House with an elephant pin on. [*Laughter*]

What happened? We produced for the American people $255 billion in spending cuts, tax cuts for 15 million working families, including 392,000 working families in the State of Michigan. We did ask 1.2 percent of the wealthiest people in this country to pay more so we could pay the deficit down, including 41,000 families in Michigan, one-tenth the number who got a tax cut. We made 90 percent of the small businesses in this State and this Nation eligible for tax reductions if they invested more to grow this economy. We made 20 million Americans immediately eligible for lower interest rates and better repayment terms on their college loans.

And what was the result? We're shrinking the Federal Government to its smallest point since Kennedy was President. We've got 3 years of deficit reduction in a row coming for the first time since Truman was President. We have 4.1 million new jobs, more jobs in a year and a half in Michigan than in the previous 4 years. We have a big drop in the unemployment rate, the largest number of new businesses formed in any single year since World War II. I plead guilty: We did it.

I just want you to remember this: In this United States Senate race, if it had not been for Congressman Carr, the plan would have gone down. We passed it by one vote. His opponent is against what we did. He is still proud of what we did. If you like where the economy

is going, elect Bob Carr to the United States Senate.

Now, let me say, we're fighting for some other things. We're going to try to pass a crime bill next week. We have to get it to a vote first. The crime bill has some controversial provisions. And a lot of Americans and some Members of Congress, in good conscience, don't agree with them. But it will put 100,000 police on the street. It will give the police a better chance to compete, because it eliminates assault weapons while protecting over 650 other hunting and sporting weapons from being fooled with, which I know is important. It says minors can't own or possess handguns unless they're under the supervision of an adult, which I think is very important. It provides funds for safe streets. It provides tougher penalties for repeat offenders, money for the States to build prisons, but money for prevention programs to give our children something to say yes to, as well as something to say no to. And we need to pass it because the security of our families and our communities and our workplaces and our schools demand it.

You know, I met a woman from Michigan out at the airport. She came to see me with her two children. Her husband was murdered in his workplace last year. He was taken to the hospital and died. And after he died, she got a $24,000 bill from the emergency room. And because her husband was a small business person who couldn't afford to buy insurance, they didn't have any health insurance. So there she was, a widow with two little kids and a $24,000 bill.

In 1943, Congressman Dingell's father introduced the first bill to provide affordable health care to all Americans. In 1945, '47, and '49, Harry Truman tried to do it. And now, here we are in 1994. We're the only country in the world with an advanced economy that doesn't provide health care to everybody. You've got the automobile industry in Michigan losing jobs and market share because they got $1,000 in every car in health care, and they're paying for the cost of people who won't even pay their own way. There are 5 million working people in America, almost all of them working people and their children, who had health insurance 5 years ago who don't have it today. We're going in reverse.

We have a clear example in the State of Hawaii, where for 20 years the employers and employees have all had to buy health insurance, where small businesses have premiums that are 30 percent below the national average. People are healthier, they're doing better, and the small business community is doing better. And we are determined to see that we do not walk away from this.

Let me tell you, when we started this health care debate, there were two dozen Senators from the other party on a bill that would provide health care to all Americans. Today, there are zero there. Every time we have moved to them, they have run the other way. It is time to stop playing politics with the health care of the people of the United States of America.

Now, I knew we had to make some changes in our plan, and we did. We made it less bureaucratic, more voluntary, gave bigger breaks to small business, and we phase it in over a longer period of time. That's what the bills now before Congress do. But the issue is this: Are we going to keep spending more than everybody else and getting less for it, or are we going to continue to let more and more money go to insurance companies and bureaucracies instead of to keep people healthy, or are we going to run the risk of imperiling this fabulous recovery in the auto industry and this recovery in the economy, or are we going to keep punishing the small business people who do provide health insurance? Or are we going to do what's right for the American people? That is the issue. It should not be a partisan political issue. In this election year we ought to forget about the election and remember the people who elected us in the first place and take care of their needs.

And let me make one final remark to you about my friend, your nominee for Governor. For 12 years I had the honor of being the Governor of my State. It was an incredible experience. And I learned a few things about doing it. And I'll tell you, if you want to succeed over the long run, you have to recognize, number one, a lot of these problems cannot be solved in Washington. I can put in place good economic policies, good health care policies, good education policies, good anticrime policies, but still, in the statehouses and in the city halls, the shape of the future will be determined by the quality of the people who are elected. The President cannot do it; the Congress cannot do it. It matters.

The second thing I want to tell you is Governors understand that partisan politics doesn't have much to do with whether kids get educated, jobs get created, streets are safer, if you're doing your job right. You need someone who can unify people; someone who believes that we don't have a person to waste, that we cannot afford to be divided; someone who will tell you hard truths but tell you hard truths in a way that will bring us together, not tear us apart; and you also need someone with an eye on the future.

This man I know well. He was the first member of your delegation to endorse my candidacy. I hope that doesn't hurt him here this year. And I can tell you, he will be a Governor you can be proud of. He will unite the people of this State, not divide them. And he will always be thinking about the future. We are living in a time when the average person will change jobs seven times in a lifetime. We cannot afford people to ever, ever, ever forget about the fact that politics can never be about what works in the moment. We have to be thinking about tomorrow. So I say to you: I want you to elect him Governor. I want you to elect Bob Carr Senator. I want you to return these Members of the House delegation, without whom this economic recovery would not be underway.

Every one of them will be attacked by their Republican opponents as being the same old tax-and-spend, blah, blah, blah, blah. [*Laughter*] The truth is, the crowd that was in there before in all the Reagan years and the Bush years, they cut taxes on the rich, raised taxes on the middle class, exploded the deficit, and the economy went downhill, and ignored things like what was happening to the auto industry.

We have an economic strategy. It includes fair taxation, but we're bringing the deficit down, investing in education and training, building the economy, and looking toward the future. I think that's what the American people want us to do. If they know what the record is, these people will all be returned. You make sure they know.

Thank you, and God bless you.

NOTE: The President spoke at 6:08 p.m. at the Westin Hotel. In his remarks, the President referred to Mayor Dennis Archer of Detroit and Michigan Democratic gubernatorial candidate Howard Wolpe.

Remarks on Presenting the Presidential Medals of Freedom
August 8, 1994

The President. Thank you very much. Ladies and gentlemen, welcome to the White House. As you might imagine, one of the great pleasures of the Presidency is selecting recipients of the Presidential Medal of Freedom, the highest honor given to civilians by the United States of America.

If I might begin on a very personal and immediate note, last fall this annual ceremony was held on a very happy day for me and for those of us who want a safer and more humane United States. It was the day we made the Brady bill the law of the land. Today as we gather here, Congress is on the verge of voting on the most comprehensive anticrime bill in history. But that bill has been held hostage for 11 days by certain special interest groups. So as we recognize the contributions of civilians to our country's way of life, I'd like to take this opportunity to call on those groups who are blocking the crime bill to let it come to a vote and ask the other citizens of the United States to ask the Congress for the same thing. Many people we honor here today have given their whole lives to enriching the fabric of the future, and we can do no less.

This afternoon we will present the Presidential Medal of Freedom to nine remarkable individuals whose service to our democracy and to humanity has advanced the common interest of freedom-loving people, not only here at home but throughout the world: Herbert Block, the late Cesar Chavez, Arthur Flemming, Dorothy Height, Barbara Jordan, Lane Kirkland, Robert Michel, and Sargent Shriver.

The medals these Americans receive today has a special history. It was established by President Truman in 1945 at first to reward notable service in the war. In 1963 President Kennedy amended the award for distinguished civilian service in peacetime. The honorees that year included the singer Marian Anderson, Justice Felix Frankfurter, diplomat John McCloy, labor leader George Meany, the writer E.B. White, playwright Thornton Wilder, and the artist Andrew Wyeth. By the time that first ceremony was held here in the White House in December of 1963, President Johnson had added to the roll of names President Kennedy and His Holiness Pope John XXIII.

Listen to this: At that time, Under Secretary of State George Ball said that the President is establishing what we can proudly call an American civil honors list. How many of our greatest citizens, who went on to achieve other things, said that the greatest thing that could ever be said about them was that they were good citizens. That is true in every way of those we honor today.

Herbert Block, or "Herblock" as we know him, became an editorial cartoonist with the Chicago Daily News in 1929, not a very good year to begin writing funny cartoons. [*Laughter*] His long and prolific career has spanned the Presidencies of 11 different Presidents. The fact that he gets to choose the targets in cartoons may have something to do with the longevity of his career. His cartoons have appeared in the Washington Post since 1946, the year I was born. [*Laughter*] He educates and persuades public opinion with effectiveness, artistry, warmth, and great good humor. He has a big heart. He sides with the little guy, people of common sense, and all who hold healthy irreverence for any sort of pretensions.

Cesar Chavez, before his death in April of last year, had become a champion of working people everywhere. Born into Depression-era poverty in Arizona in 1927, he served in the United States Navy in the Second World War and rose to become one of our greatest advocates of nonviolent change. He was, for his own people, a Moses figure. The farm workers who labored in the fields and yearned for respect and self-sufficiency pinned their hopes on this remarkable man, who with faith and discipline, with soft-spoken humility and amazing inner strength led a very courageous life and in so doing brought dignity to the lives of so many others and provided for us inspiration for the rest of our Nation's history. We are honored to have his wife, friend, and longtime working partner, Helen Chavez, to be with us today to receive the award.

Arthur Flemming served every President from Franklin Roosevelt to Ronald Reagan as the Republican member of the Civil Service Commission, as a member of the Hoover commission on the executive branch established by President Truman, as Director of Defense Mobilization and a member of President Eisenhower's National Security Council, and as Secretary of Health, Education, and Welfare. In addition to being an able administrator, Dr. Flemming is also a respected educator and former journalist. Over the course of his long and eminent career in public service, he contributed to the struggles for Social Security, civil rights, and most recently health care reform, something for which the First Lady and I are particularly in his debt. These three struggles he calls the greatest domestic crusades of his lifetime.

James Grant is the remarkable executive director of the United Nations Children's Fund, UNICEF, where he has tirelessly waged a global crusade on behalf of the world's children. Like his father before him, he was born and raised in China, where he took up his family's tradition of offering assistance abroad and first went to work for the United Nations at the end of World War II. In the fall of 1992 he helped to broker a brief cease-fire during the siege of Sarajevo and personally directed the safe passage of a convoy carrying winter supplies of clothing, blankets, and food. As the international community's guardian of innocent children in troubled regions, he oversees the delivery of humanitarian assistance that without him might otherwise never reach those in need.

Dorothy Height is one of the world's most tireless and accomplished advocates of civil rights, the rights of women, and the health and stability of family and community life. From the days when she helped Eleanor Roosevelt to organize the World Youth Conference in 1938, she has remained engaged in the public arena for 60 years and more. As a leader of the National Council of Negro Women and the Young Women's Christian Association, she's been a powerful voice for equal opportunity here and in developing nations around the world. In recent years, her Black Family Reunion celebrations have reminded our society that self-help and self-reliance within loving extended families are the dominant cultural traditions of the African-American community.

For 20 years Barbara Jordan has been the most outspoken moral voice of the American political system, a position she reached soon after becoming the first black Congresswoman elected from the deep South from her native

Texas in 1972. From national platforms she has captured the Nation's attention and awakened its conscience in defense of our Constitution, the American dream, and the commonality we share as American citizens. As professor of ethics and public policy at the Lyndon B. Johnson School of Public Affairs, she ensures that the next generation of our public servants will be worthy of the legacy she has done so much to build.

Lane Kirkland has been at the center of the American labor movement for almost 50 years. After serving in the merchant marine during the Second World War and his subsequent graduation from the School of Foreign Service at Georgetown University, he became a researcher for organized labor in the same year that he worked as a 26-year-old speechwriter in the 1948 campaign of Harry Truman and his running mate, Alben Barkley. Throughout the cold war, when some leaders saw only the threats to our freedom overseas and neglected the barriers to freedom and inequality within our own land, Kirkland showed America that you can stand up to communism abroad just as forcefully as you can stand up for working men and women here at home. As president of the AFL–CIO for the last 15 years, he has helped to teach us that solidarity is a powerful word in any language and that a vibrant labor movement is essential to every free society.

Robert Michel has served in the United States House of Representatives since 1957. That is the second longest tenure of any Republican in American history. As minority leader in the House for the last 13 years, he has served his party well, but he has also served our Nation well, choosing the pragmatic but harder course of conciliation more often than the divisive but easier course of confrontation. In the best sense he is a gentleman legislator who, in spite of the great swings in public opinion from year to year, has remained always true to the midwestern values he represents so faithfully in the House. He retires at the end of this year, generally regarded by Democrats and Republicans alike as one of the most decent and respected leaders with which any President has had the privilege to work.

Sargent Shriver is the man who launched the Peace Corps 33 years ago. Because of his creativity, his idealism, his brilliance, the Peace Corps remains one of the most popular Government initiatives ever undertaken. From the time he and his wife, Eunice, helped to organize a conference on juvenile delinquency for the Attorney General in 1947 to his efforts for public education in Chicago in the 1950's, to his leadership of Head Start and legal services and now the Special Olympics, Sargent Shriver has awakened millions of Americans, including many in this administration, to the responsibilities of service, the possibilities of change, and the sheer joy of making the effort.

These recipients of the Presidential Medal of Freedom represent different political parties, different ideologies, different professions, indeed, even different ages. Their different eras, different races, different generations in American history cannot be permitted to obscure the fact of what they share in common: an unusually profound sense of responsibility to improve the lives of their fellow men and women, to improve the future for our children, to embody the best of what we mean by the term "American citizen." By their remarkable records of service and by their incredible spirit, we have all been enriched.

And now I would ask the military aide to read the citations as I present the Medal of Freedom.

[*At this point, Major Leo Mercado, Jr., USMC, Marine Corps aide to the President, read the citations, and the President presented the medals.*]

The President. Ladies and gentlemen, in closing let me say that I couldn't help thinking, as the citations were read and I looked into the faces of our honorees and their families, friends, and admirers here, that we too often reserve our greatest accolades for our citizens when they are gone. I wish that Cesar Chavez could be here today. I am grateful that his wife is here, and I am so grateful that all these others are here.

Let us remember today that the greatest gift any of us can give the Founders of this Constitution and this Republic is to emulate the work of these citizens whom we honor today, every day, each in our own way.

Thank you for being here. God bless you all.

NOTE: The President spoke at 4:40 p.m. in the East Room at the White House.

Remarks at a Democratic Senatorial Campaign Committee Fundraiser
August 8, 1994

Thank you. Thank you very much, Senator Graham. Ladies and gentlemen, I hope you'll forgive me. I have my annual August ragweed voice. If you don't have allergies and you can't tell whether ragweed has come out in Washington, DC, you just wait for me to get my sort of, you know, raspy—surely there's a role for me in the movies when I talk like this. I could be the guy that delivers the bad news, and that wouldn't be any role change I would have to take. [*Laughter*]

I want to thank many people. I thank the incumbent Senators who are here, Senator Graham and the others who have worked so hard. I also want to congratulate the nominees who are here. We have an exceptionally outstanding group of people: Bob Carr, Alan Wheat, Tom Andrews, Sam Coppersmith, Jim Cooper, all from the House of Representatives, and former

Congressman Jim Jontz, all of whom have real records of fighting for the interests of ordinary Americans in trying to build this country and all of whom have a real chance to be elected to the United States Senate if we work hard for them.

Joel Hyatt from Ohio is not here tonight, but he and I were in law school together. He's younger than I am. Most people are these days. [*Laughter*] And those who aren't look younger now. Joel Hyatt began a program when we were in law school for undergraduates to tutor inner-city kids and then went on to become famous by making legal representation available to ordinary middle class folks. The program he started when we were in law school is still operating there, a real tribute to his capacity to innovate.

Richard Fisher from Texas is also not here tonight, but he is another longtime friend of mine who worked with me in the Democratic Leadership Council and tried to bring new ideas into the party. And believe it or not, in Texas, no matter how much the Republicans crow, he's got an excellent chance to win there, and we're going to work hard for him.

The attorney general of Delaware is here, Charles Oberly, who—now, that's the job I used to have. That's the best job I ever had. I don't know why he wants to be in the Senate. When you're attorney general, you don't have to hire people or fire them, except your own staff; you don't have to raise taxes or cut spending; and when you do things that are unpopular, you can blame it on the Constitution. [*Laughter*] Nonetheless, he wants to leave that wonderful institution. And we were together in Delaware a few months ago. It was apparent to me, not only from what I read in the Delaware papers but from what I saw of him on the stump and the reaction of the people of Delaware, that he had an excellent chance to win that race.

I also want to note the presence here of Jack Mudd from Montana who, like me, was a law professor. But unlike me, he became the youngest law school dean in America. And it hasn't seemed to do him much harm; he's here running for the Senate. Everybody I know in Montana believes that he has a great chance to win. That State went Democratic in the last election. And it's a very tightly fought State, a very closely contested one, but I think he's got an excellent chance to win.

I'd like to mention three other folks who are here, two from the State legislature, Linda Kushner of Rhode Island and Ken Harper of Mississippi, and Pat Shea of Utah who used to be counsel for the Senate Foreign Relations Committee, a committee that I worked for when I was trying to work myself through college here in the 1960's. I have had the occasion to meet and be with all three of them over the years, and I highly recommend them to all of you.

Most of you have heard me speak before. The last thing you need to hear is me give another speech, except when I'm hoarse. But I want to make a couple of points. I ran for President as an underdog, as a challenger. I was buried two or three times before the final vote came in. One of the things that I know is that you can't win a race unless you want to win for something bigger than yourself and that if you do want to win for something bigger than yourself, you have always got a chance to

win. I know that you can't win in a tough time if you don't fight, but if you do fight, you're always in the race. And I know that the American people are basically ambivalent about most things in their politics today. I think it is largely because of the time in which we live. And I think it is an enormous opportunity for us to show conviction and direction.

And I might say—I don't want to single out just one of the Senators here, but I am very, very proud of the conviction, direction, and strength that Chuck Robb is showing in his heroic fight to be reelected to the United States Senate from Virginia. And I want to begin with a story from one of his debates, and then I'll end with another one to illustrate what this election is all about.

When I entered the race for President in late 1991, when President Bush was at 70 percent approval in the polls and most people, aside from my mother, thought I had lost my mind, I did it because I was very worried that this National Government had become more about words than deeds and that we had become addicted to seeing the Presidents always worried about how they were positioned, rather than what they were doing, and that we were moving toward the 21st century at a breathtaking pace with the economy going down, the deficit going up, the middle class being squeezed—genuinely in danger of losing our position of energy and leadership and direction in the world. It seemed to me that to keep the American dream alive, we had to do some simple things that were not being done. We had to restore the economy, empower individuals to compete and win in it, rebuild our communities and support our families, and make Government work for ordinary people again.

When I started running for President—I was looking out there—Jerry McEntee came out for me fairly early, and a lot of people thought he had lost his mind, because some people said, "Well, Clinton's not enough of a Democrat; he's always working with Republicans and trying to get things done." I plead guilty: I did that. I was even popular with the previous administration until I filed. [*Laughter*] I believed, you know, that we had all these problems that did not fit very neatly within the categories that the Democrats and the Republicans had used in the past, and I still believe that.

But I want to tell you what the problem is and why these races are so important with two stories. I'll begin and end with one. The one I'll begin with was from Senator Robb's first debate on the Larry King show. The other three guys were just pounding, you know, and Marshall Coleman looked at him and said, "You come from conservative Virginia, and you pretend to be a conservative, but you are one of the top 10 Democrats supporting Bill Clinton in the United States Senate." Chuck Robb looked at Marshall Coleman and smiled, and he said, "Yep, and I was one of the top 10 Democrats supporting George Bush in the United States Senate. I do not believe the purpose of politics is to destroy the President, and I've finally got somebody who is trying to get the deficit down instead of just talk about it, and so I supported him." And I never will forget that.

Now, what's that got to do with anything? You have to decide what the purpose of your public life is. Is it to do things that genuinely respond to the needs of people, or is it to posture? You remember one of the Republican House Members that's leaving the House, Fred Grandy, said the other day that his colleagues had been told not to work with us on health care. Senator Dole was quoted a few weeks ago as saying, well, he understood that some of the Republican Senators wanted to work with us on health care and work something out, but "I've got a party to think of."

Now, all I know is, when we showed up here, the deficit was going up and the economy was going down. And with no help from them, we passed an economic program that cut spending by $255 billion, cut taxes on 15 million working Americans, made 90 percent of the small businesses eligible for tax cuts, raised taxes on 1.2 percent of the people but devoted all the money to paying the deficit down, made 20 million Americans eligible to refinance their college loans at a lower interest rate. And not a one of them helped us. They said the sky would fall. They said the deficit would go up and the economy would go down. I never heard so much Chicken Little talk in my life as we heard a year ago this month.

And they all talked about how we were the tax-and-spend party and they were against big government. You just remember this: The Democrats alone, with not a single, solitary vote from the opposition party, adopted a budget which will shrink the Federal Government to fewer than 2 million people for the first time

since John Kennedy was President—something they say they're for but couldn't or wouldn't do—that will give us 3 years of deficit reduction in a row for the first time since Harry Truman was President—something they said they were for but couldn't or wouldn't do—and has produced 4.1 million new jobs in 18 months.

Now, that's why I want these people to win, not because I am an abject partisan—my whole record shows that I'm always willing to work with people from the other side—but because the voters have to send a message to all of us that they expect problems to be solved. If the message they send is they'd rather have hot air than firm action to advance the cause of middle class people, then the Democrats will start behaving the same way.

We must keep our eyes on doing things, and then we need to stand up and do them. Today I had the pleasure of presenting the Presidential Medal of Freedom to nine distinguished Americans, one of whom was Barbara Jordan from Texas, and I wish she were here tonight. She said, "I just don't get it." You can just imagine. She said, "The Democrats have a wonderful record; what they need is to fight for it." Barbara Jordan said that.

We need this crime bill. It's being held up by people who know if it comes to a vote, it'll pass overwhelmingly. So they think they can beat it on a technicality—and the American people won't understand it—called a rule. It's the House equivalent of the filibuster: Beat it, but act like you're not.

The Democrats have put together a bill the Republicans said they were for for 6 years but couldn't produce, that every one of us can be proud of: 100,000 more police, a 20 percent increase; tougher penalties; a ban on assault weapons; a ban on ownership of handguns by children; and billions of dollars in prevention programs to give our kids something to say yes to. We cannot walk away from it.

In the health care debate, we have on the floor of both Houses of Congress, for the first time in the history of the Republic, bills that would provide health care to all Americans—never been done before, never even got on the floor before. And yes, there's a lot of controversy about it. There's a lot of information and a lot of misinformation, some genuine difference of opinion. But we do know some things about which there is no dispute. And the burden should be, therefore, on those who have no plan.

We know we spend more on health care than anybody else, 40 percent more of our income. We know that even though we do that, we're the only country in the world with an advanced economy that hasn't figured out how to cover everybody. We know that we're the only country going in reverse. There are 5 million Americans today, almost all of them working Americans and their children, who don't have insurance who did have insurance just 5 years ago. That's not happening anywhere else in the world, only here.

So by what reasoning is it that we say, "This is good that we spend 40 percent more than anybody else, do less"? We're the only ones losing ground, and we spend billions and billions on paperwork, bureaucracy, and administrative costs that no one else spends. We say we are a pragmatic people. But we know that in Hawaii, small business insurance rates are 30 percent lower than the rest of the country because everybody's covered and everybody bears some of the burden.

Should we try something else? I'm willing to try something else for 4 or 5 years. I think it ought to be phased in. I think we ought to be careful. I think we ought to give the market a chance to work. But I think we also should not walk away from what we know works.

The main thing I want to tell you is this: When we enter this debate, what I hope it will be about is the health care of the American people, their pocketbooks, the pocketbook of the Federal Government, the quality of care, the ability to choose your doctors, and the ability to meet the legitimate needs of middle class working people, and not politics.

Last week—and this is the story I want to end with—last week I had the honor of doing something that Presidents have done for 44 years: that is to present awards every year, with the Attorney General, to four young Americans who have either shown great heroism or great public service. One of the public service winners was a young woman from Keyes, Oklahoma, who was paralyzed in 1990 from the chest down in a car accident and since then has spent her time trying to organize children not to drink and drive, not to ride with people who drink and drive, and always to wear their seatbelts. In other words, instead of being bitter, this beautiful child is trying to make sure other people don't have the experience she did.

And so there I was, just totally captivated with this young woman and her little sister and her fine father and mother. And her daddy was a farmer from Keyes, Oklahoma, way out in western Oklahoma. And we just got to talking about health care. And he said, "You know, I was paying $3,400 a year for a limited policy. And my daughter's bills, they were all over 2 years ago. We hadn't had any bills in 2 years. But they told me I had used up my wellness quotient, and my premium is going to $9,600 in 2 weeks. So in 2 weeks, we'll be out of insurance." And he said—he tickled me—he said, "It's not a political deal." He said, "I'm a Republican, Mr. President." But he said, "If somebody's working as hard as I'm working and can't even have health insurance for their kids, something is wrong somewhere."

And so as we begin this debate, there are legitimate differences of approach. I welcome them. Nobody's smart enough to know everything about this issue. But let us remember that farmer from Keyes, Oklahoma, and his fine wife and his two beautiful daughters and ask ourselves, how will he send them to college if he can't even pay their health insurance? And when we go into these fall elections, let us proudly say, "Yes, we're Democrats." And when they attack us for being tax-and-spend, say, "We cut taxes on 10 times as many people as we raised them on. You guys had a bigger Government than we're having. We're just trying to solve the problems of the people of the country. We put 100,000 police on the street without a tax increase, by shrinking the Federal bureaucracy."

We can win the partisan debates if we'll fight. But the main thing we need to do is to remember that this is a difficult and confusing time for our people. The cold war is over. We're moving to a new era. It has not been defined. Every time this happens, the American people become vulnerable. At the end of World War I, we were vulnerable to the first Red scare and to the Ku Klux Klan. At the end of World War II, the same thing happened all over again. The only difference was Harry Truman gladly let his popularity drop from 80 percent to 36 percent to keep our eye on the ball, to rebuild the country and recapture the rest of the world. And in the end, the American people worked through their confusion and came back to their better nature. And they will now if we can make this election about them, not about an argument between Republicans and Democrats, not about all these rhetorical hard balls. Let's just stand up and defend what we've done, defend what we believe in, and fight for the American people. If we do, the crowd we've got in this room can win these elections in November.

Thank you, and God bless you.

Note: The President spoke at 7:54 p.m. at the Hyatt Regency Hotel. In his remarks, he referred to Gerald W. McEntee, international president, American Federation of State, County and Municipal Employees.

Exchange With Reporters Prior to Discussions With President Levon Ter-Petrosyan of Armenia
August 9, 1994

Anticrime Legislation

Q. Mr. President, on the crime bill, the Republicans have written a letter to you asking for a last-minute compromise to eliminate the money for crime prevention and then they would go ahead with the 100,000 new police officers. Is it too late to do anything like that? Are you inclined to go ahead with the compromise?

President Clinton. Republicans in the House or the Senate?

Q. In the House.

President Clinton. Well, the House voted a great amount of money for crime prevention, and all of the law enforcement groups asked for it. The people who are out there on the front lines of law enforcement want to give these kids something to say yes to as well as something to say no to. We provide tougher penalties, more money for jails. Surely we can also provide some money in these areas that have been devastated economically, devastated by the breakdown of family and community, to give these kids a future.

And somebody's always got a reason not to do this. As Leon said earlier today, there's something wrong when the Congress takes 6 years to pass a crime bill and the average violent criminal is out of prison in 4 years. We have debated all this. Let's vote on it, vote the bill, and not take any more time getting it implemented.

Q. What are you telling House Members in your phone calls to them, sir? And do you think you've got it nailed down? Do you think you have the vote nailed down tomorrow?

President Clinton. I don't know; we're working hard. You know, we've got the NRA against us, and we've got a lot of other issues out there.

But we're doing our best to win. And the American people are with us. The future of the country clearly would be better if we passed this crime bill.

Nagorno-Karabakh

Q. Mr. President, how do you feel about— [*inaudible*]—Russian peacekeeping troops in Nagorno-Karabakh——

President Clinton. It depends on what they want. If the parties agree to it, and there were clear CSCE safeguards so that we had the right sort of oversight in the process, and the parties agreed to it, then the United States would not object.

Q. What do you think about that, President Ter-Petrosyan? Would you favor Russian peacekeeping troops in Nagorno-Karabakh?

President Ter-Petrosyan. We are interested in the soonest establishment of peace. And I think that the most important in this issue is the establishment of peace itself and not who will do that.

[*At this point, one group of reporters left the room, and another group entered.*]

Q. Are you happy with the Russian role as mediators in Nagorno-Karabakh? Are you happy with the American role, or anything you would like to be changed?

President Clinton. Well, what I'm happy about is that the parties have agreed to a cease-fire and they're talking directly. And if they agree among themselves to a peace arrangement, if it involves the Russians, if it involves the CSCE, the United States would be inclined to support the ultimate agreement if the parties agree. What we want is to have a peace, and we want to then help to rebuild Armenia and to support the development of the entire area.

Aid to Armenia

Q. President Clinton, will you be continuing humanitarian aid to Armenia?

President Clinton. Yes, the United States will have a very significant aid package this year.

NOTE: The exchange began at 5:45 p.m. in the Oval Office at the White House. In his remarks, the President referred to Chief of Staff Leon Panetta. A tape was not available for verification of the content of this exchange.

Statement on Most-Favored-Nation Trade Status for China
August 9, 1994

I am committed to pursuing a sensible policy towards China that vigorously promotes the full range of U.S. interests in China, including improved human rights. We look forward to working with Congress toward these ends in the future.

NOTE: This statement was included in a statement by the Press Secretary on House of Representatives action to continue most-favored-nation trade status for China.

Message to the Senate Transmitting the Convention on Pollock Resources in the Central Bering Sea
August 9, 1994

To the Senate of the United States:

With a view to receiving the advice and consent of the Senate to ratification, I transmit herewith the Convention on the Conservation and Management of Pollock Resources in the Central Bering Sea, with Annex, done at Washington on June 16, 1994. The Convention was signed on that date by the People's Republic of China, the Republic of Korea, the Russian Federation, and the United States. Japan and the Republic of Poland, the other participating countries in the negotiation of the Convention, are expected to sign the Convention in the near future. I transmit also, for the information of the Senate, a report of the Secretary of State concerning the Convention.

This Convention is a state-of-the-art fishing agreement that will aid in ensuring the long-term health of pollock stocks in the central Bering Sea on which the U.S. pollock industry in the Pacific Northwest in part depends. Its strong conservation and management measures will be backed up with effective enforcement provisions. The agreement will require that each vessel fishing for pollock in the central Bering Sea carry scientific observers and use real-time satellite position-fixing transmitters. All vessels of the Parties fishing in the central Bering Sea must consent to boarding and inspection by authorized officials of other States Parties for compliance with the provisions of the Convention.

I recommend that the Senate give early and favorable consideration to the Convention and provide its advice and consent to ratification.

WILLIAM J. CLINTON

The White House,
August 9, 1994.

Remarks on Health Care Legislation and an Exchange With Reporters
August 10, 1994

The President. I'd like to make a brief statement and then ask Governor Waihee and Mr. Bowles to say a thing or two.

This is a very important week for our country. You know, it's the first time in our history that we've ever had a debate on the floor of either House of the Congress on the question of health care coverage for all Americans. Something that in other advanced nations people take for granted, we've never even been able to debate on the floor of our Congress. And I'm very hopeful that in both Houses they'll be able to work out enough of a consensus to pass a bill that will enable us to go to conference and come out and ultimately have legislation that does provide universal coverage.

We wanted to ask you here today to talk about Hawaii for a couple of reasons, first of all because so much of this debate—I think way too much—has turned on the question of the requirement that employers share the cost of buying private insurance with their employees. And a lot of very dramatic claims, dire claims have been made about that. Hawaii has been doing it for 20 years. It works. Businesses have thrived. Jobs have not been lost. And the most important thing is that you can see that in addition to having lower costs for small business premiums, the closer you get to full coverage, the closer you get to the other goals of health care: cost control, better health care outcomes. These are the things, it seems to me, that cannot be refuted by the people on the other side of this argument.

What it ultimately boils down to is they're saying, "Well, we have this evidence in Hawaii," or "We have evidence in Germany, but we don't want to deal with it. We still don't want to pay." And it just seems to me that—there's another issue I want to bring up that I keep talking about that's very important. Health coverage for people under 65 has dropped from 88 to 83 percent in the last 10 years. There are 5 million Americans today who had coverage 5 years ago who don't have it today. Almost all of them are working people and their children. I do not think that Congress ought to send a message to the country that it is fine with us if this deplorable development continues, if we just see a continuing erosion of the health care system in America, more and more people without coverage.

So I'm looking forward to the week and next week and the months ahead in the hopes that we can really get something done. And I think that this example of Hawaii is important because it is not refutable; it actually happened. And it's not like Germany; they can't say, "Well, it didn't happen here." It actually happened in the United States.

[*At this point, the President called on Gov. John Waihee of Hawaii and Small Business Administrator Erskine Bowles, and each made brief remarks.*]

Health Care Legislation

Q. Mr. President, the employer mandate aside, there seems to be an increasing frustration among some members of the business community about the way the health care reform bills are shaping up on Capitol Hill. Specifically, there are concerns that employers may lose control of ability to negotiate with insurance companies and, therefore, control their costs. This is directed specifically at the Mitchell bill, although they have problems with the Gephardt bill as well. Are there some changes that you would be willing to accept to meet some of the concerns being expressed now by the business community?

The President. I hope they'll get in there and make these concerns known in the whole debate.

My bottom line is what it has always been. I think we have to have a system that, over a period of time, will lead to universal coverage, because I do not believe, number one, that you can do right by the American people without it, and number two, that you can achieve the other goals we have, which are cost control—cost containment, maybe, is a better word—and better health care. Those are my principal goals.

There are a lot of members of the business community that I would urge to get into this debate with both feet. One of the reasons that the bills are in the position that they're in today is that the people who were against this from the beginning and wanted to wreck it over the mandate were out there focused like a laser beam on beating it. I think one of them was quoted in the press today talking about how great they were getting votes against things. Whereas all the people who were for it and knew it had to be done took a more wait-and-see attitude, hoping that this little change or that little change might make it a better bill. Now that it's actually on the floor, I think it's incumbent on everybody to get in there and participate in the debate.

I do believe that the more you move to universal coverage, the more all the objectives of these employers who do cover their employees will be met, because it will stop cost shifting; they won't have to bear the burden of anybody else's cost. And it will have more employers, even the small business groups, in there negotiating to keep health care costs down, which I think will help them very much.

Q. Mr. President, how do you feel the debate is going so far? And do you have any feeling on when you think it will come to a vote in the Senate?

The President. I think it's going pretty well. It may take a few more days to start having critical votes, depending on what happens in the House on the crime bill. I just don't know enough about the timing of the bodies to be sure, but we're going to try to resolve the crime bill in the House this week and move it over there, and so they may take a little longer. I think they still want to go on their August break at the end of the following week. So I hope we'll have some action before then.

Q. Are you disappointed that more members of the business community who you feel favor your ideas and proposals have not gotten involved in this debate and come to your defense, because as you know, the Washington Post reported this morning that several large business groups are now coming together to jointly oppose the Mitchell bill, the Gephardt bill? Are you disappointed that these people haven't spoken out?

The President. I met yesterday with a dozen or more business leaders who went outside the White House and once again reaffirmed their support for universal coverage. And if you read between the lines in the—at least my reading, to go back to Donna's [Donna Smith, Reuters] question, my reading of the Washington Post story today is that a lot of those people disagree with the NFIB, think they're dead wrong, want

a requirement that employers and employees provide for health care through private insurance. And they're worried that the necessary changes that Senator Mitchell has made to try to get the bill through the Senate may not meet their needs.

Well, the answer for them is to come in and try to fix the bill and stay with universal coverage. That would be my counsel. The business leaders—I met with several yesterday—told me they were terribly worried that if we passed up this opportunity to have universal coverage, we would continue to see what has happened so dramatically in the last 5 years where you've lost—you know, 5 million people don't have coverage who had it 5 years ago. More and more businesses are dropping their coverage. All those costs are being shifted on to the employers who are taking care of their employees, which makes the small businesses even more vulnerable and the big businesses even less competitive in the global economy, which will mean further aggravation.

That's one thing that I think that Congress has got to come to grips with. We just can't allow the kind of disinformation that Mr. Bowles talked about and the intense, almost hysterical fear that's been bred in some of the small business community, and has been therefore felt by the Congress, to ignore the fact that we have a system that is breaking up. We're losing ground on the coverage. We've got millions more people without coverage and millions more at risk of losing it than we had just a few years ago. So, we're going in reverse.

That, it seems to me, is a great argument for the Hawaii system. You've got something you know will work, you know won't hurt business, and you know won't go in reverse. And we can build on it and move to full coverage.

Q. Have you been disappointed with the lack of support in the business community to date——

Q. But you're asking them now to come forward at this critical time. Where were they before, and aren't you disappointed?

The President. First of all, we had a press conference here and announced 600,000 small businesses had joined our coalition. That's more members than NFIB has. We put this coalition together around health care. Therefore, unlike the NFIB, they don't have the mailing lists, the political action committees, the way of putting pressure on people at the local level. But we've shown business strength.

We've also had very large numbers of large businesses supporting our position. Do I wish they had come out stronger earlier? Of course I do. But this is nothing new. The AARP has now come out strongly in favor of what we're doing, but they ran ads for a long time which said, "Don't support a health care plan that doesn't have prescription drugs and long-term care." Our plan did, but somebody—not we but somebody else did research which showed that people thought, "Well, why didn't Bill Clinton's plan have prescription drugs and long-term care?"

So this is what always happens. Some of you may have heard me quote this before. Machiavelli said 500 years ago that there is nothing so difficult in all of human affairs than to change the established order of things, because people who are afraid they're going to lose fight you like crazy and people who will win are always uncertain of the result until the very end. And in that vacuum the antis, even if they're less numerous than the pros, can acquire a strategic advantage. That's plainly what happened in the last 4 months, 5 months in the House and in the Senate where there was just this "kill it, kill it, kill it, kill it, kill it" drumbeat coming out of the ones who were negative. But there are more American citizens, more American businesses who know we ought to have universal coverage and who support it. It's not too late to rescue that. That's why we have a debate.

And I would remind you, in spite of all that, this is the first time in history we ever even got bills to the floor of both Houses of Congress. Truman couldn't do it. President Nixon couldn't do it. Nobody who's tried to do it has ever been able to do it. So I feel good about where we are, and I think now the public voices of reason from the business community and elsewhere have a chance to be heard.

Administrator Bowles. The Governor and I will stay for questions. The President is going to have one more question and then he has to leave.

Q. We're getting very close to a vote on a bill that would restructure 15 percent of the national economy, yet Wall Street seems to be completely ignoring the debate right now. Why do you think that is?

The President. You would have to ask them. I think partly because they know it wouldn't

fully restructure 15 percent of the economy. It would simply build on what we have. The things the Government's doing wouldn't change, except we would be more efficient in the management of the Medicare and Medicaid programs. But that would stay there. We would still fund Medicare. We would still fund Medicaid. Almost all the people in the country today who are providing health insurance would have the decision, the freedom just to keep doing what they're doing now.

Only the most limited and inadequate plans would have to be substantially changed, so they could go into a different plan or stay in the one they've got. That's why this plan shouldn't bother Wall Street very much because under all the scenarios we've been discussing, what we're basically trying to do is to close that gap of people who work but don't have coverage and people who don't work but are above the poverty line and don't have coverage. That's basically what we're trying to do. The whole rest of the system will stay intact. And a lot of the structural changes which are occurring for the better, enabling a better cost control for some, will now be available for all.

I think it's important to point out—Erskine pointed out that the small business rates went up 14 percent last year; health care costs went up 4.8 percent last year. So what we're trying to do is to make this available for all, the cost containment as well as the coverage.

Q. Your wife yesterday seemed to suggest that she thought the Gephardt bill might have a better chance of producing the results you want. Do you have a similar feeling of that?

The President. I don't know. I haven't talked to her about it. And I read a couple of stories, and one seemed to suggest that, and one didn't. I can't comment on it. All I can tell you is the device for achieving universal coverage in both bills meets the criteria that I have. And I think it's quite interesting that the CBO thinks that Senator Mitchell could get to 95 percent by 1997, which is a very rapid uptake and would indicate that we could go on then and cover everybody.

Whitewater Independent Counsel

Q. Mr. President, what do you think of about the Starr nomination——

The President. Everybody else has talked about that. I'll cooperate with whoever's picked. I just want to get it done.

Health Care Legislation

Q. Mr. President, which of the two plans, the Mitchell or the Gephardt plan, most closely resembles the Hawaiian model?

The President. Ask Governor Waihee, he's an expert on that.

Q. Thank you, Mr. President.

The President. They both resemble it in different ways, that's my read. They're both different, and they both have things in common.

NOTE: The President spoke at 10:45 a.m. in the Roosevelt Room at the White House.

Letter to the Chairman of the Senate Committee on Armed Services on the Arms Embargo on Bosnia-Herzegovina
August 10, 1994

Dear Mr. Chairman:

I am writing to reaffirm my Administration's support for lifting the international arms embargo on Bosnia and Herzegovina imposed by United Nations Security Council Resolution 713 of September 25, 1991. It has been my long-held view that the arms embargo has unfairly and unintentionally penalized the victim in this conflict and that the Security Council should act to remedy this injustice.

At the same time, I believe lifting the embargo unilaterally would have serious implications going well beyond the conflict in Bosnia itself. It could end the current negotiating process, which is bringing new pressure to bear on the Bosnian Serbs. Our relations with our Western European allies would be seriously strained and the cohesiveness of NATO threatened. Our efforts to build a mature and cooperative relationship with Russia would be damaged. It would also greatly increase American responsibility for the outcome of the conflict. The likelihood of greater U.S. military involvement in Bosnia would be increased, not decreased.

The July 30 Contact Group ministerial was an important step in our strategy of giving negotiations a chance and, at the same time, building an international consensus in support of multilateral action on the arms embargo, should the Bosnian Serbs continue to reject the Contact Group's proposal.

Contact Group unity has been key to the effectiveness of our approach to date, which has brought new pressure to bear on the Bosnian Serbs. This unity will be especially critical as we approach the Contact Group's final option of lifting the arms embargo. As Secretary Christopher made clear in Geneva, we will not allow the process leading to a Security Council decision on the arms embargo to be delayed indefinitely.

In this regard, if by October 15 the Bosnian Serbs have not accepted the Contact Group's proposal, of July 6, 1994, it would be my intention within two weeks to introduce formally and support a resolution at the United Nations Security Council to terminate the arms embargo on Bosnia and Herzegovina. Further, as my Administration has indicated previously, if the Security Council for some reason fails to pass such a resolution within a reasonable period of time, it would be my intention to consult with the Congress thereafter regarding unilateral termination of the arms embargo.

I hope this clarification of my Administration's policy and intentions is helpful. I would consult promptly with the Congress should unforeseen circumstances arise. I also want to express my gratitude for your leadership and support on this important issue which affects our national security.

Sincerely,

BILL CLINTON

NOTE: This letter was made available by the Office of the Press Secretary but was not issued as a White House press release.

Remarks Announcing the Appointment of Abner Mikva as White House Counsel and an Exchange With Reporters
August 11, 1994

The President. Good afternoon. I am delighted to announce that Chief Judge Abner Mikva of the U.S. Court of Appeals for the District of Columbia will become the new White House Counsel, effective October 1st.

I am very pleased to have a man of Judge Mikva's stature, integrity, judgment, and experience join us in our efforts. He's had a long and distinguished career in public service, and he will make a vital contribution to the operations of this White House. A World War II veteran, and a member of the Illinois Legislature for 10 years, Judge Mikva was elected to the Congress in 1968. He served with distinction on the House Judiciary and Ways and Means Committees and built a reputation as a remarkably thoughtful, fair, and progressive public servant. In 1979, Judge Mikva went to the Federal bench on the highly regarded Court of Appeals here in Washington, where he has served as Chief Judge for the last 2 years. During the time that he served on this court, he's come to be regarded, justifiably, as one of our Nation's leading jurists.

With his new post Judge Mikva will have served his country now in all three branches of our National Government. I expect that his broad experience, his deep understanding of our country, our people, and our institutions will make him an extremely valuable member of the White House team.

He is a man of great decency who loves his country very much. And I am very grateful that he's willing to give up his lifetime appointment to the Federal bench to serve the White House as Counsel.

The White House Counsel advises the President on matters of law and justice, ranging from the appointment of judges to the application of law throughout our society. He must ensure that the White House meets the highest standards of ethics and trust. Judge Mikva, a man of uncompromising integrity and judgment, is the right person for this job.

Let me also say a special word about the man whom Judge Mikva will replace. Lloyd Cutler came to the White House 5 months ago for the second time in his distinguished career

to serve for a limited time as my Special Counsel. Once again, he has served his Nation magnificently. Mr. Cutler is a wise counselor, and I and all of us have benefited immensely from his contributions here at the White House. I thank him for all he has done here, and I look forward to his continuing good advice in the years to come.

It's a measure of the seriousness with which we view this office that we have turned to Abner Mikva as Lloyd Cutler's successor. And so I want to say to Judge Mikva, welcome to the White House.

Before I call Judge Mikva up, I'd like to make a special note of the debate now underway in the House of Representatives on the crime bill. As you know, this has been very hard fought. And there are many interest groups arguing that the Members of Congress should vote against the so-called rule to keep the crime bill from coming to a vote in the first place so that they can kill the crime bill without getting credit for killing the crime bill.

The choice is still the same: Are we going to put another 100,000 police officers on the street? Are we going to ban assault weapons? Are we going to ban ownership of handguns by minors? Are we going to make our schools safer? Are we going to give our young people something to say yes to, even as we make punishment stiffer and build more prisons?

The average violent criminal goes free in 4 years. This crime bill has been taking shape and has been up to the gate and thwarted for 6 years. There is something wrong with out national institutions when we can't do that. And I want to urge the House to pass the rule and the bill and do it today.

Judge Mikva, the microphone is yours.

[At this point, Judge Mikva made brief remarks.]

Baseball Strike

Q. Mr. President, can you tell us about the baseball strike which is about to start? As a fan, is there any reason why these negotiators should not be sitting down and at least trying to resolve this? They're not even meeting.

Would you call upon them to at least sit down and have some talks?

Q. And don't go away, Mr. President. [*Laughter*]

The President. I've got to go away, because I've got to get back on the phone. If I don't—I'll have lots to talk to you about if we pass the rule today, but if I don't make some more calls, then I'll always wonder.

Let me make one comment about the baseball strike. First of all, I think that you should know that since the Secretary of Labor first contacted both sides, we have been in continuous contact with both sides and have done what we could to make some constructive suggestions about how to avoid the strike. It appears that both parties are determined to let the strike proceed. We will do what we can to be of help and to get things back on track if there is anything we can do.

Today I would like to speak on behalf of the country because this is an unusual situation. You know, when a company goes on strike, the right to strike is protected and the workers go on strike because they and the management can't reach agreement. But they always have to consider in the end their customers and what will happen if they lose their customers. In a great event like the baseball strike, I think there's an assumption that the customers are always there. But the only thing I'd like to say to both sides is that there are a lot of little kids out there who don't want to see this season come to a close. And there are a lot of not-so-little kids out there who know it's the most exciting baseball season in 40 years.

And I hope that in the days ahead they will search for a way to get back together, finish this season, extend it by a few days so that all the games can be played, and the feelings of the American people that this could be one of those seasons that occurs once every four or five decades could be vindicated. I think the people really ought to be taken into consideration here, and I hope they will be.

NOTE: The President spoke at 4 p.m. in the Rose Garden at the White House.

Remarks and an Exchange With Reporters on Anticrime Legislation
August 11, 1994

The President. Ladies and gentlemen, under any circumstances I would be disappointed if the House of Representatives turned its back on the toughest and largest attack on crime in the history of our country, at a time when the American people say it is the most important issue to them. But it is especially disheartening to see 225 Members of the House participate in a procedural trick orchestrated by the National Rifle Association, then heavily, heavily pushed by the Republican leadership in the House, and designed with only one thing in mind, to put the protection of particular interests over the protection of ordinary Americans.

I don't know how many people in the run up to this vote—of both parties, unfortunately—told me, "I'll vote for that bill, but I just have to vote against this procedural bill." "Oh, I'll vote for it if it ever gets to the floor, but I just have to vote against this rule," because of the assault weapons ban or because they had decided, many of them after the fact, that there was too much money in here for preventing crime and to give our children something to say yes to instead of something just to say no to, even though two-thirds of this money is for police and prisons and punishment.

Well, tonight a majority of the House attempted to take the easy way out. But they have failed the American people. And now I say to them, the easy way out is not an option. Fear and violence, especially among our children, will still be there tonight when they go home to bed. So I want them to come back tomorrow and the day after that and the day after that and to keep coming back until we give the American people the essential elements of this crime bill, until we put 100,000 police on the street and take our children and the guns off the street with the assault weapons ban and with the ban on ownership of handguns by juveniles, until we make "three strikes and you're out" the law of the land.

We have got to do these things. And yes, we have to both build more prisons and give our kids something to say yes to, not just something to say no to. The amazing thing is that this prevention money was supported by every major law enforcement organization in the United States, representing over a half a million police officers who know something about fighting crime and putting their lives on the line.

Today's vote is a vote against all of them, those people in law enforcement who stand out day-in and day-out and try to make our streets safer. It's a vote against their organizations who pleaded for this bill, the sheriffs, the police chiefs, the prosecutors, the attorneys general, a vote against the teachers and the others who work to keep our kids safe and secure, a vote against the Democratic mayor of Chicago and the Republican mayors of New York and Los Angeles. It's a vote against the families of children like James Darby and Polly Klaas who have been killed.

Now, we can do better than this. And I want the Congress and the House to go back to work tomorrow and figure out how to save the elements of this crime bill. This is about the American people. It is their number one concern. And the American people are not foolish enough to be conned into believing that people are really for doing something about crime, but they had to pull a political trick to keep the bill from being voted on.

Q. Mr. President, where do you go from here? Some of the main supporters of the bill say it's dead.

The President. Oh, I don't think so. But of course, that's what we were all worried about. We were afraid that this would be like Humpty Dumpty, you know. And of course, that's what they want, the people that are fighting against it. But they're going to be given a chance.

You know, for the last few days, all they heard from were the special interests and people that had been stirred up by a lot of the disinformation that had been put out. But tonight I think they've got a lot of explaining to do, because we know—you all know—that there were a majority of votes in the House for this, and the bill still went down on the rule because they thought they could pull a political trick and satisfy particular pressures on them without aggravating the rank-and-file citizens of this country. I think they're wrong. I think the people will figure it out.

Q. But there were 58 Democrats, Mr. President——

Q. Mr. President, are you saying that you will keep the Congress in session until this is done? Are you going to keep the Congress in session?

The President. I don't think they ought to go home. You know, the people who are committing these crimes are not going to take a vacation. They're going to be out there working overtime.

Q. Mr. President, there were 58 Democrats, including 10 members of the Black Caucus, one Republican member of the Black Caucus. What do you say to them? They went against you on this issue.

The President. Well, I say first of all let's look at the whole thing. There were 20 fewer Democrats voting against the rule than those who voted against the assault weapons ban. So there were 20 Democrats, probably 30, who said, "Okay, I lost that fight. But the safety of the people in my district is more important than my view on this particular issue and certainly more important than my killing this bill on a procedural vote." They were very brave. They stood up and took a lot of heat.

Now, there were 10 members of the Black Caucus whose opposition to the death penalty was so strong that they could not overcome their personal opposition. At least they had a principled position. But almost 3 times that many, including many who were disappointed because they didn't get what they wanted in that bill, still voted for it.

There were 11 brave Republicans who weathered enormous pressure. But there were 38 who voted against the assault weapons ban, and there were 65—65—who voted for the crime bill with about the same amount of prevention money in it when it passed as it has today. Now I hear them say, "Well, there's just too much prevention money here. We're doing too much in these programs to help these kids who are in trouble." Well, all I know is when it passed the first time at about this same dollar amount, there were 65 Republican votes for it. But I can tell you, they were put under a lot of pressure.

Now, they can figure out how to do this. I'm not in the Congress; I'm not a part of it. But they can figure out how to get this done. They know what the elements are. There is a majority now in both Houses for all of the elements of this crime bill. To let special interests use parliamentary maneuvers to undermine what is clearly the will of the majority of the American people and a majority of the Congress on each discreet element is a bad mistake, and I don't think the people will forget about it.

Q. Mr. President——

Q. Mr. President——

The President. One at a time. One at a time. Wolf [Wolf Blitzer, Cable News Network].

Q. Mr. President, on the issue of the specific complaints that the opposition made, that there was too much money—pork, if you will, they claim— on crime prevention and the ban on 19 kinds of assault weapons, are you prepared to compromise on those two points, the crime prevention programs and the gun control, in order to get the more prisons, the 100,000 police, and everything else you want?

The President. First of all, I believe that all of these elements can pass, and I believe that they will. Let's wait and see what they have to say. There were—let me say again—there were 11 votes, Republican votes, for this rule today. There were 38 Republican votes for the assault weapons ban. There were 65 Republican votes for the crime bill with about the same dollars' worth of prevention programs we had. So I don't see how, when we're spending two-thirds of the money in this bill on prisons, police, and punishment, we can possibly walk away when we've got the toughest punishment that any Federal bill ever had—"three strikes and you're out," tougher penalties for serious offenders, tougher penalties for serious juvenile offenders—how we can walk away from the pre-vention programs when the police have told us that that's what we have to do?

Q. What's your response to those who will say that this is an enormous personal defeat for you?

The President. I can say that I worked my heart out on it, and I did everything I could. And on this day, the NRA and the Republican leadership had their way. The American people have to decide whether they think this is about which politicians are winning and losing in Washington or about kids like James Darby and Polly Klaas who are still alive.

I believe the American people will not like viewing this as some sort of political circus up here. I'm on their side, and I think we better see who's on what side. That is the only thing that matters, what happens to the American people.

Did I lose tonight? You bet I did in the sense that I wanted it to pass. But what happens to me is not important. If everybody in America had the security I had, we wouldn't need a crime bill.

Look at—what happens to me is not it. What matters is all these kids that are going to be out on the street tonight that could just get shot. That's what's important. And I think that in the end if that is felt in the heart of the Members of the House, we'll still get this crime bill.

Thank you.

NOTE: The President spoke at 6:15 p.m. in the Briefing Room at the White House.

Remarks on Anticrime Legislation
August 12, 1994

Ladies and gentlemen, last night when 225 Members of Congress voted with the NRA and the Republican congressional leadership, under enormous pressure, they decided that their political security was more important than the personal security of the American people. They said no to 100,000 police on the street, no to getting guns and kids off the street, no to protecting our police forces and our citizens against gangs with assault weapons, no to giving our kids some things to say yes to as well as something to say no to, no to "three strikes and you're out" and the toughest punishment laws ever passed by the United States Congress.

We are going out now, the Cabinet, mayors of both parties, citizens of both parties all across this country, to say that this crime bill cannot die. Congress has an obligation to the American people that goes way beyond politics and way beyond party. The American people have said over and over this is their first concern. If we can't meet this concern, there is something badly wrong in Washington. And we are going today, starting now, to the National Association of Police Officers conference to carry this battle back. We are going to fight and fight and fight until we win this battle for the American people.

Thank you very much.

NOTE: The President spoke at 8:12 a.m. on the South Lawn at the White House, prior to his departure for Minneapolis, MN.

Remarks to the National Association of Police Organizations in Minneapolis, Minnesota
August 12, 1994

Thank you. Thank you very much, Sergeant Ganley, for your introduction and for your life of commitment. I'm glad to be here again with Mayor Sayles Belton and Mayor Coleman in the Twin Cities area. I want to thank Senator Wellstone and Congressman Vento for flying home with me. And I want to thank Congressman Vento along with Tim Penny, David Minge, Martin Sabo, Jim Oberstar, and Jim Ramstad for voting for safer streets and a brighter future last night in the United States House. I want to thank Tom Scotto and my longtime friend Bob Scully and the other members of NAPO, Dennis Flaherty and others, for their support for all the elements of this crime bill. And I'd like to thank especially the two mayors who flew here with me today, one a Republican, one a Democrat, both former prosecutors, people who believe in the promise of our country and our future and understand that unless we do something about crime we're never going to fulfill it. Ed Rendell and Rudolph Giuliani represent what this country ought to be about, people belonging to the political party of their choice but when the time comes putting party aside and putting people first. And I thank them, and I wish we had more like them, in the United States Congress.

Now folks, you all know what happened last night. The House of Representatives tried to take the easy way out, tried to walk away from the crime bill. Because of organized, intense, and highly political pressure, a majority walked away, away from the police patrolling our streets, away from the children and the senior citizens afraid to walk on those streets, away from all the hard-working middle class Americans who were not organized into any group but who have told us over and over again that

crime is their first concern and pleaded with us to do something about it.

The people of Minneapolis know that taking the easy way out is no longer an option. Two years ago next month, Officer Jerry Haaf was shot in the back in a restaurant by gang members. Today his wife, Marilyn, their two children, and their two grandchildren and one son-in-law came to be with me and to meet with me. I'd like to ask them to stand up and be recognized. [*Applause*] Their husband, father, grandfather gave everything he had to the Minneapolis police force for 30 years, and he and his family deserve better than what they got from the House of Representatives last night.

You know, we had a wonderful visit in there. It never occurred to me or to Mayor Giuliani or to Mayor Rendell or to Congressman Vento or Senator Wellstone, who were in there visiting with his family, to ask them whether they were Republicans or Democrats or independents. I don't have a clue. And I don't care. They're entitled to better than they got from the House of Representatives last night.

Every day, the police of this country, including those in this wonderful national organization who are convening here, put on uniforms and badges and walk on streets, into problems, risking their lives to serve people they're sworn to protect. They don't run from their responsibilities. They don't hide behind tricks. And they don't walk away from their folks. If they did, think what would happen to the United States.

That's why the walk-away last night in Congress is so disturbing. The first responsibility of government is law and order. Without that, freedom can never really be fully alive. Without that, people can never really fully pursue the American dream.

The police here know that. That's what their lives are all about. Most ordinary Americans, without regard to their party, know that, deep down in their bones. Last night we had a vote on democracy's most fundamental responsibility, and law and order lost, 210 to 225.

Two hundred and twenty-five Members of the Congress participated in a procedural trick orchestrated by the National Rifle Association and intensely promoted by the Republican congressional leadership, a trick designed with one thing in mind, to put the protection of partisan and special interests over the protection of ordinary Americans and still leave what Mr. Scotto called the Jackie Mason trick: "Well, I would have voted for it if only it had been there for me to vote on."

It's the same old Washington game: Just stick it to ordinary Americans, because special interests can keep you in Congress forever and special interests can beat you because they're organized and they have money and they can confuse God-fearing, hard-working, ordinary Americans.

Well, goodness knows, I've seen a lot of that in my time, as your President and even before. But the time has come for those of you to say that the only way for Congress to make their seats safe is to make the rest of America safer.

When I ran for this office and when I went to Washington, I had dreams that many said were naive. I really dreamed that we could govern in Washington the way most mayors and Governors do, that somehow we would be able to go beyond the labels that colored our view of the past, beyond Republican and Democrat and liberal and conservative and whether you were for punishment or prevention in this case.

Those old left-right deals, they make great headlines, but they often don't do anything to solve people's problems. They're great in 30-second ads, throwing those rhetorical bombs over the wall at your opponent, but they don't keep any kids alive or help any families to get through the day. And we're in a whole new era in which everything in the world is changing, and we cannot afford to be bound by the categories of the past.

The thing I like so much about this crime bill—Mayor Giuliani's right, if he sat down alone and wrote it, it wouldn't be just like it is. If I sat down alone and wrote it, it wouldn't be just like it is. But the thing that's so good about

it is that it rejects all those false choices that the politics of the past always tries to impose on ordinary people in our complicated lives. It says, no more false choices; let's do what common sense dictates. And the reason it does is that this bill was largely the handiwork of people in law enforcement. We never had a bill before that was endorsed by every major law enforcement group in the entire United States. So it puts 100,000 police on the street. It says "three strikes and you're out" is the law of the land and makes available more funds for prisons to house serious offenders. It bans handgun ownership for juveniles and bans assault weapons that gangs and thugs use to outgun the police. But it also protects 650 specifically named hunting and sporting weapons, something the American people too often are not told. It imposes tougher penalties for violent crimes, all right. There is a death penalty for killing an officer of the law in the line of duty. But it also has the prevention funds in there. You heard these people in law enforcement talking about it.

It makes my blood boil when I hear people talking about pork. Because you see, I have seen the eyes of schoolchildren after the D.A.R.E. officer has talked to them. I remember when the D.A.R.E. program came into my child's elementary school and how it affected the way she looked at the whole issue of drugs and her personal responsibility and how it affected all those kids who never had a daddy at home to say, "This is right" or "This is wrong," who didn't have a job in the home to say, "This is the future you can have."

Who are we trying to kid with all of this rhetoric? Talk to people like us, who have been to the funerals of police officers gunned down in the line of duty, and I dare you to find one person who knows anything about this who's not for tougher punishment and more prevention.

Just imagine what would be happening in America today if Congress had yesterday voted to take 100,000 police officers off of the street, to put 19 more kinds of assault weapons on the street, to get rid of prison space for 100,000 criminals. Well, that's what they did: no to 100,000 police, no to the juvenile ownership of handguns ban, no to the assault weapons ban, no to "three strikes and you're out," no to the prisons, no to the prevention.

You know, this is the kind of political mess Congress has been caught in over this crime bill for 6 years, before I ever showed up, under two previous Presidents, just politics. Everybody talked about crime; nothing ever got done for 6 years. The average violent criminal only stays in prison 4 years. We let a whole generation go by with nothing getting done.

Now, last night, we gave the Congress a chance, a chance to put people ahead of politics, to go with police and punishment and prevention. And until last night, I really thought they would. Until last night, this crime bill was a bipartisan effort to the core.

The first time the bill came up in the House of Representatives, the assault weapons ban wasn't in it, but there was even more prevention money in it, and 65 Republicans voted for the crime bill last April with the prevention money they now attack in the bill.

In May, 38 Republicans voted for the assault weapons ban with the 650 hunting and sporting weapons protected. But when the crime bill came back to the House, it had even more police, more prisons, tougher penalties, and the assault weapons ban they had already adopted.

Then, instead of 65 Republicans or even 38, only 11 brave Republicans, including Jim Ramstad from Minnesota, stood up and did the right thing. The rest, including 19 Republicans who voted for everything in this bill and more than 50 who voted for the prevention programs they now attack, walked away and turned it into a partisan issue.

Yes, they were joined in voting no by some Democrats, a handful of whom were, on grounds of conscience, opposed to the death penalty, most of whom came from places like my home. They come from smalltown, rural America where hunting is important, where the crime rates tend to be lower, where the NRA is very successful at scaring people with misinformation.

But you know something, there were a lot of Democrats who voted against the assault weapons ban who came back and voted for the crime bill last night. There were some Democrats who were deeply opposed to capital punishment, and they still voted for the crime bill

last night because they put the safety of the people of this country first.

We need more Democrats, and we need more Republicans to follow the lead of those 11 brave Republicans and the Democrats who put aside their differences with certain specific provisions to put the American people first. That is what we must have, more people like that, people who believe in you and your future and will not take the easy way out. The walk-away crowd has got to change.

You know that we didn't get you a crime bill yesterday. But we're going to get you a crime bill. We are going to get you a crime bill.

To all the police officers in this country who walk out there for us every day, Washington cannot walk away from you. And all the ordinary Americans who are just out there watching this unfold, hearing all the rhetorical wars back and forth, who know there's no "American association for ordinary citizens" up there walking the halls of Congress, we're not going to walk away from you either.

Yes, it was a defeat yesterday, and I felt terrible about it. But this morning I woke up feeling good because that's a vote I'd much rather be on the losing side of than the winning side. I am glad I will never have to explain to my wife, my daughter, my grandchildren, and the people who sent me to Washington why I did something like what was done to the American people yesterday. Let us turn it around and put the people of this country first.

Thank you, and God bless you all.

NOTE: The President spoke at approximately 1:30 p.m. at the Marriott City Center. In his remarks, he referred to Sgt. Mick Ganley, president, and Dennis Flaherty, executive director, Minnesota Police and Peace Officers Association; Mayor Sharon Sayles Belton of Minneapolis, MN; Mayor Norm Coleman of St. Paul, MN; Tom Scotto, president, and Robert T. Scully, executive director, National Association of Police Organizations; Mayor Edward Rendell of Philadelphia; and Mayor Rudolph Giuliani of New York.

Nomination for United States District Court Judges
August 12, 1994

The President today nominated three individuals to serve on the U.S. District Court: David A. Katz for the Northern District of Ohio; and Robert J. Cindrich and Sean J. McLaughlin for the Western District of Pennsylvania.

"These nominees will bring exceptional legal talent to the Federal bench," the President said.

"I know they will serve our country with distinction."

NOTE: Biographies of the nominees were made available by the Office of the Press Secretary.

The President's Radio Address
August 13, 1994

Good morning. As I'm sure you know, a couple of days ago the House of Representatives had a chance to pass the toughest attack on crime in our history, and they tried to take the easy way out. But the terrible threat of crime and violence is too great for us to let them get away with it. The easy way out is not an option.

Two hundred and twenty-five Members of Congress participated in a procedural trick orchestrated by the National Rifle Association and intensely pushed by the Republican congressional leadership, a trick designed with one thing in mind: to put the protection of partisan and special interests over the protection of ordinary American families. They ought to be ashamed of themselves.

The American people have been very clear on this. The most important job is to keep the streets and the neighborhoods of America safe. The first responsibility of Government is law and order. Without it, people can never really pursue the American dream. And without it, we're not really free. And the American people have said over and over again, today they're worried about crime. They're fighting for their personal security.

The House of Representatives has a responsibility to do something about it, but this week the House walked away from that responsibility. They had a vote on law and order, and law and order lost. But that can't be the end of this fight. The hard-working, law-abiding citizens of the United States deserve better.

Yesterday I went to Minnesota where I addressed the National Association of Police Organizations. This group represents more than 160,000 police officers across the country. They strongly support the crime bill. Earlier in the week, I met with the heads of every major law enforcement group in America. Together they represent over a half-million law enforcement officers. They don't walk away from their responsibility. They put their lives on the line every day for us. And we can't let Congress walk away from them.

The crime bill we're fighting for is a crime bill America's police officers and law enforcement officials want. Our prosecutors, our teachers, our principals, our parents, our attorneys general, our community leaders, they've all joined these police organizations in endorsing this crime bill. For 6 years, Congress has bickered and battled over a crime bill when the average violent felon only serves 4 years in prison.

This crime bill departs from all those labels of the past, from liberal or conservative or tough or compassionate. This crime bill emphasizes punishment, police, and protection.

Some people in Congress say it's time for their August vacation. Well, the crime plaguing ordinary Americans is not about to take a vacation, and it's only fitting that Congress stay in Washington until they get this job done. They can't walk away on a procedural trick.

I want a crime bill that puts 100,000 new police officers on the street, one that makes "three strikes and you're out" the law of the land, one that builds prisons to lock up violent criminals where they belong, one that takes handguns away from minors, one that provides prevention programs that police officers demand to help steer our kids in troubled areas away from crime and drugs in the first place. And the bills must be paid for not by raising taxes but by cutting the Federal bureaucracy.

I gave the Congress a plan to reduce the Federal bureaucracy by 250,000 and more over the next 5 years, to bring the Federal Government to its lowest level in 30 years, and to put all the savings in a trust fund to pay for the crime bill. And let me be clear about this: The crime bill must ban the assault weapons that have no place on our streets.

We don't need any more Washington, DC, games like the House of Representatives played last week. Up until that vote, this crime bill was bipartisan all the way, with Republicans and Democrats voting for everything that must be included. Now the Republicans say, well, there's too much money for prevention in this bill. They call it pork. Well, all I know is, all the police officers in this country know we need to give kids something to say yes to. I know that 65 Republicans voted for a bill that had even more prevention funds back in the spring, but only 11 would stand up to the withering pressure of their leadership when the bill came back and was ready to pass just this week.

The American people have to make it clear to Members of Congress from both parties that even if they disagree with a particular measure in this crime bill, the overall bill is the best, the smartest bill we have ever had in this country, and the American people need it. It's time to put politics aside and finish the job. Help our Nation's police officers make our streets safer.

This fight is not over. I am continuing it. I want you to fight with me. Our children, our families, our future deserve no less.

Thank you for listening.

NOTE: The President spoke at 10:06 a.m. from Camp David, MD.

Statement on the Death of NATO Secretary General Manfred Woerner
August 13, 1994

It was with deep sorrow and regret that I learned today of the death of NATO Secretary General Manfred Woerner. On behalf of the American people, I convey the United States' most heartfelt condolences to Mrs. Woerner and the Woerner family.

As Secretary General of NATO for the past 6 years and as a distinguished German statesman over the two preceding decades, Manfred Woerner's heroic leadership made an enduring contribution to democracy and security in Europe. He was a true and loyal friend of the United States and provided wise counsel to me and other Alliance heads of state and government. Even while he bravely fought his illness, Manfred Woerner worked tirelessly to transform our Alliance to meet the new challenges of the post-cold-war era and to direct its critical involvement in the search for peace in Bosnia. Manfred Woerner's central role in forging NATO's partnership with the new democracies of Eastern Europe and the former Soviet Union was a major contribution to our common effort to build an integrated transatlantic community.

I will miss the candor, the friendship, and the good humor that Manfred Woerner displayed to the very end of his life. The transatlantic community has lost one of its finest citizens and leaders.

Remarks at the Full Gospel A.M.E. Zion Church in Temple Hills, Maryland
August 14, 1994

The President. Thank you so much. If you've been listening to the news the last few days, you know that the President has had his annual loss of voice. [*Laughter*] But when I heard the choir today I kind of got my voice back.

First, Pastor and Mrs. Cherry, on behalf of my wife, my daughter, and all of our company here, thank you so much for making us feel at home today. This was a beautiful, wonderful day for us. We've brought some old friends of ours that we've known for many years and several members of our White House staff. Our good friend Congressman Albert Wynn joined us; we're glad to see you. Thank you so much, sir.

I came here today of two minds. Usually, on summer Sundays like this, Hillary and Chelsea and I go up to Camp David, and we go to the beautiful little chapel in the woods there. And instead of being in a vast church, we worship at 9 o'clock on Sunday morning with about 50 people and about six or seven people singing in the choir including the President, who gets to sightread the music when he can talk. [*Laughter*]

I wanted to come here today for two reasons. First of all, because, as it turned out, I needed to hear the sermon. [*Laughter*] Next week, Pastor, I'll try to be a little more like Jehoshaphat. Maybe I won't have to ask you to face all our enemies all at once. [*Laughter*] The second reason I wanted to be here is that this church to me symbolizes what America should be all about right now. And it also, I believe, came about because of all the things that America should not be about right now. I mean, let me ask you, how is it that a church in 1981 could start with 24 members and in 1994 could have 16,000 members? How could an African-American church, with all of the cliches people say about the black community in America, have 16,000 members and over 40 percent of them be males?

God has worked through this pastor and his wife and his family and all of you. But why did you have to come into being? Because of this great hole that's in our country now. Because of the breakdown of the families and the communities and the loss of the things which hold people together inside and out, not just the spiritual problems but the jobs, too, and the opportunities and the things which make people believe in the future on this Earth.

And in that great vacuum, look what has usually happened, when people lose hope and lose their families and lose their communities and lose their sense of right and wrong, what has so often happened: 70 percent increase in America in 10 years in the number of children being born out of wedlock. And let's get the whole record on, today the fastest growth is among young white women giving birth out of wedlock. Soon, if we don't do something about it, we'll all be equal—too high. In 10 years, a doubling of the rate of murder among teenage young people—65 people in America get killed every day. While we've been in church, another teenager has been murdered. Every 2 hours a teenager gets murdered in America. And in this great vacuum, you have teen pregnancy and drugs and crime and, worst of all, violence.

I wanted to come here because you are filling that void from the ground up and from the inside out. And I believe that this church could never have come into existence and exploded the way it has if everybody had been in a church, in a family, in a community, in a job and had hope and direction, inside and outside, and structure. You've filled a vacuum with something good and pure and wonderful. And I thank you for it. It's beyond the reach of any President to do. It is God's work through a religious ministry.

But the Bible says that the rest of us have ministries, too. Do you remember when Martin Luther King said if you're just a streetsweeper, just sweep the streets as if you were Michelangelo painting the Sistine Chapel? Everybody has a job to do. And today, I don't think we have a bigger job than trying to keep our children alive and rebuild our families and rebuild our communities and to try to communicate some sense of right and wrong and to give our kids something to say yes to as well as something to say no to. It's two sides of the same coin.

And I'll tell you, before I got here, I've been pretty down the last 2 or 3 days because the Congress voted that crime bill down, not because it's the answer to all life's problems, here is the answer to all life's problems, but because this country is literally coming apart at the seams for millions of our young people and because there are too many streets where old folks are afraid to sit and talk and children are afraid to play, because we're not really free anymore and people aren't free to pursue the American dream anymore as long as we feel like we can just tear each other apart, because our police officers go out on the streets where the gangs are better armed than they are, and things are all mixed up now in our country. And so often it seems that petty political things or superficial divisions keep us from doing what in our heart we know is right.

And I have been so troubled at the thought that at least those of us who have been given this authority by you, the President, the Congress—the least we can do is to help you to save the lives of your children. There are children in this church who have been gunned down; I know it. The least we can do is to help you to be protected. The least we can do is to put people on the streets who cannot only catch criminals but prevent crime as good law enforcement officers. The least we can do if people are totally hopeless is to get them out of your hair so they won't be bothering you. And the least we can do is to, yes, give your children more things they can say yes to, not just things they can say no to.

That's what all that debate was about in the crime bill. It really wasn't about whether if you had written the crime bill or I had or anybody else, it would have been just the way it turned out to be. What is a democracy, after all, but people getting together and putting their different ideas and then arguing it out and having a bunch of votes and a majority rules?

Alexis de Tocqueville said many years ago, this was a good country, and as long as it was a good country it could be a great country. We're around after 218 years because more than half the time more than half the people have been right, and God has permitted us to stay and go and flourish. I believe that. Do you?

Audience members. Yes.

The President. Well, that's what this is all about. We don't have a bigger problem than the violence which is eating the heart out of this country and the breakdown of the basic fabric of values that says it is wrong to hurt other people, it is wrong to act in an instant from some momentary advantage in ways that will devastate other people's lives, it is wrong to take this kind of advantage. And we have to find a way out of this that punishes wrongdoers, yes, but that also offers the hand of hope, that rebuilds our people from the grassroots up.

And in a political moment, the Congress walked away from that last week. There are people in my part of the country, good people—they are in their churches today just like we're here—who say, "We don't break the law, and we go hunting every time they open the season, and we don't want any weapons being banned." These 19 assault weapons, folks—I had a .22 when I was 12; you don't need an assault weapon to shoot a deer or to kill a quail. If you're that bad a shot, you ought to be doing something else. [*Laughter*] You shouldn't be hunting. But their fears are all welled up in them, and they scare some of their Members of Congress.

Then there are people who represent places where all the children can go to the ballpark, where they've got a place to go swimming in the summertime, where they're in church two or three times a week, and they literally cannot imagine what it is like for some of our children. And so they say, "Oh, these programs to let these kids play basketball at midnight instead of walk the streets are pork."

I tell you, folks, I will have to, like the rest of you, answer to God for everything I have done, right or wrong. We all will. I have been a Governor. I have presided over the execution of criminals. I have built prison cells. I believe in punishing wrongdoing. I think when people go out and deliberately hurt each other, somebody ought to do something to them and stop it. I believe that. And that's what this bill does. But I also know that there are countless little children out there and they could go one way or the other. You know what the best thing about this day to me was? When everybody was asked to come up here, there were all those beautiful young people standing here. They've got a chance now. And we have to give more of them a chance now.

I came here because I needed to hear the sermon. I came here because your church stands for what our country ought to be and where it ought to go. I came here because the Bible says that good Christians are also supposed to be good citizens. And I ask you this whole week to pray for me and pray for the Members of Congress, ask us not to turn away from our ministry.

Our ministry is to do the work of God here on Earth. And that starts with giving our children and our families a place in which at least they can be safe and secure. It starts with standing up against this mindless violence which has torn the hearts out of people who are at this church and nearly every church in the United States. It starts with trying to put families back together. And it is not the province of even any one race. It is increasingly not the province of any region or any economic group. But it

savages the poor the worst because that is where the families are most broken.

And I ask you to pray and to speak to your friends and neighbors and to hope somehow we will all find the wisdom and the judgment to come back and do the will of God in our ministries, which is to make you as safe as we possibly can.

Thank you so much for giving us this wonderful day with you. God bless you all.

NOTE: The President spoke at 1:25 p.m. In his remarks, he referred to Rev. John A. Cherry, pastor of the church, and his wife, Rev. Diana P. Cherry.

Remarks on Signing the Social Security Independence and Program Improvements Act of 1994
August 15, 1994

Thank you very much. Thank you, Senator Moynihan, Chairman Gibbons, Secretary Shalala. To all the distinguished Members of Congress who are here, especially Senators Mitchell and Dole and the Speaker and to one who is not here, Andy Jacobs, who worked so hard on this endeavor, let me thank you all. Let me especially thank Senator Moynihan, who identified the need to reestablish the Social Security Administration as an independent agency 11 years ago. I was sitting here thinking, when I saw him up here so full of pride that this day had finally come to pass, of two things. First of all, about 8 months ago, Senator Moynihan said to me, "We have a lot of important business to do this year. And we'll have to fight like crazy on all of it. But if you will just come out and say you're for an independent Social Security agency, I think we can do this unanimously. And that would be a very good thing for Congress to do." [*Laughter*] And then I was wondering whether, if we waited 11 years we could be unanimous about every issue that comes before us. [*Laughter*] I want to thank Senator Moynihan for his persistence and guidance and all the others who have worked so hard on this legislation.

When Franklin Roosevelt made a speech to the New York legislature in 1931, he said this: "The success or failure of any government must

be measured by the well-being of its citizens." That was the goal that moved him 59 years ago yesterday. On that day, in a ceremony in the Cabinet Room, just behind us, he signed the Social Security Act into law. And that is what guides us today.

With an independent Social Security Administration, we are reinventing our Government to streamline our operations so that we can serve the American people better. We are strengthening those things which Social Security ought to do and taking precautions to make sure it does not do things which it ought not to do. It is proving that Government can still work to improve people's lives. And now Social Security, we know, will work even better.

For millions of Americans, that signature 59 years ago transformed old age from a time of fear and want to a period of rest and reward. It empowered many American families as well, freeing them to put their children through college to enrich their own lives, knowing that their parents would not grow old in poverty. Nine years ago, thanks to that effort, for the first time in the history of the United States, the elderly had a lower poverty rate than the rest of the population.

In fighting for Social Security and for so much else, President Roosevelt knew that the American people always would have a personal stake in overcoming the status quo when the need was great enough. That is something we should all remember as we go into the next few weeks, as we delay the August recess, as we struggle to come to grips with the challenges of this age, the challenge of crime, the challenge of health care.

These kinds of changes are difficult, but they always have been. In 1935, even Social Security as we know it nearly died in a congressional committee, as Senators considered stripping away the old-age pension. Congress almost left town with this and other critical work unfinished. But they found the grit to work on through the summer of 1935, when they didn't have as much air-conditioning as we have today. And they accomplished so much in that period now known as the Second Hundred Days. Presi-

dent Roosevelt said then that that session of Congress would be regarded as historic for all time.

What we do here today maintains that historic commitment. If we keep focus on the work we are sent here to do, what we do here today can be but the precursor of things that we also can do to benefit the American people that will be historic for all time.

Now I'd like to ask the folks here to join me as I sign this bill. In the beginning, I will for a letter or two at least, use the pen that President Roosevelt used 59 years ago yesterday.

Thank you very much.

NOTE: The President spoke at 10:40 a.m. in the Rose Garden at the White House. H.R. 4277, approved August 15, was assigned Public Law No. 103–296.

Statement on Signing the Social Security Independence and Program Improvements Act of 1994
August 15, 1994

Today I am pleased to sign into law H.R. 4277, the "Social Security Independence and Program Improvements Act of 1994." Fifty-nine years ago, President Franklin Delano Roosevelt signed the original Social Security Act, creating one of the most important and successful Government programs of all times. With the enactment of H.R. 4277, we are beginning a new chapter in the history of the Social Security program, one which recognizes the program's importance by elevating the stature of the agency responsible for its administration. Once combined with a genuine reform of our health care system, we will have fulfilled the vision of the original architects of the Social Security system to provide Americans protection against the vicissitudes of old age and ill health.

Establishing the Social Security Administration as an independent agency within the executive branch reflects my commitment to maintain the confidence of all Americans in the Social Security program. I sincerely hope that it will reassure those currently paying into the system that they too will receive benefits when they retire. For nearly 60 years, the Social Security

Administration has done an admirable job of carrying out its principal mandate: ensuring that Americans receive the Social Security benefits to which they are entitled. The agency's new status recognizes and strengthens our commitment to this tradition of public service.

As I have stated many times, my Administration is committed to "putting people first." Consistent with this philosophy, I issued Executive Order 12862 directing public officials to "embark upon a revolution within the Federal Government . . . to provide service to the public that matches or exceeds the best service available in the private sector." Establishing an independent Social Security Administration will enhance its ability to meet this goal and provide "world class service" to all Americans.

I also want to highlight that H.R. 4277 includes important provisions designed to strengthen the integrity of the disability programs administered by the Social Security Administration. For example, recipients disabled due to substance abuse will now only receive benefits for a limited time (generally 36 months). These recipients must also undergo appropriate, available treatment.

Finally, I must note that, in the opinion of the Department of Justice, the provision that the President can remove the single Commissioner only for neglect of duty or malfeasance in office raises a significant constitutional question. I am prepared to work with the Congress on a corrective amendment that would resolve this constitutional question so as to eliminate the risk of litigation.

Again, I am pleased to approve H.R. 4277 and to reaffirm my commitment to carrying out the Social Security program for the benefit of our Nation's citizens.

WILLIAM J. CLINTON

The White House,
August 15, 1994.

NOTE: H.R. 4277, approved August 15, was assigned Public Law No. 103–296.

Remarks on Anticrime Legislation
August 15, 1994

Thank you. Thank you very much, Marc, Janice, Steve, and Dewey, and to all the rest of you who are here. We have just heard from the real American interests in the crime bill.

Last week, the House of Representatives walked away from Polly Klaas and Jody Sposato and James Darby and all the law enforcement officials in this country who have worked so very hard for this crime bill. When you walk away from our police officers and from our kids, from our hard-working citizens with their futures before them or our senior citizens who have given their lives to make this a better country, and you do it on a procedural trick so you can still go back home and pretend that you didn't vote against the crime bill and you would even have voted for it had it only come to a vote, there's something wrong with the American system of Government. And it finds its way into the lives of people that are still around. Polly's sister, Annie, told me she's still afraid of being kidnapped, so she's built an elaborate alarm system in her room with ropes and bells. There's something wrong when James Darby and his classmates who are still living were so afraid of violence that they had to participate in a special program to help them cope with it. And the worst part of their fears is that there's truth behind them.

Yes, this is the greatest country in the world and the longest lasting democracy in the world. And none of us would live anywhere else for anything. But we have to face the fact that we have the highest murder rate in the world and that our children are more at risk here than they would be in most other countries and all other advanced countries because we have simply failed to act with the discipline and determination necessary to preserve democracy's most fundamental obligation, the maintenance of law and order, without which freedom and progress cannot proceed.

The crime bill makes "three strikes and you're out" the law of the land, puts 100,000 police on the street, builds more prisons to lock up serious offenders, takes handguns away from juveniles and bans assault weapons and provides investments and prevention to give our kids a better start in life, deals more sensibly with the terrible scourge of drugs that are responsible for so many of the crimes we have. These are things which ought to be done.

How can the House explain to Marc Klaas why the law that might have saved his daughter's life, had it been enacted years ago, couldn't come up for a vote? How could a politician go to a little child like Meghan Sposato and explain that, well, they just couldn't figure out a way to bring to a vote a law that would have taken the deadly weapon that killed her mother out of the hands of a deranged person? And how could a Member of Congress explain to James Darby's mother why they won't put police on the street who might have allowed little James to complete his last walk home?

If Washington had acted 6 years ago, some of these lives might have been saved. If Washington will act this week, a whole lot of lives can still be saved.

Last Friday I met with some police officers in Minnesota. I told them that they had never walked away from us and that Washington should not walk away from them. Well, the parents of this country should have the same pledge, and the children of this country should have the same pledge. You heard Janice say that in James Darby's wonderful letter to me, which I have read over and over and over again since last Mother's Day, he said, "I know you could do something about this, and I'm asking you nicely to do it."

Well, my fellow Americans, we have asked the Congress nicely long enough. There should be no more excuses, no more tricks, no more delays, and no more discussion about whether this bill is a Democratic bill or a Republican bill or a Clinton bill. I don't know when I will ever be able to get it across to people here that what we do here is not about us, it is about the rest of America. So let Congress hear this: Pass the Darby-Klaas-Sposato crime bill, and do it now.

Thank you.

NOTE: The President spoke at 1:55 p.m. in the Rose Garden at the White House. In his remarks, he referred to Marc Klaas, father of kidnap-murder victim Polly Klaas; Janice Payne, whose son, James Darby, was killed shortly after he wrote to the President about crime in his community; Steven Sposato, whose wife, Jody, was killed in a shooting; and Dewey R. Stokes, national president, Fraternal Order of Police.

Nomination for United States District Court Judges
August 16, 1994

The President today nominated four individuals to serve on the U.S. District Court: Elaine F. Bucklo, David H. Coar, and Robert W. Gettleman for the Northern District of Illinois, and Paul E. Riley for the Southern District of Illinois.

"These nominees will bring legal talent and dedication to the Federal bench," the President said. "I know they will serve our country with distinction."

NOTE: Biographies of the nominees were made available by the Office of the Press Secretary.

Statement on Signing the General Aviation Revitalization Act of 1994
August 17, 1994

I am pleased to sign into law S. 1458, the "General Aviation Revitalization Act of 1994." It is before me today as a result of bipartisan support in the Congress, and the hard work of many who have labored long to achieve passage of such legislation. The result is legislation that accommodates the need to revitalize our general aviation industry, while preserving the legal rights of passengers and pilots. This limited measure is intended to give manufacturers of general aviation aircraft and related component parts some protection from lawsuits alleging defective design or manufacture after an aircraft has established a lengthy record of operational safety.

In 1978, U.S. general aviation manufacturers produced 18,000 of these aircraft for domestic use and for export around the world. Our manufacturers were the world leaders in the production of general aviation aircraft. By 1993, production had dwindled to only 555 aircraft. As a result, in the last decade over 100,000 well-paying jobs were lost in general aviation manufacturing. An innovative and productive American industry has been pushed to the edge of extinction. This Act will allow manufacturers to supply new basic aircraft for flight training, business use, and recreational flying.

The Act establishes an 18-year statute of repose for general aviation aircraft and component parts beyond which the manufacturer will not be liable in lawsuits alleging defective manufacture or design. It is limited to aircraft having a seating capacity of fewer than 20 passengers, which are not engaged in scheduled passenger-carrying operations.

In its report to me and to the Congress last August, the National Commission to Ensure a Strong Competitive Airline Industry recommended the enactment of a statute of repose for general aviation aircraft. The report indicated that the enactment of such legislation would "help regenerate a once-healthy industry and help create thousands of jobs." I agree with this assessment; this is a job-creating and job-restoring measure that will bring good jobs and economic growth back to this industry. It will also help U.S. companies restore our Nation to the status of the premier supplier of general aviation aircraft to the world, favorably affecting our balance of trade. Therefore, as I sign into law the "General Aviation Revitalization Act of 1994," I am pleased to acknowledge the bipartisan work done by the Congress and by all the supporters of the general aviation industry.

WILLIAM J. CLINTON

The White House,
August 17, 1994.

NOTE: S. 1458, approved August 17, was assigned Public Law No. 103–298.

Message to the Congress on Trade With Belarus and Uzbekistan
August 17, 1994

To the Congress of the United States:

I am writing to inform you of my intent to add Belarus and Uzbekistan to the list of beneficiary developing countries under the Generalized System of Preferences (GSP). The GSP program offers duty-free access to the U.S. market and is authorized by the Trade Act of 1974.

I have carefully considered the criteria identified in sections 501 and 502 of the Trade Act of 1974. In light of these criteria, and particularly the level of development and initiation of economic reforms in Belarus and Uzbekistan, I have determined that it is appropriate to extend GSP benefits to these two countries.

This notice is submitted in accordance with section 502(a)(1) of the Trade Act of 1974.

WILLIAM J. CLINTON

The White House,
August 17, 1994.

NOTE: The related proclamation is listed in Appendix D at the end of this volume.

Message to the Congress on Continuation of the National Emergency With Respect to UNITA
August 17, 1994

To the Congress of the United States:

Section 202(d) of the National Emergencies Act (50 U.S.C. 1622(d)) provides for the automatic termination of a national emergency unless, prior to the anniversary date of its declaration, the President publishes in the *Federal Register* and transmits to the Congress a notice stating that the emergency is to continue in effect beyond the anniversary date. In accordance with this provision, I have sent the enclosed notice, stating that the emergency declared with respect to the National Union for the Total Independence of Angola ("UNITA") is to continue in effect beyond September 26, 1994, to the *Federal Register* for publication.

The circumstances that led to the declaration on September 26, 1993, of a national emergency have not been resolved. The actions and policies of UNITA pose a continuing unusual and extraordinary threat to the foreign ·policy of the

United States. United Nations Security Council Resolution 864 (1993) continues to oblige all Members States to maintain sanctions. Discontinuation of the sanctions would have a prejudicial effect on the Angolan peace process. For these reasons, I have determined that it is necessary to maintain in force the broad authorities necessary to apply economic pressure to UNITA to reduce its ability to pursue its aggressive policies of territorial acquisition.

WILLIAM J. CLINTON

The White House,
August 17, 1994.

NOTE: The notice is listed in Appendix D at the end of this volume.

Letter Accepting the Resignation of Roger Altman as Deputy Secretary at the Department of the Treasury
August 17, 1994

Dear Roger:
I have received your letter of today's date resigning as Deputy Secretary of the Treasury. I believe you have taken the right step under the circumstances, and I regretfully accept your resignation, effective upon the confirmation of your successor.

I agree with Secretary Bentsen that you have made many valuable contributions to this administration as Deputy Secretary. You played a vital role in the passage of NAFTA and the deficit reduction plan, both critical steps for the American economy. I hope that in due course you will be able to return to public service. Meanwhile, I look forward to the benefit of your continuing advice and assistance.

Sincerely,

BILL CLINTON

Dear Mr. President:
I am resigning today as Deputy Secretary of the Treasury. Under the circumstances, this is the proper step to take. With your permission, the resignation would become effective upon the confirmation of my successor.

As I explained to the Senate, I regret any mistakes or errors of judgment I may have made. For them, I apologize. And, hopefully, my stepping down will help to diminish the controversy.

I am proud to have served in your Administration. It has laid a foundation for improving the security and standards of living of the American people. From the Economic Plan to NAFTA to health care, you have consistently made courageous decisions. And, I believe that history will regard them as such.

It has been a special privilege to serve you, Secretary Bentsen, and the American people over the past year and a half. Thank you very much for the opportunity you gave me. I believe fervently in the Administration's agenda and hope to advance it in other capacities.

Sincerely,

ROGER ALTMAN

NOTE: Mr. Altman's letter of resignation to Secretary of the Treasury Lloyd Bentsen and the Secretary's letter of acceptance were also released by the Office of the Press Secretary.

Letter Accepting the Resignation of Jean Hanson as General Counsel at the Department of the Treasury
August 18, 1994

Dear Jean:

I have your letter of August 18, tendering your resignation as General Counsel of the Department of the Treasury, and I accept your resignation effective on the confirmation of your successor.

Secretary Bentsen tells me that you have performed your duties with great skill and devotion. You have my thanks for your valuable service to the nation, and my best wishes for your future legal career.

Sincerely,

BILL CLINTON

Dear Mr. President:

I am resigning today as General Counsel of the Treasury. My former law partners have asked me to rejoin them in the private practice of law in New York and I believe this is the right time to accept their offer, upon the effectiveness of my resignation. I understand that, with your concurrence, my resignation will take effect upon the confirmation of my successor.

I was honored to be nominated by you and grateful for the opportunity to serve in your Administration. You have repeatedly demonstrated your willingness to tackle the difficult issues of our time and I admire your vital leadership. I consider myself fortunate to have been able to work with, and for, Secretary Bentsen and Roger Altman.

While the decision to leave government is not an easy one, I look forward to returning to New York to resume my personal and professional relationships there. I wish you well in your continued efforts and want you to know that my support for your policies and programs remains strong and resolute.

With every best wish.

Sincerely,

JEAN E. HANSON

NOTE: Ms. Hanson's letter of resignation to Secretary of the Treasury Lloyd Bentsen and the Secretary's letter of acceptance were also made available by the Office of the Press Secretary.

Letter to Congressional Leaders Transmitting a Report on the Partnership For Peace
August 18, 1994

Dear Mr. Chairman:

In accordance with section 514(a) of Public Law 103–236 (22 U.S.C. 1928 note), I am submitting to you this report on implementation of the Partnership for Peace initiative.

The adoption of the Partnership for Peace initiative at the NATO Summit last January marked an historic milestone in the relationship between NATO and the nations of Europe recently emerged from decades of communist domination. The reaction of the new democ-

racies to NATO's opening to the East has been energetic. In the 6 months since the Summit, 22 countries, including Russia, have joined the Partnership. In their enthusiastic response to NATO's invitation, these countries have undertaken to respect existing borders and to settle disputes by peaceful means. Moreover, they will engage in practical cooperation with the armed forces of NATO countries and continue to absorb our culture of democracy, individual freedom, and the rule of law. As the attached report indicates, the Partnership established offices in Brussels and Mons, and a full program of military exercises this fall will serve to demonstrate NATO's commitment to immediate implementation of the Partnership initiative. The first Partnership exercises are scheduled for this September, with Poland the first former Warsaw Pact nation to host an exercise on its territory.

The end of the Cold War presented the United States and our allies with a tremendous opportunity to establish real security in Europe. Through the Partnership, the United States can work toward NATO's expansion to democracies in the East. The Partnership for Peace provides a dynamic instrument for transforming former adversaries into lasting partners and for consolidating, strengthening, and extending peace for generations to come.

Sincerely,

BILL CLINTON

NOTE: Identical letters were sent to Claiborne Pell, chairman, Senate Committee on Foreign Relations, and Lee H. Hamilton, chairman, House Committee on Foreign Affairs.

The President's News Conference
August 19, 1994

Cuban Refugees

The President. Good afternoon. In recent weeks the Castro regime has encouraged Cubans to take to the sea in unsafe vessels to escape their nation's internal problems. In so doing, it has risked the lives of thousands of Cubans, and several have already died in their efforts to leave.

This action is a cold-blooded attempt to maintain the Castro grip on Cuba and to divert attention from his failed Communist policies. He is trying to export to the United States the political and economic crises he has created in Cuba, in defiance of the democratic tide flowing throughout this region.

Let me be clear: The Cuban Government will not succeed in any attempt to dictate American immigration policy. The United States will do everything within its power to ensure that Cuban lives are saved and that the current outflow of refugees is stopped.

Today, I have ordered that illegal refugees from Cuba will not be allowed to enter the United States. Refugees rescued at sea will be taken to our naval base at Guantanamo, while we explore the possibility of other safe havens within the region. To enforce this policy, I have directed the Coast Guard to continue its expanded effort to stop any boat illegally attempting to bring Cubans to the United States. The United States will detain, investigate, and, if necessary, prosecute Americans who take to the sea to pick up Cubans. Vessels used in such activities will be seized.

I want to compliment the Coast Guard and the Immigration and Naturalization Service for their efforts. And I want to thank Florida's officials, including Governor Chiles and the Florida congressional delegation, for their help in protecting and saving the lives of Cubans who seek to escape the regime.

Anticrime Legislation

Now I'd like to speak just for a moment about the crime bill. In the last week I have fought hard to put this crime bill back on track. After extensive talks with members of both parties, I have indicated my support for strengthening the provisions that require sexual predators to report to the police and make sure their communities are notified of their presence. And I support cutting overall spending in the bill by 10 percent.

These cuts will ensure that every dollar authorized in the bill will actually be paid for, not with new taxes and not by diverting dollars from other needed programs but, as I have always insisted, with the savings we will gain from reducing the size of the Federal Government by over a quarter of a million people over the next 6 years, to its lowest size in over 30 years, since President Kennedy was here. And all of these historic savings will go back to the American people to make their streets and their homes, their schools safer.

I have insisted that we keep the most profoundly important elements of the crime bill, to keep it tough by putting 100,000 police officers on the street, building more prisons, putting violent criminals away for good, by making "three strikes, you're out" the law of the land, and by other stronger provisions on sentencing. And we're going to keep it smart, with the sensible crime prevention programs that steer our kids away from drugs and gangs and give them things to say yes to.

The crime bill must ban handguns for juveniles and take deadly assault weapons off our streets. Even though we've come under intense pressure from forces that will apparently say anything to take the assault weapons out of the bill, I have refused to do so.

Let's keep in mind what this crime bill is all about. It's about removing fear from our streets, our schools, and our home. Innocent Americans should not have to fear being preyed upon, as so many do today. Innocent children should not have to fear losing their childhoods, as so many do today. We owe it to the American people that do the work and pay the bills in this country to make sure that people who commit crimes get caught, that those who are guilty get convicted, and those who are convicted serve their time. We also owe it to them to do whatever we can to prevent crime in the first place. That's what the police and the prevention programs are all about.

That's why it is so important and why I have worked so hard to make sure that we do not turn this crime issue into yet another Washington partisan issue. This is a grassroots, mainstream, nonpartisan issue, and so it should remain. It must be an American crime bill. We have worked hard on it, and I call upon Congress to pass it without delay.

Helen [Helen Thomas, United Press International].

Cuba

Q. Mr. President, on behalf of all the press corps, we want to wish you a happy birthday.

The President. Thank you.

Q. And now——

The President. Well, you could all do a lot to make it happy. [*Laughter*] That is not a guilt trip; feel no pressure. [*Laughter*] Thank you.

Q. Mr. President, in the last 35 years we've had an embargo against Cuba and increased the economic burden on them. I understand that's

why the refugees are coming in. What is the problem with taking a few small, albeit brave steps to negotiate a possible movement toward democracy with Cuba? We've dealt with many Communist countries through the last 35 years, and we're dealing with them now.

The President. There aren't many left.

I support the embargo, and I support the Cuban Democracy Act, which was passed in 1992. And I do not believe we should change our policy there.

The fundamental problem is, democracy is sweeping the world; democracy and freedom are sweeping our hemisphere. In the Caribbean alone, and in Central and South America, in all of this region, there are only two countries now not democratically governed with open societies and open economies. The real problem is the stubborn refusal of the Castro regime to have an open democracy and an open economy. And I think the policies we are following will hasten the day when that occurs, and we follow those policies because we believe they are the ones most likely to promote democracy and ultimately prosperity for the people of Cuba.

Q. But that's not true of North Korea or China, and you're dealing with them every day.

The President. I think the circumstances are different, and I think our policy is correct.

Q. Mr. President, recognizing that you're slowing down the process, do people fleeing Cuba still get automatic entry to the United States as political refugees if they're not criminals or ill?

The President. No.

Q. You're ending——

The President. The people leaving Cuba will not be permitted to come to the United States. They will be sent to safe havens.

Q. The people who reach here?

The President. The people who reach here will be apprehended and will be treated like others. They will be—their cases will be reviewed. Those who qualify can stay, and those who don't will not be permitted to. They will be now treated like others who come here.

Brit [Brit Hume, ABC News].

Q. Mr. President, under the law it has always been clear that the Cuban refugees had a certain priority on staying here. The policy, of course, has been that anybody who got here got to stay. What restraints are you operating under in terms of the law in changing this policy? Or are you likely, sir, to be sued over this?

The President. No—let me—I'm glad you asked that question in contradistinction to the one you asked right afterward. The Cuban Adjustment Act will continue to be the law of the land. But we are doing our best within that—we will detain the Cubans who come here now. They will not simply be released into the population at large. And we will review all their cases in light of the applicable law, including the Cuban Adjustment Act.

Q. Do you know how long it will take, how long——

The President. It depends on how many there are, of course. And we don't know.

Andrea [Andrea Mitchell, NBC News].

Q. Can you give us some more details? Are these people going to be taken to Guantanamo? What kind of strain might this place on our naval forces, the Coast Guard? Already we're being told that drug interdiction is being cut back. And can you respond to criticism already from Bob Dole and Newt Gingrich? In particular, Mr. Gingrich said that your new policy is appalling, it's an example of mixed morality, and that he thinks it is illegal under the act.

The President. Well, first, let me answer the factual questions. The refugees, those who are fleeing, will be taken first to Guantanamo where we will seek safe havens for them. That is plainly not illegal under international law, nor do we believe it is illegal under the Cuban Adjustment Act.

Secondly, as to whether it is immoral, I just would say it is my belief that the American people and that the Cuban-American people and the people of Florida, but the people of the entire United States, do not want to see another Mariel boatlift. They do not want to see Cuba dictate our immigration policy. They do not want to see Mr. Castro able to export his political and economic problems to the United States.

Now, that is what is plainly being set up. We have gone through that once. We had 120,000 people sent to this country as a deliberate attempt—not because they themselves initially wanted to flee; they were encouraged to flee, they were pushed out; we had jails open; we had mental hospitals open—all in an attempt to export all the problems of Cuba to the United States. We tried it that way once. It was wrong then, and it's wrong now. And I'm not going to let it happen again.

Q. Can you respond to the rest of the question?

The President. Yes, that's my answer to them.

Q. What about the naval forces, the Coast Guard? Are they up to this? Will it affect drug——

The President. I think the Coast Guard is plainly up to it. We may have to have a little more Navy support. I met with the Secretary of Defense this morning; we discussed it at length. He is confident that we can do what we have to do without undermining our fundamental mission.

Anticrime Legislation

Q. President Clinton, previously you said that the crime bill was something that you supported, that you wanted to sign as it was. Now you're saying you can take 10 percent out of it. Why shouldn't the American people believe that there's still a lot of fat that can come out of it?

The President. First of all, anytime you start a—I've never seen a bill that started new programs that you couldn't cut some and maintain its fundamental integrity. I said that crime bill was a strong and good bill as it was, and it was a strong and good bill.

But one of the things that happened in conference that has, I think, been largely overlooked is that in an attempt to get as much money as possible for police officers and law enforcement and for prisons and for border patrol, funds were appropriated or were authorized in the crime bill that came out of conference in an amount greater than we could provide in the trust fund. Keep in mind, the great beauty of this crime bill is it's the first major program in American history that's being financed entirely by reducing the size of the Federal bureaucracy and taking all the savings from the Federal Government and putting it in a trust fund to help grassroots Americans get better control over their own lives.

The practical impact of what we are doing by cutting 10 percent of this will be to be able to put everything that's left into the trust fund. So, in terms of real dollars, I believe there will be more money actually appropriated and spent for tough law enforcement and for police officers. And I believe that all the fundamental, important things in the prevention strategy will be maintained at a very high level and dramatically higher than now.

The principles of the bill are intact: It's the biggest increase in police in the history of the country; it's the toughest increase in punishment in the history of the country; it's the biggest increase in prevention programs in the history of the country.

I am not a Member of the Congress. They have to work out all the details. If they produced this bill out of the conference, I would have happily supported this, as I did the other one.

Q. Wouldn't you just be getting into politics then, by accepting the original bill?

The President. Now, that's one of those questions designed to spoil your birthday—[*laughter*]—because it's something else, it's designed to confuse the American people about what really goes on up here.

The President is not a Member of the Congress. The Congress made a decision that they had a bill that they all wanted. They accommodated the interest as best they could. It met all my fundamental criteria: assault weapons ban, ban on handgun ownership by kids, tougher penalties, longer imprisonment, more prevention. So does this bill. This bill has the added virtue of being able to be fully funded in the trust fund that we are creating by reducing the Federal Government to its lowest size in 30 years.

And if, in fact—let me just say, Rita [Rita Braver, CBS News], there has been no conference. If, in fact, the conference proceeds along the lines that I generally believe it's going on, and it has the added virtue of some strengthening of the language which was put in involving this whole sexual predator issue—so, in that sense, I think it is a fine bill that meets all the criteria, and it doesn't just gut the prevention programs, which I was determined to see not happen.

Yes, Wolf [Wolf Blitzer, Cable News Network].

Cuba

Q. Mr. President, you say that you're not going to allow Fidel Castro to dictate U.S. immigration policy. But hasn't he just done that by forcing you to reverse three decades of a policy? And secondly, what do you say to Cuban-Americans, especially in Florida, who feel betrayed by this change in policy?

The President. Well, I believe that most Cuban-Americans want us to be very firm. The Cuban-Americans that I know, without regard to their party, supported the Cuba Democracy Act, and they remember how awful it was for the United States when the Mariel boatlift occurred. They remembered what it did in this country and the feelings it engendered in this country. And I do not believe they want another Mariel boatlift. And I do not believe we can afford to do that. And so my own view is that most Cuban-Americans will support what we're trying to do and wish us to be firm.

I would remind you that the Attorney General, who is in charge or oversees the INS, who has done a lot of work on this, and who will have a press conference, I think, when I finish to answer some of the details of this policy, was the prosecuting attorney in Dade County. I talked to the Governor last night at some length about this—of Florida.

I think my own feeling is—and I've talked to Cuban-Americans, of course, exhaustively for years now, and we've been in touch with them and with the Florida congressional delegation—I believe this policy will have broad support. I will be surprised if it does not have broad support.

Yes, Cragg [Cragg Hines, Houston Chronicle].

Q. By telling Cubans basically to stay home and at least temporarily to stomach conditions there, does that make it incumbent on you to be more active in seeking to oust Castro?

The President. Well, what we are telling Cubans is that we have a provision for their coming to the United States through in-country processing. And at least as of this date, we have no evidence that the Castro government has done anything to discourage Cubans from coming to the in-country processing, applying for the visas if they're eligible to come here, and getting them. That's what we're saying to them. That is, we do not have any evidence that would justify believing that that process won't work in Cuba as it has in other places. And indeed, the Castro government has encouraged Cubans to go down and apply to come here. But we don't object to that. That's the policy we have everywhere, and that's the policy we should have there.

Q. But doesn't that make it incumbent on you to unilaterally or multinationally press for the ouster of Castro in some way—military, economic, whatever?

The President. The United States had done more than any other country to try to bring an end to the Castro government. We have done it through the Cuban Democracy Act. We have done it through the embargo. We have worked hard, often laboring almost alone to that end. And we will continue to do that by whatever reasonable means are available to us.

Health Care Reform

Q. Mr. President, one of your fellow Democrats in the Senate, Sam Nunn of Georgia, said yesterday that it would be months if not years before a health care reform bill is produced. And the Congressional Budget Office said that a possible moderate compromise didn't cost out. There's a growing feeling in Washington that this health care crusade is hopelessly bogged down in Congress at this point. What is your view of the situation?

The President. That they should keep working at it; that if we don't move now there's a chance that it won't happen at all. You know, the congressional timetable is often different from the American timetable. I mean it took 7 years to pass the Brady bill and 7 years to pass family leave.

But for 60 years people have acknowledged that not covering all Americans and having no system for dealing with the explosive costs and the inequalities in the health care system were a problem. They have reached a significant crisis stage here, with 5 million more Americans losing their health insurance in the last 5 years alone, with the costs exploding in the last 12 years. And I believe that the time has come to deal with this.

Now, Senator Nunn simply observed what I think is clearly a fact, which is that in the Senate there is unlimited debate and you can have unlimited amendments. But a lot of these issues do need to be worked through.

I think the comments Senator Kennedy and Senator Mitchell made today about the fact that this bipartisan group was at least attempting to work with them, and in the process of so attempting, finding out how hard it is. It's easy to stand on the sideline and lob brickbats at these efforts and quite another thing to produce your own effort. But their comment made me believe that there is still a chance that people will work together and resolve this. So I would say to them, keep working, keep working at it, because if you delay, you may lose it altogether.

Q. Well, at this point, would you take something less than what Mitchell or Gephardt has proposed just to keep the process moving, since as you say if we don't get it now, we probably won't get it.

The President. I think that, for one thing, that's not so easy to do, because as we've also seen from the studies of the Catholic Health Association and others, the so-called "something less" approach often does more harm than good; that when you just try to patchwork this, often you lead to more people without insurance and higher insurance rates.

What I would say to you is, give the process time to unfold. I know for you it's been going on a long time, since we first began to debate this a year and a half ago. I think for the American people, it's almost like the baseball season, the pennant's just begun. I hope we can have the pennant in the other one, too, and the series. But I think we need to let this thing unfold a little more. I wouldn't prejudge it yet.

Ron [Ron Brownstein, Los Angeles Times].

Anticrime Legislation

Q. Mr. President, back to the crime bill. If the approach you're offering now, the changes you're offering now, does not produce enough votes to pass the bill, will you under any circumstances agree to sever the assault weapon ban for a separate vote in the House and the Senate?

The President. I won't agree to that because I think it's a mistake. And let me say—I don't want to overly comment on it, but let me try to describe what the problem is. The bill has already passed the House. But in the Senate, as you know, we could have 55, 56, 57, 59 votes for that bill in the Senate and it could still be filibustered. And we should not permit that to happen.

I also believe that there is a chance that this whole process in the last few days—we may look back on this in a year or so and think that this was the beginning of an effort, again, in other areas to work in good faith across the party lines. I have shown my good faith. I have taken the risk that all people take when they talk to people who are opposed to them of, well, being asked the questions like Rita asked me. But in this town it won't work if we have American problems unless we try to reach out across party lines. A lot of these issues don't work like that.

So if we can work through this in good faith, my view is that we'll maybe be setting the stage to have more things like NAFTA and the Brady bill and the education bills and then this one where we can work together. So I don't believe we will have to do that, and I am against doing it. I think it would be a real error.

Cuba

Q. Mr. President, Fidel Castro has been very high on the list of American demonology because he was a national security threat. I think of the Cuban missile crisis; he would provide a base for the Soviet Union. That's all ended now. Do you foresee a form of government, democratic government, in Havana with free elections that includes Fidel Castro? Or is it a case that Castro must go before there's any normalization?

The President. Well, in any democracy it's up to the people to make their own decisions. The United States does not pick leaders or delete leaders for other countries. We let people make their own decisions.

I don't want to get into that. I think what we need is a movement toward democracy and a free economy.

President's Legal Defense Fund

Q. Mr. President, when the legal defense fund was set up for you to handle the costs of defending against the litigation, Lloyd Cutler said he was intervening in that as Presidential Counsel because it threatened the Presidency, these tremendous costs. Since then, the fund has decided it cannot legally solicit, leaving no explanation since then of (a) how will the money be raised to pay these bills? And two, in lieu of enough funding to do it, what other options do you have to protect the Presidency from the threat that he was talking about?

The President. I don't know. I don't know the answer to that. I'll just have to let you ask Mr. Cutler that. I'm just trying to stay way from that whole issue of the fund, and I can't answer those questions.

Yes, go ahead, Mike [Mike McKee, CONUS].

Bipartisanship

Q. Mr. President, I hate to ask you one of those questions that might spoil your birthday again, but in light of problems that you have been having up on Capitol Hill, many people are wondering if changing your communication strategy, shuffling your staff might not be really addressing the problem; that perhaps I was wondering if you've thought about this, that as a President elected with 43 percent, you may be trying to do too much too fast. And Democrats on Capitol Hill may be trying to take too much of a partisan advantage of having control of the entire Government and perhaps exceeding your mandate.

The President. Well, first, I don't want the Democrats to take partisan advantage; I just want us to get what's necessary for the country done. I do not believe the country believes that we should sit still up here.

And for all your talk about trouble, let me remind you that every objective survey says that in 1993 this administration got more support from Congress than any administration since World War II except President Eisenhower in 1953, when he had a less ambitious agenda, and President Johnson in 1965, when he had a bigger mandate and more support from the Congress. So I think we're doing quite well with the Congress if you look at it in any kind of historic pattern.

Now, I realize the fights and the conflicts and the delays endure more than the achievements. But we reversed Reaganomics. We passed an economic program that was part of a strategy that has given us 3 years of deficit reduction for the first time since Truman, over 4 million jobs. We have the most advances in trade than we've had in a generation, in the last year and a half. This economic program is working. We broke 7 years of gridlock with the Brady bill. We passed NAFTA, which was deader than a doornail when I became President; we revived it and passed it.

So I believe this Congress is capable of working together, often on a bipartisan basis. And they still have some great opportunities here. They have the crime bill, the campaign finance reform bill, the lobby reform bill, the bill that passed the House last week that has not yet passed the Senate to require the Congress to live under the laws it imposes on the American people, which I think is a very good bill, and of course, the health care challenge.

But I believe what I have to do is to keep trying to change things. Anytime you try to provoke as much change as I have, you're going to have resistance. And you will be criticized. Is it more difficult that I had 43 percent of the vote? Perhaps it is. But I think you can make another argument, which was that 62 percent of the American people voted for fundamental change in the things that we were doing and in the way Government works.

If anything, I would say that I've been most disappointed, looking back, not so much in my inability to get things done, because once people look at the list it's a very long and impressive list, but I haven't been as successful in changing the way it works, that is, in trying to get the Democrats and Republicans to reach across to each other in good faith and work through these things. That's why I think this crime bill could be an important thing. It could be a way of people in both parties saying, "We're putting you first for a change, not ourselves."

Interest Rates

Q. Mr. President, the Federal Reserve raised interest rates again this week. Some Democrats are saying that it could cause an economic slowdown. How many more rate increases will you take before you also criticize the Fed?

The President. Well, when the Federal Reserve raised rates this week, the Chairman, Mr. Greenspan, said that he thought that this would be sufficient for a time. The truth is that our economic strategy has produced more rapid growth than they thought it would and that we thought it would. We are even doing better than we thought we would. We have got over 4 million jobs already in the last year and a half, and we've got rapid growth in the economy, dramatic new investments in the private sector. So they're worried about inflation. When it is apparent to me that the drag on the economy will be more about slowing the economy down than stopping inflation, I will do what I can to influence that policy. But I think my policy of letting them do their job and having me do mine has worked out rather well.

And I would remind you that from the time we announced—let me just go back through a little history here—from the time we announced that we would have a serious assault on the deficit after the election in November, from that day for a very long time thereafter, we had dramatic drops in interest rates which fueled last year's expansion. So I think that we have to recognize that the Fed did respond to the efforts we made and what they're responding to now is a robust and growing economy. Of course, it could be slowed down too much,

but we don't have any evidence at this time that that has, in fact, occurred.

Mexico

Q. Mr. President, happy birthday. Next Sunday, Mexico is going to have Presidential elections. Can you give us your assessment? What do you think? What do you expect, and what is going to be the impact in the relations of Mexico and the United States? Do you expect continuity?

The President. I expect the elections to be free, open, and fair. And I expect them to produce a result which will be accepted by the people of Mexico. And I expect the United States to continue its deepening friendship with Mexico. I think that our relationships are growing. I think, in spite of the political changes and the economic difficulties of Mexico in the last 2 years, we have had great success. I think NAFTA clearly was a great success if you look at the economic benefits to the United States and what has happened. So I'm looking forward very optimistically to the future with Mexico.

Middle East Peace Process

Q. Mr. President, on the Middle East, sir, progress continues between Israel and the Palestinians, but there is still violence. But I wondered, sir, if you have an assessment on that. Is there any update on the Syrian front? Have you heard recently from President Asad? And also, has any progress been made in countering worldwide terrorism?

The President. You've asked me a lot of questions there. Let me try to answer them all. I believe we are still on a path of steady progress in the hope of achieving an agreement that resolves the differences between Israel and Syria. Serious problems remain, but I would say significant advances are being made.

With regard to the Palestinian agreement, I think everyone always knew there would be some operational difficulties because the PLO had, to be fair to them, never had been in charge of a country. That is, they had never had to operate a government and to deal with all the mundane and maybe sometimes even boring day-to-day problems that, unless they are properly managed, you can't keep a society together. I think we're making some headway there. I don't want to minimize the difficulties, but I do not expect them to be so great as to derail what we're doing.

On the terrorism front, I can tell you that every week, several times a week, I get an update on our efforts. And while, as you could appreciate, I cannot discuss many of them in great detail, I believe that we are making progress. But I believe this is a problem we'll all have to be very vigilant about for years to come.

Trude [Trude Feldman, Trans Features].

President's Birthday

Q. Mr. President, can we turn the subject to your birthday today? What stirs within you as you celebrate another birthday? And if you could have three wishes fulfilled today, what would those three wishes be?

The President. Well, I woke up this morning just grateful to be here. That's what I'm feeling—I mean, grateful to be alive, grateful to have my health, grateful to have my family, grateful to have the chance to serve. And you know, I like the tough fights, so this is an exhilarating period for me. I like the big challenges. I think we're all put on this Earth to try to make a difference.

If I had three wishes, I would wish for the crime bill to pass—[*laughter*]—one; I would wish that I would make more progress on the way we do things around here as well as on the substance, because if we can open our minds and hearts to each other and play a little less politics, we can solve the health care problem, too, and other things. And I would wish that I won't have to give up my whole vacation because I still have dreams of breaking 80 on the golf course before I'm 50. [*Laughter*]

Let me say, I feel that I—you know, this is not an easy job for you either. So since it's my birthday, if we adjourn here, let's go into the dining room, and we can have some cake and whatever else is in there.

Thank you very much. Come on, let's have some cake.

NOTE: The President's 69th news conference began at 1:30 p.m. in the East Room at the White House. In his remarks, he referred to Gov. Lawton Chiles of Florida and President Hafiz al-Asad of Syria.

Message to the Congress on Continuation of Export Control Regulations
August 19, 1994

To the Congress of the United States:

Pursuant to section 204(b) of the International Emergency Economic Powers Act, 50 U.S.C. 1703(b), I hereby report to the Congress that I have today exercised the authority granted by this Act to continue in effect the system of controls contained in 15 C.F.R., Parts 768–799, including restrictions on participation by U.S. persons in certain foreign boycott activities, which heretofore have been maintained under the authority of the Export Administration Act of 1979, as amended, 50 U.S.C. App. 2401 *et seq.* In addition, I have made provision for the administration of section 38(e) of the Arms Export Control Act, 22 U.S.C. 278(e).

The exercise of this authority is necessitated by the expiration of the Export Administration Act on August 20, 1994, and the lapse that would result in the system of controls maintained under that Act.

In the absence of controls, foreign parties would have unrestricted access to U.S. commer-

cial products, technology, technical data, and assistance, posing an unusual and extraordinary threat to national security, foreign policy, and economic objectives critical to the United States. In addition, U.S. persons would not be prohibited from complying with certain foreign boycott requests. This would seriously harm our foreign policy interests, particularly in the Middle East.

Controls established in 15 C.F.R. 768–799, and continued by this action, include the following:

—National security export controls aimed at restricting the export of goods and technologies, which would make a significant contribution to the military potential of certain other countries and which would prove detrimental to the national security of the United States.

—Foreign policy controls that further the foreign policy objectives of the United States or its declared international obligations in such widely recognized areas as human

rights, antiterrorism, regional stability, missile technology nonproliferation, and chemical and biological weapons nonproliferation.
—Nuclear nonproliferation controls that are maintained for both national security and foreign policy reasons, and which support the objectives of the Nuclear Nonproliferation Act.
—Short supply controls that protect domestic supplies, and antiboycott regulations that prohibit compliance with foreign boycotts aimed at countries friendly to the United States.

Consequently, I have issued an Executive order (a copy of which is attached) to continue in effect all rules and regulations issued or continued in effect by the Secretary of Commerce under the authority of the Export Administration Act of 1979, as amended, and all orders, regulations, licenses, and other forms of administrative actions under the Act, except where they are inconsistent with sections 203(b) and 206 of the International Emergency Economic Powers Act (IEEPA). In this Executive order I have also revoked the previous Executive Order No. 12923 of June 30, 1994, invoking IEEPA authority for the prior lapse of the Export Administration Act of 1979, as amended, extended on July 5, 1994, by Public Law 103–277.

The Congress and the Executive have not permitted export controls to lapse since they were enacted under the Export Control Act of 1949.

Any termination of controls could permit transactions to occur that would be seriously detrimental to the national interests we have heretofore sought to protect through export controls and restrictions on compliance by U.S. persons with certain foreign boycotts. I believe that even a temporary lapse in this system of controls would seriously damage our national security, foreign policy, and economic interests and undermine our credibility in meeting our international obligations.

The countries affected by this action vary depending on the objectives sought to be achieved by the system of controls instituted under the Export Administrative Act. Potential adversaries may seek to acquire sensitive U.S. goods and technologies. Other countries serve as conduits for the diversion of such items. Still other countries have policies that are contrary to U.S. foreign policy or nonproliferation objectives, or foster boycotts against friendly countries. For some goods or technologies, controls could apply even to our closest allies in order to safeguard against diversion to potential adversaries.

WILLIAM J. CLINTON

The White House,
August 19, 1994.

NOTE: The Executive order is listed in Appendix D at the end of this volume.

Message to the Congress Transmitting a Report on United States Activities in the United Nations
August 19, 1994

To The Congress of the United States:

I am pleased to transmit herewith a report of the activities of the United States Government in the United Nations and its affiliated agencies during the calendar year 1993. The report is required by the United Nations Participation Act (Public Law 264, 79th Congress; 22 U.S.C. 287b).

WILLIAM J. CLINTON

The White House,
August 19, 1994.

The President's Radio Address
August 20, 1994

Good morning. This morning I want to talk with you about crime and violence. All of us know it's too familiar a threat to Americans in almost every neighborhood in our country.

Right now, just as I'm delivering this address, the family, friends, and neighbors of a 13-year-old boy are gathered in a church not far from the White House to lay him to rest. His name was Anthony Stokes. He was shot last Saturday night apparently by another boy about the same age.

Later this morning, as Anthony Stokes' family buries him, House and Senate negotiators will meet to finish work on the crime bill. Soon after, each Member of the House of Representatives will face a simple choice, to pass the toughest attack on crime in history or to block it one more time. We must not walk away from the American people in the fight against crime.

Anthony Stokes was killed just 2 days after Congress succumbed to intense political pressure and allowed the crime bill to be derailed. We fought hard over the last 10 days to get it back on track. And it is back on track because Members of Congress of both parties have worked together in good faith, determined to deliver a crime bill for the American people.

Now Congress must finish the job and pass the crime bill I've been fighting for for nearly 2 years now. When they do, it's going to make a difference in every town, every city, every State in our country.

It's a tough bill. It'll put 100,000 new police officers on our street, a 20 percent increase in the number of officers walking the beat, protecting our neighborhoods, and preventing crime as well as catching criminals. It will shut down the revolving door on our prisons and make violent criminals serve their time. Police officers and law-abiding citizens should no longer have to watch in fear and frustration as dangerous criminals are put right back on the street. It will stiffen penalties for criminals who prey on children. It will protect unsuspecting families from sexual predators in their communities by requiring local authorities to alert them to their presence. It will lock the most dangerous criminals up for good by making "three strikes and you're out" the law of the land.

But this crime bill is smart as well as tough, because our approach recognizes what the law enforcement community has been saying for years and years. There isn't a single victim of crime who wouldn't trade the toughest sentence in the world for some way to have prevented the crime from happening in the first place.

That's why this bill includes an unprecedented effort in crime prevention, to help kids stay away from crime and drugs and gangs. It gives them something to say yes to. At the same time, we make it clear there are some things young people must say no to. The crime bill bans juvenile ownership of handguns. There's no reason why kids should be carrying guns to schools instead of books.

Finally, it bans deadly assault weapons that were designed to be used in war for rapid-fire combat. Today they are the weapons of choice for gangs and drug dealers who use them to outgun police officers and to kill innocent people. They don't belong on our streets, and the crime bill will take them off.

And the entire crime bill will be paid for—and this is important—not with a new tax, not by taking money away from some other needed service but by reducing the size of the Federal bureaucracy to its lowest level in 30 years.

This crime bill answers the call of every parent afraid that random violence will harm a child, of every police officer who's been hurt or killed by the terrible fire power of an assault weapon, of every innocent, law-abiding man, woman, and child in America. The crime bill offers this pledge: From now on, our Government will do everything we can to make sure that people who commit crimes get caught, that those who are guilty are convicted, that those who are convicted serve their times, that those who can be saved from a life of crime are found when they're young and given a chance to do better.

For all these reasons, and for a young man named Anthony Stokes who's being laid to rest today, we must not let this chance pass us by. We must seize the opportunity before us to make a dramatic difference in every neighborhood. And as we do, I hope we can make a difference in the way our Government works.

Let today mark the beginning of a determined effort on the part of all of us to work in good faith across party lines. I have shown my good faith, and in so doing I have taken the risk that all people take when they talk to people who have opposed them.

Soon the Congress will have a chance to show the risk was worth it. And once they pass the crime bill, the way will be clear for us to attack other problems together, across party lines, as the American people want us to do and as we should.

Thanks for listening.

NOTE: The President spoke at 10:06 a.m. from the Oval Office at the White House.

Statement on Cuba
August 20, 1994

Over the past 2 weeks, the Government of Cuba has taken actions to provoke a mass exodus to the United States. These actions have placed thousands of Cuban citizens at risk in small boats and rafts and have had a direct impact on our national interest.

I want to thank the Cuban-American community for their courageous restraint in not taking their own boats to Cuba to fuel the exodus and thank the officials of Florida, Governor Chiles, the congressional delegation, the people from Dade County, and others, who have worked so closely with us.

Yesterday I announced steps to counter Castro's efforts to export his problems by provoking an exodus. Today I'm announcing additional actions consistent with the Cuban Democracy Act to limit the ability of the Cuban Government to accumulate foreign exchange and to enable us to expand the flow of information to the Cuban people.

Specifically, cash remittances to Cuba will no longer be permitted. Family gift packages will be limited to medicine, food, and strictly humanitarian items and transfer of funds for humanitarian purposes will require specific authorization of the Treasury Department. Second, the only charter flights permitted between Miami and Havana will be those clearly designed to accommodate legal immigrants and travel consistent with the purposes of the Cuban Democracy Act. Third, the United States will use all appropriate means to increase and amplify its international broadcasts to Cuba.

The solution to Cuba's many problems is not an uncontrolled exodus; it is freedom and democracy for Cuba.

The United States will continue to bring before the United Nations and other international organizations evidence of human rights abuses, such as the sinking of the tugboat *13th of March.* Meanwhile we will pursue this course with vigor and determination.

Remarks on Anticrime Legislation and an Exchange With Reporters
August 21, 1994

The President. The vote in the House of Representatives tonight is a great victory for all law-abiding Americans. It's also a victory for all Americans who have longed to change the way Government works here in our Nation's Capital, who have wanted us for a long time to go beyond labels and partisan divisions and false choices to commonsense solutions to our most profound national challenges.

For 6 long years, under two previous Presidents, our families were under siege; violence on our streets increased. Washington talked a lot about crime during these years but did not act.

Well, tonight Democrats and Republicans joined together, and they acted. They reached across party lines to pass the toughest and smartest crime bill in the history of the United

States. The House moved beyond politics as usual to assume responsibility for protecting our citizens and for punishing those who prey on them and for giving our children a better future.

I am very grateful for the cooperation in this effort of several Members of the House in the Republican Party who worked hard with the Democrats in the House and with our administration to make improvements in this bill over the last few days. This is the way Washington ought to work, and I hope it will work this way in the future.

Let me remind you: This crime bill will put 100,000 police officers on our streets. It will keep repeat violent criminals off our streets with longer sentences and with the "three strikes and you're out" law and with funds to build prisons to hold those criminals. It will prohibit juveniles from owning handguns and ban deadly assault weapons and provide prevention funds to our local communities to give our children something to say yes to and to give people the opportunity to teach our children who need it right from wrong.

And the entire crime bill was fully paid for—and I want to emphasize this again—this major attack on crime is fully paid for not with new taxes, not by taking money away from current expenditures but by reducing the Federal Government to its lowest level in 30 years, by over 270,000, a major focus of our reinventing Government efforts. And all that money will be taken from the Federal budget and given to local communities to empower them to keep the American people safer.

Still, in spite of the great strengths of this bill, many of the same forces that prevented a crime bill from passing for 6 years were also present here, especially over the assault weapons issue. We received great pressure after the crime bill stalled in the House to simply remove the assault weapons ban. But we held firm, though the opposition was intense and the outcome was uncertain. We held firm because we owed it to the brave men and women in police uniforms who go out and risk their lives for the rest of us every day, and we owed it to the law-abiding citizens of this country. We must never walk away from our fundamental responsibilities in this area.

Let me remind you now that this fight is far from over. We now move to the Senate, which must pass the bill this week. But I hope that the Senators watched this debate, and I

hope they watched the events of the last few days. And I hope they watched the Republicans and the Democrats working together for the safety of the people of the United States. After all, as I said the other day, this must not be a Democratic crime bill or a Republican crime bill; this crime bill must belong to the American people. And I urge the Senate to pass it without delay.

Q. Mr. President, as you know, there are many opponents in the Senate who are already threatening a filibuster. Do you believe there are 60 Senators who will vote in favor of this package?

The President. Well, I would remind you that there were over 90 Senators who voted for a crime bill that was about this expensive, cost about this amount of money. I have given them a way to pay for it without new taxes and without taking away from other Government expenditures. The crime bill the Senate passed the first time had the assault weapons ban in it. It had prevention funds in it. It had tougher punishment in it. So, since this bill is essentially what they passed before—because the Senate also passed 100,000 police officers—those who change their vote will have to explain it and will bear the burden of doing so.

We've seen enough politics on this crime bill. The time has come to pass it. And yes, I believe that when the time comes there will be 60 votes to pass a crime bill.

Q. Mr. President, you said you hope this vote changes the way Washington works. Will you change the way you work and tone down your partisan rhetoric and reach more quickly out to the Republicans?

The President. Well, Mr. Fournier [Ron Fournier, Associated Press], I disagree with you. I have always sought first on every major bill to reach out to the Republicans. And the minute it became obvious that we had a chance to do so here, I did it.

I do want to say that that group which worked so closely with the administration and with some of the Democrats who were working on this bill proceeded in good faith. I appreciate what they did. I know they, too, were under partisan pressure on their side not to do it.

But as long as we can have a working bipartisan majority to get something good done for America, I'm going to be there leading the charge. And I'm hopeful that this represents a change in attitudes across the board. It's what

I had hoped to bring to Washington when I came here. And I think it's what the American people want us to do.

Health Care Reform

Q. What lessons have you learned from this exchange on the crime bill that you think might be useful in going forward with health care reform?

The President. That's hard to say——

Q. Specifically on the matter of the mainstream version now in the Senate, is that something you would support?

The President. The issue—but the issue in every case is, are the people involved willing to look at what actually will work?

What happened to us here in this crime bill in the last couple of days is that we even had people meeting with us who voted against the assault weapons ban. We had people meeting with us who thought that the bill was too costly but that there did need to be some money put into prevention to give these kids a better future. And the discussion was unfailingly about what was reasonable, what was practical, and what would work. What gets Washington all jammed up is when ideology and labels overtake what is the clear reality of a circumstance.

And I think that that would be possible in the health care debate. But everybody would have to be willing to sort of leave their preconceived positions at the door, at least be pre-

pared to moderate them some in order to achieve the goal that we all say we want. Everybody says we want two things, to keep the health care system we have but (a) achieve coverage for all Americans and (b) do it in ways that control costs in the years to come. The issue is, will we really look at that? And I hope we will. I am very hopeful.

All I can tell you is, I'm going to bend over backwards, even though I am not a Member of the Congress; I do not control the procedures in the Congress. I think the fact that this procedure worked well should auger well for the future. And I hope people in both parties will at least seek this opportunity on major pieces of legislation.

Thank you.

Q. Sounds like you support the mainstream proposal in the Senate.

The President. That's not what I said. I don't know what it is. I haven't had a chance to study it.

President's Vacation

Q. Will you get your birthday wish and go on vacation?

The President. I hope so. I don't know yet. I missed my other one by one stroke yesterday. [*Laughter*]

NOTE: The President spoke at 8:16 p.m. in the Oval Office at the White House.

Letter to Congressional Leaders on Bosnia-Herzegovina
August 22, 1994

Dear Mr. Speaker: (*Dear Mr. President:*)

I last reported to the Congress on April 12 on our support for the United Nations and North Atlantic Treaty Organization (NATO) efforts to achieve peace and security in Bosnia-Herzegovina. I am informing you today of recent developments in these efforts, including the use of United States combat aircraft on August 5 to attack Bosnian Serb heavy weapons in the Sarajevo heavy weapons exclusion zone.

Since the adoption of United Nations Security Council Resolution 713 on September 25, 1991, the United Nations has actively sought solutions to the humanitarian and ethnic crisis in the

former Yugoslavia. Under United Nations Security Council Resolution 824 (May 6, 1993), certain parts of Bosnia-Herzegovina have been established as safe areas. Sarajevo is specifically designated a safe area that should be "free from armed attacks and from any other hostile act."

A mortar attack on Sarajevo on February 4, 1994, caused numerous civilian casualties, including some 68 deaths. The United Nations Secretary General thereafter requested NATO to authorize, at his request, air operations against artillery or mortar positions determined by the United Nations Protection Forces

(UNPROFOR) to have been involved in attacks on civilians.

On February 9, 1994, NATO responded to the Secretary General's request by authorizing air operations, if needed, using agreed coordination procedures with UNPROFOR. The North Atlantic Treaty Organization's decision set a deadline for the withdrawal of heavy weapons within 20 kilometers of the center of Sarajevo or for the regrouping and placement of such weapons under United Nations control. As of February 21, 1994, all heavy weapons found within the Sarajevo exclusion zone, unless controlled by UNPROFOR, would be subject to NATO air strikes. In response to the NATO ultimatum, heavy weapons were removed from the exclusion zone or placed in collection sites under UNPROFOR control.

On August 5, 1994, Bosnian Serb forces entered an UNPROFOR heavy weapons collection site near the town of Ilidza and removed several heavy weapons—a tank, two armored personnel carriers, and a 30mm anti-aircraft system. An UNPROFOR helicopter dispatched to monitor the situation was fired upon and was forced to make an emergency landing. UNPROFOR troops were unsuccessful in attempting to regain custody of the weapons. As a result, UNPROFOR requested assistance from NATO forces in finding the weapons so they could be retrieved or destroyed. NATO responded by making various French, Dutch, British, and U.S. aircraft available for air strikes, if necessary.

Unable to locate the specific weapons removed from the collection site, UNPROFOR and NATO decided to proceed against other targets in the Sarajevo exclusion zone. Accordingly, on August 5, a U.S. A-10 aircraft strafed a Bosnian Serb M-18 76mm self-propelled anti-tank gun located inside the exclusion zone. No U.S. personnel were injured or killed nor was U.S. equipment damaged in connection with this action. Later on August 5, the Bosnian Serbs called the UNPROFOR Commander, General Rose, and asked him to call off the attacks. They offered to return the heavy weapons that they had taken from the storage site. General Rose agreed and the weapons were returned to UNPROFOR's control.

I took these actions in conjunction with our allies in order to carry out the NATO decision and to answer UNPROFOR's request for assistance. As I earlier reported to you, our continued efforts are intended to assist the parties to reach a negotiated settlement to the conflict. I have directed the participation by U.S. Armed Forces in this effort pursuant to my constitutional authority to conduct the foreign relations of the United States and as Commander in Chief and Chief Executive.

I am grateful for the continuing support the Congress has provided, and I look forward to continued cooperation with you in this endeavor. I shall communicate with you further regarding our efforts for peace and stability in the region.

Sincerely,

WILLIAM J. CLINTON

NOTE: Identical letters were sent to Thomas S. Foley, Speaker of the House of Representatives, and Robert C. Byrd, President pro tempore of the Senate.

Letter to Members of the Senate on Anticrime Legislation
August 22, 1994

Dear _____:

This week, the Senate has an historic chance to move us beyond old labels and partisan divisions by passing the toughest, smartest Crime Bill in our nation's history.

I want to congratulate members of Congress in both houses and both parties who have reached across party lines and worked in good faith to produce this Crime Bill. This isn't a Democratic Crime Bill or a Republican Crime Bill—it's an American Crime Bill, and it will make a difference in every town, every city, and every state in our country.

The Crime Bill produced by House and Senate conferees and passed yesterday by Democrats and Republicans in the House achieves all the same objectives as the bipartisan Crime

Bill which the Senate passed last November by a vote of 95 to 4.

Many of the central provisions of this Crime Bill were included in the Senate bill:

° Nearly $9 billion to put 100,000 new police officers on our streets in community policing;

° An additional $4.6 billion for federal, state and local law enforcement (a 25% increase above the Senate bill);

° $9.9 billion for prisons (a 30% increase above the Senate bill), coupled with tough truth-in-sentencing requirements that will shut the revolving door on violent criminals;

° Life imprisonment for repeat violent offenders by making three-strikes-and-you're-out the law of the land;

° Federal death penalties for the most heinous of crimes, such as killing a law enforcement officer;

° A ban on handgun ownership for juveniles;

° Registration and community notification to warn unsuspecting families of sexual predators in their midst;

° A ban on 19 semiautomatic assault weapons, with specific protection for more than 650 other weapons; and

° Innovative crime prevention programs, such as the Community Schools program sponsored by Senators Danforth, Bradley, and Dodd, and the Violence Against Women Act sponsored by Senators Biden, Hatch, and Dole.

One of the most important elements of this Crime Bill is the creation of a Violent Crime Reduction Trust Fund, which ensures that every crime-fighting program in the bill will be paid for by reducing the federal bureaucracy by more than 270,000 positions over the next six years. The idea for the Trust Fund came from Senators Byrd, Mitchell, Biden, Gramm, Hatch, and Dole, and the Senate approved it by a vote of 94 to 4. The Trust Fund will ensure that the entire Crime Bill will be fully paid for, not with new taxes, but by reducing the federal bureaucracy to its lowest level in over 30 years.

The Senate led the way in passing these important anti-crime proposals last November, and I urge you to take up this Crime Bill in the same bipartisan spirit that marked that debate. The American people have waited six years for a comprehensive Crime Bill. It's time to put politics aside and finish the job. After all the hard work that has gone into this effort by members of both parties acting in good faith, we owe it to the law-abiding citizens of this country to pass this Crime Bill without delay.

Sincerely,

BILL CLINTON

NOTE: Identical letters were sent to Senators of the 103d Congress. This letter was released by the Office of the Press Secretary on August 23.

Remarks on Signing the King Holiday and Service Act of 1994
August 23, 1994

Good morning. Thank you. Please be seated. It was such a beautiful and, for August, a cool summer day, we thought we ought to move to the Rose Garden today and give us all a chance to enjoy this wonderful beauty.

Senator Wofford, Congressman Lewis, Martin Luther King III, Mr. Segal, ladies and gentlemen, we're here for the signing of the King Holiday and Service Act of 1994. And I have some words I want to say about that, but if I might, I'd like to mention a few things about the service that the Congress is engaged in performing at the present moment with regard to the crime bill.

On Sunday evening Democrats and Republicans in the House produced a victory for all Americans by passing the bill. They showed that with a little faith and a lot of hard work, they could reach across the partisan divide that have held this country back for too long to pass a bill that is both tough and smart, that is firm and compassionate, that gives us a chance to lower the crime rate and make our people safer.

Many of the best ideas in the bill were ones contributed by both Democrats and Republicans: to put 100,000 police on the streets, to keep violent offenders off the streets with longer sentences and "three strikes and you're out," to prohibit juveniles from owning handguns, to ban assault weapons, to provide innovative and proven prevention programs to give our children a chance to have a better future—programs, I want to emphasize, that were sponsored in this legislation by members of both parties.

And one of the best ideas in the bill was also supported in both Houses by members of both parties, that is, to establish a trust fund funded by the reductions in the Federal work force over the next 6 years, 270,000, to bring our Federal Government to its smallest size in over 30 years and to give all that money back to our local communities for police, for punishment, and for prevention, not by raising taxes, not by cutting other services but simply reducing the size of the Federal Government to its lowest point in 30 years. This trust fund was sponsored by leaders from both parties, including Senators Byrd, Mitchell, and Biden for the Democrats, Senators Dole, Gramm, and Hatch for the Republicans. It passed the Senate by a vote of 94 to 4 the first time.

When this bill comes back, it will be a little different from the bill that passed the Senate, but not much. It lasts 6 years instead of 5 years. It has some more money for border patrol and other problems. But it's not much bigger on an annual basis, and it's all paid for in the same way. Every Senator, without regard to party, ought to continue the bipartisan spirit that was established in the House for an American approach to an American problem. That is the service we ought to be performing today, to make this an American crime bill and to do it without delay.

The King Holiday and Service Act of 1994 in this bill combines for the very first time our national holiday in honor of Dr. King with a national day of service. Nothing could be more appropriate, for it was Dr. King who said everyone can be great because everyone can serve. I always think of the great line he said, that if a person was a street sweeper, he ought to sweep the streets as if he were Michelangelo painting the Sistine Chapel and try to be the best one in the whole world. That is what I think all of us ought to be about doing.

Dr. King taught us that our faith can redeem us, that the sacrifices of individuals can sustain us, that moral courage can guide us. He dedicated himself to what was in his time and what remains the most difficult challenge we face as a democratic people: closing the great gap between our words and our deeds.

Now we are attempting in this bill and in this administration to accept this challenge for those who are still barred from the American dream and for those who worry that their children will have less of it than they had. We're doing our best here to give Government back to ordinary citizens, with an administration that is really more like America than any ever has been, not only in terms of its racial and gender diversity but also in its commitment to excellence, with 4 million new jobs, 20 million young people eligible for reduced college loans, 15 million working families getting tax cuts, and 3 years of reduction in our deficit for the first time since Mr. Truman was the President.

We demanded fairness in all public services and especially in housing, not only in Vidor, Texas, but all across the United States. We fought to empower the next generation of our working people, beginning with Head Start and world-class educational standards, and apprenticeship programs for those who don't go to college, and more and less expensive college loans and national service for those who wish to pursue higher education. We fought to strengthen our communities with empowerment zones and community development banks. And we fought to make our people safer with the Brady bill and hopefully with this crime bill.

But we know and we learn here every day that laws alone cannot restore the American family, cannot give individuals the sense of self-worth and purpose, cannot make the American community what it ought to be. It takes the miracle that begins with personal choices and personal actions and that cuts through the fog of cynicism and negativism that grips every American from time to time and has often gripped this country too much.

Giving every citizen at the grassroots a chance to make a difference in his or her own life is a big part of what our efforts are all about. This law helps us to do that by linking the observance of Dr. King's birthday to a day of national service, an extraordinary idea and a timely one because just next month we will launch AmeriCorps in full-blown initiative, with 20,000 young people serving their communities at the grassroots level and earning some credit to further their education while doing so. Nothing could better serve the legacy of Dr. King. He was apathy's sworn enemy and action's tireless champion.

The King Commission has already sponsored seven national youth assemblies where young people address issues for themselves, such as drug abuse, illiteracy, and the importance of staying in school. The largest and most recent assembly took place in the capital of my home State, Little Rock, where Governor Tucker hosted 1,300 young people. Overall, the Commission has already helped to recruit 4½ million young people to sign a pledge where they say no to violence and drugs and yes to serving in their communities. That is a truly revolutionary achievement.

With today's action we can broaden that effort. We can give many more an opportunity to make a difference, to respond to the needs of their communities, whether through tutoring children or housing the homeless, improving parks or keeping our people safer. As Senator Wofford has said in what I think is one of his best statements, "The King holiday should be a day on, not a day off."

Dr. King's time with us was too brief. But his vision was so great, his moral purpose was so strong that he made us believe that we could be better than we are and that someday we would be able to walk hand in hand together into a brighter tomorrow.

He said, and I quote, "Every man must decide whether he will walk in the light of creative altruism or the darkness of destructive selfishness. Life's most persistent and urgent question is what are you doing for others?"

Today we can say with some pride we have given all Americans a better chance to work together and to help others. This celebration of Dr. King will now be a celebration of his vision of community, his vision of service. And his life proves that it will work for all Americans and for our country.

Thank you very much.

NOTE: The President spoke at 11:30 a.m. in the Rose Garden at the White House. In his remarks, he referred to Eli J. Segal, Assistant to the President and Director of the Office of National Service. H.R. 1933, approved August 23, was assigned Public Law No. 103–304.

Statement on Signing the Federal Aviation Administration Authorization Act of 1994
August 23, 1994

I am pleased to sign into law H.R. 2739, the "Federal Aviation Administration Authorization Act of 1994." It is exceedingly satisfying when legislation is presented for enactment that reflects both of the things the American people want from their Government—action by the Government when clearly needed and action to eliminate Government regulation when it proves counterproductive.

When I came into office, the aviation industry was struggling with large losses, reduced airline travel because of the recession, and a loss of aircraft orders at many of our biggest manufacturers. The problems ran deep. I know because I visited businesses to get an idea of the extent of the problems. In the face of these problems, the Government did not sit back.

With the support of the industry and other interested groups, we enacted amendments to the law that created the National Commission to Ensure a Strong Competitive Airline Industry.

Building on the Commission's recommendations, the Administration acted quickly, setting forth in our "Initiative to Promote a Strong Competitive Aviation Industry" a comprehensive strategy to address the basic issues and problems.

That initiative has borne fruit. Of course, our successful economic program is the foundation for the much better financial results we see in the aviation sector. But now the Congress has acted to translate specific Commission recommendations and those we offered in January into effective legislation, giving the industry a stable basis for further recovery.

The legislation that I am approving today sets in place a solid, multi-year authorization for Federal aviation activities. This authorization will serve as a foundation for concerted action on important and varied matters, such as quickly implementing the new Global Positioning System in the aviation sector. This bill also fulfills part of my pledge to emphasize economically valuable infrastructure investment as the way to keep our Nation competitive across the board. This year, we will have committed nearly $1.7 billion to new airport development and planning grants. Overall, I believe the legislation sends the right signal—that the aviation sector continues to be a prime contributor to this country's economic health.

Just as important, this legislation is proof that we can end Government activities when they have outlived their usefulness. My Administration strongly supported Title VI of the bill, which was designed to remove conflicting State laws, unrelated to safety, that impede efficient intermodal freight transportation. We also urged that Title VI be expanded to increase the efficiency of all commercial truckers. Fortunately, the Congress did expand it.

State regulation preempted under this provision takes the form of controls on who can enter the trucking industry within a State, what they can carry and where they can carry it, and whether competitors can sit down and arrange among themselves how much to charge shippers and consumers. Taken together in the 41 States that do this, this sort of regulation costs consumers up to $8 billion per year in extra expenditures by increasing the freight transportation cost of everything we buy. That doesn't even count the costs of additional inventories and extra miles as companies try to escape the unnecessarily high cost of hauling their products

on an intrastate basis by locating their plants far away from their consumer markets and criss-crossing State lines. Many firms have done so just to take advantage of interstate freight rates made cheaper due to the deregulation proposal of President Carter in 1980.

I fully expect that this legislation will have effects similar to those of the 1980 deregulation law. New carriers will be able to enter the trucking industry, particularly women- and minority-owned carriers who may have been "frozen out" in the past by strict entry controls. Freight rates will become more competitive, truck service will become better and more reliable even in small, out-of-the-way communities, and employment in the trucking services industry will increase substantially.

Thus, the current legislation is not only a significant addition to our economic stimulus program, it will also save consumers billions of dollars every year.

For these reasons, I am pleased to sign into law the "Federal Aviation Administration Authorization Act of 1994."

WILLIAM J. CLINTON

The White House,
August 23, 1994.

NOTE: H.R. 2739, approved August 23, was assigned Public Law No. 103–305.

Statement on Apple Exports to Japan
August 23, 1994

I am pleased to announce that the Government of Japan has agreed to take the first steps to open its market to American apples. This is good news for Washington's apple industry and for those workers whose jobs depend on it.

As many of you may know, American apples have been totally banned from the Japanese market for the past 23 years. After months of negotiations, however, we have cleared away obstacles to the export of apples from the State

of Washington. Right now, apples are being inspected in preparation for export.

Exports mean jobs, and that is why we will continue to work to open markets in Japan and elsewhere. I appreciate Japan taking this step toward greater liberalization of trade and closer economic relations between our two countries. As we move ahead, I look forward to building on this achievement to open Japan's markets to more of America's competitive goods and services.

Address to the People of Ukraine on Ukrainian Independence Day
August 24, 1994

It's a privilege to speak directly to you, the Ukrainian people, and congratulate you on your third Independence Day.

In the short span of 3 years, Ukraine has shown the world that a nation can rapidly set down the roots of democracy. This year's elections for President and Parliament are strong evidence of your commitment to a democratic future, and we congratulate you on them.

As Vice President Gore told President Kuchma when he visited Kiev earlier this month, the United States places a high value on our relationship with Ukraine. The American people strongly support your country's independence, its sovereignty, its territorial integrity. We believe in a stable, strong, and prosperous Ukraine.

To help achieve those goals, the United States will support you as Ukraine proceeds down the difficult path of economic reform. At the recent meeting of the Group of Seven, I worked hard to secure a pledge of $4 billion in assistance for your nation. Those funds will be put to work when your government takes practical steps to reform Ukraine's economy and introduce the free market. As you face the hard work of modernizing and rebuilding your economy, be assured that the United States stands ready to help.

The fruits of cooperation between our two nations can already be seen in our historic achievements on military and nuclear security matters. The leadership that Ukraine demonstrated when it became the first country to join NATO's Partnership For Peace is showing other nations the path to new security arrangements that will promote a truly unified Europe. Your nation's critical role in creating the trilateral statement on denuclearization will not only remove a source of great danger to you and people all over the world but also ensure that you receive fair compensation for the value of the nuclear warheads on your territory.

And I am confident that when Ukraine joins the 164 nations that have acceded to the Nuclear Non-Proliferation Treaty, you will witness a range of new opportunities for your high-technology industries. These industries will have the chance to flourish in both government-to-government projects and through expanded international commerce.

Here in the United States, as you know, we are especially proud of the Ukrainian-Americans who have helped to build our democracy and contribute so much to our society. I join with them in today's celebration of Ukraine's reborn statehood and in recognition of Ukrainians the world over who have given so much for the cause of freedom and democracy.

The coming years pose many challenges, but I am confident that we are laying the foundation to meet them. Working together, I am convinced that my country and yours will continue to develop a deep and abiding relationship that serves our mutual interests. We look forward to working with your new President and Parliament to find new ways to strengthen the friendship between our peoples.

On this day, we should all recall those who fought for independence before us. Your great poet Taras Shevchenko, a man born into serfdom, a contemporary of my Nation's Great Emancipator, President Lincoln, dreamed that one day his countrymen would enjoy the fruits of independence. Today, on behalf of all the American people, I congratulate you on realizing Shevchenko's dream and on the great years of freedom that lie ahead for all of you.

NOTE: The address was videotaped on August 4 at approximately noon in the Roosevelt Room at the White House, and it was released by the Office of the Press Secretary on August 24. A tape was not available for verification of the content of this address.

Teleconference Remarks With B'nai B'rith
August 24, 1994

The President. Thank you very much, President Schiner, distinguished guests, ladies and gentlemen. Thank you for that very warm greeting. And I certainly can identify with the tension of waiting for election results to come in. I'm very glad to be with you today, if not in body then very much in spirit.

It's an honor to address the international convention of an organization that has done so much for our country. I understand that, along with delegates from 40 of our 50 States, there are among you representatives from 36 nations. I want each of you to know this country's gratitude for the extraordinary work B'nai B'rith has performed since its founding in 1843. Your tireless dedication to community service, health, education, and housing for the elderly, and your staunch opposition to bigotry of any kind long ago earned our respect and our thanks.

Allow me to add my voice to the chorus saluting Kent Schiner as he steps down after 4 distinguished years as your president. Kent joined Hillary—or hosted Hillary and me—at the Jefferson Memorial last October when B'nai B'rith celebrated its 150th anniversary. I admire anyone who survives and thrives for a full term as president. So congratulations to you, Kent, on a job well done.

This is a remarkably exciting time, both at home and abroad for issues of particular concern to B'nai B'rith and to me. At home we're on the verge of winning the fight to make our streets safer for law-abiding Americans. We're closer to the day when health care will no longer be a privilege for some but a right for all. Our economy is recovering—over 4 million new jobs in the last year and a half. We're moving in the right direction at home. Abroad we've witnessed progress in one year toward peace in the Middle East that can literally take our breath away. And let me say a few words on these subjects.

This past weekend, Democrats and Republicans in the House of Representatives joined in an unprecedented effort to set aside the petty concerns of partisan politics and acted quickly to address the real concerns of real people about crime. Not only did they pass a crime bill that the American people desperately want and need, but they showed the bipartisan spirit and good faith we desperately need here in Washington to make this National Government work again.

Now the Senate has a chance to follow suit, to pass the toughest, smartest, most bipartisan crime bill in our Nation's history, a bill built on bipartisan roots of the crime bill that Republicans and Democrats in the Senate passed late last year by a vote of 95 to 4.

This bill is centrist and bipartisan to its very bones: 100,000 new police officers, billions more for prisons, "three strikes and you're out," prohibiting juveniles from owning handguns, a ban on deadly assault weapons, and much needed and working crime prevention programs, and a massive cut in the Federal bureaucracy to pay for these crime-fighting efforts. That's right. We're reducing the Federal bureaucracy to its smallest size since the Kennedy Presidency and putting all the savings into a trust fund to pay for the crime bill. These aren't Democratic or Republican ideas; they are commonsense solutions that the American people support because they can really make a difference against crime and violence now and in the future.

For 6 years, the American people have waited while Congress debated a crime bill, even as they watched the average violent criminal go free in just 4 years. It's time to act now. This is about keeping faith with the millions upon millions of American families who work hard, pay the taxes, obey the laws, and don't ask very much from our Government, but they do want to raise their children in a country that is safe and secure.

The American people don't want a criminal justice system that makes excuses for criminals. They also are tired of a political system that makes excuses for politicians. It's time to put away the excuses, the blames, and the politics and join forces to pass this crime bill now. And I urge all of you to call your Senators, without regard to party, and tell them just that.

For many years now, B'nai B'rith has been a leader in providing health care to all kinds of Americans. When I spoke to you at the Jefferson Memorial I described the hospital you opened in my home town of Hot Springs, Arkansas, some 90 years ago. The Leo N. Levi

Hospital still cares for hundreds of people every year without regard to their ability to pay. That same generous spirit should animate our national health care system.

After 60 years of trying, we're closer than ever to providing health security for all Americans. For the first time in our history, both the House and the Senate are considering comprehensive and effective health reform measures. These efforts are long overdue. Health costs are too high and rising too fast. Coverage is actually shrinking in America. Millions in the middle class are losing their insurance every year, many of them for good. There are 5 million working Americans and their children who don't have health insurance today who had it just 5 years ago.

Meeting this challenge requires more from us than politics as usual. This again shouldn't be about politics or special interests. It should be about putting the interests of our families, our Nation, and our future first. I believe we can do it if we'll leave aside ideology and partisanship and follow the example that the House did Sunday in passing the crime bill. To do it, we'll have to join together to stand up to some intense pressures to guarantee that every American has solid, affordable, private health insurance. Every other major advanced country has done it. It's time for America to do the same.

Lastly, let me say I know you share the joy that I feel in the progress that's been made toward peace in the Middle East. For more than four decades, Americans have identified with and supported Israel's struggle for survival and acceptance in a hostile region. Now, after so much bloodshed, so many lost opportunities, Arabs and Israelis are reaching out to each other to settle their differences through conciliation, compromise, and peaceful coexistence.

Some of you were on the South Lawn of the White House to witness the historic handshake between Chairman Arafat and Prime Minister Rabin. And some of you joined us in the Rose Garden when King Hussein and the Prime Minister showed the world what warm peace can mean in the Middle East. I hope and I believe that the time is not far off when we'll see a comprehensive peace in the region, a peace that binds Israelis, Palestinians, Jordanians, Syrians, and Lebanese so that all their children can know a better future.

The United States has been proud to serve as a full partner in the search for peace, not by imposing peace or making life-and-death decisions for others; that must be the responsibility of the leaders and the people of the region. Rather, our role is to facilitate negotiated compromise and to underwrite reasonable risk-taking. And that is exactly what we've done.

I applaud the bold steps that Israel has taken, and I salute the courage of the Arab leaders who have stood up to the scurrilous charge that they are somehow selling out the Arab cause by securing for their own people a future of peace, prosperity, and hope.

Now we must demonstrate that the international community supports this courage and ensure that the people of the region realize the full benefits of these peacemaking efforts. At the same time, we have a right to expect that all the participants in the peace process live up to the commitments they've made. In this regard, it's heartening to hear from many Palestinians their genuine desire for democratic elections, representative government, and transparent and accountable institutions. These things they need, and they deserve nothing less.

As we move ahead in the peace process, we need to keep in mind some basic principles. First, peace must be real, not just the absence of war but a qualitative change in the relations between Israel and its neighbors: full diplomatic ties, an end to the boycott, open borders for people in trade, joint economic projects. And it would be inconsistent with real peace for any of the parties to host or sponsor those who reject accommodation with Israel, especially terrorist groups.

Second, peace must be secure. The parties themselves must reach agreement that provides for mutual security. In the case of the Israel-Syria negotiations, this administration, following consultations with Congress, stands ready to participate in the arrangements these parties reach. And just as this administration has acted to sustain and enhance Israel's qualitative military edge, so, too, it will help to compensate for any strategic advantages Israel may choose to give up for peace.

Finally, peace must be comprehensive. We will work hard to achieve breakthroughs in the Syrian and Lebanese tracks. And when we do, we'll also expect the wider Arab and Muslim worlds to normalize their relations with Israel. Let me emphasize here that we're committed to bringing the Arab boycott of Israel to an end now.

First of all, the boycott harms American companies, and it has no place in the peace process. Through the Gaza-Jericho accord and the transfer of authority elsewhere in the territories, the Palestinians have entered into a new economic relationship with Israel. Continuing the boycott harms not only Israel but the Palestinians as well. At the same time the Washington Declaration affirms that the abolition of all boycotts is the shared goal of Israel and Jordan. With serious progress being made on the Syria negotiating track, retaining this relic of a bygone era cannot possibly be justified. The boycott must be ended.

Building peace is extraordinarily hard work. We know that the dark forces of hatred and terror remain deeply entrenched. In recent weeks, terrible attacks against Jews in Argentina, Panama, and England have underscored the heinous acts some will commit to undermine this peace process.

Among you today are members of those communities, including Joseph Harari from Panama, who lost a nephew on the plane that was bombed from the skies over his country. Mr. Harari, I pledge to you and to everyone else in this room, we'll do all that we can to help bring the perpetrators of this crime and the other crimes to justice. Our policy is clear: to weaken and isolate those who reject a more peaceful future for the peoples of the troubled region.

Two key obstacles of that future are Iraq and Iran and the radical groups they continue to support. In the case of Iraq, we must maintain the international consensus in favor of strict sanctions. This clear expression of international will has compelled Saddam Hussein finally to begin to cooperate with U.N. weapons inspectors. But the true nature of Saddam's regime remains clear. Relief workers and weapons inspectors face constant harassment and intimidation. Terrorism plagues the Iraqi people. Witness last month's tragic death of a prominent Shiite leader, the summary executions of bank managers, and the recent assassination of an Iraqi dissident in Beirut by Iraqis credited as diplomats. Baghdad still refuses to recognize the sovereignty and borders of Kuwait. And the regime continues to destroy the lives of the marsh Arabs of southern Iraq. These facts serve as

reminders of why we must and why we will maintain the sanctions.

Of equal importance is our effort to contain Iran, the world's leading state sponsor of terrorism, the pledge to work with like-minded countries to meet the challenge of Iran's support for terrorist groups, its efforts to acquire weapons of mass destruction, and its campaign to subvert moderate regimes that have opted for peace. We must do this. We call upon all our allies to recognize the true nature of Iranian intentions and to help us convince Tehran that we will not tolerate rogue behavior.

Now let me conclude on a happier and more positive note. It's been said that unless a person is a recipient of charity, he or she should be a contributor to it. Your work through B'nai B'rith gives life to that generous thought. So this week, as you reflect on your wonderful acts of community service and plan new ones, let me once again express the gratitude of our Nation for all you've done and all that you will do.

Thank you very much.

Terrorism

[*At this point, Kent Schiner thanked the President for his efforts to promote peace in the Middle East and to address the problems of health care and crime. Jorge Serejski, president of B'nai B'rith in Argentina, then asked about administration efforts to combat domestic and international terrorism.*]

The President. Let me tell you what we are doing. First of all, you can see from the results of our efforts to solve the World Trade Center bombing case that we are very aggressive in pursuing these cases. We are intensifying our international cooperation, working with Argentina, Great Britain, and Panama, and other countries, to try to help resolve who did these terrible acts of terrorism and apprehend the perpetrators.

In addition to that, we are increasing our cooperation through intelligence and law enforcement services with countries throughout the globe to try to prevent such acts from occurring in the first place. So we're trying to intensify our efforts at prevention and intensify our efforts at catching people when they do these terrible things.

And I think we will have some considerable success. But we must not be naive. There are a lot of people who have a big, vested interest in the continued misery of people in the Middle East, the continued anxiety of Arabs, and particularly Palestinians and others. And they hate the fact that peace is winning converts and making progress.

So as we move through the peace process, if we continue to have success, the enemies of peace will continue to look for opportunities to make innocent people pay the price, so that they can continue to make money and accumulate political power on the human misery that has dominated the Middle East for decades. So they'll be there, but we're doing what we can, and we are putting more resources into the effort to stop them before they do it and to catch and punish them if we're unsuccessful in stopping them in the first place.

Health Care Reform

[*Health care consultant Janet Weissberg asked about the President's commitment to health care coverage for long-term care and prescription drugs.*]

The President. Well, my commitment is just as broad as it ever was. I think the provision of the prescription drugs, the long-term care is very important.

But let me inject a little political reality here. The real problem is that we have Members of the United States Senate, including some people who've been very good friends of B'nai B'rith, who are walking away from what is the only known way to provide universal coverage, control cost increases in the out years, and still generate enough money to provide these services, which is simply to require all employers and employees to provide insurance and then provide discounts to those who can't afford to pay the full cost.

Once you say we're giving up on the requirement that employers provide health insurance and their employees help to pay for it—even in 5 years or 6 years from now, in the so-called hard trigger that Senator Mitchell advocated—once you walk away from that, then you find the Senate basically getting into taxes and Government regulation to try to raise a huge amount of money from people who are already paying for their health insurance and already have good health insurance to go throw it at people who have insisted on not being asked to do anything on their own in the hope that

they can induce them with somebody else's money to do something they ought to do anyway. And that leaves less money for prescription drugs and long-term care.

Now, that's basically what's happened. This whole debate has been mischaracterized. I think that our position is the essentially conservative one, where we simply ask everybody to do their part, since they're benefiting from the health care system, and buy private health insurance and then help them if they can't afford to buy it at the full price. But everybody's asked to do something.

The so-called moderate and conservative people are trying to find ways to raise money from people who are already doing their part to basically overly subsidize people who don't have insurance and employers who could afford to pay and don't, in the hope that they can plead with them to do something that they're unwilling to require in the law. And that is the nub of all of our other problems.

If you're asking me where I am, I am still where I always was. I will do my very best to provide it. I talked to a Member of the Congress today who needed some long-term care at home for an ailing parent. We need to do this. We need it desperately. But I would urge you to talk to the Members of Congress in both parties who have been your friends and ask them to look at the real world, instead of the kind of ideological box that they have put themselves in, and do something that will work.

The main thing we must do is we must do something that will work. And it would be better not to do anything at all than to adopt a program that would actually increase costs of health care and reduce coverage. That's what we don't want to do.

Middle East Peace Process

[*Irving Silver, chairman of the B'nai B'rith Center for Public Policy, asked what the administration was doing to impress upon Yasser Arafat and the Palestine Liberation Organization that its agreement with Israel can only succeed if the PLO accepts the spirit as well as the letter of the agreement's provisions.*]

The President. Well, we're telling him just what you said, and we're doing it on a regular basis. The Secretary of State's in constant contact with Mr. Arafat. We are working with the PLO people. We understood all along that because they had never actually run a country before and operated a government and all of its manifestations, with all of its problems, that there would be more difficulties here, operational difficulties, in making the agreement actually work. But we are working hard on that. And we're also trying to provide assistance and support as well as pressure when that will help to get them to do what they're supposed to do.

We've also been very blessed in having a group of Jewish-American and Arab-American business people who are working together and are prepared to make some investments in those areas if we can get the PLO in a position where they can actually effectively function and implement this.

So I believe that the biggest problem is one of capacity. And I think the limited capacity is undermining the question of will from time to time. We just have to keep the pressure on and also have to keep working practically to increase the capacity for this agreement to be implemented by the PLO.

Mr. Schiner. Again, Mr. President, on behalf of the half million people and members who affiliate with B'nai B'rith in 51 countries, on 6 continents, we thank you for your warm greeting and your important message. Thank you again.

The President. Thank you very much, Kent. Thank you.

NOTE: The President spoke at 3:40 p.m. from Room 459 of the Old Executive Office Building.

Interview With Gene Burns of WOR Radio, New York City
August 24, 1994

The President. Glad to be here, Gene.

Mr. Burns. Do you feel like Daniel in the mouth of the lion's den? You and talk radio these days seem to have this running battle.

The President. We were talking before we went on the air; I really have always enjoyed talk radio and I've done a lot of it, particularly when I was Governor, and in my campaign I did a lot. I find that there's a certain immediacy to it that I like. I like the interviews and I like people being able to call in a question.

Accomplishments and Goals

Mr. Burns. George Stephanopoulos was here earlier, and he says in his view—and I assume he mirrors your own—your accomplishments in your first almost 2 years as President have not gotten through the screen of the media to the American people. Do you feel any sense of isolation here in terms of what you like, you've told us, that sort of one-on-one relationship with constituents?

The President. Oh, yes. I think part of it is the nature of the Presidency and the whole security bubble that's around the President. Part of it is the demanding nature of the job and

the fact that Washington, DC, and its inner workings are a long way from the average life of most Americans. And part of it is the way news is reported today. News basically tends to be—a lot of studies have shown that the way news is reported tends to be more negative and more editorial, more commentary rather than what's going on.

A lot of the research shows that the American people are surprised to find out that in 1993, for example, I had more success in getting a very big program through Congress, with the economic program and NAFTA and family leave, the Brady bill, than any President since the end of World War II except President Eisenhower's first year and President Johnson's second year.

So we're doing well here, I think, in moving forward in an extremely contentious environment. And I just have to find ways to communicate better with the American people not only what we're doing wrong—the press will tell them that—but also what we're doing right and where we're going.

Mr. Burns. From your side of the table, what's the nature of that contentious environment? I know that you, yourself, have pointed to a deep cynicism on the part of the American people. You feel in some respects the media drives that cynicism. But there does seem to be a sense of social disconnect. I mean, Jefferson said, Americans have the power; from time to time they give it to folks like yourself to exercise for them. And the first amendment ends with, "and they'll always have a direct route for the redress of grievances." A lot of Americans don't think they have that direct route.

The President. I agree with that. I was reading this morning, interestingly enough, James Madison's "Federalist Papers." And he was arguing why a republican form of government, meaning representative form of government, was better for big countries, that you had to elect representatives and then they'd do what they thought was right. Then they'd report back, be held accountable, and be elected or defeated by the voters.

I think today there is so much—there's a lot of information about what we're doing up here, but I don't think there's a lot of basic understanding that we impart. And I think that voters know that too many decisions get made here on the basis of organized interest which may or may not be the same as the public interest.

And I think that at a time of real change, when people are uncertain about where we're going, it's just easy for negative impulses, for fears, for cynicism to overcome hopes in looking toward the future.

I also believe, and many astute people in the press have pointed this out lately, that voters themselves feel a certain ambivalence. That is, they want us to do things up here. I got elected to take action, to deal with the economy, to deal with crime, to deal with the breakdown of family, to promote welfare reform, to deal with the health care crisis. But people still basically are very skeptical about the Government's ability to do it. So we want, in a way, a Government that is more active but basically that is active in empowering the private sector to do things, rather than active in doing things directly. I think that's where the voters are.

And a lot of times that explains the apparently contradictory feelings people have about what we're doing here, that they want us to be active and address the problems but they don't necessarily trust the Government to do it. Or as we say at home, a lot of people think Government would mess up a one-car parade. [*Laughter*]

Mr. Burns. You're a student of history. Do you think that's because Camelot was illusory in the last analysis, that it's a mythical thing and that people are disappointed with both the Congress and various holders of your office? Is that the problem?

The President. Oh, only partly. I think, first of all, the American people have always, always had a deep-seated skepticism about government generally and especially their National Government. I think that we've also been told for years that government was bad. And I think that we need a clearer definition; this is partly my job. I've got to do a better job of telling the American people in very clear terms, often through a fog of people, you know, disagreeing with me or with my characterization of it—I've got to do a better job of saying, okay, look, here is what we can do, here are our problems, here are our opportunities, here's what the National Government should do and here's what we cannot do, here's the partnership we have to have. That's what I called my new Democratic philosophy when I ran in 1992.

I share what I think is the feeling of a majority of our fellow citizens, that the government should be limited in many ways and that government should do those things which it is required to do but no more than it is required to do.

Mr. Burns. I mean, that's an excellent point. The Wall Street Journal reports this morning that Al From of the Democratic leadership conference just sent you a big memo, five or six pages long. I'm not trying to invade your private correspondence, but one of the things they say he said to you was, rightly or wrongly, you have become too identified with liberal causes on Capitol Hill and therefore don't appear to some of the people who supported you initially as this centrist Democrat, which you said you were.

The President. I think that's right. And I think some of that may be my fault in terms of characterization. But if you look at what we've actually done, if you look at the economic program that I've put in place, it's bringing the deficit down for 3 years in a row, it's reducing the Federal Government by 272,000—certainly not a traditional liberal thing to do—to the smallest Federal Government we've had since Kennedy was President. We're taking all the savings and putting it into the fight against crime, which is basically money to people at the grassroots local level. We're addressing the issues like welfare reform partly with tax cuts for working families with lower incomes and tougher child support enforcement—not traditional liberal programs.

I think what happened was, more than anything else, the health care program has been characterized as a big Government program, even though it took what, at the time I proposed it, was the moderate course, which is not having a Government-financed health care program but simply having a program in which the Government requires everybody to buy private insurance and then gives tax breaks or discounts to people who can't afford it on their own. That was the moderate proposal when we started. And every time we've sought to compromise, the other guys have always moved kind of further and further to the right.

But I think that the health care debate more than anything else—we've had $140 million now spent in lobbying and advertising on health care by organized interests, the largest amount in American history, far more than was spent by the candidates in the Presidential campaign last time.

When that happened, I think that that—I have been portrayed as sort of the apostle of big Government. Actually, that is not an accurate portrayal. I'm about reinventing Government. I'm trying to bring the Federal Government down. My Republican predecessors never attempted to do anything as ambitious as reducing the Federal Government to its smallest size in 30 years. I have fought for things that Democrats often don't fight for, including all these trade agreements to expand trade. I have fought to put the Government in partnership with our business interests overseas. Yesterday, just to give you a little example, we announced that for the first time in over 20 years, farmers in the Pacific Northwest will be able to sell their apples in Japan. For the first time ever, farmers in California are selling rice in Japan. These are the things that I have worked on.

But there are some things that I believe—and this is worth debating—that the Government has to do. And when we have to do something, it should be as limited and efficient as possible. But there are some things that if we don't do it, it won't get done.

Mr. Burns. Well, Mr. President, on the lobbying money, John Connally spent $10 million because he wanted to be President of the United States, and it was all wasted money, as we both know.

The President. He got one delegate——

Mr. Burns. He got one delegate——

The President. ——from my home State. I know her.

Mr. Burns. Well, there you are.

The President. I know her well.

Mr. Burns. That's a pretty high delegate, you know. So all of this money being spent by the special interests on health care, which has to be conceded has been spent, is not going to get a warm reception unless there is a general fear of the growth of Government in the first place.

The President. I think that's right. I agree with that. I think—one of the things that Al From said to me with the Democratic Leadership Council—not in this memo, but I think it captures in one sentence the dilemma I face as President in trying to move into a post-cold-war world and take this country into the 21st century with a strategy for growth and opportunity, where the Government is not either just sitting on the sidelines or trying to solve problems but is being a partner with the American people—he said we are basically back in 1965 in what we want Government to do, but we're about in 1980 in what we trust Government to do, that is, the year President Reagan was elected.

So people have high aspirations for what they wish us to do, but they don't trust us to do much. And they're afraid we'll mess it up. So it's easy to derail almost any initiative by saying, well, this thing is wrong with it or that or the other thing. We are a people of—a democratic government requires some flexibility and compromise and people working together. And somehow, we've got to find a way to recreate that spirit. Now, it happened on the NAFTA debate, and it happened last week on crime in the House. It was wonderful to see these Democrats and Republicans sitting down together, cutting unnecessary spending, redirecting the programs, making sure we only told the American people we were going to spend what we could, in fact, spend from reducing the size of the Federal Government. That's what we need more of, that sort of thing.

Anticrime Legislation

Mr. Burns. George Stephanopoulos answered this question. I guess this is a test as to whether he's really reflecting what you believe as President of the United States. Why not break out the component parts of the crime bill? You and I both know that many of those components would fly through the Congress with no opposition—more police, more prisons. You might even win the assault weapons ban issue. Why doggedly say it's all or nothing?

The President. Well, for one thing, I'm not sure that it would all pass. There is an answer to that. The first answer is, the House adopted them separately and together. The Senate, 95 to 4, before this issue got politicized, voted for a crime bill that is very much like the crime bill now before it that is so far not being permitted to come to a vote—95 to 4. They voted for a bill that had prevention, punishment, prisons, police——

NOTE: The President spoke at 4:18 p.m. from Room 459 of the Old Executive Office Building. The broadcast of this interview was terminated by the station's scheduled 4:30 newscast.

Statement on the Observance of International Literacy Day
August 24, 1994

On International Literacy Day, I am delighted to salute the many men and women who work so diligently to empower all people with the invaluable ability to read.

If our world is to meet the challenges of the twenty-first century, we must harness the energy and creativity of all our citizens. Nearly half of American adults lack many of the basic literacy skills so essential to success in today's complex and ever-changing world. Literacy is not a luxury; it is a right and a responsibility. And in an international community increasingly dedicated to the principles of equality and opportunity, illiteracy is unacceptable.

It takes great courage and hard work to overcome illiteracy. But with the help of dedicated teachers, tutors, and volunteers, everyone can learn the joys of reading and writing. These caring partnerships are the essence of community service, bringing hope and inspiration to all of us.

As people around the world celebrate International Literacy Day, I stand with you in working toward the goal of universal literacy. I am proud to extend my heartfelt appreciation to the countless individuals whose tireless efforts are helping to put this dream within our grasp.

WILLIAM J. CLINTON

NOTE: International Literacy Day was observed on September 8, 1994. An original was not available for verification of the content of this statement.

Remarks on Anticrime Legislation and an Exchange With Reporters
August 25, 1994

The President. Good afternoon. For 6 long years, the American people have watched and waited as Washington talked about stemming the tide of crime and violence in this country but did not act. Today Senators of both parties took a brave and promising step to bring the long, hard wait for a crime bill closer to an end.

I want to salute the Senators of both Republican and Democratic ranks who put law and order, safety and security above politics and party.

Ordinary Americans all across our country ought to take heart today. In the last 2 weeks, Members of Congress in both Houses and from both parties have thrown off the bonds of politics-as-usual to do the people's business. That's what the people sent us all here to do. I hope this crime bill will now rapidly pass the Senate and that we can move on doing the people's business across party lines, unencumbered by the labels of the past and the false choices of the past, moving to a better future for all Americans.

Thank you.

Cuba

Q. Mr. President, Fidel Castro says there's a simple way to stop the exodus of Cuban refugees, and that is to open up a high-level dialog between Washington and Havana. What's so bad about that?

The President. Well, I think, first of all, we have asked that we resume our talks, as you know, or we have offered a resumption of talks on the whole issue of immigration. And I have been doing a careful study over the last few days of the nature of our immigration laws and their implementation, especially since the 1984 agreement signed in the Reagan administration. But that is what this issue is about.

The other issues—I think President Castro or Premier Castro needs to be in consultation with his own folks. The people of Cuba want democracy and free markets. And that's always been our policy, and that will continue to be our policy. But I would urge the American people to be firm and be calm about what is going on here now. We must not let any nation, even a nation as close to us as Cuba, even with so many American citizens of Cuban descent, control the immigration policy of the United States and violate the borders of the United States. We have to be firm in this. And we will work this through to a successful conclusion, I believe.

Q. Mr. President, what's wrong with talking to Cuba and Fidel Castro when we talk with other so-called outlaw nations like North Korea?

The President. Well, we have a different policy of 30 years standing. And I think Mr. Castro knows the conditions for changing that policy. The discussions that have been held on a regular basis for several years now between our two countries have been limited to matters of immigration. They can be held, and we would support that.

Health Care Reform

Q. Mr. President, is health care dead this year?

The President. I wouldn't say that, no. I don't think you can say that because—and I don't think the recess will kill it—was that what you were going to—and the reason I say that is because, like most of you, I have watched with great interest what has happened and what has not happened in the Senate and the House. I told you all when we started this issue a long time ago, now over a year ago, that it was a very complicated issue, that it's no accident that Presidents of both parties for 60 years have tried to find a way to solve the health care crisis and have never been able to do it, particularly in the face of intense, organized, and expensive efforts to stop it.

But I think the less I say the better right now, as long as Senator Mitchell and Senator Chafee and Senator Breaux and others are doing their best to continue this dialog. I spoke to another Democratic Senator today who said that she felt there's still a good chance that a bill could come out that people would want to vote for and think was the right thing to do. So I think we just have to let this thing develop a little bit and see what happens in these dialogs. And again, I think the less I say about it, the better.

Thank you very much.

President's Vacation

Q. When do you go on vacation?

The President. It's still up to the Congress, isn't it?

Q. Will you wait until the Senate goes into recess?

The President. Oh, absolutely. I want to wait until the crime bill is over for sure.

Thank you.

NOTE: The President spoke at 5:36 p.m. in the Rose Garden at the White House.

Statement on Senate Action on Anticrime Legislation
August 25, 1994

The United States Senate made history today. The long, hard wait is finally over, and the American people are going to get the action against crime they have been demanding for over 6 years.

I want to thank the members of both parties, in the House and Senate, who answered the call of ordinary Americans to get this job done.

With a little good faith and a lot of hard work, Republicans and Democrats overcame the partisan divisions and false choices that have blocked anticrime efforts time and time again.

And because they did, children will be safer and parents will breathe a little easier. Police officers will no longer be threatened by gangs and thugs with easy access to deadly assault weapons designed only for war. Violent criminals are going to learn quickly that the revolving door on our prisons has been locked and bolted shut.

This crime bill is going to make every neighborhood in America safer, and the bipartisan spirit that produced it should give every American hope that we can come together to do the job they sent us here to do.

Nomination for Court of Appeals and District Court Judges
August 25, 1994

The President today nominated Fred I. Parker to the U.S. Court of Appeals for the Second Circuit. The President also nominated six individuals to serve on the U.S. District Court: Helen Gillmor for the District of Hawaii; John R. Tait for the District of Idaho; Okla Jones II and G. Thomas Porteous, Jr., for the Eastern District of Louisiana; James A. Beaty for the Middle District of North Carolina; and David Briones for the Western District of Texas.

"These nominees will bring legal talent and dedication to the Federal bench," the President said. "I know they will serve our country with distinction."

NOTE: Biographies of the nominees were made available by the Office of the Press Secretary.

Statement on Signing Transportation Legislation
August 26, 1994

I am very pleased today to sign H.R. 2178, the "Hazardous Materials Transportation Authorization Act of 1994." This accomplishes two important objectives of my Administration— reducing outmoded and unnecessary Government regulation and enhancing public safety on our Nation's roads.

This is the second piece of important legislation that I have approved this summer to reduce unnecessary government regulation of the trucking industry, thereby helping to keep our economy strong and competitive. Title VI of the Federal Aviation Administration Authorization Act of 1994 (Public Law 103–305) removed the heavy burden of inconsistent State regulation of the trucking industry, which costs consumers up to $8 billion a year in added freight transportation costs for virtually everything we buy. Title II of the Act that I am signing today provides additional regulatory reforms at the Federal level.

Title II will greatly reduce the massive Interstate Commerce Commission (ICC) paperwork burdens faced by the trucking industry, while preserving existing Federal safety regulations. The Act also continues the process of streamlining the ICC's programs, and requires a study of how to do even more to reduce further the scope of regulatory requirements that have outlived their usefulness. I expect the Secretary of Transportation and the Chairman of the Interstate Commerce Commission to be both deliberate and thorough in identifying the remaining reforms that are necessary.

In addition to streamlining regulatory requirements, this Act authorizes a strong Federal program to regulate hazardous materials transportation. It authorizes additional appropriations for the training of emergency response personnel; makes Indian tribes eligible for emergency response planning grants; and ensures that the National Intelligent Vehicle Highway System

Program addresses the use of its technologies to promote hazardous materials safety. These measures will promote the continued safe transportation of hazardous materials and aid in our efforts to increase the safe operation of all commercial motor vehicles.

WILLIAM J. CLINTON

The White House,
August 26, 1994.

NOTE: H.R. 2178, "To amend the Hazardous Materials Transportation Act to authorize appropriations for fiscal years 1994, 1995, 1996, and 1997, and for other purposes," approved August 26, was assigned Public Law No. 103–311.

Statement on Signing the Energy and Water Development Appropriations Act, 1995
August 26, 1994

Today I have signed into law H.R. 4506, the "Energy and Water Development Appropriations Act, FY 1995."

The Act provides a total of $20.5 billion in discretionary budget authority for various programs in the Departments of Energy and the Interior, the Army Corps of Engineers, and several smaller agencies.

I am pleased that the Act substantially funds most of my budget requests for priority investment programs within the Departments of En-

ergy and the Interior and the Army Corps of Engineers, including full funding for the renewable energy portions of the Climate Change Action Plan.

WILLIAM J. CLINTON

The White House,
August 26, 1994.

NOTE: H.R. 4506, approved August 26, was assigned Public Law No. 103–316.

Teleconference With Mayors on Anticrime Legislation and an Exchange With Reporters
August 26, 1994

The President. Hello? I'm just listening to your war stories; you sound good. I think they did help, all those calls you mentioned. They made all the difference.

The Attorney General and I are here on the phone, and we want to begin by just thanking you for everything you have done. I think, you know, it's obvious that this was a very tough battle in the House and in the Senate, that the outcome was often in doubt, and you guys

hung in there tough. And you made a huge difference, and we are very, very grateful to you.

I know that you know well that among the things that this crime bill does is to create 100,000 new police officers, a 20 percent increase in police on the beat in the United States in communities all over this country. And in just a few minutes, I'm going to sign an appropriations bill here that makes available the first round of resources to make the crime bill a reality next year. We've already put some new police officers on the street through the funds we provided last year as a downpayment on the crime bill. The bill I'm about to sign will provide funds to train and hire 15,000 more police within the next 12 months. I know that some of you put police officers on the streets with last year's funds, but you probably all know that we received 10 times, 10 times as many applications for police hiring as we could afford, including many that were well-qualified. That is a real rebuke to those who say that there's no real need for this police funding. In the next 2 months alone, we're going to give you the resources to hire 2,500 more police officers in cities that were only turned down last year and this year because we didn't have enough money.

Let me emphasize, too, that this appropriations bill, consistent with the crime bill, provides significant money to fight violence against women, to lock up criminal aliens, for prisons, and for boot camps and drug courts and the other prevention programs that we believe so strongly in and also to help enforce the Brady bill. This is the downpayment. We're looking forward to seeing you all here when we sign the crime bill and celebrate it, but now I think we all know that the responsibility is on those of us who fought so hard for this to make sure the money is well spent, to make sure the implementation works, and to make sure that we make people safer and more secure on our streets.

General Reno, would you like to say something?

[*Attorney General Reno expressed her appreciation to the mayors for their hard work on the legislation and said she looked forward to working with them to implement it. During her remarks, one of the mayors indicated that they were not receiving the transmission. When the problem was resolved, the teleconference resumed.*]

The President. Mayor Giuliani, are you on? Go ahead, Mayor.

[*Mayor Rudolph Giuliani of New York City commended the President and the other mayors for their efforts on the legislation.*]

The President. Thank you, Mayor. I have to say, I think the fact that you and Mayor Riordan

and some of the other Republican mayors were willing to stand up and be counted on this made it easier for the House and the Senate Members of your party who wanted to join in this endeavor or to stay with it. And I can't thank you enough for that.

I think, you know, we have got to find a way to do the public's business on issues that affect all Americans without regard to their party. And there is nothing more profoundly significant than this. I just—I can't say enough to thank you. We tried to take this crime bill beyond the debates of the past, beyond what I like to call the false choices that have been imposed too often on political debates.

This bill has got prevention and prisons and punishment and police in it, and I think will help to empower communities to make their streets safer. And as the Attorney General said, that's what, to me, was the compelling attraction of this bill. And as the days and weeks ahead unfold, the American people will learn more and more about what's in this bill, and I think they will like it even better than they do. And you will always, I think, be very proud of what you did.

Mayor Daley.

[*Mayors Richard Daley of Chicago, IL, Norman Rice of Seattle, WA, Richard Riordan of Los Angeles, CA, and Emanuel Cleaver II of Kansas City, MO, each made brief remarks praising the President's efforts. Mayor Cleaver then said he hoped the President would be able to take a vacation.*]

The President. Well, I'm going to oblige you later today. Are you still running, Mayor?

Mayor Cleaver. Yes.

The President. You've gotten so thin you're making me look bad. [*Laughter*] Stay after it.

Mayor Cleaver. All right.

The President. Mayor Rendell, I just want to say before you speak that I think you and Mayor Daley and Mayor Giuliani and the other mayors who are former prosecutors, were able to make a unique contribution to this debate because we tried to keep always in the public mind and in the minds of the Members of Congress that the law enforcement concerns were driving this bill and that even the prevention programs, as the Attorney General said repeatedly, were pushed and inserted into the bill with the insistence of people who had been in law enforcement who knew that they were a critical part of this strategy. So I want to thank you for that especially because your conviction here was rooted in your experience as is the case of the mayors—the other mayors who are former prosecutors.

[*Mayor Edward Rendell of Philadelphia, PA, thanked the President for not backing down on the key components of the bill despite the difficulties he encountered.*]

The President. Just another day in paradise here. [*Laughter*]

[*Mayor Rendell discussed the importance of crime prevention programs and the bill's provision to prevent Federal courts from controlling the number of prisoners placed in State or local prisons.*]

The President. Well, I can tell you, as a former Governor, that's one provision I wanted in there in the worst way, because I went through all those lawsuits as an attorney general and Governor; I know what it's like. I spent millions and millions of dollars of our taxpayers' money at home building prisons. I didn't begrudge that, but I also thought a lot of those requirements on spacing and population were excessive. And this is a very good piece of legislation on that. I thank you for that.

Mayor Abramson, I think you get the prize for making the most telephone calls. You must have a cauliflower ear; they tell me you made over 200 calls on this bill.

[*Mayor Jerry Abramson of Louisville, KY, thanked the President for allowing mayors and police chiefs to help develop a balanced bill.*]

The President. Thank you very much. General, do you want to say anything? I think they can all hear you now.

Attorney General Reno. They just did a wonderful job from the very beginning, and I think the bill is strong because of them.

The President. Thank you so much.

The Mayors. Thank you, Mr. President. Have a good vacation.

The President. Let's go to work on this thing now and implement it right.

The Mayors. All right, we'll do that.

The President. Goodbye.

[*At this point, the teleconference ended, and the President then took questions from reporters.*]

Health Care Reform

Q. Mr. President, Senator Mitchell all but said today that he's not going to be able to get comprehensive health care reform through and that he'll spend the recess looking for ways to make progress on health care. Is that acceptable to you? Is there any point at which you would accept, or which you would take off your veto threat?

The President. Well, he's coming over here to see me today, and I think I better talk to him. I have talked to, oh, four or five other Senators in the last day or so since the crime bill passed last night. And a number of them who are strong supporters of health reform think that we ought to give this break a few days to occur and give Senator Mitchell and Senator Chafee and a couple of others a chance to talk before we make any decision.

I certainly don't want to embrace an approach that will do more harm than good and that won't achieve our objectives. But let's see what they're doing; let's see what people are feeling like after they get a night's sleep or two. These folks went through an awful lot here the last couple of weeks, and it may be that the long road they had to walk through—crime—was in part made longer by people who were working the timetable.

But they did it, and they deserve a lot of credit. And one of the things that this crime bill shows—this is a big, sweeping, complex piece of legislation that's really good for America. And it shows that it is possible to do something like this in what has been too often a too partisan environment. So I'm not prepared to make a final judgment on that at this time.

Q. Mr. President, you said just a moment ago that you didn't want to embrace an approach that would do more harm than good. That sounds like you'd be willing to wait.

The President. Well, I think the less I say right now, the better. Let me talk to Senator Mitchell. This debate is now going on in the Congress. It depends on what Congress is capable of producing. And I think we need to wait on that. That's the counsel I've been given by a number of Senators who do want health care reform and want it as quickly as we can get it. They think we ought to let the dust settle a couple of days and give Senator Mitchell a chance to do a little talking with some others for a couple of days, and then we'll see where we are.

Cuba

Q. Mr. President, do you think you've stemmed the tide of the Cuban refugees?

The President. Well, we're working at it, that's all I can tell you. I'm encouraged that the numbers are down. The weather may or may not have something to do with that. We have made it clear that we're willing to discuss, through the appropriate channels, the whole issue of immigration. And we do have laws on the books which will permit us to do some more on legal immigration than we have done. So we're working at this.

And I just want to say what I said yesterday: The Attorney General's doing a great job; the Immigration and Naturalization Service folks are doing a good job. We just need to be calm, steady, and firm, and I think we'll work through it just fine.

Thank you.

NOTE: The President spoke at 3:20 p.m. from the Oval Office at the White House. H.R. 4603, approved August 26, making appropriations for the Departments of Commerce, Justice, and State, the Judiciary, and related agencies, was assigned Public Law No. 103–317.

Statement on Signing the Departments of Commerce, Justice, and State, the Judiciary, and Related Agencies Appropriations Act
August 26, 1994

Today I have signed into law, H.R. 4603, the "Departments of Commerce, Justice, and State, the Judiciary, and Related Agencies Appropriations Act, FY 1995, and Supplemental Appropriations for FY 1994."

This Act provides funding for the Departments of Commerce, Justice, and State; the Judiciary; and several smaller agencies.

This Act marks a bold first step in our effort to combat violent crime in America. In this Act, the Congress has provided $2.3 billion in funding to support the key new programs in the newly-passed Crime Bill. Foremost, the bill makes good on the promise of the Crime Bill by providing $1.3 billion to begin putting 100,000 new police officers on the street over the next 6 years.

The Act will enable the Justice Department to escalate its efforts to secure the border and to control illegal immigration. Resources are provided to expand the number of agents at high-risk crossing points to deter illegal immigration, improve the equipment available to agents to increase their effectiveness, expedite deportations of criminal illegal aliens, and increase asylum adjudications. The Act also provides, for the first time, a funding source to help States that are burdened by large numbers of criminal illegal aliens in their prisons. This $130 million

initiative highlights the Federal Government's commitment to share the responsibility for reducing the fiscal impact of illegal immigration with affected States.

A total of $100 million is provided to States to upgrade their criminal records databases, continuing implementation of the Brady Bill to ensure that handguns stay out of the hands of criminals. Innovative programs such as boot camps and drug courts are supported to promote cost-effective methods of dealing with young nonviolent offenders. Finally, funds are provided to stop or penalize those criminals who prey, intentionally, on women.

This Act, coupled with the Crime Bill, will provide the foundation for our bold new strategy of fighting crime in the United States.

The Act also provides important funding for some of my investment priorities, including development of the information highway, the defense conversion projects of the Economic Development Administration, and projects to foster high technology at the National Institute of Standards and Technology.

In addition to providing important funding for fiscal year 1995, the Act provides urgently needed emergency funding for fiscal year 1994. Due to an increased need for disaster assistance, stemming primarily from the Northridge earthquake in California and the recent flooding in the Southeast, the Disaster Loan Program of the Small Business Administration (SBA) is out of funds. This Act provides $470 million for SBA's Disaster Loan Program. Concurrently with signing H.R. 4603 into law, I am informing the Congress of my designation of these funds as an emergency requirement, thereby making them available.

Finally, this Act provides important funding for our contribution to United Nations international peacekeeping efforts around the world. These efforts are essential to reducing regional tensions and preventing or stopping the horror of war.

Unfortunately, the Act does not provide sufficient funding for the Securities and Exchange Commission (SEC) for fiscal year 1995. If the Congress does not provide additional funds for the SEC before adjourning in October, the SEC will have to shut down before the Congress returns next year. To avoid this, I urge the Congress to enact legislation providing the necessary budgetary resources for the SEC prior to the start of the new fiscal year.

WILLIAM J. CLINTON

The White House,

August 26, 1994.

NOTE: H.R. 4603, approved August 26, was assigned Public Law No. 103–317.

Appointment for the President's Committee on Mental Retardation
August 26, 1994

The President today announced the appointment of Ann M. Forts of Center Harbor, New Hampshire, as a member of the President's Committee on Mental Retardation (PCMR).

Ms. Forts will become the second self-advocate [a person with mental retardation] to serve as a member of the President's Committee on Mental Retardation and the second self-advocate appointed by the President to serve on the Committee.

In appointing Ms. Forts, the President praised the contribution that she will make as a self-advocate on the PCMR Board: "Ann Forts represents the goal of my administration in meeting the needs of citizens with disabilities. By listening to citizens with disabilities, as experts about their lives and what they need to live healthy and productive lives, we will be able to pursue our common vision of moving from exclusion to inclusion, from dependence to independence, from paternalism to empowerment. I look forward to the insight and wisdom Ann Forts will share with the members of the President's Committee on Mental Retardation."

NOTE: A biography of the appointee was made available by the Office of the Press Secretary.

The President's Radio Address
August 27, 1994

Good morning. This has been an historic week for the American people. After 6 years of talking about crime, Members of Congress in both Houses from both parties overcame their partisan divisions and the false choices of the past to pass the toughest attack on crime in history. With a little good faith and an awful lot of hard work, both Democrats and Republicans took a stand against crime as the American people had demanded they do for years.

For all those Americans who want Washington to work for them, passing the crime bill shows we can break the stranglehold of politics-as-usual and solve the problems you sent us all here to solve.

Crime and violence have been increasing for a long time. Too many law-abiding citizens have been killed on their streets and in their homes. Too many of our children have been terrified on their streets and in their schools. Too many police officers have been killed in the line of duty, too many families torn apart. But for 6 years, Washington just talked about the crime problem and failed to act. But this week, Congress acted. The special interests lost. The public interest won. Democrats and Republicans came together without regard to party to make America safer, and every American can take heart.

This is how Washington should work. It's how I wanted a Washington to work when I came here as President, and how I hope it will work in the future. All the elements of an anticrime program I talked about in my campaign for President are present in this bill and a lot more good things as well.

This crime bill will put 100,000 more police on our streets in community policing, walking the beat, preventing crime, as well as catching criminals. That's a 20 percent increase in the number of police officers in America. It will provide more prisons and longer sentences for violent criminals. It will lock up the most dangerous criminals for good by making "three strikes and you're out" the law of the land. It will provide greater protection to women and children by imposing tougher penalties on those who prey on them. It will say to anyone who kills a police officer, "You, too, can pay with your life."

The crime bill answers the call of police officers everywhere to do more to prevent crime from happening in the first place. It will help to steer young people away from gangs and drugs by helping them learn right from wrong and giving them something to say yes to as well as something to say no to.

This bill does make it clear that some things are very wrong and young people must say no to them. That's why it prohibits juveniles from owning handguns and prohibits them from using them except under the supervision of a qualified adult. And this bill does something else that police officers have wanted us to do for a very long time. It bans assault weapons that were designed for soldiers to use in war but that have been used instead by gang members and gangsters to make war on police and innocent citizens.

And in another dramatic departure from politics as usual, this entire crime bill will be paid for not with new taxes, not by increasing the deficit but by reducing the Federal work force by over a quarter of a million people to its lowest level in 30 years and taking all that money to empower people to make their lives safer. More police on the street, less Government in Washington, that's a good deal for the American people.

Let's remember why this bill finally passed. It passed because half a million police officers who risk their lives every day stood up and made their voices heard. It passed because the families of innocent victims like Polly Klaas stood up and made their voices heard. It passed because parents and teachers and senior citizens who want their streets back stood up and made their voices heard, the ordinary voices of ordinary Americans that Washington so often ignored. This week, they weren't ignored. This week they were heard, and they made all the difference.

We know many challenges remain. We waited 6 years for a crime bill. Now we have to implement that bill and make it work in the lives of the American people. But the American people have waited 60 years for Washington to do something comprehensive about health care. It's a difficult challenge; there are even more interest groups irate against making real change. But we have to meet it because it affects our children, our families, and our future, our human quality of life and our ability to pay for the basic things in life as well as to run the Federal Government without increasing the deficit.

Already we've made more progress on health care than ever before. Members of both parties are trying hard to work out their differences. And health care will be the first order of business when Congress returns. We have to continue this fight; we have to win it.

The crime bill shows we can. It shows that when we put aside the rhetoric and the partisanship, we can solve any issue and meet any challenge. Its narrow victory also shows the damage, the danger that partisanship can bring to our deliberation. But we can get past the partisan static that drowns out the voices of ordinary Americans. We can put cooperation over confrontation. We can move America forward. We can put the American people first, and we proved it this week.

Thanks for listening.

NOTE: The address was recorded at 5:35 p.m. on August 26 in the Roosevelt Room at the White House for broadcast at 10:06 a.m. on August 27.

Statement on the Death of Drug Enforcement Administration Agents
August 30, 1994

I join the American people in mourning the deaths of five young agents of the Drug Enforcement Administration, lost when their plane crashed in Peru this past weekend. Agents Frank Fernandez, Jay Seale, Meredith Thompson, Frank Wallace, and Juan Vars demonstrated a true devotion to duty and a commitment to ridding our country of the scourge of illegal drugs.

Every day, dedicated men and women risk their lives in the international war against drugs. Working with officials from many nations, our DEA agents have made great progress in this struggle. But, as we have seen this week, this war is not an easy one. Even our most valiant young soldiers fall victim.

These courageous agents served to make America's streets safer for our children, and, in their names, we rededicate ourselves to fighting drug production, trafficking, and use.

On behalf of a grateful nation, I extend deepest sympathies to the families of these heroic individuals. Their bright lives will remain inspirations to all of us.

WILLIAM J. CLINTON

NOTE: An original was not available for verification of the content of this statement.

Letter on Appointments for Presidential Emergency Board No. 225
August 30, 1994

Dear Mr. Twomey:

Pursuant to section 10 of the Railway Labor Act, as amended, I established by Executive order an Emergency Board to investigate a dispute between the Soo Line Railroad Company and certain of its employees represented by the United Transportation Union. The functions and the duties of the Emergency Board are set forth in the Railway Labor Act, as amended, and in the Executive order creating the Board.

I am pleased to learn that you are willing to serve on this Emergency Board, and I hereby appoint you as Chair. This letter will constitute your appointment and your authority to act in that capacity. Each Member of the Board is to receive compensation at the rate of $429.00 per day for each day that you are actually engaged in the performance of your duties or in travel in connection therewith. In addition, each Member of the Board will be allowed per diem in lieu of subsistence while so engaged away from your home or your regular place of business.

Sincerely,

WILLIAM J. CLINTON

NOTE: This letter was sent to David Twomey, board Chair, and similar letters were sent to Richard P. Kasher and Elizabeth Neumeier, board members. This letter was released by the Office of the Press Secretary on August 31. The Executive order of August 29 is listed in Appendix D at the end of this volume.

Letter to Congressional Leaders on the Revised Pay Schedule for Federal Employees
August 31, 1994

Dear Mr. Speaker: (Dear Mr. President:)

Action on the FY 1995 Treasury, Postal Service, and General Government Appropriations Bill, will not be completed before the August 31st deadline for an alternative pay plan. Therefore, as a protective measure, in order to ensure that a substantially larger pay increase does not go into effect automatically by operation of law, it is necessary for me to transmit an alternative pay plan.

Under section 5303(a) of title 5, United States Code, the rates of basic pay of the statutory pay systems would be increased by 2.6 percent effective in January 1995.

Section 5303(b) of title 5, however, provides me the authority to implement an alternative pay adjustment plan if I consider the pay adjustment that would otherwise be required by law to be inappropriate because of "national emergency or serious economic conditions affecting the general welfare." As you know, alternative pay plan authority has been used many times over the past 15 years. "Serious economic conditions" are defined in the statute to include consideration of economic measures such as the Index of Leading Economic Indicators, the Gross National Product, the unemployment rate, the budget deficit, the Consumer Price Index, the Producer Price Index, the Employment Cost Index, and the Implicit Price Deflator for Personal Consumption Expenditures.

The budget discipline put in place by my Administration has contributed to sustained economic growth and low inflation. To continue this budget discipline and its favorable impact on economic conditions I have determined that an alternative pay adjustment is appropriate for the 1995 pay raise under section 5303.

The 1995 budget I submitted to the Congress proposed a modest pay increase of 1.6 percent for Federal employees. I believed that this was an appropriate increase in view of the other disciplines we have worked with the Congress to put in place that have reduced the Federal budget deficit and improved our Nation's economy. Further, we are currently making substantial reductions in Federal employment pursuant to the Federal Workforce Restructuring Act enacted by the Congress this year. To achieve these reductions, many agencies are offering Federal employees early retirement and incentives of up to $25,000 to leave Federal service. These considerations, as well, lead me to conclude that the substantially larger pay increase that would otherwise automatically go into effect is not appropriate at this time.

The House version of the 1995 Treasury, Postal Service, and General Government Appropriations Bill includes a provision offered by Representative Steny Hoyer that provides a section 5303 pay raise of 2.0 percent and a limited section 5304 locality pay raise. The Senate version of the bill has no pay raise provision. The Administration has informed the conference committee that it would not object to the pay raise in the House version of the bill if military personnel receive a pay raise higher than the 1.6 percent proposed in the 1995 budget. It appears likely that the 1995 Defense Authorization Bill will provide military members a 2.6 percent raise.

Consistent with the provisions of the House-passed Treasury, Postal Service, and General Government Appropriations Bill, the pay raise will be made in accordance with the following plan:

In accordance with section 5303(b) of title 5, United States Code, the pay rates for each statutory pay system shall be increased by 2.0 percent, effective on the first day of the first applicable pay period beginning on or after January 1, 1995.

The statute also provides me alternative plan authority for locality-based comparability payments, or locality pay, under section 5304 of title 5. The deadline for transmitting this alternative plan to Congress is November 30. In the absence of legislation, it would be my intent to provide Federal civilians with locality pay raises that equal 0.6 percent of civilian payroll.

In my opinion, this alternative pay plan for a 2 percent pay increase under section 5303 will not materially affect the Government's ability to recruit or retain well-qualified employees. Federal hiring rates and attrition rates are very low. In addition, most employees will receive other pay increases, such as locality pay and within-grade increases. Thus, we have every reason to believe that these pay increases, coupled with appropriate use of pay flexibilities such as recruitment bonuses and retention allowances, will allow the Federal Government to continue to be competitive in attracting and retaining quality employees.

Sincerely,

WILLIAM J. CLINTON

NOTE: Identical letters were sent to Thomas S. Foley, Speaker of the House of Representatives, and Albert Gore, Jr., President of the Senate.

Statement on Withdrawal of Russian Forces From Eastern Europe
August 31, 1994

Today marks the completion of the withdrawal of Russian military forces from the Republic of Estonia and the Latvian Republic, under terms of bilateral agreements concluded between Russia and each of these sovereign states. Russian military forces are also completing their withdrawal today from the Federal Republic of Germany, in accordance with the agreements reached between Germany and the Soviet Union in October 1990. These withdrawals constitute the final departure of Russian troops that have been present in Eastern Europe since 1945.

This effectively brings to an end a chapter in post-World War II European history, opening the door to a new era of regional stability and cooperation. I congratulate the people of Estonia, Germany, Latvia, and Russia on this historic occasion and salute their leaders for the vision and statesmanship they have demonstrated on behalf of European integration. The United States will continue its active support for this process with the goal of a brighter and more peaceful future for all of our people in the next century.

Statement on the Northern Ireland Peace Process
August 31, 1994

I welcome today's watershed announcement by the IRA that it has decided to end the 25-year campaign of violence and pursue the path of peace. While much work remains to be done, the IRA's decision to join the political process can mark the beginning of a new era that holds the promise of peace for all the people of Northern Ireland.

I have just spoken with Prime Minister Albert Reynolds of Ireland and Prime Minister John Major of the United Kingdom to congratulate them for their persistent efforts to bring this day about. Their joint resolve to end the violence and pursue a negotiated settlement has been crucial to the progress made to date. Their historic joint declaration last December, together with the Anglo-Irish agreement of 1985, have built the foundation for the new hope we have today. I am pleased that the United States

has been able to contribute to this process of reconciliation.

We join with the Governments of Ireland and the United Kingdom in the hope and expectation that today's step will help bring a lasting and just peace to Northern Ireland. I urge the IRA and all who have supported it to fulfill the promise of today's announcement to end the use and support of violence, just as we continue to call on all parties who have sought to achieve political goals through violence to cease to do so. There must be a permanent end to the violence.

The United States continues to stand ready to assist in advancing the process of peace in Northern Ireland. We hope that both traditions, unionist and nationalist, will support the only real avenue to peace, that of a negotiated settlement to the conflict.

Remarks on the Northern Ireland Peace Process to the Irish Media on Martha's Vineyard, Massachusetts
September 2, 1994

Let me say first of all, I am so pleased to have Dick Spring here. And I'm pleased that he came across the ocean to visit with me and others in the United States who very much want this process to succeed.

I am delighted by the developments of the last several days and by all the efforts that have been made in the last few months. The United States is strongly supportive of this peace process. We want to reach out and work with all the elements in Ireland, in Northern Ireland. We want all the communities to feel a part of the peace process and to feel that there is a peace dividend. We want to continue to work with and support the work of the Government of Ireland and the Government of Great Britain. And we are prepared to take some steps to do whatever we can to help that now.

Dick is going to talk at greater length about some of the specific things we talked about here today, but the United States has tried to be a friend of peace in Ireland, and we will continue to do that. And we're very, very pleased by the developments.

NOTE: The President spoke at approximately 11 a.m. at the Friedman Guest House. In his remarks, he referred to Foreign Minister Richard Spring of Ireland. A tape was not available for verification of the content of these remarks.

Message on the Observance of Labor Day, 1994
September 2, 1994

As Americans celebrate our nation's 100th Labor Day holiday, we take time out of our busy schedules to recognize and to appreciate the importance of America's working men and women. We as a people strive to put our talents and interests to use every day. We find joy in learning new skills and in making new discoveries. It is in no small measure the many rewards we find in labor that make America's workers the finest in the world.

As our country faces an increasingly competitive international marketplace, America's tradition of innovation and progress is more important than ever. Today's world demands that we reinvent the compact between labor and management, guided by a firm commitment to ongoing dialogue and cooperation. It requires that our nation make use of the tools at hand: our abundant land, our diverse and determined people, and our shared belief in the values of hard work and fair play.

Working together, we have the power to build a new partnership for prosperity. We know how to improve quality and efficiency, to reduce production costs and to increase profits—knowledge that will serve to benefit employer and worker alike. With a renewed dedication to providing education and re-training, we can craft a work force ready to meet the challenges of the twenty-first century and beyond.

This year, we resolve to press forward in our efforts to promote new growth and opportunities, creating safe and healthy working conditions that enable our citizens to be good workers and good parents. For at the heart of the American Dream is the American family. And our goal must be to make the Dream a reality for all of our families. Indeed, as we celebrate Labor Day this centennial year, that common vision inspires us still.

Best wishes to all for a memorable holiday.

BILL CLINTON

NOTE: The message was made available by the Office of the Press Secretary on September 2 but was not issued as a White House press release.

The President's Radio Address
September 3, 1994

Good morning. For most Americans, this Labor Day weekend is our last chance to catch our breath before the hustle and bustle of the fall. I'm on vacation with my family, and many of you may be driving to the beach or the lake for the last long weekend of summer. Maybe you're planning to do some back-to-school shopping or have a backyard barbecue for your family and friends. Or perhaps you're one of the unsung heroes of Labor Day, the police officers, the health care workers, who have to be on the job this weekend. Whether you're working or relaxing, let's take a few minutes to remember the story of Labor Day and what it says about the promise of American life.

One hundred years ago, America created this national holiday to honor our working men and women. A hundred Labor Days later, its founders would be proud to know that the vast majority of our working people have lifted themselves into the great American middle class. We didn't do it with handouts but by working, hard working, smart working.

The American way is to offer opportunity and challenge people to make the most of it. We have a unique partnership between government, business, labor, and individual citizens. It's given us the public school system, the State universities, collective bargaining, the GI bill, to name just a few, all partnerships that have given Americans the tools to build better lives for themselves.

For the past two decades, however, more and more people have had a harder time achieving the American dream. Too many Americans have found themselves working longer and harder for stagnant wages. Crime and terrible social problems have rendered our quality of life more tenuous. Global economic competition and serious, serious problems at home have really complicated our lives.

The American people have suffered and, too often and in too many ways, the National Government has ignored these problems or even made some of them worse. We have actually managed to quadruple our national debt in the decade of the eighties, while reversing and declining in our commitment to invest in our people and our economic future.

I ran for President because I think our Nation's mission at the close of the 20th century must be to keep the American dream alive in the 21st century. We need a plan for the future that puts our people first, that has a partnership that creates opportunity, insists on more personal responsibility for our people, and enables us to rebuild our communities.

We face tough challenges, and change is always hard. The status quo has always had powerful friends. But the families we honor on Labor Day deserve better.

Last year we began to put into place this strategy for the future, beginning with an effort to renew our economy and put our economic house in order with the biggest budget deficit reduction package in history, including $255 billion in spending cuts, tax increases for the wealthiest 1.5 percent of Americans, and tax relief for 15 million working families with children to encourage them to keep working and not fall back into welfare.

We pried open new markets around the world for American workers with NAFTA, a worldwide trade agreement, new openings to Japan and the rest of Asia, serious efforts to sell American products, everything from airplanes to apples.

While we cut spending, we actually invested more in the lifelong education and training that our people will need in the global economy, from Head Start to apprenticeships for young people who don't go on to college to constant job-training opportunities for people once they're in the work force.

The friends of the failed policies of the past—the people who raised taxes on the middle class, lowered them on the wealthy, reduced investment in our people, and exploded our deficit—they predicted this economic strategy would fail. They said it would produce disaster. But instead, in just 19 months, our economy has created more than 4.2 million new jobs, 93 percent of them in the private sector.

Yesterday we got more good news. We reached 2 million new jobs this year, and the year still has 4 months to go. And that total includes 135,000 new manufacturing jobs created this year. For the first time in 10 years, manufacturing jobs have increased for 8 consecutive months.

In addition, 20 million young Americans are already eligible to refinance their college loans at lower interest rates with longer repayment terms. And we're going to have 3 years of deficit reduction for the first time since Harry Truman was President, creating a more stable future for our children.

Restoring opportunity, honoring work and family and community, that's what this administration and our mission are all about. A big part of that is personal security, and all of you saw that as the debate over the crime bill unfolded in the last several weeks. We have reduced the size of the Federal bureaucracy by over 270,000 over the next 6 years and taken all that money to give it back to local communities to make children and families safer, 100,000 more police, more prisons, longer sentences for serious offenders, programs to help young people have something to say yes to, to prevent crimes: drug courts, boot camps, education and job-training programs, jobs and activities for young people, and a ban on juvenile ownership of handguns and on assault weapons. Again, there was bitter opposition. The status quo had powerful friends, but the American people and the American future won.

In everything we do, we must honor work and family and community. That's why we're fighting for health security for working Americans by providing universal coverage and controlling costs, why we're working to reform the welfare system to help people move from public assistance to productive jobs, and why we're changing the unemployment system to a reemployment system to help people continuously get the training, the counseling, the information they need about new jobs.

Our work won't be done until all Americans enjoy the dignity of work, the security of world-class skills, and the opportunity to build a life

for themselves and their children that is better. That can only be done by taking a new direction—not a Government which says we can do it alone and certainly not a Government that sits on the sidelines but one that works in partnership with business and with our individual working men and women and their families.

On Labor Day, Monday, I'll be visiting with workers at a shipyard in Bath, Maine, where that partnership is taking place, where labor and management have made a uniquely American covenant with themselves and with their Government: with themselves, to share the responsibility and rewards for the company's success, and with their Government, to take a little help to move from a defense-based economy to prove that they can compete and win in a global economy that involves far more than defense. Those shipyard workers in Maine exemplify the best in the American spirit, the understanding that when we pull together for the common good we are unstoppable.

This Monday, Labor Day, you'll see that spirit all across our country: Milwaukee, at the Labor Day Parade; and Little Rock, at the Old-Time American Union Picnic; in Michigan, as they have on every Labor Day since 1958, you'll see tens of thousands of people walking the 5 miles across the Mackinac Bridge connecting the State's Upper and Lower Peninsulas.

Next Sunday, in Washington, DC, there will be a special Labor Day Mass at the National Shrine of the Immaculate Conception to bear witness to the timeless truth that work gives structure and meaning to our lives and is divinely ordained.

Whatever you're doing this weekend, I wish you all the best for yourselves and your families. I thank you for listening and for your dedication to our country.

NOTE: The President spoke at 10:06 a.m. from the Tisbury School on Martha's Vineyard, MA.

Remarks on Labor Day in Bath, Maine
September 5, 1994

Ladies and gentlemen, I know it's raining here today, but you have brought a lot of sunshine into my life by the example you've set

and the work you've done. And I want to thank you for coming out in the rain to stand up for the interests of the working families of

America on this Labor Day. Thank you for being here.

I thank our great labor leaders Tom Donahue and George Kourpias for being here. I want to thank Buzz Fitzgerald and Stoney Dionne. Tom talked about the ironworks being run by two guys named Buzz and Stoney. It sounded like a television series. [*Laughter*] If you do what I expect you to do here, we may get a television series out of this yet.

I also want to say a special word of thanks to my good friend Joe Brennan for being here and for presenting himself as a candidate for Governor again, to Senator Dutremble and Senator Baldacci for being willing to run for Congress at a time when it's not a very popular place to be, but it's still an important place to be. And I want to say a special word of thanks to Tom Andrews for his leadership in the United States Congress to help us rebuild the shipbuilding industry in America and help turn this economy around.

And of course, most of all I want to thank my good friend George Mitchell. You know, if George had been commissioner of baseball, they'd be back playing again now. And I might say on this Labor Day, there's still time for them to go back to work and finish the best baseball season in 50 years, and I hope they will.

Folks, most of what needs to be said here today has been said. But for a century now people have been gathering on Labor Day to celebrate the dignity of work, its importance to our lives, and to have that last long weekend before school starts again and we all go back to work full-time.

I ran for President because I thought this country was in danger of going in the wrong direction and because I thought that our people had it within them to keep the American dream alive into the 21st century for our children and our grandchildren. And I believed then just as strongly as I believe today that we have to have a plan, a strategy, a vision of what we wish our country to be like and how we're going to get there.

If we're going to keep the American dream of opportunity alive for everybody who's willing to work hard and play by the rules, I believe we must do three things: We have to have an economy that works, we have to empower our people to succeed and win in that economy, and we've got to come together again as a com-

munity and work together. We cannot afford in a global economy to be divided again, Government and business and workers fighting each other all the time, people in this country finding ways to get in fights with each other instead of ways to pull together and make this country great again.

And our administration has fought for change against some very, very powerful enemies of change, against people who often don't seem to understand what the stakes are because that's what I want for you and your families and your children.

You heard Senator Mitchell say that we began with an economic strategy to get this terrible deficit down. The debt of this country was quadrupled in 12 years. We are bringing the deficit down for 3 years in a row for the first time since Harry Truman was President. We are doing it by cutting spending, asking the wealthiest 1.5 percent to pay more taxes, and providing tax breaks to 15 million working families that are hovering just above the poverty line because we want them to keep working and raising their children, not going into the welfare system. In the State of Maine alone, almost 61,000 families got a tax cut, and only 3,700 got a tax increase. It was a good deal for Maine. It was a good deal for America. And if it hadn't been for Tom Andrews and George Mitchell, the plan would have failed, because we passed it by the narrowest of margins over the enemies of change.

We have expanded trade. We have expanded educational and training opportunity. But maybe most important of all on this Labor Day, we have called for new partnerships in shipbuilding, in airplane building, in automobiles, in agriculture. The partnership here that you've heard these people detail between labor and management is the thing I came here to highlight. Even in the driving rain, the rest of America should know that if you can take a 110-year-old company and redesign the relationship of labor and management in a new partnership and ask the National Government to help you to build a commercial future as well as a defense future, then every manufacturing facility in America can do the same, and we can rebuild this economy on the strength of your example.

For the first time in 10 years, manufacturing jobs in America have increased now for 8 months in a row. They're a part of that 4.1 million jobs that George Mitchell talked about. And as we look ahead from this Labor Day, let us leave here rededicating ourselves to meet the other challenges that face us, to keep this economic recovery going, to keep this partnership between business and labor and a partnership with Government going, to keep working until every American can have the education and training opportunities he or she needs to compete and win, to keep working until we turn the terrible situation we have in health care around where we're spending more and covering less.

This is the only advanced country in the world that spends 40 percent more than everybody else, and we're still losing people with health insurance. There are 5 million people in working families just like yours who had health insurance a year ago, 5 years ago, who don't have it today. My friends, we can do better. And until we do better, we will pay the price.

And let us continue our efforts to change the way the political system works. We need more examples of what we had with the crime bill, where we broke through gridlock and a few brave Republicans stood up to their leadership and said, "The American people want a solution to the crime problems. It's not a partisan problem. It's an American problem, and we're going to work on it together." We need that in other examples as well. We need the Congress to pass the laws reforming the lobbying practices and the campaign finance practices in Washington, to help to free people to make the courageous decisions that have to be made.

And finally let me say this, and I want to close with this because I want you to think about this as you leave. We've got to get out of here, or we're going to raise health care costs by staying in the rain too long. [*Laughter*] We can create more jobs. We can empower you to seize those jobs. But unless we get back to

good, old-fashioned American values of working together in partnership, we're still not going to do what we ought to do. Everybody is for change in general, but they can always find a reason to be against it in particular. Believe me, there will never be a bill in Congress that is perfect, because we are not perfect people. There is always some reason we can find to say no, to turn away from tomorrow, to be divided from our friends and neighbors.

This Bath Iron Works is coming back because Stoney and Buzz and all the other people put aside their differences to find something they could say yes to. This is going to happen in America because this administration is working with the tools we have to rebuild the American economy in partnership, not sitting on the sidelines and not promising you miracles but promising you progress.

And I ask you as you leave here today to reward people in public life who will say yes to America, who will look for ways to come together, not be divided, who will ask you to be courageous enough to face the tough decisions. That's the real way to make sure we have a 21st century where the rain brings the sunshine.

Thank you, and God bless you all. Thank you.

NOTE: The President spoke at 11:25 a.m. at the Bath Iron Works shipyard. In his remarks, he referred to Tom Donahue, secretary-treasurer, AFL–CIO; George Kourpias, international president, International Association of Machinists and Aerospace Workers (IAM); Duane (Buzz) Fitzgerald, president and chief executive officer, Bath Iron Works Corp.; John (Stoney) Dionne, president, IAM Local S6; John E. Baldacci, Maine State senator; and Dennis L. Dutremble, president, Maine Senate.

Statement on the Observance of Rosh Hashana, 1994
September 5, 1994

Warm greetings to all who are celebrating Rosh Hashana in this promising year of renewal.

The high holidays, the most solemn and hallowed days of the Hebrew calendar, mark the beginning of a new year. Jews around the world

pause to reassess their lives and their relationships with others and with God. Most important, Rosh Hashana celebrates change—bidding farewell to an old year and welcoming the new.

During last year's high holy days, the world rejoiced as Prime Minister Rabin and Chairman Arafat took the first brave steps toward peace in the Middle East. This year, in the same courageous spirit, we have seen new, bold steps in the peace process. Together, we watched the determined leaders of Israel and Jordan turn away from the sorrow of generations of hostility, blood, and tears to embrace the promises of hope and prosperity.

As the shofar sounds this Rosh Hashana, let it be a summons to build on this long anticipated foundation—a summons to nourish the seeds of peace that have finally been planted on both sides of the River Jordan.

Best wishes to all for a joyous Rosh Hashana and a peaceful new year.

NOTE: A message identical to this statement was also made available by the White House. Rosh Hashana was observed on September 6.

Statement on the Observance of Yom Kippur, 1994
September 6, 1994

I am pleased to extend greetings to all who are observing Yom Kippur, the most solemn of Jewish holidays.

The holy day of Yom Kippur recognizes that all human beings are capable of transgression and of atonement. Judaism teaches that every person, from time to time, fails to act in accordance with his or her highest principles. Yom Kippur offers worshippers the chance to seek forgiveness for sins committed during the past year and to reassess personal behavior. Beyond this, the Day of Atonement urges the repair of torn relationships and encourages treating all people with kindness. It is a day intended for rectifying mistakes and for recommitment in a journey leading from thought to deed.

As we strive to recognize changes that must be made in our own lives and for our entire world, we turn to each other for the strength we seek. Though the challenges of our world are formidable, and ancient animosities are not easily overcome, the past year has shown us time and again that peace is within our power.

Let this day serve as a call to make the changes in our lives and in our communities that peace and prosperity require. Let us rededicate ourselves to caring for others and to teaching our children the lessons of compassion. In the spirit of reconciliation and renewal that were so evident in the Israeli-Jordanian peace initiative, let us work toward building a brighter world for the generations to come.

Best wishes to all for an observance full of meaning and hope.

NOTE: A message identical to this advance text was also made available by the White House. Yom Kippur was observed on September 15.

Remarks at the Presentation Ceremony for the All-American Cities Awards
September 8, 1994

The President. Thank you very much, and welcome to the Rose Garden on this beautiful day. I want to acknowledge the presence of Secretary Cisneros, who was once director of the National Civic League and whose city, San Antonio, a few years ago was an All-American City under his leadership. Congresswoman Johnson, Con-

gressman Borski, Congressman Blackwell, Congressman Thomas, and Congressman Sharp are here.

I also want to say a word of special appreciation for the National Civic League because this is its centennial year. When the league was founded, Theodore Roosevelt said, "There are many ways in which a man or a woman can work for the higher life of American cities." Well, judging by what the mayors here and their citizens have shown us, that is just as true if not more true today than it was 100 years ago. We know, given the complex challenges that our cities face, we need that kind of commitment now even more than we needed it 100 years ago.

We are here to celebrate success on many fronts. Some of the cities are being honored for designing programs to get our children off the streets and into better lives. Others have expanded downtown business areas, opened free health clinics for the poor, smoothed the economic impact of a base closure. These 10 cities represent regions all over America, and they're of different sizes, with different problems and different challenges and different opportunities. They do teach us, however, one thing in common: when our citizens work in partnership, when they work business and labor and government, when they find ways to come together instead of being divided, they can do miraculous things.

The partnerships we celebrate here are a reminder that government can and must help, that businesses and volunteer organizations working with citizens themselves must do the hard work of restoring America's communities. Each and every one of us must be personally responsible for working in our communities and making a difference. No one else will ever care about a community half as much as those who live there and raise their children there, who look forward to growing old there and being remembered there. And who knows how to solve the problems of a place better than those who call it home?

That's not to say that you should do all the work on your own. Our Federal Government must and will continue to help. Everything we do, even here, should ultimately be about empowering people at the grassroots to assume responsibility for their own lives, their own communities, their own families; to be able to compete and win, to succeed in the complicated but exhilarating world toward which we are moving in the next century.

We've worked hard over the last 19 months to create that kind of framework, in strengthening our economy, in reforming our education system, in following some of the initiatives Secretary Cisneros has set out for cities and for communities within cities all across America.

We have another great opportunity for partnership now that the crime bill has at last passed. If ever there was an example of the Federal Government reaching out to empower people at the grassroots level, the crime bill is it. It's paid for by reducing the size of the National Government by 270,000 over the next 6 years, giving all the money back to local communities to hire police, to build prisons, to build prevention programs, to reach out to young people, to give people something to say yes to, to put people to work and put people in responsible play as well.

These things can work in miraculous ways, but we're going to depend upon you to make them work. Getting the crime bill through Congress was difficult, all right. It took 6 years. But you don't have 6 years to make it work at the grassroots. The money is flowing in this fiscal year, and we have to depend upon all of you to reduce crime and violence and to increase the number of young people who have a better future.

The partnerships that we celebrate today and the ones our administration is committed to creating tomorrow, all of them are the backbone of our future. The cities are leading the way, and those of you who are being honored today are truly outstanding. I can't wait to present the awards. I have already read the reasons why all of you are being acknowledged. It reminded me of a lot of the things that I did as a Governor. It reminds me, too, here in Washington that very often the most important things we do receive the least publicity, especially if we do them hand in hand instead of fist against fist. But you keep on doing it, because in the end the results will be the ultimate reward.

Now I'd like to introduce a person that it's my great honor to present, one of our country's most distinguished citizens, the chairman of the National Civic League, John Gardner.

[*At this point, Mr. Gardner and Wayne Hedien, chief executive officer, Allstate Insurance Co., sponsor of the awards, each made brief remarks. The awards were then presented.*]

The President. Thank you very much. Let me just say a word of thanks to Allstate and to its chairman for their leadership. And thanks again to John Gardner. Thanks to all the Members of Congress for coming here. And thanks to all of you.

The most important thing I think we can take away from here is what John Gardner said: This is a can-do country. This is fundamentally an optimistic country. Just 2 days ago the international economic experts who every year rank the countries of the world in terms of how productive they are, ranked the United States number one again for the first time in nearly 10 years.

That happened because of what people are doing in the heartland and because we're getting our act together up here. And you should feel very hopeful about the future because of what you have done and because of what you have done.

Thank you, and God bless you all. We're adjourned. Thank you.

NOTE: The President spoke at 2:10 p.m. in the Rose Garden at the White House.

Appointment for the National Cancer Advisory Board
September 8, 1994

The President today announced his intention to appoint Barbara K. Rimer, Dr. P.H., of Duke University, as Chair and member of the National Cancer Advisory Board (NCAB).

"The NCAB plays a critical role by providing advice on the Federal cancer research effort," the President said. "Dr. Rimer has demonstrated her ability to meld insight from the biological and behavioral sciences into new approaches to cancer control, and I look forward to her leadership of the NCAB."

NOTE: A biography of the appointee was made available by the Office of the Press Secretary.

Appointment for the President's Cancer Panel
September 8, 1994

The President today announced his intention to reappoint Harold P. Freeman, M.D., of Harlem Hospital Center, New York, as Chair and member of the President's Cancer Panel. The President's Cancer Panel is a 3-member group providing advice to the President on various aspects of the National Cancer Program. Dr. Freeman has chaired the Panel since 1991.

"The President's Cancer Panel plays an essential role in monitoring the Nation's cancer program and guiding its progress into the future," the President said. "I admire Dr. Freeman's commitment to reducing death and suffering from cancer during this time of significant progress and considerable challenge in cancer research. The National Cancer Program is vital to our Nation's health."

NOTE: A biography of the appointee was made available by the Office of the Press Secretary.

Remarks to the 1994 Seeds of Peace Representatives
September 9, 1994

The President. I want to welcome all of you here to the White House, young people from all across the Middle East. We have here Israeli, Palestinian, Egyptian, Moroccan, and Jordanian young people coming together to our country as ambassadors of peace for an entire generation.

A year ago, almost to the day, we had the signing of the Israeli-PLO accord here. And there were young people from Seeds of Peace here. And when they were here, I saw them and asked that all present dedicate themselves to peace for the next generation. Since then we have seen an agreement between Israel and Jordan. We have seen further peace on the other Middle East fronts, further progress on the other Middle East peace fronts. And we have seen just last week Morocco and Israel take the first step toward establishing diplomatic relations.

But ahead of all that is the simple magic of the person-to-person relationships that you are building and a future you are building for yourselves. I hope so much that by the time all of you are my age the problems of the Middle East will be a distant memory, and all of you will celebrate the unity and strength, the harmony and prosperity of a region of people working together just as you have sung together today and come together in the United States.

This is a time of peace as well as trouble in the world. We see progress in the Middle East. We see progress in Ireland. We see de-

mocracy taking root in Russia. There is a great deal to hope for and a great deal of work to do. I think it is fair to say that for me and for all of us who have seen you here in the United States, the image of your smiling together, of you singing together, of you being together will spur us on to try to make sure that the future that you share will be a future you share together.

Thank you very much.

[*At this point, John Wallach, president, Seeds of Peace, and Tamer Nagy Mohamed, an Egyptian participant in the program, made brief remarks and presented gifts to the President.*]

The President. Thank you. [*Applause*] That's terrific. Good luck to you. Thank you.

Mr. Mohamed. Thank you very much.

The President. Let's give him another hand. Didn't he do a good job? Thank you. Thank you.

NOTE: The President spoke at 8 a.m. on the South Lawn at the White House, prior to his departure for New Orleans, LA.

Remarks to the National Baptist Convention, U.S.A., in New Orleans, Louisiana
September 9, 1994

If I could sing like that, I would have never gotten into politics. [*Laughter and applause*] Reverend Jemison; your president-elect, Dr. Lyons; to Dr. Richardson, Reverend James, Dr. Mary Ross; to all the distinguished Louisianians here present, including Reverend Governor Edwards—I thought he did very well today—Senator Breaux and Congressman Jefferson and Mayor Morial and all your State officials and legislators; Reverend Jackson; to all the members of my staff and Cabinet who are here— where are the people here with the administration? They're all here somewhere.

I want to say many things, but first we have a duty, I think, as Americans to take a moment of silence now for the 131 people who were killed in that awful air crash in Pittsburgh. Hillary and I send our deepest sympathies and our prayers to the friends and the loved ones of

the crash victims. And I know that all of you and all Americans also send your prayers to the grieving.

Our Secretary of Transportation, Secretary Peña, is there in Pittsburgh. I have talked with the mayor and the Governor this morning and with Senator Wofford. All Americans should know that we will do whatever we can to assure their safety in travel. But let us today, in the painful recognition of our fallibility as human beings, mourn with a moment of silence those who lost their lives.

Amen.

Well, Dr. Jemison, I thank you for that warm introduction. I have known you as a friend for a long time. When we were standing outside, about to come up, he was reviewing his more than 50 years in the leadership of this great church. That's a long time, worthy of honor, and I give it.

Two years ago I had a great moment with all of you in Atlanta when I was running for President. And last year I was invited to appear, and I couldn't. I had to give my regrets. I sort of felt like the boy who skipped Sunday school. [*Laughter*] I promised Dr. Jemison I'd be here this year no matter what, so I showed up, and I hope you have forgiven me because I feel at home.

Two years ago I came to you, and you responded. I asked you to work with me to give us at least a chance to change the direction our country was headed in. We had too much debt and too few jobs. We seemed to be going in the wrong direction, where ordinary Americans were ignored and people with money and organized power were heeded, but somehow the thing was not working. As the Vice President used to say, "What ought to be up was down, and what ought to be down was up." And that was a problem. I wanted a chance to try to move this country forward again and to try to pull our country together again.

Today, having served now for not quite 2 years, I guess what I want to say to you is I think we're doing a pretty good job of moving forward but not nearly a good enough job of coming together.

I have here in the front some of my friends and former employers from the State of Arkansas. Would you all stand up? Thank you and bless you for being here.

I lived in a little State to the north of here for a while, you know. And I learned that it was not healthy to say one thing to one group and one to another. You had to say the same thing to everybody and mean it every day.

I never will forget when I was running for President, one of the most memorable days I had was speaking on one day of the weekend in Macomb County, Michigan, the prototypical, what they used to call "Reagan Democrat county," where there was a lot of what they used to call "white flight." And then the next day I went to a black church in Detroit where half the people were from Arkansas. And I gave the same speech I had given the day before, and people thought that was strange. And I said, "Is it so strange that we should say the same thing to all Americans and try to come together?"

I want to talk to you today about that. I still believe what I believed 2 years ago, that the Government has a role to play in the future of this country and the future of our families and our hopes and our dreams, not as savior but not on the sidelines, just as a partner in progress. I still believe that, together, we can meet every challenge, that we can fulfill the hopes of our children. I still believe there are a lot of things we have to do that go way beyond the reach of Government into the depths of the human spirit.

Today I say to you again, I think we're making a lot of progress, and I feel good about that. But I don't think we're doing as well as we should in coming together. And I don't feel good about that, and I want to examine that and what I could do better and what you can do better.

I noticed a columnist wrote the other day in the newspaper, he said, "There's lots of things going right in this country. The economy is booming. We've got over 4 million new jobs. The stock market is up. The deficit is down. Things look good in the future. Our country was just rated the most productive country in the entire world for the first time in nearly 10 years." We've got over 4 million new jobs, as I said, the unemployment rate is down. A lot of things are going well.

We see around the world real progress: peace in the Middle East, in the Holy Land, something that should gladden the heart of every Christian. We see peace prospects are moving forward in Northern Ireland, something many of us thought we would never see. We see the majesty of peace and democracy and freedom unfolding in South Africa. And I want to thank Reverend Jackson for his leadership of our election team over there in South Africa, during that process.

And, so the writer said—he was writing about me—he said, "If things are going so well, why are people still mad at the President?" Well, what he might have said is, you remember that old saying, "If I'm so rich, why am I not happy?" [*Laughter*]

Well, there are a lot of reasons for that. But let me offer one. I just got back from vacation, and when I was on vacation, I went to church and I heard a minister I'd never seen before from a little town in New Jersey called Red Bank. You know where Red Bank, New Jersey is? [*Applause*]

The first thing he did was give us dispensation for being on vacation, which I felt good about. He said, "Life is not all work. It is also play and rest and worship." But he went on to say, it's not only important to do all those things but to get them right. And if you don't have faith, you won't have the rhythm right. You will find yourselves working at play and playing at worship, and you'll have it all messed up.

Well, that's kind of what's going on in our country today. We still haven't quite got the rhythm right. So that even though we are facing a lot of our most profound problems and even though we are clearly making progress in areas too long ignored, which many of you have mentioned here, we have to say: What is the real deal here? Why aren't we happier about it?

There are many reasons, but let me offer three. One is, whenever periods of profound change occur in the lives of individuals or nations, they are unsettling. Isn't that right? Can't you think of times in your own life when you were making a change, and every day you woke up and it was like there was this scale inside your body. And on one side of the scale was hope, and on the other side of the scale was fear, and it seemed like every day, the scales would be in a little bit different balance until you finally got through this change you were going through.

We can all identify with that. That's what's going on in this country today. It's happened before. At the end of the First World War, we won this great battle, and we didn't know what to do with ourselves, and so we just came home and folded up our tents. We thought we could withdraw from the world. And what happened? That's when the Ku Klux Klan first started rising up. At the end of the First World War, when we lost our concentration, and we lost our way, and we didn't know who the enemy was anymore. It's also when we had the first Red Scare, when everybody began to be accused of being a Communist if they had unconventional opinions.

Then, at the end of the Second World War, the same sort of thing happened, except we knew better than to withdraw from the world. Harry Truman said, "No, no, we're going to rebuild the country here at home for the soldiers and their families, and we're going to rebuild our enemies, Germany and Japan, and our Allies in Europe. And we know who the enemy is. It's the Soviet Union and communism. So we're going to have a great wall against communism, and we're going to fight this cold war."

But still, there was uncertainty. There was a new Red Scare, which came to its height under Senator McCarthy. And Harry Truman had a hard time getting people to change. You know, he was at 80 percent approval in the polls after he dropped the bomb which ended the war, but by the time he sent the second health reform legislation to Congress—that's how long we've been trying to fix the health care system—by the time Harry Truman did it the second time, he was down to 36 percent in the polls. Now, everybody talks about him like he ought to be on Mount Rushmore. [*Laughter*] But I was for a family who supported him when he was living, and I know what happened.

Change is difficult. And when you're going through a period of change, we are vulnerable to getting out of our rhythm.

The second problem is, we live in a time which almost seems to glorify the negative, the cynical, don't we? [*Applause*] It's the old story. There's a lot more people prone to see the glass of water is half empty than half full than there used to be, and to tell all the rest of us we're just fools if we see it half full; it's really half empty.

And then, frankly, let's face it: We still have some problems that are real deep in this country that all the progress we're making does not necessarily touch. We have 4.1 million new jobs. The work force is expanding more rapidly than it did 10 years ago, the last time we had any kind of economic recovery, but lots of folks still out of work. A lot of folks live in places where they don't believe new jobs are coming. A lot of people are working harder; they have their job, but they don't think they'll ever get a raise. Five million, five million people live in working families who had health insurance 5 years ago, who do not have it today.

So we have some real problems. Governor Edwards alluded to the most heart-breaking of all, those that involve the children of this country, their sins and their abuses and their loss of their childhood and their innocence, and our loss of their future: The 11-year-old boy in Chicago, Robert Sandifer, who sprayed gunfire at a group of kids and killed a 14-year-old girl and then was killed himself, his grandmother saying, "I could not reach you." And then in New Jersey, the 13-year-old who stole a gun to end a petty argument and the life of his 11-year-old friend. In Detroit, Rosa Parks was attacked by a crack addict for $53. In my home-town, an 82-year-old woman, attacked by two teenagers, brutalized and sexually molested—82 years old.

These aren't Baptist problems or Catholic problems or Jewish problems. Contrary to what some people say, they're not black or white problems. No, the 11-year-old in Chicago was black, but the teenager in New Jersey who killed and the victim were both white. Rosa Parks is a hero to African-Americans and a hero to people who have been oppressed throughout the world, but the 82-year-old woman in my home-town was a white lady, and so were the people who attacked her.

These problems and the problems behind them that brought the children to the miserable point in life where they did what they did, these are the things that are gnawing at our spirit that we have to address so we can get the rhythm right, we can go on and face the chal-lenges of this time, all the changes. And we can make change our friend if we know that we are grounded. That is what your faith is about. But it is also now what our citizenship must be more about.

I note that there are many voices from all sectors preaching to us today about the decline in our values. In a way I welcome them all. And whether they are traditionally our allies or our adversaries, we should listen for the truth of their words, and if they are true, we should heed them.

On the other hand, I would issue two caution-ary notes: We should not let the voices of de-spair make our insecurities even deeper. That is wrong. That is wrong. There have always been problems in every society, and there will be until the end of time. That is the lesson of the Scripture. So for all the people who try to use the difficulties of the moment to dampen the energies of Americans, to defeat our spirits, I say, that is wrong. The Scripture says, "Let us not grow weary in well-doing, for in due season we shall reap if we do not lose heart."

The darkness of every storm provides a new chance for renewal, every storm. And so does this one. So to all those who preach that we need to return to the values of our faith, I say, we do. But the real issue is, what are we going to do about it? Not what are we going to say about it, but what are we going to do

about it? The saying is important, for we in words come to visualize the future. And we need the vision so that we do not perish. But we must act on the vision. And that's where all the problems come.

You know the old story about the preacher who was preaching his best on Sunday morning and thought he had finally reached everybody in the service? And he said, "I want everybody who wants to go to heaven to stand up right now." And everybody in the whole church stood up except Sister Jones, who had not missed a day in church in 40 years. And he was crest-fallen. It broke all his concentration. He stopped the sermon. He said, "Sister Jones, you have not missed a sermon in 40 years. Do you mean to tell me you do not want to go to heaven when you die?" And she popped right up, and she said, "Oh, I'm sorry, preacher, I thought you were trying to get up a load to go right now." [Laughter]

Now that's a big problem, isn't it? We all want to do it somewhere down the road, but if we have to do something right now, well that's something we better think about. So the challenge is, what are we going to do right now? Not later, but now, right now.

I say this to the people who always say the glass is half empty, always being pessimistic, al-ways being negative. They have it easy. That lets you out of any responsibility at all. You adopt a pessimistic, negative attitude; you be cynical. It just relieves you of any responsibility for doing because then doing doesn't matter. Right? All I can tell you is, there would be no free Americans sitting in this place today if the pessimists and the cynics and the negative people had ruled this country all along the way.

Our obligation and our power flows out of two simple lessons I was taught about our whole civilization many years ago in college. One is that the future can be better than the present, not perfect but better. And the second is that each of us has a personal, moral responsibility to make it so. That is the simple lesson that will get our rhythm back, that will put us back in harmony, that will enable us to enjoy our progress and still keep working on the deep and profound things that are challenging us and dealing with the unsettling impact of this chang-ing time.

My vision is that we will go into the 21st century as a country more free, more prosperous, more united, and more open to making change our friend than we have ever been.

Yes, we are beginning to see results. Yes, the economy is doing better. Yes, we are seeing more fairness as well as more progress. We did raise taxes on the wealthiest 1½ percent of Americans to bring the deficit down, but we also gave tax cuts to 15 million working families just above the poverty line to say, "You got off welfare; you're working; we're going to reward you being a parent and a worker." We did that. We are making progress.

We got 180,000 more kids in Head Start. We're going to immunize a couple of million more children so that by 1996 all the kids 2 years of age and less, like this little kid here, will have their shots. We're doing more to provide job training for people who lose their jobs, and we made 20 million Americans eligible to refinance their college loans at lower interest rates with a longer repayment term. These things are important. They matter.

Work, the dignity of work is central to our ability to build a future. The second thing we have to do is not just talk about how we need stronger families but think about what I can do and you can do to make them stronger. We didn't cut taxes for those 15 million working families for just political reasons. We did it because people have got to be able to succeed today as workers and as parents. And if we want people to work and parent, we have to reward work. That's why the Family and Medical Leave Act was so important. How can you say you want people to be good family members and then fire them if they have to take a little time off to have a baby or take care of a sick parent?

There's a bill in the Congress I really believe in, sponsored by Senator Metzenbaum, to make adoptions easier and to make it possible for people to adopt children across racial lines if nobody else is there wanting to adopt the children. Don't leave kids in the limbo of foster care for years and years and years. Give them a chance to do it.

The third thing we have to do is to make our communities stronger. We have to act as if we believe what we talk about all the time, that we're all in this together. The Secretary of Housing and Urban Development is here today. Henry Cisneros has done more to come up with a program to end homelessness than anybody in the last 10 years. We've been talking

about it. He's trying to do something about it. It makes us stronger as a community.

The welfare reform bill is about community, empowering everybody to participate. The enterprise zones are about giving poor communities the incentive to draw capital to put people to work. These things will make our communities stronger.

And the crime bill was about communities. Because if your streets aren't safe, if people don't feel secure, it's hard to call them to higher citizenship. What did Edwin Everett say, "If you've got the right to vote but you're scared to go to the polling place, it's hard to talk about citizenship." That's why it was important.

We're also trying to change the way Government works, reforming the way we finance our campaigns and try to at least tell you what the lobbyists are doing in Washington with new disclosure requirements, a bill that would make Congress live under all the laws it imposes on you. That's not a bad idea, I think. These things are important.

We're trying to prove something that I always believe, that you can have diversity and excellence at the same time. Look at our Cabinet: five African-Americans, more than twice as many as ever served; 15 percent of all appointments, more than twice as many appointments to the Federal courts as the last three Presidents combined are African-Americans. But what really ought to make you clap is that these judges have the highest percentage of "well-qualified" ratings by the American Bar Association since they have been giving out the ratings. They're not just from different racial groups and men and women; they're well-qualified.

So there are things that Government can do. This crime bill I want to talk about because it runs into the question of harmony. There are a lot of things the Government can't do, or there are things the Government can do, and it's still not enough. I know that crime bill wasn't perfect. And I know it imposed great, great challenges for the African-American Members of Congress and for many people and religious faiths because it contains capital punishment provisions. And many people oppose capital punishment for everyone, and many others say that African-Americans are more likely to get the penalty because poor folks are more likely than non-poor folks to be convicted and sentenced to death. I know that there are those who say that when we build more prisons and make sentences for repeat offenders longer and tougher, that will have a disproportionate impact on the African-American community.

But to that, I say this: Every time you look at the evening news, there's another funeral. And there's a disproportionate number of black kids lying in those pine boxes, too. And that's wrong. That's what's really wrong. And we have got to find a way, imperfect though it is, to get all the Americans together, with all their different perspectives, and move forward on this issue, because if people are not safe, we're in trouble.

And if we put the 100,000 police on the street and do it right, they'll prevent crime, not just catch criminals. If we get these assault weapons off the street—and it's now illegal for kids to own handguns—if we start enforcing that law, and if we do something with that prevention money, if we give these kids something to say yes to, if we do something with the job money, with the job training money, with the drug treatment money, with the recreation money, if we give people at that time of their lives when they've got all this energy some constructive outlet for it, it will make a difference.

But if you really want it, to lower the crime rate, reduce violence, and save more kids' lives, all the work is still to be done. All the work is still to be done. And it's like asking Sister Jones to go to heaven; we've got to do this right now. If we believe there is a crisis of the spirit, a crisis of values in this country, we have to do something about it right now. And we've got to do it where we live.

I would like to suggest just four simple things that go beyond Government programs. And you know them all, and many of you are doing them all. But every American can make a contribution. We are raising a whole generation of kids who aren't sure they're the most important person in the world to anybody.

Now, consider this: Today, about 40 percent of all children are born in the homes where there was never a marriage. Twenty-seven percent of all pregnancies end in abortion. I don't care what your position is, whether you're pro-choice or anti-; that's too many. That's not about serious health problems or emotional problems. So when the miracle of conception occurs, less than half of those miracles wind up being babies born into homes where there's a mother and a father and where the kid's got a better-than-even chance of having the life that most of

us have, or we wouldn't be here in our neckties and nice dresses today. Now, that's just a fact.

Dr. King once said, "Whom we wish to change, we must first love." And I know not everybody is going to be in a stable, traditional family like you see in one of those 1950 sitcoms, but we'd be better off if more people were. I was raised by a wonderful mother who worked, who cared for me, who was a widow when I was born, went through a difficult marriage. And at least every now and then I find somebody who thinks I turned out all right, so it can happen. But we have to say, who is going to care for these children? In every single study that's ever been done of young people who did well against all the odds with terrible circumstances and all the things that could have gone wrong, it is always, always, always the case that they had a relationship with somebody who cared about them, somebody.

I don't think we ought to give up on families. Yesterday I met with a number of ministers. And one friend of mine who pastors a massive church in the Washington area, an African-American church, has made the mission of his church the rebuilding of the family. Over 40 percent of the members are male, and he left our breakfast to go back to meet with 150 couples who had split up or never married. Some of them were divorced. Sometimes people had flown in from thousands of miles away. He was trying to get them back together for the children's sake and because it was the right thing to do. We need to do more of that. But he's not just talking about it, he's doing something.

If that's not an option, then somebody's got to love these children. When I was in Des Moines, Iowa, in the campaign, I saw a white lady holding an African-American baby that had AIDS. She was from Iowa. The kid was from Miami. She had been abandoned by her husband. She had two children of her own. She was living in an apartment house, working at a meager job. She thought it was God's will that she take a child who was sick and abandoned. And she did it. If she could do it, a lot of the rest of us should as well.

Someone has got to care for these children. I've heard Reverend Jackson talk about this. I think about it all the time as my daughter grows up. We have to find—in families where the mother is doing all the work, then there needs to be somebody outside the family, a male figure, who can at least relate to children, who can say things like, "What are you reading?" and "How are you doing in class?" "This is right, and this is wrong." "I'd like to see your report card." "What do you want to do 5 years from now?"

You know, how many children do we know—how many children, how many of these kids that are shooting one another never think about 5 years from now? The future to them is 5 minutes from now. Why is that? Because no one is asking them about it. Where there is no vision, people perish. They cannot visualize 5 years from now. So that's the first thing.

The second thing we've got to do is help these kids at least grow up without fear, which means we've got to keep them from getting shot and stop them from shooting. And laws can help, and policemen can help, but every 2 hours in this country another kid under the age of 19 dies from gunfire. A 9-year-old boy wrote me from this city right here in New Orleans and said, "Please do something about this. I'm afraid I could get killed." And on Mother's Day, a month after he wrote me, he got killed just walking home from school.

Now, there are things people can do in their neighborhoods to stop this. We are giving you more tools in terms of the laws and the police, but we've got to have help. Schools can be made safer. Walking routes can be made safer. Use the crime bill funds—the churches are eligible to participate—and give kids something to do after school to get them off the street where they can be in recreation. I got so tired, when we were debating that crime bill, hearing people badmouth midnight basketball. I'd a lot rather have somebody shooting hoops than shooting bullets. But you have to make that work.

The third thing I would say is, we have to be more honest. Sometimes it is almost embarrassing, I know, but we've got to be more honest with our young people in teaching them to respect themselves, their bodies, their souls, and their futures. And we always talk about how irresponsible it is for young men to father these children and run off, but we've got to get more young women to make a different choice in life, too. We have simply got to find a way to deal with this.

Thirty years ago one of 40 white births was out of wedlock; now it's one in 5. Thirty years ago, one in five African-American births was out of wedlock; now, over half. But the white out-of-wedlock birthrate is growing much faster

than the African-American rate. So, we are going to have equal opportunity for all before you know it. [*Laughter*]

You're laughing to keep from crying, but it's not funny, is it? We're going to see a merger of this. No more race discrimination; more than half of everybody's babies will be born where there was never a marriage. That is a disaster. It is wrong, and someone has to say, again, "It is simply not right. You shouldn't have a baby before you're ready, and you shouldn't have a baby when you're not married. You just have to stop it." We've got to turn it around.

Now I want to make it clear we shouldn't stigmatize these babies, and when they're born, we should take care of them. We ought to love the babies. We ought to love the parents. We ought to give them the best future we can, but we have to tell people, look at the facts. Look at what happens to people. Look at their incomes, their education levels, their future. We've got to get people out of thinking that the future is 5 minutes away and to realize it is 5 years or 10 years or 20 years away. And you have to do that. I'll try to do my part, but this is not a Government deal. This is the way people are behaving, as if there was no respect for themselves and no future. We have to stop.

Finally, let me say, I ask you to help lead us in bringing back an ethic of service to this Nation. We're going to kick off our national service program on Monday, which will this year involve 20,000 young Americans in serving their community, many of them in church groups. The Congress of National Black Churches is an active participant in national service. We want kids working with churches to solve a lot of these problems and earning credit for their college education. Year after next we'll have 100,000 young people. You can put them to work. When people are serving one another, when they're acting as role models, they'll be better people themselves. And you can do that.

All these things you can do: help our kids be safer, help make sure every child is loved by somebody and disciplined by somebody and cared for by somebody, and help our kids change this culture which is ending family life and childhood as we know it and bring us back to the spirit of service.

Finally, let me say this: I came here to say this because I don't believe in preaching at people. I believe you are the heroes of this whole thing. A lot of you have been out there like the little Dutch boy with your thumb in the dike against all these forces for years. A lot of you have been doing these things. A lot of you have run the day care centers and run the recreation programs and run the prison ministries and counseled the young people. You have done this. But America now knows that we must all do this.

So I say, I honor you. I honor the members of your church that get up and go to work every day and follow the law and pay their taxes and do their best to raise their kids. And let us say for the record, since all America is watching this, most of the members of your church do exactly that. They play by the rules, and they work hard, and they do their best.

But let's not kid each other, folks. I'm going to go back to Washington. And I'll keep trying to create jobs. And we'll do a good job of that. And we'll open America to the world. I'll keep working for peace and freedom around the world. I'll keep working for better education and training opportunities. I'll keep trying to solve this terrible riddle of why we can't get jobs in the inner city and poor rural areas. And we'll try to find ways to do that. But in the end, if we're going to get the rhythm right, if we're going to enjoy the progress we're making, even in an imperfect world, we have to

get the bedrock right. We have to know that the spirit that we believe in is rifling through this country and is going to work.

You know, Paul, St. Paul, was not Timothy's father, but he was his spiritual father. And he said, "When I call to remembrance the unfeigned faith that is in thee, I put thee in remembrance that thou stir up the gift of God which is in thee." I believe and you believe that every child has a gift of God within them. When the gift dies, it is our sin as well as theirs and our loss as well as theirs.

So let us leave here resolved to stir up the gift of God that is within us and do those things that will enable us to go forward with joy and confidence to make the future what it ought to be.

Thank you, and God bless you all.

NOTE: The President spoke at 11:10 a.m. in the Ernest N. Morial Convention Center. In his remarks, he referred to National Baptist Convention, U.S.A., officers Rev. Theodore J. Jemison, president, Rev. Henry J. Lyons, president-elect, Rev. W. Franklyn Richardson, general secretary, Rev. A. Lincoln James, Sunday School Congress president, and Dr. Mary O. Ross, Women's Auxiliary president; Mayor Marc H. Morial of New Orleans; and Rev. Jesse Jackson, District of Columbia shadow U.S. Senator.

Statement on the Cuba-United States Agreement on Migration
September 9, 1994

This agreement, when carried out, will help ensure that the massive flow of dangerous and illegal migration will be replaced by a safer, legal, and more orderly process.

NOTE: This statement was included in a statement by the Press Secretary announcing the agreement reached in the New York migration talks.

Memorandum on the 1994 Combined Federal Campaign
September 9, 1994

Memorandum for the Heads of Executive Departments and Agencies

I am delighted that Secretary of Energy Hazel R. O'Leary has agreed to serve as the chair of the 1994 Combined Federal Campaign of

the National Capital Area. I ask you to support the campaign by personally chairing the campaign in your Agency and appointing a top official as your vice chair.

The Combined Federal Campaign is an important way for Federal employees to support thousands of worthy charities. This year our goal is to raise more than $38 million. Public servants not only contribute to the campaign but assume leadership roles to ensure its success.

Your personal support and enthusiasm will help guarantee another successful campaign this year.

WILLIAM J. CLINTON

The President's Radio Address
September 10, 1994

Good morning. Let me begin by saying that Hillary and I send our deepest sympathies and our prayers to the friends and loved ones of the 132 people killed in the air crash near Pittsburgh on Thursday. I know all Americans will send their thoughts and prayers to the grieving this weekend. Meanwhile, we're working to get to the bottom of what happened in the crash, and we're working to continue to assure the safety of American passengers.

All across our country this week, Americans came back from vacation. Our children are back in school, and for many families this is what they regard as the real new year. As we get back to the business of our lives, it's a good time to stop and think about the work we have ahead of us as a nation.

Unfortunately, that work includes a stark fact about our children. Too many of them are growing up in fear. All too many are growing up without the values of mainstream society, without knowing the difference between what's right and wrong, and without believing that it makes a difference whether they do right or wrong.

By now, nearly all of us know the story of Robert Sandifer, known as Yummy to his friends. He was first arrested when he was 8 years old. A couple of weeks ago, when he was only 11, he became a suspect in the gang shooting of an innocent girl named Shavon Dean. Several days later, that boy died himself in what Chicago police say was yet another gang-related killing.

The number of gang homicides has nearly tripled since 1980 in Robert and Shavon's hometown. And all across America, too many decent people have felt the anguish of losing a child to the meanness of the streets. At younger and younger ages, boys and girls are turning to gangs and to guns.

For a child without an involved family, a gang offers a feeling of belonging. For a young person without options for tomorrow, a gang offers a sense of purpose. For anyone born in a home barred and chained off from danger, life on the streets seems like a taste of freedom they've never known.

But America knows how to use its freedom better than that. We see it every day in big cities and small towns as Americans do come together to take up their responsibilities and to put the spirit of community to work. And I believe we have many opportunities right now to do just that and to turn around the scourge of violence in the lives of our children.

Much of that work begins with what each of us can do as caring Americans. Today I'll sign a proclamation designating next week as National Gang Violence Prevention Week. I'm asking Americans to address this profound problem, each of them in their hometowns, to save a generation of our children. Every parent, every teacher, every person who has the chance to influence children must force a change in the lives of our kids. We have to show them we love them, and we have to teach them discipline and responsibility. Robert Sandifer's grandmother despaired at his funeral because, she said, "I couldn't reach you." We must keep doing everything we can to reach those children. And we must help them respect the law and keep them safe.

Next week I'll sign into law the historic crime bill that will be a tough but smart tool in every community's fight for our children's safety. It'll punish hardened young criminals with stronger penalties, and it will expand boot camps, drug courts, and other sanctions to stop first-time offenders from beginning lives of crime. It bans 19 assault weapons and goes a long way toward keeping the guns out of the hands of our children. And with prevention programs, the crime law will take on the sickness of gangs and drugs and give our young people a chance at a new and better life.

Finally, we have to show our children before they enter gangs that they already belong to a community larger than themselves, in which they can feel important and serve a larger purpose. On Monday, here at the White House and at sites all across America, we'll kick off AmeriCorps, our national service effort.

AmeriCorps is America at its best, people rolling up their sleeves and assuming responsibility to make our country better. At a time when so many of our people feel alienated or alone, the 20,000 new members of AmeriCorps will work closely with neighbors and fellow citizens all across this country to make our communities places where children can grow up to realize their God-given potential. They'll help make schools safe in Los Angeles, tutor second graders from Kentucky, repair neighborhoods in Philadelphia. Instead of just talking about problems, they'll be solving them. AmeriCorps will call upon the best of a generation to reclaim what has always been best about America.

All these things will help us make this time a year and a season of renewal. It's a time in which I'll keep working to bring greater prosperity to our hard-working people. We already have over 4 million new jobs in this economy, but we've got a good ways to go. It's a time, with our new crime law, when we will send not just a legal but a moral message across America, that Americans have a right to be secure in their homes, on their streets, in their schools and places of work. And it's a time, with AmeriCorps, when we will renew the ethic of service that has always been a key to our greatness, offering first 20,000 and, in 2 years, 100,000 of our young people a chance to earn some credit against a college education in return for serving their country at the grassroots level.

In all these ways, we'll be helping to fulfill our obligations to our children, to our Nation, and to our future.

Thanks for listening.

NOTE: The President spoke at 10:06 a.m. from the Oval Office at the White House.

Remarks to AmeriCorps Volunteers in Aberdeen, Maryland
September 11, 1994

Thank you very much. Chaplain, and General and Mrs. Tragemann, General Monroe, General Scott, Colonel Bosley, Senator and Mrs. Sarbanes, ladies and gentlemen.

I guess I'll start by saying happy birthday—[*laughter*]—and happy anniversary. A commitment of 43 years is something the rest of this country could do more to emulate, sir. And we thank both of you for what you've done.

Hillary and I are delighted to be here today with all of you and especially with our young AmeriCorps volunteers. [*Applause*] A quiet, reticent group. [*Laughter*]

This is a special service that reaffirms our relationship to our God and our God-given responsibility to serve our fellow human beings. The Scripture from Isaiah that is the basis of this service today is something we would all do well to read and live by on a regular basis and to echo the words of Isaiah, "Here am I, Lord; send me." Because as all of you who are here know already, service to others is something everyone can do and something everyone should do because of our relationship to our God, our responsibility to others, and our responsibility to ourselves.

This chapel is filled with people who have answered the call to service. In every case, you embody what service means to America, Americans coming together and moving forward. In three words that I have always believed embodied what was best about this country—opportunity, responsibility, and community—your country has given you the opportunity to serve. You have assumed the responsibility. And our American family is much stronger and better and richer as a result.

Many of you are civilians who have spent a lifetime fulfilling the public trust in and around Aberdeen and supporting our Nation's military. And for that we are all very grateful. Many of you have spent your entire careers in uniform, your service profound, often putting you at risk of providing what President Lincoln called "the last full measure of devotion." We honor you more than we can say.

And many of you are the young people here in AmeriCorps. When I was inaugurated President, I called America to a season of service, and I asked our young people to lead the way. Thankfully, Congress has given them that opportunity, and they have responded with their responsibility in the national service program. And so we honor them for their service as well.

Later today, 40 of these young people, those in the yellow outfits, will be leaving to fight the forest fires that are raging in the West, that have already claimed so much of our natural heritage and, unfortunately, the lives of some of our finest citizens. To them and to all the other corps members who are here and to the tens of thousands who will take the pledge of service with us tomorrow at the White House and all across America as we formally kick off the first full year of AmeriCorps with 20,000 young people across this country, let us say to them, we honor your service as well, and we thank you for the high calling you have answered.

These young people will be doing a lot of things, working in education, working to help the environment, working to deal with people's human needs, working to help to increase the safety and security of our neighborhoods and our schools and our streets. Some may be working with the veterans now at Perry Point Hospital or connecting young students to the world of knowledge in Baltimore classrooms right here in Maryland. Some will be tying service and science together as they work to reclaim the Chesapeake Bay or deal with the problems of the Anacostia down in the District of Columbia.

Every one of you represents the oldest and best of America's traditions. This country really got started by a bunch of volunteers. Nobody made them do what they did. They all had to sign up on their own accord. Now we are run, from our national security all the way down to our most elemental function in every community in this country, by a nation of volunteers, not by Government edict, not by large bureaucracies but by the spirit of service and devotion that burns within the heart of every American.

So for all of you, and especially for these young people who may launch a whole generation of renewal of service all across this country, I say God bless you and all who serve, and thank you from the bottom of my heart.

Thank you very much.

NOTE: The President spoke at 10:25 a.m. in the base chapel at Aberdeen Proving Ground, where AmeriCorps volunteers in the National Civilian Community Corps had received training. In his remarks, he referred to Chaplain (Lt. Col.) O. Wayne Smith; Maj. Gen. Richard W. Tragemann, commander, Aberdeen Proving Ground, and his wife, Kathy; Maj. Gen. James Monroe, chief of ordnance and commander, U.S. Army Ordnance Center and School; Brig. Gen. Don Scott, USA (Ret.), president, National Civilian Community Corps; James M. Bosley, deputy installation commander, Aberdeen Proving Ground; and congregation members celebrating special occasions.

Remarks to Organizations of the Jewish Community
September 12, 1994

Prime Minister Rabin, ladies and gentlemen, I'm very pleased to have this chance to address all of you, gathered from some 70 communities across the United States.

It is with thanks for the remarkable year we have just lived and optimism for the New Year that I wish you peace, health, and happiness in the months ahead. *Shana Tova!*

What a year it's been. Twelve months ago tomorrow I was privileged to host Prime Minister Rabin and Chairman Arafat on the South Lawn of the White House. Many of you were there to witness their historic handshake, which marked the dawn of a new era in the Middle East, one of conciliation and hope. Their brave, historic act paved the way for others.

This summer, King Hussein of Jordan and Prime Minister Rabin at the White House came here to end the state of war between Israel and Jordan and to start down the road of warm friendship and cooperation. As Prime Minister Rabin stated then so eloquently, "A million eyes all over the world are watching us now with great relief and great joy. Yet another nightmare of war may be over. At the same time, millions of eyes in the Middle East are looking at us now with great hope, heartfelt hope, that our children and grandchildren will know no more war."

I applaud Israel's courage, and I salute the Arab leaders—including the King of Morocco, who last week began the process of establishing diplomatic relations with Israel—for standing up for the naysayers and embracing change. By working to secure a future of peace and prosperity, these far-sighted statesmen will fulfill their people's hopes and their yearnings for the quiet miracle of a normal life.

Already we see the fruits of their efforts. Palestinians and Israelis are learning every day how to live side by side in peace. Jordanian planes may now fly over Israel. Tourists visiting the Dead Sea can cross from Eilat to Aqaba. These are small steps, but they lay the foundation for much greater strides to come.

Now, the international community must do all it can to ensure that Arabs and Israelis realize the full benefits of peace. At the same time, we have a right to expect that the participants in the peace process live up to their commitments. And we also hope that all those in the region who have been urging us to continue to play an energetic role will do their part, too, in particular by taking steps now to dismantle the Arab boycott of Israel.

As we look to the year ahead, I hope and I believe that we'll see even greater progress toward a comprehensive peace in the region, a peace that joins Israelis, Palestinians, Jordanians, Syrians, and Lebanese so that all their children will come to know a better future. More than 100 of these children, participants in the 1994 Seeds for Peace program that have met at the White House this past Friday before returning to their homes, they just spent a month together in Maine, learning about one another, breaking down barriers, building ties.

These young men and women told me that in just a few short weeks, first names replaced ethnic and religious labels. Mistrust turned into curiosity. Fear gave way to friendship. These kinds of person-to-person relationships, multiplied thousands of times through business ventures, joint projects, trade, and regional cooperation, will help ensure that the olive branch of peace stretches its bough across the entire Middle East.

Nurturing peace is hard work. The dark forces of terror remain deeply entrenched, as horrible attacks against Jews in Argentina, Panama, and England recently demonstrated. But despite these terrible acts, it's essential that the American Jewish community continue its support for peace and the peace process.

As we move ahead, I urge you to keep the faith, because Israel, for the first time in its history, has the opportunity to achieve real peace. And I pledge to you that we will do our part to make sure that it is a lasting and secure peace.

I understand that in a few moments my friend Prime Minister Rabin will speak to you from Jerusalem. I want to reiterate to him my admiration for all he's done for his people and for the cause of peace.

Yitzhak, I wish you and your people a very Happy New Year. And remember, you've got an open invitation to visit the White House, because every time you come here we seem to move a step closer to lasting peace in the Middle East.

My fellow Americans, I hope that 12 months from now when we take stock of the year ahead, we'll have even more happy events to celebrate. Working together for peace, I believe we will.

Thank you.

NOTE: The address to the Council of Jewish Federations and the Conference of Presidents of Major Jewish Organizations was taped on September 10 at 10:45 a.m. in the Roosevelt Room at the White House and was released by the Office of the Press Secretary on September 12. A tape was not available for verification of the content of this address.

Remarks in a Swearing-In Ceremony for AmeriCorps Volunteers
September 12, 1994

The President. Good afternoon. In just a moment, I'll speak to thousands of you young people and those of you who are young in spirit around the country about our national service program, AmeriCorps. But before I do, let me say just a few words about what occurred here this morning.

As you know, a plane came down here early this morning, and the pilot lost his life. An investigation is taking place that will determine how and why this happened. We take this incident seriously because the White House is the people's house. And it is the job of every President who lives here to keep it safe and secure.

On his second night in the White House, our second President, John Adams, wrote: "I pray heaven to bestow the best blessings on this house and on all that shall hereafter inhabit it." That prayer has been answered. In times of war and peace, in hard times and good, the White House is an enduring symbol of our democracy. It tells our people and those around the world that the mission of America continues, as it does on this happy and important day. So let me assure all Americans, the people's house will be kept safe, it will be kept open, and the people's business will go on.

We stand at the start of America's new season of service. For 20,000 Americans this year all over our great land, this moment marks the beginning of a journey that will change their lives forever. For our Nation, the moments of service that will follow will change our lives for many seasons to come.

Service is never a simple act, it's about sacrifice for others and about accomplishment for ourselves, about reaching out, one person to another, about all our choices gathered together as a country to reach across all our divides. It's about you and me and all of us together, who we are as individuals and what we are as a nation.

Service is a spark to rekindle the spirit of democracy in an age of uncertainty. We hear a great deal about values now. I encourage America in that conversation. But all the lofty talk comes down to three simple questions: What is right? What is wrong? And what are we going to do about it?

Today we're doing what is right. Just look around you. You're what is right with America. Twenty thousand of you this year and 100,000 over the next 3 years will be getting things done in hundreds of places around the country. You will be saving babies in south Texas, walking the police beat in Brooklyn. You will work on boats to reclaim the Chesapeake Bay and work on new housing to rebuild parts of Roxbury. You will take seniors safely to the doctor in St. Louis and teach children in Sacramento to read.

Every generation in our history has learned to take responsibility for our future, and your generation is no exception. We look at you now, and we know you are no generation of slackers. Instead, you are a generation of doers. And you want to give something back to the country that has given so much to you. The only limit to our future is what we're willing to demand of ourselves today. Generations of Americans before us have done the groundwork. Now it falls to all of us to build on their foundations.

In just a minute, I'll lead nearly 20,000 AmeriCorps members gathered across America in a pledge. I ask all Americans to reflect on the words they will say, because with words like "action" and "commitment," "community" and "common ground," this is much more than a pledge of service. It's a creed for America as we move forward to renew our great country. And to all of you who will help to lead us in that journey, I say God bless you, and thank you from the bottom of my heart.

And now it's my great pleasure to swear in the first members of AmeriCorps around the Nation, including these fine young people who are here with me. Would you all raise your right hand and repeat after me:

I will get things done for America to make our people safer, smarter, and healthier. I will bring Americans together to strengthen our communities. Faced with apathy, I will take action. Faced with conflict, I will seek common ground. Faced with adversity, I will persevere. I will carry this commitment with me this year and beyond. I am an AmeriCorps member, and I am going to get things done.

[*The AmeriCorps volunteers repeated the pledge line by line after the President.*]

The President. Thank you, and good luck.

NOTE: The President spoke at 2:46 p.m. by satellite from the Oval Office at the White House.

Remarks in a Swearing-In Ceremony for AmeriCorps Volunteers
September 12, 1994

The President. Thank you. Thank you so much. Thank you, Mr. Vice President. Thank you, Eli Segal, for your wonderful work. This is a very, very happy day for Hillary and for me, especially, to see all of you here with all of your enthusiasm, your energy, your dreams.

There are so many things I would like to say, but before we go on, I feel that I ought to give you some explanation about what occurred here this morning and why we had to delay this event and move it to the front of the White House.

As you know, a plane came down here on the South Lawn, and a pilot lost his life. The investigation is now in place that will determine how and why this happened. We take this incident seriously because this house is the people's house. It's the job of every President to keep it safe and secure.

On his second night here, our second President and the first person to live in the White House, John Adams, wrote: "I pray heaven to bestow the best blessings on this house and on all that shall hereafter inhabit it." That prayer has been answered. In times of war and peace, in hard times, in good times, the White House has remained an enduring symbol of our democracy. It tells our people and all those around the world that the mission of America continues. And that is the message that you send out here today as well. So I pledge to you that we will continue that, and I'm sorry we had to move to the front, but maybe we ought to be in the front of the White House today for something this important.

This year 20,000 Americans, most of whom are young, some of whom are young in spirit and determined to serve and also go on to further their education, mark the beginning of a journey that will change their lives forever. It will also change the life of this Nation for many seasons to come.

This day is part of a long journey for me, personally, and for many others who have long harbored the dream that national service embodies. I want to say a special word of thanks to someone who worked with me through this whole process and who dreamed of national service even before I did, and that is Senator Harris Wofford of Pennsylvania. I thank you especially, sir, today. Like the Vice President's fine sister, Senator Wofford started out with the Peace Corps 30 years ago.

One of the main reasons I ran for President is that I felt that we as Americans needed to make our life's journeys together rather than apart. I felt that we not only needed to change our direction and make more progress but that we had to do it by coming together instead of drifting apart. Today we begin to fulfill that mission.

For many of us, this journey of service reaches back to life growing up in places we called home, back to our classrooms, our church basements, our backyards, with the American traditions of community and service. So for many of us, today is just one step on what has been a lifetime journey.

But what we do today and what we will do in the days and years ahead will give new life to the values that bind us as Americans. For service is about sacrifice for others and about accomplishment and fulfillment for ourselves, about reaching out, one person to another, about all of our choices gathered together as a country, to reach across all those things that divide us, about you and me individually and about all of us together, who we are as individuals and who we are as a nation.

Service is a spark to rekindle the spirit of democracy in an age of uncertainty. We hear a great deal today about values, and so we must. I encourage America in that conversation. But when it is all said and done, it comes down to three simple questions: What is right? What is wrong? And what are we going to do about it?

Today you are doing what is right, turning your words into deeds. In my Inaugural Address, I called upon America to a new season of renewal, a new season of service. And I said then what I firmly believe: There is nothing wrong with America that cannot be fixed by what is right with America.

Well, all of you that are about to embark on this journey, as far as I'm concerned, you're what's right with America. Let's just look at a couple of our AmeriCorps volunteers. Laura Sullivan, who's here at the White House today, is helping people put their lives back on track and start their own businesses in Baltimore. Leo Negron out in Chicago is teaching construction skills to teenagers and offering them a role model for taking pride in their work. Sara Wittenberg in Seattle is showing us how to be stewards of our Nation's natural beauty.

Twenty thousand more this year and 100,000 over the next 3 years, all of you will do things like this in hundreds of places all around our country: saving babies in south Texas, walking police beats in Brooklyn, working on boats to reclaim the Chesapeake Bay and working on new housing projects in Roxbury, taking seniors safely to the doctor in St. Louis, and helping children to learn to read in Sacramento.

Every generation in our history has learned to take responsibility for this country, and yours is no exception. We look to you and know that you are no generation of slackers but instead a generation of doers who want—[*applause*]— we are grateful for those of you who wish to give back something to the country that has done so much for you and to the parents and loved ones who are with you today and who taught you that these values are important.

Our greatness, after all, has never come from those who went in search of distant riches or personal glory. The people who really made this country great for over 200 years are ordinary people who make extraordinary sacrifices for the common good: the farm boys on the beaches of Normandy, the police officers walking the dark beats, the schoolteachers staying up late to help students from troubled homes to lead better lives.

And you, the people of AmeriCorps, will be America's next generation of heroes. We need you now more than ever. So many of our people are alone and cut off from one another. So many others are deeply divided from each other, resentful, skeptical, even cynical about the possibilities of their own lives and the life of their country. You will devote your own potential to helping other people live up to their God-given potential.

You remind us how America has always worked best: by offering opportunity and demanding responsibility. We've seen over the last 20 years that you can't have one without the other and expect the American community to grow and flourish.

AmeriCorps says: Come together, citizens and businesses, schools and churches, come together as partners in progress to solve our problems and reach our promise. We know we will succeed not by Government edict, not by large bureaucracies but by the spirit of service and devotion that burns within the heart of every American.

With AmeriCorps you are building your country's future and helping to build your own. For your hard work, those of you who serve will earn money for your education and the chance to do even more with your God-given abilities, earning something that money can never buy as well. For you know now that you are helping to breathe new life into the spirit of the American Republic.

Benjamin Franklin once said that if we don't hang together, we will surely hang separately. At the time he said it, he was worried about a foreign invader. But as the old comic strip character says, "Today we have met the enemy, and it is us." We better hang together, folks, or we're going to hang separately. You are the glue that will enable us to hang together.

We cannot go on as a nation of strangers, mistrusting one another because we've never had the chance to work side by side or had the chance to walk in one another's shoes. If we just stand only on our own ground, we will never find common ground. When I mentioned three of you, Leo, Laura, and Sara, before, I didn't tell you about their backgrounds. Laura is from a suburb of Boston. Leo is from the inner city of Chicago. Sara is from the farmlands of Wisconsin. Each will bring something special and different and unique from those places to their service of America.

But each will surely learn, along with all the rest of you, that with all of our differences, we can belong to something larger than ourselves. I hope the nation that you serve will learn this as well from your shining example. We are all part of the American family joined by a common purpose, bound by a common sense of responsibility, challenged by common possibilities that know no limits.

The only limit to the future of this country and to the future that all of you hope to have is what we are willing to demand of ourselves today and in the future. Generations before us have done the groundwork, and now we must build on those foundations.

In just a moment, I will lead the 20,000 volunteers who are here, and some who have already done this a couple of hours ago across America, in a pledge. But I want to ask you and all Americans who will learn of this event to reflect on the words of that pledge, words like "action" and "commitment," "community" and "common ground." It's more than a pledge of personal service; it's a creed for America, a creed we desperately need as we move forward to renew our great country in the 21st century.

To all of you who have taken the pledge to join, who have entered this season of service, who have redeemed the most important commitment your President ever tried to make to the American people, to give us a chance to come together, to move forward together, I say thank you, and God bless you.

Now let me ask all the AmeriCorps volunteers here to raise your hand and repeat after me:

I will get things done for America to make our people safer, smarter, and healthier. I will bring America together to strengthen our communities. Faced with conflict, I will seek common ground. Faced with adversity, I will persevere. I will carry this commitment with me this year and beyond. I am an AmeriCorps member, and I am going to get things done.

[The AmeriCorps volunteers repeated the pledge line by line after the President.]

NOTE: The President spoke at approximately 4 p.m. on the North Grounds at the White House. In his remarks, he referred to Eli Segal, Assistant to the President for National Service, and Nancy Gore, late sister of the Vice President.

Statement on the Nomination for Supreme Allied Commander, Atlantic
September 12, 1994

I will look to General Sheehan to continue the innovative efforts of Admiral Miller in defining the role of allied military power in forging a safe and secure world.

NOTE: This statement was included in a statement by the Press Secretary announcing that the President nominated Gen. John J. Sheehan, USMC, to succeed Adm. Paul D. Miller as Supreme Allied Commander, Atlantic, and to serve as commander in chief, U.S. Atlantic Command.

Statement on Implementation of the National Voter Registration Act of 1993
September 12, 1994

This law creates the opportunity to include millions of Americans in the political process who have previously been excluded because of difficult and confusing voting rules. I urge all Americans of all political parties to register to vote, and I urge the voter registration groups to continue and expand their efforts to ensure as many of our citizens as possible are registered.

NOTE: This statement was included in a White House statement announcing the Executive order of September 12 on implementation of the National Voter Registration Act of 1993. The Executive order is listed in Appendix D at the end of this volume.

Remarks on Signing the Violent Crime Control and Law Enforcement Act of 1994
September 13, 1994

I think we ought to give the Vice President a hand for all the work that he has done. [*Applause*] Thank you, Mr. Vice President, for your introduction and for your labors on this bill.

Most of the introductions have been made, but I want to join what has been said. I want to thank the members of my Cabinet, General Reno and Secretary Bentsen and all the others who worked so hard on this. I want to thank all these mayors here, Mayor Giuliani, Mayor Webb, Mayor Rice, Mayor Daley, Mayor James, Mayor Rendell, all the other mayors. I'd like to ask—and there are some county officials here—I'd like to ask all the local leaders who are here to please stand up; they didn't all stand—I'd like to ask them all to stand and be recognized. Mayor Golding, Susan, good to see you. Mayor Schmoke, Mayor Helmke, Mayor Abramson who got cauliflower ear from making his phone calls. [*Laughter*] I'd also like to ask, even though many of them have been introduced, I would like to ask the people without whom we would not be here today, all the Members of the Congress who are here, Republicans and Democrats, to please stand and be acknowledged; every one of them, I'd like for them to stand up. Thank you.

And let me say to all the representatives of the victims groups and the citizens groups how grateful we are to you; to all the leaders of the law enforcement groups; to all the rank-and-file folks who worked so hard; to all the leaders of the community groups of people who wanted to give our kids something to say yes to and to prevent crime before it occurs; to all the ministers—to all of you, I thank you for being here and for making this day possible.

The American people have been waiting a long time for this day. In the last 25 years, half a million Americans have been killed by other Americans. For 25 years, crime has been a hot political issue, used too often to divide us while the system makes excuses for not punishing criminals and doing the job, instead of being used to unite us to prevent crime, punish criminals, and restore a sense of safety and security to the American people.

For the last 6 years, children have become the most likely victims of violent crime and its most likely perpetrators. And for 6 years, Washington debated a crime bill without action while more and more children died and more and more children became criminals and foreclosed a productive life for themselves.

In the last 2 years, Meghan Sposato lost a mother she had only begun to know; Polly Klaas lost her life to a felon who should never have been back on the streets; and James Darby wrote his President a letter because he was so afraid, only to lose his life walking home before anybody could erase his fears. And still, some people in this town tried to keep this day from happening. But today, at last, the waiting ends.

Today the bickering stops, the era of excuses is over, the law-abiding citizens of our country have made their voices heard. Never again should Washington put politics and party above law and order.

From this day forward, let us put partisanship behind us, and let us go forward—Democrats, Republicans and independents, law enforcement, community leaders, ordinary citizens—let us roll up our sleeves to roll back this awful tide of violence and reduce crime in our country. We have the tools now. Let us get about the business of using them.

One of the reasons that I sought this office is to get this bill, because if the American people do not feel safe on their streets, in their schools, in their homes, in their places of work and worship, then it is difficult to say that the American people are free.

Not so long ago, kids grew up knowing they'd have to pay if they broke a neighbor's window playing ball. I know; I did it once. [*Laughter*] They knew they'd be in trouble if they lied or stole because their parents and teachers and neighbors cared enough to set them straight. And everybody knew that anybody who committed a serious crime would be caught and convicted and would serve their time in jail. The rules were simple, the results were predictable, and we lived better because of it. Punishment was swift and certain for people who didn't follow the rules, and the rewards of America were considerable for those who did.

Now, too many kids don't have parents who care. Gangs and drugs have taken over our streets and undermined our schools. Every day we read about somebody else who has literally gotten away with murder. But the American people haven't forgotten the difference between right and wrong. The system has. The American people haven't stopped wanting to raise their children in lives of safety and dignity, but they've got a lot of obstacles in their way.

When I sign this crime bill, we together are taking a big step toward bringing the laws of our land back into line with the values of our people and beginning to restore the line between right and wrong. There must be no doubt about whose side we're on. People who commit crimes should be caught, convicted, and punished. This bill puts Government on the side of those who abide by the law, not those who break it; on the side of the victims, not their attackers; on the side of the brave men and women who put their lives on the line for us every day, not the criminals or those who would turn away from law enforcement. That's why police and prosecutors and preachers fought so hard for this bill and why I am so proud to sign it into law today.

When this bill is law, "three strikes and you're out" will be the law of the land; the penalty for killing a law enforcement officer will be death; we will have a significant—[*applause*]— we will have the means by which. we can say punishment will be more certain. We will cut the Federal work force over a period of years by 270,000 positions to its lowest level in 30 years and take all that money to pay for this crime bill. The savings will be used to put 100,000 police officers on the street, a 20 percent increase. It will be used to build prisons to keep 100,000 violent criminals off the street. It will be used to give our young people something to say yes to, places where they can go after school where they are safe, where they can do constructive things that will help them

to build their lives, where teachers replace gang leaders as role models. All of these things should be done and will be done.

This bill makes it illegal for juveniles to own handguns and, yes, without eroding the rights of sports men and women in this country, we will finally ban these assault weapons from our street that have no purpose other than to kill.

But my friends, let us be frank with each other: Even this great law, the toughest and smartest crime bill in our history, cannot do the job alone. By its own words, it is still a law. It must be implemented by you, and it must be supplemented by you. Even when we put a new police officer on your block, the officer can't make you safe unless you come out of your home and help the officer do his or her job. Even when we keep our schools open late and give our children an alternative to drugs and gangs, your children won't learn the difference between right and wrong unless you teach them and they're in those schools when they're open. Our country will not truly be safe again until all Americans take personal responsibility for themselves, their families, and their communities. This day is the beginning, not the end, of our effort to restore safety and security to the people of this country.

Here in Washington there is more that we can do. Today I am naming Vice President Gore, whose reinventing Government report first proposed the cuts in the bureaucracy that will pay for this bill, to head the President's Prevention Council. I want him to work with every Department to make this a coherent and cost-effective effort to give communities the tools they need to prevent crime from occurring in the first place. In a few weeks I will name the head of our program to put 100,000 new police on the street. And early next month, the Justice Department will award grants to put new police on the street in 150 more cities and towns that applied last year.

Last Sunday, I was in Maryland, and Senator Sarbanes told me that already one of our community policing grants had resulted in the capture of a serious felon in a community in his State. This will make a difference. And I want to commend the Attorney General and the Justice Department for being determined to do this right, to get this money out to the grassroots so that we can hire the police and get on with the job.

Thirdly, in the coming months the Vice President and I will hold forums on crime and violence all across our country, with all kinds of people from all walks of life, leading up here to a meeting at the White House next year to launch a national effort at the grassroots level in each and every community to implement the crime bill properly, to enshrine the values and common sense the crime bill represents, and to do something about this terrible scourge of violence that is especially gripping our children and robbing them of their future. We intend to continue the fight, and we want you to keep working with us.

Today we remember the thousands of officers who gave their lives to make our Nation safer, whose names are inscribed in a stone memorial just a mile away from here. We remember the innocent victims whose lives were lost and whose families were shattered by the scourge of violent crime. We remember three, James Darby, Polly Klaas, and Jody Sposato, whose deaths literally galvanized this Nation and shamed our political system into action. It is in their memories that I dedicate this bill. I hope this law will always be remembered in their names. And I hope, too, that we will remember what the Vice President said, "The ultimate victory of this law will be in the salvation of the children whose names we will never know."

Early in 1992, I was walking through one of the countless kitchens of a hotel lobby in New York on my way to a dinner when a waiter working there came up to me and grabbed me, and he said, "Mr. President"—he didn't call me Governor then—he said, "My 10-year-old boy is studying this election in school, and he says I should vote for you." But he said, "I want to tell you something first. I came here as an immigrant, and the place where I lived was very poor, and we were very poor. But at least we were free. Now we live here, and we have more money, but we are not free. We are not free because my boy can't walk across the street and

play in the park unless I am with him. We are not free because my boy cannot walk to school unless I am with him. Make my boy free."

On the day after the crime bill was signed, I received a letter carefully typed from a very young man who is the son of a member of our administration. It was so eloquent. He said, "I live in a good neighborhood. I go to a nice school. You wouldn't think people like me would care about this crime bill, but I have been keeping up with it every day because every time I go out with my friends at night to a movie or to a game, I think someone might shoot me before I get home. Now I feel so much better."

My fellow Americans, this is about freedom. Without responsibility, without order, without lawfulness, there is no freedom. Today the will of the American people has triumphed over a generation of division and paralysis. We've won a chance to work together.

So in that spirit, let us rededicate ourselves today to making this law become the life of our country, to restoring the sense of right and wrong that built our country, and to make it safe, not in words but in fact, in the lifeblood of every child and every citizen of this country who believes in the promise of America. Let us make it real.

Thank you, and God bless you all.

NOTE: The President spoke at 10:48 a.m. on the South Lawn at the White House. In his remarks, he referred to Mayors Rudolph Giuliani of New York City; Wellington E. Webb of Denver, CO; Norman Rice of Seattle, WA; Richard M. Daley of Chicago, IL; Sharpe James of Newark, NJ; Edward Rendell of Philadelphia, PA; Susan Golding of San Diego, CA; Kurt Schmoke of Baltimore, MD; Paul Helmke of Fort Wayne, IN; and Jerry Abramson of Louisville, KY. H.R. 3355, approved September 13, was assigned Public Law No. 103–322.

Memorandum on the Ounce of Prevention Council
September 13, 1994

Memorandum for the Vice President, the Secretary of the Treasury, the Attorney General, the Secretary of the Interior, the Secretary of Agriculture, the Secretary of Labor, the Secretary of Health and Human Services, the Secretary of Housing and Urban Development, the Secretary of Education, the Director of the Office of Management and Budget, the Director of National Drug Control Policy, the Assistant to the President for Domestic Policy

Subject: The Ounce of Prevention Council

The Federal Government must administer its programs and deliver services to the American people in the most efficient, effective, and economical ways possible. To that end, this Administration is committed to streamlining, coordinating, and integrating the related responsibilities, programs, and functions of our various executive branch departments and agencies and to designing solutions to traditionally local problems in a manner that provides greater flexibility to those who implement these solutions—our State and local governments.

It gives me great pleasure to sign into law today the Violent Crime Control and Law Enforcement Act of 1994 ("Act"), which attacks this country's crime and violence problems through a comprehensive, responsible, and bottom-up approach. This Act establishes, among other things, new programs designed to address some of the root causes of criminal and violent behavior. All of these prevention programs are being fully funded through the reduction of the Federal bureaucracy—which was accomplished under the Vice President's National Performance Review. (Specifically, these reductions were effectuated by Executive Order No. 12839 of February 10, 1993, my memorandum of September 11, 1993, and the Federal Workforce Restructuring Act, approved March 30, 1994, which together directed executive branch departments and agencies to reduce the Federal workforce by 272,900 positions.)

The Act also empowers States and localities by providing these governmental entities with maximum flexibility in administering the Act's prevention programs. But, unlike similar programs established in the past and in the true meaning of "reinventing government," this law sets strict guidelines that ensure that these programs are administered in a manner that is consistent with the Act and fulfills the goals of the programs. Finally, the Act creates the Ounce of Prevention Council (the "Prevention Council" or "Council") to, among other things, oversee and coordinate the various crime prevention programs governed by the Act.

In order to continue our efforts to streamline, coordinate, and integrate the work and activities of the Federal Government, I hereby order the following:

(i) The Vice President, who leads the National Performance Review and chairs the President's Community Enterprise Board (the "Board"); the Assistant to the President for Domestic Policy, who is responsible for overseeing the implementation of the Crime Bill; and the Director of the Office of Management and Budget shall be members of the Prevention Council;

(ii) The Vice President shall serve as the Chair of the Council and shall appoint a staff to support the work of the Council, and the Assistant to the President for Domestic Policy shall serve as the Council's Vice Chair;

(iii) The Vice President, to the extent appropriate and permitted by law, shall coordinate and integrate the work of the Prevention Council with the work of the President's Community Enterprise Board, which is responsible for coordinating across agencies various Federal programs available to distressed communities;

(iv) The Prevention Council shall report to the Board on its activities, which shall include assisting communities in developing bottom-up crime prevention strategies that are sufficiently tailored and flexible to meet the security needs of the communities and evaluating the effectiveness of the programs governed by the Act;

(v) To the extent permitted by law, Prevention Council members shall cooperate with the Vice President in coordinating all of the Administration's crime prevention programs and in integrating the work of the Council and the Board; and

(vi) Each executive branch department and agency represented on the Council shall dedicate the personnel and administrative support necessary for the Council to fulfill its missions and responsibilities.

With this structure, I am confident that we will be able to provide communities in distress with a single Federal forum dedicated to helping them address their economic and security needs.

WILLIAM J. CLINTON

NOTE: H.R. 3355, approved September 13, was assigned Public Law No. 103–322.

Statement on Senate Action on Banking Legislation
September 13, 1994

Today this country took an historic step, one that has been delayed for much too long, to help American banks better meet the needs of our people, our communities, and our economy. By joining the House in passing the interstate banking bill, the Senate has gone beyond gridlock to eliminate unnecessary barriers to the competitiveness and efficiency of our banking system while preserving essential prerogatives of the States.

We also welcome the bill's requirement that the Treasury, with the assistance of a broadly representative advisory committee, study and make recommendations on the future shape of financial services in the United States. American banks have shown over the last several years that they can combine high quality service for all with strong financial performance. Enactment of the interstate bill and the community development and regulatory improvement legislation will help them continue that record.

Remarks on the Reinventing Government Initiative
September 14, 1994

Thank you. You know, when the Vice President opened this occasion by saying that he would have to wear his full body suit for 2 years and that the Speaker of the House had been restored to full powers after his surgery came out all right, I couldn't help thinking, it took reinventing Government to get him on David Letterman—[*laughter*]—and now this terrible accident—but he's actually become the funniest person in the administration as a result of these two projects.

There is no effort that he has spared to promote this project. You remember he even went on the Letterman show to smash an ashtray. And he has now been invited, as part of our followup to show we're making progress, to go on the show again, where he will read a top five list; showing that we can do more with less, he will make each one of them twice as funny as any top 10 list that was there. [*Laughter*]

I want to thank Dr. Mendoza, Mr. Torno, Ms. Holstein for traveling here to tell your stories. For all the facts and figures and charts about the success of reinventing Government, the thing that really counts is that the benefits are being felt the way they ought to be by the American people, in a very personal and immediate way. And of course, we hope as a result of this occasion today and the followup report, that the rest of the American people will see that we are changing the way the Federal Government works.

I want to thank the successful teams who made these particular stories possible: Erskine Bowles and the "Low Doc" team from the Small Business Administration who cut a 100-page application down to one page; Customs Commissioner George Weise, the Assistant Commissioner Samuel Banks, and Lynn Gordon for their team in the Miami office, who realized that becoming partners with airlines and shippers is a win-win situation; my old friend James Lee

Witt and Bea Gonzales and the team that completely reorganized FEMA so that all its resources are available to respond to any emergency.

When I took office, the National Academy of Public Administration said this about FEMA: "FEMA is like a patient in triage. The President and the Congress must decide whether to treat it or let it die." There was even a bill pending in Congress to abolish FEMA. And in 1992, as I traveled the country, I never went a place that somebody didn't say something disparaging about it. Well, the bill is gone, and it may be the most popular agency in the entire Federal Government.

There's nothing that makes an ordinary taxpayer madder than to feel that those of us who work for the Government don't value their hard-earned dollars. One single, simple example of the waste of taxpayers' money can erase in the public mind thousands and thousands and thousands of examples of devoted service to the same taxpayers. That's especially true in these perplexing times when people have such conflicting feelings. We're going through a period of profound change. And by large margins, Americans say they want Government to address our great national problems. But by equally large margins, they say they don't trust our ability to do it right, or as we say down home, most of our folks think that the Government would mess up a two-car parade. [*Laughter*]

Now, this reinventing Government effort grew out of several sources: first, out of my experience as a Governor, where we tried to begin this effort; second, out of the encounters that the Vice President and I had with each other and with citizens all during the campaign, with the literature we read and the things we learned that were going on in the private sector; thirdly, with the enormous energy and desire we got out of Federal employees themselves; next, with the leadership that was already coming out of the Congress—Senator Glenn and Congressman Conyers have already been acknowledged, and there were others who really thought that we ought to do it.

But finally we did it because it was necessary, because without it we could not fulfill the mission of the administration. The mission of this administration from day one has been to increase economic opportunity and maintain national security; to empower the individuals of this country to assume personal responsibility for their own futures; to strengthen the sense of community in America, to make our diversity a cause of celebration and unity, not division; and to change the way Government works for ordinary citizens.

Unless we can do the last thing, we cannot achieve the other three. Why is that? Well, one of the reasons we have so much economic opportunity today is that we reduced the budget deficit. You couldn't reduce the budget deficit and not hurt the public interest unless you're reinventing Government.

We want to empower individuals. One of the things that we did with our empowerment program is, through the Department of Education, to completely reform the college loan program so that 20 million Americans now with outstanding loans are eligible to refinance them with longer repayment schedules at lower interest rates. And starting this year, large numbers of new students will be able to do the same thing. We couldn't afford to do that except we actually save money by doing it, by converting the old expensive, cumbersome student loan program into, at least largely, a direct loan program and increasing our ability to recover delinquent loans, which is dramatically increasing.

If you want to strengthen the American community, people have to feel like we care about each other. If every place there is a disaster people think that FEMA has failed them, it's hard to say they're part of an American community. But from the people in California who suffered from the earthquakes and the fires, the people all up and down the Mississippi River that were flooded out last summer, to the people in the Southeast that suffered drought last year and floods this year, I think they will tell you that FEMA is on the job.

Yesterday the Vice President mentioned national service. It is not a Government bureaucracy; it is a movement that the Government has made possible. None of this would have happened if we hadn't had a serious approach to reinventing Government. And none of that would have happened if we hadn't reinvented the relationship between the President and the Vice President.

Some people take it as a sign of weakness that I try to get the most out of everybody that lives around here or works around here— [*laughter*]—and that I try to find people who do things better than I do. I thought that was my job. The Vice President—whether it is leading our efforts in the environment to develop a clean car or performing with such superb leadership to get a compromise at the very important Cairo conference, dealing with reinventing Government or difficult foreign policy issues—is plainly the most active, productive, constructive Vice President in the history of this Republic. And that is a very important thing.

Historically, this argument about Government that politicians had was something designed to play into that feeling I just gave you when you all chuckled, when I said most folks think Government would mess up a one-car parade. For example, when we had meetings on our health care reform initiative, people would come in opposition, and they would say, "I don't want Government getting into this. I'm afraid Government will mess up my Medicare." [*Laughter*] We actually had people say this sort of visceral thing. So any politician worth a flip can figure out how to develop four or five one-liners that will make 90 percent of the voters shout hallelujah.

The problem is that this debate has normally stopped at the rhetorical level. Politicians garner the votes; Government grows in a sort of piecemeal fashion; Government employees and the citizens get more frustrated every year, and real problems aren't solved. We had an idea that we could make Government smaller, but also different: that we could do more and cost less, that we could have more responsibility with less bureaucracy if we empowered the people who work for this Government and paid attention to the people who pay for it. We didn't see Government as the savior of America, but we knew our Government couldn't sit on the sidelines in a period of such profound change. So we tried to develop a partnership that makes sense.

This vision is at the heart of everything we're trying to do. It's at the heart of the national service program. It's at the heart of the crime bill that we signed yesterday where we made a pretty good swap: We would take all the savings from reducing the size of the Federal Government and just give it to the American people to make themselves safer on their streets, in their homes, in their schools.

This has been a very important endeavor. A lot of people were very skeptical when we began. But if you just look at what's happened in the time we've been in office, as evidenced by those charts over there, since I became President, the size of the Federal work force has been reduced by 71,000 positions. In 3 years we'll have the smallest Federal work force since President Kennedy was here, to go with 3 years of deficit reduction in a row for the first time since President Truman was here.

The savings already enacted by Congress or undertaken by the executive branch will amount to $47 billion in this budget cycle, and we're on the way to saving $108 billion. Most of these savings will pay for the crime bill and help to put 100,000 more police officers on the street, 100,000 serious criminals behind bars. There were those who said that these things would never pass through the Congress. But Congress has already enacted more than 20 bills that will save money and improve services by reinventing Government, and 50 percent of the items needing congressional action are already pending in Congress, many with real bipartisan support.

I'm proud to announce some more good news today. At the General Services Administration, Administrator Johnson saved $1.2 billion by carefully reviewing construction projects that had been approved and not yet built, in other words, buildings we really didn't need. And just today, the GSA is announcing it saved $23 million simply by managing the Government's motor pools more efficiently.

Today the Secretary of Defense set a goal to cut in half the time it takes to complete internal business processes, from hiring workers to building new weapons systems. This is very important. Senator Glenn has worked for years on procurement reform. If we are going to maintain the national security at a time when we have to impose budget discipline, we must find ways to make these dollars go further. We can't simply abandon our technological lead, our readiness, our preparedness, all the things that have been so carefully built up over the last 16 or 17 years.

At the Office of Management and Budget, Director-designate Rivlin tells me the Federal Government will offer buyouts to another 40,000 employees at the beginning of the new fiscal year next month. And next Tuesday the Vice President and I will release a report on the first-ever consumer service standards for the Federal Government. Over 100 agencies have prepared more than 1,700 specific pledges to the taxpayers of this country to improve the services that they provide.

I am more convinced now than ever that we have to keep doing this, that we have to make this reinventing Government a permanent process, and that there are serious structural issues which still have to be addressed. Washington needs to work for ordinary middle class Americans. And in order to do that, we have got to find a way to open this process up so that the public interest can always overwhelm particular interest in matters of great importance.

That's why Congress must also finish the job it has begun, passing a tough campaign finance reform bill, a lobbying reform bill, and the bill that requires Congress to live under the laws it imposes on the rest of Americans, before the end of this session. All three of these actions have broad bipartisan support in both Houses. Two of the bills have passed both Houses and await conference resolution. The House of Representatives has overwhelmingly passed the third one. We need to move forward. These are actions that Americans deserve and demand, and they will help them to believe that the rest of these things are also occurring, as well.

Meanwhile, I assure you that we will be unrelenting in our efforts to continue reinventing Government, to give you a Government that costs less, does more, empowers employees, and listens to the people who pay for it. We will measure our progress not only in terms of bills passed and money saved but in terms of people better served. You met some of those satisfied citizens today. We're committed to making a lot more satisfied citizens in the months and years to come.

Thank you very much.

NOTE: The President spoke at approximately 10:45 a.m. on the South Lawn at the White House. In his remarks, he referred to Emilio Mendoza, president/CEO, Galactic Technologies, Inc., San Antonio, TX; Art Torno, managing director, American Airlines, Miami, FL; Alameda Holstein, disaster victim, East Northridge, CA; and Beatrice Gonzales, FEMA disaster assistance employee praised by Ms. Holstein for her help.

Remarks to United States Attorneys on the Violent Crime Control and Law Enforcement Act of 1994
September 14, 1994

Thank you very much, General Reno, ladies and gentlemen. Welcome to the White House, and I want to begin by just thanking you, all of you, for the work you did to help us pass the crime bill. It was one of the more interesting and rigorous legislative exercises we've had around here in a long time. I believe that you fought for this crime bill because you knew that there was so much in it that would actually work for this country.

And I'm encouraged as I saw some of the coverage on the crime bill last night that people are finally beginning to look at a lot of the provisions that weren't so hotly debated during the campaign for and against the crime bill that are really going to help us to make a difference to lower the crime rate and make the American people safer. We know that some of these things will work. We have example after example in America that more police, properly deployed in community policing settings, will actually lower

the crime rate. We have example after example that if you can figure out how to lock up the repeat offenders and give the first-time folks a chance to build a better life, you can lower the crime rate. We know that if you can keep guns out of the hands of schoolchildren, you can make the schools and the streets safer, you can save a lot of victims, and you can save a lot of potential criminals, too, for a more constructive life.

But the hard work of passing the crime bill, as I said yesterday when I signed it, was only the beginning. It's up to those of us who are charged with executing the laws to roll up our sleeves and put the crime bill to work as quickly as we possibly can.

One of the most important provisions of this crime bill is one which has been largely overlooked, I think, in this debate. I want to discuss it with you today because I think it can make a huge difference. And that is the ban on juvenile possession of handguns. Except when hunting or target shooting with a parent or other responsible adult, young people simply shouldn't be carrying guns. Period. This provision is critical to our ability to make our schools and neighborhoods safer. It is so critical that I am directing you today, each of you, to prepare a plan in your districts for enforcing this law over the next 100 days. We need to work with local law enforcement officials and other local officials as you have been doing.

And I want to compliment all of you and compliment the Attorney General for bringing this group in on a repeated, disciplined basis and working closely with you on policy. And then I want to thank you for the work you've done with State and local officials.

But we have to make this work. If this law turns out to be just a law on the books that is widely ignored and never enforced, it will be a terrible shame, because this law can save our children's lives. This law can make a huge difference, but we obviously have to have a strategy to enforce it, and the means by which it is enforced may not be the same, as a practical matter, in every district in the country. So I want to urge you to do that. By January the 1st, we should have a strategy in every community to get guns out of the hands of violent teens and away from young criminals. Anybody can talk tough on crime; this law gives you a chance to be both tough on criminals and successful in making your community safer. We must—we must—implement it vigorously and promptly.

I also want to discuss the penalties which are in the laws, which are now available to you, to make sure that people who do commit serious crimes are punished, people who commit violent crimes are punished severely, people who repeat their offenses are punished even more severely.

This crime bill gives you the ultimate punishment, capital punishment, for most heinous crimes, including murdering a police officer. It makes it possible to keep repeat violent offenders off the street for good with the so-called "three strikes and you're out" law. It stiffens the penalty for criminals who lure children into the drug trade. And from now on, if you use a child to sell drugs, the penalty will automatically be tripled.

It tells young people that if you commit a serious crime or belong to a gang, you can get more time in jail automatically. It not only helps

to protect communities by notifying them of people who have committed crimes which qualify them as sexual predators, but from now on, the penalty for these offenses has doubled. The bill has some remarkable provisions in the violence against women section, which I urge all of you to read, become familiar with, and use. Violence in and around the home is still a terrible problem in this country, and it gives us the tools to do something about it. It has some innovative provisions for boot camps and drug courts, and other innovations which we know have worked to lower the crime rate and to give people the chance to live a safer and more secure life.

These are just some of the examples of what is in the crime bill. Much of America does not know everything that's in the crime bill yet, but many people in the law enforcement community don't know everything that's in the crime bill yet. The penalties for selling drugs to residents of public housing are doubled. There are increased penalties for felons who commit crimes with guns, for criminals who use assault weapons, for those who sell guns to minors.

All of these things have to be implemented in order to work. The most important thing I want to emphasize today is the sweeping ban on handgun possession by minors. If we can enforce this, it will make a massive difference in the problem of youth violence. So let's come back here in 100 days with a plan to do it, and let's start the next year, 1995, with a system in place that will prove that the confidence of the people in this crime bill is not misplaced, and that we are going to lower crime, reduce violence, and increase security in the United States with your leadership.

Thank you very much.

Now I would like to introduce Mary Jo White and Michael Stiles, and they're going to speak, and maybe they'll ask me to do something, since I asked you to do something.

The Attorney General said that's dangerous; they'll ask for money. I've gotten good at saying no to that. [*Laughter*]

Let me also say, just as I introduce Mary Jo and Michael, because I know they are the leaders of this task force representing you in working with the Attorney General, we have worked very hard here at the White House and in the Justice Department in the appointment of United States Attorneys, in the appointment of Federal judges, and we are proud of the job that we have done because of the job that you are doing and the job you will do. And I want you to know that that is also, to me, a very important part of the President's job, and I spend a great deal of time on it.

So I want to emphasize again, as I ask Mary Jo and Michael to come up here, that one of the things that I have been so pleased about the Attorney General's performance in doing is bringing you here on a regular basis and involving you in a regular way in making the policy of the Justice Department. Because for most Americans, the policy of the Justice Department is not the decisions we make about what appeals to enter into or what position to take on appeals; for most Americans, the policy of the Justice Department is what you do all day every day, and we thank you for that.

NOTE: The President spoke at 2:40 p.m. in the State Dining Room at the White House.

Interview With Wire Service Reporters on Haiti
September 14, 1994

The President. I asked you in here today because I want to talk a little about Haiti. As you know, I am going to address the country tomorrow night, and I will have more to say then. But I wanted to emphasize the interests of the United States and the values of the United States that are at stake in this situation and to just remind you and, through you, the American people of what the United States has done here for the last 3 years.

Let me begin by saying that the report of the Assistant Secretary of State for Human Rights, John Shattuck, yesterday highlights the interest we have there that has gotten so much worse. This is plainly the most brutal, the most violent regime anywhere in our hemisphere. They have perpetrated a reign of terror in Haiti, and it is getting worse.

I just had a long meeting with John Shattuck, and he left me, just for example, these pictures as illustrative of what is going on there that you may want to look at, of people who have been killed: This man killed in the slums, in Port-au-Prince, disemboweled in the—[*inaudible*]; this man, a distinguished supporter of the elected President, dragged out of church and murdered; this woman horribly disfigured. And we have examples now of the slaughter of orphans, the killing of a priest, in small towns killing people and dismembering them and then burying them and leaving parts of their bodies to stick out to terrify people. We have clear examples of widespread use of political rape, that is, rape against wives and daughters to intimidate people, children included. We now

know there have been over 3,000—well over 3,000 political murders since the military coup occurred.

So the human rights violations and the situation there, right on our back door, is very, very significant.

The second point I'd like to make is that the United States clearly has an interest in preventing another massive outflow of refugees, which are plainly going to flow from this if the international community does not act to put an end to it. We already have over 14,000 Haitian refugees at Guantanamo; many thousands of others have come——

Q. How many?

The President. Over 14,000. Many thousands of others had come to the shores of the United States or attempted to, as you know. We're going to have a massive immigration problem that we will have to pay for, with thousands of dislocated people.

The third thing I want to emphasize is a point that has been made repeatedly to me by leaders in the region, in the Caribbean, and has been echoed by the person who was in charge of Latin American policy under the previous administration, and that is that we have a decided interest in seeing democracy succeed in Haiti. We have now 33 of the 35 countries in the Caribbean, Central America, and South America are democratic governments. Cuba is not and has not been for a very long time. But Haiti is the only one where there was an election and then a military coup negated it. Ninety percent of the people in Haiti voted;

67 percent of the people voted for President Aristide.

As the leaders in the region, particularly in the Caribbean, have pointed out to me repeatedly in my conversations with them, democracy is not a done deal all over this region. And if this is allowed to stand after all this brutality, all this evidence of violations of international law and human conscience, then democracies elsewhere will be more fragile.

That is important to us, not only because of security concerns. We look toward the 21st century, and we know what our problems are going to be. We know we're going to have problems with small-scale weapons of mass destruction. We know we're going to have problems with terrorism. And we know that democracies are far less likely to tolerate that sort of thing than dictatorships are. Furthermore, we know that an enormous percentage of our economic growth and prosperity is tied to the growth of democracy and an open trading system south of our borders. And we have to keep it going. So those three things, human rights, immigration, democracy, are very important.

I'd like to mention just one other thing that is equally important, and that is the reliability of the United States and the United Nations once we say we we're going to do something. And let me go through the chronology here. You will remember, first of all, when this coup occurred, President Bush said that this was a serious threat to our national security interests. Secretary of State Baker said that the coup could not be allowed to stand.

We worked hard on a nonviolent solution, on a peaceful solution to this with the United Nations called the Governors Island accord, which was signed in the United States. It was an agreement, in effect, all the parties made with the United States and the United Nations. On the day it was supposed to be carried out, the military leaders broke their word to the United States and to the United Nations.

We then went back and pursued sanctions and the tightening of sanctions. We did everything we could to avoid any kind of confrontation of force. And what has happened? The sanctions have made the Haitians poorer. They have not undermined the resolve of the dictators to keep milking the country dry in perpetrating their reign of terror. They have instead led to continued terrorism, the expulsion of the U.N. human rights monitors, the refusal of the dic-

tators to see the representative of the Secretary-General of the United Nations. All that has happened.

Meanwhile, the Security Council Resolution 940 has approved all necessary measures to restore democracy and has called for a two-phase process, one in which the leaders would be removed and there would be an immediate beginning of retraining the police force and a period when a multinational force would attempt to stabilize the situation there, restore President Aristide, and establish a security force that is reliable. And then within a matter of a few months, the mission would be turned over to the United Nations itself to stay until the Presidential election in '95 and the inauguration of a new President in '96. The multinational force mission, in other words, that the United States is called upon to spearhead is a limited one.

The international community is exhausted. Not very long ago—I mean, their patience is exhausted. The Secretary-General of the U.N. himself said the time for diplomacy had finished.

Now, just in the last few weeks, we have had more than 20 countries say that they would participate with us in the first stages of this, in the multinational force, in retraining the police force, operating as police monitors, trying to maintain security while we normalize the situation there. More countries are willing to come into the U.N. mission to stay for a longer period of time, until the election is held and a new President is installed.

The United States has an interest, it seems to me, in the post-cold-war world in not letting dictators break their word to the United States and to the United Nations, especially in our backyard. We have supported other countries taking the lead in other areas of the world where their interests are directly at stake. The Europeans overwhelmingly, principally aided by the Canadians, have been in Bosnia. The Russians sent a force into Georgia at the request of the Government of Georgia but willing to abide by United Nations standards.

Here is a case where the entire world community has spoken on a matter in our backyard involving horrible human rights violations, the threat of serious immigration dislocation in the United States, the destabilization of democracy in our hemisphere when it's going along so well, and the total fracturing of the ability of the world community to conduct business in the post-cold-war era. Those are the things that are at stake here. And it seems to me that we have literally exhausted every available alternative. And the time has come for those people to get out of there.

Now, there is still—they can still leave. They do not have to push this to a confrontation. But our interests are clear; the support is astonishing. We have countries all over the world on every continent willing to come to be a part of this because they are appalled by what's going on.

But the flipside of this is that the United States must not be in a position to walk away from a situation like this in our backyard while we expect others to lead the way in their backyard, as long as the United Nations has approved of an operation. And yet, people are coming from all over the world to be a part of this, to rebuild Haiti because they understand the significance of it.

That is my case. There is no point in going any further with the present policy. The time has come for them to go, one way or the other.

Q. Why give them the pass, Mr. President, if they're responsible for such horrific deeds as this, to allow them at this stage free passage out of Haiti?

The President. Well, I happen to have two answers to that. First of all, we are interested in bringing an end to the violence; violence may tend to beget violence. And secondly, President Aristide himself supports this. Keep in mind, President Aristide has been willing all along to follow the spirit and the letter of the Governors Island Agreement. In the Governors Island Agreement the military leaders and the police leaders were promised safe exit. And yes, this is horrible, but the most important thing we can do is to quickly create a spirit of reconciliation and to try to move to a point where we can do that.

Now, if they don't leave, of course, then they are vulnerable to being handed over to the authorities and being held accountable for whatever their role was, their respective roles were, in the kinds of things that have occurred. But anyway, those are my two answers.

Q. Mr. President, are you going to fix a deadline by which they must leave or the United States is going to take action? How imminent is something?

The President. Well, I'll have a little more to say about that tomorrow night. But I don't want to talk about any specific date. All I can

tell you is that the time is at hand. They need to leave, and they're going to leave one way or the other.

Q. Does that mean you are going to give a deadline?

The President. That means that it wouldn't be responsible for me to discuss that question at this moment.

Q. Is it a matter of days or weeks?

The President. I don't want to get into the time.

Q. Are you going to—is this an ultimatum? You've said they must go, they have to go, they have—and so forth. All of these words amount to, in fact, that you have made a decision to invade Haiti.

The President. No, that decision is up to them. My decision is that it's time for them to go. We have tried every other option. We now have an enormous array of international support for a problem that is on our doorstep.

Q. But you don't have any support in this country.

The President. Well, you know, it's interesting. When we had the—let me just remind you about the—let me say first of all what's important.

I am concerned about that, and I am sorry that the polls are the way they are. But my job as the President is to take the information that I have and the facts that I know and do what I believe is best for our national security interests. And I believe it is best—in fact, I think it is very important, for the reasons I have stated, for us to resolve this matter and to do it now. That is what I believe. And I hope that I can persuade the American people that I am right. But my job in this case, where I have access to a lot of facts and evidence, is to make that decision and to go forward.

I also would remind you that these polls come and go. There was a poll at the height of the immigration crisis which said, by 51 percent to 17 percent, the people of America would support our going in there to restore democracy if it were part of a United Nations effort. And clearly, when the immigration crisis abated, it abated not simply because we established safe havens outside the United States, it abated because it was part of a process that the Haitian people thought was going to lead to a resolution of this crisis.

If we walk away from this and these things keep happening, you're going to see another explosion of immigration, I am convinced, with far, far more people than the 14,000 that are at Guantanamo today that the American taxpayers are supporting, that are in a terrible situation. And we will have to see—it's going to be a very difficult situation.

Q. So you'll move even if you don't have Congress or the American people behind you because you think that they will rally once you have made them?

The President. No, I think my job—look, I have taken on a lot of tough fights since I have been here, and I believe that the country is going to be better off because of them. And in a matter like this, I believe that if the American people knew everything that I knew on this—and I think as they know more, I think more of them will agree with me. But regardless, this is what I believe is the right thing to do. I realize it is unpopular. I know it is unpopular. I know the timing is unpopular. I know the whole thing is unpopular. But I believe it is the right thing. I have been working on this hard since the day I took office. Indeed, I began to work on it before I took office. I was trying to continue the policy not only that I felt was right but that my predecessor said was right. He said it was a serious threat to our security.

We were very reasonable. We went through that whole Governors Island thing. We agreed, because they wanted it, to lightly arm our soldiers and the French and the Canadians, the others that were part of Governors Island. And then we showed up to implement the Governors Island Agreement. And because we were lightly armed, because we had agreed to do that, and because we had agreed to come on conditions of mutual willingness, they broke the deal while we were literally on the point of landing, the United Nations.

We did not invade them then; we did not resort to violence then. Instead, we went back and got a consensus of the international community. We dealt with the refugee crisis. We ended the policy of direct return of refugees. And we went to the sanctions, and we did everything we could. And all of our efforts resulted in more of this, more of this. And it is wrong for us to permit more of this when the United Nations authorized us 50 days ago to act—50 days ago they authorized us. I have tried for 50 more days. And when we got support from countries—we will talk about it some more to-

morrow, but we have an amazing array of countries who believe this is right.

I think when the American people know the facts of this, they will be supportive. And as I said, no decision has been made to use force. That decision is in the hands of the people in Haiti; they can still leave. But they've got to go.

Q. Is there any signal from Port-au-Prince saying that General Cédras could leave?

The President. What?

Q. Is there any signal coming out of Port-au-Prince saying that he could leave?

The President. I don't know what's going to happen there.

Q. Have you had any signals?

Q. Before the Persian Gulf war, President Bush sent Secretary Baker for one final, last meeting, an emissary, with Tariq 'Aziz and said, "This is it. You've got to go within"—I think he prescribed some kind of deadline. Some of your supporters say that you should make one last stab at this; send an emissary. Is that something—do you endorse that idea?

The President. I don't want to say anymore today about all of that. I just want to say that I think I have shown already extreme good faith and forbearance in the face of dictators who broke their word to America, broke their word to the United Nations, permitted gross brutalization of their own people, and are exercising a destabilizing force in our region when we need to be supportive of democracy. I have shown forbearance.

We will deal with those questions—that question and questions like it—in an appropriate fashion. And they, I hope, will make the right decision.

Q. Well, are you sending President Carter, by any chance, who seems to be a world peacemaker? I mean, giving him a chance to meet with Cédras?

The President. There is nothing to meet about, unless they are leaving. If they are leaving and they want to discuss things, well, that's a different issue.

But the time has come for them to go. I am not interested in sending anybody down there to try to talk them into doing something that they plainly will not be talked into doing in a reasonable, fair, humane way.

They broke their word on Governors Island. I was prepared, fully committed, to see that the amnesty provision was honored, that they and the people that they were associated with were protected. I had no intention of supporting any international aid to Haiti if the Governors Island Agreement was not honored. We still are committed to a spirit of reconciliation and to putting an end to this. I know that there will be pressures for other kinds of violence when the change occurs. People don't suffer this kind of thing and not want to retaliate. We are committed to—the international community is, the U.N. is, all these countries that are willing to go in are committed to trying to put an end to this.

Q. Even at the price of American lives?

The President. Well, I hope there won't be a loss of American lives. But the United States went into not only Desert Storm but went in— in our hemisphere, where we have a special interest—went into both Panama and Grenada in a conflict without United Nations support, without United Nations—an outright request and certainly without 20 other countries supporting an endeavor.

I think that, therefore, our interests are clear and certainly as compelling here as they were there.

Q. Have there been any signals at all, any feelers from—[*inaudible*]

The President. You've seen enough from the films to know that we have been doing preparations. And we will do everything we can under all circumstances always to minimize any risk to American lives.

Q. Have there been any signals at all, any feelers from Cédras and the others, that at long last they're ready to go?

The President. All I can tell you is that the issue as we stand tonight is how I have presented it to you. And I'll have more to say tomorrow night.

Q. What about a congressional vote? If that happens, if there is a congressional vote and it goes against you, would you ignore that?

The President. Well, we've had—first of all, I'm not convinced that that's going to happen, but secondly, we have had seven debates about it. The 1994 appropriations bill actually provided—if you will remember—provided a procedure by which the United States could move, along with the U.N., and file a detailed report about what was going on.

I do want to emphasize this, because I think this is a legitimate concern of Congress and the American people: What is our mission? If we lead this multinational force, what is our mission? Our mission is to get the dictators out; bring the police monitors in from these other countries to help maintain the peace; begin to retrain a Haitian police force to be responsible, supportive of democracy, and to prevent violence, not participate in it; restore the elected President; and turn the mission over to the U.N. as quickly as we can. Then there would be a U.N. mission in which the United States would participate but at a much reduced level, which would stay there until the election occurs next year and the new President is inaugurated early '96.

In other words, we have very limited objectives. We are not trying to win military conquest. We have no interest in that at all. And we are not responsible in any way, shape, or form for rebuilding Haiti. This is not a nation building operation. It is not a traditional peacekeeping operation. Our responsibility would be limited to removing the dictators, bringing in the police monitors from other countries, retraining the police force, restoring the President, turning it over to the U.N.

The nation building, so-called nation building, would have to be done by the international aid institutions. You should know, by the way—because one of the questions that will be asked is, how do we know that we'll be on a more positive path—there was a meeting in Paris a few days ago. There was a commitment to give over $1 billion in aid to Haiti when democracy is restored, when the dictators leave, if conditions of reconciliation exist.

Q. If force has to be used, how many troops would be involved and how long would they have to——

The President. I'm not going to discuss the details of that. It would not be responsible. I'll have some more to say about it tomorrow night.

Q. Your exit strategy?

The President. Absolutely.

Q. I was going to say that——

The President. Absolutely, a disciplined and clear one. There is. That's what I'm trying to say. This is, there is—first of all, the whole U.N. mission will be over when the next Presidential election is held in '95. That's when the U.N. mission is over. The U.S. responsibility as head of a multinational force would be over in a couple of months, as soon as we could do those things I said, remove the dictators, retrain the police, let the police monitors maintain order, restore the President, turn it over to the U.N. It could be done in a matter of a couple of months.

You know, it is very important that it be limited. The nation building must done by the international financial institutions. They have a plan that I think will work.

Baseball Strike

Q. Mr. President, a purely domestic issue, as you probably know, Bud Selig has announced that the baseball season is over with no World Series. Do you think the antitrust exemption should be removed from baseball at this point because of the situation?

The President. I don't want to give you a definite answer, but it's something that I think ought to be looked at. The reason I don't want to give you a definite answer is that I have not had a chance to study that issue in detail or to get any kind of advice from the Justice Department. But I think that if for the first time in history we're not going to have a World Series, and if we have ended what could have been the best baseball season in 50 years—I might say, you know, we tried. We had the Federal Mediation Service in there. The Secretary of Labor worked very hard. The White House worked very hard. We did everything we could. If this has just turned into another business in America, then that's an issue, it seems to me, that has to be examined. But I cannot give a definitive answer at this moment for the simple reason that I have not had adequate time to study it or get a recommendation from the Attorney General, so I should not do that. But I don't see how we can avoid a serious examination of it in light of what has happened now to the American people.

Press Secretary Myers. Next question.

Haiti

Q. You sound very angry.

The President. Well, I believe that the United States—I think there's no question, about what you said, about the whole issue about the public support—but that's because immigration has gotten off the front page and the nature of the U.N. commitment got off the front page. And I understand that, and I'm sympathetic, and we were doing a lot of other things in America, you know, a lot of things at home. But, you know, we asked for this report from the Assistant Secretary for Human Rights. He gave it to me. Just in the last few days we had the New York Times story on the orphans being killed. It's just getting worse, and I am— I am very angry.

Those people gave their word to the United States and the United Nations at Governors Island. And we gave our word to them. We kept our word to them. They broke their word to us. They went about committing this kind of atrocity. And I have bent over backwards. I have used sanctions and everything else. I have also not had the United States be the Lone Ranger. We had the U.N. come in here. The United Nations has asked us to move, and we have all these other countries. And it is—this is senseless, and it needs to stop.

NOTE: The President spoke at 4:45 p.m. in the Oval Office at the White House. Participants in the interview were Helen Thomas of United Press International, Terence Hunt of Associated Press, Gene Gibbons of Reuters, and Sophie Huet of Agence France-Presse. A reporter referred to Bud Selig, acting commissioner of baseball.

Message to the Senate Transmitting a Protocol to the Canada–United States Taxation Convention
September 14, 1994

To the Senate of the United States:

I transmit herewith for Senate advice and consent to ratification the Protocol Amending the Convention Between the United States of America and Canada with Respect to Taxes on Income and on Capital Signed at Washington

on September 26, 1980, as amended by the Protocols signed on June 14, 1983, and March 28, 1984, signed at Washington August 31, 1994. Also transmitted for the information of the Senate is the report of the Department of State with respect to the Protocol.

The Protocol further amends the Convention to reflect changes in U.S. and Canadian law and treaty policy and to make certain technical corrections to the existing Convention that are necessary because of the passage of time. It also improves the operation of the Convention and facilitates the flow of capital and technology between the United States and Canada.

I recommend that the Senate give early and favorable consideration to the Protocol and give its advice and consent to ratification.

WILLIAM J. CLINTON

The White House,
September 14, 1994.

Message to the Senate Transmitting the Ukraine-United States Taxation Convention and Protocol
September 14, 1994

To the Senate of the United States:

I transmit herewith for Senate advice and consent to ratification the Convention Between the Government of the United States of America and the Government of Ukraine for the Avoidance of Double Taxation and the Prevention of Fiscal Evasion with Respect to Taxes on Income and Capital, with Protocol, signed at Washington on March 4, 1994. Also transmitted for the information of the Senate is the report of the Department of State with respect to the Convention.

The Convention replaces, with respect to Ukraine, the 1973 income tax convention be-tween the United States of America and the Union of Soviet Socialist Republics. It will modernize tax relations between the two countries and will facilitate greater private sector United States investment in Ukraine.

I recommend that the Senate give early and favorable consideration to the Convention and related Protocol and give its advice and consent to ratification.

WILLIAM J. CLINTON

The White House,
September 14, 1994.

Message to the Senate Transmitting the Sweden-United States Taxation Convention
September 14, 1994

To the Senate of the United States:

I transmit herewith for Senate advice and consent to ratification the Convention Between the Government of the United States of America and the Government of Sweden for the Avoidance of Double Taxation and the Prevention of Fiscal Evasion with Respect to Taxes on Income signed at Stockholm on September 1, 1994, together with a related exchange of notes. Also transmitted for the information of the Senate is the report of the Department of State with respect to the Convention.

The proposed Convention with Sweden re-places the present income tax regime between the two countries. In general, the proposed Convention follows the pattern of other recent U.S. income tax treaties and the 1981 U.S. Model Income Tax Convention, as well as the OECD Model Tax Convention on Income and Capital.

I recommend that the Senate give early and favorable consideration to the Convention and the related exchange of notes and give its advice and consent to ratification.

WILLIAM J. CLINTON

The White House,
September 14, 1994.

Nomination for Court of Appeals and District Court Judges
September 14, 1994

The President today nominated Karen Nelson Moore to the U.S. Court of Appeals for the Sixth Circuit. The President also nominated the following seven individuals to serve on the U.S. District Court: Roslyn Moore-Silver for the District of Arizona; Maxine M. Chesney for the Northern District of California; Alvin W. Thompson for the District of Connecticut; James Robertson for the District of Columbia; Thomas B. Russell for the Western District of Kentucky; William H. Walls for the District of New Jersey; and Sidney H. Stein for the Southern District of New York.

"These nominees will bring excellence to the Federal bench," the President said. "Their commitment to public service and to equal justice for all Americans is outstanding."

NOTE: Biographies of the nominees were made available by the Office of the Press Secretary.

Letter to Congressional Leaders Transmitting a Report on Cyprus
September 8, 1994

Dear Mr. Speaker: (Dear Mr. Chairman:)

In accordance with Public Law 95–384 (22 U.S.C. 2373(c)), I am submitting to you this report on progress toward a negotiated settlement of the Cyprus question. The previous report covered progress through May 20, 1994. The current report covers the remainder of May through July 31, 1994.

During this period both sides in the Cyprus dispute said that they accept the U.N. proposed package of confidence-building measures. We will be working closely with the United Nations to reconcile the remaining differences concerning the modalities of implementation.

I would also like to take this opportunity to express my sincerest gratitude for the efforts of Robert Lamb, who retired as Special Cyprus Coordinator on June 1 after 32 years of distinguished service in the U.S. Foreign Service. Special Cyprus Coordinator Lamb's dedication and commitment to finding a solution to the Cyprus problem was unbending. He worked diligently to bring both sides closer together and is responsible for the recent significant progress. We are actively searching for a replacement for Robert Lamb.

Sincerely,

WILLIAM J. CLINTON

NOTE: Identical letters were sent to Thomas S. Foley, Speaker of the House of Representatives, and Claiborne Pell, Chairman of the Senate Committee on Foreign Relations. This letter was released by the Office of the Press Secretary on September 15.

Message to the Senate Transmitting the France-United States Taxation Convention
September 15, 1994

To the Senate of the United States:

I transmit herewith for Senate advice and consent to ratification the Convention Between the Government of the United States of America and the Government of the French Republic for the Avoidance of Double Taxation and the Prevention of Fiscal Evasion with Respect to Taxes on Income and Capital, signed at Paris on August 31, 1994, together with two related exchanges of notes. Also transmitted for the information of the Senate is the report of the

Department of State with respect to the Convention.

The Convention replaces the 1967 income tax convention between the United States of America and the French Republic and the related protocols and exchanges of notes. The new Convention more accurately reflects current income tax treaty policies of the two countries.

I recommend that the Senate give early and favorable consideration to the Convention and related exchanges of notes and give its advice and consent to ratification.

WILLIAM J. CLINTON

The White House,
September 15, 1994.

Message to the Senate Transmitting the Portugal-United States Taxation Convention and Protocol
September 15, 1994

To the Senate of the United States:

I transmit herewith for Senate advice and consent to ratification the Convention Between the United States of America and the Portuguese Republic for the Avoidance of Double Taxation and the Prevention of Fiscal Evasion with Respect to Taxes on Income, together with a related Protocol, signed at Washington on September 6, 1994. Also transmitted for the information of the Senate is the report of the Department of State with respect to the Convention.

The Convention is the first income tax convention between the United States of America and the Portuguese Republic. The Convention reflects current income tax treaty policies of the two countries.

I recommend that the Senate give early and favorable consideration to the Convention and related Protocol and give its advice and consent to ratification.

WILLIAM J. CLINTON

The White House,
September 15, 1994.

Message to the Senate Transmitting the Kazakhstan-United States Taxation Convention and Protocol
September 15, 1994

To the Senate of the United States:

I transmit herewith for Senate advice and consent to ratification the Convention Between the Government of the United States of America and the Government of the Republic of Kazakhstan for the Avoidance of Double Taxation and the Prevention of Fiscal Evasion with Respect to Taxes on Income and Capital, together with the Protocol and the two related exchanges of notes, signed at Almaty on October 24, 1993. Also transmitted for the information of the Senate is the report of the Department of State with respect to the Convention.

The Convention replaces, with respect to Kazakhstan, the 1973 income tax convention between the United States of America and the Union of Soviet Socialist Republics. It will modernize tax relations between the two countries and will facilitate greater private sector U.S. investment in Kazakhstan.

I recommend that the Senate give early and favorable consideration to the Convention, Protocol, and the two related exchanges of notes and give its advice and consent to ratification.

WILLIAM J. CLINTON

The White House,
September 15, 1994.

Message to the Senate Transmitting a Protocol to the Mexico-United States Taxation Convention
September 15, 1994

To the Senate of the United States:

I transmit herewith for Senate advice and consent to ratification the Additional Protocol that Modifies the Convention Between the Government of the United States of America and the Government of the United Mexican States for the Avoidance of Double Taxation and the Prevention of Fiscal Evasion with Respect to Taxes on Income, signed at Washington on September 18, 1992. The Additional Protocol was signed at Mexico City on September 8, 1994. Also transmitted for the information of the Senate is the report of the Department of State with respect to the Additional Protocol.

The Additional Protocol will amend the tax treaty provisions to broaden the scope of tax information exchange with Mexico. The Protocol will authorize the exchange of tax information under any tax information exchange agreement between the two countries and will provide for information exchange under the treaty for taxes at all levels of government.

The current Agreement Between the United States of America and the United Mexican States for the Exchange of Information with Respect to Taxes, which now applies only to Federal taxes, is also being amended by a protocol to provide for the exchange of information to administer and enforce tax laws at all levels of government. This protocol, which was also signed at Mexico City on September 8, 1994, will enter into force only after the Protocol to the Convention has been ratified.

I recommend that the Senate give early and favorable consideration to the Additional Protocol and give its advice and consent to ratification.

WILLIAM J. CLINTON

The White House,
September 15, 1994.

Letter to Congressional Leaders on Ordering the Selected Reserve of the Armed Forces to Active Duty
September 15, 1994

Dear Mr. Speaker: (*Dear Mr. President:*)

I have today, pursuant to section 673b of title 10, United States Code, authorized the Secretary of Defense, and the Secretary of Transportation with respect to the Coast Guard when it is not operating as a service within the Department of the Navy, to order to active duty any units, and any individual members not assigned to a unit organized to serve as a unit, of the Selected Reserve. The deployment of United States forces to conduct operational missions to restore the civilian government in Haiti necessitates this action.

A copy of the Executive order implementing this action is attached.

Sincerely,

WILLIAM J. CLINTON

NOTE: Identical letters were sent to Thomas S. Foley, Speaker of the House of Representatives, and Albert Gore, Jr., President of the Senate. The Executive order is listed in Appendix D at the end of this volume.

Address to the Nation on Haiti
September 15, 1994

My fellow Americans, tonight I want to speak with you about why the United States is leading the international effort to restore democratic government in Haiti.

Haiti's dictators, led by General Raoul Cédras, control the most violent regime in our hemisphere. For 3 years, they have rejected every peaceful solution that the international community has proposed. They have broken an agreement that they made to give up power. They have brutalized their people and destroyed their economy. And for 3 years, we and other nations have worked exhaustively to find a diplomatic solution, only to have the dictators reject each one.

Now the United States must protect our interests, to stop the brutal atrocities that threaten tens of thousands of Haitians, to secure our borders, and to preserve stability and promote democracy in our hemisphere and to uphold the reliability of the commitments we make and the commitments others make to us.

Earlier today, I ordered Secretary of Defense Perry to call up the military reserve personnel necessary to support United States troops in any action we might undertake in Haiti. I have also ordered two aircraft carriers, the U.S.S. *Eisenhower* and the U.S.S. *America* into the region. I issued these orders after giving full consideration to what is at stake. The message of the United States to the Haitian dictators is clear: Your time is up. Leave now, or we will force you from power.

I want the American people to understand the background of the situation in Haiti, how what has happened there affects our national security interests and why I believe we must act now. Nearly 200 years ago, the Haitian people rose up out of slavery and declared their independence. Unfortunately, the promise of liberty was quickly snuffed out, and ever since, Haiti has known more suffering and repression than freedom. In our time, as democracy has spread throughout our hemisphere, Haiti has been left behind.

Then, just 4 years ago, the Haitian people held the first free and fair elections since their independence. They elected a parliament and a new President, Father Jean-Bertrand Aristide, a Catholic priest who received almost 70 percent of the vote. But 8 months later, Haitian dreams of democracy became a nightmare of bloodshed. General Raoul Cédras led a military coup that overthrew President Aristide, the man who had appointed Cédras to lead the army. Resistors were beaten and murdered. The dictators launched a horrible intimidation campaign of rape, torture, and mutilation. People starved; children died; thousands of Haitians fled their country, heading to the United States across dangerous seas. At that time, President Bush declared the situation posed, and I quote, "an unusual and extraordinary threat to the national security, foreign policy, and economy of the United States."

Cédras and his armed thugs have conducted a reign of terror, executing children, raping women, killing priests. As the dictators have grown more desperate, the atrocities have grown ever more brutal. Recent news reports have documented the slaying of Haitian orphans by the nation's deadly police thugs. The dictators are said to suspect the children of harboring sympathy toward President Aristide for no other reason than he ran an orphanage in his days as a parish priest. The children fled the orphanages for the streets. Now they can't even sleep there because they're so afraid. As one young boy told a visitor, "I do not care if the police kill me because it only brings an end to my suffering."

International observers uncovered a terrifying pattern of soldiers and policemen raping the wives and daughters of suspected political dissidents, young girls, 13, 16 years old; people slain and mutilated, with body parts left as warnings to terrify others; children forced to watch as their mothers' faces are slashed with machetes. A year ago, the dictators assassinated the Minister of Justice. Just last month, they gunned down Father Jean-Marie Vincent, a peasant leader and close friend of Father Aristide. Vincent was executed on the doorstep of his home, a monastery. He refused to give up his ministry, and for that, he was murdered.

Let me be clear: General Cédras and his accomplices alone are responsible for this suffering and terrible human tragedy. It is their actions that have isolated Haiti.

Neither the international community nor the United States has sought a confrontation. For nearly 3 years, we've worked hard on diplomatic efforts. The United Nations, the Organization of American States, the Caribbean community, the six Central American Presidents all have sought a peaceful end to this crisis. We have tried everything: persuasion and negotiation, mediation and condemnation. Emissaries were dispatched to Port-au-Prince and were turned away. The United Nations labored for months to reach an agreement acceptable to all parties.

Then last year, General Cédras himself came here to the United States and signed an agreement on Governors Island in New York in which he pledged to give up power, along with the other dictators. But when the day came for the plan to take effect, the dictators refused to leave and instead increased the brutality they are using to cling to power.

Even then, the nations of the world continued to seek a peaceful solution while strengthening the embargo we had imposed. We sent massive amounts of humanitarian aid, food for a million Haitians and medicine to try to help the ordinary Haitian people, as the dictators continued to loot the economy. Then this summer, they threw out the international observers who had blown the whistle on the regime's human rights atrocities.

In response to that action, in July the United Nations Security Council approved a resolution that authorizes the use of all necessary means, including force, to remove the Haitian dictators from power and restore democratic government. Still, we continued to seek a peaceful solution, but the dictators would not even meet with the United Nations Special Envoy. In the face of this continued defiance and with atrocities rising, the United States has agreed to lead a multinational force to carry out the will of the United Nations.

More than 20 countries from around the globe, including almost all the Caribbean community and nations from as far away as Poland, which has so recently won its own freedom, Israel and Jordan, which have been struggling for decades to preserve their own security, and Bangladesh, a country working on its own economic problems, have joined nations like Belgium and Great Britain. They have all agreed to join us because they think this problem in

our neighborhood is important to their future interests and their security.

I know that the United States cannot, indeed we should not, be the world's policemen. And I know that this is a time with the cold war over that so many Americans are reluctant to commit military resources and our personnel beyond our borders. But when brutality occurs close to our shores, it affects our national interests. And we have a responsibility to act.

Thousands of Haitians have already fled toward the United States, risking their lives to escape the reign of terror. As long as Cédras rules, Haitians will continue to seek sanctuary in our Nation. This year, in less than 2 months, more than 21,000 Haitians were rescued at sea by our Coast Guard and Navy. Today, more than 14,000 refugees are living at our naval base in Guantanamo. The American people have already expended almost $200 million to support them, to maintain the economic embargo. And the prospect of millions and millions more being spent every month for an indefinite period of time loom ahead unless we act.

Three hundred thousand more Haitians, 5 percent of their entire population, are in hiding in their own country. If we don't act, they could be the next wave of refugees at our door. We will continue to face the threat of a mass exodus of refugees and its constant threat to stability in our region and control of our borders.

No American should be surprised that the recent tide of migrants seeking refuge on our shores comes from Haiti and from Cuba. After all, they're the only nations left in the Western Hemisphere where democratic government is denied, the only countries where dictators have managed to hold back the wave of democracy and progress that has swept over our entire region and that our own Government has so actively promoted and supported for years.

Today, 33 of the 35 countries in the Americas have democratically elected leaders. And Haiti is the only nation in our hemisphere where the people actually elected their own government and chose democracy, only to have tyrants steal it away.

There's no question that the Haitian people want to embrace democracy; we know it because they went to the ballot box and told the world. History has taught us that preserving democracy in our own hemisphere strengthens America's security and prosperity. Democracies here are more likely to keep the peace and to stabilize our region. They're more likely to create free markets and economic opportunity, and to become strong, reliable trading partners. And they're more likely to provide their own people with the opportunities that will encourage them to stay in their nation and to build their own futures. Restoring Haiti's democratic government will help lead to more stability and prosperity in our region, just as our actions in Panama and Grenada did.

Beyond the human rights violations, the immigration problems, the importance of democracy, the United States also has strong interests in not letting dictators, especially in our own region, break their word to the United States and the United Nations. In the post-cold-war world, we will assure the security and prosperity of the United States with our military strength, our economic power, our constant efforts to promote peace and growth. But when our national security interests are threatened, we will use diplomacy when possible and force when necessary.

In Haiti, we have a case in which the right is clear, in which the country in question is nearby, in which our own interests are plain, in which the mission is achievable and limited, and in which the nations of the world stand with us. We must act.

Our mission in Haiti, as it was in Panama and Grenada, will be limited and specific. Our plan to remove the dictators will follow two phases. First, it will remove dictators from power and restore Haiti's legitimate, democratically elected government. We will train a civilian-controlled Haitian security force that will protect the people rather than repress them. During this period, police monitors from all around the world will work with the authorities to maximize basic security and civil order and minimize retribution.

The Haitian people should know that we come in peace. And you, the American people, should know that our soldiers will not be involved in rebuilding Haiti or its economy. The international community, working together, must provide that economic, humanitarian, and technical assistance necessary to help the Haitians rebuild.

When this first phase is completed, the vast majority of our troops will come home, in months, not years. I want our troops and their families to know that we'll bring them home just as soon as we possibly can.

Then, in the second phase, a much smaller U.S. force will join forces from other members of the United Nations. And their mission will leave Haiti after elections are held next year and a new Haitian government takes office in early 1996.

Tonight I can announce that President Aristide has pledged to step down when his term ends, in accordance with the constitution he has sworn to uphold. He has committed himself to promote reconciliation among all Haitians and to set an historic example by peacefully transferring power to a duly elected successor. He knows, as we know, that when you start a democracy, the most important election is the second election. President Aristide has told me that he will consider his mission fulfilled not when he regains office but when he leaves office to the next democratically elected President of Haiti. He has pledged to honor the Haitian voters who put their faith in the ballot box.

In closing, let me say that I know the American people are rightfully concerned whenever our soldiers are put at risk. Our volunteer military is the world's finest, and its leaders have worked hard to minimize risks to all our forces. But the risks are there, and we must be prepared for that.

I assure you that no President makes decisions like this one without deep thought and prayer. But it's my job as President and Commander in Chief to take those actions that I believe will best protect our national security interests.

Let me say again, the nations of the world have tried every possible way to restore Haiti's democratic government peacefully. The dictators have rejected every possible solution. The terror, the desperation, and the instability will not end until they leave. Once again, I urge them to do so. They can still move now and reduce the chaos and disorder, increase the security, the stability, and the safety in which this transfer back to democracy can occur.

But if they do not leave now, the international community will act to honor our commitments; to give democracy a chance, not to guarantee it; to remove stubborn and cruel dictators, not to impose a future.

I know many people believe that we shouldn't help the Haitian people recover their democracy and find their hard-won freedoms, that the Haitians should accept the violence and repression as their fate. But remember, the same was said of a people who more than 200 years ago took up arms against a tyrant whose forces occupied their land. But they were a stubborn bunch, a people who fought for their freedoms and appealed to all those who believed in democracy to help their cause. And their cries were answered, and a new nation was born, a nation that ever since has believed that the rights of life, liberty, and the pursuit of happiness should be denied to none.

May God bless the people of the United States and the cause of freedom. Good night.

NOTE: The President spoke at 9 p.m. from the Oval Office at the White House.

Remarks and an Exchange With Reporters on Haiti
September 16, 1994

The President. Thank you for coming in; I'm glad to see you. I wanted to make three quick points. One is, we had a detailed briefing this morning from General Shalikashvili, and I feel good about the extraordinary work and preparation that our military leaders have done. Second, we're up to 24 nations now participating in the coalition, and I feel very good about that. I think there will be more; I think we'll have more before very long. And the third thing that I want to say is, I've seen a copy of the remarks that President Aristide is going to deliver today, and I'm pleased with that. I think it is very important, in light of all the things that have occurred from the time he was elected forward, that this message of reconciliation be genuine, sincere, and straightforward. And I think it will be, and I feel good about that.

And I know some of you have been somewhat skeptical of that. And I would remind you that there's one event which has occurred in recent times which I think will reinforce it, and that is the meeting in Paris which got together the proposed aid package for Haiti to create the economic opportunity for the Haitians, which I think is clearly premised on the right sort of spirit of going forward down there and the whole promise of reconciliation being realized. So I feel good about it. And Admiral Miller's done a marvelous job. I thank you, sir, for what you've done.

Anyway, I didn't mean to interrupt the briefing—[*laughter*]—see so many——

Q. Are you nervous?

The President. Am I nervous? No, I feel good about it. I don't know if good is the right word. I think the policy is right, and I think that I have done the best I could to present it to the American people and we have done the best we could to prepare. And I have enormous confidence in the work that others have done. I think they have done the best they could.

We don't live in a risk-free world, and there are risks associated with anything we did or didn't do. But I think we're doing the right thing, and I think we have the right people doing the right thing. That's all I could ever ask for. And I've made the decision, so if it doesn't go right, I'm responsible.

Q. Secretary Christopher says that he expects more public support and more support on the Hill now, Mr. President. Do you expect to get fairly strong support in Congress now?

The President. I don't know; I can't answer that. I hope so. But he may know more about it than I do. All I can tell you is I've done the very best I could, and I hope they'll be supportive for it. I'm encouraged by the indications that the American people are more supportive. My sense is that the important things to a lot of Americans about last night were—first of all, I think more and more are learning about the human rights abuses and how that reinforces the arguments we made about immigration and democracy. But I think most of the people are focused on that.

But the two things I think that a lot of Americans got last night from an informational point of view were, one, the extraordinary efforts we have made in the diplomatic area and the patience we've shown and the rebuffs we've received over a long period of time. And two, I think a lot of Americans had forgotten about the Governors Island Agreement and that it was broken. And most Americans think when you make a deal with this country, you ought to keep it. And so I feel—all I can tell you is I feel good about it.

Q. Why did you wait so long to make your case to the American people?

The President. Well, I've been talking about this all along, you know. I waited so long to make an Oval Office address because you can only make—I mean, it's only appropriate to make one Oval Office address on a subject like this. And we have done the best we could. We exhausted all other alternatives. I thought this was the right time. I did the best I could with it.

Adm. Paul Miller. Mr. President, before you leave, can I just report one thing to you? Yesterday I was at Fort Drum up in New York; that's the 10th Mountain. And one of the commanders mentioned that a battalion of troops are going to be involved. There was 50-some that could leave the Army before the projected time was

up, and 21 of them said, "We want to stay." So that shows support from the uniformed side, from the practitioner, the youngster. They want to be there, and that's what the call to duty was. I just wanted to mention that.

The President. Thank you very much. Two young men—when we were in Berlin a few months ago and cased the colors of the Berlin Brigade and I met with some of the young soldiers there, two of them asked me to please delay any action in Haiti until they got home so they could go. That's very rewarding. Thank you, sir.

Goodbye.

NOTE: The President spoke at 12:02 p.m. in the Roosevelt Room at the White House. Adm. Paul D. Miller was Supreme Allied Commander, Atlantic. A tape was not available for verification of the content of these remarks.

Remarks at a Meeting of the Multinational Coalition on Haiti
September 16, 1994

President Aristide, Prime Minister Arthur, distinguished Prime Ministers, Deputy Prime Ministers, Foreign Ministers, Ambassadors, Chargés, the Representative of the United Nations, my colleagues in the United States, I begin by saying a simple thank you. Thank you to all the nations here represented for joining an international coalition to restore democratic government to Haiti as called for by United Nations Security Council Resolution 940.

Your presence here demonstrates that this international coalition is strong, diverse, and growing. We have countries from the Caribbean, countries from Latin America, countries from Europe, Asia, Africa, and the Middle East, united in our insistence that the enemies of democracy who now terrorize Haiti leave and leave now and that democratically elected government be returned.

And thank you, President Aristide, for your remarks, for your commitment to democracy and your commitment to reconciliation, for your commitment to the long, hard work of rebuilding your economy and your society, and for your commitment to the future of democracy as evidenced by your comments about the next elec-

tion. I think your statement that in a democracy the most important election is always the second one may become a staple of civics books in our country and perhaps throughout the world.

For 3 years, the international community has done everything it could think of to do to restore Haiti's democratic government peacefully, to end this brutal reign of terror in our hemisphere. We have tried everything. Often our envoys have been rebuffed. Often just a simple request for talk has been denied.

On one occasion an agreement was reached here in the United States, where General Cédras came and actually signed the Governors Island Agreement, committing the military dictators to give up power in return for the spirit of reconciliation about which President Aristide spoke. When the day came for that plan to take effect, the coup leaders went back on their word and refused to leave. And all our efforts since have failed to budge them. As all of you know, the atrocities have only gotten worse. And recently, the leaders even refused to meet with the U.N. Special Envoy.

We have an interest, obviously, in many things: the importance of spreading democracy;

the importance of dealing with the immigration problem about which President Aristide spoke; clearly, the importance of dealing with the horrible human rights violations; and also the importance in not allowing dictators to break their word to the international community, the United Nations, the Caribbean community, the Organization of the American States.

As I look around this room, I am struck by the fact that our common goal is shared by nations not only here in the neighborhood we all share but in those well beyond our hemisphere, from all over the Earth. Some of the countries here represented have been struggling so hard with economic difficulties of their own. Some of the countries here represented have been struggling for decades for peace in their own region. Some of these countries here represented have only recently come to know their own freedom and democracy. And yet, you are all here in this international coalition because of the unusual and the terrible developments in Haiti.

Our goals are clear, but they are limited. Once the military regime is removed from power, the coalition will then help the democratic government to establish basic security. It will begin the process of placing Haitian police under civilian control and monitoring them to ensure respect for human rights. This will enable the Haitian Government to provide the security necessary for international institutions and private institutions to resume the delivery of basic humanitarian assistance. Then, in months, not years, the coalition will pass the baton to the United Nations. The U.N. mission in Haiti will take over the peacekeeping effort and continue to professionalize Haiti's police and military. It will leave Haiti no later than 18 months from now, after the next elections are held and a new government takes office.

Over time, all of us here, and the international financial institutions as well, will be involved in helping Haiti to recover, in providing Haiti with the economic and humanitarian and technical assistance that will be required to keep the country on the path of progress and democracy. But all of us realize, none more than President Aristide, that in the end, the job of rebuilding Haiti belongs to the Haitian people. I think they ask for nothing more than the opportunity to meet that challenge.

And sir, I say again to you today, the spirit of reconciliation, the hand which you have reached out, even in this hour, to those who have taken democracy away, is critical to your success, and I applaud you for what you have said.

Our international coalition goes to Haiti to give democracy a chance—we cannot guarantee it; to remove cruel and brutal dictators, but not to impose a future on Haiti. We cannot do that; that is for the Haitians to make themselves. But I hope and believe that what we are doing will not only be successful but will generate support from even more nations. I think as we go along, you will see more and more countries from all over the world coming to be a part of this. I invite them to do so.

Together, we can help to ensure that the bright light of democracy once again burns in Haiti; that we have taken a stand that helps to restore human rights and end an almost unimaginable brutality; and that we will send a clear message that people who keep their word to the international community—who give their word—should keep it.

Ladies and gentlemen, there are some more things which I believe we all need to discuss and certainly things which our coalition partners are entitled to know and questions they might want to ask. So I have asked the Chairman of our Joint Chiefs of Staff, General Shalikashvili, to discuss in more detail the military and security aspects of our efforts.

Let me say, if I might, to all of you, I appreciate the fact that you have given us your people to serve as a part of this effort. I know you appreciate the fact that in this world, dealing with difficulties, there is no such thing as a risk-free effort. But I will tell you that General Shalikashvili and the other leaders of our military have worked and planned and done everything they possibly could to maximize the chances of success and minimize the risks to your people and the risks to human life generally, consistent with the spirit outlined in President Aristide's remarks.

With that, I leave you with General Shalikashvili and the Secretary of State. And I thank you all again very, very much. Thank you.

NOTE: The President spoke at 2:15 p.m. in the East Room at the White House.

Remarks Honoring African-American Veterans of World War II
September 16, 1994

Thank you very much, Congressman Rangel, Secretary Brown, Chairman Mfume, other members of the Congressional Black Caucus, and to all of the veterans of our Armed Forces who are here, to your family members and friends, my fellow Americans. I am proud to be here to honor the African-American veterans of World War II.

This is a distinguished generation in the history of African-American military service. But you belong to a legacy older than the Declaration of Independence, one that includes the legendary service of the Massachusetts 54th in our Civil War, the Buffalo Soldiers in the West, the 92d Division in World War I.

Congressman Rangel, I'm sure most of you know, is a decorated veteran of the Korean war, and he had a son who served in the United States Marine Corps. I want to recognize his service and that of the other veterans of the Congressional Black Caucus: Congressmen Blackwell, Bishop, Clay, Conyers, Dellums, Dixon, Jefferson, Rush, Stokes, Scott, and Towns.

I also want to acknowledge our Secretary of Veterans Affairs, Jesse Brown. I'm grateful to have him in my Cabinet not only because he is the first African-American Secretary of Veterans Affairs but because he is a genuine hero of our military service and someone, as Congressman Rangel said, who has been a Secretary of Veterans Affairs and a secretary for America's veterans. I was telling him on the way over here, I had just gotten another one of his letters reminding me that there was something else I should have done that I had not yet done for the veterans of this country. [*Laughter*] I told him, when we had our little interview before I became President, that I expected him not only to be loyal to me but loyal to you and that as long as he were honest and straightforward with me, he could fulfill both loyalties. I can honestly say he is doing his best to follow my admonition. [*Laughter*]

I want to note that today is also POW/MIA Recognition Day, a day to recognize those Americans who were held prisoner of war or those who remain unaccounted for, the missing who never received their proper welcome home.

They are not forgotten. The United States stands firmly resolved to help their young loved ones find the answers they deserve. And even today, we are working hard and investing a significant amount of money in that endeavor in Southeast Asia.

For decades, African-American veterans were missing in our Nation's memories of World War II. For too long, you were soldiers in the shadows, forgotten heroes. Today it should be clear to you, all of you, you are forgotten no more. I'm very proud of your service to our country. You've protected and expanded the freedoms that all the rest of us enjoy today. Our Nation's debt to you can never be fully repaid, but we can certainly honor your service, as we do today.

Americans endured much during World War II, the terrible loss of lives, the separation of families and loved ones, the interruptions of life on the homefront. All our people felt some of that. But no group of Americans endured what African-Americans endured in uniform. You had to win the right to fight the enemy we faced in common. You endured the indignities of double standards for black troops, the put-downs, the segregated units and bases, some of which gave you less freedom to move than German prisoners of war. You defended America with no guarantees that your own freedom would be defended in return.

I'm just reading the new book by Doris Kearns Goodwin about World War II and President and Mrs. Roosevelt, war on the homefront, war abroad. She was constantly urging her husband to try to do something about the double standard accorded to African-American people in the military and demanded, among other things, that people who wanted to enlist in the Navy ought to be able to do something besides work in the mess.

We've come a long way since then, largely because of you and many tens of thousands like you who disproved the false stereotypes, who showed that American troops were, are, and always will be the best trained, the best prepared fighting force in history, regardless of the color of their skin. In fact, units comprised entirely or mostly of African-Americans performed remarkably, groups honored today such as the

famed Tuskegee Airmen. This is something—
[*applause*]—to the Tuskegee Airmen, stand up
there. When I was in Europe recently to celebrate the 50th anniversary of the liberation of
Italy and Rome and D-Day, I was escorted on
part of my journey by a Tuskegee Airman from
my home State who told me what is now in
my notes here—[*laughter*]—that Tuskegee Airmen flew 1,578 combat missions and they were
the only fighter group in the Mediterranean,
black or white, never to lose a single, solitary
bomber under escort.

The Red Ball Express, they landed at Normandy in the wake of D-Day and rushed materiel to supply the rapid Allied advance. The U.S.
Army's 761st Tank Battalion, the first black armored unit to see combat in World War II—
are they here? [*Applause*] Thank you. They
fought bravely at the Battle of the Bulge and
did so while in combat for 183 days in a row.

In Europe, North Africa, the Pacific, or state-
side, in the Army, the Navy, the Air Force,
the Marines, the Coast Guard, more than a million African-American men and women helped
to win this century's greatest fight for freedom.
In helping to show the world what America was
against, you helped to show America what
America is for. You helped to liberate all of
us from segregation. The civil rights marches
were already underway every time you marched
in a uniform. And today, at the end of the
cold war, we should do everything we can to
pay back the debt we owe, to move forward
as a nation as you helped America to move
forward after World War II.

Most of you were born in the years after
World War I, a time when America came home
from victory and retreated from the world, a
time in which insecurity arose. As Hitler's hate
spread overseas, the Red Scare and the Ku Klux
Klan grew up here at home. But after World
War II, we avoided a lot of those mistakes.
We turned our old adversaries into new allies.
We brought prosperity into our own economy,
even as we built the global economy. We educated our people for new work and propelled
a movement for civil rights that lifted millions
of Americans into equal dignity and gave all
Americans at least some chance to join the middle class.

Now we have to do what your generation
did for us, to guide new democracies into an
era of security and prosperity, to renew our
own economy, to give hope to our communities,

to give every individual the tools they need to
assume personal responsibility for themselves
and their families, to prepare our young people
for life in the 21st century. And perhaps still
most difficult of all, we have got to find a way
to work together in this country to make a
strength out of our diversity, to prove that in
a global economy where the Earth is smaller
and smaller, the fact that we are nations of
many races and faiths and many backgrounds
is a great source of strength if we will tap it
with open minds and open hearts.

Here in the Government, the President and
the Congress, we have some power to bring
more jobs and lower the deficit. We have the
power to pass laws that will help people to combat crime and will help to open trading opportunities all around the world. We have the power
to pass laws that will give communities the tools
they need to rebuild and give families the breaks
they need to succeed at work and at home,
like the Family Leave Act.

But one thing I've learned here now in nearly
2 years as President: No matter how much
progress we make in passing the laws, what goes
on in the hearts of our countrymen is still the
most important thing. And there is still too
much in our country that divides us, too many
who see the glass as half-empty instead of half-
full. We can win the battles before us. There
is no problem we face today that America cannot overcome. But we have to have the spirit
and the character and the sheer endurance and
faith that so many of you demonstrated by the
dignity and courage of your service in the Second World War.

Before I turn the microphone over to Congressman Sanford Bishop of Georgia, who will
read the awards as Secretary Brown and I congratulate the honorees, let me say just a word
about Haiti, since Congressman Rangel was kind
enough to mention it.

As all of you know now, it is a place where
terrible atrocities have occurred. After a democratic leader was thrown out and dictators took
over, people were murdered, slashed, raped,
anything to intimidate them into submission. It
is a place where democracy has been taken
away, the only place in our entire hemisphere
where an elected government was supplanted
with a dictatorship. Because of the oppression
and the difficulties, it is a place where we have
had many immigrants streaming out of it, look-

ing for freedom and relief. And unless we act, there will be more.

I hope you also know that we have bent over backwards now for 3 years to avoid this confrontation. We have sought a peaceful solution, repeatedly. Last year we made an agreement here in the United States; the dictator, General Cédras, came here and signed an agreement in which he promised to leave power in return for a spirit of a reconciliation and humanity, putting the country back together. And then when the day came to keep the deal, he broke it, turned the United Nations away, and now they're even refusing to talk to representatives of the United Nations.

Well, here in our neighborhood, that level of human rights abuse, the loss of democracy through robbery, the continued threat of the instability of immigration, and breaking your word to the United States, United Nations, and all your neighbors, those things are things which cannot stand.

I also want to say, as all of you know, our military is as good as it's ever been, perhaps better than it's ever been. It's more united, more flexible, more modern, and yet more skilled in the old-fashioned virtues and abilities perhaps than ever before. Our leaders have prepared well for this moment, while hoping that

it would not be necessary. But as all of you know, as well as any American, there is no such thing as a risk-free journey in this area.

We have done everything we can to be deliberate and fair. Even at this hour, just a few minutes ago, we had all the members of our coalition, including the Prime Ministers of several of the Caribbean countries, into the White House. President Aristide made a speech in which he said, "No violence, reconciliation. Let's don't do this; let's don't take retribution on each other anymore." This is a right cause, with a country that is near, in our own neighborhood, where the mission is plain and limited and achievable.

And I just want to say to all of you that I honor your contributions, and I know you honor the contributions of all those young men and women in uniform who now are able to achieve their God-given abilities in the service of their country without regard to their race because of what you did.

Thank you, and God bless you all.

NOTE: The President spoke at 4:59 p.m. at the Longworth House Office Building. The National POW/MIA Recognition Day proclamation of September 14 is listed in Appendix D at the end of this volume.

Memorandum on the Federal Plan To Break the Cycle of Homelessness
September 16, 1994

Memorandum for the Secretary of Housing and Urban Development

Subject: Federal Plan to Break the Cycle of Homelessness

The Federal Plan to Break the Cycle of Homelessness is a pathbreaking document. The Federal Plan sets forth a comprehensive strategy to create a continuum of care system, consolidate duplicative programs, and more comprehensively address the needs of homeless families and individuals by doubling the Housing and Urban Development's homeless budget.

In short, the Federal Plan is a vital first step in addressing one of my top priorities as President. Because of our deep commitment to ending homelessness and the importance of this

issue to America, I hereby direct you to work towards building and solidifying support across this Nation for the Federal Plan. Our citizens must understand the principles of the Federal Plan. They must be convinced of the importance of our proposed legislation to reorganize HUD's homeless programs, and they must be persuaded of the critical importance of doubling HUD's homeless budget. Most of all, they must understand our eagerness to work in partnership with local governments, not-for-profit providers, advocates, and others to create a comprehensive continuum of care in all our cities and towns.

I am counting on you and the Department to help create the support that the Federal Plan to Break the Cycle of Homelessness deserves.

WILLIAM J. CLINTON

The President's Radio Address
September 17, 1994

Good morning. The night before last, I spoke with you about why America's interests compel us to help restore democratic government in Haiti.

For 3 years, the United Nations, the Caribbean community, and the Organization of American States have pursued every diplomatic avenue possible. But the dictators rejected all of our efforts, and their reign of terror, a campaign of murder, rape, and mutilation, gets worse with every passing day. Now we must act.

Our reasons are clear: to stop the horrific atrocities that threaten thousands of men, women, and children in Haiti, here in our own neighborhood; to affirm our determination that we keep our commitments and we expect others to keep their commitments to us; to avert the flow of thousands of more refugees and to secure our borders; and to preserve the stability of democracy in our hemisphere.

Today I'd like to speak with you about the steps we are now taking to ensure that these brutal dictators leave and leave now. The preparations of the extraordinary international coalition we have assembled are proceeding without delay. Even as I speak with you, our Armed Forces, in coordination with personnel from 24 other nations from all around the world, are poised to end the reign of terror that has plagued Haiti since the military coup 3 years ago. I have great pride and confidence in our troops. Our leaders have prepared their mission very, very carefully, and our forces are clearly the finest in the world.

At the same time, it is the responsibility of any American President to pursue every possible alternative to the use of force in order to avoid bloodshed and the loss of American lives. That is why this morning, at my request, President Carter, former Chairman of the Joint Chiefs of Staff General Colin Powell, and chairman of the Senate Armed Services Committee Senator Sam Nunn left for Haiti. Their mission is to make one last best effort to provide a peaceful, orderly transfer of power, to minimize the loss of life, and to maximize the chances of security for all Haitians and, of course, for our own troops in the coalition force.

On Thursday night, I stated that the Cédras regime's time is up. Their time is up. The remaining question is not whether they will leave but how they will leave. They can go peacefully and increase the chances for a peaceful future and a more stable future for Haiti in the near term, not only for all those whose democracy they stole but for themselves as well. They can do that, or they will be removed by force.

Yesterday leaders of the international coalition gathered at the White House. They come not only from our hemisphere and from our neighborhood here in the Caribbean but also from Europe, Asia, Africa, and the Middle East, from countries as diverse as Israel and Poland, Belgium and Bangladesh, countries with problems of their own, economic problems, political problems, even security problems. But each and every one of them believes it's important enough for them to come here to participate, to stand united with us in insisting that the dictators who terrorize Haiti must be removed and that the democratically elected government must be returned to power now.

As Prime Minister Owen Arthur of Barbados stated so eloquently yesterday, "The Haitian people have wished for democracy. They have suffered for it. They have voted for it. And now they are dying for it."

The goals of the international coalition are clear and limited. Once the military regime is removed from power, the coalition will help the democratic government establish basic security. It will begin the process of placing the Haitian police under civilian control and monitor them to help ensure that they respect human rights. Then, in months, not years, the coalition will pass the baton on to the United Nations. The U.N. mission in Haiti will take over and continue to professionalize Haiti's police and military. It will leave Haiti no later than 18 months from now, after elections are held and a new government takes office.

Over time, the coalition countries as well as the international financial institutions will provide Haiti with economic, humanitarian, and technical assistance that the country needs to stay on the democratic track, to put people back to work, and to begin the work of progress.

They can get assistance from other countries, but we all know that in the end the job of rebuilding Haiti belongs to the Haitian people.

Yesterday at the White House, President Aristide took a long step toward the job of rebuilding, in the spirit of reconciliation. He put it very well when he said, "We say and we will be saying again and again, no to vengeance and no to retaliation; let us embrace peace." President Aristide also reiterated his pledge to transfer power peacefully to a duly elected successor. He said that in the formative years of any democracy, the most important election is not the first one but the second. That's a senti-ment that should become a staple of civics books in our country and throughout the world.

My fellow Americans, at this very hour, we are taking important steps in the journey back to democracy in Haiti. We still hope to end this journey peacefully. But let me say one last time: The cause is right, the mission is achievable and limited, and we will succeed. The dictators must leave.

Thank you for listening.

NOTE: The President spoke at 10:06 a.m. from the Oval Office at the White House.

Remarks at the Congressional Black Caucus Foundation Dinner
September 17, 1994

Thank you. Thank you so much, Cardiss Collins, for your introduction, your support, and your two decades in the United States Congress, making you the longest serving African-American woman in the history of the Congress. Congressman Payne, thank you for your leadership here and for so much that you do, but especially for cochairing, along with C. Payne Lucas, our mission to Rwanda to see the fine work done by the United States in that beleaguered land. And thank you, Congressman Mfume, for your brilliant leadership of the Congressional Black Caucus. It has been an honor and a privilege to work with you to move this country forward and to bring this country together.

There are so many distinguished Americans here tonight. But I can't help acknowledging the presence here—and to say I am so glad to see her able to be here tonight—of Rosa Parks. Thank you, ma'am. I also want to say I'm a little jealous that I didn't see the rest of the program, also all the things for the young people, and especially Reverend Flake's sermon this morning. The Vice President came in this morning when we had our meeting, and he said, "You know that verse in Ezekiel about the dry bones?" And I said to him, I said, "Can there be life in these dry bones?" He said, "Yes, that one. Floyd Flake just gave one of the three or four best sermons I ever heard in my entire life about that." So I would like a tape or a transcript next week, if I could.

I want to congratulate you, too, on your message, embracing our youth for a new tomorrow. You know, when I ran for President, I did so out of a sense of obligation to the next generation. I often said in 1992 I did not want my daughter to grow up in a country in which she was part of the first generation of Americans to do worse than her parents and in which her beloved land was coming apart when it ought to be coming together.

The theme song of our campaign was "Don't Stop Thinking About Tomorrow." In order to do that, this country needs a clear mission and a good spirit. Our mission clearly has been to strengthen our economy and to preserve our security, to empower our people to seize the opportunities the future offers, to rebuild our American sense of community, to find strength in all this diversity we have rather than division and weakness, to try to make our Government work for ordinary citizens again, not as a savior but as a sure partner, to try to summon Americans to the idea that we can do better and that we are doing better.

Now, in just a year and a half or so, we have seen over 4 million jobs come into this economy, a 20 percent drop in the African-American unemployment rate. We have seen 3 years of reduction in our terrible national deficit in a row for the first time since Mr. Truman was President of the United States. We have seen investments in new technologies and dramatic increases in trade. And just a few days ago, a distinguished panel of international economists for the first time in 9 years said that the United States was once again the number one productive economy in the entire world.

We have begun the hard work of empowering our people, everything from increasing the quantity and quality of Head Start programs to apprenticeship programs for young people who don't go to college, to dramatic increases in the availability of lower interest college loans, to job training programs for those who lose their work.

We have begun the work of rebuilding our community. By 1996 we should be able to immunize every child in America under the age of 2. We passed the family leave bill and gave 15 million working families just above the poverty line a tax break so that people could be successful workers and successful parents.

We dealt with all aspects of the crime problem and tried to give our young people something to say yes to as well as something to say no to. We banned assault weapons against enormous odds, passed the Brady bill after 7 years of delay.

We began to rebuild our communities and pull ourselves together. Just last week, we kicked off AmeriCorps, the national service program, with now 15,000 and soon to be 20,000 young Americans all over this country like this young lady here, Erika Lomax, who's a teacher in the Teach For America corps. We can revolutionize this country from the grassroots up if we just give more people like Kweisi was when he was 16 or 18 or 20 something to do that is good and wholesome and pure and true that will lead to a better tomorrow. And we are making a beginning at that. Now our young people will be working in everything from helping our elderly people to be more secure, to improving our environment, to tutoring kids, to keeping our streets safer, to dealing in drug prevention and education and treatment programs.

We passed the empowerment zone proposal, and we're about to finish the process of reviewing those. It's been the most remarkable thing I have ever seen, how communities have come together across racial and economic lines to try to find a way to get investment in jobs to those people who have been totally left behind in every economic recovery for the last 20 years. We are making a beginning at that.

And I want to say a special word of thanks for one proposal to three of your members. Soon we will have ready for my signature the community development bank proposal, thanks in no small measure to Congressman Rush, Congressman Flake, and Congresswoman Waters. And I thank them for that.

We're also trying to pull this country together in other ways, proving that an administration can be both diverse and excellent. One of the things I am proudest of is that as of this night, it has been my privilege as your President to appoint more than twice as many African-American judges to the Federal bench than the last three Presidents combined and more than twice as many Hispanic judges to the Federal bench than the last three Presidents combined. The really important thing is that the American Bar Association has given "well-qualified" ratings to a higher percentage of this administration's appointments than in any of the last five Presidencies.

I say that because unless we can find a way to go forward into the future together, all of our particular successes will not have the general result we want. Still it is so easy to see the glass as half-empty instead of half-full. And it is the spirit that burns within each of us that tells us we can get up every day and do a little better that really keeps this country going. Our Nation has always been made great because of the efforts of its people, the spirit of its people.

Yesterday Congressman Mfume and Congressman Rangel and others invited me over to the Capitol, where we gave awards to a large number of African-American veterans of World War II. And I couldn't help thinking as I looked out at those fine people the extraordinary lengths to which some of them had to go simply to serve their country. The Tuskegee Airmen flew nearly 1,600 missions, and they were the only fighter group never to lose a bomber in Europe in World War II.

Well today, we need all of our people, and we do not have a person to waste. And yes, we can do better. We must, and we will. But it is important to know that democracy is on the move in this country in no small measure because of the contributions of the members of the Congressional Black Caucus.

Before I go, I have to say a few words about Haiti. As you know, I had looked forward to being here tonight in a more jovial mood. I even like to—I've gotten finally to the point in my life where I like to wear one of those tuxedos. When I used to complain about it, my mama used to tell me that I came from a family where she could still remember the first time anybody ever had a necktie. And I was not to complain about wearing a tuxedo; I should be proud to have the opportunity to do so. So I look forward to doing that sort of thing. And I always love to be with you, and there are hundreds of my friends here. But I came late and a little out of style because, as you might imagine, I have been preoccupied today with the events in Haiti and the preparations we have been making at the Pentagon.

I just want to say a word or two about that and how it relates to everything I have said before. Just because the cold war is over does not mean the United States can withdraw from the world. Just because it is almost always not necessary to resort to force, and we must always do everything we can to avoid it, does not mean there are never circumstances in which it might be necessary.

What I want to say to you tonight is this: Our security interests in the world are many and varied. We must first finish the work of the cold war and remove the nuclear threat from our children's future. And we are making real progress there. We must try to limit the spread of all weapons of mass destruction and contain terrorism and the truly astonishing new threat of global organized crime. We must also try to spread a system of free economies and open trading so that as people work together and deal with each other, their suspicions and animosities and hatreds go down, and their sense of the practical benefits of being more open and more free and more democratic come to them.

But we also have a special responsibility here in our own neighborhood, even as other countries do in their own neighborhoods, to deal with things which the world community condemns. And that is why we have sought for 3 years to restore democracy to Haiti, to end violence and terrorism and human rights violations, to see that all parties lived up to their commitments, to keep democracy on the move in our hemisphere and encourage those fledgling democracies to be brave and to go forward, to stabilize the borders and the territorial integrity of all countries, including ours.

I have done everything I could to that end, along with the United Nations, the Caribbean community, and the Organization of the American States. Now there is an international coalition committed to implementing United Nations Security Council Resolution 940. Twenty-four other nations from around the world, with more to come, have already said they would come here to be with us to help to bring democracy back. I have great pride and confidence in our troops. And we are honored to have the support of these nations and of the United Nations.

Yesterday the international coalition gathered at the White House and heard a very moving address by President Aristide in which he said that there should be no violence; there should be no retaliation; there should be no recrimination; everyone should simply lay down their arms and go to work at building a country that has suffered for too long from hatred and violence and recrimination. If it can be done in South Africa, surely it can be done in Haiti.

And then yesterday evening, as all of you now know, I asked President Carter and General Powell and Senator Nunn to go to Haiti and try our last best effort to have a peaceful transition, to follow the will of the international community to end the bloodshed, to restore democracy.

Tonight, whatever your feelings and wherever you're from, I ask you to remember this simple statement made by Prime Minister Arthur of Barbados yesterday when he said, and I quote, "The Haitian people have wished for democracy. They have suffered for it. They have voted for it. And now they are dying for it." The time for idle discussion has ended. There is still a little time for serious discussion.

Tonight, as we move toward Sunday, our worship day for those of us who are Christians, I ask all of you to say a prayer for all the people of Haiti, for the members of our Armed Forces, and for the cause of peace. We are doing our duty, and I am doing mine, as I believe it to be plain and evident. But we all must hope every day and every way that we can go forward in peace.

My decisions are firm and clear. The mission is still in Haiti. Let us hope for its success. But whatever happens, let us resolve that we will stand against violations of human rights and terrorism in our neighborhood. We will stand for democracy, and we will keep our commitments and expect those who make commitments to us to keep theirs.

I ask you now as I leave to remember these things and each in your own way, as hard as you can, say a prayer for peace and for the success of our effort there. It is a part of the future we wish to build for our young people and for our country into the 21st century.

Thank you, God bless you, and good night.

NOTE: The President spoke at 9:45 p.m. at the Washington Convention Center. In his remarks, he referred to civil rights activist Rosa Parks, who had been hospitalized after having been attacked in her home.

Address to the Nation on Haiti
September 18, 1994

My fellow Americans, I want to announce that the military leaders of Haiti have agreed to step down from power. The dictators have recognized that it is in their best interest and in the best interest of the Haitian people to relinquish power peacefully, rather than to face imminent action by the forces of the multinational coalition we are leading.

Our objective over the last 3 years has been to make sure that the military dictators leave power and that the democratically elected government is returned. This agreement guarantees both those objectives. It minimizes the risks for American forces and the forces of the 24 nations of the international coalition. And the agreement maximizes the orderly transfer of power to Haiti's democratically elected government.

This is a good agreement for the United States and for Haiti. The military leaders will leave. The United States and coalition forces will arrive beginning tomorrow. And they'll do so in conditions that are less dangerous, although still not without risk. It will be much easier to preserve human rights. And there is a real chance of a more orderly and less violent transfer of power.

And to the supporters of President Aristide, he will be returned. I ask that all Haitians remember what President Aristide said just a couple of days ago: no vengeance, no violence, no retribution. This is a time for peace. That is what the United States is going, along with our coalition partners, to work for.

As all of you know, at my request, President Carter, General Colin Powell, and Senator Sam Nunn went to Haiti to facilitate the dictators' departure just yesterday. I have been in constant contact with them for the last 2 days. They

have worked tirelessly, almost around the clock. And I want to thank them for undertaking this crucial mission on behalf of all Americans. Just as important, I want also to thank the men and women of the United States Armed Forces. It was their presence and their preparations that played a pivotal part in this agreement.

Under the agreement, the dictators have agreed to leave power as soon as the Haitian Parliament passes an amnesty law, as called for by the Governors Island Agreement, but in any event, no later than October 15th. They've agreed to immediate introduction of troops from the international coalition, beginning, as I said, as early as tomorrow. They have also pledged to cooperate fully with the coalition troops during the peaceful transition of power, something we have wanted very much.

I have directed United States forces to begin deployment into Haiti as a part of the U.N. coalition. And General Shelton, our commander, will be there tomorrow. The presence of the 15,000 member multinational force will guarantee that the dictators carry out the terms of the agreement. It is clear from our discussions with the delegation that this agreement only came because of the credible and imminent threat of the multinational force. In fact, it was signed after Haiti received evidence that paratroopers from our 82d Airborne Division, based at Fort Bragg, North Carolina, had begun to load up to begin the invasion, which I had ordered to start this evening. Indeed, at the time the agreement was reached, 61 American planes were already in the air.

Because of this agreement, the United States and other coalition troops going to Haiti will now be able to go under much more favorable conditions than they would have faced had the generals not decided to leave power.

But let me emphasize that this mission still has its risks, and we must be prepared for them. Haiti is still a troubled country, and there remain possibilities of violence directed at American troops. But this agreement minimizes those risks and maximizes our chance to protect the human rights of all Haitians, both those who support President Aristide and those who oppose him, and to create an environment in which President Aristide can return, as he said, without violence, without vengeance, without retribution.

Under the terms of United Nations Security Council Resolution 940, an international coalition from 25 nations will soon go into Haiti to begin the task of restoring democratic government. President Aristide will return to Haiti when the dictators depart.

On Thursday night I told you that the United States must act here to protect our interest, to stop the brutal atrocities that threaten tens of thousands of Haitians, to secure our borders and preserve stability and promote democracy in our hemisphere, to uphold the reliability of commitments we make to others and the commitments others make to us. This agreement furthers all these goals.

From the beginning I have said that the Haitian dictators must go; tonight I can tell you that they will go. And to our troops tonight who are headed to Haiti under less risky conditions, I am confident you will carry out your mission as you already have, effectively and professionally. We depend upon you to do well tomorrow as you have done so very well today and in the weeks and days before, when you planned this exercise, prepared for it, and then began to carry it out. To all of you I say, thank you, your Nation is proud of you.

Good night, and God bless America.

NOTE: The President spoke at 9:30 p.m. from the Oval Office at the White House. In his remarks, he referred to Lt. Gen. Henry H. Shelton, USA, commander of U.S. forces in Haiti.

Letter to Congressional Leaders on Deployment of United States Armed Forces to Haiti
September 18, 1994

Dear Mr. Speaker: (Dear Mr. President:)

I am providing this report, consistent with the sense of Congress in section 8147(c) of the Department of Defense Appropriations Act, 1994 (Public Law 103–139), to advise you of the objectives and character of the planned deployment of U.S. Armed Forces into Haiti.

(1) The deployment of U.S. Armed Forces into Haiti is justified by United States national security interests: to restore democratic government to Haiti; to stop the brutal atrocities that threaten tens of thousands of Haitians; to secure our borders; to preserve stability and promote democracy in our hemisphere; and to uphold the reliability of the commitments we make and the commitments others make to us.

From the very beginning of the coup against the democratic government of Haiti, the United States and the rest of the international community saw the regime as a threat to our interests in this hemisphere. Indeed President Bush declared that the coup "constitute[d] an unusual and extraordinary threat to the national security, foreign policy, and economy of the United States."

The United States' interest in Haiti is rooted in a consistent U.S. policy, since the 1991 coup, to help restore democratic government to that nation. The United States has a particular interest in responding to gross abuses of human rights when they occur so close to our shores.

The departure of the coup leaders from power is also the best way to stem another mass outflow of Haitians, with consequences for the stability of our region and control of our borders. Continuing unconstitutional rule in Haiti would threaten the stability of other countries in this hemisphere by emboldening elements opposed to democracy and freedom.

The agreement regarding the transition between the *de facto* government and the elected government, negotiated by former President

Jimmy Carter, Senator Sam Nunn, and General Colin Powell, will achieve the objective of facilitating the departure of the coup leaders. Their departure will substantially decrease the likelihood of armed resistance.

(2) Despite this agreement, this military operation is not without risk. Necessary steps have been taken to ensure the safety and security of U.S. Armed Forces. Our intention is to deploy a force of sufficient size to serve as a deterrent to armed resistance. The force will have a highly visible and robust presence with firepower ample to overwhelm any localized threat. This will minimize casualties and maximize our capability to ensure that essential civil order is maintained and the agreement arrived at is implemented. The force's rules of engagement allow for the use of necessary and proportionate force to protect friendly personnel and units and to provide for individual self-defense, thereby ensuring that our forces can respond effectively to threats and are not made targets by reason of their rules of engagement.

(3) The proposed mission and objectives are most appropriate for U.S. Armed Forces, and the forces proposed for deployment are necessary and sufficient to accomplish the objectives of the proposed mission. Pursuant to U.N. Security Council Resolution 940, a multinational coalition has been assembled to use "all necessary means" to restore the democratic government to Haiti and to provide a stable and secure environment for the implementation of the Governors Island Accords. The deployment of U.S. Armed Forces is required to ensure that United States national security interests with respect to Haiti remain unchallenged and to underscore the reliability of U.S. and UN commitments.

This crisis affects the interests of the United States and other members of the world community alike, and thus warrants and has received the participation of responsible states in the coalition to redress the situation. The United States is playing a predominant role because it is the leading military power in the hemisphere, and accordingly, has the influence and military capability to lead such an operation. The coalition is made up of representatives from 25 member nations, including the United States. During the initial phase of the operation, the force will be of sufficient size to overwhelm any opposition that might arise despite the existence of the agreement. In the follow-on, transitional phase,

forces from other members of the coalition will assume increasingly important roles. At all times when U.S. forces are deployed in whatever phase, they will be equipped, commanded, and empowered so as to ensure their own protection.

(4) Clear objectives for the deployment have been established. These limited objectives are: to facilitate the departure of the military leadership, the prompt return of the legitimately elected President and the restoration of the legitimate authorities of the Government of Haiti. We will assist the Haitian government in creating a civilian-controlled security force. We will also ensure the protection of U.S. citizens and U.S. facilities.

(5) An exit strategy for ending the deployment has been identified. Our presence in Haiti will not be open-ended. After a period of months, the coalition will be replaced by a UN peacekeeping force (UNMIH). By that time, the bulk of U.S. forces will have departed. Some U.S. forces will make up a portion of the UNMIH and will be present in Haiti for the duration of the U.N. mission. The entire U.N. mission will withdraw from Haiti after elections are held next year and a new Haitian Government takes office in early 1996, consistent with U.N. Security Council Resolution 940.

(6) The financial costs of the deployment are estimated to be the following. A conservative, preliminary estimate of Department of Defense and Department of State incremental costs for U.S. military operations, U.S. support for the multinational coalition, and the follow-on U.N. peacekeeping operation is projected at $500–$600 million through February 1996. This covers potential costs to be incurred in FY 1994, FY 1995, and FY 1996. Final deployment-related costs could vary from this estimate depending on how operations proceed in the first few weeks, how fast civic order is restored, and when the operation is replaced by a U.N. peacekeeping operation. A preliminary estimate of U.S. nondeployment-related costs—migrant operations, sanctions enforcement, police training, and economic reconstruction—will be provided separately. The Congress will be provided more complete estimates as they become available.

Sincerely,

WILLIAM J. CLINTON

NOTE: Identical letters were sent to Thomas S. Foley, Speaker of the House of Representatives, and Albert Gore, Jr., President of the Senate. This letter was released by the Office of the Press Secretary on September 19.

Remarks Prior to a Breakfast With President Jimmy Carter, General Colin Powell, and Senator Sam Nunn
September 19, 1994

Good morning, ladies and gentlemen. Let me—before we sit for breakfast, let me just make a couple of points very briefly. First of all, our deepest thanks as a nation should go to President Carter, General Powell, and Senator Nunn. They have had about 4 hours' sleep in the last 2 or 3 nights. They have worked very hard, and they have, I think, made a major contribution toward helping us find a peaceful solution to the problem in Haiti.

I also want to say to you, I think that a significant measure of credit goes to the United States military forces for their preparation, their readiness, and their eminence. And finally, let me say that we have, this morning, the first peaceful introduction of our forces there to begin to carry out the mandate of the United Nations.

So it has been, so far, a good day, thanks in no small measure to the extraordinary labors of this delegation. I know that you join me in thanking them for all they've done.

We're going to have a press conference in just a minute, so there's no point in having two. [*Laughter*]

Thank you.

NOTE: The President spoke at 10:21 a.m. in the State Dining Room at the White House. A tape was not available for verification of the content of these remarks.

The President's News Conference With President Jimmy Carter, General Colin Powell, and Senator Sam Nunn on Haiti
September 19, 1994

President Clinton. Good morning. I'd like to begin by thanking President Carter, General Powell, and Senator Nunn for their extraordinary work in Haiti. They got in very early this morning; they have had hardly any sleep for the last 2 nights, as they have worked virtually around the clock. The peaceful solution they helped to work out is another major contribution in all their careers, which have been devoted to the pursuit of peace and democracy. They have done a great service to our country, as well as to the people of Haiti, the people in our hemisphere, and the efforts of the United Nations, and we owe them a great deal of gratitude. I also want to thank the men and women of our United States armed services, who are beginning their operations in Haiti even as we meet here today. Their preparation and pres-ence made a crucial difference in convincing the Haitian leaders to leave power.

In the end, two things led to the agreement to leave. The first was this delegation's appeal to the Haitians to do the right and honorable thing for their own people in accordance with the United Nations Security Council resolutions. The second was the clear imminence of military action by the United States.

This is a good agreement. It will further our goals in Haiti. General Cédras and the other leaders will leave power no later than October 15th. After 3 years and a series of broken promises, American steadfastness has given us the opportunity to restore Haiti's democratically elected government and President Aristide.

American troops are beginning to take up their positions in Haiti today, and they will be there to make sure that the leaders keep their word. The agreement means that our troops do not have to invade. They have entered Haiti peacefully today. It minimizes the risks to American forces and to our coalition partners.

But I want to emphasize that the situation in Haiti remains difficult, it remains uncertain. The mission still has risks. But clearly we are in a better position to work for peace in a peaceable way today than we were yesterday.

My first concern, and the most important one, obviously, is for the safety and security of our troops. General Shalikashvili and Lieutenant General Hugh Shelton, our commander in Haiti, have made it clear to all involved that the protection of American lives is our first order of business.

Let me repeat what I said last night and what I said on Thursday night: This mission will be limited in time and scope. It is clearly designed to provide a secure environment for the restoration of President Aristide and democracy, to begin the work of retraining the police and the military in a professional manner, and to facilitate a quick handoff to the United Nations mission so that the work of restoring democracy can be continued, the developmental aid can begin to flow, Haiti can be rebuilt, and in 1995 another free and fair election for President can be held.

I also have to say again that we remain ready to pursue our interests and our obligations in whatever way we have to. But we hope that good faith and reasonableness will prevail today and tomorrow and in the days ahead, so that this will not be another violated agreement that the United States has to impose and enforce. We believe that, because of the work of this delegation, we have a chance to achieve that kind of good faith and cooperation.

And I want to thank, again, President Carter, General Powell, and Senator Nunn and ask them each in turn to come and make an opening statement, and then we will be available for your questions.

[*At this point, President Carter praised the balanced use of military power and diplomacy, described the goals of the diplomatic mission, and expressed his appreciation for the President's support and the contributions of General Powell and Senator Nunn. General Powell thanked the President and expressed his satisfaction that with the administration's support and guidance, the* delegation's discussions with the Haitian leaders helped bring about a peaceful solution. Senator Nunn then thanked the President for his strong leadership, discussed the roles played by General Powell and President Carter, and stressed the importance of free and fair parliamentary elections to Haitian democracy.]

President Clinton. Terry [Terence Hunt, Associated Press].

Q. Mr. President, you accused the military leaders in Haiti of maintaining a reign of terror; you said that they were responsible for 3,000 deaths. Why did you accept an agreement that allows them to stay in Haiti and perhaps run for elected office there? And can you tell us, is President Aristide satisfied with this agreement?

President Clinton. Well, first of all, I'm not entirely sure that they will stay in Haiti, but that was not the charge of this mission. They only had about a day and a half to stay down there, and they worked for probably 21 or 22 hours during that time they were there. Their charge was to assure that they would leave power.

Secondly, I don't take back anything I say about what has happened there in the last 3 years and the absence of any effort by the authorities to stop it and sometimes some direct responsibility for it. But with regard to the amnesty provision, that was a part of the Governors Island Agreement. And we had always felt that we should follow through on the agreements to which we had all been a part and we had to demonstrate a willingness to do that.

I cannot answer all the questions that you have asked about what will happen in the future and what decisions people will make in the future and where they'll wind up living. I don't know the answers to all that. But I do believe that this agreement substantially furthers our objectives there and dramatically increases the chances of a peaceful transition of power, a peaceful restoration of democracy, a peaceful restoration of President Aristide. He will have to determine for himself what he thinks about it, but it won't be very long before he'll have the opportunity to be back in Haiti, governing as President. And it won't be very long before we'll have new parliamentary elections, which I think everyone on all sides in Haiti believes is a very important thing.

Q. Mr. President, granted that victory has 1,000 fathers and defeat is an orphan, but do you intend to make as a pattern using military action without the consent of Congress or the approval of the American people?

President Clinton. Well, those are two different things. And with regard to the consent of Congress, I think that every President and all my predecessors in both parties have clearly maintained that they did not require, by Constitution, did not have to have congressional approval for every kind of military action.

I obviously think the bigger and more prolonged the action, the better it is to have congressional approval. If you look at the pattern of my two immediate predecessors, there was congressional approval sought in the Desert Storm operation where there was a 5½ month buildup and a half a million troops facing hundreds of thousands of troops on the other side. There was not congressional approval in advance of the actions in Panama and Grenada. So I think that we will have to take that on a case-by-case basis.

In terms of popular approval, the American people, probably wisely, are almost always against any kind of military action when they first hear about it, unless our people have been directly attacked. And they have historically felt that way. And obviously at the end of the cold war, they may be more inclined to feel that way.

The job of the President is to try to do what is right, particularly in matters affecting our long-term security interests. And unfortunately, not all of the decisions that are right can be popular. So I don't believe that the President, that I or any other President, could conduct foreign policy by a public opinion poll, and I would hope the American people would not wish me to.

Q. You would grant that you would have to have the support of the people in the long run for any engagement——

President Clinton. Any sustained endeavor involving our military forces requires the support of the people over the long run. We have learned that mostly in good ways and sometimes in sad ways in our country's history.

Q. Mr. President, you and your aides said repeatedly last week there was only one thing about which you would be willing to discuss anything with the leaders in Haiti and that was the modalities, as it was repeatedly called, of

their departure. As President Carter has made clear today, it became necessary for him to conduct a somewhat more extensive negotiation. And I just wanted to ask you, sir, what prompted you, what made you decide to change your mind and go along with that?

President Clinton. Well, I think if you look at this agreement, the details of the agreement are consistent with the modalities of their leaving power. What I told President Carter and General Powell and Senator Nunn was—and I think we talked three times each before they went—was that I basically did not care what was discussed as long as there was no attempt to change the timetable of the administration for action or to derail the ultimate possibility of action.

And if the objective of their departure from power was achieved, then, if other things had to be discussed, I did not object to that. In fact, it was obvious to me that one—let me just back off and say, one of the things that will determine whether this United Nations sanction mission, that is, to restore democracy, is successful and one of the things that will determine whether we can do it with a minimum of risk to our people is whether there can be an orderly transfer of power and an orderly retraining of police and military forces, rather than a total collapse of the structures of Haitian society which could cause a much more violent set of activities, perhaps involving us only peripherally. They have avoided that, I think, by the terms of this agreement if it can be implemented, which of course is what I hope will happen.

Q. Did President Carter say something to you that made you decide that it would be well to allow him to conduct a broader discussion? Was that his suggestion, sir?

President Clinton. No, we never—what we discussed, what I said to him was—and I said to each of the three gentlemen—was, "I want you to pledge to me, number one, that the objective is removing them from power; number two, that there will be no attempt to change the timetable that I will set unilaterally for doing so forcibly if we have to; and number three, that there'll be no attempt to derail the possibility of taking that kind of action if it becomes necessary. Beyond that, whatever you feel you should discuss, feel free to discuss it within those three criteria."

Q. President Clinton, there have been a lot of reports that you and President Carter have had some tension in the past, and I wondered if you might comment on that. And in particular, was there a point at which President Carter wanted to go to Haiti and the administration was not ready for him to go at that time? And was there a point when you wanted him to come home and he wasn't ready to come home? And if President Carter would comment on that as well, I'd appreciate it.

President Clinton. The answer to the first question is no, there was not a point where he wanted to go and I didn't want him to go. The answer to the second question is maybe, but not for the reason you think. And let me try to answer what I mean by that.

President Carter and I have discussed Haiti, I think beginning before I became President, on a regular and repeated basis. And he has a deep interest there because, among other things, he's not only been there many times but he and his group monitored the election which resulted in President Aristide's election.

I have also discussed Haiti repeatedly with General Powell, both when he was the Chairman of the Joint Chiefs of Staff in my tenure and after he left office. I have called him at least two and maybe more occasions and said, "I'm tearing my hair out about this problem; what do you think? What about this, that, or the other thing?" And Senator Nunn and I have discussed it before.

When President Carter called me and told me that he had heard from General Cédras, we began to talk about this and about the prospect of a mission. We talked about General Powell, Senator Nunn. I picked up the phone, and I called General Powell and Senator Nunn to find out if they would be willing go there. It wasn't the first item on their list of what they had planned to do last weekend, but they were open. A number of other calls ensued. We had to determine (a) that they would be received and (b) that there was a serious chance of at least affecting this agreement, because there was no agreement in advance by them, by the Haitians, to leave. Once all that was worked out, we decided it was quite a good thing and certainly worth the risk for them to go. Any kind of mission like this is full of risk.

In answer to your second question, there was never a point when I wanted him to leave in the sense that I wanted him to stop talking.

There was a point last evening, as you know, when I became worried that we needed to get them out of there because of the timetable of the mission. In other words, I was just beginning—was concerned about—I wanted them to be safe, I wanted them to be secure, I wanted them to be out of Haiti in a timely fashion. That is the only issue about their leaving.

And the last time we talked, he said, "Well, we're almost there. We've about got this nailed. We're going over to the Presidential Palace." And I said, "Okay, you have 30 more minutes, and then I will have to order you to leave," because I was worried about their personal security. There was no political debate at all. They were making progress. But the time was running out on the hourglass.

Q. Mr. President, President Carter was quoted today as saying that the launching of the first wave came while they were still negotiating peace. And he said that that was very disturbing to us and to them, to the Haitian leaders with whom he was negotiating. Could I ask both of you to comment on that, and whether you felt that the launching of the 82d Airborne was, in fact, interfering with their attempts to negotiate?

President Clinton. I think I'll let him answer that.

Q. Could we ask you to comment?

President Clinton. Yes, I'll be happy to, but I'll let him answer it first.

President Carter. The key to our success, to the extent it is successful, was the inexorability of the entry of the forces into Haiti. And we spent the first hours of discussion with the military leaders to convince them that this was going to happen, it would be with an overwhelming capability, and that the schedule was set and that we had no intention or authority to change the schedule. And it was that inevitability that was a major factor in that decision.

Another one, I should hasten to say, was their quandary about what to do that was right and honorable. Haiti, I think, is perhaps one of the proudest nations I have ever seen because of their long history and because of the turmoil in which they have often lived. And it was very difficult for Haitian military commanders to accept the proposition that foreign forces could come on their soil without their fighting. But we all worked to convince them that this was the best thing to do for their country and for their people.

Now, we recognized the difficulty of this. And we were down to the last stages of negotiating which involved the last date that the military leaders could stay in office. At that time, General Biamby received a report from Fort Bragg, he told us, that the initial operation had already commenced. And they were on the verge of saying, "We will not negotiate anymore; this may be a trick just to keep us occupied, all of us military commanders in the same room while the invasion takes place." We obviously assured them this was not the case. And the thing was about to break down. They finally decided, let's go over to the President's house, the Presidential Palace. President Jonassaint, we have been led to believe—and I believed it ahead of time—was a figurehead. This proved to be absolutely incorrect. When we got to President Jonassaint's office with his ministers sitting in front of him and the commanders of the military in front of him and I sitting next to him and Senator Nunn and General Powell there, he said—very quickly to summarize my answer—"We will take peace instead of war; I will sign this agreement." All of his people in the room disagreed. One of his ministers, a minister of defense, said, "I resign tomorrow." The others belabored the point. But there was no doubt that his decision was what brought about the consummation of the agreement. All the time through this, we were consulting fervently and constantly with President Clinton.

So the inexorability of the force coming in made it possible. There was a setback when we found, to my surprise, that the initial stages had begun; as soon as President Clinton knew that President Jonassaint and I had reached an agreement, so as far as I know, the planes reversed their course.

Q. Mr. President, can you comment on that?

President Clinton. Yes.

Q. Did he ask you why they had taken off and asked you to turn them back?

President Clinton. No. No, when they went, I told them that we needed to conclude the negotiations by 12 o'clock Sunday. Then I said, but they could clearly stay until 3. And then the thing kept getting put back. They were very dogged; they didn't want to give up.

I frankly had come to the conclusion that we were not going to reach an agreement. What I—and let me say, there had never been a plan to have them talking while American planes were flying. That was never a plan. The infer-

ence—because I wanted them out of there, I wanted them safe. And I think President Carter has made it clear what—to the extent that it was disrupted, it was because they thought the whole thing maybe had been pointless, a ruse.

To the extent it was helpful, it was the final evidence that President Jonassaint needed to push the agreements. But it was one of those things that happened. It was not a thing that we calculated, because I would never have put the lives of these three men in any kind of jeopardy. They were just determined to stay until the last moment. And they had, literally, when they reached that agreement, they had 30 more minutes before I—I told President Carter, I said, "This is uncomfortable for me; we've been friends a long time; I'm going to have to order you out of there in 30 more minutes. You have got to get out." They had to get out before dark. So they worked it out.

Press Secretary Myers. Last question.

Q. Mr. President, there still is this very sensitive issue, as you well know, involving the so-called status of exile for Generals Biamby and Cédras. They maintain that there is no commitment, no need, and that they don't want to leave their country forever. Now, a senior administration official last night suggested that while there is no formal commitment, the U.S. anticipates that they will leave once President Aristide returns and they do receive amnesty. What exactly do you believe will happen?

President Clinton. First, let me say that our objective is twofold as a part of restoring democracy and President Aristide. The first was to have them step down. The second is to retrain and to help professionalize the army and the police forces so that they can never be either a participant in or a bystander while gross human rights violations occur, and so that they can help to secure the country and preserve order.

It has been our feeling that that was the most important thing. And, therefore, that was not an issue that I was ready to let this mission founder on, as long as they could achieve that. I think they should leave, and I think they probably will leave at some point. But that is something that still has to be worked out and something that subsequent actions by all the actors in the Haitian drama will have to be heavily relied upon.

General Powell made a comment to me—he might want to comment about this because

I think it's very important that we not let this issue cloud the enormity of what has occurred and the practicality of what is likely to occur.

General Powell. I'd just like to add to that, that I am very pleased this morning—the thing I was looking for, would General Cédras be cooperating with General Shelton for real—signing an agreement last night was one thing, but what would happen today—he is cooperating. And so the transition of power has begun. And sometime over the next month or so, either as a result of parliamentary action or the October 15th date arriving, General Cédras will step down, having done what I believe is the right and honorable thing in these circumstances.

It will remain an issue for President Aristide and General Cédras and others to consider where he should go or what he should do. But I don't think we need to spend a lot of time on that at this point. Let that flow out, and we will see what happens. He is stepping down from power, which I think is the important point.

Q. Last week you told America that these people treated their own people shamefully, that they've massacred them and raped them and tortured them and did all these frightful things. And now, all of a sudden, we've appealed to their military honor. I wonder how you detected that, and they're our partners and presumably our friends. It's a little abrupt——

President Clinton. No, that's not accurate. But we did say—I did say last week that they had one last chance to effect a peaceful transfer of power. And you know, when you've got a country deeply divided, I mean, think of the things which have happened in South Africa when reconciliation was possible.

Remember what President Aristide himself said when he came here—after I spoke—the next day—he said, "We have to say no to violence, no to vengeance, yes to reconciliation." What this delegation did, and all this delegation did, was to give these people the chance to do something that is, to use their words, was right and honorable and to do it in a peaceful way and to have a peaceful transfer of power. And I think that was an appropriate thing to do. In terms of the amnesty issue, I would remind you that was an issue raised and agreed to by all the parties in Governors Island. So that is something that has been on the board for quite a long while now.

Thank you very much.

NOTE: The President's 70th news conference began at 12:02 p.m. in the East Room at the White House.

Message to the Congress Transmitting the Jamaica-United States Investment Treaty
September 19, 1994

To the Senate of the United States:

With a view to receiving the advice and consent of the Senate to ratification, I transmit herewith the Treaty Between the United States of America and Jamaica Concerning the Reciprocal Encouragement and Protection of Investment, with Annex and Protocol, signed at Washington on February 4, 1994. Also transmitted for the information of the Senate is the report of the Department of State with respect to this Treaty.

This bilateral investment Treaty with Jamaica is the second such Treaty between the United States and a member of the Caribbean Community (CARICOM). This Treaty will protect U.S. investors and assist Jamaica in its efforts to develop its economy by creating conditions more favorable for U.S. private investment and thus strengthening the development of the private sector.

The Treaty is fully consistent with U.S. policy toward international and domestic investment. A specific tenet of U.S. policy, reflected in this Treaty, is that U.S. investment abroad and foreign investment in the United States should receive national treatment. Under this Treaty, the Parties also agree to international law standards for expropriation and compensation for expropriation; free transfer of funds associated with investments; freedom of investments from performance requirements; fair, equitable and most-favored-nation treatment; and the investor or investment's freedom to choose to resolve disputes with the host government through international arbitration.

I recommend that the Senate consider this Treaty as soon as possible, and give its advice and consent to ratification of the Treaty, with Annex and Protocol, at an early date.

WILLIAM J. CLINTON

The White House,
September 19, 1994.

Appointment for the President's Committee on the Arts and the Humanities
September 19, 1994

The President today announced he is revitalizing the President's Committee on the Arts and the Humanities and intends to name Dr. John Brademas to chair the Committee. The President also announced his intention to name 32 private citizens to serve as members of the Committee, and he announced that First Lady Hillary Rodham Clinton will serve as Honorary Chair.

In making these appointments the President said, "The Federal, State, and local governments together provide only a small percentage of the support essential to our cultural life. These appointments underscore the vital partnership between the government and the private citizens who do so much to enrich and preserve the arts and humanities in our country. I am pleased that John Brademas, who has been a vigorous champion of learning and culture both in Congress and as a university president, has agreed to chair the Committee. At a time when our society faces new and profound challenges, when we are losing so many of our children, and when so many people feel insecure in the face of change, the arts and the humanities are fundamental to our lives as individuals and as a nation."

NOTE: The following individuals were appointed to the Committee: Peggy Cooper Cafritz, vice chair; Cynthia Perrin Schneider, vice chair; Terry Semel, vice chair; Susan Barnes-Gelt; Lerone Bennett, Jr.; Madeleine Harris Berman; Curt Bradbury; John H. Bryan; Hilario Candela; Anne Cox Chambers; Margaret Corbett Daley; Everett Fly; David P. Gardner; Harvey Golub; Richard S. Gurin; Irene Y. Hirano; David Henry Hwang; William Ivey; Quincy Jones; Robert Menschel; Rita Moreno; Jaroslav Pelikan; Anthony Podesta; Phyllis Rosen; Ann Sheffer; Isaac Stern; Dave Warren; Shirley Wilhite; Harold Williams; Emily Malino; and Timothy Wirth. Biographies of the appointees were made available by the Office of the Press Secretary.

Nomination for a United States Court of Appeals Judge
September 19, 1994

The President today nominated Sandra L. Lynch to serve on the U.S. Court of Appeals for the First Circuit.

"Sandra Lynch has an extraordinary record of dedication, excellence, and achievement in the legal profession and in public service," the President said today.

NOTE: A biography of the nominee was made available by the Office of the Press Secretary.

Remarks Prior to a Meeting With Congressional Leaders
September 20, 1994

Good morning to all of you, and welcome. In just a moment Secretary Perry and General Shalikashvili will brief you on the status as of this morning of Operation Uphold Democracy and the situation in Haiti as we see it unfolding.

But before they begin, I'd like to touch on just a few points. This is a very different and a much better day than it would have been had we not been able to successfully combine the credible threat of force with diplomacy. I want to thank President Carter, General Powell, and Senator Nunn again for their mission to Haiti and for their work in securing an agreement that will permit the peaceful departure of the military leaders.

Our troops have already entered Haiti peacefully. Under the command of Lieutenant General Hugh Shelton, our troops are working with full cooperation with the Haitian military. We must be prepared for the risks that remain to the troops, but we should recognize that we are in a much stronger and safer position to achieve our goals in Haiti today. The de facto leaders are leaving power, and the democratically elected government will be restored.

I want to emphasize that, in a matter of months, the United States troops will hand over to the United Nations the responsibility for completing this mission and for maintaining basic security. A much smaller contingent of United States forces would take part in the United Nations mission which will end after the next elections in Haiti in 1995.

I was gratified by the action of the House of Representatives yesterday, and I hope the Senate will follow in providing its support today. It's important, I think, that we also keep this in proper context. We have much other important business to do in the relatively small number of days that remain with the Congress.

First, we have to continue to meet the challenges of the global economy. I hope that you will pass GATT. It is the largest world trade agreement in history. It will provide a global tax cut of $740 billion, reducing tariffs worldwide by more than a third. It means more jobs and growth and higher incomes for ordinary Americans. GATT was started under President Reagan, continued under President Bush, completed under our administration. It has been a bipartisan effort all the way, and I hope it can be completed in a speedy and bipartisan fashion this year.

I also would urge you, as we reform the global economy, to take these last few days to reform the way we do business here in Washington. That means passing campaign finance reform, lobby reform, making laws that now apply to the private sector apply also to Congress. The American people clearly want these actions, and they deserve them. And again, I believe they want them on a completely nonpartisan or bipartisan basis.

Lastly, let me say I know that Senator Mitchell, in rapidly accelerating his aging process, had further meetings yesterday on health care reform, and I look forward to hearing a progress report from him on that, and I know that all of you do, too.

Now I'd like to recognize Secretary Perry and General Shalikashvili. Let me say, General Shalikashvili has to go back to the Pentagon; Secretary Perry does, too. So we can't take any questions here this morning, but he will be in the Briefing Room soon.

NOTE: The President spoke at 10:29 a.m. in the Cabinet Room at the White House.

Remarks Announcing the Report on Customer Service Standards
September 20, 1994

Ladies and gentlemen, I want to thank all of you for being here. Under Secretary Frank Newman and all those who were on the subcommittee on customer service to the President's Management Council, in particular, I thank you for your work.

Today we are releasing a report that I think is literally unique in the annals of the Federal Government. It is called "Putting Customers First: Standards for Serving the American People." It contains specific new commitments for more than 100 agencies to improve the way Government serves the American people.

The Vice President released a report of the National Performance Review a year ago this month. It included dozens of extremely important reforms that have already had a profound impact on our Federal deficit, on funding the crime bill, and on making Washington work better for ordinary citizens. Of all the recommendations it contained, however, one I chose to enact immediately by Executive order was designed to force the Government to respect the needs of ordinary citizens again by treating them as valued customers. This report describes what has taken place as a result of that order.

The order called for a fundamental change in Government. It set forth a requirement that Government services shall be equal to the best in business. And it commanded the agencies, for the first time, to set and publish specific standards for the services they provide to the public. Over the past two decades, there has been a renaissance in quality and customer service in corporate America. There's no reason these same principles cannot apply with equal force in our Government. There's no reason for an application to Government agencies to take months or for a phone call to go unanswered.

We face many great challenges as a nation, and we can and will meet them. But in order for Government to do the big things well and in partnership with the American people, it must do the small things better as well, in ways that increase the confidence of the American people. It must earn that confidence in many ways, one customer at a time. This report will help us to do that.

Better customer service will also save us money. For example, Veterans Affairs is already redesigning the way it handles benefit applications so that veterans get faster and more personalized service. The new system takes 8 steps instead of 25, requires fewer people, costs 20 percent less. When the IRS stopped generating puzzling form letters in response to taxpayers' questions and—[*laughter*]—I used to be one of those taxpayers that got those published—and

let their employees write and sign sensible answers instead, believe it or not, the cost decreased by $600,000. That's the equivalent of what 100 average families pay in Federal taxes each year.

These examples demonstrate a larger truth. That is, employees of the Federal Government have become partners in the search for better service. They also are fed up with the redtape. They, too, want to serve customers better, and the National Performance Review has empowered them to do so.

Let me give you another example closer to home. This report recounts the story of Jackie Collins-Miller, the branch manager of Baltimore's Social Security office. Not long ago, she got a call from a woman who had received someone else's check by mistake. Jackie Collins-Miller jumped in her car, picked up the check, mailed it to the rightful owner, and called a few days later to make sure it had arrived. That's service that rivals anything you'll see in the private sector.

This story reflects the work that has been done throughout the Government, simply to listen to the people who pay the bills and are supposed to receive the service. When taxpayers said they wanted forms and instructions that were easier to understand, the IRS listened. When businesses going through customs in Miami said they wanted to get in and out quicker, the U.S. Customs listened. When veterans said they wanted more personal attention, Veterans Affairs listened.

This report contains more than 1,500 new standards for customer service that reflect the direct input of the American people. The standards are promises and commitments. In the days ahead, we'll measure our performance against these standards and report back to our customers.

The principles represent a major step toward the goal that Congress set in the Government Performance and Results Act to promote a new focus on results, service quality, and customer satisfaction in Government. And these standards help to fulfill the promise that the Vice President and I made a long time ago, to put the American people first again.

Again, this report was not written to sit on a shelf; it's meant to be read, used, and followed. Its written and organized to be customer-friendly, with chapters labeled Business, Veterans, and so on. Its contents are arranged not by agency or department but by customer group. It's organized for those who use Government, not for those in Government.

Finally, if you're wondering where the Cabinet Secretaries are and the agency heads are while I am bragging about what they're doing, they're not hiding in a bunker and hoping this will go away. [*Laughter*] Instead, they're busy. We have declared this day Customer Service Day all over the United States. And our Cabinet Secretaries are out there serving their customers. In Chicago, the Veterans Affairs Secretary, Jesse Brown, will help veterans file benefit claims in the regional office. In New Britain, Connecticut, HUD Secretary Henry Cisneros will help renovate the home of Steven and Rachel Rival, recent recipients of a loan which allows people with low or moderate incomes to renovate distressed property. Altogether, there are 24 Customer Service Day activities taking place across our Nation today.

Let me close by thanking the Vice President for the extraordinary work that he and the National Performance Review folks have done since

we embarked upon this task. Most people gave our efforts to reduce and improve Government service little chance to succeed. But he has proven them wrong; all of you have proven them wrong; events have proven them wrong. We just have to keep doing what we've been doing.

I want to thank him for the job he's done in general, and specifically for this report, which he will discuss in a moment.

I said when we introduced the NPR on March 3d, 1933—1993, I'm not that old—[*laughter*]—although I feel that old today—[*laughter*]—and I quote, "We must change the way Government does business and make the taxpayer the valued customer and the boss again." We have made a very strong beginning. And with the energy and dedication of the people in this room and the leadership of the Vice President, we intend to keep on doing that as long as we are here.

Thank you very much.

NOTE: The President spoke at 11:50 a.m. in the Roosevelt Room at the White House.

Message to the Congress Reporting on the National Emergency With Respect to Angola
September 20, 1994

To the Congress of the United States:

I hereby report to the Congress on the developments since March 26, 1994, concerning the national emergency with respect to Angola that was declared in Executive Order No. 12865 of September 26, 1993. This report is submitted pursuant to section 401(c) of the National Emergencies Act, 50 U.S.C. 1641(c), and section 204(c) of the International Emergency Economic Powers Act, 50 U.S.C. 1703(c).

On September 26, 1993, I declared a national emergency with respect to Angola, invoking the authority, *inter alia*, of the International Emergency Economic Powers Act (50 U.S.C. 1701 *et seq.*) and the United Nations Participation Act of 1945 (22 U.S.C. 287c). Consistent with United Nations Security Council Resolution No. 864, dated September 15, 1993, the order prohibited the sale or supply by U.S. persons or from the United States, or using U.S.-registered vessels or aircraft, of arms and related materiel

of all types, including weapons and ammunition, military vehicles, equipment and spare parts, and petroleum and petroleum products to the territory of Angola other than through designated points of entry. The order also prohibited such sale or supply to the National Union for the Total Independence of Angola ("UNITA"). United States persons are prohibited from activities that promote or are calculated to promote such sales or supplies, or from attempted violations, or from evasion or avoidance or transactions that have the purpose of evasion or avoidance, of the stated prohibitions. The order authorized the Secretary of the Treasury, in consultation with the Secretary of State, to take such actions, including the promulgation of rules and regulations, as might be necessary to carry out the purposes of the order.

1. On December 10, 1993, the Treasury Department's Office of Foreign Assets Control ("FAC") issued the UNITA (Angola) Sanctions

Regulations (the "Regulations") (58 *Fed. Reg.* 64904) to implement the President's declaration of a national emergency and imposition of sanctions against Angola (UNITA). There have been no amendments to the Regulations since my report of April 12, 1994.

The Regulations prohibit the sale or supply by U.S. persons or from the United States, or using U.S.-registered vessels or aircraft, of arms and related materiel of all types, including weapons and ammunition, military vehicles, equipment and spare parts, and petroleum and petroleum products to UNITA or to the territory of Angola other than through designated points. United States persons are also prohibited from activities that promote or are calculated to promote such sales or supplies to UNITA or Angola, or from any transaction by any U.S. persons that evades or avoids, or has the purpose of evading or avoiding, or attempts to violate, any of the prohibitions set forth in the Executive order. Also prohibited are transactions by U.S. persons, or involving the use of U.S.-registered vessels or aircraft relating to transportation to Angola or UNITA of goods the exportation of which is prohibited.

The Government of Angola has designated the following points of entry as points in Angola to which the articles otherwise prohibited by the Regulations may be shipped: *Airports*: Luanda and Katumbela, Benguela Province; *Ports*: Luanda and Lobito, Benguela Province; and Namibe, Namibe Province; and *Entry Points*: Malongo, Cabinda Province. Although no specific license is required by the Department of the Treasury for shipments to these designated points of entry (unless the item is destined for UNITA), any such exports remain subject to the licensing requirements of the Departments of State and/or Commerce.

2. FAC has worked closely with the U.S. financial community to assure a heightened awareness of the sanctions against UNITA—through the dissemination of publications, seminars, and notices to electronic bulletin boards. This educational effort has resulted in frequent calls from banks to assure that they are not routing funds in violation of these prohibitions. United States exporters have also been notified of the sanctions through a variety of media, including special fliers and computer bulletin board information initiated by FAC and posted through the Department of Commerce and the Government Printing Office. There have been no license applications under the program.

3. The expenses incurred by the Federal Government in the 6-month period from March 26, 1994, through September 25, 1994, that are directly attributable to the exercise of powers and authorities conferred by the declaration of a national emergency with respect to Angola (UNITA) are reported at about $75,000, most of which represents wage and salary costs for Federal personnel. Personnel costs were largely centered in the Department of the Treasury (particularly in the Office of Foreign Assets Control, the U.S. Customs Service, the Office of the Under Secretary for Enforcement, and the Office of the General Counsel) and the Department of State (particularly the Office of Southern African Affairs).

I will continue to report periodically to the Congress on significant developments, pursuant to 50 U.S.C. 1703(c).

WILLIAM J. CLINTON

The White House,
September 20, 1994.

Message to the Congress Transmitting the China-United States Fishery Agreement
September 20, 1994

To the Congress of the United States:

In accordance with the Magnuson Fishery Conservation and Management Act of 1976 (16 U.S.C. 1801 *et seq.*), I transmit herewith an Agreement between the Government of the United States of America and the Government of the People's Republic of China Extending the Agreement of July 23, 1985, Concerning Fisheries Off the Coasts of the United States, as extended and amended. The Agreement, which was effected by an exchange of notes at Beijing on March 4 and May 31, 1994, extends the 1985 Agreement to July 1, 1996.

In light of the importance of our fisheries relationship with the People's Republic of China, I urge that the Congress give favorable consideration to this Agreement at an early date.

WILLIAM J. CLINTON

The White House,
September 20, 1994.

Nomination for a United States District Court Judge
September 20, 1994

The President today nominated Kathleen M. O'Malley to serve on the U.S. District Court for the Northern District of Ohio.

"I am proud to nominate Kate O'Malley to the Federal bench," the President said. "She has an outstanding record of excellence and achievement in the legal profession and in public service."

NOTE: A biography of the nominee was made available by the Office of the Press Secretary.

Remarks Honoring Representative Bob Michel
September 20, 1994

Thank you very much, ladies and gentlemen. Please be seated; relax. Dr. Brazil, Speaker Foley, Congressman Gingrich, distinguished Members of the House, Senator Dole and Senator Mitchell are here or will be, and other Members of the Congress who are here, to Bob and Corinne and ladies and gentlemen.

It occurs to me that after 19 terms in the House, 13 years as minority leader, it's a real shame for a man with Bob Michel's distinguished reputation to have it destroyed at the end by having a Democratic President brag on him. [*Laughter*] I asked him if he didn't have some really crazy and sort of kooky-sounding criticism I could lob so you would all stand up and cheer for him, but he said I could just say what was on my mind and heart.

You know, you never know what's on a person's mind and heart. I understand we now have the sayings of Mr. Michel in a little red book, which will doubtless get ideologically vetted. I expect Mr. Gingrich to have it reprinted in blue within a day or two. [*Laughter*]

I want to say that it's a real honor for me to be here tonight. And I say in all sincerity, I'm going to miss Bob Michel. I know in theory he's reached an age where he's earned retirement, but I have found him remarkably young and vigorous. He's as addicted to golf as I am. He's survived at least one car wreck since I've been here and a lot of other wrecks in the Congress that could do more damage to you inside. He still sings like he did 30 years ago. I leave it to your own interpretation what that means—[*laughter*]—beautifully, as you know. He's spent his whole life serving this country, from being a genuine hero when he wore our uniform in the Second World War to being a genuine patriot in the United States Congress.

It was a great honor for me just a few days ago to exercise one of the few things I can do without the approval of Congress when I awarded him the Presidential Medal of Freedom. I shouldn't have said that. I saw Congressman Gingrich raise his eyebrow. He's going to make a note, "Surely we can restrain his discretion there." [*Laughter*]

You know, when I was a kid growing up in Arkansas, even there, even there in the fifties, the saying about how will it play in Peoria was alive and well. And after I got to—and, of course, I married a woman from Illinois, so I used to hear it about every 3 days when I was about to do something my wife thought was nonsensical. But after I got to know Bob Michel, I understood the genesis of the saying, because in a very real sense he represents in my view the heart of America, the values of America, and the sense of fairness of America.

I enjoyed working with him when we fought against enormous odds with most of you here to pass the NAFTA agreement. I enjoyed it when we were on opposite sides and he thought I was absolutely wrong but was still fair and decent. I even enjoyed it when we were on opposite sides when he was sympathetic with what I was trying to do but couldn't quite get there. Those are three things that often happen in the course of people's relationships in this town. And I can tell all of you who come from his hometown and his home district that he is just as highly thought of here as he is there. And we will miss him.

We had a joint leadership meeting this morning, and we talked about, obviously, the issue of Haiti and then what we would do between now and the end of the Congress. By the time the meeting was over, I can tell you this: I wasn't sure where everybody in the room was on every outstanding issue, but I knew where he was on the issues that really counted. And I think we'll always know where he is, trying to do what's right for this country in a way that is right for this country.

And let me just close with that. This is a time in which the negative often outweighs the positive, in which people are so overwhelmed with things that are discouraging, from the news to the political campaigns, that very often all half-full glasses are seen as half-empty. I think in the end, the thing that enabled Bob Michel to succeed as the leader of his party in Congress, to keep his good humor, to keep his character, to keep his integrity, and to earn the respect of those who are in different camps on different issues and even in different parties was the fact that he believed that America was a place where the glass should always be half-full and where we could do the right thing, move forward to a brighter tomorrow, and fulfill our obligations in an atmosphere of mutual respect even when we differ.

It is the genius which has taken the theory of the Constitution and made it real in the life of this country. And it's why we're still around here after more than 200 years, because of people like Bob Michel.

Thank you very much.

NOTE: The President spoke at 8:13 p.m. at the Grand Hyatt Hotel. In his remarks, he referred to John Brazil, president, Bradley University, and sponsor of the dinner; and Corinne Michel, wife of Representative Michel.

Remarks to the President's Committee on the Arts and the Humanities
September 21, 1994

Thank you very much, the First Lady and my old friend John Brademas, and to all of you who have agreed to serve and your friends and supporters who are here. I thank you for coming.

Before I make the remarks that I want to make to you, I believe, in view of the events of the last few days and particularly the events of the last 24 hours, I should make a short statement about the situation in Haiti.

The deployment of our forces there is now going quite well. As a result of the agreement we have reached last weekend, we now have 8,500 United States troops who have entered Haiti peacefully without any resistance. The multinational force, which was enhanced today

by the decision of Australia to join, will soon be in a position to carry out its overriding mission, to ensure the transfer of power from the de facto military leaders to the democratically elected government of Haiti by October 15th.

I must also tell you how strongly we condemned yesterday's police violence there. Such conduct cannot and will not be tolerated. General Shelton, our commander on the ground, has met with the Haitian military and police officials today and made clear our policy to them.

During this transition period, the Haitian military will carry out basic police functions. Our Armed Forces cannot and will not become Haiti's police force. But we can work to see that the Haitian military and police operate in a responsible and professional manner. Today we are deploying on schedule 1,000 United States military police who will monitor the Haitian police and by their own presence help to deter violence. In the days ahead we will reintroduce into Haiti human rights monitors who were expelled several weeks ago and bring in police monitors as part of the multinational force.

Today is only the second day of this mission. The situation in Haiti will not change immediately. But today is better than yesterday, and yesterday was better than the day before. We will keep going. We will make steady progress. We will restore democracy.

As we move toward the 15th of October, we will also work to moderate the conduct of Haitian security forces without assuming the responsibilities. Then after the democratic government returns to power, the coalition will help it to devise a long-term plan of police and military reform, including retraining people so that they can perform to their fullest capabilities in an appropriate manner for a democratic society.

We went into Haiti to help stop the senseless, tragic terror that has plagued the nation since the democratically elected government was forced from power. The habits of violence will not be shed overnight. But during the coming weeks, we will work to help stop the violence and to begin the process of reconciliation.

I thank the American people for their understanding and increasing support for this endeavor. And again, let me say my special word of appreciation to our troops there and to their families and all those who have supported them. [*Applause*] Thank you.

Now let me thank you all again, all of you who've agreed to serve on the President's Committee on the Arts and Humanities, to underscore the vital partnership that must exist between your Government and the private citizens who do the work of the arts and humanities in our Nation. I want to thank the First Lady for agreeing to be the Honorary Chair, although this is a job she wanted, unlike some of those I've asked her to take on. [*Laughter*] You couldn't have a much more appreciative or informed friend.

I am also very, very pleased that John Brademas has agreed to serve as the Chairman. I have known him for many years since his distinguished career in the United States Congress and through his brilliant presidency of

New York University. I think he is one of our Nation's most outstanding citizens and will certainly be one of the most eloquent advocates imaginable for the cause you are here to further. He also happens to have been an original cosponsor of the bill that created the National Endowment for the Arts and Humanities, and he wrote the bill that established the Institute of Museum Services. He also promised to give me free congressional lobbying advice on the side in return for this appointment. [*Laughter*]

I have charged the President's Committee with advancing public understanding of the arts and humanities, which is so important to our democracy, and to establish new partnerships between the Federal agencies and the private sector. As a sign of our commitment to the arts and humanities today, we have here with us members of the Cabinet and the administration, including Secretary Riley, Sheldon Hackney, Jane Alexander, Joe Duffy, and a number of other Government officials.

I appointed, as all of you can see, an extraordinary group of Americans to this Committee—artists, scholars, writers, thinkers, leaders in the corporate world and the philanthropic community, committed citizens, activists recognized in their communities—people who represent outstanding achievement and a commitment to the cultural life of our Nation, a commitment to keep it alive and to make it more accessible.

By this time next year, I want you to deliver to me a report on the progress we're making in furthering America's cultural life. For 200 years the arts and humanities have helped to bridge American differences, learned to appreciate differences—they helped Americans to learn to appreciate differences, one from another, and to build strong and vibrant institutions across our country. You must help us explore ways to do this better.

The most disturbing thing to me about American life today is not the problems we have, although we have problems aplenty; it is the lack of unity among Americans and the lack of optimism we feel in dealing with those problems.

Just a couple of weeks ago, a distinguished international panel of economists said that the United States was the most productive country in the world. They said that for the first time in almost a decade because of the remarkable resurgence of our economy, because of the number of jobs we're creating, because we accounted for almost all the job growth and three-quarters of the economic growth in the seven great industrial nations of the world in the last year and a half, and because we are taking on a lot of our biggest challenges—bringing our Government deficit down 3 years in a row for the first time since Mr. Truman was President, the only country of all the advanced economies to do that. And yet, so many Americans still feel that we're kind of adrift and falling apart from one another.

Maybe even more important as you look toward the 21st century, isn't it interesting that in the last year and a half the South Africans wanted us to spend $35 million and send our best people to South Africa to work on making that election a success? The Irish and the English have been fighting for eight centuries now; they wanted the United States to be involved in the process of reconciliation that is now taking hold in Northern Ireland. After decades of brutal struggle, the Israelis and the Arabs working together to make peace in the Middle East want the Americans to be centrally involved. Even in the moment of our greatest tension a few days ago in Haiti, one of the military leaders said, "Well, if the President is determined to do this and the world community is absolutely determined to go ahead, we want the Americans here."

Why is that? We have Haitian-Americans, Jewish-Americans, Arab-Americans, Irish-Americans, English-Americans. You think of it: This diversity we have which cuts across racial and religious and philosophical and regional and income lines, it is the source of our great strength today in a world that is ever more interdependent.

And people look at us and say, "You know, with all their problems—yes, their crime rate's too high; and yes, they're too violent; yes, too many of their kids drop out of school; and yes, there's too much income inequality, especially for working people. But you know, they pretty well get along. And people from all different kinds of backgrounds wind up pursuing their chosen path in life and living up to their God-given potential. And they're adaptable; they work their way through the changes that time and circumstance are imposing on them." That's what others think about us.

We somehow have to begin to think that about ourselves again. And I cannot help but believe that the arts and humanities must play a central role in that task. How we imagine our own lives and our own future and how we imagine ourselves as a country will have as big an impact on what it is we ultimately become as anything in the world.

I said the other day, I will just say again, a lot of you have been involved in various enterprises, great business enterprises, great art enterprises, great entertainment enterprises. Just imagine how you would function if every day in all the important years of your life you showed up for work and two-thirds of the people you were working with thought that your outfit was going in the wrong direction and nothing good could happen. [*Laughter*] Imagine what would happen if the National Gallery of Art were given the most priceless collection of Impressionist paintings uncovered after having been thought destroyed for 50 years, and two-thirds of the people said, "I don't believe they're Impressionist paintings. I know Monet; he was a friend of mine. That's not him. Don't bother me with the facts." [*Laughter*] You're laughing because you know that it's true, don't you? There is a grain of truth in this.

Somehow we have to not sweep our problems under the rug and not sweep our differences under the rug, for that is also what makes America great. But we only find energy for dealing with our problems and the heart and the hearing to deal with our differences when at least we have a realistic appreciation of where we are, what we're doing, and where we're going. And I feel so good about the work we've done to move America forward in the last 20 months, but we'd all have to admit we've still got a lot of work to do in bringing America together, in giving our people a realistic feeling about where we are in the world and where we're going. You can do that. You can make a huge difference. The arts and humanities have always helped to do that work.

So I urge you to continue in this work. I urge you to make your progress report to me. I urge you to remember what we are trying to do in our schools in helping to improve our children's education with the arts and humanities. I urge you to work to expand private philanthropy. We all know that the Government in this country provides a crucial measure but only a tiny measure of the support that the arts and humanities need.

I urge you to promote international cultural exchange and understanding, not only because we need desperately to know more about others throughout the world but because I believe that we'll learn a lot more about ourselves if we just come in contact with people from other walks of life and other paths of the world.

Thanks to phones, faxes, Internet, E-mail, CNN, we can see the power of our cultural traditions as they are exported around the world. And sometimes they come back to us. We're the first White House to communicate with huge numbers of people from all over by E-mail. And I'm trying to do a sociological analysis now of whether there's a difference between the E-mail communication and the mail communication—or the female communication. [*Laughter*]

I am very hopeful that you will make a remarkable contribution to this country. I went over this list of people with great care. I tried to get a very different group of people. I tried to imagine all the different things that I hope that this Committee could deal with and all the different challenges I hope you could assume. If I haven't done a good job, it's not your fault. It's mine in picking you, but I think you're pretty special.

Let me say in closing that I hope that in addition to the schools, you can think about how we can increase access to the arts and humanities all across America to people who might otherwise be isolated from them, people who are homebound, people who live in very isolated areas, people who now don't even know how to speak the language that would be necessary to ask for something that might change their lives forever. I ask you also to think of that.

We've faced a lot of challenges as a country, but I'm actually pretty optimistic about it, based on the objective evidence. What remains is whether we can develop a vision that will sustain us as a people as we move through a period of change, without a known big enemy, into an uncertain future. It requires courage, but courage comes from having something inside that you can connect with what you see outside.

You can help us as we work our way through this in this remarkable time in our country's history. I hope you enjoy it. I thank you for serving. And I thank you for being here today.

Thank you.

NOTE: The President spoke at approximately 5 p.m. in the East Room at the White House.

Remarks at a Democratic Senatorial Campaign Committee Dinner
September 21, 1994

Thank you so much, Senator Graham, Senator Mitchell, Secretary and Mrs. Bentsen, Members of the Congress, my fellow Democrats and my fellow Americans.

I couldn't help thinking, as I listened to George Mitchell talk, that he is always so cool, calm, collected, and still intense and eloquent. He always seems to have such a great sense of balance. He did make one huge mistake this year: People wanted to see a resumption of baseball and a cessation of the Senate, and he got it in reverse. [*Laughter*]

I want to thank Senator Graham first for his leadership of the DSCC and his long friendship to me, his long personal friendship to me. We used to sit near each other in the Governors' Association, and both of us sometimes think that's the best job we ever had. And I have loved working with him. I admire him immensely. I have a lot to be grateful to him for on a very personal basis, but especially I thank him tonight for his support, steadfast and longstanding, for our attempts to end the human rights violations and restore democracy in Haiti. I thank you, Senator Graham, for that.

I'd like to say a few words about Haiti tonight, and then go back to my remarks. I think, just as Americans, you ought to know where we are and what happens next. We had a good day there. Our troops are carrying out their mission. To date, we now have 8,500 American troops in Haiti. All of them have entered peacefully. They have not shot at any Haitians. No one has shot at them. They are about the business of bringing back human rights and peace and decency and restoring democracy.

Of course, this is only the second day of the mission. The situation will not change immediately. But today was a better day than yesterday; yesterday was better than the one before. We are making steady progress.

The habits of violence which are so deeply ingrained there will not be shed overnight. But in the coming weeks we will be working to stop the violence, to begin the process of reconciliation, to say no to revenge and yes to peace, in the words of President Aristide. We will finally have accomplished a mission that began 3 years ago under the previous administration, to restore democracy and to have the de facto military leaders step down no later than October 15th.

Haiti is really evidence of the kinds of problems that are gripping the world at the aftermath of the cold war. An example of one of the challenges we face as we move from a world in which all the rules of activity as a society were clear and the one in which we have to take a new direction. I want to talk a little about that tonight, but I'd like to begin by saying a special word of thanks to George Mitchell for the leadership that he has given to the United States Senate and to our administration over the last nearly 2 years now.

Before I ran for President, I hadn't had the opportunity to spend a lot of time in Maine. And after I became President, I didn't need to spend a lot of time in Maine because George Mitchell brought one or two people from Maine to the White House every time he showed up. [*Laughter*] I was the most surprised person in the world when he told me he wasn't running for reelection. And when I finished crying and got up off the floor—[*laughter*]—I said, "Well, George, you're the only guy in the Congress that never comes to the White House without bringing somebody from your home State." I said, "You have literally brought enough people to the White House just since I've been President to secure reelection for the next 18 years." [*Laughter*] And he said "Well, I didn't know, but," he said, "I would have done it anyway."

I cannot imagine how we could have done what we have done—and I'll talk a little about that in a moment—if it hadn't been for George Mitchell. I cannot tell you what it means to have somebody you work with who always understands every issue, who always knows where the votes are, who always has a good sense of what can and can't be done, who will always

tell you respectfully when he thinks you're all wet, and then will go out and fight like crazy to win every time against all odds. He is a good, honest, and brave man, and I will miss him terribly. But he has earned whatever future he chooses for himself.

Senator Mitchell talked about what it was like to be a Democrat. And I guess, you know, I saw that poll today that said 53 percent of the American people thought we needed another party, and most people don't identify with the parties, and young people don't identify with the parties. I guess I'm an anachronism. I'm a Democrat by heritage, instinct, and conviction. I was raised until I was four by a grandfather whose politics were forged in the Great Depression. I had to have a new outfit every Easter because I still remember my grandfather telling me about how he couldn't afford an Easter dress for my mother that cost a dollar in the 1930's, in the middle of the Depression.

But I always thought the main thing about the Democratic Party was that we had constant values and the capacity to change with the times. Our country has been astonishing because we have kept this Constitution that the Founders crafted; amended it, really, a fairly small number of times; held absolutely fast to its fundamental principles; and still proved ourselves capable of changing over more than two centuries, showing the kind of flexibility and dynamism that guarantees the existence of a society. So has our party. It is the oldest political party in all of democracy anywhere.

Our principles are pretty much what they were when they were first articulated by Thomas Jefferson, with the obligation of government to help do affirmative good, as articulated by Andrew Jackson. But we have always been able to change. Now, for a while people thought we couldn't. And for a while the American people seemed to have made a decision that they would leave the Democrats permanently in control of Congress and give the White House to the Republicans so the Republicans could tell them what they wanted to hear and the Democrats could do the work they wanted to have done and keep the Republicans from actually doing what they threatened to do. [*Laughter*]

The problem is, that worked fine except when we actually had to change. And in 1992, there was a sense out there among the American people that we were not making the changes we needed to adapt to the changes in the world, to take this country into the 21st century, to guarantee a future for our children that would enable all of our kids to live up to the fullest of their God-given potential and guarantee that America would be the greatest country in the world well into the next century.

I ran for this job because I could see that, sitting out in the middle of the country where I was. I also had very little illusion about how the politics at the national level in this country had been often paralyzed because it had become so abstract, so rhetorical, and so subject to distortion, so totally divorced from the real life experiences of real Americans, that change had become very difficult, indeed. And so we embarked on that great journey in which I said what I would like to do is to change the Democratic Party's direction a little bit, not its values but its direction. Why? Because in the post-cold-war world, we can't have a Government that sits on the sideline and shouts at people. That's what the Republicans wanted to do. But the deficit is so big and the private sector is so important, we can't have a Government that actually solves all people's problems as we once thought it could under President Roosevelt. We have to have a new idea of partnership and empowerment, of opportunity and responsibility. And we have to rebuild this country from the grassroots up. And so we began.

In the last 12 years, our respectful opponents talked about the balanced budget amendment, bad-mouthed Government, told everybody how terrible spending was, went home and issued press releases about the money they'd gotten for their States or their districts, quadrupled the national debt, cut taxes on the wealthiest Americans, and raised payroll taxes on the middle class. We reduced our investment in the future and exploded our debt at the same time. And we were getting more and more polarized. It seemed to me simple enough to say that if we wanted to make it into the 21st century and guarantee that tomorrow for our kids, we had to move America forward, and we had to bring America back together. And somehow we had to divorce this enormous gulf between the word wars of Washington and the real-life experience of Main Street all over America.

If you look at what we've done in the last 20 months, I think we've done an amazing job of moving the country forward. And we're having a terrible time of reducing the gap between where we are here and Main Street America

because the obstacles are so profound. So let's talk tonight about that, because that's what this election ought to be about. And I'm here tonight to tell you that if we have the courage of our conviction, if we will listen to people, and if we will explain to them the difference between what is said here and what is done, these elections can be our friends, not theirs.

If I had told you 20 months ago that by Labor Day we would have passed an economic plan that cut spending by now over $300 billion, eliminated 100 Government programs, increased investment in education and training from Head Start to apprenticeship programs to college loans, that we would reduce the deficit 3 years in a row for the first time since Truman was President, reduce the size of the Federal Government to its lowest level since Kennedy was President, provoke an economic regrowth that would generate now almost 4.5 million new jobs, make 20 million young people eligible to refinance their college loans at lower interest rates at longer repayment terms, pass a national service program that in its first year would have more kids in a domestic Peace Corps than the Peace Corps did in its biggest year, break the gridlock on the Brady bill, family leave, motor voter, the crime bill, finance the crime bill totally by reducing the size of the Federal Government, and pass a crime bill that would have the support of every single law enforcement association in the entire United States of America—if I had told you that, and for good measure said that in a year and a half we would expand trade by more than any period in our history in 35 years, that for the first time in over two decades we'd actually have a policy to rebuild automobiles, airplanes, and ships and their international competitiveness, that we would have worked with Russia to get all the nuclear weapons out of all the other states of the former Soviet Union, that all the Russian troops would be gone for the first time since World War II from Eastern Europe and the Baltics, that we'd be actively involved in peace in the Middle East with two-thirds of the job done, actively involved in peace in Northern Ireland, actively involved in helping the election process in South Africa—if I had told all that, I'd say, "What do you think about that?" You'd say, "Well, that sounds pretty good, Bill, but you won't get that done." But we did, and that ought to be what we're running on out there.

I ask you, if we have a good economy, if we face the challenges of trade and crime, if we have reached out to families who are trying to keep their families together and raise their kids with the family leave bill and by giving 15 million working families tax cuts—we've put on the table a welfare reform program that is both compassionate and tough—why would anyone think there will be any problem? Because a lot of people don't know what has happened, number one. And number two—I don't know if you want to clap about that or not, it's partly our fault. A lot people don't know what has happened, number one. And number two, in addition to the jobs problem in America, we've got an income problem because as we go into the global economy, more and more people are working harder for static wages.

We're all happy there's no inflation with this economic revival. What that means among other things is, most people's wages aren't going up because they're set in a competitive global economy. And number three, the other guys aren't near as good as doers as we are, but they are better talkers, especially when they're saying no, as George Mitchell said. And they've got a whole talking apparatus here; they built it up over the last 12 years. And now that they have no responsibility in the executive branch, they've got a lot more free time to talk—[laughter]—and to find a thousand different ways to say no. One of them was quoted in the newspaper the other day, saying, "Now we've killed health care, let's just don't get our fingerprints on it."

So why is it that if for the first time in 9 years the annual meeting of the international panel of economic experts said America has the most productive economy in the world; for the first time in a decade we have 8 months of manufacturing job growth in a row; we have a 1.5 percent drop in the unemployment rate, a 20 percent drop in the minority unemployment rate; why is it that more than half the people say the country's going in the wrong direction? First of all, they do not know these things. That's why George Mitchell gave his little economic sermon up here. They do not know. And secondly, they are still profoundly concerned that maybe, if all this happened, it won't make a difference. They've been told for so long that Government can't do anything but mess up a one-car parade, it's hard to imagine that what we do here can make a difference. But it does. It does.

Every time I leave this place and go out into the country, I meet somebody who has a job that wouldn't have one if it weren't for the policies of our administration; I meet somebody with an opportunity to pay his or her way to college; I see a parent with a child in Head Start; I see a family that's benefited from the family leave program; I see whole industries—shipbuilding, airplanes—moving forward because of the efforts we have made to strengthen this economy. It makes a difference.

And what we have to do is to make this election our friend. We have to go home and say, "Look, you know, we've done a lot of stuff up there. You may not have liked it all, but we're finally getting something done."

I'll tell you something else, one of Clinton's nine laws of politics: Everybody is for change in general, but they're scared of it in particular. [Laughter] It always happens. It always happens. Five hundred years ago Machiavelli said, "There is nothing so difficult in all of human affairs than to change the established order of things." Why? Because those who will be disadvantaged by the change know it and fight you like crazy. And those who will benefit are uncertain of the result until they finally see it. Woe unto you if you have to run for reelection in the interim. [Laughter] Machiavelli didn't say that, I sort of added that one. [Laughter]

But I want you to understand what we're up against. But it is not right, and it is not rational. The American people are not by nature pessimistic people. Let's face it, we do have some problems. We're still the most violent country on Earth, but we passed the crime bill. We're going to lower the crime rate. We've given the communities of this country the tools to deal with it. We do have too many kids who are born where there was never a marriage and there was never an intact family, but we're trying to do something about it. We do have many communities where there was no economic recovery, but we have tried to do some things about that with the empowerment zones, the community development banks, and other things.

We have real problems. But consider this, every one of you, whatever it is you do for a living, how could you function if every day you showed up for work, two-thirds of the people in your place of business were in a deep funk and thought nothing good has happened? That's what they're asking today. Could you get anything done if two-thirds of the people you work with said, "Our business is going in the wrong direction. Nothing good's going to happen. Nothing can happen"?

How did the American people get in this fix? Well, the election is something we have to use to work them out it. You can analyze it nine ways from Sunday, but no one can repeal the facts. The facts are, they said we would bankrupt the economy, when all we tried to do was to cut spending, ask the wealthiest of Americans, including a lot of you in this room—and thanks for sticking with us—to pay a little more taxes so that we could give a break to 15 million families that had not gotten a pay raise in forever and a day and were hovering above the poverty line. And we said we didn't want them to go into welfare; we wanted them to stay right there and raise their children and go to work everyday. We put another 200,000 kids in Head Start. We did these things. We must talk about them. They matter. People must know. These elections can be our friend.

Now, in every election you have to be relevant. If you're not, even if you're right, you're beat. But if you are relevant and all you do with your relevance is play on the resentments and the fears of the people, you can win the election and harm the country terribly. They are out there with all their pie-in-the-sky schemes and all their no-saying and now a lot of their denial about what they did and didn't do when they were up here. We have a record.

And if I had told you 20 months ago we could amass this record, you would have said hallelujah. What you never imagined was what could happen to that record and those actions between the time it happened here and the time it got to them out there in the country, and all the static in between. Heck, half the time I watch the evening news, I wouldn't be for me, either. [*Laughter*]

But let me tell you something. I'm trying to get you to laugh about this because if you can get people to laugh about it and listen, we can do very well here. Three times in this century has the President's party not lost seats in one or both Houses. Only one time in this century has the President's party actually gained seats in both Houses at mid-term. But we have a record here, and they got the rhetoric. And they had 12 years to build up an apparatus of no-saying and bad-mouthing and positioning, and they are brilliant at it. Give them their due.

They are good at it. But we're not bad at it when we can clear our heads.

So you have raised this money tonight so our people can get on television and get on the radio and be in the newspapers and travel in their States and tell the truth.

You know, it was never going to be easy. Everybody can talk about a balanced budget amendment. You start bringing down the deficit, and you actually have to make decisions. That gives people a headache. Everybody could talk about doing something about crime, but if you really looked at it, it required some difficult choices. Everybody could talk about expanding trade, and everybody could talk about reducing the deficit and still spending more on children. But when you really got down to doing it, it required some decisions.

Meanwhile, we had to go through the static between here and where all of you live. And I'm telling you, the American people are smart, and they are fair, and they do not like being pessimistic. And we can use this election like the sunshine breaking through the clouds. And I want every one of you to go out there and not just think about winning and not just think about how crazy it is to have the politics of resentment and all this sort of name-calling and division and agitation dominating our people; don't even think about it in personal terms.

Just remember why we came here, every one of us. This is the greatest country in human history. We have won two World Wars and a cold war in this century. We are going through a period of change, and every time we do as a country—we're just like people going through changes—we're in a period of insecurity and uncertainty. And it is for the Democrats to lead the way out and to take the licks to do it. That's what Harry Truman and the other people did after World War II. That's what gave us the rebuilding of the American economy at home, the growth of the middle class, NATO and the cold-war edifice abroad, and rebuilding Germany and Japan in a worldwide trading system. It's what gave us the last 50 years without a war that threatened our very existence. And now we have to do the same thing for the people who will live in the next century. We can do this. We can do it. We can do it.

I'll just close with this. You tell people this wherever you're from: If things are going so bad in this country, why is it that after 800 years of fighting between the Irish and the English, the people of Northern Ireland would still like the United States involved, along with Great Britain and Ireland in trying to work through this? John Hume is here tonight in the United States, the symbol of peace and hope and decency. Where are you, John? Stand up. [*Applause*]

If things are so bad here, why did the people of South Africa want the United States to go there and help them ensure that their election was free and fair and honest and nonviolent? Why did the people in the Middle East want to come here to sign their peace agreement and want us involved in what they are doing? Why, even at the tensest moments of our negotiations down in Haiti, did the de facto leaders say, "Well, if the President is determined to do this and the world community is determined to do this, at least we want the Americans here. We trust them."?

I'll tell you why: Because this is a good country which is changing as it has always changed. We have problems. But in order to have the energy to face our problems and overcome them, we have to have the necessary attitude that says we are doing some things right, we are going in the right direction, and the last thing we need to do is to go back to the politics of resentment and rhetoric and diversion and division. Go out there and fight for the future, and you will all win in November.

Thank you, and God bless you all.

NOTE: The President spoke at 9:25 p.m. at the Washington Sheraton Hotel. In his remarks, he referred to Beryl Ann Bentsen, wife of Secretary of the Treasury Lloyd Bentsen, and John Hume, Member of Parliament from Northern Ireland.

Letter to Congressional Leaders on Deployment of United States Armed Forces to Haiti
September 21, 1994

Dear Mr. Speaker: (*Dear Mr. President:*)

On September 18, I reported to the Congress that an agreement was successfully concluded by former President Jimmy Carter, Senator Sam Nunn, and General Colin Powell regarding the transition between the *de facto* government and the elected government in Haiti. On September 18, I also directed the deployment of U.S. Armed Forces to Haiti as part of the multinational coalition provided for by U.N. Security Council Resolution 940 of July 31, 1994. I am providing this report, consistent with the War Powers Resolution, to ensure that the Congress is kept fully informed regarding this action to support multilateral efforts to restore democracy in Haiti and to protect democracy in our hemisphere.

On September 19, at approximately 9:25 a.m. e.d.t., units under the command of the Commander in Chief, U.S. Atlantic Command, were introduced into Haitian territory, including its territorial waters and airspace. United States Armed Forces participating in the deployment include forces from the U.S. Army's 18th Airborne Corps, including the 10th Mountain Divi-

sion; U.S. Naval Forces from the U.S. Atlantic Fleet, including the U.S. Second Fleet and U.S. Marine Forces and amphibious ships; U.S. Air Forces, including the 12th Air Force; and various units from U.S. Special Forces.

Air-landed and seaborne U.S. forces successfully secured initial entry points at Port au Prince International Airport and the Port au Prince port facilities. Approximately 1,500 troops were involved in these initial efforts. No resistance was encountered and there were no U.S. casualties. Over the next several days, it is anticipated that U.S. troop strength in Haiti will increase by several thousand in order to ensure the establishment and maintenance of a secure and stable environment.

As to the duration of the mission, our presence in Haiti will not be open-ended. As I indicated on September 18, the coalition will be replaced after a period of months by a U.N. peacekeeping force, the U.N. Mission in Haiti (UNMIH). By that time, the bulk of U.S. forces will have departed. Some U.S. forces will make up a portion of the UNMIH and will be present in Haiti for the duration of the U.N. mission.

The entire U.N. mission will withdraw from Haiti after elections are held next year and a new Haitian government takes office in early 1996, consistent with U.N. Security Council Resolution 940.

The military operations I have directed are conducted under U.S. command and control. As I reported to the Congress on September 18, the departure from power of the coup leaders will substantially decrease the likelihood of armed resistance. There has not been armed resistance to the deployment. However, the forces are equipped for combat and ready to accomplish their mission and to defend themselves, as well as to ensure the safety of U.S. nationals in Haiti.

I have taken these measures to further the national security interests of the United States: to stop the brutal atrocities that threaten tens of thousands of Haitians; to secure our borders; to preserve stability and promote democracy in our hemisphere; and to uphold the reliability of the commitments we make, and the commitments others make to us, including the Governors Island Agreement and the agreement concluded on September 18 in Haiti.

I have ordered this deployment of U.S. Armed Forces pursuant to my constitutional authority to conduct foreign relations and as Commander in Chief and Chief Executive.

Finally, I remain committed to consulting closely with the Congress, and I will continue to keep the Congress fully informed regarding this important deployment of our Armed Forces.

Sincerely,

WILLIAM J. CLINTON

NOTE: Identical letters were sent to Thomas S. Foley, Speaker of the House of Representatives, and Albert Gore, Jr., President of the Senate.

Message to the Congress Transmitting a Report on Emigration Policies of Russia
September 21, 1994

To the Congress of the United States:

I hereby transmit a report concerning the emigration laws and policies of the Russian Federation as required by subsections 402(b) and 409(b) of Title IV of the Trade Act of 1974, as amended (the "Act"). I have determined that the Russian Federation is in full compliance with the criteria in subsections 402(a) and 409(a) of the Act. As required by Title IV, I will provide the Congress with periodic reports regarding the Russian Federation's compliance with these emigration standards.

WILLIAM J. CLINTON

The White House,
September 21, 1994.

Remarks at a Rhythm and Blues Concert
September 22, 1994

Thank you. Please be seated. Well, we're a little late and a little wet, but I hope that you're as glad to be here as Hillary and I are glad to have you here, even though a little late. I want to thank Marilyn Bergman and Frances Preston for their leadership in promoting American music and for their help in making this evening possible.

In this tent tonight, there are representatives of many creative disciplines: lyricists, composers, authors, photographers, film makers, dramatists, and others. All of you have heightened the way the rest of us experience beauty, pleasure, pain. I can't even begin to contemplate a world without the gifts that you have given. I'm also glad you've brought some great performers with you. The theme of tonight's program is "Soul Tree," a celebration of the roots and reach of American music, soul music, in all of its forms: blues, gospel, jazz, country, pop, rhythm and blues, and rock and roll. It was all born and bred in America, from Memphis to Motown, from New Orleans to New York.

In Ken Burns' new PBS series on baseball, Gerald Early, a professor at Washington University, says that 2,000 years from now when people study our civilization, there are only three things America will be remembered for: the Constitution, baseball, and jazz. [*Laughter*] Now, he says they're the three most beautifully designed things our culture has produced and the three greatest tributes to American improvisation.

Well, wonderful as it is, and even though I used to teach it, you probably don't want to hear my lectures on the Constitution tonight, and sadly there is no baseball. So we're left with music: jazz, rhythm and blues, all the sounds of America's soul.

Let's get on with the show. Thank you, and welcome to the White House.

NOTE: The President spoke at 10:36 p.m. on the South Lawn at the White House. In his remarks, he referred to Marilyn Bergman, president, American Society of Composers, Authors, and Publishers, and Frances Preston, president and chief executive officer, Broadway Music, Inc.

Nomination for United States District Court Judges
September 22, 1994

The President today nominated the following three individuals to serve on the U.S. District Court: John D. Snodgrass for the Northern District of Alabama, Sven E. Holmes for the Northern District of Oklahoma, and Vicki Miles-La-Grange for the Western District of Oklahoma.

"These nominees will be outstanding additions to the Federal bench," the President said. "They bring experience and excellence in the legal profession."

NOTE: Biographies of the nominees were made available by the Office of the Press Secretary.

Remarks on Signing the Riegle Community Development and Regulatory Improvement Act of 1994
September 23, 1994

Thank you so much, Reverend Lawson and Dave Lollis, for your stories. Thank you, Secretary Bentsen, for your work on this, and thank you, Secretary Espy and SBA Administrator Erskine Bowles, for your work on this important project.

Ladies and gentlemen, Secretary Bentsen and I were lamenting when he was up here that he didn't have a complete list of all of the Members of Congress who were here. I'm going to try to name everyone I saw. And then I'm going to ask everybody who is here to stand up so that you can pick out who you think should be angry at me for missing. [*Laughter*] I see Senator Riegle, who has been mentioned, and Senator Sarbanes, Senator Mathews, Senator

Kerry, Senator Bennett, Congressman Bacchus, Congressman Fingerhut, Congressman Flake, who had so much to do with this legislation, Congressman Kanjorski, Congressman Kennedy, Congressman King, Congressman Menendez, Congressman Neal, Congressman Orton, Congressman Pickle, Congresswoman Lucille Roybal-Allard, Congressman Rush, who had a lot to do with this legislation, also. I know Congresswoman Velázquez, Congressman Watt. And I doubtless missed somebody, but would everybody here from Congress please stand so we can acknowledge your presence? Who did I miss? Oh, Congresswoman Waters, Congressman Bereuter, Congressman Fields. I missed five; I apologize to all of you. [*Laughter*]

Let me also say that this is the only public appearance I will make today, and I have an update that I feel I should give to the American people about the situation in Haiti. So I'd like to make a couple of remarks about that and then return to the subject at hand, which has been an important one to me for nearly 10 years now.

First, let me say that I'm pleased to report that we're making good progress in our efforts in Haiti. Our troop contribution to the international coalition will soon be up to full strength, about 14,000 American servicemen and women. But we have already begun to pull back or replace units who took part in the initial deployment, consistent with our original plan.

Among our men and women in Haiti are 1,000 military police. They're making contact with police precincts, where they'll keep a close watch on the police to see that there is professional action there with restraint. In the coming weeks, they'll be joined and ultimately replaced by hundreds of international police monitors from all around the globe, now having over 26 countries participating in this effort.

The United Nations human rights monitors will be returning to Haiti as soon as possible. We're beginning a weapons confiscation and buy-back program. Heavy weapons that were in the Haitian military's control are being turned over to our Armed Forces. At the same time we'll be working with Haitian authorities to buy back light weapons from the militia and civilians and to help them to institute a licensing program for gun ownership. All these steps should help to reduce the level of violence there.

Already, the situation on the ground has become calmer and more peaceful, and as a result the first shipload of Haitian migrants from Guantanamo will go home to Cuba on Monday, carrying between 200 and 300 Haitian citizens. We expect more will return next week.

I'd also like to announce that it's planned to—the U.S. Agency for International Development is increasing the food program so that we will be supplying, instead of 1 million, 1.3 million meals per day there. The first shipment will arrive on the 26th.

In short, our mission is going well. Of course, difficulties remain; they are part of any military undertaking. But I am very proud of the competence and the discipline our troops and their commanders have demonstrated. They are executing a complex operation with tremendous

skill. They deserve our thanks and our admiration and our persistent support. Thank you.

Let me say to all of you that I have dreamed of this day for a long time. The possibility to sign this act into law and, more importantly, to unleash the energies of millions of Americans too long denied access to the mainstream economics of our country, was one of the things that drove me into the campaign of 1992. Anyone who ever heard me give a talk anywhere probably knows that in almost every speech I talked about the South Shore Bank in Chicago, a place that I visited, got to know, and got to understand.

I've long admired the way they steered private investments into previously underprivileged neighborhoods, to previously undercapitalized and underutilized Americans, proving that a bank can be a remarkable source of hope and still make money in the free enterprise system.

Long before I ran for President, the founders of Shore Bank in Chicago helped us to launch the Southern Development Bank Corporation in Arkansas. My wife and I and our administration, including Bob Nash, who now works with Secretary Espy at the Agriculture Department, worked to make an idea that had worked in an urban community in the north take roots in rural communities all over the southern part of our State.

In 1992 I visited an awful lot of places where I thought these same things would work. I'll never forget the first time we had people up to the Governor's conference room to talk about what it was like when they got their first loan, when they thought their lives had ended and that they were going to be consigned to public assistance or living off welfare, but instead were starting businesses and making money, some of them even able to hire other people. It made an impression on me that I will carry with me always.

Today, the $4.8 billion in credit for new businesses and new jobs into communities and into people who need it the most is the beginning of those stories, countless thousands of them, all across this country. It's also good for our economy.

This bill is an example of what I hope and believe must be the goal of Government in the future. Nobody seriously believes that Government can be society's savior anymore. But very few people seriously believe that Government can sit on the sideline anymore. In the world of the 21st century, what Government will have to do is to be a more effective partner and to find ways to clear away barriers so that people can be empowered to live up to the fullest of their own capacities.

This bill is not about bureaucracies, and it's certainly not about distributing handouts. It's about new opportunity for people to assume responsibility to make good lives for themselves by making the private sector work in places where it had not gone before. That is what this bill is about.

This is a campaign commitment I am especially glad to be able to keep today because of what it says about what Americans will be able to do for themselves and what other Americans in the private sector will do for them and still make money.

Secretary Bentsen and I have worked hard, along with everybody else in this administration, to change the way Government works, to bring the deficit down, to shift our budget priorities from consumption to investment, to expand trade and to open markets. Secretary Espy has been especially active in the effort to change the way Government functions here by increasing our ability to help the agricultural sector and redevelop rural America while drastically reducing the size of the Agriculture Department.

Ninety-three percent of the over 4 million new jobs which have been created since I became President have been in the private sector. I am very proud of that. That's a higher percentage of jobs coming in the private sector than had been the rule in the previous decade. We need to do more of that, and if we do our jobs well in Government, we'll continue to be able to do more with fewer of us to create more of you in the private sector.

But our national economy clearly is not so much a national economy as a large number of regional and local economies. I was talking with a friend of mine last night who is an economist who said, "You know, it's even become more difficult to talk about the inflation rate. In 93 percent of the industries in America, there is no inflation. The overall inflation rate sometimes obscures the fact that there is serious inflation in one or two sectors and none anywhere else."

The overall unemployment rate similarly obscures the fact that the unemployment rate may be under 3 percent in some States in our coun-

try and still be very high in some isolated rural areas and inner cities where capital has not flown, where enterprise has not worked. But I believe that every American who is willing to work hard and learn can succeed in the free enterprise system. I do not believe that it is necessary to have 20 percent unemployment rate in inner cities and rural areas to keep this economy from overheating. I do not believe that.

And just as I have strongly supported our efforts to develop economic opportunity in our trading partners because I believe, for example, a wealthier Mexico, a wealthier Caribbean is good for America and builds our strength and builds jobs here, surely it must be even more true that if there were no American willing to work without a job, if there were no American willing to start a small business and able to start a small business, who cannot do so—if none of those people existed, our economy would be stronger. We would have more growth with less inflation, less social tension, fewer crime problems, fewer problems with broken families and broken homes. We have got to find ways to reach into the isolated areas of America to bring the promise of America. Ultimately, that is what this whole idea of community development financial institutions are all about. And I know that we can do that.

I want to say again, too, especially in view of the people who are here today from the Congress, I am very proud of the fact that this was an all-American effort, that this had broad bipartisan support in the Congress, this had broad support in the country, from traditional banking institutions, traditional business institutions, and community organizers who for years felt that no one noticed the efforts they were making. Since this issue was put on the Nation's agenda, more and more communities have become organized.

And let me close with just giving you a few examples. Reggie White, the all-time NFL defensive leader in sacks, has now gone on the offensive, investing his earnings in community development banks. Richard Dent, the all-pro defensive player for the Bears—I think Richard is here today, but he's injured, so he can't stand up. Can you? Good to see you. Richard is now with the 49'ers. But if he hadn't sustained his injury, he couldn't be here today; so I'm not glad he's injured, but I am glad he's here. He is joining in, too. Private sector involvement in these institutions is up almost a third, even before a single public penny has been spent, in anticipation of the impact of this bill.

Today I'm proud to announce commitments from two of the Nation's leading banks to help us in this effort: $25 million from NationsBank and $50 million from the Bank of America over the next 4 years. Their representatives are here. Would they please stand and receive our thanks, wherever they are? Thank you so much. [*Applause*]

I hope very much that in the days ahead we can find other ways to bring new ideas into a spirit of partnership and empowerment with Government. That, after all, was the idea behind reducing the size of the Federal Government and giving the money to the communities to hire police and to build prisons and to start prevention programs in the crime bill. It was the idea behind AmeriCorps. It was the idea behind reorganizing the student loan program so that it actually costs less than it used to and still provides lower interest loans that 20 million young Americans are already eligible to refinance their present obligations to achieve, the idea behind the empowerment zones that we will announce this fall.

This is the sort of thing we ought to be doing up here, helping people out of the grassroots to chart their course into a brighter future. I am proud to sign this bill, and I want, again, to say my profound thanks to all the Members of Congress who are here and those who are not, in both parties, for making this such an all-American effort. Thank you very much.

I'd like to invite the Members of Congress who are here to come up and be here at the signing. After all, you did it.

[*At this point, the President signed the bill.*]

The President. Thank you. Thank you very much.

NOTE: The President spoke at 11:29 a.m. at the U.S. Department of Agriculture. In his remarks, he referred to Rev. Philip Lawson, president, Northern California Ecumenical Council, and founder and director, Community Bank of the Bay; and David Lollis, director, Appalbanc. H.R. 3474, approved September 23, was assigned Public Law No. 103–325.

Statement on the Nomination of Philip Lader To Be Administrator of the Small Business Administration
September 23, 1994

I have today announced my intention to nominate Philip Lader as Administrator of the Small Business Administration.

Upon Mr. Lader's confirmation by the Senate, the SBA Administrator will hold Cabinet rank and serve as a member of my Cabinet.

The elevation of the SBA Administrator to Cabinet status reflects my firm commitment to address the interests and concerns of the Nation's small business community. By sitting as a member of the Cabinet, the SBA Adminis-

trator can ensure that the views of our small business community are expressed and heard in the most senior levels of Government.

Small business is the backbone of our economy and the driving force behind economic growth. We have already taken major strides in making the SBA an effective agency for enhancing the strength of our Nation's small businesses. In giving the Administrator Cabinet status, we will accelerate that progress.

Nomination for the Small Business Administration
September 23, 1994

The President today announced his intention to nominate Philip Lader as Administrator of the Small Business Administration. He also announced that he would make the SBA Administrator a member of his Cabinet, effective when Mr. Lader takes office. The SBA Administrator is also a member of the National Economic Council.

"Phil is a great manager and motivator, and he knows business," the President said. "His extensive private sector experience as well as his work at OMB and in the White House make him an ideal candidate to head the SBA. Erskine Bowles turned SBA around after years of neglect. Phil is going to make it even better."

"I think it's well known how much I respect Phil Lader. My selection of Erskine Bowles and now Phil Lader for this job reflects my firm commitment to a strong SBA. This appointment and the elevation of the SBA Administrator to Cabinet status reflect my equally firm commitment to address the interests and concerns of our Nation's small business community."

NOTE: A biography of the nominee was made available by the Office of the Press Secretary.

Message to the Senate Transmitting the Belarus-United States Investment Treaty
September 23, 1994

To the Senate of the United States:

With a view to receiving the advice and consent of the Senate to ratification, I transmit herewith the Treaty Between the United States of America and the Republic of Belarus Concerning the Encouragement and Reciprocal Protection of Investment, with Annex, Protocol, and related exchange of letters, signed at Minsk on January 15, 1994. Also transmitted for the information of the Senate is the report of the Department of State with respect to this Treaty.

This bilateral investment Treaty with Belarus is the sixth such Treaty between the United States and a newly independent state of the former Soviet Union. This Treaty will protect U.S. investors and assist the Republic of Belarus in its efforts to develop its economy by creating conditions more favorable for U.S. private investment and thus strengthening the development of the private sector.

The Treaty is fully consistent with U.S. policy toward international and domestic investment.

A specific tenet of U.S. policy, reflected in this Treaty, is that U.S. investment abroad and foreign investment in the United States should receive national treatment. Under this Treaty, the Parties also agree to international law standards for expropriation and compensation for expropriation; free transfer of funds associated with investments; freedom of investments from performance requirements; fair, equitable and most-favored-nation treatment; and the investor or investment's freedom to choose to resolve disputes with the host government through international arbitration.

I recommend that the Senate consider this Treaty as soon as possible, and give its advice and consent to ratification of the Treaty, with Annex, Protocol, and related exchange of letters, at an early date.

WILLIAM J. CLINTON

The White House,
September 23, 1994.

Nomination for a United States District Court Judge
September 23, 1994

The President announced today the nomination of Patrick J. Toole, Jr., for the U.S. District Court for the Middle District of Pennsylvania.

"Patrick Toole has a profound commitment to public service," the President said. "He will serve Pennsylvania well on the Federal bench."

NOTE: A biography of the nominee was made available by the Office of the Press Secretary.

Appointment of Deputy Chief of Staff for White House Operations
September 23, 1994

The President today named Erskine B. Bowles, currently the Administrator of the Small Business Administration, as his Deputy Chief of Staff for White House Operations. Mr. Bowles, who will also be an Assistant to the President, will take over his new responsibilities on October 3.

In the new White House staff structure, also announced today by Chief of Staff Leon E. Panetta, Mr. Bowles will be responsible for internal White House operations as well as the day-to-day activities of the President and will oversee access to the Oval Office.

The offices reporting to him will be the Office of Scheduling and Advance, the Office of Management and Administration, the Office of Presidential Personnel, and the Office of the Staff Secretary, as well as the Director of Oval Office Operations.

"I am very excited that Erskine is coming to the White House," the President said. "As SBA Administrator, he turned around an agency that previous administrations had neglected. It has become a beacon of support for the Nation's small businesses, and it now responds with incredible speed and sensitivity to major disasters. Erskine will undoubtedly bring to the White House the same vigor and creativity with which he has headed the SBA."

NOTE: A biography of the appointee was made available by the Office of the Press Secretary.

Nomination for Chair of the Council on Environmental Quality
September 23, 1994

The White House today announced a plan to reorganize the environmental operations within the Executive Office of the President by merging the White House Office on Environmental Policy (OEP) with the Council on Environmental Quality (CEQ). In a move that will give continued strength to environmental policymaking in the administration, environmental activities will be consolidated under the Chair of the CEQ.

The President will nominate Kathleen A. (Katie) McGinty, currently Director of the Office on Environmental Policy, as Chair of the CEQ.

"I am pleased to nominate Katie as my new chair of the Council on Environmental Quality," the President said. "She has served this administration, the American people, and most of all the environment with skill and dedication. I am confident that Katie will continue to reflect my commitment to the environment in her new, expanded role."

The President continued, "This merger will enable us to advance our environmental agenda sensibly and effectively. Joining these two teams will make it easier to achieve the goals of economic growth and environmental protection."

NOTE: A biography of the nominee was made available by the Office of the Press Secretary.

Remarks at a Democratic Senatorial Campaign Committee Dinner in Chicago, Illinois
September 23, 1994

Thank you very much. Senator Graham, Senator Simon, Senator Moseley-Braun, Senator Biden, Senator Leahy, Mrs. Daley, Secretary Babbitt, Secretary Shalala. Joe Cari, thank you for doing such a wonderful job tonight. Let me say a special word of thanks to David Wilhelm for his heroic efforts over the last 2 years on behalf of the Democratic Party. David and I were flying in tonight on the helicopter, and we flew across the lake and we were coming in, and I said—I looked at him, and I said, "Lord, I love Chicago, and I miss being here." And we went through all of our history together. And I remember so well the night at the Navy Pier when I named him my campaign manager and all the things that happened and the night of St. Patrick's Day in 1992, when the votes in Illinois and Michigan pretty well ensured the nomination of our campaign in the election. I am so glad to be back here, and I want to say a special word of thanks to David and to Degee, who is also here. And I wish them well. They're about to give us one more Democrat in a couple of months—[*laughter*]—which is the most important thing of all.

We're looking forward to being back here for the convention as well, and I know you'll be a good host. And we will show Chicago to the world in a way that is very, very good.

Let me say—I want to say some political things. I'd like to start by thanking the people who have spoken already so much for what they have said but more importantly for their service to our country and their leadership. Every one of them has rendered enormous service to this Nation and stood up for the ordinary citizens of this country and has been willing to take on the real problems of this country.

But before I get into my remarks about the election and about what's at stake I think I ought to say a few words to you about our mission in Haiti. I'm pleased to report that we're making good progress. I had the opportunity to talk on the plane coming out here with General Shelton, General Meade, and our Ambassador there, Bill Swing, who has done a magnificent job under incredibly adverse circumstances.

Soon our coalition will be at full strength, including about 14,000 American service people, about a thousand military police who will keep a close watch on the Haitian police to see that we do keep order with professionalism and restraint. Soon they'll be joined and then replaced by hundreds of international police monitors from now well over two dozen countries, many of them coming from all over the world because they believe in what we are trying to do there in ending human rights abuses and restoring democracy.

The Haitian military, so far, has cooperated very well with our Armed Forces. They're turning over their heavy weapons. We're helping to buy back light weapons from the militia and the civilians. The situation is already calmer and more peaceful than it was when we got there.

On Monday, the first shipload of Haitian migrants from Guantanamo will go home to Haiti to begin to build a peaceful and a free life, and we expect more to follow soon. Of course, difficulties remain; they are always part of any military undertaking. But I want you to know you can be very proud of the men and women in the armed services that are down there executing a complex and exceedingly difficult task. They deserve our praise, they deserve our prayers, and they deserve our support.

I also want to welcome the three candidates who are here tonight in Chicago: Congressman Sam Coppersmith from Arizona; Jack Mudd, I think clearly one of our most promising challengers from the wonderful State of Montana that was good enough to vote for the Clinton-Gore ticket in 1992; Bob Carr, who's in a tight race in Michigan but who I am convinced is going to win that race and going to be the next Senator from Michigan. Each of them has something important to contribute to the future of this country. And thanks to you, they've got a lot better chance to make that contribution.

I want to talk to you tonight a little bit about what's at stake in this election and what I hope you will do besides give your money between now and November.

Like most of you here, I'm a Democrat by heritage, instinct, and conviction. I was raised by my grandfather until I was 4. He had a fourth-grade education, and he thought when he died, he'd meet God first and FDR second. [*Laughter*] I was raised to believe that the party to which I belong stood up for ordinary people in extraordinary times and was always looking toward the future for all Americans, not just for a few.

Our party and our Nation has survived for two centuries and more now because we've always found a way to meet the challenges of the moment and to fulfill our goals and to help people move forward in fulfilling their own God-given potential. We've always believed that our country could do better and that we had to do our best to call forth what is best within us. Always we believed that we had to be an engine of change, even when it was tough and even when it would cause us to be misunderstood. Always we believed that government had a responsibility not necessarily to give people anything except an opportunity to make the most of their own lives and that people in turn, all of our citizens, had a responsibility to follow the American dream and to make our community stronger. Those are the values that have defined us as a party and a people for quite a long while now. They are summed up for me in the three simple words I used all across this country in the '92 campaign: opportunity, responsibility, and community.

Two years ago, the American people knew clearly that we had to make a change, that we couldn't keep going in the direction we were and expect to move to the 21st century with a strong America, a more united America, an America where our children had a chance to make a future better than their parents enjoyed. You sent me to Washington to reverse a dozen years of failed policies that brought higher taxes on the middle class, lower taxes on the wealthy, higher unemployment, reduced investment in our people, and less ability to compete and win in the global economy.

Often I came to Chicago in that campaign, and always I received a rousing reception and always I looked into the heart of America here, because there are all kinds of people here from all racial and ethnic groups, from all walks of life, people who know what it's like to live in a community where you can find unity in diversity and strength across differences. And I told you what I would try to do.

Now, if I had told you then not only what I would try to do but if I'd told you on election night, for example, that within 20 months we would have cut our deficit by over $250 billion, eliminated over 100 Government programs outright, raised income taxes only on the wealthiest 1.2 percent of our people, cut taxes for 15 million working families, made 90 percent of our small businesses eligible for a tax cut—thereby bringing 3 years of deficit reduction in a row for the first time since Truman was President, producing 4.3 million new jobs, including 8 months in a row of increasing manufacturing jobs for the first time in a decade; that we would be voted by the annual roll of the international economists as the most productive country in the world for the first time in 9 years; that we would increase spending on Head Start, on job training, on apprenticeships for people who don't go to college, and still reduce the Federal payroll, as Senator Biden said, by 270,000 so that by the end of this century we will have—and by the end of this budget cycle—in 5 years we'll have the smallest Federal Government we've had since John Kennedy was President. You know, the Republicans always bad-mouthed the Government, but they expanded it. We say we're going to make it work, and we have shrunk it.

If I had told you all that, if I'd told you that here in Illinois there'd be 125,000 new jobs, taxes would be cut for 600,000 families and raised for 79,000 of the wealthiest people of this State to bring that deficit down; if I had told you that in 20 months we'd have more expansion of trade than in any comparable time period in a whole generation, that we would have targeted automobiles, airplanes, ships, and defense conversion into new technologies for special treatment and had helped to revive all those industries; if I had told you that today we would sign a bill modeled on the South Shore Bank in Chicago to put $4.8 billion into inner-city neighborhoods and devastated rural areas, in banks to loan money to poor people under circumstances that will make the banks money and put free enterprise into devastated economic areas; that we would pass more education reform in any year since 1965; that we would make 20 million Americans eligible to refinance their college loans at lower interest rates and longer repayment terms; now, if I had told you all that and said, Oh, and by the way, after 7 years of delay we would pass the family leave law, after 7 years of delay we would pass the Brady bill, after 7 years of delay we would pass the motor voter bill, after 6 years of delay we would pass a crime bill that puts 100,000 more police on the street, 100,000 more jail cells for serious criminals, prevention programs for kids to have something to say yes to, that takes assault weapons off the streets, even though we had a brutal battle on that with the NRA and the Republican leadership; if I had told you that our national service program would start this year with more people in the first year serving America at the grassroots level than the Peace Corps had at its peak year and that year after next we'd have 100,000 more young people earning some money for their college education by solving the problems of America here at home, you would have thought that I had slipped a gasket. [*Laughter*] Wouldn't you? You would not have believed that.

The fact is, that is the record of this administration in the first 20 months, and more. And we've got more to do. But there is a larger purpose behind all these details that sometimes can get lost, and we have to stand back from it.

When I ran for President I said that my goal would be putting the American people first. And Al Gore and I wrote a little book called "Putting People First" that we put our heart into with the best ideas we could come up with from all over the country. We decided we could make Government work for ordinary people and that we could restore the American dream. And if I had told you 20 months ago that we would do all this, you would say, "I do not believe it, but you ought to go try." But that was done with the help of the people standing behind me in the Cabinet and, importantly, in the Congress. It happened because we were willing to say yes to America, we were willing to say that Government should not be on the sidelines, that Government should not be the prisoner of special interests, that Government could not ever

be the savior of this country but that we could be a good partner and we could empower the American people to seize control of their destiny and make something of their lives.

And that is exactly what we have done. And we have done it all along the way with the Republican leadership and most of their allies in the Congress voting no on every tough vote and painting an increasingly distorted picture of what happened.

Our economic plan, they say, was the biggest tax increase in history. It raised income taxes on 1.2 percent of the people, cut income taxes on 15 percent of the working people so they wouldn't fall into poverty and wouldn't go on welfare. It brought the deficit down after they quadrupled our national debt in 12 years. But they all voted no.

They think if they can keep the noise up and keep saying no and confusing the American people and playing on their frustrations and their anger and the fact that there are an awful lot of people out there that have justifiable worries still, they may have a job, but they're not ever going to get a raise, it seems like. They may have a job, but they're scared they're going to lose their health care. They may have a job, but they're worried about crime in their neighborhoods and the pressures on families. They believe if they can just keep people in a state of high anxiety they can actually fool the people into voting for the very people who did the things that they're against. That is what they believe.

But, you know, Abraham Lincoln, who was their first and their greatest President, said—it must be disheartening for them; it's been all downhill since then. [*Laughter*] He said—what did he say? "You cannot fool all the people all the time. You cannot fool—you can fool all the people some of the time, and some of the people all of the time, but you cannot fool all the people all the time."

This election is going to give us a chance to get that record out there. When the American people know it, when we say it over and over and over again, and when they see it, they will wonder what the no-sayers have been doing and why they have been filling their ears, their minds, and their hearts with a vision of America that is inadequate to the present and woefully short of what we have to do for the future.

They don't want the American people to know that we've been helping business and creating jobs, that we've been helping working people to get the education and training they need, that we've been helping families to get their kids in Head Start, that we've been giving kids a chance to go to college without regard to their income and that we're actually doing something for middle class kids for a change on college aid. They don't want them to know any of that.

And they sure don't want the American people to know what they've been doing. When we gave the middle class a fair shake in that economic plan by asking the wealthiest Americans to pay their fair share, every Republican in the Congress said no. When we reformed student loans to benefit millions and millions and millions of middle class students, every Republican in the Congress said no. When we gave 15 million working families a tax cut and made—and I want to say this again—90 percent of the small businesses in the entire United States of America eligible for a tax reduction, every Republican in the Congress said no. When we banned assault weapons, when we fought for health care reform, when we fought for campaign reform, when we fought for the Brady bill, most of the Republicans and their leaders said no. They said yes to the narrow interests, no to the national interests. They don't want you to see that big picture because if they did, you wouldn't like what you saw.

Sure, people are suspicious of all political claims. They've been disappointed, manipulated, and had reality distorted for years now. And their lives are full of negative messages and genuine concern. But I'm telling you, Abraham Lincoln was right. You cannot fool all the people all the time. And your contributions tonight are a sword of truth that these Senate candidates can use to cut through the fog and tell the truth of the record we are making to change America and to put the people of this country first again. And I thank you for it.

I just want you to think about this. When you go home tonight, I want you to think about this. This country has been around a long time now, longer than any other big democracy in human history. And it's here because when we went through tough times and had big challenges, we relied on the people who said yes, yes to the challenge, yes to the change, yes to making the most of the difficult situations. That's why we're still here.

And you know, all around the world, it's amazing, people see us, and they sometimes ask me as I travel the world why we're so agitated, because they would give anything to have an economy with our strength. They would give anything to see people from so many different races and religious backgrounds and ethnic groups living together, working together, voting together, disagreeing together. The things we take for granted about this great country are things other people would literally give their lives for.

Let me just give you a couple of examples, just since I've been your President. Why did the South Africans want the United States to contribute $35 million and our best experts to help them conduct an election that was free, fair, open, honest, had slews of candidates, and produced Nelson Mandela, who, after 27 years in jail, is coming here for a state visit with the President of the United States in the next few days?

Why did the people of Northern Ireland, after the English and the Irish and the Protestants and the Catholics had been fighting for 800 years want the United States to help to bring peace to Northern Ireland? Why do the people of the Middle East, Israeli and Arab alike, after they have fought for decades and their very existence has been at risk, want to come to the United States and have us play a part of their peacemaking process? Why do these things happen?

Why, even in the 11th hour at the moment of highest tension in Haiti a few days ago, when it was not clear whether there would be an invasion or not, the de facto military leaders said, "Well, if the President is determined to do this, and if the United Nations is determined to proceed, at least we want the Americans here. We trust them." Why? Because they know we stand for freedom and democracy and fairness and opportunity, and we know this is the greatest country on Earth.

So here's what I want to ask you to do— in the rhythm of American politics, in almost every election in the 20th century—I haven't checked back in the 19th century—the sitting President's party has lost some seats in the Congress at midterm. The only time in this century when the sitting President's party did not lose seats in at least one section of Congress was in 1934 when all the Republicans killed Social

Security, and the Democrats won seats in both Houses.

If the American people knew the litany I gave you tonight, we would win seats in both Houses, wouldn't we? Wouldn't we? In spite of all of the pundits and all the polls, if they knew that we had 4.3 million new jobs, if they knew we had 3 years of deficit reduction for the first time since Truman, if they knew we had the smallest Federal Government since Kennedy, if they knew that we had passed family leave and the Brady bill and the crime bill, and if they knew that so much we had done was done against overwhelming bitterly partisan opposition, that is what would happen again, wouldn't it? Therefore, you must conclude they do not know. And if you want Abraham Lincoln to be right, then you have a personal responsibility to go beyond your checkbook to your voice and your heart.

Do not let this election go by and let the American people inadvertently vote for the very things they're against. Do not turn back. Keep going. We are moving in the right direction; we are turning the corner. This is a great country, and we are looking to the future. Let's keep doing it.

Thank you, and God bless you.

NOTE: The President spoke at 7:40 p.m. at the Ritz-Carlton Hotel. In his remarks, he referred to Maggie Daley, wife of Mayor Richard M. Daley of Chicago; Joseph A. Cari, dinner chairman; David Wilhelm, chairman, Democratic National Committee, and his wife, Degee; Lt. Gen. Henry H. Shelton, USA, commander, U.S. forces in Haiti; and Maj. Gen. David Meade, commander, 10th Mountain Division.

The President's Radio Address
September 24, 1994

Good morning. This week I'm in Chicago, where my radio address is carried live each week by radio station WMAQ.

One week ago, America stood ready to use force if necessary to help restore the democratically elected government in Haiti. American power marshaled in pursuit of our national interest enabled American diplomacy to succeed. Haiti's military leaders agreed to leave power no later than October 15th. And our troops entered Haiti peacefully and without bloodshed, leading an international coalition of 28 nations that will work to bring greater security to the people and restore to power Haiti's democratically elected government.

Today I am pleased to report on the progress of our mission. The U.S. contribution to the international coalition will soon be at full strength, some 14,000 American service men and women. Our troops include nearly 1,000 military police, who are working to help ensure that the Haitian police act with restraint toward the Haitian people. Police monitors from our coalition partners, Argentina, Jordan, and Bolivia, are expected to arrive next week. And the United Nations human rights observers expelled

from Haiti 2 months ago will soon return. We've also have begun programs to confiscate heavy weapons controlled by the Haitian military and to buy back light weapons from the militia and civilians.

Our presence, in short, is helping to restore civil order in a country wracked by violence and instability. Perhaps the best evidence of our success is that 200 to 300 Haitian refugees who we sheltered at our base in Guantanamo will go home on Monday. And we expect more to follow soon.

This remains a difficult undertaking, as with all military operations, and as I speak to you, Secretary of Defense Perry and General Shalikashvili, Chairman of the Joint Chiefs of Staff, are traveling to Haiti to review our progress on the ground. I am proud of our troops and their commanders there. They deserve our thanks, our prayers, and our praise.

Our success in Haiti to date shows what the international community and American leadership can achieve in helping countries in their struggle to build democracy. Our mission, however, is limited. We must remember, as I plan to tell the United Nations General Assembly on Monday, that it is up to the people in those countries ultimately to ensure their own freedom. This is the great challenge and opportunity of democracy.

That's also one of the lessons I hope Americans will learn as Russian President Boris Yeltsin and South African President Nelson Mandela visit our country in the next 2 weeks. Their visits will be occasions to reflect on the remarkable democratic transformations of Russia and South Africa, which the United States has done a great deal to promote.

America should be proud of our leadership in helping to build open societies around the world. By supporting democracy and promoting economic growth, we are actively helping others, but we're helping ourselves at the same time.

Despite this, some people in our country question the importance of American engagement in the post-cold-war world. They say we should hide behind the walls of protectionism and isolationism. But they're wrong.

That's why early next week I'll submit to Congress legislation to implement the GATT world trade agreement, the largest trade agreement in history. By cutting tariffs around the world, GATT will mean a $36-billion tax cut for Americans over the coming 10 years. It will also generate between 300,000 and 700,000 permanent new jobs in those years and in time many, many more for our children. And most of all, it will mean that we are facing this moment of decision with the confidence we need to meet the challenges of the post-cold-war world, tearing down walls that separate nations instead of hiding behind them.

As we've learned again this week, when we approach our responsibilities around the world with the same sense of purpose, we can indeed accomplish great goals.

Thanks for listening.

NOTE: The President spoke at 9:06 a.m. from the Ritz Carlton Hotel in Chicago, IL.

Remarks at a Reception for Senatorial Candidate Ann Wynia in Minneapolis, Minnesota
September 24, 1994

The President. Thank you very much. Thank you. Thank you, Ann Wynia, for that wonderful introduction and for your fine speech and for what you represent for the State of Minnesota and for the prospects for our country. Thank you, Senator Wellstone, and thank you, Congressman Sabo and Congressman Vento, for helping me to keep my commitments to the American people to move this country forward and for your outstanding leadership. And thank you especially, Senator Graham, for your brilliant leadership of the Democratic Senate Campaign Committee and for being such a good and wise and trusted adviser to me on so many issues. I wish Bill Luther luck. And Bruce Vento reached over and whispered in my ear and said, "Now, even though he's running for Graham's seat, he's really going to win, Bill." [*Laughter*] Thank you, David Wilhelm, for that rousing speech, for reminding us what we are against as well as what we are for.

Ladies and gentlemen, I came here to ask you to help Ann Wynia get to the United States

Senate, not because, as she said, she would agree with me on every issue but because she would bring common sense and common decency to the United States Senate, something we need more of.

You know, half the time when you see what's going on in Washington, you must wonder what is really going on. A lot of us who come from the States and then go to Washington are amazed by the level of political rhetoric and how abstract and almost artificial it seems. We need more people in the United States Congress like Ann Wynia who actually served the folks at the grassroots level, who actually did things to help real people take responsibility for their own lives like the children's health care plan here in Minnesota, which provided health care to 35,000 Minnesota children. That's a lot of families that have been helped to do something in their own lives.

I have been interested in and working on the whole subject of welfare reform for nearly 15 years, and I know that the further you go away from the welfare recipients, the more likely you are to hear hot air and see no results. Ann Wynia I would like to have in the Senate when we pass welfare reform next year because, as commissioner of human services, she didn't just talk about it, she actually moved people from welfare to work, not talking about it but doing it.

I want to talk with you today about what this election is all about, especially from my point of view as your President, someone who has tried hard to be President of all people, without regard to their party or their region or their race or their economic standing.

Two years ago, I ran for President because I wanted to lead this country into the 21st century with the American dream still alive for my daughter and for all the children here, because I thought the Republican leadership in the White House was taking our country in the wrong direction. Their economic policy was not working; it was increasing inequality in our country. And their social policy seemed to be to divide us by race, by religion, and other ways, to preach at us instead of to practice and to move forward.

I thought, frankly, we needed a new direction in Washington that came from the grassroots, that we needed to go beyond these partisan fights that had dominated both parties too much. I didn't think that the Government could be the savior of the American people the way we Democrats believed during the New Deal when it was very nearly so then. But neither did I think that Government could just sit on the sidelines when all of our competitors all around the world were taking a different approach. And I didn't think our Government could come off of the sidelines only when the special interests needed help, as opposed to ordinary, middle class Americans.

I thought that we ought to run this country the way most of us try to run our families, our lives, our businesses, our grassroots efforts; that there ought to be a partnership; that the Government, after all, was no more than us. You all pay the bill. Everybody that works up there is your hired hand. Every now and then you have elections and get a chance to not renew contracts or vote for new people if you want. The Government ought to be our partner and ought to do its best to provide economic opportunity, to challenge citizens to assume personal responsibility to make the most of their own lives, and to try to rebuild the frayed bonds of our American communities.

For the last 12 years before I showed up, the leadership in Washington talked about a balanced budget amendment and quadrupled the national debt; talked about helping the middle class, but taxes went up on the middle class and down on the wealthiest Americans; talked about making us competitive but reduced investment in the things which make us competitive, including the education and training of our people; talked a lot about our social problems but didn't do very much about them.

I wanted to bring more jobs to America and help people to begin to raise their incomes again. I wanted to bring more educational opportunities and health care opportunities for people who didn't have them and to do something to control the spiraling costs of health care. I wanted to rebuild our families and our communities. I wanted to see this country have a Government that worked for ordinary people again. And I desperately wanted it to occur without the kind of partisan rancor that I had seen for the past several years.

Well, after 20 months, I can tell you that we're doing a good job of moving America forward, but we need some help at ending the partisan rancor, and you can't reward it in this election.

Here is why you ought to stick with the direction in which we are going. Two years ago I came here; we had the end of our bus trip here—5,000 miles. And after 5,000 miles, we were running late because there were people on the side of the road at every little crossroads. And a lot of you waited a long time for us to finally show up. There were tens of thousands of people here. And we were all caught up in the excitement of the moment and the promise of a new direction and change for America.

But even with all that optimism, if I had told you 2 years ago that if you elected me President and we got to work up there, within 20 months the following things would happen, you ask yourself, even then, would you have believed? If I had told you that we'd put our economic house in order, $255 billion worth of spending cuts, scores of programs eliminated outright, raising tax rates on only the top 1.2 percent of the income groups, cutting taxes for 10 times as many people, 15 million in working families to keep them above the poverty line so they didn't give up their jobs and sneak into welfare; if I had told you that it would be a Democratic, not a Republican administration that would make 90 percent of the small businesses in this country eligible for a tax cut, that would reduce the Federal bureaucracy to its smallest size since John Kennedy was President and would reduce the deficit 3 years in a row for the first time since Harry Truman was President, you wouldn't have believed it then, but it happened.

If I had told you then that we would expand trade for America's products and services, more in 20 months than had been done in any comparable period for the last 35 years—with NAFTA; with trade with Mexico up 17 percent this year; with the GATT worldwide trade agreement, which will produce between 300,000 and 500,000 jobs for us in the next few years; with new outreaches in Asia and in Latin America; with $35 billion more in high-tech exports eligible to be sold all across the world; with new initiatives to rebuild shipbuilding and aerospace in this country and build a clean car and sell things all across the world—if I had told you we would do that, that we would launch a major defense conversion program and take the technologies of the cold war to create high-wage jobs in a peacetime economy, and if I had told you that those results would produce $4.3 million new jobs, 8 months of manufacturing job increases in a row for the first time in a decade, America rated the most productive country in the world for the first time in 9 years, 88,000 new jobs in Minnesota, the unemployment rate dropping here from 5.1 percent to 3.4 percent, tax cuts for 155,000 working families, 26,000 small businesses, tax increases for less than 23,000 families—if I had told you that, you might not have believed it, but it's so, and it happened.

If I had told you that we would make 200,000 more children eligible to be in Head Start programs, immunize 2 million more kids so that all the children under 2 will be immunized by 1996, that we would have a national education strategy in a bill that set world-class educational standards and promoted grassroots reforms like those pioneered right here in Minnesota, that we would launch a national effort to have apprenticeships everywhere to help young people who don't go to college move into high-wage jobs, that we would reform the college loan program to make 20 million people eligible to refinance their loans with lower fees, longer repay-

ment periods, lower interest rates, you might not have believed it, but it happened.

If I had told you that after 7 years of deadlock we would pass the family and medical leave law to enable people to take a little time off, protecting 845,000 people right here in Minnesota; that after 7 years of deadlock we would have passed the Brady bill; that after 6 years of deadlock we would have passed a crime bill that gave you 100,000 more police, 100,000 more jail cells for violent offenders, "three strikes and you're out," yes to those good prevention programs, a ban on juvenile ownership of handguns, and a ban on assault weapons, you might not have believed it, but it happened.

If I had told you that the national service program I talked so much about would pass the Congress, be the law of the land, provide opportunities for young people all across America to rebuild their communities at home and earn money to go to college as well, 20,000 this year, 100,000 3 years from now, you might not have believed it, but it happened.

If I had told you that around the world we would keep democracy and economic growth as our foremost goal in Russia and we would stop pointing our nuclear weapons at each other; that they would withdraw their troops from Eastern Europe and the Baltics for the first time since World War II; that we would make a new partnership all over Europe with 21 nations to have defense security as one, not being divided; that we would make real headway, dramatic progress on peace in the Middle East, a breakthrough on peace in Northern Ireland, we would be actively involved in conducting the first free and fair and totally multiracial elections in South Africa, you might not have believed it, but it all happened. We are moving this country forward.

And if I had told you we would do that not with a Government that is bigger but one that is smaller, that began with a White House with the biggest work load in decades cutting its own size by 25 percent, a 272,000 reduction in the size of the Federal work force over the next 5 years to finance the crime bill out of savings, taking money from Washington and giving it to you at the community level and reorganizing vast sizes of the Federal Government to cut through redtape and promote reforms—we have given 17 States permission to embark on their own welfare reform programs, numerous States permission to try to find ways to cover all their citizens with health care coverage—if I had told you these things, you might not have believed it, but it happened. That is the record, the truth, and the facts.

Now, yes, to be sure, there is still more to do. We've had $100 million spent against us in the health care battle, and we haven't won that one yet. But we will if we keep fighting. We still have to pass the welfare reform bill next year. We still have to pass the trade legislation, campaign finance reform, lobby reform. We have lots to do. But the issue is, are we going to keep doing it, or are we going to become more partisan, more divisive, and more hot air and less real-people oriented in Washington? That is what this election is all about.

We are making progress. The economy is stronger, the deficit is lower, taxes are fairer, trade is greater, working families and communities are safer and building a new security. We are making real progress on hard problems against intense, organized opposition from the other party and from the special interests. That is the fact.

Now, what is our challenge? Our challenge in this election is that many Americans are still profoundly upset with the political system, profoundly disillusioned, even cynical. And they are in the mood to throw the rascals out without distinguishing who the rascals are. But what are the problems?

Number one, most Americans don't know what I just told you, do they? Most of you didn't know a lot of what I just told you, did you? [*Laughter*] What's the second problem? A lot of people have not felt these things. Why? The social problems we have, crime, the family breakdown problems, the violence among young people, they've been developing for 30 years. The economic problems we have, static wages for working people and troubles for farmers and people living in rural areas, they've been developing for 20 years. And the bad political policies that we've had, dividing us, the wealthy against the middle class, different races, different religions, all these political and economic and social problems we have, we had those for the last 12 years.

I have just been there 20 months. We are going in the right direction. Do not turn back. Do not turn back.

I went there, I went to Washington with the fondest hope of reaching out to Republicans on all kinds of issues—health care?

[*At this point, there was a disturbance in the audience.*]

The President. Is there a doctor here?

Audience member. No.

The President. Help. CPR?

Audience member. We have a doctor over here.

The President. We need CPR, though. Who knows CPR? No, wait, wait. Make plenty of room. We okay?

Audience member. Okay.

The President. Give him a hand; he made it up. [*Applause*] I appreciate his support for the urgency of health care reform, and we're glad to see him up and around. [*Laughter*]

Let me ask you something. I want you to know this, too. Keep in mind, I came to Washington not as a creature of Washington. I came to Washington with the fondest hope that we would be able to work together across party lines where we had honest agreements, that we would have to give a little and work a little and we'd work things out. Once in a while we did that.

We had the—the debate over NAFTA was an honest debate where most people just voted their conscience for and against. But it's about the only example I can give you. You look at the economic program. I was not there a week in Washington as your President before I was informed by one of the leaders of the other party that there would be no votes for our economic plan, no matter what changes we made.

So, look what they did. When we gave the middle class a fair break on taxes and cut the taxes for those low-income working families and asked the wealthiest Americans to pay their fair share, every Republican in the Congress said no. When we reformed the loans to benefit middle class college students, not just poor kids, middle class kids, every Republican in the Congress said no. When we gave 90 percent of the small businesses in this country an eligibility for a tax cut, all the Republicans said no. When we banned assault weapons, when we put 100,000 police on the street, when we reduced the size of the Federal Government by 270,000 to pay for that crime bill, when we protected victims in that crime bill, when we had a great section on violence against women and children, most of the Republicans voted no. And all the leaders did, and those who didn't were told they were being traitors to the Republican Party.

And when they got up and said that our prevention programs were pork, I just want to remind you that a crime bill with the prevention programs in it passed the Senate about a year ago with the votes of the Republicans 42 to 2 for. When we got close to the election and they saw that their obstructionist tactics and their negative tactics were having a positive impact on them in the poll, the 42 to 2 for changed to 6 to 34 against in the United States Senate. A friend of mine George Mitchell, the Senate Democratic leader, said, "If you took the word 'no' out of their vocabulary, they would be mute." [*Laughter*]

Let me tell you something, friends, we do have problems. And we must face them. But the issue is this administration has got a good record. We have kept our commitments. We are going in the right direction. We must see the glass is half full, not half empty.

Yes, we still have to change more of the way Government works. But after years with the Republicans badmouthing Government, we are the ones who have reduced the size of Government, we are the ones who've changed regulations of bureaucracy and slashed it and given more power back to State and local governments; we're the ones that gave the small business people the opportunity to walk into the SBA today and apply for a loan on a one-page form and get an answer in 3 days. Those are the kinds of things that we are doing.

And I just want to say this: If we're going to have the energy to keep solving our problems, we have to have our heads on straight and we have to stay with the policies that work. And when we're making progress, we have to know it and we have to get with it. This election is an opportunity for you to reassert what is best about our country, people pulling together and working together and moving forward. It's an opportunity for you to say, by the people you vote for, people like Ann Wynia, to send a signal to America that look, when the Congress gets together again, we don't care whether you're Republican or Democrat, roll up your sleeves and go to work. Don't say no to the other party, say yes to America. It's time to say yes to America.

This is the greatest country in human history. Every time I leave the borders of America and represent you in another land, I just swell with pride. People would give anything to have the diversity of our economic strength. They would give anything to find the diversity we have in our society. There are counties in America with people from 150 different racial and ethnic groups living in peace, even as people from just 2 or 3 different groups continue to kill each other with abandon in other parts of the world.

And I want you to think about that when you walk out of here. You think about what you can do for a person like Ann and how you want to feel when you see your United States Senator on television coming back from Washington. Do you want one more slogan, one more hot-air rhetoric, one more divisive statement, or do you want to look at somebody you think is imagining what your life is like, imagining how you feel when you put your kids to bed at night, imagining how you feel when you go out to work in the field or at your office the next day? That's really what this is about.

I'm telling you, other people sometimes may have a better fix on us than we do on ourselves. But it is no accident that the South Africans wanted us to spend $35 million and help them conduct their successful elections. It is no accident that the Israelis and the Arabs want us to help them work out a lasting peace in the Middle East. It is no accident that after hundreds of years of fighting, the turbulence in Northern Ireland may be coming to a close, and they want us to be involved.

And let me say this. Even at the most difficult moment of our encounter last week in Haiti, the military leaders looked at the delegation that I sent down there and said, "Well, if the President is determined to do this, and if the United Nations is determined to go forward, then at least we want the Americans in here; we know we can trust them."

That is what we are to the rest of the world. So let us be that to ourselves by voting for people who can bring out the best in us and say yes to America, people like Ann Wynia.

Thank you very much, and God bless you.

NOTE: The President spoke at 2:16 p.m. at the Minneapolis Convention Center.

Remarks at a Reception for Senatorial Candidate Alan Wheat in Kansas City, Missouri
September 24, 1994

Thank you very much, Governor Carnahan, for your leadership on so many fronts, on health care and welfare reform and for being a good friend and a good leader of this State. To you and Mrs. Carnahan, it's good to see you again. I have been here to Missouri and to Kansas City so much that the Governor and Mayor Cleaver told me that if I came one more time I would get a tax bill. [*Laughter*] But I have such a good time it might be worth it.

I'm honored to be here with your Mayor and Mrs. Cleaver. I thank him for his leadership on the crime bill especially. He made a real difference in the work that he and the other mayors did. I'm honored to be here with Chairman McCarthy, who will be an able replacement for Alan Wheat, and with all your other distinguished supporters of Alan Wheat and Yolanda.

I really wanted to come here tonight, and I hope you will give me a few moments to tell you why I think this is an important race to our country in terms of what it is I have been trying to do as your President.

Two years ago, I ran for President at a time in my life when I didn't really want to do it. I was having a wonderful time as Governor of your neighboring State. Things were going very well for me and for my wonderful family. Our friends, our work, everything, was just perfect. And it didn't look like much of a race. At the time when I entered the race the incumbent President was at 70-some percent approval. So I not only was disrupting a job that I loved and my family life and my friends and the routines and the rhythm of normal life out here in the heartland, but it looked like it was a fool's errand.

I did it for a pretty simple reason. I felt very strongly that our country was in trouble, that we were going in the wrong direction, and that we were coming apart when we ought to be coming together. I thought there was a serious chance that we would not go into the next century in a position to preserve the American dream for my daughter and for the children of this country.

I thought the leadership that the other party had provided in the White House had followed economic policies that were unfair, but more importantly didn't work, and talked about the social problems in this country in ways that divided us in order to get them votes and turn the Democrats into aliens, making voters feel that we didn't somehow share their values. But they didn't much do anything about the social problems of the country.

I thought both parties in Washington were guilty of being a little too partisan and used rhetoric, throwing at each other these words that we heard in sound bites on the evening news that didn't mean much to folks that are just living out here in the country, trying to make a living and raise their kids and deal with all the problems they face. And I thought we needed to take a new direction.

I believed strongly that we needed to try to form a new consensus in America about what the National Government ought to do; that no one felt in this global economy, where more and more of our future is determined by our competitive ability, that the Government could be a savior, as people once felt. But neither, clearly to me, could we afford to have a National Government that just sat on the sidelines and preached at us except when they were called into play for the special interests. And we were given these two different models of what the National Government ought to do, and neither one of them made any sense. We really needed somebody to go up there and bring common sense, common decency, compassion; say, "Hey, let's identify our problems, identify what the National Government has to do, and get after it. Let's be a good partner with the American people. Let's create opportunity where we can. Let's demand responsibility for the American people to do what they have to do. And let's recreate this American community, because when we're together, nothing can stop us." And I ran on that for President.

I ran against what had happened for 12 years, more division, more diversion, more distraction. The other crowd talked about the balanced budget amendment and quadrupled the debt. They told us how much they hated Government, and they hung on for all they were worth.

[*Laughter*] A lot of the ones that bad-mouthed Government couldn't bear to live outside Washington, DC. They told us how terrible the Government was, and they kept drawing their check every month from the Government. [*Laughter*] They railed against taxes as if they were protecting the middle class, but middle class taxes went up and taxes went down on the wealthiest Americans. Inequality got worse, and we didn't have much of a policy.

I believed we could do better, so 2 years ago I set out to travel this country and try to prove it. Thanks to the leadership that I enjoyed here in our campaign in Missouri, and thanks to the fact that I had a lot of friends and roots here, and maybe because I was your neighbor, you gave me a resounding victory in that election. And I'm grateful for that.

Here's what this is all about right now. And I want you to listen to this because this is important. On the night I was elected President, with a 10-point margin in Missouri, let me ask you, if I had gotten up in my acceptance speech and I had said, "Folks, thank you for electing me. I'm going to keep my pledge to you to get this country moving again and to pull this country together again, and within 20 months we will have put our economic house in order with the biggest budget cutting in history, with the elimination of scores of Government programs; we will raise tax rates on only the top 1.2 percent of the people and ask them to pay the deficit down, but we'll give a tax break to 10 times that many people, 15 million working families who are raising children just above the poverty line, because we don't want them to go back into welfare, we want them to keep working; we'll make 90 percent of the small businesses in this country eligible for a tax cut; we will reduce the size of the Federal bureaucracy to its lowest point since John Kennedy was President; and we will have 3 years of deficit reduction for the first time since Harry Truman was President," if I had told you that on election night, you would not have believed it. But it has happened.

If I had told you on election night that within 20 months we would have done more to expand trade for American products than in any comparable time period in 35 years; that NAFTA would lead to a 17-percent increase in exports to Mexico and help to fuel the boom in the auto industry, adding more employees; that we would have a worldwide trade agreement, new initiatives in Asia, new initiatives in Latin America; that we would have a real effort for the first time in decades to rebuild our shipbuilding industry, our aerospace industry; that we would be converting defense industries into engines of commercial resurgence with a remarkable innovative, high-tech-oriented defense conversion program; if I had told you that we were going to do all that, that we would target the inner cities and the poor rural areas, not for Government handouts but for free enterprise with community development banks designed to put almost $5 billion in loans to people who can go into business for themselves, and help make the banks make money as well; and that all of this together would produce 4.3 million new jobs in 20 months, 8 months of manufacturing growth for the first time in a decade in a row, that for the first time in 9 years the United States would be voted the most productive country in the world, that there would be more than 115,000 new jobs in Missouri, tax cuts for 300,000 Missourians, with tax increases on only 21,000; if I had told you that, you would not have believed it. But it happened. It's so.

On top of all that, we have passed the most comprehensive education legislation in any comparable time period since 1965, increased the people in Head Start by 200,000. We're going to immunize 2 million kids; by 1996, all kids under the age of 2 will have their shots. We're going to have a national program to help States have apprenticeships for young people who don't go to college but do want to have good jobs. And we have reformed the student loan program so that already 20 million young Americans, including over 300,000 right here in Missouri, are eligible to refinance their college loans with lower fees, longer pay-out terms, lower interest rates. That is so. That has happened.

If I had said, after 7 years of gridlock in Washington we're going to pass the family and medical leave bill, giving 900,000 Missouri families the security of knowing that they can be successful parents and successful children, as well as successful workers because they won't lose their job if they have to take a little time off from work; that we would pass the Brady bill after 7 years of obstinate refusal, that the crime bill we pass would have every single element I pledged in the campaign—100,000 more police officers, that's a 20 percent increase of on-street police officers, 100,000 more jail cells for serious offenders, tougher penalties for violent offenders, prevention funds that work, and drug treatment funds, and drug education funds to keep these kids out of trouble in the first place, a ban on juvenile ownership of handguns and the assault weapons ban, and a ban that protects, contrary to what the NRA says, protects 650 hunting weapons by any encroachment by the Federal Government whatever, you would not have believed it. But that is exactly what has happened in the last 20 months.

All the while it has been the Republicans who say they hate Government; we've got too much Government. And all the while when they had it, Government got bigger and less responsive and less effective. But under the Democratic administration, we voted to reduce the size of the Federal bureaucracy by 270,000 over 6 years and to put all the money into paying for the crime bill to make people safer at the grassroots. Under this administration, we made the Emergency Management Agency go from the most unpopular to the most popular agency in the Federal Government. Ask Governor Carnahan and anybody that dealt with the horrible flood in the Federal Government.

I could keep you here all night doing this. But I want you to know the point. The point is, we have taken on tough issues that were important to the American people. We have brought real change, and we are moving in the right direction. We don't want to turn back now and give it back to the other people.

Of course, there is still work to do. We still have to find a way to control health care costs and provide health care security to all Americans. We can't go on. In just the last day or so, one of our major newspapers carried one more horrible article about how we were spending more on health care than any country in the world by light years, and we were losing coverage, and small businesses were going broke, and families were being left behind. I will never forget the million people who wrote to me and to my wife and said, "Help us. We need health care," or "We want to provide it for our employees," or "Somebody's got to give us a chance to buy it at affordable rates." Yes, we still have to do that.

Yes, we still have to pass welfare reform at the national level. But on our own, we've given 17 States, including Missouri, waivers to do what they can do at the grassroots level to move people from welfare to work. We've made a good beginning.

Yes, we have to pass campaign finance reform, lobby reform, a whole spate of environmental initiatives that are important to the future of this country. We still have to pass the world trade agreement in the Congress.

But look what's happened: The economy is stronger; the deficit is lower; the tax system is fairer; trade is greater. We are moving forward. We are doing it with an administration that is both diverse and excellent in terms of geography, race, gender, background. We are in a situation where working families, because of the initiatives we have taken, are going to be able to be more secure, more safer, in stronger communities.

That is the real record. Now, what is the problem? I'll tell you what the problem is. Number one, nobody knows it. Even you didn't know some of this stuff, right? [*Laughter*] You have no way to find out.

I saw an article the other day where some fellow had done a focus group with some people that voted for Mr. Perot in the last election, after my press conference, and they heard me reel off some of this. And they said, "You know, I never thought the President was dishonest, but I just don't believe that. That couldn't be true. We'd know it."

Well, it is true. And you don't know it because you can't find out in the fog that surrounds what we do. But it is true. And you must take that truth to the voters because it relates directly to why Alan Wheat should be a Senator.

Now, let's be honest. People have real reasons to still be frustrated and feel negatively about the Government. They still have problems. Many of these initiatives have passed, but people haven't felt them yet. The social problems we have in our country, the drugs, the breakdown of the family, the rising violence, they've been developing for 30 years. The problems working people are having, never getting a raise, even when they work harder, because of the global economy, they've been developing for 20 years.

The wrong-headed policies that Washington pursued were in place for 12 years, and all that anti-Government rhetoric and that negativism and that predisposition to believe the worst about anybody that shows up in Washington, DC, that's been developing for 12 years.

I have only been there 20 months, but we're going in the right direction, and we do not want to turn back now.

While we have been doing—more jobs, lower deficits, more trade, more opportunity, more education, more training, tougher crime bill, smaller Government—while we have been doing, they have been talking. And they are great at talking. And they have peddled fear and division and diversion with unconscionable distortion for so long they feel no guilt whatever in whatever they say. And they are good at it. They are good at it. Sam Rayburn once said, "Any old jackass can kick down a barn, but it takes a carpenter to build one." [*Laughter*] It also takes longer to build one than it does to kick one down.

While we've been saying yes to the American people—here's where Alan comes in. I wasn't in Washington a week before they started trying to turn me into one of them to all of you. I wasn't in Washington a week until one of the Republican leaders said to me, "You will not get one, single, solitary vote for your economic plan, no matter what you do to it—nothing." And so every one of them voted no when we gave the middle class a fair shake in that economic plan, cut taxes for 15 million working families. They did it because we asked the top 1.2 percent, including some of you in this room, to pay a little more. Every one of them voted no.

When we said, "Let's do something for the middle class for a change and reform this student loan program and give middle class families a break so they can borrow the money to go to college," every one of them voted no, every one. When we said, "You say you're the small business party. Let's lower taxes on 90 percent of the small businesses in this country by increasing their expensing provision by 70 percent," every one of them voted no, every one of them. When we said, "Let's reduce the size of the Federal Government," which we did first in that bill, every one of them voted no.

Then when we got to this crime bill, last year the crime bill passed with 95 votes in the Senate; 42 to 2, the Republicans voted for it. And it was a lot like the bill we ultimately passed—had a few more police officers, some more money for prisons. But remember that pork speech they gave you? You know how it works: They pass a bill; the House passes a bill; you put them together; the final bill comes back. Well, from the time they voted 42 to 2 for the crime bill until it came back, there was not a lot more money on an annual basis

for prevention programs in there. In fact, in 4 of the years, there was less money than they had already voted for. And many of the programs in there for prevention had been cosponsored by Republicans. It was a total bipartisan effort last year before the election started. But when they got to talking instead of doing, and telling everybody how terrible we all were and how, you know, nothing was happening, and they saw it was helping them in the polls, they changed like that, and they went from 42 to 2 for it to 6 to 38 against it. And the six brave people who voted for it, including the person that Alan is trying to replace, were excoriated by their leaders for betraying the Republican Party who said that the party was far more important than bringing the crime rate down in America and saving people's lives.

Now, when we started this health care debate, there were 24 Republican Senators, 24, on a bill to provide coverage for health care for all Americans and to control costs. I didn't agree with the way they wanted to do it, but we had the same objective. They said, "We're for covering everybody, too. We want to control costs. Mr. President, we think we've got a better idea." I said, "This is wonderful. This is what I wanted to do. We'll have a bipartisan consensus. We'll work this through."

But then they got a memo from their political boss, not elected by anybody, who said, "You must defeat health care at all costs. You will give the Democrats too big a victory for the middle class, and we won't be able to keep middle class voters by scaring them about values and telling them the Democrats aren't like them. You must defeat it." So by the time the health care legislation got to the floor, how many Republicans in the Senate were still for universal coverage and controlled costs? Zero. It went from 24 to zero.

Now, that is what is going on there. We say yes; they say no. You hear conflict; conflict and defeat is what you hear. You don't know what has been done, and it's hard to assess responsibility. And I went there, folks—you remember—I went there saying both parties had been at fault in the past. We needed less partisanship, not more. I wanted to reach out my hand in this crime bill. I did reach out to the Republicans in the House and the Senate. And we got a few of them who were brave enough and good enough and cared enough about you to pass that thing.

But I am telling you, this is the most intense partisan atmosphere—and why? Because they think they are about to be rewarded for their obstreperous tactics. They believe they can sucker the American people into voting for what the American people are really against, which is too much partisanship, too much gridlock, too much special interest politics. And they believe they can do it because folks can't quite figure what's going on, and they can say, "We've got a Democrat in the White House and the Democrats in the House and the Senate have more than we do." Now, that is what is going on.

So Alan Wheat is important to Missouri. But he's important to the country, not because we will always agree, not because we will always agree but because he will show up for work in the morning. [*Laughter*] Too many of them show up for talk; or when their leaders say turn right instead of left, go back instead of forward, they say, "Yes, sir, tell me where to stand and when to walk." Now that is a fact. So I ask you to think about that.

The greatest Republican President, some of us think the greatest President we ever had, Mr. Lincoln, once said that you can fool all of the people some of the time, and you can fool some of the people all of the time, but you cannot fool all of the people all the time. This election is going to test that proposition.

I think Lincoln was right. You can't do it unless people don't know the facts. So I am asking you to do more than give money to Alan Wheat. I am asking you to go out and tell people the facts. They will peddle fear; we will peddle hope. They will say no, and we will say yes.

Harry Truman said, "America was not built on fear. It was built on courage, imagination, and an unbeatable determination to do the job at hand." The job at hand is just what it was 2 years ago, to get this country into the 21st century with a good future for our children, in a world that is more secure, more peaceful, and more democratic, and to do it by enabling all of us together to live up to the fullest of our God-given capacities. That is the job at hand.

We are doing the job at hand. Go tell the people of Missouri that, and send Alan Wheat to the Senate.

Thank you, and God bless you all.

NOTE: The President spoke at 6:24 p.m. at the Ritz-Carlton Hotel. In his remarks, he referred to Gov. Mel Carnahan of Missouri and his wife, Jean; Mayor Emanuel Cleaver II of Kansas City and his wife, Dianne; and Karen McCarthy, Democratic candidate for Congress. A tape was not available for verification of the content of these remarks.

Remarks at the Bethel A.M.E. Church in New York City
September 25, 1994

The President. Thank you so much.

[*At this point, the President was interrupted by the sound of a siren.*]

The President. That's my introduction there, you hear it? [*Laughter*] Pastor Mackey, thank you. Thank you very much. Pastor Mackey, first let me say on behalf of my family, we are glad to be here in this church with its great history going back to 1819, running the Underground Railroad to help people to freedom. I'm also glad to be here in this African Methodist Episcopal church because your church has a long history with my home State, Arkansas, and my hometown, Little Rock, where Bishop Allen came a long time ago as part of his effort to

found this church. I also want to thank you, if I might, for just letting us come here and worship. And I would like to say that for Hillary and for Chelsea and for me, this has been a great morning. And I'm sure I can say that all three of us are very grateful to all of you just for letting us come in here and to be with you.

I got a good lesson out of the briefest sermon I've heard in a long time. [*Laughter*] And I got a good lesson out of one of the most beautiful songs I have heard in a long time. I loved all the music. You know, I like music and even as I get older and I can't sing quite in tune anymore—I heard that fine man singing, "Work on Me." [*Laughter*] So I need to be here, and I need to hear that. And then I heard your pastor say, "There is always a word from the Lord."

I am grateful to be here with all these people who are my friends, with the Governor, about whom I will say more in a moment, and Carl McCall and my dear friend Ruth Messinger and Mark Green and Denny Farrell and Senator Paterson, Assemblyman Wright, and Karen Burstein who wants to be your attorney general. That's the best job I ever had. I was attorney general of my State, and you don't have to hire people or fire them. You don't have to raise taxes or cut programs. And if she ever does anything unpopular, she can just say the constitution made her do it. [*Laughter*] I hope you'll give her the chance to do it. And I want to say a special word of thanks about my friend Charlie Rangel, for what he said. You know, Charlie talked about Haiti. Let me say that for Hillary and for me, for both of us, he has been a wonderful friend and partner in so many ways. But I want to use him today in a way to get into what I want to talk about briefly.

Charlie mentioned Haiti and how the people were defenseless and poor and how hard it is for me to convince some people that our interest is at stake there, although I think more and more Americans are seeing that what we are doing there is good and supports democracy throughout our hemisphere—which is nothing more than saying our neighborhood—helps to end human rights violations that we find intolerable everywhere but unconscionable on our doorstep, and offers them a chance at stability.

But it is an example of what I ran for President about. I thought I had two jobs to get us into the next century. One is to move this country forward, just to get us to face our problems again—jobs, education, drugs, violence, crime, health care—just to face the problems and go to work on them instead of just talking about them all the time. And the other was to bring this country together instead of letting it drift apart and to try to bring the world together across the lines of race and region and income and religion.

I have just finished reading, late last night, a book about World War II and President and Mrs. Roosevelt. And I am reminded, as I think of our brave soldiers from all over the country and all their backgrounds doing their work today in Haiti, that in World War II, African-Americans were kept segregated in units in the Army until the Battle of the Bulge at the end of the war, when they had so many casualties that blacks and whites had to fight together. And they didn't do it very long before they found out they liked it very well. And the only complaint recorded in this book I read was that some of the white officers said that their black comrades were so ferocious they could hardly get them to quit fighting even when they needed to rest. I am reminded that in World War II we put Japanese-Americans in concentration camps, and then we let their children serve. And a Japanese outfit had the highest casualties of any American outfit in World War II. And in this book, I saw the picture painted by the author of the military people going to the concentration camps to give the parents of the dead boys their medals while they were keeping them behind bars because we were fighting Japan, a country they had given up.

When I was fighting to build an economic partnership with Mexico, I was reminded in so many of our endeavors, Mexican-American soldiers have had the highest rate of casualties. I look at Charlie Rangel who served his country in uniform bravely and his son who served as a United States Marine, and I think to myself, this is a country that, if we can figure out how to live together, will be strong all the way through the next century; because the world is getting smaller, and if people who are different can find oneness, there is nothing that can stop them.

That is why the South Africans wanted the United States to help run the election and spend a few million dollars for an honest election that produced the President, Nelson Mandela, who is coming here to see me in a few days. That is why the people in Ireland, having fought for 800 years against one another, wish the people of the United States to be involved in trying to bring an end to their conflict. That is why the Israelis and the Arabs wish the United States to be involved in bringing an end to that horrible, horrible period of violence in the Middle East. This is a very great country.

Even in the moment of great tension one week ago today in Haiti, when I did not know whether we would actually have to shoot our way in there, the de facto military leaders told our delegation there, President Carter, General Powell, and Senator Nunn, "Well, if the President is determined to do this, if the United

Nations is determined to do this, we want the Americans here because we trust them." I say that because if we can just face our challenges and move forward and come together, we're going to be all right.

Now, when the pastor said, "There is always a word from the Lord," I looked at the program and I saw the word from the Lord, Isaiah 40:31, "They that wait upon the Lord shall renew their strength. They will mount up with wings as eagles." But I want to talk to you about the rest of the verse, "They shall run and not grow weary. They shall walk and not faint."

Now, I have a simple message for you today. The people who don't want us to get together and who have a very different idea about moving forward than most of us do are hoping and praying that you will grow weary, that you will not run, that you will not walk, that you will just grow weary.

Look at Mr. McCall here. How many times do people all over America say, "If only our children had more role models, if only men would take responsibility for their families and their communities and set a good example and lift our children up." Oh, how many times do you hear it said? Well, folks, you've got a chance to send a message to this entire country that people who make something of themselves and who stand for something good and who work for what is right will be rewarded without regard to their background, that we are going to go forward and we are going to do it together. And if you will not grow weary, you can do it.

And let me say something about Governor Cuomo. His greatest failing is he speaks about me better than he speaks about himself. [*Laughter*] By the time he got through nominating me for President in New York, he had me convinced I ought to have the job. [*Laughter*] I grew 3 inches sitting out there in the pew today just listening to him talk.

They say, "Well, the Governor will have a hard time getting reelected; after all, he's running for a fourth term." I know about that. I did that one time. And I was out in a little booth in the State fair in Little Rock—I want you to listen to this, this could be about him instead of me, this is how it happened—and every year at the State fair in my little rural State, I would go to the fair and have a Governor's Day. And anybody could come up and talk to the Governor and say whatever they

wanted. And I lived in a rural State where most people call me by my first name, including my enemies, and they said whatever they wanted. [*Laughter*] And so I listened to this all day. And I was having to decide whether I would run for reelection. I had been Governor a long time. And along toward the end of the day, an old man in overalls came up to me, and he said, "Bill, you going to run again?" I said, "I don't know. If I do, will you vote for me?" He said, "Yes, I will. I always have." And I said, "Well, aren't you sick of me after all these years?" He said, "No, but everybody else I know is." [*Laughter*] And then he said, "But what do you expect? All you have done is nag us. You're always trying to get us to do something else, always pushing us on jobs and education and taking care of kids." And he said, "You know, it's just hard to take all that. But you know something? It's beginning to work, and I'm going to stick with it." And I went all across my State and told that story on myself. But I told the last part, too, and the people sent me back.

How many times in the Bible—I think two or three times—does our Saviour say, "A prophet is not with honor except in his own land"? Most places would give anything to have a leader like Governor Cuomo. And you can say, "Well, he's been there a long time." Let me tell you something: In a lot of ways, this is his first term and it just started, because it's the first time we've had a chance to work together as partners.

I ask you to consider the problems of America, the breakdown of community, the breakdown of family, the rise of drugs and violence and gangs, the things that grip you here every day. Do you think that just started yesterday? That's been going on for 30 years. I told my wife and daughter as we were coming up here today that when I was a young man living in England, I used to come back to the United States when I was sent over there for a couple of years, and I would land in New York. And unlike most people like me, I mean, here I was—and I had an even bigger accent back then—I took the transportation, and I got off at 125th and Lennox—[*laughter*]—every time I came back here, and I walked alone through Harlem because I was fascinated by it. I wanted to see the people. I wanted to talk to the people. I wanted to see what they were up against. Even then I can remember some people, back when the drug of choice was heroin, leaning in corners with needles in their arms. This didn't just happen overnight, friends.

And these economic problems that we've got, they've been going—the social problems, 30 years. What are the economic problems? Not only do we have a lot of people out of work, we've got a lot of people working like crazy never getting a raise, right? And they are worried about losing their health care, or they're worried about losing their pensions. How long has that been going on? Twenty years. Twenty years we have been struggling to organize ourselves and to educate ourselves and to be competitive in a global economy.

And then our governmental policies, how long did we hear from our Government that the real answer was, to all of our problems, bad-mouth the Federal Government, lower taxes on the wealthiest of Americans, burden the middle class, reduce investment in our future, and explode the debt? And all the time, the people that were in cussed the Government as they were doing their best to stay in the Government and keep drawing those checks. That happened for 12 years, right?

I have been President for 20 months, not 30 years, not 20 years, not 10 years. When Mario Cuomo became Governor, it was all he could do to stand up against the tide of walking away from the States, walking away from the cities, walking away from the people. And in 20 months, because we're working together— my partner Mr. Rangel and I, my partner Governor Cuomo and I, we're all working together with people in the private sector—we brought our national deficit down for 3 years in a row for the first time since Mr. Truman was President. We've done something the other party said they were for, but never did: We have reduced the size of the Federal Government. It's going to be as small as it was when Mr. Kennedy was President, at the end of my term. But we gave all the money back to you to pay for the crime bill the Governor talked about. We empowered the communities and the States to hire the police, to build the prisons, to have the drug education, the drug treatment, the other programs for the kids, the job programs. We at least got the health care debate into both Houses of Congress and on the floor for the first time in American history, and we've got to keep doing that.

We've had 4.3 million new jobs, manufacturing jobs increasing for almost a year now, the longest period they've increased in a decade. Our country was voted the most productive country in the world by a panel of international economists just the other day for the first time in 9 years. Just this week, I signed a bill that will help Harlem, that will help New York City, that will point $4.8 billion into special banks to loan money to poor folks who can't borrow money to go into business, just this week, something I specifically pledged to do when I ran for President.

Now what's happening? We're having an election in which there are 30 years of social problems, 20 years of economic problems, and 12 years of politics bad-mouthing the Government. And we've done more in any 20-month period than anybody has in a month of Sundays. But a lot of people have not felt it yet, and they cannot know it, as the Governor said, because there's no way for them to get the information except in an election where we tell people.

So we now find a situation in which the people may actually go out and vote for the very things that they are against, because they don't know what has happened in 20 months and they see the wake of the last 30 years; an election which depends largely, on its outcome, on those same people's ability to bad-mouth those of us that are trying to move the country forward and bring the country together, so you will be weary and stay home and not mount up with wings as eagles, not run or walk without growing weary or fainting.

One day a long time ago, I suffered a terrible setback in my public life. I was trying to do something for the people of my State. It was a very bad day for me, not personally but because I had failed to help hundreds of people I had worked to help. And my secretary, who was a great woman of faith, kept one of those Scripture calendars on her desk. And I was alone in my office, almost in tears, and she looked at the calendar for the first time and ripped off the calendar piece and brought it into me and gave me what has ever since been my favorite verse of Scripture from St. Paul's letter to the Galatians: "Let us not grow weary in doing good, for in due season we shall reap if we do not lose heart."

I say to you today, my fellow Americans, we've just been here 20 months. We're 4.3 million jobs better. We're a crime bill better. We're the immunization bill better; 2 million kids are going to get their shots by '96. We're 200,000 more children in Head Start better. We're coming together more.

Do not lose heart. Show up. Talk to the people in your neighborhoods; tell them to show up. Scripture says we're supposed to be good citizens, too. Mario Cuomo is the heart that you must not lose. Mr. McCall is the heart that you must not lose. These people are the heart that you must not lose. Do not let a moment pass. When the movement is in the for-ward direction and the feelings are not there yet, stay strong, mount up, go forward.

God bless you.

NOTE: The President spoke at 12:39 p.m. In his remarks, he referred to Rev. O'Neil Mackey, Sr., pastor, Bethel A.M.E. Church; H. Carl McCall, New York State comptroller; Ruth W. Messinger, Manhattan Borough president; Mark Green, New York City public advocate; Herman D. (Denny) Farrell and Keith L. Wright, members, New York State Assembly; and David Paterson, New York State senator.

Statement on Haiti
September 25, 1994

We regret any loss of life in connection with our mission in Haiti, but it must be clear that U.S. forces are prepared to respond to hostile action against them and will do so. We will continue to work with Haitian military authorities for a peaceful transition.

Remarks at a Democratic Congressional Campaign Committee Dinner in New York City
September 25, 1994

Thank you very much. Congressman Fazio, thank you, first of all, for the absolutely wonderful job you have done in the leadership of the Democratic Congressional Campaign Committee. That is very often a thankless task. It requires a Member of Congress to travel a long way from home, even when he or she may need to be home. And Vic has done it; Judy has worked hard; they have been brilliant. And I am very, very grateful for what they have done. I'd also like to thank Sumner Redstone and Phyllis and all the rest of you who have done your part to make this night a success. And I thank all the Members of the Congress who are here who are my partners in this effort to change our country and move it forward.

I want to talk a little tonight about why this election is important and why we need not simply your contributions but your commitment to work and to talk and to reach your friends in the next several weeks.

Two years ago, I was involved in a campaign for President that started almost 3 years ago now. Up until that time, I was living at home, doing my job as Governor of my State, serving my fifth term. Our economy was finally beginning to grow much more rapidly than the Nation's, after a decade of working to turn it around. I was as happy as I had ever been, personally and professionally, and I felt immensely committed to the work I was doing.

I left that job and embarked on what a lot of people thought was a fool's errand. The incumbent President was then at 70 percent in the polls or more. I did it because I did not believe our country was facing up to the challenges of the post-cold-war world. I did not believe we were doing what we needed to do to move into the 21st century the strongest and greatest country in the world, keeping the American dream alive for our children. I thought the leadership of the other party was taking us in the wrong direction.

I watched for 12 years while we talked about how terrible Government spending was and quadrupled the national debt. I watched people talk about how they wanted term limits and then be willing to say anything in the wide world to get elected so they could keep drawing a Government check. I watched people talk about the idea of America and then try to divide Americans by race, by region, by religion. I watched people say they represented the interests of ordinary Americans and then raise taxes on the middle class, lower them on the wealthiest Americans, and still not invest in our country, in fact, reduced investment in education and training and the things that will enable ordinary Americans to compete and win in the global economy.

And I also believed there needed to be some change in the way both parties worked in Washington. I would, like most Americans do, get a lot of my news by sitting at home at night and looking at the television news or reading the newspaper. And I would often think that the sound bites, the clips that came across the airwaves, didn't bear much relationship to the world I live in and the people I lived around and the concerns that the people I represented had.

Politics in Washington seemed to me to be unduly negative, unduly partisan, and frankly, unduly abstract and divorced from the way people are. I thought that we needed a conception of the role of our National Government in our lives that was somewhat different than the debate often seemed to be. I didn't think that Government could answer all the problems or be a savior, but neither did I think Government could sit on the sidelines or just sort of enter the game when there were particular interests that needed to be protected.

It seems to me that we ought to learn to believe in our Government again as an extension of ourselves, as our partner, that in a world that is properly and thankfully dominated by private sector and free markets, the Government ought not to do things that others can do as well or better. But there are some things the Government has to do to ensure opportunity for Americans, to enable Americans to assume personal responsibility for their own welfare and that of their families, and to rebuild this almost mystical thing we know as the American community.

We're going into a period of profound change, and the dimensions of the future are not fully clear to anybody. But it is obvious to me that the success of this country will depend as much as anything else on our spirit, on our attitude, on whether we believe we can make change our friend and not our enemy, on whether we believe that our diversity is a source of strength and unity and not weakness and division, and on whether we are willing to have the discipline as well as the courage and vision to pay the price of time, because many of the conditions with which we must deal did not arise overnight and cannot be erased overnight.

After 12 years in which I thought this country was not led very well, because we were divided instead of united and because we weren't going forward, we were going backward economically, I thought we could change all that. So I ran for President. And I got elected. And I have to tell you that if you ask me to evaluate how well we've done in the last 20 months, I think we have done an excellent job of moving the country forward. But I still haven't figured out how to bring the country together given the obstacles to honest, open, clear debate and the obstacles of people even getting the information about what is going on.

If on the day I was inaugurated President I had given an Inaugural Address that said, 20 months from now, folks, consistent with my campaign commitments, we will put our economic house in order; we will have cut the deficit by a record amount, over $500 billion, much more than it was going to be cut under the previous administration in their plans; we would have way over $250 billion in spending cuts; we would abolish scores of Government programs outright; we would raise taxes on the wealthiest 1.2 percent of Americans, including virtually everybody in this room—thanks for sticking with us—[*laughter*]—but we would lower taxes on more than 10 times as many Americans, 15 million of them living in families where people are working and raising children just above the poverty line, and we don't want them to give up on work and go on welfare, we want them to succeed as workers and parents; that we would make 90 percent of the small businesses in this country eligible for a tax cut; that we would reduce the Federal bureaucracy to its smallest size since John Kennedy was President—the other guys always talked about hating the Government, but it got bigger under them—we made it smaller; and that we would have 3 years of deficit reduction in a row for the first time since President Truman was in office, if I had told you that 20 months ago, you'd say, "There's another one of those politicians making promises that he can't keep." But that is exactly what we have done. That is the record of this administration and this Congress.

If I had said, in 20 months we will have more expansion of world trade than at any time in the last 35 years; the Federal Government will get back on the side of American business and American workers in trying to compete and win in the global marketplace; we'll have a strategy for aerospace, a strategy for shipbuilding, a strategy for automobiles, a strategy for high tech; we will take $30 billion off the list of things we can't sell overseas and start selling them; we will sell in California everything from rice to apples in Japan for the very first time; we will pass NAFTA and trade will increase to Mexico 17 percent in one year alone, we'll actually be adding autoworkers in America because of our expansion of trade with our neighbor to the south; if I had told you all that, you'd say, "Well, that sounds good, but you can't do it." But that is in fact the record of this administration, and that is what has been done.

And the result has been—if I had told you this, you'd have really thought I was nuts: 4.3 million new jobs in 20 months, over 90 percent of them in the private sector in contrast with the record of the previous decade; 8 months of manufacturing job growth in a row for the first time in 10 years; and for the first time in 9 years America was voted in the Annual Review of International Economists as the most productive economy in the world, the number one economy in the world, for the first time in 9 years. That is the record of the last 20 months that this Congress has helped this administration to make, working with the American people.

If I had said that in 20 months we will pass more education and training reform legislation than in any comparable period in the last 20 years—200,000 more young people in Head Start; the Goals 2000 bill which establishes national standards for the performance of our schools and promotes grassroots reforms to achieve them; a national program to help every State have a system for moving the kids who don't go to college into high-wage jobs with extra training and apprenticeships; a dramatic reform of the student loan program which has made 20 million Americans eligible to refinance their college loans at lower fees, lower interest rates, and longer repayment terms; 100,000 young Americans over 3 years in national service solving the problems of America at home and earning money against their college education— if I had told you that, you might not have believed it, but that is the record of this Congress. That's exactly what they've done in just 20 months, and the American people need to know it. And when they do, they will reward them for having done it.

Now, if I had said, while we weren't doing those other things, we broke 7 years of gridlock and passed the family and medical leave law so people can have a little time off from work when their kids are born or when their parents are sick without losing their jobs; 7 years of gridlock and passed the Brady bill; 6 years of gridlock and passed a crime bill that had, almost to the specifics, everything I recommended in the campaign of 1992: 100,000 more police on the street—there are only 550,000 of them there today—100,000 more police on the street, 100,000 more prison cells for violent criminals, prevention programs to give kids something to say yes to, drug treatment, drug education programs, alternative punishments for first offenders like drug courts and boot camps; if I had told you all that, and I said, "Oh, by the way, we're going to ban juvenile ownership of handguns, and nobody thinks that anybody can ever beat the NRA in the Congress, but we will actually pass an assault weapons ban," if I had said that, you would have said, "Nice try, but it's another bunch of political promises." That is exactly the record of this Congress and this administration in the last 20 months.

And let me say again, we did this by making the Government smaller. Our White House is the most active in a generation. We cut the White House staff when I came in office to set an example. We are cutting the Federal bureaucracy over 6 years by 272,000 people and giving every last red cent of the money back to communities to pay for the crime bill. We have really reinvented the Government. The other guys always talked about the terrible Federal bureaucracy.

When I became President, the most unpopular agency in the Federal Government was the Emergency Management Agency because every time there was a disaster, they made it worse. [*Laughter*] It is now the most popular agency in Federal Government because I appointed somebody to run it who'd actually dealt with disasters before. And you can talk to the people in California, the people in the Middle West, the people in the Southeast, everybody who's dealt with it.

They're supposed to be the party of small business. Now, because I've put somebody in the Small Business Administration who had actually spent 20 years starting small businesses instead of losing elections, which is how it's usually filled, you can now go to the SBA and fill out—if you want a loan, you fill out a one-page form, and you get an answer, yes or no, in 3 days. That is stuff they talked about, but we did.

And I could give you lots of other examples. Vic's from California. When they had that earthquake in southern California and the busiest highway in America was shattered, right, what did we do? We had an innovative contract out there. We said, "If you can beat the deadline and you will work around the clock 7 days a week, we'll give you a premium." And we beat the deadline by more than half of what they said it would take to finish it. We opened it months early, the highway. The American people who have to ride on that road in California know that we are delivering.

So this is a very different image, right, than you hear when our adversaries talk about this administration. And while we were doing all this, we made a remarkable partnership for democracy and economic growth with Russia. We've worked with them as the Russian troops have been withdrawn from the Baltics and Eastern Europe for the first time since World War II. We've got 21 new nations in a new security partnership with NATO, trying to unite Europe for the first time since nation states have existed there. We are working with the Irish and the British on peace in Northern Ireland. We worked to help conduct free and fair elections that produced Nelson Mandela's miraculous victory in South Africa. We have worked hard to make dramatic steps forward on peace in the Middle East and, I believe, in what we are doing tonight in Haiti.

Now, that is the record of the last 20 months. Do we have a lot of work to do? Sure, we do. We've still got a lot of things we could do back in Washington now: pass the GATT

worldwide trade agreement, pass campaign finance reform, pass the lobby reform bill. There's a whole spate of environmental legislation still waiting to be passed in the Congress right now. And I will never give up until we have finally joined the ranks of other nations and found a way to provide health care to all Americans and to bring the cost in line with inflation, because if we don't do that the deficit will start to go up again, and being in Congress will be a matter of writing health care checks for the same old health care with no money to invest in America's future.

Yes, there is work to do. But the fact is, the economy is stronger, the deficit is lower, taxes are fairer, trade is greater, working families and communities have a chance to be secure and safer. That is the record of this Congress and this administration in the last 20 months. The American people don't know it, but thanks to your help, they will by election day, and the results will be there.

Now, you might ask, "Well, Mr. President, if you're so smart, why don't they know it?" First of all, many people—let's deal with the real world—many people have not felt these changes in their own lives. When they have, I can tell you who they're voting for—when a person comes up to me and says, "I have doubled my business in international trade; thank you. I never thought I'd be a Democrat, but I am now." And a man in the White House came up to me on a Sunday morning several months ago and he was going through a tour, which is very unusual on Sunday morning, with his three children, and I noticed one was in a wheelchair. This man came up and grabbed me and he said, "I want to tell you something. My little girl here is sick, and she's probably not going to live. And her wish was to see the White House. But because of that family leave law, which your predecessor vetoed twice, I can take time off from work and spend this precious time with my daughter without losing my job and hurting my other children and my wife. Don't you ever think what you do up here does not make a difference; it does." But most people haven't felt it.

And look at the problems of the country. We have social problems that we have had now developing for 30 years, the crime, the drugs, the family breakdown. We have economic problems that working people feel in the form of stagnant wages and fragile benefits that have been developing for 20 years. We had a political climate that said that the Government would mess up a one-car parade, that Democrats were aliens, and that tried to divide us and frighten us for 12 years.

We've just been here 20 months, folks, but we are going in the right direction. And the thing that we must not permit to happen is to have the American people, out of their frustration and out of our failure to tell them what we've done, vote for that which they are against. That is why your presence here is important tonight.

Also, let's face it, the guys we're running against are good at talking. And they have a simple system: rule or ruin. They've not much interest in doing. So they're not only good at talking, they've got more time to work on it than we do. We show up for work every day; they show up for talk. You think I'm kidding? Every single Member of the other party in Congress, every last one, voted against that economic program. And you say, "Well, maybe they just didn't like it." No, no, no, no, I was told the first week I was President by one of the Republican leaders that there would not be a single vote for the economic program, no matter how we changed it. He said, "We want to be in a position to blame you if it doesn't work. And if it doesn't work, we'll still blame you, and we'll convince people that you taxed them even if you didn't." That's what I was told the first week I showed up.

So when we gave the 15 million working people a tax break, every one of them said no. When we made 90 percent of small businesses—supposed to be their constituents—when we made 90 percent of them eligible for a tax break, every one of them said no. When we gave 20 million Americans a break on their college loans and all the middle class kids to come, not just poor kids, middle class kids, every one of them voted no, every single one of them. When we made the first big cut in the size of the Federal Government in three decades, every one of them voted no. George Mitchell, our Democratic leader, said that if you took the word no out of their vocabulary, a bunch of them would be stone mute. [*Laughter*]

Then, we moved to the crime bill. When we banned assault weapons, passed a dramatic bill to deal with the problems of violence against women and children in the homes, passed a bill that protected the rights of victims in the criminal justice process, put 100,000 more police on the street, put 100,000 more prison cells out there, toughened the penalties, all their leaders and most of them voted no. And the ones that didn't were absolutely excoriated for putting their country ahead of their party.

Now, these are facts. When I showed up in Washington, I really believed that we would be able to do what we did with just a few Republicans on the crime bill and more on trade. I thought we would be able to have a more nonpartisan or bipartisan spirit of governance because so many of these problems are new problems. They don't fit within the proper categories of Democrat and Republican that you could tell right off in the forties, fifties, or sixties, well, who would vote which way. These are new and different problems. So I said to myself, I will reach out to them. But I already gave you one example. On the budget bill they told me in advance.

On the crime bill, let me tell you what happened. Last year the Senate passed the crime bill with the assault weapons ban and a vote among the Republicans was 42 to 2 for the crime bill. My ratings in the polls were high at the time. It was a long way from the election at the time, and they never dreamed the House would pass the ban on assault weapons because they knew they'd have to vote on it separately. Lo and behold, the House, stunning me, passed it by two votes. I thought that the NRA would beat us like a yard dog in the House on that. Lo and behold, they passed it. So the bill goes to conference. And it comes out, and then all of a sudden they start making all these speeches about pork.

Let me tell you something, when the Senate passed the bill, it was 4½ years long. When we passed it, it was 6 years long. We put more money in it for 100,000 instead of 50,000 police and a little more money in it for prisons, but the prevention programs were actually slightly higher on an annual basis in the bill the Republicans voted for 42 to 2 than they were in the bill they voted against 6 to 38. Nothing had changed except the politics. In their conference, they were told, "Our job is not to lower the crime rate and make the American people more secure. Our job is to stiff anything that the other party and that administration tries to do."

I'll give you a third example, health care. When I introduced our health care bill, I said, "Look, this may not be a perfect bill. It's the best I can do. But what we ought to do is do what other sensible countries have done. We ought to find a way to cover everybody in a way that brings cost more in line with inflation. And we ought to do it by keeping the system as private as possible, private health care providers. And I don't want to eliminate private health insurance, and this is my idea." I was so happy; there was a bill introduced in the Senate by 24 Republican Senators that did the same thing, provided coverage for everybody and controlled costs, universal coverage and cost control. It wasn't the way I would have done it, but I was elated. I thought, this is what I came to Washington to do. We're going to have a debate, and they'll say, you know, they'll characterize my plan unfairly, they'll brag on theirs, and we'll get together and work it out. We'll solve this problem for the American people and everybody will share the credit. By the time our bill got to the floor, do you know how many Republican Senators were left on that bill to provide universal coverage? Zero. Not a single solitary one. Why? Politics. One of them was quoted in your local paper here the other day saying, "Well, we killed health care. Now the trick is not to have our fingerprints on it."

I just gave you a list of all those things that are back in Washington awaiting action. In the House where all these folks work, you can't delay action. We may or may not get any of those things voted on now because for the first time in the history of the Republic—never has this happened before, ever—the Republican Senators are requiring the Democratic majority to jump through procedural hoops that take 30 hours just to get a vote on procedural things to take up bills. And then when they run through this exhausting 30 hours, half of them jump on the bandwagon and vote for it so they won't get caught doing what they did. It has never happened before, ever.

Those are just four examples. I'm telling you, I came here running, saying the Democrats had problems, too, we had to change the partisan environment. But I want the American people to know that the no-sayers in this crowd are the leaders of the Republicans in Congress.

There are a lot of good Republicans in the Congress that would like to work with us on a lot of issues, and most of the time they are threatened with their very lives. You see the Congressman from Iowa was threatened; he was

told, under no circumstances could he cooperate with any of us on health care.

Now, the American people need to know that. Why? Because this is a time of change. We're moving away from the cold war into a new era. I am convinced the 21st century can be the best time this country ever had. I believe that. I believe that. But we have to be able to face our challenges in an open and honest way. We have to be able to make change our friend, and that requires a certain level of security.

And all the American people here with this sort of partisan, negative stuff pounding on them day in and day out, they do not know what we have done. We haven't had time to talk; we've been busy doing. So we're going to go out now and talk. But if you think about your organization, whatever it is, we live on people-power today. And people-power depends on spirit as well as it does brains. You cannot get anything done in a world where people determine the course of history unless people are in a good frame of mind. You think about whatever it is you do and wherever it is you work, and how well would you do if two-thirds of the people showed up every day convinced what you were doing was in the wrong direction and nothing good could ever happen; they were in a deep funk. Wouldn't be very pleasant to go to work, would it?

That is what our political adversaries actually try to create every day in the minds of the American people. They say no; they play on their fears; they try to turn us into aliens. And frankly, they do a very good job at it. And when we can't get out there and talk to them, they do it. But the bad thing is not what happens to me or whether I get reelected or Vic gets reelected. In the big line of history, that's not as important as whether the American people face the future with confidence and hope and are willing to take on their challenges and are willing to find strength in our diversity. That is what we have to do.

And I am telling you, that's what this election is all about. It's not about seats in Congress and everything else, except as they reflect whether we are going into the future with fear or hope. If you think about this time in our history, it's most like the times at the ends of the wars. At the end of the First World War, the American people were tired, distracted, they got inward looking. They said, "We're just going to walk away from everything." What happened?

We elected three Presidents, starting with Mr. Harding who promised us normalcy, whatever that is. What was normalcy? Normalcy was the rise of the Ku Klux Klan, the Red Scare, and a global depression.

Then at the end of the Second World War, Harry Truman found himself as President. He was at 80 percent approval in the polls the day after he dropped the atomic bomb that ended the war. Two years later, when he sent national health reform to Congress for the second time, he was at 36 percent in the polls. Why? He was an instrument of change, and it was disruptive to the established order of things. But, he said, "We've got to rebuild Japan and Germany and rebuild Europe and have international mechanisms for growth." He carried through on Roosevelt's vision of the United Nations, where I will speak tomorrow. He said, "We have to stand up to the Communist threat and limit it, and we have to rebuild America at home." And it required change, and it was difficult and uncomfortable. But when he finally got out there on that train and told the American people the truth, they stuck with him. And now most people think Harry Truman ought to be on Mount Rushmore.

But I'll tell you something. I come from a family that was for him when he was living, and it wasn't so simple back then. Because when countries go through periods of change, they are just like people. You think about every period of change you've been through in your life, when you went off to college, when you got married, when you had your first child, when you took your first job, when you started your first business. Every period of change is marked by hope and fear, isn't it? And when you're going through the change as opposed to the beginning or the end of it, when you're going through it, every day you wake up and it's like there are these scales inside, and some day hope's winning and some day fear's winning. Right? In your personal life.

That is what our country is going through today. And all these dire predictions about the election and all these polls showing how sour and frustrated the American people are—let me tell you something, the people of this country are good people. And if you give them a chance, they will do the right thing 99 times out of 100. And they desperately want to believe in the future of this country, but they have been bombarded with everything that's wrong. They have not heard what is right. And there are real objective problems still out there. Our job is not always to win but to be the party of hope over fear, to be the party of big over little, to be the party of change over the status quo, to be the party of the children's future, not yesterday's vision. And I believe, since this is a time of change, that also, in the end, is the right thing to do politically. The right thing to do morally for our kids and their future is the right thing to do politically.

And I want you to look around this room. Every Member of this Congress that's here—there were bills that we won by one vote, by two votes, bills that passed by the narrowest of margins—they deserve credit for stepping up to the plate and voting for the future of this country and for our children instead of for their momentary interests, and they deserve to be rewarded in this election. And if you want the changes for this country to continue until all Americans feel them, then I ask you not to quit with your check tonight but to keep speaking for them and working for them and talking to your friends and getting them to help all the way until election day, because they are about the future of this country.

Thank you, and God bless you all.

NOTE: The President spoke at 8:45 p.m. at the Waldorf-Astoria Hotel. In his remarks, he referred to Representative Vic Fazio, chairman, and his wife, Judy, finance director, Democratic Congressional Campaign Committee; and Sumner Redstone, chairman, Viacom, and his wife, Phyllis.

Remarks to the 49th Session of the United Nations General Assembly in New York City
September 26, 1994

Mr. President, Mr. Secretary-General, distinguished delegates. First, let me congratulate you, Mr. President, on your election as President of the 49th General Assembly. The American people look forward to working with you to celebrate the United Nations 50th anniversary.

We meet today in a time of great hope and change. The end of the cold war, the explosion of technology and trade and enterprise have given people the world over new opportunities to live up to their dreams and their God-given potential. This is an age of hope.

Yet, in this new world, we face a contest as old as history, a struggle between freedom and tyranny, between tolerance and bigotry, between knowledge and ignorance, between openness and isolation. It is a fight between those who would build free societies governed by laws and those who would impose their will by force. Our struggle today, in a world more high-tech, more fast-moving, more chaotically diverse than ever, is the age-old fight between hope and fear.

Three times in this century, from the trenches of the Sommes to the island of Iwo Jima to the shattered wall of Berlin, the forces of hope were victorious. But the victors of World War I squandered their triumph when they turned inward, bringing on a global depression and allowing fascism to rise and reigniting global war.

After World War II, the Allies learned the lessons of the past. In the face of a new totalitarian threat and the nuclear menace, great nations did not walk away from the challenge of the moment. Instead they chose to reach out, to rebuild, and to lead. They chose to create the United Nations, and they left us a world stronger, safer, and freer.

Our generation has a difficult task. The cold war is over; we must secure the peace. It falls to us to avoid the complacency that followed World War I without the spur of the imminent threat to our security that followed World War II. We must ensure that those who fought and found the courage to end the cold war, those from both East and West who love freedom, did not labor in vain.

Our sacred mission is to build a new world for our children, more democratic, more prosperous, more free of ancient hatreds and modern means of destruction. That is no easy challenge, but we accept it with confidence. After all, the walls that once divided nations in this very chamber have come down. More nations have chosen democracy than ever before, more have chosen free markets and economic justice, more have embraced the values of tolerance and liberty and civil society that allow us all to make the most of our life.

But while the ideals of democracy and free markets are ascendant, they are surely not the whole story. Terrible examples of chaos, repression, and tyranny also mark our times. The 20th century proved that the forces of freedom and democracy can endure against great odds. Our job is to see that in the 21st century these forces triumph.

The dangers we face are less stark and more diffuse than those of the cold war, but they are still formidable: the ethnic conflicts that drive millions from their homes; the despots ready to repress their own people or conquer their neighbors; the proliferation of weapons of mass destruction; the terrorists wielding their deadly arms; the criminal syndicates selling those arms or drugs or infiltrating the very institutions of fragile democracy; a global economy that offers great promise but also deep insecurity and, in many places, declining opportunity; diseases like AIDS that threaten to decimate nations; the combined dangers of population explosion and economic decline which prompted the world community to reach the remarkable consensus at the Cairo conference; global and local environmental threats that demand that sustainable development becomes a part of the lives of people all around the world; and finally, within many of our nations, high rates of drug abuse and crime and family breakdown with all their terrible consequences. These are the dangers we face today.

We must address these threats to our future. Thankfully, the end of the cold war gives us a chance to address them together. In our efforts, different nations may be active in different situations in different ways. But their purposes must be consistent with freedom and their practices consistent with international law. Each nation will bring to our common task its own particular strengths, economic, political, or military.

Of course, the first duty of every member of the United Nations is to its own citizens, to their security, their welfare, and their interests. As President of the United States, my first duty is to the citizens of my country. When our national security interests are threatened, we will act with others when we can, but alone if we must. We will use diplomacy when we can, but force if we must.

The United States recognizes that we also have a special responsibility in these common endeavors that we are taking, the responsibility that goes along with great power and also with our long history of democracy and freedom. But we seek to fulfill that responsibility in cooperation with other nations. Working together increases the impact and the legitimacy of each of our actions, and sharing the burdens lessons everyone's load. We have no desire to be the world's policemen, but we will do what we can to help civil societies emerge from the ashes of repression, to sustain fragile democracies, and to add more free markets to the world, and of course, to restrain the destructive forces that threaten us all.

In every corner of the globe, from South Africa to Asia, to Central and Eastern Europe, to the Middle East and Latin America, and now to a small island in the Caribbean, ordinary citizens are striving to build their own future. Promoting their cause is our generation's great opportunity, and we must do it together.

A coalition for democracy—it's good for America. Democracies, after all, are more likely to be stable, less likely to wage war. They strengthen civil society. They can provide people with the economic and political opportunities to build their futures in their own homes, not to flee their borders. Our efforts to help build more democracies will make us all more secure, more prosperous, and more successful as we try to make this era of terrific change our friend and not our enemy.

In my Nation, as in all of your nations, there are many people who are understandably reluctant to undertake these efforts, because often the distances are great or the cultures are different. There are good reasons for the caution that people feel. Often, the chances of success

or the costs are unclear. And of course, in every common endeavor there is always the potential for failure and often the risk of loss of life. And yet our people, as we have seen in the remarkable global response to the terrible crisis in Rwanda, genuinely want to help their neighbors around the world and want to make some effort in our common cause.

We have seen that progress can be made as well. The problem is deciding when we must respond and how we shall overcome our reluctance. This will never be easy; there are no simple formulas. All of us will make these decisions, in part, based on the distance of the problem from our shores or the interests of our nation or the difference we think we can make or the cost required or the threat to our own citizens in the endeavor. Hard questions will remain and cannot be erased by some simple formula.

But we should have the confidence that these efforts can succeed, whether they are efforts to keep people alive in the face of terrible tragedy, as in Rwanda, or our efforts to avert a tragedy, as in the Horn of Africa, or our efforts to support processes that are literally changing the future of millions. History is on our side.

We should have confidence about this. Look at the march of freedom we have seen in just the last year alone. Who, a decade ago, would have dared predict the startling changes in South Africa, in the Middle East, in Ireland: the stunning triumph of democracy and majority rule; the redemption of the purpose of Nelson Mandela's life; the brave efforts of Israel and its Arab neighbors to build bridges of peace between their peoples; the earnest search by the people of Northern Ireland and Great Britain and Ireland to end centuries of divisions and decades of terror. In each case, credit belongs to those nations' leaders and their courageous people. But in each instance, the United States and other nations were privileged to help in these causes.

The growth of cooperation between the United States and the Russian Federation also should give us all great cause for confidence. This is a partnership that is rooted in democracy, a partnership that is working, a partnership of not complete agreement but genuine mutual respect.

After so many years of nuclear terror, our two nations are taking dramatic steps to ease tensions around the world. For the first time since World War II, foreign troops do not occupy the nations of Central and Eastern Europe. The Baltic nations are free. Russian and American missiles no longer target each other's people. Three of the four nuclear members of the former Soviet Union have agreed to remove all nuclear weapons from their soil. And we are working on agreements to halt production of fissile materials for nuclear explosives, to make dismantling of nuclear warheads transparent and irreversible, and to further reduce our nuclear weapons and delivery vehicles.

The United States and Russia also recognize that we must cooperate to control the emerging danger of terrorists who traffic in nuclear materials. To secure nuclear materials at their sources, we have agreed with Russia to stop plutonium production by the year 2000, to construct a storage facility for fissile materials and buying up stocks of weapons-grade fuels, and to combat the criminals who are trying to smuggle materials for nuclear explosives.

Our two nations and Germany have increased cooperation and engaged in joint terrorist training. Soon, under the leadership of our Federal Bureau of Investigation, we will open a law enforcement training academy in Europe, where police will learn how to combat more effectively trafficking of nuclear weapons components as well as the drug trade, organized crime, and money laundering.

The United States will also advance a wide-ranging nonproliferation agenda, a global convention to halt production of fissile materials, efforts to curb North Korea's nuclear ambitions, transparent procedures for dismantling nuclear warheads, and our work to ban testing and extend the Nuclear Non-Proliferation Treaty.

And today I am proposing a first step toward the eventual elimination of a less visible but still deadly threat: the world's 85 million anti-personnel land mines, one for every 50 people on the face of the Earth. I ask all nations to join with us and conclude an agreement to reduce the number and availability of those mines. Ridding the world of those often hidden weapons will help to save the lives of tens of thousands of men and women and innocent children in the years to come.

Our progress in the last year also provides confidence that in the post-cold-war years we can adapt and construct global institutions that will help to provide security and increase economic growth throughout the world. Since I

spoke here last year, 22 nations have joined NATO's Partnership For Peace. The first joint exercises have been conducted, helping to give Europe the chance to become a more unified continent in which democratic nations live within secure borders. In Asia, security talks and economic cooperation will lead to further stability. By reducing nations' fears about their borders and allowing them to spend less on military defenses, our coalition for democracy can give nations in transition a better chance to offer new freedoms and opportunities to their own people.

It is time that we think anew about the structures of this global economy as well, tearing down walls that separate nations instead of hiding behind them. At the Group of Seven meetings in Naples this year we committed ourselves to this task of renewal, to reexamining the economic institutions that have served us so well in the past. In the interest of shared prosperity, the United States actively promotes open markets. Though still in its infancy, the North American Free Trade Agreement has dramatically increased trade between the United States and Mexico, and has produced in the United States alone an estimated 200,000 new jobs. It offers a model to nations throughout the Americas which we hope to build on.

And this week, I will send legislation to the Congress to implement the General Agreement on Tariffs and Trade, the largest trade agreement in all of history. GATT and its successor, the World Trade Organization, hold the promise for all of us of increased exports, higher wages, and improved living standards. And in the months and years to come, we will work no less to extend the reach of open markets, starting with the Asian-Pacific cooperation forum and the Summit of the Americas later this year.

Here, at the United Nations, we must develop a concrete plan to meet the challenges of the next 50 years, even as we celebrate the last 50 years. I believe we should declare next year's 50th anniversary not just a year of celebration but a year of renewal. We call on the Secretary-General to name a working group so that, by the time we meet next year, we will have a concrete action plan to revitalize the U.N.'s obligations to address the security, economic, and political challenges ahead, obligations we must all be willing to assume.

Our objectives should include ready, efficient, and capable U.N. peacekeeping forces. And I am happy to report that as I pledged to you last year, and thanks to the support in the United States Congress, $1.2 billion is now available from the United States for this critical account.

We must also pledge to keep U.N. reform moving forward, so that we do more with less. And we must improve our ability to respond to urgent needs. Let me suggest that it is time for the members of this Assembly to consider seriously President Menem's suggestion for the creation of a civilian rapid response capability for humanitarian crises. And let us not lose sight of the special role that development and democracy can play in preventing conflicts once peace has been established.

Never before has the United Nations been in a better position to achieve the democratic goals of our Founders. The end of the cold war has freed us from decades of paralyzing divisions, and we all know that multilateral cooperation is not only necessary to address the new threats we face but possible to succeed.

The efforts we have taken together in Haiti are a prime example. Under the sponsorship of the United Nations, American troops, now being joined by the personnel of an ever growing international coalition of over two dozen nations, are giving the people of Haiti their chance at freedom. Creative diplomacy, the influence of economic power, the credible threat of military force, all have contributed to this moment of opportunity.

Essential civil order will be restored. Human rights violations will be curbed. The first refugees are returning within hours on this day. The military leaders will step down; the democratic government will be restored. President Aristide will return. The multinational mission will turn its responsibilities over to the United Nations mission, which will remain in Haiti throughout 1995 until a new President is elected. During this time, a multinational development effort will make available more than $1 billion to begin helping the Haitians rebuild their country.

In the spirit of reconciliation and reconstruction, President Aristide called yesterday for the immediate easing of sanctions so that the work of rebuilding can begin immediately. Accordingly, I intend to act expeditiously within the Security Council Resolutions 917 and 940, to enable us to restore health care, water, and electrical services, construction materials for humanitarian efforts, and communications, agricultural, and educational materials.

Today I am also announcing that the United States will suspend all unilateral sanctions against Haiti except those that affect the military leaders and their immediate supporters. This will include regularly scheduled air flights when the air support becomes available, financial transactions, and travel restrictions. I urge all other nations to do the same.

In Haiti, the United States has demonstrated that it would lead a multinational force when our interests are plain, when the cause is right, when the mission is achievable, and the nations of the world stand with us. But Haiti's people will have to muster the strength and the patience to travel the road of freedom. They have to do this for themselves. Every new democratic nation is fragile, but we will see the day when the people of Haiti fulfill their aspirations for liberty and when they are once again making genuine economic progress.

United Nations actions in Bosnia, as those in Haiti, demonstrate that progress can be made when a coalition backs up diplomacy with military power. For the first time ever, NATO has taken, since we met last year, military actions beyond the territory of its members. The threat of NATO air power helped to establish the exclusion zone around Sarajevo and to end the Bosnian Serbs' spring offensive against Gorazde. And NATO's February ultimatum boosted our mediation efforts which helped to end the war between the Bosnian Government and the Bosnian Croats and forged a federation between those two communities.

The situation in Bosnia, to that extent, has improved. But in recent weeks, the situation around Sarajevo has deteriorated substantially, and Sarajevo once again faces the prospect of strangulation. A new resolve by the United Nations to enforce its resolutions is now necessary to save Sarajevo. And NATO stands ready to act.

The situation in Bosnia is yet another reminder of the greatest irony of this century we are leaving: This century so full of hope and opportunity and achievement has also been an age of deep destruction and despair. We cannot help but remember the millions who gave their lives during two World Wars and the half-century in struggle by men and women in the East and West who ultimately prevailed in the name of freedom. But we must also think of our children and the world we will leave them in the 21st century.

History has given us a very rare opportunity, the chance to build on the greatest legacy of this century without reliving its darkest moments. And we have shown that we can carry forward humanity's ancient quest for freedom, to build a world where democracy knows no borders but where nations know their borders will always be secure, a world that gives all people the chance to realize their potential and to live out their dreams.

Thank you very much.

NOTE: The President spoke at 11 a.m. at the United Nations Building. In his remarks, he referred to United Nations Secretary-General Boutros Boutros-Ghali; United Nations General Assembly President Amara Essy; and President Carlos Menem of Argentina.

Remarks at a Luncheon for Heads of State in New York City
September 26, 1994

Mr. Secretary-General, distinguished heads of state and government, your Excellencies, guests: First, I think I can speak for all of us in thanking the Secretary-General for his remarks, for his hospitality, and most important of all, for his very strong leadership of the United Nations.

Mr. Secretary-General, you have taken the ideas of peace, help, and security that are at the heart of the U.N.'s mission and worked hard to make them a reality. As the cold war has ended, the world has looked to the U.N. for even more assistance and leadership. You have met this challenge by effectively placing the U.N. at the forefront of international affairs. Your leadership has been particularly apparent in the improvements of the U.N.'s peacekeeping operations. There are now approximately 70,000 peacekeepers deployed around the world, some 5 times the number when you took office. Collaboration among nations is improving, and the operations are growing more efficient.

Your initiatives at the Cairo conference, your efforts to improve coordination of development assistance, the establishment of an independent inspector general and meaningful cost controls and your work to improve the U.N.'s field operations, all these are testaments to your outstanding leadership.

Above all, you have focused on the use of diplomacy to prevent bloodshed and conflict and on building the kinds of permanent institutions that lead to long-term stability within and, as you have so eloquently stated, among nations. For these things and more, all of us applaud you.

Today, opportunities abound to build a world in which democracy reigns, respect for human rights is the rule, political stability expands, economic prosperity is shared by all. These things will not occur, however, unless we commit ourselves to a cooperative spirit unmatched in all human history. That is our challenge. As leaders of member states, we must take responsibility for making the U.N. more responsive and more effective than it has ever been. Only in this way can the U.N. remain a positive force for change and a symbol of justice and hope for the world.

Mr. Secretary-General, you have kept our focus on building the kind of organization that can effectively turn our ideals into reality. We thank you for your vision.

As the United Nations approaches its 50th birthday, let us all pledge to continue to work together for the promise of a better tomorrow. And let us raise our glasses in toast to the Secretary-General and to that promise.

NOTE: The President spoke at 1:45 p.m. at the United Nations Building.

Remarks at a Reception for Heads of State and United Nations Delegations in New York City
September 26, 1994

Thank you very much, Mr. Secretary; and thank you, Ambassador Albright, and thank you for your outstanding leadership in the United Nations.

Most of what I have to say I have already said to the United Nations today. And we did not ask you to come here to listen to speeches but simply to enjoy yourselves and to give us a chance to say thank you for your friendship to the United States and your cooperation with the United States.

I'm very glad to be here in one of our Nation's truly outstanding institutions, this magnificent museum, and particularly in this place. When I walked in, the Foreign Minister of Egypt rolled his eyes at me because here we are. I do want to say that I am here out of respect for Egyptian culture, not because I am a candidate for pharaoh.

I would just leave you with this one thought. We have an enormous opportunity today. Every day we get up and we read about all the problems we have in the world, and most of the discussions in the United Nations are focused on those problems. But the way that we talk about them is made possible because of the triumph of democracy, the triumph of freedom, the end of the cold war, the possibilities opened to us by the global spread of technology and enterprise and opportunity. And so I ask you all to maintain a very hopeful outlook. Even as we are careful and calculated about what we can do and we don't reach into those things we cannot, let us look to the future with real confidence.

I feel very, very hopeful about the next 50 years for the United Nations, and especially about the next 10 years as we prepare the way for the 21st century, in which, as I said, I hope we will prove that freedom and democracy can not only endure but can actually triumph and change the lives of ordinary people all across the world.

Thank you very much, and welcome.

NOTE: The President spoke at 7:15 p.m. at the Metropolitan Museum of Art.

Statement on Health Care Reform Legislation
September 26, 1994

Today Senator George Mitchell reported that he sees no way to pass health care reform in this session of Congress. He and the bipartisan group of Senators have been doing their best. But he cannot find the 60 votes needed to overcome the Republican filibuster.

I am very sorry to say that this means Congress isn't going to reform health care this year. But we are not giving up on our mission to cover every American and to control health care costs.

When I addressed Congress a year ago, I said our journey to health care reform would have some rough spots in the road. Well, we've had a few. But this journey is far, far from over.

Some Republican leaders keep saying, "Let's put this off until next year." I am going to hold them to their word. We have reached out to Republicans, and we will continue to do that. But we are going to keep up the fight against the interests who spent $300 million to stop health care reform. We will fight for campaign finance and lobby reform, so these special interests do not continue to obstruct vital legislation, and we will return to the fight for health care reform. There is too much at stake for all the American people, and we have come too far to just walk away now.

Although we have not achieved our goal this year, Hillary and I are proud—and our allies should be proud as well—that we were able to bring this debate further than it has ever progressed before. For solid, smart, and important reasons, the ordinary working families of America expect their elected leaders to pass health care reform:

—If we don't act, the deficit we have worked so hard to contain will balloon again over time.

—And, most important, millions of Americans still won't be able to count on coverage when their families need it. Every month that we don't act, 100,000 more Americans will lose their coverage. They will join the 5 million Americans who lost theirs in the last 5 years.

For their sake, and for the sake of those who touched us during this great journey, we are going to keep up this fight and we will prevail.

Nomination for the Environmental Protection Agency
September 26, 1994

The President announced today that he intends to nominate Fred Hansen to be the Deputy Administrator of the Environmental Protection Agency.

"Through his accomplished State leadership, Fred Hansen brings real environmental expertise and commitment to this position," the President said. "I am confident that his service at the E.P.A. will be marked by the same excellence and leadership he has shown in Oregon as a long-time environmental leader there."

NOTE: A biography of the nominee was made available by the Office of the Press Secretary.

Remarks Welcoming President Boris Yeltsin of Russia
September 27, 1994

President and Mrs. Yeltsin, members of the Russian delegation, distinguished guests. On behalf of the American people, it is my great honor to welcome President Boris Nikolayevich Yeltsin and Mrs. Naina Yeltsin to Washington for this state visit.

Mr. President, it wasn't so long ago that Russian-American summits were moments of high drama and sometimes disappointing results. The people of our countries and from around the world watched nervously as their leaders met in a heavy atmosphere of mutual suspicion and fear. The fate of the world seemed to hang in the balance of those encounters. And success was defined as the avoidance of confrontation or crisis.

Our moment is quite different but no less important. For these are exciting times, times of great opportunity. And we are cooperating to seize them for the good of all Russians, all Americans, and all the people of the world. Today we meet not as adversaries but as partners in the quest for a more prosperous and a more peaceful planet. In so many areas, our interests no longer conflict, they coincide. And where we do disagree, we can discuss our differences in a climate of warm peace, not cold war.

The Russian-American relationship is at last, remarkably, a normal one, full of real accomplishments and genuine promise. Mr. President, this evolution in our relations is due in no small part to the peaceful revolution you are leading in Russia, one that the United States has fully supported. Your steadfastness and courage in the face of difficult odds have inspired millions of Americans.

And you have proved the pessimists wrong. Far from falling backward, Russia, under your leadership, is coming together and moving forward. Your efforts, of course, could not be successful if you did not have the support of a great and courageous people. Here in America, we have known the trials and tribulations of history, but the Russian people have survived invasions and wars, deprivation and dictatorship.

And through it all, the Russians have endured, producing uplifting poetry and songs, great novels and films, ingenious science and path-breaking technology. Now, the free and open society you are building will allow the Russian people finally to reach their full potential. Russia's greatest hours lie before her.

Mr. President, we are privileged to share a great moment, an historic opportunity. When we met in Vancouver over 18 months ago, and again in Moscow last January, we vowed to seize that opportunity by creating and building upon a new partnership between our two nations, a partnership that works. And we have kept that commitment.

As a result, our missiles no longer target each other's people for destruction; instead, they are being dismantled. Our soldiers no longer face each other as deadly adversaries; instead, they work together as partners for peace. Young Russians and Americans no longer learn to be fearful and mistrustful of each other; instead, they study together in record numbers. Trade between our countries is no longer stifled by export controls and prohibitions; instead, it is growing every day to the benefit of both our peoples. In short, our nations are growing closer together, replacing suspicion and fear with trust and cooperation.

Mr. President, this summit of ours, unlike its predecessors, is about the future, a future in which we will strive to integrate Russia and the West, to build a new century of peace in Europe, and a future of shared responsibility that comes with vast territory, large populations, great power, and democratic values, to use our combined influence and authority for the good of the world beyond our borders.

Together, we have agreed to safeguard nuclear materials and to shut down plutonium production reactors. Together, with Ukraine, Kazakhstan, and Belarus, we will rid your region of thousands of nuclear warheads. Together, we must ensure that all the new independent states achieve their rightful place as strong and independent nations in Europe, able to chart their own destinies. For that reason, all Americans rejoiced and deeply respected your decision to withdraw your troops from the Baltic nations.

Together, we are working to bring peace to Bosnia, to the Middle East, to Nagorno-Karabakh. Together, we will build an international space station and explore the solar system. Together, we will carry the fight against transnational problems like terrorism, environmental degradation, and organized crime. Together, we can and we will make a difference not only for our own people but also for men, women, and children all around the world.

Mr. President, it is an honor to have you with us. Together, we have done well in laying the foundation of trust and security between our two peoples. Now let us build on it to secure a future of peace.

Welcome to the United States.

NOTE: The President spoke at 10:15 a.m. on the South Lawn at the White House.

Remarks Prior to Discussions With President Yeltsin of Russia and an Exchange With Reporters
September 27, 1994

President Clinton. Well, let me say before you start that this is a very important meeting for both of us and for our country as we're looking forward to having the opportunity to discuss a lot of things, particularly issues relating to the remaining nuclear matters we're trying to resolve between us and a lot of our mutual concerns about organized crime, which I think will take a good deal of work over the years ahead. As you know, the FBI Director has already been to Moscow, and we're working closely on that. So we're looking forward to the meeting.

Bosnia

Q. President Yeltsin, can we ask you, if Congress forces the President, and he has promised he will do this, to lift the arms embargo if the Serbs don't comply, what will be your response if the United States lifts the arms embargo and lets the Bosnian Muslims arm themselves?

President Yeltsin. My response would be negative, of course. But we will discuss this issue with the President of the United States.

Q. Mr. President, do you want to comment? Do you want to comment on what you think can be accomplished?

President Clinton. Well, as you know, the—at least for the moment, this may be a largely academic discussion for two reasons. One is, the legislation now pending commits me to pursue a multinational, multilateral lifting of the embargo through the U.N., and we received word just in the last couple of days from the Bosnian Government that they may be interested in deferring any action on that for 4 to 6 months. It's something they brought to us, so we're all working through that.

I think the most important thing is we have to keep pressing the Bosnian Serbs to end the conflict, to accept the Contact Group's proposal. And I want to emphasize that the United States and Russia have worked very closely together on Bosnia to this point. We have been together every step of the way. We're going to do our best to stay together.

Q. Haven't they stopped you from further air strikes? Haven't they opposed some of your policies?

President Yeltsin. Very impressive. [*Laughter*]

President Clinton. That's very impressive, right?

Q. It's my job.

President Clinton. She does it well. She does it well. [*Laughter*]

[*At this point, one group of reporters left the room, and another group entered.*]

President Yeltsin's First Visit

Q. Mr. President, do you remember your first meeting with President Yeltsin 2 years ago in Blair House here in Washington?

President Clinton. Yes, I do. I remember it well. We had a fine visit. It was more than 2 years ago, I think, wasn't it?

Q. Yes, it was in June.

President Clinton. Yes, that was before I had even been nominated for President formally. I remember it well. He was very kind to receive me. You know, then as I remember, I was running third in the polls, and no one thought I would be elected President. So I was very pleased that he saw me. And we got off to a good start.

Russia-U.S. Partnership

Q. You say that the main task is unification of the West and Russia, and at the same time you want to be closer—you want to broaden NATO. Don't you see that there's a contradiction in that?

President Clinton. We're going to discuss all those things. We've made a remarkable partnership, and I think it's been based on real mutual respect for the interests of each other and for our shared goals in the world. And I believe we can continue that partnership. We're going to work at it.

NOTE: The President spoke at 11 a.m. in the Oval Office at the White House. A tape was not available for verification of the content of these remarks.

Remarks Honoring Russian and American Veterans of World War II
September 27, 1994

President Yeltsin, Mrs. Yeltsin, members of the Russian and American delegations. We say a special word of welcome to the Red Star Red Army Band that has come all the way from Russia to be with our Marine Band today. To the Members of Congress who are here, honored veterans, distinguished guests: We welcome you all to the White House.

We gather to celebrate the bonds between the Russian people and the American people

forged during World War II. And we gather to pledge that the opportunity we lost five decades ago to build a better world will not be lost again.

A half century ago, half a world away, brave men and women from our nations fought as allies for a common cause and an uncommon sacrifice. In April 1945, as the greatest war of this century drew to a close, they embraced on the banks of the Elbe River. Their meeting held the promise not only of the war's end but also of an enduring peace that sadly was deferred for decades. Today we honor the Russian and American veterans who risked their lives, and sometimes gave their lives, to defeat that tyranny. We are deeply honored to have some of those veterans here with us at the White House. Theirs was a partnership on land, air, and sea but also in heart, mind, and spirit.

To our children, their stories sound like the stuff of novels and movies, but they are real. Some American heroes helped win the war not by fighting on the front lines but by ferrying tons of supplies to Russia, everything from boots to locomotives. It was very dangerous work. Fifty years ago this week, the Liberty ship S.S. *Edward H. Crockett*, carrying 68 members of the merchant marine and the naval armed guard, left the Russian port of Archangel to return home. Fifty years ago to the day on Thursday, it was torpedoed by the enemy and sank in the icy Bering Sea. Miraculously, most of the crew survived. Six of those survivors are here with us today, and we welcome them. [*Applause*]

In the deserts of Iran, thousands of American soldiers delivered gasoline and munitions to Russian units. Many, like Robert Patterson, drove in heat so intense that the steering wheels of their trucks burned their bare hands. And American nurses, like Anna Connelly Wilson, tended to the wounded in primitive field hospitals with no blankets or running water.

In 1944, Joseph Beyrle parachuted into France with the 101st Airborne Division, only to be captured and taken to a prison camp in Germany. But he escaped, joined advancing Russian troops, and fought as a member of a Russian army unit as it drove toward Berlin. While manning a Russian tank gun, Joseph Beyrle was wounded, but Russian doctors saved his life. I'm especially grateful to them because Joseph survived the war and went on to have a son. His son, John Beyrle, works here at the White House as one of my advisers on Russian affairs. I'd like to ask them both to stand and be recognized here: the Beyrles. Thank you, Mr. Beyrle, thank you. [*Applause*]

We're also joined today by Russian veterans of the war, including Alexsandr Olshansky. Then a young corporal, he was one of the Russians who went, who met American troops at the Elbe River. Now, he is a major general in the Russian Army. In a few minutes, I will be honored to present to Major General Olshansky, as the Russian veterans' representative, a medal commemorating our wartime partnership.

Let us now pause for a moment to applaud all the Russian and American veterans of World War II who are here today. [*Applause*] Each of their stories, in different ways, teaches the same lesson. Once before, Russians and Americans shared a just cause and prevailed. Today, we are partners in peace, not war. Now we have a responsibility to work together for our own good and for the good of the world beyond our borders.

Two men symbolize the renewed bond between Russians and Americans: Ambassador Malcolm Toon and General Dimitri Volkogonov. World War II veterans both, they are the cochairmen of the U.S.-Russian Joint Commission on POW's/MIA's. They spent the last 2½ years on a mission to account for U.S. servicemen missing from the Second World War, the cold war, and the conflicts in Korea and Vietnam and for Russian soldiers missing in Afghanistan.

President Yeltsin, you first proposed this Commission. It has become an important part of our bilateral relationship. The recent repatriation of the remains of U.S. Air Force Captain John Dunham is an example of your commitment to this Commission's work.

Our feelings today are perhaps best expressed by the great Russian poet Yevtushenko. He wrote with great emotion in words that many Russian citizens know by heart, "We remember those who joined us in battle, who embraced us at the Elbe River. And we are faithful to this memory."

To the veterans of our two great nations, we say thank you for the inspiration of your example. We will learn from it, from your courage and your sacrifice. And we vow, finally, to redeem the promise of that embrace at the Elbe.

Thank you very much.

NOTE: The President spoke at 3:26 p.m. in the Rose Garden at the White House.

Letter to Congressional Leaders on the Compact of Free Association With the Republic of Palau
September 27, 1994

Dear Mr. Speaker: (Dear Mr. President:)
(Dear Mr. Chairman:)

In my letter of July 26, 1994, I reported that the voters of Palau had approved the Compact of Free Association with the United States, opening the way, 7 years after its approval by the Congress, for the Compact to be brought into force.

Along with my letter, in accordance with section 101 of the Compact of Free Association with Palau Act, Public Law 101–219 (December 12, 1989), section 101(d)(1)(C) and (2) of the Compact of Free Association Approval Act, Public Law 99–658 (November 14, 1986), and section 102(b) of the Compact of Free Association Act of 1985, Public Law 99–239 (January 14, 1986), I submitted the Economic Development Plan of the Republic of Palau, copies of certain subsidiary agreements between the United States and Palau, and an agreement between Palau and the United States establishing October 1, 1994, as the effective date for the Compact, provided that all lawsuits in Palau challenging approval of the Compact had been resolved by that date.

I have been advised by the Government of Palau that approval of the Compact is now free from any legal challenge in the courts of Palau and that the time for filing additional challenges has expired. Therefore, in addition to the findings and determinations that I reported in my July 26 letter, I am pleased to advise you that:

1. Pursuant to section 101(1) of Public Law 101–219, I have determined that the Compact was approved by the requisite percentage of votes cast in a referendum conducted pursuant to the Constitution of Palau and that such approval is free from any legal challenge.

2. Pursuant to section 101(2) of Public Law 101–219, the requisite 30 days in which either the House of Representatives or the Senate of the United States was in session have elapsed since my July 26 notification to the Congress

of the October 1, 1994, effective date of the Compact.

3. Pursuant to section 101(d)(1)(A) of Public Law 99–658, I hereby certify that the Compact has been approved in accordance with section 411(a) and (b) of the Compact and that there exists no legal impediment to the ability of the United States to carry out fully its responsibilities and to exercise its rights under Title Three of the Compact.

4. Agreements have been concluded with Palau that satisfy the requirements of section 101(d)(1)(C) of Public Law 99–658.

5. The period of congressional review provided in section 102(b)(2)(B) of Public Law 99–239 having elapsed, the United States hereby concurs with Palau's Economic Development Plan.

Therefore, all statutory conditions for implementation of the Compact having been met, I have issued the attached proclamation terminating the trust relationship between the United States and Palau and the entry into force of the Compact of Free Association between the United States and the Republican of Palau, effective October 1, 1994, at one minute past one o'clock p.m. local time in Palau.

Sincerely,

WILLIAM J. CLINTON

NOTE: Identical letters were sent to Thomas S. Foley, Speaker of the House of Representatives; Albert Gore, Jr., President of the Senate; Claiborne Pell, chairman, Senate Committee on Foreign Relations; J. Bennett Johnston, chairman, Senate Committee on Energy and Natural Resources; Lee H. Hamilton, chairman, House Committee on Foreign Affairs; and George Miller, chairman, House Committee on Natural Resources. The proclamation is listed in Appendix D at the end of this volume.

Message to the Congress on the General Agreement on Tariffs and Trade
September 27, 1994

To the Congress of the United States:

I am pleased to transmit legislation and a number of related documents to implement agreements resulting from the General Agreement on Tariffs and Trade (GATT) Uruguay Round of multilateral trade negotiations. The Uruguay Round Agreements are the broadest, most comprehensive trade agreements in history. They are vital to our national interest and to economic growth, job creation, and an improved standard of living for all Americans.

When fully implemented, the Uruguay Round Agreements will add $100–$200 billion to the U.S. economy each year and create hundreds of thousands of new, well-paying American jobs. They provide for a reduction in worldwide tariffs of $744 billion, the largest global tax cut in history.

The United States will be the biggest winner from the Uruguay Round Agreements. We are the world's largest trading nation with the world's most dynamic economy. In 1993, the United States exported $660 billion in goods and services, accounting for more than 10 percent of the U.S. GDP.

These agreements are the result of bipartisan cooperation and reflect the consensus supporting market-opening trade policies that the United States has enjoyed for decades. The Uruguay Round was launched by President Reagan, continued by President Bush, and concluded by this Administration. Each Administration consulted with the Congress and welcomed congressional participation and guidance throughout the negotiations. Similarly, this Administration has worked closely with the Congress to ensure that the implementing legislation that I am now forwarding enjoys broad bipartisan support.

The United States has led the world on a path of open markets, freer trade, and economic growth. Now we must lead the way in implementing these agreements. The leaders of every major industrialized nation have pledged to take action so that the Uruguay Round Agreements can be implemented by January 1, 1995. Any delay on our part would send a negative signal to our trading partners at a time when their economies are just beginning to recover.

Our economic recovery is now fully underway. As the economies in Europe and Japan begin again to grow, we must be positioned to reap the benefits of their expansion. As a result of the Uruguay Round Agreements, our major trading partners in Europe and Asia will cut their tariffs to historic lows.

The Asian Pacific economies are the fastest growing economies in the world and are currently the largest market for U.S. exports. United States exports to Latin America, the second fastest growing region in the world, have grown 60 percent since 1989. The Uruguay Round Agreements will ensure that these fast-growing markets will be open to international competition and that all of our trading partners will play by international trading rules.

The Uruguay Round Agreements enjoy very broad and deep support in the United States. Forty of our Nation's governors, numerous eminent economists, and the vast majority of U.S. industrial, agricultural, and services firms support the agreements, as do an array of former Presidents, Secretaries of State, Secretaries of the Treasury, and U.S. Trade Representatives.

Americans are at their best when they face the challenges of their time. Our predecessors did so after World War II when they created a new international trading system that guided global growth for 50 years. Now we must do the same to foster sustained prosperity for the decades to come.

The end of the Cold War and the rise of the global economy have created new challenges and new opportunities. Implementation of the Uruguay Round Agreements will ensure that we rise to the challenges of this new era and lead the world on a path of prosperity.

WILLIAM J. CLINTON

The White House,
September 27, 1994.

Remarks at the Congressional Hispanic Caucus Reception
September 27, 1994

Thank you, Congressman Serrano, and to all my colleagues up here on the stage, and the Congressional Hispanic Caucus, and to Secretary Babbitt, Secretary and Mrs. Cisneros, Secretary and Mrs. Peña. I know the Attorney General is coming. I haven't seen her here, but I think she's here somewhere. And I thank her and all of them for serving our Cabinet and our country so well. To Rita Elizondo, and all the others who work at the Institute, and to all of you, first, let me thank you for receiving me so well, and thank you for letting me come early and leave early. You know I have a date with President Yeltsin tonight. [*Laughter*] And I don't want to stiff him, so I'm going to have to leave here in just a moment. I do want to— I wish I could take the mariachis back with me to entertain him. [*Laughter*]

I want to say a special word of thanks to a couple of people here: First, to Congressman Ron de Lugo who's retiring after two decades representing the Virgin Islands. We will miss him very much. And thanks—next I would like to say a special word of thanks to the chief deputy whip, Congressman Bill Richardson, for his wonderful efforts in Haiti, to help us make peace and restore democracy in Haiti.

Congressman Serrano went over some of the accomplishments of this administration, but I want to do it again to ask you to do something for all of these Members who are up here, because they have worked very hard—very, very hard—to make this country work again. And our biggest problem—the thing you laughed about there, about not getting credit—I don't really care who gets the credit, as long as the country is going forward. But when the congressional elections come up, the people who are getting credit for moving the country forward need to be rewarded, so the voters don't wind up inadvertently voting for the very things they are against.

And that's what I want you to think about. If someone had told you 20 months ago that in 20 months we would see the biggest deficit reduction passed in history; the biggest spending cuts in history; scores of Government programs eliminated outright; the smallest Federal bureaucracy since Kennedy was President; 3 years of deficit reduction in a row for the first time since Truman was President; and still more money being spent to put 200,000 more kids in Head Start, to immunize all the children in America under the age of 2 by 1996; for education and training for people who are unemployed, for young people who want to go into good jobs when they get out of high school, but don't want to go on to college—you need apprenticeships; that we would reform the student loan program and make 20 million Americans eligible for student loans at lower interest rates, lower fees, and longer repayment terms; and that these things would produce 4.3 million new jobs, a 1.5 percent decline in the Hispanic unemployment rate, you'd say that was pretty good, wouldn't you?

We are moving this country in the right direction. The guys that voted against us said if we did this, it would wreck the economy. They were wrong; we were right; the American people should know it. It's important, and you need to make a commitment not simply to support these folks here with the Institute and with your presence at this dinner but with your voice and your heart and your spirit and getting people out to vote between now and November 8th. They were wrong; we were right.

They should be rewarded because we are moving this country in the right direction. Since NAFTA was ratified, we have increased exports to Mexico by 19 percent, 3 times as much as our exports are going up elsewhere. Automobile and truck exports are up 600 percent. We've got folks in those auto factories working overtime for the first time in more than 10 years. And I might say, that's why I hope we can pass the GATT agreement before we leave, because that will bring another 300,000 to 500,000 jobs into this economy. We had 8 months in a row this year where manufacturing employment increased for the first time in 10 years. And for the first time in 9 years, the annual vote of the panel of international economists, the United States was voted the most productive economy in the entire world. We're moving in the right direction. They need to be rewarded for it, these people in Congress who have made it possible.

Because of the Hispanic Caucus, we're closer to reenacting the Elementary and Secondary Education Act to help give educationally disadvantaged children a better chance. Congressman Becerra worked especially hard on that.

In addition to passing, in this economic plan, a tax cut for 15 million working families with children, who are working and hovering just above the poverty line—who are disproportionally Hispanic, I might add—we cut their taxes. We raised tax rates on the top 1.2 percent of Americans, cut taxes for 15 million working families so they wouldn't fall into poverty while they were working, so they could succeed as parents and workers, so they wouldn't choose welfare over work. We did it; they all voted against it. You ought to reward the people who did it and not the reverse.

We also passed the motor voter bill after several years of gridlock, the Brady bill and the family and medical leave bill after 7 years of gridlock, the crime bill after 6 years of gridlock. We're about to announce the communities, sometime this year, who won the empowerment zone competition, the enterprise community competition. We have more coming forward.

Last week I signed the community development banking bill, which will put $4.8 billion into poor communities, urban and rural, in this country so poor people can borrow money to put themselves in business in ways that will make a profit. This has been proven to work in other countries. It is wrong that America has not done it before, but we're going to bring free enterprise to the inner city and the isolated rural areas of America and prove that poor people want to work as well, and they can and will and will succeed. And I want to say a special word of thanks to Chairman Gonzalez and Nydia Velázquez, Luis Gutierrez, and Lucille Roybal-Allard for their leadership on this community development initiative; it was very important.

This administration has also kept its commitment to look more like America. With 302 Hispanic-American appointments, we have now appointed more than twice the number of Hispanic-Americans as my predecessor and, even better than that, of all those that went before. And I might add, in the area of Federal judges, we have appointed twice the number of Hispanic-Americans appointed by the last three Presidents, Democratic and Republican, combined, and I am proud of that.

One other thing I want to mention, because some of you were there, but one of the greatest honors I have had as President was the opportunity that I was able to take to give the Medal of Freedom to Cesar Chavez. I only wish he had been there to receive it in person.

Let me close with this. I had the opportunity to have a great meeting, when I spoke to the United Nations yesterday, with President Salinas. And he said to me, "Mr. President," he said, "I follow American politics very closely, and we've had a wonderful partnership." And he said, "I understand many things about America, but I do not understand how, with your economy booming, with so much progress being made, with all these bills flying through Congress, most Americans say when they're polled they think the country is going in the wrong direction." I said, "Well, you just have to live here to understand that." [*Laughter*]

But you think about it. Every one of you works in some working group; maybe it's a big one, maybe it's a small one. How well could you do at your job if every day two-thirds of the people who showed up to work with you were convinced nothing good was going to happen and, when something good did happen, denied that it did? [*Laughter*] That is the environment you ask these people to come to work every day in. You ask them to take brave decisions, vote for change, stand up to interest groups, push the country forward, when they know that there's better than a 50 percent chance that the people they're fighting for may not even get the message. That is what elections are for.

The fact is that against enormous odds from interest groups and enormous political odds and relentless opposition, the people on this stage with me have been responsible for an economic revival, for seriously addressing many of the greatest social problems facing this country. The deficit is down; the economy is up; jobs are up; trade is up. We have seriously addressed the crime problem. The American people are going to be more secure. We have done things for children, too long deferred, on immunizations, Head Start, the family leave policy, the policy of giving a tax break to working families on low incomes. We are moving the country forward and pulling it together. What remains is to get the message of the record of the last 20 months to the voters in the next 5 weeks.

You can do it; they need it. I will be out there doing my part. But if you liked what has happened before, you must ratify it by getting your friends and neighbors to say, "We are not going to be fooled, we are not going to be divided, and we are certainly not going back to the old policies of the past which wrecked the economy and divided this country. We're going forward together."

Thank you very much, and God bless you all.

NOTE: The President spoke at 6:46 p.m. at the Washington Hilton Hotel. In his remarks, he referred to Rita Elizondo, executive director, Congressional Hispanic Caucus Institute. A tape was not available for verification of the content of these remarks.

Remarks at a State Dinner Honoring President Boris Yeltsin of Russia
September 27, 1994

Ladies and gentlemen, President Yeltsin, Mrs. Yeltsin, distinguished guests: It is a great pleasure for Hillary and I to welcome Boris and Naina and all the Russian delegation to the White House. We're glad for this opportunity to return the generous hospitality that you bestowed on us in Moscow last January at the magnificent state dinner in the Kremlin's Hall of Facets and St. George's Hall. It was a magnificent evening that brought home to me, to Hillary, and to all the Americans there the vast richness of Russian culture.

Mr. President, our fellow Americans know you as the man who has led one of the most peaceful and hopeful revolutions of our time, the second Russian revolution. We were all inspired when you stood up for freedom in the streets of Moscow. And we have admired your patient, persistent, and successful efforts to build the institutions of democracy.

We know reform has been difficult, and there is a hard road yet to travel. But as I said this morning when you arrived at the White House, you have already proved the pessimists wrong. Under your leadership, Russia is coming together and moving forward. Her best days are still to come. And we are proud of our partnership with your great country.

At one of our previous meetings you were kind enough to give me a copy of your autobiography. It's a remarkable story, a story still in progress, of a man dedicated and determined to give his fellow Russians the opportunity to reach their full potential. I know there are many more volumes yet to be written, but one part of your book made a particular impression on me.

In your autobiography you tell the story of your father's ambition to invent a brick-laying machine. Time and again, he would describe in intricate detail how it would work, how it would mix mortar, lay the bricks, clean off the excess mortar, and move on to keep building. He had all sorts of sketches and calculations for this machine, which he believed would better the lives of the Russian people.

Mr. President, you have realized your father's dream, and on a scale he could never have imagined. Brick by brick, through your tireless and steadfast efforts, you have laid the foundation for a democratic Russia. Your nation has now an elected President and Parliament, a Constitution, an increasingly free economy, and an open society. In just a few short years, you have accomplished the work of a lifetime.

And so it is with great admiration for your historic achievements, confidence in our new partnership, and a belief that working together we will help to make a better world, that I, and I ask all of you to join me, in raising a glass to you, Boris Nikolayevich Yeltsin, President of the Russian Federation.

NOTE: The President spoke at 8:35 p.m. in the State Dining Room at the White House.

Remarks on Opening the Library of Congress Exhibit on the History of the Russian Orthodox Church in North America
September 28, 1994

Thank you very much. President and Mrs. Yeltsin, Mr. Speaker, Senator Stevens, distinguished Members of Congress and other guests: I'd like to say a special word of commendation to Dr. Billington. I don't have an informed opinion about his Russian, but his English was impeccable this morning.

I'm honored to be joined by the President of the Russian Federation in opening the exhibit on the 200th anniversary of the Russian Orthodox Church in North America. We gather in a new era of cooperation between our countries, but this exhibit reminds us that the ties between our peoples are old and deep.

Two centuries ago, eight Russian priests arrived in North America to minister to Russian traders and the native peoples of Alaska. Together they forged a partnership, a new Russian and native American community that eventually would stretch down the Pacific coast. Though born on different continents, they were all resourceful, brave, and faithful people.

A century later, another Russian came to Alaska, Archbishop Tikhon. He soon presided over all the new Russian communities that had grown throughout the entire United States. He oversaw the completion of St. Nicholas Cathedral in New York City and returned to his mother country to become the first patriarch of Russia since the time of Peter the Great.

In the years since, countless Russian immigrants to America have formed churches and cultural associations in many of our great cities and farming communities. They have strengthened American industry, education, science, and most notably, the arts: literature, music, and dance. As this exhibit shows, our Nation's history has long been enriched by the Russian people, their fortitude, their culture, and their faith.

President Yeltsin, this library is a fitting place for this exhibition, for the Library of Congress first grew out of the personal library of our third President, Thomas Jefferson, the author of the Declaration of Independence and one of our first champions of religious tolerance and freedom. Today, the spirit of respect and understanding thrives in the exchange programs offered to the brilliant minds of young people from Russia and the United States. And we are joined here today by 30 of those students who have benefited from the exchange programs that our two Governments support so strongly. I'd like to recognize especially the efforts of our USIA Director, Joe Duffey, and Senator Bill Bradley, who have worked so hard to make these exchanges a reality. Thomas Jefferson would be proud of them both.

As we remember the ties between Russia and America of two centuries ago, let us welcome our new ties and the new spirit of cooperation and a new century of partnership that lies ahead, remembering that much of it began on one of the most important principles of our entire existence in America, the principle of religious liberty. When our Founders fought for the freedom of this country, they pledged their lives, their fortunes, and their sacred honor for the right of every American to worship as he or she chooses.

Thank you very much.

NOTE: The President spoke at 10:28 a.m. in the Great Hall of the Library of Congress. In his remarks, he referred to James H. Billington, Librarian of Congress.

The President's News Conference With President Boris Yeltsin of Russia
September 28, 1994

President Clinton. We will begin the press conference now with opening statements, after which we will have, obviously, questions from the press. And we will do our best to alternate between the Russian and American press corps.

Hillary and I and our entire delegation have very much enjoyed having President and Mrs. Yeltsin with us, along with all the Russians who came with them. When President Yeltsin arrived yesterday, I spoke of the new partnership between our two nations. After our talks, one thing is clear: Relations between our nations are moving forward at full speed.

Both our countries, as President Yeltsin said yesterday, are sometimes not so easy to deal with, but we're succeeding in tackling some hard challenges. Over the past 2 days we've made good progress on security, economic, and diplomatic issues.

I'm pleased to announce today that President Yeltsin and I have agreed that as soon as the START I treaty takes effect and the START II treaty is ratified by both of our countries, we will immediately begin removing the nuclear warheads that are due to be scrapped under START II, instead of taking the 9 years allowed. There will be no adverse impact on the United States or the Soviet Union. Indeed, by shaving several years off the timetable, we will make the world safer for all of us.

We also plan to work together to encourage Ukraine to join the Nuclear Non-Proliferation Treaty this year. As the world's two largest nuclear powers, we recognize our special responsibilities to ensure the security of nuclear weapons and materials, even as we keep dismantling them. This is one of the most urgent security challenges all the nations of the globe face as we enter the next century.

President Yeltsin and I spent a lot of time on this issue. We understand we won't solve the problem overnight, but the steps we've taken in areas such as inspecting each other's storage facilities and information sharing are an important start. We are personally committed to seeing this issue through.

Today President Yeltsin and I have signed an agreement that will gradually normalize our economic relations by removing major barriers to trade and investment. American support for Russian economic reform has been constant, and over the last 2 days American and Russian businesses have signed deals worth nearly $1 billion, ranging from agriculture to telecommunications. We met several American and Russian business leaders this morning, and we're determined to advance America's investment in and trade with Russia. We will transfer $100 million in aid funds to directly support trade and investment

through OPIC and the Commerce Department. And we will also devote $30 million to help in the fight against crime in Russia through cooperation between the FBI and the Justice Department and appropriate Russian authorities.

On the diplomatic front, we've made progress on the difficult issue of Russian arms sales to Iran. We agreed to continue to work on this problem in the near future. We also agreed to work more closely together to help resolve the tragic conflict over Nagorno-Karabakh. On Bosnia, we repeated our commitment to work within the Contact Group to compel the parties to accept the settlement that has been worked out. Once again, I congratulated President Yeltsin on his historic decision to withdraw Russian troops from the Baltic nations.

No area better captures the potential for our emerging partnership than Russian-American cooperation in space. President Yeltsin and I first discussed this idea in Vancouver last year and decided we needed to go forward. Today I have signed into law a bill that will help to fund the international space station. This bill is the result in no small measure of the extraordinary cooperation between Vice President Gore and Prime Minister Chernomyrdin, as well as the strong bipartisan support we received in the United States Congress. Like so much that we've accomplished in the past 2 days, this space station symbolizes the potential for progress when we work together.

This is the fifth time President Yeltsin and I have met since I came into office. I think I've spent more time with him than with any other world leader. We've made real progress over the last few days, in no small measure because we've worked together, we've learned to be open and candid with each other about our differences, we've built an atmosphere of mutual trust. And I'm confident that our partnership is working and will continue to work, not only between our two governments but increasingly between the people of Russia and the United States.

Mr. President.

President Yeltsin. Thank you.

Ladies and gentlemen, first of all, I would like to express the feeling of great thanks and appreciation to President Bill Clinton, to his wife, Hillary, and also to the American people and you, the journalists, for a very warm welcome and for very fine conditions which were created to make our very tough and difficult visit, to make it very productive.

We always start these meetings by saying that we've really done a tremendous amount of work. We always say this at these press conferences. But we can't say that this meeting, as well, doesn't deserve this kind of characterization. In fact, we have accomplished a lot of work. And if we planned at one time that we were going to have one 30-minute one-on-one session, it turns out it lasted for 3 hours. So you can judge for yourselves how many issues we touched upon and discussed and what a wide scope we really worked on.

Although I have a trip to Seattle coming up where I want to familiarize myself with the West—I had never been out West, out on the West Coast of the United States. I want to familiarize myself and get to know the Boeing Company, the city of Seattle, and just to see what kind of Americans live out there on the West Coast and how they work and how they are.

We, of course, with Bill now, it's—we are interlocutors who know each other and partners in our discussions and negotiations. We know each other very well, and more than that, we this time don't have to come and start warming up. We've had phone conversations; we talked ahead of time. So we started from the word go, right from the very beginning. We say that our partnership has to be pragmatic and not declaratory. And right away from the very beginning, we agreed to that.

I'm sure that neither Russia nor the United States needs all kinds of sharp deviations from having good, normal communications and ties. We don't need a situation where the whole world is in trepidation. We don't need to waste a lot of words and chew a lot of fat, but we have to get down to basics and start working in a very pragmatic style.

Of course, I say these words—now I think Bill has confirmed that the United States is a very complex partner, and Russia also is, too. But look, what family doesn't have some kind of squabbles occasionally which, eventually, they kind of work out. It's not always that simple, right? I mean, here are two great humongous, almost half billion member family who, too, has sometimes its own little approaches, if you will. But the most important thing is the ability to listen, to have patience, to have humanity, respect to each other. And then, absolutely, we will be able to find solutions.

I just want to tell you, to be short about it, these little introductory words—I just want to give you literally that very list that those issues that we discussed. Here we go, and then later on, you'll be able to ask questions. It will be a lot easier to ask questions. [*Laughter*]

The most important talks and subjects of these talks are the strategic partnerships between Russia and the United States; international issues; external political coordination of our efforts so that we two great powers, two countries, constantly coordinated everything that we do so that nothing happens in the world that might ruin peace on our planet—we have to support peace; the Big-8; peacekeeping; CIS; the role of Russia in the CIS; NATO and Russia; coordination in the United Nations Security Council; reforming United Nations; cooperating in the United Nations and the CIS; the situation all around the world, Bosnia, Middle East, Caribbean Basin, North Korea, Rwanda, Islamic extremism, Iran, Libya, Iraq, Trans-Dniester, Nagorno-Karabakh, Abkhazia, Tajikistan, the Baltics; military issues; START III—START I, START II, now III, START III now—we're talking about three—[*laughter*]—nonproliferation; harmonizing our—you're not catching up? You can't think fast enough? [*Laughter*] You can't think fast enough? Well, okay, then I'll go a little slower. All right? [*Laughter*] Apparently we're not on the same wavelength here, you and I, in terms of the pace here, okay.

Non-pro-lif-er-a-tion of weapons—[*laughter*]—harmonizing military doctrines, harmonizing, since today doctrine in the United States, the military doctrine, is one; Russia has a different one. How are we going to be able to have a partnership, friendly partnership, and work together if we have such disparate military doctrines?

New initiatives of the great five powers on strategic stability; ABM systems, strategic and tactical ABM systems; biological weapons; chemical weapons; destruction and elimination of nuclear weapons, the safe elimination of nuclear weapons; exchange of information on nuclear arms and fissile materials for the first time; banning nuclear testing; participation of Russia in the regime of rocket technology—and we attach ourselves to this, we are joining where the United States is the initiator; banning the export of mines, antipersonnel mines—I fully support the proposal of the United States of America in the U.N., when he spoke about getting rid of these antipersonnel mines; incidents with submarines.

Economic issues; investments; getting rid of discriminatory limitations on Russia and opening up the American market to Russian goods; the status for Russia of an economy in transition; post-COCOM economic and trade projects; free trade status; GATT; finally, we got together and agreed on the so-called Jackson-Vanik amendment. I've already said that every single kid in Russia knows who these people are, Jackson and this guy Vanik. [*Laughter*] The President, by my decree—I mean, by his decree—well, maybe it's temporary, but he has stopped it, all right, the actions of this amendment. And I am grateful that this was a huge window, a bright window that appeared here between us. I'm very grateful.

Questions of crime; cooperating in the field of education, culture, ecology, environment, national minorities, the north; cooperation on tariffs, duties.

And the President has already said that, of course, for all mankind, this is very important, so that in place of the year 2003, after the ratification of START II by Russia and the United States we simultaneously remove all those weapons from alert status that were mentioned in the treaty, immediately. In other words, we save at least 7, maybe more, years by doing it right away. And we give mankind hope that our generation will be, for sure, living in peace.

At the center of our negotiation was the strategy of partnership between Russia and the United States. And I've already said that we've agreed on the fact that it should be more pragmatic.

Discussions of partnership for economic progress as well—we agreed here, also. In the United States now we have a large group of Russian businessmen. In New York I met with the captains of industry, big industry in the United States and with Russia. And today, as a matter of fact, with President Bill Clinton, we met also with representatives of big business here. And we came to terms and decided, well, what, after all, is standing in the way of investments and attracting investments and capital to Russia, on the part of private capital. And I have to say that we, in general, came to terms with this.

Looking into the future, we, at the same time, tried not to sort of float above this sinful Earth. Specifically, we agreed on fighting crime. And there are other specific things, protecting the environment in the north of Russia, protecting the environment; communications systems, developing communication.

After all, I mean, I just have to say that even though many people predicted that this is going to be not just tough negotiations but they're going to fall through in the ultimate analysis, I have to really be very sorry and express my condolences to these people. We agreed to almost practically on every single one of these issues. Sometimes the United States stepped forward and compromised a little; sometimes Russia compromised. But the most important thing is for peace, for humanity, for mankind, for our whole planet, we have agreed.

Thank you. Now, please, questions. He is the host, so he calls the shots. [*Laughter*]

President Clinton. Helen [Helen Thomas, United Press International]. Let me say, one of the things I would do—I've always wanted to be on the other side of this microphone, and if I were on the other side of the microphone today, my question would be, "And what were your agreements on issues 15, 27, and 43?" [*Laughter*]

Go ahead, Helen.

Q. Well, I have a question for each of the Presidents, and I've narrowed it a bit. You covered the waterfront, and I'm sure you have all the answers. I would like to ask President Clinton, are you going to call a special session on GATT?

President Yeltsin, I think the American people are very happy to find out that Russia will never attack the United States, as you said today, that you would never fight. But we are a little bit concerned——

President Clinton. Excuse me, Helen. Apparently the Russian interpreter is not coming through the microphone. No, no, no—he can hear you. It's the Russian—we need the Russian. We need someone to say this in Russian.

Q. Oh, okay, I'm sure the United States is very happy to hear you say that Russia will never attack the U.S. You said that today, and that's very good. But there is some concern that Russia may still have some feeling that it has a sphere of influence over former Soviet republics, and that when you intervene, you don't feel it necessary to go through international institutions. Is that true?

General Agreement on Tariffs and Trade

President Clinton. So we have two separate questions. I'll answer mine first.

I think it is the responsibility of the United States and the United States Congress to pass the GATT this year. And I hope that the Congress will do it before they leave. Our information is that there are more than enough votes to pass it in the House and that we have a majority in the Senate if we can get the bill to the floor. That's so often the question in the Senate. So we'll keep trying to pass it. If for some reason the Senate does not pass it, then I will urge that they stay in session and simply go on recess for the election break and then come back after the recess and pass GATT.

This is the biggest trade agreement in history. It's the biggest worldwide tax cut in history by reductions of tariffs, $36 billion in this country alone. It will give us 300,000 to 500,000 new high-wage jobs in the next few years alone. I think it is important to pass it.

Our country has established, even in what has been a reasonably or very partisan atmosphere in the last couple of years, a real commitment during our administration to work in a bipartisan way toward expanded trade. So I urge the Congress to pass the GATT before they go home. If it passes the House and doesn't pass the Senate I will urge that the Senate stay in session, take a recess for the election, come back afterward, and pass this. It's very important.

We have the APEC meeting coming up; we have the Summit of the Americas coming up. We're trying to break down our barriers with Russia and many other countries. The United States has to lead on this, and I intend to do everything I can to see that we do lead.

President Yeltsin.

Russian Foreign Policy

President Yeltsin. Well, of course, we're not planning to avoid and go walk around the decisions of the United Nations. Moreover, as you know, I'm appearing at the General Assembly session and I came out and talked for strengthening it, for widening this organization, so this organization would be strengthened in the future. Maybe they need it now more than ever, more than 20 years ago.

So, now, as far as the CIS countries, how do you feel, I mean, are you close to the neighbor that you live next to, or not? Of course—are you? [*Laughter*]

Well, these are our neighbors. Yesterday, we all were in the same—we lived in the same house in the Soviet Union. There is no Soviet Union, but these republics stay. They're our blood, right? Come on, let's be honest. We've helped them financially just as you help other countries, you financially help other countries, Latin America, Africa, et cetera, et cetera. It's only natural that we would have contacts and ties. They should be good. As a matter of fact, now we're planning some kind of centripetal forces pulling them inward, those tendencies. Everybody wants to be close to Russia, and we will be friendly with them, and we will support them, but in no way—not to contravene any international norms of behavior which are established or which shall be established. No.

President Clinton. Call on a Russian, Mr. President.

COCOM and Russia-U.S. Trade

Q. Now, COCOM and antidumping campaign, are there any specific decisions, any specific time lines and schedules and solutions?

President Yeltsin. Well, probably, it's the first time now that we have—for a long time we marched along this path. It took us a long time to get here. There were many problems along the way, but we've come to terms. The conditions—I think Bill will probably agree with me—I can tell you very frankly that for us the one condition that was set was that—we supply weapons to Iran, and so we were not allowed to this so-called kitchen in the creation of the post-COCOM regime where they were cooking up whatever this regime was going to look like.

Now, how have we come to an agreement? Now, there was a contract signed by the former Soviet Union with Iran. We are solid citizens, great power; we cannot but satisfy the terms of that contract. So the old contract, which had been signed years ago, back in '88, will be honored. But no other new contracts, no other new supplies, no other new shipments of weapons and weapons goods will be shipped. Those are the grounds upon which Bill Clinton agreed that we are going to participate in the post-COCOM era.

President Clinton. You asked another question. Let me say that is generally accurate where there are some—we reached a conceptual agreement in principle about how we would proceed, and then we agreed to let our experts on this matter work through it. And so we are working through it now, and we hope to resolve it soon. But we cannot say that it is resolved because in this matter, as you might understand, for both of us the details are quite important. So that while we reached a conceptual agreement, we have to work through the details.

Now, with regard to the antidumping, I think what you're referring to is my attempts to get the Congress to pass legislation which would declare Russia an economy in transition, which would facilitate more two-way trade. I have proposed such legislation to the Congress; it has not yet passed. We are working on a package of initiatives which would include the reduction of trade barriers in Russia and some more initiatives on our part so that we could get that kind of economy-in-transition status, which I think responds to the question that you asked.

General Agreement on Tariffs and Trade

Q. Mr. President, as you know, it's within your authority to call Congress back into session should it leave without passing GATT. Are you prepared to take that step if necessary, sir?

President Clinton. Well, I thought I made that clear. Yes, my preference would be, and what I believe we can do, based on our soundings today, is, if Congress leaves without passing GATT, I will ask that the Senate not adjourn but simply to go in recess and then return afterward. I will do whatever I can within the law to do everything I can to pass the GATT this year. I think it is important that it pass. It's important that it pass this year. It's important for the United States and our leadership, our efforts to get others to drop their trade barriers, to open their markets, to move forward. We have to set an example here.

I might say that a lot of the people who were opposed to NAFTA—let me just point out, our trade with Mexico has increased by about 19 percent in the last year. Our sales of autos and trucks have increased by 600 percent. And that's one of the reasons that a lot of those folks are working overtime for the first time in a decade. So this is plainly in our interest. It will create hundreds of thousands of jobs. And I'm going to do whatever I can, Brit [Brit Hume, ABC News], within the law to get this done this year.

Security and Stability Initiative

Q. Appearing at the United Nations, you proposed to immediately work out a treaty on stability and security. Apparently, you discussed this, too, with the President. How much do you feel that the approaches of Russia and the United States are similar in terms of coming up with a treaty? How would they coincide?

President Yeltsin. Well, in principle, the President of the United States agreed with the formulation that I made. Although he did say that the President of Russia has put forth too many initiatives there at the Assembly, and we're going to have to have some time to study all of these new initiatives that I've put forward.

Bosnia

Q. President Yeltsin, sir, you said again today that you oppose lifting the arms embargo on Bosnia. Would Russia veto a resolution to lift that arms embargo if the Serbs don't agree to a settlement within a certain amount of months?

And to President Clinton, what's your understanding of—is there any agreement between the two of you on this contentious issue?

President Yeltsin. Well, first of all, it's made easier for us by the decision, in solving this issue, the fact that the Bosnians themselves have asked a delay for, say, 4 to 6 months altogether, even to take it off of the agenda for discussion. But in 6 months we'll take a look and see.

President Clinton. What we did agree to do was to take some new initiatives to try to get the thing worked out as quickly as possible. And we still have a potential difference over that issue; there's no question about it. But we have—let me say, the remarkable thing here is how closely we have worked together on Bosnia for many months now. And I think a lot of the good things that have happened in that whole sad case have come about because we have worked together with Russia and with our NATO allies as well as with the United Nations.

Russia-U.S. Investment and Trade

Q. What are you planning to do in improving the investment climate for American companies after your discussions here that you had all day? And an additional question to President Bill Clinton regarding the antidumping legislation. Does it mean giving Russians the transition economy status, the Section 4.06 on trade?

President Yeltsin. I answer by saying that in meeting with businessmen, every one of them when he speaks said one and the same thing, taxes, taxes. We, ourselves, understand that in '91 a reborn Russia rather quickly prepared legislation on taxation, and it was full of mistakes, both for our own businessmen and for outside businessmen. And so now, what we're preparing—and among this is also, very kindly Bill proposed the use of our American 200-year history and experience in tax legislation, that we send a group of tax specialists here to take a look at how all these things are formed in the United States. But we're preparing a tax code which will, I feel, be adopted in the first 6 months, the first half of 1995. And it, of course, is substantially going to be different from the situation today and, of course, will make life a lot more easy for the foreign investors as well.

President Clinton. Let me respond very briefly to the question you asked. If Russia were granted under Federal law an economy-in-transition status, then the rules for judging whether products are being dumped or not would be somewhat different. The United States has made a great effort to trade more with Russia. Since I've been President, we've tripled our trade in 1993 over 1992; we doubled our purchases in 1994 over 1993. So we are working ahead. But we also have to have some tariff relief on things that we can sell in Russia in certain critical areas, including aerospace, automobiles, confectionery, a lot of other things we've talked about. So we're going to try to work through that and get a resolution.

Go ahead, Andrea [Andrea Mitchell, NBC News].

Russian Foreign Policy

Q. I'd like to ask both President Yeltsin and President Clinton: The United States has been concerned about what Russia will do in the former CIS countries, particularly Nagorno-Karabakh. You've spoken to that, but can I ask you, how is that any different from the sphere of influence that the United States claims to have over Haiti? And I'd like your comment as well.

President Clinton. Fair question.

President Yeltsin. Well, you know, in general, the President of the United States and we personally never really got into the details of this issue and only now we dedicated a lot of time at this session. As a matter of fact, we haven't

even finished in one day; we carried it over until today. Today we discussed it again, on Nagorno-Karabakh. And finally, in principle, the principle approach, we sort of brought them together. But in order to implement these, we're going to need some time to prepare documents, to look at the U.N. documentation. In short, the most important thing is that we have come to an understanding on this.

Q. President Yeltsin, I'm interested in whether you feel that the U.S. objections to Russian intervention with your neighbors is any different than what the United States has done in intervening in Haiti, which we claim is part of our sphere of influence. Do you think there is some hypocrisy here on the part of the United States?

President Yeltsin. No, I cannot say that, because Russia voted for the Resolution 940 in the United Nations and thereby we supported the actions of the United States of America.

Now, as Nagorno-Karabakh, this is our neighbor. They asked us that we help them, that we participate in the resolution of this conflict, just like we resolved it in Moldova, just like we set up peacekeeping forces between Abkhazia and Georgia, and there bloodshed stopped. Now we have to get the refugees back, et cetera. We're helping our neighbors.

President Clinton. Let me answer that question. First of all, the United States does not object to Russia taking an active role in the resolution of the problem in Nagorno-Karabakh. What we have discussed with the Russians, and what Boris and I finally had a chance to discuss personally together at some considerable length, is how that could be made more like Haiti, that is, how whatever Russia does should be done in a manner that is consistent with and within the framework of a United Nations resolution.

I think that Russia plainly does have an interest, a significant interest, in what happens on its borders and what happens in countries on its borders. In all of our discussions, President Yeltsin has acknowledged that he respected the sovereignty, the independence, and the territorial integrity of all those countries, but that what happened there affected what happened within his country and that there were things that he might be able to do there in pursuit of stability, without being inconsistent with sovereignty and territorial integrity and independence, that were appropriate.

What we did in Haiti, as you know, was not to act on our own, although the United States has in the 20th century acted on its own many times in this hemisphere. We went to the United Nations. We amassed an international coalition that has 28 nations for the first phase of this operation and then even more for the second phase. And I think that's the way we ought to proceed.

It may be necessary for other nations with military or other capacity to handle other problems or to at least take the lead on other problems in their areas. But when it is done, it should be done within the framework of the United Nations wherever possible and with respect for territorial integrity. And I think we are moving forward in that direction.

Press Secretary Myers. Last question.

ABM Treaty

Q. Based on the reports of the U.S. press sources, the United States aimed at making additions to the ABM Treaty which substantially changes its content. Was this discussed at the negotiations and talks? And what is your impression?

President Yeltsin. Well, apparently you didn't catch—I was reading so fast this list of mine, you didn't—I mentioned there the ABM. In other words, we did discuss the ABM issue, but there, taking into the account the professional difficulties, we handed that over to a joint commission which is now working so that it can make its recommendations. Right?

President Clinton. Thank you.

NOTE: The President's 71st news conference began at 3:45 p.m. in the East Room at the White House. President Yeltsin spoke in Russian, and his remarks were translated by an interpreter. In his remarks, President Clinton referred to Prime Minister Viktor Chernomyrdin of Russia. H.R. 4624, the Departments of Veterans Affairs and Housing and Urban Development, and Independent Agencies Appropriations Act, 1995, approved September 28, was assigned Public Law No. 103–327.

Remarks at a Reception for Business Leaders
September 28, 1994

Ladies and gentlemen, after about 2 days of solid meetings, President Yeltsin and I are talked out. [*Laughter*] But we're delighted to see you.

We just came from our joint press conference where President Yeltsin listed about 40 things, or maybe 50, that we discussed. I never thought I would see anyone exhaust the American press corps, but he did it. [*Laughter*] So then I got up to answer the first question, and I said, before any questions, I want you to know our positions on items 13, 27, and 32. [*Laughter*]

Ladies and gentlemen, when I became President, I was absolutely convinced our country had to redefine the role of its National Government as we move toward the 21st century and that one of the things we had to do is to move away from the extreme views of Government as a savior for all the problems of society on the one hand or Government as sort of sitting on the sidelines while history goes by on the other. It was obvious to me that we needed a new idea of partnerships between our National Government—partnerships with other countries, partnerships with the business community, partnerships with all ordinary Americans as they seek to fulfill their dreams and their abilities.

This meeting represents two of those partnerships. I want to thank the Vice President for the work he has done with Prime Minister Chernomyrdin in cementing our partnership with Russia on an economic basis and on a scientific basis. And I want to thank Bob Strauss and all the rest of you who have been a part of our partnership between the American Government and the American business community reaching out for new opportunities all around the world.

The depth and the durability of the relationship between the United States and Russia will affect the future of every person in our two countries and every person in the world over the next 10 years. We have to make it right. And one of the ways we can make it right is by a deep economic partnership rooted in trade and investment. We are committed to that. And

I know you are committed to that. And I can tell you that Boris Yeltsin is committed to that.

Let me close by thanking some of the people who will turn our words into reality. Besides the Vice President, as he has already noted, the Secretary of Commerce, Ron Brown, the head of our Export-Import Bank, Ken Brody, Ruth Harkin, who runs OPIC for us. I thank all of them. And I also thank Ambassador Tom Pickering, who along with the Secretary of State and so many others in the State Department have totally changed the direction of our American diplomacy so that now the American State Department is known all over the world as being interested in doing business and helping Americans do business, instead of being uninvolved.

I thank Secretary O'Leary and all the other Cabinet members who have been to Russia. And again, I close with pledging my full partnership to you and to my friend Boris Yeltsin. Together, we can make the future what it ought to be for all our people.

Thank you.

NOTE: The President spoke at 4:50 p.m. in the Atrium at the Corcoran Gallery of Art. In his remarks, he referred to Robert Strauss, chairman, U.S.-Russian Business Council.

Partnership for Economic Progress: Joint Statement on Principles and Objectives for the Development of Trade, Economic Cooperation, and Investment
September 28, 1994

The United States of America and the Russian Federation,

Believing that strong economic ties and cooperation can contribute significantly to the building of strong, friendly relations and acceleration of the development of free markets, economic growth and job creation in both countries,

Based on continuing progress by the Russian Federation in steps to create a market economy and more open commercial and investment environment, including the necessary legal and financial conditions,

Desiring to build a strategic economic partnership between the two countries and accelerate and give vibrancy to the efforts of their private and commercial sectors to develop commercial projects on the basis of trade, joint ventures, and foreign direct investment,

Noting the positive trends and developments in the legal, commercial, and financial frameworks for bilateral trade, economic cooperation and investment,

Positively assessing steps by the Russian Federation in creating a market economy, and by the United States of America in extending technical assistance to support, on a bilateral and multilateral basis, market reforms in the Russian Federation and the development of bilateral commercial relations,

Noting the complementarity of the American and Russian economics for the development of key economic sectors and the significant potential for development of mutually beneficial commercial ventures between the two countries,

Reaffirming their commitment to the purposes and principles of the Charter for American-Russian Partnership and Friendship of June 17, 1992, and the principles of the Vancouver (April 1993) and Moscow (January 1994) Declarations by the presidents of both countries,

Noting the important role of the joint Commission for Economic and Technological Cooperation in creating the conditions for strengthening U.S.-Russian economic cooperation,

Have adopted the following Principles and Objectives for the development of trade, economic cooperation and investment relations:

Trade

The United States of America and the Russian Federation seek to establish a normal trade relationship as quickly as feasible, to support a rapid increase in bilateral commerce. Great value is placed on the Agreement on Trade Relations in force between the United States of America and the Russian Federation and both countries are committed to carry out fully the provisions of this Agreement.

The United States recognizes the significance of the removal of Russia from application of the provisions of Title IV of the U.S. Trade Act of 1974 (the Jackson-Vanik Amendment). The U.S. Administration has made a positive determination that Russia is in full compliance with Title IV criteria and will consult with the U.S. Congress at an early date concerning legislation to remove Russia from application of Title IV.

Both countries welcome the work of the U.S.-Russia Joint Commission for Economic and Technological Cooperation and its various bilateral committees, including the U.S.-Russia Intergovernmental Business Development Committee to contribute to the expansion of bilateral trade and investment and will utilize the Business Development Committee as a means for frequent consultation on the means of improving the environment for commercial growth. Each side will use its best efforts to implement measures supporting trade expansion and to remove obstacles to trade development.

The United States and Russia note that as of September 30, 1993, the United States has extended to qualifying Russian exports eligibility for duty-free entrance into the United States under the U.S. Generalized System of Preferences program covering 4,400 products, and that during 1994 U.S. technical experts will provide information to Russian officials and entrepreneurs on effective utilization of the GSP program.

The United States expects to extend the benefits of the GSP program to Russia for so long as its program authority and Russian eligibility under authorizing legislation permit. Russia will review the possibility of removing certain tariff barriers impeding development of trade.

Both countries will facilitate trade and investment expansion through the dissemination of reliable and comprehensive economic data, transparent and stable commercial laws and regulations, and active promotion of business contacts and facilitating access to commercial market information. Noting the provisions of the U.S.-Russia Agreement on Trade Relations concerning transparency of new laws and regulations, the United States believes it would be useful if Russia adopted procedures for public comment on proposed changes to commercial laws and regulations, as well as advance notification and publication of proposed changes. Until such procedures are in place, both countries through

the Business Development Committee will facilitate the timely exchange of information on legislation and regulations as they are adopted.

Market Access. Each country desires to provide liberal access to its market for the other's goods and services. They are committed to avoid trade frictions and facilitate access consistent with fair trade practices and their respective trade laws.

The U.S.-Russia Business Development Committee is an important forum for discussions of current and potential market access issues and for the development of recommended policies and regulations which would support expanded trade and investment.

Recognizing that Russia is an economy in transition to a free market, the United States will give priority attention to the special market access problems Russia faces as it continues its economic transition. The U.S. Administration will consult with the U.S. Congress on this subject.

Market access issues will be addressed from a broader bilateral perspective through the Business Development Committee's Market Access Working Group. This group will consider initiatives designed to reduce barriers to mutual market access, taking into account the unique problems Russia faces as an economy in transition.

The United States and Russia will immediately work to address Russia's concerns with U.S. antidumping laws, beginning with procedures to disseminate information designed to prevent unfair trade and procedures designed to facilitate participation in antidumping proceedings if unfair trade occurs. They agree to discuss changing market trends resulting from Russia's transition to a market economy and integration into the global trading system.

Both countries recognize that tariff-reducing measures, consistent with GATT/WTO principles, will provide an important stimulus to bilateral trade and investment. They also intend to review and seek prompt removal of technical barriers to trade through both bilateral cooperation and unilateral measures. The reduction of such tariff and technical barriers to trade will lead to increased investment and promote the development and growth of economically healthy, globally competitive domestic industries.

Both countries consider cooperation in international standardization and openness of conformity assessment indispensable to eliminating or avoiding the creation of technical barriers to trade and intend to proceed vigorously with the program of work agreed upon in the Joint Communique on Cooperation in Conformity Assessment issued in Moscow on December 16, 1993, at the conclusion of the meetings of the Joint Commission for Economic and Technological Cooperation led by Vice President Albert Gore and Prime Minister Victor Chernomyrdin. They consider progress in product certification, testing and quality assurance to be of priority for telecommunications equipment, drugs, pharmaceuticals and medical devices.

The United States looks forward to the implementation by Russia of a trade regime that would speed its accession to the GATT/WTO and open the way to application of GATT/WTO principles in their bilateral trade. The United States supports Russia's accession to the GATT/WTO and expresses its readiness to extend appropriate technical assistance and to consult concerning the process of accession.

Intellectual Property Rights. The United States and Russia look forward to continued cooperation under the working group on intellectual property matters, established by the Agreement on Trade Relations between the United States of America and the Russian Federation.

The United States recognizes Russia's considerable progress in enacting intellectual property rights legislation. Both sides consider effective enforcement of those laws to be important. In particular, the United States considers protection for pharmaceuticals, computer software, sound recordings, books, and integrated circuit layout designs to be of primary importance. The U.S. side looks forward to Russia's rapid accession to the Berne Convention on the Protection of Literary and Artistic Works.

Closer Economic Cooperation and Commercial Partnership. The two countries share the view that their two economies are complementary in many ways and that the extent of economic cooperation currently existing between the two is only a small fraction of its potential. They agree that the two economies could benefit strongly from the elimination of trade and commercial barriers between them.

The United States and Russia concur that Russia must take additional market-oriented steps for trade and commercial cooperation to reach its potential. Both agree that closer economic cooperation will have a beneficial effect on bolstering the continued market transformation of Russia's economy.

The elimination of barriers to trade and investment and increased commercial cooperation will emphasize the totally changed nature of the relationship between the two countries to one of strategic economic partnership.

In this context, the United States and Russia at an appropriate time could consider future arrangements to enhance their bilateral economic relationship. They also will work through the Business Development Committee forum to identify measures for achieving closer commercial integration.

Investment and Finance

The two sides note favorably the June 1992 Treaty on the Encouragement and Reciprocal Protection of Investment that has been signed by the heads of both States and that has been approved by the U.S. Senate. They agree that ratification by the Russian Federation Federal Assembly and its prompt entry into force is a critical goal to be achieved in improving the Russian investment environment for American companies.

They also agree that the steps taken by Russia pursuant to President Yeltsin's Decree 1466 of September 27, 1993 form the basis for moving forward with administrative and legislative actions to further improve the investment climate in Russia. They share the opinion that bilateral discussions that include the business communities of both countries will be the most rapid way of identifying the precise actions that are needed.

Support for Reform. The United States reaffirms its support for Russia's efforts to establish a market economy and offers continuing active assistance to the process of reform.

In particular, the United States welcomes Russia's intention to establish new incentives, consistent with international standards and agreements including the GATT/WTO, to attract foreign direct investment, to continue its highly successful privatization program, to take additional steps to liberalize the economy and foreign trade by freeing prices and opening up its markets to the world at large, and to enforce the right of private land ownership.

Russia acknowledges and welcomes the support of the United States for its reform efforts and will continue to cooperate closely to identify ways in which the two nations can work together to expedite Russia's transformation into a market system.

Russia is committed to a continuous process of market reform. The United States and Russia recognize that trade and investment activities between the two countries, based on private sector commerce, will provide the foundations for sustained growth now and in the future. Such trade and investment activities will help both nations acquire new technology and know-how and the resulting capital flows will be an important source of financing for both nations that will support reform, create new jobs and improve the quality of life in both countries.

The United States and Russia agree that the development of a climate hospitable toward foreign direct investment could result in tens of billions of dollars of new direct investment in Russia, and could generate a much closer commercial relationship between the business communities of both countries. The United States and Russia will work through the Business Development Committee to identify and eliminate barriers to investment, including sector-specific issues.

"Commercial Partnership Program". The United States and Russia undertake to establish a "Commercial Partnership Program" to enhance existing bilateral and multilateral agreements by providing detailed guidelines and milestones based on the principles outlined in this document for achieving closer commercial cooperation. The Commercial Partnership Program will be developed in several stages, based on continuing progress in political and economic reforms by Russia and in the flow of commerce between the two nations. Each stage will involve implementation and expansion of specific programs to encourage company-to-company cooperation and expanded trade and investment. The Business Development Committee will co-ordinate the identification and implementation of specific steps toward this goal.

Industry Cooperation. The two countries believe that private sector efforts are vital to the success of Russia's creation of a market economy. Industry cooperation in key sectors will provide the necessary capital and business expertise to support economic development. Economic competition generated through private sector cooperation will benefit both countries by improving product quality and manufacturing efficiency and by creating jobs.

The United States and Russia agree that investment and trade in the oil and gas sector provide Russia with an opportunity to attract U.S. capital and technology on a vast scale, far beyond resources available from foreign assistance. They understand the desirability of taking earliest possible steps in Russia to attract foreign capital and to provide an attractive investment climate, including realization of production sharing agreements, stable and reasonable tax and export regimes, and equal and predictable access to pipelines, in line with the European Energy Charter Treaty.

The United States and Russia declare that investment and trade in other industry sectors, as well, are essential to overall economic development. Agribusiness and food processing, aerospace, mining, medical devices and pharmaceuticals, telecommunications, transportation, environmental equipment, housing, and defense conversion are priority sectors for cooperation. Both countries will consider appropriate measures for supporting joint ventures in designated sectors.

NOTE: An original was not available for verification of the content of this statement.

Joint Statement on Cooperation in Promoting the Rule of Law and Combating Crime
September 28, 1994

President Boris Yeltsin and President William Clinton, during their meeting in Washington on September 27 and 28, 1994, noted the threat which crime poses to the Russian and American societies and to the entire international community. Of particular concern to the Presidents was the rise in financial crime, nuclear materials smuggling, organized crime, and drug trafficking. They agreed that bilateral and international cooperative efforts would be necessary to combat this growing threat.

The Presidents noted that cooperation in law enforcement between their two countries could in a substantial way help to resolve the problem of crime and should be institutionalized through bilateral agreements. To this end, delegations from the United States and the Russian Federation held a first round of negotiations for an Agreement on Cooperation in Criminal Matters which commits each country to assist the other in criminal investigations and crime prevention. The Presidents expressed their intention to sign and bring into force as quickly as possible this Agreement. The Presidents also announced their intention to enter into negotiations for a broader Mutual Legal Assistance Treaty.

President Clinton announced the intention of the United States to offer an expanded program of assistance to the Russian Federation, including technical assistance and training of personnel to support cooperation between the Russian Federation and the United States in promoting the rule of law and combating crime.

NOTE: An original was not available for verification of the content of this statement.

Joint Announcement on Environmental Protection in the Arctic
September 28, 1994

President William Clinton and President Boris Yeltsin announced at their summit meeting on September 27 and 28, 1994, that cooperation in the resolution of the problems of processing and storage of Russian liquid radioactive wastes in the North of Russia is considered by both sides as an important component of more effective protection for the environmental quality and natural resources of the Arctic.

The Russian Federation and the United States of America confirm their readiness to cooperate in consistently preventing dumping of liquid radioactive wastes, in accordance with the London Convention, and to proceed to a solution of the problem of Arctic pollution from all sources. To this end, the Russian Federation and the United States of American agree to undertake immediately, in cooperation with other inter- ested countries, a step-by-step expansion and upgrading of a treatment facility for liquid low-level radioactive waste in Murmansk. Both sides hope that a speedy implementation of this project, which is in the interests of all states of the region, will become the focal point of efforts to create the infrastructure for ecologically safe processing and storage of liquid low-level radioactive wastes in the North of Russia. At the same time, Russia intends to continue its present policy of voluntary commitment to the prohibition on dumping liquid radioactive wastes under the London Convention with a view to eventual formal adherence to the prohibition.

NOTE: An original was not available for verification of the content of this statement.

Statement on Signing the Departments of Veterans Affairs and Housing and Urban Development, and Independent Agencies Appropriations Act, 1995
September 28, 1994

Today I have signed into law H.R. 4624, the "Departments of Veterans Affairs and Housing and Urban Development, and Independent Agencies Appropriations Act, FY 1995."

The Act provides funding for the Departments of Veterans Affairs (VA) and Housing and Urban Development, Environmental Protection Agency, National Aeronautics and Space Administration, and National Science Foundation and various other agencies. This Act will fund important activities in the space program, housing programs, environmental protection, and programs for our Nation's veterans.

I am pleased that the Act provides funding for a number of my high-priority investment proposals, including both the National Service and Community Development Financial Institutions initiatives. The National Service Initiative will provide an opportunity for young people to obtain funding for a college education while serving the country in areas of great need such as education, environment, public safety, and human services. Funding for the Community Development Financial Institutions fund will increase the flow of capital to distressed neighborhoods and their currently underserved low-income residents, and provide financing for neighborhood redevelopment and revitalization efforts.

The Act also provides funding for the redesigned Space Station and other programs that will set a new direction for the Nation in space exploration, science, and technology. The Act includes about $260 million for cooperative activities with Russia, with about half of that going directly for joint space station, human space flight, and scientific cooperation.

The Act includes $7.2 billion in funding for the Environmental Protection Agency (EPA). The Act provides funds for EPA programs that protect our environment through enforcement of our environmental laws, cleanup of hazardous waste sites, and construction of needed water and waste water treatment facilities.

The Act meets the needs of our Nation's veterans by providing $16.2 billion in funding for the VA medical care program, an increase of $0.6 billion over the FY 1994 enacted level.

The Act includes $25.7 billion in funding for the Department of Housing and Urban Development, including funding for programs such as the HOME block grants for housing, Community Development Grants, and Severely Distressed Public Housing. These programs will assist communities and individuals in revitalizing neighborhoods and increasing opportunities for home ownership.

The Act provides $3.4 billion in funding for the National Science Foundation (NSF), a $343 million increase over the FY 1994 enacted level. NSF programs will promote basic research that is vital to enabling our Nation to compete in world markets.

The Act includes a requested FY 1994 emergency supplemental appropriation of $225 million to finance housing repairs in areas affected by the Northridge earthquake ("ghost towns") to be derived by transfers of previously appropriated emergency funds from the Departments of Education and Transportation.

Concurrently with signing this bill, I am transmitting to the Congress a request to make available $14.5 million for FEMA, which I am designating as an emergency requirement. These funds will provide additional resources to address consequences of the Northridge earthquake. The funds, which were appropriated in Public Law 103–211, the Emergency Supplemental Appropriations Act of 1994, will be transferred from the Unanticipated Needs account within Funds Appropriated to the President. These funds will provide $150 million in additional emergency disaster loans to the victims of the Northridge earthquake.

WILLIAM J. CLINTON

The White House,
September 28, 1994.

NOTE: H.R. 4624, approved September 28, was assigned Public Law No. 103–327.

Remarks on Signing the Riegle-Neal Interstate Banking and Branching Efficiency Act of 1994
September 29, 1994

Thank you very much, Dick Kovacevich, for your fine words and your strong support of this endeavor. Thank you, Tom Labrecque, for what you said. Thank you, as always, Secretary Bentsen, for your remarks and your stellar leadership. I thank all the Members of Congress for coming and the Members of the House who are out voting; you were all introduced by name in absentia. [*Laughter*] But I do want to say a special word of thanks to retiring Congressman

Steve Neal for his wonderful leadership on this bill, and I thank him. I thank the Senators, those who are here especially, Senator Dodd, Senator Sarbanes, Senator Bennett, and of course, Senator Riegle. We will miss you, and we thank you for this very important part of your legacy.

I thank Chairman Greenspan and Mr. Blinder and Chairman Levitt for coming and for their role in stabilizing and strengthening our economy. I never comment on these things, but I'm awfully glad this bill is taking effect at a time when banks will still be able to make loans at reasonable interest rates. [*Laughter*]

There are a lot of other people here—I'll live to regret this, I know—[*laughter*]—a lot of other people here that could be introduced, but I think I would be remiss if I did not say something about someone who fought for this issue when he was in Congress and is now the distinguished Governor of the State of Connecticut, Lowell Weicker. We're delighted to see you here, sir. Thank you for coming. We're delighted to see Sarge and Eunice Shriver here; thank you for coming.

And now, there are two other people I would be personally remiss if I did not introduce because they had a lot to do with my interest in this issue. The thing that sparked my interest in this issue, first of all, was being Governor of a State when banks were dropping like flies all around the country, and we were determined to protect ours. And I began then to seriously think what was structurally wrong with the financial system in this country. There is a gentleman here from my home State who has been my banker, my adviser, my supporter, and was the last person who served as my chief of staff as Governor of Arkansas. I'd like to ask him to stand up, Mr. Bill Bowen, former chairman of the Commercial National Bank. [*Applause*] And the other person here, who stayed up with me half the night once—you may think you can't stay up half a night talking about interstate banking. [*Laughter*] You may think it would put you to sleep even though—but you have never heard Hugh McColl talk about it. Will you please stand up? Thank you so much. [*Applause*] I figured if he could be rhapsodic about this at 2 a.m., I ought to be for it, strong for it. [*Laughter*]

You've already heard how important this legislation is and what it will do for the banking industry. I'd like to just take a few moments to describe to you, from my point of view as President, how this fits into our comprehensive economic strategy. You've already heard people say it will make us stronger economically; it will be better for consumers; it will make us more efficient. It represents another example of our intent to reinvent Government by making it less regulatory and less overreaching and by shrinking it where it ought to be shrunk and reshaping it where it ought to be reshaped.

The people who are here up on this stage with me represent the economic team who worked with me to try to develop a strategy that would put the American people first and enable us to compete and win in the 21st century and enable us to stay together and go forward in spite of all of our differences, to restore prosperity, and to renew the American dream.

The economic strategy we have crafted, while it may have critics in every corner from point to point, still should be recognized for what it is: a serious attempt by the national administration to systematically address the problems of the American economy and the opportunities of the American economy that enable us to increase our capacity to work together for opportunity for all.

Secretary Bentsen has been my wise counsel and strong leader. Secretary Brown is with President Yeltsin in Seattle today, probably still trying to make another sale. [*Laughter*] As all of you know, he's traveled from South America to South Africa to promote American businesses and exports and has been the most active Commerce Secretary certainly in my lifetime. Secretary Reich has been tireless in his advocacy for a skilled work force and for changing our whole unemployment system into a reemployment system. Alice Rivlin and before her Leon Panetta have played a central role in shaping tough and responsible budgets and in giving us 3 years of declining deficits for the first time since Mr. Truman was the President of the United States. Ambassador Kantor has given us more leadership on trade in the last 20 months than in any comparable period in the last 35 years. Erskine Bowles is not here, but the Acting Administrator of SBA is here, Sandra Pulley. And let me say, among other things, they have proved that if you put people in charge of the Small Business Administration whose job it is or has been in the past to create and expand small businesses, it makes a remarkable difference. The agency is less political but more effective than it has ever been. One of the things they did was to take the small business loan form, which was that thick, and cut it to one page and give you a decision in 3 days, yes or no, which is something that interstate banking will probably make possible for every bank in America to do, before you know it. I want to thank Laura Tyson, the Chair of our Council of Economic Advisers, who has done so much to help us analyze the economy and strategize long-term. But most important of all, I want to thank the most self-effacing but talented person I've ever had the privilege to work with in the area of the economy, Bob Rubin, for coordinating this entire team. And I'd like for him to stand up, because he never gets any recognition. [*Applause*]

Our strategy was pretty simple: Get our fiscal house in order; bring the deficit down; do it and find a way to invest more in the skills of our people, the technologies of the future, defense conversion; expand trade; open markets; be more aggressive in appropriate ways in having a partnership outside our borders between the United States Government and our economic interests; and work to find ways to make the Government more efficient.

We have committed ourselves to that. And among other things, the budget we are about to adopt—we're in the process of adopting now—combined with the budget last year, represent only the first time in 17 years when a President's had two budgets in a row adopted by Congress substantially intact. They will give us 3 years of deficit reduction in a row for the first time since the Truman Presidency. But also somewhat less known, they will over this 6-year period, because we adopt 5-year budgets, reduce the size of the Federal Government by 270,000 to its smallest size since Mr. Kennedy was President. All of that money is being given to the American people in their own communities to fight crime. That's how the crime bill was funded. This is a remarkable change. We have already reduced the size of the Federal Government in 20 months by more than 70,000 people. And so I thank all of them for that.

The result of these comprehensive efforts and our disciplined coordination with other aspects of the public and private sector is that our economy is healthy and growing, inflation is moderate, trade is expanding, the deficit is dropping, and the Government is shrinking. There have been 4.3 million new jobs. And in contrast to the pattern of the eighties, when much of the job growth in times that were slow was in State and local government, 93 percent of the new jobs for the last 20 months have been in the private sector.

According to a recent annual survey by international economists, America has now been ranked the most productive economy in the world for the first time in 9 years. We've also had 8 months in a row of manufacturing job growth, something others had all but given up on, for the first time in 10 years.

Our challenge now is to keep moving in the right direction, to keep creating new partnerships between business, Government, and citizens. And this legislation is a good step in that direction.

Under this law, as you've already heard, banks will be able to operate in more States with less trouble. We wipe away obsolete Government-created restrictions, something I'm determined to do in many other areas. And you'd be amazed how many areas these exist in.

Just for example, in the last year and a half, we have given 17 States permission to try new ways to move people from welfare to work. In every case, we had to wipe away Federal restrictions to allow States to do things that nearly 100 percent of the American people without regard to race or income want done to find a way to put people in the work force and take them off the dole. So we are working hard. We know we can save billions of dollars if we do that. Some estimates suggest the efficiencies in this bill alone in reducing paperwork and regulation will save this industry about $1 billion a year.

We know this bill is good for consumers for reasons that have already been stated. I wish I had thought of Tom's line myself: It's easier for a New York bank to expand in Kuala Lumpur than Jersey City. So, since he's already said that, I won't give you what they wrote for me, which is longer and not nearly as graphic. [*Laughter*]

I also want to thank the Congress for working on this bill in a bipartisan spirit. You know, I get very frustrated, as all of you know, that it takes so long to do big things around here. I went back and read "The Federalist Papers" the other night, I was so frustrated by it. And then, lo and behold, some of our brilliant framers organized this Government to slow things down. Even they couldn't be right about everything, but anyway, we took our time on this bill.

And there are so many things that we've been able to do in the last year and a half that were just sort of hanging around for 6, 7, or 8 years. But when the bill did pass, when we had the confluence of forces and energy and vision to pass it, it passed with overwhelming bipartisan support, which should increase the confidence of the American people that this is a good thing for our country and that it will help all of us to do better.

Let us all acknowledge that this work is far from over. You've already heard the previous speaker say there was more to be done in the banking area, even though we have had a very good year and a half with trade. And NAFTA, by the way, is having a very positive effect on our economy. We've had a 19 percent increase in exports to Mexico, a 600 percent increase in the exports of automobiles and trucks to Mexico since NAFTA passed. Jobs are up to both Canada and Mexico because exports are up. Still, the really important thing to do is to pass the GATT.

I am going in November to Indonesia to meet with the leaders of the big Asian economies. I will then go back to Florida in December to have all the leaders of the democratic governments in the Caribbean and Latin America there at the Summit of the Americas that Mr. McLarty, who is here, is coordinating for us. We need to be able to continue to be the leader in opening up the global economy to efficiency and to competition and to expansion.

This is not a zero-sum game, this economy. But the only way it cannot be that is to keep pushing back the limits of the possible. And the only way you can do that is to have global economic growth. So we will keep hoping and working for GATT. I think we need to create it and pass it as quickly as we can. The American people will be a winner there.

All of you know that every serious economic study of the GATT has estimated that it will create hundreds of thousands of high-paying American jobs over the next decade and ultimately add between $100 billion and $200 billion to our GDP every single year. It will cut foreign tariffs by a third. It will provide a global tax cut of $744 billion. So I hope that the bipartisan support the GATT has will result in the same thing that happened with the banking bill,

that we will pass it and pass it in a prompt way.

Yesterday the House Ways and Means Committee approved the GATT by a vote of 35 to 3. This morning the Senate Finance Committee approved it by a vote of 19 to 0. The fact is, these folks have figured out that this is good for our economy, good for our country, good for our global leadership to continue to be pointing the way for other countries, to keep them looking upward and outward and reaching out to each other instead of drawing inward and giving in to the difficult pressures that all of us face.

I want Congress to pass the GATT this year. If it passes the House but not the Senate, I'll urge the Senate to return after the election recess and pass it then. We have come too far on this journey, making our Government more efficient, our economy more productive, and working together, to back off now.

You know, this week I've had the honor to represent you at the U.N. and to meet with President Yeltsin here in Washington and to watch as our courageous soldiers are working to bring democracy back to Haiti in a peaceful fashion. I am reminded that the world, with all of its difficulties, has never really had greater opportunities and that our very existence now is not threatened, as it once was, because of the progress we have made in trying to learn to live together.

People everywhere who yearn for political freedom and for economic opportunity are having more chances to realize both than ever before. We have a chance to help them. Sometimes we are called upon to help them in definite and specific ways, as we were early in the process of Russian reform or as we have been in Haiti. But I always believe that the most powerful way we help is by setting the right example.

We have set a good example today. Passing the GATT is setting a good example. Reaching out to the rest of the world, being unafraid to compete and determined to contact people and to work with them and to keep doing what we do better is the best way to set that kind of example. To me, that's what this bill represents, and I'm honored to be here to sign it today.

Thank you very much.

We don't have enough room on the dais for every Member of Congress who's here, but I would like to ask at least Mr. Neal to come up here. He and Senator Riegle should be in this picture. It may get them so many write-in votes, they won't be able to retire.

NOTE: The President spoke at 3:05 p.m. at the Treasury Building. In his remarks, he referred to Richard Kovacevich, president and chief executive officer, Norwest Corp. of Minneapolis; Tom Labrecque, chairman and chief executive officer, Chase Manhattan Bank; Alan Greenspan, Chairman, Federal Reserve Board; Alan S. Blinder, member, Council of Economic Advisers; Arthur Levitt, Chairman, Securities and Exchange Commission; Robert Sargent Shriver, Jr., first Director of the Peace Corps; Eunice Shriver, director, Special Olympics; and Hugh McColl, Jr., chairman of the board, NationsBank Corp. H.R. 3841, approved September 29, was assigned Public Law No. 103–328.

Joint Statement on Strategic Stability and Nuclear Security
September 29, 1994

Joint statement on strategic stability and nuclear security by the Presidents of the United States of America and the Russian Federation

Presidents Clinton and Yeltsin underscored that, with the end of the Cold War, major progress has been achieved with regard to strengthening global strategic stability and nuclear security. Both the United States and Russia are significantly reducing their nuclear forces. Important steps have been taken to detarget strategic missiles. Multilateral negotiations on a comprehensive nuclear test ban have begun. The Presidents noted the key role of the Non-Proliferation Treaty in ensuring global stability.

President Yeltsin outlined the initiative Russia presented to the UN General Assembly for a treaty among the five permanent members of the UN Security Council for a halt to the production of fissile materials for weapons, a ban on the reuse of fissile materials in weapons, further elimination of nuclear warheads, and reduction of strategic delivery systems.

President Clinton outlined the ideas he described at the UN General Assembly for cooperation in advancing nuclear non-proliferation, particularly to enhance the security of nuclear materials and to prevent nuclear smuggling.

The Presidents discussed these initiatives, of which they had informed each other in advance and which reflected shared goals and certain common proposals designed to contribute to nuclear non-proliferation. In this regard, the Presidents agreed that the permanent members of the UN Security Council, given their responsibilities as nuclear powers, have a special role to play.

The United States and Russia will work with the other permanent members, as well as other countries, to ensure a successful outcome at the 1995 Non-Proliferation Treaty conference that produces an indefinite and unconditional extension of the NPT, to conclude a comprehensive nuclear test ban treaty at the earliest possible date, and to achieve a global prohibition on the production of fissile materials for nuclear weapons. The Presidents also agreed on the desirability of continuing their respective moratoria on nuclear weapon tests.

The Presidents welcomed the ongoing deactivation and dismantlement of strategic nuclear systems by the parties to the START I Treaty and the implementation of the January 14, 1994 Trilateral Statement. They welcomed the real possibility to bring the START I Treaty and the Lisbon Protocol into force in the very near future and pledged full cooperation to this end. The Presidents agreed that their defense ministers would exchange information every three months on strategic systems that have been deactivated and eliminated.

The Presidents confirmed their intention to seek early ratification of the START II Treaty, once the START I Treaty enters into force, and expressed their desire to exchange START II instruments of ratification at the next U.S.-Russia summit meeting.

In an important new development, the Presidents concurred that, once the START II Treaty is ratified, the United States and Russia would proceed to deactivate all strategic delivery systems to be reduced under START II by removing their nuclear warheads or taking other steps to remove them from alert status.

The Presidents instructed their experts to intensify their dialogue to compare conceptual approaches and to develop concrete steps to adapt the nuclear forces and practices on both sides to the changed international security situation and to the current spirit of U.S.-Russian partnership, including the possibility, after ratification of START II, of further reductions of, and limitations on, remaining nuclear forces. They also discussed the prospect for confidence-building and transparency measures in this area. The Presidents consider that, as the political partnership develops, there will be new opportunities to strengthen stability through openness and transparency.

President Clinton described to President Yeltsin the unilateral adjustments the United States will make in its strategic and non-strategic nuclear forces and safety, security and use control practices as a result of the recently completed nuclear posture review. President Yeltsin noted these U.S. changes as a manifestation of the new relationship between the United States and Russia and described the comparable review of measures underway in Russia to reduce Russian nuclear forces and improve their safety. The Presidents agreed that each side would independently consider further unilateral steps, as appropriate, with regard to their respective nuclear forces.

The Presidents discussed the benefits of reduction and enhancements to the security of non-strategic nuclear forces.

The Presidents agreed on the fundamental importance of preserving the viability and integrity of the ABM Treaty. Noting the recent progress made on the issue of ABM/TMD demarcation and multilateralization of the ABM Treaty, the Presidents instructed their respective delegations, working with the other participating states, to complete agreement on remaining issues in the shortest possible time.

Both sides have an interest in developing and fielding effective theater missile defense systems on a cooperative basis. The Presidents agreed that the two sides will conduct a joint exercise of theater missile defenses and early warning of missile launches. This exercise would contribute to providing a basis for U.S. and Russian forces to operate together, for example, in peacekeeping operations.

Proceeding from the principles of partnership and reciprocity, the Presidents agreed to work together to develop broad bilateral and multilateral cooperation on assuring nuclear security as follows:

Cooperate on a bilateral and multilateral basis, including through the exchange of appropriate information, to prevent illegal trade in nuclear materials and undertake measures to strengthen the regime of control and physical protection of such materials.

Exchange detailed information at the next meeting of the Gore-Chernomyrdin Commission on aggregate stockpiles of nuclear warheads, on stocks of fissile materials and on their safety and security. The sides will develop a process for exchanging this information on a regular basis.

Direct their joint working group on nuclear safeguards, transparency and irreversibility to pursue by March 1995 further measures to improve confidence in and increase the transparency and irreversibility of the process of reducing nuclear weapons.

Facilitate broad cooperation among appropriate agencies in both countries to ensure effective control, accounting and physical protection of nuclear materials.

Facilitate cooperative programs between U.S. and Russian national laboratories in the areas of safety, physical protection, control and accounting of nuclear materials.

Deepen cooperation between the U.S. Department of Defense and the Russian Ministry of Defense in the area of ensuring nuclear security.

Implement a joint plan to expedite construction of a new, long-term storage facility for fissile materials from dismantled nuclear weapons at Mayak.

Taking a broad view of strategic stability and bearing in mind the need to control all types of weapons of mass destruction, the Presidents agreed on:

The importance of continued, full, mutual and reciprocal implementation of the September 1992 U.S.-Russian-UK statement on Biological Weapons as a means of gaining confidence that offensive biological weapons programs have been terminated.

The need for adherence by all states to the Chemical Weapons Convention and for universal application of its provisions, as well as the need for adoption without delay of measures that make it possible to bring the CWC into force; and the need to resolve without delay the outstanding issues related to the Bilateral Destruction Agreement and the Wyoming Memorandum of Understanding.

NOTE: This joint statement also included a report of September presummit meetings on U.S.-Russian security issues.

Statement on the 1996 Democratic National Convention
September 29, 1994

I am pleased with Chairman Wilhelm's decision to name Debra DeLee to head the 1996 Democratic National Convention. I am confident her energy and enthusiasm as well as her political expertise will make the 1996 convention an exciting and rewarding experience for those inside the convention hall, throughout Chicago, and across America.

Statement on Lobby and Campaign Finance Reform Legislation
September 29, 1994

The American people have made it clear that they want a change in the way Washington works. From the beginning of my administration, I have called upon Congress to enact tough political reform legislation. Today Congress made real progress in the effort to return Government to the people. It is now time for Congress to finish the job and enact lobby reform and campaign finance reform, so that narrow interests are never able to obstruct the national interest.

The House of Representatives took a major step toward changing the culture of the Capital when it voted for lobby reform. This legislation will, for the first time, require lobbyists to fully disclose their activities, their clients, and the sources of their funding. And it will bar lobbyists from providing gifts, meals, and entertainment to lawmakers. I call on the Senate to quickly pass lobby reform and send it to my desk. We must take the political system away from the lobbyists and the narrow interests in Washington and give it back to the American people.

I am also heartened by the agreement between House and Senate leaders on campaign finance reform legislation. This bill will limit congressional spending, curb the PAC's and lobbyists, open the airwaves to debate, and ban the use of soft money in Federal elections. Make no mistake: this is real reform. Tomorrow the Senate will vote to end a filibuster and appoint conferees on this bill. I call on Senators from both parties to put aside partisanship and move forward with this legislation. There is simply no excuse for delay.

Remarks at a Reception for Senator Edward M. Kennedy in McLean, Virginia
September 29, 1994

Thank you so much. Senator and Mrs. Kennedy, the Kennedy family, Senator Mitchell and Members of the Senate, Congressmen, Con- gressman-to-be Patrick Kennedy, and Marvin Rosen, and all those who made this night possible, I thank you so much for your help for our friend. Chevy Chase, thank you for making us laugh.

I'll tell you a story about Chevy Chase. I never told this story in public before. Don't get that excited, it's not that good. [*Laughter*] I had never met Chevy Chase in my entire life, except on a movie screen. And in 1988 or '89, I went up to Long Island in the summertime. Hillary and I were up there visiting our friend Liz Robins, who's here tonight. And every summertime there's a softball game to raise money between the artists and the writers. And they asked me if I would be an umpire in this game. And once I realized there were some members of the press there and I'd be able to give them grades instead of the other way around, I eagerly accepted. Now, at that time— a lot of you won't remember this; I hope, at least, you won't remember it, and I hope you'll forget after I tell you tonight. [*Laughter*] I had given a speech for Governor Dukakis at the Democratic Convention, which I intend to complete here this evening. [*Laughter*] Anyway— I can't believe I said that. [*Laughter*] The announcer for the ball game was Jim Brady, the guy that does that "Brady's Bits" in Parade magazine every Sunday, you know? He's a delightful man, but when he saw me out there on the mound about ready to call balls and strikes, he said—he introduced me—he said, "This is Governor Clinton from Arkansas. He's up here visiting, and if he takes as long to make the calls today as he did to speak in Atlanta, we'll never get out of here." [*Laughter*] I really appreciated that. [*Laughter*] Anyway, so the game starts, and the next time the sides change, I look up in the stands, and this tall guy stands up and walks down, comes out to the pitcher's mound, shakes my hand, and says, "I'm Chevy Chase." And he said, "I may be the only person in America besides your mother who feels this way, but I liked that speech. Tell him to go to hell." [*Laughter*] That's verbatim what he said. [*Applause*] You just applauded for the next ambassador to Great Britain. [*Laughter*]

Ladies and gentlemen, you know we all do a lot of these events, and a lot of you are the backbone of our party. And sometimes we do them with great energy; sometimes we do them with interest; sometimes we do them because we know it's the right thing to do and we do them. I am here tonight because there is no place else in America I would rather be tonight than here in this cause for this good man.

You know, before I got here I really didn't understand how things so often came across in the country so different than they are up here. I was another alienated American, even though I was the Governor of my State. And I was terribly worried that this country was going in the wrong direction, that the people that were running our country were just telling the voters what they thought they wanted to hear and avoiding all the tough problems—we had had profound social problems building up for 30 years, we'd had serious economic problems building up for 20 years—that we had finally come to the end of the cold war, a time when we had an opportunity to take a fresh look at both the opportunities and the difficulties of this country at this time, and that we had a window here in which we could either secure the American dream for our children and our grandchildren and the strength of this country as we move into the 21st century, or we could walk away from the responsibilities of our generation.

When I talked to Hillary about running for President, I—in a very personal way, I didn't really want to do it. First of all, most of my friends thought it was a fool's errand because the incumbent President was at over 70 percent approval. Secondly, things were going pretty well for us at home, with our family, our friends, and our work. But I did it because I thought that we all have an obligation to try to make a difference and that we had to change the direction of the country.

Tonight we come here to honor someone who has always fought to keep us going forward in the right direction, who has always fought for hope over fear, for reconciliation over division, to bring out the best in us instead of to bring out the worst in us. Well, when I came here I knew it wouldn't be easy, but I was determined to see that we work together to move this country forward, to address our problems, to get things done for ordinary Americans.

Well, it hasn't been easy. There have been some tough times and some really brutal fights. But you know, we've made a good start. And now, as always happens in these midterm elections, with the issue hanging fire, the American people will have to decide whether we will continue this rigorous transition into tomorrow.

Every time we reach a point in history where we're going through big changes and the future is not clear, we fight a battle within ourselves.

In that sense, our Nation is very much like a person. If you think about your own life, whenever you did anything really different and took on a new challenge, it was always with a mixture of hope and fear, when you went to school the first day or first went off to college or had your first job or first sought elective office or married or had your first child. No matter how good a thing is, if it is really big, it is also a little scary. Countries are the same way. A delicate balance always has to be maintained between hope and fear. And every day we all get up and we see things that are happening that we don't like or we're unsure what will happen to us. And it's almost as if we have a scale inside us, with blind justice holding it, and hope is on one side and fear is on the other. And each day it may take a little different balance.

The job we have between now and election day is to make sure that when people wake up on election day, they vote their hopes instead of their fears, they vote for tomorrow instead of yesterday, they vote to keep going forward, and they vote for Senator Ted Kennedy for re-election in Massachusetts.

We still have a lot to do, but we've made a good start. And we've done some very important things by putting our economic house in order, giving the American people their first serious attack on crime in a long time, and beginning to make this Government work for ordinary citizens.

If you look at the last 20 months, this Congress—I might add, without one single, solitary vote from a member of the other party—the Democrats, who were so often attacked as being for big Government and spending, voted for a budget that cut $255 billion in Federal spending, that reduced the deficit by more than any plan ever adopted in the history of the country, that gave us 3 years of deficit reduction in a row for the first time since Harry Truman was President. I might add, they did it by raising tax rates on only the top 1.2 percent of Americans, including most of you in this room tonight. And we thank you for staying with us. [*Laughter*]

This administration—and it's a great rebuke to those who think people only vote their own short-term self-interests; all of you are. And I honor you for your presence here tonight and for caring about your country and the long-term health and discipline and economic direction of what we're trying to do.

Our administration expanded trade by more than any in the comparable time period in the last 30 years. Exports are up, sales are up, and jobs are up in export-related areas. And what has all this produced: 4.3 million new jobs, 93 percent of them in the private sector, unlike the ratio in previous years when it's been mostly Government jobs created to try to help people deal with the problems of economic fallout. We've had 8 months of manufacturing job growth in a row for the first time in a decade. And just last week, at the annual vote of International Economists, for the first time in 9 years, it was the United States of America that was voted as having the most productive economy in the world. We've got a long way to go, but we've made a good beginning.

Senator Biden is here. And Senator Kennedy for years has been interested in this whole crime issue from his service on the Judiciary Committee. But Joe Biden will tell you they talked about crime around here for 6 years, but we finally passed the crime bill that is tough with punishment, tough in terms of putting 100,000 police on the street, but also smart in providing prevention and giving people a chance to turn away from lives of crime and giving our young people a chance to have something to say yes to. Also, for the first time in my memory we put together back-to-back victories with the Brady bill and the assault weapons ban, in spite of the ferocious opposition of the NRA. That's a pretty good beginning. We've got a long way to go, but it's a pretty good beginning.

If you look at what was done to make Government work for ordinary people, in the economic plan, we reformed the college loan program—the Secretary of Education is here tonight—making 20 million Americans, including over 840,000 in the State of Massachusetts, eligible for low-interest loans at longer repayment terms, a stunning benefit for middle class kids, not just poor kids, so that no one need ever walk away from the challenge of paying for a college education again—you can clap for that; Ted Kennedy was for it. [*Applause*] We have 200,000 more children in Head Start; hundreds of thousands of people in Massachusetts alone affected by the family leave law which says that if you've got a sick parent or you're about to have a child, you can take a little time off work without losing your job. We are going to have 2 million more children immunized by 1996, so that all the kids under 2 will be immunized and parents can go to work not worrying about whether their children are going to be safe from preventable childhood diseases. Fifteen million working people and their children are going to get income tax cuts because they work hard and they raise their kids but they're hovering just above the poverty line, and we do not want them to fall into the poverty line and quit working and go on welfare. This is a pro-work, pro-family administration making this Government work for ordinary citizens again. And it's a good start.

Finally, let me say to our friends in the other party, I sat out there in the heartland of America as the Governor for years and years and years, and I heard them talk about how terrible the Federal Government was and how big and bloated it was. But we, the Democrats, voted to reduce the size of the Federal Government by 272,000, to make it the smallest it's been since President Kennedy was in office. We have already done over 70,000 of those reductions. And every last red cent of reduction in the Federal Government is going to local government and to local communities to help them fight crime. That is the record of the Democrats in the last 2 years.

Now, if you compare that to what our opponents have done and what they have said, it's a pretty big difference. In the name of partisanship, they tried to stop the crime bill. They voted entirely against the economic program, a program that gave college loan breaks to millions of kids, a program that made 90 percent of the small businesses in this country eligible for tax cuts and gave tax reductions to 15 million working families. They have done everything they could to keep us from addressing the health care reform issue in a serious way. You needn't take my word for it, only listen to them: Congressman Grandy from Iowa saying that they had all been ordered not to cooperate and compromise on health care; a Republican Senator quoted in one of our big newspapers the other day saying, "We killed health care, now if we can just not get our fingerprints on it"; their political adviser, Mr. Kristol, telling them the one thing they must not do is to cooperate to bring down health care costs, make health insurance secure for those who have it, and cover those who don't because that would be a political benefit for the other party. That is their record.

Now we know what they wish to do if they get the majority. They put out their Contract With America, and you know what they did? It looks like a contract; it looks like they took out a contract against the deficit, a contract against Medicare, a contract against paying for the crime bill, a contract against all the gains we have made for ordinary Americans in the last 2 years. They want to go back to the way they did it before, explode the deficit, tell people what they want to hear, and stick it to ordinary Americans. We can do better than that. We have to go forward. We have to reelect the people and elect the people who want to keep going forward.

If you just look at the things that Senator Kennedy has been involved in just since I have been President—the Head Start program, 200,000 more children; reforming the education loans; working on changing the whole unemployment system to a reemployment system, something we haven't finished yet; the Goals 2000 bill, which for the first time in the history of America commits us as a nation to world-class standards of educational excellence and commits the Federal Government not to have a bureaucracy but to give help to local grassroots efforts at reform; the national service program, which this year has 20,000 young Americans and 2 years from now will have 100,000 young Americans earning their way to a higher education by serving their communities at the grassroots level, not in a bureaucracy but in people power that can truly change the course of our country's future—he led the way in all of those endeavors. And he deserves a lot of credit for it.

But elections are about the future. If we do a good job, it's just what we were hired to do. So why should he be reelected? Because if you ever want this country to be able to bring the deficit down without breaking the backs of our senior citizens; if you ever want to see a time when working people will be secure in their insurance, instead of the situation which exists today—this is the only advanced country in the world where working families are losing ground in insurance coverage. There are 5 million Americans in working families today who had health insurance 5 years ago who do not have it today, even though we spend 40 percent more of our income than any other country on health care. If you want to preserve the integrity of our great medical institutions of higher learning, if you want to see health insurance for all Americans and stability in our economy long-term and in our Federal budget long-term, we have got to address the health care issue.

So what if we couldn't do it in a year. Look what's happened since I've been here. It took 7 years to pass the Brady bill, 7 years to pass family leave, 7 years to pass motor voter, 6 years to pass the crime bill. I signed a banking reform bill today that they've been working on longer than anybody can remember. We can do this. We will do this. The people of Massachusetts, I don't believe, want to send a signal to Washington, DC, that they have abandoned health care. I think they want to tell us to keep at it until we get it right. And the only way to do that is to say, "Senator Kennedy, stay on the job; keep doing it until we get it right."

My friends, you will see this election everywhere in America played out. Look at Patrick Kennedy's race in Rhode Island. He's running against someone who signed the contract, a contract against health care reform, for cutting Medicare, for exploding the deficit, for putting the Federal budget in a place where they won't even be able to fund the crime bill—the same old promises, tell them what they want to hear, bad-mouth Government, bad-mouth the people who are the instruments of change, and hope you don't get caught. I think the American people are smarter than that.

You know, Ted Kennedy said tonight that he was not the youngest man in the Senate race. He was once the youngest man in the Senate for quite a long time. Well, I was once the youngest Governor in America by 9 years. Time has a way of curing those problems—[*laughter*]—and of changing your perspective. But I would like to say something about Senator Kennedy and about the United States. He's made enemies in his life because he has fought for things. But the things he has fought for are things that would help people who are very different from him. Ninety-five percent of the people that would have been given the things that he was given in life never would have spent

their life trying to get all that for everybody else in the country. Most of us, given the opportunities he had, would have enjoyed them in a very different way. They wouldn't have put themselves on the line day in and day out, year in and year out.

This country is also very old as a democracy, but it is forever young. When people say they worry about whether we've still got it as a country, I say to them: Why do you think the Israelis and the Arabs want to come here and have us work with them to end the decades of horrible fighting in the Middle East? Why do you think that after literally hundreds of years of fighting, the Catholics and the Protestants in Northern Ireland, and the British and the Irish wish the Americans to be involved in the peace process? Why did Mr. Mandela and Mr. de Klerk want the United States to spend a few million dollars of our tax money to help them develop an election that would really work? Even in the 11th hour of our crisis in Haiti a little over a week ago, when the delegation was down there meeting with the military leaders and they realized finally that we meant business, one of them said, "Well, if the President is determined to do this and the United Nations is determined to act, at least we want the United States here; we trust them, we know they can be trusted. We know what they represent." Why? Because the right things, my fellow Americans, never get old.

And I was sitting here looking at Ted Kennedy give that speech tonight, and I saw it literally moving his entire being. And I said to myself, let the people who disagree with him disagree. Let the people who say he's wrong on the issues say that. But let no one doubt that he may be the youngest person running for the Senate in any State this year, because he believes in things that are forever young.

Thank you, and God bless you all.

NOTE: The President spoke at 9:30 p.m. at the Kennedy residence. In his remarks, he referred to host Marvin Rosen and comedian Chevy Chase.

Message to the Congress on Measures To Restrict the Participation by U.S. Persons in Weapons Proliferation Activities
September 29, 1994

To the Congress of the United States:

Pursuant to section 204(b) of the International Emergency Economic Powers Act (50 U.S.C. 1703(b)) and section 301 of the National Emergencies Act (50 U.S.C. 1631), I hereby report to the Congress that I have exercised my statutory authority to declare a national emergency and to issue an Executive order, which authorizes and directs the Secretary of Commerce, in consultation with the Secretary of State, to take such actions, including the promulgation of rules, regulations, and amendments thereto, and to employ such powers granted to the President by, the International Emergency Economic Powers Act, as may be necessary to continue to regulate the activities of United States persons in order to prevent their participation in activities, which could contribute to the proliferation of nuclear, chemical, and biological weapons, and the means of their delivery.

These actions are necessary in view of the danger posed to the national security, foreign policy, and economy of the United States by the continued proliferation of nuclear, biological, and chemical weapons, and of the means of delivering such weapons, and in view of the need for more effective controls on activities sustaining such proliferation. In the absence of these actions, the participation of United States persons in activities contrary to U.S. non-proliferation objectives and policies, and which may not be adequately controlled, could take place without effective control, posing an unusual and extraordinary threat to the national security, foreign policy, and economy of the United States.

The countries and regions affected by this action would include those currently identified in Supplements to Part 778 of Title 15 of the Code of Federal Regulations, concerning nonproliferation controls, as well as such other countries as may be of concern from time to time due to their involvement in the proliferation of weapons of mass destruction, or due to the risk of their being points of diversion to proliferation activities.

It is my intention to review the appropriateness of proposing legislation to provide standing authority for these controls, and thereafter to terminate the Executive order.

WILLIAM J. CLINTON

The White House,
September 29, 1994.

NOTE: This message was released by the Office of the Press Secretary on September 30. The Executive order of September 29 is listed in Appendix D at the end of this volume.

Interview With Alan Colmes
September 30, 1994

Mr. Colmes. President Clinton, very nice to meet you. I've been an unabashed supporter of yours for a very long time, to the point where my listeners call me up and accuse me of being on your payroll. I'd like to dispel any such myth right now. [*Laughter*]

The President. You're not on the payroll, but I appreciate what you've said.

National Public Opinion

Mr. Colmes. Thomas Jefferson said of democracy that "democracy is cumbersome, slow, inefficient, but in due time, the voice of the people will be heard and their latent wisdom will prevail." How latent is that wisdom at this point in our evolution?

The President. Well, I think what's going on in our country today is that people desperately want circumstances to change for themselves in their own lives, and they see things going on around them they don't like: high rates of crime and violence and drug abuse and family breakdown, the continued economic uncertainty and insecurity, a lot of working people worried about their incomes, their ability to finance their kids' education, the stability of their health care, their retirement. And they are not sure that the Government ever works for ordinary people. And I think that that plus the atmosphere in which we operate up here, which is so contentious and so full of the conflicting messages spawned by all the interest groups, make it difficult for anybody to communicate through that. But what I have to do is to just keep working for the American people, keep fighting for change.

You know, we've made a remarkable start, I think. It's just the beginning, but we've made a good beginning in restoring the economy and fighting crime and making this Government work for ordinary people. That's what I got sent here to do, and that's what I'm trying to do.

Midterm Elections

Mr. Colmes. Midterm elections are coming up, and just the other day the Republicans had a photo-op at the Capitol and they gave a 10-point plan. I wonder if you feel the American people will buy this and change the balance of power legislatively this November?

The President. Well, the Republican contract, it's—I'm so glad they did it because they finally told the American people what I knew all along, which is what they're for. What they're for is to go back to trickle-down economics. They made over a trillion dollars worth of promises to the American people in this contract. And how they're going to pay for it is either to explode the deficit again, after we brought it down, or to cut Medicare or Social Security or never pay for the crime bill.

It's the same old thing they did in the 1980's, and it poses a stark choice for the Americans in this election: Do you want to keep going forward with an economic plan that has brought the deficit down for 3 years in a row for the first time since Truman, helped to produce over 4.3 million new jobs, has got America ranked the most productive country in the world for the first time in 9 years, that's provided college loan relief for millions of Americans and done a lot of other things that are growing this economy? Or do you want to go back to the same old trickle-down economics that exploded the debt, reduced investment in people, and nearly

wrecked this economy? I mean, that's basically what the choice is in this election.

And their contract, basically, is a contract on America, puts out a contract on the deficit, puts out a contract on Medicare, puts out a contract on the crime bill. I mean, they're going to wreck it all if they got to implement these ideas. It's just—it's unbelievable, but it's really where they are.

Mr. Colmes. How successful do you think they'll be in their attempt to take over Congress?

The President. Well, if we can get out there and tell the American people the truth about our record, the fact that we have made a good start, that we've got a long way to go and this is no time to turn back, I think we've got an excellent chance to defy the experts and the pundits.

In all but three elections in this century, the incumbent President's party has always lost seats in at least one House of Congress. And I think there's only been one election, in 1934, when the incumbent President actually picked up seats in both Houses. So this is a natural rhythm, but what's going on now is the country is going through a lot of changes. People are having a tough time. They do not know what this administration has done to make our good first start. I'm going to get that out there. And they need to know that it's just the beginning, because a lot of people haven't felt it yet.

Health Care Reform

Mr. Colmes. You've had an incredible string of accomplishments and perhaps the best first year legislatively of any President since Eisenhower. You've also cited Johnson's second year as a very successful year for him.

The President. Yes.

Mr. Colmes. But even your detractors, like Newt Gingrich, said you've had a great first year legislatively. Is it going to be more difficult in the second half of your first term, if there are more Republicans in Congress, for you to get things forth, like health care?

The President. Well, sure it is, unless they decide that they want to get something done for America instead of something done for their party.

Mr. Colmes. Is health care dead?

The President. No, not at all. Look, we didn't get it in the first year, and I think the main reason we didn't get it is that the Republicans decided they didn't want it to happen. I was willing to compromise; I reached out to them. But let me just give you the evidence.

When I introduced my plan, I said, "Look, folks, all I want to do is to help people control health care costs, protect the health insurance of people who have it so they don't lose it, and provide coverage for those who don't. Here's the best way to do it, I think. If you've got a better idea, let me know." When we started, there were 24 Republican Senators on a bill to provide health care for all Americans; they did it in a different way. When we got to the end of the legislative debate, that number 24 had dropped to zero.

Meanwhile, a Republican Congressman from Iowa said that the Republican leader in the House, Mr. Gingrich, had threatened them all that they must not cooperate. A Republican Senator was quoted in a major newspaper saying, "We killed health care; now we can't get our fingerprints on it." And the guy who gives them all their ideas, Mr. Kristol, said that the one thing you can't do is to pass health care reform while a Democrat is President; it'll ruin the party. So they put party ahead of the health care interests of the country.

But we can still get it. You know, things sometimes take longer around here. You just quoted Thomas Jefferson. I got the family leave bill on my desk to give people some time off from work without losing their job if a child is born or a parent is sick; it took 7 years for that. I had the opportunity to sign the Brady bill, which took 7 years to pass. The crime bill was around for 6 years. I signed a banking reform bill yesterday that's going to cut a billion dollars a year in regulatory costs, and it was around for 10 years. So sometimes these bills take longer. I think we can get health care reform, but the Republicans are going to have to be willing to cooperate and put their country ahead of politics.

President's Approval Rating

Mr. Colmes. Given these lists of accomplishments, is it incredibly frustrating for you when you see approval ratings not being where you feel they should be?

The President. Well, I think—no, I think it's absolutely understandable, because people can only vote on what they know and what they feel. And you know, this country—I'll say again, these social problems that we have in our country, the crime, the family breakdown, the violence, the drugs, they've been developing over 30 years. The economic problems have been developing over 20 years. And the other party was in power for 12 years. I've been here 20 months. So, we've made a good step, but a lot of people haven't felt it.

And because I have tried to change so much so fast, all the news the American people get is dominated by the conflicts, the process, the interest groups and all that kind of stuff, and the intense partisanship of the opposition. This election gives us an opportunity, gives me an opportunity to go out there and say, "Hey, here's our record; here's what we've done; here's a good first start. They want to go back to trickle-down economics. You decide." Then the American people are the boss; let them decide.

Republican Opposition

Mr. Colmes. Do you feel the intense opposition you talk about is stricter or more strident against you than it's been against other Presidents, and why?

The President. Well, I don't know the—a lot of the studies have said that this is the most highly partisan opposition that's ever been recorded. All I can tell you is what they've done. The Republican Senators voted 42 to 2 for the crime bill last year, when it wasn't an election year. And it came back this year, and they said all these prevention programs were pork. Well, they all voted for them last year, and they went from 42 to 2 for it, to 38 to 6 against it.

We've got an important piece of environmental legislation right now pending in the Senate—it's passed the House of Representatives—the Superfund bill for cleanup of toxic dumps. Everybody in America, believe it or not, from the Sierra Club to the chemical companies, is for this bill, from the most extreme environmental groups to the industry groups. The only people who are against it are the Republican Senators who don't want us to have one more legislative accomplishment before the election. That is the fact.

What I've got to do is just keep fighting for change, keep going forward. The American people are going to have to decide whether they want to keep going on a path that is bringing the deficit down and the economy up, that's addressing crime, that has—unlike the Republicans who talked about this, we've actually reduced the size of the Federal Government, the

Government's already 70,000 smaller than when I got here, and the law requires us now to take it down 270,000—or whether they're going to just go for that same old rhetoric where you promise everybody the Moon and explode the deficit and run the economy into the ditch. Now that's the clear choice in this election, and it's the—I think the American people, once they have a chance to think about it, will have a different view.

Haiti

Mr. Colmes. I would guess the most difficult decision a President would ever have to make would be whether or not to send young people in this country into war. As you've struggled over this, vis-a-vis the Haiti situation, what kind of internal conflict have you gone through?

The President. Well, I think first of all, the President's first responsibility is to the security and safety of the American people. At the end of the cold war when our interests, our—excuse me, our security doesn't seem so imminently threatened by nuclear weapons, I still have to work hard on that. That's what I worked hard with President Yeltsin on; that's why we're so engaged in these very tough negotiations with the North Koreans.

But there are other things that affect our interests as well as our values. And one of the things that makes us secure today is that nearly everybody in our neighborhood, that is, in the Caribbean and Latin America, are democracies, and they're trading with us and working with us, and they're going to help us move into the next century. There are only two exceptions, and Haiti is the only country where a democratically elected President was overthrown by military dictators who proceeded to launch a reign of terror.

So, I'd thought about it for a long time, and I worked for over a year and a half to give those people every single solitary opportunity to leave power peacefully, to restore democracy, to stop a flood of refugees coming for this country, and to give that country a chance. Meanwhile, we fed a million Haitians every day, we sent medicine down there, and we exhausted all diplomatic alternatives. So that's—when I decided to use military force there, it was because I thought there was no other alternative. Having made the decision, I decided that I would give the peace mission a chance to go down there and tell them, "The President has made this

decision. Now you have a decision about which way you are going to leave and under what circumstances and whether you are going to try and keep the country peaceful and whole."

I'm glad that the peace mission worked out, although, as you know, we already had over 60 planes in the air at the time that they finally agreed to leave. It was a difficult decision, but I thought in light of the human rights violations and the interest that we have in protecting our own borders and the interest we have in stability and democracy and growth in our area, it was the right one. And I might say, I'm very, very proud of what our soldiers have done there. If you look, just this week, we've got the Parliament meeting, the mayor has returned from hiding, electricity has been doubled, we've got refugees going back from Guantanamo to Haiti, and we started the gun buy-back program. So I feel good about what they're doing. You ought to be proud of them.

Mr. Colmes. What will happen if Cédras refuses to relinquish power, or if the Parliament doesn't vote the amnesty which is part of the pact that was made? What happens then?

The President. Well, the pact said that we would do our best to reconstitute the Parliament and encourage them to vote an amnesty bill but that, in any case, they would have to leave on October 15th, they would have to give up power, whether or not they got the amnesty bill in fact passed.

We committed to support the amnesty bill last year when Mr. Cédras came here and made his agreement with the United States and with Haiti and with the United Nations. And when the time came—and President Aristide put out the amnesty proclamation and told the Parliament he expected them to vote for it, and he would sign it. And when the time came, he wouldn't leave. So a lot has happened between now and then, and they've got to work through this.

But I think the Parliament will do the right thing. I think that they will work through—they're debating not only whether to give it but what the terms of it ought to be, what the reach of it is. All these things are for the Haitians to resolve. But regardless, they are going to have to leave power.

Mr. Colmes. Is there a contingency plan in case Cédras doesn't leave, once again?

The President. Well, the contingency plan is that they will leave power on the 15th, regardless. That's what the United States is doing there.

Mr. Colmes. But there's no chance that Cédras will refuse to leave power?

The President. Well, I believe he will honor his agreement, but if he doesn't, he'll have to leave anyway.

Mr. Colmes. A lot of people who otherwise are supportive of taking democracy and helping to install it in a place like Haiti have problems with the fact that the spearhead at the top of this is Aristide and that he does not represent the best hope for democracy—he's been called a Marxist, he's been accused of necklacing—and that even those who might support such a policy toward Haiti have a more difficult time because of who the person is who's President of Haiti.

The President. I think he would say that given the long history of violence and bloodshed and all the animosity that existed in Haiti at the time he became President, he may have said some things, or his supporters may have said some things that they would just as soon not have said. But the international human rights monitors who have been in Haiti say that during the months when he was President, the human rights record in Haiti was better than it was before he became President and much better than it's been since he left office.

Moreover, in the years he's been out of Haiti, he has made repeated, consistent commitments to avoid violence, avoid retribution, avoid human rights violations. Furthermore, keep in mind, this time when he goes back into power, he will have forces from 29 or 30 countries there monitoring the situation, preventing human rights violations. And if he wants to succeed as President, which I believe he does, he needs the international aid package and the help in conducting parliamentary elections, all of which require an observance of human rights and not abusing the rights and interests and the lives of the minority.

So I think the American people and the people of the world can have a pretty high level of confidence that President Aristide will do what he says. So far, in all my dealings with him, he has kept every commitment he has made. And that's all you can ask of anybody. And he's made an ironclad commitment that he will not support violence.

The Presidency

Mr. Colmes. Mr. President, I know your time is limited, and I thank you very much for spending some time with us, but you know, I do have to in conclusion ask a really tough question. Is being President fun? Are you having a good time doing this?

The President. Yes, I am. Believe it or not, it's not all—when people's lives are at stake, it's not always fun. When you're fighting a tough battle where you think you're fighting for something good and you're willing to compromise with the other side and they're playing politics, that's not always fun.

But it is a real joy and a profound honor to just have the opportunity to come into this office every day and try to stick up for ordinary Americans and fight their fight and make their lives a little better. And whether they know it or not is not so important; it's not so important what they think of me on a daily basis. What is important is that I think of them on a daily basis, that I keep fighting for them. And I think the end will bring us out all right.

Mr. Colmes. How do you get them to know that, though, so they appreciate what they may not know about your day-to-day machinations?

The President. In part, that's what the elections are all about. That's what interviews like this are all about. I have to—I may have worked too hard on too many things for the last 2 years and spent too little time trying to directly communicate. I've worked hard at it, but I'm going to work even harder.

But the main thing is that I show up for work every day and fight other people's fights. And then when elections come, I go out and make a report to the people; they make their own judgment.

Mr. Colmes. Thank you very much, sir, for communicating here with us and our audience.

The President. Thank you.

NOTE: The interview began at 2:40 p.m. in the Cabinet Room at the White House.

Message to the Congress on Continuation of the National Emergency With Respect to Haiti
September 30, 1994

To the Congress of the United States:

Section 202(d) of the National Emergencies Act (50 U.S.C. 1622(d)) provides for the automatic termination of a national emergency unless, prior to the anniversary date of its declaration, the President publishes in the *Federal Register* and transmits to the Congress a notice stating that the emergency is to continue in effect beyond the anniversary date. In accordance with this provision, I have sent the enclosed notice, stating that the Haitian emergency is to continue in effect beyond October 4, 1994, to the *Federal Register* for publication.

Resolution of the crisis between the United States and Haiti is in sight as a result of the September 18 agreement reached in Port-au-Prince by the delegation led by former President Carter. Pursuant to that agreement I have announced that all unilateral United States sanctions against Haiti will be suspended with the exception of the blocking of the assets of any persons subject to the blocking provisions of Executive Orders Nos. 12775, 12779, 12853, 12872, or 12914 and Haitian citizens who are members of the immediate family of any such person as identified by the Secretary of the Treasury.

At the same time, the United Nations Security Council, with our support, has decided that the sanctions established in Resolutions 841 and 917 should remain in force, consistent with the provisions of Resolutions 917 and 940, until the military leaders in Haiti relinquish power and President Aristide returns to Haiti. That may well not occur before October 4, 1994. Therefore, I have determined that it is necessary to retain the authority to apply economic sanctions to ensure the restoration and security of the democratically elected Government of Haiti.

While the UN Security Council sanctions remain in force and in order to enable the multinational forces to carry out their mission and to promote the betterment of the Haitian people in the interval until President Aristide's return, I have directed that steps be taken in accordance with Resolutions 917 and 940 to permit supplies and services to flow to Haiti to restore health care, water and electrical services, to provide construction materials for humanitarian programs, and to allow the shipment of communications, agricultural, and educational materials. This will allow the Haitian people to begin the process of reconciliation and rebuilding without delay.

WILLIAM J. CLINTON

The White House,
September 30, 1994.

NOTE: The notice and related memorandum on the Economic Support Fund for Haiti are listed in Appendix D at the end of this volume.

Statement on Congressional Completion of Appropriations Legislation
September 30, 1994

I want to thank the House and Senate leadership, Senator Byrd and Congressman Obey, the chairmen of the Appropriations Committees, and their colleagues for their leadership and assistance. And I would be remiss if I didn't say how sorry I am that Congressman Natcher could not be with us to enjoy this achievement.

We are making a start at putting our country's fiscal house in order. After years of partisan bickering, after years of rising deficits, it was time for Washington to get Federal spending under control. Our economic plan adopted by Congress last year gave us this start.

Our 5 year deficit reduction plan put into place rigid controls on Government spending. It has produced 2 years of declining deficit for the first time in 20 years. We are reducing Federal employment by 272,000 positions, placing us on a path to the smallest Federal Government since John Kennedy was President. We are making a start on running Washington the way Americans run their households at home, within budget limits, paying the bills on time.

For the first time since 1948, the Congress has adopted all 13 Appropriations for signing by the President before the end of the fiscal year, all 13 bills, on time, within the rigid spending restraints required by our economic plan.

The economic recovery gathering strength across our country is being built on this kind of progress. We have embarked on a journey to rebuild and renew the American economy. We haven't finished the job, but we are going to keep moving forward, keep cutting spending, and we're not going back.

Appointment for the National Cancer Advisory Board
September 30, 1994

The President today announced his intention to appoint three new members to the National Cancer Advisory Board (NCAB).

"We welcome the new NCAB members and appreciate their willingness to serve as advisers for the National Cancer Institute and the National Cancer Program," the President said. "I look forward to continuing reports of progress

against these diseases, which affect the health of so many people in our country."

The following new Presidential appointees will serve 6-year terms on the NCAB: J. Michael Bishop, Philip S. Schein, and Vainutis K. Vaitkevicius.

NOTE: Biographies of the appointees were made available by the Office of the Press Secretary.

Statement on Signing the Treasury, Postal Service and General Government Appropriations Act, 1995
September 30, 1994

Today I have signed into law H.R. 4539, the "Treasury, Postal Service, and General Government Appropriations Act, 1995."

The Act provides a total of $11.6 billion in discretionary budget authority for various programs in the Department of the Treasury, the U.S. Postal Service, the General Services Administration, the Office of Personnel Management, the Executive Office of the President, and several smaller agencies.

I am pleased that the Act appropriates $39 million from the Violent Crime Reduction Trust Fund to several Treasury agencies to fight crime and promote gang resistance programs.

The Act also provides important funding for the United States Customs Service to support the commitments made to enhance the enforcement of trade laws and regulations related to NAFTA. This initiative remains an Administration priority.

This Act funds the IRS tax compliance initiative, which is essential in ensuring that everyone pays his or her fair share of their Federal taxes. This initiative is expected to have deficit-reducing potential by strengthening audit and debt collection activities, thereby generating additional revenue without raising taxes.

Several other provisions in H.R. 4539 condition the President's authority—and the authority of certain agency officials—to use funds appropriated by this Act on the approval of congressional committees. The Administration will interpret such provisions to require notification only, since any other interpretation of such provisos would contradict the Supreme Court ruling in *INS* vs. *Chadha*.

Regrettably, the Congress has continued its past practice of including personnel floors and other restrictions in several of the Treasury agencies funded by the enrolled bill. Such measures run counter to our efforts to reduce the number of Federal employees, as recommended by the National Performance Review and mandated in the Federal Workforce Restructuring Act of 1994. These restrictions would exclude over 20,000 Treasury employees from reduction, thereby imposing a greater burden on other agencies. While we have made a start on deficit reduction, we cannot fully achieve our goals without making reductions in the Federal workforce, fairly apportioned among *all* departments and agencies.

WILLIAM J. CLINTON

The White House,
September 30, 1994.

NOTE: H.R. 4539, approved September 30, was assigned Public Law No. 103–329. This statement was released by the Office of the Press Secretary on October 1.

Statement on Signing the Agricultural, Rural Development, Food and Drug Administration, and Related Agencies Appropriations Act, 1995
September 30, 1994

Today I have signed into law H.R. 4554, the "Agriculture, Rural Development, Food and Drug Administration, and Related Agencies Appropriations Act, 1995."

The Act provides $13.4 billion in discretionary budget authority for programs of the Department of Agriculture, including the special supplemental feeding program for women, infants, and children (WIC); food safety programs; and various programs to protect and support rural communities.

The Act also provides a total of $39.2 billion for the Food Stamp program, the Commodity Credit Corporation, and other mandatory programs.

The Act includes authority for providing disaster assistance for losses to 1994 crops due to natural disasters. The Administration is currently reviewing estimates of the need for this assistance. I will be transmitting to the Congress requests for the release of these emergency funds in the near future.

The Act also includes the following appropriations that I hereby designate as emergency requirements pursuant to section 251(b)(2)(D)(i)

of the Balanced Budget and Emergency Deficit Control Act of 1985, as amended:

Emergency community water assistance grants, $10,000,000;

Very low-income housing repair grants, $15,000,000;

Agricultural credit insurance fund program account: For the cost of emergency loans, $7,670,000; and

Emergency conservation program: Transfer from Watershed and flood prevention operations, $23,000,000

These funds will be used to provide needed assistance to victims of natural disasters, including flooding victims of Tropical Storm Alberto in south Alabama, south Georgia, and north Florida.

WILLIAM J. CLINTON

The White House,
September 30, 1994.

NOTE: H.R. 4554, approved September 30, was assigned Public Law No. 103–330. This statement was released by the Office of the Press Secretary on October 1.

Statement on Signing the Department of Transportation and Related Agencies Appropriations Act, 1995
September 30, 1994

Today I have signed into law H.R. 4556, the "Department of Transportation and Related Agencies Appropriations Act, 1995."

The Act provides funding for the Department of Transportation and several smaller agencies, including the Interstate Commerce Commission and the National Transportation Safety Board.

This Act provides funding for a number of my high-priority investment proposals within the Department of Transportation. These include the core highway programs of the Intermodal Surface Transportation Efficiency Act, the Intelligent Vehicle Highway System research pro-gram, Mass Transit Formula Capital Grants, Next Generation High-Speed Rail, and the Penn Station Redevelopment Project.

WILLIAM J. CLINTON

The White House,
September 30, 1994.

NOTE: H.R. 4556, approved September 30, was assigned Public Law No. 103–331. This statement was released by the Office of the Press Secretary on October 1.

Statement on Signing the Department of the Interior and Related Agencies Appropriations Act, 1995
September 30, 1994

Today I have signed into law H.R. 4602, the "Department of the Interior and Related Agencies Appropriations Act, 1995."

H.R. 4602 provides funds for various programs of the Departments of the Interior and Energy, the Forest Service (Department of Agriculture), and the Indian Health Service (Department of Health and Human Services). Funding for various independent agencies such as the Smithsonian Institution and the National Foundation on the Arts and the Humanities is also included.

The Act provides important funding to further the protection and rehabilitation of America's inventory of natural and cultural assets, including our national parks and forests.

I am pleased that the Act includes funding to support a number of my energy conservation initiatives. These investments are important for our Nation's energy and environmental future.

The Act also provides $200 million in additional emergency funding for Forest Service fire-fighting activities and $250 million in additional contingent emergency firefighting funds, reflecting the severe 1994 fire season affecting national forests in many western States.

There are several provisions in the Act that purport to require congressional approval before executive branch execution of aspects of the bill. The Administration will interpret such provisos to require notification only, since any other interpretation would contradict the Supreme Court ruling in *INS* vs. *Chadha.*

WILLIAM J. CLINTON

The White House,
September 30, 1994.

NOTE: H.R. 4602, approved September 30, was assigned Public Law No. 103–332. This statement was released by the Office of the Press Secretary on October 1.

Statement on Signing the Departments of Labor, Health and Human Services, and Education, and Related Agencies Appropriations Act, 1995
September 30, 1994

Today I have signed into law H.R. 4606, the "Department of Labor, Health and Human Services, and Education, and Related Agencies Appropriations Act, 1995."

This Act provides funding for the Departments of Labor, Health and Human Services, and Education; the Corporation for National and Community Service; the Corporation for Public Broadcasting; and several smaller agencies. Programs within these agencies address the training and employment needs of our Nation's work force, the Federal role in our education system, and fundamental elements of our health care network.

This Act provides funding for a number of my high-priority investment proposals within the Departments of Labor, Health and Human Services, and Education, and the Corporation for National and Community Service. These include the Head Start program, Goals 2000 program, School-to-Work Opportunities program, dislocated workers assistance, education for the disadvantaged, AIDS treatment programs authorized under the Ryan White CARE Act, and the National Institutes of Health.

I am pleased that the Act provides my full request for childhood immunizations. This program will ensure that all children who do not have health insurance coverage for immunizations have access to immunizations at the appropriate age.

The Act provides funding for investment initiatives for automation and disability processing within the Social Security Administration (SSA). This will help SSA improve the quality of service to millions of Americans.

WILLIAM J. CLINTON

The White House,
September 30, 1994.

NOTE: H.R. 4606, approved September 30, was assigned Public Law No. 103–333. This statement was released by the Office of the Press Secretary on October 1.

Statement on Signing the District of Columbia Appropriations Act, 1995
September 30, 1994

Today I have signed into law H.R. 4649, the "District of Columbia Appropriations Act, 1995." This Act provides $712 million in Federal appropriations for the District of Columbia.

The Act requires the District of Columbia to reduce total FY 1995 spending from District funds by $140 million. The Act includes enforcement mechanisms that require a reduction in the FY 1996 Federal payment if the District fails to balance its FY 1995 budget. The Act also includes a provision that requires the District to reduce its total employment level by 2,000 full-time equivalent positions in FY 1995.

Consistent with the Administration's request, the Act directs the Army Corps of Engineers to conduct a study that addresses the longer-term capital improvements and operation and maintenance requirements of the Washington Aqueduct facility. The study will consider alternative methods of financing such operation and maintenance and capital improvements, as well as alternative arrangements for ownership of the Washington Aqueduct facility. The study will be conducted in consultation with the Environmental Protection Agency, the Office of Management and Budget, and the nonfederal public water customers of the Washington Aqueduct.

WILLIAM J. CLINTON

The White House,
September 30, 1994.

NOTE: H.R. 4649, approved September 30, was assigned Public Law No. 103–334. This statement was released by the Office of the Press Secretary on October 1.

Statement on Signing the Department of Defense Appropriations Act, 1995
September 30, 1994

Today I have signed into law H.R. 4650, the "Department of Defense Appropriations Act, 1995." H.R. 4650 supports the Administration's major defense priorities and reflects a spirit of cooperation between the Administration and the Congress to provide for a strong national defense. My number one defense priority remains the training and readiness of our military forces. I am very pleased that the Congress has resolved difficult budget issues in such a manner that supports this priority. I also appreciate the support the Congress has given to key defense investment and modernization proposals.

The Act provides $299 million in urgently needed supplemental FY 1994 funding for emergency relief for Rwanda and for emergency migrant processing and safe haven costs in and around Cuba. I designate the $299 million provided as an emergency requirement pursuant to section 251(b)(2)(D)(i) of the Balanced Budget and Emergency Deficit Control Act of 1995, as amended. I am concerned, however, with the inflexibility of the provisions concerning the U.S. mission and military participation in Rwanda. I will interpret this legislation consistent with my constitutional authority to conduct the foreign relations of the United States and my re-sponsibility as Commander in Chief and as Chief Executive.

I am also concerned about section 8118 of this Act, which limits the Administration's flexibility to make reductions in certain personnel categories. This provision runs counter to the recommendations of the National Performance Review and this Administration's efforts to streamline Federal activities. It will hamper DOD's ability to manage its civilian personnel efforts efficiently.

I would point out that section 8136, which relates to changes in obligations under the Treaty on Conventional Forces in Europe (CFE Treaty), cannot restrict the constitutional options for congressional approval of substantive modifications of treaties, and I sign this bill with that understanding.

WILLIAM J. CLINTON

The White House,
September 30, 1994.

NOTE: H.R. 4650, approved September 30, was assigned Public Law No. 103–335. This statement was released by the Office of the Press Secretary on October 1.

The President's Radio Address
October 1, 1994

Good morning. As we come to the end of this congressional session in 1994, it's clearer than ever that Americans still want to change the way Washington works, and they should.

We've worked hard here for 20 months to make sure Government responds to ordinary citizens, not to organized pressure groups; responds to the national interests, not narrow interests. And we've made some good progress, but there's still a lot more work to do.

Since I became President, we fought to change the culture of our Capital City. We first imposed the toughest ethics rules ever on our own officials. Then we moved to close the tax loopholes that lets lobbyists deduct the costs of their activities. And then our initiative to reinvent Government, led by the Vice President, is already making progress in making Government work better and cost less. We're cutting the size of the Federal Government by 270,000, to its lowest level since John Kennedy was President. Already in our 20 months, there are 70,000 fewer people on the Federal payroll. And we're giving every dime of the money we save in reducing the Federal payroll back to local communities to fight crime. We've also slashed regulations and bureaucracy, speeded up the time Small Business Administration loans get answered. We've changed the way Government buys products to make it cheaper and more efficient. We've given 17 States permission to change the rules so they can move more folks from welfare to work.

Despite all these steps forward, our political system is still too often an obstacle to change, not an instrument of progress. One big reason is that here in Washington there are some 80,000 paid lobbyists who work to influence the Government. In the last year, we've certainly seen how well-organized, lavishly funded campaigns by people protecting their narrow interests work.

The gun lobby nearly derailed the crime bill strongly supported by police and prosecutors, just because it banned 19 assault weapons from our streets, weapons designed only to kill people, and in spite of the fact that the crime bill protected 650 hunting and sporting weapons from any Federal restrictions.

The foes of health care reform have spent $300 million, by most estimates, to oppose change. By all accounts, this was the most intense lobbying campaign in history. But rest assured, we're not giving up on our fight for health care reform, for universal coverage, cost controls, and protecting small businesses and the people who have health insurance now from losing it.

This week we're working to pass a major reform bill that Congress still has time to act on, a bill that will go a long way toward taking Government out of the hands of the influence industry. The legislation, for the first time ever, would require lobbyists to fully disclose who they work for, how much they're paid, and what they're seeking to get out of Government. That's not all it does. It also prevents lobbyists from buying Members of Congress meals, gifts, or vacations. All in all, it's very tough, and it will change the way Washington does business.

Not surprisingly, a lot of Washington's lobbyists don't like this bill very much. It takes away their special access and puts ordinary people on a more equal footing. And now at the last minute, some are trying to defeat lobby reform with bogus arguments.

Last Thursday, the House of Representatives stood up to intense pressure and passed lobby reform by a large margin. This week, it's the Senate's turn. The lobbyists and their allies will throw up a lot of rhetoric about how this bill hurts ordinary people. Don't you believe it. It's bad news for people who use paid professional lobbyists to influence legislation and don't want

you to know what they're doing. That's all it does, and that's why the Senate should pass it immediately.

I've fought for reforms like this my entire public career. When I was Governor of Arkansas, after years of trying to pass lobby reform through the legislature, I went to the people of my State, and we passed a tough bill by a popular vote. I advocated this measure when I ran for President, and I've worked for it ever since. I am confident it will become law.

There's another bill Congress should pass before it goes home. This would apply the laws Congress passes to govern the rest of America to Congress itself. That's just common sense, and it's only fair. But believe it or not, it doesn't always hold up today. The people who make laws for the private sector should be willing to live under the laws they make. That's what this law would require.

Even these important changes, however, won't complete the task of political reform. The way we fund campaigns gives too much power to special interests and too often drowns out the voice of the people. We had a good chance to change that. But yesterday, once more, a Senate filibuster defeated campaign finance reform. I was very disappointed by this result. The campaign finance reform bill was a strong bill. It gave real reform. It would have limited spending in congressional races, curbed the political action committees, opened the airwaves to honest debate, and closed the so-called soft money loophole in our Presidential election system.

The fight for campaign reform isn't over, either. We'll return to it next year with redoubled determination to get this job done. The American people demand it.

Since I became President, we've made real progress in turning our country around, in getting our economic house in order, fighting crime, making Government work for ordinary people. Our comprehensive economic strategy cut our deficit drastically and for 3 years in a row for the first time since Mr. Truman was President. We've expanded trade with Mexico, negotiated a worldwide trade agreement, improved the education and training of our work force. We've got 4.3 million new jobs in just 20 months, and our country's rated the most productive in the world for the first time in 9 years. We've also enacted a tough crime bill. And we've begun with reinventing Government, the effort to make Government work for ordinary people.

But to finish this work, we need to keep changing the way Government does the people's business. Let's keep forward in the fight for political reform. We need your help on that.

Thanks very much.

NOTE: The address was recorded at 3:36 p.m. on September 30 in the Roosevelt Room at the White House for broadcast at 10:06 a.m. on October 1.

Radio Address to American Troops in Haiti
October 1, 1994

I wanted to take this opportunity to say a few words to those of you who are part of Operation Uphold Democracy. For the last 2 weeks, your efforts to bring peace and stability to Haiti have moved all of us here at home. I want you to know just how proud and grateful I and all other Americans are for what you're doing.

Your Nation has asked you to take responsibility for a difficult but important mission. The work you're doing is helping the Haitian people win their fight for freedom and democracy. It's making possible the return of an honestly elected government. It's proving to the world that the United States will stand up for democracy in our hemisphere, will honor its own commitments, and expects those who make commitments to us to honor them.

You have responded brilliantly to the call of duty. In less than 2 weeks, your presence and your professionalism have helped curb the violence in Haiti, given hundreds of refugees the confidence to return home, permitted the Haitian Parliament to resume its work, and restored the mayor of Port-au-Prince to his office. These are the kinds of steps that will help the multi-

national force you are leading do its job and do it right.

As you carry out your demanding mission, you should know that your safety remains our number one concern. General Shalikashvili, Lieutenant General Shelton, and your other commanders have assured me that they are taking every possible precaution to ensure your welfare as you carry out your mission.

You're the finest fighting force in the world, the best trained, the best equipped, the best prepared. I share the pride of every American in your efforts on behalf of peace and democracy. You're performing a difficult mission with extraordinary skill. You have our thanks, our praise, our admiration, and our prayers.

On behalf of the American people, I wish each and every one of you Godspeed in the service of our Nation.

NOTE: The address was recorded at 3:43 p.m. in the Roosevelt Room at the White House on September 30 for broadcast on October 1. In his remarks, the President referred to Lt. Gen. Henry H. Shelton, USA, commander of U.S. forces in Haiti.

Remarks Welcoming Crown Prince Hassan of Jordan and Foreign Minister Shimon Peres of Israel
October 3, 1994

Good morning. I'm happy to welcome back to the White House both Crown Prince Hassan and Foreign Minister Peres. We've had a productive session today. Jordan and Israel have taken further and very specific steps on the road

to building a warm peace between their two nations.

Almost exactly a year ago, Crown Prince Hassan and Foreign Minister Peres and I met to launch this trilateral process. What a difference a year makes. Since then, intensive bilateral and trilateral negotiations culminated just 2 months ago in the historic meeting I hosted here between King Hussein and Prime Minister Rabin when they signed the Washington Declaration and put an end to war between their two nations.

Since then, peace treaty negotiations have made considerable progress, and steps to implement the warm peace all three of our nations want have already been taken. Jordan and Israel have already opened a border crossing for citizens of other nations at Aqaba and Eilat. And trilateral discussions on tourism, communications, and economic development are proceeding.

These discussions take place at a time when the economic and trade barriers of the past are dissolving before our eyes. It's heartening that the Gulf Cooperation Council states, led by Saudi Arabia, have now declared that they will no longer enforce the secondary and tertiary aspects of the economic boycott and will support a move in the Arab League to end the primary boycott of Israel. Promoting trade, development, and cooperation, rather than restraining and hindering normal economic relations, should be the hallmark of the new Middle East, and Jordan and Israel are leading the way.

Today the Crown Prince and the Foreign Minister have reached agreement on a variety of issues that will help develop the Jordan Rift Valley, increase tourism, and assure future economic and social progress in the region. They have agreed to adopt basic principles to guide the future development of the Jordan Rift Valley, including projects dealing with the environment, water, energy, and tourism; to open a new northern border crossing for third-country nationals by October 15th; to establish a Red Sea marine peace park with assistance from the United States Government; to convene a conference on exploring constructing a canal between the Red Sea and the Dead Sea; to explore

the establishment of a free trade zone in the Aqaba-Eilat area with a view to making it an economic hub for the northern peninsula of the Red Sea; to conduct, together with the United States, feasibility studies to expand the availability of water and to undertake joint financings of dams on the Yarmuk and Jordan Rivers to alleviate water shortages.

That's quite a lot of work for them in this session. They are solid evidence that Jordan and Israel have not only ended their state of war but are following through on their commitment to cooperate with each other and negotiate as rapidly as possible a final peace treaty. Our goal remains a comprehensive peace between Israel and all its Arab neighbors. We're hopeful that a breakthrough can be achieved in the negotiations underway between Israel and Syria and Israel and Lebanon.

In their ongoing talks, Israel and Jordan have looked to the trilateral discussions to help establish a comprehensive, lasting, and warm peace. The steps we announce today are the building blocks of a modern peace between these ancient lands. The United States is proud to be a partner and facilitator in this extraordinary endeavor.

Crown Prince Hassan and Foreign Minister Peres, on behalf of the American people and personally, let me say that I salute your vision, your courage, and your persistence. This has been a relationship that has meant a great deal not only to me but to all of us in this country because of the incredible openness that you have displayed and the creativity you have brought to these negotiations. I am grateful that the United States has been able to play a role in this process, grateful for the opportunity that we have had to try to facilitate an extraordinary coming together between two extraordinary nations and very extraordinary leaders.

NOTE: The President spoke at 10:52 a.m. in the West Lobby at the White House.

Remarks to Business Leaders on the General Agreement on Tariffs and Trade
October 3, 1994

Thank you very much. Senator Mitchell, I was thinking even before you spoke how much

I would miss you. Now, after that introduction, I feel it even more keenly. Ambassador Hills, thank you for your steadfast support and your leadership on GATT. Ambassador Kantor, thank you for what you have done on this, and congratulations on the agreement with Japan, too, by the way. You did a fine job, and we're proud of you. To all the distinguished Members of Congress who are here and those who would like to be here who cannot be, and all the members of the business community and others supporting the GATT today, I thank you for coming here. To the distinguished leaders of previous administrations who are here, including Larry Eagleburger, Brent Scowcroft, Herb Stein, and others, I thank you for being here.

Much that needs to be said about the GATT has already been said. Mickey Kantor reminded me this morning of something I confess I had not thought of on this day. It was 3 years ago today that I announced my candidacy for this job. And he did it because there is a line here on the first page of the talk which said, "I refuse to be part of a generation that fails to compete in the global economy and so condemns hard-working Americans to a life of struggle without reward or security."

The great challenge of our age economically is to figure out how we can create jobs and increase incomes for people who work hard, without having too much inflation. It is obvious to me that in order to do that we have to do three things: We have to bring the deficit down; at the same time, increase investment in education, training, and technology; and expand trade and investment. If we can do those things and if our neighbors do those things— in short, if we do them together, then we will be able to create more jobs and find productive lives for our people without unacceptable inflation. We will also be able to end what is now nearly two decades of people working harder and longer without ever getting much of a pay raise.

I'm encouraged that in just this year we see incomes rising at about 6 percent in the United States with nowhere near that sort of inflation. Why? Because of productivity, investment, and trade. That is what we have to do. In the end, that needs to be our bipartisan commitment to our children and to our grandchildren and to our future. Our commitment to make America great in the 21st century involves a commitment to make America a good leader but a good partner as well.

We have cut the deficit with $255 billion in spending cuts and revenue increases, and 3 years now in a row the deficit will go down for the first time since Mr. Truman was here.

We have shrunk the Federal bureaucracy. It's already more than 70,000 people smaller than it was when I came. But the Congress has adopted a bill to reduce it by 270,000 over 6 years. That will make the Federal Government the smallest it was since President Kennedy served here.

We have increased our investment in education and training, and we are opening the doors of trade, removing barriers to the sales of $35 billion in high-tech export items and of course working hard with trade initiatives like NAFTA and GATT.

Carla already alluded to this, but I think it's worth pointing out to those who said that NAFTA would be a disaster that our trade with Mexico is growing at 3 times the rate of our overall trade in the world, that exports of automobiles and trucks to Mexico have increased by 600 percent. At a lot of those auto factories, people are working overtime for the first time in a very long while.

So I feel very good about the direction in which we are going. In the last year and a half, 93 percent of all the new jobs in this country have come in the private sector. That means that the strategy will work, but we have to keep it going.

A lot of tribute has been paid to the people in the three previous administrations who have worked hard on this. I just want to add my words to those who have spoken before and to say a special word of thanks not only to Ambassador Kantor but to all those in the administration who worked so closely with him, to Secretary Espy, who is here and whose agriculture reform bill just passed the Congress, to Secretary Bentsen, to Secretary Brown, and to Laura Tyson, the Chair of our Council of Economic Advisers, and others.

We know, we know this is in our national interest. You might wonder, since we all know it, what are we doing here today? We all know this. I'll tell you what we're doing here today. We're trying to do this with the least possible delay. We're trying to do this in the shortest possible time.

We know that when the GATT is finally implemented, it will add $1 billion to $2 billion to our economy every year. We know the GATT plays to our strengths for the reasons Ambassador Hills has already mentioned. We know that our pharmaceutical and computer software firms can harness America's brainpower and now put it to work all over the world. We know our tractors can plow the soil of every nation. We know that from cars to computers, from furniture to frozen foods, we can still make the things the world wants to buy, and when GATT is fully implemented, we'll be selling those things everywhere in the world.

The GATT passed the House Ways and Means Committee by 35 to 3, the Senate Finance Committee by 19 to 0; has a phenomenal amount of support from business, consumer, labor groups, over 400 economists. But the point I want to make is, we need to do it now. Secretary Bentsen has estimated that even a 6-month delay will cost our economy up to $70 billion in extra economic growth over the decade, a 6-month delay.

So we are here today to say: The work has been done. The path to the future is clear. Our obligations are plain. We thank all of you for your support, and let's do it now and do it this year.

Thank you very much.

NOTE: The President spoke at 12:14 p.m. at the West Wing Portico of the White House.

Statement on the Resignation of Mike Espy as Secretary of Agriculture
October 3, 1994

I have accepted with regret Secretary Mike Espy's offer to resign effective December 31, 1994. This decision will permit me to name a successor efficiently. It will facilitate the work of the Department, and it will enable Secretary Espy to leave his post with an outstanding record of accomplishment that will outlast the uncertainty that exists today.

Secretary Espy has been a relentless champion for American farmers and consumers. Because of his leadership, legislation enabling USDA to reinvent its management and modernize the services it provides farmers and farm communities is nearing completion in Congress. When lives and livelihoods were threatened by natural disasters in rural communities, Mike Espy was our steward for relief efforts. As Agriculture Secretary, he was an advocate for ensuring that people who were hungry in an abundant America were fed by the food we grow here. He fought for agriculture exports, the environment, and for a Department that was service-friendly to farmers and taxpayers. In these duties and others, he served well.

Over the last few weeks, however, the Office of the White House Counsel has reviewed information about Secretary Espy and the actions he took while in office. Although Secretary Espy has said he has done nothing wrong, I am troubled by the appearance of some of these incidents and believe his decision to leave is appropriate. During the remainder of his tenure, Secretary Espy will recuse himself from meat and poultry inspection issues. And I have asked Judge Abner Mikva, the White House Counsel, to continue his review of the Espy case until that review is complete.

Message to the Congress Reporting on the Unblocking of Panamanian Government Assets
October 3, 1994

To the Congress of the United States:

1. I hereby report to the Congress on developments since the last Presidential report on November 9, 1993, which have resulted in the termination of the continued blocking of Panamanian government assets. This is the final report with respect to Panama pursuant to section

207(d) of the International Emergency Economic Powers Act, 50 U.S.C. 1706(d).

2. On April 5, 1990, President Bush issued Executive Order No. 12710, terminating the national emergency declared on April 8, 1988, with respect to Panama. While this order terminated the sanctions imposed pursuant to that declaration, the blocking of Panamanian government assets in the United States was continued in order to permit completion of the orderly unblocking and transfer of funds that the President directed on December 20, 1989, and to foster the resolution of claims of U.S. creditors involving Panama, pursuant to 50 U.S.C. 1706(a). The termination of the national emergency did not affect the continuation of compliance audits and enforcement actions with respect to activities taking place during the sanctions period, pursuant to 50 U.S.C. 1622(a).

3. The Panamanian Transactions Regulations, 31 CFR Part 565 (the "Regulations"), were amended effective May 9, 1994, to foster the resolution of U.S. persons' claims against the Government of Panama arising prior to the April 5, 1990, termination date. (59 *Federal Register* 24643, May 12, 1994.) A copy of the amendment is attached. The amendment, new section 565.512, includes a statement of licensing policy indicating that the Department of the Treasury's Office of Foreign Assets Control ("FAC") would issue specific licenses authorizing the release of blocked Government of Panama funds at the request of that government to satisfy settlements, final judgments, and arbitral awards with respect to claims of U.S. persons arising prior to April 5, 1990. In addition, FAC stated that it would accept license applications from U.S. persons seeking judicial orders of attachment against blocked Government of Panama assets in satisfaction of final judgments entered against the Government of Panama, provided such applications are submitted no later than June 15, 1994.

4. No applications were received pursuant to this amendment for the purpose of obtaining judicial orders of attachment against blocked Government of Panama assets. Since the last report, however, specific licenses were issued at the request of the Government of Panama to unblock about $4.4 million to satisfy settlements reached with the vast majority of U.S. creditors by the Government of Panama. On

September 9, 1994, the FAC gave notice to the public that the remaining blocked Government of Panama assets, approximately $2.1 million, would be unblocked effective September 16, 1994. (50 *Federal Register* 46720, September 9, 1994.) A copy of the notice is attached. Half of the $2.1 million had been held at the Federal Reserve Bank of New York at the request of the Government of Panama. The remaining amounts were held in blocked commercial bank accounts or in blocked reserved accounts established under section 565.509 of the Panamanian Transactions Regulations, 31 CFR 565.509. The remaining known claimants were informed that, prior to the unblocking, the Government of Panama and Air Panama had directed the transfer of $400,000 into a trust account administered by counsel to the Republic of Panama and Air Panama, as escrow agent, to be utilized toward resolution of the few remaining U.S. claims. This sum exceeds the face amount of the total of the known remaining claims.

5. With the unblocking on September 16, 1994, of Government of Panama funds that had been subject to the continued blocking, the sanctions program initiated to deal with the threat once posed by the Noriega regime in Panama is completed. However, enforcement action for past violations may still be pursued within the applicable statute of limitations.

6. The expenses incurred by the Federal Government during the period of the national emergency with respect to Panama from April 8, 1988, through April 5, 1990, that are directly attributable to the exercise of powers and authorities conferred by the declaration of a national emergency with respect to Panama are estimated to total about $2.225 million, most of which represents wage and salary costs for Federal personnel. Personnel costs were largely centered in the Department of the Treasury (particularly in the Office of Foreign Assets Control, the U.S. Customs Service, the Office of the Under Secretary for Enforcement, and the Office of the General Counsel), and the Department of State (particularly the Bureau of Economic and Business Affairs and the Office of the Legal Adviser).

WILLIAM J. CLINTON

The White House,
October 3, 1994.

Message to the Congress Transmitting Transportation Department Reports
October 3, 1994

To the Congress of the United States:

I transmit herewith the 1993 calendar year reports as prepared by the Department of Transportation on activities under the Highway Safety Act and the National Traffic and Motor Vehicle Safety Act of 1966, as amended (23 U.S.C. 401 note and 15 U.S.C. 1408).

WILLIAM J. CLINTON

The White House,
October 3, 1994.

Message to the Congress Transmitting the Report of the Federal Labor Relations Authority
October 3, 1994

To the Congress of the United States:

In accordance with section 701 of the Civil Service Reform Act of 1978 (Public Law 95–454; 5 U.S.C. 7104(e)), I have the pleasure of transmitting to you the Fifteenth Annual Report of the Federal Labor Relations Authority for Fiscal Year 1993.

The report includes information on the cases heard and decisions rendered by the Federal Labor Relations Authority, the General Counsel of the Authority, and the Federal Service Impasses Panel.

WILLIAM J. CLINTON

The White House,
October 3, 1994.

Remarks at a Reception for California Gubernatorial Candidate Kathleen Brown
October 3, 1994

The President. Thank you very much. Why don't we just vote right now? [*Laughter*] You do that for 30 more days, and you're in like Flint. That was terrific. Thank you, Kathleen. And thank you, Governor Bayh, for your leadership.

You know, I really resent Evan Bayh. He's young and handsome, manages to avoid controversy and stay popular. And he's done a lot better as head of the Democratic Governors than I did when I was there. [*Laughter*]

Gov. Evan Bayh. Well, that's because I have a great President helping out.

The President. Not only that, but he's a wonderful tribute to our party, and he has a terrific future.

I came here tonight to speak for Kathleen Brown. I want to thank the members of our administration who are here, the members of the Cabinet. Their presence here should tell you how important we think this race is.

I was listening to Kathleen speak a moment ago, and I want to just tell you a few things from the heart about this. First of all, I declared for President 3 years ago today. At the time I was Governor; I had just been reelected to a fifth term, two 4-year terms, three 2-year terms. I was happy as a clam at home. I got into the race basically because I didn't want to see our victory in the cold war be squandered in the aftermath, because I didn't want to see America move to the 21st century not able to compete and win, and because I didn't like the fact that our country was coming apart when it ought to be coming together.

And when I began that race, most people thought I needed my head examined because the incumbent President was over 70 percent approval in the polls. My mother thought I could win; that's about it. [Laughter] That's about it.

I say it to make two points. One, in the moment the polls are not as important as the public official, the candidate, and the conviction. And secondly, the choice that Kathleen Brown just posed to you is a choice we're going to have to be making over and over and over and over again, until we get out of what we got ourselves into over a very long period of time.

And all along the way, at various times, the choice will be more difficult for people. But when I look at what her opponent's tried to do to her out in California and how he's tried to sort of define her, it's classic Republican politics. And they're very good at it. Let's not kid ourselves. They are very good at demonizing their opponents, at turning their opponents into aliens, and making people at the local Kiwanis Club think that they wouldn't share a piece of apple pie with their opponents. That's what they're good at. That's how they stay in.

They always think that, given the contentious and divisive nature of the way people communicate and the way they are communicated to today, they can exalt blame over responsibility, they can exalt division over unity, they can exalt fear over hope. That's what they believe. Once in a while we prove them wrong, when we can communicate with discipline and conviction and persistence and when we are not ground down.

I'd have come over here tonight just to hear her give that speech, because now she's got me in a better humor, too. [Laughter and applause] I'm telling you.

So you heard it, and it's the same thing everywhere. I mean, I ran for President because we were in the midst of 30 years of social problems, 20 years of economic problems, and 12 years of the kind of stuff she's going through now, where the leadership of this country would always tell the American people what they thought they wanted to hear. They would talk tough and get the image that they are tough—Presidential, national message—and they would act weak. They would talk like our parent and then act like our child, telling us exactly what we wanted to hear as if it were tough medicine and then writing us a check and never worrying about who was going to pay the bill. Now, that

is what has happened for 12 years. And always escaping responsibility by placing blame. Now, that is exactly what they have done. And that's what you see in California.

I just want to say something personally to the people of California. I may not have an opportunity to say it out there. I've been to California about a dozen times since I've been President, would have been once more if it hadn't been for the events in Haiti that kept me away from going out there for Kathleen a few days ago. I love the place. It's a fascinating place. And everything that America has everywhere is also there.

They have had two huge problems. One is, since they're the biggest State in the country economically, when we had a recession, they got hit harder with it. The second is that with about 12 percent of our population, they had 21 percent of our defense investments. So that when we cut defense in this country at the end of the cold war, starting back in '87—that's when defense peaked—it was absolutely predictable that it would have double the impact in California that it would have anywhere else because of the concentration and that the impact might be highly weighted in high-wage jobs. Therefore, turning it around takes a little more time because the hit was bigger there.

And so I went all over California in that election trying to figure out what was going on in southern California, what was going on in northern California, what was going on for the farmers, what was going on in the inland empire, what was going on in San Diego—how were the border problems, the immigration problems going to be aggravated and exacerbated and people's sense of insecurity going to be reinforced by all these terrible economic problems. If you had 150 different racial and ethnic groups in Los Angeles County, that meant that it could be the beacon of the whole future for the United States, but how were they going to get through all the tensions that would be caused by the economic contraction of the moment until we could turn it around.

I have really given a lot of thought to this. And when we put together an economic strategy, it was pretty simple. It was: reduce the deficit; increase investment in education, training, and new technologies; expand trade and investment; and try to empower individuals and communities to succeed, which means that the places that are in the worse shape need some extra help.

How did that play itself out in California? Well, we removed restrictions on $35 billion worth of high-tech exports where California has a decided interest greater than any other State in the country. We spent hundreds of millions of dollars, as Kathleen said, on defense conversions, helping to turn bases over to local communities so they could get businesses in there to put people to work and actually investing with companies in new technologies of the future. I visited the Rockwell plant out there, and you were there, too, the day we went there to talk about that.

When the earthquake came, when the fires came, we were there with emergency aid in a hurry. We rebuilt the world's busiest highway quicker than anybody thought we could by literally reinventing, to use the Vice President's term, the way we spend the money out there.

In spite of all this talk about immigration, it was our administration that for the first time recommended and got through Congress Federal assistance to pay for the criminal justice costs of illegal immigrants. We increased by 30 percent, by 30 percent, the amount of aid—in a tough time when we were reducing spending overall, we increased by 30 percent the amount of money going to California to deal with their costs of immigration, 30 percent over what happened when the previous President was here and the present Governor was a Member of the United States Senate. That's what we did. That's our record on that issue.

We have done a number of other things. We are backing Senator Feinstein's desert bill. Last weekend we turned the Presidio over to you so you folks can do something great with it. We are doubling the border guards for enforcement on the border. We have worked hard for California. We're selling California rice to Japan for the first time in history.

I met a walnut farmer last month from California said, "It just kills my farmer friends because they're all Republicans, but they have to admit that you have done more for us than any President in the last 30 years." So we are working for California.

Now, I say that to make this point—and why it's so important that you're here—all that can still be washed away by the deliberate, concerted effort of our opponents to place blame over responsibility, division over unity, fear over

hope, can wipe away all the details and all the facts. And what you have to do to help Kathleen Brown win is to contribute now and then talk and work between now and the election, to prove that what really counts is what will build that State.

I'm really proud of the fact that in 20 months we have made a good start on bringing this country back. But don't kid yourself, it's just a good start. I'm proud of the fact that we have 3 years of deficit reduction in a row for the first time since Truman; we're going to the smallest Federal Government since John Kennedy was President—the Republicans badmouth the Government, but we shrunk it with no help from them; that there are 4.3 million new jobs in this economy; and that for the first time in 9 years the United States was rated a couple of weeks ago by the panel of international economists as the most productive country in the world. I am proud of that. But it is just a beginning.

You look at what is happening in California, and you will see the combined impact of 30 years of social problems, 20 years of economic problems, 12 years of neglect and a disproportionate impact of the defense cutback. The people out there cannot be blamed if they are still frustrated and full of anxiety. That is not their fault. It is our job to tell the people of California that Kathleen Brown and Dianne Feinstein are builders, people who are trying to make things better and that they should not be diverted from the urgent task of building the country and building the State.

If I might just say a word about crime, Kathleen's already said that. You know, a picture of Kathleen Brown and Jerry Brown and Rose Bird is not worth near as much as the assault weapons ban, 100,000 police, 100,000 jail cells for criminals, thousands and thousands of prevention programs, and a tougher approach to crime. And I'll tell you something else, I know something about this; I started out as attorney general of my State. I have a different position than she does on capital punishment, but our crime bill had 60 different specific statutes on that. She supported our crime bill, and he didn't. Who are we kidding with these ads about who's weak on crime or not? She had the record when we needed it.

So I say to you, you have to make up your mind. You can cheer tonight, but tomorrow all those ads will still be out there on television, and everybody will be writing about this as if it's a horse race instead of a fight for the spirit and the soul of that State and what happens to the future of little children. And you have to decide whether you feel some sort of personal responsibility to affect the outcome.

I'm telling you, it is a wonderful place. It has enormous potential. This country will never fully recover until California recovers. And we have work to do. And the people out there cannot be blamed for voting on what they know. That's the way all the rest of us are, too. We can only act on what we know. We can only see the world through the prism of our own experience. And while all of us have been up here working for them, the other guys have been out there talking about us. So now when the Congress goes home, the election should be our friend because we can go tell the truth. And what you have to do is make a personal commitment to do that.

The economic plan that Kathleen Brown has outlined will help to do what only the State can do to rebuild California. The Federal Government and a partnership that we are building between the private sector and the Federal Government cannot do it alone. There must be State initiatives. There will always be in California things that can only be done by people who know the problems the best, who understand the opportunities most clearly. The economic strategy that I have outlined cannot fully succeed anywhere without aggressive leadership at the State level to rebuild the economy. And believe me, we can continue to make progress on education and training; we can continue to build this economy; we can drive down the crime rate; we can make progress on immigration. But to do it, it's going to require a tough, disciplined, concerted, long-term partnership between the White House and Washington and the people who live and work in California, starting in the statehouse in Sacramento. That's what this election is about.

So the country has a big interest in who wins here—not the political system, not the political pundits but the welfare of the average man and woman and child all across America. You just heard her case for why she should win. Let us exalt hope over fear. Let us exalt unity over division. Let us prove that responsibility still beats blame in commonsense America by making sure that no voter goes to the polls in California unaware of the real facts.

Thank you, and God bless you all.

NOTE: The President spoke at 6:45 p.m. at the Sheraton Carlton Hotel. In his remarks, he referred to Gov. Evan Bayh of Indiana and Rose Bird, former justice, California Supreme Court.

Remarks at a Victory Rally for Senator Charles S. Robb in McLean, Virginia
October 3, 1994

The President. Thank you. Thank you so much. You have already answered one of my questions—[*laughter*]—and that is whether you were going to take this laying down or whether you were going to stand up and fight for the future of your State.

I am so delighted to be here with all of you, and I'm glad to see Lieutenant Governor Beyer here tonight and all of the other local officials. Toddy, you did a terrific job introducing us, and you ought to be better known than we are. Thank you. And I'm glad to be here with my good friend Senator Robb and with my good friend Lynda and their children. You know, we have been friends a long time. And we have

seen a lot of things happen in this country. And Chuck Robb and I, during most of the eighties, were Governors. You heard Toddy talking about what he did for education here, how hard he worked to build Virginia's economy.

I want to say two things about our common experience because it really will craft what the differences are in this race. And whether you can get this across to the other voters in Virginia will determine what they do. The first thing was that all during the eighties, we thought, Chuck and I and a number of others, that the Democratic Party had to change, that we had to be identified with mainstream issues, that we had to reach out to a broad base of supporters, that we could never give up our devotion to the rights of individual citizens, to the obligation to fight for equal opportunity, but that we also had to be prudent in spending for economic growth, tough on crime, and facing the relevant problems of the country. That's how we got into the whole Democratic Leadership Mainstream Forum group, to try to move this country forward beyond left and right and beyond all the partisanship that had paralyzed Washington, DC, for too many years.

But the other thing that both of us had to do, even to make a career in public life, was to fight against what has been the brilliant strength of the Republicans, particularly the Republicans on the right, for many years now, and that is that they are better talkers than we are and—and listen to me now—and they raise more money than we do to turn their opponents into aliens. Right? [*Laughter*] How do they do that? They do that by exalting fear over hope, by exalting blame over responsibility, by exalting division over unity. That is what they do. And they are brilliant at it. They sort of try to turn you into a space alien. I tell people—and they are devoted to it. And they are brilliant at saying one thing and doing another.

So Chuck Robb and I, for most of our lives, tried to change two things: We wanted to change the Democratic Party from a left-right debate to a forward-backward debate, to broaden our base and move forward; and we wanted to break the stranglehold that the national Republican Party had on ordinary Americans because they were not acting in their interest; they just told them what they wanted to hear and demonized their opponents. Now, here in this election, you see it all being played out again here in Virginia and throughout the country.

Three years ago today, I announced for President. And I must say, my mother was the only person who thought I could win that day. [*Laughter*] The incumbent President was over 70 percent in public approval. But what I didn't like was that we had won the cold war and we were in danger of losing the peace, that the economy was going down, the country was becoming more divided. I did not want my child and the children of this country to grow up to be the first generation of Americans to do worse than their parents. I saw an opportunity for this country to enjoy peace and prosperity, to build a unity out of our diversity, to move into a relationship with the rest of the world

unknown in all of human history if only we had the courage, the wisdom, and the good old-fashioned common sense to line up our problems and take them on one at a time and go on into the future. That's why I ran.

And I had these grand dreams that I would come to Washington and not only be able to move the country forward but that we would launch—people like Chuck Robb and others and I would launch a new bipartisan debate where people of good faith in both parties would argue about what ideas would best take America into the future and would wind up cooperating on the important issues of the day to move the country forward, knowing that at election time, there would always be enough to argue about. [*Laughter*]

Well, let me tell you what has happened instead. We came here with America suffering from terrible social problems, crime, violence, drugs, family breakdown. They had been developing for 30 years, folks. We came here with America suffering from serious economic problems where many, many wage earners were working longer and longer and longer and never getting a wage that kept up with inflation and often losing jobs and taking lower paying jobs because of the pressures of a global economy.

And we came here after 12 years in which Presidents of the other party had talked tough about our problems but acted soft. They railed about the deficit and quadrupled the debt. They railed about the Government and put their folks in all the Government jobs they could get. They talked tough about crime, but all they did was talk. Every single issue was talk.

We've been here 20 months, folks. And now the Republicans are saying, "Well, if your problems aren't all solved, it's just because the aliens have taken over Washington." [*Laughter*] Isn't that right? "They don't share your values. They're for big Government." You know all the things they say.

Well, look at the record. We have made a good beginning that matters to America. The next time you hear their space invaders speech—[*laughter*]—you ask them this: Well, how do you explain the fact that we have passed the biggest deficit reduction package in history, the largest number of spending cuts in history, and tax rates went up only on the top 1.2 percent of our people; that we made 90 percent of the small businesses in this country eligible for a tax cut and reduced taxes on 15 million working families to keep them out of welfare and in the work force; that while were cutting spending, we increased investment in education and training and new technologies and defense conversion; we expanded trade by more than any comparable period in 35 years.

And what has that produced? They said the sky would fall. You remember? The same crowd that is campaigning against Chuck Robb said the sky would fall. Well, instead, we have 4.3 million new jobs, 130,000 in Virginia alone; 330,000 families in Virginia alone were eligible for income tax cuts; 600,000 people in Virginia alone, today, already eligible for lower interest college loans. We've had 3 years of deficit reduction in a row for the first time since Harry Truman was President. And we have reduced the size of the Federal Government already by more than 70,000—270,000 over 5 years. The Federal Government will be the smallest that it has been since John Kennedy was President. That is the record of this administration.

Now, that is why Chuck Robb pleads guilty to voting for that economic plan: It produced for the people of Virginia. Republicans and Democrats got those jobs. Republicans and Democrats got those tax cuts. Republicans and Democrats will get those lower interest college loans. It was good for the people of Virginia.

Chuck Robb hates deficit spending. And when I reeled off all this to him in private, he said, "It's a good start, but you've got to keep going." [*Laughter*] The difference is the other guys want to go back.

Let me give you the second example. We have made a good start in fighting the crime and the social problems that are gripping America: 100,000 more police on the street; 100,000 more jail cells for violent criminals; "three strikes and you're out"; the assault weapons ban, over the opposition of the NRA. And we've made a start in making Government work for ordinary Americans again.

Now, what have they done?

Audience members. Nothing!

The President. They have done—oh yes, I wish that were the answer. [*Laughter*] I came to Washington with all my dreams that we'd be able to work together. The first week I was here, I was told by the leader of the other party in one of the Houses of Congress—listen to this—I was told, "You're going to have to pass this economic plan without one single, solitary vote. It doesn't matter how you change

it. We're not going to vote for any tax increases on the wealthy. And if it fails, we'll be able to blame you. And if it works, we'll attack it and call it a tax increase anyway," which is exactly what happened. But he said, "No point in you even talking to us. You won't get a vote." So I sort of waited 8 months; we passed it anyway. They said the sky would fall, and the economy is booming.

Then last year they voted 42 to 2 for the crime bill. Last year they voted for the assault weapons ban; they voted for prevention programs—all those things they call pork, they voted for, they sponsored a lot of them—42 to 2. Why? They did not believe the House of Representatives would pass it.

So then, when the crime bill comes back this year in the Senate—I want you to understand what you're thinking about doing here, what the consequence of this race is—all of a sudden, all of those prevention programs they voted for, they sponsored, that on an annual basis they were spending more on in their bill than in the one we finally passed, they went from 42 to 2 for it, to 6 to 38 against it. Why? Because they were told the objective was not to lower crime but to hand a political defeat to the administration and to the Democrats. That's why.

Let me give you another example. On health care, when I introduced the health care bill, I said, "Look, I don't have a monopoly on truth. You may have a better idea." And I was so happy. I thought, finally, we're going to get there because 24 members of the other party, 24 Republican Senators, were on a bill that would have provided coverage for everybody and would have controlled costs. So, anyway, so they had 24 Republicans on this bill. So I said, "Great, we're going to get health care." That's right. I said, "We're going to get health care." And I thought, they'll have ideas; we'll have ideas; we'll get together and we'll work out a deal. We'll have health care—24. By the time the bill got to the committee process, do you know how many of those 24 were left? Zero. Why? Why? Why? Because—because—don't take my word, take their word. Republican Congressman says, in print, "We were ordered not to cooperate on health care." Republican Senator says, in print, "We have killed it. Now the trick is to keep our fingerprints off of it"— in print; Republican idea person says, in print— passed it out, proud of it—to the Republicans, "The one thing you must not do is pass any health care reform. It will help the Democrats too much."

Now that is what we are facing. That is the national context in which you must see this election. But far more important than that is they have now told us what they will do. They have put their contract out. And what is it? Trickle-down economics; eighties promises; a trillion dollars worth of unfunded promises, \$1 trillion.

Audience members. Boo-o-o!

The President. I'll tell you what that contract is. It's a contract on America's future. It's a contract on our deficit reduction. It's a contract on Medicare. It's a contract on paying for the crime bill. It will take us right back down the road that we were on before if you do not change the direction of the country. So I say to you, let's don't quit. We have made a good start in 20 months on 30 years of social problems, 20 years of economics problems, and 12 years of neglect.

I want to say something else. If you say, "I want the same thing from Chuck Robb today that I did when I voted for him for Governor: I want a mainstream, progressive, bipartisan, commonsense effort to move this country forward"; if you say, "I am sick and tired of this demonization; I am sick and tired of this distortion of a good man's record and a good man's life and a good person's public service"; if you say, "I will not reward people who talk tough, just tell me what I want to hear, pander to my every whim, and act weak when they have power; I will instead reward people who make tough decisions and think about my children's future, and Chuck Robb has done that every day he was in public office from the first day I elected him"; if you say, "We don't want to demonize our opponents either, but we have values, too, and we can read the rules, too, and we know that one of the rules that sometimes the other side forgets to mention in their litany of values is 'Thou shalt not bear false witness'"—let me tell you something, the people of this State are good people. They are good people, regardless of their party or their background or their experience. They can only vote in this election based on what they know, what they see, what they feel.

Now, let me end where I began. We've made a good start in 20 months on 30 years of social problems, 20 years of economic problems, 12 years of neglect. But most people have not felt it yet. And while we have been working, they have been talking, blaming, dividing, turning us into aliens.

You, you can decide whether we go forward or backward. We've moved the economy; we've taken a serious step on crime; we've begun to make Government work for ordinary people again. They have put out their contract on America. They want more of trickle-down economics, more of inequality, more of division. You can decide.

But the voters who are not here at this rally tonight can only vote based on what they know. There is a mountain of money raining down on them at home tonight while you're here with us, coming through the television screen, playing on people's paranoia, their disillusionment over the years, their frustration, their cynicism. You have to break through it. And you can do it.

But paying to come to this rally is not enough. You've got to talk at work. You've got to talk on the weekends. You've got to talk to your friends. You've got to talk. You've got to work. You've got to walk. Do not take this lying down. Do not take this lying down.

This is your State. It is your country. It is your children's future. Go take it back.

Thank you, and God bless you all.

NOTE: The President spoke at 7:53 p.m. at the McLean Hilton Hotel. In his remarks, he referred to Lt. Gov. Don Beyer of Virginia and Toddy Puller, Virginia House of Delegates member and widow of author Lewis Puller.

Remarks at a Victory Dinner for Senator Charles S. Robb in Vienna, Virginia
October 3, 1994

Thank you so much for that wonderful welcome. Thank you, Senator Robb, and thank you, Lynda, for the years of friendship and the years of service, the years of wise counsel and the years of shared joy, and all the rest of it that goes along with this work.

Congressman Moran and Congressman Scott, I'm delighted to see you here tonight. Lieutenant Governor Beyer, you gave a magnificent talk, and I thank you for what you said about your Senator and your President. I'm sure neither of us will ever forget it. Thank you, Mark Warner, for your work here. And Senator, I think one of your colleagues is here; I think Senator Daschle is here from South Dakota. Are you here? Stand up. [*Applause*] Thank you.

Ladies and gentlemen, this is a special day for me and for Hillary and for our family and close friends. It was 3 years ago today that I announced my candidacy for President. I was trying today, in the midst of meeting with the Vice Premier of China and the Foreign Minister of Israel and the Crown Prince of Jordan and dealing with a lot of our domestic issues, I was trying hard to remember exactly how I felt on October 3, 1991, in front of the Old State House in Little Rock. I know one thing: My mama was the only person there who thought I had a chance to win. And I don't think she was so sure. [*Laughter*] The incumbent President was at over 70 percent approval in all the polls, and most people though it was a fool's errand. But I thought that the race was worth making, no matter what the outcome, because at least I would never have to explain to my child why I didn't do my part to sound the alarm about what I thought was going on in America.

It was all part, really, of what I had been working on for several years before I ran for President, part of a political heritage that I shared with people like Chuck Robb and Tom Daschle, who's from South Dakota, a place that makes Arkansas look like a metropolitan center. [*Laughter*] I say that to make this point: Several years ago Chuck and I and a number of others helped to found a group called the Democratic Leadership Council, after the Democrats just

kept on getting beat in the Presidential race. We did it with two goals in mind, and both of them are important and both of them bear directly on the choices Americans face in this election and especially on the choice Americans have here in Virginia.

The first thing we wanted to do was to broaden the base and change the rhetoric and the substance of a lot of the policies of the Democratic Party. We thought we had been typecast too much as the big Government, pro-tax, Government-can-solve-all-the problems party. We needed to broaden our base and prove that we could spend tax money with discipline, grow the economy, be tough on crime, and bring the American people together across regional and racial and party lines, and move the country forward. Instead of always having a left-right argument, in a time of transition you need to be moving ahead.

The second thing we wanted to do is equally important. We wanted to challenge people in the other party to do the same thing. We were sick and tired of seeing the other party be rewarded in national elections primarily for their ability to talk rather than to act, primarily for their ability to turn us into aliens instead of tell the people of the country what they were for. And they are very good at that, I know.

And so we began to work on that. And to me, that's what the 1992 campaign was all about. I knew at the end of the cold war, we were in danger of squandering our opportunities, of not meeting the challenges of the 21st century, of raising the first generation of children not to do better than their parents. I also felt then, and I feel even more strongly today, that the best days of this country are still before us; this is by far the strongest country in the world; that if we can learn how to live together in harmony and take responsibility for our problems and listen to each other instead of scream at each other, we can take our challenges one by one and take this country into the next century with the greatest era of peace and prosperity and opportunity for all our people the world has ever known.

We face in this election many dilemmas. But there are two we can't do anything about except to address. The first is one to which Senator Robb alluded. We are living in a time of historic change. The cold war is over. Shimon Peres, the brilliant Foreign Minister of Israel, said to me today, he said, "It is a great challenge you face, Mr. President, in foreign policy, where the American people have to now stop thinking about the threat of immediate destruction and start thinking responsibly about just dealing with their problems, because if you don't deal with your problems, then eventually your security will be threatened again."

Similarly here at home, we have to deal with the realities of a new global economy where what we earn depends largely on what we learn; where the average 18-year-old will change jobs six times in a lifetime; and where, with all of our strengths, we still have to confront a bewildering array of problems. And whenever a country goes through a period of change, it's just like when a person goes through a period of change. I ask each of you tonight to think about that when you think about the state of the American people's mind in this election. Think about the first day you ever went to school or the first day you went to college or the first day you showed up for your first job or the first day you started your first business or the day you got married or the day your first child was born. Those are all good things, but I'll bet you anything you were scared to death, if you were really thinking about it.

And these are good things. If you think about the other challenges you faced—were you going to get fired, were you going to go broke, what was it like in the line of fire, what was it like when you had your first crisis in your family—whenever you go through a period of great change, inside you, hope and fear are at war. It's almost as if you had a big scale inside, and every day hope and fear—hope would be one side, fear would be on the other, and every day they'd be in a little bit different balance until you actually get through the period of change and things level out.

That is where we are today. And we are at midcourse in this term the American people gave me, where we have made a terrific start on our country's problems but a lot of people have not felt it yet. That is compounded today by the fact that the other party, being relieved of power in the Presidency, has gone back to what it does best, which is to talk instead of do, to blame instead of to assume responsibility, to divide instead of unite, to play on fear instead of hope. So they try to turn the President or the Senator from Virginia into an alien in the minds of ordinary voters and hope they can clog the information channels enough so that that will guarantee that in the scales inside us all, fear will outweigh hope on election day, and we will actually do that which we do not wish to do: We will make a choice which will undermine the very path which we wish to walk.

Now, I have to tell you, folks, we have done a lot of things in the last 20 months. It doesn't solve all the problems, but we've made a good start. We have made a good start. And I ask you to see this Senate race not just in the terms that Mr. Robb presented them but in these terms. We have had 30 years of social problems building up in this country: the breakdown of the family, the rise of crime, the rise of drugs, the rise of gangs, the loss of opportunity in many of our inner cities and our rural areas, a whole generation of children being raised without the kind of discipline and love they needed to grow up to be productive citizens. For 30 years that has been coming.

We have had 20 years of serious economic problems where, when the economy was booming or when it was sinking, wages of hourly wage earners tended to be stagnant, and people had to change jobs more and more, and those who would work hard but didn't have high levels of skills were having to struggle just to hold on to their income. That has been developing for 20 years.

We had 12 years where we tried it their way, where they talked tough but acted soft, where they tried to pretend to be so strong—and they were very good at it—but they just really told us what we wanted to hear. They cursed the deficit and quadrupled the debt. They lambasted Government, but they didn't shrink it; they got all their friends in Government jobs as quick as they could. They talked about investment and free enterprise, but they tried to spur economic growth by massive deficit spending instead of by investment and productivity.

We have had 20 months to deal with 30 years of social problems, 20 years of economic problems, and 12 years of trickle-down. And here is what has happened in 20 months: We have made a good start on the economy; we have made a good start on crime; we have made a good start on making Government work for ordinary Americans. Our economic strategy involved bringing the deficit down, increasing investment in education and training and new technologies, expanding trade, and trying to empower individuals and communities to grow.

You tell me how it's worked. We've had more trade expansion in the last year and a half than in any comparable period in 35 years. The economic plan for which Chuck Robb has been criticized for voting had $255 billion in spending cuts; the biggest deficit reduction package in history; a tax increase, a rate increase, yes, on the top 1.2 percent of the American people, including most of you in this room, and I thank you for staying here. [Laughter] But you can take some pride in knowing that every red cent went to reduce the deficit, not for new spending.

That economic plan also made 90 percent of the small businesses in this country eligible for a tax cut. It made 15 million working families, including 330,000 working families in Virginia who were working hard, raising children, and still hovering just above the poverty line, eligible for an income tax cut so that they would never have any incentive to give up work and go into welfare, and so instead we would reward their being good parents and good workers.

That's what that plan did. That plan made 20 million Americans eligible for lower interest, longer repayment on their college loan so that no young person again should ever decline to go to college because of the cost, because now if you want, you can pay back that loan over 25 years as a percentage of your income with a lower interest rate than used to be available. That's what that economic plan did, 600,000 people in Virginia alone eligible for that. That is what Chuck Robb pleads guilty to voting for.

Now, what did they say would happen if we passed our plan? They said the sky would fall. They said the economy would come to an end. All their leaders in the United States Senate said the deficit would go up, the economy would go down, things would be terrible. That is what they said. And what has happened: 4.3 million new jobs in 20 months, 93 percent of them in the private sector; 3 years of deficit reduction in a row for the first time since Harry Truman was President; the United States was rated number one of all the countries in the world in productivity by the annual vote of international economists for the first time in 9 years; and

after they have cursed the Government, lo and behold, it was the Democrats that shrunk the Government. There are 70,000 fewer people working for the Federal establishment than there were on the day I was inaugurated. And under our law, there will be 270,000 fewer 4 years from now. That is our record, and it is a good start.

And 100 percent of them voted against it. That was their response. I was told the first week I came here—I came here with the philosophy I just explained; Chuck Robb, we had this philosophy. He lost his position on a budget committee because he was for bigger deficit reduction. He wasn't some clone of the Democratic establishment; he stood up to everybody. Even when I presented this program, he said, "Well, I'll vote for it, but you ought to cut it more." That was our philosophy.

You know what I was told the first week I got here by the leader of the other party in the Senate? "Well, you'll have to pass this without a single Republican vote. In either House you won't get a vote. And it doesn't matter how you change it, because we want to be in a position to condemn you if you fail. And if you succeed, we will obscure it by just reminding people that you raised taxes. And even if you just raised them on the wealthiest Americans, we'll convince everybody you did it to everybody." That's what I was told the first week I got here. I said, what happened to all this bipartisan cooperation? What happened to this 90-day honeymoon I was promised? What happened to all these words that I kept hearing? But we did it anyway, and we made a good beginning. We made a good beginning.

Now we come to the crime bill. Everybody says it's the biggest problem in America. The crime bill puts 100,000 police on the street; builds 100,000 jail cells to hold violent criminals; has the power to remake communities with community-based—not bureaucracies—community-based programs to prevent crime from occurring in the first place, that the law enforcement community of this country demanded be in that crime bill. It did ban assault weapons. And it did pass, in spite of the brutal efforts of leaders in the other party to defeat it.

Now, here's what you may not remember. When they talked about Chuck Robb and the assault weapons ban—let me just remind you of something. Late last year this crime bill, in only a slightly different form, passed 95 to 4, and the Republicans voted for it 42 to 2 in the United States Senate. It had the assault weapons ban in it. It had prevention programs in it. The only reason it didn't cost quite as much is it was a 4½-year bill instead of a 6-year bill. But in all the years that this crime bill has in common with the bill that was passed last year, they voted for a bill that had more prevention funds per year in it than the one they voted against. And they called it "pork"—the funds, the programs they had already voted for, the programs many of them had cosponsored. It went from 42 to 2 for, to 6 to 38 against. Why? Because they were told that the job they had to do in the Senate was no longer to lower the crime rate in America, to make the American people safer; the job they had to do was to defeat the Democratic President and the Democrats in Congress. That is not what I came to Washington to do; I came to try to help you be safer.

But we've still made a good start on crime. And we've made a good start in making Government work for ordinary people. I already mentioned we passed a bill to reduce the size of the Federal Government by 270,000 and give all the money back to local communities to fight crime. We're bringing the deficit down. We're making Government work again in all kinds of interesting ways. The Small Business Administration finally has a director in Erskine Bowles, whom I just brought into the White House, but for the last 2 years—he spent his whole life starting small businesses. So, lo and behold, he wasn't a politician over there, like what you usually have; he was a guy who was used to starting small businesses. So, now, you can go to the SBA, and if you want a loan, you can fill out a one-page form instead of one that's 100 pages long, and you get an answer in 3 days, yes or no. That's not the Government that started it.

I'm about to sign a procurement bill that will put an end to $10 ashtrays and $80 hammers and all that stuff you've been hearing about. You may not have heard about it because it passed quietly, but we passed a bill that will reform all the purchasing practices of the Government. The things, in other words, that people who were alienated from Government and who voted for Ross Perot wanted, we are doing.

I supported campaign finance reform. I supported lobby reform. I support the bill that's in the Senate now that would require Congress to live under the laws it imposes on the private sector. It's already passed the House; let them pass it in the Senate now. But you ask Senator Daschle or Senator Robb what happened to campaign finance reform. People who don't want us to have a bill killed it.

Now—so, you have a choice. We made a good start on economic recovery, on crime, making Government work for ordinary people. Is there a lot to be done? You bet there is. Is the answer to go back to trickle-down economics? They now have a plan. We now know that in addition to being obstructionists, if you give them enough votes, they've got a plan. And what's the plan? The same thing they did before, tell them what they want to hear but act tough doing it, so nobody catches you being soft.

You know, the mature thing to do if you're taking responsibility for your family, your kids, your business, or your country is just to tell people what has to be done and take a deep breath and get about doing it. And it's never quite as hard or as difficult or as painful as you think it's going to be. That is what we are doing.

Now, after 3 years of deficit reduction, for the first time since '48, after robust job growth, after the weakest job growth since the Great Depression, their crowd has now given us a trillion dollars' worth of unfunded promises, which they call a Contract With America. Folks, it's a contract on America. They have put out a contract on the deficit. They have put out a contract on Medicare. They have put out a contract on ever paying for the crime bill. But they're going to promise you everything, "We're going to have a balanced budget amendment, but we're going to cut everybody's taxes. And we're going to spend more on defense; we're going to start Star Wars up again. Don't worry, we'll do it." Hey, I heard that before. They quadrupled the debt, reduced their investment in America, and nearly drove this country into the ditch. And I don't think we want to do it again.

So you've got a clear choice, and you have to decide. You have to decide: What do you believe in? And here in Virginia, you have this stark, graphic example of how really good they are at making down, up; up, down; square, round; and turning us into aliens. I will tell you, they are better than we are at this. They are. They have turned me into an alien with a lot of voters in Virginia so I can be in the ads. But that is a true ad, that I'd rather have Robb in the Senate. I knew if they ran enough ads, they'd finally run one that was true. That's true.

But what I want to say to you is that the people of this State are good people, but they are just like the rest of the country. We're going through this period of change, and change is hard. And we all are for change in general, and then we're all against it in particular, as soon as it requires any rigor at all or when it takes time to wait for.

That's another thing that makes politics really hard today. Look at the way we communicate: these pounding messages—right?—the 30-second ads, a trauma on the news every night, the dynamics of how we get our information.

Now, Don Beyer said it the best, he said, "Everything that really counts in life takes time." Everything that you really care about in life takes time. But we're not given much time to digest here, to digest; we just have all this stuff crammed at us in a time of uncertainty and change. And the other guys are better talkers. I've been busy up here doing. And since they gave up all doing and didn't want to work with me, they had more time to talk. And mercy, they're good at it. And they've got plenty of money to do it.

So we now have a stark choice. We're clearly making progress on the economy, on crime, on making the Government work for ordinary people, clearly. We clearly have a long way to go. Is the answer to turn around and do what failed us before? That is the choice we're being given. And here, you have a little extra gloss on it. Here, it is more stark.

So I know how you feel, because you showed up and you made this contribution to Chuck Robb. But what I want to tell you is that your contribution, as much as I appreciate it, is not enough, because you cannot give $20 million. And the voters in Virginia can only vote on what they know, just like voters everywhere. You don't want them to wake up a year from now, saying, "Oh, my goodness, what have I done?" There have to be enough who will make the right decision now.

That's what happened to Mr. Truman in '48, by the way. A lot of people have forgotten this. You know, if you took a poll today, everybody wants Harry Truman on Mount Rushmore. But I came from one of those families who was for him when he was still alive. And I'm telling you, those of you who are old enough to remember that know that he just barely won that race and that he was a figure of positive change in a difficult time. And he fought, and enough Americans listened to him to stay the course and enable our country to be a responsible power in the world, to stand up to the cold war, to rebuild Europe and Japan, and to build the middle class in this country, because we made the right decision.

That's the decision you're being called upon to make. You cannot walk out of this fundraiser and say, "I have done my part for Chuck Robb." You cannot do it.

Chuck Robb has served you well and honorably as a Lieutenant Governor, as a Governor, as a Senator. I have known him a long time. He has stood—I'm proud of what he did in the Marine Corps and in the war, and I can't believe anyone would ever question it, but I'm really proud of what he's done in public life since he's been back home, too. And you should be, too.

And I know it is easy when things are tough and you're frustrated to say, "Just throw them out if they're in. Let me see if I can't find something I don't like about them and X them off." But this is a choice. This is a choice. And I know this man. I have seen him work year-in and year-out with very high standards of discipline and integrity, standing up and taking unpopular positions. I know what he did as Governor. I know what he's done as Senator. And the idea that they could be trying to turn him into some sort of space alien who is from the far left, when he has done something that they talked about but never did—fight for lower deficits, fight for a more responsible economic policy, and fight for the future of Virginia and America—is a travesty, and you must not allow it to happen. You must not. You must not allow it to happen.

Now, I'm going to tell you something, folks— just stand right there, because I'm finishing. Don't even sit down; I'm nearly done, and it won't encourage me to go on. Just stand right there. [Laughter] I want you to think about this. Every one of you knows somebody else you can call. You know somebody else you can talk to. There's somebody at work. There's somebody in your civic club. There's somebody you spend your time on the weekends with. There's somebody you meet at the school meeting. There's somebody you can talk to, somebody whose scales are going up and down between hope and fear. And you can tell them that this is about going forward, not going back. It's about assuming responsibility, not pointing the finger of blame. It's about bringing people together, not dividing them. It's about playing to our hopes, not our fears. That is what you have to do. You cannot let Chuck and Lynda and the people that work in the campaign headquarters do it all, and say, "I've paid for the television ads. I quit." That is not enough.

And I want every one of you to pledge to yourselves tonight that if you want this country to keep turning around and you want your children to reap the benefits of the 21st century and you want to do right by your country in this period of change, the way our forebears did at the end of World War II, you will send Chuck Robb back to the Senate.

Thank you, and God bless you all.

NOTE: The President spoke at 9:20 p.m. at the Sheraton Premiere. In his remarks, he referred to Mark Warner, Virginia Democratic Party chairman.

Remarks Welcoming President Nelson Mandela of South Africa
October 4, 1994

President Mandela, members of the South African delegation, distinguished guests, my fellow Americans, we are here to welcome Nelson Mandela back to the United States, but first, to the United States as the President of his nation.

Now, all over the world, there are three words which spoken together express the triumph of freedom, democracy, and hope for the future. They are "President Nelson Mandela." In you, sir, we see proof that the human spirit can never be crushed. For a half century, you pursued your ideals, keeping your promise never to surrender, risking all, despite danger. For 27 years, we watched you from your prison cell inspire millions of your people with your spirit and your words. And when you emerged, instead of retribution for past wrongs, you sought peace and freedom and equality for your people.

You are living proof that the forces of justice and reconciliation can bridge any divide. Every day, you teach the world that those who build triumph over those who tear down, that those who unite can actually prevail over those who would divide. Your presence here and the growth of a new South Africa are stern rebukes to both the destroyers and the cynics of this world.

The struggle in South Africa has always had a special place in the heart of America. For after all, we fought our own most terrible war here in our own land over slavery. And our own civil rights movement has taken strength and inspiration from and given aid to your fight for liberty. Americans take great pride in the role we played in helping to overturn apartheid and in supporting the free elections which produced your Presidency.

Now we are working with you to build the new South Africa. The challenges you face, poverty, joblessness, homelessness, the despair born of long years of deprivation, are as large as they are difficult. But we know you will forge ahead, and we know that we here in the United States will also be better for your progress. For a thriving South Africa, spurring greater prosperity throughout the region, opening new markets, that makes us more prosperous, too. And a stable and democratic South Africa, working with its neighbors to restore and maintain the peace, that makes us more secure as well.

And perhaps most important of all, in this age of ethnic, religious, and racial strife the world over, you can be our partner, and together our two nations can show the world that true strength is found when we come together despite our differences. We know and you know that diversity and progress can go hand-in-hand, indeed, that they must do so if we are to give all our people the chance to fulfill their God-given potential.

Mr. President, you have brought forth a new nation, conceived in liberty and dedicated to equality. Today the American people welcome you here, and we salute your stunning achievement. We pledge, as you have pledged, that we will walk every mile with you and that we will not grow weary on the way.

I say to all of you here, *Nkosi Sikelel' i Afrika.* God bless Africa. And God bless America.

NOTE: The President spoke at 11:15 a.m. on the South Lawn at the White House.

Statement on Unfunded Federal Mandates Reform Legislation
October 4, 1994

I want to state today my continued support for efforts by Congress to restore balance to the intergovernmental partnership between the Federal Government and State, local, and tribal governments. Since my days as Governor of Arkansas, I have spoken out on the need to address the burgeoning growth of Federal unfunded mandates. As President, I have taken action to resolve this problem within the executive branch by issuing Executive Order 12875, "Enhancing the Intergovernmental Partnership."

However, more needs to be done. Therefore, I want to reiterate my endorsement of and strongly encourage the Congress to send to my desk before the session ends, the bipartisan "Federal Mandate Accountability and Reform Act of 1994." This legislation, drafted by Senator Glenn and Senator Kempthorne in close consultation with my administration, will curtail the imposition of Federal mandates on State, local, and tribal governments without adequate Federal funding and will promote informed and deliberate decisions by Congress on the appropriateness of Federal requirements in any particular instances.

Nomination for the Defense Base Closure and Realignment Commission
October 4, 1994

The President today intends to nominate Alan Dixon, former U.S. Senator of Illinois, to be Chairman of the Defense Base Closure and Realignment Commission.

"I am pleased to nominate Alan Dixon to the Defense Base Closure and Realignment Commission. His record of dedicated public service, extensive background in defense matters, and tested leadership will contribute greatly to the valuable work of this Commission," the President said. "I look forward to his confirmation."

NOTE: A biography of the nominee was made available by the Office of the Press Secretary.

Appointment for the President's Committee on Mental Retardation
October 4, 1994

The President today announced his intention to appoint the final eight members to the President's Committee on Mental Retardation. The appointees are Gisselle Acevedo Franco, Tom Smith, Robert Dinerstein, Cathy Ficker Terrill, Deborah Spitalnik, Lorenzo Aguilar-Melancon, Ruth Luckasson, and Virginia Williams.

"We have now assembled a strong and dynamic group of advocates, self advocates, family members and professionals who share our common vision of moving from exclusion to inclusion, from dependence to independence, from paternalism to empowerment," the President said. "I look forward to the leadership that these dedicated appointees will provide to the committee."

NOTE: Biographies of the appointees were made available by the Office of the Press Secretary.

Remarks at a State Dinner for President Nelson Mandela of South Africa
October 4, 1994

President Mandela, members of the South African delegation, distinguished guests, my fellow Americans. Mr. President, the American people welcome you to the White House on this, the occasion of your first state visit to the United States. You've been an inspiration to the American people. You have been a genuine inspiration to the American people and to freedom-loving people around the world, people who still marvel at the price you paid for your conviction, a conviction that our country embraces but still struggles to live up to, the conviction that all men and women are created equal and therefore ought to have a chance to live up to the fullest of their God-given potential and to have an equal say in the affairs of their land.

Your captivity symbolized the larger captivity of your nation, shackled to the chains of prejudice, bigotry, and hatred. And your release also freed your nation and all its people to reach their full potential, a quest too long and so cruelly denied.

But your story, thankfully, for all South Africans and for the rest of us as well, does not end with your freedom; it continues into what you have sought to do with your freedom. Because you've found within you the strength to reconcile, to unite, to make whole a country too long divided, you are giving real life to the magnificent words that begin the Freedom Charter you helped to draft nearly 40 years ago: "South Africa belongs to all who live in it, black and white."

Now, instead of focusing on the past 342 years, when South Africa did not belong to all who lived in it, you are building a future of trust and tolerance. White South Africans might have fled in fear of retribution, but instead, they have had the courage to stay and to join you in building a new future for all the people of your land. I would say to a world too often torn apart by racial and ethnic and religious strife: Watch South Africa as it comes together, and follow South Africa's example.

As an American, and as a child of the southern part of our country who grew up in a segregated environment and saw firsthand its horror and its debasement of all of us who lived in it, I must add that, as you well know, Mr. President, your presence here has special significance for Americans. We have been especially drawn to the problems and the promise of South Africa. We have struggled, and continue to struggle, with our own racial challenges. So we rejoice, especially, in what you have accomplished, and we hold it out. And as we hold it out as an example to others, so we also hold it out as an example to ourselves.

Mr. President, I know how proud you are to have your daughter, Zinzi, with you on this trip, and I am proud to have her as my dinner partner tonight. I know that during your years in captivity you were a prodigious letter writer and your daughter was one of your favorite correspondents, not least because of her own writing talent. In one letter, written from your cell at Robben Island Prison, you counseled her as follows: "While you have every reason to be angry with the fates for the setbacks you may have suffered from time to time, you must vow"—excuse me. Let me read it again; it's so beautiful, it shouldn't be marred by my voice. "While you have every reason to be angry with the fates for the setbacks you may have suffered from time to time, you must vow to turn those misfortunes into victory. There are few misfortunes in this world you cannot turn into personal triumph if you have the iron will and the necessary skill."

President Mandela, you have shown us the iron will and the necessary skill. And I might add, you have done it with genuine compassion for others. We are honored by your presence here. We are honored by the promise that your leadership offers your country. We are committed to your success and proud of the partnership we have already established.

And so I ask all my fellow Americans to raise their glasses to you and to all those who have led South Africa into the bright light of freedom.

NOTE: The President spoke at 8:50 p.m. in the East Room at the White House.

Remarks at a Congressional Black Caucus Luncheon for President Nelson Mandela of South Africa
October 5, 1994

Good afternoon, ladies and gentlemen. Mr. President, Members of Congress, ladies and gentlemen, welcome to the White House. Welcome to this occasion marking what Martin Luther King once called "a joyous daybreak to end the long night of captivity."

Most of you in this room, through your prayers and your actions, helped to keep freedom's flame lit during the dark night of apartheid in South Africa. Now here we are: South Africa is free; Nelson Mandela is President. Some dreams really do come true.

We are also here because of our own ongoing struggle against racism and intolerance and division. Over the years South Africans and Americans have shared ideas and drawn strength from one another. The NAACP was founded just a few months before the African National Congress, and close bonds were forged between two of the greatest leaders our two countries have produced, Nobel Prize winners Albert Luthuli and Dr. King.

Over the years Americans raised a powerful, unified voice for justice and change in South Africa that would not go unheard. A diverse coalition spread the word: churches, universities, human rights organizations; ultimately, banks, businesses, cities, and State governments. The tools they wielded, cultural and economic sanctions, divestment, international isolation, ultimately helped to force the apartheid regime to end more than four decades of repression.

At the center of this movement stood the Congressional Black Caucus. The caucus helped to raise the consciousness of all Americans to the terrible injustice of apartheid, and it consistently acted upon a deep-rooted commitment to South Africa's freedom. Representative Ron Dellums introduced the first antiapartheid legislation in 1972, the year the CBC was founded. It took 14 more years, the unbending will of the CBC, and ultimately the willingness of Congress to override a veto. But you persevered, you prevailed. And today we can say, South Africa's triumph is your triumph, too. And we thank you.

Now that freedom and democracy have won, they must be nurtured. And that is the ultimate purpose of President Mandela's visit to us in the United States. Working with Congress and the private sector, our administration is helping to promote trade with and investment in South Africa, not only for the good of South Africans but in our own interests as well. The private sector, which made its weight felt in the fight against apartheid, must now lead the effort to build a prosperous South Africa. This is not, I say again, about charity. It's about opportunity, opportunity for South Africans, opportunity for Americans.

We must also help South Africa to create jobs, housing, and schools; to improve health care; to fight illiteracy and poverty. These are challenges with which the new South Africa must contend, now and vigorously. And rising to meet them, South Africa will become a model for all of Africa.

Let me add that our concern must not end with South Africa. For all its problems, Africa is a continent of tremendous promise and progress. I reject the Afro-pessimism, as it's been called, that is often expressed around this city. That's why we'll provide some $3 billion to Africa this year, directly and through international organizations, for economic assistance and humanitarian relief; why we've had the first-ever conference on Africa recently that many of you have participated in; why we're working through sustainable development and debt relief, through peacekeeping and conflict resolution, through diplomacy and military conversion, to take advantage of the opportunities for democracy and development on the African Continent.

We owe our new partnership with South Africa to the man I have been privileged to host in Washington this week. President Mandela, by the simple justice of your cause and the powerful force of your example, you have inspired millions of Americans and millions more throughout the world. We are in your debt, not only for what you have done for South Africa but for what you have done for us, for what you have made us believe again about what we might become and what we might do here at home.

Let me close with the words of the poet Jennifer Davis, which she wrote in tribute to Albert Luthuli. They apply equally well to you: "Bounded, you gave us knowledge of freedom; silenced, you taught us how to speak."

President Mandela.

NOTE: The President spoke at 12:46 p.m. in the State Dining Room at the White House.

Remarks Prior to Discussions With President Nelson Mandela of South Africa
October 5, 1994

Hello, everybody. Let me say very briefly—as you know, President Mandela and I will have statements and answer questions after we have our meeting. But I do want to say again how pleased we are to have him here. This has been both a summit meeting and a celebration for so many Americans who have so strongly supported South African democracy. And now we're in the process of working on the future, planning for the future, and seeing what we can do to be of help.

And I'm looking forward to this meeting. And as I said, we'll be glad to answer your questions after it occurs.

NOTE: The President spoke at 2:30 p.m. in the Oval Office at the White House. A tape was not available for verification of the content of these remarks.

The President's News Conference With President Nelson Mandela of South Africa
October 5, 1994

President Clinton. Ladies and gentlemen, for the last 2 days, President Mandela and I, joined by the American people, have celebrated freedom and democracy in South Africa. We also have begun to assume our historic opportunity to join with the people of South Africa to ensure that their new democracy grows stronger.

Since before President Mandela's election, the United States has played an aggressive role in helping South Africa to shape its democratic future. We supported that historic balloting with $35 million in aid. Following the elections we reaffirmed our commitment with a $600 million trade and investment package. In the 5 months since then, we have already delivered $220 million of that package. Americans have always invested, and will invest more, in private capital in South Africa to help that country's economy grow.

We have moved forward on a range of issues, and let me just mention a few of the new initiatives within our aid program. First, we will form a joint binational commission to promote cooperation between our nations. Vice President Gore will lead this commission, along with Deputy President Mbeki. This is important to America. Russia is the only other country with which we have such a commission. The commission will give a high-level boost to projects involving energy, education, and development.

Second, to help heal the legacies of apartheid, American loans will be used to guarantee nearly a half-billion dollars of new housing in South Africa. We will also contribute $50 million to help bring electricity to the townships and $30 million to support basic health care.

We are taking several actions to help advance President Mandela's goal of expanding trade and investment. The Overseas Private Investment Corporation is launching its second $75 million fund to promote investment in South Africa. Commerce Secretary Ron Brown has created, with his South African counterpart, the U.S.-South Africa Business Development Committee. It will seek to expand the $4 billion trade which already exists between our countries. We will also promote private-sector participation in a conference the South Africans are hosting in early 1995 to support the nation's pragmatic program for reconstruction and development.

Mr. President, yesterday you asked for our geniuses to help to build your land. Today I can tell you we're going to send you some of our best. The Peace Corps will establish a presence in South Africa next year, and we are prepared to help you to develop, through Peace Corps volunteers, small enterprises to train nurses and teachers, to create South Africa's own volunteer corps.

President Mandela and I also discussed other issues, ranging from educational exchange programs promoted by the USIA, to rural development and school lunch programs developed with the leadership of Secretary Espy, to cooperation in the battle against drug trafficking under the leadership of our Drug Policy Director, Lee Brown, who's just returned from South Africa, to building roads and highways, to energy projects which Secretary O'Leary is working on.

President Mandela and I discussed, finally, the broader problems of southern Africa. I salute President Mandela not only for the remarkable work he has done within his own country; his leadership has also been instrumental in resolving crises in Mozambique and Lesotho. He's played a vital role in trying to solve the conflict in Angola, as well.

To help the entire region, we're establishing a $100 million development fund for all of southern Africa. I'm happy to welcome today to the White House Ambassadors from 10 of those countries. And I'm also pleased to announce that Ambassador Andrew Young, who has long worked to improve conditions in the region, has agreed to chair this fund.

The new South Africa, with Nelson Mandela's wise leadership, has won the fight for freedom. Now it stands at the crossroads of hope. The problems it has inherited, the old and deep wounds of apartheid, are not small ones. But President Mandela, you can be certain that the United States will continue to do everything in our power to support the new nation you and your South African people have created and now seek so strongly to build. After a half century of struggle, you've proved to people on every continent that justice and reconciliation can prevail. In a world where too many tear down, you and the South African people have proved that there are those who build up and create. You have shown us the way, and we look forward, sir, to walking down the road with you.

President Mandela. It would be remiss of me to use this opportunity to express my gratitude and that of my delegation for the hospitality that has been extended to us during our visit to the United States. I think I missed out the word "not." I should have said, it would be remiss of me not to use this opportunity—[*laughter*]—to express my gratitude and that of my delegation for the hospitality that has been extended to us during our visit to the United States.

I hope journalists will report the second version of my statement. [*Laughter*]

A special note of thanks should go to my good friend Bill Clinton. The level of engagement by the United States in South Africa is largely attributable to the personal interest that Bill Clinton and his administration have in ensuring that Africa does not become a forgotten continent. The recently organized White House Conference on Africa is evidence of this. We are particularly appreciative of the sensitivity and willingness to assist that has been shown by the Clinton administration. Powerful leaders with a common touch are in great demand in the world today. President Clinton is one of these.

It goes without saying that a great deal has happened in the world, and particularly in South Africa, in the 15 months since I last had the occasion of addressing remarks to the media after meeting President Clinton here at the White House. During that earlier meeting, President Clinton and I agreed on the importance of underpinning the political changes that occurred in South Africa with economic reconstruction. The government of national unity has to demonstrate to our communities disadvantaged by apartheid that democracy has tangible economic as well a political benefits. We can only accomplish this by improving the material well-being of our disadvantaged communities through economic growth and the promotion of increased trade and investment.

You will no doubt have noticed that this has been a recurring theme during my visit here. In this regard, I am highly appreciative of efforts by President Clinton to encourage American trade with and investment in South Africa and for the support that has been pledged for our reconstruction and redevelopment program. Success will not only underpin the consolidation of democracy in South Africa but will also enable South Africa to play its role as the powerhouse of the South African region in a mutually beneficial partnership with our South African Development Community neighbors.

South Africa, and no doubt our neighbors too, welcome continued U.S. engagement in the region. The announcement that the United States Government-sponsored South Africa Enterprise Development Fund will promote small to medium sized business enterprises throughout the region is tangible evidence of this. I believe that the whole South African region, and Africa, in general, can also benefit from these efforts.

South Africa's transition to democracy has created an historic opportunity for South Africa to play its rightful role for the first time on the world stage. Resuming our place in the international arena has been a challenging experience, none more so than rejoining world and regional bodies promoting world peace, democracy, and human rights and participating in humanitarian relief operations in Africa, the most recent being Rwanda. The United States and, indeed, all countries that participated in making the efforts in Rwanda a success are to be commended. This helped to avert a human tragedy.

We attach significance to the crucial role that the United States can play in the promotion of democracy and human rights worldwide. South Africa will undoubtedly be called upon to participate in United Nations peacekeeping missions. We will not be found wanting, within the constraints imposed by budgetary and other considerations. In addition to humanitarian aid, another area which warrants further consideration by the South African Government is the provision of such nonmilitary assistance as is monetary.

There is already a great deal of commonality in the goals and interests of South Africa and the United States, ranging from the promotion of human rights and the strengthening of democracy, to the nonproliferation of weapons of mass destruction. Coupled with active U.S. engagement in South Africa, this partnership can only grow from strength to strength.

There are many areas in which practical relations are unfolding, such as joint and structured efforts to mobilize funds for investments in and trade with South Africa, cooperation in dealing with environmental issues, increased aid to South Africa in the context of our reconstruction and development program, and lastly, assistance by the United States in restructuring the judicial system in South Africa as part of broader efforts to strengthen democracy and deepen the culture of human rights.

I thank you.

President Clinton. Let me say, if I might, before the question, we would like to alternate between American and South African journalists. And so President Mandela will call on the next journalist. So those of you from South Africa, or representing South Africa media outlets, we will hear from you next. And then we'll alternate back and forth.

Haiti

Q. I believe you both share an interest in Haiti, and I'd like to ask you about that. Increasingly, American officials say that they expect General Cédras and his chief of staff to leave Haiti by October 15th. General Cédras says that he's not going to leave. Why are American officials so confident that they will leave? And will American troops make life unpleasant for them if they stay?

President Clinton. Well, let me say, first of all, I have left that question to the Haitians to resolve, as you know. The important thing for the American people is that the situation with great difficulty has remained calm overall, that Parliament has reopened and is considering amnesty and other things, that the mayor of Port-au-Prince, Evans Paul, has come back to his responsibilities after years of hiding, that we've turned the lights back on in Cap Haitien and there's more electricity available in Port-au-Prince, that almost 1,500 refugees have left Guantanamo and gone back to Haiti. President Aristide now has a transition office—I remember those—in Port-au-Prince. And General

Shelton and our military people there, I think, have done a superb job under difficult circumstances. They are working through that. The political questions in large measure involve what the Haitians decide themselves. I was very, very impressed with President Aristide's most recent speech, and I'm very committed to continuing on the course we're on.

That's all I know to say. I feel very good about where we're going. I think we'll wind up in a good place if we just stay steady and realize that our young men and women down there are doing a terrific job under difficult circumstances. Their work is certainly not free of danger, but you have to give them credit, I think, so far for the work they have done.

Mr. President—President Mandela, would you like to call on one of the South African journalists?

President Mandela. Yes.

South Africa-U.S. Trade

Q. President Mandela, did you ask President Clinton if he would lift U.S. restrictions on trade with South Africa, in particular the denial order on the Rooivalk helicopter deal?

President Mandela. Well, we have discussed this matter both with Mr. Clinton alone and also with his delegation. The President has shown a great deal of sensitivity towards this question, and he has undertaken to do what he can to resolve this problem. I have confidence that if he has a chance to assist in this regard, he will do so.

President Clinton. Jill [Jill Dougherty, Cable News Network].

Haiti

Q. Mr. President, President Aristide reportedly is resisting signing an agreement that would define the status of U.S. troops and what their mission is in Haiti. Is that the case, and does this create a danger that the mission could be ill-defined or spread farther than it should?

President Clinton. Well, no agreement has yet been signed. But I wouldn't let that concern you too much. We think the mission is clearly defined in terms of scope and time. We always knew there would have to be some flexibility in the early weeks until we got the police monitors in and until we began to retrain people to assume police and military roles, and that the nature of the mission would depend upon three things: to what extent the police were

willing to stay at their posts and observe the rules of professional encounter; second, to what extent things beyond our control would occur; and third, how quickly we could get the training programs up and going.

So there has been—there has had to be some flexibility there. But essentially, we are on the same mission that we went there with. We're going to stay with that mission, and we're going to complete it, turn it over to the U.N., and bring our people home. And whether and exactly how we work out an understanding with President Aristide, particularly after he reassumes authority, I think will be something that will not present insurmountable obstacles. And I feel comfortable that the American people will be comfortable with the definition of the mission just as it is, and I'm not particularly worried about that.

Mr. President.

President Mandela. Can I make an appeal that in view of the interest in this question, could we deal with it if any South African journalist would like to put the question, so that we can put it at rest for the purpose of this press conference.

Yes.

Q. President Mandela, President Clinton apparently asked you in the past to perhaps send South African troops to help in the police efforts in Haiti. Have you made a decision to send South African troops to Haiti? Will they be part of the peacekeeping mission?

President Mandela. Our attitude on this question is that the operation, which is essentially a United Nations operation although it has been carried out at this stage by American troops, that operation is intended to restore democracy in that country, a worthy objective which we fully support.

Secondly, without in any way prescribing to the leadership of Haiti, we sincerely hope that they will realize the crucial importance of national reconciliation and to heal the wounds of the past by involving all the parties which may have been at cross purposes with one another.

Now, as far as our own participation is concerned, we regard this, as I say, as an operation of the United Nations of which we are a part. But we are busy discussing the matter. And we are keen to act and not unilaterally as South Africa; we are keen to act collectively as a region, especially because we have a tradition which we have to change of our country having been involved in the military destabilization of our neighboring states and economic sabotage. If we're involved in an operation anywhere in the world, we would like this to be a collective decision from our region. And therefore, we are now busy with consultations on this question——

President Clinton. Rita [Rita Braver, CBS News].

President Mandela. ——and will come back to the President in due course.

President Clinton. Thank you, sir.

GATT

Q. President Clinton, while you have been meeting with President Mandela, it looks like there's been another hangup in GATT. It seems to be once again slowed down. Do you still have the confidence that you had last week when we talked to you that this will go through? And why do you think you're having so much trouble with it?

President Clinton. The people that are holding it up now are people who have always supported the GATT. Let me just say that, first of all, I won't know until sometime tonight—I think they're going to have a vote or at least consider having a vote on the rule in the House on the GATT. I've never come to the end of a full congressional session before, so for all I know this often happens.

But there's still time for Congress to act on this, for the House to act on GATT, for the Senate to act on lobby reform, on the elementary and secondary education act, on the Superfund legislation, which has the support of everybody from the chemical companies to the Sierra Club. There is no one against it anymore. It's an important piece of legislation. I can't imagine why it shouldn't pass. So I'm hopeful that it will.

The GATT, it has always been a bipartisan issue. It's a huge job-gainer for America, just like NAFTA was, except more so over the long run. And it's the biggest world tax cut in history. It's over a $700 billion tax cut. So I think, as we get closer to it, I would expect the people who have always supported it to support it and there to be a majority support for it. We'll continue to push it.

Haiti and South Africa

Q. President Mandela, a question for you and then a question to President Clinton. First of all, we understand that you might be meeting President Aristide or deposed President Aristide tomorrow. If that is happening, how will that change South Africa's stand towards what you have just described as consultation at the moment about Haiti?

And secondly, President Clinton, when are you coming to South Africa?

President Mandela. Well, the consultations that we are having are not going to be directly affected by my meeting with President Aristide. I do not know, of course, what he is going to raise with me, but I know what I am going to say to him. [*Laughter*] And so it is premature for me to answer your question fully. We will be going back to South Africa—if I don't meet you after this meeting, I'll brief you fully as to what the President will say to me. [*Laughter*]

President Clinton. Let me say, first of all— I'll answer the other question, but first of all, I am personally very grateful to President Mandela for making time in what has been an unbelievably busy schedule to see President Aristide. The most important thing South Africa can do for Haiti has been accomplished by President Mandela coming to the United States at this historic moment and then, on top of that, agreeing to meet with President Aristide. Why? Because here is President Mandela and here is President Mandela's delegation. And the Haitian people will see that you can bring a country where there have been deep, even bloody divisions together and work together in a spirit of freedom, reconciliation, democracy, and mutual respect. It must be very encouraging to President Aristide; it also should be very encouraging to those who have opposed him.

So this is—I assure you that this was not planned or calibrated in terms of the action the United States took there. But as it happens, this is a very good thing for the cause of democracy in Haiti.

Secondly, the President, as you know, has invited me to South Africa very publicly and also privately. I would like very much to go. I hope I can go there. I have made no final commitments on travel outside the United States for next year, so I can't announce a commitment now, but I would like to do it very much. We're proud of our association with your country, and we hope we can do more.

Thank you very much.

President Mandela. Can I just add that I have met President Aristide twice, and I have discovered that he has a very serious weakness, which I intend to exploit to the full: He is a man who can think. He is flexible. He is broad-minded. And I have no doubt that if I put a reasonable argument with him, I am unlikely to come out with empty hands. That I can say to you.

President Clinton. Thank you very much. Thank you.

NOTE: The President's 72d news conference began at 3:43 p.m. on the South Lawn at the White House.

Statement on Signing the National Defense Authorization Act for Fiscal Year 1995
October 5, 1994

Today I have signed into law S. 2182, the "National Defense Authorization Act for Fiscal Year 1995." This Act authorizes appropriations for Department of Defense and Department of Energy national security activities and extends and amends other programs. This Act, which authorizes most of the Administration's major defense priorities, will provide for a continuing strong national defense during fiscal year 1995.

In signing this Act, it is important to clarify the interpretation of several provisions related to the President's authority and responsibility in the area of foreign affairs.

First, with respect to section 1404, which relates to Bosnia and Herzegovina, I note that the language on international policy leaves flexibility to calibrate our actions as events develop. Similarly, the provisions on reporting to and consulting with the Congress on training and the unilateral termination of the Bosnia arms embargo leave flexibility to determine the content of these reports and consultations and the extent to which such proposals would be implemented. This flexibility is critical for ensuring that the United States remains in a position to react to developments in the manner that best serves our Nation's interests.

Moreover, with respect to the provision on use of funds, I note that the limitation in section 1404(f)(2) applies only when appropriated funds are used "for the purpose" described therein. I sign the bill with the understanding that it therefore would not affect the United States' ability to participate in activities in the Adriatic that are needed in order to avoid impeding enforcement of sanctions against Serbia, or for other purposes, even if doing so provides indirect or incidental support or assistance for the

embargo. Also, I further understand that the waiver authority in paragraph (3)(A) applies to U.S. military personnel serving in headquarters positions for NATO's Supreme Allied Commander, the Commander in Chief, Allied Forces Southern Europe, and subordinate headquarters staffs, such as those for the Commander, Joint Task Force Provide Promise and his subordinate headquarters staffs.

To the extent that section 1404 could be construed to require the President or other executive branch officers or employees to espouse or refrain from espousing certain substantive positions, it would be inconsistent with my constitutional authority for the conduct of foreign affairs. I will accordingly interpret the provision as not applicable to efforts that are diplomatic in nature.

In the Classified Annex, incorporated into S. 2182 by reference, section 101 directs that the Secretary of Defense provide a weekly National Operations Summary to the Committees on Armed Services of the House and Senate. Implementation of this provision must be consistent with my constitutional authority as Commander in Chief and my constitutional responsibility for the conduct of foreign affairs. While I understand the interest of the two Defense oversight committees in receiving this sensitive information, there are questions of scope that need to be resolved. In this regard, I note that the joint explanatory statement of the conferees indicates their intent to provide maximum flexibility to the Department of Defense and the committees to work out the details of the content of the National Operations Summary.

I also point out that section 232, relating to modifications to the Anti-Ballistic Missile Treaty, cannot restrict the constitutional options for congressional approval of substantive modifications of treaties.

Finally, I note that section 1304 could be interpreted as specifically directing the President how to proceed in negotiations with European countries regarding cost-sharing arrangements for U.S. military installations in host nations. I support the policy underlying section 1304 to encourage these countries to increase their contributions, direct and indirect, of the

nonpersonnel costs described in the provision. However, my constitutional authority over foreign affairs necessarily entails discretion over these and similar matters.

WILLIAM J. CLINTON

The White House,
October 5, 1994.

NOTE: S. 2182, approved October 5, was assigned Public Law No. 103–337.

Statement on Senate Action on Education Legislation
October 5, 1994

I am gratified by the broad bipartisan support in the Senate for final passage of the elementary and secondary education act (ESEA). This act is good news for students, teachers, families, and communities across our country. It represents a commitment to world-class standards of academic achievements for all students and to adequate preparation for every teacher. It brings added help to the schools that need it the most and offers new flexibility to States and local communities. It reinforces our national commitment to schools that are safe and drug-free and that offer young people a disciplined environment for learning. It encourages parental involvement in the education of their children. And it puts the Federal Government squarely on the side of public school choice, innovative charter schools, and character education.

Final passage of the ESEA is the capstone of 2 years of efforts to improve the entire system of lifelong learning. In an economy in which, more and more, what we earn depends upon what we learn, these efforts are the key to our future. Head Start reform, national goals for elementary and secondary education, new bridges between schools and workplaces, national and community service that allows citizens to help their country while expanding educational opportunity, loan reform that lowers costs and allows students to repay their debts as a percentage of income over time—these reforms mean increased opportunity, a more productive economy, and a more inclusive society. Future generations will look back on this period as years of historic accomplishment that began the task of renewing our Nation by investing in our people.

Statement on Unfunded Federal Mandates Reform Legislation
October 5, 1994

I want to commend Chairman John Conyers and the House Government Operations Committee for adopting today the bipartisan "Federal Mandate Relief for State and Local Government Act of 1994" (H.R. 5128). This legislation, which I strongly support, will control the growth

of Federal unfunded mandates and restore balance to the intergovernmental partnership between the Federal Government and State, local, and tribal governments. I encourage the House of Representatives to act on this legislation expeditiously.

Letter to Congressional Leaders Transmitting a Report on Vietnam
October 5, 1994

Dear Mr. Speaker: (Dear Mr. President:)

Pursuant to the authority vested in me by section 522 of the Foreign Relations Authorization Act, Fiscal Years 1994 and 1995 (Public Law 103–236), I hereby transmit the attached report on Sanctions on Vietnam.

Sincerely,

WILLIAM J. CLINTON

NOTE: Identical letters were sent to Thomas S. Foley, Speaker of the House of Representatives, and Albert Gore, Jr., President of the Senate.

Nomination for the Federal Trade Commission
October 5, 1994

The President today announced that he has nominated Christine Varney of the District of Columbia as a member of the Federal Trade Commission (FTC).

"I have thoroughly enjoyed working with Christine these past 20 months, and I am delighted to nominate her to the FTC," the President said. "Her commitment to public service and firsthand experience in the areas of trade and regulation will serve the Commission well. I look forward to her confirmation."

NOTE: A biography of the nominee was made available by the Office of the Press Secretary.

Nomination for United States District Court Judges
October 5, 1994

The President today nominated three individuals to serve on the U.S. District Court: Lacy H. Thornburg for the Western District of North Carolina; and David Folsom and Thadd Heartfield for the Eastern District of Texas.

"These individuals have records of achievement in public service and the legal profession," the President said. "I am confident that they will continue to distinguish themselves as members of the Federal judiciary."

NOTE: Biographies of the nominees were made available by the Office of the Press Secretary.

Remarks at a Reception for the Africa Prize for Leadership for the Sustainable End of Hunger
October 5, 1994

Thank you so very much for that warm welcome. I've had a great 2 days; I like being on Nelson Mandela's coattails.

I was sitting there listening to the Secretary of Commerce introduce me, and it got more and more and more generous. And for a mo-

ment, I was almost carried away. Then I remembered what a sterling example that was of Clinton's third law of politics, which is, whenever possible, be introduced by someone you've appointed to high office. [*Laughter*] I am delighted to be here with President Mandela, Her

Majesty Queen Noor, Mr. Secretary-General, Mr. Kakizawa, Madam President, Mr. Chester, Chief Anyaoku, and all of you. I want to say a serious word of thanks to Ron Brown not only for his introduction but for the work he has already begun to do with his counterpart in South Africa, with the U.S.-South Africa Business Development Committee, with the work he has done all across the world to promote the interest of our country. I think it is no exaggeration to say, as many business people of both parties have said to me, that he is the finest Secretary of Commerce in decades; and we appreciate him very much.

Secretary Brown and several of you whom I see here, along with the Vice President and Mrs. Gore and the First Lady, were part of the delegation that represented the United States and the President at the swearing-in of President Mandela last spring. It was a triumphant moment for him and for his country. To see someone who had sacrificed so much for so long in the fight for freedom finally wind up in the driver's seat really made all of us believe, as I said today to the Congressional Black Caucus, that some dreams really do come true.

I think it important to say, as I felt again today when President Mandela and I were at our press conference and I looked at him there with his delegation from all segments of South African society, that his victory was a victory for all South Africans, without regard to race or political party, for they were all freed of the oppression, they were all freed of the division, they were all freed of apartheid. It made slaves of them all, and now they are all free.

I'm honored to be here with you tonight because of this award you have given so deservingly to the President. Clearly as South Africans go forward, they face many, many challenges, the legacy of over three centuries of apartheid, the challenge of illiteracy, the challenge of homelessness, the challenge of joblessness, the challenge to improve the health care system. But one of the most profound challenges, clearly, is the challenge of hunger. Perhaps America's greatest champion of this cause in recent history was the late Congressman Mickey Leland, who was a good friend of mine. He was once asked what a guy from Texas was doing spending so much time trying to end hunger in Africa. And he said, and I quote, "I'm as much a citizen of this world as I am of my country."

Clearly, that applies with equal force to many of you who are here tonight, explains why you're so devoted to this project and why your work is so important. Your programs have made us more aware of the persistence of starvation in all corners of the globe. Already you are helping people in more than 25 nations to help themselves to end their hunger and, as you say in your prize here, on a sustainable basis. The United States is in your debt for your work.

Now President Mandela, having won the victory of freedom, must see that it bears fruit. And all of us must do what we can to see that he succeeds. As we work to support his efforts and the efforts of all South Africans to build a new nation, we know that dealing with hunger is an important part of their mission.

In my meetings with President Mandela this week, we outlined the steps we would take to increase our strong support for South Africa, including helping to fight the problem of hunger. We will support South Africa's plans for nutrition programs, for school lunch programs, for land reforms, for expansion of clean water and sanitation efforts, for rural development. Peace Corps volunteers will help to provide assistance with agriculture and food production projects. We know that the people of America must act on the pride and the stirrings that were awakened in us by what has occurred in South Africa. We know that we cannot confine our attention to South Africa alone, that we have for too long in this Nation ignored the vast potential as well as the solvable problems of the African Continent.

Our country has shown its concern by the actions we took in Somalia, the work we have done so recently in Rwanda, by the conference on Africa which we held at the White House recently, by all the things that we are trying to do to heighten the awareness of the problems and promise of Africa here in the United States.

We are also committed to work on trying to avert some tragedies before they occur. Most recently, we have worked a lot on planning what we might do to avert what many predict will be a terrible crisis in the Horn of Africa. This is the sort of thing the United States ought to be doing. It will make us a better partner with the Hunger Project because we cannot approach Africa without dealing with this issue.

I have said from the beginning of my administration that our mission in the world was to promote freedom and democracy, that that

1707

would increase our own security because free people with democratic governments do not have time or the inclination to go to war with each other, to break their word, or to otherwise meddle in things that undermine human potential. They are always too busy trying to increase the human potential of those whom they represent. But it has been said that a hungry man is not a free man. So if we seek freedom and democracy, we must first also seek to meet the basic needs that God meant for all people to have met in this world, wherever they live, whatever their race, whatever their station, especially the children.

Let me say to you that I have had a marvelous time with President Mandela. We have talked about a lot of things. We have told stories. One of the things that I find that our cultures have in common is the compulsion of its politicians to tell good jokes, often on themselves. [Laughter] We've even discussed the history of boxing in the world over the last 60 years, something the President knows a good deal more about than I do, although I knew enough to keep up.

Let me close with this thought. Nelson Mandela, perhaps his most remarkable achievement was that he spent 27 years as a prisoner and came out the freest of all people.

And so I say to you, Mr. President, as we part for the last time and I go about my business and you go about yours, this morning I awoke before dawn, thinking about the meeting we would have today. And I asked God to free me of all the petty resentments, the negative thoughts, all the things that crowd in on all of us who believe from time to time that life is not exactly as it should be and get frustrated when we cannot make it that way. Because neither I nor anyone else I have ever known has ever faced the spiritual crisis you must have faced so many times, and with each succeeding week and month and year, you reached deeper and deeper and deeper in yourself for the ultimate truth. As you have fed your spirit, let us feed the world.

Congratulations, sir, and thank you.

NOTE: The President spoke at 6:56 p.m. at the Omni Shoreham Hotel. In his remarks, he referred to Queen Noor of Jordan, member, and Robert Chester, chair, board of directors, The Hunger Project; former United Nations Secretary-General Javier Perez de Cuellar, chairman, and Koji Kakizawa, member, Africa Prize international jury; Joan Holmes, president, The Hunger Project; and Emeka Anyaoku, Secretary General of the British Commonwealth.

Remarks at the Senator George Mitchell Scholarship Fund Dinner
October 5, 1994

Thank you very much. Senator Cohen, Senator Dole, Senator Mitchell, my fellow Americans. I've already heard enough tonight to build the speeches for the next year on. [Laughter]

First of all, I come here in all sincerity to say that I believe if the decision were made on the merits, Bob Dole and not George Mitchell would be the baseball commissioner, because Bob Dole is much better at keeping his team out on strike. [Laughter] I also have to tell you that I really admire Bill Cohen. They call me Slick Willie—[laughter]—I mean, he's so erudite, you know, he writes all these books—stands up there and smiles at Senator Dole with that little twist of the head and says, "I'm one of those errant ones." That's right, I have gotten one vote out of him in the last 2 years. [Laugh-

ter] Bill's last book was called "Murder in the Senate." The longer I stay here, the more appealing that book gets. [Laughter]

I will never forget the night George Mitchell said he just had to tell me something. I thought he was going to give me another piece of advice, tell me how I was messing up, talk about how we were going to achieve the Elysian Fields. And then he said he wasn't going to run for reelection. It's really—it's not very pleasant to see a grown man cry anytime, especially when it's the President. [Laughter] I begged; I pleaded; I wept. I called him back in the middle of the night, and I got him up, and I thought maybe he would be in a weakened condition, you know, if I woke him up. [Laughter] I have one last idea. I will ask Ken Burns to do a special on the Senate and scrap "Baseball" if Mitchell will stay in the Senate, and then he can be the star. [*Laughter*] And I called Burns about it today. And he said, "I like this. You know," he said, "when I did this baseball thing, it was a retrospective on decade after decade. But I could do one on the Senate in real time, and it would just seem like decade after decade." [*Laughter*]

Well, anyway, I'm about adjusted to the fact that George won't be around next year, but I want to say seriously, I don't believe that any of us would function very well in this town if we tried to do anything on our own. One of the reasons I ran for President is I thought this country was too divided. I thought we needed a greater spirit of partnership. I thought people had either excessive or too restricted notions about the Government and that we didn't work together very well.

Ironically, I was elected to President of this country without knowing the majority leader of the Senate very well. But I could never have asked for a better partner. Last year, despite all the smoke and mirrors and conflict, according to Congressional Quarterly, it was the most successful year of partnership between a President and a Congress since the end of World War II, except for 1953, President Eisenhower's first year, and 1965, President Johnson's first year after his election.

Now, that was in no small measure because of George Mitchell. And there are a lot of things that we can rejoice about, even where we disagreed with the methods. The country's deficit's gone down 2 years in a row for the first time in 20 years, and next year will make 3 years in a row for the first time since Mr. Truman was here. We passed NAFTA. We passed national service, something that I'm convinced may revolutionize America from the grassroots up. We reorganized the student loan program, and now millions of middle class young people can afford to go to college and need not shy away from it. In every State in this country and every community, there is somebody who's got a job or access to an apprenticeship program or a better student loan or a place in a Head Start program or a childhood immunization because of the labors of George Mitchell in the last year and a half alone.

I cannot tell you what it has meant to me to have the honor of working with him on a daily basis. He has this almost magical blend of ability and discipline, of pragmatism and principle, of flexibility and fight. His powers of concentration and persuasion are legion. He really does bring a sense of balance to every debate. No matter how strongly I feel something, if he thinks I'm wrong, I'm afraid to talk to him because I think there's a 90 percent chance he will convince me that I had it all wrong all along. I don't know why he's not that persuasive with Senator Dole. [*Laughter*]

He is truly a leader in the best sense. He has vision. He tries to get things done that he believes are right. He has the skill to do it, but because he's never lost the common touch, he's able to keep the trust and the confidence of the people who sent him here.

You know, I was watching that film, and there was a picture of George along toward the end of the film sitting at a plant in his shirtsleeves, talking to the workers. Now, every one of us who ever ran for office in any State in America has had a picture taken like that. But if you've looked at as many of those films as I have, you can tell the people who went there for the first time when they were in the shot and the people who just do it all the time and would just as soon be there as on the floor of the Senate. George Mitchell is the latter category.

I have made a joke to many of you that of all the Members of Congress, from the freshmen to the most senior, the Republicans and the Democrats, George Mitchell is the only person who never comes to the White House without some young person from his home State in tow. I honestly believe—you know, Maine's not a very big State, and I can appreciate that. Mitchell's been here 14 years; I believe he has personally brought enough people to the White House that he could never be defeated, just because of them, their parents, their spouses, and their siblings. He couldn't lose. I don't know how he's ever had time to go to the meetings; he's always so busy making sure I don't miss my picture with a person from Maine. [*Laughter*] Just this week he was here, and I almost got back in the White House, and I thought, "He forgot." And I was walking to the door, and he said, "Wait a minute, wait a minute, Mr. President. Here's somebody from my home State I want you to meet." [*Laughter*] And it's become a joke between us now. And we're all laughing about it, but I tell you, the most important thing for all of us is to never forget who sent us here. And if you're President in this day and age and you try to do anything, you've got to be willing to be misunderstood from time to time. I often tell people, and I try to actually feel this way every day, that the important thing for us is not what the American people think of us every day but whether we think of them every day. George Mitchell has thought of the people who sent him here every day he has been here for 14 years. I have no doubt of that.

Let me just say one last thing. A lot of the things that we say around here, we say so often that they seem trite-sounding, and then we stop saying them because they lose their feeling. But you cannot be an immigrant's child in this country and become majority leader of the Senate; you cannot rise from the roots that Senator Dole came out of in Russell, Kansas; you can't be somebody like me who had the privilege—and I mean this sincerely—for a brief period in my early childhood to live in a place that didn't have any indoor plumbing, so I never got to forget what other people had to live like, and have the gifts that we have been given without knowing that our primary obligation is not to solve every problem that is before us but to leave this country well enough off that the American dream is still alive for everybody that comes after us.

And that is why this scholarship tonight is so important to me, because you could not do anything for George Mitchell that would be more fitting. It's better than a statue. It's better than a plaque. It's better than an endowment for some other purpose, because what you are doing is giving him a chance in his name to create other George Mitchells, to give other young people a chance to live out their dreams, and to prove that the dream that made him what he is is still alive and real in this country today.

I thank you for that, because I have known very few Americans that remotely embodied the qualities of this country in their purest sense as well as George Mitchell does. And this gift you have given him does that as well.

Ladies and gentlemen, please welcome Senator Mitchell.

NOTE: The President spoke at 9:13 p.m. at the Hyatt Regency Hotel.

Remarks Aboard the U.S.S. *Eisenhower* in Norfolk, Virginia
October 6, 1994

The President. Thank you very much, Secretary Perry, Admiral Miller, Admiral Owens, Admiral Flanagan, Admiral Murphy, Captain Gemmill, and to all of you who are here. It's a great honor for me to be here. I asked to see the person responsible for decorating the F-14 with my name and the Vice President's name there. I guess I'm going to have to take flying lessons.

Audience member. He's right here, Mr. President, Skipper Al Myers.

Comdr. Alan Myers. Al Myers, sir.

The President. Thank you very much. I appreciate it. I told someone to take a picture of that, and I'm going to take it back to the Vice President when I see him this afternoon and suggest that we both take flying lessons. [*Laughter*] Admiral Miller said, "You understand on that plane, you would still control the eject seat." [*Laughter*] And I told him, "I don't be-

lieve in ejecting. I'd never bail out." But I was glad to know that.

I thank you all for your service. I'm pleased and honored to be with you today. I understand that some of you have actually chosen to come back from your leave to be a part of this ceremony, and I'm deeply grateful for yet another expression of your devotion to your country. I am proud of the job you have done, proud of the great work that all of our troops are doing in Haiti. And on behalf of the American people, the most important message I have to you today is a simple, straightforward, heartfelt thank you.

I also want to thank, especially, Captain Gemmill and the crew of this magnificent carrier for the "I Like Ike" button. You know, you may think that's funny, since he was a Republican and I'm a Democrat, but—[*laughter*]—when I was born, President Truman was President. But obviously, I was an infant; I didn't have much consciousness of it. President Eisenhower was elected in the year I went to the first grade, so he was the first President I really ever knew anything about. And all of us, regardless of our party, liked Ike. I can still remember when the country was united in a way that it's not now and when political arguments were a little more civil than they tend to be now. President Eisenhower's life of service to our country and his incredible leadership throughout his military career, culminating in his leadership in World War II and of course ultimately in his election to the Presidency, was an inspiration to me and to every other young American and I know is a continuing inspiration to all of you who are privileged to serve on this great carrier and in this group.

Much has been asked of you, and you have delivered. Thanks to your efforts, the Haitian people are moving from fear to freedom. Thanks to your efforts, the democratically elected government will soon return to power. Thanks to your efforts, the world knows that the United States will stand up for human rights and against slaughter, stand up for democracy, honor our commitments, and expect those who make commitments to us to honor them as well. We gave our word, and you, the men and women of the *Eisenhower* Battle Group, kept the word of the United States. And for that, we are all in your debt.

The stories from Port-au-Prince and elsewhere in Haiti have inspired all Americans. We have seen the moving images of Haitians approaching and thanking American troops for their new-found freedom. We have seen the joy in their eyes and the hope in their faces. Operation Uphold Democracy is not over yet, and you know well that it still presents dangers to the men and women of our Armed Forces.

But look what has happened in less than 3 weeks. In less than 3 weeks, you've disarmed FRAPH, the attachés, and the other militia who terrorized thousands of Haitians. In less than 3 weeks, you took heavy weapons away from the military and made the cities and the towns more secure. In less than 3 weeks, you helped 1,900 refugees return home from Guantanamo, no longer afraid for their lives. In less than 3 weeks, you permitted Parliament once again to open its doors for business. And today, they're having a good, old-fashioned debate down there, about like what happens in Congress every day in Washington. In less than 3 weeks, you re-

turned Port-au-Prince Mayor Evans Paul, a man in hiding in his own country for 3 years, back to his office. In less than 3 weeks, you put state radio and television back into the hands of people who want democracy. In less than 3 weeks, you even turned the lights back on in Cap Haitien after 2 years of darkness. In less than 3 weeks, you showed the world what the men and women of the American military can do.

All of us owe these achievements to the fact that you are the best trained, best prepared, best equipped, most highly motivated fighting force in the world. Your reputation preceded you to Haiti. When the military rulers learned that you were on your way, they agreed to step down. The awesome force you represent is the steel in the sword of America's diplomacy.

The success of the mission in Haiti to date also shows how flexible our military has become. Thanks to careful planning by the U.S. Atlantic Command and the joint task force, we were able to quickly recall the massive assault force that was on its way. In its place, and within just hours of reaching agreement with Mr. Cédras and the other military leaders, we sent in troops, carried by the *Eisenhower* Battle Group, to keep the peace in Haiti.

Operation Uphold Democracy demonstrates the value of mixing our four services together and drawing on the special capabilities of each of them, what Admiral Miller calls adaptive force packaging. You prepared the first-ever infantry air assault from a carrier. Had it not been for such innovation, it would have taken many more hours, if not days, for our troops to be on the ground there. I salute Admiral Miller and the members of his staff who developed this innovative plan, which will change our military planning and make it possible for us to do remarkable things well into the 21st century. You have laid the groundwork for a dramatic forward movement in a military planning and execution. You should be proud, and the Nation owes Admiral Miller and his staff a great deal.

Of course, even the best strategists can only make a difference if they have the resources to do the job. That's why I was pleased yesterday to sign the fiscal year '95 defense authorization bill, which was passed with strong bipartisan support including the support of Virginia's two fine Senators, Chuck Robb and John Warner, and the two able Congressmen from this area, Norm Sisisky and Bobby Scott. This bill will assure that you remain better trained, better equipped, and better prepared than any other military in the world, and I am determined that it will always be that way. [*Applause*] Thank you. I know that one piece of this defense bill will be especially welcome news for all of you, the $3.6 billion we will spend on a new aircraft carrier, CVN–76. That carrier will be built right here in Norfolk by thousands of hard-working Virginians. Like the *Eisenhower*, it will give us the capability to project our power around the world, to support peacekeeping and humanitarian relief missions, and, if necessary, to fight and to win regional conflicts.

In 2 weeks, just 2 weeks, you set sail for the Adriatic, to carry on your work of protecting our country's national interests around the world. I know you will demonstrate the same skill and professionalism on this journey that you have shown in Haiti.

In a few moments, I'll have the distinct honor of presenting Navy commendation medals for meritorious service in Haiti to several of you. But I want every one of you to know that in my book, each and every one of you is a medal winner, an example of what is the very best

in our country. You serve with distinction, you serve in a selfless way, you serve in a way that will help us to build a peaceful and freer and stronger world for yourselves and your children as we move into the next century, and we are all in your debt.

Men and women of the *Ike,* you have proved your capabilities time and again. In Haiti, you brought a new day to a people who thought they would never get it. You answered the call; you did the job; your country is proud of you.

Thank you. God bless you, and God bless America.

NOTE: The President spoke at 11:51 a.m. In his remarks, he referred to Adm. Paul D. Miller, commander in chief, U.S. Atlantic Command; Adm. William A. Owens, USN, Vice Chairman, Joint Chiefs of Staff; Adm. William J. Flanagan, Jr., commander in chief, Atlantic Fleet; Adm. Daniel J. Murphy, Jr., commander, Cruiser Destroyer Group 8; Capt. Mark Gemmill, commanding officer, U.S.S. *Dwight D. Eisenhower*; and Comdr. Alan Myers, commanding officer, Fighter Squadron VF–32, Oceana Naval Air Station, Virginia Beach, VA.

Message to the Congress on North American Free Trade Agreement Transportation Provisions Concerning Mexican Motor Carriers
October 6, 1994

To the Congress of the United States:

In November 1993, in preparation for the implementation of the North American Free Trade Agreement (NAFTA) on January 1, 1994, I informed the Congress of my intent to modify the moratorium on the issuance of certificates of operating authority to Mexican-owned or -controlled motor carriers that was imposed by the Bus Regulatory Reform Act of 1982 (49 U.S.C. 10922(l)(2)(A)). The modification applied to Mexican charter and tour bus operations. At that time, I also informed the Congress that I would be notifying it of additional modifications to the moratorium with respect to Mexican operations as we continued to implement NAFTA's transportation provisions. In this regard, it is now my intention to further modify the moratorium to allow Mexican small package delivery services to operate in the United States provided that

Mexico implements its NAFTA obligation to provide national treatment to U.S. small package delivery companies.

Prior to its implementation of the NAFTA, Mexico limited foreign-owned small package delivery services, such as that offered by United Parcel Service and Federal Express, to trucks approximately the size of a minivan. This made intercity service impractical and effectively limited small-package delivery companies to intracity service only. Mexico has no similar restriction on the size of trucks used by Mexican small package delivery services. Because Mexico did not take a reservation in this area, the NAFTA obligates Mexico to extend national treatment to U.S. small package and messenger service companies. Mexico must allow U.S. small package delivery services to use the same size trucks that Mexican small package delivery companies are permitted to use.

Mexico, earlier this year, enacted legislation that addresses the small package delivery issue. Amendments to the *Law on Roads, Bridges, and Federal Motor Carriers* authorize parcel delivery and messenger services to operate without restriction so long as they obtain a permit from the Secretariat of Communications and Transportation and direct that such permits be granted in a timely fashion. The law includes no restrictions on the size and weight of parcels nor on the dimensions of the vehicles that small package delivery services will be permitted to use.

At the North American Transportation Summit hosted by the United States on April 29, 1994, Mexico's Secretary of Communications and Transportation Emilio Gamboa reaffirmed his government's commitment to permit unrestricted operations by foreign-owned providers of small package delivery services in Mexico. In return, even though the United States does not have a similar obligation under the NAFTA, Secretary of Transportation Federico Peña stated the United States Government's intention to grant Mexican small package delivery service companies reciprocal operating rights in the United States by modifying the moratorium imposed by the Bus Regulatory Reform Act. Mexico and the United States agreed to establish a joint working group to specify the details of this arrangement by September 1, 1994.

The U.S. small package delivery service industry is supportive of United States Government efforts to eliminate Mexico's restrictions on small package delivery operations. Provided Mexico implements its NAFTA obligation to extend national treatment to U.S. small package delivery companies, the U.S. industry would not object to a modification of the moratorium that would provide Mexican small package delivery companies reciprocal treatment in the United States.

Provided that Mexico meets its NAFTA-imposed national treatment obligation to allow U.S.-owned small package delivery services unrestricted operations, I intend, pursuant to section 6 of the Bus Regulatory Reform Act, to modify the moratorium imposed by that section to permit Mexican small package delivery services to operate in the United States in exactly the same manner and to exactly the same extent that U.S. small package delivery services will be permitted to operate in Mexico. The Bus Regulatory Reform Act requires 60 days' advance notice to the Congress of my intention to modify or remove the moratorium. With this message, I am providing the advance notice so required.

WILLIAM J. CLINTON

The White House,
October 6, 1994.

NOTE: This message was released by the Office of the Press Secretary on October 7.

Message to the Congress Transmitting the Railroad Retirement Board Report
October 6, 1994

To the Congress of the United States:

I hereby submit to the Congress the Annual Report of the Railroad Retirement Board for Fiscal Year 1993, pursuant to the provisions of section 7(b)(6) of the Railroad Retirement Act and section 12(1) of the Railroad Unemployment Insurance Act.

WILLIAM J. CLINTON

The White House,

October 6, 1994.

NOTE: This message was released by the Office of the Press Secretary on October 7.

Remarks at the Blue Ribbon Schools Ceremony
October 7, 1994

Thank you very much for that wonderful welcome, increasingly rare around here these days. I just wanted to hear the Vice President say those lines from "A Man For All Seasons." [*Laughter*] They're wonderful, aren't they?

Let me say, as you know, we're about to wind up this session of Congress today, tomorrow—sometime in our lifetime, it will end—and that's why I couldn't be here earlier today. But I did want to come by and say a heartfelt congratulations to all of you.

The Vice President and the Secretary of Education have already talked about what we're trying to do here, but I would like to put in a couple of sentences what I think is very important. It's hardly ever discussed in the common discussion, at least, of what goes on in Washington. But we have been quietly, but effectively, trying to create a dramatic change in the relationship of the National Government to the schools of this country and to the teachers and to what is going on in education. It is a change rooted in the experiences that Secretary Riley and Deputy Secretary Kunin and I had as Governors and the hours and hours and hours that we all spent in public schools, listening to teachers, watching people work in the schools, listening to parents.

We have made the Federal Government both more active in education and, yet, less meddlesome in trying to support what you are trying to do. We have tried to put the National Government on record in favor of globally competitive national standards of excellence in education but also in favor of getting out of the way and letting you achieve those standards of excellence in education. And this is a substantial departure. The elementary and secondary education act that just passed the Congress, overcoming the perennial filibuster problem, does just that. It provides targeted funding, more directed toward the areas of real need, but also provides for an enormous amount of flexibility for the schools so that every school can be a blue ribbon school. That, in the end, ought to be our objective in America.

So we will keep trying to do our job here. It will make a real difference that no child should ever walk away from going to college because of the cost, because under this new student loan program, you can have lower interest rates and longer repayment terms, and it can be geared to your salary so that if you want to be a schoolteacher or a police officer, something where you're not going to be rich, you can still afford to pay back that student loan. That will make a difference. It will make a difference in hundreds of thousands of more kids in Head Start; that by 1996, every child in this country under the age of 2 will be immunized; that'll make it easier for the kindergarten and the first grade teachers to do their job. Those things will make a difference.

But in the end, we know what will make the difference is you, the teachers, the parents, the principals, the people at the grassroots level. All the magic of education is still in the human interplay that is a long way from Washington, DC. So we'll keep trying to do our job, but a big part of our job is making sure that you have, to use the new Washington buzzword, the empowerment necessary to do your job. That is our commitment to you; we will keep it. And I am glad to see your smiling faces here today.

Bless you all, and thank you very much.

NOTE: The President spoke at 12:15 p.m. on the South Lawn at the White House.

The President's News Conference
October 7, 1994

The President. Good afternoon. Ladies and gentlemen, 20 months ago I came here to make a start and to make America work for ordinary citizens again, to take on some tough issues too long ignored and to get our economic house in order. There have been some tough fights along the way, but I believe they were the right fights for our future.

We came here with an economic strategy that was comprehensive and direct: reduce the deficit, expand trade, increase investment in people and technology, and reinvent the Government to do more with less. We pursued this strategy with discipline. Now we have fresh evidence that the national economic program we put into place last year is beginning to work for America.

The Department of Labor reported today that the unemployment rate fell to 5.9 percent, a 4-year low. And the economy has created about 4.6 million jobs since I took office. More jobs in high-wage industries were created this year alone than in the previous 5 years combined. It's not enough, of course. As the census report makes clear, there are still too many Americans working for low wages, living in poverty. There are places in rural and urban America where the recovery has not yet reached.

But if you look at the changes since just a few short years ago, when we were exporting jobs and exploding the deficit, there's a great difference. We're getting our economic house in order. Jobs are being created at home. We're moving in the right direction.

This Congress, as it concludes a difficult session, showed that it could make a difference for ordinary people when it put people and progress ahead of narrow interests and partisan obstruction. It didn't always happen, so let's begin with a look at the record, what's been done, what hasn't been done, where do we go from here. Let's begin with what was accomplished.

The economic plan passed, putting our house in order. It was historic deficit reduction led by cutting over $255 billion in spending; cuts in 300 separate Government programs; raising taxes—or tax rates—on only the top 1.2 percent; cutting taxes for 15 million working families with 50 million Americans in them, people who work full-time but still hover just at the poverty line, so that people will always be encouraged to choose work over welfare and won't have to raise their children in poverty if they do.

We've broken down trade barriers, eliminated barriers to exports, passed NAFTA. Exports to Mexico are up 19 percent, exports of cars and truck up 600 percent in the last year.

They talked for more than a decade around here about making Government smaller, but it never seemed to happen. Well, now it is. Under

our legislation we are shrinking Federal positions and cutting the Federal work force by 272,000, to its smallest size since the Kennedy administration. And now, again I say, private sector jobs are going up; the deficit is going down.

For the first time in a generation, we have taken a serious assault on crime, passing the Brady bill and the crime bill with its 100,000 prison cells, its 20 percent increase in police on the beat, its ban on assault weapons, its "three strikes and you're out," and other penalty laws.

The Government is beginning to work for ordinary citizens in important ways. That's what the family leave law was about. That's what the law which will provide immunizations for all children under 2 by 1996 is about. That's what Head Start for 200,000 more kids is about. That's what the national standards of educational excellence with more local control; apprenticeships for kids who don't go to college; national service, so people can earn money for college and serve their communities; and making college loans more affordable for 20 million people who can now have lower interest rates, lower fees, longer repayment schedule; it's what the empowerment zones and the community development banks to bring free enterprise to poor communities are about.

All of this was real progress. It's only a beginning, and more could have been done. But too many times, an idea for creating jobs, reforming Government, educating students, or expanding income, fighting crime, or cleaning up the environment, or reforming the political system was met by someone trying to stop it, slow it, kill it, or just talk it to death.

A lot of the same people just recently signed that so-called Contract With America, a commitment to taking us back to the Reagan-Bush years when we exploded the deficit, cut Medicare, cut taxes for the wealthiest in America, divided our citizens, and sent our jobs overseas. My contract with the American people is for the future: grow the economy, fight crime, take on the tough problems, make Government work for ordinary people.

Congress is leaving town without passing GATT, the world's largest trade agreement. It will cut global tariffs and, over the next decade, means a $744 billion tax cut. It will generate hundreds of thousands of new jobs for American workers. It will keep our recovery going and sustain growth all around the world. We must not retreat on GATT. That's why I've asked Congress to return and pass it after the election, and I believe they will do that.

But Congress had a chance to do a lot of other things which it should have done but didn't do. It should have passed significant environmental legislation, much of which has the support of both American people and industry and environmental groups. It should have passed health care reform instead of watching another million Americans lose their coverage, as the new data points out happened just last year, while costs increased faster than inflation and more citizens lose the right to chose their doctor. And it certainly should have passed political reform. I think the American people were appalled by the spectacle of lobbyists hiding who they work for, what they get paid, and by Members of Congress accepting their gifts and then walking away from lobbying reform. There's something wrong when a Senator can filibuster this bill and walk off the floor of the Senate and be cheered by lobbyists. Well, the Congress is the people's Congress. The lobbyists may have been cheering in the filibuster last night, but the American people were not.

So Congress has done well on the economy, on crime, on tax fairness, on education and training, on trade, on loans for the middle class, on family leave, on reinventing Government. Congress has not done well on political reform, on environmental legislation, on health care, and on an unprecedented record of using the filibuster and other delaying tactics to try to keep anything from being done.

We have to now resolve to give the American people a choice as Congress leaves town and we move into the next few weeks before this election. Do they really want this contract which is a trillion dollars of unfunded promises, a contract which certainly will lead to higher deficits, cuts in Medicare, and throwing us back to the years of the eighties when we lost jobs and weakened our country? Or do we want to face up to the challenges which were not met in this Congress and use the next Congress to keep the economic growth going, to pass health care reform, to pass welfare reform, to pass political reform, to deal with these environmental issues?

You know, countries all over the world want America to succeed and want to follow our lead. We saw it just in the last few days when the elected democratic Presidents of South Africa

and Russia were here working with us on their common futures and their aspirations. We see it in the help we've been asked to give to the peace process in Northern Ireland. We see it in the help we've been asked to give to the peace process in the Middle East. We see it in the enthusiastic reception our young men and women in uniform have been given by the people of Haiti who want their democracy back.

I am proud of the work America has done around the world in the cause of democracy. I am proud of what our troops have done in the last 3 weeks in Haiti. As I said, and I caution you again, their job is still difficult and dangerous, and we still have a lot of work to do. But the violence is down, the Parliament is back, the refugees are returning, the electricity is burning again, and democracy is coming back. This is the direction we ought to be taking at home as well as abroad, fighting for the future, not going back to the past.

Helen [Helen Thomas, United Press International.]

Administration Accomplishments

Q. Mr. President, while acknowledging your accomplishments, the Republicans are savoring a big-time victory in November. You also have had some major setbacks in legislation. And some of the pundits are counting you out in '96. How do you account for this very dark picture, political picture, and what are you going to do about it?

The President. Well, what I'm going to do is go out and make sure the American people understand what the choice is. If the American people had been told 20 months ago that we would have had a historic first year with the Congress, that we'd have 4.6 million new jobs, the lowest unemployment rate in 4 years, an unusual number of high-wage jobs coming back into the economy, a serious assault on crime, that I would have presented major reform legislation in all the areas I've mentioned, plus the welfare reform bill I sent to Congress that I expect to pass next year to end welfare as we know it, I think they would have been well pleased. And I think when they see what has been done and that we are going in the right direction and then they see the alternative, the clear alternative, partisan gridlock by the Republican congressional leadership—I know you may say, "Well, some Democrats didn't vote with you, Mr. President, on campaign finance reform and lobby reform," and you would be right. But look at the record. Most Democrats, on these filibuster votes, voted for campaign finance reform; most Republicans voted against it. Most Democrats voted for political reform; most Republicans voted against lobby reform.

So the American people have to make a choice first about what direction they want. Do they really want this Republican contract on America? Do they really want somebody to just tell them what they want to hear one more time, instead of someone who'll take over the tough problems? Do they really want someone to make a trillion dollars in promises that means higher deficits, cuts in Medicare, the crime bill won't be funded, the economy will be back in the dumps? I don't believe they do want that. They haven't had much of a chance to see the big picture here; they just follow the daily march of events. In the end, this is a decision for the people to make in '94 and in '96.

When I showed up here, I knew that there was always a great deal of enthusiasm for change in the beginning. But the process of change is difficult, exacting; it requires discipline and confidence, and you have to stay at it. And there are always dark times. There has never been a time when the organized forces of the status quo haven't been able to drive down the popularity of a President who really fought for change. I'm not worried about that. I am not at issue here. The real issue is what is the future the American people wish for themselves. And I am looking forward to having a chance to go out and say what I think the direction should be and then let the people make their decision.

Iraq

Q. What can you tell us about the mobilization of Iraqi troops on the border with Kuwait? Do you think this is just bluster or do you think it's a real menace? And what's the United States prepared to do?

The President. Well, first let me say we are watching it very closely, and we are watching the troop movements as well as the threats that the Iraqis have made to the U.N. mission there. I spoke with General Shalikashvili just before I came over here today. We are taking the necessary steps as a precaution to deal with this issue. I don't believe I should discuss them in any greater detail, but let me say, I think they are appropriate and necessary, and we are fully in agreement on the course we are taking.

Iraq should not be able to intimidate the United Nations Security Council and the U.N. mission there. They should not be misled into thinking that they can repeat the mistakes of the past. If Iraq really is trying to say in some insistent way that what they want is relief from the U.N. sanctions, there is a clear way for them to achieve that relief, simply comply with the United Nations resolutions. If they comply with the United Nations resolutions, they can get relief from the sanctions. There are clear rules, clear standards. This is not a mystery.

So we have taken this matter seriously. We have responded with necessary precautionary steps. I cannot say more than that now, and I don't want to read more into it than has actually happened. But I am confident we are doing the right thing.

Yes, Andrea [Andrea Mitchell, NBC News].

Foreign Policy

Q. Over the past 20 months, Mr. President, some people would say that you have made very strong threats against the Bosnian aggressors; that you have warned North Korea not to build even one nuclear bomb, yet now there's acknowledgement that they at least have one, if not more; there have been threats against aggressors in Haiti and compromise, leaving the option for the leaders to stay there. To what extent would you say that it is fair criticism that Saddam Hussein might be testing you because this country has not been strong enough in responding to aggression and to aggressive threats?

The President. Well, first of all, I think that if he were testing me based on the facts that you outlined, he would have a very gross misapprehension of the facts. When I ran for President and when I became President, I never said that the United States would take any unilateral action in Bosnia. And I defy you to find the time when I did say that. I said that we would work with our allies. The actions of force which have occurred in Bosnia have been largely as a result of the initiatives of the United States; the creation of the safe havens, the use of NATO air power out of its area for the first time in history have largely been the results of the constant and insistent pushing of the United States.

Secondly, with regard to Korea, I think that our actions in Korea and our policies to date have been appropriate. They have been firm;

they have been deliberate. The implication of your remark was that they had a bomb-making operation going on during this administration. The evidence that has been cited in some press reports is quite different. It is that before I became President, they may have accumulated enough nuclear material to make a nuclear device or two. That has been the press reports. I fail to see how that shows a lack of resolve on our part since we have been here. I think we have pursued this course quite firmly. We were pushing the sanctions option if there was not a return to serious negotiations. There has been, and I hope those negotiations will succeed.

In the case of Haiti, I think it is absolutely apparent to everybody that it was the literal imminence of the military invasion which is leading to a peaceful transfer of authority there. We have, after all, 19,000-plus troops in Haiti. We are proceeding with the transfer of authority. It plainly was the result largely of the credible threat of force that a diplomatic solution permitting that threat of force to be instituted into the country in a peaceful rather than a warlike manner that resulted.

So if those are the examples, I would think that Saddam Hussein would draw exactly the reverse conclusion than the one you have outlined. Secondly, I would remind you that when we had clear evidence that the Iraqis were involved in an attempt to kill former President Bush, the United States took decisive and appropriate action.

Health Care Reform

Q. Mr. President, we haven't really had a chance to hear from you since last week Senator Mitchell declared that there just could be no resolution of the health care issue. I wonder if you could give us a sense of how you're regrouping on health care, if you are, and whether or not you now think that you made a mistake by proposing such broad changes and whether you're now willing to accept something more incremental in the next Congress.

The President. Well, I haven't had a lot of chance to think about exactly where we should go with this except to say that no sooner had Senator Mitchell issued his statement than the press reports were then full of, "Oh, my goodness, we have all these problems; 1.2 million Americans lost their health insurance last year, 1993; the cost is still going up at twice the rate of inflation; people are still losing their choice of doctors." So this problem will not go away.

I am very proud of the fact that we did get as much broad-based support as we did for comprehensive reform and that the basic elements of this reform were supported for the first time in history, I might add, by a heavy majority of medical providers, that—doctors and nurses and others—that for the first time in history we got a bill to the floor of both Houses of Congress. So what we will do after Congress goes out of session is to assess where we are and how we ought to go about this next year. But I fully intend to keep after it.

Let me just say one other thing. Let me try to put this into perspective. We worked hard on health care for a year and a half. It's the most complex issue facing the Congress but one that has to be addressed because of its human and its budgetary and economic implications not only for the Government, where it's the primary fueler of the deficit, but for the private sector as well. We worked on it for a year and a half. Since I have been here, we have broken gridlock and passed family leave after 7 years, motor voter after 5 years, the Brady bill after 7 years, the crime bill after 6 years, the banking reform bill after 7 years. Those are just five examples of how long fundamental reform took in areas that were more limited and less comprehensive. I think we can do health care—we must do health care in less time than that. But if it takes one more year, I'm not discouraged by that.

Q. Can you accept incremental reforms?

The President. I think in the end we will have to do—we will have to address this comprehensively. I think the principles I outlined have to be addressed by the country or we'll never solve the deficit or deal with the problems in the private sector. And I have not had any chance to think about how to approach the Congress with that. I will, but I—no one came forward with a convincing case that we could control costs, for example, which is imperative, without having a mechanism to cover everybody.

But there may be some other way to do it. I have always been open to any kind of new idea. I was disappointed that there weren't more bills introduced into the Congress in this last session that actually offered the promise of doing that. But I still think we can get it next year. I hope there will be a less partisan atmosphere. I hope the needs of the American people will be put first. And I intend to come back full force trying to do that.

Yes, Peter [Peter Maer, NBC Mutual Radio].

President's Approval Ratings

Q. Mr. President, going back to the upcoming campaign, as you yourself joked, I guess, at a reception earlier today, warm welcomes are increasingly rare. How do you analyze your own low approval ratings? And what's your advice and reaction to members of your own party who are running away from the administration's very record?

The President. Well, the record is a good one. And there is ample evidence that if people know the record, they respond to it. I think what— a lot of them are frustrated by the fact that the American people don't know it. All I can tell you is, you analyze it. You figure it out. Generally, there is a period of drag that sets in on Presidents at midterm. It happened to President Reagan in '82; it's happened in other cases. But also I think when people know what the choices are, they're in a better position to make those choices. I don't think they know that today.

My only concern is that the American people not go out and vote against what they're for and vote for what they're against. I think the American people wanted us to bring this deficit down. I think the American people wanted us to invest more in the education and training of the work force. I think the American people wanted us to make college more affordable for middle class people. I think the American people wanted us to pass the crime bill. I think the American people wanted us to pass campaign finance reform and lobby reform. That's what I think they wanted.

So what the American people should do is to say, "Who voted which way? What do I want for the future? Do I want to keep fighting in these directions?" and say, "Okay, Congress did some good things, and they failed to do some things they certainly should have done." Or do they want to go for this contract that the Republicans have put out on America, a trillion dollars in promises, just like we had in the eighties, which explodes the deficits, cuts Medicare, shifts jobs overseas, and puts us back in the ditch? I don't think that that's the choice they'll make if they understand the choice before them.

Iraq

Q. Mr. President, getting back to the situation in Iraq, could you tell us: How many Iraqi troops are moving? How many troops are involved? Which are those troops? Are they members of the Republican Guard? How far north of Kuwait are they right now? And the second part of that question: Tariq Aziz, the Deputy Prime Minister of Iraq, said today that Iraq is complying with all of these U.N. sanctions. What specifically has Iraq not done that you wanted to do that would result in its being allowed to export oil?

The President. Well, I think the Iraqis are well aware of what the United States believes in terms of their sanctions compliance and to the extent to which they are working with the United Nations mission there. And I would remind you that there are other United Nations resolutions over and above the weapons inspections ones that are usually discussed. So I think that the Iraqis are quite well aware of what the United Nations expects them to do to lift the sanctions. And if they will do it, then no one will stand in their way of lifting the sanctions.

In terms of the military situation, I think I have said all it is appropriate for me to say at this moment. We know what they're doing. We have responded with necessary steps. We will watch it very closely. We will report more as events unfold.

Yes, Sarah [Sarah McClendon, McClendon News Service].

Arkansas Airbase

Q. Sir, the Republicans are trying to blame you for the existence of a small airbase at Mena, Arkansas. This base was set up by George Bush and Oliver North and the CIA to help the Iran-*contras*, and they brought in planeload after planeload of cocaine there for sale in the United States. And then they took the money and bought weapons and took them back to the *contras*, all of which was illegal, as you know, under the Boland act. But tell me, did they tell you that this had to be in existence because of national security?

The President. Well, let me answer the question. No, they didn't tell me anything about it. They didn't say anything to me about it. The airport in question and all the events in question were the subject of State and Federal inquiries. It was primarily a matter for Federal jurisdiction; the State really had next to nothing to do with it. A local prosecutor did conduct an investigation based on what was within the jurisdiction of State law. The rest of it was under the jurisdiction of the United States Attorneys who were appointed successively by previous administrations. We had nothing, zero, to do with it. And everybody who's ever looked into it knows that.

Iraq

Q. Saddam Hussein has misread the intentions of American Presidents before. Without going any further than you care to into what may be the nature of these particular troop movements, what can you say to him today to make sure that he does not, because of your situation in Haiti, believe that you are perhaps vulnerable in the way that he thought your predecessor was vulnerable and do something that you don't want him to do?

The President. First of all, let me—I rarely do this to any of you, but I thank you for asking the question in that way because I do think President Bush's intentions were misunderstood, not because of anything President Bush did. And perhaps our position here might be misunderstood, not so much for the reasons that in your question were implied but because we do have troops in Haiti and we are otherwise occupied.

Saddam Hussein should be under no illusions. The United States is not otherwise occupied. We remain committed to the United Nations resolutions. We remain committed to the policy we followed before. The mistakes of the past should not be repeated. On the other hand, I would encourage you not to inflame this situation beyond the facts. Let us deal with this on the facts. We are monitoring what has actually happened. We are taking what we believe is factually appropriate steps, the necessary steps that any prudent administration would take under the same circumstances.

So let us watch this concern, but let us not blow it out of proportion. Let's just deal with the facts as they unfold. But it would be a grave mistake for Saddam Hussein to believe that for any reason the United States would have weakened its resolve on the same issues that involved us in that conflict just a few years ago.

The Economy

Q. Mr. President, to go back to domestic matters for a moment. You mentioned looking at the record. I want to ask you about one part of the record that does not look so good. The Census Bureau reported that through the first year of your term, through the end of 1993, median income has gone down. The rich have continued to get richer, the poor have continued to get poorer, income inequality has grown, precisely the trends that you singled out as the reasons you were opposed to what happened in the eighties. Do you believe that you can reverse these trends in the next 2 years of your term? And if you cannot, how do you think you'll be able to convince the American people that your Presidency has been a success?

The President. Well, first of all, let me—let's put this in context. And that was a fair question, I think, properly asked. These trends have been developing for nearly 20 years, as you pointed out. I don't think anyone thought I could turn them around in a year or that I alone could turn them around.

And let me try to be clear about where I think responsibility lies here, because I don't think it's fair to just say that the previous administration is completely responsible for these trends. I think their policies aggravated them to some extent but, more importantly, did not address them, which I think is the most important thing.

What is happening in America that would lead incomes to go down or be stagnant among people who actually work full time? And how could it continue even in a period of economic expansion? Indeed, how could it have continued through expansions for 20 years? That is the question. The answer, it seems to me, is to be found in the following facts.

Number one, for about 30 years we have had a problem developing primarily in our urban areas and our very rural areas where there was disinvestment of economic opportunity coupled with the breakdown of traditional family structures and community structures, so you had a lot of people growing up and living in places where the only jobs available were low-wage jobs or where there were relatively—there were too few good jobs. That's been going on for about 30 years.

Number two, compounding that, for about 20 years, American jobs overall, certainly hourly wage jobs, have been set more and more and more in the context of a global economy, so that to whatever extent a person has a job in America that can also be done by somebody somewhere else living on a much, much lower wage, that person will be under great pressure either to lose the job or to have the wage lowered or at least never to get a wage increase.

What is the answer to the problem and how might it be fixed? I think there are three answers, and we're pursuing all of them as best we can. First, increase the level of education and training of the work force and make it more permanent for a lifetime. That's why we had the apprenticeship program; that's why we have the college loan program; that's why I'm trying to pass the reemployment system legislation that I introduced this year, but I think it will pass next year. In other words, develop a system to raise the skill level of the work force and the wages will rise.

Secondly, follow policies that will change the job mix in America, that will tend to get more high-wage jobs here. That's why I believe so strongly in expanding trade. In the United States when we expand trade, it drives the wages up, up.

The third thing we have to do is to bring free enterprise to the inner cities and the isolated rural areas. That's what the empowerment zones are about; that's what those community development banks to make loans to low income people are about. Will that all change the income distribution in 2 years or 3 years? I don't know. I know we've been going in this direction for 20 years, and we can certainly change it back the other way in less than 20 years. But again I will say, we have to stay on this course. If we change course in this midterm election and decide that instead of investing in education, expanding trade, and empowering the inner cities and poor people, we're going to explode the deficit, give another tax cut we can't pay for, and cut Medicare—and, by the way, cut all other programs, including education and training and the crime bill—we'll be going in the wrong direction.

So the voters are going to decide whether this is the right direction, and I hope that they will decide that it is.

HUD Secretary Henry Cisneros

Q. Did you know when you nominated Secretary Cisneros that he was making payments to a former mistress? If you did, did you ask any questions about them? And finally, do you think the recent controversy about them undermines his effectiveness in your Cabinet?

The President. We knew what the facts were at the time and the legal counsel or the people—excuse me—who were handling it for me reviewed it, decided that there was nothing illegal or inappropriate about what was done by Secretary Cisneros, something that was fully known by his family. And no, I don't think it undermines his effectiveness. I mean, what he did in his past he's dealt with, and he's been pretty forthright. He's been, in fact, I think painfully forthright. And I think he has been an extraordinarily gifted HUD Secretary. He has proposed initiatives heretofore unseen to house the homeless, to empower people who are stuck in these public housing projects, to sweep the projects of weapons and drugs. He is doing the job that I hired him to do for the American people. And as long as he is doing that job at a high level, I think he ought to be permitted to continue to do it.

Cuba

Q. Mr. President, the Haitians in Guantanamo at least knew that you were working hard to get them out of there. What is the hope for the Cubans in Guantanamo?

The President. I'm sorry, what was the first part of your question?

Q. The Haitians in Guantanamo, they knew that you were working hard to get them out of there. What is the hope for the Cubans in Guantanamo?

The President. Well, we're working on that, and we're talking to them about that. As you know, some of them are going to Panama; some of them will have to decide what it is they wish to do. Of course, any of them who go back to Cuba would be eligible to apply to come to the United States legally now under a much higher ceiling. And we think a substantial number of them would be in the category of people who could get in because of their family connections in the United States and the broadened definition of family connections under the new agreement, which raises the ceiling to 20,000 people we're taking in. Also, some of them are children or otherwise vulnerable, and we're looking at them to see whether there should be any special considerations for them.

Yes, Mike [Mike McKee, CONUS].

Middle Class Tax Cut

Q. Mr. President, you promised the middle class a tax cut 2 years ago during the campaign. Will you be able to keep that promise in the next 2 years?

The President. I can't give you an answer today because it depends upon how well the economy goes and what other considerations there are with the budget. And let me just give you an example of that.

In this budget, because we began with a deficit that was bigger than we expected, the middle class tax cut essentially was capped at 15 million families, comprising about 50 million Americans or only about 20 percent of our population. Would I like to do better than that? Yes, I would, but not at the expense of the economic recovery for the same middle class. So what we are looking at now in the context of the welfare reform legislation, the child support enforcement legislation, the other things we're trying to do to strengthen families is whether and to what extent we can address that issue. What are the revenue projections for the next 2 years? What are the other demands on State spending—Government spending, I mean? How much can we control the other costs? What do we absolutely have to do for defense? Because that's very important, as we've all seen in the questions you've asked me in this press conference.

So I cannot give you an answer. Do I think it should be done? I still do. I don't think—the Federal tax system is much fairer than it was when I became President because of the tax cut for the working families just above the poverty line and also because something we often forget: We made 90 percent of the small businesses in this country eligible for a tax cut last year in the economic plan. Any small business with a taxable income below $100,000 was also eligible for a tax cut.

So I think we're doing better. But the Tax Code is not where it ought to be. And middle class families, especially those with children, I think should look forward to a little more fairness, but I can't say how and how much yet.

Midterm Elections

Q. Despite the economic expansion and the record you've been citing here today, the political mood in the country remains extremely sour. Your poll ratings are very low, but you're far more popular than the people up on Capitol Hill. How can you go out to the public, as you're going to do in the next couple of weeks, and argue that given the rate of failure, the record of failure you cited today, the people up there should be reelected and that staying the course that is underway right now is good for the country?

The President. Well, it's easy to argue that staying the course we're underway right now is good for the country because these 2 years compare so favorably with the previous several in terms of economic direction, investment in people, and making Government work for ordinary folks. That's easy to argue.

What I think is important is to take the message to the American people in terms of what's good for them and what changes they want. In other words, the election should be about them and their future and what changes they want, not necessarily about whether the parties are ideal or perfect or whatever.

We're going through a period of change. The American people are not satisfied either with the rate of change or with the certainty that it will occur. And they, like everybody else—I mean, after all, you can't—the people are of more than one mind on more than one issue. That is, all these interest groups that everybody reviles when they want campaign finance reform or lobby reform are the same people that have the money and the organized communications ability to change the attitudes of the people out there on issue after issue after issue.

So the important thing, the message I have to say is, what is the direction you want? Do you want continued progress in the economy? Do you want a Government that takes on tough problems like crime and welfare reform and health care? Do you want a Government that does things for ordinary people, like the family leave law or making college loans more available to middle class people? Or do you want this contract, which says clearly, "Give us power, and we'll take you back to the eighties. We'll give you a trillion dollars' worth of promises. We'll promise everybody a tax cut. We'll explode the deficit. We'll cut Medicare. We'll never fund the crime bill. But we will have told you what you wanted to hear." I think the American people will vote for the future and not the past, and that's my hope and belief.

Health Care Reform

Q. Mr. President, a question about bipartisanship. Looking back on the health care reform effort, is there anything you think you could have done differently to forge a consensus? For instance, do you think it would have helped if you'd brought Republicans earlier on in the process up to the White House to negotiate the way you did at the end of the crime bill fight? And looking ahead to next year when you're going to be pushing health care reform and other issues through a more Republican Congress, is there anything that you plan to do differently to forge a coalition for governing?

The President. Well, let me say, I'm sure that there are some things I could have done differently. You know, I never dealt with Congress before last year, and I'm still learning all the time. I would point out that the Congressional Quarterly said that last year that the Congress and the President worked together more successfully than at any time since World War II, except in President Eisenhower's first year and President Johnson's second year. So I felt that we accomplished quite a great deal.

When we were putting this health care bill together, there was a lot of consultation with Republicans. When we wanted to present a proposed bill and say, "Now, how would you like to change this?" we were told that they had their own group working on health care, and they wanted to present a bill, and then we would get together. So I said, that's fine; I understand that. Then Senator Chafee, to his everlasting credit, came up with a bill that had two dozen Republican Senators on it that would have covered all Americans and controlled costs. By the time we got down to serious negotiations, instead of two dozen Senators for universal health care and controlled costs, there were zero. They all left. I mean, Senator Chafee was still there, but everybody had abandoned his bill. We had one Republican Congressman saying they'd all been instructed not to work with us. We had one Republican Senator quoted in one of your papers saying that they had killed it, now they had to keep their fingerprints off of it.

So I am more than happy to work with them in any way I can. I do not believe we have a monopoly on wisdom. Let me say, let me give you some evidence of my good faith on being flexible about changing. I have given State after State after State waiver from Federal regulations to pursue universal coverage and health care costs control on their own. Tennessee has done some very exciting things and, by the way, gotten some very impressive results, I understand. We just approved Florida to do this. We're in the process of approving more States to move forward. I am very flexible on how we get this done. And if the American people are worried that the Federal Government has too much emphasis and they want more for the States, fine, let's talk about that. But if there's going to be a bipartisan effort, it has to be good faith on both sides.

I like working with Republicans. I proved that in the NAFTA fight, proved it in the crime bill fight. I will prove it in the health care fight. But it can't be a kind of situation where every time I move to them, they move further the other way. That's the only thing I would say.

Yes, sir, last question.

Secretary of Agriculture

Q. Mr. President, for Secretary of Agriculture, will you be looking for someone with farm experience, or will you be looking for somebody like Secretary Espy, who has heavy congressional experience?

The President. Well, the most important thing, I think, is someone who really understands how to deal with the agriculture community, understands the interests, and is committed to agriculture and to farmers and to rural development. And let me say that, if I might, in closing, that I also want somebody who will faithfully implement the reforms that Secretary Espy has started.

We passed a dramatic restructuring of the Department of Agriculture. We're going to take down the number of employees by at least 7,500. We have seen an Agriculture Department that has been extremely active in helping farmers deal with disasters, that has tried to help the farmers in the Middle West with their production problems, that has given an enormous amount of emphasis to rural development. So this Agriculture Department, under this Secretary of Agriculture, has established a lot of credibility with the American people who are in agriculture, including selling rice to Japan for the first time, selling apples from Washington to Japan for the first time, doing things that haven't been done for a long time for hard-working, grassroots farmers, whether they're Republicans or Democrats or independents.

And when I came here, out of a rural background, out of a farming background, that's what I desperately wanted to do for the agricultural community. And so when I pick another Agriculture Secretary, that is a standard that Mike Espy set that must be met for the next Agriculture Secretary.

Thank you very much.

NOTE: The President's 73d news conference began at 2 p.m. in the East Room at the White House.

The President's Radio Address With President Nelson Mandela of South Africa
October 8, 1994

President Clinton. Good morning. This week I'm honored to be joined by President Nelson Mandela of South Africa, a man who has been a hero for people in every corner of the world. For a long time, the name "Nelson Mandela" has stood for the quest for freedom. His spirit never bent before the injustice of his 27 years of imprisonment. Apartheid could not silence him. And when he was freed, Americans all across this country who had fought for justice in South Africa rejoiced.

After his long struggle, Nelson Mandela found in himself the strength to reach out to others, to build up instead of tear down. He led his country forward, always choosing reconciliation over division. This is the miracle of the new South Africa. Time and again, President Mandela showed real wisdom and rose above bitterness. President Mandela and the South African people, both black and white, have inspired others around the world.

In our own hemisphere today, the people of Haiti are emerging out of fear into freedom. Now Haitians have the chance to do what South Africans have done, to bring together a country where there have been deep and bloody divisions. It can be done, and the United States stands ready to help.

We must do all we can to help civil societies free themselves from the shackles of repression, to sustain their fragile democracies, and to defeat the forces of destruction that threaten all of us. That's why America stands with Nelson Mandela and the South African people through economic assistance, through trade and investment to help them to build the thriving democracy they so richly deserve, and why we're working to help the Haitian people stand up and reclaim their freedom and their future, too.

Now I'd like to ask President Mandela to speak with you.

[*At this point, President Mandela discussed his visit to the United States and thanked the American people for their friendship.*]

President Clinton. Thank you, Mr. President. This week I pledged to President Mandela that the United States will continue to support his nation just as we have since before his election. And I want to encourage all of our citizens and especially our businesses to accept the President's invitation to invest, to build in his country, to visit his country. A flourishing South Africa involved in the rest of the world is in our interest.

President Mandela was right the other day when he called the transformation of his country an achievement of all humanity. The kind of peaceful development we're seeing in South Africa will inspire progress all around the world. Now South Africa is a model for building the open, tolerant societies that share our values. And when we look around the world at the stirring changes in Russia, the moving developments in Northern Ireland, the stunning achievements of the peace initiatives in the Middle East, we see the prospects for democracy and peace growing. Our mission is to build a new world for our children, more democratic, more prosperous, more free of ancient hatreds and modern means of destruction. This is no easy task. But more nations than ever are choosing democracy, and more are embracing the values of tolerance that allow each of us to make the most of our God-given potential. Freedom is on the march, and that is good news for all of us.

Once again, let me thank the symbol of freedom for the world, President Mandela, for visiting us here in the United States. And thank you all for listening.

NOTE: The address was recorded at 4:53 p.m. on October 7 in the East Room at the White House for broadcast at 10:06 a.m. on October 8.

Remarks on Iraq
October 8, 1994

Before I leave today I just wanted to say one thing. I have been briefed by the National Security Adviser on the situation in Iraq. We have discussed the measures I have ordered to deal with the situation. And I want to make it clear one more time, it would be a grave error for Iraq to repeat the mistakes of the past or to misjudge either American will or American power.

Thank you very much.

NOTE: The President spoke at 1:05 p.m. on the South Lawn at the White House, prior to his departure for Camp David, MD.

Statement on California Desert Legislation
October 8, 1994

Today's passage of the California desert bill is a clear-cut victory for the people of California and everyone across America who cares about this Nation's great natural heritage. We all owe a debt of gratitude to Senator Dianne Feinstein for her tireless efforts to bring together a bipartisan coalition in Congress that ensured its passage.

The passage of this important environmental legislation is a testament to Dianne Feinstein's skillful leadership, perseverance, and determination to do the right thing for the people of California.

Address to the Nation on Iraq
October 10, 1994

Good evening. Tonight I want to speak with you about the actions we are taking to preserve stability in the Persian Gulf in the face of Saddam Hussein's provocative actions. But first, let me take just a minute to report to you on today's events in Haiti.

Three weeks ago today, our troops entered Haiti. They went there to keep America's and the world community's commitment to restore the democratically elected government to power by October 15th. Today Lieutenant General Cédras and Brigadier General Biamby, the two remaining coup leaders, have resigned. They have said they will leave Haiti shortly. I am pleased to announce that President Aristide will return home to resume his rightful place this Saturday, October 15th.

I want to express again my pride in what our men and women in uniform have done in Haiti and how well they have measured up to their difficult mission. In just 3 weeks, the level of violence is down, the Parliament is back, refugees are returning from Guantanamo. And now the military leaders are leaving.

But I also want to caution again, the job in Haiti remains difficult and dangerous. We still have a lot of work ahead of us. But our troops are keeping America's commitment to restore democracy. They are performing their mission very, very well with firmness and fairness, and all Americans are proud of them.

The strength of America's foreign policy stands on the steadfastness of our commitments. The United States and the international community have given their word that Iraq must respect the borders of its neighbors. And tonight, as in Haiti, American troops with our coalition partners are the guarantors of that commitment, the power behind our diplomacy.

Three and a half years ago, the men and women of our Armed Forces, under the strong leadership of President Bush, General Powell, and General Schwarzkopf, fought to expel Iraq from Kuwait and to protect our interests in that vital region. Today we remain committed to defending the integrity of that nation and to protecting the stability of the Gulf region.

Saddam Hussein has shown the world before, with his acts of aggression and his weapons of mass destruction, that he cannot be trusted. Iraq's troop movements and threatening statements in recent days are more proof of this. In 1990, Saddam Hussein assembled a force on the border of Kuwait and then invaded. Last week, he moved another force toward the same border. Because of what happened in 1990, this provocation requires a strong response from the United States and the international community.

Over the weekend I ordered the *George Washington* Carrier Battle Group, cruise missile ships, a Marine expeditionary brigade, and an Army mechanized task force to the Gulf. And today I have ordered the additional deployment of more than 350 Air Force aircraft to the region. We will not allow Saddam Hussein to defy the will of the United States and the international community.

Iraq announced today that it will pull back its troops from the Kuwait border. But we're interested in facts, not promises, in deeds, not words. And we have not yet seen evidence that Iraq's troops are in fact pulling back. We'll be watching very closely to see that they do so.

Our policy is clear: We will not allow Iraq to threaten its neighbors or to intimidate the United Nations as it ensures that Iraq never again possesses weapons of mass destruction. Moreover, the sanctions will be maintained until Iraq complies with all relevant U.N. resolutions. That is the answer to Iraq's sanctions problems: full compliance, not reckless provocation.

I'm very proud of our troops who tonight are the backbone of our commitment to Kuwait's freedom and the security of the Gulf. I'm also proud of the planners and the commanders who are getting them there so very quickly and in such force. They all are proof that we are maintaining and must continue to maintain the readiness and strength of the finest military in the world.

That is what we owe to the men and women of America who are putting their lives on the line today to make the world a safer place. And it is what we owe to the proud families who stand with them. They are protecting our security as we work for a post-cold-war world of democracy and prosperity.

Within the last 2 weeks, America hosted two champions of post-cold-war democracy. South African President Nelson Mandela came to thank the United States for our support of South Africa's remarkable democratic revolution and to seek a partnership for the future. And Russian President Boris Yeltsin came to further the partnership between our two nations so well expressed by the fact that now Russian and U.S. missiles are no longer pointed at each other's people and we are working to reduce the nuclear threat even more.

In short, we are making progress in building a world of greater security, peace, and democracy. But our work is not done. There are difficulties and dangers ahead, as we see in Iraq and in Haiti. But we can meet these challenges and keep our commitments. Our objectives are clear, our forces are strong, and our cause is right.

Thank you, and God bless America.

NOTE: The President spoke at 8 p.m. from the Oval Office at the White House.

Remarks on Iraq
October 11, 1994

Good morning. Our deployments in the Gulf region are continuing today. There has been no change in the pattern of Iraqi activity from yesterday, so we will continue our deployments.

We received strong support from the international community for this approach. I talked with several world leaders yesterday. The British are already sending more troops, planes, and ships. So I'm quite encouraged about the direction of the events. We will just simply stay on course and judge what we should do as events unfold. But today I can tell you that we are continuing with our deployment and that there has been no change in the pattern of Iraqi activity to date.

Thank you.

NOTE: The President spoke at 9:24 a.m. on the South Lawn at the White House, prior to his departure for Detroit, MI.

Remarks to Ford Motor Company Employees in Dearborn, Michigan
October 11, 1994

Thank you very much, Alex, for your introduction and for your work. And especially, thank you for not giving up on the Mustang.

I'm delighted to be here with Alex Trotman and Owen Bieber. And I want to thank all the people from Ford and from the UAW who made it possible for me to be the first President ever to visit this plant and to take the tour and to see the new Mustangs and to sort of regret I couldn't drive out of here with one. [*Laughter*]

Mayor Archer, it's good to see you. Mr. McNamara, ladies and gentlemen, thank you all so much for coming here today.

I guess it's not much of a secret to you that I own a 1967 Mustang, so I have been out of the market for a while. When I left Arkansas 20 months ago, I think it was the thing I most regretted leaving behind. Of course, all the drivers in my State were elated, but I miss it anyway. [*Laughter*]

I want to tell you how very proud I am of Ford, of the UAW, the American auto industry generally for what you have done to put America on the move again, to rebuild our position globally in auto manufacturing, to strengthen manufacturing in America, and to give us a better chance to move into the 21st century. Ten years ago, a lot of people were willing to throw in the towel on the auto industry. But you fought back, labor and management, together. And now for the first time in a good long while, you are number one again, not only here but in the entire world, and you ought to be proud of yourselves.

I want to say to you that the fight you have fought is the fight I am fighting for America. I want us to be number one again. I want us to be able to compete and win in the 21st century. I don't want our children to be the first generation of Americans to do worse than their parents. And I believe the future can be the best time America has ever had if we have the discipline and the courage and the vision to stick with it and go forward and do what we know we ought to do.

I've been in a lot of tough fights in my life and none so tough as the one I've been in in Washington for the last 20 months. But it's been a good fight. It's a fight to give Americans the power to compete and win and to empower all Americans to live up to their God-given potential, and we have made a good start.

No one would want to go back to the days when we exported jobs, not products. No one would want us to go back to the days when our deficit was exploding and our economy was going downhill. That is exactly the decision that all of you are going to have to make on November 8th, whether we keep going in the right direction or go back to the 1980's trickle-down economics.

You remember the folks in the other party; they talked a good game. But trickle-down economics gave us an economy stuck in reverse: tax breaks for the wealthiest Americans, higher taxes on the middle class, a quadrupled deficit, jobs going overseas. Most manufacturing jobs that were ever lost in this country were lost in that period. And in their last 4 years, we had the worst job growth since the Great Depression. Michigan alone lost almost 70,000 manufacturing jobs during that time. Well, I don't think we want to go back to that, where families struggle longer and harder for less, where we come apart when we ought to be coming together.

The American people really hired me to try to change all that. It wasn't easy, and I knew it wouldn't be. But I ask you to remember this: We've had 30 years in which we've been developing serious social problems with our families, our communities, the crime problem, the gang problem, the drug problem. We've had 20 years when most working people have worked harder for stagnant wages. And we tried 12 years of trickle-down economics. After 20 months, I think it's plain that we've made a beginning in turning this country around. And I hope you'll say it's plain that you don't want to go back, you want to go forward into the 21st century.

I ask every American in the next 4 weeks not just to think of their discontents with the political system, although there's plenty of good reason to be discontented, but remember the problems we found 20 months ago. Remember the progress we're making. Remember how many of them fought us every step of the way. And remember now what they want to do to take us back, when we have so much to do to keep going forward.

We cannot turn back again. We're headed in a new direction, with a new idea about what our National Government ought to do: not a Government that ignores our problems but not one that promises to solve all the problems for us either, but instead, a Government that empowers citizens to build good lives of their own; not more Government but less Government that works better for ordinary Americans. Look at the start that's been made:

The family leave law, which in Michigan alone provides extra protection for 1.5 million working people so they can succeed as parents and workers; it's a very important thing. Nobody should lose their job when a baby is born or a parent's sick.

Immunization for all American children under the age of 2 by 1996, 2 million kids that are going to have a better chance at a better life. That's something that ordinary American families ought to be able to expect of their Government.

Apprenticeships for young people who don't go to college but want good jobs. Every young American ought to have a chance to train for a good job in a 21st century economy.

College loans affordable for 20 million people, almost 600,000 right here in Michigan, eligible for lower interest, longer term, better repayment college loans so that now no young person should ever decline to go to college because of the cost of a college education, the burden on the student, the burden on the parents. It's the most important thing that's been done for middle class Americans in a very long time by the National Government, and we ought to stick with it.

We sent a welfare reform plan to Congress to end welfare as we know it, to move people from welfare to work. And while it hasn't passed yet, it will. And we've already given 17 States permission to get rid of all Federal regulations that undermine their ability to move people from welfare to work.

For the first time in a generation, we've also begun a serious assault on crime, passing the Brady bill and the crime bill with "three strikes and you're out," a 20 percent increase in the number of police officers on the beat in America—already in Taylor, nearby here, they're getting more police officers, and you will see it in every community in this country—100,000 more prison cells to hold serious offenders, and prevention programs to give young people a chance to avoid a life of crime.

We've begun, finally, to put our economic house in order. When I took office, we had had 12 years of exploding deficits and declining incomes; we had quadrupled the national debt. Before I could do anything else, folks, I had to get our economic house in order, and we had to do something about this terrible deficit. It was choking the economy and robbing our children of their future. So we fought for historic deficit reductions, $255 billion in Federal spending cuts. We did raise tax rates on the top 1.2 percent of Americans, but we cut taxes for 15 million working Americans. In Michigan alone, that means 41,000 families had higher income tax rates and 390,000 families had lower income tax rates to encourage those people to work instead of going on welfare.

Now, when I proposed this economic program, the same folks that exploded our deficit in the eighties said if this passes, the sky would fall; the deficit would go up more; the economy would collapse; it would be the end of the world. And so every last member of the Republican Party in the Congress voted against that program, every single one, against the deficit reduction, against the college loan program, every single one.

So what happened when they said the world would come to an end? Well, for the first time since Harry Truman, we're bringing the deficit down 3 years in a row. We had more jobs created in high-wage industries this year than in the previous 5 years combined. We've had 9 months now of growth in manufacturing jobs in a row for the first time in 10 years. America was voted the most productive country in the world by the annual panel of international economists for the first time in 9 years. And we have 4.6 million new jobs in America in the last 20 months.

Our exports are up around the world. We're selling all kind of things we never sold before, not just automobiles; we're selling rice to Japan for the first time, something I'm very proud of—and Mustangs to Japan, I might add. Exports to Mexico are up 19 percent; exports of cars and trucks are up 500 percent, 500 percent. If we pass the world trade agreement, it will enable us to get more high-wage jobs tied to exports. We are doing that.

So what are we doing? Putting our economic house in order, making a serious assault on crime, making Government work for ordinary people again. The other thing we're trying to do is to do it with less Government, not more. Republicans talked forever about how much they dislike the Federal Government and how they wanted to cut bureaucracy and inefficiency, and they're saying it again this year. I just want to remind you that it was our Democratic administration that passed laws to reduce the size of the Federal bureaucracy by 272,000, to make it the smallest it's been since John Kennedy was President, and to give every last dollar of the savings to you in your local community to fight crime. That is the record that we have made in reducing the Federal Government.

Now, you may say, "Well, that's all fine, Mr. President, but my life is still pretty tough," or "My neighbor still doesn't have a job," or "I'm still not sure what the future holds." Well, no one can promise you to repeal the laws of change that are sweeping through the world today. What we have to do is to make change our friend.

What are the problems we still have in America? Too many people still haven't gotten a raise in a long time. A million Americans lost their health insurance last year. We have too many people who are trapped in the cycle of welfare. We have social problems that are profound. These are legitimate problems. The political system needs some internal reforms. That's right, we have problems. What you have to say to yourself is, "Who is more likely to meet these problems? Who is more likely to seize these challenges?"

Look at what the strategy of our administration is. It's to create more high-wage American jobs, train more Americans to do those jobs, bring free enterprise to poor inner-city areas and rural areas that have been ignored for too long, continue to fight for political reforms, and meet the challenges of America that have not yet been faced in health care, in welfare, and in so many other areas. That is our strategy, fighting for the future.

Now, consider instead what their strategy is. Look what they've done just in the last year. Whenever they were faced with an idea that created jobs or educated students or fight crime or reform the political system, no matter how good it was, no matter even if they had already supported it, what did they do? You remember what they did, just in the last couple of weeks. They tried to stop it, slow it, kill it, or just talk it to death.

Congress should have passed a bipartisan health care reform bill with private insurance, consumer choice, cost constraints, and universal coverage. Instead, we watched another year go by where health care costs rose faster than inflation, over a million Americans lost their coverage, the cost of health care exploded the Federal deficit. Why? Because the other guys walked away from every attempt we had to compromise this issue.

Congress should have passed a lobbying reform and a campaign finance reform bill and made all the laws that they apply to private employers and employees apply to themselves. And they passed both Houses. Why did those laws fail? Because in the end the Republican congressional leadership delayed them to death. It is wrong when a Senator of the other party can filibuster lobbying reform, which Senator Levin has worked so hard for for so long, and then walk off the floor of the United States Senate and be cheered by a crowd of lobbyists for killing it. But it happened. Well, the lobbyists may be cheering, but I don't imagine you are.

The Republican leadership blocks change in Washington, and then they go home and tell you how hard they're fighting the Democrats to change the way things are. They say one thing in one place and another in another.

Look what else they blocked that affects Michigan. In the 11th hour they blocked the passage of the Superfund legislation to clean up toxic waste dumps. You know who was for that? Every industry group, the labor groups, and the Sierra Club. It's the only time in history the chemical companies and the Sierra Club have agreed on anything. There was nobody in America against passing Superfund except the Republican leadership. Why? So we wouldn't be able to stand up here and celebrate the passage of Superfund.

There's a bill you care a lot about in Michigan that was blocked that would give local folks some control over the interstate transportation of solid waste. Not very many people were against it, but it was blocked. Why? For political reasons. The same can be said for a lot of other bills.

Well, now the same folks that blocked these bills have come forward with what they'll do if you give them control of Congress. They call it their Contract With America. Three hundred and fifty Republicans stood on the steps of the Nation's Capitol with the leadership and one by one signed this contract. I'll give them credit for at least doing that. For 2 years, I couldn't get them to say anything they were for. [*Laughter*]

But if you read this contract, it's not a contract with America, it's really a contract on America. It takes us back to the 1980's, to trickle-down economics. Look at what they do: They promise everybody a tax cut, although 70 percent of it goes to the wealthiest Americans; they promise to increase defense and to start up Star Wars; they promise a trillion dollars' worth of things. I wish I could come here and do that today, just tell you exactly what you want to hear. "Here's a trillion dollars. Go spend it."

You give me a trillion dollars, and I'll show you a good time, too. [*Laughter*]

But since it's just a bunch of promises, what does it mean? Same thing it meant in the 1980's. It means exploding the deficit, shipping our jobs overseas, cutting Medicare and veterans benefits, not funding the crime bill. It means a lot of terrible things, because you simply cannot go around this country making idle promises to people that you cannot keep. We must not go back to that sort of politics.

So I hope the American people will have a simple answer to this contract. We've been there. We've seen that. We've tried it. And we will not be fooled again. I offer you a difficult and more challenging contract, but the only one that can work. It's the contract that had always worked for America. It is fighting for the future, making the most of the potential of every American. It is doing whatever it takes to compete and win in the global economy of the 21st century. It is doing with our Nation what you have done here at this Mustang plant. That is what I offer you: more jobs, a lower deficit, more education for our kids, competing in the global economy, doing the things that will make America work again so that these fine young people in their musicians' uniforms will be able to grow old, when they're like me and they have to give up their horns, and they'll still have a life they'll be proud of.

Look, I read all these stories about how angry the voters are and how fed up. Well, let me tell you something: I showed up in Washington to work 20 months ago, and since then I have been amazed and often angered at some of the stuff I see. I have been bewildered at the resistance to change from time to time. And I know that both parties bear some burden, and I know that even the President is not perfect. But remember this: When it came to change, we were on the side of the future.

When we offered a plan to cut the deficit and provide college loans to the middle class, they all voted against it. When campaign finance reform and lobbying reform came up to change the way the political system worked, most of our party voted for it. Most of them voted against it. On the crime bill, which had always been a bipartisan effort, where over 90 percent of both parties' representatives voted for it last year when there were no politics, most of our folks were still for it, just where they were last year. But they changed and voted against it for politics.

So you have a choice. We are fighting for a 21st century in which America goes forward, competes, wins, every American lives up to the fullest of his God-given potential. We refuse, even though it's tempting, I guess, from time to time, to take the easy way out and give you a trillion dollars' worth of unfunded promises. That is their contract.

We have a covenant for the future. They put out a contract on the future. I think the choice is clear. I want to ask you to help ensure America, through all the frustration and anger, does not inadvertently vote for what you're against and against what you're for.

Look to the future. Think of your children. Stand up for tomorrow. And remember, it's not so different building a country than it is building a car. You have to think about the tasks, you have to face the hard jobs as well as the easy ones, you've got to work together, and you've got to always be thinking about tomorrow.

Thank you, and God bless you all.

NOTE. The President spoke at 11:45 a.m. at the assembly plant. In his remarks, he referred to Alex Trotman, chief executive officer, Ford Motor Co.; Owen Bieber, president, United Auto Workers; Mayor Dennis W. Archer of Detroit, MI; and Edward McNamara, county executive, Wayne County.

Exchange With Reporters Prior to a Meeting With Auto Industry Leaders in Detroit, Michigan
October 11, 1994

Iraq

Q. Mr. President, are you encouraged by developments in the Gulf?

The President. Well, I'm hopeful. It's a little early yet to reach a final conclusion. We're watching it very closely.

[*At this point, one group of reporters left the room, and another group entered.*]

Auto Industry

Q. Mr. President, why do you meet with the auto industry as often as you do?

The President. Why do I?

Q. Yes.

The President. Because it's an important part of our economy, an important part of our strat-

egy for economic revival, and because we've had a good partnership in working on a lot of issues.

I'm very encouraged and Americans should be, not just the people of Michigan but the people of the United States, that the auto industry is back, clearly, leading the world now in sales of cars at the cutting edge and rebuilding our manufacturing base here at home. That's a big part of the objective of my administration. So I'm encouraged by it. I want to keep working with them.

Q. How did you feel about your reception?

The President. It was great.

NOTE: The exchange began at 2:06 p.m. at the Westin Renaissance Hotel. A tape was not available for verification of the content of this exchange.

Remarks Announcing Community Policing Grants
October 12, 1994

Thank you very much, General Reno, for your remarks and your tireless work on this and for really a brilliant effort on the part of the Justice Department employees to move this grant

money, only 12 days after the bill became effective, out into our communities.

Thank you, Chief Massey, for your testimony and for your work, and I want to thank all your forces. When I was introduced to his community policing recruits, I mean, just look at them, they're going to lower the crime rate by walking the streets. [*Laughter*]

I want to thank the other law enforcement officers from Maryland who are up here and all of you who are out in the audience today. I thank the Members of Congress who are here, Congressman Pallone, Congressman Moran, Congresswoman McKinney. And especially I thank Senator Sarbanes for telling me Chief Massey's story a few weeks ago and bringing this whole issue to my attention as an illustration of how we can fight crime and lower the crime rate through community policing.

It was just a month ago that we were here on the South Lawn of the White House to sign the crime bill. We came back today to show determination to implement this law without delay.

I want to make three points, if I might. One is, I think all Americans know that we can never be strong abroad unless we are first strong at home. As we are very proud of the work our armed forces are doing today in Haiti and in the Gulf, we know that they are able to be there doing what they're doing because they come out of a strong, good country with strong basic community ties and values. And our ability to make our people secure is the critical element of personal freedom that rests at the root of our strength as a nation.

The second point I want to say is that we know we've got an issue here we have to deal with, and we're determined to hit the ground running. And we want all of you to help us keep hitting the ground running, not just now but over the entire life of this crime bill.

And the last point I want to make has already been made more graphically and powerfully by the story Chief Massey told. This is not a problem that can be fought in Washington, DC. The genius of this crime bill is that it empowers people at the community level in big cities like San Francisco, whose mayor is represented here today, and in smaller communities like Ocean City to take control of their own destiny, to drive down the crime rate, and to catch criminals. The genius of this bill in the end may be that we really did say, "We're going to pay for this by shrinking the size of the Federal Government and giving every last dollar of the shrinkage to local communities to fight crime, to prove that they can bring the crime rate

down," not we in Washington but you out there. This is a bill which gives you the power to take control of the destinies of your people. And I know that you will do it.

Today we have rejected decades of excuses that crime is a local problem that Washington can do nothing about. However, Washington can do a lot to help you fight crime. And if you look at the crime bill and the grants for local police and the prevention programs and the help to build prison cells for serious offenders and the supportive work coming out of the extra help for Federal law enforcement authorities, this is an enormous step forward in a national partnership to help people fight crime at the grassroots level. We have to prove here in America that we can make progress on this. We have to prove that we can make a difference.

Yesterday I was in Detroit celebrating the revival of our automobile industry. For the first time in 15 years, it's now clearly number one in the world in sales worldwide. And it's wonderful to see that the biggest problem in Michigan is now how much overtime they have at the auto industry, a story you wouldn't have heard 10 years ago. But you build a country the same way you build a company like that. You have to face your problems, face your challenges, get people together, empower people to take control of their own destinies and get after it. And that's what we're trying to do.

After I did the event in Detroit, I went by and met with the editorial board of the Detroit Free Press, and they read a letter that a 9-year-old girl named Porsha had written to me and asked to be delivered. And she said, "Please, please make me free from fear." That is what we're here about. We can talk about all the details, and we can glory in all the specifics, but the bottom line is that we together have made a commitment to make the American people freer of fear. It is a great tribute to the Members of Congress who voted for this bill, a tribute to the Attorney General and all the people who work with her who worked so hard for it, a tribute to all of you, without whom we would not have passed it.

Let me say again that 100,000 police officers is a number that doesn't mean a lot to the average American. Most Americans don't know how many police we have now. They don't know how many that is. They're not sure what it means on their block. There are 550,000 police

officers in America today; 100,000 police is nearly a 20 percent increase. And if they are all
put into community policing as they are supposed to be, then it will be at least a 20 percent
increase in the effective police presence on the
street in the United States. That is the message
we need to get out to the American people,
so they can imagine what this means. This is
something of profound magnitude, not only in
catching criminals but, as every officer here will
tell you, in reducing the rate of crime in the
first place by deterring crime, by the simple,
effective presence of community policing.

I am very, very proud of all of you for your
support. I am very proud of Chief Massey for
coming here to tell this story.

I want to emphasize one other thing that the
Attorney General said before I close. The more
we got into this problem, the more we realized
that big city crime was going down in some
cities but that the inevitable consequence was
that it was being exported to smaller towns and
rural areas nearby, that as many of our larger
cities perfected their capacity to do community
policing and to drive down the crime rates, was
actually putting inordinate pressure on the
smaller towns who were in the vicinity. And
one of the things we were absolutely determined
to do is to make sure—I might add, with the

support of all the big city mayors—that this
would not simply be a big city bill. So now,
as you know, we have already put out over 2,000
police officers in 250 different communities of
all sizes in the country, and the Attorney General gave you the figures on what we're doing
today. I can assure you that over the life of
this crime bill, we will not lose focus on the
fact that crime is a problem for all Americans
in all size communities—400 communities today,
hundreds and hundreds and hundreds of more
to follow.

So I ask all of you now, as we leave this
place, not only to celebrate what we have done
but to redouble our efforts. We're getting off
to a quick start. We're making our country
strong at home, just like we have to be strong
abroad, and we know that it starts at the grassroots level. This is something Washington has
done to give you the power to change the future
of your communities, so that all the little
Porshas in this country can think they are truly
free.

Thank you, and God bless you all.

NOTE: The President spoke at 10:50 a.m. on the
South Lawn at the White House. In his remarks,
he referred to David Massey, police chief, Ocean
City, MD.

Interview With Ellen Ratner
October 12, 1994

Ms. Ratner. I just want to say, President Clinton, on behalf of all the radio stations I work
with and the Talk Radio News Service, it's really
a pleasure to have an opportunity to meet with
you. And I recently read your interviews in Talkers magazine. I'm delighted and glad that things
are better with talk radio.

The President. I like talk radio. I just think
that it's like anything else; it depends on how
you communicate. What I'm more concerned
about is the way communication in America has
stopped being communication and started being
more not just advocacy but just sort of attack,
attack, attack. I think that radio is kind of an
intimate medium. People can imagine being
there talking with you when they're listening
to us. And I think it ought to be used to explore

what we have in common as well as what divides
us.

Foreign Policy

Ms. Ratner. I would agree with that. And
in terms of what we have in common, it's interesting, the last 2 weeks I've been around the
White House covering what you've been saying.
We've had President Mandela here, Gerry
Adams has been in the United States, what's
going on in the Mideast, I mean, this has really
been an amazing time. What's it feel like?

The President. Well, it has been a truly amazing time just to be here in the last 10 days.
You mentioned that. It's a great tribute, in a
way, to the United States that we're working
for peace and making progress in so many areas.

We had President Mandela. We had President Yeltsin. We had Gerry Adams. We had the Arab boycott lifted by Saudi Arabia and the other GCC countries. We had the Chinese Foreign Minister here, and we made some real breakthroughs there on getting their agreement not to sell missiles. We made a new trade agreement with Japan that I think is better than anything we've done with them in a very long time. It's been a very exciting 10 days.

Religion and Politics

Ms. Ratner. You're also a man of faith. I know lately you have been meeting with religious leaders across the country, and they've been coming to the White House. What's going on? What is being accomplished? What are you trying to find out?

The President. Well, ever since I've been here, I have met on a periodic basis with either ministers and rabbis or scholars about a number of questions but mostly relating to the concerns of religion and the concerns of the political sphere and how they overlap and what the role of faith is for citizens today. And we talk about it, because I think that on balance most people who have strong religious convictions are good citizens. Most of them pay their taxes, obey the law, raise their kids well, and show up when their country needs them in war or peace.

And it bothers me that the only way that we think about religious people being active in politics is now under the guise of what's been called the Christian Coalition and involves people sort of signing off on an agenda, a certain agenda of political positions. Whereas I believe that people of faith come in all sizes, shapes, colors, political convictions and ought to be able to bring their concerns and their attempts to do God's will into the public arena. And so I just tried to do what I could both to gain more personal insight for myself but largely for my fellow Americans, to encourage people to get into being good citizens and to be active but also to be tolerant of those who have views that are different from theirs.

President's Inauguration

Ms. Ratner. This has been a question that I've personally wanted to ask you since the Inauguration. You had the song "Simple Gifts" sung at your Inauguration. It's a personal favorite of mine. Why did you select that? What does it mean?

The President. I think most of the great things in life are pretty simple and straightforward. And even though I guess I had a reputation as a policy wonk, which was probably well-deserved, I ran for President to do some fairly simple things. I wanted to restore the dreams of our children that they could be or do whatever they wanted to be or do. And I wanted people to believe that this was a country where we could come together instead of come apart. And that song seemed to capture that, the idea that the great things in life which flow from God are simple, profound, and they may be difficult to achieve, but they're simple and that we need not overcomplicate them to appreciate them and revel in them.

Administration Accomplishments

Ms. Ratner. The print media now has begun slowly, I think, to discuss some of your successes.

The President. Yes, it's amazing, reassessment or something.

Ms. Ratner. The legislative session now is coming to an end. How would you evaluate it?

The President. It's almost like a tale of two Congresses. The first one, Congress was one of the most productive in modern history. And it occurred mostly but not entirely last year, where we adopted a new economic plan which reversed trickle-down economics, brought the deficit down, asked the wealthiest 1.2 percent of our people to pay higher tax rates but lowered taxes on about 15 percent of our working families, 15 million people. We brought the deficit down dramatically 3 years in a row for the first time since Mr. Truman was President because of that economic plan, with $255 billion worth of tax cuts—I mean, spending cuts and cuts in over 300 Government programs.

Last year produced a dramatic expansion of trade with NAFTA and with the GATT agreement we got, which the Congress hasn't passed yet, but they will after the election. They'll come back and pass that.

The third thing we tried to do was to increase investment in people and technology, and the Congress did a good job of that. We put 200,000 more kids in Head Start. We're going to immunize 2 million children under the age of 2 by 1996. We passed a bill called Goals 2000 to have national world-class standards education for our classes, but have more local control of the schools at the same time. We passed a bill to improve apprenticeships in every State, so that more kids could leave high school and go to work and get good jobs if they didn't go to college. Perhaps the most important thing we did was we reformed the student loan program and made 20 million people eligible for lower interest student loans at longer repayment. And we, of course, passed national service, which allows young people to earn college credit by doing community service or earn money to go to college. So that was very, very good.

We passed this crime bill after 6 years of haggling. And it's very tough in terms of "three strikes and you're out" and 100,000 more jail cells and 100,000 more police on the street. But it also has some good prevention programs that give our kids something to say yes to, drug treatment, drug education, job training, wholesome and constructive community-based recreation programs. So that was very good.

With this reinventing Government initiative, it's been astonishing. We're reducing the size of the Federal Government to its smallest point since Kennedy was President. That's something Republican conservatives always said they were for, but we did that.

Ms. Ratner. When I talk about it on talk radio, people say it doesn't happen. I mean, why doesn't this message sink in?

The President. I don't know. I think because—that's why I think talk radio should be important to educate people, because so much of the press that comes out of here is based on conflict, process, the emergency of the moment. So a lot of the big things we do doesn't get a lot of press.

But anyway, we reduce the size of the Federal Government by 272,000 over this budget cycle. Now, we've already reduced it, already, just in 20 months, by more than 70,000. But in the 5-year period, 270,000 will be taken off. That's the smallest Federal Government since Kennedy. We're giving all the money to local communities to fight crime, every cent of it. We adopted a procurement reform bill I'm going to sign in a couple of days, which means the end of the $500 hammer. It says Government gets to buy things at the cheapest, best price, and must do it.

Ms. Ratner. I know. I saw it; it was great.

The President. We just adopted a reform of the Agriculture Department to reduce it by thousands and thousands of people. You can apply for a small business loan now on a one-

page form and get an answer in 3 days. These are things that were unheard of before. So that's been very good.

So I would say in the area of the economy, in the area of crime, in the area of reinventing the Government, in the area of education and training, and finally in the area of just making Government work for ordinary people—we adopted the family and medical leave law, the motor voter bill to make it easier to vote, the Brady bill—things that matter, we have done a very good job.

For the cities—a lot of your listeners live in urban areas—we've been trying to bring free enterprise to cities. The other party talked about it all the time, but they never did much. We have passed two major bills, one to create——

Ms. Ratner. Actually, I've seen the results of that in Cleveland, Ohio, recently.

The President. Yes, and it's beginning to work. We passed bills for empowerment zones. We passed bills to reform the way public housing works. We passed initiatives to set up community development banks to make loans to poor people. So all of that's been good.

Now, what's the second part of Congress? What did we fail to do? We didn't pass health care reform; we didn't pass lobby reform; we didn't pass campaign finance reform; we didn't pass a bill to make Congress live under the laws they imposed on private employers. We haven't passed the safe drinking water act; we haven't passed the California desert bill; we haven't passed the Superfund bill, which is supported by everybody from the chemical companies to the Sierra Club.

Why have we not passed those bills? Because there's strong special interest opposition, of course, but also because the leaders—the congressional leaders of the other party decided they wouldn't permit any of those bills to pass. And we've had—there's never been as many filibusters ever as there have been in the last 2 years. There have never been as much delaying tactics. So next year, we're going to have to come back on political reform, health care reform, welfare reform, and keeping the economy going.

Midterm Elections

Ms. Ratner. Do you think if there's that slight possibility that Republicans gain control of the House or the Senate, that you're going to be seen more as a man of the people whose agenda really needs to——

The President. Yes, in a funny—[*laughter*]—I suppose in a funny way, if people really got a dose of the alternative, they'd like me better, but that's just a part of the process of politics.

But what I want the American people to focus on in this election coming up is the choice for them: not between Democrats or Republicans or Bill Clinton or not, it's what's good for them. The fact is that I set out to do three things: to get the economy going again, to take on the tough problems, and to make the Government work for ordinary people. We have made real progress in all those areas. We have the lowest unemployment rate in 4 years; 4.6 million new jobs; the highest number of high-wage new jobs in this last year, more than in the previous 5 years.

Ms. Ratner. More manufacturing, as I understand it.

The President. Yes. We've got more high-wage jobs in this recovery than in the past 5 years combined. We've got 10 years of manufacturing job growth—10 months, excuse me, of manufacturing job growth in a row for the first time in a decade. So we're moving that way; we're making progress.

Now if you look at what the Republicans have promised, they signed this little contract. They call it a Contract With America. I call it a contract on America.

Ms. Ratner. That's what some people in talk radio are calling it also.

The President. It's amazing. I mean, it's just what they did in the eighties. They promised everybody the Moon. They tell them what they want to hear. It's a good way to get popular and a bad way to wreck the country. I mean, it's a trillion dollars in unfunded promises. So if they give everybody these tax cuts, if they start Star Wars again, if they increase defense again, if they do all the stuff they promised to do, what will happen? The deficit will go up instead of down, Medicare will have to be cut drastically, the crime bill will never be funded, and jobs will be lost.

Now, right now, we've got the deficit going down and the economy going up, a tough assault on crime, and a real attempt to deal with people's problems. Sure, we have not done everything; yes, we have a long way to go. But the answer is to keep going toward the future, not to go back to the eighties. That's what these

people want. And I think that—what I want to do in the next month is to have an honest conversation about that. Why should we go back and try what failed before when what we're doing now is working and we need more change, not less?

President's Management Style

Ms. Ratner. In closing, Mr. President, the broadcast media, some of them have been, I would say, almost brutal about your management style, but it's clearly working. I mean, there are some things that are happening. Some other people are saying that your management style actually reflects sort of a new philosophy of management. What is your management philosophy?

The President. I believe in, first of all, delegating to my Cabinet Departments decisions that are made consistent with my policies but which don't need to be made here. I believe in making big policy decisions myself, after you get everybody in with the best possible ideas and let them argue them out. I think the idea that somehow a President should be able to know off the top of his head and be able to make a snap decision on how to reverse 12 years of economic policies, 20 years of stagnant wages, and 30 years of social decline is a naive way of looking at things.

And if you look at people—whatever people want to say about my management style, last year, according to Congressional Quarterly, we got more done with Congress than any administration since World War II, except for President Eisenhower in '53 and President Johnson in '65. We have reduced the Federal Government when the Republicans couldn't. We have increased the performance of the Federal Government. And we got the economy going again. So I think our management style is producing pretty good results. We've got Russian missiles that are no longer pointed at the United States for the first time since World War II.

Ms. Ratner. Some people are saying it's a new model.

The President. We've got a lot of things going. And I just think that part of it is, people think in patterns, and they think with preconceived notions of how decisions should be made. And a lot of our preconceived patterns are rooted in the organization of our thoughts and attitudes and actions that came out of World War II and the cold war. Now we're moving toward the 21st century, when things are changing much more rapidly, when it requires a whole lot of knowledge from different sources to make good decisions, and when you're dealing with problems that developed over a long period of time and therefore may need some period of time to solve. In that sort of environment, a whole different decisionmaking process has to take hold. And you need to deal with different kinds of people and work in different ways to make things happen.

But I think if I get scored based on what we actually did, I'll be satisfied. I just want the American people to know what kind of changes we're trying to effect. And I don't want them to turn back; I want them to keep going with us. Give us 2 more years to make these changes; then they can make a judgment about whether we did what we said we'd do.

Life in Washington, DC

Ms. Ratner. One last question: How's it been living in Washington? You're new to this area; I'm fairly new to the area. I find it a tough place to be sometimes.

The President. Well, you know, Harry Truman said if you want a friend here, you ought to buy a dog. [*Laughter*] But I must say first, it's a beautiful place; it's a magnificent place.

Ms. Ratner. It certainly is.

The President. Secondly, it is an honor—with all the difficulties, it is still an honor and a joy to come to work in this office every day. Next, my wife and I have a lot of good friends here. And our daughter has done wonderfully well. She's been blessed with a terrific school, a very difficult, challenging, but good school and wonderful friends. So I have no complaints about living here. I've enjoyed it very much, and I'm just trying to get up here every day and do the job the American people hired me to do.

Ms. Ratner. Thank you very much, Mr. President.

The President. Thank you.

NOTE: The interview began at 3:23 p.m. in the Oval Office at the White House. A tape was not available for verification of the content of this interview.

Nomination for Controller of the Office of Management and Budget
October 12, 1994

The President today announced his nomination of G. Edward DeSeve as Controller of the Office of Management and Budget (OMB).

"Ed DeSeve is a financial innovator with financial management expertise in both the public and private sectors," the President said. "He is a welcome addition to OMB and will help the administration meet its goal of strengthening financial management throughout the Federal Government."

NOTE: A biography of the nominee was made available by the Office of the Press Secretary.

Remarks on Signing the Federal Acquisition Streamlining Act of 1994
October 13, 1994

Thank you very much. Ladies and gentlemen, let me begin by thanking all of you for all your work on these projects and thanking the Members of Congress who are here. Let me also begin with a story that's not in my notes but I think is important to you to understand all this.

When Vice President Gore and I showed up here 20 months ago, we had talked about a lot of things. There were even cartoons making fun of us for being policy wonks. I've got one in there in the White House with everybody falling asleep while I talked to them about more new ideas. [*Laughter*] But one of the things that I learned as a Governor, even though we had kept our State and local tax burden when I was Governor in the bottom two or three in the country every year, I still found that there was massive frustration among taxpayers and among public employees with the way our government worked, which was much smaller than almost any other State government and obviously much smaller than the National Government. And we began this process of trying to reinvent our efforts there.

I thought that something like this on the national scale was much more necessary if we were ever to make public employment rewarding, if we were ever to reduce defense and maintain our national strength and national security, if we were ever to regain the confidence and trust of the American taxpayers. And when I talked to the Vice President about it, he thought so, too. I said, "You know, the problem with this sort of deal is, everybody is for it. It's a 100 to nothing deal, but nobody wants to take responsibility for it because it is a real pain to get it done." He was willing to take responsibility for getting it done, and the American people owe him a great debt of gratitude for the work that he has done on it.

I kind of hate to sign this bill today. What will Jay Leno do? There will be no more $500 hammers, no more $600 toilet seats, no more $10 ashtrays. Al Gore will never get on David Letterman again. [Laughter] It's sort of a sad moment—[laughter]—the passing of Government purchasing as the butt of all the jokes on the evening shows. But it is a very important moment for the American people who are out there working hard and need to keep as much of their money as they can, and if they give us any of it, they're entitled to know that we're spending it properly.

This Government cannot ignore problems with our operations. We have tried to get those problems into the open and to deal with them and in the process to make it part of our ongoing effort to have the actions of our National Government mirror what should be happening in all of our society, decentralizing, empowering people, relying more on people who are closest to the action.

We've done a lot of other things like that. I signed a bank reform bill the other day which will remove a billion dollars in regulatory compliance; the trucking deregulation bill, estimated to save $8 billion in compliance with Federal regulations. We built a new highway in California after the earthquake in less than half the time we were told it could be built because we just changed the rules and the incentive structure there. The SBA now can give you a 3-page form—or a one-page form for a loan instead of one that's 100 pages long, and you can get an answer in 3 days. This is all part of that. We've given 17 States—17 States in 2 years, more than in the previous 12 years—permission to design their own welfare reform systems to move people from welfare to work.

So this procurement reform legislation we are signing today is a way to build the confidence of the American people in Government but also empower the people who work for the Government to make the most of their jobs and make the most of taxpayers' dollars.

This is the kind of thing I'm convinced that we'll be called upon to do more and more, not to do things for people but to empower people to do things for themselves, both within and beyond the Government. If you think about it, that's what the family leave law is all about. You've got to be a parent; you've got to be a worker; you might as well be good at both. That's what the family leave law is about.

That's what the college loan law is about, where the Secretary of Education and Deputy Secretary of Education and others designed a way that actually costs the taxpayers less to figure out how to give people college loans at lower interest rates and longer repayment terms; 20 million Americans already eligible to refinance their loans. We're not giving anybody an education; we're just making it possible for them to get it and make a contribution to our country.

And that's really what this whole reinventing Government effort is all about. It's a big challenge. One of the reasons it's a big challenge is that we've committed to reduce the size of this Government by 272,000, to its smallest size since the Kennedy administration, within a 6-year period. That means that we have to reform all of our other systems. If we don't reform the procurement system, we'll have too many people working in procurement to ever make that reduction. If we don't redefine the functions of the Government, we'll never get there.

That's why I'm so proud—and I want to say a little more in a minute—but I am so proud of the work that Secretary Espy has done at the Agriculture Department, where they have—in this Agriculture Department reform legislation that I just signed, they've reduced the number of their agencies by a third within the Agriculture Department; they've reduced their employment by 7,500; they've done a whole lot of other things that are profoundly important. All of this will enable us not only to downsize the Government, to do it without reducing the services we're giving to the American people.

One of the things that I found kind of nice is—you know, it's hard for a fellow like me to ever find anything in print I want to hold up anymore—[*laughter*]—but the Financial World, which is not the house organ of this administration, has written a letter to me in their present issue. And it says, with regard to running the Government, "We think you're making real progress. We've taken a close look at 10 of your major executive branch Departments and agencies to see how well they're managed. And we can report that most of them have improved under your leadership." Well, I appreciate that, but you guys get the credit, and I thank you for doing it.

I know that a lot of Americans have heard all these stories, but in addition to the ones that the Vice President told on the Letterman show, I think it's important to realize that there were real consequences to some of these problems that went beyond money.

A lot of you remember the story that Lt. Col. Brad Orton told us from Operation Desert Storm, when the Air Force tried to buy 6,000 of these high-tech, two-way radios from Motorola that were on the commercial market. They couldn't do it, and we were embarrassed. We had to go to the Japanese and ask them to buy the radios because we didn't have time to go through our procurement processes when we were out there trying to fight a war and stop a tyrant. You know, it's not as funny as the stories you hear, but it is terribly important.

Well, a highly competitive company like Motorola, frankly, didn't have time to spend all the money and effort it would take to comply with the inane regulations that kept Government employees from buying these. One of the things that I'm really pleased about is that, Senator Glenn, we now have, and Congressman Conyers, a letter in our file to me from the president of Motorola saying that you guys did a good job on this procurement reform, and we can now buy all of these that we need. [*Laughter*]

You know, one other thing I would like to say is that very often little things have big con-

sequences. I was pleased to see that the Vice President introduced Michelle Cradduck, and you see she got a good little article in the local paper here today. We would like to have your advice about how to get this kind of press on a more regular basis. Now, that would be a real reinvention of Government. [*Laughter*]

But you think about this. This law cuts redtape for purchases under $100,000, but it lets, maybe most important of all, front-line managers decide on purchases of less than $2,500. They can shop for the best deal without being bogged down in any bureaucracy. This will save—this is amazing—this will save, we estimate, $50 on every single purchase of items under $2,500. That's how much money we have been paying to comply with our own rules and regulations. Fifty dollars, you think about it; you add that up. That's a lot of children in Head Start. That's a lot of high school graduates going into apprenticeship programs. That's a lot of middle class kids getting college loans. That's a lot of money that's just been flushed away because we didn't change with the times. Gone are the days when a $4 stapler will require $50 worth of paperwork—never again, thanks to people like Michelle Cradduck. We thank you very much.

Today I am signing an Executive order that will go a little beyond the law. It will actually give people who use these products the authority to make small purchases, so the managers don't have to do it either.

These reforms, as I said, by illustrating this, will also strengthen our national security. Under the old system, defense contractors were virtually forced to develop practices and products unique to the military. The procurement process itself defied the development of modern technology in requiring the American industry to divide into defense and nondefense sectors. It meant our military paid higher prices, often couldn't get state-of-the-art technologies, and it meant also that we were dividing American industry at a time when emerging technologies were unifying processes across the lines of defense and nondefense economic sectors.

With these reforms and the ones that Secretary Perry announced last June, our men and women in uniform will have the best equipment in the world. They will be able to operate in this post-cold-war world which, as we all know, is still a dangerous place. The private sectors will be able to provide the equipment they need, and they will be able to do it in a way that strengthens the commercial sector as well as the defense sector instead of dividing them both and weakening them both. This will help us to compete and win in the global marketplace as we build our national security, not forcing company after company after company to choose between one or the other path. It is a very important but little noticed consequence of this reform.

Let me also say that this law also builds on our commitment to small businesses. It allows small businesses to learn more about and bid on Government contracts through electronic information that works, they can reach through their own computers. It continues to increase purchases for minority-owned businesses. It sets a goal that at least 5 percent of the purchases will come from businesses owned by women.

As I said earlier in reference to the Agriculture Department bill, there are a lot of other things which should reinforce what we're doing today. I signed a bill which helps HUD to improve the management of apartment buildings and helps the Department of Energy's laboratories to develop peacetime technologies. The Agriculture Department bill, as I said earlier, closes 1,200 unneeded offices, fights fraud and abuse in the crop insurance program, cuts the number of divisions in the Department by a third, reduces employees by 7,500. Pretty soon, we'll be able to move the rest of the Federal Government over to the Agriculture Department. [*Laughter*]

I also signed before I came out here the Government Management Reform Act. Again, a little noticed bill, but it will be very important to all of you as we seek to keep this process going. It will help to eliminate waste, fraud, and abuse by developing reliable financial statements on cost and performance. Within 4 years, for the first time ever, believe it or not, the Government will publish, just like any good company would, an annual consolidated financial statement covering every executive branch agency. We are going to do that as well.

There's one more step I want to take today, and this may be somewhat controversial, but

it's important. You know, these signing ceremonies are fun. Everybody forgets there are a lot of hard work and tough tradeoffs and difficult decisions that leads to these things.

Congress recently passed two spending bills that prevent several Government agencies from making the personnel cuts that must be made to continue reinventing Government and to finance the crime bill. Today, I'm asking Congress to get rid of those restrictions on our ability to cut back big government and to do more with less. This is a matter of principle as well as practice. No agency anywhere should be exempt from doing its job as efficiently as possible. The Federal employees don't want it that way. It's not fair to some and not others, and it won't permit our system to work as it should.

Finally, let me say this. Most of you here care a lot about all this. But a lot of people don't get very excited about it, and far too many can't imagine that Government could ever change itself. But bit by bit, the things we are doing, like the thing we are doing today, we'll be able to prove by actions, not words, that we can use taxpayers money wisely and with respect, in an appropriate way. After all, the American people own this place. They are our employers as well as our customers. They deserve the same honesty and efficiency from their Government they demand from the private sector. They should settle for nothing less. With this historic law, we are taking another big step in meeting their expectations and in doing our duty.

To all of you who have made this day possible, I say a profound thank you.

NOTE: The President spoke at 11:30 a.m. in the Rose Garden at the White House. In his remarks, he referred to Michelle Cradduck, contract specialist in the Public Health Service's Division of Acquisition Management. S. 1587, approved October 13, was assigned Public Law No. 103–355. The Executive order and related memorandum on Federal procurement are listed in Appendix D at the end of this volume.

Statement on Signing the Federal Crop Insurance Reform and Department of Agriculture Reorganization Act of 1994
October 13, 1994

Today I have signed into law H.R. 4217, the Federal Crop Insurance Reform and Department of Agriculture Reorganization Act of 1994. As the name implies, this Act has two purposes. The first is to reform Federal crop insurance and the second is to reorganize the U.S. Department of Agriculture (USDA).

H.R. 4217 provides the Secretary of Agriculture with the critically needed authority to reorganize USDA so that the Department can meet the challenges of the 21st century. It will be the most ambitious reorganization proposal ever undertaken by the Department. Guided by the principles articulated in the Vice President's National Performance Review, this legislation grants the Secretary authority to pursue more efficiently the goals of improving the prospects for farmers, enhancing the quality of life in rural America, better ensuring food safety, strengthening conservation efforts, and improving nutritional programs.

The Secretary will reorganize USDA around six basic missions, improve the Department's accountability and service to customers, reform its field structure, and reduce personnel and costs. Indeed, during 1994–1999, USDA will save $2.4 billion in personnel costs and about $1.3 billion in other costs. The end result will be a more streamlined and responsive Department.

This Act also reforms Federal crop insurance to address the frustrations of farmers with the inadequacies of the current system. Many farmers have not participated in the program and others have found that their losses for prevented planting were not covered. Those who relied on ad hoc disaster assistance did not know until weeks or months after their loss whether such assistance would be provided, leaving many fearful of losing their farms and livelihood.

The need for reform became apparent during last year's devastating flood in the Midwest and drought in the Southeast. Out of that experience, the Administration made a commitment to reform the current program, and began consultations with Members of the Congress, farmers, insurance providers, lenders, and others on developing a legislative proposal.

The Administration proposal was included in the 1995 Budget submitted to the Congress last February. The Administration and many Members of the Congress have spent several long months fine-tuning this proposal so that it would meet budget-scoring requirements and other considerations.

This Act is substantially similar to the Administration proposal. It provides for a minimal level of catastrophic coverage for most crops, greater incentives for producers to buy additional coverage, payment assistance for other crops where insurance is not available, and reforms to the disaster payment system that should greatly reduce the incidence of fraud. It requires producers who participate in USDA's farm income support and credit programs to sign-up for catastrophic coverage on their insurable crops, and eliminates the use of emergency legislation for agricultural crop disaster assistance. Producers will be able to obtain catastrophic insurance coverage for a nominal processing fee. Yet, taxpayers will save money compared to the current approach of enacting ad hoc disaster assistance year after year.

I want to thank Secretary Espy for the tremendous and tireless work he and his staff have put into developing a reorganization plan that will make USDA more farmer-friendly, improve customer service, and save taxpayer money. I also wish to thank the chair and ranking member of the Senate Committee on Agriculture, Nutrition, and Forestry, Senators Patrick Leahy and Richard Lugar, and the chair and ranking member of the House Committee on Agriculture, Representative "Kika" de la Garza and Pat Roberts, as well as Representative Charles Stenholm, for their leadership in guiding the bill through to passage.

The Administration is committed to reinventing the Federal Government, so that it works better and costs less for all Americans. By authorizing the reinvention of USDA, this Act sets the standard for the rest of the Federal Government to follow and is a victory for American taxpayers.

WILLIAM J. CLINTON

The White House,
October 13, 1994.

NOTE: H.R. 4217, approved October 13, was assigned Public Law No. 103–354.

Statement on Signing the Government Management Reform Act of 1994
October 13, 1994

Today I have signed into law S. 2170, the "Government Management Reform Act of 1994."

In September of last year, Vice President Gore and his team at the National Performance Review (NPR) stated this simple fact in their report entitled, "From Red Tape to Results":

"Management isn't about guessing, it's about *knowing*. Those in positions of responsibility must have the information they need to make good decisions. Good managers have the right information at their fingertips. Poor managers don't."

By passing the Government Management Reform Act of 1994, which is largely based on ideas developed by the NPR, the Congress has helped ensure that the Federal Government's managers will have the financial information and flexibility they need to make sound policy decisions and manage resources.

The Act expands the coverage initially mandated by the Chief Financial Officers Act so that 24 major Government departments and agencies will now provide annual audited financial reports of all their activities, spending, and revenues. Not later than 1998, the Federal Government will produce a consolidated financial statement covering virtually all of the $1.5 trillion annual budget authority of the Government and the revenues it receives.

The NPR report also stated that "we believe Americans deserve numbers they can trust" and recommended that the Federal Government provide an annual accountability report to our citizens. This Act's requirement for an audited consolidated financial report is a step in achieving this goal. To advance the process of accountability, I have requested that the Secretary of the Treasury, with the Director of the Office of Management and Budget (OMB), also produce an Annual Accountability Report to the Citizens in 1995, as recommended by the Vice President in the NPR report. The Accountability Report will be a straightforward description of the money spent and its effects on achieving results.

Measuring results is an important management goal of this Administration. The financial statements promise to be an excellent tool for providing agency performance and financial data, so we can have a closer look at results and whether Government indeed works better and costs less.

S. 2170 contains a number of other significant provisions. These include: the establishment of pilot programs to create franchising operations that will consolidate administrative support services, improve competition, and cut costs; expansion of the use of electronic funds transfers for Federal payments; and authority for the OMB Director to streamline management reporting to the Congress.

The Franchise Fund Pilot Program authorized by this Act will create internal markets through "franchising" common administrative support services to many agencies so the service providers may compete with one another. Injecting competition and market forces into the delivery of these services will reduce duplication, lower overhead costs, and better serve the American people.

Starting on January 1, 1995, S. 2170 promotes the use of direct deposit through electronic funds transfer for Federal wages, salaries, and retirement payments. The costs of disbursing money electronically are considerably less than the costs of printing, mailing, and processing paper checks.

The Act also provides tools to the OMB Director to consolidate and streamline management reporting processes. In particular, the Director will have the flexibility to determine the most meaningful timing and presentation of financial management reports from agencies to OMB and the Congress.

By expanding the scope of the financial statement requirements, the Act ensures the American people will have financial information they can trust. We will be better able to show the taxpayers what they are getting for their dollar. In short, this law means greater accountability. I commend the Congress for passing the Government Management Reform Act of 1994, and I am pleased to sign this legislation into law.

WILLIAM J. CLINTON

The White House,

October 13, 1994.

NOTE: S. 2170, approved October 13, was assigned Public Law No. 103-356.

Teleconference Remarks to Broadcasters Associations
October 13, 1994

Thank you, Marcy. Good morning to you and to the hundreds of distinguished members of the broadcast journalism industry gathered there with you. I'm honored to help kick off the very first joint undertaking of the Radio Television News Directors Association and the National Association of Broadcasters Radio.

You know, I've talked a lot about building new partnerships all over America; I must say that after the last 20 months I never expected it would be the journalists who would be the first to take me seriously. But I'm glad you're leading the way.

I've had the chance to review the ambitious agenda you've had for this week—discussing issues involving programming, ethics, technology, marketing—in one of the most dynamic industries on Earth. I applaud you for accepting these challenges as well as for the decades of leadership in your industry. I know Reed Hunt, our Chairman of the FCC, will join many of you soon for an in-depth discussion of these and other issues.

I'm delighted that you're honoring Charles Kuralt with the Paul White Award for lifetime achievement. I've admired him for a long time. "On The Road" was a true celebration of the unsung heroes and the enduring values of America. I'm told he got the idea for the show one night when he was on a plane looking down at the lights below. He said he thought the following: "There are a lot of Americans who don't live in cities and don't make headlines. I was interested in finding out about them." Well, for most of my life I was one of them, and I'm proud that Charles Kuralt found out so much about them. He taught us about the steadiness and the joys of daily life that are so often masked by the daily headlines.

Before I get into the body of my remarks today, I'd like to give you an update on the situations in the Persian Gulf and Haiti. First, let me say how very proud I am of the men and women of our Armed Forces who are serving in both areas. We've asked an awful lot of them, and they're delivering with great skill and professionalism. They are the power behind our diplomacy.

Last week, in the face of Iraq's threatening troop movements on the Kuwaiti border, I ordered the deployment to the Gulf of an aircraft carrier battle group, cruise missile ships, Marine and Army troops, and several hundred attack aircraft. Our policy is clear: We will not allow Iraq to threaten its neighbors or to intimidate the United Nations as it ensures that Iraq never again possesses weapons of mass destruction.

I'm pleased to say that Iraq heard our message. Its forces have begun a broad retreat from the border area. Only a few Republican Guard units remain in southern Iraq, and they are withdrawing, too. But the withdrawal is not yet complete, and it's too soon to say where all the troops are going. So we're watching the situation very, very carefully, and we'll continue to deploy our forces in the Gulf until we're satisfied that Iraqi troops no longer pose an immediate danger to Kuwait.

At the same time, Ambassador Albright has proposed a very strong resolution in the United Nations to prevent Iraq from threatening its southern neighbors now or in the future. We're working closely at the Security Council to win broad international support for that resolution.

Now let me add a few words about Haiti. Our troops went there to keep a solemn commitment by the United States and the international community to restore the nation's democratically elected government and to help bring an end to terrible human rights problems. We're keeping that commitment.

I'm pleased to say that General Cédras and his closest followers have arrived in Panama. On Saturday, President Aristide will return home to resume his rightful place. Haiti's remarkable journey from fear to freedom continues. And given the outstanding performance of our troops there and in Iraq and elsewhere, we should be confident of our ability to rise to the new challenges we surely will be called upon to meet.

You know, I came to Washington 20 months ago to try to really change this country, to change the direction in which we were going and the attitude we had about our present and our future. Quite simply, I wanted to move the country forward and bring it together so that we could compete and win in the 21st century and so that every one of us could live up to the fullest of our God-given capacities.

In the last 20 months, we followed a disciplined strategy to try to create more jobs, bring the deficit down, improve education and training, invest in new technologies, assist the conversion from a defense to a commercial economy, reach out to the rest of the world and have more trade and more peace and security, help the American people at home by having the Government work for ordinary people again.

In short, what I offered the American people was not a set of gifts or promises but a real challenge and the opportunity to take responsibility for their own lives, if we had the courage to make the changes on the difficult issues that we had ignored for years and years and years.

I knew we were facing a big task. We'd had, after all, 30 years of serious social problems relating to the breakdown of communities, neighborhoods, families, the rise of crime and drugs and violence and gangs. We've had 20 years of serious economic problems for working people, where most hourly wage earners have had no gain in wages, even though the cost of living has gone up. We had 12 years of a different theory of how we ought to deal with these problems, the trickle-down Reaganomics years in which from my point of view we were making things worse, not better.

Well, after 20 months, we've made a good beginning. We passed an economic plan that brought the deficit down at a record rate with $255 billion of spending cuts, a tax increase

in the rates on 1.2 percent of our people, tax breaks for 15 million working families who work for modest wages and raise children and shouldn't be in poverty if they're working. That economic plan, along with our aggressive trade strategies with NAFTA, GATT, and other areas, has helped to bring our economy back, and we've got 4.6 million more jobs now than we did 20 months ago. We've had more high-wage jobs come into this economy in the last year than in the previous 5 years combined. We've had 9 years of manufacturing job growth for the first time in a decade. The annual vote of international economists said that America is now the most productive country in the world for the first time since 1985. So we're making a good beginning.

We've taken a serious stand against crime with the passage of the Brady bill and the crime bill which will increase police on the street by 20 percent, build 100,000 prison beds for serious offenders, stiffen punishment, ban assault weapons, and provide prevention funds to give our young people another chance to avoid a life of crime.

And we've begun to make Government work for ordinary people again, literally to empower them to take responsibility for their own lives. That's what the Family and Medical Leave Act was all about. Most people are workers and parents; they ought to be able to succeed as both. That's what expanding Head Start so 200,000 more children can be enrolled is all about. That's what providing immunizations for 2 million children so that all our kids under the age of 2 will be immunized by 1996 is all about. It's what a national network of apprenticeships for young people who graduate from high school and don't go to college but do want good jobs is all about. It's what the college loan reform is all about, making 20 million young Americans eligible to refinance their college loans at longer repayment terms and lower interest rates. And it's what our reinventing Government effort, spearheaded by the Vice President, is all about.

We worked very hard to reduce the size of the Federal Government, to slash regulations, to provide more flexibility to local government. Just in the last few days, I signed a banking reform bill which will reduce compliance with Federal regulations by a billion dollars. We signed the trucking deregulation bill which will save another $8 billion. When California had its earthquake, we changed the way we rebuilt roads in ways that cut the time for rebuilding the Nation's busiest freeway by more than half. These are the kinds of things we're trying to do to literally reinvent the way Government works. Today the Small Business Administration can give you a loan application that's only one page long, and you can get an answer, yes or no, within 3 days.

One of the most important things we've had to do is to face the mind-boggling difficulty of procurement reform. That's what you know when you think about the $500 coffee pot bought by the Pentagon or the $4 stapler that costs $50 in paperwork to procure. The bureaucracy that was supposed to shrink in the last decade instead grew like Godzilla. Eliminating these kinds of abuses and excesses has been in my plan since the day I came to Washington.

You'll all remember the Vice President going on the David Letterman show to try to break the ashtray and show you how incredible the regulations were there. That's just one of thousands of examples of things we have to change to rebuild the confidence of the American taxpayers that we're spending their money wisely and also to empower Federal employees to give their taxpayers good value for the dollar.

Well, today at the White House I've taken a series of very important steps toward that goal, and I want you to hear about them. First and foremost, I signed today a bill to completely restructure the way Government buys $200 billion worth of goods and services every year. It's called the Federal Acquisition Streamlining Act of 1994.

Let me try to put this again in larger context. Everything we're trying to do here has been about making Government work better for ordinary people, giving taxpayers the value they deserve, empowering people to live up to the fullest of their potential. We cannot do that until the Government spends taxpayer money wisely and responsibly. We have to do better. We don't have the time or the money now to waste on bad government. And the place to start making Government work better is to cut it to an effective size and at the same time to make it more efficient so that we can do more with less.

The Vice President's done a very good job in leading this fight. We're cutting the Federal work force by 272,000 people. We've already reduced it by more than 70,000. And when we finish, the Federal work force will be smaller than at any time since President Kennedy

served. We're taking the savings and we're giving it all back to our local communities to fight crime.

We're also insisting that Government institute the same kind of management reforms that have made the private sector more productive and competitive in recent years. And I'm proud to say that's working. Financial World magazine just published an open letter to me in which they said, "We think you're making real progress. We've taken a close look at 10 of your major executive branch departments and agencies to see how well they're managed, and we can report that most of the 10 agencies have improved under your stewardship." Now, like all change, this has not been easy, and a lot of times it occurs in smaller steps that are easy to overlook when they do occur.

When I took office, this Government was literally riddled with rules and regulations that made absolutely no sense. Let me give you one example. In the midst of the Gulf war, our troops couldn't buy two-way Motorola radios they badly needed because Motorola didn't keep detailed enough books to meet the procurement regulations. No sensible company in the international marketplace would have done what it took to meet these regulations. So what happened? The Japanese had to buy them for us. It was pretty embarrassing. Today the historic law I signed will ensure that this never happens again. The chairman of Motorola wrote me a letter saying that we could buy his products now, and we'd be buying a lot more things at lower cost with better value.

This law eliminates a great deal of the redtape in the Federal procurement system. For the first time, the Government will be able to shop off the shelf for the best values they can find, just like everybody else. In short, $500 coffeepots or $600 toilet seats, the $50 ashtrays, all these things, as a matter of Government policy, are history.

In addition, this reform will cut out the excessive need for separate industries, one for civilian products and one for defense products. That will help to diversify our economy. It will allow defense industries to compete and win in the global marketplace. The world is still a very dangerous place, and this procurement reform ensures that our fighting men and women will have the highest quality weapons and equipment they need, while encouraging the same companies to compete in commercial enterprises.

This morning I also signed two other measures to cut the size of Government and improve its operations. One bill reorganizes the Department of Agriculture. It closes or combines 1,200 unnecessary offices, reduces the number of divisions in the Agriculture Department by a third, and reduces employment by over 7,500. The Secretary of Agriculture and all those who worked on this deserve a lot of credit for this important step forward.

The other bill requires the Government to publish a complete financial statement every single year for every executive branch agency. Believe it or not, complete consolidated financial statements weren't required before this.

Finally, I'd like some help from you and others to get another change or two along this line. Congress has just passed two spending bills that protect several agencies from the personnel cuts that have to be made in order for us to meet the reinventing Government target of 270,000 and to fund the crime bill. So today I'm asking that Congress get rid of these restrictions on our ability to cut back big Government. This is a matter of principle. No agency anywhere should be exempt from doing its job as efficiently as possible.

The American people deserve a Government that works. For most Americans, good Government means a timely Social Security check or better police protection or a tax burden that doesn't suffocate them. Democracy means little to them if it can't meet these basic needs except with a Government that costs too much or is too big or too slow or too unresponsive. We can, we must do better, and we are doing better. It's a part of bringing America back, restoring economic growth, making a serious assault on crime, making Government work for ordinary people again, having a Government that does more with less.

I'd like to close on this note. More than 30 years ago, President Kennedy addressed the members of the Radio TV News Directors Association. About that time, he said this about the press: "Even though we never like it and even though we wish they didn't write it and even though we disapprove of it, there isn't any doubt at all that we could not do the job in a free society without a very, very active press." The fundamental truth is that for all the profound changes that have taken place in world affairs, technology, and markets, his words are still as accurate as they were on the day he said them.

Every day, the national dialog that helps to sustain our freedoms is begun by you. Every day I have the opportunity to discuss the work we're doing directly with the people we're doing it for because of you. We share fundamental ideals for a free and open society where all can reach their God-given potential and pursue the American dream.

I wish you the best of luck this week and in the months ahead. These are exciting and challenging times, and I think we should enjoy them together. Yes, there are problems, but nothing, nothing we cannot face if we roll up our sleeves, pull together, and look to the future.

Now, Marcy, I'll turn it back to you with a warm thank-you to all of you for the opportunity to speak with you today. Thank you very much.

NOTE: The President spoke at 12:37 p.m. by satellite from Room 459 of the Old Executive Office Building to the Radio Television News Directors Association and the National Association of Broadcasters NAB Radio Show, meeting in Los Angeles, CA. In his remarks, he referred to Marcy Burdick, chair, Radio Television News Directors Association.

Statement on Signing the Uniformed Services Employment and Reemployment Rights Act of 1994
October 13, 1994

I am pleased to sign into law H.R. 995, the "Uniformed Services Employment and Reemployment Rights Act of 1994."

Today there are members of the National Guard and Reserve, including Coast Guard Reservists, on active duty supporting operational missions. As their Commander in Chief, it is timely for me to sign a bill that will clarify and strengthen their right to return to the civilian positions they held before going on active duty without any loss of seniority, status, or pay.

The "Uniformed Services Employment and Reemployment Rights Act of 1994" revises, improves, and clarifies the existing veterans reemployment rights statute, which was first enacted in 1940. Since that time, a confusing and cumbersome patchwork of statutory amendments and judicial constructions have made the law difficult for employers to understand.

Among other changes, H.R. 995 extends coverage for the first time to the Coast Guard and Public Health Service Reserve components.

It also entitles service members to continued health insurance coverage under their employer's plan for up to 18 months of military leave and makes explicit the rights of reemployed service members under their pension plans.

My Administration is committed to enforcing the reemployment rights of service members. This Act is key to the achievement of that goal.

WILLIAM J. CLINTON

The White House,
October 13, 1994.

NOTE: H.R. 995, approved October 13, was assigned Public Law No. 103–353.

Statement on the Cease-Fire in Northern Ireland
October 13, 1994

I welcome today's announcement by the Combined Loyalist Military Command in Northern Ireland declaring an end to its campaign of violence. The cease-fire announcement by the IRA on August 31 and today's announcement by Loyalist paramilitaries present the best hope for peace in a generation in Northern Ireland. The parties must now build on this historic step forward and enter into negotiations for a lasting settlement.

Prime Minister John Major of the United Kingdom and Prime Minister Albert Reynolds of Ireland deserve great credit for their leadership and persistence in pressing for progress.

The principles put forward in their Downing Street Declaration provide an important foundation for a just and lasting peace. I look forward to the next steps in the process, including the Forum for Peace and Reconciliation proposed by Prime Minister Reynolds and the roundtable talks convened by the Irish and British Governments with all involved parties.

I am pleased that the United States has been able to contribute to the peace process in Northern Ireland. We continue to stand ready to assist in achieving a negotiated, democratic settlement supported by both communities in Northern Ireland.

Statement on Disaster Assistance for Georgia
October 13, 1994

I am pleased that we can provide additional assistance to the people of Georgia in their efforts to rebuild their communities. I look forward to working in cooperation with them in the recovery.

NOTE: This statement was included in a White House statement announcing the President's decision to authorize an increase in the Federal Government's part of the cost-share program for repairing flood-damaged public property.

Statement on the Arts and Humanities Awards Recipients
October 13, 1994

These extraordinary and talented individuals have borne eloquent testimony to the enduring power of the arts and the humanities in our everyday lives. They have contributed profoundly to the richness and variety of our Nation's cultural life, and so it is with enormous gratitude that we pay them national tribute.

NOTE: This statement was included in a White House statement announcing the awards ceremony for the National Medal of the Arts and the Charles Frankel Prize scheduled for October 14. Biographies of the honorees were made available by the Office of the Press Secretary.

Statement on the National Award for Museum Service
October 13, 1994

This national honor is a tribute to the power of museums to engage children, families, and communities, in towns and cities all across America.

NOTE: This statement was included in a White House statement announcing the presentation of the National Award for Museum Service to the Brukner Nature Center, Troy, OH; the Cummer Museum of Art and Gardens, Jacksonville, FL; and the Missouri Historical Society, St. Louis, MO.

Letter to Congressional Leaders Reporting on the National Emergency With Respect to Haiti
October 13, 1994

Dear Mr. Speaker: (Dear Mr. President:)

1. In December 1990, the Haitian people elected Jean-Bertrand Aristide as their President by an overwhelming margin in a free and fair election. The United States praised Haiti's success in peacefully implementing its democratic constitutional system and provided significant political and economic support to the new government. The Haitian military abruptly interrupted the consolidation of Haiti's new democracy when, in September 1991, it illegally and violently ousted President Aristide from office and drove him into exile.

2. The United States, on its own and together with the Organization of American States (OAS), immediately imposed sanctions against the illegal regime. The United States also actively supported the efforts of the OAS and the United Nations to restore democracy to Haiti and to bring about President Aristide's return by facilitating negotiations between the Haitian parties. The United States and the international community also offered material assistance within the context of an eventual negotiated settlement of the Haitian crisis to support the return to democracy, build constitutional structures, and foster economic well-being.

As a result of continuing military intransigence in the face of these efforts and of worsening human rights abuses in Haiti, the conclusion was reached that no political settlement of the Haitian crisis was possible as long as the three principal military leaders remained in power. Therefore, beginning in early May 1994, a series of steps were taken to intensify the pressure of sanctions on the military leaders and their associates in order to bring the three leaders to step down. With U.S. leadership, the U.N. Security Council on May 6, 1994, enacted Resolution 917, imposing comprehensive trade sanctions and other measures on Haiti. This was followed by a succession of unilateral United States sanctions—banning scheduled air service and financial transactions to or from Haiti or between Haiti and third countries through the United States and blocking the assets in the United States or under United States control of Haitians resident in Haiti. Additionally, under authorities not related to the IEEPA, all visas that had been issued to Haitians at Port-au-Prince or Curacao before May 11, 1994, were revoked. Several other countries took similar actions.

The continued resistance of the illegal regime to the efforts of the international community also prompted the United States to augment embargo enforcement. The United States and other countries entered into a cooperative endeavor with the Dominican Republic to monitor that country's enforcement of sanctions along its land border with Haiti and in its coastal waters.

As the reporting period progressed, it became apparent that the Haitian military leaders, even under the pressure of intense worldwide sanctions, were determined to cling to power and to block the restoration of democracy and return of President Aristide. Internal repression continued to worsen, exemplified by the expulsion in July of the U.N./OAS-sponsored International Civilian Mission (ICM) human rights observers. As a result of this deterioration and the threat it posed to peace and security in the region, the U.N. Security Council enacted Resolution 940 on July 31, 1994, authorizing the use of all necessary means to bring about the departure of the military leadership and the return of the legitimate authorities including President Aristide. In the succeeding weeks, the international community under U.S. leadership assembled a multinational coalition force to carry out this mandate.

On September 18, 1994, I directed the deployment of U.S. Armed Forces to Haiti to remove the military leaders and restore democracy. However, I remained deeply committed to achieving our goals peacefully if possible. Therefore, on the previous day I had sent former President Jimmy Carter, Senator Sam Nunn and retired General Colin Powell to Haiti on a final diplomatic mission. The combination of an imminent military operation and determined diplomacy led to an agreement on September 18, that portends the early achievement

of our and the international community's goals in Haiti. The military leaders have relinquished power and the legitimate authorities will be restored by October 15 at the latest. As a result of the agreement reached in Port-au-Prince on September 18 U.S. forces in the vanguard of the multinational coalition force drawn from 26 countries began a peaceful deployment to Haiti on September 19.

In a spirit of reconciliation and reconstruction, President Aristide called on September 25 for the immediate easing of sanctions to further the mission of the coalition forces and begin without delay the work of rebuilding. In response to this request, on September 26, in an address before the United Nations General Assembly, I announced my intention to suspend all unilateral sanctions against Haiti except those that affect the military leaders and their immediate supporters and families. I also directed that steps be taken in accordance with Resolutions 917 and 940 to permit supplies and services to flow to Haiti to restore health care, water and electrical services, provide construction materials for humanitarian programs, and allow the shipment of communications, agricultural, and educational materials.

Regulations to accomplish those objectives were published in the *Federal Register* on October 5. In addition, the U.N. Security Council on September 29 enacted Resolution 944 directing that all U.N. sanctions be terminated the day after President Aristide returns to Haiti. Finally, the national emergency with respect to Haiti was extended on September 30, 1994, to allow the continued enforcement of those sanctions that are to remain in force until the restoration of democracy to Haiti is completed as will be signified by President Aristide's return to his country.

3. This report is submitted to the Congress pursuant to 50 U.S.C. 1641(c) and 1703(c). It is not a report on all U.S. activities with respect to Haiti, but discusses only those Administration actions and expenses since my last report (April 25, 1994), that are directly related to the national emergency with respect to Haiti declared in Executive Order No. 12775, as implemented pursuant to that order and Executive Orders Nos. 12779, 12853, 12872, 12914, 12917, 12920, and 12922.

4. Economic sanctions against the *de facto* regime in Haiti were first imposed in October 1991. On October 4, 1991, in Executive Order

No. 12775, President Bush declared a national emergency to deal with the threat to the national security, foreign policy, and economy of the United States caused by events that had occurred in Haiti to disrupt the legitimate exercise of power by the democratically-elected government of that country (56 Fed. Reg. 50641). In that order, the President ordered the immediate blocking of all property and interests in property of the Government of Haiti (including the Banque de la Republique d'Haiti) then or thereafter located in the United States or within the possession or control of a U.S. person, including its overseas branches. The Executive order also prohibited any direct or indirect payments or transfers to the de facto regime in Haiti of funds or other financial or investment assets or credits by any U.S. person, including its overseas branches, or by any entity organized under the laws of Haiti and owned or controlled by a U.S. person.

Subsequently, on October 28, 1991, President Bush issued Executive Order No. 12779, adding trade sanctions against Haiti to the sanctions imposed on October 4 (56 Fed. Reg. 55975). This order prohibited exportation from the United States of goods, technology, and services and importation into the United States of Haitian-origin goods and services, after November 5, 1991, with certain limited exceptions. The order exempted trade in publications and other informational materials from the import, export, and payment prohibitions and permitted the exportation to Haiti of donations to relieve human suffering as well as commercial sales of five food commodities: rice, beans, sugar, wheat flour and cooking oil. In order to permit the return to the United States of goods being prepared for U.S. customers by Haiti's substantial "assembly sector," the order also permitted, through December 5, 1991, the importation into the United States of goods assembled or processed in Haiti that contained parts or materials previously exported to Haiti from the United States. On February 5, 1992, it was announced that specific licenses could be applied for on a case-by-case basis by U.S. persons wishing to resume a pre-embargo import/export relationship with the assembly sector in Haiti.

5. On June 30, 1993, I issued Executive Order No. 12853 that expanded the blocking of assets of the de facto regime to include assets of Haitian nationals identified by the Secretary of the Treasury as providing substantial financial or material contributions to the regime, or doing substantial business with the regime. That Executive order also implemented U.N. Security Council Resolution (UNSC Resolution) 841 of June 16, 1993, by prohibiting the sale or supply by U.S. persons or from the United States, or using U.S.-registered vessels or aircraft, or petroleum or petroleum products or arms and related materials of all types to any person or entity in Haiti, or for the purpose of any business carried on in or operated from Haiti, or promoting or calculated to promote such sale or supply. Carriage of such goods to Haiti on U.S.-registered vessels was prohibited, as was any transaction for the evasion or avoidance of, or attempt to evade or avoid, any prohibition in the order.

6. As reported earlier, apparent steady progress toward achieving the firm goal of restoring democracy in Haiti permitted the United States and the world community to suspend economic sanctions against Haiti in August 1993. With strong support from the United States, the U.N. Security Council adopted Resolution 861 on August 27, 1993, suspending the petroleum, arms, and financial sanctions imposed under UNSC Resolution 841. On the same day, the Secretary General of the OAS announced that the OAS was urging member states to suspend their trade embargoes. In concert with these U.N. and OAS actions, U.S. trade and financial restrictions against Haiti were suspended, effective at 9:35 a.m. e.d.t., on August 31, 1993.

Our work to reach a solution to the Haitian crisis through the Governors Island Agreement was seriously threatened by accelerating violence in Haiti sponsored or tolerated by the de facto regime. The violence culminated on October 11, 1993, with the obstruction by armed "attachés" supported by the Haitian military and police of the deployment of U.S. military trainers and engineers sent to Haiti as part of the United Nations Mission in Haiti. The Haitian military's decision to dishonor its commitments made in the Governors Island Agreement was apparent. On October 13, 1993, the U.N. Security Council issued Resolution 873, which terminated the suspension of sanctions effective at 11:59 p.m. e.d.t., October 18, 1993.

As a result, effective at 11:59 p.m. e.d.t., October 18, 1993, the Department of the Treasury revoked the suspension of those trade and financial sanctions that had been suspended, so that the full scope of prior prohibitions was reinstated (58 *Fed. Reg.* 54024, October 19, 1993). The reinstated sanctions in the Haitian Transactions Regulations, 31 C.F.R. Part 580 (the HTR), prohibited most unlicensed trade with Haiti, and blocked the assets of the *de facto* regime in Haiti, and of the Government of Haiti. Restrictions on the entry into U.S. ports of vessels whose Haitian calls would violate U.S. or OAS sanctions had they been made by U.S. persons were also reinstated.

Also effective at 11:59 p.m., October 18, 1993, I issued Executive Order No. 12872 (58 *Fed. Reg.* 54029), authorizing the Department of the Treasury to block assets of persons who have: (1) contributed to the obstruction of UNSC Resolutions 841 and 873, the Governors Island Agreement, or the activities of the U.N. Mission in Haiti; (2) perpetuated or contributed to the violence in Haiti; or (3) materially or financially supported either the obstruction or the violence referred to above. This authority was in addition to the blocking authority provided for in the original sanctions and in Executive Order No. 12853 of June 30, 1993, and ensured adequate authority to reach assets subject to U.S. jurisdiction of military and police officials, civilian "attachés" and their financial patrons meeting these criteria. A list of 41 such individuals was published on November 1, 1993, by the Office of Foreign Assets Control of the Department of the Treasury (FAC) (58 *Fed. Reg.* 58480).

On October 18, 1993, I ordered the deployment of six U.S. Navy vessels off Haiti's shores. To improve compliance with the ban on petroleum and munitions shipments to Haiti contained in UNSC Resolutions 841 and 873, the United States succeeded in securing the passage of UNSC Resolution 875. UNSC Resolution 875 called upon the United Nations Member States, acting with national or through regional agencies or arrangements, to halt inbound maritime shipping for Haiti in order to inspect and verify that the Haiti-bound cargo does not contain UNSC prohibited petroleum or arms. A multinational Maritime Interdiction Force, including elements of the U.S. Navy and the U.S. Coast Guard, was established.

7. The declaration of the national emergency on October 4, 1991, was made pursuant to the authority vested in the President by the Constitution and laws of the United States, including the International Emergency Economic Powers Act (50 U.S.C. 1701 *et seq.*) (IEEPA), the National Emergencies Act (50 U.S.C. 1601 *et seq.*) and section 301 of title 3 of the United States Code. The emergency declaration was reported to the Congress on October 4, 1991, pursuant to section 204(b) of IEEPA (50 U.S.C. 1703 (b)). The additional sanctions set forth in Executive Orders Nos. 12779, 12853, and 12872 were imposed pursuant to the authority vested in the President by the Constitution and laws of the United States, including the statutes cited above, as well as the United Nations Participation Act, 22 U.S.C. 287c, and represent the response by the United States to the U.N. Security Council and OAS directives and recommendations discussed above.

8. Since my report of April 25, 1994, in order to implement UNSC Resolution 917 of May 6, and to take additional steps with respect to the actions and policies of the *de facto* regime in Haiti, I issued Executive Order No. 12914, dated May 7, 1994. Effective at 11:59 p.m. e.d.t., on May 8, 1994, the order blocks all funds and financial resources of three categories of individuals that are or hereafter come within the possession or control of U.S. persons, including their overseas branches. These groups include (a) all officers of the Haitian military, including the police, and their immediate families; (b) the major participants in the coup d'état in Haiti of 1991 and in the illegal governments since the coup d'état and their immediate families; and (c) those employed by or acting on behalf of the Haitian military, and their immediate families. The Executive order also bans arriving and departing flights, and overflights stopping or originating in Haiti, except regularly scheduled commercial passenger flights. A copy of E.O. No. 12914 (59 *Fed. Reg.* 24339, May 10, 1994), is attached for reference.

9. Subsequently, on May 21, 1994, in implementation of UNSC Resolution 917 of May 6, and in order to further strengthen sanctions in response to the actions and policies of the *de facto* regime in Haiti, I issued Executive Order No. 12917. Effective at 11:59 p.m. e.d.t., on May 21, 1994, the order prohibits (1) the importation into the United States of any goods originating in Haiti or services performed in Haiti, that are exported from Haiti after May 21, 1994, or any activity by any U.S. persons or in the United States that promotes, or is intended to promote, such importation; (2) any activity by U.S. persons or in the United States that promotes the exportation or transshipment of any

goods originating in Haiti that are exported from Haiti after May 21, 1994; (3) any dealing by U.S. persons or in the United States, or using U.S.-registered vessels or aircraft, of any goods originating in Haiti that are exported from Haiti after May 21, 1994; and (4) the sale, supply, or exportation by U.S. persons or from the United States, or using U.S.-registered vessels or aircraft, of any goods, regardless of origin, to Haiti, or for the purpose of any business carried on in or operated from Haiti, or any activity by U.S. persons or in the United States that promotes such sale, supply, or exportation.

Exemptions from the foregoing prohibitions include: (1) informational materials, such as books and other publications, needed for the free flow of information; (2) the sale, supply, or exportation of medicines and medical supplies, as authorized by the Secretary of the Treasury, and rice, beans, sugar, wheat flour, cooking oil, corn, corn flour, milk and edible tallow, provided that neither the *de facto* regime in Haiti nor any person designated by the Secretary of the Treasury as a blocked individual or entity of Haiti is a direct or indirect party to the transaction; and (3) transactions specifically licensed or otherwise authorized by FAC. A copy of E.O. No. 12917 (59 *Fed. Reg.* 26925, May 24, 1994) is attached for reference.

10. Again, on June 10, 1994, in order to take additional steps with respect to the actions and policies of the *de facto* regime in Haiti, I issued Executive Order No. 12920. Effective at 11:59 p.m. e.d.t., on June 10, 1994, the order prohibits, first, any payment or transfer of funds or other financial or investment assets or credits to Haiti from or through the United States, or to or through the United States from Haiti, with the following exceptions: (1) payments and transfers for the conduct of activities in Haiti of the United States Government, the United Nations, the OAS, or foreign diplomatic missions; (2) payments and transfers between the United States and Haiti for the conduct of activities in Haiti of nongovernmental organizations (NGOs) engaged in the provision in Haiti of essential humanitarian assistance as authorized by the Secretary of the Treasury; (3) payments and transfers from a U.S. person to any close relative of the remitter or of the remitter's spouse who is resident in Haiti, provided that such payments do not exceed $50.00 per month to any one household, and that neither the *de facto* regime in Haiti nor any person designated

by the Secretary of the Treasury as a blocked individual or entity of Haiti is a beneficiary of the remittance; (4) reasonable amounts of funds carried by travelers to or from Haiti to cover their travel-related expenses; and (5) payments and transfers incidental to shipments to Haiti of food, medicine, medical supplies, and informational materials exempt from the export prohibitions of this order. The order also prohibits the sale, supply, or exportation by U.S. persons or from the United States, or using U.S.-registered vessels or aircraft, of any goods, technology, or services, regardless of origin, to Haiti, or for the purpose of any business carried on in or operated from Haiti, or any activity by U.S. persons in the United States that promotes such sale, supply, or exportation. Exportations of the following types are exempt from the foregoing provision: (1) informational materials, such as books and other publications needed for the free flow of information; (2) medicines and medical supplies, as authorized by the Secretary of the Treasury, and rice, beans, sugar, wheat flour, cooking oil, corn, corn flour, milk, and edible tallow, provided that neither the *de facto* regime in Haiti nor any person designated by the Secretary of the Treasury as a blocked individual or entity of Haiti is a direct or indirect party to the transaction; and (3) donations of food, medicine, and medical supplies intended to relieve human suffering. A copy of E.O. No. 12920 (59 *Fed. Reg.* 30501, June 14, 1994), is attached for reference.

11. Once again, on June 21, 1994, in order to take additional steps with respect to the actions and policies of the *de facto* regime in Haiti, I issued Executive Order No. 12922. Effective at 10:09 p.m. e.d.t., on June 21, 1994, the order blocks all property and interests in property that are or come within the United States or within the possession or control of U.S. persons, including their overseas branches, of (1) any Haitian national resident in Haiti; or (2) any other person subject to the blocking provisions of Executive Order Nos. 12775, 12779, 12853, 12872, or 12914 and Haitian citizens who are members of the immediate family of any such person, as identified by the Secretary of the Treasury. This provision does not apply to property of nongovernmental organizations engaged in the provision of essential humanitarian assistance in Haiti or in the conduct of refugee and migration operations in Haiti, as identified by the Secretary of the Treasury.

Payments and transfers previously authorized by Executive Order No. 12920, of June 10, 1994, may continue to be made in a manner directed by the Secretary of the Treasury. A copy of Executive Order No. 12922 (59 *Fed. Reg.* 32645, June 23, 1994), is attached for reference.

12. A policy statement, effective January 31, 1994 (59 *Fed. Reg.* 8134, February 18, 1994), was published to extend until March 31, 1994, the expiration date for all current assembly sector licenses issued by FAC pursuant to the HTR, and a second policy notice, effective March 29, 1994, was published on April 1, 1994 (59 *Fed. Reg.* 15342), extending these licenses through May 31, 1994. These licenses provided an exception to the comprehensive U.S. trade embargo on Haiti under which the "assembly sector" continued to receive parts and supplies from, and supply finished products to, persons in the United States.

Assembly sector trade with the United States accounted for a significant portion of Haiti's imports, and a substantial majority of its exports, prior to the institution of the OAS-requested embargo in November 1991. Although initially suspended due to the embargo, assembly sector imports from and exports to the United States were allowed to resume on a case-by-case basis beginning in February 1992 in order to keep poorer segments of the Haitian population employed and to reduce their incentive to attempt illegal and dangerous migration by sea to the United States and other countries. However, the continuing uncertainties of the Haitian situation led to a sharp decline in assembly sector activity, with such employment estimated by the spring of 1994 to be no more than 10 percent of pre-embargo levels.

As noted above and as mandated by UNSC Resolution 917, Executive Order No. 12917 further restricted imports from and exports to Haiti after May 21, 1994. Consequently, all FAC licenses for importation into the United States from the Haitian assembly sector were withdrawn effective May 22, 1994. The FAC is continuing, in close coordination with the Department of State, to evaluate license applications from U.S. companies seeking to repatriate capital equipment, parts, and components previously exported for use in assembly sector activities.

Following the successful deployment to Haiti of U.S. forces serving as the vanguard of the multinational coalition force, and as promised

in my September 26 address before the United Nations General Assembly, amendments to the HTR were published on October 5, 1994, suspending, effective 10:28 a.m. on October 5, 1994, the sanctions that the United States had imposed on Haiti unilaterally, with the exceptions noted below. Section 580.211 of the HTR, which was added to the HTR in June 1992 to deny entry into U.S. ports to vessels engaged in certain trade transactions with Haiti, was removed. A new section, 580.518, was added to license generally the export from the United States to Haiti of all food and food products.

Section 580.519 was added to the HTR to remove the prohibition (which I had imposed in Executive Order No. 12920 on June 14) on payments or transfers of funds or other financial or investment assets to Haiti from or through the United States, or to or through the United States from Haiti. Section 580.520 was added to unblock the property and interests in the United States of Haitian nationals resident in Haiti, which I had blocked in Executive Order No. 12922 on June 23; however, section 580.520 provides that the property and interests in property of certain persons, listed in the revised "Appendix A" to the HTR, will remain blocked until further notice. The HTR were also amended by the addition of section 580.521 to permit the specific licensing of exports to Haiti of fuel and equipment for electric power generation, telecommunications materials, media and educational supplies, agricultural supplies, and construction and transportation supplies for humanitarian purposes. Section 580.522 was added to authorize the case-by-case licensing of charter flights between the United States and Haiti for use by humanitarian relief agencies to transport needed personnel and supplies, or for journalists covering events in Haiti. The HTR were also amended to provide, in new section 580.523, a general license authorizing the export to Haiti from the United States of equipment needed for reporting and broadcasting from Haiti and for documentary film making in Haiti, provided that such equipment is removed from Haiti when the reporting, broadcasting, or filming has been completed.

Each of the new sections added to the HTR provides that no transaction authorized thereunder may result in a payment or transfer to, from or through a person listed in the revised "Appendix A" to the HTR. In the revised "Appendix A" are set forth, in section I, the names of individuals who, until further notice, will remain "Blocked Individuals of Haiti," and in section II, entities of the *de facto* regime in Haiti whose assets will remain blocked.

On September 29, I directed the Secretary of Transportation to issue the necessary directives to terminate the ban on regularly-scheduled air passenger service between the United States and Haiti that had been imposed on June 24.

The HTR will be further amended upon the return of President Aristide to Haiti to provide that, in accordance with U.N. Resolution 944 of September 29, 1994, on the day following his return, the U.S. sanctions imposed pursuant to U.N. Resolutions 841, 873, and 917 will be terminated. At that time, I will also direct the Secretary of Transportation to rescind the ban on all other air transportation (all cargo and charter) between the United States and Haiti that I imposed on May 7, 1994.

13. *Humanitarian Shipments.* Executive Order No. 12917 revoked an earlier exception to the export ban permitting the exportation to Haiti of "donated articles to relieve human suffering." A substantial amount of humanitarian aid, such as clothing or shoes, had previously been shipped to Haiti pursuant to this exception. The exception of donated foodstuffs was not affected. However, the Executive order provides an exemption from its trade prohibitions for the sale, supply, or exportation of certain basic commodities essential to humanitarian assistance programs serving Haiti's urban and rural poor, *i.e.,* medicines and medical supplies and certain nutritional staples of the Haitian diet, as well as for informational materials. The FAC developed procedures to facilitate U.N. Sanctions Committee approval for humanitarian shipments to Haiti that do not fall within the narrowly-defined U.N. exemption categories. Specific authorizations have also been issued on a case-by-case basis for commercial deliveries to certain "blocked individuals of Haiti," in order to allow the continued supply in Haiti of essential foodstuffs, while retaining the ability to closely monitor such transactions. Food supplies and prices are being monitored for profiteering by Haitian food importers. Between issuance of Executive Order No. 12917 on May 21, and September 1, 1994, FAC issued 94 specific licenses for such humanitarian exports.

Humanitarian Services. Executive Order No. 12920 exempts from its financial prohibitions payments and transfers between the United States and Haiti in support of the conduct of activities in Haiti of NGOs engaged in the provision in Haiti of essential humanitarian assistance. The FAC immediately issued a specific license to the U.S. Agency for International Development (AID), permitting it to continue uninterrupted its essential services in Haiti. Subsequently, based on recommendations by AID and the State Department, FAC developed a system of registration for NGOs engaged in relief efforts such as the delivery of food, medicine and medical supplies, as well as refugee and migration operations, to assure that approved payment orders are neither rejected nor blocked by U.S. banks in implementing the financial prohibitions of recent Executive orders. Since June 10, FAC has registered 156 NGOs, of which 16 have been issued specific licenses authorizing provision of their services in Haiti. One application has been denied. Others are under review by the Department of State and AID.

Air Transportation Services. Executive Order No. 12914, effective 11:59 p.m. e.d.t., May 8, 1994, banned arriving and departing flights and overflights stopping or originating in Haiti, except regularly scheduled commercial passenger flights. On June 10, an order was issued by the President to the Secretary of Transportation that terminated, effective June 24, 1994, regularly scheduled air service between the United States and Haiti by U.S. and Haitian carriers.

Specific licenses have been issued to authorize air ambulance services for medical evacuation flights to and from Haiti. Licenses have also been issued to authorize certain cargo flights for the delivery of humanitarian shipments, including food and medicine, by registered NGOs, as well as passenger service for NGO personnel and a congressional delegation wishing to assist in food distribution. The FAC also has licensed a U.S. air carrier to continue paying its Haitian employees in Port-au-Prince. In addition to providing support for the airline's Haitian employees and their families, the license aimed to position the airline to resume service speedily in the event of an emergency or when sanctions were lifted. Effective on the date of the rescission of the June 10, 1994, unilateral ban on scheduled air service between the United States and Haiti, carriers are authorized to resume such in coordination with the commander of the Multinational Force who controls the Haitian airports.

More than 35 requests have been received from news organizations for specific licenses to charter flights to Haiti in connection with newsgathering activities, ranging from personnel rotation and equipment transportation to proposals from nationally known television anchors to conduct interviews. Licensees include major U.S. and foreign networks.

Blocked Haitian-Owned Vessels. Several dozen Haitian-owned vessels in the United States were blocked by Executive Order No. 12922 on June 21, 1994. Nearly all such vessels were old, small-capacity vessels (many wood-hulled) that formerly loaded and discharged cargoes along the narrow Miami River. These vessels that had previously delivered the bulk of humanitarian assistance shipments to Haiti, were moored at the facilities of their U.S. agents and presented a serious hazard to navigation (particularly with the onset of the hurricane season), clogging the channel and occupying needed docking space. Most Haitian-owners were unable to finance the costs of a long-term lay-up. Some 170 crew members, who were confined to the vessels, were faced with diminishing provisions and maintenance supplies, and dependency upon donations from the local community.

Specific licenses have been issued to U.S. agents for the blocked vessels to authorize the provisioning, maintenance and repairs necessary to ensure seaworthiness to facilitate the lawful return of crew members to their home countries. No debits of U.S.-blocked funds were authorized by such licenses. The FAC has also issued licenses effectively unblocking the Haitian vessels by authorizing them to engage in trade transactions consistent with sanctions, particularly the carriage of authorized humanitarian supplies to Haiti. In some cases, where appropriate, the vessels were licensed to depart the United States but not return for the duration of the sanctions.

14. Following the issuance of the blocking order in Executive Order No. 12922 on June 21, more than 1,200 Haitian accounts were blocked totaling in excess of $79.1 million as of August 30, 1994. This success was due, in part, to FAC notices about the new Executive orders posted to banks through the Federal Reserve, the New York Clearing House, the Council on International Banking and the International Banking Operations Association in Miami. Notices also were posted to other electronic bulletin boards such as the Federal Bulletin Board of the United States Government Printing Office and the Economic Bulletin Board of the Department of Commerce. These notices were passed on to family remittance forwarders by banking oversight authorities in New York and Florida. The FAC launched an aggressive compliance initiative to identify family remittance forwarders in the Miami area who route funds to Haiti. This review revealed that one of the largest companies in south Florida handling remittances to Haiti (previously valued at about $500,000 per month) is owned and controlled by a Haitian national resident in Haiti. The company's accounts, with combined balances of more than $1 million, were blocked and other enforcement actions involving them were undertaken.

15. Continued close coordination between FAC special agents and the U.S. Customs Service in Miami has resulted in the interception of substantial quantities of checks and currency transported from and to Haiti through the United States, as well as the seizure of merchandise valued at $1.5 million. Numerous other enforcement matters are under active investigation.

During the reporting period, the multinational Maritime Interdiction Force (MIF), which contains elements of the U.S. Navy and U.S. Coast Guard, continued to patrol offshore Haiti and to conduct ship boardings, inspections of cargoes bound for Haiti, identification of suspected violators and referrals for investigation. The MIF boardings resulted in numerous vessel diversions to non-Haitian ports after MIF boarding parties determined that cargo was not fully accessible for inspection or that vessels were attempting to enter Haiti with cargo prohibited by UNSC resolutions and U.S. sanctions. The FAC acted on MIF boarding reports by subsequently denying entry into the United States of several vessels that had attempted to violate the sanctions. With assumption of control of Haitian ports by the Multinational Force following its September 19 deployment to Haiti, enforcement of the maritime sanctions in the ports became possible. The MIF operations therefore were terminated on September 28, 1994.

16. Since my report of April 25, 1994, in consultation with the Department of State and other Federal agencies, FAC has issued General Notices No. 5, No. 6, No. 7, No. 8, No. 9, and No. 10, "Notification of Blocked Individuals and Blocked Entities of Haiti." The Notices (issued June 2, June 17, June 22 (two Notices),

August 2, and September 14, 1994, respectively) identify a total of 372 additional individuals and 94 companies and banks determined by the Department of the Treasury to be Blocked Individuals and Blocked Entities of Haiti. These are persons (1) who seized power illegally from the democratically-elected government of President Jean-Bertrand Aristide on September 30, 1991, or who have since the effective date of Executive Order No. 12775, acted or purported to act directly or indirectly on behalf of, or under the asserted authority of, such persons or of any agencies, instrumentalities or entities of the *de facto* regime in Haiti or any extra-constitutional successor thereto; (2) are the immediate family members of an individual who is (a) an officer of the Haitian military, including the police, (b) a major participant in the coup d'état in Haiti of 1991 or in the illegal governments since the coup d'état, (c) employed by or acting on behalf of the Haitian military, or (d) a Haitian national resident in Haiti; or persons subject to the blocking provisions of Executive Orders No. 12775, No. 12779, No. 12853, No. 12872, or No. 12914, or a Haitian citizen who is member of the immediate family of such person. United States persons are prohibited from engaging in transactions with these entities and individuals and with all officers of the Haitian military unless the transactions are licensed by FAC. All assets owned or controlled by these parties that are or come within the United States or that are or come within the possession or control of U.S. persons, including their overseas branches, are blocked. United States persons are not prohibited, however, from paying funds owed to these entities or individuals into blocked Government of Haiti Account No. 021083909 at the Federal Reserve Bank of New York, or, pursuant to specific licenses issued by FAC, into blocked accounts held in the names of the blocked parties in domestic U.S. financial institutions. Copies of General Notices No. 5 – No. 10 are attached for reference.

On August 18, 1994, in consultation with the Department of State and other Federal agencies, FAC identified three additional entities of Haiti, whose property and interests in property are now blocked pursuant to Executive Order No. 12922. On the same date, FAC removed the name of one individual from the list of Blocked Individuals of Haiti. These actions bring the total number of entities so blocked to 128 and the number of individuals to 916.

Since March 1994, FAC has collected 49 civil monetary penalties, totaling in excess of $133,000 as of August 30, 1994. Penalties were imposed pursuant to FAC enforcement investigations, U.S. Customs Service referrals, and FAC compliance audits of reports required pursuant to specific licenses. The enforcement investigations dealt with violations of the HTR by vessels carrying unauthorized and nonexempt cargo to Haiti. The Customs Service referrals all involved import and export violations of the embargo. Compliance audits related to licenses issued to U.S. participants in Haiti's assembly sector.

17. The expenses incurred by the Federal Government in the 6-month period from April 4 through October 3, 1994, that are directly attributable to the authorities conferred by the declaration of a national emergency with respect to Haiti are estimated at about $3.7 million, most of which represent wage and salary costs for Federal personnel. Personnel costs were largely centered in the Department of the Treasury (particularly in FAC, the U.S. Customs Service, and the Office of the General Counsel), the Department of State, the U.S. Coast Guard and the Department of Commerce.

The combination over time of mediation among the Haitian parties and steadily intensified sanctions proved, in the end, ineffective in budging the Haitian military leaders from their stubborn and illegal hold on power. Only the imminent threat of force combined with determined diplomacy was in the end successful in making it possible to achieve our objectives and further our national interests regarding Haiti. With the return of Haiti's democratically-elected President near, it is my hope and expectation that those U.N. and unilateral sanctions that remain in effect, as detailed in this report, can soon be terminated, and that I will shortly have the privilege of sending to you my final report, pursuant to 50 U.S.C. 1641(c) on implementation of the national emergency regarding Haiti declared 3 years ago by the previous Administration in Executive Order No. 12775.

Sincerely,

WILLIAM J. CLINTON

NOTE: Identical letters were sent to Thomas S. Foley, Speaker of the House of Representatives, and Albert Gore, Jr., President of the Senate.

Remarks to the National Association of Police Organizations
October 13, 1994

Thank you. Thank you so much, Tom and Bob. Thank you for the kind words. Thank you for the "Top Cop" honors. Before we came out, Tom also made me a New York City detective. So now, after 2 years, I finally have an excuse for all the traffic I stop when I go up there. [*Laughter*]

I'd also like to say what a signal honor it is for me just to be on the stage with these 12 fine officers behind me who will be recognized later and who put their lives on the line every day, as so many others do. But I am profoundly honored to be here with them, and I honor their achievements.

I also want to say a special word of thanks to the Members of Congress who are here who supported the crime bill and especially to all of NAPO's members and all the law enforcement community who fought so hard with us to pass that crime bill. Dennis Flaherty and Mick Ganley, who hosted me in Minneapolis, are here, and they deserve some special thanks, too, because I think we sort of jump-started the effort to pass the crime bill in Minneapolis that day, when those who wanted to kill it on a technicality thought we were dead and gone and expected us to give up. We didn't because you didn't. And now we have the crime bill, thanks to you, to all of you, and I thank you for that.

There are some other folks here from the Law Enforcement Steering Committee I want to recognize: John Pitta of the Federal Law Enforcement Officers Association; Jim Rhinebarger, Johnny Hughes of the Troopers Coalition; Chris Sullivan with the International Brotherhood of Police Officers. I thank all of them for their support as well.

You know, I came here 20 months ago, having lived in Washington only when I was a young man, as a college student. I was never part of the political environment here. I found, looking at it from a distance, things to admire, but much to question. And I must say, having gone through this crime bill debate, I have a lot of admiration for those people in both parties who hung in there with us, but still much to question.

You know, around here, people talk a problem to death, and then when the time comes to do something about it, everybody looks for a reason not to do it. I saw it happen with the deficit; I saw it happen with crime. But there are real things in this crime bill, as Tom said. And I guess that's what I really want to emphasize.

Yesterday at the White House, we had the kickoff of the crime bill. Just 12 days after I signed it, we released the first round of police grants to 400 communities of all sizes, all across the country, all the way from little bitty towns in our most rural States to our largest cities. And I saw smalltown mayors and smalltown police chiefs come up to me and say, "You know, finally someone has done something to help us keep our streets safer, our schools safer, our neighborhoods safer."

I met a young officer from Ocean City, Maryland, who was hired last year in one of our police hiring grants—you know, we started this last year and have already put about 2,000 more police officers on the street. Already, this young man had apprehended a serial rapist on his bicycle beat as a community police officer. That one officer has already made a difference in countless people's lives who will never know him, because they will not be victimized by the person he caught.

Over the next 5 years, another 100,000 police officers, just like him and just like you, will join you on the beat around the country because of the crime bill which has passed. If all of them are actually put into direct patrol, that will amount to a 20 percent increase in the direct police coverage the American people have. It will lower the crime rate. It will make people safer. It will make them feel more secure. It will make them feel greater confidence in their Government and in the way their tax dollars are being spent. And if it hadn't been for you, fighting like crazy in the 11th hour, it wouldn't have happened. So I thank you for those efforts.

You know, somebody asked me when we started this why I felt so strongly about this, why I wanted to do this so much. And there are a lot of reasons. The first job I ever had as an elected official was as attorney general of my State. And I have worked with police officers and in the criminal justice system for a very long time now. For a dozen years, I served as a Governor. I had to build a prison system, run a parole and probation system, carry out the capital punishment law of my State, develop boot camps and other alternatives for first-time nonviolent offenders, and generally watch as this country became more violent and our response to it was clearly inadequate. I've also been to quite a few funerals of law enforcement officers who lost their lives in the line of duty. And it only takes one to make an indelible impression and to impose on every other citizen a terrific obligation to do what we can to turn this situation around.

A lot of you probably saw when I was campaigning for the crime bill, I often read from a letter a 9-year-old boy from New Orleans sent me, named James Darby, saying that he and his classmates were afraid to walk on the street in New Orleans and would I please make his life safer. He just knew I could do it; after all, I was the President. A couple of weeks after James Darby wrote me that letter, he was shot dead on the streets, just because he happened to be in the wrong place, not because he did anything wrong. A couple of months ago, a young 13-year-old honor student here in Maryland, right across the District line, was shot standing on the street—with his whole life before him.

And we think sometime, well, only kids who live in violent neighborhoods are affected by this. That's not true. The day after the crime bill passed, I found a note on my desk at the White House which almost made me cry, a carefully typewritten note from the son of a member of my administration who is 10 or 11 years old. And he said, "You know, I have been following this crime bill all summer long, and I know you may think that a kid like me wouldn't worry

about it. I know I live in a nice house in a nice neighborhood, and I go to a nice school. But every time I go downtown to the movies, I think there is a good chance I'll be shot with my friends on the street. And now that this crime bill has passed, I'm going to sleep better tonight." Think about it: in your country, in 1994, a 10-year-old kid writing a letter to the President like that.

And just a couple of days ago, I was in Michigan and I met with the editorial board of the Detroit Free Press. And they got all these letters from children, because they've got a great children's project in the newspapers out there, trying to save kids and give them a better future. And they read me a letter from a young girl named Porsha, who just said she wanted me to make her feel free again. And as long as she felt in danger, she wasn't free.

So I don't think what I did as your President was so remarkable; it was my plain duty. What I thought was remarkable was that people would be looking all over town to find excuses not to do it. We shouldn't have had to work as hard as we did to do it, but that's something I've learned about coming to Washington: Every change is twice as hard as it ought to be. But then again, when you get it done, it feels twice as good as it would have otherwise. So I thank you all for that.

You know, tonight I can't leave here without noting that thousands of our American forces are standing up for our Nation's mission in Haiti and in the Persian Gulf. And I hope that our prayers will be with them. We should be so proud of them; they are astonishingly remarkable, able men and women. But it's also important that the American people know that today the most dangerous work of our society is done in trying to contain violence here at home. And the men and women who put on a uniform every day and try to give girls like little Porsha a sense of security and real freedom, who try to make sure that there won't be any more James Darbys, who keep on going even when people they work with have been shot or wounded, who deal with all the frustrations and anxieties that come along with thinking that problems can never be solved, we owe you an enormous amount.

And let me just say to all of you, you mustn't give up. The truth is, we're making progress in this fight. And we're fighting against big, deep, sweeping trends. For 30 years or more,

America's neighborhoods have been growing more violent as families have broken down and community institutions have broken down and traditional avenues of opportunity and education and work have broken down and the vacuum has been filled by guns and gangs and drugs and violence. This has been happening a very long time. But we are actually learning things that we can do about it, things that people in uniform can do not only in punishment but in prevention, things that community leaders can do. And there is city after city after city, town after town after town in this country where the crime rate is going down.

The big problem we have to face now is that the rate of random violence among children, people under 18, is still going up. But what I wish to say to you is that America now knows that we can't ask you to do all the work alone. People are willing to go shoulder-to-shoulder with you in your communities. Public opinion in this country demanded that this crime bill be passed, and we are going to keep going until we get the crime rates down, not holding the line, driving them down—driving them down.

The things that are in this bill, starting with the police, the 100,000 more jail cells for serious offenders, the stiffer penalties, the prevention money, the assault weapons ban, the ban on handgun ownership by juveniles, these things are important, and they will help you to drive the crime rate down. I hated to step on the applause line on the assault weapons ban— [*laughter*]—but I thank you for doing that. All these things will matter. We now have enough

experience with the Brady bill to know that because of the Brady bill, thousands and thousands of people who had no business being able to buy handguns have not gotten them. We know that now.

So what I ask you to do is to go home, make sure this crime bill works. If you think it's not working, you let me know. We are going to reduce the size of the Federal Government by a quarter of a million and more over the next 6 years and take every last red cent, in reducing the size of the Federal Government to its lowest level since President Kennedy was here, and pay for the crime bill. That's how we're paying for it. All the money is going from the Federal bureaucracy to communities to help fight crime. We have got to spend this money properly. We have got to do honor to the people we honor tonight and to all of you. Help us spend the money right. Convince the people back home we did the right thing, and convince them to look forward with hope and optimism. We know what to do. We have the tools to do it. We can make America a safer place. And with your leadership and God's grace, we will.

Thank you, and God bless you all.

NOTE: The President spoke at 7:52 p.m. at the Capital Hilton. In his remarks, he referred to Tom Scotto, president, and Robert Scully, executive director, National Organization of Police Officers; Dennis Flaherty, executive director, Minnesota Police and Peace Officers Association; and Sgt. Michael Ganley, Minneapolis Police Department.

Remarks on the Restoration of Haitian Democracy
October 14, 1994

President Aristide; distinguished Haitian guests; to the distinguished Members of Congress who are here, Senator Dodd, Congressman Rangel, Congressman Conyers, Congressman Oberstar, Congressman Combest; to the members of the United States military and their families who are here; to the friends of Haiti and the process of peace and reconciliation:

Three years ago, the international community, led by the United States, set out to restore Haiti's democratically elected government.

Today, on the eve of President Aristide's return to his beloved nation, we mark the end of one stage of the long and difficult journey and the beginning of a new era of hope for the people of Haiti.

Halfway around the world, America's armed forces are also bringing a message of hope and confidence to the people of Kuwait. Our troops have responded rapidly to the threat from Iraq, and I have ordered that the deployment of personnel and equipment to the area continue. Let there be no mistake: The United States will not allow Iraq to threaten its neighbors.

In Haiti, the men and women of our Armed Forces have protected our national interests and advanced the democratic values we Americans hold so dear. We've helped to curb the violence that threatened tens of thousands of Haitians, to secure our own borders, to bring democratically elected government to the 34th of our hemisphere's 35 nations, to uphold the reliability of our own commitments and the commitments others make to us. In so doing, we have helped to give the people of Haiti a chance to remake the democracy they earned, they deserve, and they so plainly wish. President Aristide's return to Haiti is a victory for freedom throughout the world.

More than 3 years have passed since a bloody coup stole the Haitian people's first elected government. But the road back to democracy, as we all know, has been strewn with obstacles and dangers. Despite exhaustive efforts, diplomatic condemnation, economic sanctions, United Nations resolutions, the brutality of the military regime and its hired guns increased day by day. Haiti sank deeper into poverty and chaos. Only the combination of the imminent American-led invasion and the skillful diplomacy by President Carter, General Powell, and Senator Nunn brought this terrible chapter in Haitian history to a close. General Powell is here today, and on behalf of the American people, sir, I thank you for your mission and for what you did. Thank you.

Just one month later, today, the generals have stepped down from power and left Haiti. The Haitian people have begun to move from fear to freedom. American troops and those of our coalition partners are restoring basic security and civil order. They have helped more than 3,700 refugees to go home from Guantanamo. The Haitian Parliament has once again opened its doors. The mayor of Port-au-Prince is back in office, and the lights are on in more ways than one.

In a few short weeks, these things have paved the way for President Aristide's return. Haiti's voyage back to reclaim its democratically elected government is surely a cause for celebration. But the days and weeks ahead will be full of arduous work, and they will not be free of danger.

Now more than ever, I urge the Haitian people to come together in a spirit of reconciliation

and peace, the spirit so eloquently advanced by President Aristide himself. As he has said, there should be no vengeance, no violence, no retribution. This is a time for peace. That is what the United States and its coalition partners are working for, and I am certain that that spirit will continue to prevail when the multinational force turns its responsibilities over to the United Nations.

President Aristide's return to Port-au-Prince sets the stage for the Haitian people to take control of their future. The task is large: to strengthen a young and fragile democracy, to build a new economy based on opportunity, small enterprise, and steady development. The international community has pledged to do all it can to help, starting with a one-year, $550 million reconstruction and recovery program to fund humanitarian relief, provide economic assistance, support the institutions that must become a permanent foundation for Haitian democracy.

To help launch the economic recovery more immediately, I am pleased to announce that today I will sign an Executive order lifting all economic sanctions against Haiti after President Aristide returns. Now that the coup leaders have departed, democracy is being restored, the sanctions have clearly served their purpose; by lifting trade, banking, and travel restrictions, we can help to give back to the Haitian people the opportunities they need to grow and to prosper and to preserve their freedom.

Ultimately, the task of rebuilding Haiti belongs to the people of Haiti themselves. Theirs will be a long and hard road. Each and every citizen must make a contribution. It will take a lot of patience, but it will be a joyous effort if it is done in the right spirit and if the rest of us do our part to help.

The progress will begin with reconciliation, as the President has said. He will go home in that spirit, vowing to oppose all who seek revenge and retribution. Tomorrow, when he resumes his duties, as he has said, it will be just the beginning. But what a beginning it is.

President Aristide has also vowed to step down at the end of his term, leaving his office to the next democratically elected President. In one of the most insightful comments about democratic government I have ever heard, he has said that when you start a democracy the most important election is the second one. This is the kind of insight that will serve Haiti so well in the years ahead.

Let me conclude by expressing my gratitude to all those who have done their part to give Haiti a second chance, something we need more for not only countries but people in this old world. I thank the 30 countries whose troops are in Haiti as part of the multinational coalition and all the nations who joined our multilateral efforts in the Caribbean community, the Organization of American States, and United Nations. Your efforts have made our hemisphere safer and sent a message of resolve around the world.

I thank the men and women of our Armed Forces who have answered the call and performed a difficult job with skill, devotion, and humanity. You are the steel in the sword of America's diplomacy. Thanks to your efforts, the world knows that we will stand for democracy, honor our commitments, and expect others to honor theirs.

I thank especially the families of our service members here at home, those who make such great sacrifices. Some of them, including the children, are here today, and I would like to ask them to stand and be recognized, the families of the service people serving in Haiti. [*Applause*]

And finally, to the American people, I say that although we are not, we cannot, and we should not be the policemen of the world, we have proved once again that America will stand up for others when the cause is clear, the mission is achievable, and our interests are at stake. The American people have done the right thing in Haiti. They have stood for what is best about America. And because of the support of the American people, democracy will be stronger tomorrow than it is today all around the world.

Finally, to President Aristide and the people of Haiti, for 3 years you have kept faith against all odds that one day a government of the people would be restored to your native land. Tomorrow will be that day. You have survived decades of violence, terror, poverty with dignity, pride, and hope. Now you and your people will have the opportunity to make democracy work for yourselves; to let all the children we are tired of seeing in turmoil on our newscasts become a part of that vast mass of humanity in free societies seeking their God-given potential. I say to you, *bonne chance, Haiti toma.* Good luck, and long live Haiti.

NOTE: The President spoke at 10:20 a.m. at the North Portico of the West Wing at the White House. The Executive order is listed in Appendix D at the end of this volume.

Letter to Congressional Leaders on Haiti
October 14, 1994

Dear Mr. Speaker: (Dear Mr. President:)

On October 4, 1991, pursuant to the International Emergency Economic Powers Act (50 U.S.C. 1701 *et seq.*) and the National Emergencies Act (50 U.S.C. 1601 *et seq.*), President Bush exercised his statutory authority to issue Executive Order No. 12775, declaring a national emergency and blocking Haitian government property. To further tighten the sanctions against Haiti, President Bush exercised his statutory authority to issue Executive Order No. 12779, and I acted pursuant to the same authorities as well as the United Nations Participation Act of 1945, as amended (22 U.S.C. 287c), to issue Executive Order Nos. 12853, 12872, 12914, 12917, 12920, and 12922.

In view of the restoration of a democratically elected government in Haiti, and taking into consideration United Nations Security Council Resolution 944 of September 29, 1994, I have determined that the unusual and extraordinary threat to the national security, foreign policy, and economy of the United States previously posed by the policies and actions of the *de facto* regime in Haiti has terminated. Today, pursuant to the above authorities, I have exercised my statutory authority to issue an Executive order to terminate the national emergency declared in Executive Order No. 12775 and revoke the Executive orders referenced above imposing additional sanctions with respect to Haiti.

I have determined to issue the new Executive order terminating all remaining sanctions against Haiti in view of the return of Haiti's legitimately elected President, Jean-Bertrand Aristide, and the adoption of United Nations Security Council Resolution 944, which rescinds mandatory sanctions against Haiti previously adopted by the Security Council with our support.

Sincerely,

WILLIAM J. CLINTON

NOTE: Identical letters were sent to Thomas S. Foley, Speaker of the House of Representatives, and Albert Gore, Jr., President of the Senate. The Executive order is listed in Appendix D at the end of this volume.

Remarks on Presenting Arts and Humanities Awards
October 14, 1994

Thank you very much. Ladies and gentlemen, Hillary and I are delighted to have all of you here today. This is the second year I've had the pleasure of honoring the winners of the National Medal of the Arts and the Charles Frankel Prize. And it's really one of the great pleasures of my job. I may or may not be the first President who's actually reviewed the recommendations of the committee when they send them to me for who should receive the prize, but it enables me to sort of relive large chunks of my life as I see the artists who have been recommended for this esteemed honor.

Today we celebrate the human imagination and its power to move us forward as a civilization. In honoring our finest artists and humanists, we honor the great American cultural traditions of pluralism, free expression, and tolerance. We honor the quality of our civic life, which for more than two centuries has offered hope and opportunities to Americans from all walks of life, even in the midst of momentous social and political change.

The arts and humanities are our bridge as a people, our bridge to one another. Whatever divisions exist among us, the arts and humanities draw us together. They enable us to celebrate our own individual identities, while also teaching us about the things we share as Americans. They give us a window on the human condition that prevents us from becoming too complacent or too numb or too fearful of the challenges and complexities of the world of today and tomorrow.

Too often we think of art and scholarship, of creative expression and the world of ideas, as the provinces of a cultural elite. Indeed, too often these very arguments have been made by those who would seek to divide us one from another, to divide those who write our songs and paint our pictures and act in our dramas from what they would call normal Americans. But the truth is that the arts and humanities don't discriminate or prejudge, they honor all of us equally. And when we listen and look and feel, they bind us together instead of giving in to those who would divide us.

Song, dance, painting, drama, books, ideas, and scholarship have never been the province of one ethnic group, one religion, one political faction in this country. They are part of our common heritage. They convey all the distinct and different voices, emotions, and images that together make up what is a uniquely American culture. That's why they can be a powerful source of our renewal and our common unity as we move forward into the 21st century.

We need only look at our own history to know that every step we have taken forward as a democracy has coincided with a period of great artistic and intellectual ferment. By fueling our own imaginations, by enlarging our understanding of human experience, the arts and humanities have always given us greater confidence to confront whatever uncertainties loom before us. We need that now, greater confidence in the face of uncertainty, because I believe more than I can convey in words that the 21st century can be our greatest time if we learn to relish and cherish and celebrate our diversity and to face our challenges with genuine confidence. [*Applause*] You know, I'm glad you clapped for that because it wasn't in the notes; it's just what I wanted to say. [*Laughter*] The president of my alma mater, Georgetown, is over there. He's very glad I'm well-educated enough to think of one coherent sentence that wasn't written for me. [*Laughter*]

Given that this is National Arts and Humanities Month, it's an appropriate time also to remember that public support for the arts and humanities, while always a minor portion of overall financial backing, remains essential today. And it will be so, as far as we can foresee. Therefore, I want to thank especially all those people who were individually introduced by the First Lady just a few moments ago. They are a powerful voice for arts and humanities within this administration, and I am very proud of each and every one of them and the service they render to the United States.

Now, I have the honor of conferring the National Medal of the Arts and the Charles Frankel Prize on a wonderful group of awardees.

First, to a man whose music I love and who I found to be one of the funniest people I ever saw perform in person, who later lived long enough to be able to encourage and on occasion rebuke me as President, Harry Belafonte. Harry Belafonte once brought tears to my eyes of laughter at one of his concerts and later brought tears to my eyes with his passion for an event which is unfolding today, the return of President Aristide to Haiti. He once said, "The role of art isn't just to show life as it is but to show life as it should be." Well, Harry Belafonte has not only brought joy to his audiences, but he's inspired people throughout the world with his dedication to freedom movements and humanitarian causes.

Singer, actor, producer, Harry Belafonte has set industry standards with many successes. His third album, "Calypso," was the first ever to sell over a million copies. We're familiar with his work on U.S.A. for Africa, which produced a Grammy award-winning album and video, "We Are The World." Today he continues to bring art and activism together to inspire all of us to live our lives with passion and with concern for others.

Ladies and gentlemen, please join me in congratulating Harry Belafonte.

[*At this point, the President congratulated Mr. Belafonte, and Hillary Clinton presented the medal.*]

The next awardee is the first person on this list whose work ever touched me personally. I'll never forget the first time when, as a high school musician, I discovered that I could actu-

ally play the saxophone lead in "Take Five." And Mr. Brubeck, I can still almost do it. [*Laughter*]

A pianist, composer, and bandleader, Dave Brubeck is truly an American jazz legend. Reaching international stardom in the 1950's, the Dave Brubeck Quartet performed with Charlie Parker, Dizzy Gillespie, Stan Getz, and others. The "Time Out" album was the first modern jazz album to go gold. A classically trained musician, Dave Brubeck is also recognized worldwide for his compositions that include ballet scores, piano concertos, oratorios, cantatas, and a mass. Merging both of his interests, he was a pioneer in combining jazz and symphony sounds.

I can also tell you that he is still playing all the time and very well. It is my great personal honor to present the next award to Dave Brubeck.

[*The President congratulated Mr. Brubeck, and Hillary Clinton presented the medal.*]

Contralto Celia Cruz is known internationally as the Queen of Salsa. Born in Havana, she began her vocal career singing her younger siblings to sleep. It wasn't long, though, before she began electrifying audiences on a larger scale. She's sung with Latin musical greats like La Sonora Matancera, Tito Puente, and Johnny Pacheco. Celia Cruz has used her powerful voice and style to transplant Afro-Cuban music to every corner of the globe. Please congratulate Celia Cruz.

[*The President congratulated Ms. Cruz, and Hillary Clinton presented the medal.*]

Since beginning her career as a violin teacher at the Juilliard School in 1948, Dorothy DeLay has inspired and instructed dozens of virtuosos and concert masters from all over the world. Instead of teaching a particular technique or a tone, her greatest achievement has been to draw out the individual talents and passions of her students. Through her guidance and encouragement, artists such as Itzhak Perlman, Sarah Chang, Nadja Salerno-Sonnenberg, Cho-Liang Lin, and Nigel Kennedy have become internationally renowned violinists. Itzhak Perlman said this: "Miss DeLay's contributions to the excellence of the arts in this country are vast, and her place in the history of classical music is secure." No one could say it better.

[*The President congratulated Ms. DeLay, and Hillary Clinton presented the medal.*]

Anyone who has ever seen our next awardee perform knows what great acting is all about. Julie Harris is a 5-time Tony Award winner, one of our Nation's most talented and versatile actresses. Her credits include "I Am a Camera," "The Lark," "Forty Carats," "The Last of Mrs. Lincoln," and "The Belle of Amherst," in which she had the starring role as Emily Dickinson. That 1976 production broke box office records here at the Kennedy Center as well as in Philadelphia and Boston. Her stage successes won her the New York Drama Critics Circle Award and the Donaldson Award. She has also, as all of you know, lent her considerable talents to television, radio, and film. Miss Julie Harris.

[*The President congratulated Ms. Harris, and Hillary Clinton presented the medal.*]

Our next honoree is truly a pioneer in his field. Erick Hawkins was the first American in George Balanchine's School of American Ballet and the first male dancer in Martha Graham's company. In 1951, he opened his own dance school and founded a dance company, both of which continue to add vitality and originality to the dance world today. As a choreographer, dancer, and teacher, Erick Hawkins' unique talent has been to place dance in a larger cultural and philosophical context. For his boldness and talent, Erick Hawkins commands a legendary place in American modern dance heritage. Erick Hawkins.

[*The President congratulated Mr. Hawkins, and Hillary Clinton presented the medal.*]

Our next honoree is Gene Kelly. Perhaps the most versatilely talented and widely admired American dancer, singer, and actor of this generation. He wanted very much to be here today and had planned to come, but at the last moment was literally forbidden by his doctors to do so. So his wife has come to receive the award for him.

All of you know that he is an award-winning director, choreographer, and producer, a household name who has inspired even the most uncoordinated among us to imitate his memorable scenes, as I must confess I tried to do for my daughter not very long ago when he was singing in the rain on television. Every one of you has probably done the same thing, if you would be perfectly honest about it. [*Laughter*]

Having performed in such timeless classics as "For Me and My Gal," "Anchors Aweigh," "On the Town," and "An American in Paris," its's no wonder that he received a Kennedy Center Award in 1982 for his lifetime contribution to the arts. Whether on stage or screen, Gene Kelly is an American treasure whose musicals entertain people of all generations. Even though he is unable to join us today, we know he's here with us in spirit. We're glad that Patricia is here to accept this award on his behalf. Mr. Gene Kelly.

[*The President congratulated Mrs. Kelly, and Hillary Clinton presented the medal.*]

The next awardee is the second person on this list who had a personal impact on my life, and I would daresay, the lives of every American citizen, at least every American who is 50 years of age or younger and maybe who's 75 or 80 or younger. Pete Seeger is an American legend. Influenced by his father, Charles Seeger, a famous American musicologist, he achieved international fame as a folk singer, songwriter, and political activist in the fifties and sixties. Among his many credits are performing with Woodie Guthrie's band and composing "If I Had a Hammer," "Where Have all the Flowers Gone," and many other songs that all of us know by heart. He has also lent his music to support the civil right movement, the protection of our environment, and the labor movement. Occasionally he still picks up his banjo, and anyone who is fortunate enough to listen will attest still to his place as one of our most enduring and endearing and important folk musicians. Mr. Peter Seeger.

[*The President congratulated Mr. Seeger, and Hillary Clinton presented the medal.*]

Catherine Filene Shouse has been a lifelong patron of the arts. Her leadership has supported the Washington Ballet, the Washington Opera, the Kennedy Center, the New York City, and Miami City Ballets. For a half century, she worked on behalf of the National Symphony Orchestra. In 1966, she donated 100 acres of her Virginia farm as well as funds for an amphitheater to the United States Government. The Wolf Trap Farm Park for the Performing Arts is America's first and only national park dedicated to the performing arts and related educational programs. It is a truly national treasure that I think we should all be grateful for. I wish we had more national parks that were for people to work in and learn in and live in. We owe her a lot, and today we recognize her for her signal gifts.

[*The President congratulated Ms. Shouse, and Hillary Clinton presented the medal.*]

Professor Wayne Thiebaud is not your average college art teacher. A professor at the University of California at Davis, he's also an internationally renowned artist whose painting are on display at the Metropolitan Museum of Art, the Museum of Modern Art, and the Whitney Museum of Art in New York, the Chicago Art Institute, Harvard's Fogg Art Museum, and the San Francisco Museum of Art.

While his works hang on the walls of the most famous American museums, his teaching allows serious art students to learn and develop from his own artistic genius. I don't know about you, but one of the things that I'd like to say is we probably ought to recognize more teachers in this world. And when a teacher has this kind of gift and decides on his own initiative to keep on teaching, that in itself is a contribution worthy of this medal. Thank you.

[*The President congratulated Mr. Thiebaud, and Hillary Clinton presented the medal.*]

Richard Wilbur has been a poet, translator, teacher, Broadway lyricist, among others, for— I have to plug one of my favorites—for the work he did with Lillian Hellman and Leonard Bernstein on "Candide." A critic and editor, an author of children's books, foremost among his literary achievements have been his poetry and his translations. He has won two Pulitzer Prizes, the National Book Award, was our second poet laureate. For his translation of French plays, he's won the Bolligen and PEN translation prizes. His translations from Moliere and Racine are the most celebrated American translations from the French theater. I think that all of us know that Richard Wilbur is, among all other things, one of the greatest poets of the 20th century, and we honor him today.

[*The President congratulated Mr. Wilbur, and Hillary Clinton presented the medal.*]

We're giving an award to an organization now that is terribly important. In a time when many schools are having to scale back or eliminate their music, theater, or dance programs, Young Audiences Incorporated is helping to make the performing arts an essential part of young people's education. Last year Young Audiences' professional artists presented nearly 50,000 performances, reaching more than 6 million public school students. Coordinating with schools and communities to establish partnerships on behalf of arts education, Young Audiences has been instrumental in bringing the enrichment of performing arts to millions of young people all across our country. That is a terrific achievement, and I am honored to present the medal to one of our most outstanding young musicians, Yo Yo Ma.

[*The President congratulated Mr. Ma, and Hillary Clinton presented the medal.*]

I now present the winners of the 1994 Charles Frankel Prize for their work in the humanities. And I begin quite proudly with a man who has been a longtime personal friend of the First Lady and of mine, whose work in education will influence educators and therefore help students well into the next century. Ernest Boyer is a distinguished scholar, educator, and administrator who has demonstrated in his life an unparalleled commitment to educational excellence.

As president of the Carnegie Foundation for the Advancement of Teaching at Princeton, he's helped lead the national education debate for more than 10 years now. He has consistently cited as one of our Nation's foremost advocates of educational reform. And I can tell you that, having worked with him myself for the better part of a decade, deep in his heart he does believe that all children can learn and that we can find a way to teach them. Mr. Ernest Boyer.

[*The President congratulated Mr. Boyer, and Hillary Clinton presented the prize.*]

A professor of English at the University of Montana and an accomplished writer, William Kittredge is considered the leading scholar of the American West. His essays, memoirs, short stories, and film screenplays about the West have reached a national audience. Helping to establish Western regional studies as an academic field, he has taken Americans beyond the sentimentalized view of the Old West, providing us with a more complex and worthy history of the American West. Mr. William Kittredge.

[*The President congratulated Mr. Kittredge, and Hillary Clinton presented the prize.*]

For the past 20 years, Peggy Whitman Prenshaw has been a champion of the humanities. A distinguished scholar of Southern literature at Louisiana State University, she has organized, conducted, or participated in dozens of public humanities forums in Mississippi and Louisiana. She has been a tireless advocate of the humanities in American civic life and has served on the Mississippi Humanities Council, the Federation of State Humanities Councils, and the Louisiana Endowment for the Humanities. She is my neighbor, and I know of her work and how much it has meant to so many of those ordinary citizens who might never have seen some of the things they saw but for her efforts. Thank you very much.

[The President congratulated Ms. Prenshaw, and Hillary Clinton presented the prize.]

It is a great personal honor for me to have the opportunity to present the next award to our good friend Sharon Percy Rockefeller, the president and chief executive officer of WETA from 1989 to 1994. She has led TV 26 in becoming the third largest producer of national programs for the Public Broadcasting Service. During her tenure, the weekly viewership of WETA TV 26 grew to an unprecedented one million viewers and WETA became a forerunner in the production of outstanding programming in the arts and humanities. Most notable among the long list of excellent programs is WETA's co-production of Ken Burns' magnificent 1990 documentary "The Civil War," the highest rated program in the history of public television.

[The President congratulated Ms. Rockefeller, and Hillary Clinton presented the prize.]

You know what she said when I gave it to her? She said, "Don't forget 'Baseball.'" And it was the only baseball we had this year. *[Laughter]*

Today, Dorothy Porter Wesley is recognized for her role as a preeminent archivist of African-Americana. During her 43-year tenure as the principal compiler of the black studies collection housed at Howard University's Moorland-Spingarn Research Center, she has set national standards for collecting, preserving, and making accessible thousands of books, pamphlets, manuscripts, portraits, and artifacts relating to blacks in America and in Africa. She was the visiting senior scholar at the W.E.B. DuBois Institute for Afro-American Research at Harvard University. She also is still in her heart a librarian. The first thing she asked me when I saw her today was whether I was using the White House Library. *[Laughter]* The second thing I did was get a reprimand for having four overdue books. *[Laughter]* Please welcome her here today.

[The President congratulated Ms. Wesley, and Hillary Clinton presented the prize.]

The final presentation is of a Presidential Citizens Medal to an invaluable ally of the arts and humanities in Congress, the distinguished chairman of the Senate Foreign Relations Committee, Claiborne Pell of Rhode Island. Senator Pell is one of the founding fathers of the National Endowment for the Arts and the National Endowment for the Humanities. He has tirelessly served this country through legislative leadership and unwavering advocacy of the arts and humanities. As chairman of the Senate Subcommittee on Education, Arts and Humanities, he's been instrumental in providing opportunities for artists in funding arts programs and preservation projects and in bringing the experience and the appreciation of the arts to communities all across this country.

Let us give him a warm round of applause. Senator Pell, congratulations. *[Applause]*

[The President congratulated Senator Pell, and Hillary Clinton presented the medal.]

Now, let's end this program with a thanks to the good Lord for keeping the rain away and a good round of applause to all of our honorees. *[Applause]*

Thank you very much.

NOTE: The President spoke at 2:52 p.m. on the South Lawn at the White House.

Message on the Observance of National Arts and Humanities Month
October 14, 1994

The arts have long been an integral part of America's cultural heritage, encouraging us to gain a deeper understanding of ourselves and of our society. In a world too often beset by hatred and incivility, the arts and humanities empower us to celebrate our individual identities, while reminding us of the values and commitments that unite us as a country.

Although the rich diversity of our nation would seem to preclude an official American culture, we have a powerful tradition of artistic expression and intellectual inquiry that honors every one of us equally. Through art, music, literature, history, and philosophy, we preserve and pass along, from generation to generation, our most cherished images, ideas, and beliefs.

For more than two centuries, the arts and humanities have helped Americans transcend political, religious, racial, and ethnic divisions by engaging us in the common task of interpreting and expressing the meaning of human experience. When we read each other's stores, discuss each other's ideas, and feel each other's emotions through dance, painting, and song, we come to understand the complexity and texture of each other's lives. In so doing, we gain a greater appreciation and understanding of the breadth of human thought and emotion. And we gain a more profound sense of our common purpose as Americans.

But if the arts and humanities are essential to appreciating and preserving our culture, they are also essential to our growth and renewal as a people. For it is only by deepening our understanding, unleashing our imaginations, and enlarging our capacities to see and to feel that we can envision a better future for ourselves, our communities, and our nation.

In the new and complicated century that awaits us, we will depend even more on our artists and humanists to help us discover the roots of our deepest beliefs and gain a vision of our most promising possibilities.

The month of October has been designated National Arts and Humanities Month, and I urge all Americans to celebrate the artistic and intellectual freedoms we enjoy and to reflect on the crucial role they play in reinvigorating and renewing our great nation every day.

BILL CLINTON

NOTE: This message was made available by the Office of the Press Secretary on October 14 but was not issued as a White House press release.

Statement on Federal Funding for the Homeless
October 14, 1994

I am pleased to announce the release of these much-needed funds to help feed, shelter, and give a hand up to America's homeless. By involving local community organizations as we decide where to best allocate these resources, we will ensure that the most urgent needs in our communities are met.

NOTE: This statement was included in a White House statement announcing the release of $130 million in funding to feed and shelter the homeless.

Statement on the Death of Corporal Nahshon Waxman
October 14, 1994

I wish to express my profound shock and abhorrence at the death of Corporal Nahshon Waxman as the result of his kidnaping by Hamas terrorists.

On behalf of the American people, Hillary and I would like to convey our deepest sympathy to the Waxman family and to the people of Israel at this dark moment. Nahshon Waxman was a son of Israel, but he was also a son of America.

Terrorists must know that these acts will not defeat the process that is bringing peace to Israel and her Arab enemies. In the face of such cowardly and evil actions, I know that it is hard to go forward. But we owe it to all those who have paid such a heavy price to persist and finally prevail in our pursuit of peace.

The President's Radio Address
October 15, 1994

Good morning. I want to begin by expressing my profound shock and abhorrence at the death of Corporal Nahshon Waxman as a result of his kidnaping by Hamas terrorists.

On behalf of the American people, Hillary and I want to convey our deepest sympathy to the Waxman family and to the people of Israel at this dark moment. Nahshon Waxman was a son of Israel, but he was also a son of America.

Terrorists must know that these acts will not defeat the process that is bringing peace to Israel and her Arab neighbors. In the face of such cowardly and evil actions, I know it's hard to go forward. But we owe it to all those who have paid such a heavy price to persist and finally to prevail in the pursuit of peace in the Middle East.

Our efforts to achieve a comprehensive peace in the Middle East are part of an overall strategy to enhance American security and broaden American opportunities in the post-cold-war world by promoting democracy, increasing trade, and reducing the threat of terror, chaos, and weapons of mass destruction.

We're making progress on all fronts. The United States and Russian missiles are no longer targeted at each other. We're expanding trade through NAFTA, the GATT world trade agreement, a new agreement with Japan. This means more jobs for Americans and less tensions with other countries. And we have to be encouraged by the recent successes of democracy or peace efforts in the Middle East, in Northern Ireland, and of course in South Africa.

Today I want to talk with you about Haiti and Iraq. In Haiti this week, we've helped to restore the democratic government of President Aristide after 3 years of brutal military rule. In the Persian Gulf, our resolve in the face of Iraq's provocative actions is preserving security in that vital region.

Even as I speak with you this morning, Haiti's first democratically elected President is flying home to resume his rightful place at the helm of his country. President Aristide's return marks the end of one leg of a long and difficult journey and the start of a new era of hope for the Haitian people.

They've come a long way since a military coup toppled the democratic government in 1991. For 3 years, the international community, led by the United States, tried diplomacy and economic sanctions to force the brutal military regime from power. They were unwilling to yield. Four weeks ago, faced with an imminent United States-led invasion authorized by the United Nations, the military regime finally agreed to peacefully give up power. Since then our troops, together with those of our coalition partners, have done a remarkable job in moving Haiti from fear to freedom.

President Aristide returns today to a more stable, less violent nation. The Parliament is once again open for business. And in the best sign that democracy is taking hold, thousands of refugees are returning from Guantanamo. But let me say, dangers still remain. We know that. Still, thanks to the men and women of our Armed Forces and the brilliant work they have done in Haiti, democracy is back on track.

Now the difficult job of rebuilding Haiti must begin. Countries from around the world have pledged to do their part, starting with a $550 million recovery and reconstruction program. In the end, though, only the Haitian people can do the job of rebuilding their country. It will be a clearly difficult task. But the people of Haiti have survived decades of violence and terror and poverty with dignity, pride, and hope. And now they have an opportunity to make democracy work for themselves and to reach their God-given potential.

Our troops have helped to give them the chance to do so, just as they are also giving the people of Kuwait the confidence that they can live in peace. It was less than 4 years ago that the men and women of Operation Desert Storm drove Saddam Hussein's troops out of Kuwait. This time we are determined not to let Iraq violate its neighbors' borders or to create new instability in the Gulf region. That is why in the face of Iraq's threatening troop movements on the Kuwaiti border last week, I ordered our troops, ships, and attack aircraft to the Gulf. Our policy is clear: We will not allow Iraq to threaten its neighbors or to intimidate the United Nations as it ensures that Iraq

never again possesses weapons of mass destruction.

Much of the force that Iraq sent to the border has retreated. But significant elements still remain within striking distance of Kuwait. We're watching this situation very carefully and continuing with the deployment of our own forces. They will remain in the area and on alert until we are absolutely satisfied that Iraq no longer poses threats to Kuwait.

At the same time, we're working to ensure that Iraq does not threaten its neighbors or the United Nations weapons inspectors in the future. We're seeking support in the U.N. Security Council for a strong resolution that would prevent renewed provocations by Iraq.

I share the pride of every American in the men and women of our Armed Forces. In both the Western Hemisphere and on the edge of the Persian Gulf, they have answered the call of duty. They have performed difficult tasks with great skill and devotion. They have shown again that the American military remains the finest in the world. And thanks to their effort, the world now knows again that the United States will honor its commitments, just as we expect others to honor the commitments they make to us.

Thanks for listening.

NOTE: The address was recorded at 5:16 p.m. on October 14 in the Roosevelt Room at the White House for broadcast at 10:06 a.m. on October 15.

Remarks to the Community in Stratford, Connecticut
October 15, 1994

Thank you so much. "Governor Curry"—that has a good sound, doesn't it? [*Applause*] I am delighted to be here with Bill Curry and Joe Ganim and all these fine people, your State officials behind me, Attorney General Blumenthal and others, and especially with my good friends and allies Rosa DeLauro and Barbara Kennelly.

Hillary and I were very pleased to be asked to come to Connecticut today to campaign for Bill Curry and, in a larger sense, to campaign for the change we're trying to bring to our country. If you will permit me, though, I'd like to

begin with a few comments about what this day means for us as Americans setting an example around the world.

Today is a day of celebration for Americans as our leadership has helped to bring peace and democracy and the restoration of the democratic President of Haiti, as President Aristide goes home there. And I have to tell you that one person who wanted to be here today with us is on that plane going back because he has played a major role in the liberation of Haiti: Senator Chris Dodd is back there today.

Today is a day of sorrow for America in our efforts around the world to bring peace, because just yesterday, as Prime Minister Rabin and Foreign Minister Peres and Chairman Arafat were awarded the Nobel Peace Prize for their progress in peace in the Middle East, a young corporal named Nahshon Waxman was murdered by terrorists who are the enemies of peace in the Middle East. He was a son of Israel, but many of you may know he was also a citizen of the United States. And our prayers and our hearts go out to the people of Israel and to the Waxman family as we say to them, the United States will stand with you in the cause of peace in the Middle East. We have come too far to turn back, and we must not let the wreckers and the killers turn us back today.

And this is a day of determination for America in the world as our men and women in uniform stand up again in the Middle East and the Gulf and say that Iraq will not be allowed to threaten its neighbors or to intimidate the United Nations in its work to make sure they never again have weapons of mass destruction. We will stay there until we are sure that the threat is gone.

What I want you to do today, my fellow Americans, as you must be filled with pride for the incredible work, the skill, the discipline, the bravery of our men and women in uniform from Haiti to the Gulf, is to understand that our overall strategy to increase our security—a strategy that Sikorsky has played a major role in—involves not just the effort to bring peace and democracy to Northern Ireland, the Middle East, to South Africa; not just our efforts to become more secure from weapons of mass destruction, as for the first time the missiles of Russia are no longer pointed at the American people; not just an effort to expand international economics, although all that is important. I came here today because I know and you know we can never be strong abroad unless we are first strong in the United States of America, in every State, every community, in every neighborhood.

You know, as I flew over the beautiful Connecticut countryside coming down here in the helicopter, and I saw those fall leaves I came to love over 20 years ago, and I thought about how proud I was to be coming down here to campaign for somebody like Bill Curry, who was outspent and counted out but never gave up because he wanted to be an agent of change to make life better for ordinary citizens, to have

sensible programs to develop the economy, to have programs to reform the Government and make it work again for average people, to give a tax break to people who deserved it. I liked the way he won the primary, and I have to say I also really admire the way his principal opponent, John Larson, came over and endorsed him and is trying to help him get elected. And I hope the rest of you will, too.

I want to talk to you today a little as a political rally and a little just as an old-fashioned visit about why this race here fits into what I'm trying to do as President and why we need your help. I went to Washington 20 months ago to try to change this country, to do some very basic things: to bring the economy back, to make the Government work for ordinary citizens, and to empower individual Americans to take responsibility for their own future. I offered the American people not so much a set of promises as a real challenge that we could compete and win in the 21st century, we could keep the American dream alive, if we had the courage to change. I asked people of all parties and persuasions to work with me to fight for the future. It's been an interesting 20 months. And what I want to talk to you about is this: As we come onto these elections, I want you to think about the problems we found when we got there, the opposition we got from the leadership of the other party on every issue, the progress we made, and the stakes in the future.

After all, we confronted 30 years of serious social problems developing—they didn't happen overnight—the loss of jobs in our inner cities and rural areas, the terrible problems of the breakdown of families and communities and the rise of crime and violence and drugs and gangs. This has been happening for three decades. We confronted 20 years in which working people have been working harder and harder just to hang on and wages have been stagnant. And we confronted 12 years of trickle-down Reaganomics, the economic theory that if you cut taxes on the wealthiest Americans, loaded them up on the middle class, exploded the deficit, you could somehow spend your way into somebody's prosperity. Now, that's what we found. The last 4 years before I took office had the slowest job growth since the Great Depression. In the city of Bridgeport alone, the average job loss was about 6,000 a year.

And so we set to work to try to make the Government work for ordinary people, to try to turn the economy around. And I think it's fair to say that we've got a long way to go, but we made a very good start. You be the judge. You be the judge.

After 7 years we passed the family and medical leave law to give people some time off when their babies are born or their parents are sick. The Congress voted at long last to put America at the front, not in the rear, of taking care of its children by immunizing all the kids in this country under the age of 2 by 1996; to put 200,000 more children in Head Start programs; to provide apprenticeship programs for young people who get out of high school and don't go to college but want to get good jobs; most important of all, to provide longer term, lower interest rate college loans to middle class Americans so that everybody could afford to go to college. Already, 20 million Americans are eligible to refinance their college loans, including about 540,000 people right here in Connecticut.

We sent genuine welfare reform legislation to Congress that would invest in education and training and make welfare a second chance, not a way of life. And we gave 18 States a chance to find ways to put people to work and get them off the welfare rolls. We gave nine States a chance to try to find ways to cover all people with health insurance.

And I want to tell you, we didn't win that battle, but just remember this: It took 7 years to pass family leave, 7 years to pass the Brady bill, 6 years to pass the crime bill, and we just started. Another million Americans lost their health insurance last year. We can find a way to give people their choice of doctors, to keep the cost coming down, and still cover all Americans. And we're going to keep going until we do it.

We passed the first serious assault on crime in a generation: the Brady bill, the assault weapons ban, the ban on handgun ownership by children, 100,000 more jail cells for serious offenders, "three strikes and you're out," and other things to strengthen laws against the victims of domestic abuse, women and children, and to protect the rights of victims in the criminal justice process. And we've provided prevention funds to give these kids who can still live a good life something to say yes to, as well as something to say no to. And the police officers asked us to do it. It was the right thing to do.

And just this week—for all those naysayers who said that the money would never get out there to make a difference—this week, only 2 weeks after the crime bill was signed, we have already given funds to Bridgeport, Bristol, East Hartford, and Norwich to hire more police officers this week.

When Barbara Kennelly and Rosa DeLauro and Senator Lieberman and Senator Dodd voted for the economic program, every Republican in the Congress voted against it. And they said that if we asked the wealthiest Americans to pay a little more, and if we cut taxes on 15 million working families who were working 40 hours a week and had kids in the home and were still fighting to stay above the poverty line, and if we cut $255 billion worth of spending, they said, the Republicans, that the economy would fall and the deficit would explode, that the world would come to an end if we reversed trickle-down economics. They said if 84,000 working people in Connecticut, who are barely above the poverty line even though they're working 40 hours a week and trying to raise their kids in a decent way, got a tax cut and we still cut spending, we brought the deficit down, the world would come to an end.

Well, we have now been here 20 months, and we have seen whether they are right. And what has happened? You heard Barbara Kennelly; the deficit's going down 3 years in a row for the first time since Truman. We have 4.6 million new jobs. The unemployment rate in Connecticut is a point and a half below what it was on the day I was elected President of the United States. Now, believe you me, this is the beginning. We have a long way to go. There are a lot of people in the Bridgeports of America who have not felt this economic recovery. But what you have to decide is, what is the best way to feel it?

We have to bring investment back into our cities. I just signed a bill to set up banks in all the cities of this country to make loans to poor people who couldn't get them otherwise, to put people in business and bring free enterprise into the cities. It has worked around the world; it will work in America. And we are going to do that. We are designating cities around the country, giving them extra incentives for people to invest in these cities to put people back to work. The answer is to do more of what we are doing, not to turn around and go back the way we came from. If you want to bring Bridgeport back, let's keep doing what we're doing, and we will do that.

Now, my message to you is this: We're trying to change things, folks, and it's hard to do in Washington, but we've made a good beginning.

Now, what are our opponents trying to do? Look what they did. Every one of them voted against reversing Reaganomics. Every one of them voted against college loans to the middle class. Most of them voted against the Brady bill, the crime bill, and family leave. Now, at the end of this last congressional session, what did they do? In the United States Senate, the Republican Senators ganged up and killed campaign finance reform; they killed lobby reform; they killed all the environmental measures that were there except the desert bill for California.

We had a bill to clean up toxic waste dumps, the Superfund legislation. Everybody in the country was for the bill; made you kind of wonder about it. We had the chemical companies, the labor unions, and the Sierra Club; they were all for it. They have never been for the same thing, ever. [Laughter] The only people in America who were against the Superfund bill were the Republican Senators. And why were they against it? Because they didn't want Rosa and Barbara and Joe Lieberman and Chris Dodd to be able to come back to Connecticut and say that they helped to clean up toxic waste dumps. There was no other reason. It was politics.

Now we know why they killed campaign finance reform and lobby reform. This week in the Washington Post, it was reported that they killed campaign finance reform and lobbying reform on the weekend, and on Monday the leaders of the Republican Party in the House and the Senate got all the lobbyists together and they said—it's quoted in the Washington Post— "We killed campaign finance reform for you. We killed lobby reform for you. We share your values. So you give us money, and don't you give the Democrats money, or else." That's what they did.

Now, what will they do if we give them power? Have you seen their contract for America? They promise everybody a tax cut, mostly the wealthiest Americans. They promise huge increases in defense spending. They promise everybody everything, a trillion dollars. And you say, "Well, how are you going to pay for this?" And they say, "We'll tell you later." [Laughter] Well, you know it's election year, folks. I'd like

to make you a trillion dollars' worth of promises, too. I could show you a good time with a trillion dollars. [Laughter] We could have a lot of fun; that's real money.

But what happened when they did it before? They quadrupled the debt of the country. They sent our jobs overseas. We're going to have to cut Medicare, veterans benefits, the crime bill for police in the cities, and we're going to run this economy in the ditch if they get their promises. This is not a contract with America, it's a contract on America. You have been there; turn away from it. You know better than that.

So they have told us what they are going to do. They are going to give us their trickle-down economics of the 1980's. They are going to give their politics of the enemies list of the 1970's. They are going to gang up with the Washington lobbyists whose values they share and run this country any way they please and try to tell you what you want to hear and give you a bunch of idle promises. We tried it before. It did not work.

We are moving this country forward. The economy's coming back. We're making the Government work for ordinary citizens. And the Congress is looking for a message from the American people.

I say to you, what is this election about? It's about all those kids in the uniforms over there that provided the music. It's about what kind of future they're going to have. That's what this election's about. Are we going forward, or are we going back? Are we going to be united, or are we going to be divided? Are we going to vote for our hopes, or are we going to vote for our fears?

That is what Bill Curry represents here, everything we are trying to do. You have got to elect him Governor. And you have got to say to America, "We have tried what they are offering, and it failed. We heard them say what the President was doing was failing, and it has succeeded."

So let's keep on going into the future with our heads held high. I'm telling you something, folks, we are just a few years from the next century. And what will really count is whether every man and woman can live up to the fullest of their God-given capacities. That's what we offer, the promise of challenge, the promise of succession, because we are doing what we can to make sure every one of you can be what God meant you to be. Don't fall for the Republican promises one more time. We don't need to go back; we need to go forward.

Thank you, and God bless you.

NOTE: The President spoke at 11:39 a.m. at Sikorsky Memorial Airport. In his remarks, he referred to William E. Curry, Jr., Connecticut gubernatorial candidate; Mayor Joseph P. Ganim of Bridgeport, CT, candidate for Lieutenant Governor; and Richard Blumenthal, Connecticut attorney general.

Remarks at a Fundraiser for Gubernatorial Candidate Bill Curry in Bridgeport, Connecticut
October 15, 1994

Thank you. You know, I've been telling the people at the White House for months, if we could just get the Congress out of town and I could get out in the country, we could have a little fun. [*Laughter*]

I am delighted to be here with two of the finest Members of Congress, Rosa DeLauro and Barbara Kennelly; and with the leaders of Bill Curry's campaign, the leaders of the Democratic Party; with the State officials, including my longtime friend Attorney General Blumenthal; with the mayor of this city and his wife; and with Bill Curry and his mother.

I want to talk a little today about two or three things that I hope will help to put this Governor's race in perspective. Let me tell you, I used to be a Governor, and it's a pretty good job. There have been a day or two in the last couple of years where I wondered why I ever gave it up. They used to tell me there were times when I could take a boat out in the middle of the Arkansas River and walk back, and the headline would be, "Clinton Can't Swim." I know what it means now. [*Laughter*]

But I want to say to you today—I want to try, if I can, from my perspective to tell you just how important a Governor's race is and just why I think Bill Curry is not only the right sort of person for this job at this time but also why I think he did a very smart thing in having a bright young mayor as a running mate. And the reason is you cannot see the role of government anymore as all divided up. You can't look at there's a little box, and that's what mayors do; and there's another little box, and that's what Governors do; and there's another little box, and that's what Presidents do at home; and another little box, and that's what Presidents do abroad; there's another little box, and that's what people in the private sector do. This country needs to stop thinking like that, because we are moving into a global society, not just a global economy but a global society, and we have to look at our work in terms of partnerships. We have got to get the best out of everybody. And we have to have as a goal how to get the best out of everybody and how everyone can live up to the fullest of their own potential.

When I was out at the airport just a few moments ago I said, looking at our role in the world, this was a day of celebration, a day of sorrow, and a day of determination: celebration in the return of President Aristide to Haiti and seeing the people dancing in the streets for democracy; sorrow, of course, because on the day that the long struggle of Prime Minister Rabin and Foreign Minister Peres and Chairman Arafat to bring peace to the Middle East was rewarded with the Nobel Prize, Corporal Waxman, an Israeli soldier and an American citizen, was killed by terrorist thugs who desperately want peace in the Middle East to fail so that they can go on and ply their craft of death; and determination because our men and women in uniform in the Gulf are standing up to one more threat from Iraq to its neighbors, one more attempt to bully the United Nations into backing off its resolutions.

There's a lot to be proud of and a lot to be happy about. Even in the terrible tragedy in Israel, you see shining through that the determination of the people there to keep working for peace and not to turn back, to give not only that troubled region but the rest of us who are so caught up in it and its future a different and a better future.

But if you look at that, and you recognize that we cannot be strong abroad unless we are first strong at home, that is the inner strength of America that permits us to lead the world in bringing democracy back to Haiti. It is the internal strength of America that gave us the power to lead the international coalition first in the Gulf war and now in standing up to what is happening there. It is the symbolic power of America and the fact that we represent the kaleidoscope of the world's cultures and ethnic groups and religions that make people wish us to be active in helping them to achieve peace in the Middle East or peace in Northern Ireland or conducting the elections in South Africa, which we celebrated recently with President Mandela's trip here.

It is very important to understand that. It is the fact that people believe that we live by our values that enables us to be trusted when we say to the Russians after decades of mistrust, "We know that the future will have differences between us, our interests will be different, our opinions will be different, but we ought to go forward as democracies," and that leads us to the point where today, for the first time since the dawn of the nuclear age, there are no Russian missiles pointed at the people of the United States. That is important to know.

So we come to this point in our history, as the First Lady said, at a point of transition, the end of the cold war, the advent of a global economy, with very serious challenges and enormous opportunities. And the question is: What must we do in our country to continue to be able to celebrate the things we just discussed? What is it that we have to do in our time to give new birth to the American dream, to rebuild this country, to empower all of our people to be what God meant for them to be? What is it that we have to do—that is the question— and how must we do it? Those are the things that dominate my thinking as your President every day. That's what I think about. That's what I work on.

It is important not only who is President but what other things are going on in this country. One of the things I'm convinced of is that Washington is very good at doing some things and not very good at all doing others. Second, people have more trust in government that's closer to them than they do in governments further away, so even if we are good at some things we need to go ahead and let a lot of that be started out at the grassroots level. And third, there are just differences from place to place.

The economic challenges faced by Bridgeport are different than the economic challenges faced by Hartford and certainly different than those faced by Laramie, Wyoming.

So I have tried to launch a kind of a revolution in the way we think about Government. I don't want a Government anymore that sits on the sidelines or just kind of comes into the game to help preserve the status quo and organized interest groups. But neither do I think the Democrats can afford to make a lot of promises we can't deliver and say that we're doing things for people, when what we really ought to be doing is empowering people to do more for themselves.

So let me give you some practical examples in why it matters who the Governor is and why it's a good thing the ticket has a mayor on it. Example number one: welfare reform. Everybody knows that we've had 30 years, not 30 months, 30 years, of developing social problems in this country. The breakdown of families, the breakdown of community structures, it started with the collapse of the economic infrastructure of many of our urban areas and rural areas, and it was accelerated by changing social patterns. But when people bemoan crime and drugs and guns and gangs and violence, it is important to recognize that these things have been developing, after all, for quite a long while.

One of the things we know we have to do is take the families that exist now that are dependent on the Government and try to make them self-sufficient. That's what welfare reform is all about, making welfare a second chance for people that really need it, not a way of life.

The truth is no one has a magic bullet. I have sent legislation to Congress which I believe will be adopted next year, but it rests upon the ability of people at the grassroots level to implement it and make it work. So we have given 18 States, including Connecticut, I might add, permission to cut through all the Federal rules and regulations and design their own ways to move people from welfare to work. Just recently I gave the State of Oregon permission to take the welfare check and just give it to employers who would hire people as an employment supplement. It may or may not work, but it's worth trying. In Connecticut, we'll know soon enough whether it did. And so will other States in the country. This is important, but if you don't have a good Governor, it's a bust.

First of all, they won't ask for the permission to do it, and secondly, they may not be able to carry it off.

We've given 9 States—in the middle of all this health care rhetoric that we've put up with in the last couple of months—9 States have gotten permission to go beyond a lot of the Federal rules and regulations to try innovative ways to provide health coverage for all their people in ways that preserve consumer choice, preserve the private health care system, but got out there in ways that would control costs and provide more coverage.

We just passed an education bill that I have worked very hard for based—it is rooted in my experience as a Governor that has strong national standards for achievement but gives all the initiatives back to grassroots schools and school districts, State departments of education. It really matters who's out there. Now those are just three examples that this Congress has worked with me on to help put decisions back at the local level.

Finally, let me say we're trying to do some things that will really bring economic opportunity back to places where it has long been lost. This is something I've worked on for a decade. When I was Governor, part of my State was the fastest growing part of America, and part of it was the poorest part of America. I understand a little about this, and I know there is no one formula that works.

So we are trying to build institutions like community development banks to make loans to poor people to start businesses where they live—proven to work all over the world, and we're way late in putting them in all the cities in America—like enterprise zones and empowerment zones and enterprise communities, all these things we're trying to do. These are important things, but I can propose all the laws and they can pass all the laws, and none of those things will change anybody's life if the people at the grassroots level don't know how to do it and aren't connected to the real problems of real people.

So if you want America's economy to be revitalized, you have to have a good Governor, everywhere; you have to have people who have a partnership; you have to have people who understand these things. This guy is a fountainhead of ideas. And he won this primary with a grassroots movement, which means that he has people in every community who understand

what is going on there. That is terribly important to whether the President and the country succeed. It really matters.

I also see a lot of partnership here, and if you'll forgive me, I want to say a special word of thanks to your major opponent in the primary, Senator Larson, for being here today and for being so strongly for you and helping you. Where is he? John, stand up. Thank you very much, sir. [*Applause*]

Now, that brings it back to what we have to do. Our mission in Washington has been to try to make the Government work for ordinary people again, bring the economy back, get the American people together, to empower people to make the most of their own lives. After 20 months—a rather interesting 20 months, I might add—I'd say we've made a good start, and we've got a ways to go. And the midterm elections offer the American people the chance to decide whether they want to go forward or whether they want to go back and try what the opposition party says they offer America. We now have clear evidence on both paths.

If you look at what we've done to make the Government work for ordinary people, and the family leave law has already been mentioned, we debated for 7 years, we passed it in a couple of months; we provided immunizations for all children under 2; another 200,000 seats in Head Start for young children; apprenticeship programs were staged to help kids who don't want to go to college but want to be in good jobs, not low-wage jobs; a dramatic reform in the college loan program that makes already 20 million middle class Americans, including over half a million in Connecticut, eligible for low interest and longer repayment terms on their college loans so that no one should ever again not go to college because of the cost of a college education; this is a dramatic thing. This is making Government work for ordinary people.

We are also—you heard Bill talking about the crime bill—you know how we paid for the crime bill? Not with a tax increase, not by cutting out other Government programs but by a commitment to reduce the size of the Federal bureaucracy over 6 years by 270,000. The National Government already has more than 70,000 fewer people working for it today than it did on the day I took office, and all the money's being spent to fight crime. And I might add, that makes the point again. We're shrinking the size of the Federal Government to do more with less, and we're giving all the money to communities to fight crime, to Bridgeport, to Bristol, to East Hartford, to Norwich. You already have these four communities, within 2 weeks after I signed the crime bill, were already given grants to hire more police officers—taking the money away from Washington, giving it to you at the grassroots. If you spend it right, the crime rate will go down. We know that.

You know, our opponents, the Republicans, always cussed the Federal Government for years, but they didn't make it smaller, they just tried to make sure their folks were in all those jobs before we took over. [*Laughter*] And they talked about Government waste, but they didn't want to do anything about it because they wouldn't have anything to run against anymore. So we passed a bill to change the way the Government buys $200 billion worth of services a year. You know that we're going to save an average of $50 on every purchase the Government makes that costs less then $2,500 by getting rid of paperwork and letting competition in; no more $500 hammers, no more $600 toilet seats. Poor Al Gore can't go on David Letterman anymore—[*laughter*]—because we did that. The Democrats did that. We're trying to make this Government work for you in a commonsense way.

And the second thing we're trying to do is to bring this economy back. The first thing I did as President, before I ever took office, the first decision I made was that we needed an economic security organization. Just like we had a national security operation and a domestic policy operation, we needed an economic operation. And I put a man from New York named Bob Rubin, who's had a distinguished business career, in charge of it, and we have worked from the get-go to make sure that everything we do is good for the American economy.

And if you really talk to people who deal with the Federal Government, they'll tell you we've got the best Commerce Department, the best Small Business Administration, the best Agriculture Department that anybody's seen around there in decades when it comes to promoting economic growth and development, the best trade negotiator, because we are trying to grow this economy.

When we put the economic plan before the Congress, which lowered the deficit and which provided tax cuts for 15 million working Americans and tax increases for the wealthiest one

and a half percent, what did our adversaries say? They said, "If this plan passes, the deficit will go up and the economy will go down." That's what they said, the world would come to an end. Chicken Little would not have been as eloquent—[*laughter*]—as they were about how bad that plan was.

Well, we passed it—thanks to Barbara, thanks to Rosa—without one of them being for it, and where are we? We've got 3 years of deficit reduction for the first time since Truman was President, 4.6 million new jobs, more high-wage jobs in 1994 than the previous 5 years combined, 9 months of manufacturing job growth for the first time in 10 years, and America rated the most productive country in the world at the annual vote of international economists for the first time in 9 years. They were wrong, and we were right.

So are we here celebrating? No, not exactly. There are still too many people who don't have jobs; there are still too many people who have worked for jobs but never get raises. A million Americans lost their health insurance last year. We still have to pass welfare reform and important environmental legislation and political reform legislation like campaign finance reform and lobby reform. And we have to keep going until our future is secure. No, we're not satisfied, but we have made a very good start.

What have they done? What is the choice? I want to make three points to you. First of all, they voted no every chance they could. Every one of them voted no against the economic plan which included, also, the middle class college loan. Most of them voted against the Brady bill. Most of them voted against the family and medical leave bill. Most of them voted against the crime bill, having once voted for the crime bill, because it was election season. In the last week of the Senate, on one day, there were four separate issues being filibustered. To give you a sense of what that means, you know, if there's a filibuster, it takes you 60 percent of the Senate to pass it. In the 1800's, we had an average of one filibuster every 6 years. In the 1900's, we've had an average of one filibuster every year. We had four in one day because the "no" crowd was trying to shut us down.

Do you know what they stopped from passing, among other things? The Superfund bill to clean up toxic waste dumps. Who was for it? The chemical companies, the labor unions, and the

Sierra Club. It's the first issue they'd ever agreed on in their lives. Every American with a breath and an opinion was for the Superfund legislation except the Republican Senators. And why were they not for it? Because they didn't want Rosa and Barbara to be able to come back to Connecticut and say, "In the closing days of the Congress, we passed the bill to clean up toxic waste dumps." They'd rather leave the dumps and deny them the credit.

In the closing days, we had big bipartisan majorities for campaign finance reform, for lobbying reform, for a bill to require Congress to live under the same laws they impose on private employers, and they killed them all with filibusters. Now that's a fact. And they give us a little inkling of where they'll go if they get a majority in the Congress. Two stunning articles in the Washington Post this week—they killed the campaign finance reform and the lobbying bill on the weekend. On Monday, the leaders of the Republican party in the House and the Senate had a little meeting with the lobbyists. And according to the news article, they said, "Look, we killed campaign finance reform for you. We killed lobby reform for you. We share your values, and you better give us money, and you better not give the Democrats money, or else." Then yesterday it was reported that if they could just get control, they'd give us a National Government by subpoena with an enemies list.

Now, you have to see that in terms of their Contract With America. Remember their contract? They all signed up; they all stood right up there and signed on the dotted line. You know what was in that contract? They promised just what they did in the eighties, the return to trickle-down economics, a trillion dollars in promises, tax cuts for the wealthy, more money for defense, bring back Star Wars, don't hurt anybody. And when we ask them, "Well, how are you going to pay for all this?" they say, "We will tell you later."

I'll tell you how they're going to pay for it. The deficit will be exploded, Medicare will be cut, veterans benefits will be cut, the police program cannot be funded, jobs will start to go overseas again just like they did before, and the economy will be in the ditch. But it will all happen after the election.

You know, I mean, this is election time. He wants to win; he wants to win; I want you to help our folks in Congress. I would love to stand up here and make you a trillion dollars' worth of promises. You know, if I could write a trillion dollars' worth of hot checks, I could show you a good time, too. [*Laughter*] That's still real money.

So they've told us what they'll do. They'll give you trickle-down economics and abuse of power politics. Now, that's what they'll do. They've had a high old time trying to stop everything and point the finger of blame. I love what Bill Curry said, what they're saying is not "What should we do?" but "Who can we blame?"

What we have done is try to turn a light on in this country, to lift people's spirits and pull people together and say: We can make the Government work for ordinary people. We can do more with less. We can empower people. We can get this economy going again. We can stand for the best of American ideals around the world. We can make ourselves more secure and more prosperous.

And it won't happen overnight. We're dealing with 30 years of social problems, 20 years of economic stagnation, and 12 years of trickle-down economics. But it can happen if we keep going forward.

So I am here to say, if you want this country to go forward, you need to elect this good man Governor. And you need to say to the people of Connecticut, in every one of these congressional races we must decide: Are we going forward, or are we going backward? What do we stand for? Do we really want to go back to a Government of idle promises where people are simply told what they want to hear, where all their fears are played upon, where a majority is created through dividing the electorate, or do we want to go forward into a future where we can compete and win in an exciting global economy where our diversity is an asset and our economic strengths are legendary and every American child has a chance to live up to the American dream? I think the answer is clear, and I want you to help make it clear in November.

Thank you, and God bless you all.

NOTE: The President spoke at 1:22 p.m. at the Holiday Inn.

Statement on United Nations Security Council Action on Iraq
October 15, 1994

I am very pleased with the strong action just taken by the U.N. Security Council on Iraq. UNSC Resolution 949, passed unanimously this evening, condemns the Iraqi effort at intimidation of its neighbors. It expresses the clear will of the international community that such threats are unacceptable. It demands that Iraq withdraw its troops to their original positions and requires Iraq not to redeploy these forces to the south or take other action to enhance its military capability in southern Iraq.

The Security Council has made clear that it will not permit Iraq to use its military to threaten its neighbors or U.N. operations in Iraq. This resolution underscores the unanimous backing of the Security Council and the broad support of the international community for our demand that Iraq take steps that would prevent it from threatening its neighbors now or in the future. This is an important step in our efforts to end the current crisis in a way that prevents such crises from recurring.

Remarks to the National Medical Association
October 15, 1994

The President. Good evening, ladies and gentlemen.

Karen Mouton. Good evening, Mr. President.

The President. It's nice to hear your voice, and I appreciate what Dr. Walton said. I'm sorry I'm not with you tonight. I know that this evening marks the beginning of a very special year in recognizing the 100th anniversary of the National Medical Association and its contribution to the health of our Nation.

I'm certainly impressed with the star-studded cast for this evening's program, and I want to give my own salute to the physician honorees, whose accomplishments touch on every area of the medical profession. And of course, I want to say I am especially pleased to note that our own Surgeon General, Dr. Joycelyn Elders, is one of your honorees. I thank you for that.

I also want to thank the National Medical Association for the key role you've played during the past 20 months in our joint effort to seek health care reform. Dr. Tracy Walton and Dr. Leonard Lawrence, your president and immediate past president, were especially effective during the health care debate. And I don't want you to be too discouraged that legislation didn't pass. After all, this was the first time in the history of the United States that comprehensive health care legislation made it to the floor of both Houses of Congress. And the problem is not going away. We now know from the census

report that over a million Americans lost their health insurance just last year. There are still challenges that have to be met, and in the end, the spirit, the leadership, the guidance of the National Medical Association is going to be rewarded with comprehensive health care for all Americans.

If you won't give up, I won't; we'll keep working. The First Lady is here with me, and we want to tell you that we're proud of you, we're grateful to you, and we want to keep working for health care reform.

Let me also thank you for supporting a lot of our other initiatives, for helping us pass the crime bill, which in itself was a public health bill to reduce violence and crime and drug addiction among our people, especially our young people; for your support of the economic program to bring the deficit down and get the economy going again. It's produced over 4½ million new jobs in the last 20 months. But most of all, I want to thank you for your partnership. We're going to keep working together. We're going to keep making progress together. We're going to keep moving America forward together.

You know this health care reform issue is literally a matter of life and death for many African-Americans, because of the higher rate of preventable diseases and the great at-risk nature of so much of the African-American population who go without primary and preventive care and health care coverage in general. But we are moving forward. And we have an opportunity now in the next few weeks to send a message to the country and to the Congress when you vote in your communities. We want to keep working forward. We want to keep going forward. We don't want to go back. We know we can make a difference in jobs and crime and the deficit, and we know we can make a difference in health care if we'll stay at the task.

So I ask you to keep doing what you're doing, keep standing for the right things, keep being a shining symbol of America at its best. I look forward to being with you and supporting you, and I am very grateful for the support you've given to me.

Thank you, and God bless you all.

NOTE: The President spoke at 5:57 p.m. by telephone from the Port Authority Terminal in Miami, FL, to the association's centennial celebration at the National Theatre in Washington, DC. Karen Mouton was assistant to program producer Debbie Allen.

Remarks at a Democratic Senatorial Campaign Committee Dinner in Miami, Florida
October 15, 1994

Thank you very much. There's nothing left for me to say. [*Laughter*] You know, Hillary kind of got into that zone that sometimes you get into, and she was just hitting on all cylinders. And I felt very much like I did the first time I ever gave a public speech as an elected official over 18 years ago. I went to a Rotary Club installation banquet in south Arkansas as attorney general. And it was the first time I'd ever spoken since I'd been elected, and I was nervous as a cat. There were 500 people there; we started at 6:30. Everybody got introduced in the whole crowd, except three people; they went home mad. [*Laughter*] And I got introduced to speak about a quarter to 10. And the only guy more nervous than me was the guy introducing me, and he said, "You know, we could stop here and have had a nice evening." And when I heard Hillary hitting her stride, I thought, we ought to stop here, we'll have a nice evening. [*Laughter*]

Let me say, first, to Hugh and to Carol, thank you, thank you so much not only for this evening but for all the days and all the nights that you have helped to advance the cause of the Democratic Party and of our administration and all the things that you have given to your country out of a genuine desire to make things better for other people. I thank you so much, and I'm honored to be here in your home tonight.

I want to thank the Members of Congress who are here, Senator Daschle, who was here, and Congresswoman Meek and Congressman Hastings, Congressman Torricelli, who's come all the way from New Jersey, and say how very glad I am to be here. I want to echo the sentiments of my wife about my fine brother-in-law; I may have a little more to say about that in a moment. And I want to thank my long-time friend Bob Graham. You know, I told somebody not very long ago, someone—I don't even know how the conversation came up, but it got around to the fact that I'd known Bob Graham a long time. And this person who was talking to me had not known him a long time and was marveling about how much money he had raised as chairman of the Democratic Senate Campaign Committee. I said, "Well, it doesn't surprise me because he gets more done than anybody I know, and secondly, he's had me at every crossroads in the United States at these fundraisers." [*Laughter*]

I was a Governor for a good long while. Some days I wish I still were—[*laughter*]—but rarely. I served with 150 American citizens, men and women, who were Governors. And I can say without any qualification that he is one of the 5 ablest people I ever served with as a Governor out of that 150. But he has a weakness that I also have, apparently, and that is that on occasion, we're better doers than we are talkers.

And the crowd we're running against are a whole lot better talkers than they are doers. And part of the reason is, they have more time to think about what they're going to say because they spend so little time worrying about what they're going to do.

And I must say, just for example, our friends here in Florida—I didn't carry Florida in the last election, but I worked hard to do a good job for Florida. We've worked hard not to let Hurricane Andrew be forgotten. We've worked hard to get Homestead rebuilt and regenerated and revitalized. We worked hard to save the space station and the space program, which is so important to central Florida; to settle the American Airlines strike, which is very important down here. Florida was one of the States that got permission to slash through all the Federal rules and regulations to try to find new and innovative ways to control health care costs and cover more people without health insurance and to reform the welfare system and to move people from welfare to work. And that's just a beginning.

I'd also remind everybody, with Mr. Torricelli here, that until I really got behind the Cuban Democracy Act, along with Democrat Torricelli and Democrat Graham, we couldn't find the Republicans and where they were on that legislation or what they were doing.

So I don't know if any of that will register in this election, because they talk very well. But I want you to think tonight about what you can do in the next 4 weeks, maybe in a nonfinancial way, in the States in which you live to change the outcome of the election, or in the cases where we're winning, to reinforce the outcome of the election.

You heard Hillary make the case, but the fact is, I ran for President to be a different sort of President. I did not expect that the environment in Washington would be as partisan as it turned out to be. I never dreamed I'd see grown people actually get up and willfully kill bills that they themselves were for, just to make sure that nobody else got credit for helping. I thought that was something that children did in a play yard. I didn't dream grownups would do it, and I sure didn't dream that anybody could get away with doing it.

I wanted to go to Washington to get this economy going again, to get our people together again, to make that Government work for ordinary citizens again. And I think we've made

a good start. We have brought the deficit down; we've got the economy up. When Bob Graham cast the decisive vote on the economic plan— all the Republicans voted against it, and they said, "If this thing passes, the economy is down the tubes; if this thing passes, we'll lose jobs and the deficit will go up." Well, they've been telling us that fairytale for 12 years. We tried it their way for 12 years, and they quadrupled the national debt and drove the economy in the ditch. We changed our policy, we reversed trickle-down economics, and we've had 4.6 million jobs and 3 years of deficit reduction for the first time since Harry Truman was the President of the United States.

When we tried to pass family and medical leave, they wanted to filibuster it. They said it would be bad for small business. Well, we passed family and medical leave, we joined over 100 other countries that had already done it, and guess what? We've had record new incorporations of small business and record small business profits. It hasn't hurt anything, but it's helped a lot of working people to be home when their babies were born or their parents were sick. That's the truth.

When we changed the whole college loan program to lower the interest rates and string out the repayment terms so that every middle class person in this country could afford to go to college, not a single one of them helped, not a one, zero. But we kept going, trying to make this thing work.

Then we got to our trade initiatives, and we actually had a bipartisan effort on NAFTA, and I thought, "This thing is turning around." And then late last year, the Senate voted 95 to 4 for a crime bill; the Republicans voted 42 to 2 for it. So we finally got it through the House, and we brought it back to the Senate, and we were going to have a vote on the final crime bill. It was really very much like what I campaigned on for President and what they voted for a year ago. But instead of being 42 to 2 for it, they were 38 to 6 against it. Why? Because it was close to election, and they cared more about defeating an administration initiative to make our streets safer than they did making the American people safer. So if they had had their way—2 weeks ago I signed that crime bill; we have already released funding for 250 more police officers for Florida, 95 of them in Dade and Broward County alone—if they had had their way, they wouldn't be here. But they are here; they are here. And there will be more.

So you have to make a choice in this election, not just to contribute but what you're going to do in the next 4 weeks. We're bringing the economy back; we're making the Government work for ordinary people; we're moving into the future. Are there still things to be done? You bet there are. There are still jobs to be created. There are still people who are working hard and never get a raise. There are still problems in our inner cities and isolated rural areas. There is still a new trade agreement that we have to adopt. We still have to have the Summit of the Americas and try to create a whole new explosion of economic opportunity in our backyard. We've still got to pass welfare reform. We still have to address the health care crisis. Another million Americans lost their health insurance this year; almost every single one of them was a worker or the child of a worker. So yes, there are problems. But we are clearly moving in the right direction.

And the alternative is about as stark as it can be. Look at what happened in the last week of the Congress. You all know what the filibuster is; if a bill gets filibustered it means it takes 60 Senators instead of 51 to pass it. In the 1800's, we had an average of one filibuster every 6 years. In the 1900's, we've had an average of one filibuster a year. In the last days of the Congress, there were four filibusters on four different issues on one day. Why?

They filibustered the Superfund bill to clean up the waste dumps of the country. You know, it's the only bill I ever saw that everybody was for. The chemical companies were for it, the labor unions that worked for them were for it, and the Sierra Club was for it. I thought there must have been something wrong with it; everybody was for it. The only people in America who were against it were the Republican Senators. Why? Because they would have rather denied a Democrat the opportunity to say from a platform like this, "I helped to clean up toxic waste dumps," even if they had to leave the poison in the ground. Nobody else was against it.

They killed campaign finance reform. They killed lobby reform. They killed a bill they've been crowing about for years, saying they wanted it, that would have required Congress to live under the same laws that Congress imposes on private employers. I always thought that

would be a great thing for Congress to pass. And if ever there was a bill that every Republican ought to hallelujah to, that was it. But they killed it. Why? Because they didn't want anybody else to say they had a role in that.

Now you have to decide not just where the check goes but what you feel in your heart about what you want for your country. I'm telling you, it's time to turn the lights on in this country. We've got to get people out of this idea that everything's going wrong and things are bad. The economy's coming back; we're assaulting our problems; we're moving into the future with confidence. The only thing that can derail us is rewarding the kind of misbehavior we saw in the last week of this session of Congress, and we have to stand up to it. And you have to decide.

What about their Contract With America? Have you seen it? It's a trillion dollars in promises: "We're going to balance the budget and increase defense and revitalize Star Wars." And when you say, "How are you going to pay for it?" they say, "We'll tell you after the election." It's just like what they did before, a trillion dollars' worth of promises. How will it be paid for? You know how it will: exploding the deficit, sending our jobs overseas, cutting Medicare, not funding those police officers you need here to fight crime and drugs and gangs. That's what will happen. And we'll have this economy in a ditch again just like they did last time if you ratify the contract, not those of you in this room but everybody you know in this country. This contract on America is nothing more than the second verse of trickle-down economics. We tried it; we saw it; it did not work.

So the choice is clear: Are we going forward, or are we going to go back? Are we going to give in to all this sort of naysaying and negativism and all the things they say? You know, they talk about how liberal and out of step the administration is. If you had a Republican administration that cut the deficit, presided over an expansion that produced 4.6 million new jobs, got tough on law and order, and began to clean up some of this country's most serious problems, they would be asking you to canonize them, wouldn't they? I don't want you to canonize me. I just want you to vote for good people for Congress so we can keep going forward and facing our problems and moving into the future.

You know, this is a very exciting time to be alive. Look at what happened in Haiti today.

Look at the progress we're making in the Middle East, even in the face of the terrible murder of that young Israeli soldier. Look at the progress in Northern Ireland. Look at the progress in South Africa. Look at the fact that all these heads of democratically elected nations are coming here to south Florida to the Summit of the Americas and they want to build a new future with us. This is a wonderful time to be alive and to be seizing this incredible array of opportunities.

And what we have to do is just simply to say in the next month: We have thought about this; we have seen it. We have a path to the future that is working and a ticket to the past that didn't work the first time. We will take what works and say no thank you to people who want to play on our fears, divide us against one another. While the Democrats are seeking to empower people in the new direction we

are seeking, they just want to grab power. We're going to say, no thank you, let's build tomorrow and make it better than today.

Thank you very much, and God bless you all.

I want you to clap one more time for Bob Graham. This is a plaque which recognizes the fact that he has done a much better job than anybody who ever held this job before him. And you've already heard that this is the first time we've ever been able to give the maximum contribution to 19 of our Senate Democratic candidates. And it's because, like everything else he ever did, Bob Graham got the job done. Thank you very much. [Applause]

NOTE: The President spoke at 10:50 p.m. at a private residence. In his remarks, he referred to dinner hosts Hugh and Carol Westbrook and Florida senatorial candidate Hugh Rodham.

Remarks on the Return of the United States Delegation to Haiti
October 16, 1994

Good afternoon. Secretary Christopher, Mr. Gray, distinguished members of Congress, and members of the delegation who went to Haiti. Let me welcome you back to the United States from your historic trip. We are here today to continue this remarkable celebration of freedom over fear that all of you witnessed yesterday in Port-au-Prince and here to look ahead to the hard work the people of Haiti now have to do in order to rebuild their nation.

But first let me say a few words about the situation this morning in the Persian Gulf. I was pleased that the United Nations Security Council yesterday passed a very strong resolution and unanimously condemned the recent provocative actions by Iraq near its border with Kuwait. The Security Council resolution makes clear that the international community will not allow Iraq to threaten its neighbors or to intimidate the United Nations as it ensures that Iraq does not again possess weapons of mass destruction.

The message is clear: Iraq must complete its withdrawal. It must not threaten its neighbors in the future. It must comply with all relevant Security Council resolutions. The troops, ships,

and attack aircraft I have ordered to the Gulf area will continue to remain there until the crisis passes.

As our troops in the Gulf are helping to enforce the will of the international community, our young men and women in uniform in Haiti are doing so as well. And as all of you saw yesterday, they're doing so in a brilliant fashion. When we sent our armed forces to Haiti just 4 weeks ago, their mission was to pave the way for President Aristide's return. Yesterday that mission was completed, as the President returned home in joyous atmosphere that we all watched so happily from here. Now Haiti is a nation where violence is down and the Parliament is back, a nation where men and women freely chosen by the Haitian people are once again leading their country, where a long night of fear is giving way to a new day of promise.

A few moments ago, I was briefed by Secretary Christopher and Bill Gray on yesterday's events. I asked a lot of questions about what happened and what would happen in the future. But let me just say, yesterday I was moved—as I know all of you were, even more moved being there on the ground—by the incredible sight of President Aristide addressing the people from the Presidential Palace and saying again and again, "No to violence, no to retribution, yes to peace, yes to reconciliation."

We know there is a long road ahead, that dangers still remain. Now that the democratic government has been restored, it must be nourished, and the country must be rebuilt. Many nations around the world are already pledging to do their part, starting with a $550 million reconstruction and recovery fund to provide humanitarian relief, development assistance, and support for democratic institutions. The United States will work with these countries, with the international financial institutions, with private organizations, all together, over the next several months to make sure this work succeeds.

In the end, of course, only the people of Haiti can rebuild their country. They have waited a long time for the chance to do so. Now, thanks to the efforts of the men and women of our Armed Forces, those of our coalition partners, and the supporters of freedom, they are being given the chance to do it.

Several of you have commented on the freshly painted signs you noticed in Port-au-Prince. I understand that the most popular one had three words: "Thank you, America." So let me conclude by saying a few thank-yous. Thank you to all of you who worked so long and hard to help to put Haiti back on the track to democracy. As he ends his mission, let me say a special word of thanks to Bill Gray, who at a critical time brought energy, focus, credibility, and great skill to this task. Thank you, sir. Thank you to the men and women of our Armed Forces and their families, from General Shelton to every last enlisted man and woman who are there. All of them are the power behind our diplomacy. Thank you to the nations from our hemisphere who have worked with us and those beyond our hemisphere who have worked with us on this project. Thank you to the people of our country who time and again have been willing to stand up for others because it is the right thing to do. And finally, thank you to President Aristide and the freedom-loving people of Haiti who never gave in to despair and who today stand in the warm, bright sunshine of freedom. Thank you all.

Thank you.

NOTE: The President spoke at 12:10 p.m. at the North Portico of the West Wing at the White House. In his remarks, he referred to Special Adviser on Haiti William H. Gray III.

Remarks and an Exchange With Reporters on the Israel-Jordan Peace Treaty at Andrews Air Force Base, Maryland
October 17, 1994

The President. I'm delighted by the announcement from Amman today that King Hussein and Prime Minister Rabin have reached agreement on the text of an Israel-Jordan peace treaty. These two visionary leaders today resolved that their nations should henceforth live in peace and as good neighbors.

This was an extraordinary achievement; it must be welcomed by the friends of peace all around the world. At a time when hatred and extremism and threatening behaviors still stalk the Middle East, this agreement reminds us that moderation and reason are prevailing, that nations can put conflict behind them, that courageous statesmen can lead their people to peace.

On behalf of the United States and all the American people, I congratulate Prime Minister Rabin and King Hussein and, even more, the people of Israel and the people of Jordan. Together they are embarking on a journey, a journey of peace that will bring a bright future for generations to come. The United States has stood by them and worked with them, and we will stand by them every step of the way.

Thank you very much.

Q. Are you going to the Middle East, sir, if a peace treaty is signed there?

The President. I have nothing to say about that yet.

Q. Does it sound a good omen for Syria, the talks with Syria?

The President. I think it is very good. We're continuing to work there, and we're encouraged.

We just have to keep working. We have to keep working until it's all done.

Thank you.

NOTE: The President spoke at 8:50 a.m., prior to his departure for Albuquerque, NM.

Remarks to the International Association of Chiefs of Police in Albuquerque, New Mexico
October 17, 1994

Thank you very much. Chief Daughtry, Chief Whetzel, ladies and gentlemen of the IACP, I am honored to be here. I love the jacket, and I love what it stands for. I thank you more than I can say for your help and support in passing the Brady bill and the crime bill.

I'd like to acknowledge in this audience today the presence of some very important people here in the State of New Mexico and throughout our Nation. First of all, behind me, the Governor of the State of New Mexico, Governor Bruce King. Bruce and I are two of the only three people serving in America who were Governors in the seventies, the eighties, and the nineties. I don't know what that means anymore. [Laughter] I can barely remember them.

I'm delighted to be here with the two Senators from the State of New Mexico, Senator Domenici and Senator Bingaman, who are out here. Congressman Steve Schiff, the Congressman from this district, is here. Thank you, sir. My good friend Congressman Bill Richardson, who was very active in passing the crime bill—where's Congressman Richardson? He's here somewhere. Thank you. And of course, the mayor, Mayor Marty Chavez, who is one of my jogging partners, is here.

I want to also say that, you know, I think I have more administration members who have been active in this outfit than previous Presidents. Your ex-president Lee Brown is now our drug czar. Your ex-vice president Tom Constantine is now our DEA Administrator. And I thank you for that. The head of the U.S. Marshals Service, Eduardo Gonzalez, was Tampa Bay chief and once active in this organization. So I feel at home here.

I think our FBI Director is here. I want to tell a story on him. Is Louis Freeh here somewhere? Tomorrow? He's coming tomorrow? It's the first time I've been ahead of him in a long time. [Laughter]

I want to tell you a story about the—since this is an international organization, one of the things that I have really tried to do as President is to build international cooperation in law enforcement. It's important in dealing with drugs. It's important in dealing with terrorism. It's important in dealing with organized crime.

Lee Brown and Tom Constantine, both of them, as you know, have major responsibilities that go beyond our Nation's borders, as you would expect, in dealing with the drug problems. But the FBI Director, Mr. Freeh, also took a very popular trip to Europe and to Russia not very long ago, and slightly after that, when I was following him instead of the other way around, I went to Riga, Latvia, to celebrate the withdrawal of Russian forces from Eastern Europe for the first time since World War II and from the Baltic States. And we had this meeting with the heads of the government of Estonia, Lithuania, and Latvia. And so help me, the first thing the President of Latvia said is, "Can we have an FBI office in Riga?" [Laughter]

Now, it's funny, and it's flattering, but it's also serious. Why? Because as these countries convert from totalitarian societies to free societies, as they become much more open, they become much more vulnerable to organized crime because they haven't developed their banking system and their trading rules and their business rules. And that relates to whether they, themselves, then become more vulnerable to drug trafficking and to terrorism and to trafficking in weapons of mass destruction or stolen nuclear materials or any of that sort of thing. So I say to you, I'll make you a prediction: For the next 10 years when you meet, more and more and more, your concentration will have to be on the international aspects of the crime problem which affects what you do on the streets in your cities and towns throughout the United States.

I'd like to talk a little today about the crime bill and what it means against the background of the crime problem in America. And the state of play, as you know, is very troubling, because the good news is that in many of our cities the crime rate is actually going down. The mayor of Odessa, Texas, was in town the other day when we handed out the first wave of grants, police grants, under the new crime bill, only 2 weeks after the bill was signed. And she said they'd had a drop in the crime rate in excess of 15 percent for 3 years running because of community policing, because of what law enforcement officers have done. The mayor of Houston was reelected with 91 percent of the vote after they had over a 20 percent drop in crime in only one year there. This is happening in many cities and towns throughout the country.

On the other hand, we know that a lot of small towns and suburban areas have rising crime because as cities clamp down on crime, a lot of times the criminals just move their base of operation, and they're not as well equipped to deal with it. We also know that even as overall crime rates drop, the rate of random violence among young people, people under the age of 18, is going up dramatically in sickening ways that we have all seen again in recent days.

The point I want to make about all this is that this is a manifestation of trends that have been developing in our country for quite a long while now. We have had really 30 years, a whole generation and more, of these trends that have been developing in a lot of the high-crime areas in America: the breakdown of families and community organizations and neighborhood organizations, the loss of economic opportunity, creating huge social vacuums into which have moved gangs and guns and drugs and crime and violence.

I wanted this crime bill to pass very badly because I believed that the National Government had a responsibility to help you deal with it. But we have to look at what we can do together within the crime bill and then what we have to do beyond the crime bill, because we're going to have to change this country from the grassroots up. We're going to have to change the culture that a lot of these kids live in. And you can do it, I can do it, parents can do it, but we're all going to have to do it. And there is clearly something for everybody to do.

The first job I ever had as an elected official was as attorney general of my State, and I began to work with law enforcement on a regular basis. Then I was Governor for a dozen years, the years when crime was exploding in America. I built prison cells. I devised work programs. I put in education programs and drug education programs and boot camps for first offenders. I enforced the capital punishment laws and tried to find ways to rehabilitate people who were getting out. I went to funerals of police officers who were friends and family members of friends of mine who died in the line of duty.

Dealing with all this has made an indelible impression on me. And when I became President, I guess I had in that sense more personal experience with the human cost and the human side of crime and law enforcement than a lot of people who have had this job. I was determined to bring an end to 6 years of political debate in Washington and to pass the Brady bill, which had been there for 7 years, to pass a crime bill, which had been debated for 6 years, because I knew that we had some things that we had to do. I am doing my best where I live and where I work to get this country together and to move our country forward again.

I think my mission as President is to keep the American dream alive and to help make sure Americans can compete and win as we move into this exciting 21st century by making Government work for ordinary people and by bringing this economy back, by making us more secure and more prosperous in our relations with the rest of the world. After 21 months, I can tell you I think that we've made a good start. America's in better shape than it was 2 years ago. We've got more jobs, low inflation, a much lower deficit. Over 70 percent of the new jobs coming into our economy this year, according to a report just published today, are higher wage jobs. We're moving away from the time when all of our new jobs were low-wage jobs.

We've got a smaller Federal Government, by more than 70,000 already, that's doing more for ordinary citizens. The Congress just passed and I signed a procurement bill which changes the way we spend your money when we buy things, and it'll put an end to the $500 hammers and the $50 ashtrays. The Vice President kind of has mixed feelings about that. He'll never get to go on David Letterman again now because of that, but it was the right thing to do. [*Laughter*]

Russian missiles are no longer pointed at the United States. We've got big increases in trade that are fueling these high-wage jobs. And now America is leading the way to peace and security and democracy, as you've seen in the last few days in the Middle East and Northern Ireland and Eastern Europe and, of course, in Haiti.

But all of us know, I think, that no matter how much economic progress we made, no matter how much progress we make in dealing with trouble spots around the world, there will be a gnawing feeling that all is not right in America until our children feel safe in their schools and on their streets and Americans feel secure in their homes and at their work.

We have to do things that will go beyond talking, that will actually reduce the rates of crime and violence in the United States, that will actually make sure that more of our children do say no to drugs and gangs and guns, and yes to books and to boys and girls clubs and to games. That's what the Brady bill was all about; that's what the crime bill was all about. It was the National Government's contribution to a national effort to really change the way Americans are living, to change the way they feel inside. And it is terribly important.

I was in Detroit the other day doing an editorial board meeting, and the Detroit Free Press had done a program with children in the area and had taken letters from children. And a little girl named Porsha, 9 years old, wrote me a letter and said, "I just want you to make me feel safer. I don't feel safe." Many of you saw the reports that I gave when we were debating the crime bill about that 9-year-old boy in New Orleans who wrote me a letter saying, "Can't you make me feel safe?" And he was killed on the street in a random shooting just a few days after he wrote me. A 10-year-old son of a member of my administration, a young man brought up in a well-to-do home, goes to good schools and lives in a beautiful neighborhood, wrote me a wonderful letter the day after the crime bill passed, a 10-year-old boy saying, "I know you think that I wouldn't be afraid of this, but every time my friends and I go downtown to a movie, I am afraid I will be shot before I get home. And I feel so much better now that this crime bill has passed."

These are the voices of the children of America, across racial and income and regional lines,

telling us that we have to do better. That is what this is about. Well, we are doing better, but there's more to be done.

The Brady bill has made a difference; all of you know it. There are thousands of people who have already been denied weapons who were not entitled to them, who had a criminal background, who would have gotten them if it hadn't been for the Brady bill.

And the crime bill will make a difference. We have evidence of that. Before the crime bill passed last year, I asked Congress to make a downpayment on our commitment to put 100,000 more police officers on the street, and the Congress funded another 2,000 police officers. Last week when we gave out the first police grants under the crime bill, Chief David Massey from Ocean City, Maryland, came with the police officers he'd hired under the first grant. One of them was an ex-linebacker at the University of Maryland, the sort of person that you just see and you want to ask permission. [*Laughter*] This young man was in a community policing program riding a bicycle in Ocean City. And very soon after he went to work, he caught a serial rapist, he did, as a community police officer. Now, all the victims that will never be preyed upon by that rapist will never know what they owe to that one young man who is a community police officer. And now we're going to be able to multiply that by 100,000 in every State in this country.

Something else I think that really needs to be pounded home over and over again is that this crime bill was fashioned largely by law enforcement officers. From the punishment programs to the policing programs to the prevention programs, it was the law enforcement officers who shaped what was in it. You said we ought to have "three strikes and you're out" because there were some violent criminals who kept getting paroled because they were lucky enough not to have severe consequences to the victims of their crime. But what they tried to do was terrible. That's what the purpose of "three strikes and you're out" was.

You said that too many people were getting out too quick because there wasn't enough prison space, so there's provision for 100,000 more prison cells in this bill—never been done before—the Federal Government had never before helped to build prison space for States. You said that we ought to have capital punishment if someone kills a police officer, and it's in the bill. You said it ought to be against the law for a minor to carry a handgun except when supervised by an adult; it's in the bill. You said we should do more for victims of crime. You said we should make a serious assault on the problems faced by women and children, the problems of domestic violence and neighborhood violence. You said we should do more to make schools safer. You said we should do more to give our kids some prevention programs, some things they could say yes to, places to go, things to do, good things to do, maybe most important, good people to look up to when they can't find that at home.

When the NRA tried to take the assault weapons ban out of the crime bill, you stood firmly in favor of leaving it in, not because you were against the rights of hunters and sportsmen but because you knew that there were 650 weapons in the bill specifically protected from any Government interference. And to those of you who come from smalltown and rural areas, you can go home and tell your sportsmen that we are not going to allow the Federal Government to interfere with the legitimate interests of hunters and sportsmen, but we do not support leaving weapons in the hands of kids thats only purpose is to kill as many people as quickly as they can.

And you said that we ought to have 100,000 more police. Indeed, we probably ought to have more, but that's all we could figure out how to pay for. For the American people now, that's a number that doesn't mean a lot. That's why last week was so important, when we had 400 communities coming up and little towns getting one police officer and bigger places getting 25 or 30, because people began to visualize what that means. There are 550,000 police officers in this country. If you add 100,000 and they all go into beat work, if they actually go into working to prevent crime and to catch criminals, it'll be about a 20 percent increase in the presence of police on the street. It will work. It will work. We've had only a 10 percent increase in police officers in the last 30 years, while we've had a 300 percent increase in violent crime. This was a critical component of the crime bill.

And today I want to announce two important steps to get those officers on the streets as quickly as possible. And you will have the release from the Justice Department here today supporting that.

First of all, we're going to make it possible for cities with at least 50,000 people to begin hiring officers immediately, by setting aside some money even before the grants are awarded so that you can know what you're going to get and you can start hiring and training now. And the grants will be there when you put the people on the payroll full-time.

Secondly, for cities and towns of fewer than 50,000 people who don't have a lot of people in clerical departments to help you deal with the Federal Government, we're going to do for you what we did for small business people applying for SBA loans. We're going to give you a one-page application with about eight questions on it, and you can start filling them out right now, so that nothing will come between America and the new police officers.

I'd like to end today by asking you to reflect on three things. One is a tribute to how the Congress funded this bill. This is a big bill. It was funded not by raising taxes, not by increasing the deficit but by reducing the size of the Federal Government by 270,000 over 6 years and giving all the money back to local communities to fight crime. That's how it was funded. I consider that to be a solemn trust with America that we must not breach. And you will have to work every year for the next 6 years to make sure that we keep that trust.

The second point I want to make is that for most of its life this crime bill enjoyed broad bipartisan support, which dissipated at the end of the debate, as all of you know. It became a political football, first, because there were some who were honestly willing to sacrifice everything in the crime bill to beat the assault weapons ban—to give up the police, to give up the prison cells, to give up the capital punishment provisions, to give up the prevention programs, to give up the violence against women section, to give up the victims against crime section, to give it all up. Second, there were some who just thought it was important to kill the bill for political reasons.

That's all in the past now. It passed. What I want to say to you is, we have got to make this crime bill work, every provision of it work. We have got to demonstrate to our people that the money is being well-spent. And we have to find a way to reach out at the grassroots level across political lines. We have to stop this. We can't tell the American people they've got to change their behavior to change this country if crime is a partisan political issue. The victims of crime are Republicans, Democrats, and independents. The people who put on uniforms every day are Democrats, Republicans, and independents. This is about America and our future. We must never again permit crime to be divisive in a partisan political way. And you can stop it, and I want you to do it.

And I have to tell you, the only thing that I really worry about now in that regard is that in this election season, there are many who are campaigning on a Contract With America which costs a trillion dollars, to balance the budget, to increase defense, to revitalize Star Wars, to give huge tax cuts. And there is no clear notion of how this is going to be paid for. But the only option to pay for it is the way it was paid for before, higher deficits and cuts in everything else from Medicare to veterans benefits to this crime bill.

So I ask you: Start today. Say, "We've fought too hard for this bill. We won it fair and square. Let's not take it away indirectly by adopting a commitment to a budgetary process that will make it utterly impossible to fund the crime bill." The lives and the future of the American people, and especially our children, are too important. This must not become a political football. The bill is long. The trust is there. We must fund this crime bill. We cannot back away, and you must see that it is done.

The third thing I want to say, and probably way the most important thing, is that we have now done a major thing with this crime bill, and you will do major things with it. But the people of this country have a job to do here, too. We're not here giving things out to the American people. We're here challenging the American people to take their streets and their schools and their neighborhoods and, indeed, their homes back. And if all of us go out here and say the right things and do the right things and we get no help from the rest of America, we'll be back here next year and the year after and the year after that, bemoaning the same problems. And you know that as well as I do.

You now have the tools to deal with this problem. But you've got a whole country out there full of people who have to help. Parents have to recognize that the real war on crime begins at home. If the first responsibility of Government is to provide law and order, the first responsibility of parents is to teach right from wrong. We've got to have more folks turning

off the TV and knowing where their kids are and spending time reading and doing homework and accepting personal responsibility. And we've got to have more folks helping them, like those wonderful police officers in the D.A.R.E. programs all across America. Kids are going to look up to somebody, and it's up to the adults in this country to decide who they're going to look up to.

What do you think about those two kids, 10 and 11 years old, in Chicago that threw that 5-year-old boy out the window? A 5-year-old kid, who knew right from wrong, lost his life at the age of 5 because he wouldn't steal candy, because he knew right from wrong. And his brother, only 3 years older, knew right from wrong and he wouldn't steal candy either, trying desperately to save his little brother's life. Who did the other two kids look up to? Who did they come in contact with who could have taught them right from wrong and didn't? Who did they come in contact with who taught them wrong? What about that little kid that was set on fire, burned over 85 percent of his body, 3 years old, not even big enough to do anything wrong? Who taught those children right from wrong?

You know, we see all these stories of these kids doing these things, and then we see that they apparently feel no remorse. At that age in their development, it is a question of where they got the message. Where did it occur to them to hang somebody out of a window in a highrise? How do they learn to pick up a gun? Where do they know that a fast buck today is better than 10 years or 12 years or 16 years of hard work and school to make something of yourself?

These kids are looking up to somebody. Who are they going to look up to? How are they going to learn this? We can hire 5 million police officers, and if we keep losing the battle for what these kids think is right and wrong, we're going to be in a lot of trouble.

I know we grownups sometimes—we're too negative sometimes; we're too cynical sometimes. A good Catholic friend of mine and I the other day were having a theological discussion, and he said, "You can never get discouraged, Bill, because the only truly unforgivable sin is despair." That's why I preach hope all the time. I am telling you, this country is coming back economically. This country has resources and character and richness and diversity that will open unparalleled opportunities to us in the 21st century. This is a good country.

When the delegation came back from Haiti yesterday, they said that all the Haitian people had these little signs in Creole, painted, and the most popular one said simply, "Thank you, America." They looked at those young men and women we sent down there in uniform, and just by walking around, these young people, our kids, they make a statement about what's right and what's wrong, what's good and what's bad, what kind of a person it's worth being, just by being there and being who they are. And it is thrilling to other people to see the best of this country.

And we need not be worried about that if we just roll up our sleeves and face our challenges and go on. But what we must be worried about is wave upon wave upon wave of these little children who don't have somebody both good and strong to look up to, who are so vulnerable that their hearts can be turned to stone by the time they're 10 or 11 years old. And when there is a good one, a 5-year-old kid in difficult circumstances, blooming like a flower in the desert, knowing that it's wrong to steal candy, he actually has his life at risk.

That's why all of you wanted these prevention programs. But I am telling you, you've got to go home, and you've got to say, "Okay, I'll wear my D.A.R.E. uniform, I'll do my part, but every last citizen in this country has got to do more than look at you and demand that you do something about crime. We have got to teach our children and lift them up."

Thank you, and God bless you all.

NOTE: The President spoke at 11:38 a.m. at the Albuquerque Convention Center. In his remarks, he referred to Sylvester Daughtry and John T. Whetzel, past president and incoming president of the association.

Remarks on the Israel-Jordan Peace Treaty in Albuquerque
October 17, 1994

I am delighted that Israel and Jordan have reached agreement on the text of their peace treaty. Earlier today, I spoke with King Hussein and Prime Minister Rabin. I congratulated them on their historic achievement and on their courage and persistence in getting there. I assured them that the United States will continue to stand with them in the days ahead and to support this peace process as we have all along.

These leaders have decided that from now on they will live in peace as neighbors. They have decided that they want to be friends. And their friendship and their peace is clearly welcomed by the friends of peace throughout the world. At a time when hatred and extremism and threatening behavior still stalk the Middle East, this is a clear signal that there can be a different future. This agreement reminds us that moderation and reason can and will prevail in the Middle East, that nations can put conflict behind them, that statesmen can lead people to peace.

On behalf of the American people, I want to say a profound word of thanks and congratulations to both King Hussein and Prime Minister Rabin, and especially to the people of Israel and the people of Jordan.

NOTE: The President spoke at 12:42 p.m. at the Albuquerque Convention Center.

Interview With Mark Riley and Laura Blackburne of WLIB Radio, New York City
October 18, 1994

Mr. Riley. Mr. President, good morning.

The President. Good morning. How are you?

Mr. Riley. Fine, thank you.

Ms. Blackburne. Good morning, Mr. President.

Mr. Riley. Thank you so much for being with us.

The President. I'm glad to do it. It's nice to hear your voice.

President's Visit to New York City

Mr. Riley. Mr. President, you're coming here to New York tomorrow to speak to issues pertaining directly to the economy at a session that was called by Governor Mario Cuomo. Tell us a bit about this particular event.

The President. Well, I was invited by the Governor to speak there on the Governor's Leadership Conference on the Future of the Economy, and I wanted to come and talk about what we have done so far in the first 2 years of our administration to try to help bring back the national economy and the New York economy.

The unemployment rate in New York has dropped 2 percentage points since I've been President. New businesses are up; the business failure rate is down about 20 percent. We're moving forward. But there are still some significant challenges for the New York economy. There are still people who want jobs who don't have them. There are people who are stuck in jobs who aren't getting raises. There are still large numbers of people without health insurance. There are still some barriers to investment in inner cities and in some of your rural areas, too.

So what I want to do is talk about the partnership that I see unfolding in the next couple of years, how New York can make the most of the enterprise zone concept that I'm pushing, how New York can make the most of the community development banks that we just created to make loans to low income people in inner cities to start their own businesses and to get investment flowing. I just want to talk about how we can bring this economy back even more and how the people who haven't been touched by the recovery can be helped.

Community Development and Job Creation

Ms. Blackburne. Mr. President, I wanted to ask you, many of the people that are in the WLIB listening area are very much affected by the fact that jobs are not available to them. We have people involved in their own entrepreneurial efforts who are being frustrated. Part of it is seen as an unwillingness on the part

of the Republican administration to target jobs to people in the African-American community. How would your partnership address that?

The President. It would do that in several ways. First of all, we're trying to make the African-American community more accessible to capital to start jobs. One real problem we have in America is that once areas get high unemployment rates and people leave it, don't invest there, it's almost impossible to get loans to start businesses and to begin them. Floyd Flake, a Congressman from Queens, has been particularly active in working to help to set up a new network of development banks around the country so that we can get money, capital, into these areas to start businesses.

If you look at the opportunities for economic growth within America, inner-city areas and rural areas, especially those that are heavily minority populated are a great opportunity for economic growth, because unemployment is high and the potential for consumer demand to grow is enormous. So the first thing we've got to do is to get some money in there.

The second thing we have to do is to try to increase direct investment in the form of infrastructure projects, community development projects. And one of the things that came out of the crime bill, for example, was a real commitment to try to put people to work at the grassroots level in neighborhoods, solving the problems of the neighborhoods there. And that will become a short-term boost in a lot of our cities throughout the country.

Over the long run, what we've got to do is get investment there. And the last thing I want to point out is that we really worked hard to increase the capacity of people in the inner cities to get the training they need to take the jobs that are opening up. Like New York, for example, has gained about 102,000 jobs in the private sector since I've been President. In the previous 4 years, New York lost 500,000 jobs. So there will still be a lot of people who once had jobs who don't now—that's 300,000 different—but it shows you we're coming back. What we've got to do is keep the jobs coming back and also make sure people who are unemployed can get those jobs.

Welfare Reform

Mr. Riley. Mr. President, I wanted to ask you about one initiative that you put forward this year, and that's specifically welfare reform.

There are a number of poor people and single mothers in our listening audience who feel demonized when the subject of welfare reform comes up, because it appears as though they are being stereotyped in terms of not wanting to work, not wanting to find a job, et cetera, when it has been the experience of many people in our community that this is not the case, that many people on public assistance want desperately to find jobs. Tell us how your welfare reform program would speak to this seeming demonization of single mothers and the poor.

The President. Well, first of all, let me say I agree with what you just said. One of the things that I try to say every time I mention this issue is that the people who most want relief from welfare dependency are the people who are on welfare. I have spent probably more time with people who are actually on public assistance rolls—who are mostly, as you know, young women and their children—than any President ever has, because I served several years as a Governor and I did a lot of work on welfare reform.

What our program would do is to, first of all, try to do more to empower people to move from welfare to work through adequate education and training and health care and child care for the children of welfare recipients, so they can facilitate their move into the workplace.

We also have lowered taxes on workers with children who work full-time for very modest wages so they won't be falling back into poverty, there won't be an incentive to go back on welfare if they get a job.

Now, the trick is going to be how to create enough jobs for people to get them. That is, once you train people for work and once you say that after 2 years they have to go to work if they're not, then there have to be jobs there available. And there are only two options: You either have to have some sort of incentive for the private sector to hire more people, or people have to go to work in public jobs, community service jobs. And we're working on both. I just approved—I've approved 18 experiments in 18 separate States to try things to put people from welfare to work. And the State of Oregon has just gotten permission from our administration to actually give welfare checks to private employers as a supplement, and then the employer puts in some pay over and above that. And the idea is that the private work force will grow a lot more because of this extra incentive, and

the welfare recipient will get more money than would have been the case just drawing the welfare check by going to work.

So we're doing a lot of things in an experimental way right now to try to make sure we have the jobs there, because I am convinced that almost all people on welfare, given the proper training and knowing that their children won't lose their health care coverage, will gladly choose work over welfare.

President's Vision

Ms. Blackburne. I agree with that, Mr. President. I wanted to ask another question, a little broader, moving away directly from the economy for a moment. You've been pretty much beat up and brutalized as the President. And many of the great things that you have done and wanted to do have been sort of made to appear frivolous and silly. What is it that you do personally—[*inaudible*]—your vision of how you see your Presidency going? How do you keep your dream alive?

The President. That's one of the best questions anybody's ever asked me. Well, first of all, I work on it a lot personally. I mean, I begin each day and I end each day talking with my wife about where we are and where we're going. I pray a lot. And I try to remember every day I'm here that there are real people out there I'm trying to help and that there may be times when a lot of Americans don't even know what I've done or tried to do because of the incredible contentious atmosphere in which public life is conducted today.

But I just try to keep my eyes on my vision for this country. I want to keep the American dream alive for every American. I want us to go into the next century with everybody being able to compete and win in this global economy. I want it to be a more peaceful world.

And I know that the economy is in better shape, that we're doing things for ordinary Americans, like family leave and immunizing children and trying to get investments into poor areas. I know that this country is a safer and more secure place because Russian missiles aren't pointed at us, and we're making peace in Haiti, the Middle East, Northern Ireland.

I know that we're moving in the right direction, and I just have to keep that flame alive inside me. I tell our staff all the time, when things get really rough around here because of the politics, that it's not important every day what ordinary Americans think about us, but it is important what we think about ordinary Americans every day and that we just keep our vision alive, and I work on it.

But you asked a good question, and it's harder some days than others, but I find that if I really follow a disciplined effort to just work at the task every day and to remember the people, the real Americans that are out there I'm trying to help, every day is still a joy to go to work.

Ms. Blackburne. That's great.

Democratic Congressional Support

Mr. Riley. Mr. President, there seems to be a perception afoot among many in the country that the Republican Party seems to be more organized around its agenda than the Democrats are around theirs. Many of your initiatives, including a jobs bill that would have brought some money to New York, were scuttled in some measure or to some extent by members of your own party. Why is that? Why does it appear to most Americans that the Republicans are organized, they know what they want, but the Democrats don't?

The President. Well, part of it is what they want to do. Sam Rayburn said, "Any jackass can kick down a barn. It takes a carpenter to build one." [*Laughter*] So it's a lot easier to kick down the barn, you know. They all voted against my economic program, for example, which brought the deficit down and brought the economy back and provided college loans to 20 million people and Head Start positions to 200,000 more kids and immunizations to all the children in this country under the age of 2. I mean, they all voted against it. They just lined up like robots and said no.

So they, at the end of this session of Congress, they killed campaign finance reform and political lobby reform and some important environmental measures to clean up toxic waste dumps, for example. They just killed them all because they didn't want anybody to be able to say that they'd done these things. So it's easier to say no than to say yes. You can always find a reason to say no, particularly if you think it's politically advantageous.

Now, the Democrats, on the other hand, if you go back 50 years, the Democratic Party has always been, particularly in the Congress, much more diverse. You know, we have very liberal Democrats; we have very conservative Democrats. We have Democrats that come from

very rural areas; we have Democrats that come from the inner city. And when you're trying to put together a program to actually do things, it's harder to do.

Now having said that, let me just say one thing in defense of the Democrats in the Congress. We haven't gotten the figures for this year, but last year, according to the Congressional Quarterly, which is a nonpartisan research service, the Democrats in the Congress supported me more strongly than any President since Roosevelt, except for one brief period when President Johnson was passing the civil rights legislation. And we had a higher rate of success in passing bills through Congress last year, even though the stimulus didn't pass, than any President except for President Eisenhower in '53 and President Johnson in '65.

So I think that the Congress has gotten a little bit of a bum rap. If they fail to do something, it's news for weeks. If they do something, it's news for 30 minutes. So, we actually—if you look at what we did, we passed an economic program that reversed trickle-down economics; we've passed major expansions in global trade; we've done an awful lot. I've mentioned a few things, family leave, the motor voter bill, tax cuts for low income working families. We passed the Brady bill, and we passed the crime bill with its ban on assault weapons and juvenile handgun ownership and prevention programs and 100,000 more police for our cities, in the face of bitter, bitter Republican opposition.

So, if you look at the overall record, we've been able to do quite a bit. Do I wish we'd done more? Yes, I do. Do I hope we'll do more next year? I wish—you know, we had another million Americans lose their health insurance this year. I want to pass health care reform. But we've done quite a lot, and I think it's important to defend the Democrats for hanging together as much as they have, because they've had to do it in the face of this blistering criticism and people distorting all out of proportion their positions and what they've done. So, I'd say, like Mr. Rayburn said, it's easier to kick down a barn than build one. And we're the barn builders, and we're going to keep trying to do it.

Haiti

Mr. Riley. Mr. President, thank you so much for being with us on WLIB this morning. On behalf of our very large Haitian listening audience, I have to say, on a personal note, thank you for what you did in Haiti.

The President. Well, I am elated so far. President Aristide has done a fine job. And our young men and women in uniform, some of whom by the way are Haitian-Americans, have performed superbly down there. I'm very, very proud of them.

Looking forward to being with Governor Cuomo tomorrow and talking about New York's future.

Mr. Riley. Okay.

Ms. Blackburne. Thank you, Mr. President.
The President. Thank you. Goodbye.
Mr. Riley. Thank you. I hope that you can come by our studio one day.
The President. Thanks.
Mr. Riley. You take care.
The President. Goodbye.

NOTE: The interview began at 9:50 a.m. The President spoke by telephone from the Oval Office at the White House.

Remarks on the Partnership for a New Generation of Vehicles
October 18, 1994

Thank you very much, Steve, and Bill Hogland, Tom Denomme, Alex Trotman. Senator Levin, Senator Riegle, welcome, we're glad to have you here today. I want to thank all those who have worked on this project: Secretary O'Leary, Administrator Browner, Dr. Mary Good, and Jack Gibbons, our science adviser, and the Vice President.

This is a perfect project for the Vice President and me to work on: all of his obsession with the environment and technology and my indiscriminate love of anything that has anything to do with automobiles. [*Laughter*]

I listened to them talking about regenerative brakes and fuel cells and ultra-capacitors. You know, there wasn't a single one of those things on the three most important cars in my life— [*laughter*]—my '67 Mustang, my '63 Buick Le Sabre, and my '52 Henry J. I could fix everything on those cars, except when the hydraulic brakes went out on the Henry J. Then I just shifted down into first gear and ran into the curb. [*Laughter*] But I'm going to have to learn all this all over again.

When I realized what we were asking the auto companies and the UAW to do in developing this vehicle that would triple fuel mileage, it reminded me of this old Chinese proverb about a businessman who goes to an oracle and says he's got a terrible problem. His abacus counters can't keep up with the workload, and he can't afford to hire any more of them. So the oracle says, "Well, it's simple. You should just have each abacus counter grow another fin-

ger on each hand." And the businessman said, "That's a wonderful suggestion. How do I get them to do that?" The oracle said, "Don't ask me. I only make policy. It's your job to implement it." That's the way the Government's been talking to the auto industry for years. [*Laughter*]

But you saw these prototypes over there, cars that weigh 1,400 pounds, 2,000 pounds, cars that can get up to 100 miles a gallon—not commercially viable yet, still a lot of technical problems, but people are working together and doing something remarkable.

I have to tell you, the reason I believed this would work—basically, there were two. One is, as Bill said or maybe it was Tom, one of them said, we have to do this. We simply don't have an option. If you look at what's happening to greenhouse gas emissions, if you look at what's going to happen to automobile growth throughout the world, we have to do it. And normally when free people with a lot of energy and intelligence have to do something, they figure out how to do it.

The second reason I believed it would happen is because of what the automobile industry has already done in the last few years. You know, 1994 marks the first time since 1979 when American auto companies will sell more cars anywhere in the world than Japanese cars. We are literally back to number one in sales for the first time in 15 years. If you look at how it's been done, there has been a remarkable partnership, a partnership which we have tried to support and enhance, and I appreciate the remarks that have been made about that.

If the auto industry can get to the point today, after what people were saying about it 10 years ago—I was in Michigan just a few days ago, and I went out to Dearborn to the Mustang plant there. And don't laugh, I didn't drive one. I was safe. They were safe. [*Laughter*] But it was amazing to me, the biggest problem that I heard in Michigan is that too many people are working too much overtime. Now, when you consider where the auto industry was 10 years ago, 6 years ago, that is what we call, where I grew up, a high-class problem. [*Laughter*]

And it is a tribute to the massive investment in technology, to the absolute determination by labor and management to work together and to increase levels of productivity to unprecedented levels, and to visionary leadership. It didn't happen overnight. It required a leap of faith that was dramatic. It required these companies to continue to invest, even in the years when they weren't making money. They did all that, and if they did that, they can do this, especially if we work together in the spirit of partnership.

I was thinking the other day, rebuilding a country is not that much different than rebuilding the auto industry. People have to get together and quit fighting. They have to agree on a common goal. You have to invest in the fundamentals, educate and train people, and have high standards. I feel very good about where the country is going, and I feel very good about where the auto industry is going, and we just have to go there together.

If you look at what's happened in the last 21 months, we have, as has already been said, dramatically expanded trade in America and dramatically increased the efforts that this Government is making to support the American business community as we go into a global economy. We brought the deficit down, reduced the size of the Federal Government, kept inflation low. We have 4.6 million new jobs now. And I'm proud to report that in 1994, more high-wage jobs have been created than in the previous 5 years combined, and well over half the new jobs coming into this economy this year have been at above-average income levels.

So America is coming back. We can do this. But if you think about the long-run economic development of the country, we can only hope to continue to grow and prosper if we find a way to do it that is friendly to the environment, that enhances our natural resources, that permits that elusive goal we call sustainable development. This car can do as much to achieve that goal as anything I can think of. And therefore, it is as major a key to our future economy, our strength and success in the global marketplace in the 21st century, as anything else we can be working on.

I am very, very proud of what these fine people have done on this project after only one year. And we're going to keep going until the job is done.

Thank you very much.

NOTE: The President spoke at 11:40 a.m. on the South Lawn at the White House. In his remarks, he referred to Steve Yokich, vice president, United Auto Workers; Bill Hogland, vice chairman, General Motors Corp.; Tom Denomme, vice chairman, Chrysler Corp.; and Alex Trotman, chairman and CEO, Ford Motor Co.

Remarks on the Nuclear Agreement With North Korea
October 18, 1994

Good afternoon. I am pleased that the United States and North Korea yesterday reached agreement on the text of a framework document on North Korea's nuclear program. This agreement will help to achieve a longstanding and vital American objective: an end to the threat of nuclear proliferation on the Korean Peninsula.

This agreement is good for the United States, good for our allies, and good for the safety of the entire world. It reduces the danger of the threat of nuclear spreading in the region. It's a crucial step toward drawing North Korea into the global community.

I want to begin by thanking Secretary Christopher and our chief negotiator, Ambassador at

Large Bob Gallucci, for seeing these negotiations through. I asked Bob if he'd had any sleep, since he's going to answer all your technical questions about this agreement, and he said that he had had some sleep. So be somewhat gentle with him. After meeting with my chief national security advisers, and at their unanimous recommendation, I am instructing Ambassador Gallucci to return to Geneva on Friday for the purpose of signing an agreement.

The United States has been concerned about the possibility that North Korea was developing nuclear weapons since the 1980's. Three administrations have tried to bring this nuclear program under international control. There is nothing more important to our security and to the world's stability than preventing the spread of nuclear weapons and ballistic missiles. And the United States has an unshakeable commitment to protect our ally and our fellow democracy South Korea. Thirty-eight thousand American troops stationed on the Peninsula are the guarantors of that commitment.

Today, after 16 months of intense and difficult negotiations with North Korea, we have completed an agreement that will make the United States, the Korean Peninsula, and the world safer. Under the agreement, North Korea has agreed to freeze its existing nuclear program and to accept international inspection of all existing facilities.

This agreement represents the first step on the road to a nuclear-free Korean Peninsula. It does not rely on trust. Compliance will be certified by the International Atomic Energy Agency. The United States and North Korea have also agreed to ease trade restrictions and to move toward establishing liaison offices in each other's capitals. These offices will ease North Korea's isolation.

From the start of the negotiations, we have consulted closely with South Korea, with Japan, and with other interested parties. We will continue to work closely with our allies and with the Congress as our relationship with North Korea develops.

Throughout this administration, the fight against the spread of nuclear weapons has been among our most important international priorities, and we've made great progress toward removing nuclear weapons from Ukraine, Kazakhstan, and from Belarus. Nuclear weapons in Russia are no longer targeted on our citizens. Today all Americans should know that as a result of this achievement on Korea, our Nation will be safer and the future of our people more secure.

Now I'd like to ask Ambassador Gallucci to come up and make a statement and answer your questions.

NOTE: The President spoke at 5:09 p.m. in the Briefing Room at the White House.

Statement on Flooding in Texas
October 18, 1994

My thoughts are with the people of Texas during this crisis. With the help of our team down in Texas, I will continue to monitor the situation closely.

NOTE: This statement was included in a White House statement announcing that the President directed Secretary of Transportation Federico Peña, Small Business Administrator Phil Lader, and Federal Emergency Management Agency officials to travel to Texas to survey flood damage.

Statement on the 1994 Malcolm Baldrige Award Recipients
October 18, 1994

The Malcolm Baldrige National Quality Award recognizes clear, proven strategies for continued American success in the global economy. These three winners demonstrate that aggressive quality management, including a clear customer focus and partnerships with employees and suppliers, equips American companies to compete and excel in the global marketplace.

NOTE: This statement was included in a statement by the Press Secretary announcing the following recipients of the 1994 Malcolm Baldrige National Quality Award for excellence in quality management: AT&T Consumer Communications Services of Basking Ridge, NJ; GTE Directories of Dallas/Fort Worth, TX; and Wainwright Industries of St. Peters, MO.

Letter to Congressional Leaders Transmitting an Immigration Report
October 18, 1994

Dear Mr. Speaker: (Dear Mr. President:)
I transmit herewith the President's Report on Immigration. This interim report is required by section 141(i) of the Immigration Act of 1990, as amended (Public Law 101–649).

Sincerely,

WILLIAM J. CLINTON

NOTE: Identical letters were sent to Thomas S. Foley, Speaker of the House of Representatives, and Albert Gore, Jr., President of the Senate.

Letter to Congressional Leaders Reporting Budget Deferrals
October 18, 1994

Dear Mr. Speaker: (Dear Mr. President:)
In accordance with the Congressional Budget and Impoundment Control Act of 1974, I herewith report seven deferrals of budget authority, totaling $3.5 billion.
These deferrals affect International Security Assistance programs as well as programs of the Agency for International Development and the Departments of Health and Human Services

and State. The details of these deferrals are contained in the attached report.
Sincerely,

WILLIAM J. CLINTON

NOTE: Identical letters were sent to Thomas S. Foley, Speaker of the House of Representatives, and Albert Gore, Jr., President of the Senate. The report detailing the deferrals was published in the *Federal Register* on October 27.

Remarks to the Governor's Leadership Conference in New York City
October 19, 1994

Thank you very much. You know, after the last several months in Washington, I'm sort of disoriented. I don't know how to react to that

sort of reception. When I came in and you were so wonderful and warm and you were cheering, I said to the Governor, I said, "Well, shall we sit down now?" He said, "No, no, no." He said, "That's part of your problem." He said, "Let them cheer. When they boo, you sit down." [*Laughter*]

When Andrew Cuomo, who as you know is a Presidential appointee, wrote his father a note and said, "Ten minutes, don't be too long," and then the Governor came up and embarrassed his son by telling you that, I wrote a note on the note. I said, "Clinton's eighth law: Blood is thicker than water, but the paycheck is thicker than blood." [*Laughter*]

I appreciated what Governor Lundine said about my supporting tourism in New York. I have supported it in two ways. I brought the Democratic Convention here, and I come here. And then when I come here, no one else can get out, so they have to spend money. [*Laughter*] And so you know, I've gotten to feeling like a thief when I come to New York. I have to leave in the middle of the night so I don't inconvenience anybody. But I love to come, and I am delighted to be here. And I am delighted to be here with so many of you.

I want to say a special word of thanks to Congressman Schumer for his work on the crime bill—thank you, sir—and to Congressman Rangel for many things, but especially for supporting our policy on Haiti before anybody else was for it. Thank you, sir.

I appreciate the presence here of my longtime friend Bob Reich and the other members of our administration who are here, and those who have been here already. I'm proud that they are a part of this.

You know, we're kind of practical people of this administration. There are a lot of folks who worked in State government and local government and the private sector who came to Washington. As a matter of fact, we think it's kind of strange that Congressman Gingrich says his goal in life is to convince you that I am the enemy of normal Americans. As somebody pointed out to me the other day, before I came to Washington I was one. [*Laughter*] And we tried to bring a lot of normal Americans to Washington who would not forget that most of what counts in this country is done somewhere else and that our job was to change the role of Government away from this back-and-forth pendulum of either trying to solve all the problem or sitting on the sidelines and acting as if they didn't exist. We have tried to bring a genuine constructive partnership to this country.

And I must say, it is a lot easier in New York State and New York City because we've had good leadership to work with, and I thank the Governor and I thank the mayor for that.

I must tell you that because I was a Governor for a good long while, I have a sympathy for people who like to be Governor for a good long while. [*Laughter*] It's the best job I ever had, in some ways. And I like it because it was a real job, dealing with real peoples and real problems and real opportunities.

I think it makes a difference whether you have a partnership for growth in New York; I really do. And whether you think that or not is a big part of whether you will make any kind of difference. I think it makes a difference who's in the partnership. It makes a difference whether you have new ideas. Long before I ever dreamed of running for President and thought it was a practical option for me, I read the first volume of the Cuomo commission report. And I remember both volumes very well, all the ideas that they had, all the suggestions they gave not only to States but to our country for dealing with these problems. To me, that's what we ought to be doing in government, being catalysts for helping people take responsibility for their own lives and get together in their communities and reach across the lines that divide them and solve their problems and seize their opportunities.

Twenty-one months ago I went to Washington, determined to do what I could to restore the economy, to make our Government work for ordinary Americans again, and to empower people to compete and win in the 21st century. After 21 months, there's a lot we still have to do. But it is clear that America is in better shape. We have more jobs, a lower deficit, low inflation, a smaller Federal Government doing much more. We're doing things that make Government work for ordinary people, valuing work and family with things like the family leave law, our initiatives in welfare reform, tax credits for working families just above the poverty line so they don't fall into the poverty line—no one who raises kids and works 40 hours a week should fail at either task—immunizing all the children in the country under the age of 2 by 1996.

We've made a serious assault on crime. You've already talked about it a lot. Let me just say that a lot of the ideas in that crime bill have been pioneered here by Governor Cuomo, including the boot camps and the after-school programs as prevention. It is a bill of punishment, police, and prevention, and it's a bill which will lower crime, not because of what the Federal Government will do but because of what the Federal Government has empowered you to do.

One of the things that we're doing is hammering over and over and over again on the need to implement this crime bill, every single part of it, in the proper way: the safe schools provision, the violence against women provision, the victims rights provision, a lot of things most people don't even know are in there. If you do them all in New York, you will lower the rate of crime and violence, not because of what the Federal Government did but because of what you will be empowered to do with the tools that are in the bill.

We also supported, as I'm sure the Secretary of Labor has already said, the idea of lifetime learning. The average 18-year-old will change jobs six or seven times in a lifetime. Many Americans today with good jobs still feel insecure because they keep reading about big companies laying people off, and they're afraid to change jobs when they're 45 or 50. We have to make these kinds of changes the friend of ordinary Americans, because nothing any public official can do will repeal the laws of global economic change. But if we are prepared to seize them and make them our own, then all these changes will make life more exciting, more interesting for ordinary people. The changes in work will be an opportunity to move up, to broaden one's horizons, not to be undermined or have your family lose their security or have people lose their sense of self-worth. So this issue of developing a system of lifetime learning is hugely important in preserving the sense of optimism and strength and inner confidence that has always been at the core of what is America's greatness.

We also clearly are working to make the world a safe and a more democratic and a freer place. For the first time since the dawn of the nuclear age, Russian missiles are no longer pointed at the United States. We have played a major role in trying to promote peace in Northern Ireland, in the Middle East, and of course, in Haiti. We have secured an agreement with North Korea to end that nation's nuclear program, which is terribly important. And we have told Iraq that we still believe the territorial integrity

of its neighbors are inviolate and that it must not be enabled to intimidate the United Nations.

All of this is exhausting work and sometimes frustrating work in a world that is ever changing. But it is clear to me that the rewards will go to people with vision and energy and discipline and an upbeat outlook on the future, and people who are not deterred.

Let me say today the saddest moment for me in the morning was reading about the horrible bombing in Israel, the deaths of innocent civilians by a terrorist determined to wreck the quest of the Arabs and the Israelis for peace in the Middle East. If you think about the kind of disappointments and obstacles those people have to face every day—and they're still out there determined to sign that peace treaty with Jordan next week, to make a comprehensive peace in the Middle East to go forward—now those are real problems.

The American people should look at the strengths and assets we have and say there is nothing that can stop us, look at strengths and assets New York has and just say there is nothing that can stop us. This is a very big deal when you see Americans feeling a little more pessimistic than the facts warrant.

So I'm glad you're here. And if you don't do anything else when you leave but to pat each other on the back and convince yourselves that if you work together you will make a difference, you will have done more than half of the good you can do by showing up in the first place. And I hope you believe that.

I want to talk very briefly about what we tried to do here. A big reason we've had some success in the last 2 years is that our administration came into office with an economic mission. We wanted to rebuild the American dream and make sure every American was empowered to take advantage of it. We had a long-term strategy as well as a short-term strategy. And we organized the White House and the administration in a completely different way.

The key figure in that reorganization was Bob Rubin from New York, my National Economic Adviser. I don't even know if he's still here. But if it hadn't been for him, this whole thing would not have worked in the proper way. We have regular, disciplined, sustained efforts involving the Secretary of the Treasury, the Secretary of Labor, the Trade Ambassador, the Council of Economic Advisers Chair, our Commerce Secretary, who's clearly the most active

Commerce Secretary in my lifetime, the SBA Director, who has changed the Small Business Administration dramatically. You now apply for an SBA loan on a one-page form and get an answer in 3 days.

We work with all the other Departments you see here: The Education Department is a part of our economic strategy; the Health and Human Services Department and welfare reform is a part of our economic strategy; HUD is a huge part of our economic strategy. And we all work together in a disciplined way to think about where America is going in the rest of the world and what America has to do at home. And we work very hard to support and cooperate with and move forward with Governors and mayors and folks in the private sector, with whom we meet on a regular basis and work through the major issues.

Now, if you look at the economy we confront, we all know what the strengths of it are. We also all know we have some problems: 30 years of accumulated social problems; 20 years of stagnant wages for hourly wage earners with limited educations, increasingly buffeted by a global economy; and 12 years of an economic theory that I don't think worked very well, except to give us a big debt and reduced investment.

Our strategy was pretty simple and straightforward: reduce the deficit; increase investment in education and training, new technologies, and defense conversion; increase trade and the sales of American products and services around the world; work with business to sell abroad when it is appropriate and proper to do so; give special incentives to forgotten areas—you heard the talk earlier about the community development banks and the empowerment zones—so that we can get free enterprise into inner cities and isolated rural areas; reduce the role of Government wherever we can, reduce regulation, reduce bureaucracy, but increase the effective leverage the Federal Government has and be a good partner. That has been our strategy.

Now, if you look at what's happened, the deficit is going down dramatically. It's about half of what it was when I took office, as a percentage of our national income. Trade has increased dramatically. Since NAFTA was ratified, trade to Mexico is up 19 percent this year; that's 3 times as much as our overall trade. The GATT world trade agreement will bring hundreds of thousands of high-wage jobs into the country, and the Congress will adopt it, I believe, in

late November. We're selling everything from rice and apples to telephones and Mustangs in Japan now, some of them for the first time. Every country in our hemisphere but one is now a democracy, and they're all going to meet in Miami in December and talk about how we can increase our common wealth and prosperity by working together. We are doing things, in short, that make a lot of sense.

We've increased our investment in Head Start and apprenticeships, in providing more affordable college loans to middle class kids, in spite of the fact that the overall deficit has been reduced on the domestic side for the first time in 25 years this year. We still were able to increase our investment in education and training.

Governor Cuomo mentioned in passing a very important thing about Long Island in defense conversion. We are investing hundreds of millions of dollars around this country to help communities where bases have closed that need to rebuild themselves and to help businesses that used to depend on defense business that's not there anymore. Defense spending's peak in 1987—it peaked in 1987. In 1993 when I took office, there was still $500 million in funds the Congress of the United States had appropriated for defense conversion that had not been spent. We were just leaving these companies and these communities out there floating in the wind with no strategy to bring them back into the industrial base of America and the industrial future of America.

We are changing that now, and it is very important. If you look at New York, if you look at the economic profile of New York, especially out on Long Island, it is criminal to walk away from these companies that helped us win the cold war just because we are reaping the benefits of the cold war by reducing defense spending. So that's a big, big part of our economic strategy.

These things are working. The community development bank legislation I just signed, but you will see when it comes out that we'll be able to create, we estimate, about 150,000 jobs in very isolated inner-city and rural areas just with the community development bank authority that has already been provided. So I am very hopeful about that.

We're also shrinking the Government. It's an unusual thing for the Democrats to be doing, but we did it anyway. We passed bank reform legislation that was hung up for 7 years—we'll save a billion dollars a year in compliance costs; trucking reform legislation that will save billions of dollars a year. There are already 70,000 fewer people working for the National Government than there were on the day I became President, and we are reducing the overall size of the Government by 270,000, and all the money's going back to you to fight crime. That's how we're funding the crime bill.

Now, what are the results? The smallest Federal Government since President Kennedy; 3 years of deficit reduction for the first time since President Truman; 4.6 million new jobs; more than half the new jobs this year above average wage; more high-wage jobs this year in our economy than in the previous 5 years combined; the first time in 15 years this year American companies will sell more automobiles around the world than Japanese companies; the first time in 9 years in the annual vote of international economists, the United States was voted the most productive economy in the world. We are moving in the right direction, and you should be proud of that.

In the State of New York, the unemployment rate has dropped about 1½ percent. There are over 100,000 more jobs. Two million New Yorkers are eligible for lower interest, longer repayment terms on their college loans; 3.1 million New Yorkers are protected by the family leave law. You'll get another 6,100 police in the crime bill; you've already gotten 108, within 2 weeks after the crime bill was signed, to New York. You've got 20 percent more funding in Head Start and $400 million for prisons. We are making a good beginning. We are moving forward, and we're doing it together. That's what partnerships are about.

Do we have more to do? Of course we do. And I want to mention just some of the things that were left undone by this Congress and some of the things we need to do in our own partnership. We walked away from some very important environmental legislation. And I'll just mention one: The Superfund bill was filibustered at the end of the Congress. The Superfund bill to clean up toxic waste dumps was supported by the chemical companies, the unions, and the Sierra Club. I never saw anything they were all for at the same time. There was no one in America against the Superfund bill except more than 40 Republican Senators who didn't want any Member of Congress who

happened to be in the other party or the President to come to New York and say, "We're helping you to clean up toxic waste dumps." So the poison is in the ground because the filibuster poisoned the political atmosphere. And we have to change that. We have to change that.

We walked away from three bills that will help to change the culture of Washington: campaign finance reform, lobbying reform, and a bill to say—and the business people ought to like this—a bill to say that when Congress imposes a requirement on private employers, the Congress has to observe the same requirement, live under the laws you impose on the private sector. And we're going to do our best to pass all three of those next year.

And then—Governor Cuomo has already talked about health care. Let me say that it was interesting to me, the day after the health care legislation was declared over for this session, all the papers were all of a sudden filled with articles about how all the problems are still there: more and more Americans losing their right to choose their doctor; '93 census shows that another 1.1 million Americans in working families, in working families, lost their health insurance; the cost of health care is still going up at well over the rate of inflation. So this will not go away.

And I also want to say—and I don't think I've ever said this in public before, but I finally made a study of this. When I came to Washington, I came to Washington from a State that was both low in per capita income and had a high percentage of poor people. So I never had to worry about the problems of New York, which is high in per capita income but has a high percentage of poor people. I am convinced now that that Medicaid formula is unfair to you, and I think we should change it. And I think that's fair. [Applause] Thank you. You all—you need to sit down, or you'll increase my mail from someplace else. [Laughter]

But it is—I will work with Governor Cuomo, with Mayor Giuliani, with others. We will work through this. It's not going to be easy, but this is an error, I think, in policy that the Congress did not make on purpose. It was something that had not been fully accounted for. I mean, in the last couple of years when Charlie's been trying to get more for New York, there were people who were on purpose trying to get more for their States. I didn't mean it like that. Rangel's eyes nearly popped out when I said that. [*Laughter*] But I think it is very important, and we will work through it.

The other thing I want to say is something about welfare. Now welfare reform has become like God, motherhood, and apple pie; everybody's for it. And that's good. Franklin Roosevelt said in the Depression that to dole out relief in this way is a subtle destroyer of the human spirit. No one ever intended for it to work this way. And I think I would be fair in saying that no President has ever spent as much time as I have had the opportunity to spend, because I was a Governor, actually talking with people on welfare. I find that the people on welfare would rather us change the system than almost any other group of people in America; they're not very satisfied with it either.

So what we have to do is to find a way that rewards work, that requires work, but that also enables people who work to be responsible workers and good parents at the same time. That is very important. I sent a welfare reform bill to Congress last spring. The Congress did not act on it this year. I hope and believe they will act on it next year. It will work to reduce teen pregnancy, to toughen child support enforcement, to educate people more, and also to give them the support they need for their kids if they go to work. And we will ask Congress to pass that plan.

In the meanwhile, we have to keep granting these waivers. I saw when all of you were clapping before that you actually know what a waiver is. If you know what a waiver is, this is the largest group ever gathered in the history of the United States that knew what a waiver was—which is amazing to me, I mean, that's something which is truly laudable. A waiver means that the Federal Government has a bunch of rules and regulations it ought not to have to tell you not to do things you ought to be able to do, but we'll let you do it anyway. That's what a waiver is. And today I guess the most important thing I have to announce is that I'm going to give one of those waivers to New York for your welfare reform proposal.

I believe very strongly in this. Everybody talks about welfare reform, but some people do it, and some people just talk about it. I want you to have a chance to prove that Jobs First works. I want you to have a chance to prove that you can either move 21,000 families off of welfare or keep them from going on in the first place.

I want you to have a chance to prove what I know, that most people on welfare want to work if it will work for them in their family situation. And so that's what this welfare reform waiver will do. And I know you will make the most of it.

I want to say again, this administration is dedicated to partnership. I am a Democrat by heritage, instinct, and conviction, but I don't believe the National Government has all the answers. I believe that we need a smaller but more effective National Government. I think that we need more activism at the grassroots level. Tomorrow I'm going to Massachusetts to sign an education bill that clears away for all States a lot of the rules and regulations that kept people from educating our children, especially our poor children, as well as they are capable of doing. This is a direction we must continue.

The last thing I want to say is that this is not entirely a job for government, and attitude and personal conduct count. You know, those kids that beat up that New York City transit detective the other night, they should have been home. They shouldn't have been out on the street beating him up. There's nothing I can do as President to change that. But all of us together, if we talk about the responsibilities of parents and neighborhoods and community groups, if we take some of that crime money and use it to provide opportunities for kids to go someplace constructive late at night and to have role models that are positive role models, if they don't have a home to go home to, that will make a difference.

And that's something you have to do. That's something you have to do. We need more people who will do what those two men did on the Upper East Side yesterday when they put their own lives at risk to help that man who was stabbed at the automated teller machine and then go get the people who stabbed him. That's what America ought to be about. We ought to lift people like that up, we ought to follow them, and we ought to do what they do. That's the last point I want to make to you. None of this is going to work unless most of us have our heads on straight.

I've become a friend of Ken Burns, the wonderful filmmaker who did the series on the Civil War and did the baseball series. And so I watched it all. It's the only baseball I got this year. Reich is going to fix that for next year, or he'll need three boxes to get up here when he comes back. [*Laughter*]

But listen to this. Listen to what your Governor said in the baseball film. Baseball—Mario Cuomo is talking about why he always liked Joe DiMaggio. He said, "Always you look for heroes. Always the people look up to see something that represents them, to something that is larger than them, and if it's perfect, something they might become." Well, we can't all be Joe DiMaggio, but we could have all done what those guys did at the teller machine yesterday, every one of us. And we can all take one kid in trouble and give that boy or girl somebody to look up to. And we can all do less bellyaching and more visionary talk about the future. And every one of us, including me, every one of us could spend a little less time placing blame and a little more time assuming responsibility. That is what is great about your country.

And I just want to leave you with this thought: When President Aristide went back to Haiti this weekend, there were all these Haitian people in the street with these little signs with their messages on it. And the most frequent message was, in Creole, a simple "Thank you, America." And if you had seen just the eyes, the faces of our young men and women down there in uniform who brought them their freedom back, some of them Haitian-Americans, Americans of all different races and sizes and both genders, it would be impossible for you not to want to do whatever you could to make this country and this State what it ought to be.

So the Governor will try to do his part. I'll try to do mine. If you do yours, the 21st century will be the best time this country ever had.

Thank you, and God bless you.

NOTE: The President spoke at 3:45 p.m. in the Imperial Ballroom at the Sheraton New York Hotel. In his remarks, he referred to Lt. Gov. Stan Lundine of New York.

Statement on the Terrorist Attack in Tel Aviv, Israel
October 19, 1994

The terrorist bombing this morning in Tel Aviv is an outrage against the conscience of the world. Our thoughts and prayers are with the Government and people of Israel at this terrible moment, especially the families of those killed and wounded in this criminal act.

This attack comes at a moment when we are rejoicing in the progress which has been made toward a real and lasting peace in the Middle East. The terrorists who committed this act are enemies of that peace and enemies of all those who are working to create a better future for the people of the region. Their violence is aimed at destroying the hopes of the Palestinian people as surely as it is directed at the people of Israel. They must not be allowed to succeed. I call upon leaders in the Middle East and throughout the world to condemn this act and to ensure that there is no haven or support for those responsible. Together, we will ensure that the promise of peace for which we have worked so long is realized.

Statement on Flooding and Tornadoes in Georgia
October 19, 1994

My heart is with the people of Georgia. I admire their courageous work in repairing their communities from the floods this summer, and my thoughts are with them as they battle these latest forces of nature.

NOTE: This statement was included in a White House statement announcing disaster assistance for Georgia due to flooding and tornadoes that began October 1.

Statement on Maritime Legislation
October 19, 1994

The American maritime industry plays an important role in our Nation's economy and security. Under Secretary Peña's leadership, we have made significant progress implementing a program that enhances the competitiveness of American shipyards in the international commercial market. But our work is not complete.

Congress still must act to ensure a maritime presence in the United States' vast international trade. It must act to ensure that a fleet of U.S.-flag merchant ships, crewed by skilled American seafarers, stands ready to serve our country's economic and military sealift needs. The administration looks forward to working with the next Congress to enact legislation that achieves these important goals.

Remarks at a Dinner for Governor Mario Cuomo in New York City
October 19, 1994

You've still got it, Mario. [*Laughter*]

Among the many things I admire about Governor Cuomo is his remarkable family. And here was his wife saying you should vote for him because he's strong and slim. Can you imagine what would happen to anybody else if someone got up and said, "You should vote for this person because he's got a good body"? I mean, it was great. [*Laughter*]

His son tells him today, Andrew says in the economic conference, "Don't speak very long, Dad." So Mario gets up and announces it and then gives his speech at twice the normal speed. [*Laughter*]

I watched him tonight, and I was thinking, why is this a race? Why is it even close?

I don't know how many of you saw my friend Ken Burns' magnificent series on baseball, but Mario was in it, and he hasn't seen it because he's been out campaigning. I'm not up, so I stay home and watch "Baseball"—[*laughter*]—the only baseball we have right now. One of the things that is in this series is the scouting report from the Pittsburgh Pirates on the promising young center fielder from St. Johns. This is what the scout said about Mario Cuomo: "Potentially the best prospect on the club; could go all the way if he improves his hitting to the point of a respectable batting average. He's aggressive; he plays hard; he's intelligent, not easy to get to know but very well-liked by those who succeed in penetrating his shell." Let me tell you something, he's still the best prospect on the club, and he ought to be sent back to the playing field. And his batting average is very, very good.

You know, when Mario was talking about how—all of his immigrant roots and doing all that, I just was virtually transported. I never get tired of thinking about that sort of thing about our country. In a much more blunt and less eloquent way, Boris Yeltsin said the same thing to me the other day when he was here—really, it was the time before last we were together. Yeltsin grew up in a house literally where the farm animals shared the living room with the children. He was in a very difficult way as a child, and he had read somewhere that I had once lived in a house without indoor plumbing. So about halfway through this banquet he looked at me one night and he said, "You know, guys like us don't get to be President very often." [*Laughter*] The truth is, guys like us do get to be President or Governor or other things in this country because this is a very great country, because we've had leaders like Mario Cuomo.

I've had a lot of time to think about this Governor's race in New York. You know, I admire your Governor so much, I like him so much, I feel that he is my real partner. I think that he has given you strong and disciplined and responsible leadership, and he's still full of new ideas and energy. But I also understand what the issues are.

You know, I was the Governor of my State for a good, long while, and I loved it better than anything. And my State was smaller, but it was the same sort of deal. My people had been there since about the time of the Civil War. I knew every country crossroads. I could still walk into counties and remember the percentage of the vote I got in 1974. Some people thought that was a character flaw, but I thought it showed I was good at math. [*Laughter*] And I want to tell you this story because it was told on me, but it's something every New Yorker ought to think about before this election.

You know, in rural States—and New York, by the way, is a big rural State with a huge agricultural sector—the State fair is about the biggest thing that happens. I'll tell you how big it is, the guy who was my chief cabinet officer left my administration and—well, he worked for my successor a while—and he left to become the head of the State fair. He got a promotion. [*Laughter*] It's a huge deal in a country place. And so I used to go out to the State fair every year and have a Governor's Day, and I'd just sit there. And people would come up and talk to me and say whatever was on their mind, which often burned my ears. And after I had completed my fourth term about—I had served three 2-year terms and one 4-year term—and I was trying to make up my mind whether I would run for 14 years and would serve longer than anybody ever had in my State. At the end of the Governor's Day, when I had heard all this stuff, this old fellow in overalls came up to me, clearly in about his seventies. He looked at me and he said, "Bill, are you going to run for Governor again?" I said, "I don't know. If I do, will you vote for me?" He said, "Yes, I guess I will. I always have." I said, "Well, aren't you sick of me after all these years?" He said, "No, but everybody else I know is." [*Laughter*] And I looked—I swear he did. And he said, "But," he said, "what do you expect? All you do is nag us to do better. You're on us day and night, talking about what we've got to do to get jobs, talking about what we've got to do to get schools, just nag, nag, nag." He said, "Nobody could live with that all the time." He said, "It just wears us out. But," he said, "you know something? I think it's beginning to work." That's what I want to tell you. It's beginning to work. Don't walk away from it when it is beginning to work.

We have a partnership now. In the last 21 months, New York State has over 110,000 new jobs; about a 1½ percent drop in the unemployment rate; 3.1 million families in this State protected by the family leave law; 2 million people eligible for lower interest college loans. Nine hundred thousand families got tax cuts because they work full time, they have kids in the house, they're just hovering above the poverty line; they shouldn't go into poverty. If people work and raise kids, they ought to be able to succeed as parents and workers. That has happened. There's a 20 percent increase in the number of kids in Head Start. You're going to get 6,100 police officers under the crime bill. That's what we can do.

But you know something? A President cannot do anything that changes the lives of people unless there are partners in the governorships, in the mayoralties, in the private sector, on every street, people who care about people, who know their people, and who will get things done. Now, that is why you should reelect this Governor. It is clear that we have a partnership that can make a difference for the people in New York.

A Governor is at his best or her best if the Governor embodies the real qualities of a State. When I see Mario Cuomo talking, I think that is New York. And I like it. And America likes it. You know, even his opponents could not have heard this speech tonight without wanting to kind of tighten their coats and sit up a little straighter and throw their shoulders back and be proud to be an American. And that's very important. So if a man has a good record, if he's got a good program for the future, if he understands how to get things done, and if he really knows his State, and if he embodies the character, the strength, the courage of the State, that's a pretty good ticket.

It's interesting today when we spoke at his conference on growth, I said something I was embarrassed I didn't know. There's a lot of things I don't know about your Governor. I was embarrassed I didn't know this. I said that no matter what the President did, no matter what the Governor did, no matter what the mayor does, no matter what the people who are supposed to be heads of great organizations do, we had to change the spirit of this country. And we had to challenge more people to take responsibility for their own children, their own friends, their own neighbors, or for somebody else's children or friends and neighbors if no one else was doing it. And I said when I saw that transit policeman come home from the hospital after being so horribly beaten by those nine kids, I thought, what in the wide world were those kids doing on the street at that hour of the night? And why didn't somebody give them some better place to go to or try to teach them right from wrong or stand up for what was right and wrong? And then, when I saw today in the paper that there were two people who put their lives on the line to help that poor guy at the teller machine last night in New York, I thought, that's what this country's all about. And more people ought to do it.

Now, after I gave this speech where everybody was clapping, a friend of the Governor's came up and said, "He did the same thing 3 years ago. He got out and chased a criminal, trying to do the right thing." That is the sort of person he is, and he would do it again tonight. He would walk through a wall to do the right thing, and you ought to do the right thing and reelect him Governor.

You know, I had 17 pages of notes, and I came up here with this—because Mario already told you what I did the last 2 years. [*Laughter*]

I want to say something else, too, about this election. It's not just—the difficulty is not just that all the stuff we've been talking about. Why is there a sort of a tight anxiety-ridden negative mood in the country today, when we're plainly better off than we were 21 months ago? I mean, we have more jobs and a lower deficit; we've got a Government that's finally doing things for ordinary people, like middle-class college loans and family leave and immunizing all the kids in the country under the age of 2. We're moving toward peace and prosperity. We've had more advancements in trade in the last year than we have in 30 years. And we have all of the movements toward democracy and freedom that the United States has been involved in, supporting the election in South Africa, the peace process in Northern Ireland, what is going on in Haiti, what is going on in the Persian Gulf, and, of course, the incredible story of peace in the Middle East against all the odds. This is a good time, and we are plainly moving in the right direction. So what is the beef? Why is there this anxiety, this tension in the country? There are a number of reasons, but I'd like to tell you a few, because dealing with them may hold the key to how this election comes out and whether people can hear the song that your

Governor sang tonight, America's song, the song we always respond to when we're at our best.

First of all, we are dealing with the accumulation of enormous problems that have been ignored for a long time. All these social problems that we see that just tear our hearts out, when we see that 5-year-old kid hung out the window and dropped to die because he knew it was wrong to steal candy, that didn't happen overnight. This stuff has been developing for 30 years, for 30 years, what's happened to the families and the communities and the loss of hope and the vacuum that has been created. Drugs and gangs and guns, that stuff just fills a vacuum. There's a hole inside people's lives, and it just goes in there, because there's a vacuum just sucking it into people.

The economic anxieties people feel has been developing for 20 years, where most wage earners who earn hourly wages have not gotten a raise. The average working person is working a longer work week today than 20 years ago. And the global economy requires people to change jobs six or seven times in a lifetime. Those of us who have knowledge and skills and can learn new things and can stay on top and dance on our toes, well, we're pretty secure. Other people are just scared.

And for 12 years, we tried a different approach. We basically had—we were governed by people who tried to convince us that we should hold our Government in contempt, that the Government would mess up a one-car parade, and that we should just sit on the sidelines and let things happen. And it takes time to turn that around. And it takes time for people who have been disappointed a long time to scrape away all that and begin to feel as well as think again that things can be better.

And there's another big issue here: We are going through a period of historic change. At the end of the cold war, the changing of our economy, moving into a new century where all the rules will be different, I honestly believe, for the reasons Mario said, the 21st century will be America's best time. All this diversity we have—if we learn to enjoy it, celebrate it, reinforce it, it is our meal ticket to the future, because the world is a small place.

But every time we go through a period of change, our democracy is tested, because people's hopes and fears are at war. Think about your own life. Think about the first day you went to school, the first day you went off to college, the day you got married, the day you had your first job. Think about only things that had more good than bad in them but were radically different—you were scared to death. One of those movies always work, where the guy walks down the aisle or the woman walks down the aisle and they say, "I don't"—[laughter]—because everybody thinks about it, that's why it works. And because anytime you put yourself on the line and try a new thing, it might not work, and it's frightening.

So you fight this battle all the time inside, between hope and fear. Countries are the same way when they go through big changes. At the end of World War I, America had done a great thing. It was the first time we had ever gone abroad to fight for values and other people without our own existence being at risk. It was a great thing. It exhausted us. And what happened? We came home, and we shrunk up, and we had the rise of the Ku Klux Klan. We had the rise of the Red Scare. And we walked away from the rest of the world and brought on an international economic collapse that gave rise to fascism and nazism and brought the Second World War.

At the end of the Second World War, we didn't do that. But there were lots of pressures to do the same thing, Joe McCarthy, the loyalty program, a Communist behind every bush. But we had strong leadership. It was tough. Harry Truman's popularity was at 80 percent when he dropped the bomb and ended the Second World War. Two years later, when he sent national health insurance to Congress for the second time, it was at 36 percent by the time people got through working on it. All of the people in the 80-to-36 crowd, they all think he ought to be on Mount Rushmore. Well, I was in one of those families that was always part of the 36. We were always for him, and we know. I was raised being told about this. It was inevitable. People were afraid. Things were changing.

And now, you just think about what life's like for the average American today and how they get their information and how they communicate about public things. What we have to do in the next 3 weeks all over the country is go out and say, "We've turned that situation around. The economy's coming back. The government's working for ordinary people. The world is more peaceful and secure. The opportunities are great. We have to vote our hopes and not our fears. We have to vote for tomorrow, not yesterday." That's what we have to do. If on election morning in New York State, most people in this State wake up and the scales inside of them are tilted toward hope instead of fear, it will be a rout for Governor Cuomo. You know it, and I know it. That is our job.

Eleanor Roosevelt once said, "You know, you can spend a lot of time fighting the darkness, and there's a lot of dark things to fight, but the quickest way to beat it is to flip the light switch on." You think about that. You think about that.

What we need is more Americans who will go take up for the people that are getting mugged at the teller machine. What we need is more Americans who will put a hand on those little 5-year-old kids and give them somebody to look up to. What we need is more Americans who will reach out to those 10- or 11-year-old kids when they're 5 so their hearts don't turn to stone before it's too late.

What we need is everybody saying that this is a very great country. If you have any doubt, if you have any doubt, just remember what happened last weekend when President Aristide went home to Haiti. President Aristide went home to Haiti, and all those people were holding those little old signs in the street that said "Thank you, America" in Creole, and they were looking at these young men and women in uniform, our kids who are black, white, brown, yellow, Lord only knows what. A lot of them are Haitian-American; we got every Haitian-American soldier we could find and sent them down there so somebody could speak Creole to those folks. It was unbelievable. And just look at their eyes, and they knew that this was a good country, standing for something good, doing something good, bringing out the best.

That's the way of the rest of us have to be. In our minds, we have to put on a uniform every day. We have to say we are not going to let this country go down; we're going up. And we are certainly not going to let this country go back; we're going forward. And if we have that feeling, that spirit, then all the facts will fall into place. And our story will be credible. And our Governor will be reelected. He is a national treasure, but he really is New York's treasure. Every one of you know. Every one of you know.

I kind of promised myself I wasn't going to mention this, but I'm going to. Every one of you know that he could have had another job with longer tenure. [*Laughter*] Every one of you know that he stayed here because he loves you, he loves that neighborhood he grew up in in Queens. He cannot imagine walking away from this fight until we have had a chance to do every last thing we can to give every kid in this State a chance at a better future. You take care of it and make sure he's reelected.

Thank you, and God bless you all.

NOTE: The President spoke at 9:09 p.m. in the Imperial Ballroom at Sheraton Centre.

Interview With Marjorie Clapprood of WRKO Radio, Boston, Massachusetts
October 19, 1994

The President. Good morning, Marjorie.

Ms. Clapprood. How are you?

The President. Great. It's a beautiful day down here.

Ms. Clapprood. I've got to tell you something, sir. I have been waiting a long time on getting you on this program.

The President. Well, it's high time.

Ms. Clapprood. It is high time. I even went down for the big old Clinton watch when you were over on the Vineyard this summer, and I'm sorry I missed you. But we sort of feel like you've made Massachusetts your second home, so we're delighted you're coming on back.

The President. I'm glad to be back; looking forward to coming up there tomorrow.

Education

Ms. Clapprood. So let's talk about a couple of things. First of all, you need to know that all the kids over at Framingham High are looking forward to your coming down with Senator Kennedy. And let's talk about this education bill. Even Jack Anderson is calling you the education President.

The President. Well, we've worked very hard on education, and Senator Kennedy has had a lot to do with it. A lot of our education initiatives have not attracted a great deal of public notice, maybe because we've been successful in getting bipartisan support for them, for most of them, all but the college loan program. The program to provide middle class college loans at lower interest rates had no Republican support because we took on some organized interest groups. But all the others did. And it's a real tribute to Ted Kennedy because he got the ex-

pansion of Head Start in, he got the national service program in.

And this education act we're signing in Boston tomorrow, or in Framingham, has an incredible amount of good things in it. It's a dramatic reform in terms of putting more responsibility back on local school districts, giving them freedom from Federal rules and regulations but giving them very high standards to shoot for. It's a really—it's a very modern, exciting, and I think, effective piece of education legislation. I'm proud to be signing it.

Massachusetts Senatorial Campaign

Ms. Clapprood. Well, you know, Mr. President, Senator Kennedy is not only delighted to have you here signing that particular bill, but as you know, this is the toughest race the Senator has ever faced in 32 years. And for many of us in Massachusetts, we're surprised to know that nationally he is one of several seats that we're looking at that could be in very serious jeopardy. Your coming out here to help him will be bringing a message to Massachusetts voters that says what? How important is Senator Kennedy and his reelection to the completion of your agenda as you go back to Washington?

The President. He's terribly important to doing it. And he's important for some reasons that people, I think, may not be aware of in Massachusetts. I mean, the rap that his critics are saying is that, "Well, he's been there long enough. He's yesterday's politician." But I can tell you, I've been talking around here the last week, just asking people, and there is a general feeling here that of all the people in the Congress, Ted Kennedy is one of the four or five who are most receptive to new ideas, to trying new things, to breaking out in new directions.

And if you just look at what we've done in education, we have changed the whole national approach to education. It's much more grassroots, local control: Have national standards, have the National Government helping, but give people the freedom at the grassroots level to try new things and to do things that will work. And he's also been instrumental in developing a national apprenticeship program for young people who don't go to college and, as I said, this college loan program. We've had the most impressive set of achievements in the last year and a half in education we've seen in the last 35 years, a lot of cutting-edge, new ideas, and Ted Kennedy has done it.

The other thing he's very good at that I think people don't appreciate is he's the best Democratic legislator at getting Republicans to support what he's doing. He's the best at getting bipartisan support.

Ms. Clapprood. So I've heard, yes.

The President. And I think that if the people of Massachusetts know that, they would be more inclined to reelect him, because he's really a very forward-looking Member of the Congress, and we need him back.

Midterm Elections

Ms. Clapprood. Well, one of the things that the First Lady said when she was in a couple of weeks back—I was happy to be at the dinner that she hosted for the Senator—she went so far as to say that Senator Kennedy's opponent, Mitt Romney, is really just another clone for Phil Gramm and another Senator "no" for you. Are you as worried about that? Do you want to make any predictions on all of these GOP threats that they are going to be taking over the Senate and taking over the Congress this time around?

The President. Well, I don't think they will if we can get the facts out there. I mean, we have made the Government work for ordinary Americans. We've passed things like family leave and the Brady bill and immunizations for all the kids in this country under 2, against ferocious Republican opposition. We've got the economy coming back. We've got more high-wage jobs coming into the economy in 1994 than the previous 5 years combined. Unemployment is down. Employment is up. The deficit

is down. If we can get the record out, we should be winning seats, not them.

But the problem is that they are great talkers, and they promise the Moon, and they will go like robots off of a cliff together. And that's what I'm worried about. It's no offense to Mr. Romney, but they all—in the last few days of the legislative session up here, we had an important piece of environmental legislation, the Superfund bill to clean up toxic waste dumps.

Ms. Clapprood. Right.

The President. Everybody in America was for it. We had the chemical companies, the unions, the Sierra Club; they were all for it—first time they had ever agreed on anything. There was no one in America against it except over 40 Republican Senators who filibustered it to death to keep people like Ted Kennedy from coming back to Massachusetts and saying we helped to clean up toxic waste dumps. They were willing to leave the poison in the ground. That's how bitter and partisan and obstructionist they are. They killed lobby reform and campaign finance reform. And all the lobbyists were cheering Senator Helms when he walked off the floor of the Senate and saying how great it was.

Now, I don't think the American people want to turn the Congress over to them. And especially, I don't think they want to go back to trickle-down Reaganomics. That's what they've promised to do, you know. They've promised to give us the economic policies that they did in the eighties that put New England in the ditch. And I don't think that the people will support it once they know that.

Ms. Clapprood. Well, you know, one of the things that I loved about your campaign, Mr. President, was the slogan "It's the economy, stupid." And it seems as though, with all the indicators macroeconomically looking so terrific—what is the deal with cynical voters? I mean, how do we get this message out? It seems to me that you can't win for losing, even when everything looks good.

The President. Well, I think there are two problems. One is a substantive one. And that is that we've had 20 years when most wages have been stagnant for hourly wage earners and when people have been changing jobs more frequently, so that makes them more insecure. The average 18-year-old, for example, will change jobs six, seven times in a lifetime now. And those feelings don't change overnight. So even though people may say the unemployment rate is dropping and new jobs are coming into America, into Massachusetts, there is still an unsettled feeling. A lot of people themselves haven't gotten a raise. A million Americans lost their health insurance last year; that's why we have to address that.

Then there's a political problem, which is that when Congress is in session, particularly with the bitter partisan obstruction we've seen, what tends to get covered is the fights, the bad news, the failures, the process. So a lot of people just don't know the facts about the economy. So what I'm going out to do now, in the last 3 weeks, is to say, "Look, we're making Government work for ordinary people. We're bringing the economy back. The world is a more peaceful, more secure place for Americans, with opportunities for prosperity. We should be very upbeat about the future, and we ought to reward the people that are building the future, not reward the people that are tearing it down."

Talk Radio

Ms. Clapprood. Do you have any further comments, other than those that you made on KMOX, about talk radio? Do you think that the right-wing conservative bashing of talk radio has done a disservice? It seems to me that's the national pastime of a lot of my colleagues on the air; that's just the "get good ratings if you kick Bill around."

The President. Well, what I think is important, let me say—one thing I like about radio is——

Ms. Clapprood. Me.

The President. Oh, I like you.

Ms. Clapprood. Good.

The President. But generally, I like radio because it's an immediate, it's almost an intimate thing. People feel like they're right there.

Ms. Clapprood. Right.

The President. And people feel that they have a chance to have their say. But a lot of these folks who are on the far right, they never have anybody on that disagrees with them, they never have an honest discussion, and they're not as careful as they ought to be with their facts. I think it's good to have your critics on there and to have honest debates. We shouldn't all agree on everything, and no one in America, including the President, is right about everything. There are always things we can learn. But what I think the American people ought to insist on from talk radio is a conversation, not a screaming match, and strict adherence to

the facts. There's plenty to argue about when we get the facts straight.

That's the only thing that bothers me. I think generally this talk radio phenomenon can be a great instrument in promoting democracy. People feel so isolated from Washington, so isolated from the bureaucracies. A lot of folks even feel isolated from their State capital. So if talk radio makes people feel like they've got a voice, they can be heard, then that's good. But it ought to be a conversation, not a screaming match, and we ought to get our facts straight.

Ms. Clapprood. Yes. And I've got this big problem—my mother always said to me, a position that is not articulated ceases to exist. And sometimes, if that other side isn't heard, people actually believe it's their reality.

The President. I agree with that.

Foreign Policy Accomplishments

Ms. Clapprood. Yes.

I wanted to ask you a little bit about international affairs, if we can. Coming on the heels now of what looks like a fairly peaceful transition and return of Jean-Bertrand Aristide to power in Haiti, you've got an awful lot on your international plate, with the Middle East, with what's happening in Kuwait, and I understand you're on your way next week to the signing of the peace accord between Israel and Jordan. Do you feel as though you've turned a major corner in your administration in terms of not only the maturity of the Clinton administration but in public perception finally cutting you a break and saying, "You know what, he's doing all right"?

The President. Well, I hope so. I think, first of all, a lot of these problems are very difficult, and they don't yield overnight. And a lot of them are things we have been working on here for 2 years. But I'm very proud of what our people, particularly our young men and women in uniform, have done in Haiti and in the Persian Gulf. I'm proud of the role the United States is playing toward peace in the Middle East and in Northern Ireland. And I'm very proud of the work that Ambassador Gallucci did in hammering out this agreement with the North Koreans, which will enable us to avoid a confrontation with them, and enable them to move toward a more normal relationship with South Korea and with the rest of the world, and take a major nuclear threat away.

But I'm feeling good about it. You know, last year we devoted ourselves intensely to two things: getting our relationship straight with the Russians and reducing the nuclear threat in that part of the world, and toward getting an international economic order set up. We worked on NAFTA, the Asian Pacific countries, the GATT world trade agreement. And then this year, we had some good success, as you have pointed out, in Haiti and the Middle East and elsewhere. So I'm very hopeful. And I'm very excited, as I know a lot of people in Massachusetts are, about the moves toward peace in Northern Ireland. And we're working hard on that as well.

President's Leisure Activities

Ms. Clapprood. You don't even have time to go bowling anymore.

The President. No. I miss bowling. I like to bowl, actually.

Ms. Clapprood. By the way, I know I heard on your birthday one of your wishes was to break 80. Did you ever do that?

The President. I never have.

Ms. Clapprood. You never have.

The President. But the last 10 games of golf I've played I had 80 once, 81 twice, 82 three times, so I'm playing——

Ms. Clapprood. Oh, man.

The President. I'm playing pretty well, for me. That's about as good as I can play. And if I lowered my handicap when I was President, the American people would never believe that I'm working as hard as I am. [*Laughter*] So I probably should not want to break 80. But still, I do.

The Presidency

Ms. Clapprood. I know. It makes you very charming and endearing, because the rest of us can all relate to that.

Let me ask you just a couple wacky questions. The thing that I remember most about you from the first time that I heard about the Governor from Arkansas that wanted to be President was a picture I saw of you with then-President John Fitzgerald Kennedy, a personal hero of mine but also someone here from Massachusetts. And I grew up in his hometown of Brookline. And I saw that picture recently on sort of a retrospective of your tenure over this last year and half as President. And I wondered, from that idealistic young man that you were, to now sitting in the Oval Office and dealing with questions like sending the 82d Airborne down to Haiti while Sam Nunn and Jimmy Carter and

Colin Powell sat there, making decisions on war and peace, is it everything that you thought it was going to be? And what are your biggest surprises now that you're actually sitting where you worked so hard to get?

The President. Oh, yes, it is that much and more. I mean, if anything, I am more hopeful, more optimistic about the future of this country than I was before I got here.

Ms. Clapprood. You never want to say, "Quit your bitching. Quit your whining. Why is everybody being so unreasonable?"

The President. Yes. Well, I do want to say that some. I mean, sometimes I think that Americans in this time are a little too prone to see the glass as half empty instead of half full. Our optimism, our unfailing faith in our ability to make the future better has been one of the great secrets to our successes over the last 200 years. And so I do feel that. I regret that at this moment in our history there is a lot of accumulated cynicism and frustration and that it is, in some ways, more difficult for the President to communicate directly to the American people than it has been in the past, because of all the indirect filters between me and the American people. The Presidency is more isolated than I wish it were, partly because of the security concerns that exist in this day and age.

But having said all that, it is a joy and an honor to go to work here every day. And I feel good about the fact that the economy is coming back. I feel good about the fact that we're facing up to problems that have been ignored for years and years here. I feel good about the fact that we're able to do things like this family leave law and to give tax breaks to working families with children to keep them out of poverty, because I don't think anybody that works full-time with a kid in the house should be there. These are things I take pride in, not for me but for our country. And to see how much America is still looked up to in other parts of the world and how people want us involved in Northern Ireland, in South Africa, in the Middle East peace process, and in Haiti, that is a source of great pride.

So with all the down sides of this job and with all its frustrations, it's still an opportunity to make America a better place. And this system of ours does work. It's worked for over 200 years. And the only thing I hope I can do is a better job of communicating with the American people about what we're trying to do and getting them to believe more in themselves and their future. We ought to be quite optimistic based on what is going on here in this country now.

Ms. Clapprood. Well, I'll tell you what, we'd like to be part of making this a regular morningside chat with you. And if it means anything, my sainted mother, who lives in fine Whiskey Point, in Massachusetts, always had a picture of John Fitzgerald Kennedy next to the praying hands and the palms from Palm Sunday. Now she's got a picture of you and Hillary there, as well.

The President. Oh, wow.

Ms. Clapprood. You've got a place of honor, sir. And I thank you very much for joining us. Can I ask one favor?

The President. Sure.

Ms. Clapprood. As you go out jogging around the Charles River Thursday morning, would you put on your little "walkwoman" and listen to Clapprood and Whitley right here on WRKO?

The President. If I can find one of those, I'll do that. Thanks.

Ms. Clapprood. Yes. You've pushed my buttons. I thank you, sir, for joining us. God bless.

The President. Goodbye. Bless you.

NOTE: The telephone interview was recorded at 11:05 a.m. in the Cabinet Room at the White House for broadcast and release at 7 a.m. on October 20.

Remarks on Signing the Improving America's Schools Act of 1994 in Framingham, Massachusetts
October 20, 1994

Thank you. You know, we wanted to come here because this school has a reputation for academic excellence and because it is so diverse, because it's a school that really looks like America. But if I had known we were going to get such an enthusiastic reception, I would have come yesterday instead of today and just waited. [*Applause*] Thank you.

I also want to say a special word of appreciation to your student council president. I thought he did a fine job up here. I can tell you this, if he continues to speak so well, so much to the point, and so briefly, he'll win a lot more elections. [*Laughter*] Very impressive.

I'd like to thank your principal, Mr. Flaherty, your superintendent, Dr. Thayer, your school board chairman, Mr. Petrini, and all the people here who made this wonderful visit possible.

I'd like to thank all the Members of Congress who have joined us. I especially want to thank those who have come from other States, Senator Pell and Congressman Reed have come from Rhode Island, and Senator and Mrs. Jeffords are here. We're glad to see them. I thank Congressman Markey for hosting us. And I thank Congressman Kennedy for coming and bringing

his wife and his mother. I'm glad they're all here. Thank you for coming.

I want to say just a brief word about those who have spoken. Governor Kunin, who was the Governor of Vermont, is now the Deputy Secretary of Education, spoke on behalf of the Department and Secretary Riley, who was the Governor of South Carolina. All three of us served as Governors together, working on these education problems. And I think we've made a real difference, bringing a whole different approach to education to Washington. We look at it from the grassroots up, from the point of view of the principals and the teachers and the school board members. And we like to think from time to time we even look at it from the point of view of the students, from the grassroots up, from education at the school level where it should be.

I want to say a special word of thanks to Senator Jeffords for what he said and to Congressman Ford and Senator Kennedy. Let me say that you read a lot and hear a lot about all the fights that go on in Washington and about how things don't get done. But when the history of this time is written, the progress we have made in education will be known chiefly for two things: One is, we really did write new ideas into the law, and secondly, we did it in a bipartisan fashion, with Republicans and Democrats, for all the children of this country.

I was sitting up here listening to these fine people speak, wondering what all of our words might mean to the students who are here, trying to remember what it was like when I used to sit over there in the band when I was their age and hold my saxophone. You did a great job today, by the way, and I thank you.

I'd like to try to tell you why this whole thing is important from your point of view, because this whole education issue is really about your future. Twenty-one months ago, when I moved to Washington to become President, I had some very clear ideas. I wanted to rebuild the American dream, to restore the health of the American economy, to make sure that your future would be the brightest future ever enjoyed by any generation of Americans, as you grow into the 21st century, a new and exciting, rapidly changing and very different time. I knew that we had to do some things that would matter to people in the short run. We had to begin to make our Government work for ordinary Americans again.

And we've done a pretty good job of that. We passed the family and medical leave law to protect parents when they need time off from work because their children are sick. And we're immunizing all the kids in this country under the age of 2 by 1996. [*Applause*] I see the nurses clapping there. Thank you.

Because we want to reward people who are trying to be good parents and good workers, we actually lowered the income taxes of 15 million working families, because they make modest wages and we don't want them to be in poverty if they're working full time and raising their kids. So we began to do these things.

And we started to work to bring the economy back, to bring the deficit down, to invest more in new technologies, to expand trade. And it is working, and the economy is coming back. But over the long run, the United States of America cannot continue to lead the world economically in a world where the average young person will change work six, seven, eight times in a lifetime, in a world where what you earn depends on not just what you know but what you are capable of learning, in a world that is incredibly fast-moving and diverse—we cannot do that unless we develop the learning capacities

of every person in this country. That is the key to the long-term survival and strength of the United States.

When I was a Governor, my administration and especially my wonderful wife and I spent most of our time working on what we could do to improve our schools: how we could get the test scores up, how we could get more kids in foreign language, how we could improve mathematics achievement, how more of our young people could be ready to learn when they come to school, how we could facilitate more young people going to college. And I learned over and over again, as I think Governor Kunin said, that there are schools in this country, including this one, that are doing a very good job, sometimes against great odds. They are still doing a good job teaching and learning.

But we have some significant challenges we have to face. First of all, we are not as good as we ought to be as a country in taking the things that work well in some school districts and seeing them spread throughout the country. Secondly, we have great challenges because of all the great nations in the world, we are by far the most diverse, racially, ethnically, religiously, economically. Thirdly, we know that schools have become the home away from home for a lot of children who have enormous personal challenges to face. And all those things mean that we have to be constantly working overtime to try to meet the challenges that we face today and the challenges we know you will face in your lives tomorrow.

That's why I worked so hard several years ago to get our country to set a mission, a national set of education goals. Most of you may not know what they are, but I think they're good goals. They're worth repeating: that we will make sure every child shows up for school ready to learn; that we will raise the high school graduation rate to at least 90 percent of all students, which is the international standard, all over the country; that we will make sure our young people learn and are proficient in, by international standards of excellence, basic subjects in English and mathematics and history and geography and languages, and we will learn how to measure whether we are doing that or not at least three times during the course of a student's career; that we will lead the world in math and science achievement, not bring up the rear; that our schools will become safe, disciplined, and free of drugs; and that we will

Overleaf: Signing the Uniformed Services Employment and Reemployment Rights Act of 1994 in the Oval Office, October 13.
Left: Swearing in AmeriCorps volunteers in the Oval Office, September 12.
Below left: Signing the Violent Crime Control and Law Enforcement Act of 1994 on the South Lawn, September 13.
Right: Taping a radio address with President Nelson Mandela of South Africa in the East Room, October 7.
Below: At the Georgetown University School of Foreign Service, November 10.

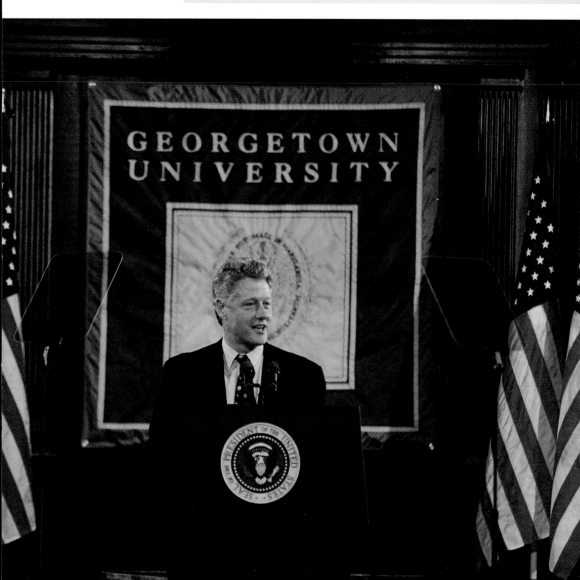

Left: Working in the Residence, December 15.

Below left: At the Full Gospel A.M.E. Zion Church in Temple Hills, MD, August 14.

Right: Meeting with National Security Adviser Anthony Lake and Chief of Staff Leon Panetta in the Oval Office, October 11.

Below: Greeting Health Security Express participants on the South Lawn, August 3.

Left: Celebrating Thanksgiving at Camp David, November 24.
Below: Meeting with Cabinet members in the Cabinet Room, August 4.
Right: With Prime Minister Yitzhak Rabin of Israel and King Hussein I of Jordan at the peace treaty signing ceremony at the Wadi Araba border crossing, October 26.
Overleaf: Meeting with President Jean-Bertrand Aristide of Haiti in the Oval Office, October 14.

develop a system of lifetime learning so that people, no matter how old they are, will always be able to develop new skills, acquire new knowledge, know what they need to know to move forward with confidence.

Those are the goals of this Nation educationally. They have been adopted by Presidents of both parties, by Governors of both parties. They have been embraced by educators all across this country. They are now the law of the land, thanks to this Congress.

The important thing about this bill is that it represents a fundamental change in the way the Federal Government looks at how we should do our job in helping you students achieve those goals. For 30 years, the Federal Government has shipped money to the States and the local school districts to try to help with problems that needed the money. But mostly, they have done it in ways that prescribed in very detailed manner the rules and regulations your schools had to follow, the rules and regulations your States had to follow in applying for the money and in complying with it. And very often, we had teachers at the grassroots level who said, "This doesn't make any sense."

This bill changes all that. This bill says the National Government will set the goals. We will help develop measurements to see whether Framingham School District is meeting the goals. But you will get to determine how you're going to meet the goals, because the magic of education occurs between the teacher and the students in the classroom, with the parents, with the principals, with the schools supporting it.

And you have to see all this stuff we're talking about up here in terms of that. We've expanded the Head Start program, as Senator Kennedy said. These goals have now been written into law, and 31 of the 50 States have asked for our help in devising a State strategy to meet the goals.

The School-to-Work Opportunities Act, which the Senator mentioned, has now all 50 States working to try to develop statewide systems of apprenticeships so the young people who don't go to college but do want to have good jobs will be able to get at least some post-high-school training in ways that help them academically, help them practically, and give them a good start into the future. And that is a very, very important thing. Our Nation is the only advanced nation in the world that does not have a system that picks up every single high school graduate who doesn't go to college and gives them some further education and training so they can make a good living, be good citizens, raise a strong family, and contribute to our future. We're going to change that with this legislation.

And the college loan program and the national service programs I want to explain in tandem. You know, in the 1980's, the gap between what a high school graduate earns in his or her first year of work and what a college graduate earns in his or her first year of work doubled—doubled. Earnings for high school graduates in their first year of work in the United States actually declined in the 1980's, under the pressure of a global economy, where there are a lot of people around the world in developing countries doing jobs for wages we cannot live on. It is clear that it is in the economic interest of the entire United States to get as many young people to go on to college as possible. At the same time, you know we face even more social challenges, especially among younger children.

So we've done two things: One is, we've changed the college loan program to say you can borrow money at lower interest rates; you can pay it out over a longer period of time; if you take a job that doesn't pay a high wage, you can tie the loan repayment to the salary you make. You'll have to pay it back over more years, but there will never be a time when because of the cost of your college education, you can't make a car payment, you can't make your rent payment, you can't meet the basic responsibilities you have.

And the national service program, which you have well represented here in Massachusetts, simply says that if you join a community service program that's part of AmeriCorps, you can earn almost $5,000 a year against the cost of a college education while helping to solve the problems of people here in the United States. It's sort of a domestic Peace Corps.

And this morning I met with a couple of hundred National Service Corps volunteers who are in the City Year project in Boston, which a lot of you probably know about, each of them telling me about what they're doing to try to help solve a human problem in the State of Massachusetts, not with some bureaucracy but from the grassroots up, just young people helping other people to make their lives better and earning some money for a college education.

That is the ticket to America's future and the ticket to your future, as well.

Now, let me just say two or three things about this bill, and then I'll go sign it, because it's getting warm in here. [*Laughter*] It's getting so warm, I'm about to think I'm in Arkansas, not in Massachusetts in October. [*Laughter*]

But I have to say a few more things because now I'm getting to the part that you have to do something about. And this bill is a challenge to you as well. This bill does many things, and I won't tell you all about them, but I want to give you just a few examples.

The first thing this bill does is to encourage schools to take kids that are from underprivileged backgrounds and instead of separating them out from other students, bring them into the classrooms, have smaller classes, work with them, have kids help kids to get everybody into the mainstream, and everybody develop to the fullest of their God-given capacities. We know now that works better than separating kids out and trying to help them, instead of bringing them in and challenging them to do the best they can do.

Let me tell you what that means. That means that every one of you has to support that, not just the teachers. The school district needs to encourage that, especially for the younger kids. But if you have a friend in your class or if you know a student who is not necessarily a friend of yours who is struggling, you ought to see whether you or somebody else can help that student. We need to have more kids helping kids to learn in this country. We've got to have that.

There are a lot of studies today—and I won't bore you with all of them—but basically there are a lot of studies on learning and how people learn that show that some people learn best by just going home at night, opening the book, and working like crazy. But some people learn best in groups, from their friends and neighbors, from being free to ask when they don't know, and from getting help and from working through problems. There are a lot of young people who think they're not very smart who maybe just don't learn very well in the way that they're being asked to learn. And you need to try to help them do better.

The second thing I want to say is something that has already been alluded to here by the previous speakers. If we can't make these schools in this country safe, if children are not free of fear when they come to school, they are not going to learn very well. And this bill has a safe schools component, but it must be implemented. All we can do is give the means to make schools safe to local school districts. We in the National Government don't do anything to make the schools safe; you do that. And you must, and every school must. The children of this country, even if they are scared to death on the streets, ought to feel safe when they're in their schools so they can learn.

The third thing I want to say is—I'm getting sort of progressively more controversial maybe here—is there's an interesting provision of this bill that had enormous bipartisan support that provides opportunities for schools to get some help from this bill to develop what are now being called character education programs, programs that basically enable schools to develop values that can be taught to students in the public schools based on a consensus of people in the community. I made this National Character Counts Week, putting Government on the side of having the schools tell children that there is a difference between right and wrong. And there are some basic things that we ought to teach. There is a bipartisan Character Counts coalition in the Congress that's been working on this.

We disagree about a lot of things, but we ought to be able to agree that our schools should say people should tell the truth. They should respect themselves and each other. They ought to be good citizens, which means that we should assume responsibility for obeying the law and for helping others to develop themselves. We ought to practice fairness and tolerance and trustworthiness. These things should be taught in our schools, and we shouldn't gag our teachers when they try to do it. We ought to applaud them instead, and I hope we will be doing more and more of that.

And now I'm going to ask you young people to do one more thing. There is a lot of evidence, and there is a new survey that's been put out today, saying that in a modest but very clear way, drug use is going up again among young people in America—I hope you're clapping because you agree with what I said, not because you agree that it's a good thing—that more and more young people simply don't believe it's dangerous to use marijuana, for example, and that it's okay to do.

Let me tell you something: Every single scientific study that has been done in the last several years shows alarming increases in the toxicity and the danger of using marijuana, especially to young women and what might happen to their child-bearing capacity in the future.

All illegal drugs are dangerous. We have to drive down usage again. It has got to be not a good thing to do, not a cool thing to do. It is a stupid thing to do, as well as an illegal thing to do, and I want you to help bring it back down.

So this bill is about you. It's not about all of us politicians up here, it's about you. It's about your future. The age in which you are growing and the world toward which you are going can be the best time America ever had. It will be exciting. And our diversity in America is a gold mine of opportunity. No other country is so well-positioned to move into the 21st century, to live in a global society that is more peaceful and more secure—no one. But it all depends upon whether we develop the God-given capacity of every boy and girl in this country, no matter where they live, no matter what their racial or ethnic or religious background is. That is your challenge. Let's do it together.

Thank you, and God bless you all.

NOTE: The President spoke at 11:25 a.m. in the John F. Kennedy Gymnasium at Framingham High School. In his remarks, he referred to Jeremy Spector, student council president; Robert Flaherty, principal; Eugene Thayer, superintendent, Framingham Public Schools; and Christopher Petrini, chairman, Framingham School Committee. H.R. 6, approved October 20, was assigned Public Law No. 103–382. The National Character Counts Week proclamation of October 14 is listed in Appendix D at the end of this volume.

Remarks at a Rally for Democratic Candidates in Framingham
October 20, 1994

Thank you so much for this wonderful, warm, enthusiastic, passionate welcome. And thank you for your commitment to reelect Senator Ted Kennedy on November 8th. I want you to send Kevin O'Sullivan and John Tierney down there to help us in the House of Representatives to move this country forward. And I want to congratulate Mark Roosevelt on giving debating lessons to the Republican Party in the last few days.

I loved Ed Markey's speech, except he said everything that Ted and I wanted to say. [*Laughter*] And he said it very well. It was a great defense of a great record by a great supporter of progress in this country. I thank Ed Markey.

I want to say one thing a lot of you may not know. This is serious. I want to thank Ed Markey because last spring he called my attention to the fact that we had one million military assault-style weapons coming into this country from China. And he said we ought to stop it, and we did. And I thank him for that. And I also want to thank him for paving the way for the information superhighway in Framingham and all along Route 128, the birthplace of high technology and the future of the information superhighway. Thank you, Ed.

Ladies and gentlemen, until the last few days this had the earmarks of an unusual election, where people were in danger of voting against what they're for and for what they're against because of the inordinate success of our opponents in talking things to death and confusing things, but the fog is beginning to clear in America.

Twenty-one months ago, you sent me to Washington to try to change this country, to make Government work for ordinary people, to bring the economy back, to make the world more peaceful and more prosperous, and basically to make us feel like we were going in the right direction again and that we were coming together again, that we could recover the American dream, that we could get to the next century with all the children in this room looking at America's best days ahead of us. And I come here to tell you that we've still got a long way to go, but America's in better shape than it was 20 months ago.

I know there are a lot of people who want jobs who still don't have them. I know there are a lot of people who are working hard who haven't gotten a raise. I know that another million Americans in working families lost their health insurance last year. I know we still have crime problems and social problems. But I ask you to think of this: the social problems, the crime, the drugs, the family breakdown, the things that are gripping this country, they've been developing over 30 years. The economic stagnation of working people, wage earners, has been a problem for 20 years. We had 12 years of trickle-down economics, of failed economic policy that ignored the problems or made them worse.

And in 21 months, we've got more jobs, lower deficit, the Government working for ordinary people, a serious assault on crime. We are moving in the right direction. We don't need to turn back now. We need to go forward into the future.

I believe most Americans, without regard to their party, support the family and medical leave law. I believe they do. In Massachusetts alone, 1¼ million working people in Massachusetts alone can now take some time off when there's a baby born or a family member sick or an elderly person in trouble in your family without losing your job. I believe most people are for it. Well, we voted for it. Most of them were against it. I believe most people in this State and this country think the Brady bill is right, think it is right that we're immunizing all the children in this country under the age of 2 by 1996, believe it is right to expand Head Start. I believe they like these things.

These are the changes we are bringing. I believe most people in this country think that Senator Kennedy's bill to provide national service to give kids a chance to work in their communities and solve problems at the grassroots level and earn money for a college education is a good thing that looks to the future. It is not a relic of the past.

I believe most people in this country like the fact that we have reformed the student loan program and made 20 million Americans eligible for lower interest rates and longer repayment terms on their college loans, for middle class Americans; 840,000 people in Massachusetts alone eligible to benefit from this program immediately. I think most Americans are for it. Every single Republican in the United States Congress voted against it. And we gave it to

the United States, and I think the people are with us and not with them.

I believe most people in the United States think it was right for us to lower the taxes of 15 million working families, people working full time with children in the home, because they had modest wages. No one should work full time and raise kids and be in poverty. We can do better than that. I think people are for that. In Massachusetts, 184,000 working families had their taxes lowered under our economic plan. And every one of the Members of Congress of the opposite party voted against it.

Now, they said if our economic approach passed, instead of what we said, the deficit would explode and jobs would go away. That's what they said. Well, we've had plenty of time now, and what have we got? It was the Democrats, not the Republicans, under our approach that reduced the size of the Federal Government, that lowered the deficit 3 years in a row for the first time since Truman, that oversaw an economic recovery that produced 4.6 million new jobs—and a 2½ point decline in the unemployment rate in Massachusetts alone. They were wrong in what they said.

Now, do we still have problems? You bet we do. There are still environmental challenges. There is still political reform. There is still welfare reform, And yes, there is still health care reform to face. But you should vote for the agents of change, not the agents of yesterday.

I want to tell you something, folks. The ironies of this election continue to abound. Imagine this: Suppose Massachusetts had a Republican Senator—no, wait, wait, wait; no, listen—suppose Massachusetts had a Republican Senator who had voted for legislation to make the Federal Government the smallest it's been since John Kennedy was President, to reduce the deficit 3 years in a row, for economic recovery that produced an explosion of new jobs, for the toughest crime bill in a generation to be paid for by reducing the Federal Government, not with new taxes. The Republicans would be building a statue to this person. They should be building one to Ted Kennedy because that's what he voted for.

So when you hear them spouting their liberal epithets, you know, "Liberal, liberal, liberal," you say, "All we know is, you guys didn't reduce the size of the Federal Government. We did. You guys talked about a crime bill. We passed one. You guys badmouthed the deficit. We lowered it. You guys talked about the economy. Our economy is coming back." Let us reward the agent of change. Let us reward people like Senator Ted Kennedy.

Now, let me ask you this. I want you to draw this clear contrast. I was talking to several people just in the last week about Senator Kennedy, you know, because they say, "Oh, he's been there too long." I'll tell you something, you talk to anybody in Washington of either party who will tell you the truth, and they will tell you two things about your Senator. Number one, there is not a single, solitary Member of the United States Senate more interested in new ideas than he is, new ideas for the economy, new ideas for education, new ideas for the future. And the second thing they will tell you is that in the most partisan atmosphere in modern history, he is absolutely the ablest Member of the Congress at getting Republicans to vote with him and work with him to make this country a better place.

Now, that is the choice you face: a program that's working, new ideas, an approach that is fair to people of all parties. What is the alternative? Look at what they did in the last week of the legislative session. They said no to environmental legislation. They said no to political reform. They, the Republican Senators, killed the Superfund bill to clean up toxic waste dumps. Everybody in America was for it, the chemical companies, the labor unions, the Sierra Club. We never had a bill that all those people agreed on. They couldn't agree on when the sun comes up in the morning. There was literally—there was nobody in America against the Superfund bill except more than 40 Republican Senators. And why? Because they would have rather left the poison in the ground than let Ted Kennedy come home and say he helped to clean it up. That is wrong. We can do better than that. We must go forward. We can do better.

And let me tell you this: You take this contract on America they put out very seriously, and you look at it. You look at what it does. They promise you—listen to this, it sounds great, made my ears perk up when I heard it—"Give us power, give us power, and we will increase defense, revitalize Star Wars, give everybody a tax cut—mostly to the wealthy, but we'll tell you about that later—and balance the budget." Presto.

Does that sound familiar? It's a trillion dollar deal. Now, folks, this is election year. It is almost election time. I would love to make you a trillion dollars' worth of promises. And with a trillion dollars' worth of hot checks, I could show everybody in this house a good time tonight. [*Laughter*] We could have a good time.

But the job of people and responsibility is to do right, not hold out false hopes. It is not to sacrifice the future of our children to give people a quick fix today. This is wrong, this contract, and we must say it is wrong, and we must vote against it, and we must stand against it. This is wrong.

If you let them do this, they will take us back to where—do you remember what it was like in Massachusetts and New England in the eighties? They will explode the deficit. You'll have cuts in Medicare. You won't have any more statements like, "I'm helping you with your water rates, or your sewer rates." They will never fund this crime bill to bring the police to the streets of your communities to make them safer. These things will not happen. We'll start shipping jobs overseas again, and they'll put the economy right back in the ditch, all the time trying to find somebody else to blame.

Stand up against this contract. Stand up against the naysayers. Stand up for somebody who said yes to America, yes to the future, yes to our children. Don't go back. Reelect Ted Kennedy. Stand up for America. Go to the future. God bless you. We can do it.

Thank you.

NOTE: The President spoke at 12:45 p.m. in Nevins Hall at the Framingham Memorial Building. In his remarks, he referred to Mark Roosevelt, Massachusetts gubernatorial candidate, and Representative Ed Markey.

Remarks on Departure From the Rally for Democratic Candidates in Framingham
October 20, 1994

Well, I'm glad to be here. You heard the speech in there. I hope you'll reelect Senator Kennedy. Thank you very much. Let's go out here and say hi to them. Thank you, and thank you for the music. Give the band a hand, U. Mass.-Lowell Band. Give them a hand. Thank you. [*Applause*]

Can you hear? The sound is back. Ladies and gentlemen, it is wonderful to be back in Massachusetts, wonderful to be the first President since Harry Truman to come to Framingham. And I thank you all for coming out here today. I thank you all for participating in this election.

I want to say, you heard what we had to say in there; it was broadcast out here. I want to make one comment that I didn't say in there, that I hope all of you will listen to, whatever your party or your predispositions. One of the things that this country has got to do always, in every age in time, is to believe in itself.

All this business about how we should be cynical and skeptical—I can tell you that everywhere I go around the world, people know the United States is leading the way to the future. They know our economy is coming back. They know we are dealing with our problems. They know we are promoting peace and prosperity all around the world.

If you looked into the faces of those young Americans who were in Haiti last weekend when President Aristide went home, you saw the best of this country. This is a great country, and

I am tired of people trying to tear it down when we ought to be building it up and moving to the future with confidence.

I believe with all my heart, if you look at the results of the last 21 months, you will have to say America is in better shape. We have adopted things that help ordinary Americans: the family leave law, the Brady bill, immunizing all the kids under 2, extending Head Start. These are things that make a difference to real people. And we have got 4.5 million more jobs. The economy is coming back, and we are moving to the future. This is a more peaceful and a more secure country than it was 2 years ago. I ask you to help us to keep the country going forward. Let us not go back to the contract our opponents have offered. They promise everybody a tax cut. They promise everybody a spending increase. They promise everybody a balanced budget. It will get Massachusetts and New England right back where we were in the 1980's, exploding deficit, compromising our children's future, and sending our jobs overseas.

We're going in the right direction. Help us continue to march into the future and keep this country the greatest country in the world, well into the 21st century, and help elect Ted Kennedy on November 8th.

NOTE: The President spoke at 1:15 p.m. outside Nevins Hall at the Framingham Memorial Building. A tape was not available for verification of the content of these remarks.

The President's News Conference
October 21, 1994

The President. Good afternoon. Ladies and gentlemen, when I became President, I did so with a commitment to help more Americans seek a higher education, because it was important for our people and important for our long-term economy.

A big part of the problem of getting more Americans into college and having them stay

there has been the broken Federal college loan program. It's too expensive, it did not provide eligibility for too many middle class people, and there were too many people who didn't go to college or, having gone to college, dropped out because they never thought they could meet their repayment options. There were others who were frustrated because they thought they couldn't take a job they might want because they simply wouldn't earn enough money to meet their repayment obligations.

Today I want to talk about what we have done to fix that system. We already give Americans looking forward to their retirement the chance to save in what we called an individual retirement account. Now we offer people at the beginning of their careers the chance to pay for college in what we call individual education accounts. Here's how it works.

The individual education account enables you to borrow money for college and then to determine how best to pay it back in the way that best fits each individual's needs as their work life changes. There will be four ways to repay the accounts, and people will be able to switch back and forth among payment options at any time and at no cost, depending on what's best for them. Under one option, you can simply pay a fixed amount back on your loan over 10 years. Two other options will permit people with very high debts to spread their repayments over a longer period of time. And as I promised during our campaign, people will be able to pay back their debts as a percentage of their incomes for the life of the loan. This income contingent repayment, or pay-as-you-can option, will give people the chance to start a business, do community service, work as teachers, police officers, or in other public-service-oriented employment and make payments in smaller amounts in the early years if their wages are lower.

Our plan eliminates the middle man in the student loan process, who used to impose enormous and inefficient transaction costs, and, in so doing, to save $4.3 billion for U.S. taxpayers and $2 billion for students in lower loan fees. It means that more people will be able to borrow in a simple, fair, and affordable way.

Over the next few years, as part of our larger school reform, named for Congressman Bill Ford who's retiring this year, every American will be eligible for an individual education account. Already, 300,000 students have taken out these new college loans. By next year, 40 percent of all of our colleges, some 1,500 of them, will be enrolled. In January, we'll announce a phased-in plan to allow millions of people who have already borrowed for their educations to consolidate their loans into an individual education account and get the benefits of these new repayment options.

As more and more middle income Americans will discover, this is a very good deal, which is a very important part of America's long-term strategy for economic health.

Unfortunately, there are those who don't support this approach and want to take us back to the days when working families couldn't afford to send their children to college. Every single one of our political opponents voted against the college loan reform plan. Most of them have now signed a contract telling us what they would do if they controlled Congress. They would give a $200 billion tax cut to the wealthiest Americans, they would explode the deficit, and to help pay for their promises, they have made a specific pledge to cut the student loan programs for 3 million American student borrowers every year. Well, our contract is with the future. I don't want to go back, and I don't believe the American people will support this approach.

Ten days ago I got a letter that shows how important this issue is. A 16-year-old boy named Artur Orkisz, who immigrated here from Poland just 4 years ago, attends Elk Grove School in Des Plaines, Illinois. Here's what he wrote me about his dream of going to college: "Since I came to the United States, my dream has been to attend a school like Harvard or Stanford. I rank number one in my class, but I know for a fact my parents are not going to be able to pay my tuition if I should get accepted to a good university. I'd like to know if students not as rich as others will get the opportunity to fulfill the American dream and graduate from a great university?" Well, Artur, if you're listening, I got your message, and the individual education account will help you get your wish.

Before I take your questions, I'd like to say just a word about the framework with North Korea that Ambassador Gallucci signed this morning. This is a good deal for the United States. North Korea will freeze and then dismantle its nuclear program. South Korea and our other allies will be better protected. The entire world will be safer as we slow the spread of nuclear weapons.

South Korea, with support from Japan and other nations, will bear most of the cost of providing North Korea with fuel to make up for the nuclear energy it is losing. And they will pay for an alternative power system for North Korea that will allow them to produce electricity while making it much harder for them to produce nuclear weapons.

The United States and international inspectors will carefully monitor North Korea to make sure it keeps its commitments. Only as it does so will North Korea fully join the community of nations.

Terry [Terence Hunt, Associated Press].

Middle East Peace Process

Q. Mr. President, when you met last January with President Asad of Syria, he said that peace with Israel was a strategic option. And you said that he was taking the risks for peace. Has he followed through on that? Do you think that he's been forthright enough? And when you go to the Middle East next week, what can you do to break this impasse between Syria and Israel?

The President. Well, I can say that there has been progress in the negotiations between Israel and Syria. Let me also say in general terms why I'm going there.

As you know, I and my administration have worked very hard for a comprehensive peace in the Middle East. It is very much in the interest of the United States. I have been invited by King Hussein and Prime Minister Rabin to be at this signing, and I think it's important that, particularly now, with the violent reaction to the efforts at peace, that the United States stand shoulder-to-shoulder with our friends and allies who are taking such terrific risks to make peace.

While I am there, I will visit Syria because it is my judgment that the visit will further the goal of an ultimate peace agreement between Israel and Syria. And until that is done, we will never have comprehensive peace in the Middle East. There has been some progress in the negotiations, which are, as you know, candid and confidential between the two. I think there will be more progress. I want there to be more progress, and I think this visit will further it.

Helen [Helen Thomas, United Press International].

Q. I have a three-part question. In the overall sense, what do you expect to achieve from this trip? In view of the recent incidents, are there real security concerns? And in the interest of reconciliation, will you try to persuade Israel to release some of the thousands of political Palestinian prisoners that it still holds?

The President. First of all, let me begin with your second question. I have confidence in the security capacity of the governments and the countries that I will visit and in, of course, the work of our own Secret Service. And I think it is terribly important, especially since there have been violent reactions from the enemies of peace, that the United States stand with the friends of peace and the champions of peace at this time. It is even more important than it would have been a few days ago that I go there and that our country stick up for this.

Secondly, what I hope to achieve is to continue to further the peace process. This peace treaty is a huge step forward. I will have the opportunity in Cairo to meet with President Mubarak and Mr. Arafat. I will have a chance there to talk about the importance of implementing fully the PLO-Israel accord. I will have the opportunity to go to Syria. As to what specific things I will discuss with Prime Minister Rabin and others, I think it's better for me to have the conversations and discuss it later.

Q. But you will be trying to move everything forward?

The President. I will definitely be trying to move everything forward. My purpose in going there is, first, to stand with our friends at this moment when they're standing up for peace and the enemies of peace are trying to derail them and, secondly, to move the peace process forward.

Q. Mr. President, how difficult a decision was this to go to Damascus, since your own State Department still lists Syria as a country that supports international terrorism? And a related question, only this morning, there were Katiusha rockets landing from southern Lebanon, an area dominated by Syrian control, landing in northern Israel. How do you believe that this will advance the peace process? And do you have any assurances in advance from President Asad that he's willing to go further now than he went in Geneva earlier this year?

The President. First, I think that with regard to the Katiusha rockets, I think that matter will be resolved between the parties involved before the trip develops. Secondly, with regard to meeting President Asad, even though Syria is on the terrorist list, that remains an issue between our two countries. It is a serious issue. It has been constantly discussed between us, and it will continue to be. But I do not believe that we can permit it to keep us from pursuing a comprehensive peace as long as nothing in our peace agreements undermines our commitment to end terrorism.

So I believe that anything I can do, just as I did when I met with President Asad in Geneva, to further the peace process is something that ought to be done. And I believe that by meeting with him and talking with him and working with him, we will continue to make some advances.

Andrea [Andrea Mitchell, NBC News].

Terrorism

Q. Mr. President, what can the United States do to make sure that Hamas is not getting money from organizations here in the United States, not recruiting people and training people here in the United States? And are you satisfied with Yasser Arafat's response so far, in his willingness to really crack down on Hamas and other terrorist groups?

The President. We can, here, do everything we can through the FBI and our other law enforcement agencies to make sure that we're handling any possible illegal activities in the United States redounding to the benefit of Hamas vigorously. And just in the last week, I have given instructions to the proper Federal agencies to redouble our efforts in that regard.

With regard to your question about Mr. Arafat, I do believe, and the Israelis believe, that he did his best to support them with good intelligence when Corporal Waxman was captured and held hostage. And I believe that in the wake of the killing of Corporal Waxman, the determination of the PLO to distance itself from Hamas and to enforce the law within its territories has stiffened, and I think it will continue to stiffen.

Q. Do think that he has cracked down sufficiently in the Gaza, especially regarding this latest incident?

The President. I think that he's moving in the right direction. One of the things that we are always trying to determine in this moment when they're taking over in the West Bank and Gaza is the capacity of the Palestinian government, the PLO government, to do that work, and we're trying to support an increase in that capacity. I can say that I believe that they're moving in the right direction.

Haiti

Q. Mr. President, having spent hundreds of millions of dollars to restore democracy to Haiti, why is it necessary for American taxpayers to spend still more, renting the homes that Raoul Cédras left behind? I realize it's a relatively insignificant sum, but isn't that adding insult to injury?

The President. Well, first of all, I don't think it's an insult that we spent the money to restore democracy to Haiti. Let's look at what has happened in the last 4 weeks. We have restored democracy. The military dictators have stepped down. The military dictators have left Haiti. President Aristide is rebuilding his government. The economy is beginning to be rebuilt. People are being put to work at rebuilding the country. This is a signal triumph for the men and women in uniform who are down there and the work that they have done, and it is a very important lesson in what can be done to promote democracy and to end human rights abuses.

Now, with regard to the houses, let me just say that the United States and other countries that are with us on the coalition are not in the business of expropriating people's property. And when you make people leave their home, something arguably should have been done. The only instruction I gave was that nothing could be done that would exceed the fair market value of the property—that was the rule under which the State Department was operating anyway—and that some use had to be made of it. So they're either going to use it or turn around and release it so that the taxpayers in this country aren't disadvantaged by it. But I think that this policy has been phenomenally successful in terms of saving lives, not putting Americans unduly at risk, and moving this country's objectives forward. And I think the American people should be very proud of it.

Iraq

Q. Mr. President, during the last Persian Gulf crisis, the Bush White House at times suggested that Saddam Hussein should be overthrown. What's your assessment of the internal situation in Iraq now, and do you think Saddam Hussein should be overthrown?

The President. Well, the Bush White House also made it clear that a condition of their international coalition was that they would not do the overthrowing. My position is that we should keep the pressure on that regime as long as it is out of compliance with U.N. Security Council resolutions. And there are obviously costs to the regime internally from that pressure, and that is the consequence of the misconduct of Saddam Hussein. And the immediate threat is receding. The withdrawal above the 32d parallel is nearly completed.

But we will maintain the deployment at the level we have it now for a while. We will watch the situation. I am gratified by the United Nations Security Council resolution unanimously condemning that conduct. There is no question that internally the pressure will continue to build up unless Saddam Hussein decides to do the right thing and fully comply with the Security Council resolutions.

Q. And your assessment of the internal situation there?

The President. Your assessment might be as good as mine. I think there are extra pressures on them. And I think that those are creating some difficulties, but I don't want to predict what would happen within Iraq.

Midterm Elections

Q. Mr. President, to change to domestic policy—or politics. For the first time in 40 years, a multitude of polls are suggesting that more Americans are prepared to vote for Republicans in congressional elections than Democrats. Can you explain why that's happening for the first time since the Truman administration and to what degree you believe your administration is responsible for it?

The President. Well, I think it's changing in the last few days, and we didn't want to peak too soon. [*Laughter*] Let me say, just on a brief, serious note, one of the things that we know is that Americans almost always do the right thing when they have all the information. We know that Americans literally don't know a lot of what went on in Congress, who was responsible for what, and what's happening now. As more and more Americans find out between now and election day that our administration, working with our allies in Congress, did things to make Government work for ordinary Americans—like the middle class college loans, the family leave law, the Brady bill, immunizing kids under the age of 2, a dozen more things—and that these things were uniformly opposed by the Republican congressional leadership and sometimes by all Republicans, that the Repub-

licans killed the Superfund law to clean up toxic dumps and all the political campaign reform laws and now have a contract that would take us back to the trickle-down economics of the eighties, explode the deficit, ship jobs overseas, and cause the cuts of Medicare and all other Government programs, including student loans, and they talk tough on crime, but they've got a plan to cut the crime bill and make sure it can't be funded and police officers can't be put out there—I think the voters will change their minds. And I think that when Congress went home and the American people now have a chance to hear the debate and hear both sides, if we can get the evidence and the arguments out there, I feel quite confident that they'll do the right thing.

Medicare

Q. You and other Democrats around the country have been complaining about the contract that—the Republicans' Contract With America—that it would cut Medicare steeply. Can you say that you would not propose to cut Medicare next year?

The President. You know what my position is. My position is that any Medicare savings that we can get from managing the program better should be put back into providing for the health care needs of our country. That was my position, that's the position that I offered in the health care debate, and that's still my position.

Virginia Senatorial Campaign

Q. President Clinton, there have been a lot of reports coming out about you meeting with former Governor Wilder. Can you tell us whether the subject of an ambassadorship for him to an African country ever came up during that recent meeting in exchange for any promise he made to endorse Chuck Robb? And what do you think of the comments that candidate Oliver North has been coming up with, suggesting that there should be some kind of investigation of the meeting, that you may have broken the law during that meeting?

The President. Well, first of all, there was absolutely no discussion along the lines you mentioned of an ambassadorship to an African country in return for his endorsement of Senator Robb. That just did not happen. I would not do that. I would never be part of that, and that did not happen. The Vice President spoke to it today. I will tell you again, that did not happen. It did not happen.

Now, you know, Oliver North says a lot of things, and you know, if you've got $17.5 million to buy your own version of the truth, then you don't have to be held, apparently, to the same standard that other people do. I noticed the other day he said that I wasn't his Commander in Chief, and someone asked me if it bothered me. I said, it didn't bother me nearly as much as the fact that he didn't act as if Ronald Reagan was his Commander in Chief, either, when he had a chance. [*Laughter*] So, I don't know what else to say about Mr. North.

Brit [Brit Hume, ABC News].

Foreign Policy

Q. Mr. President, you've been able to report advances in foreign policy across a number of fronts, some that you've mentioned here today. I doubt anyone here would have anticipated 2 years ago you would be spending next week, the week before the election, out of the country. Obviously, historic events have something to do with that, but I wonder if your attitude toward the role of foreign policy in your Presidency and your absorption with it and interest in it has changed or grown.

The President. I wouldn't say that, but what is happening now with regard to Haiti and Korea and Iraq in the sense that Iraq is an example of our increased mobility as a result of commitments we made in the defense budgets, what happened with the Chinese commitment to comply with the missile control regime and not to sell dangerous missiles to its neighbors, a lot of these things are the accumulation of 2 years of hard work, trying to fashion the national security of the United States and advance the economic interests of the United States and advance democracy in the post-cold-war world. And it is all—a lot of these things have come together in a short time. But we have been working on them for quite a long time now, and it's just, I think, to some extent, a simple coincidence that the benefits of these long efforts are coming to fruition now.

You're right, I never would have anticipated going to the Middle East at this particular season, but I think it would be wrong for me not to go, particularly for the reasons I just said at this moment. I think it's important.

And one of the things I tried to say in the election campaign that I'd like to reiterate—

I wish it were possible for the American people to believe what I believe about this, which is that there is no simple and easy dividing line between domestic policy and foreign policy, that in a global economy, a global society where everything is so interrelated, we can't be strong abroad if we're not strong at home. But we cannot maintain our internal strength and our values unless we are secure and strong beyond our borders.

Washington, DC

Q. Mr. President, Washington is becoming an issue in this campaign. The latest thing is that a candidate in Oklahoma says there are no normal people here. [*Laughter*] You've lived here almost 2 years now. I wonder what you think of Washington?

The President. I would be glad to testify in court that I think you are a normal person. [*Laughter*] I don't know. I think there is a bunch of normal folks here, but I think this atmosphere is sort of abnormal. The thing that I think is bizarre, though, is I think the American people need to have their antenna up when they hear that, especially since Mr. Gingrich had already said in his meeting with the Republican professional politicians that his mission in life was to convince people that I was the enemy of normal Americans. So I would just caution the voters everywhere in this country, and when they hear somebody say there's no normal people in Washington, a lot of the people that are saying it are the people that have done their best to hang on to every last job they could get in Washington in the executive branch for two, three decades now. So the atmosphere is abnormal, and that makes the people sometimes do and say weird things. But there's a lot of fine folks here, and what we ought to do is kind of get together and do better.

Deborah [Deborah Mathis, Gannett News Service].

Social Problems

Q. Mr. President, notwithstanding the problems all around the world, there are pernicious social problems here in the United States. And many of these problems, in many views, are breaking down along racial lines. Indeed, some people say that the progress of the sixties has been upset and overturned, that the great divide between black and white is worsening, widening. And lately, there is a new book out that suggests that these problems, these conflicts may be inherent, and we may be doomed to them. What do you think about race as it applies to the social problems? And what can you do, what can a government do to try and fix some of it?

The President. Well, if you're asking me first of all about Mr. Murray's book, I haven't read it. But as I understand the argument of it, I have to say I disagree with the proposition that there are inherent, racially based differences in the capacity of the American people to reach their full potential. I just don't agree with that. It goes against our entire history and our whole tradition.

I also think if you—let's just take the social problems. And I guess—I don't want to overly digress; I know a lot of you have a lot of questions, but this is a huge deal. I don't know if you saw the piece in the Wall Street Journal not very long ago where black Americans and white Americans were polled about the social problems generally, crime, family breakdown, drugs, gangs, violence, welfare dependency, the aggregate of them, overwhelming majorities agreed that these were the great problems of our country. And they've been developing for 30 years now. Then, overwhelming majorities agreed that we needed to reform the welfare system to move people from welfare to work. The great divergence came when one group said that this was caused because of the loss of economic opportunity, and the Government had a responsibility to rebuild it. And the other group said, no, this is caused by an escalating amount of personal misconduct, and people needed to change their personal behavior. In other words, the Government can't do anything about it.

I would like to make the following points: I think both groups are right and both groups are wrong, number one. Number two, there's not as much racial difference here as you think there is. And let me try to illustrate it by starting at the second point.

The out-of-wedlock birth rate in the aggregate in the United States is today about 30 percent. It is higher for African-American young women—that is, a birth where there was never a marriage—than it is for white young women, but it is rising faster among whites than among blacks, markedly faster. And it seems to be far more tied to poverty and lack of education and lack of being connected to the future than to race. Number two, it is plain that we are dealing

with both the loss of economic opportunity and a changed set of social mores, a changed sense of what is right and wrong, what is acceptable and unacceptable. And I believe we need to change both.

What can the Government do about it? What can the President do about it? First, we can try to bring this economy back. In 1994, we've had more high-wage jobs created in our economy than in the previous 5 years combined. This is the first year when over half of the jobs coming into our economy are above average wages. Number two, as all of you know, I have signed laws to create community development banks and empowerment zones in our inner cities to try to get investment back there, to give hope to people who have been left behind, to try to do the economic mission. But having said that, to try to rebuild a society that has been pressured both in our inner cities and our isolated rural areas for a generation now—we're talking about 30 years of serious pressure—is going to take a concerted effort that starts with parents and churches and community groups and private business people and people at the local level. The Federal Government cannot be the salvation of that. We have to rebuild the bonds of society.

And everybody has a role to play. That's why—I want to compliment—Deputy Secretary Kunin is here, Governor Kunin from the Department of Education. We signed the elementary and secondary education act today; we're kicking off the college loan program—yesterday—we're kicking off the college loan program today. One of the things in that act that Secretary Riley fought so hard for was the so-called character education provision, so that the schools can explicitly work with their communities and agree about what values need to be transferred to children through the schools and promote them.

This is a very serious and complicated issue. I think it is a quick fix to try to break it down by race. I believe that the evidence is clear that what we ought to be working on is a way for every kid in this country to live up to the fullest of their potential. And that potential is quite extraordinary, and they will do quite well without regard to race if we can attack these problems.

North Korea

Q. Mr. President, a question on the North Korean nuclear arms accord. Even before the ink is dry on that accord, officials of the international atomic energy association are complaining it denies them of a key right, that of special inspections. Doesn't this set a bad precedent for other countries with nuclear ambitions, such as Iran?

The President. I don't think it does deny them special inspections. It commits North Korea first to freeze and then to dismantle, something they'd never committed to do before and something they weren't required to do under the NPT. It also commits them to ship out their spent nuclear fuel, to get it physically out of the country so they cannot do anything with it. The question of special inspections, whether and when, is put off from the present, and that bothers some people. But if you consider the fact that the waste sites are not going anywhere, that the IAEA is going to be in the country, and that we have a commitment for a freeze and then a dismantling and that if they ever violate it they won't get the benefits that they seek from it, it seems to me this is still a very good deal indeed. And I think that what we have to do is to work with the IAEA people who will be on the ground and work out the practical details of this.

Racial Diversity

Q. Mr. President, related to Deborah's question, several years ago a Piscataway, New Jersey, school board had to lay off teachers. And it came to a white female teacher and a black female teacher. And rather than flipping a coin—as it turns out, both had been hired on the same day so they had equal experience—the school board fired the white teacher because of the color of her skin. Now, your Justice Department originally opposed the school board in court, but has flipped recently. And I was wondering if you agree with that decision, if you think that we need more affirmative action acts like this or whether that's a case of reverse discrimination.

The President. I support the position as finally articulated, but I'd like to say it's a very narrow case. That is, if you have a school district where the children are overwhelmingly of one race or another and the faculty is as well and you have two equally qualified people and you stipulate

that—in this case, both sides in the lawsuit stipulated they were absolutely equally qualified—then can trying to preserve some racial diversity on your faculty be a ground for making the decision, as opposed to flipping a coin? As long as it runs both ways, or all ways, I support that decision; that is, there are other conditions in which if there were only one white teacher on the faculty in a certain area and there were two teachers, they were equally qualified, and the school board or the school administrator decided to keep the white teacher, also to preserve racial diversity. That is the position the Justice Department has taken. And on those very narrow grounds, I support it, because both sides stipulated, both teachers and their lawyers stipulated that there was absolutely no difference in their qualifications for the job.

Midterm Elections

Q. Mr. President, this is a political season, and you've been out on the stump a fair amount. What is your prediction of how many seats the Democrats will lose in the House and the Senate? And do you think if the Republicans manage to win the House, given all the mean things that have been said this year, could you work with a Speaker Newt Gingrich? [*Laughter*]

The President. Well, you know Newt's the person that said I was the enemy of normal Americans. I didn't say that about him. The American people have to make a judgment in the election. I can tell you this: I believe with all my heart if the American people knew the record of our administration in making advances, making this Government work for ordinary people, if they knew that; if they knew what we'd done to restore the economy, bring the deficit down, shrink the size of the Federal Government; if they knew what we'd done in passing the crime bill; and if they knew the extent to which the Republican leadership had opposed this every step of the way; if they understand what's in this contract; then if they know we have a contract with the future, that my only interest is in moving this country into the future in a stronger position, I don't believe we would lose seats at all.

Now, almost always at midterm the incumbent President's party loses seats. That's partly because there's a lag between when you do something and when people feel it. And of course, this is an extremely contentious time. But I believe that that will happen. So what

I'm going to do in the next 2½ weeks is to do everything I can to get as many voters as possible to know exactly what the facts are and what our vision for the future is. Then they will make their judgment. After they make their judgment, I will do everything I can to honor their judgment by fulfilling my responsibility, which is to challenge every Member of Congress without regard to party and especially the leaders to work with me to make this country a better place. That's what I have always done, and that's what I will do.

Northern Ireland

Q. Mr. President, now that the IRA and the loyalists' paramilitaries in Northern Ireland have called a cease-fire, which has been today accepted by Prime Minister Major, can you say how soon the administration will have ready a package of economic incentives to help a peacetime Northern Ireland economy? And can you characterize the package? And can you also say what is now the United States role in the talks that are going to take place regarding Northern Ireland?

The President. Let me first congratulate the action which was taken and Prime Minister Major's response to it. I think both are very hopeful. And I am very glad that the United States has been able to be involved in this peace process in Northern Ireland. We will continue to be involved in it. And we certainly want to contribute to the development of Northern Ireland in ways that go beyond even what we've done already with the Irish-American fund. And there are a lot of private citizens in this country who are also really committed to that. And in the end, they will have the most to say about it because we need private enterprise development in Northern Ireland. We have looked at a number of options. We have not finalized any of them because obviously we want to wait for developments to unfold, until the appropriate point. We're a lot closer to the appropriate point today because of the announcements that have been made.

Bill [Bill Plante, CBS News].

Bosnia

Q. Mr. President, are you still committed to lifting the arms embargo against Bosnian Muslims unilaterally if you can't achieve it in the U.N. Security Council by November 15th, even though that might mean the evacuation by peacekeeping forces, a buildup by the Serbs, and alienation of our relations with the Russians?

The President. Well, let's go back to the timetable first. Under the law that our Congress adopted that I agreed to, the compromise we worked out between the administration and the Congress, because the October 15th deadline has passed without an acceptance of the peace plan by the Bosnian Serbs, we are obliged to go to the United Nations with a resolution to lift the arms embargo through the United Nations, but at the request of the Bosnian Government to delay it for 6 months, to give us 6 more months to work on the peace. That is our commitment. If that fails, we are then obliged to go back and consult with Congress to discuss whether we should have a unilateral lift.

I still believe that is a mistake. I have believed for more than 2 years that would be a mistake, because if we lift unilaterally it will cause the collapse of the United Nations mission. The people of the United States don't want our soldiers to go there alone to engage in a battle that is essentially a civil war. I am convinced that the United Nations troops, or most of them, will withdraw if there's a unilateral lift. And I am convinced that it will undermine our ability to work with other countries within the United Nations to resolve this. So I don't support that. But under the law I am obliged to bring that back to Congress and work it through. But keep in mind, we still have 6 months to work through this in the United Nations at the request of the Bosnian Government itself. So that's what we'll keep working on.

Hillary Clinton's Role

Q. I want to ask you about Mrs. Clinton, if I may. What is Mrs. Clinton's professional role at this point? Will she be fully engaged in the health care bill after the next Congress? And does she have any other professional or political portfolio right now?

The President. You bet she does. I mean, I think if you follow her schedule every day, you know what she's doing. And of course, she will continue to be involved in health care. I would never call it a professional role except insofar as everything she does as First Lady is professional. But we intend to continue to work on the health care issue.

I would remind you that another 1,100,000 Americans in working families lost their health insurance this year, that the new estimates are that unless we do something about the rising cost of health care, we will be spending well over 25 percent of our Federal budget on health outlays early in the next century or the next decade now. So we're going to have to face this. This is not a problem that's going to go away. It's going to keep rearing its head.

Immigration

Q. A year ago, you took a position on a California ballot initiative. Do you have any advice this year for Californians facing Proposition 187, which would deny benefits to illegal aliens, and services? And do you have any concerns about the strong tide of anti-immigrant feelings that are in California right now?

The President. Yes, I have concerns about it. I spoke about this briefly with USA Today a couple of days ago, but I'd like to talk about it a moment.

First, let me say the people of California and the people of the United States are right in wanting to eliminate illegal immigration and increase our ability to protect our own borders, even against people that we welcome to our shores when they are legal immigrants. That was a part of the tension recently with regard to Cuba when we made the agreement to stop illegal immigration there. It was part of the early tension last summer with regard to Haiti. The people of California, therefore, are right to want that.

It is, on the other hand, a great mistake to be against immigration generally. We are a nation of immigrants. Practically all of us have forebears who came from somewhere else. And from time to time, we have been greatly strengthened by immigrants. The fact that we have so many different people of different races and ethnic groups and religious backgrounds will be, I might add, an enormous strength for this country as we move into the next century and we get into a global economy.

Let me just give you one small example, and I will come back to 187. What other country besides the United States could have undertaken the operation in Haiti and sent Haitian-American soldiers in uniform to Haiti to speak Creole to the citizens of that country? That's just one example. We're having the Summit of the Americas here in December. We can do that because

Spanish is the second language of America now and because of our growing involvement in the rest of the world. So we—in being against illegal immigration, we should not be against immigration and the incredible source of strength that immigrants bring to our borders.

Now, what to do about it. I guess I've spent as much time working on California and the problems of California, the economic problems of California, as any President ever has. It was my duty to do so. They've had so many problems, caused by the decline of defense spending, caused by the recession generally, coupled with the explosion of immigration and a whole range of other problems they have out there.

Look at what we have done: We have increased spending on the States to deal with the immigration problems by 32 percent since I've been President, even though we've been cutting overall spending. We've increased border guards by 30 percent. We put 1,000 more border guards on. We have doubled the border guards in San Diego. We've had—San Diego and El Paso and Arizona. We've had very successful initiatives to slow the influx of illegal immigrants. We have toughened the penalties. We're beginning to send criminals who are illegal immigrants out of the country. We are the first administration ever to give money to the States to deal with the criminal justice costs. We're spending money on health care and education never before spent. So we are doing things that have not been done.

Barbara Jordan just issued her commission's report. We have those recommendations under advisement. We are going to do some things that will continue to increase our capacity to reduce illegal immigration. That's what I think the right thing to do is.

I have some problems with 187. One is, even its supporters admit that it's unconstitutional. And I don't think as a matter of practice it's a good thing to condition an election referendum, much less other elections in California, on a measure that even the supporters say is unconstitutional. Secondly, I think it presents significant risks. If you don't give the children health care, you can create health risks for the society generally. If you don't give the children education, and they're still in the country and you can't get them out, then they'll be on the street, and the increased risks of crime or other antisocial behavior will go up. If you turn the teachers and other educators into instruments of a sort of a State police force, it's like bringing Big Brother into the schools.

I guess what I'm saying is, I sort of agree with what Jack Kemp and Bill Bennett said in their article about it. And I applaud them for saying it. I mean, this is an issue again where our parties ought to be together. Historically, both Republican and Democratic parties have been strengthened by our immigrants. And I think—if the people of California would be fully candid, they would have to say that leadership decisions made in the past in California have actually facilitated illegal immigration, when they were called undocumented immigrants, in ways that people in California thought were supporting the economic growth of California in good times.

So we need to back away and change our policy. But we don't need to do it in a way that is overbroad, that runs the risk of these problems, and that is plainly unconstitutional, in my judgment. And I have fought harder, I think, than any President to help California deal with the problems of illegal immigration. I just don't think that's the way to do it.

Thank you very much.

NOTE: The President's 74th news conference began at 2:32 p.m. in the East Room at the White House. In his remarks, he referred to Charles Murray, co-author of "The Bell Curve"; former Secretary of Housing and Urban Development Jack Kemp; former Director of the Office of National Drug Control Policy William J. Bennett; and Barbara Jordan, Chair of the Commission on Immigration Reform.

Memorandum on World AIDS Day, 1994
October 21, 1994

Memorandum for the Heads of Executive Departments and Agencies

Subject: World AIDS Day, 1994

As you know, December 1, 1994, is World AIDS Day—a day set aside for our Nation and for the world to reflect on the scope of the HIV pandemic, to honor those we have lost, and to renew our commitment to fight this disease on all fronts.

It is my hope that all departments and agencies once again will plan significant activities to recognize World AIDS Day, as so many did last year. I was touched by the outstanding programs many of your agencies presented for employees, and I appreciated the acts of personal service a number of you performed for people living with HIV and AIDS. These activities exemplify what we have worked to make hallmarks of this Administration: leadership by example and putting people first.

The theme of World AIDS Day, 1994, "AIDS and Families: Protect and Care for the Ones We Love," recognizes that HIV is a challenge to families, not just individuals. Family members must work together to protect their loved ones from becoming infected. And all family members share responsibility for those who have become ill.

In order to begin planning for December 1, I request that each agency head designate an appropriate individual to plan and coordinate World AIDS Day, 1994, activities for the agency. Please inform the White House Office of the National AIDS policy coordinator by November 1 of the individual you have selected who will act as the coordinator for your agency's activities, and keep the office informed of the activities you plan for that day. The Office also will sponsor a meeting of coordinators from all the agencies and will inform your World AIDS Day coordinator of the time and place.

WILLIAM J. CLINTON

Remarks at the Kennedy-King Dinner in Alexandria, Virginia
October 21, 1994

The President. Thank you very much, Governor Wilder, especially for that introduction. You know, you mentioned the PLO-Israel signing. It put me in mind of Arafat and Rabin when you and Chuck were shaking hands then. Peace is breaking out all over. [*Laughter*]

Let me thank Margo Horner and Mame Reiley and Mark Warner for their leadership and for having us here, thank my good friend Jim Moran for that magnificent speech from the heart. Leslie Byrne had to go and win her debate, but I ask you to help her come back. She is a fine woman and wonderful Congresswoman. And Don Beyer, thanks for reminding everybody how we're doing in auto sales and— [*laughter*]—how well we are doing in our heart. You were great tonight, and I thank you for that. He can really give a talk.

You know, I want to say a few words about two friends of mine, people I serve with, Governor Wilder and then-Governor Robb. And I want to try to get you to think about this election beyond the cheerers here. First, let me say that I thank Doug Wilder for what he said about our administration and our efforts. I thank him for being a longtime friend and colleague and a worthy adversary when we were campaigning in the snows of New Hampshire. I thank him for being an example to a lot of young people in this country, that you really can get there if you have real big dreams and you work hard and you do what you ought to do. Maybe that's the most important thing of all. And I thank him for being here tonight, because what he said here tonight is a genuine expression of love and concern for the future of the people he had served for so many years in the Commonwealth of Virginia.

Let me say to Chuck and Lynda Robb, I am really sorry they've had to take so many licks for being friends of mine. [*Laughter*] That goes with the territory, I guess, but I'd never have believed it if you'd told me a year or two ago that it would have happened. I can tell you that I have known them a long time. We served together. We've been overseas together. We've been up and down together before. And I have watched Chuck Robb go through this campaign. I have watched him attacked, vilified.

I've seen his record distorted and outright falsified. I've seen him labor on in good cheer in the face of the richest campaign in the history of the United States to buy the hearts and minds of the people in any State. He had a magnificent record as a marine officer in Vietnam. He was a terrific Lieutenant Governor and a wonderful Governor of this State. Under Republican Presidents, he was telling people of both parties we had to do something about this awful Government deficit that was robbing our children of their future. But this is his finest hour.

Anybody can run and do well in the good times. Anybody can keep on going when you know you are solidly anchored in the spirit of the people. But when a tidal wave comes along, venom and anger and misrepresentation fueled by unlimited money, to stand strong, to not cut and run, to be brave enough to defend what you know is right, to risk it all for the people you really love, those of you who are voting for him and the people who ought to be voting for him who aren't yet, that is his finest hour.

You know, I've been giving a little bit of thought about this election that's going to come up and all the stuff's being said and how I have become the poster boy for Mr. Gingrich and his crowd. [*Laughter*] Now they don't even sort of sneak around about it, you know. The other day after they killed the lobbying bill and one of their number walked off the floor of the Senate and was cheered by the throngs of lobbyists for killing the lobbying bill on a Saturday—on Monday they met with the lobbyists and said, "Okay, we share your values and you better give us money, and don't give the Democrats money, or else." And then the next day, the House leader, Mr. Gingrich, said that their goal, the Republican goal, was to convince the American people that I was the enemy of normal Americans. I always thought my problem was I was too normal, you know. [*Laughter*]

I know Virginia is modernizing and growing and diversifying and all of that stuff. And it's magnificent. When I was a Governor and I served with Doug and Chuck, I used to resent how rich Virginia was getting. [*Laughter*] But I applaud your successes, and I have now contributed to them with some of the defense decisions that have been made in this administration.

But to get right down to it, this is a Southern race, this whole deal. You think about it. Most of us remember—going back to what Jimmy said—where we were on April 4, 1968, and June 6, 1968, when Martin Luther King and Robert Kennedy were killed. It was like somebody tearing a big piece out of our heart because they made us better than we would otherwise have been, not because they were, as they are now painted by our adversaries, the apostles of some liberal, insensitive big Government. Quite the contrary. Read what they said. Both of them wanted Government's power to be used to help ordinary people without regard to their race. But both of them preached the gospel of personal responsibility and cautioned against overreliance on Government.

Robert Kennedy went into Indiana and talked to blue-collar workers who thought they were for George Wallace and got them to be for him because he was both tough on crime and compassionate on civil rights. Martin Luther King didn't say, "No matter who you are, you're entitled to a handout." He said, "No matter who you are, you have to do your job as well as you can. And if your job is to be a street sweeper, you ought to sweep the streets like Michelangelo painted the Sistine Chapel"—not an apostle of some sort of overweening Government but to use the power of the people to help ordinary folks without regard to their race to live up to the fullest of their God-given potential. And each of them confronted people who tried to demonize them.

Now, let's face it, folks, I'm a son of the South, and they have tried to demonize me in the South. And they've done a pretty good job of it, haven't they? [*Laughter*] They've done a pretty good job of it.

Let's think tonight about the next 17 days and who is not for Chuck Robb for the Senate, and why. What is it that they object to that we have done together that is not normal? Let's talk about it. Let's talk about it. And I want you to think about it, because it's not enough for you to stand up here and shout hallelujah. You've got to go out and get some other folks when you leave here. So you talk about it.

Now, I want you to think about this. I came to Washington to revive the American dream, to do three things: to put the Government back on the side of ordinary Americans, to bring the

economy back, and to make the world more peaceful and prosperous for Americans to live and work in. Now, what is it that they object to that is not normal? Is it that we honored work and family with the family and medical leave law? Is it that we're going to immunize all the kids in this country under the age of 2 by 1996? Is it because another 200,000 kids are going into the Head Start program over this period? Is that what they don't think is right? Is it the fact that we gave tax cuts to 15 million working families because they're working 40 hours a week and they've got kids in the house and they still live on modest wages and we don't think that anybody that works full-time and is raising kids should live in poverty? Is that not normal? What is it that they object to about that? Well, their leaders opposed every single one of those initiatives. And I think that is not normal. Most normal Americans want it.

This is Virginia. Do you know what's on Thomas Jefferson's tombstone? "Author of the Declaration of Independence, the Statutes of Religious Freedom for the State of Virginia, founder of the University of Virginia." Now, were we abnormal to totally revamp the expensive and inefficient college loan program, saving over $4 billion in tax money, saving students $2 billion in excessive fees so that we could loan college money to more students, to middle class students at better terms and lower interest rates, so that by the time we're done we will have 20 million more Americans eligible for lower interest college loans? In the State of Virginia I say to you, that is normal. And every single one of them opposed it.

Is it abnormal to recoil in fear and disgust and horror at the crime and violence that is gripping our people and to say, "You folks have been talking about a crime bill for 6 years. Why don't we do something strange and surprise the American people and actually pass one, instead of talking about it?"—to put the police on the street—and we've already started in Northern Virginia putting police on the street—to build more prison cells, to have those prevention funds to give the kids something to say yes to, to have tougher penalties. Is that abnormal? I think that was normal.

What is abnormal is that you could convince the people that it wasn't normal in this strange time. Tell the truth. This was a good thing for the people of Virginia.

What about the way we ran the Government? They say that we're too liberal and they're so conservative. They quadrupled the debt in 12 years. For them, 2 and 2 was always 5. [*Laughter*] They railed against the Government, and they railed against the deficit, but they could not afford to do anything about it because it required a decision instead of tough talk.

So was that abnormal that we're bringing the deficit down, that we're actually reducing the size of the Federal Government they always complained about but never did anything about? Was it abnormal when we passed the procurement bill that changes the way we buy goods and services and will save billions of dollars—the end of the $500 hammer and the $50 ashtray—a Democratic initiative, not a Republican initiative? I think that is normal, and we should be for it.

This State is supposed to be pro-business. You ask any business person that's dealt with the Federal Government over the last 20 years, and they will tell you that this administration has done more to help people sell their goods and services all around the world, done more to expand trade, done more to create jobs, done more to revitalize manufacturing, done more to help defense conversion than any administration in recent history. That's why we have 4.6 million new jobs. I don't think that's abnormal. I think that is normal and good and right for America.

Let me ask you this: If Chuck Robb were a Republican—now, listen. No, don't boo; think. [*Laughter*] Remember, you've got to leave here and reach somebody that's not for him yet. Now, listen to this: If Chuck Robb were a Republican and he had voted to shrink the Federal Government to its smallest size since Kennedy, to get rid of the $500 hammers and the $50 ashtrays, to reduce the Federal deficit to its smallest size in a long time and to do it 3 years in a row for the first time since Truman, to support economic policies that created 4.6 million new jobs, to pass a crime bill that had the toughest penalties in the history of the United States, the Republicans in Virginia would be erecting a statue to him tonight.

So what is their beef? Why are we too liberal? Because we have more minorities on the Federal bench and in the Cabinet, more women on the Federal bench and in the Cabinet? Because we have—look at the world. Is it abnormal that for the first time since the dawn of the nuclear age Russian missiles are no longer pointing at American children at night? I think that is normal, not abnormal. Is it abnormal that we have worked so hard to get North Korea to now commit to be inspected, to say, "We're going to freeze our nuclear program; we're going to give it up"? Here's one thing our kids won't have to worry about if we implement the agreement that was signed today. I think that is normal and good and wholesome, and I think we ought to be supporting it. Were we abnormal by proving that Mr. North was wrong and the American military could, yes, lickety-split, get into the Gulf and stand up to Saddam Hussein and stop aggression again? I don't think so.

What is going on? I'll tell you what's going on. I am a Southerner. I love this part of the country. I love my roots. I love my family. I can take you into every county in my State and to every country crossroads and show you something that I know personally. I like to hunt ducks in duck season, in spite of what the NRA thinks. [*Laughter*] I like to ride horses and go to rodeos. I like country music. I am a Southerner. But I know one thing. You look at our past, the past that Doug Wilder had to overcome. How have we lived through these contradictions all this time? Sometimes we were like Thomas Jefferson, we faced the truth and we moved forward. Sometimes we had to go into a shell because we couldn't live with the challenges of the moment. And the way we did it was by finding somebody to demonize. And a lot of the time, before it became unfashionable, we demonized black people. Now, we elect them Governor.

What are we demonizing? We're demonizing liberals. Never mind if it doesn't fit. Never mind if the facts aren't right. The people are upset; they are exercised. They're anxiety-ridden; they're cynical and skeptical about the Government. So spend $17 million and tell it to them anyway. If it's not true, who cares? That is what is going on, isn't it?

Audience members. Yes.

The President. That is what is going on. They say they are strong and we are weak. They say they are for conservative principles and we are liberal. But we reduced the Government. We reduced the deficit. We made your money go further. We stuck up for ordinary working people. We began to grow this economy again and to bring this country together again.

Now what they want to do is to put in this contract—oh, but it sounds so sweet. In all the crossroads where they think we are not normal, they say, "Here is what is normal: I'll give everybody a tax cut, I will raise defense spending, I will bring back Star Wars, and I will balance the budget. But it costs a trillion dollars." How will you pay for it? "I'll tell you about that after the election." [*Laughter*] You know how they'll pay for it, don't you? The same way they paid for it before. We will explode the deficit and put it right on our kids and lower their standard of living. We will cut Medicare. We will cut veterans benefits. We will never fund the police in this crime bill. We will start shipping jobs overseas again. We will put this economy in the ditch. But they won't care. They'll have the election.

You know, it's 17 days until the election. Chuck Robb's in a tough fight. I'd love to be able to stand up here with him here and make you a trillion dollars' worth of promises. If I could write you a trillion dollars' worth of hot checks, I could show everybody in this room a good time. [*Laughter*] But it is not the responsible thing to do. It is wrong, and you know it's wrong. It is wrong to treat voters like they are children and make them promises that will undermine their own lives and the future of their children. That is not right just because it sounds good. And it is wrong to say that your opponents are not normal Americans just because they've done things you wish you'd done when you had the chance and you can't think of any way to get around it. [*Laughter*]

Now, I'm going to tell you what I really think is going to happen in this election. What I really think is going to happen is that sometime in the next 17 days the psychological balance inside the heart and spirit of the people of Virginia will be set, either by the spirit we come here to honor tonight that animated the lives and the sacrifice of the lives of Robert Kennedy and Martin Luther King, or by that old, dark spirit that often grabs us in the history of those of us who are Southerners, where we are compelled to identify ourselves against someone else, to see other people as our enemies, alien, not normal.

Folks, that's what this is all about. And what you have to do is not just shout here. We've all got our good lines against Oliver North. And

I do think it's more important—more important than that he doesn't consider me his Commander in Chief was that he didn't act like President Reagan was his Commander in Chief. That is more important.

But what is really at stake in this election is what is in the heart of the people of Virginia. Are we going to go forward, or are we going to go back to trickle-down economics of the eighties? Are we going to empower people and challenge them to assume responsibility, or are we going to make them a bunch of cheap promises in a power grab? Are we going to bring out the best in each other, or are we going to keep right on dividing people and letting them vote their fears? That is what is at issue.

This is a period of profound historic change for America. You cannot blame people for being upset and angry and confused. And frankly, it's hard for them to get the facts about what's going on half the time. And what you have to do in the next 17 days is not so much to bash your adversaries, although, goodness knows, you need to answer them back. You need to turn the light on in Virginia and let the light shine and let people feel the future flowing through their veins, in their hearts, in their minds, and their spirits.

If you will give the people of Virginia the vision of the future that is symbolized by the lives of the people we come here to honor tonight, Chuck Robb will win, Jim Moran will win, Leslie Byrne will win. But that's not what's really important: the Commonwealth of Virginia will win.

Go do it. Don't leave a stone unturned. Don't leave a person untouched.

God bless you, and goodnight.

NOTE: The President spoke at 8 p.m. at the Radisson Hotel. In his remarks, he referred to Yasser Arafat, Chairman, Palestine Liberation Organization; Prime Minister Yitzhak Rabin of Israel; Margo Horner, Eighth Congressional District chair, Democratic National Committee; Mame Reily, chief of staff and campaign manager for Representative Jim Moran; Mark Warner, chairman, Virginia Democratic Party, and Lt. Gov. Don Beyer of Virginia.

The President's Radio Address
October 22, 1994

Good morning. As the autumn leaves begin to reach the height of their color, students all across our country are hard at work preparing for math tests and spelling bees, history papers and midterm exams. Their knowledge and skills are being tested. Their report cards will be a measure of their success.

Well, just like those students, America is also being tested. We're facing difficult questions about how we should guide our children in today's world and whether we'll prepare them for the challenges they'll meet. It's not an easy test, perhaps one of the most difficult we have ever undertaken. But the right answers are before us, and our children will be the measure of our success. We've found a number of right answers already. Our national report card shows some exciting progress.

When I became President, I knew the only way we could continue to lead the world would be if we developed the learning capacities of as many of our citizens as possible. That's why the progress we've made on our lifelong learning agenda is so vital to the long-term strength of the United States.

In all our education proposals, we've tried to make a fundamental change in the way the Federal Government helps students to meet their goals. Instead of prescribing detailed rules and regulations that schools have to follow, as the Federal Government has done in the past, we've tried to show that it's the responsibility of individual teachers and students and communities, with the help of our National Government, to work hard to make good lives for themselves.

In everything from an expanded Head Start program to new youth apprenticeships for young people who don't go to college, we've worked to build on those principles. In our Goals 2000 law, which I signed last spring, we set tough world-class standards in the basic subjects for students and schools, but we made it clear that students and teachers at the school level have to decide how to meet those standards. We made it clear that we have to keep guns and drugs out of our schools, that we have to encourage our parents to stay involved with our children's education.

Now this past week, I had the opportunity to sign into law the elementary and secondary education act. That bill says that while the National Government will set the standards and help to develop the measurements of whether schools are meeting them, it is fundamentally the responsibility of people at the grassroots to make sure those standards are met. We are encouraging what we know is the true magic of education, that which occurs between teacher and student, with the help of parents and principals and communities.

This new law does another thing. It supports programs that teach our young people that character does count, that helps them to learn the difference between right and wrong, based on standards developed in our local communities.

We also have to work to make sure more Americans have the higher education they need to compete and win in the global economy. One of the biggest obstacles has been soaring college costs and an inadequate national system of college loans. We've started two new programs to help fix those problems. Our national service program, AmeriCorps, is already giving 20,000 people the chance to serve their country and earn money for higher education. Within 3 years, 100,000 people will be participating in this domestic Peace Corps. To give you some idea of how many that is, the largest number of young people who ever participated in the Peace Corps in a single year was 16,000.

Over and above the national service program, this week I announced that Americans will be able to open what we call individual education accounts. We already have individual retirement accounts that help people direct the growth of their own retirement benefits, and now all Americans will be able to have individual education accounts, so that they can pay back college loans over time in ways that meet their own needs and the requirements of their own working lives. This program will save the Government money, reduce defaults, lower fees for everyone. With these reforms, we're helping to make sure that America can embrace the challenges we face in the world economy as we look to the next century.

But you should know that there are those who would take us in a very different direction, back to the policies of the past which have failed. Our political opponents have signed what they call a contract that tells us what they would do if they control Congress. They'd give a $200 billion tax cut to the wealthiest Americans. They would explode the deficit. That would mean cutting many of the education reforms we've worked so hard to pass, along with Medicare and other programs. Our opponents have even made a specific proposal to cut college aid for 3 million American student borrowers each year to pay for their trillion dollar package of promises in tax cuts, defense spending increases, revitalization of Star Wars, and an allegation that they can balance the budget. Well, we tried that before, and it didn't work out very well.

My contract with America is for our future and for the future of our children. I don't want us to go back. To guarantee that we keep moving forward, we have to be willing to meet the tests of our time, to keep doing everything we can for young Americans who are looking to us for help in meeting the world's demands. We can't give in to easy promises. We have to embrace the challenges of the future. And if we do, we'll be rewarded. The world places many demands on us, but I'm sure you believe, as I do, that that's a test we can pass with flying colors.

Thanks for listening.

NOTE: The address was recorded at 5:55 p.m. on October 21 in the Roosevelt Room at the White House for broadcast at 10:06 a.m. on October 22.

Remarks to Students at Carlmont High School in Belmont, California
October 22, 1994

It's nice to be back in California. It's nice to be here in Belmont. It's nice to be here at Carlmont High School. I'm honored to be the first President to come here. And it's only fair that I came here to see your principal, since he didn't get to come and see me. Now that should not be interpreted as a sign of dissatisfaction with the lady who got to be the principal of the year, but he would have made an awful good one. [*Laughter*] And he sounds to me like the principal of the year here.

I want to say how very honored I am to be here with all of you. I thank Mayor Rianda for her welcome, Mayor Davids for what he said. I thank them for their leadership and their devotion to public service at the grassroots level, where so many of our problems and challenges have to be met. I thank Congressman Lantos and Congresswoman Eshoo for not only being my friends but for their extraordinary service in Washington. I can tell you that there is this popular feeling, I think, that nearly everybody who goes off to Washington has something bad happen to them and forgets about the folks back home; they do not. And they represent you well, and you should be very proud of them. I'm also very pleased to be joined today by your State treasurer, Kathleen Brown, and your State

insurance commissioner, John Garamendi. Thank you, John. I'd like to introduce one other person, too, who is my partner in these education endeavors, a former colleague of mine and former Governor of Vermont and now the Deputy Secretary of Education, who's come all the way from Washington with me today, Governor Madeleine Kunin. Please make her feel welcome. [*Applause*] I want to say a little more about Senator Feinstein in a moment, in connection with this work, but I appreciate what she said today.

But let me begin by saying that, as all of you know, I had the opportunity to spend a great deal of time in this magnificent State of yours a couple of years ago. And since I have been President, I think I've been back here a dozen times. I've worked on emergencies for California, like the earthquake and the fires. I've worked on trying to get the economy of this State going again, to sell computers overseas, to sell the farmers' rice to Japan for the first time, to start the shipbuilding industry in the southern part of the State, to help the defense conversion momentum really get going here so we could build a lot of jobs out of this defense downsizing and not just lose them. I've tried to do things that would help you deal with the crime and the immigration problems, real, concrete steps, not just talk about it. Ten thousand more police officers will come to California under the crime bill. We have doubled the number of immigration officers along the southern border of the State. We've begun to have a real impact in dealing with the problem of illegal immigration.

But what I want to say to you is that over the long run, if we are going to have a bright future for the people of the United States, and if California is going to work—and it can work, you look around at the students here, look at all the different ways they found to say welcome to me up there—if this country is going to work, and this State is going to work, then schools like this school have to work all across America. We have to prove that there is strength, not weakness, in our diversity. We have to prove that all children can learn. And we have to prove that with all the changes that we're going through in America today, we can still give our kids an old-fashioned, safe upbringing and a good education, because that is the key to the future of the global economy.

One of the least known stories, perhaps, of the recent concluded session of Congress is that it was the best session for education in at least three decades. [*Applause*] That's worth clapping for. I appreciate that. This Congress expanded the Head Start program, making more children eligible and making younger children eligible. This Congress passed the Goals 2000 bill, writing into national law our national education goals, world-class standards, and saying that we would help to develop means of measuring whether we're meeting those standards but emphasizing that education reform has to come from the grassroots, school by school.

Just a couple of days ago I signed the elementary and secondary education act, which dramatically reduces the Federal regulations telling schools how to spend the money we give them to help kids who need extra help in school and encourages schools to do things that will actually prove that children can learn without regard to their racial or economic background. The bill also, as Senator Feinstein said, helps to support safe schools initiatives and promotes the concept of character education when basic civic values to be taught in the schools are developed at the community level.

We also passed a bill for young people who don't go to college but do want to get good education, an apprenticeship bill to help every State in the country develop a system to guarantee that even those who don't go to college will have a chance to get some further education and training and get a good job with a prospect of a growing income.

Finally, and perhaps most important, we dramatically reorganized the system by which the National Government makes college loans available, not only to low income but also to middle class young people.

One of the things that's always bothered me in the last couple of years is seeing the cost of a college education go up faster than any other essential part of a family's budget, even more rapidly than health care costs. In my own State, I saw young people start college and then drop out because they either couldn't get loans or they were convinced they would never be able to repay them. Then I saw young people get out of college with big debts and take jobs that paid higher wages, not because they wanted them but because they were afraid they couldn't afford to do something they really wanted to do, like work with people in the community to help kids get a better start or be schoolteachers or police officers or do other things, because they were afraid they could never repay their college loan.

Under this system, you won't have to worry about that anymore when you become of age and you get out of high school. You'll be able to choose to borrow money and pay it back over a longer period of time at a lower interest rate as a percentage of your income, so that if you choose to serve the public and you choose not to get rich, you at least won't be driven into the poor house by the cost of your college education.

The last thing the Congress did was to pass a program that's already being felt here in California, the national service program, AmeriCorps, to give young people the chance to serve their communities and earn money for their college education. This year, 20,000 young Americans are doing it; year after next, 100,000 young Americans are doing it. If the Congress will continue to support it, I am convinced we can have as many as a half a million young Americans paying their way to college by solving the problems of this country one on one, person by person, at the grassroots level all across America. And I thank the Congress for that record of education reform.

Now, having said that, let me come to the point. Education still does not occur in Washington. Education occurs school by school, class by class, student by student. The magic of education is in what happens between the teachers and the students, what the role of the principal is, whether the parents are supportive at home, what is going on inside the student. None of that can happen in an atmosphere of fear.

We all know stories, horrible stories of children being shot or cut or terrorized. When I was in California last year, I did a town meeting and a young man from northern California told me that he and his brother changed schools because they thought the school they were in was so dangerous. And then when they lined up to register in the new school they thought was safer, somebody just came in the school door and shot his brother, standing right there in line to register. He just happened to be in the wrong place.

You would not believe the letters I get from children of all ages begging me to do something about the violence that terrorizes their lives. You may have seen me read a letter that I got from a young man from New Orleans, when the crime bill was being debated, who said, "I know you can do something about crime, and I am frightened." That young man was shot a couple of weeks after he wrote a letter to me.

I got a letter after the crime bill was signed from the son of a friend of mine in my administration who said, "I have a nice family. We have a high income. We live in a good neighborhood. I go to a good school. My friends and I are still scared every time I go downtown to the movies. I feel better now that the crime bill has been signed."

We cannot operate in a country where children are afraid and cannot feel, much less think. You cannot learn in that kind of atmosphere. That is why, as the principal said, we're trying to be tough and firm and strong in some of these critical areas. That's why we had to pass the Brady bill. That's why we had to pass the crime bill. That's why we adopted Senator Feinstein's amendment to ban assault weapons on the streets of our cities. And that's why we come here today to sign this executive order. I know here in this high school you already have a zero tolerance policy for guns, and I applaud you for it. I applaud your principal, and I applaud the students who support it. Now students all over the country, their parents, their teachers,

their principals will be required to meet the challenge that you have met, to follow your example. Students have to take the lead to take responsibility for this. We can do better, and we must.

"Zero tolerance" is a commonsense policy. Why does anybody need to have a gun in school? That's why this order directs the Secretary of Education to withhold funding the States that don't comply with the law. Young people simply should not have to live in fear of young criminals who carry guns to school.

And again I will say, just like the assault weapons, this bill is in the Federal law because Senator Feinstein sponsored it and demanded it. And we got it thanks to her efforts and those of Senator Dorgan, and I thank them both.

As I sign this order, just before I do, I want you to think about it, all of you students here. What are you going to do? What are you personally going to do about what's going on? That's really what counts. We can have this rule, and fewer people will bring guns to schools. We also need fewer guns on our streets. One of the things in the crime bill is the banning of juvenile possession of handguns unless the juvenile is under the supervision of an adult. We are doing all we can to pass laws. But in the end your future will be decided by what is inside you, what you decide to do.

I think all Americans have been very moved— I know I certainly have—by the sight of the Haitian people getting their freedom back and President Aristide going back, to bring democracy back to Haiti. You know, one of his biggest challenges after all the violence that those people have suffered is to make sure that his own supporters now do not resort to violence to retaliate. Why is violence going up so much among young people in our country? Violence begets violence, begets violence, begets violence. It has to end somewhere.

And if you watched President Aristide back in Haiti, perhaps the most gripping thing was when he stood there—having had many of his friends killed, having had children that he tried to help terrorized—standing there saying to the masses of his people, "No to violence, no to retribution, yes to peace, yes to reconciliation." And if they are saying that inside their heart, that will do more than any law.

So I say to you, as your principal said, we've done some tough things to try to give you a bright future. And we're not ashamed of them;

we're proud of them. If we can think of other things to do, we will do them as well. But in the end, what you say inside is even more important. You must say no to guns, no to gangs, no to drugs; yes to education, yes to hope, yes to your own future.

The 21st century can be the best time this country and this State ever knew because of all of you, because of our diversity, because in a global society we will be the great global nation, because everybody can be an American. You don't have to be of a certain race or ethnic background or religious conviction. You just have to come here and share our land and share

our values and make the most of your own life. That is what you have to do.

But in the end, you will have to do it. So I say to you, I'm proud to sign this order to give you the chance to say yes to your future. And I hope and pray you will do it.

Thank you, and God bless you all.

NOTE: The President spoke at 12:11 p.m. In his remarks, he referred to Carlmont High School principal Michael Johnson, Mayor Pam Rianda of Belmont, CA, and Mayor Tom Davids of San Carlos, CA. The memorandum on implementation of safe schools legislation was released by the Office of the Press Secretary on October 25.

Statement on Safe Schools Legislation
October 22, 1994

The single most important thing we can do to improve education for everybody in this country is to make schools safe. Violence against young people is a terrible national problem.

Every other day, enough young people to fill a classroom are killed with guns. In California alone, two children are killed with guns every single day. We have got to put an end to this madness. And the first thing we need to do is to get those guns out of the hands of young people where they don't belong.

The crime law makes it a Federal crime for a minor to carry a handgun except when supervised by an adult. Goals 2000 set a national standard for school safety and requires school districts to take the measures necessary to reach that standard.

The elementary and secondary education act (ESEA) takes it a step further by making it

clear that we simply cannot tolerate guns in our schools, and anyone who brings a gun to school just doesn't belong there.

ESEA requires that States adopt a simple law: If somebody brings a gun to school, they'll be expelled for one year.

This is common sense: There should be zero tolerance for guns in school. That's why I am directing the Secretary of Education to withhold funding to States that do not comply with this law.

It's really very simple: Young students should not have to live in fear of young criminals who carry guns instead of books.

NOTE: The memorandum on implementation of safe schools legislation was released by the Office of the Press Secretary on October 25.

Remarks at a Dinner for Gubernatorial Candidate Kathleen Brown in San Francisco, California
October 22, 1994

The President. Thank you so much. I'm just curious, can you hear me in the back of the room? [*Applause*] Good.

I was listening to Kathleen give that speech——

Audience members. Louder, louder.

The President. I know, there's something wrong with the sound system, isn't there? Can someone turn the sound up? There's something wrong with it.

Well, I'm sorry, you'll just have to listen. [*Laughter*]

I was thinking when Kathleen was speaking that I was glad that she didn't run against me in 1992. And then I was thinking when she was speaking, we will now know what happened when "Mrs. Wilson" gets a lot of write-in votes from Modesto on election day.

You know, I really looked forward to this, to coming out to California and giving you a progress report, talking about what this election is all about. I care a lot about this Governor's race. I used to be a Governor. In some ways it was the best job I ever had. At least I had an easier time defending myself. [*Laughter*] The truth is, I wouldn't trade this for anything.

But if you will bear with me, even in this festive atmosphere, I want to talk tonight pretty seriously to you about what is at stake in these national elections, including Senator Feinstein's race and the congressional races, and then why what is at stake here in California is just like that and why, even though it's a different issue and a different race, what is underlying the contest is the same and why you have to make the same decision. And I want to do it because, after all, for the next 2 weeks and some odd days, you need to spend more time talking to the people who aren't in this room than the people who are if you want to make a difference in this election.

When I was elected President, thanks in no small measure to the overwhelming support of the people of the State of California, I went to Washington determined to do everything I could to rebuild the American dream and to bring the American people together, to make sure that we move into the next century able to compete and win, to make sure that our children are not the first generation to do worse than their parents, to make sure that all this incredible diversity we have in America was the engine of our strength and unity, not the instrument of our undoing. That is why I wanted to be President. And I went there hoping, because I was determined to take our Democratic Party in a different direction, that the Republicans would at least meet me halfway, or would you believe 5 percent? [*Laughter*]

Well, we've been there 21 months. And here are the facts: We have made a real start in making the Government work for ordinary Americans, in bringing the economy back, in making the world more peaceful and more secure for Americans to live and to grow and to flourish in. And in this election we do not pretend that there is nothing left to be done. We ask only that the American people look at what has been done, look at what our opponents have done, look at what they offer for the future. We ask them not to go back to the dark days of trickle-down economics and divisive social policy but to go forward into the 21st century with confidence.

I got tickled, the Republican House leader, Mr. Gingrich, in a rare moment of candor the other day said that his whole—that their whole mission in life, all of them, the Republicans in Washington, the leaders, was to make sure Americans thought I was the enemy of normal people. Well, you know, the truth is he's done a pretty good job of that in a place or two. [*Laughter*] I thought to myself, now, what does that mean? I understand it partly because I grew up in the South, like a lot of you who are immigrants to California from that part of America. And I mean, I was raised on that kind of politics. If you couldn't think of anything to be for and you wanted to get in, just demonize your opponent. And if people are mad and angry and upset about something else, maybe they could just transfer all that onto the election. And just like a kid in a snit on a playground, if you make a decision when you're mad, normally you don't know what you're doing. So you run the risk of being for that which you're against and being against that which you're really for.

Now, that's the risk in the California Governor's race, that's the risk in the California Senate race, and that's the risk in these Congress races all over the country. If you can get people all mad and then transfer their anger and frustration to somebody with a "D" beside of their name and make them the enemy, then you wind up doing that which you would not do if you were thinking.

It reminds me—you know, one of the primary jobs of any parent is to try to raise their children not to make important decisions when they're just stomp-down furious. And in my part of the country—you know, I was born in a little town in south Arkansas about 20 miles from the Louisiana border. And I don't know how many of you have ever been down there, but there are a lot of Cajuns in Louisiana who literally came from Acadia before and populated the State. And they developed a special way of speaking and even a sort of a hybrid language and an incredible body of humor. And when I was a young man, I used to make a habit of collecting these Cajun jokes. But I remember one which illustrates what we are in danger of seeing happening in this election if we don't turn it around and get people to thinking and not just feeling anger, a story about these two Cajun fellows named René and Jacques. And Jacques walks down the street, and he meets his friend Jean. And Jean says, "Jacques, I always see in your pocket your $5 cigars. And they ain't there today. Why ain't they there anymore?" And he said, "You know, that no-good René, every time he sees me, he says, 'Hey, Jacques, how you doing?' He hits me in the pocket. He ruins my $5 cigars." He said, "Yes, I understand that, but how come you replace the cigars with dynamite?" He said, "Don't you know the next time he does that, you'll get killed?" He said, "Yeah, I know that, but I'll blow his hand off, too." [*Laughter*] You think about that. That's what's going on here. That's what's going on here.

We have made a beginning for a change in having the National Government honor work and family. That's what the family leave law was all about, so people could take a little time off when their kids were born or their parents were sick without losing their jobs; in immunizing 2 million children under the age of 2 by 1996; in expanding Head Start; in giving 19 States permission to try their own plans to move people from welfare to work with dignity; in giving tax cuts to 15 million working families with children, so nobody who works full-time will raise their children in poverty. I think that's a pretty good beginning.

We've made a major, major start in developing a system of lifetime learning and training, so people don't stay unemployed for a long time and so young people can live in a world where they may have to change work seven times in a lifetime.

We've signed just a couple of days ago the new elementary and secondary education act, which cuts off—[*applause*]—there are some educators here. You know why the educators are clapping? Because this act recognizes that all the real magic in education occurs in the classroom. And instead of having the Federal Government send a check to California with a string on it 3,000 miles long, accompanied by a gazillion rules, this act says: Here are the standards you must meet, here are the people you must help, here is the money; you figure out how to do it and be accountable for it. We're going to empower you to educate our children.

In our budget we changed the system of student loans to save $4.3 billion in tax money, to cut student fees by $2 billion to enable 20 million Americans over the next couple of years to have lower interest, longer repayment options on their student loans so everybody can borrow the money to go to college who needs it in this country. And I think that's a pretty good beginning. And I don't think it's bad for normal Americans.

We passed the crime bill and the Brady bill, and they tried to stop us. The Republicans cussed the Government for years. You know, that used to be how they made their bread and butter. Before immigration and crime, there was how bad the Government was. But they never shrunk it because all their crowd wanted those jobs in Washington. Also they knew if they ever made it smaller they wouldn't have anybody to kick around anymore.

So we made it smaller, the Democrats. We reduced the size of the Federal Government, already more than 70,000 fewer people working in Washington bureaucracies than when I became President. And when our plan goes through, it will be the smallest Government since John Kennedy was President of the United States.

And here's the really important thing: What did we do with the money? We gave it to you to fight crime. It's going to California; it's going to New York; it's going to Texas; it's going to Montana. It's going back to the grassroots of America to hire those police officers, to have those prevention programs, to build those prison cells, to give the American people a chance to be safer on their streets. That's what we did with the money. I think it was a pretty good swap. I wish they'd helped us do it.

Now, when we lowered the Federal deficit 3 years in a row for the first time since Truman and exploded opportunities for trade and exports for California and a lot of other places and increased our investment in education and training and provided for increased incentives for people to put free enterprise into isolated urban and rural areas, 4.6 million new jobs—in 1994 we've had more high-wage jobs come into this American economy than in the previous 5 years combined. Is California slower than the rest of the country at coming back? Yes. Why? Well, you had the earthquake, and you had 21 percent of America's defense budget. So it's taking a little longer. But your unemployment is one percentage point lower than it was when I became President. And I'll say a little more about the things we've done to try to make sure that 1995 and 1996 are even better years for California. The point is not that we have done everything that needs to be done, but we are plainly moving in the right direction and the country is better off than it was 21 months ago.

Now, we did it in a different way, too. I don't think this was abnormal. I have more than twice as many women and more than twice as many minorities in my Cabinet as ever served any other President. I didn't think that was abnormal. At this point in our Presidency, we've appointed more than twice as many women, more than twice as many African-Americans, and 3 times as many Hispanics as well as more Asians to the court than all the three previous Presidents combined at this point in their Presidency. But since our judicial appointees have a higher percentage of them rated well-qualified by the Bar Association, I don't see what's so abnormal about that. Why shouldn't the bench look like America? Why shouldn't the administration look like America?

And let me ask you this. Is the fact that Russian missiles are not pointed at your children for the first time since the dawn of the nuclear age an abnormal thing? I think that's pretty good. I think it's a good thing for America that we reached agreement with China not to export missiles that are dangerous. I think it's a good thing that we're making progress there. I think it's a good thing that we are contributing to peace in the Middle East and we helped the South Africans with their elections and we're contributing to peace in Northern Ireland. I think it's a good thing. I think it's a good thing that we did not let Saddam Hussein again become an aggressor. And a good thing—I think it's a good thing that President Aristide went home to Haiti.

Do we still have problems in this country and in this world? You bet we do. But we are moving in the right direction. The last thing

in the wide world we need to do, because there are people who have not yet gotten a raise or people who still feel insecure in their jobs, because another one million Americans lost their health insurance last year and they're all in working families——

Audience member. What about 186?

The President. ——because of all these things, there are problems. So what's the answer? Turn around and go back where we came from? I don't think so. Give it to the people that haven't tried to solve the problems? I don't think so.

Audience member. Help us out on 186.

The President. You, look——

Audience member. Help us out on 186.

The President. Do you want to give this speech?

Audience member. No, but I——

The President. Do you know the first thing about manners?

Audience member. We need your help.

The President. Let me tell you something, I made a statement about it yesterday and if you will just be quiet, I'll talk some more. But I cannot talk if you're going to talk.

I tried to solve the health care problem in a way that I thought was right. If the people want to solve it in California, you can do it. [*Applause*] Thank you.

Now, what's all that got to do with this election? You think about it. What did they do? I want you to know what they did, because it's just like what the Governor is doing here. If you like the fact that we passed family leave and the Brady bill and the crime bill and the college loans, their leadership fought against every one of them, and now they're coming back to people and saying we ought to do something about crime and all the other problems in America.

They had their chance, and they were against them all. At the end of the legislative session, they blocked campaign finance reform, they blocked lobby reform, they killed the Superfund bill. You know, the Superfund bill cleans up toxic dumps. In the Superfund bill we had chemical companies, labor unions, and the Sierra Club wanting to pass it. I never saw those folks for the same thing in my life. I never thought they would be for anything. Do you know who was against the Superfund bill? Slightly more than 40 Republican Senators. That's it. And do you know why? Because they would rather have left the poison in the ground than let Dianne Feinstein come home to California and say, "I helped to clean it up." That's the truth. That is the truth.

And now they've got this contract. I want you to see if you can remember if you've ever heard this before. Here is their deal—you heard Senator Boxer's litany here—"Let that crowd run the Senate and make Mr. Gingrich Speaker, and here is what we'll do for you"— this is great, this sounds great—"here's what we'll do. We'll give everybody a tax cut, and if you're rich we'll give you a huge tax cut. And we will revitalize Star Wars, and we will increase defense spending, and we will balance the budget." Does that sound familiar? And what happened the last time we did that? We exploded the deficit. We face cuts in Medicare, veterans benefits, everything else. We ran the economy into the ditch and sent our jobs overseas, and it'll happen again. You have to say no, no, no, no, no. No!

Audience members. No! No! No!

The President. The cynicism of these people, it's unbelievable. It's unbelievable.

I've got to tell you about one more filibuster. They tried to filibuster the California desert bill. They almost got that done, and finally, there were some Republican Senators who cared enough about the environment and were so overcome with embarrassment at what the rest of them were doing that they bailed out and broke the filibuster. But it was weird. We had a guy from Wyoming leading a filibuster against the California desert bill so he could help that guy from Texas buy the California Senate seat. [*Laughter*] I mean, it was amazing. That's what was going on. That's what goes on up there. You've got to say no to that.

Now, what's that got to do with this race? Kathleen and I were talking about it the other day. Listen to this. Five million Americans who live in California benefit from the family leave bill; 1,650,000 Americans who live in California will be eligible for lower interest college loans. The crime bill will bring another $900 million to California for 10,200 police officers, among other things. Over 2 million California families got tax cuts. And they fought it all.

Now, if you look at what's happened in California since I became President—I didn't come out here and point the finger at Governor Wilson. I just sort of said, "These folks are in trouble, and I ought to help." The first thing we did was to take off all the controls on a lot

of high tech exports so we could sell more. And California benefited more than any other State from that.

And then we started a program that the previous administration had literally refused to start, to help places where bases had closed or where companies had lost defense contracts to do defense conversion. And California has gotten more than one-third of all the defense conversion money given out by the Federal Government in the last 2 years to help rebuild this economy for the 21st century.

When the earthquake came along, you wound up with $11 billion. And unlike the last earthquake in northern California, this time the Government paid for 90 percent of it from Washington, not 75 percent, because we knew that you needed the help. And we did it in record time.

They talk about immigration. What have we done? We are cutting spending overall, and yet we increased funding to help the States deal with immigration costs by a third. We doubled the border guards along San Diego's border. We have for the first time paid for some of the criminal justice costs. And we have paid to ship some people who have been convicted of crimes out of the country. And your Governor calls my effort pathetic? He made the problem happen when he was in the Senate. And when he came back here and he had his President in Washington, he never issued a peep for more money or a peep of blame or responsibility. Never.

And when I took office, I knew this was a problem. I didn't care if you had a Republican Governor. You could have had somebody in the "purple party" for all I cared. You had a problem. And I have tried to help you solve it. The Attorney General has been to southern California. We have also started dealing with the sewage problems down there. We have done a lot of other things. We never sought to place any blame on anybody else. We were just trying to help. That's what Governors should be doing, building people's lives, building the economy, building people's future. That's the kind of partner I would like to have in Sacramento so we could do even more things. Now, you think about that. You think about that.

What else has happened since our administration came in? Well, we're selling California rice to Japan for the first time in history. We got enough shipbuilding contracts to NASCO at San Diego to save 4,000 jobs, and the Livermore labs just got a $2 billion research contract to help to build a high tech future here. I never thought of trying to blame somebody else. I just knew you needed help and you had great resources and it was time to start moving forward. And that's the kind of Governor you need.

I want to say one thing about this immigration proposition. You know, I also came out against it yesterday. But I want to talk to you about this. I want to make two points about it. And I want—again, remember, you've got to spend the rest of this election talking to people outside this room. I want to make two points about it. Number one, I have really tried to help you with this problem, and we are making a difference. But why should we punish the kids because we're not smart enough to figure out how to stop their parents for coming here looking for work? And what does it do, really, for your treasury if kids are out of school so they'll be free to get in trouble? What does it do if kids don't go to the clinic so they'll be free to communicate diseases and other problems to other people? I don't know that you're going to save a split nickel on this deal.

Now, let's solve the problem. We already deny welfare benefits to immigrants who are not here legally. There is a problem in the work place; there is a problem in enforcement. Let us go after it in a responsible way. It is a legitimate problem. When people don't have jobs themselves, they don't want someone else having a job who didn't even wait in line like all the other immigrants do every year to come here in a legal fashion. There is a problem. But this problem was largely created by politicians in previous years who wanted this to happen. And a lot of them are now trying to benefit from the very situation they created, and that is wrong. That is wrong.

Now, let me say something else. If you've got a bunch of friends who are going to vote for that anyway, you ought to still talk them into voting for Kathleen Brown. And here is the argument you ought to use. Why in the wide world would you vote for Pete Wilson because he says he's for that if you are? Why would you waste two votes on that proposition when one will do just as well? [Laughter]

Now, listen to this. What is the argument against Governor Wilson? What is Kathleen Brown's argument? That she represents vision and energy and ideas and she has a plan for the future. Not that the last 4 years would not

have been challenging, no matter who had been Governor. There was defense cuts coming; there was a recession in the economy. What is the charge? Not that there were tough times but that the response was inadequate. It didn't reflect energy and compassion and leadership and planning.

Now, if this election turns on an issue that will be over on the morning of November 9th, you will be giving another 4 year contract, this time with an explicit permission to lift not one finger to solve the real problems of California or to help build its future. That would be a mistake. That would be a mistake.

So tell your friends, "Look, I'm not for this thing. I wish I could talk you out of it. But if I can't, don't shoot yourself in the foot and vote twice when once will do." [Laughter] If you make a mistake on this, you're going to need a Governor even more than I do. You need a good Governor. Go do it right. And every time you worry about it and you get frustrated, you think about the story I told you about the guy that swapped cigars for dynamite. It happens all the time.

Now, let me close by just saying this. Let me tell you what I really think will turn this election. I think it depends what frame of mind the people are in when they wake up on election day. This is an old-fashioned election, right? Hope versus fear, the future versus the past, plan versus a wedge. That's what this is about. And you cannot blame people for being exercised and frustrated and angry. Most people in California have not felt the benefits of the recovery, in spite of the fact that we have put billions in here, every last thing I could think of to do. A lot of people have not felt it in their lives. They still feel uncertain and insecure.

We have social problems in this country, the crime, the gangs, the drugs, the guns; this stuff has been building up for 30 years. Most hourly wage earners have had stagnant wages in America for 20 years. California has been through this trauma. These problems have been with us. And for 12 years we had this trickle-down economics approach and this divide-them-and-conquer social policy approach, which I have had 21 months to work on. Now we're making a good start, but we have a ways to go before people can feel it inside.

So you have got to leave this room and do two things. One is, if you can give her some more money so she doesn't get blown away on television, you ought to do it. The second thing is to go out and talk to people about what this election is really all about and get them to unload all their frustration and their anger and try to get them to relax. And get them into a conversation, get them into a dialog.

What I really think you ought to do is go out there and try to turn the lights on in California. If the lights are on, if people are up, if they're looking to the future, they will vote for Kathleen Brown because she's got a plan; she's got energy; she symbolizes the future. Turn the lights on! Turn the lights on! Turn the lights on!

Thank you, and God bless you all.

NOTE: The President spoke at 8:53 p.m. at the Fairmont Hotel.

Remarks at a Rally for Democratic Candidates in Seattle, Washington
October 23, 1994

The President. Thank you so much. Thank you.

Audience member. Give them hell!

The President. You're going to help, aren't you?

Thank you, Governor Lowry, for your friendship and your support and your leadership here. Thank you for all the things you said. Thank you, ladies and gentlemen, for making me feel so very welcome today.

I hope all the folks who have joined us here who will tell the rest of the world about what we did, took notice of Larry Brown from Boeing and Sergeant John Manning and Mikelle Mathers. You see, they represent the real Washington and the real America we ought to be concerned about in this country. They're the kind of people that my friend Norm Rice works for every day. They're the kind of people that the members of this congressional delegation support.

I want to say a special word of thanks to the ones who are here, to Norm Dicks, for his friendship to me and his leadership, especially on defense issues; to Jim McDermott, for his courageous and never-flagging struggle to get all Americans health care; to Mike Kreidler, who in his first term has worked so hard to combat violence and to cut the deficit while the Republicans just talked about it. I want to thank Maria Cantwell for a lot of things, but especially for working so hard, along with Senator Murray, to make sure Washington continues to be a center of innovation in software and computer technology, to work with government and industry partnerships to make sure that this is part of our 21st century economy and part of your 21st century future. Before he leaves the Congress, I want to thank Al Swift for being a good friend and a good supporter and ask you to replace him with Harriet Spanel.

And I want to say, every time I am around Ron Sims, I like him more and more and more. I was sitting there listening to his speech today, in the place where we were just before we came over here, thinking about, you know, this will be a real dose for the U.S. Senate, I mean, a real person. Instead of somebody that postures about being tough on crime and then votes against the crime bill, you've got a guy who goes out and puts his life on the line to try to fight crime and violence and give kids a better chance at life. Instead of pontificating about family and work, you've got a man who's worked all his life, raised a good family, and then spent a fair amount of his time trying to make sure everybody else could raise their family, too. So I hope you will bring him home in the next 2 weeks, and I want to say more about that. But I can tell you it will not only be good for you, it would do the rest of the United States Senate, especially the crowd on the other side, a world of good to have to deal with somebody who's actually lived about the things they spout off about all the time.

Folks, I think it would not be an overstatement to say that this is kind of an unusual election. [*Laughter*] And the psychology is sort of strange. And there is a huge gap between what is actually going on and what people have been told for 2 years is going on, a huge gap. Now, this is a very great country and a very good country. And given the information and the facts, the people will nearly always do the right thing.

But I want you to think about this: I went to Washington 21 months ago to restore the American dream, to get our country together, to take up problems too long ignored because my predecessors didn't want to deal with all the heat that would come down, to seize opportunities that we had too long walked away from.

My mission was pretty simple: I wanted to put Government on the side of ordinary Americans. I wanted to do it by supporting work and family with things like family leave and tax cuts for working people who work full time and have kids in the home that are just barely above poverty, and they ought never to be in poverty if you work full time and you got kids in your house. I wanted Government to be on the side of ordinary Americans by empowering people so they could assume responsibility for their own lives. That's what our bill to have school-to-work apprenticeships was about, so that young people that don't go to college can at least train for good jobs. That's what the middle class college loan program was all about, to give lower interest rates and longer repayment terms so that nobody—I mean, nobody—ever walks away from a college education because they're afraid they can't afford to go or will never be able to pay their debts back.

With 30 years of accumulated social problems, I wanted a serious attack on crime and violence. That's what the Brady bill and the crime bill and all of its facets was all about. That's what our welfare reform efforts, to liberate people so they can succeed as parents and workers and won't be on the dole for a lifetime—that's what that is all about.

I wanted to get this economy going again. That's what bringing down the deficit and investing more in new technologies and expanding trade for Washington State and all the other States in the country—that's what that was all about, to get the economy going again. And I wanted to change the way the Government works. I wanted us to do more with less. There are more than 70,000 fewer people working for the National Government than there were the day I took office. There will soon be a reduction in the life of this budget of about 270,000. Our Government will be the smallest it's been since John Kennedy, and every cent of the savings will go back to you at the grassroots to help you fight crime and build a more just society.

I wanted to make a world more peaceful and prosperous. That's what all these trade expansions are all about. That's what's selling all this high-tech material and products and the airplanes and the apples—that's what it's all about, letting people prosper in a global economy. I wanted you to be safer. And that's why I'm so proud of the fact that these little children are the first generation of Americans since the dawn of nuclear power that do not have Russian missiles pointing at them. I am proud of that, glad they will not have to worry about a North Korean nuclear power threatening their future, glad the Chinese have agreed not to sell their dangerous missiles.

I wanted a world in which we could have a more peaceful and prosperous and democratic future. I'm proud of what we did in helping the election in South Africa and the peace process in Northern Ireland and standing up to Saddam Hussein and bringing Father Aristide back to Haiti. I am proud of what we've been able to do to contribute to peace in the Middle East. And I hope you will pray for me and all those in the Middle East next week as we try to take the next big steps.

Now that I told you this, let me ask you this: If Jim McDermott and Norm Dicks and Maria Cantwell and Mike Kreidler were Republicans running for reelection, and they said, "Look, I gave you the smallest Federal Government since Kennedy, 3 years of deficit reduction for the first time since Truman, an explosive amount of economic growth, and finally some high-wage jobs coming back into our economy and the toughest crime bill in history," the Republican Party in Washington would be building a statue to each of them, not running against them. What is this? Isn't that right? Isn't that right? [Applause]

What is going on here that they say these people are the apostles of big Government and they're wildly liberal and they're for taxes? Eight times as many Washington citizens got a tax cut as a tax rate increase in our economic program. Don't you forget that.

How could people believe this? What is going on? Well, I'll tell you something, we live in a time when the negative is louder than the positive. The American people will nearly always, nearly always do the right thing if they know what it is. It used to be people didn't have enough information; now they have too much. And sometimes the people—and it's not all true, and it's hard to know what's relevant and what's irrelevant and what's important and what's not important. And people are just screaming at them all the time, trying to keep them in a turmoil, upset, agitated, disoriented. That's what our adversaries try to do. They figure if they can make people mad enough and disoriented enough, they'll just lash out at whoever's in and they will forget about what's happening.

I was telling some folks this morning that a few months ago in one of my rarer times when I had a little time to reflect, I sat down with a pencil and a piece of paper, and I made out a list of everything I'd ever done in my life to make a living, from the time I went to work in a grocery store when I was 13, to clearing land, to cutting grass, to building houses, to having a wholesale comic book operation. I've done a lot of interesting things. And the thing I was trying to think of, is there any job I ever had that's like the job I've got now? [*Laughter*] And was it Governor? Well, Governor was a little like it, but the job that's most like the one I've got now was one I didn't ever make any money at. It was when I was in civic clubs in high school, and we used to do car washes to raise money. Kids still do that, don't they? And I liked to be the guy that wiped off the windshield. That's kind of what we need to do now.

You think about it: If you're driving a car around and the windshield's all dirty, you'll think it's about to storm if the sun's shining bright. And if there are lots of things on the window, you'll think there's all kind of problems in the road, and it's just as clear as can be. And if it's really messed up, there may be a problem out there, and you won't see it, and you'll run smack dab into it. [*Laughter*] That's what I've got to do. We've got to wash America's windshield off in the next 2 weeks so they can see the light coming in.

I look at Ron Sims; I think of the life he has lived and the values that virtually pour out of him when he talks. And I think, I don't believe most people in Washington State want a Senator who voted against family leave, against college loans, against tax breaks for low-income working people, against deficit reduction, voted for the crime bill and then against it when it became a political deal. I don't think they want that.

Audience members. No-o-o!

The President. These people—you know, I don't think they want a Government that just screams and shouts and says no, no, no, no, a Government of fear, not hope; a Government of blame, not responsibility.

You know, look what happened in the Senate at the end of this session. In the 1800's we had a filibuster, that is, a talkathon, about once every 6 years. And people said, well, once every 6 years something will come along, and you don't want to rush it; you just ought to talk it to death to make sure you're doing the right thing. And then in the 1900's we got more verbose, and we've had about one a year. The partisan atmosphere has gotten so intense that in the last week, on the last weekend of this session of Congress, we had four filibusters on four different issues in one day. That is what they are doing.

You take—let me just give you one example, the Superfund bill that their delaying tactics killed. There was nobody in America against the Superfund bill, hardly. We had the chemical companies and the labor unions and the Sierra Club. Shoot, those folks never agreed on anything. You couldn't get them to agree on what time the Sun was coming up tomorrow morning. [*Laughter*] But they agreed on the Superfund bill. They wanted to clean up those toxic dumps. Nobody in America was against it except slightly more than 40 Republican Senators. And they knew that no way we could ever get it up. And why were they against it? Because they would have rather left the poison in the ground than let Maria Cantwell and Mike Kreidler and Norm Dicks and Jim McDermott come back here and say they helped to clean it up. That is the truth.

And so I say—and now they say, "Give us power and we'll—give us power, we'll give everybody a big old tax cut, especially if you're really rich. And we'll spend lots more on defense, and we'll spend lots more to revitalize Star Wars, and we'll balance the budget." [*Laughter*] Does that sound familiar?

Now, that costs a trillion dollars. You say, "Well, how are you going to pay for this?" They say, "We'll tell you after the election." [*Laughter*] You know how it'll be paid for? You know what it would take? It would take a 30 percent across-the-board cut in every program in America. What will happen is just what happened before. It will explode the deficit. It will lead to unwise cuts—and we have cut Government;

they haven't—and it will lead to shipping our jobs overseas instead of bringing them back home to Washington State.

We have to say, "We tried that once. Thank you very much. We don't want to go back to the trickle-down economics and the divisive social policies that you gave us before. We don't want to go back. We don't want to go back."

I want you to think about this. I want you to think about this in the 2 weeks and a few days that remain. We've still got a lot of challenges in this country. We've got economic challenges. We've got social challenges. We've got important political reform and environmental and health care and welfare challenges to face. But this country's in better shape than it was 21 months ago. We have a Government that's done some important things for ordinary Americans. We've taken a serious stand against crime. There are more jobs. There is a lower deficit. It is a more peaceful world. We are in better shape.

What we need to do now is to say to the American people and to say to the people in Washington, "Look, it's up to you now. You've got to keep going into the future. You don't want to turn back now. You've got to choose hope over fear. You've got to empower people, not let somebody grab power with a bunch of cheap promises from yesterday. You have got to look at the future as it is and look at the facts as they are."

We've got to have everybody here thinking about what I did as a little boy. If you'll go out and you'll wipe off the windshields, if you will turn the lights on in Washington State, you will have Ron Sims for a United States Senator, and you will have these Congressmen back, and we'll have America going forward into the future.

Thank you, and God bless you all. Thank you. You can do it. You can do it.

One more thing. Don't you dare walk out of here and just think about the cheering. Spend your time for the next 2 weeks talking to people who weren't here. Go have a cup of coffee with your neighbor. And if they're mad and upset and fuming, ask them to relax, take a deep breath, look at the pretty fall coming on, and talk about your country. The people of this country will do the right thing if they know the facts. And each of you should make a personal commitment to doing that, not only for them but for these kids here. You can do it. Turn the lights on. You can do it.

NOTE: The President spoke at 2:36 p.m. in the Flag Pavilion Room at the Seattle Center. In his remarks, he referred to Larry Brown, Boeing machinist; John Manning, Seattle police officer; Mikelle Mathers, AmeriCorps volunteer; Mayor Norman B. Rice of Seattle; and Harriet Spanel and Ron Sims, congressional candidates.

Remarks on the Office of Management and Budget Memorandum in Seattle
October 23, 1994

I'd like to make a very brief statement about the Alice Rivlin memo on the options for deficit reduction.

First of all, my position is what it was in the campaign of '92 and what it has been through the first 2 budget years. I do not support cuts in Social Security, and I believe any savings we achieve in the Medicare program should be used in health care. That has always been my position.

The memo was a list of options that grew out of a consideration of what might be the recommendations of the Kerrey commission,

what might come out of the budgeting process next year, and the kinds of problems that might be created if the Republican contract that the Republican House leader and the Senate leader and others have embraced. We have serious problems with the deficit still, in the future because of the escalating costs of health care. And if they were to have a huge tax cut for the wealthy, increase defense, increase Star Wars, we would be looking at an explosion in the deficit that could only be dealt with with massive cuts in other programs, all other programs.

But there is nothing in that memo and nothing in the record which should indicate that I have changed my position on these two fundamental issues.

Thank you.

NOTE: The President spoke at 3:13 p.m. at the Seattle Center.

Remarks on the Office of Management and Budget Memorandum in Seattle
October 23, 1994

I've been—when I gave my statement over there, one of you asked me a question—and I left—about Mr. Gingrich's charge that it was hypocritical for someone to have a memo which speculated about the recommendations that the Kerrey commission and others might have.

Now, I've told you what my position is. And my position is, I haven't and don't support cuts in Social Security, and I would support savings in the Medicare program only if they're used to advance the cause of health care.

Now, Mr. Gingrich has leveled a charge which is not right. It doesn't have anything to do with how the list came about. But he can solve this whole problem if he would say what I said. So just ask him if he and Senator Dole will say what I said. Will they say they support—they don't support cuts in Social Security, and they won't support using Medicare savings for anything other than helping health care?

If they have the same position, they can make this issue go away. Then they have to answer, what about their trillion dollar contract, because they will explode the deficit by a trillion dollars and start sending jobs overseas again.

The answer to this is for him to say what I have said to you today. So ask him if he'll take the same position. And then the only question is whether he's going to abandon his contract for all these tax cuts and spending increases.

Thank you.

NOTE: The President spoke at approximately 3:45 p.m. at the King County Airport. In his remarks, he referred to House Republican whip Newt Gingrich. A tape was not available for verification of the content of these remarks.

Statement on Signing the Bankruptcy Reform Act of 1994
October 22, 1994

The "Bankruptcy Reform Act of 1994," H.R. 5116, stands out as a significant achievement of the 103rd Congress, and I am pleased today to sign this measure into law. Breaking through years of gridlock that prevented the enactment of meaningful bankruptcy reform legislation, the chief sponsors of this measure worked tirelessly on a bipartisan basis with the Justice Department and other agencies of this Administration to pass this bill. Senator Howell Heflin, Chairman of the Senate Judiciary Subcommittee on Courts and Administrative Practice, Senator Charles Grassley, Ranking Member of that Subcommittee, House Judiciary Committee Chair-

man Jack Brooks, Congressman Hamilton Fish, Jr., Ranking Member of that Committee, Congressman Mike Synar, and their respective staffs are to be commended for their efforts.

This is the most broad-based bankruptcy reform measure to be signed into law in 16 years. Bankruptcy plays a pivotal role in the dynamic American economy and is a critical element of our civil justice system. The Act will update the bankruptcy system so that it may better serve the needs of debtors and creditors, from individuals and small business owners to large corporations and financial institutions. The role of government agencies in bankruptcy proceedings will also be clarified, assuring enhanced collection of debts owed to the public treasury.

Of particular significance are the provisions of this Act directed at accelerating the reorganization process for small businesses. The current version of chapter 11, which embodies a single set of procedures for all types of reorganizations, has proven to be particularly burdensome and time consuming to both small business debtors and creditors, resulting in unnecessary costs and delays. The Act will create a simplified "fast-track" system for businesses with debts totaling less than $2 million, meaning far quicker and less costly disposition of approximately 70 percent of the business reorganizations handled by the bankruptcy system. This is precisely the kind of reform that will restore public faith in the ability of our courts to perform in a timely and cost-effective manner.

This Act also expands the use of "consumer reorganizations," allowing individuals with debts up to $1 million to file for bankruptcy under chapter 13. This provision provides an alternative to the harsher process of liquidation while maintaining safeguards against fraud and abuse.

I am also pleased to note the enactment of new bankruptcy fraud measures. Creation of a criminal bankruptcy fraud offense will enhance the integrity of the bankruptcy process and give prosecutors new tools to use against those who would abuse the system.

Finally, and perhaps of the greatest, long-range importance, is the creation of a National Bankruptcy Review Commission to study and report on the issues and problems relating to bankruptcy. Beyond the numerous specific deficiencies in the Bankruptcy Code, it is also time to look at critical policy issues concerning the bankruptcy system. These issues include the relationship of the bankruptcy system to the health of the economy in general and of individual communities, the interaction between bankruptcy law and other legal disciplines, and encouraging the use of alternatives to litigation. I look forward to the expeditious appointment of members of the Commission, drawn from diverse backgrounds of legal, academic, business, and practical experience.

WILLIAM J. CLINTON

The White House,
October 22, 1994.

NOTE: H.R. 5116, approved October 22, was assigned Public Law No. 103–394. This statement was released by the Office of the Press on October 24.

Interview With Chuck Meyer of WWWE Radio in Cleveland, Ohio
October 24, 1994

Mr. Meyer. President Clinton, good morning, and welcome to Cleveland. President Clinton, can you hear me?

The President. I can. Can you hear me?

Mr. Meyer. Yes. This is Chuck Meyer, and welcome to Cleveland. Good morning to you, sir.

The President. Thank you, Chuck, it's nice to hear your voice.

OMB Memorandum

Mr. Meyer. Now, let's clear up a matter here of this budget memo. This story broke yesterday in the Washington Post, and your reaction to it came on the West Coast yesterday. And some people in Cleveland may not be caught up on it, but apparently there was a budget memo that was leaked to the Washington Post indicating that one of your administration's options in the future might be a reduction in Social Security benefit COLA's and a raising of some taxes. What's the straight story on that?

The President. The straight story is that that was not an options memo for us, it was a memo which simply cataloged all the things that we might be confronted with over the next couple of years by this commission on entitlements that's meeting, this bipartisan commission, as well as if the Republicans make substantial gains in the Congress and try to implement their Contract With America. You know, they've made a trillion dollars' worth of commitments to the American people: big tax cuts for the wealthy, and they've promised to balance the budget while cutting taxes to the wealthy and increasing defense and increasing Star Wars again. They won't say how it's going be paid for. Our calculations indicate that it would require a 30 percent cost cut in everything else. So you're going to have exploding deficits, Medicare cuts, and other things if this contract goes in. This memo was simply designed to show us the kind of problems we were going to confront over the next few years if those sort of things came up.

The truth is, we're doing a good job right now in bringing the deficit down. Today I'm going to speak at the Cleveland City Club and talk about the deficit reduction. We brought it down from $290 billion-plus to $203 billion this year in 2 years. That's $100 billion less than it was projected to be when I took office. And we've done it by cutting the size of Government, by eliminating Government programs, by cutting others, while still being able to increase our investment in education and training and new technology. And that's what I want to keep doing, managing this thing in a very disciplined way to give us a smaller Government that does more. And if we do that, we can maintain our commitments to our senior citizens and do what we have to do to grow this economy. The main thing we can't do is to throw our economy in a tailspin by going back to trickle-down economics.

Administration Accomplishments

Mr. Meyer. Mr. President, I'm looking at a political cartoon that appeared in the Cincinnati Enquirer the other day, and it's a couple sitting on their front porch and she says, "I know I'm mad at Clinton. I just can't remember why." And the whole question comes up here, while Ronald Reagan was the "Teflon President" and nothing stuck to him, everything is sticking to you. And you're getting blamed for just about everything going on in the country today, including the heartbreak of psoriasis. Why is that?

The President. Well, I don't know. I think part of it is the skill of the Republican congressional leadership and the far right in this country in just continuing to keep the American people in a turmoil and obscuring the facts. I mean, what I've got to do is to spend more time communicating with the American people about what we've done and where we're going.

Take Ohio, for example. The unemployment rate has dropped 1½ percentage points since I've been President. Business failures have

dropped by 24 percent; jobs are up. The economic plan that the Congress passed has given us 2 years of deficit reduction already for the first time in more than 20 years, and next year it'll go down again; it'll be the first time since Truman was President. Eleven times as many Ohio families got a tax cut as a tax rate increase under our economic plan, 509,000 families. The Family and Medical Leave Act that we passed gives 2 million families in this State opportunities for the working people to take a little time off when their babies are born or their parents are sick. That bill was something we supported that the Republican leadership opposed. The same is true of college loans for middle class kids, immunizing all the kids in this country under 2, things that will strengthen work and families.

So I believe if the people of Ohio and the people of this country knew what we've done to empower working people, to increase our investments in education, to shrink the size of the Federal Government, shrink the deficit, and grow the economy, they'd be pretty well pleased with this administration.

But if you look at the environment in which we've operated, which has been highly contentious, highly negative, and almost no opportunity to get through the positive achievements, it's not surprising. People can only act on what they know.

Crime

Mr. Meyer. But, Mr. President, don't you play into those hands sometimes yourself? For instance, the crime rate's been going down now for several years, and yet crime seems to be the number one issue in this campaign, if there is such a thing as a top issue. We have a lot of politicians running around the country ready to throw everybody in jail, and yet the crime rate's going down. Doesn't that—isn't that a non-issue?

The President. No, it's not a non-issue for a couple of reasons. The crime rate is going down in some categories in some places because we know that local police and community groups have figured out how to lower the crime rate with community policing and having neighbors work with law enforcement. We know that. But we also know that the crime rate is going up in two ways that are very troubling. First of all, it's going up among teenagers and people under 18. And secondly, the amount of random violence is going up among children under 18. And that's very disturbing to people, and it makes for a more insecure society.

Now, what happens about whether people know the crime rate is going up or down is a function of what they see on their local and national news. But there is still way too much crime and violence in this country. How can you say we made our own problem? I gave the Congress a comprehensive crime bill, which the first time around both Republicans and Democrats voted for it, and the second time around all the Republicans bailed out and tried to make it a political issue—or most of the Republicans bailed out. Some of them stayed on and showed good citizenship.

But that crime bill will increase police presence by 20 percent in the communities of this country. It offers strategies to help prevent crime, and it has much tougher punishment for seriously violent offenders. So I think it's a very good crime bill. It makes a real start in the right direction.

So if you look at what we've done here in the last 2 years, we've strengthened the economy, we've made a serious assault on crime, and we've done a lot of things for ordinary working people like the family leave bill, the middle class college loans, and things of that kind. But I think most people in Ohio support the Brady bill, support the crime bill, support the things we've done and regret the fact that it became a political football in Washington.

Health Care Reform

Mr. Meyer. Mr. President, we've had some calls this morning asking about health care. I know it was a big disappointment that it did not pass, and I read where the White House is gearing up for a more aggressive health care plan to pass next year. And yet, the other day I read where that 30-some-odd million people in this country who don't have health care has grown to nearly 40 million people now.

The President. That's right.

Mr. Meyer. I think these people want to know why health care didn't pass and why the debate got so bogged down when this was clearly a top issue that Americans wanted and were willing to pay for 2 years ago.

The President. Well, it got bogged down because the people who are making a huge amount of money out of the system that we have spent a lot of money to terrify the people

who do have health care today into thinking that if our bill passed it would make it worse and it would lead to more Government intervention in the health care system.

That was not the truth. And what we've got to do is to come back and find a way to demonstrate to the American people what we want to do is to protect the plans that they have now that they like, but to make sure we cover the people who don't have health insurance and we control the costs better.

But here's the fundamental problem. Every other country in the world with an advanced economy, every other wealthy country, spends between 9 and 10 percent of its income on health care to cover everybody. We spend 14 percent of our income, or another $240 billion, and we have almost 40 million people without insurance. Another million Americans in working families lost their health insurance last year.

Well, the people that are making that extra $240 billion by and large don't want us to change. And they spent somewhere between $200 million and $300 million lobbying against our health care plan. Then again, the Republican congressional leadership operated on the theory that they could not permit any kind of health care to pass because it would be politically beneficial to the Democrats and to the administration. I wanted them to have half the credit. I wanted this to be bipartisan. And we've just got to keep dealing with this.

The health care problem is the main cause of the big Government deficit. It is a main source of insecurity for working people who have jobs. And we're going in reverse. We're the only major country where we're actually losing ground in providing coverage to people. So I'm going to come back and try to find a way that the American people will support and will not be frightened by, to cover the people who don't have coverage, to protect the coverage of the people who do have coverage, and to slow the rate of cost increases.

Midterm Elections

Mr. Meyer. Mr. President, I'd like to ask you another political question. My 17-year-old daughter, Andrea, told me to pass along the message to you that she intends to vote for you in 1996 when she is allowed to vote in a Presidential election for the first time. And that's the good news.

The bad news is, why isn't Tom Foley as excited about you as my daughter?

The President. Well, what are—Tom Foley has done a pretty good job.

Mr. Meyer. Well, he wasn't by your side in Seattle yesterday.

The President. Well, he shouldn't have been. You know why he wasn't? He had a debate last night, and he was preparing for it, and he was doing exactly what he should've done. He was over in the part of the State where his district was, doing exactly what he should have done. The Seattle Congressmen were all there. And I think he—I would have been disappointed if he had come all the way over there and then turned around and gone back and taken away 3 or 4 hours from his debate preparation time. He's in a tough fight. He's been in tough fights consistently in his district for the last 15 or 20 years, and he's over there paying attention to the people of his district, which is what he ought to be doing.

Mr. Meyer. Okay. Well, there is some logic to that explanation. But there are Democrats around the country this year who don't want you to come and campaign for them. And you're reduced to helping get votes for Mario Cuomo and Ted Kennedy, and these guys should be winning easy reelection, shouldn't they?

The President. I don't know why you would say that. It's very hard for any Governor to get elected to four terms, very, very difficult. And Governor Cuomo had a pretty close race 4 years ago. I think he is going to win, but it's a very combative environment in New York. And I was asked to come in there because it was a difficult case and because I think he's an important leader for our country and I hope he can be reelected.

Senator Kennedy has been in office 30 years, and there's a big anti-incumbent feeling out in the country this year. I think he will be reelected because he's been willing to change, embrace new ideas, and take a different approach in the last few years. I think he's really become an instrument of a lot of the new ideas the American people would like to see adopted by the Congress, and I think that's why they'll reelect him.

But I don't think you should assume that because somebody is well known they'll have an easy reelection. Sometimes that makes for a tough reelection, particularly given the harsh feelings people have about the Congress.

Middle East Peace Process

Mr. Meyer. I know that you have to go in a moment, but I wanted to ask you a quick question about Syria. You're making the trip to the Middle East this week, and you're visiting Syria, a country that we still consider a renegade nation, a country that has not done enough, say some, to control radical elements in the region. What do you hope to accomplish there this week?

The President. I don't expect a dramatic breakthrough, and I want to caution the American people about that going in. I mean, the primary purpose of going to the Middle East is to stand shoulder-to-shoulder with Israel and Jordan, particularly given the difficult events of the last couple of weeks and the violence that they've undergone. I was asked to come there and witness the signing because the United States played a major role in this peace agreement.

But I'm going to Syria because achieving a full peace in the Middle East requires a peace between Israel and Syria, which will make possible a peace between Israel and Lebanon. And that would be a huge plus for the United States and all the world to have a comprehensive peace there. I'm going because progress has been made. Terrorism is still an issue with Syria, and it will continue to be. But it seems clear to me that the best way to end terrorism in the Middle East is to have a comprehensive peace settlement there. And I do believe we're making progress. And I think if I go to Syria we will make further progress. Since I am in the region, I think that I ought to keep working and not just celebrate what we've done already, but to keep making progress toward the future.

Mr. Meyer. Mr. President, thank you very much for your time, and enjoy your trip to northern Ohio today.

The President. I'm looking forward to it. Thank you.

Mr. Meyer. I'm sure that was the chilliest jog you've had in a while, but I hope it was okay this morning.

The President. To tell you the truth, I got in late so I slept in. I was a derelict this morning, I didn't go jog. [*Laughter*]

Mr. Meyer. Well, shame on you, but we'll give you this one.

The President. Thanks.

Mr. Meyer. Thanks again for your time.

The President. Goodbye.

NOTE: The interview began at 8:35 a.m. The President spoke by telephone from the Sheraton City Centre.

Remarks and a Question-and-Answer Session at the Cleveland City Club
October 24, 1994

The President. Thank you. It's kind of nice to be out of Washington. And it's very nice to be back here for my third appearance. On the way in I told Steve, I said, "Shoot, if I show up again, you're going to have to start charging me dues." He said, "You've forgotten Senator Metzenbaum's already paid your dues." [*Laughter*] So I thank you, Senator, for paying my dues.

I'm glad to be joined here by so many guests and especially by some of your distinguished political leaders. I want to thank Howard Metzenbaum, as he leaves the Senate, for the things he's done for Ohio and for the United States over the years.

This is not what I came to talk about, but I want to mention in particular a bill that he got into the very last set of bills that passed in the filibuster-wild Senate at the end of the session. It's a bill that has achieved, finally, some long overdue national notice, to make it easier for parents to adopt children and to make it easier to get these kids out of long-term interminable delays in foster homes and into solid adoptive homes. And it's a great contribution to what I think ought to be the pro-family position of the United States of America. I thank you for that, sir. It was great.

I'm glad to be here with Senator Glenn and Congressman Fingerhut, Congressman Stokes, Congressman Sawyer, Congressman Hoke. Former Congressman Mary Rose Oakar is here and as an Arab-American is going to the Middle East with the American delegation. I'm glad to see you here. Mayor White, I thank you for meeting me at the airport last night at midnight. I thought, now, there is a guy who is leaving no stone unturned. I thought Cleveland already had all the Federal money the law allowed, and there was Mike at the airport at midnight. [*Laughter*]

Your ex-treasurer, our new Treasurer, Mary Ellen Withrow is here. [*Applause*] Thank you.

The only person happier than I was when Mary Ellen Withrow was appointed was Lloyd Bentsen, the Secretary of the Treasury, because you can't print a new dollar bill until you've got a Treasurer, and he didn't have his name on any dollar bills. So after Mary Ellen was confirmed, Lloyd Bentsen sent me the first dollar bill with his name on it and with her name on it, which is framed in the White House.

I'm glad to see my friend Joel Hyatt here, and so many other friends of mine here in Ohio. I thank you for coming.

Eighteen months ago I had the privilege of speaking here at your club and outlining our economic programs to get the economy moving again. That was on May 10th of 1993. Ninety days after I spoke to this distinguished gathering, Congress passed that economic program by a landslide, you may remember, one vote in both Houses. [*Laughter*] As the Vice President always says, he's the most successful member of my administration; whenever he votes, we win. [*Laughter*]

Today I wanted to come back here to discuss with you the progress that's been made and what we still have to do and the decisions that lie before you as citizens of this great country. We have made an important beginning with a comprehensive economic strategy designed to empower American workers to compete and win in the 21st century. That is, after all, our mission.

The key elements of the strategy are simple and direct and important: First, reduce the deficit; second, expand trade and intensify the efforts of the United States Government to be a partner with American business in doing business beyond our borders; third, increase our investment in education and training, in technology and defense conversion; fourth, bring the benefits of free enterprise to areas which have been isolated from it, in our inner cities and rural areas, with new strategies, including but not limited to welfare reform; fifth, reinvent the Federal Government, make it smaller, more effective, less regulatory, more efficient.

These strategies have all been implemented. And I want to go through them point by point, but I want to say what is clearly obvious. The implementation of these strategies required a reversal of the policies of the past 12 years. It required much more aggressive, innovative partnership with the private sector. We recognized that Government's role cannot be either to save the economy, because we don't have the capacity to do that in the global economy, or to sit on the sidelines but instead to do everything we can to create the right climate, the right conditions and to empower people so that they can compete and win by taking responsibility for themselves and their families. The increasing changes in the world make this imperative.

The course of the last 21 months is very different from the previous course, as I have said, and one of the great questions in this election season is whether we will press on this course or return to the course we abandoned just 21 months ago, a course with easy promises and superficial attraction but which is a proven failure. We cannot afford to bankrupt the country when we need to invest and grow the economy.

Let's look at the record. Business leaders here and all around the country understand that a nation, like any successful enterprise, needs a clear mission, a strategy to achieve the mission, the determination and the patience to implement the strategy, and a willingness to look at the bottom line, to measure success and failure and to make adjustments as indicated by results. The mission is clear, to empower the American people to compete and win. The strategy is sound; I just outlined it. We clearly have pursued it with determination, and the bottom line is getting stronger every day.

Let's look at the elements of the strategy, starting with the national deficit. You all know that the deficit exploded in the 1980's and that the aggregate debt of the United States quadrupled in only 12 years from what had been accumulated in the previous 190-plus years.

Last year we began to change that. We passed huge reductions in Federal spending, cuts in over 300 Federal programs, outright eliminations in scores of programs, a 5-year freeze on domestic discretionary spending, restrictions on entitlements. In the budget I just signed we not only reduced defense spending, we reduced discretionary domestic spending for the first time in 25 years.

The Congress enacted the reinventing Government program in which the Vice President has taken such a lead and in which we committed to reduce the size of the Federal Government by 272,000 over a 6-year period, bringing the Government to its smallest size since President Kennedy served in this office. Already there are more than 70,000 fewer people working for the Federal Government than there were on the day I became President. One hundred percent of this money is going to help you and people like you all over America fight crime at the grassroots level. That is how the crime bill is paid for. That is how we are going to increase the police forces of this country by 20 percent, build another 100,000 jail cells for serious offenders to enforce the tougher penalties in the bill, and pay for the preventive strategies that the law enforcement officers and the community leaders and the mayors say will work, not by increasing the deficit, not by raising taxes but by shrinking the Government.

One other part of this strategy that I think is terribly important, especially in Ohio, to mention is the procurement reforms. The United States spends about $200 billion a year buying goods and services under rules and regulations that would give anybody a headache. It was the rules and regulations, not outright venality, which caused the famous stories you've all heard of the $500 hammer and the $50 ashtray, rules and regulations which literally added $50 to every Government purchase that cost $2,500 or less—$50. If it was a $50 purchase, it cost $100. If it was a $1,000 purchase, it cost $1,050. After years of haggling about it, we have finally passed procurement reform which will save hundreds of millions of dollars a year and put an end to the policies which brought us the $500 hammers, thanks largely to the leadership of Senator John Glenn, and I thank him for that.

Well, all this has led to deficit reduction. When I spoke here last year the Federal deficit for 1994, the fiscal year that ended on the last day of September, was estimated to be $305 billion. Today the Treasury has announced its preliminary estimate, $203 billion, $102 billion less than was projected before the plan was passed. The decline in the deficit since 1992 is the largest 2-year decline in our history and the first time in 20 years the deficit has gone down for 2 years in a row.

Let me go over here and try to illustrate what this means, and I hope this microphone works. It does. That's the technology wizards in our administration having their way.

So you can get a feel for this, the deficit, which was very small in 1979, began going up dramatically. It was at about $60 billion, or $65 billion in 1980, and then it began really rising. It had gone to $220 billion by 1990; you see where it was in 1992. Our budget took quite a bit off of it last year. And what these figures mean is that now we are drawing the line on the deficit down to $200 billion, a dramatic change.

So you can get an idea of the difference, if we hadn't passed that deficit reduction plan last year, the deficit would have been off the charts, up here at $305 billion. And because we did, next year it will be off the charts down here at about $170 billion. And when that happens, it will be the first time that the deficit's gone down 3 years in a row since Harry Truman was the President of the United States. The Congress deserves credit for doing this and helping to lift a burden of debt from our children and helping to free up funds that would otherwise have been consumed in financing Government debt to finance homes and businesses all across the United States.

The second thing I want to emphasize is that the remarkable thing about this budget is that while reducing the deficit and reducing spending, we have actually been able to increase our investments in education and training and technology. We increased Head Start. We increased funds to help all States develop apprenticeship training programs for young people who don't go to college but do want to get good jobs. With the new individual education accounts that I announced on Friday, we are reorganizing the college loan program to provide lower interest loans, lower fees on the loans, longer repayment options for young people who get jobs when they get out of college with modest wages and should not have to pay more than a certain percentage of their income. Over the next few years, this will make 20 million Americans, including almost a million in Ohio, eligible for lower interest, longer term repayment on their college loans. At a time when what you earn depends upon what you can learn, these invest-

ments are very, very important for the economic future of the entire United States.

In addition to that, we have increased our investments in defense conversion, including in several sites here in Ohio. This is especially important because defense has come down rather dramatically since 1987, and we had built a huge high-wage, high-tech infrastructure around the defense industries that can make a major contribution to our moving into the 21st century if we have the kind of partnerships to help them make the transition.

The third thing we did was to expand trade and to intensify America's efforts to promote the sales of American products. We passed NAFTA. We negotiated a new trade deal with Japan which has opened markets for everything from cellular telephones to American rice and apples for the first time. We have negotiated the GATT agreement. And I believe Congress will pass it after the election when they come back in a special session to do that. That will add $100 to $200 billion a year to the gross national product of the United States.

We've also changed the time when the American Government thought that it should be totally passive in helping American companies pierce foreign markets when other governments were doing everything they could to help their companies do the same. We've worked hard from Saudi Arabia to South Africa to China to open up contracts for American businesses that they can win on the merits.

The fourth thing I mentioned I want to take a minute of time to talk about because it relates to the kind of things that Mayor White has tried to do here in Cleveland. We know that even as the economy grows, there are pockets of our country that have not been affected by the economic recovery, where investment has not come, where jobs have not come, where people are still despondent, places where free enterprise has not reached. This is true, by the way, in every advanced country, but it's more true in the United States, in our inner cities and in some of our isolated rural areas. What are we to do about it?

The first thing we have to try to do is to change the job mix, keep getting more good jobs here, which we're doing. The second thing we want to do is to try to provide special incentives for people to invest in isolated areas, the empowerment zones, the enterprise community concept, all of which offer incentives for people to put their money into areas that are otherwise not so attractive. You know, for years we've had special incentives for our business people to invest in the Caribbean. I don't quarrel with that, but we ought to have the same sort of advantages for people who invest in places in the United States that have no jobs and no hope and no future.

I signed a bill not very long ago that will set up a network across the country of community development banks, modeled on successful experiments in Chicago and even in rural areas in our country and in other parts of the world, to make small loans to lower income people at a profit to generate capital in areas that otherwise don't have it. There are markets all across this country in areas where people live but there aren't very many jobs. And we need to bring capital investment to development banks there.

The last thing I'd like to say is, we've tried to make Government a better partner with deregulation of banking and trucking and exports of high-tech products and by just having our Government work better. The Small Business Administration when I took office was, for most small business people, kind of a bureaucratic pain. We have reorganized it now so that the loan applications are one page long and you're supposed to get an answer, yes or no, if you put the documents in, within 72 hours. That's the kind of service the American people ought to get if we're going to have an agency of that kind.

Now, this strategy of ours has a lot of critics. When the deficit reduction plan passed, there were speech after speech after speech saying, "Gosh, if we do this the economy will collapse; the deficit will explode; middle class taxpayers will be bankrupted. This will be the end of the world." I heard it all. Then when NAFTA passed, we had a different set of critics who said there would be a giant sucking sound—I think that was his phrase—[*laughter*]—do you all remember that?—to destroy our industry. Well, the economic program passed, and jobs went up, and the deficit went down. Middle class families did not have their tax rates hiked. The wealthiest Americans and corporations with incomes of over $10 million did, but all the money went to deficit reduction. And we built a new partnership with business by things like deregulation of banking and deregulation of intrastates trucking, which saves billions of dollars a year which then can be freed up to invest in this economy.

Since NAFTA passed, exports to Mexico are up 21 percent. The Big Three automakers report their exports are up 500 percent to Mexico. NAFTA isn't a year old, and I just got back from Detroit where the biggest problem in Detroit is now complaints by autoworkers working overtime. That is a high-class problem.

So that's the strategy; that's what we've done. What are the results? We are in the midst of the first investment-led, low-inflation, productivity-driven economic expansion in over three decades. New businesses are up. Exports are up. Jobs are growing. The deficit is falling. In the last 21 months there have been 4.6 million new jobs in the American economy, 90 percent of them in the private sector. In 1994 something perhaps more fundamental and important has finally begun to happen. More than half the new jobs created by our economy in this year are above average wage, more high-wage jobs in this year than in the previous 5 years combined. And that is good news for the American working people.

Investment in new equipment is 8 times what it was in the last 4 years. And the Federal Government's purchases are down almost 8 percent. This is not a Government-inspired, deficit-driven recovery. This is more enterprise and less Government, better for the long run.

For the first time since 1979 America leads the world in the sales of automobiles. For the first time in a decade we've had 9 months of manufacturing job growth in a row. For the first time in 9 years the annual vote of international economists said America, not Japan, was the most productive economy in the entire world.

Now, you might say, if all that's so, why aren't we happier? [*Laughter*] Well, partly because the atmosphere in which we operate today is particularly contentious and, I believe, entirely too partisan. Partly because the way we get our information guarantees that we'll know more about our failures than our successes, guarantees that we'll know more about our conflicts than when we cooperate. Partly because we're dealing with long-term problems that haven't really affected a lot of real people's lives yet.

If you look at the problems of crime, violence, family breakdown, drugs, gangs, and guns, they are a complex of social problems that have been developing over 30 years. You can't just wipe away their reality in a few months. If you look at the economic anxieties of people—average hourly wages in this country actually peaked about 20 years ago, and working people have been losing their health insurance steadily for about 10 years, the only advanced country in the world where this is the case. Another million Americans in working families lost their health insurance last year. So there are real reasons that a lot of hard-working Americans don't feel more secure or more happy with good statistics and growth rates. They're still not sure that guarantees them a good future and a good job, the ability to keep their kids' health insurance or put aside money for their college education. They're still not sure that we're going to be able to solve a lot of the problems that violate our values and our conscience in our society. They're still not sure that they're going to be able to achieve the American dream or that their children will be able to.

I want to say to you, the only way to do that is to keep facing our problems and facing our challenges and moving into the future with a strategy we know has the best chance to work and to resist easy promises, quick fixes, and things that have already caused us trouble in the past. The realities of the modern world are that the economy is so globalized and change is so institutionalized that no government of any nation can promise to protect people from the changes of the world economy. You can't make the world go away, to use the phrase from the old song. You cannot do that.

So if change is inevitable and if we will never have a single economy anymore—we'll have a local economy in Cleveland and a State economy in Ohio and a regional economy in the Middle West and a national economy in America and a global economy in the whole world—if that is the reality, then what do we have to do? We have to facilitate people making the changes that will make change our friend and not our enemy, that will make change a source of security for us, not a source of insecurity. And we have to do it in a way that promotes those institutions of society that are most important to us, principally our families and our communities.

Companies are making changes like this all the time. And the changing nature of work is placing enormous demands on working people. The average worker today in every kind of work has to be able to work with more information,

to be more creative, to solve more problems on his or her own initiative. We have to see more responsibility being devolved down to workers at the grassroots level. And they have to learn more skills and information than ever before because the average worker will change jobs six or seven times in a lifetime, even if he or she stays with the same firm. This is the law of change with which we all will live and which we will either use to help make us more prosperous or walk away from and pay the penalty.

Since every American has to face these forces, and every American family does, the job of the Government ought to be to try to empower people to make the most of them.

A family can't treat these problems just like a business can. You know, if a family's under economic stress, you can't divest yourself, although some people with teenagers would like to from time to time. [Laughter] You can't really downsize. You can't restructure. I mean, you're sort of stuck with who shows up at the dinner table at night. [Laughter]

So when the family is under economic stress, what are their options? You either have to learn and to become more productive or get a better job or you face increased competition by hunkering down, working harder for less, and just trying to be as tough as the times are.

Now, that is what has happened to millions and millions of American families for the last 20 years, that latter alternative, working harder for less. The average working family is spending more hours at work today than 25 years ago for about the same hourly wages, adjusted for inflation. When working families are doing everything they can and small business people are and they lose their health insurance or their health insurance deductibles are so high that all they really have is the insurance that if they get sick they won't lose their home, it's tough on them. It's hard to maintain the sense of security and optimism that a country like ours needs to lead the world into the future and to keep our own dreams alive.

So what are we are going to do about that? Well, we need more pro-family policies, like family and medical leave. We need to pass welfare reform that enables people to move from welfare to work, to be successful parents and successful workers. And we can do that. I sent a bill to the Congress last spring. We've given 19 States permission to get out from under all the crazy Federal rules that keep them from moving people into the workplace. And we're going to pass it next year.

We need to set up a national network of these manufacturing extension centers, like the Great Lakes Manufacturing Technology Center here in Cleveland, to help small firms to accommodate new challenges, to compete, and to get new technologies. We need to pass the telecommunications reform bill which died at the end of this Congress, which will help us to get along that information superhighway and provide unbelievable numbers of high-wage jobs for our people.

We need to reform our job training programs, especially our unemployment system, and transform it into a reemployment system. We are still stuck with the same unemployment program we've had for 40 years. It's not fair to working people, but it's not fair to employers either to pay a FUTA tax which you pay to somebody when they're unemployed so that they have enough money to get along on. It's less than they were making at work but more than they'd be making on welfare. The whole assumption is they're going to be called back to work. Eighty percent of the people who lose their jobs today don't get called back to their old jobs. We are stuck with the 1950's system, when we need one for the 21st century that will encourage continuous retraining and placement in the work force. So these are some of the things that we have to do.

Let me just say one last word about health care. By the time the people who like the system the way it is got through spending between $200 and $300 million to convince the rest of you that I was trying to have the Government take over your health care and take away your choice of doctors, you didn't like my plan too much. That didn't happen to be what I was trying to do, but there was nothing I could do to stand against that.

Here is the problem that we'll have to face. No country in the world spends more than 10 percent of its income on health care except us. We spend 14 percent. That is $260 billion more than the other most expensive system in the world. Now, if we were just buying better health care, who would complain? The problem is no other advanced economy in the world—the other countries that are about as rich as we are, they cover everybody. Their costs are more nearly in line with inflation, and people don't

lose their health care when they move from job to job, all of which happens here.

I will say again, the 1,100,000 people who lost their health insurance last year, almost all were in working families. They weren't people who were on welfare; they were in working families. So we have to find a way that you folks can accept and feel comfortable with that lets you keep what you've got if you've got it and you like it, gives people the security that they won't lose their health insurance when they change jobs or if they happen to have a baby born with an illness, and still brings costs in line with inflation and provides coverage to the people who don't have coverage now, 85 percent of whom are workers. We've got to find some way to do that.

Now, keep in mind, we have reduced defense about all we can. We have reduced domestic spending for the first time in 25 years. The only thing driving the Federal deficit now is Medicare and Medicaid costs going up at 3 times the rate of inflation. This is a serious problem. We'll have to face it.

Now, having said all that, I hope that you are optimistic about the future. I hope that you will make a decision in these coming elections that is consistent with keeping on this course, because it is working.

This is not necessarily a partisan issue. There are a lot of Republicans who have good, serious ideas for how we keep bringing the deficit down and be discriminating about what we invest in. But I don't think this contract is a good idea because it promises everybody a tax cut, it promises a defense increase, promises to revive Star Wars, and promises to balance the budget. Now, that will indulge the present instead of preparing for the future. It will cut college loans explicitly, when we ought to be educating more people. It won't reduce the deficit; it will explode it. But it sounds good; it's a trillion dollars in promises. We're just 2 weeks away from the election. After all I've been through, I'd love to make you a trillion dollars' worth of promises. I could show everybody here a good time on that. [*Laughter*] We could have a good time. But it wouldn't be the responsible thing to do.

The responsible thing to do is to take your licks and say, look for the long run. Look for the long run. You know, I know people are frustrated and angry. One of the first things that every parent learns to try to teach your children is not to make decisions based on frustration and anger but to make decisions based on what you really know, when you're thinking, is best for the present and for the future.

So I ask you to think about this. We have made a substantial start at building the kind of America that will be strong in the 21st century. There are reasons for Americans to still feel uncertain and worried. But the reasons can be addressed only if we keep going forward, not if we go back.

And the last thing I want to say is this—[*applause*]—thank you. Sometimes we have to see ourselves as others see us. Sometimes where you get discouraged or so caught up in the day-to-day business that it's hard to make our contract with the future, our commitment to the long run, our covenant to revive the American dream, we need to remember how other people see us.

Other people think, folks, this is a pretty great country. It's no accident that when they want to have elections in South Africa, they ask us to come help put them on, or when after hundreds of years of fighting in Northern Ireland, they want the United States to bring people here who are on opposite sides and let them come to America and see people who share their roots and try to work through this. It's no accident that when Saddam Hussein reared up again in the Gulf, the countries there that want to be free look to the United States for quick leadership. It's no accident that in the Middle East, it was the United States that was asked to witness this historic peace agreement between Israel and Jordan. That is not an accident. It was no accident. If you could have looked into the eyes of those young men and women we sent to Haiti in uniform when President Aristide went back and all the Haitian people had those signs in Creole saying "Thank you, America"—they know, other people know, this is a very great country.

It is our job to build on that greatness, even when it requires difficult decisions and looking toward tomorrow and not giving in to the easy path today. That is what is before us. And I believe that today you can see that we are a very different place than we were 21 months ago. We're in better shape than we were 18 months ago. We are going in the right direction. We should stay on this economic course and make it a bipartisan commitment to a strong America and a global economy that keeps the American dream alive into the next century.

Thank you very much.

Steve Smith. Thank you, President Clinton. We now turn to our traditional question-and-answer period, a long tradition of the City Club. But because there were so many members who wished to ask questions today, we selected questioners by lottery a few minutes before the President arrived. In front of this audience, in fact, the names were drawn.

The questions, however, have not been submitted either to the President or to the City Club in advance. We'll both be hearing them for the first time. Please, those of you who are asking questions, please remember that President Clinton is the only one authorized to give a speech today so be sure your questions are, in fact, succinct questions. [*Laughter*]

And President Clinton, if you'll come back up here, I want to tell you that our membership director handed me a note while you were speaking, indicating that your renewal for City Club membership is now due. [*Laughter*] First question.

Republican Contract With America

Representative Martin R. Hoke. Mr. President, my question is about the Republican Contract With America which includes several of the same proposals that you campaigned for 2 years ago, like the line-item veto, a middle class tax cut, requiring welfare recipients to work. But you have called this contract, on at least a half a dozen occasions, a contract on America. Your advisers may think that this is cute rhetoric, but I think it's outrageous because as one of its signers——

Audience members. Boo-o-o!

The President. Let him finish. Let him finish. He wanted to do this; let him finish.

Representative Hoke. Thank you, Mr. President. [*Laughter*] Because as one of its signers, your suggestion that I would take out a contract on my constituents is a suggestion that I take very, very personally. My question is this: At a time when the public is so concerned about violent crime, why would you resort to using such talk, in such an inflammatory way, especially when you have spoken yourself saying that you personally want to reduce the amount of partisanship in the debate?

Audience member. Ignore him.

The President. No, I don't want to ignore him. First of all, I agree with the line-item veto. I agree that we still should have some tax relief for middle class taxpayers. The earned-income tax credit relief that we provided went to 15 million middle class families, including a half a million families in Ohio—10 times as many people here as got a tax increase—and it went up to $27,000. I think we should do more; I agree with that. There are some things in there I agree with. I certainly agree with welfare reform.

And so I do agree with that. What I do not agree with is saying, "Put us in control, and we will cut everybody's taxes, balance the budget, increase defense, and increase Star Wars. And we'll tell you how we're going to do it after the election." That's what I don't agree with. And I do think that's a contract on our future.

And let me say this. And you may think that partisan rhetoric is rough, but I see Mr. Fingerhut over there. It was the Republicans, not the Democrats, that killed lobby reform and campaign finance reform in the last week of the session. And I appreciate your concern about crime and violence. I wish you hadn't voted against the Brady bill and the crime bill.

Q. Mr. President, it's an honor to be able to ask a question of the President of the United States. You have indicated your dislike for the Contract With America. In particular, what do you dislike about the balanced budget amendment, requiring welfare recipients to work, a middle class tax credit, or reducing the size of Government, which all American people want?

The President. Okay. Stand there. Let's go through them all. First of all, I proposed welfare reform not all that different from the Republican plan. My bill was there, been in the Congress since March.

Secondly, I'm strong for the line-item veto, and I recognize that some members in my party in the Senate prohibited it from passing, and I'm going to do everything I can to pass it. I've always been for it.

Thirdly, I believe that we should do more to provide tax relief to middle class families, especially with children, although I would remind you that we did provide substantial relief last time with no help from members of the other party. And—wait a minute—70 percent of the tax relief in the contract goes to upper income people.

But my fundamental problem is how it all fits together. On the balanced budget amendment, I've lived under a balanced budget amendment. The problem with the way the balanced—it depends on how it's written. But no matter how it's written you've still got to lower the deficit, I mean—and cut the size of Government. It was the Democrats, we've cut the size of the Government. When the Republicans were in, they didn't cut the size of the Government. The Federal Government has 70,000 fewer people working for it today than it does on the day I became President. It's going to have 270,000 fewer people working over a 6-year period. It will be the smallest Federal Government since Kennedy. We are shrinking the Federal Government. We are doing that, and we are doing it in a good way. So yes, I'm for that.

And insofar as those ideas are in there, I am fine on them. But here is the problem. My problem is it doesn't add up. You cannot promise that in a fixed period of time you're going to cut everybody's taxes, raise defense, bring back Star Wars, and balance the budget. That is exactly what we heard before. It is almost exactly what we heard before. And what did we get? The debt of this country was quadrupled in 12 years.

A lot of the isolated elements are very popular, and they sound wonderful. But when you add it up, you wind up with more deficits, which will take the economy down, cause massive—I'm talking massive—cuts in all Government programs, including education and Medicare and other things. We're not talking about minor things. We're talking about huge cuts. You'll still have a bigger deficit. The economy will be weaker, and we'll go right back where we were when we tried this before. That's my problem, not the specifics. The specifics sound great. But the package is cynical because when you say, "How are you going to pay for it?" "I'll tell you later." And it's the same thing as it was before. It's more red ink when we ought to be investing and growing. That's the way to put the American people first.

Q. First of all, I'd like to say, I think you're doing a great job, and I'm proud that you're my President.

The President. Thank you.

Let me say before you ask your question, I'm glad to have this opportunity to have this kind of discussion. And I want people who disagree with me to ask their questions. And I don't believe that any party or group has a monopoly on political wisdom. But I'll tell you something, when you hired me to be President, you knew that no matter who was President, this country had a lot of serious problems and we had to face them and that all the solutions wouldn't be popular. If it were easy, somebody would have already done it. The only thing I don't want you to do is to fall into the path of just taking another easy way out.

Go ahead. I'm sorry.

Q. That's okay. [*Laughter*]

The President. Go ahead.

Middle East Peace Process

Q. In light of the recent events that are going on in Israel and your upcoming trip, what kind of assistance will you give to or pressure will you put on Arafat to control what's going on in terms of the violence coming out of the territories?

The President. That's an excellent question, first of all. Let me tell you a little about my trip, so I can answer that question. The King of Jordan and the Prime Minister of Israel are going to sign this peace agreement in a couple of days, and they've asked the United States, the President, to be the witness of it because we worked so hard on it.

I'm going to go to Cairo to see President Mubarak, who's been a real partner of ours in this Middle East peace process, and to visit with Chairman Arafat there in Egypt about all the issues you just raised. I'm also going to Syria, as you know, to hope to make further progress there because until we have a peace with Syria, we can't get a peace with Lebanon and a comprehensive peace in the area.

There are two questions in the question you asked. One is the question you asked, what are you going to do to see that Chairman Arafat keeps his commitments under the agreement he made with Israel? The second question is, what can we do to increase his capacity to keep those commitments?

Keep in mind, the really difficult thing in this Middle East peace package is, if Israel makes an agreement with Jordan, they are two nations, with two systems of law enforcement, two armies, two sets of borders. They can—they have a real capacity to enforce their agreement, the same as if we can ever get this agreement with Syria or with Lebanon; you will have borders, armies, institutions, law enforcement.

With the agreement with the PLO in the West Bank and—I mean, in Gaza and Jericho—I mean, in Jericho and the West Bank, you

have only the beginnings of the capacity to honor this. Now, when Corporal Waxman was kidnapped, I believe that Mr. Arafat really made an effort to help find out where he was and to share intelligence with the Israelis, and it was a good first step. But I will press him to honor the agreements in spirit and letter, but we also have to develop his capacity to honor the agreements. That is very important because, keep in mind, the PLO had never—not only never run a police force or an army before but never had to see the lights come on or do all the things Mayor White has to worry about: does the sewer system work; does the water system work; what is the order and structure of events?

So the challenge is not only to get them to want to keep their commitments but to ensure that they can keep their commitments.

Q. Good afternoon, Mr. President. First of all, I'd like to say I'm a native of Camden, Arkansas, a Razorback, 45 miles from Hope, Arkansas.

The President. Thank you.

Q. Watermelon capital of the world. [*Laughter*]

The President. The chamber of commerce thanks you.

Public Awareness of Administration Accomplishments

Q. All right. I am a staff rep with the international union of Communication Workers of America—President Morton Bahr, out of Washington, DC, headquarters; Jeff Rechenbach, our newly elected vice president here in district 4.

My question is—and you already alluded to most of what I'm going to say—all the good things you're doing leading our country, good things, signing the bill, the family leave bill, the crime bill, and also you just signed the education bill the other day. Why—I'm getting to the question—[*laughter*]—I want to know why you're not getting that—the media, rather, is not getting that out for all the good things. All we are hearing is the negative side of it.

The President. Well, I told my press conference the other day in Washington that I arranged it that way because I didn't want to peak too soon. [*Laughter*]

It's a complicated thing, really it is. Let me—it is a complicated thing. First of all, there is a highly political chain of communication on the other side of people that disagree with me about everything, and they have their own kind of media outlets. And the Democrats really never developed such a thing in the time when we didn't have the White House and I think didn't appreciate it because the—the national media tends to be—during the—while Congress is there, the things that go on longer get more coverage than the things that go on shorter. So if you pass a bill and it's good news, it's news for one day or maybe one night on the television, and then it's gone. If you have a bloodbath over health care for 4 months, you hear about it every day. And you remember what Mark Twain said, that there are two things people should never see, sausage and laws being made. [*Laughter*]

And I think sometimes just the—it's hard to see the forest for the trees sometimes. And I think that, you know, I need to give more thought about what my responsibility in this is, how I can do a better job of communicating with the American people, getting this information out. But it's always easier when the Congress goes home because then I can go out and have meetings like this, we can talk, and we can communicate.

It is one of the great frustrations of the job, you know, because all the research shows that only a very small percentage of the American people know about the family leave law or the middle class college loans or the apprenticeship programs or immunizing all the kids in the country under 2 or the Head Start program. Senator Glenn showed me an excerpt from Time magazine which said that this Congress had enacted a higher percentage of my proposals than any Congress had done for a President since the end of World War II, except for President Eisenhower's first 2 years and President Johnson's first 2 years. And I dare say nobody in America knows that.

So I would say I have to do a better job of that. I think sometimes, you know, I get so busy working on things I forget that the American people hired me to communicate with them as well as to work. And frankly—and our adversaries, if they just want to stop us from doing things, then they don't have to do as much work as we do because all they have to do is just keep saying no out in the country, so it's easier. They have an easier burden than I do because they don't have to get anything done if they just want to stop things.

So I just have to do a better job. And any of you got any good ideas about how I can do a better job of communicating, I'd like to have them. I'm not as good a talker as I thought I was when I got this job. [*Laughter*]

Thank you.

Q. Mr. President, I'm Tom Corey from Brook Park, Ohio. And I want to add our welcome to you, as well.

The President. Thank you.

Middle East Peace Process

Q. My question is the Middle East again, back to that, Lebanon, and how soon do you think we can expect a treaty between Lebanon and Israel? And the second part of the question is, can we get the travel ban to Lebanon lifted? And then, I believe you are more than a candidate for the Nobel Peace Prize.

Thank you.

The President. First of all, I think there will be a peace with Lebanon, for reasons that you clearly understand by the question you asked. Peace with Lebanon will probably come about the time peace with Syria does. I think we have some chance of getting there. I wouldn't expect some sort of immediate breakthrough; I don't want to unduly raise expectations. But we are making good, steady progress. And I think it is very much in the interests of the people and the governments of Syria, Lebanon, and Israel to keep going with the peace process. I cannot set a time for you on that. If I knew, I probably couldn't say, but I don't know.

But I can tell you, we're making good progress. The travel ban is an issue which will come up. We are trying to take these issues one by one, as we can. I'm encouraged by the travel that's going back and forth in other countries now, especially between Israel and Jordan. I'm encouraged by the lifting of the embargo against Israel by the GCC countries. So this is another barrier that will surely fall; even though I can't tell you when, I think it'll be sooner rather than later because we seem to be on a pretty good roll here.

If the people of Israel can keep their courage up and the people of the Middle East can keep their courage up and we won't be intimidated by these terrorists and enemies of peace, I think we'll get there in a reasonable time. And I thank you for your question.

Q. Mr. President and ladies and gentlemen, this will be the last question.

Health Care Reform

Q. President Clinton, my question is about health care and how it might be paid for. My proposal is that to keep the taxpayers constantly informed as to the cost of health care, that a national sales tax be put on every purchase at the retail level, and that this—if the expenditures on health care increase or if they decrease, then that this is—as quickly as possible be reflected in the amount of the percent of the tax; also that tax stamps be put out—Ohio wants to do that—so the people knew they were paying for the program. So, sir, to keep the taxpayers informed, I think the regular tax and that sort of thing should be adjusted as a function of time and as a function of the total expenditures.

Would you comment, sir? [*Laughter*]

The President. Well, there are—I know you're laughing, but there are some people in the Congress who think that health care should be funded that way, too, with a national—some sort of national sales levy.

Let me tell you what my problem with it is. My problem with it is that we are already, let me say again, we are already spending 14 percent of our income on health care. Canada spends 10; Germany and Japan are a little under 9 percent of their income.

Now, part of the reason we spend more is that we have higher rates of AIDS and higher rates of violence and higher rates of some other health problems than they do. So if we had more people showing up at the emergency rooms in Cleveland that are cut up or shot or have drug problems, just to take three, we're going to pay more for health care.

But a lot of it is because our system is so incredibly inefficient in so many ways. And the problem I've always had with just passing some sort of a tax to cover the uninsured is that you just build in all the inefficiencies into the system and you force the people who are already—many of whom are already paying more than their fair share for health care to pay for everybody else's health care as well, without knowing whether they're going to pay their fair share.

So there are a lot of people, good people, who agree with the proposal that you have outlined. But I'm just reluctant to embrace it until I believe we've done more to build in some competitive pressures to take waste out of the system and to make sure the people who can pay their own way are doing their own part before we ask the rest of Americans to do anything for them.

Thank you very much.

NOTE: The President spoke at 12:40 p.m. at the Statler Tower Building. In his remarks, he referred to Steve Smith, club president; Mayor Michael R. White of Cleveland; Representative Eric Fingerhut; King Hussein of Jordan; Prime Minister Yitzhak Rabin of Israel; President Hosni Mubarak of Egypt; and Yasser Arafat, Chairman, Palestine Liberation Organization.

Remarks at a Reception for Representative Tom Sawyer in Akron, Ohio
October 24, 1994

Thank you. Thank you so much for being so enthusiastic. I thank Congressman Sawyer and Joyce and Mayor Plusquellic and Deputy Mayor Jackson. Thank you for helping us get through this today. Bless you. Joel and Susan Hyatt and our wonderful Senators here, Howard Metzenbaum and John Glenn. I'm glad to be here with all of you.

The last two times I've been to Akron, I've been in two of the most interesting buildings I've ever been in. You know, we had the campaign rally in the air dock. Do you remember that? I am sure—it was really good for me. It was calculated both to make me ecstatic and to keep me humble because we were ecstatic that we had 50,000 people there and humbled that the building was 80 percent empty. [*Laughter*] It was amazing. And this place is magnificent and a great treasure for you. And I'm honored to be here.

I've had a great day today with Tom already. We've been to Inventure Place. And I'm looking forward to coming back when the Inventure

Place is open, full of inventions that I can come play with.

As all of you know, I am here in behalf of Tom Sawyer tonight and in behalf of Joel Hyatt and so many others who want to make this country a better place. I have much to be grateful for in the incredible contribution and support that Senator Glenn and Senator Metzenbaum have provided. And I want to thank them, as well.

You know, this is an unusual election. I think that's putting it mildly. [*Laughter*] I went to Washington 21 months ago with a charge from you to try to change this country, to try to get America into the 21st century able to compete and win, to rebuild the American dream, to help us go through this period of remarkable change in a way that would bring this country and our people out on top, to forge a new partnership between our National Government and our citizens and our businesses, not with the Government pretending to be able to solve all the problems or with the Government sitting on the sidelines but walking hand-in-hand into a brighter and better future.

And I committed to you that I'd try to do three things if you voted for me: I'd try to make the Government work for ordinary Americans again, to reward work and family, to make a serious stab in the fight against crime and our social problems, and to build up the strength of our people; I'd try to bring back the economy, to reduce the deficit and increase jobs and move us forward; I'd try to make the world a more prosperous and a more peaceful place. And I leave it to you to decide how well we've done. But here are the facts, thanks to the leadership of the people on this stage.

We passed the family and medical leave law. It helped almost a million people in this State to take a little time off when they need it. We passed an expansion of Head Start and immunizations for all children under the age of 2 by 1996. We gave tax relief to a half a million Ohio families who have children in the home, work full-time, but are just above the poverty line because we don't think anybody who's working full time and raising their kids should fail and should be in poverty. We think people should succeed as workers and succeed as parents. That's rewarding work and family.

We passed the Brady bill and the crime bill to make a serious assault on crime. And I might say, I want to thank the mayor for his support.

I want to thank the Congressman for his support. And I want you to know that I signed that bill only about 3 weeks ago, and the city of Akron has already received assistance to hire more police officers to go on the street, to lower the crime rate here in Akron because of the crime bill.

And perhaps most important, and thanks in no small part to Tom Sawyer, we have begun to give the American people the kind of educational help they need to develop a system of lifetime learning, so that when places like Akron get hit with what you faced in the 1980's again, we will have a system that will enable people to continuously learn and relearn new skills from the get-go so we will not have to pass through a dark night of despair.

Congressman Sawyer deserves reelection if for no other reason than his contribution to this education Congress. In 1991 he was the principal sponsor of the National Literacy Act. Look what happened in this Congress. We expanded Head Start. We passed the Goals 2000 legislation to establish national education goals but to support grassroots reform because we know he knows, since Joyce is a teacher—[*applause*]— yes, you can clap for her, she probably deserves more credit than the rest of us do. This is a very important point. For the first time in a long time, the Federal Government recognized that the magic of education occurs in the classroom, between the teacher and the parents and the students. That's what works. And we passed the elementary and secondary education bill which cuts out all kinds of Federal rules and regulations and lets the schools decide how best to spend Federal money to make sure all of our children learn. It is a very important piece of legislation.

We passed legislation to help make our schools safer, to give schools the opportunity to get together with grassroots community leaders and decide what basic values of citizenship and character they want to teach in the school and not run away from that but run toward it to give all of our kids a common foundation of good citizenship. We passed legislation to have every State in the country set up a national system, State by State, of apprenticeships for young people who don't go to college but want to get good jobs. And finally, we made 20 million Americans eligible for lower interest, longer-term college loans so the middle class of this country need never walk away from a college education again. And he was a leader in all that.

On the economy, as I told the Cleveland City Club today, we brought the deficit down, we increased investment in new technologies and in education and training. We've had 4.6 million new jobs. The unemployment rate in Ohio has dropped 1½ percent since I have been President. Ninety percent of those jobs are in the private sector. And this year, here's the real good news, for the first time in a very long time more than half the new jobs coming into the American economy were above the national average in wages, above the national average.

If you look at the world, this is a more prosperous and peaceful place. We passed NAFTA. We negotiated the GATT world trade agreement. We are reaching out to Asia. We are reaching out to Latin America. We took controls off all kinds of exports so we could sell more high-tech products. We are reaching out to the rest of the world. And this is plainly a more peaceful place because of what the United States has been involved in. For the first time since nuclear weapons were developed, no Russian missiles are pointed at the children of Ohio and the United States this year. We are leading the fight for democracy in Haiti, for freedom in the Persian Gulf, for an end to the war in Northern Ireland, and yes, for peace in the Middle East. The United States is making this world a more peaceful place.

We've got a long way to go, folks. And we've got a lot of problems to solve. But this country's in better shape than it was 21 months ago, and you should reward the people who are helping.

Now, here's the real rub. If all this is true, why aren't we happier? What is going on here? I'll tell you one thing, one thing Thomas—I mean, Mark Twain once said that the American people—[laughter]—I started to say Tom Sawyer. Maybe it was Huck Finn. Maybe it was old Jim. [Laughter] But Mark Twain once said, "You know, the American people should never have to see two things, sausages and laws being made." And sometimes I think all we do is concentrate on the negative. And then there are people in this country today who only communicate with us through what is known as attack journalism, unconstrained by the facts, designed to destroy arguments, credibility, to make people more cynical, to get them upset. And to be fair, our opponents have had more time to bad-mouth than we have had to defend, because

we've been working. And when they're not trying to help, they have a lot of free time. [Applause] That's right.

What do they offer? I want you to think about this. When you think about Joel Hyatt and his opponent for the Senate—and you ask John Glenn and Howard Metzenbaum if I'm not telling the truth—I want you to think about this, what have they offered? They have offered "No." Right? They all voted against the middle class college loans. They voted against the tax relief to working people. Their leaders tried to beat and mostly voted against the family leave law, the Brady bill. They did everything they could do to kill the crime bill. They said no.

And at the end of this session of Congress—this is important, because they just stepped on things important to our country and to your legislators—they decided that they would kill every living thing they could. Right before they decided that, we did get through John Glenn's procurement bill to change the way the Government buys things. We're going to save hundreds of millions of dollars—no more $500 hammers, no more $50 ashtrays—thanks to Senator Glenn.

But then they decided they would say no. And they brought up the filibuster, which means 41 Senators can kill anything the rest of America wants. They killed campaign finance reform. They killed lobby reform that a freshman Congressman from Ohio, Eric Fingerhut, had so much to do with. He ought to be reelected, if for no other reason than carrying on this courageous fight to reform the lobbying practices in Washington, DC.

They killed all the environmental legislation. They even killed the Superfund bill. You know, the Superfund bill, folks, is designed to clean up toxic waste dumps. I want you to listen to this. You think about this every time you think about Joel Hyatt and his opponent between now and election day, his opponent who said he can't wait to get up there and get in with that crowd so he can stop things, too. Now, the Superfund bill was supported by the chemical companies, by the labor unions, and the Sierra Club. They've never been for anything together before. [Laughter] You could not get that crowd to agree on when the Sun's coming up tomorrow morning. But they were for this. As a matter of fact, no one in America was against the Superfund bill except more than 40 Republican Senators. And why were they against it? Because they would have rather left the poison in the

ground than let Tom Sawyer come home to
Akron and tell you he helped to clean it up.
That is wrong, and we should stop it. That is
wrong.

And if you don't like what they did to kill
campaign finance reform, lobby reform, the
Superfund bill, all the other environmental legislation, you have a way to send the message.
You can send Tom Sawyer back to the House,
and you can send Joel Hyatt to the United
States Senate. And you will tell the American
people that Ohio wants things to be done, not
things to be stopped.

Now let me just say this. Today in Cleveland,
I had the opportunity to engage a Member of
the House of the other party and his administrative assistant, who apparently by lottery out of
hundreds of people drew questions one and two
to get to ask me—[laughter]—and it was fine,
but they wanted to talk about their contract
for America and to complain that I had called
it a contract on America. And they said, "Well,
there are things in this contract that you like.
You're for the line-item veto." And I am.
"You're for welfare reform." I am; I sent legislation to Congress in March to change the whole
welfare system and move people from welfare
to work. "You're for giving more tax relief to
the middle class. You're for shrinking the Government. Why aren't you for our contract?" I
want you to know why. That was a very clever
question they asked. They took all the popular
things out of their contract. But what their contract does is to promise a huge tax cut, a big
defense increase, an increase in Star Wars, and
a balanced budget. And when I said, "Well,
how are you all going to pay for this?" They
said, "Well, we'll tell you that after the election."
[Laughter]

It's a trillion dollar promise they've made. And
it sounds familiar, doesn't it? "Vote for me. I'll
cut your taxes, raise spending, and balance the
budget, with no consequences." We tried that
once. It didn't work out too well.

You know what it means. It means we're
going to explode the deficit after we got it down,
coming down 3 years in a row for the first
time since Truman was President. It means that
we are going to ship our jobs overseas. It means
we're going to have to gut a lot of programs.
They specifically call for cutting the college loan
program 3 years in a row, when we need more
kids going to college, not fewer. This is a bad
idea, this contract. This is a bad idea.

So what is going on? We don't want to go
back. We need to go forward. We don't want
to reward the blame crowd. We want to reward
the crowd that wants to take responsibility for
this country. We want to reward people that
want to empower Americans, not people that
want to grab power by telling us what we want
to hear. Shoot, I'd like to promise you a trillion
dollars' worth of stuff. It's 2 weeks before the
election. I mean, we could have a good time
on a trillion dollars worth of hot checks. [Laugh-
ter] But it would be wrong. She would pay
the bill. We would set up the risk of setting
us right back where we were in the trickle-
down eighties. It would be wrong. You need
to think about this in terms of what you do
between now and the election for Senator and
Congressman.

You know, if Tom Sawyer were a Republican
running for reelection and he had voted—
[laughter]—now, listen, this is serious because
you—we're preaching to the saved here; you've
got to go out and convert—[laughter]—so you
need to listen to this. If he were a Republican
running for reelection who had voted to reduce
the Federal Government to its smallest size
since Kennedy was President, to give us 3 years
of deficit reduction for the first time since Truman was President, for the toughest crime bill
in the history of the country, and for economic
policies that literally exploded the economy and
drove down unemployment in Akron and
throughout Ohio, the Republican Party would
be building a statue to him and saying no one
should run against him. That's what they should
be doing anyway because that's what he voted
for. Now, that's the truth.

So what is all this rhetoric? It's just a bunch
of stuff. But if you talk loud enough, long
enough, and people are upset enough, maybe
it gets across. I want you to think about this.
This is the last point I want to make, because
I want you to do something besides stand here
and cheer me. I like that, and it's a new experience for me, having been in Washington—
[laughter]—but that's not what I want you to
do. I want you to think about all your friends
and neighbors in Ohio who don't have their
minds made up or even think maybe they're
going to vote against the Congressmen or not
vote for Joel or anybody else you know in these
other districts, like young Mr. Fingerhut who
has done so much.

I want you to think about this. I got to thinking, what's my job like today, and is it like any job I ever held before? And I thought, well, you know, I've done a lot of things for a living. I mean, from the time I was a little kid, I've worked in a grocery store; I had a wholesale comic book business; I've mowed lawns, cleared land, built houses. I mean, I've done a lot of different things. I was a Governor. And I thought, well, maybe it's like being a Governor, but it's not really. The job that I think I should be doing now that is most like what I've done before was something I didn't make money for. It was when I was in junior and senior high school. When I was in little clubs, we would raise money by doing car washes. And I was the guy that liked to clean the windshield. That's about what I need to do today.

You think about that. If you're driving a car and the windshield is real dirty, it could be sunshine outside and you'd think it was about to storm. It could be clear way ahead, and you would think that there are all kind of obstacles in the way. Or there could be a real obstacle in the way, and you'd run smack dab into it because you couldn't see it. That's where we are in America today. We need to clean the windshield off. We need to turn the lights on in this country. This is a very great country,

and we are moving in the right direction. And we need to reward that, not punish it. And that's what you need to do. That's what you need to do.

So I want you to think about that. And I want you to clean the windows for Tom Sawyer and clean the windows for Joel Hyatt. Most importantly of all, clean the windows for your fellow Ohioans and your fellow Americans. You cannot blame people for being torn up and upset. Look at how they get their information and what they hear. Go out and find people that you know and tell them to take a deep breath. Tell them a joke; buy them a cup of coffee; get them to where they think. And remember that even parents don't let their children make decisions when they are angry. You almost always make a mistake. And imagine that between now and November 8th, everybody you see is an opportunity for you to clean the windshield and turn the lights on. America deserves it, and so do you.

Thank you, and God bless you.

NOTE: The President spoke at 6:05 p.m. at the Akron Civic Theater. In his remarks, he referred to Mayor Donald L. Plusquellic and Deputy Mayor for Intergovernmental Relations Dorothy Jackson of Akron, and Representative Martin R. Hoke.

Statement on the Presidential Election in the Former Yugoslav Republic of Macedonia
October 24, 1994

I congratulate President Gligorov on his election to a second term as President of his country. Under his able leadership, I am confident the Former Yugoslav Republic of Macedonia will continue on its path toward full integration into the international community of nations. The Former Yugoslav Republic of Macedonia has upheld the principles of democracy and has courageously embarked on a bold program of economic reform and renewal. Despite strong external economic pressures which have caused great hardship, President Gligorov and his countrymen have shown a determination to continue on the path to free market democracy.

I am pleased that international observers to the recent elections concluded that the first round of elections were conducted in an overall free and fair manner. The second round of parliamentary elections, scheduled for the end of this month, will be the next important step in the FYROM's democratic development. It is our hope that they will take place in a free and peaceful environment.

The Former Yugoslav Republic of Macedonia's peaceful political and economic development is essential to stability in the Balkans. The United States has taken numerous steps to support that development, including sending U.S. troops to participate in a U.N. peacekeeping mission there, establishing a liaison office in Skopje, and increasing our economic assistance under the SEED program in fiscal year 1995. I have instructed my Special Envoy, Matthew Nimetz, to redouble his efforts in the weeks ahead, in tandem with U.N. mediator Cyrus Vance, to help Skopje and Athens resolve their differences. We will continue to work with other friends of the Former Yugoslav Republic of Macedonia in the months ahead to try to help bridge the country's balance-of-payments gap so that programs prepared by the IMF and World Bank can go forward.

Memorandum on Implementation of Safe Schools Legislation
October 22, 1994

Memorandum for the Secretary of Education

Subject: Implementation of the Gun-Free Schools Act of 1994, and the Safe and Drug-Free Schools and Communities Act

Our schools are increasingly plagued by violence and crime that is abhorrent to all law-abiding citizens. It is of paramount importance that this Nation's schools be safe, disciplined, and conducive to learning.

Several laws passed this year will promote our effort to make schools safe for learning. The Gun-Free Schools Act of 1994 provides that within one year, every State receiving Federal aid for elementary and secondary education must have a law requiring school districts to expel from school for at least one year any student who brings a gun to school, subject to certain exceptions. The Safe and Drug-Free Schools and Communities Act funds comprehensive violence prevention programs, including those that enhance school security.

To ensure vigorous enforcement, I am directing you to coordinate implementation of these anti-violence measures with appropriate local authorities to the maximum extent possible. Your collaborative efforts should include the States, school districts, law enforcement agencies, and educators. In the case of the Gun-Free Schools Act, enforcement should include termination of Federal assistance if you determine that a State is not in compliance.

You should report to me in writing by December 31 on the specific steps you have taken to implement these statutes.

WILLIAM J. CLINTON

NOTE: This memorandum was released by the Office of the Press Secretary on October 25.

Statement on Signing the Small Business Administration Reauthorization and Amendments Act of 1994
October 22, 1994

Today I am pleased to sign S. 2060, the "Small Business Administration Reauthorization and Amendments Act of 1994." This Act will reauthorize programs of the Small Business Administration (SBA) for fiscal years 1995 through 1997, make meaningful program revisions, and authorize important new initiatives. By doing so, the Congress and my Administration are carrying out the plans we began in 1993 to make the SBA a leaner, more efficient, more effective organization that is focused on meeting the needs of all small businesses.

The Act will allow the SBA to continue to meet the growing demand for its loans and loan guarantees. This will help ensure that our Nation's small businesses have access to capital, which will enable them to prosper and create new jobs. The Act will also enable the SBA to expand and improve its innovative Microloan program, under which relatively small loans are provided to entrepreneurs by nonprofit intermediaries. Microloans are an important tool in the One-Stop-Capital-Shops that the SBA is establishing to bring relief to disadvantaged communities in the Empowerment Zones and Enterprise Communities.

With the changes provided by this legislation, the SBA will be able to harmonize its export loan program with that of the Export-Import Bank to carry out its role in the trade agenda I outlined in the Trade Promotion Coordinating Committee. Also of great importance is the new emphasis the legislation places on assistance to women business owners, who are now creating businesses at a faster rate than their male counterparts.

Finally, S. 2060 will allow the SBA to provide relief from high prepayment penalties to borrowers under some of its programs. By revising the prepayment penalties and allowing the refinancing of these loans at more favorable interest rates, we will unleash the productive power of these companies by freeing up their resources for new production, new employment, and new contributions to our economy and tax base.

Again, I am pleased to sign this legislation, which is of great significance to our Nation's small business women and men.

WILLIAM J. CLINTON

The White House,
October 22, 1994.

NOTE: S. 2060, approved October 22, was assigned Public Law No. 103–403. This statement was released by the Office of the Press Secretary on October 25.

Remarks on Departure for the Middle East
October 25, 1994

Good morning. Today I embark on a mission inspired by a dream of peace, a dream as ancient as the peoples I will visit, a dream that now, after years of struggle, has a new chance of becoming a reality.

Tomorrow, in the desert between Israel and Jordan, two neighbors will agree to lay to rest age-old animosities and give a new future to their countries and their children. King Hussein and Prime Minister Rabin will enter into an historic peace treaty. By their courage, they help their peoples, their region, and the entire world. They help to begin a final journey to peace in one of the most perilous conflicts of our age. By taking part in that ceremony, I will help to fulfill a mission pursued vigorously by the United States, by Presidents of both parties, since the end of World War II.

Peace in the Middle East is in our fundamental interests, and our continued participation in the peace process is crucial to its success. The signing ceremony I will witness grows out of the peace process we have helped to build.

The treaty between Israel and Jordan will be only the second full peace treaty between Israel and one of its Arab neighbors and the first ever signed in the Middle East itself. The roots of this process reach back to the Camp David accords between the late Anwar Sadat of Egypt and Menachem Begin of Israel, in which President Carter played such a pivotal role, and to the historic peace treaty they signed here 15 years ago.

But this trip is more than a celebration of another important step toward peace, it's an opportunity to pursue new steps. Israel and Jordan have shown that contact can overcome conflict and that direct talks can produce peace. My goal is to make clear that the time has arrived for all parties to follow the brave and hopeful inspiration of Israel and Jordan. With so much at stake, it is more important than ever for the United States to stand shoulder-to-shoulder with those who are taking risks for peace.

For all the progress toward peace, indeed, because of that progress, we have witnessed a new wave of terrorism and violence. No step on this long journey requires more patience, more discipline, more courage than the steps still to come. At this crucial moment, the people of the Middle East stand at a crossroads. In one direction lies the dark past of violence, terrorism, and insecurity that desperate enemies of peace seek to prolong. In the other lies a brighter future, a brighter future that Israel and all her Arab neighbors can achieve if they have the courage to stand up to violence, to terrorism, to mistrust, to build that future.

Above all else, I go to the Middle East to deliver one clear message: The United States stands by those who, in the words of the Psalms, "seek peace and pursue it." And we stand up to those who threaten to destroy the dream that has brought us to this historic moment.

Standing up for peace in this region includes countering the aggressive acts of Iraq's toward its neighbors. Like our troops around the world, the men and women of our Armed Forces stationed in Kuwait are the strength behind our pledge to support peace and security. They are doing a magnificent job, and I want them to know how proud all Americans are of their efforts. When I visit them on Friday, I know I'll carry the good wishes of all their fellow Americans, just as I know all Americans will pray this week for the progress toward peace as we witness this historic treaty and carry the peace process forward.

Thank you very much.

NOTE: The President spoke at 7:42 a.m. in the Rose Garden at the White House.

Statement on Signing the Immigration and Nationality Technical Corrections Act of 1994
October 25, 1994

I am pleased to sign H.R. 783, the "Immigration and Nationality Technical Corrections Act of 1994," which will reauthorize the Visa Waiver Pilot Program, assist new refugees coming to the United States, improve laws relating to naturalization and citizenship, and speed the deportation of alien felons.

The Visa Waiver Pilot Program was established in 1988 to allow visitors from certain countries to travel to the United States without a visa. The countries participating in this program grant reciprocal privileges to American visitors. In 1993, more than nine million international tourists and business people from 22 nations traveled to the United States under this program. This Act will help to promote U.S. tourism by extending the Visa Waiver Pilot Program for 2 years.

The Federal Government provides approximately $400 million annually to States and voluntary agencies to help provide for health, employment related services, English language training, and other resettlement needs of refugees. H.R. 783 will continue the authority for this program.

The Act also corrects a decades-old injustice to certain persons born outside the United States before 1934 of one U.S.-citizen parent and one noncitizen parent. Prior to the enactment of this Act, such persons could become U.S. citizens if the father was the citizen, but not if the mother was the citizen. H.R. 783 corrects this inequity and makes persons born before 1934 to a U.S. citizen mother and alien father eligible for U.S. citizenship.

The Act allows for more rapid deportation of undocumented aliens who are convicted of serious crimes in the United States. The Act also adds certain crimes to the definition of aggravated felony. I sign this legislation with the understanding that convictions for crimes included in the existing law will be governed by the current effective date provisions, and that the effective date provision related to the expanded definition applies only to convictions for those crimes that have been added by this Act.

Finally, I note that section 221 of the Act, relating to visits to the United States by Taiwan officials, is in potential tension with my constitutional authorities concerning receipt of Ambassadors, recognition of governments, and the conduct of foreign policy. Section 212 of the Immigration and Nationality Act of 1952 ("INA") permits the Secretary of State to exclude aliens where admission would have potentially serious adverse foreign policy consequences. Were section 221 of the Act read to restrict this authority, section 221 would impermissibly impinge on my constitutional responsibilities.

Section 221 can be read in a manner consistent with the Constitution, however. Because the Congress has chosen not to modify section 212(a)(3)(C) of the INA, 8 U.S.C. 1182(a)(3)(C), I will construe section 221 as expressing the

Congress' own view that in the six circumstances enumerated, our foreign policy is better served by admitting these individuals, but ultimately leaving this determination to the Secretary of State under section 212 of the INA. It is in this manner, consistent with the Constitution, that I intend for this statute to be construed.

Accordingly, I am hereby directing the Secretary of State to weigh particularly carefully the foreign policy interests of the United States in considering any application by Taiwan's leaders to visit the United States in the six designated circumstances. These interests include maintaining the present peaceful conditions and robust economic climate in the Taiwan Strait region and the successful balance struck between our unofficial relations with Taiwan and our relations with the People's Republic of China.

WILLIAM J. CLINTON

The White House,
October 25, 1994.

NOTE: H.R. 783, approved October 25, was assigned Public Law No. 103–416.

Statement on Signing the Veterans' Compensation Cost-of-Living Adjustment Act of 1994
October 25, 1994

Today, I have signed into law S. 1927, the "Veterans' Compensation Cost-of-Living Adjustment Act of 1994."

In signing S. 1927, I am pleased to extend a most deserved benefit to our Nation's service-disabled veterans and the surviving spouses and children of those who gave their lives in defense of our beloved freedoms. This Act not only maintains the value of benefits so dearly earned, but underscores a debt of gratitude that we can never fully repay.

S. 1927 provides a 2.8 percent increase in compensation and dependency and indemnity compensation benefits, effective December 1, 1994. This is the same percentage increase that Social Security beneficiaries and veterans' pension recipients will be receiving in January.

I salute the more than two and one-half million individuals who will directly benefit from this increase and all veterans and their families. Moreover, to those proud men and women still in uniform, our actions today bear witness to our Nation's commitment to you for your contributions to our security and well-being.

WILLIAM J. CLINTON

The White House,
October 25, 1994.

NOTE: S. 1927, approved October 25, was assigned Public Law No. 103–418.

Letter to Congressional Leaders on Additional Measures Against the Federal Republic of Yugoslavia (Serbia and Montenegro)
October 25, 1994

Dear Mr. Speaker: (Dear Mr. President:)

On May 30, 1992, pursuant to the International Emergency Economic Powers Act (IEEPA), 50 U.S.C. 1701 *et seq.*, and the National Emergencies Act (NEA), 50 U.S.C. 1601 *et seq.*, President Bush exercised his statutory authority to issue Executive Order No. 12808, declaring a national emergency with respect to the actions and policies of the Governments of Serbia and Montenegro and blocking Yugoslav Government property.

On June 5, 1992, pursuant to the above authorities, as well as section 1114 of the Federal Aviation Act (49 U.S.C. App. 1514), and section

5 of the United Nations Participation Act of 1945, as amended (UNPA), (22 U.S.C. 287c), the President exercised his statutory authority to issue Executive Order No. 12810, blocking property of, and prohibiting transactions with, the Federal Republic of Yugoslavia (Serbia and Montenegro). This latter action was taken to ensure that the economic measures taken by the United States with respect to the Federal Republic of Yugoslavia (Serbia and Montenegro) conform to United Nations Security Council Resolution 757 of May 30, 1992.

On January 15, 1993, President Bush exercised his statutory authority under IEEPA, the UNPA, and the NEA to issue Executive Order No. 12831 to impose additional economic measures with respect to the Federal Republic of Yugoslavia (Serbia and Montenegro) in accordance with United Nations Security Council Resolutions 757 of May 30, 1992, and 787 of November 16, 1992. Those additional measures prohibited transactions related to transshipments through the Federal Republic of Yugoslavia (Serbia and Montenegro), as well as transactions related to vessels owned or controlled by persons or entities in the Federal Republic of Yugoslavia (Serbia and Montenegro).

On April 25, 1993, I exercised my statutory authority under IEEPA, the UNPA, and the NEA to issue Executive Order No. 12846 to impose additional economic measures with respect to the Federal Republic of Yugoslavia (Serbia and Montenegro) in accordance with United Nations Security Council Resolutions 757 of May 30, 1992, 787 of November 16, 1992, and 820 of April 17, 1993. These additional measures blocked the property of businesses in the Federal Republic of Yugoslavia; charged owners or operators of property blocked under Executive Orders Nos. 12808, 12810, 12831, or 12846 all expenses incident to the blocking and maintenance of such property; ordered the detention; pending investigation, of all nonblocked vessels suspected of violating United Nations Security Council Resolutions 713, 757, 787, or 820 and the blocking of such conveyances or cargos if a violation is determined to have been committed; prohibited any vessel registered in the United States from entering the territorial waters of the Federal Republic of Yugoslavia; and prohibited United States persons from engaging in any dealings relating to the shipment of goods to, from, or through the United Nations Protected Areas in the Republic of Croatia and areas in the Republic of Bosnia and Herzegovina under the control of Bosnian Serb forces.

On September 23, 1994, the United Nations Security Council adopted Resolution 942, which requires the imposition of additional measures on the areas of the Republic of Bosnia and Herzegovina under the control of the Bosnian Serb forces due to their refusal to accept the proposed territorial settlement of the conflict in the Republic of Bosnia and Herzegovina.

On October 25, 1994, pursuant to the above authorities, I expanded the scope of the national emergency declared in Executive Order No. 12808 to address the unusual and extraordinary threat to the national security, foreign policy and economy of the United States posed by the actions of the Bosnian Serb forces and the authorities in the areas of the Republic of Bosnia and Herzegovina under their control and imposed additional measures in those areas to conform to United Nations Security Council Resolution 942 (1994).

The new Executive order:

—blocks all property and interests in property of (and transactions with): (1) the Bosnian Serb forces and authorities in those areas of the Republic of Bosnia and Herzegovina under the control of those forces; (2) any entity organized or located in the Bosnian Serb-controlled areas; (3) any entity, wherever organized or located, which is owned or controlled directly or indirectly by any person in, or resident in, the Bosnian Serb-controlled areas; or (4) any person acting for or on behalf of any person mentioned above;

—prohibits the exportation or provision of services by United States persons to Bosnian Serb-controlled areas or to any person for the purposes of any business carried out in those areas;

—prohibits vessels registered in the United States or owned or controlled by United States persons from entering the riverine ports of the Bosnian Serb-controlled areas; and

—prohibits any transaction that evades or avoids or has the purpose of evading or avoiding, or attempts to violate, any of the prohibitions of the order.

In addition, this order authorizes the Secretary of the Treasury, in consultation with the Secretary of State, to take such actions and to employ all powers granted to me by the International Emergency Economic Powers Act and the United Nations Participation Act as may be necessary to carry out the purposes of the order, including the issuance of licenses authorizing transactions otherwise prohibited. The sanctions imposed in the order apply notwithstanding any preexisting contracts, international agreements, licenses or authorizations.

The new Executive order is necessary to confirm our commitment to a negotiated settlement of the conflict in the former Yugoslavia that preserves the territorial integrity of all the states there within their internationally recognized borders; to respond to the continued refusal of the Bosnian Serb party to accept the proposed territorial settlement accepted by the other parties; and to implement mandatory United Nations Security Council measures imposed on the Bosnian Serbs under Chapter VII of the Charter of the United Nations in order to urge them to accept the proposed territorial settlement unconditionally and in full.

The declaration of the national emergency made by Executive Order No. 12808 and the controls imposed under Executive Orders Nos. 12810, 12831, and 12846, and any other provisions of those orders, to the extent that they are not modified by or inconsistent with this new order, remain in full force and are unaffected by this order.

Sincerely,

WILLIAM J. CLINTON

NOTE: Identical letters were sent to Thomas S. Foley, Speaker of the House of Representatives, and Albert Gore, Jr., President of the Senate. The Executive order and the related proclamation of October 25 on immigration measures with respect to U.N. Security Council Resolution 942 are listed in Appendix D at the end of this volume.

Statement on Technology Reinvestment Awards
October 25, 1994

Today, commercial firms are the source of many of the advanced technologies that are needed to keep our military the most powerful in the world. The winning projects I am announcing link commercial industry and defense needs to keep America strong, militarily and economically.

NOTE: This statement was included in a White House statement announcing the winners of Federal matching grants from the Technology Reinvestment Project.

Statement on Signing the Dietary Supplement Health and Education Act of 1994
October 25, 1994

Today I am pleased to sign S. 784, the "Dietary Supplement Health and Education Act of 1994." After several years of intense efforts, manufacturers, experts in nutrition, and legislators, acting in a conscientious alliance with consumers at the grassroots level, have moved successfully to bring common sense to the treatment of dietary supplements under regulation and law.

More often than not, the Government has been their ally. And the private market has responded to this development with the manufacture of an increasing variety of safe supplements.

But in recent years, the regulatory scheme designed to promote the interests of consumers and a healthful supply of good food has been used instead to complicate choices consumers have made to advance their nutritional and dietary goals. With perhaps the best of intentions agencies of government charged with protecting the food supply and the rights of consumers have paradoxically limited the information to make healthful choices in an area that means a great deal to over 100 million people.

And so, an historic agreement was finally reached in the Congress this year that balances their interests with the Nation's continued interest in guaranteeing the quality and safety of foods and products available to consumers. This agreement was embodied in S. 784, legislation sponsored in the Senate by Senator Orrin Hatch and Senator Tom Harkin, in the House by Congressman Bill Richardson, and passed with the help of Senator Edward Kennedy, Congressman John Dingell, Congressman Henry Waxman, and scores of cosponsors in the House and Senate.

Simply said, the legislation amends the Federal Food, Drug, and Cosmetic Act to establish new standards for the regulation of dietary supplements including vitamins, minerals, and herbal remedies.

The passage of this legislation speaks to the determination of the legislators involved, and I appreciate their work. But most important, it speaks to the diligence with which an unofficial army of nutritionally conscious people worked democratically to change the laws in an area deeply important to them. In an era of greater consciousness among people about the impact of what they eat on how they live, indeed, how long they live, it is appropriate that we have finally reformed the way Government treats consumers and these supplements in a way that encourages good health.

WILLIAM J. CLINTON

The White House,
October 25, 1994.

NOTE: S. 784, approved October 25, was assigned Public Law No. 103–417. This statement was released by the Office of the Press Secretary on October 26.

Exchange With Reporters Prior to Discussions With President Hosni Mubarak of Egypt in Cairo
October 26, 1994

Middle East Peace Process

Q. What's your message for Chairman Arafat this morning, Mr. President?

The President. Well, first of all, I'm delighted to start this trip with President Mubarak. After all, Egypt has been the leader in the peace process all the way and has set a standard for many years now and has helped all the parties, including the United States, to pursue this peace process.

I'm looking forward to having a chance to talk with the President. And then we're going to talk with Chairman Arafat about what we can do to keep the process going and the importance of condemning terrorism and working together to go forward.

Q. Do you have any ideas on the subject?

The President. A few. We'll be talking about it.

Have you been to sleep, Helen [Helen Thomas, United Press International]? Have you all had any sleep?

Q. No.

Note: The exchange began at 8 a.m. at El-Qubbeh Palace. A tape was not available for verification of the content of this exchange.

The President's News Conference With President Hosni Mubarak of Egypt in Cairo
October 26, 1994

President Mubarak. Good morning. It is a source of great pleasure for me to welcome President Clinton and his able assistants in Cairo on behalf of the people of Egypt. We look upon President Clinton with great admiration and esteem. He's a man of courage and conviction, a man of ideals and action alike.

Since he has assumed his awesome responsibilities, he has demonstrated an exceptional ability to combine his evident concern over domestic matters with a genuine interest in foreign policy. Under his leadership, the United States has played a pivotal role in the maintenance of world peace and security. Such a role is indispensable in an era of profound change and—*[inaudible]*. It was only natural that the Middle East received much attention from the President and the American people.

During the past 2 years, much has been achieved on the road to peace. To a great extent, this was due to the active role the Clinton administration undertook with vigor and perseverance. And it has been a success story all along.

We are not unmindful of the obstacles that remain on the road to a comprehensive and lasting peace. But we are determined to pursue that goal with vigor and determination. As you move to consolidate the steps which were taken on the Palestinian and Jordanian tracks, we cannot lose sight of the centrality of the Syrian and Lebanese track. Today I discussed with President Clinton the necessity of making meaningful progress on these tracks. I assured our guests that President Asad is wholeheartedly committed to a just and honorable peace. So is the Lebanese leadership. Hence, we should spare no effort in order to reach that goal without delay. In the weeks ahead, we shall work together and more in harmony toward that end.

We must rekindle hope in the hearts of the peace-loving forces in the region. And with the same goal we must fight despair and violence. We deplore the killing of innocent people and attempts to spread fear and hatred. The time has come for healing all wounds of the past and of creating a better future for Arabs as well as Israelis.

President Clinton, you have made a great contribution to the solidification of the ever-growing friendship between our two nations. Through your words and deeds alike you have cemented our partnership for peace and development. This role is highly appreciated by our people.

In our discussion this morning we explored new ways and means for strengthening our cooperation even further. We are determined to make it a stable and everlasting aspect of our policy.

In short, we are in agreement that this relationship, which is based on mutual respect and mutuality, is a constant element of progress and stability, a model for cooperation and solidarity among nations.

Much credit goes to you, Mr. President, and your vision and sound judgment. I wish you success in the efforts you are exerting during this trip. Your decision to make Cairo your first stop is a good omen, for it is here in this proud city that the first and most difficult steps and decisions towards peace were taken.

May God Almighty bless your endeavor and guide your steps. And thank you.

President Clinton. Thank you. Thank you, President Mubarak.

It is fitting that we begin this day, which will include the celebration of a new peace between Israel and Jordan, in Egypt with President Mubarak. Egypt's courageous example set at Camp David and President Mubarak's tireless leadership in the peace process have paved the way to the historic progress we celebrate on this day. Mr. President, this region, indeed, the entire international community, owe to you and your nation a deep debt of gratitude. Egypt led the way. And I am proud to stand here with you, the United States is proud to stand with Egypt as partners in the pursuit of peace.

Today I reaffirmed to President Mubarak my commitment to do all I can to achieve a comprehensive settlement. The peace we seek calls on the parties to do more than lay down arms. We seek reconciliation between peoples, cooperation between governments joined by a vision of shared destiny. The United States has walked each step with Egypt. Despite many sacrifices, the journey to peace has brought Egypt to better times. After so many years of conflict and so many casualties, no Egyptian has died in battle against Israel since 1973.

Now we're on the verge of seeing those and other benefits extend throughout the region. I salute President Mubarak for the crucial role he has played in bringing the Palestinians and the Israelis together. Your work helped make possible the historic handshake between Prime Minister Rabin and Chairman Arafat in the White House last year.

To keep moving on that front, President Mubarak and I have just met with Chairman Arafat. We had a useful discussion about the need to fully implement the Declaration of Principles between the Palestinian Liberation Organization and Israel. We reviewed the progress toward elections and the early empowerment of Palestinian authorities in the West Bank.

I made it clear that the United States places great importance on establishing strong and accountable democratic institutions. I also told Chairman Arafat that as the Palestinian administration starts to work on setting up a system to raise revenues, the United States will lead an international effort to support the Israeli-Palestinian agreement on early empowerment in the West Bank.

We also discussed a matter of great urgency, the absolute necessity to combat Hamas and all other extremist groups using terror to perpetuate hatred. We agreed that the same courage is needed to fight the enemies of peace that Chairman Arafat showed in making peace.

I want to reaffirm that the United States will stand with all friends of peace. Terrorists must not be allowed—must not be allowed—to intimidate the peoples of this region into abandoning the peace process. At this moment of opportunity, those who perpetuate violence pose the greatest threat to the Palestinian people and to all Arab people. The enemies of peace are desperate, but they must not defeat the hopeful forces of the future.

President Mubarak and I discussed our determination to stand as partners in this and many other efforts. We have worked on many things around the world in the past; we do in the present. I congratulated him again on the success of the remarkable population conference here at Cairo. We will continue to work together on many fronts, including the need to stand up and repel the Iraqi threat to Kuwait.

Our countries share a commitment to promote economic growth in Egypt as well. At my request, the Vice President met with President Mubarak when he was in Cairo in September, and they initiated a new partnership for economic growth. Earlier this week our two countries agreed to establish new committees to support this partnership. The Vice President will be saying more about that in the next few months. I believe he'll have the opportunity to come back here.

Again, let me thank President and Mrs. Mubarak for their gracious reception. And let me thank President Mubarak especially again for his leadership in this process. I am confident we would not be where we are today had it not been for him.

Thank you, sir.

Middle East Peace Process

Q. I'd like to ask both President Mubarak and President Clinton how Chairman Arafat responded to your saying that it is an absolute necessity to combat Hamas and other groups of terror and how both of you interpret Chairman Arafat's comment about the Israel-Jordan agreement, saying that those who support it should drink sea water?

President Mubarak. Chairman Arafat is very keen to put the violence of Hamas to an end. I remember when one of the events took place a couple of weeks ago, he did his utmost and he captured several of the people of Hamas when he heard that the man—the soldier is still in Gaza, although it proved that the man was not in Gaza. He came here the second day, and Secretary Christopher was here, and he told him about the effort which Arafat did to avoid this trouble. Hamas needs cooperation between both sides, so as not to spoil the peace process and the progress of peace in the area.

President Clinton. I felt that we got a very firm and unambiguous response. Certainly, the position that I took, the position that President Mubarak took was very firm and unambiguous. And Chairman Arafat said he would continue to do all he could to combat terrorism, specifically Hamas but other groups as well. And I am satisfied with the response that he gave, and I believe he will attempt to implement it.

We discussed that and a whole range of other issues. But I believe, on this issue, he will continue to do that. He understands, I think, clearly that Hamas is his enemy now, that once you become a partner in the peace process you have to fight for peace and those who seek to undermine it are seeking to undermine you. I think he clearly understands that. And I was satisfied with the answer I received. And we will have to now proceed to achieve the results. But I think the understanding there is clear.

Q. And what about the Israel-Jordan treaty, his response——

President Clinton. We did not discuss his comments yesterday. I can tell you this: I think that this is a great day, and I think that it will continue the process. And I agree with President Mubarak, we have to also move on with Syria and with Lebanon. But clearly, the peace process is moving in the right direction.

Q. U.S. President, you are the first American President to visit Syria in 20 years. Do you expect to narrow the gap between the Israeli and the Syrian viewpoints or produce a breakthrough on this track before the end of 1994?

President Clinton. I expect that we will make some progress. I expect that we will narrow the gap. I do not expect this trip to Syria to produce a dramatic breakthrough in the immediate aftermath of the trip, but I believe we have made a good deal of progress in the last few months. I have been quite encouraged by that, and it is on that basis and my conviction that both President Asad and Prime Minister Rabin and their two peoples want to continue to work for peace that I go to Syria.

In terms of the timing of a breakthrough, I don't want to commit myself to that because that really is up to the parties. They must determine the substance and the timing. But I believe we should move as quickly as possible, and I am pushing it as quickly as possible. I cannot give you a date.

Q. President Clinton, earlier this week your Secretary of State spoke in Washington, and he talked about putting international pressure on Iran to deal with Hamas. He didn't name the Western states, but it's clear that there are some, perhaps including Germany and France, that are believed to be trading with Iran. What kind of international effort do you plan to lead to crack down on Iran? And I'm wondering whether President Mubarak can talk about perhaps what the Arab world might be willing to do to put pressure on other terrorist states as well.

President Clinton. Well, first of all, let me say that what we want to do with regard to Hamas and these other terrorist groups is to try to move to put pressure on all points of support for them that we are able to determine. And that would include an effort that would go beyond Iran.

Obviously, there are things that can be done that are well-known to all of you in the form of refraining from having economic relations. And we're going to ask all of our friends throughout the world to support this, all the people who are the friends of peace and the enemies of terrorism. We ask them to recognize that they cannot have it both ways.

Q. President Clinton, in connection with terrorism, and also Chairman Arafat, how will the U.S. objectively evaluate what he is doing to combat terrorism? And is there any plan that the U.S. would have to peg the amount of money that it would raise for the implementation of the agreement between Israel and PLO to his cracking down on terrorism?

President Clinton. Let me answer the second part of that question first, because I think it's important to get this out. There was absolutely no discussion of tying any effort—of aid by the United States or the international community to this effort. The effort to combat terrorism is the first step that is the precondition to making the whole peace process work.

So we did discuss the need that we have always acknowledged and supported to continue with elections in the territories, to have economic development assistance. But there was no quid pro quo discussion. Chairman Arafat started the discussion himself with his desire to combat terrorist groups and with his willingness to do all that he could.

I think that we would all admit that it is impossible to guarantee 100 percent success in any effort. I mean, in the United States we're not 100 percent successful in combating crime or organized crime. What we want is 100 percent effort. And I think it will be obvious to the Israelis, who are partners in the peace process with the PLO, and to the United States and to the other parties whether that effort is being made. I must say that from my own observation, based on what our own people have told me, there has been an increasing effort in the last several weeks on the part of Chairman Arafat and the authorities in the territories to do what they can on this front. And I think it will continue to increase. And I think President Mubarak agrees with that.

President Mubarak. Yes, I agree with that.

Q. President Clinton, sir, what is the statement you're making after speaking so strongly against terrorism by visiting Syria, a country which the U.S. still labels as an advocate of terrorism?

And President Mubarak, please, did you discuss the issue of the sanctions imposed against Libya with President Clinton, and if so, do you hope for a lifting—a complete or partial lifting of these sanctions soon?

President Clinton. Let me answer the Syrian question first and then defer to President Mubarak.

Terrorism is still an issue between our two countries, and it cannot be ignored. But the most successful way to end terrorism in this part of the world is to have a comprehensive peace in the Middle East. Syria is a partner in the peace process. We are making progress in that process. I believe President Asad wants a comprehensive peace and wants an end to terrorism as a part of that. And therefore, I think it would be a mistake for me not to take this opportunity, since I'm in the region, to try to go to Syria to further the peace process.

President Mubarak. Concerning the sanctions in Libya and Iraq, we just touched these two issues in general. They were on my agenda. We just had a very short discussion about it.

Q. Are we still at the status quo now as it is, or will there be developments with regards to these sanctions?

President Mubarak. This needs further discussions with the United States.

Q. The question from Egyptian television is addressed to the two heads of state. President Clinton, President Mubarak, what's the American viewpoint and the Egyptian viewpoint re-spectively on the delay on implementation of self-rule in the territories?

President Clinton. The American viewpoint is that we should proceed as quickly as we can. We want to have—we want to support the elections process, and we want to support the multinational development process in the territories. And we do support that. We also are very sensitive to and understand the security concerns of Israel. So one of the things that I had hoped to do in my meeting with Chairman Arafat, and again in my meetings in Israel, is to try to work through the differences on both sides about that so we can proceed with the elections and proceed with the development process. I think we should do it sooner rather than later, giving proper concern to the security needs of Israel.

President Mubarak. Concerning the Egyptian point of view toward this, we are with the continuation of the implementation of the declaration principles. But if we are going to respond to terroristic action, this will delay the peace process and this will not lead to any security and any comprehensive peace in the whole area.

Thank you very much.

Q. And Mr. President, please, did Chairman Arafat ask your assistance or mediation to solve the problem of the holy places in Jerusalem between Jordan and Palestine?

President Clinton. No, we did not discuss that at all.

President Mubarak. Let's just leave it at that.

NOTE: The President's 75th news conference began at approximately 9:45 a.m. at El-Qubbeh Palace. In his remarks, he referred to Yasser Arafat, Chairman, Palestine Liberation Organization.

Remarks at the Signing Ceremony for the Israel-Jordan Peace Treaty at the Border Between Israel and Jordan
October 26, 1994

King Hussein, President Weizman, Prime Minister Rabin, Prime Minister Majali, Crown Prince Hassan, Foreign Minister Peres, Foreign Minister Kozyrev, Mr. Secretary of State; to the people of Jordan and Israel, with a special thanks to those who are our cheering section up there—[*laughter*]—we thank you all.

At the dawn of this peace of a generation, in this ancient place we celebrate the history and the faith of Jordanians and Israelis. But we break the chains of the past that for too long have kept you shackled in the shadows of strife and suffering. We thank those who have worked for peace before. We celebrate the efforts of brave leaders who saw the bright horizon of this dawn, even while the darkness lingered.

This vast bleached desert hides great signs of life. Today we see the proof of it, for peace between Jordan and Israel is no longer a mirage. It is real. It will take root in this soil. It will grow to great heights and shelter generations to come.

Today we honor the constant and devoted work of two courageous leaders, two who have risked everything so that their children and their children's children need fight nor fear no more.

King Hussein, today in this arid place, you bring to full flower the memory of the man who taught you to seek peace, your grandfather, King Abdullah. When he was martyred four decades ago, he left you with a great burden and a great dream. He believed that one day, on both sides of the River Jordan, Arab and Jew would live in peace. How bravely you have shouldered that burden and carried that dream. Now after so much danger and so much hardship, Your Majesty, your day has come. Truly, you have fulfilled your grandfather's legacy.

Prime Minister Rabin, you have spent a lifetime as a soldier, fighting first to establish your country and then for so long to defend it. For a lifetime, you have fought with skill and tenacity and courage, simply to achieve a secure and lasting peace for your people. Now you have given them the hope of life after the siege. In your own words, you have now given them the challenge to furnish the house of Israel and make it a home. As a general, you have won many battles through strength and courage. But now, through strength and courage, you command the army of peace, and you have won the greatest victory of all. We salute you.

As has been said before, this treaty is the product of many hands. Crown Prince Hassan and Foreign Minister Peres know better than any of us that peace does not spring full-grown. It requires cultivation. It requires patience and care. We salute their devotion and persistence, and the wise and determined counsel of Secretary Christopher. We are in all their debt, and we thank them.

I say to the people of Israel and Jordan: Now you must make this peace real, to turn no man's land into every man's home, to take down the barbed wire, to remove the deadly mines, to help the wounds of war to heal. Open your borders. Open your hearts. Peace is more than an agreement on paper. It is feeling. It is activity. It is devotion.

The forces of terror will try to hold you back. Already they take deadly aim at the future of peace. In their zeal to kill hope and keep hatred alive, they would deny all that peace can bring to your children. We cannot, we must not, we will not let them succeed.

The United States stands with you. Since President Truman first recognized Israel, we have wished for and worked for comprehensive peace between Israel and all of her neighbors. On behalf of all Americans, including millions of Jewish and Arab Americans for whom this day means so much, I thank you for trusting America to help you arrive at this moment. The American people are very proud of the opportunity we have had.

And now let the work of progress bear fruit. Here at the first of many crossing points to be open, people from every corner of the Earth will soon come to share in the wonders of your lands. There are resources to be found in the desert, minerals to be drawn from the sea, water to be separated from salt and used to fertilize the fields. Here where slaves in ancient times were forced to take their chisels to the stone, the Earth, as the Koran says, will stir and swell and bring forth life. The desert, as Isaiah prophesied, shall rejoice and blossom.

Here your people will drink water from the same well and savor together the fruit of the vine. As you seize this moment, be assured that you will redeem every life sacrificed along the long road that brought us to this day. You will take the hatred out of hearts, and you will pass along to your children a peace for the generations.

Your Majesty, Mr. Prime Minister, here in the Great Rift Valley you have bridged the tragic rift that separated your people for too long. Here in this region, which is the home of not only both your faiths but mine, I say: Blessed are the peacemakers, for they shall inherit the Earth.

NOTE: The President spoke at approximately 1:50 p.m. at the Wadi Araba border crossing. In his remarks, he referred to King Hussein, Crown Prince Hassan, and Prime Minister Abd al-Salam al-Majali of Jordan; President Ezer Weizman, Prime Minister Yitzhak Rabin, and Foreign Minister Shimon Peres of Israel; and Foreign Minister Andrey Kozyrev of Russia.

Remarks to the Jordanian Parliament in Amman, Jordan
October 26, 1994

Your Majesties, Prime Minister Majali, Mr. President, Mr. Speaker, Members of the Parliament, citizens of Jordan, citizens of the United States:

Mr. President, thank you for that generous introduction. Your Majesty, thank you for welcoming me to your beautiful country and for giving me the opportunity to accept your kind hospitality after your many visits to our Capital.

I thank you all for the honor to address this assembly and to reflect with you on this historic day of peace. On this day, Your Majesty, descendent of the Prophet Mohammed, in making peace with your neighbor has done even more than fulfill the legacy of King Abdullah. You have sent a signal to the entire Arab world that peace is unstoppable.

On this day, in the desert of the Great Rift Valley, the people of Jordan stepped out of the shadows of strife. You made a bold choice: You rejected the dark forces of terror and extremism. You embraced the bright promise of tolerance and moderation. You spurned those who would drag you back into the hostile past. You chose instead a future of opportunity and tranquillity for your children. The United States admires and supports the choice you have made. And we will stand with you in months and years ahead.

Today the people of Jordan pay homage to those who led the great Arab revolt for freedom, independence, and unity. You honor the memory of three generations of Jordanians who gave their lives in defense of your country, what Your Majesty has called the shattering toll in blood and tears, the waste of youth, and the grief of our forefathers.

In your address to our Congress 2 months ago, Your Majesty called for an end to the unnatural and sinister state that has spread fear and isolation. You urged your people to commit themselves to establishing a new, humane, and natural order. Now the people of Jordan have said: Enough of blood, enough of tears. It is time to move on. In the words of Your Majesty, they have said, "Let us make what is abnormal, normal."

All over the world people of different faiths and all walks of life celebrated this day. All over the world people of good will rejoiced at the leadership of King Hussein, who, with his courage, discipline, and vision, honored King Abdullah's wish as he embarked on his last journey to Jerusalem, when he said, "Do your very best to see that my work is not lost. Continue it in the service of our people." Now it can be said, Your Majesty has met King Abdullah's charge, and in so doing you are meeting the challenge of history and advancing the cause of peace throughout the Arab world.

Today's victory is also in keeping with the history of Jordan, which has long been a model for progress and a voice of moderation in the Arab world. From the beginning, when King Abdullah brought together disparate peoples in a united kingdom, following this path has never been easy for you. Yet in the midst of hard times and conflicts, you are building a society devoted to the growth of pluralism and openness. You have established a Parliament where all voices can be heard. You have nurtured a growing partnership between Your Majesty and all Jordanian citizens.

Your nation's commitment to pluralism has been matched by a remarkable generosity of spirit, for you have opened your doors to millions of your Arab brethren. And they have come here, year after year, seeking refuge in your nation, and here they have found a true home. In return, they have enriched your economy and your culture.

My country, a nation of immigrants from every area of this world, respects your openness and your understanding that diversity is a challenge but it can be a source of strength. America's commitment to Jordan is as strong tonight as it was when Your Majesty traveled to the United States for the first time 35 years ago and met President Dwight Eisenhower, the first of eight Presidents you have known.

The President and Your Majesty discussed the great threat that communism then posed to America and to the Arab world. And when President Eisenhower asked what America could do to help, Your Majesty said then, "We need more than anything else the feeling that we do not stand alone." Now, at a time when those who preached hate and terror pose the greatest threat to the cause of peace, President Eisenhower's response still holds true. Thirty-five years ago he told Your Majesty, "Our country knows what you have done. Believe me, we won't let you down."

Both of us, Jordan and America, are fighting the same battle. Today, that battle is the struggle for peace. And I say again, on behalf of the United States, we will not let you down.

From the outset, America's commitment to a comprehensive peace in the Middle East has been backed by a strong pledge that whenever Arabs and Israelis turned the page on the past, the United States would work with them to write a real, practical future of hope. Those who take risks for peace must not stand alone. We will work with Jordan to meet your legitimate defense requirements and to give you the security you deserve.

But for peace to endure, it must not only provide protection, it must produce tangible improvements in the quality of ordinary citizens' lives and, in so doing, to give those citizens a real stake in preserving the peace. The United States understands the need for peace to produce real benefits, and we are taking steps to meet that goal.

We have pledged to forgive all of Jordan's debt to our own Government, and we have encouraged, indeed urged, other countries to do the same. From one end of your border with Israel to the other, the U.S.-Jordan-Israel Trilateral Economic Commission is preparing to invest in progress. Visionary designs to develop the Great Rift Valley, ambitious projects to produce more energy and fresh water, new efforts to extract minerals from the Dead Sea, and exciting plans to encourage visitors to share the wonders of your lands, all these are being brought to life.

Making these dreams real, of course, will require new investment and new capital. To that end, the United States supports the creation of a Middle East bank for cooperation and development. And we will take the lead in consultations with governments within and beyond the region to ensure that the bank is properly structured. Our Government's Overseas Private Investment Corporation is establishing a $75 million regional investment fund to encourage American investment in projects like those in the Rift Valley. And the United States will actively pursue practical means of expanding trade and investment opportunities with Jordan. We will consider a wide array of measures, including a bilateral investment treaty, other trade arrangements, and other initiatives that will lessen barriers to trade and increase prosperity in your area.

These critical steps, and others to provide your citizens with the economic opportunities they deserve, are vital to building peace in Jordan and throughout the Middle East. If people do not feel these benefits, if poverty persists in breeding despair and killing hope, then the purveyors of fear will find fertile ground. Our goal must be to spread prosperity and security to all. After all, the chance to live in harmony with our neighbors and to build a better life for our children is the hope that links us all together. Whether we worship in a mosque in Irbid, a Baptist church like my own in Little Rock, Arkansas, or a synagogue in Haifa, we are bound together in that hope.

Yet, though we know in every corner of the world people share that hope, there are those who insist that between America and the Middle East there are impassable religious and other obstacles to harmony, that our beliefs and our cultures must somehow inevitably clash. But I believe they are wrong. America refuses to accept that our civilizations must collide. We respect Islam. Every day in our own land, millions of our own citizens answer the Moslem call to prayer. And we know the traditional values of Islam, devotion to faith and good works, to family and society, are in harmony with the best of American ideals. Therefore, we know our people, our faiths, our cultures can live in harmony with each other.

But in the Middle East, as elsewhere across the world, the United States does see a contest, a contest between forces that transcend civilization, a contest between tyranny and freedom, terror and security, bigotry and tolerance, isolation and openness. It is the age-old struggle between fear and hope.

This is the conflict that grips the Middle East today. On one side stand the forces of terror and extremism, who cloak themselves in the rhetoric of religion and nationalism but behave in ways that contradict the very teachings of their faith and mock their patriotism. These forces of reaction feed on disillusionment, on poverty, on despair. They stoke the fires of violence. They seek to destroy the progress of this peace. To them, I say: You cannot succeed. You will not succeed. You must not succeed, for you are the past, not the future.

The people of Jordan and all those throughout the Arab world who are working for peace are choosing progress over decline; choosing reason, not ruin; choosing to build up, not tear down; choosing tomorrow, not yesterday. The people of Jordan on this day, through King Hussein, have pledged themselves to a treaty based on a fundamental law of humanity, that what we have in common is more important than our differences.

This was the message of Moses' farewell address to the children of Israel as they gathered to cross the River Jordan, when he said, "I have set before you life and death, blessings and curses. Choose life so that you and your descendants may live." And it is the message the Prophet Mohammed brought to the peoples of other faiths when he said, "There is no argument between us and you. God shall bring us together, and unto him is the homecoming."

Today the people of Jordan and the people of Israel have reached across the Jordan River. They have chosen life. They have made a homecoming. And tonight we say, thanks be to God, *Ilham du Illah.*

NOTE: The President spoke at 9:32 p.m. in the Chamber at the Parliament. In his remarks, he referred to Ahmad Lowzi, President of the Senate, and S'ad Ha'il Srour, Speaker of the Lower House.

Exchange With Reporters Prior to Discussions With President Hafiz al-Asad of Syria in Damascus
October 27, 1994

Q. Gentlemen, do you think you will be able to agree on new steps toward peace today? President Asad?

President Asad. We hope so. If we don't have this desire, we wouldn't have any incentive for such a meeting. And so the peace process needs efforts, and it always has its own difficulties. People think that with a magic word they might be able to achieve peace, but this is not possible.

President Clinton. Thank you. We're working hard.

NOTE: The exchange began at approximately 9:15 a.m. at the Presidential Palace. A tape was not available for verification of the content of this exchange.

The President's News Conference With President Hafiz al-Asad of Syria in Damascus
October 27, 1994

President Asad. President Clinton, ladies and gentlemen, I am pleased to welcome President Clinton in Damascus, the oldest continuously inhabited city in the world, in the heart of a region which witnessed the dawn of human civilizations and the cradle of divine religions. This region, whose peoples have long suffered, especially throughout this century, from the horrors of wars, the bitterness of conflict and bloodshed, hopes at last to enjoy peace and stability.

The visit of President Clinton at the head of the high-level American delegation to our country and the positive and fruitful talks we had today constitute an important step towards the realization of this noble objective to which the people of the region and the world at large aspire.

Our talks today have focused on the different aspects of the peace process and its developments. In this regard, I would like to express my deep satisfaction with the fact that our views were identical regarding the importance of achieving a comprehensive peace on the basis of Security Council Resolutions 242 and 338 and the principle of land for peace and that the solution we seek has to be just in order to be stable and lasting.

I have reaffirmed to President Clinton the continued commitment of Syria to the peace process and her serious pursuit of a comprehensive and just peace as a strategic choice that secures Arab rights, ends the Israeli occupation of the Arab land in conformity of the Security Council Resolutions 242, 338, and 425, and enables all peoples of the region to live in peace, security, and dignity.

I also stressed to President Clinton—emanating from the principle, full withdrawal for full peace, I stressed to President Clinton the readiness of Syria to commit itself to the objective requirements of peace through the establishment of peaceful, normal relations with Israel in return for Israel's full withdrawal from the Golan to the line of June 4, 1967, and from the south of Lebanon.

In this context, the statement of President Clinton on the eve of his trip to the region asserting that no comprehensive peace can be achieved in the region without Syria is a realistic expression that reflects an international consensus regarding this fact. Our nation has sacrificed hundreds of thousands of martyrs, not out of love for war or fighting but in defense of its rights, dignity, and land. That's why we aspire today to transform the region from a state of war to a state of peace: a peace that renders to each party its rights, ends occupation, saves the blood of the innocent, and preserves man's dignity; a peace that prevails throughout the region and enables its peoples, both Arabs and Israelis, to live in security, stability, and prosperity.

Finally, I would like to convey greetings to the American people through President Clinton and to thank President Clinton for his personal efforts and the efforts of his aides. I would like to express my readiness to work with him for achieving a real, comprehensive, and just peace in the region.

Thank you.

President Clinton. I am glad to have had the opportunity to stop in Syria to meet with President Asad. After yesterday's signing of the peace treaty between Israel and Jordan, I came to Damascus today to continue working for our common goal of peace in the Middle East.

During our meeting this morning, President Asad and I affirmed our common commitment to that goal and want to accelerate progress toward our objective. Yesterday's signing represents an important step forward. But our job will not be done and we will not rest until peace agreements between Israel and Syria and Israel and Lebanon are achieved.

A Syrian-Israeli agreement is key to achieving a comprehensive peace. Given Syria's important regional role, it will inevitably broaden the circle of Arab States willing to embrace peace. And it will build confidence throughout the area that peace will endure.

My talks here with President Asad are a sign of our mutual determination to achieve a peace of the brave as quickly as possible. The United States will do everything possible to help make that a reality.

For peace to endure, it must also be just. Peace between Israel and Syria must be based on United Nations Security Council Resolutions 242 and 338 and the principle of land for peace. Peace must also be real, more than mere words on paper, more than just the absence of war. Nations must establish normal, peaceful relations.

Peace must also be secure for both sides. Security for one side should not come at the expense of the other's security. Peace must guarantee security against surprise attack by any side. And peace must enable the parties to invest in economic development, rather than military might.

All sides must enjoy stability and tranquillity. Violence must cease. Borders must no longer be subject to aggression, terrorist infiltration, violent acts, or bombardment. The murderous acts of terror that we have witnessed over the past weeks have two targets: first, innocent people who have been killed and wounded; and second, the very peace that President Asad supports. All who work for peace must condemn these terrorist acts. President Asad and I agree that the peace process allows no place for the killing of innocent civilians.

I also told President Asad of my desire to see the relations between our two nations improve. In an era of peace, improved relations would benefit both countries and improve regional stability and security.

Finally, I want to tell the Syrian people how very glad I am to have the opportunity to visit your country, if only briefly. Like your neighbors in Israel, you have waited too long and have suffered too much to be further denied the hope for a new and better future.

On behalf of the American people, I pledge that I will work with President Asad to do everything possible to make real this new and peaceful future.

Thank you.

Middle East Peace Process

Q. President Asad, you do seem to hold, in the minds of many, the key to a comprehensive peace in the Middle East, and you have now expressed the bottom line of what will be true peace in the Middle East. How do you intend to go about getting it? And how soon will it occur?

And President Clinton, do you agree that there should be a full withdrawal of Israeli troops from the Golan Heights to Lebanon and Syrian troops from Lebanon to make a real peace in the Middle East?

President Clinton. I think I answered the question in my statement. We believe that the peace between Israel and Syria must be based upon the United Nations Security Council resolutions. And we made some progress today in our own talks, the details of which, as you would expect, I am not free to discuss. But we are moving forward today, consistent with the United Nations Security Council resolutions, and we will continue to do it until we have a peace that is based on those resolutions.

President Asad. For a long time we've been moving according to a mechanism that pushes us to achieve the peace process. We are relying in this, as President Clinton said, on Security Council resolutions and on different activities undertaken by all the parties, particularly the United States of America. We achieved a few

things, and we didn't achieve other things. We are going to continue our pursuit in order to reach there, in this way or in any other more effective way, in order to achieve peace sooner.

[*At this point, a question was asked in Arabic, but a translation was not provided.*]

President Clinton. I didn't get the translation. Am I on the wrong channel?

Q. [*Inaudible*]—security and stability of the region?

President Clinton. Well, first, as I said, I think the role of Syria in the security and stability of the region is absolutely critical. I don't think we can finish a comprehensive peace or maintain peace in the region unless there is peace between Syria and Israel. And I think the benefits that would come to the people of both countries over the next several years are enormous if such a peace can be achieved.

My view of President Asad, based on our two meetings and our many conversations over the telephone and his constant willingness to receive the Secretary of State and other representatives of the United States, is that he is committed to achieving a peace. He is clearly a very effective and determined advocate for the interests of his country and its people. But I believe he wants peace, and I believe we will achieve it.

Q. President Asad, the majority of the Israeli public, according to the polls, does not believe it is physically safe to give up the Golan Heights. This mistrust has been added by the fact that you haven't visited Israel; you haven't met with Mr. Rabin; there's no direct talks; you haven't spelled out the exact terms of peace; your support for 10 rejectionist groups in Damascus and Hezbollah. All this taken together, sir, I want to know what assurance can you give the Israeli public—now that you are able to address them through this press conference, they could hear you—what assurance can you give them that withdrawal will indeed lead to true peace and not to the next war? Thank you very much.

President Asad. The concern of any country in the world about its security does not justify for that particular country to preserve the lands of other states, of other countries. And countries which fought throughout history did not put conditions for achieving peace that one party should visit the other or should not visit the other.

The issue is not concerning rhetorical or formal issues, not with a visit. There are people who visited Israel before, but he himself complained—when he was in office, he complained and went on for a long time before being able to reach a peace agreement with Israel.

The important point is that the assumptions or the attempts to confine the peace process to small things, to formal things concerning the visit of one party to the other, or that one of us is concerned about security and that he should arrive there or we should take them there—to be secure and not to have any concern from anything—this was never there in reality or in books.

There's nothing we have that proves our desire for peace except our saying that we want peace. And anyone who does not believe what we are saying, he would have no other way for peace. It would be him who doesn't want peace.

What also makes us believe that they want peace? We have many proofs which we have against them that they do not want peace and not us who don't want peace. Such matters to a certain extent were the subject of discussion and contemplation between me and President Clinton, and we are both convinced, as I believe, we are convinced that the United States is serious in pushing the peace process forward.

And as I've heard from President Clinton, he has proved that we are serious. Why the others are not convinced that we are serious— although I heard statements from Israeli officials which say that Syria is serious in the peace process—and probably what I remember is that Rabin was in the front, he was in the front of those people who said a short while ago that Syria is serious in wanting peace. And I hope I remember quite well, I hope my memory is accurate in this. I heard him saying and asserting that Syria is serious in the peace process. So of whom is he afraid?

Q. Mr. President, in your speech today you emphasized the significance of security for both sides, i.e., Syria and Israel. On numerous occasions, Israeli leaders have sought preferential and rather advantageous security arrangements as a precondition for any peace pact with Syria. It's common knowledge that Israel possesses a huge arsenal of both conventional and mass destruction weapons, refuses to sign the nuclear arms nonproliferation treaty. How do you explain your endorsement of any future package of security arrangements in view of Israel's illogical and unacceptable precondition?

President Clinton. Well, first of all, I don't have to explain it because there won't be a peace agreement until both sides agree on security measures. And these are measures that to some extent are objective and to some extent are based on intuition, the feeling about what the possible future threats to Syria and to Israel are. But the United States has absolutely no hesitation in facilitating an open and straightforward exchange on those issues. Both sides will have to be satisfied that their security needs are met. And it's been my experience that countries, and particularly their leaders, are the best judge of what those security requirements are.

I don't believe for a moment that President Asad or Prime Minister Rabin would agree to a peace that would undermine the security of either nation. I think both of them will feel that they're more safe after the agreement rather than less safe. And that, to me, is the ultimate answer to this question.

Q. Mr. President, Secretary Christopher said that leaders, Presidents like yourself, are capable of bold moves that negotiators and diplomats aren't able to make. Can you tell us, were there any bold moves made today that you can report in terms of agreements on the Golan Heights or peace or terms of security?

President Clinton. Well, let me restate what I said earlier. First of all, I respect and I welcome the statement that President Asad has made here today, which goes beyond, in my judgment, the public diplomacy initiatives which have been made in the past. And I think that that statement should be reassuring to the people of Israel and should encourage more dialog and a greater willingness to pursue the peace process.

Secondly, in our private discussions there was some progress made, the details of which I will not and I should not discuss at this time. But we are moving forward. I will obviously see Prime Minister Rabin. We will have a frank and open discussion, as we always do, and we'll do what we can to keep moving forward.

Q. Mr. President Clinton, I have a question for you please. On numerous occasions the United States has stressed commitment to Israel's security and has provided Israel with all forms of financial and military support. How would you, Mr. President, reconcile your role as an honest intermediary in the peace process and your different way of dealing with Syria, which since the outset of the peace process has confirmed her seriousness and positive attitude to make the process successful?

President Clinton. The commitment of the United States to the security of Israel is something that goes back a long way, is of long standing, and is a given as a part of our foreign policy. I think that, notwithstanding that commitment, President Asad and all others in the Middle East who have dealt with us in this peace process would say that we have done our best, not just me but especially the Secretary of State, Mr. Ross, and others, to be an honest intermediary, to carry the legitimate concerns of the various parties, to try to help them make peace.

I would say to you, if I might, what I said in the previous answer: This peace agreement will never occur unless Israel and Syria sign with the absolute conviction that they will be more secure for signing it, not less secure. So whatever the details of the ultimate security arrangement are in this peace treaty, if it is signed by the leaders of both countries it will only be because they are both convinced that they will be safer after they sign than they are before. And we will support that in any reasonable way that we can.

Q. President Asad, President Clinton referred to terrorism earlier. As you are aware, the United States keeps Syria on its lists of countries that sponsor terrorism. Did you in this discussion promise not to sponsor terrorism anymore? Did you acknowledge that you, in fact, do? And can you tell us what the Syrian view is of terrorist activities?

President Asad. We did not discuss terrorism as a separate title. And the context of our discussions mentioned some of the examples of the discussions which took place between me and some of the senior American officials, these discussions which are related to accusing Syria of supporting terrorism. I said in these discussions to the American senior official, whom I asked then to mention for me one incident in which Syria has committed a terrorist action, and he was helpless. He was not able to mention one single incident in which Syria supported terrorism.

Terrorism—but as it is known, the problem of terrorism is an accusation, allegation because of the conflict between us and Syria. This is a fact. None of you, in my opinion, neither an Arab nor an American, who doesn't know that the reason for accusing Syria of terrorism—it's not because that Syrians and those who are in Syria are practicing terrorism but for reasons which are related to our stand regarding Israel. That's why this accusation went on for a very long time. And regardless of the desire of many people, both in Syria and the United States, at different times to solve this problem, we did not reach until now such a solution.

But at any rate, this was not one of the topics on the agenda in my discussion with President Clinton, and we are discussing what is more important. And our concern and focus was on the peace process.

If the time allows, I would have asked all of you, does any one of you have anything that proves that Syria has done a single terrorist act. But I don't want this to be a question to you because time does not allow such a question.

President Clinton. I'll make two points. First of all, in our meeting I said, and I believe President Asad agrees, that if we are going to have peace in the region and a peace agreement is made, then supporting those who try to undermine a peace that is made is inconsistent with that, particularly if they try to undermine it with terrorist tactics.

Secondly, we do not, we cannot, and we will not support the killing of innocent civilians. And President Asad has said repeatedly and said to me in our meeting today that he thought that was wrong as well, wherever it occurred, whether in the bus incident or in Hebron. So we did discuss it in that context.

I am here because I believe strongly that the best way to bring an end to terrorism in this part of the world is to achieve a comprehensive peace. And I believe we should keep working at it until we get the job done.

Q. President Clinton, you said many times that achieving a progress on the Syrian track is the basis for achieving a just and comprehensive peace in the region. And incidents have shown that the stalemate in this track now is caused by the rejection of Israel to fully withdraw from the Golan and from the south of Lebanon. Do you believe, Mr. President, that it is possible to overcome this obstacle during this visit of yours to Syria? Thank you.

President Clinton. No, I don't believe we'll announce a peace treaty on this visit. I don't believe we will finish the job on this visit. I do know we have made some progress here, and I expect to make some progress in Israel.

I believe, and I have told all the parties in the Middle East this, that we should build on what has happened and try to accelerate this peace process, not slow it down.

The people of Israel have been shaken by the incidents in the last couple of weeks. But I also think they must have been lifted up by the signing yesterday with Jordan. And they also should have been encouraged by President Asad's speech to the Parliament, by Foreign Minister Shara's interview on Israeli television, by the statement President Asad made here today.

So no, I wish we were signing a peace treaty on this trip. We won't do it, but we are making progress.

Thank you.

NOTE: The President's 76th news conference began at 12:55 p.m. in the Great Hall at the Presidential Palace. In his remarks, President Clinton referred to Dennis B. Ross, Special Middle East Coordinator, and Foreign Minister Farouk al-Shara of Syria. President Asad spoke in Arabic, and his remarks were translated by an interpreter.

Letter to Congressional Leaders Reporting on Iraq's Compliance With United Nations Security Council Resolutions
October 27, 1994

Dear Mr. Speaker: (*Dear Mr. President:*)

Consistent with the Authorization for Use of Military Force Against Iraq Resolution (Public Law 102–1), and as part of my effort to keep the Congress fully informed, I am reporting on the status of efforts to obtain Iraq's compliance with the resolutions adopted by the U.N. Security Council.

In light of the crisis on the Iraqi-Kuwaiti border that began in early October, this report begins with a brief account of the Iraqi provocation and U.S. responses through the U.N. Security Council vote of October 15. Subsequent developments in this crisis will be covered in the next report.

Iraq's recent behavior with respect to Kuwait has shown the world that it has not changed its threatening ways and cannot be trusted. In early October 1994, elements of the Hammurabi Division of the elite Iraqi Republican Guard were detected relocating to positions at Shaihah airfield in southern Iraq. This was the southernmost deployment of Republican Guard forces since the 1990–1991 Gulf War. By October 8, the 15th Mechanized Brigade of the Hammurabi Division had deployed to approximately 20 kilometers from the Kuwait border. Its artillery assets were oriented south toward Kuwait. At the same time, the Al Nida Division of the Republican Guard began moving from the Mosul rail yard and the Baghdad area to positions in south-ern Iraq. All these units were fully equipped with ammunition, food, and fuel, leading us to conclude that this was no mere exercise.

By October 8, these troop movements, combined with forces already in southern Iraq, brought Iraqi troop strength in southern Iraq to 64,000, organized into 8 divisions. By October 9, indications were present that logistic sites were being established in the vicinity of these deployments. Iraqi movements to the south continued, and by October 11, it was assessed that Iraq would be capable of launching an attack by October 13.

This provocation required a strong response. Accordingly, on October 8, 1994, I ordered the immediate deployment of additional U.S. military forces to the Persian Gulf. These deployments included the USS *George Washington* Carrier Battle Group and its accompanying cruise missile ships, a U.S. Marine Corps Expeditionary Unit, a U.S. Army Mechanized Task Force, and personnel to operate two additional Patriot missile batteries. On October 10, I further ordered the deployment of over 500 U.S. Air Force and Marine Corps combat and supporting aircraft to the region.

In response to these measures, the Iraqi government began ordering its forces to move to positions in the rear, around Nasariyah and Qalat Salih, north of Basra, but still within several hours of the Kuwaiti border. Had these forces remained deployed around Nasariyah, it would have constituted a significant enhancement of Iraq's capabilities in southern Iraq. By October 15, there were clear indications that most Iraqi forces that had been moved south since late September were being redeployed to their original locations. On October 15, 1994, the international community also demonstrated its strong resolve regarding this latest provocation when it passed unanimously U.N. Security Council Resolution (UNSCR) 949, which condemned Iraq's provocative behavior and demanded that Iraq immediately withdraw the units deployed in the south to their original positions, not utilize its forces to threaten its neighbors or U.N. operations, not redeploy or enhance its military capacity in southern Iraq, and cooperate fully with the U.N. Special Commission (UNSCOM).

As this recent episode shows, we continue to witness an Iraq that has failed to demonstrate its readiness to comply with the will of the international community. We will continue to insist that Iraq not threaten its neighbors or intimidate the United Nations as it takes steps to ensure that Iraq never again possesses weapons of mass destruction. The sanctions will be maintained until Iraq complies with all relevant provisions of U.N. Security Council resolutions. Indeed, these recent provocative Iraqi actions underscore the wisdom of the Security Council's September 14 decision not to modify the existing sanctions regime.

Cooperation by Iraq with the United Nations since 1991 has been meager, sporadic, selective, and opportunistic. Taken as a whole, Iraq's record represents a stunning failure to meet the standard set by the Council when it set the terms for ending the Gulf War in UNSCR 687: to assure the world community of its "peaceful intentions." The purpose of the drafters of Resolution 687—to ensure that Iraq could never again pose a threat to its neighbors or to regional peace and security—remains unfulfilled.

Nonetheless, UNSCOM and the International Atomic Energy Agency (IAEA) are working hard, with the help of the United States and other supporting nations, to put in place a comprehensive and effective monitoring regime for Iraq. During the month of August alone, UNSCOM and IAEA had seven different teams in Iraq building and testing monitoring capabilities. This effort must be carefully designed if it is to be so thorough that Iraq cannot rebuild

a covert nuclear program, as it did before the Gulf War, when it claimed to be in compliance with the nuclear Nonproliferation Treaty. Continued vigilance is necessary because we believe that Saddam Hussein is committed to rebuilding his weapons of mass destruction (WMD) capability.

Indeed, significant gaps in accounting for Iraq's past programs for WMD continue. There are unresolved issues in each of the four weapons categories (nuclear, long-range missile, chemical, and biological). This has been particularly true in the chemical and biological weapons areas, where Iraq claims to have destroyed large amounts of documentation. It is, therefore, extremely important that the monitoring regime be effective, comprehensive, and sustainable. A program of this magnitude is unprecedented and will require continued, substantial assistance for UNSCOM from supporting nations. Rigorous and extensive trial and field testing will be required before UNSCOM can judge the program's effectiveness.

Rolf Ekeus, the Chairman of UNSCOM, has told Iraq that it must establish a clear track record of compliance before he can report favorably to the Security Council. We strongly endorse Chairman Ekeus' approach and reject any attempt to limit UNSCOM's flexibility by the establishment of a timetable for determining whether Iraq has complied with UNSCR 715.

The U.N. Sanctions Committee continues to consider and, when appropriate, approve requests to send to Iraq materials and supplies for essential civilian needs. The Iraqi government, in contrast, has continued to maintain a full embargo against its northern provinces and has acted to distribute humanitarian supplies throughout the country only to its supporters and to the military.

The Iraqi government has refused to sell $1.6 million in oil as previously authorized by the Security Council in UNSCRs 706 and 712. Talks between Iraq and the United Nations on implementing these resolutions ended unsuccessfully in October 1993. Iraq could use proceeds from such sales to purchase foodstuffs, medicines, and materials and supplies for essential civilian needs of its population, subject to U.N. monitoring of sales and the equitable distribution of humanitarian supplies (including to its northern provinces). Iraq's refusal to implement UNSCRs 706 and 712 continues to cause needless suffering.

Proceeds from oil sales also would be used to compensate persons injured by Iraq's unlawful invasion and occupation of Kuwait. Of note regarding oil sales, discussions are underway with Turkish officials concerning the possible flushing of Iraqi oil now in the Turkish pipeline that extends from Iraq through Turkey. The objective is to prevent physical deterioration of the Turkish pipeline as a unique asset. Discussions continue as to how to conduct the flushing in a manner consistent with the U.N. sanctions regime.

The "no-fly zones" over northern and southern Iraq permit the monitoring of Iraq's compliance with UNSCRs 687 and 688. Over the last 3 years, the northern no-fly zone has deterred Iraq from a major military offensive in the region. In southern Iraq, the no-fly zone has stopped Iraq's use of aircraft against its population.

However, the Iraqi government continues its harsh campaign against its perceived enemies, both in the north and south. Baghdad's campaign of economic warfare against the people of northern Iraq continues. Last month the Iraqi regime cut electrical power to the Aqrah/Shirwan districts of Dohuk Governorate. Three hundred fifty thousand people now confront a lack of water, sanitation, and hospital services. Also in northern Iraq, in the vicinity of Mosul, we are watching Iraqi troop movements carefully; Iraq's intentions are still unclear. In the south, Iraq's repression of the Marsh Arabs and the implementation of a policy of environmental devastation represent a clear intent to target a specific area for reprisals without regard to the impact on innocent civilians. Further, Iraqi forces still wage a land-based artillery campaign in the marshes, and the shelling of marsh villages continues. In the last few years, the population of the region, whose marsh culture has remained essentially unchanged since 3500 B.C., has been reduced by an estimated three-quarters.

Iraq still refuses to recognize Kuwait's sovereignty and the inviolability of the U.N. demarcated border, which was reaffirmed by the Security Council in UNSCRs 773 and 833. Indeed, Iraq continues to view the issue of Kuwaiti sovereignty as an object of tactical moves rather than an opportunity to demonstrate peaceful intentions. Further, it has not complied with Security Council demands to resolve the issue of Kuwaiti MIAs, return Kuwaiti property stolen

during the occupation, and renounce terrorism. Iraq also has not met its obligations concerning Kuwaiti and third-country nationals it detained during the war and has taken no substantive steps to cooperate fully with the International Committee of the Red Cross (ICRC), as required by UNSCR 687, beyond agreement to participate in a technical committee being organized by the ICRC.

The Special Rapporteur of the U.N. Commission on Human Rights (UNHRC), Max van der Stoel, continues to report on the human rights situation in Iraq, particularly the Iraqi military's repression against its civilian populations in the marshes. The Special Rapporteur asserted in his February 1994 report that the Government of Iraq has engaged in war crimes and crimes against humanity, and may have committed violations of the 1948 Genocide Convention. Regarding the Kurds, the Special Rapporteur has judged that the extent and gravity of reported violations place the survival of the Kurds in jeopardy. The Special Rapporteur has noted that there are essentially no freedoms of opinion, expression, or association in Iraq. Torture is widespread in Iraq and results from a system of state-terror successfully directed at subduing the population. The Special Rapporteur repeated his recommendation for the establishment of human rights monitors strategically located to improve the flow of information and to provide independent verification of reports. We are pressing for the deployment of human rights monitors.

Special Rapporteur van der Stoel will file additional reports to the U.N. General Assembly in the fall and to the UNHRC in early 1995. We are also considering efforts to investigate and publicize Iraqi crimes against humanity, war crimes, and other violations of international humanitarian law.

Examples of Iraqi noncooperation and noncompliance continue in other areas. Dozens of Shi'a clerics are still imprisoned in Iraq without charge. Reliable reports have indicated that the Government of Iraq is offering reward money for terrorist acts against U.N. and humanitarian relief workers in Iraq. For 3 years there has been a clear pattern of criminal acts linking the Government of Iraq to a series of assassinations and attacks in northern Iraq on relief workers, U.N. guards, and foreign journalists, including a German journalist murdered in northern Iraq last spring. Ten persons have been injured and two have been killed in such attacks this year. These acts are indicative of Iraq's continuing disdain for the United Nations and, in our view, also constitute violations of UNSCRs 687 and 688.

The U.N. Compensation Commission (UNCC) has received about 2.4 million claims so far, with another 100,000 expected. The United States Government has now filed a total of 3,100 individual claims with a total asserted value of over $215 million. Earlier this year, one panel of UNCC Commissioners submitted its report on the first installment of individual claims for serious personal injury or death. The UNCC Commissioners' report recommended awards for a group of about 670 claimants, of which 11 were U.S. claimants. The Governing Council of the UNCC approved the panel's recommendations at its session in late May. This summer the first U.S. claimants received compensation for their losses. The UNCC Commissioners are expected to finish reviewing by the end of the year all claims filed involving death and serious personal injury.

In October the Governing Council will consider reports from the UNCC Commissioners on two other groups of claims. The first group involves approximately 50,000 persons, including approximately 200 U.S. claimants, who were forced to depart suddenly from Kuwait or Iraq during the invasion and occupation. The second group will involve claimants who sustained itemized individual losses, e.g., lost salary or personal property.

The United States Government also has submitted a total of approximately $1.5 billion in corporate claims against the Government of Iraq, representing about 140 business entities. Those claims represented a multitude of enterprises ranging from small family-owned businesses to large multinational corporations. In addition, in late July, the United States Government filed five Government claims with the UNCC. The five claims were for nonmilitary losses, such as damage to Government property (e.g., the U.S. Embassy compound in Kuwait) and the costs of evacuating U.S. nationals and their families from Kuwait and Iraq. These Government claims have an asserted value of about $17 million. In the future, the United States Government also expects to file one or more additional Government claim(s) involving the costs of monitoring health risks associated with oil well fires and other environmental damage in the Persian Gulf region. The UNCC expects to begin processing corporate claims and government claims later this year or early 1995.

It is clear that Iraq can rejoin the community of civilized nations only through democratic processes, respect for human rights, equal treatment of its people, and adherence to basic norms of international behavior. Iraq's Government should represent all of Iraq's people and be committed to the territorial integrity and unity of Iraq. The Iraqi National Congress (INC) espouses these goals, the fulfillment of which would make Iraq a stabilizing force in the Gulf region.

Neither in its words nor its deeds has Iraq convinced us it is no longer a threat to regional peace and security. Any discussion of lifting the oil embargo and other sanctions cannot be limited to future Iraqi cooperation in the area of WMD, but must take into account all the issues that comprise the true test of Iraq's peaceful intentions. Full Iraqi compliance with all relevant U.N. Security Council resolutions remains the objective of U.S. policy.

The Congress' continued support of our efforts is especially gratifying.

Sincerely,

WILLIAM J. CLINTON

NOTE: Identical letters were sent to Thomas S. Foley, Speaker of the House of Representatives, and Albert Gore, Jr., President of the Senate.

Remarks on Arrival in Tel Aviv, Israel
October 27, 1994

Thank you very much. Mr. President, Mrs. Weizman, Prime Minister Rabin, Mrs. Rabin, to all the people of Israel, it is wonderful for Hillary and for me to be back in Israel and especially to come here in this capacity and at this momentous time.

Yesterday was an historic day for the people of Israel and for the people of Jordan. It was also a wonderful day for the rest of the world, for we gained a glimpse yesterday of the future of a new Middle East.

Like all Americans, I have been inspired by Israel's long struggle to survive and to flourish. Today, Israel is strong and growing stronger. You stand on the threshold of a new era of peace and security. America, as always, is proud to stand with you. We intend to remain by your side in the years ahead.

Your new peace treaty points the way toward a goal we have all sought for a very long time: a comprehensive peace in the Middle East. This goal, as we all know, will require all Israelis to continue to demonstrate the awesome courage and vision and determination that have brought you this far. But we have seen the bright promise of the future.

I would like to say, on a very personal level, how much I have enjoyed working with the Prime Minister, the Foreign Minister, and all the others on the Israeli team; how much it has meant to the Secretary of State and to all of the rest of us to have the opportunity to be a part of a genuine commitment to lasting peace.

I look forward to meeting with the Prime Minister, to speaking at the Knesset. I hope to have the chance to meet as many citizens of this magnificent country as possible. I thank you for making us feel very welcome.

Thank you.

Note: The President spoke at 4 p.m. at Tel Aviv Ben Gurion International Airport. In his remarks, he referred to Israeli President Ezer Weizman and his wife, Ruma, and Prime Minister Yitzhak Rabin and his wife, Lea.

Remarks to the Knesset in Jerusalem, Israel
October 27, 1994

Mr. President, Mr. Prime Minister, Mr. Speaker, Mr. Netanyahu, ladies and gentlemen of the Knesset: Let me begin by thanking the Prime Minister and the people of Israel for welcoming me to your wonderful country, and thanking all of you for giving me the opportunity to address this great democratic body where, clearly, people of all different views are welcome to express their convictions. I feel right at home. [*Laughter*]

Yesterday Israel took a great stride toward fulfilling the ancient dream of the Jewish people, the patriarchs' dream of a strong and plentiful people living freely in their own land, enjoying the fruits of peace with their neighbors. Nearly 17 years after President Sadat came to this Chamber to seek peace and Prime Minister Begin reached out in reconciliation, and just over a year after Israel and the PLO declared a pathway to peace on the South Lawn of the White House, Israel and Jordan have now written a new chapter.

Tonight we praise the courage of the leaders who have given life to this treaty, Prime Minister Rabin and Foreign Minister Peres. They have shown the vision and the tenacity of other leaders of Israel's past whose names will be remembered always for their devotion to your cause and your people: Ben Gurion, Meir, Begin.

In your life, Prime Minister, we see the life of your country. As a youth, you wished to fulfill the commandment to farm the land of Israel, but instead you had to answer the call to defend the people of Israel. You have devoted your life to cultivating strength so that others could till the soil in safety. You have fought many battles and won many victories in war. Now, in strength, you are fighting and winning battles for peace. Indeed, you have shown your people that they can free themselves from siege, that for the first time they can make real a peace for the generations.

For the American people, too, this peace is a blessing. For decades, as Israel has struggled to survive, we have rejoiced in your triumphs and shared in your agonies. In the years since Israel was founded, Americans of every faith have admired and supported you. Like your country, ours is a land that welcomes exiles, a nation of hope, a nation of refuge. From the Orient and Europe and now from the former Soviet Union, your people have come, Ashkenazim and Sephardim, Yemenites and Ethiopians, all of you committed to living free, to building a common home. One of nearly four of the citizens of this country is an Arab, something very few people know beyond your borders. Even without the blessings of secure borders, you have secured for your own people the blessings of democracy. With all of its turmoil and debate, it is still the best of all systems.

In times of war and times of peace, every President of the United States since Harry Truman and every Congress has understood the importance of Israel. The survival of Israel is important not only to our interests, but to every single value we hold dear as a people. Our role in war has been to help you defend yourself by yourself. That is what you have asked. Now that you are taking risks for peace, our role is to help you to minimize the risks of peace.

I am committed to working with our Congress to maintain the current levels of military and economic assistance. We have taken concrete steps to strengthen Israel's qualitative edge. The U.S.-Israel Science and Technology Commission, unprecedented Israeli access to the U.S. high-technology market, and acquisition of advanced computers, all these keep Israel in the forefront of global advances and competitive in global markets.

I have also taken steps to enhance Israel's military and your capacity to address possible threats not only to yourselves but to the region. F–15 aircraft are being provided and F–16's transferred out of U.S. stocks. We work closely with you to develop the Arrow missile, to protect against the threat of ballistic missiles.

As we help to overcome the risks of peace, we also are helping to build a peace that will bring with it the safety and security Israel deserves. That peace must be real, based on treaty commitments arrived at directly by the parties, not imposed from outside. It must be secure. Israel must always be able to defend itself by itself. And it must be comprehensive. We have worked hard to end the Arab boycott, and we've had some success. But we will not stop until it is completely lifted. There is a treaty with Jordan and an agreement with the PLO. But we must keep going until Syria and Lebanon

close the circle of states entering into peace and the other nations of the Arab world normalize their relations with Israel.

This morning in Damascus I discussed peace with President Asad. He repeated at our press conference what he had earlier said to his own Parliament: Syria has made a strategic choice for peace with Israel. He also explained that Syria is ready to commit itself to the requirements of peace through the establishment of normal peaceful relations with Israel. His hope, as he articulated it, is to transform the region from a state of war to a state of peace that enables both Arabs and Israelis to live in security, stability, and prosperity.

We have been urging President Asad to speak to you in a language of peace that you can understand. Today he began to do so. Of course, it would take more than words, much more than words. Yet I believe something is changing in Syria. Its leaders understand that it is time to make peace. There will still be a good deal of hard bargaining before a breakthrough, but they are serious about proceeding.

Just as we have worked with you from Camp David to Wadi Araba to bring peace with security to your people, so too we will walk with you on the road to Damascus for peace with security.

There are those who see peace still as all too distant. Surely, they include the families of those burned in the rubble of the community center in Buenos Aires, those in the basement of New York's World Trade Center, the loved ones of the passengers on bus number 5, and of course, two people who, as been noted, are in this Chamber with us tonight. And we honor the parents of Corporal Nahshon Waxman, a son of your nation and, I proudly say, a citizen of ours.

We grieve with the families of those who are lost and with all the people of Israel. So long as Jews are murdered just because they are Jews or just because they are citizens of Israel, the plague of anti-Semitism lives, and we must stand against it. We must stand against terror as strongly as we stand for peace, for without an end to terror there can be no peace.

The forces of terror and extremism still threaten us all. Sometimes they pretend to act in the name of God and country. But their deeds violate their own religious faith and make a mockery of any notion of honorable patriotism.

As I said last night to the Parliament in Jordan, we respect Islam. Millions of American citizens every day answer the Moslem call to prayer. But we know that the real fight is not about religion or culture. It is about a worldwide conflict between those who believe in peace and those who believe in terror, those who believe in hope and those who believe in fear.

Those who stoke the fires of violence and seek to destroy the peace, make no mistake about it, have one great goal. Their goal is to make the people of Israel, who have defeated all odds on the field of battle, to give up inside on the peace by giving in to the doubts that terror brings to every one of us. But having come so far, you cannot give up or give in. Your future must lie in the words of a survivor of the carnage of bus number 5 who said, "I want the peace process to continue. I want to live in peace. I want my children to live in peace."

So let us say to the merchants of terror once again: You cannot succeed. You must not succeed. You will not succeed. You are the past, not the future. The peacemakers are the future.

I say to you, my friends, in spite of all the dangers and difficulties that still surround you, the circle of your enemies is shrinking. Their time has passed. Their increasing isolation is reflected in the desperation of their disgusting deeds.

Once, in this area, you were shunned. Now, more and more, you are embraced. As you share the waters of the River Jordan and work with your neighbors, new crops will emerge where the soil is now barren. As you join together to mine the Dead Sea for its minerals, you will bring prosperity to all your people. As you roll up the barbed wire and cross the desert of Araba, the sands will yield new life to you. As you dock in each other's ports along the Gulf of Aqaba, more and more people will have the chance to experience the wonders of both your lands, and more and more children will share the joys of youth, not the dread of war.

This is the great promise of peace. It is the promise of making sure that all those who have sacrificed their lives did not die in vain; the promise of a Sabbath afternoon not violated by gunfight, a drive across the plains to the mountains of Moab where Moses died and Ruth was born, a Yom Kippur of pure prayer without the rumble of tanks, voices of fear, or rumors of war. After all the bloodshed and all your tears,

you are now far closer to the day when the clash of arms is heard no more and all the children of Abraham, the children of Isaac, the children of Israel will live side by side in peace.

This was, after all, the message the prophet Mohammed himself brought to peoples of other faiths when he said, "There is no argument between us and you. God will bring us together, and unto Him is the homecoming." And this was the message Moses spoke to the children of Israel, when for the last time he spoke to them as they gathered across the River Jordan into the Promised Land, when he said, "I have set before you life and death, blessings and curses. Choose life so that you and your descendants may live."

This week, once again, the people of Israel made a homecoming. Once again, you chose life. Once again, America was proud to walk with you.

The Prime Minister mentioned a story in his remarks that he never asked me about. Wouldn't it be embarrassing if it weren't true? [Laughter] The truth is that the only time my wife and I ever came to Israel before today was 13 years ago with my pastor on a religious mission. I was then out of office. I was the youngest former Governor in the history of the United States. [Laughter] No one thought I would ever be here; perhaps my mother, no one else. [Laughter] We visited the holy sites. I relived the history of the Bible, of your Scriptures and mine, and I formed a bond with my pastor. Later, when he became desperately ill, he said he thought I might one day become President. And he said, more bluntly than the Prime Minister did, "If you abandon Israel, God will never forgive you." He said, "It is God's will that Israel, the biblical home of the people of Israel, continue forever and ever."

So I say to you tonight, my friends, one of our Presidents, John Kennedy, reminded us that here on Earth, God's will must truly be our own. It is for us to make the homecoming, for us to choose life, for us to work for peace. But until we achieve a comprehensive peace in the Middle East and then after we achieve comprehensive peace in the Middle East, know this: Your journey is our journey, and America will stand with you now and always.

Thank you, and God bless you.

NOTE: The President spoke at 9:25 p.m. in the Chamber at the Knesset. In his remarks, he referred to Shevach Weiss, Speaker of the Knesset, and Beinyamin Netanyahu, Lekud Party leader.

A tape was not available for verification of the content of these remarks.

The President's News Conference With Prime Minister Yitzhak Rabin of Israel in Jerusalem
October 27, 1994

Prime Minister Rabin. Mr. President, ladies and gentlemen, I believe that we experienced during the visit of President Clinton in the region a real move towards peace. No doubt that the visit of President Clinton was crowned yesterday by the second peace treaty between an Arab country and Israel, the first one after the convening of the Madrid's peace conference.

We look, from Israel's point of view, to President Clinton as a friend of Israel and a President that works very hard to bring about what we dream for, aspire to: to achieve comprehensive peace, that is to say, peace with our four neighboring Arab countries. With two, it has been accomplished. And no doubt, the visit of the President in Damascus, I believe that will bring about, through certain changes, a movement toward better negotiations, better possibilities to overcome the gaps between the positions of Israel and Syria.

No doubt in my mind that during the term of you, Mr. President, as the President of the United States, we have seen dramatic change in the relations between those Arab partners with whom we negotiate. We signed the Declaration of Principles between us and the PLO on the lawns of the White House. It was followed by the negotiations to bring about the first phase of its implementation in the Gaza-Jericho first. We are engaged today in continuation of our negotiations with the Palestinians about early empowerment, elections. And no doubt, yesterday we signed a peace treaty that the President helped to bring about and witnessed.

For 2 years, to reach two agreements, one with the Palestinians, with which we have a long story of suspicion, hatred, prejudice, bloodshed, and with the Jordanians, that I remember over 46 years ago that in this city I fought them and they fought me. And we look forward to make it possible to overcome yet the differences between Syria and Lebanon and us.

It might take time. One has to be patient. One has to understand that there are problems. And I believe that it will not take long, and hopefully, we'll find ways and means by which to overcome these gaps.

I hope, Mr. President, that you will continue sending Secretary Christopher, that worked very hard and tried in your name to move between Damascus and Jerusalem with the purpose to find ways to overcome the differences.

Allow me also to add that the Government of Israel of today is determined, on one hand, to continue all our efforts to bring about comprehensive peace. But at the same time, we are fully aware that there are enemies of peace. For us, the enemies of peace are the extreme Islamic radical terror movements. Among the Palestinians, they are the Hamas and the Islamic Jihad. Ninety percent of the terror activities against us are carried by them. And there is a tendency for oversimplification, to identify those part of the Palestinians with whom we reach an agreement and we try to implement it and the extreme radical Islamic elements that are enemies of peace and enemies of the Palestinians that reach agreement with us. From Lebanon, Hezbollah, which is a part of the ugly wave of Khomeinism without Khomeini that is all over the Arab world and the Islamic world. Whatever happens in Algeria is not related whatsoever to the Arab-Israeli conflict, or in Sudan, or in fighting within Egypt. It's an ugly wave that threatens not only the peace. They are the infrastructure of the international terrorism. And behind it, to a certain extent there are certain parties, to a larger extent is Iran. And therefore, Mr. President, we support your policy of dual containment. We believe it's vital to the peace in the Middle East, to stability among the Arab and the Muslim world, and to prevent international terrorism.

We thank you very much. You heard today in our Knesset the government and the opposition together joined in the support of the peace treaty with Jordan, in expressing thanks to you, Mr. President, for the way that you have stood and stand in support of Israel's security while trying your best to bring about advancement, which was successful so far in bringing about peace to the region.

Therefore, today here in Jerusalem, the united city, the capital of Israel, and, no doubt, the heart of the Jewish people, we thank you.

Thank you very much.

The President. Thank you, Prime Minister.

Ladies and gentlemen, because I had the opportunity to speak at length at Knesset this evening and to outline my position on a number of matters, I will be very brief. I would like to make just a couple of points.

First of all, at my first meeting with Prime Minister Rabin shortly after I became President, he told me he was prepared to take risks for peace. And I told him that that being the case, the job of the United States was to minimize those risks. For 20 months now, we have both done our best to do our jobs, and I think it's fair to say that we have had a reasonable amount of success in which the people of Israel can be proud and in which they can feel secure and one in which I hope the American people take pride.

Secondly, I would like to congratulate him and the people of Israel again on the peace treaty with Jordan. We have responsibilities there that relate to the security of both Israel and Jordan, and I have been working on that even since the peace treaty has been signed. I was in conversations with the King well past midnight last night. We are attempting to do our part to make sure this peace is as wildly successful as everyone believes that it can be.

Thirdly, I thank the Prime Minister for his comments about terrorism and his support for our policies. Especially I think I should mention something I did not mention in my speech tonight, which is the steadfast support of Israel for our policies in the Gulf and for our recent action in the Gulf. I will be going to Kuwait tomorrow to see our troops and on to Saudi Arabia. I appreciate the support of Israel.

Finally, with regard to what the Prime Minister said about Syria and my trip there today, I went there because I was convinced we needed to add new energy to the talks. And I come away from Syria convinced that we have, that some significant progress has been at least made

possible, that there has been some change in positions that offer the hope of more progress. And I have instructed the Secretary of State to return to the region within a few weeks to continue. Meanwhile, other discussions continue at other levels. And I am confident that we can be successful by simply pushing ahead.

So on all these fronts, I feel better tonight than I did when I came here. And again, I thank the Prime Minister for this welcome and for the opportunity to address the Knesset.

Middle East Peace Process

Q. Mr. President and Prime Minister Rabin, you are talking about significant developments coming from Damascus. From what we heard publicly until now, your visit to Damascus seems a disappointment for the Israelis. I mean, you gave the Syrians maybe one of the biggest gestures America has, a personal visit of the President of the United States. And President Asad responded publicly in his general words of peace which we heard in the past. So what else is new, Mr. President? And Mr. Rabin, what did you hear maybe privately from the President about this visit?

The President. Well, I would like to make three points if I might. First of all, I don't think it's accurate to say that he had ever said to me and to the rest of the world and to the people of Israel that he wanted to make peace with Israel and wanted to have normal, peaceful, constructive relations with Israel.

Secondly, he made some statements in our private conversations about the details of this process which I would be wrong to discuss because the essence of these negotiations is that they can proceed in some confidence. But they did show some forward movement in ways that I believe are not insignificant.

Thirdly, there's one thing I do regret about the press conference today. I regret that President Asad did not take the opportunity to say in public what he said to me in private about his deep regret about the loss of innocent lives and, particularly, the bus bombing. He said to me, "You know, we have to end the killing of innocents wherever it occurs, whether it was on that bus or in Hebron. I deplore it all. And I am convinced that only by making peace can we end it. And when we do make peace, it will end." That is what he said to me.

I think the way the question was posed to him, I think, led him to give an answer which may have been somewhat misleading, not intentionally but because he did not say that. I also want to reaffirm that there was absolutely no discussion in our private meeting, as he said, about the question of the United States removing Syria from the terrorist list. He did not ask for that; he did not bring it up. And I certainly did not bring it up. There has been no mixing of those two issues.

So, I think that his statement did break some new ground. I know that his private conversations broke some new ground. And I was particularly encouraged by what he said in private to me about the killing of innocent people. I regret that that was not said in public, but I can tell you that it was said in private. And what I said in the press conference is now, as I understand it, even being rebroadcast on a regular basis in Syria tonight to reaffirm that that is in fact what happened.

Prime Minister Rabin. I am accustomed to the prolonged and sometimes difficult period of negotiations. If one would have told us 2 years ago that we'd make a strategic understanding with Chairman Arafat and the PLO, people would not believe.

In the process towards peace, we have to overcome on both sides certain perceptions, certain sometimes prejudices, one about another. Therefore, I believe that all the partners to the Madrid peace conference—and by now remain the Palestinians with which we reached an agreement in principles; Syria and Lebanon would like to have peace—I don't know any one of the partners who don't want to have peace. The only question is, what is the meaning of peace? What is the price of peace? It takes time to overcome differences. And whatever I heard is, first, that Syria strategically decided for peace. Second, they are ready to continue the negotiations, not in the best way to my opinion, but as long as there is any avenue of negotiations, we should follow it. Thirdly, I don't believe it will be right on the part of Israel, regardless what he said or didn't say on the press conference today in Damascus—which I would like that he would say different things, but it doesn't discourage me to continue our negotiations.

And this is the essence of the peacemaking process, to be patient, to be determined, and not to be misled by ups and downs of public statements. Therefore, we will continue the way that it will be possible in negotiations with Syria.

I am aware that there are gaps between our positions. But I can't recall any negotiations in the past that there were no gaps. And whenever we succeeded to reach an agreement, came about as a result of the capability to make the compromise that bridged the gap.

Q. Mr. Prime Minister, if you'll forgive us, we're going to keep pressing still. The President is speaking of change in positions; you're speaking of change in perception. We have the issues tattooed on our forehead. The issues have been here for 3 years. We know there are major gaps. Are you talking about new atmospherics 3 years after Madrid, or have you been told something about Syria's position on Golan, on security, on the terms of peace? Have you heard sufficiently for you to reverse your election stand and surrender the Golan Heights?

Prime Minister Rabin. Well first, I believe that whoever sees what has taken place in the last over 3 years, he cannot ignore the tremendous change as a result of the Declaration of Principles between the PLO and us, the signing of the peace treaty, the openness in the Arab world that the Foreign Minister of Israel can fly to Bahrain, that multilateral negotiations can be taking place in Oman and Qatar and who knows where else, the decision of the six members of the Gulf Community Council about ignoring, not counseling, the Arab boycott. There is a trend, a move that no doubt will have its implications in other Arab countries, I hope in the short run or in the long run, even on the issues that have not yet been solved between Syria and Israel.

I believe that the mere fact that there is a continuation of negotiations with all the partners, it creates new realities in the region. From Maroc tomorrow, our big mission headed by the Foreign Minister will go to the Casablanca meeting. When did you expect that such a meeting will take place in an Arab country? We have to see, beyond technical or tactical or certain important issues between us and one of our partners, the changes that have taken place in the whole region in the attitude, a change of attitude. This is what realities speak about.

And therefore, don't ask me today about details of this part or that part of the negotiations. The fact that we are moving—Palestinians, yesterday Jordan, openness in the Arab world, different kind of relations, Maroc, Tunisia, and I believe there will be other Arab countries—this is the importance. You don't have to look at it on a limited point of view. You have to look at it: Are there changes in the region? Are there changes in the attitude of so many Arab countries towards relations to Israel, or not? This is the issue. And it will continue. And we will continue, regardless to the terrible atrocities of the Islamic radical terror groups against us. I believe you'll see more changes and more in the right direction.

Q. Mr. President, the restoration of Israel's exact fulfillment of over 300 Bible prophecies proves the Bible is God's true word. Genesis 17:8 says God gave Israel "all the land of Canaan for an everlasting possession." And Leviticus 25:23 forbids her ever to sell it. How can it produce real peace to induce Israel to defy God by selling Judea and Samaria for Arafat's or Asad's paper promises of peace?

Prime Minister Rabin. Do you ask the President of the United States this question? He is not representing Israel, to the best of my knowledge.

The President. That was the answer I was going to give. [*Laughter*]

The people of Israel, through their elected leaders, will decide what they are required to do for their own existence, their own security, their own future, and for their patience and peace with God.

Q. Mr. Prime Minister, in the agreements you signed with some of your Arab neighbors, the issue of Jerusalem remained unresolved, the whole status of east Jerusalem. And that's also true at the U.N. and in most of the world, it's unresolved. Why did you assert such absolute control? Were you trying to put President Clinton on the spot tonight?

The President. You mean in his speech to the Knesset?

Q. Yes.

Prime Minister Rabin. First, we are independent states. And we have our positions, and the United States has got its position. I can speak only on the Israeli position. We believe that Jerusalem must remain united under Israel's sovereignty. But we did not reject that the Palestinians, once we negotiate permanent solution, will raise the issue. We know their position; they know ours.

I believe that in the long run, the Jerusalem problem should be solved on two levels, the political one, that is to say, what will be the sovereignty over the united Jerusalem—which we have no doubt that it must be Israeli sov-

ereignty—and the question of the holiness of Jerusalem to the other two religions. And you'll see a sign in the Washington Declaration, in the peace treaty that we signed between Jordan and Israel, that we distinguished between the holy shrines to the Muslims that in the last 27 years we allowed free access, free practice. But even beyond that, the administration of the holy shrines to the Muslims and the Christians is done by the respective churches. We don't intervene. In that way that they run something within the holy shrines that derived from their own religion, as long as it doesn't affect the security of the area. It works for 27 years. And I believe we have in Hebrew an expression, *Jerusalem shall maala, Jerusalem shall matta,* Jerusalem in the heavens, and Jerusalem on the ground.

I believe this is the key to the real solution in the long run of Jerusalem. But we are committed if they want to raise this issue. We know our position when we negotiate the permanent status between us and the Palestinians. We negotiate the solution to the refugee problems of much wider scope not only with one partner, on a regional basis. Therefore, from my point of view, it's very clear.

[*The following question was asked and answered in Hebrew and translated by an interpreter.*]

Q. Mr. Prime Minister, I should like to take this opportunity to ask you a question in Hebrew. President Clinton and the Secretary of State have spoken about progress in Damascus. Following your meeting with President Clinton, do you share their estimation that, indeed, there is progress towards peace? And if so, in what areas?

Prime Minister Rabin. To begin with, I heard from President Clinton about his meeting with President Asad. His impression, whereby on certain subjects there has been some progress, is relevant. We must bear in mind that we are now negotiating with the Syrians. In fact, this has been going on for 3 years, ever since the Madrid convention. And we are advancing in tiny steps, inch by inch.

In the talks between us, we reached an agreement whereby Secretary of State Christopher, within a period of 3 or 4 weeks, would examine the progress being made in order to implement or to put into practice what we hope will be done. In other words, we are interested in reaching peace with Syria. We do want a peace treaty with Syria. In principle, we have agreed to a withdrawal. There is no agreement between us and Syria as to the final borders of peace, and there are other areas which have not yet been resolved.

President Clinton did not tell me that there was a historic breakthrough. He said that there was some progress on certain areas. Therefore, we must pursue these efforts. We must continue along the road on which the negotiations have been taking place so far. In other words, Secretary of State Christopher will continue shuffling between Damascus and Jerusalem. And indeed, we have agreed that this will be taking place within 3 or 4 weeks from today, if I'm not mistaken.

Q. [*Inaudible*]—have another day yet before the trip is over, and I know I'm getting you while you're somewhat tired. But even so, I'd like to ask you if you could to reflect a little bit, since this is the last press conference before you go home, if you could tell us a little bit about what have you learned on the trip the last couple of days? What will you take home with you that's different from what you came here with? And what do you feel has changed for yourself from the experiences that you've had in the last however many hours it's been?

The President. Well, this has been my first opportunity to see first-hand the potential for a new Middle East, the real potential for peace, and the yearning that I see everywhere.

In Damascus today, when I was riding along the road and people would stop their working or children would crowd around their buildings,

their play yards, and wave a greeting, they did it because they see the United States as the instrument of peace to bring these two nations together or at least to make it possible for them to come together. These are all things that you know, but until you see it, it's a very different thing, indeed.

I also come away from this trip profoundly grateful to the leaders of Israel and Jordan for setting an example that I think will give confidence and conscience to the efforts that others will make now to resolve the problems in the Middle East.

I also came away, frankly, with a much clearer idea of what things the United States can do and indeed what we must try to do to help make peace successful from a security point of view and from an economic point of view.

So all these things I leave with. But the most important thing is the deep yearning for this to work. I saw it in the energy in the Knesset tonight. We saw it in the energy and the passion in the Jordanian Parliament last night. And I have seen it on the streets of every place I have been, in the eyes of the people. I think we are on the right historic mission, and we need to redouble our efforts until we finish.

Prime Minister Rabin. May I, Mr. President? [*Inaudible*]—in the last 15 years, the President of the United States did help and attended signing of the peace treaty between an Arab country and Israel.

NOTE: The President's 77th news conference began at 10:44 p.m. in the Convention Center.

Statement on Signing Legislation Regarding United States Policy Toward Haiti
October 25, 1994

Today I have signed into law S.J. Res. 229, "Regarding United States policy toward Haiti."

In signing this joint resolution, it is important to clarify the interpretation of a provision related to the President's authority and responsibility as Commander in Chief.

Section 2 of the resolution calls, *inter alia*, for a detailed description of "the general rules of engagement under which operations of the United States Armed Forces are conducted in

and around Haiti." I interpret this language as seeking only information about the rules of engagement that I may supply consistent with my constitutional responsibilities, and not information of a sensitive operational nature.

Let me take this opportunity to associate myself unreservedly with the joint resolution's commendation of the professional excellence and dedicated patriotism with which the men and women of the U.S. Armed Forces are performing their mission in Haiti.

The combination of determined diplomacy and military resolve achieved, just 1 month ago, an agreement that permitted the peaceful deployment of U.S. and multinational forces to Haiti pursuant to the provisions of United Nations Security Council Resolution 940. And on October 15, culminating 3 years of international efforts led by the United States, Haiti's democratically elected President, Jean-Bertrand Aristide, stood on the steps of the Presidential Palace in Port-au-Prince and addressed tens of thousand of his countrymen and women in an atmosphere of joy, reconciliation, and rebuilding.

That historic achievement capped a breathtaking month of democratic restoration and the beginnings of Haiti's economic recovery, all made possible by the dedicated efforts of our service men and women in Haiti. The Haitian people no longer live in fear; they now have hope. The coup leaders are gone from Haiti and the thugs are no longer in control. Haiti's parliament is open. It has enacted an amnesty law and is busy laying the legislative groundwork for stronger democratic institutions. The Mayor of Port-au-Prince has been restored to office after 3 years of internal exile, the legitimate Prime Minister and Cabinet have reclaimed their offices, and the state media are back at the service of the people. The lights are on again in Cap-Haitian after 2 years of darkness as electrical service is expanded throughout the country. With the lifting of all U.S. and international sanctions upon President Aristide's return to Haiti, commercial fuel and food shipments and airline service have resumed.

The full restoration of democracy opens a period of hope for the Haitian people. Only they can reconcile their country. As the international community supports them with a major program of economic assistance, our military personnel participating in the multinational force will maintain the climate of basic security in which those goals can be achieved. Through police monitors and trainers, the multinational force will lay the groundwork for the transition of the Haitian army to a professional defense force and for the creation of a civilian police force.

We expect that within months, the bulk of our military personnel will leave Haiti. The multinational coalition will transfer responsibility to the United Nations Mission in Haiti in accordance with United Nations Security Council Resolution 940. Our forces' accomplishments in the last month have been superb. I am confident they will maintain their outstanding record and leave a Haiti poised to consolidate its hard-won democracy, create a brighter future for all its people, and become a factor for stability in the region and hemisphere.

WILLIAM J. CLINTON

The White House,
October 25, 1994.

NOTE: S.J. Res. 229, approved October 25, was assigned Public Law No. 103–423. This statement was released by the Office of the Press Secretary on October 28.

Exchange With Reporters in Jerusalem
October 28, 1994

Holocaust Memorial

Q. Mr. President, Voice of Israel, live—a word if I may. What did you put in writing in the guestbook, sir? May I bother you to approach the mike, sir, please?

The President. I wrote that today we are one step closer to the time when the people of Israel can live together in peace with all of your neighbors, the time when people of Israel will never again suffer death and destruction—the events that are memorialized here—simply because of their race or their faith, and may God let it come to pass.

President's Visit

Q. Mr. President, how would you summarize your visit in Israel?

The President. It was a wonderful visit. I was deeply touched by the reception of the people, grateful for the opportunity to address the Knesset. I leave redoubled in the support of the American people for the people of Israel and redoubled in my determination to continue until we have a comprehensive peace.

Q. What will be your message to your troops in Kuwait, sir?

The President. I'm very proud of them.

NOTE: The President spoke at 8:49 a.m. at Yad Vashem, the Holocaust Memorial. A tape was not available for verification of the content of this exchange.

Remarks to United States and Coalition Troops at Tactical Assembly Area Liberty in Kuwait
October 28, 1994

The President. Who said, "Go, hog" there?

Audience members. Go, hog!

The President. There's a reward for you somewhere. That's good.

General Peay, General Taylor, Crown Prince Saad. Thank you all for your service. Thank you, Crown Prince Saad, for your fine words. I'm delighted to be here in Kuwait with all of you, with General Peay, with General Taylor, with General Ali, with the Kuwaiti Armed Forces, with our coalition partners from the United Arab Emirate and from Great Britain.

I'm especially glad to be here with all of you Americans in uniform. I understand—when I was getting briefed to come over here, I was being briefed by an earnest young person who said that I just didn't understand what you had been up against, that in addition to dealing with Iraq, you've been plagued by a pretty severe case of *shamal,* the desert sandstorm that can make life pretty rough around here. That has been offered to me as the explanation for why one of the young officers preparing for my visit, Second Lieutenant Rowe, took your brigade commander's personal communications system the other day to report that he had spotted Elvis. [*Laughter*] Well, there have been times in my life when I wanted to be Elvis, but I'm not. And thanks to *shamal,* Lieutenant Rowe will not become the only third lieutenant in the entire United States Army. [*Laughter*]

I want to say to the men and women of Operation Vigilant Warrior, the men and women of the 24th Mechanized, the Victory Division, a division that liberated the Philippines, fought from Korea to the Gulf war, I am honored to be with all of you here in Tactical Assembly Area Liberty. I am proud of the work you're doing for your country.

More than anything else, I came here, after a couple of fascinating, very important days for your country and Egypt and Jordan and Israel and Syria, to say a simple thank you. Thank you for what you have done for Kuwait. Thank you for what you have done for the United States of America.

Nearly 4 years ago, your tanks rolled across these dunes with mighty force. You were the Desert Storm. Then you expelled Iraq from Kuwait. Now we were determined to stop Iraq before it could violate its neighbor's borders and create new instability. So once again, we called upon you, the Army, the Navy, the Air Force, the Marines. Well, one of the things that will go down in the history of this encounter is that you got here in a very big hurry, and because of that, Iraq got the message in a very big hurry. It withdrew its forces that were massed near the Kuwait border.

You know, when this crisis began, there were a few back home who questioned our military preparedness. To them, I say, they ought to come here and take a look at you, and they would know better.

Our policy in the Gulf is clear. We will not permit Iraq to enhance its capabilities below the 32d parallel. We won't permit Baghdad to intimidate the United Nations teams making sure that Iraq never again possesses weapons of mass destruction. The United States and the international community will not allow Baghdad to threaten its neighbors now or in the future. That is not our threat, that is our promise. You, you here, are keeping that promise. The force you represent is the steel in the sword of American diplomacy. You are the best equipped, best trained, best prepared military in the world and in our Nation's history. You have proved it again here in the Gulf. We are all proud of you.

I know that no monetary value can fully reflect your service to our country. I know that all of you serve for higher reasons. But I am pleased to say today that I have just signed an Executive order to right a wrong in your military pay concerning your subsistence allowance. I think you ought to be rewarded, not penalized, for doing this important job.

If I may say just a serious word for a moment, your country needs you for America to be strong. We are a peace-loving nation, but President Truman once said, "The will for peace without the strength for peace is to no avail." You are that strength. You and your commanders are bringing hope and stability around the world, from Port-au-Prince to the Persian Gulf.

Our ultimate goal is peace, and that requires even more than military might. It requires the courage to go beyond conflict to reconciliation. Two days ago I witnessed a brilliant example of that along the border between Israel and Jordan. I applaud the leaders of Israel, Jordan, and others in the Middle East who are turning away from a violent past toward a future of peace. This is difficult and dangerous work, as the vicious terrorist attacks in recent days have shown. The people behind those acts want to prevent peace. They want to perpetuate hatred. They want to undermine your mission. They cannot succeed. They must not succeed. And they will not succeed.

If you ever wonder, sometime out here in the desert, whether what you do makes a real difference, just consider what has happened in the last few weeks. I am honored, as I know all of you are, that America was able to play a role in ending 47 years of conflict between Israel and Jordan, in restoring President Aristide and democracy in Haiti, in helping to make real progress toward an end to the violent conflict in Northern Ireland, in helping South Africa's democracy to succeed, in building a new partnership with Russia that enables us to say for the first time since the dawn of the nuclear age, there are no nuclear missiles pointed at the children of the United States. And I am also proud of what you have done to stand up to aggression here in the Gulf.

We stand with the people of Kuwait, people who have rebuilt their army and their economy since the difficult days of 1990. The people of Kuwait should be proud of their accomplishments and proud of their tough reactions to Iraq's provocation. The international community will assure that Iraq never threatens your nation again. The proof of that commitment is here in the brave men and women of Operation Vigilant Warrior.

Let me say, too, that we have no quarrel with the people of Iraq. We know the suffering they endured in the war with Iran, a war that blighted an entire generation. Just 2 years after that horrible conflict, Iraq sent its sons to war again, and we know the price they paid for their leader's folly here. But the pain of the people of Iraq is the result of one thing only, the path their leadership has chosen.

So we say again to Iraq: Comply fully with the resolutions of the United Nations. Obey the will and the law of the international community. That is the only way to have a normal life. It is the way the rest of us have followed, and you should try it as well.

My fellow Americans, you're making sacrifices to defend your country, its values, and its interests. I know the demands on you are great. I know your love of country takes you away from home and the family that you love for long stretches of time. I know when you cheered about the announcement I made on pay, part of the cheering was for the folks back home, the children, and the hope that you have for your own families and for their future.

What you are doing is assuming America's burdens in this new and challenging time, to maintain our national security, to maintain our national commitments, to help the world move toward peace and freedom. I hope you will always take the pride in your contributions that I see in your faces today, that I hear in your voices today.

Our country is the land of the free and the home of the brave, as the song says. Because of your bravery, we're spreading that freedom to others. Because of your bravery, we will remain forever free.

So I thank you, I thank you for your service. I thank your families back home. God bless you all, and God bless America. Don't forget to go Christmas shopping.

NOTE: The President spoke at 3:19 p.m. In his remarks, he referred to Gen. Binford J.H. Peay III, USA, commander in chief, and Maj. Gen. James B. Taylor, USA, deputy commander, U.S. Central Command; Crown Prince Saad Al Sabah, Prime Minister of Kuwait; and Maj. Gen. Ali Al-Mumen, commander in chief, Kuwaiti Armed

Forces. The Executive order changing the definition of "Field Duty" to ensure parity of pay among deployed troops is listed in Appendix D at the end of this volume.

Remarks on Receiving the Mubarak Medal in Kuwait City, Kuwait
October 28, 1994

First, let me thank you, Royal Highness, and the people of Kuwait for this high honor. Mubarak the Great, your grandfather and the modern-day founder of this proud nation, symbolizes the determination to defend your independence against all aggression.

I accept your honor on behalf of all the American people and especially the men and women of our Armed Forces. They are the strength behind our commitment to Kuwait and to peace and security in the entire Gulf region. They are the steel in our determination never again to allow Iraq to threaten its neighbors. They have stood shoulder to shoulder with your men in arms and once again have said no to aggression and yes to peace.

As the men and women of our Armed Forces work to make peace in the Gulf, far-sighted leaders are making peace elsewhere in the Middle East. I am encouraged by the effort of Arabs and Israelis to live together in peace. As Jordan and Israel have demonstrated, a peace for the generations is now before us.

I want to thank Kuwait especially for the important contribution you have made to the peace process. By helping lead the way to end the boycott of Israel, Kuwait is saying, let us close the door on the past and open a new page to the future, a future of peaceful coexistence and prosperous commerce for all the people in this region.

Your Royal Highness, the United States stands with those who seek to ensure the triumph of hope over fear. It was just a few years ago that President Bush sent our troops here to defend your very existence. Since that time our friendship has grown and our military cooperation has increased.

Our determination is clear: Kuwait shall remain free. And the United States and Kuwait will remain partners into the future.

I thank you again.

NOTE: The President spoke at approximately 7 p.m. in Bayan Palace. In his remarks, he referred to Amir Jabir Sabah of Kuwait.

Remarks on the Economy and an Exchange With Reporters in Kuwait City
October 28, 1994

The President. As I think you know, we had good news from the home front today: Economic growth in the third quarter was at 3.4 percent and inflation a very low 1.6 percent. This sustained economic expansion is producing jobs—this year, more high-wage jobs than not, more high-wage jobs this year than in the previous 5 years combined.

This is the result of a remarkable partnership between the private sector and our policies: the efforts of all of our companies and people to be competitive in the global economy, coupled with our determination to lower the deficit, increase investment in critical areas, expand trade,

and aggressively promote United States economic interests all around the world.

I'm very, very encouraged by this. We have growth, better jobs, low inflation. That's the right path to be on. That's the path we need to continue.

U.S. Troops in the Persian Gulf

Q. Mr. President, when do you think you'll make a decision on bringing the troops home by Christmas, and how many?

Mr. President. Well, I will make a decision on that essentially based on the facts as they exist. If our military people tell me that their judgment is that we can handle that, then I expect that decision will flow in a prompt fashion. But we're going to wait a little while longer to make sure we have all the evidence, we know exactly where we are, we know what the range of risks are. And we'll make a decision pretty soon.

Q. Sir, are you feeling a little unplugged from your domestic matters here?

The President. No. No. I haven't been gone long enough to be unplugged.

NOTE: The President spoke at 7:44 p.m. at Bayan Palace. A tape was not available for verification of the content of these remarks.

Exchange With Reporters Prior to Discussions With Prince Bandar in Hafal-Batin, Saudi Arabia
October 28, 1994

King Abdul-Aziz Medal

Q. Your Majesty, would you care to tell us what the decoration was, what its purpose was, Prince Bandar?

Prince Bandar. This is the highest medal in the kingdom, that His Majesty awarded the President for his gratitude for the President of the United States of America and the people of the United States.

The President. You all are holding up well?

Q. No, are you?

Q. What are you going to do with all your medals now? Put them in your library?

The President. No, I'm going to wear them to my press conference and hope that I'll get more respect. [*Laughter*] I'll just wait until a difficult question arises, and I will put it on and hope it serves as a shield.

NOTE: The exchange began at 9:43 p.m. at the Royal Compound Reception Hall. Prince Bandar was Saudi Ambassador to the United States. A tape was not available for verification of the content of this exchange.

Joint Communique of the United States of America and the Kingdom of Saudi Arabia
October 28, 1994

The Custodian of the Two Holy Mosques, King Fahad Bin Abdul-Aziz Al-Saud, King of the Kingdom of Saudi Arabia held a meeting with his excellency President William Clinton, during his Excellency's current visit to the Kingdom of Saudi Arabia, on Friday the 23d of Jumda Al-Awal, 1415, A.H., corresponding to the 28th of October, 1994.

In this meeting, the two leaders reviewed bilateral relations along with regional and international issues of common interest. In this regard, there was an expression of deep satisfaction at the level of bilateral relations and a mutual readiness to promote and develop their relations in a way that serves the common interests of the two countries and the well-being of the

two peoples as well as contribute to the security and development of the whole region.

In addition, the two leaders discussed recent developments related to the peace process in the Middle East. On this matter, the Custodian of the Two Holy Mosques, with great satisfaction, noted the relentless efforts of President Clinton and his government to move ahead the peace process and emphasized support for all the agreements already reached. On his part, President Clinton expressed his appreciation for King Fahad's support for the Israel-PLO agreements and the Israel-Jordan Peace Treaty and for his promotion and enhancement of the peace process. In particular the President expressed appreciation to him and his counterparts in the

Gulf Cooperation Council for ending their enforcement of the secondary and tertiary boycotts. Both leaders emphasized their commitment to continue efforts to achieve concrete progress in the Israeli-Syrian and Israeli-Lebanese track. The two leaders took cognizance of the fact that a permanent and comprehensive peace in the area must be based on the Security Council Resolutions 242, 338 as well as the Principle of Land for peace.

During the talks, the two leaders also examined current threats that endanger regional peace and security, notably, the recent Iraqi violation of Security Council Resolutions and confirm the ill intentions of the Iraqi Government and its continued aggressive policies that threaten the security and stability of the Gulf area.

They also noted the provisions of Security Council Resolution number 949, underscoring their firm resolve to prevent Saddam Hussein from again posing a threat to Iraq's neighbors, particularly, the security of the State of Kuwait and future stability of the region. The two leaders voiced their view that any attempt to lift or alleviate the sanctions on Iraq will continue to be premature as long as Iraq does not comply fully and comprehensively with all the Security Council Resolutions that pertain to its aggression on the State of Kuwait. Consequently, any other efforts, inconsistent with the Security Council Resolutions, would only result in encouraging the Iraqi regime to continue its aggressive policies and to flout the will of the international community.

The two leaders emphasized that they had no quarrel with the Iraqi people with whose plight they sympathize. They drew attention to the humanitarian provisions of the UNSC resolutions which the Iraqi regime has failed to take up. The responsibility for the hardship of the Iraqi people lies entirely with the Iraqi regime.

The United States and Saudi Arabia condemn all terrorist activities. We are united against all the enemies of peace, those who threaten aggression and those who kill innocent people and whose real target is peace itself. In this way, we will widen the circle of peacemakers and promote reconciliation between them.

Remarks on Returning From the Middle East
October 29, 1994

Thank you very much, and good morning. Less than 24 hours ago, I stood with the brave men and women of our Armed Forces stationed at Tactical Assembly Area Liberty in the desert sands of Kuwait. I went there to express my pride and the pride I know all Americans share in the job our military is doing to protect our interests in the Persian Gulf.

Our troops are living in difficult conditions. But I saw in their faces the pride they have in their work and the work of our coalition partners. And I can tell all Americans, their morale is high and they are prepared and ready to do their job, to do what they must to stand up for freedom. Anyone who doubts it should go and see what I saw in the sands of Kuwait.

I also wish that all Americans could have been with me in the Wadi Araba, on the border between Israel and Jordan. There, in the middle of the Great Rift Valley, soldiers of the nations of Israel and Jordan reached across 47 years of hostility to shake hands in a true, genuine gesture of reconciliation, just as their leaders found the courage to sign a peace treaty, a crucial step on the road to a comprehensive peace in the Middle East.

Israel and Jordan looked to America to help them to make peace. And they and other nations in the Middle East look to America as we travel the difficult road ahead, until we achieve peace throughout the Middle East. And as I said in every one of the six nations I visited, the United States will continue to stand shoulder-to-shoulder with those who seek the peace, with those who take risks for peace, with those who stand up for change in the face of terrorists and extremists who seek to destroy the peace by killing the innocent. They cannot, they must not, they will not succeed. They are the past; the peacemakers are the future.

My trip to the Middle East is a reminder that we live in times when the spirit of America—our freedom, our vitality, our strength, our respect for others, our commitment to the future—this is a driving force in the lives of millions and millions of peace-loving people all around the world. That is why we're trusted to support the people of the Middle East and the people from South Africa to Haiti to Northern Ireland to the former Soviet Union in their courageous efforts to escape the shackles of the past and realize their dreams for tomorrow.

Our efforts in these places, of course, also advance our own interests, for their successes strengthen our security and promise us more prosperity in a world that daily grows more interdependent.

As we support others in renewing themselves, we must continue the work of renewal here at home. For the source of our ability to lead beyond our borders is the strength of the American dream in the minds and hearts of our own people. In every community, every school, every workplace, we must deal with the changes and challenges, with the great problems and the much greater promise of the times in which we live. We must turn from the past and embrace the future, a future where ordinary Americans build strong families with good jobs and safe communities, served by a Government that neither interferes with our lives nor walks away from us but empowers us and challenges us to make the most of our God-given potential.

That is exactly what we have begun to do here. We've made a start in putting Government on the side of ordinary Americans, creating jobs and stimulating growth, in building a world more secure, more free, more prosperous for ourselves and for our children.

Like people all over the world who are drawing on our strength and our spirit to make their dreams real, we Americans must renew our own faith in the greatness and unlimited potential of our country. We must keep moving forward here at home with no thought of turning back. I have looked into the faces of millions of people elsewhere. I have seen how much they love our country, how much they share our dreams. We must do that as well.

Thank you all for coming out this morning. It's been an exciting trip, but it's great to be home.

Thank you.

NOTE: The President spoke at 8:08 a.m. on the South Lawn at the White House.

The President's Radio Address
October 29, 1994

Good morning. This week I'm speaking to you from Tactical Assembly Area Liberty in the sands outside Kuwait City, Kuwait, in the Persian Gulf, where I am visiting the brave men and women of our Armed Forces who are working here to defend freedom.

Three weeks ago, I ordered them and other members of the military to come here because Iraq was massing tens of thousands of troops on Kuwait's border. Our soldiers, sailors, pilots, and marines got here in a hurry, and Iraq got the message in a hurry. Its forces stopped dead in their tracks, and now they have withdrawn. On behalf of all Americans, I came to Kuwait to tell our troops two simple but deeply felt words: Thank you.

I can tell you the men and women of our Armed Forces are doing well. They are working well with their coalition forces, the Kuwaitis, the British, and the other allies who have come here to help to defend this country. Their morale is high; their commitment to their mission is unquestioned. Of course, they'd rather be home with their loved ones, and we'll do everything we can to get them back there soon. But they're here to do their jobs, and nobody does it better. In places from Haiti to Korea, our troops are the great source of our national strength.

As our military helps to secure peace in the Gulf, our diplomacy is also helping to make peace between Israel and its Arab neighbors. I wish all Americans could have seen what I had the privilege to witness this week. The leaders of Israel and Jordan, enemies for 47 years, found the courage to put aside their past to come together in a moving ceremony in the desert between their two countries. They made peace after a generation of war so that this generation and the next generation of their citizens could enjoy their lives, not live in dread.

I know you were moved, as I was, by what Jordan's King Hussein and Israel's Prime Minister Rabin said about America. They said they couldn't have made this peace without our support. One member of a delegation of Americans who went with me put it best when he said, "It made me so proud to know that my country was responsible for helping to build this peace."

The United States, at this moment in history, is uniquely blessed. We are blessed with great power and a heritage and commitment not to abuse that power but instead to seek peace, freedom, and democracy as well as our own security. We are using our role to do that in the Middle East to build a comprehensive peace.

A year ago, leaders of Israel and the Palestine Liberation Organization came to the White House for another historic peace accord. This week I made it clear to them that the PLO must do everything it can to end terrorism against Israel so that the peace process can create a better future for this region. And I met with President Asad of Syria to say it's time he, too, follow the example and inspiration of Israel and Jordan. We made progress on this trip, and we'll continue to do our part to bring peace to this long-troubled part of the world.

All over the world, nations look to us for leadership, whether it's in the peace process between Israel and its Arab neighbors or the South Africans asking us to help them hold their first successful democratic elections or leaders in Northern Ireland asking the United States to help end their terrible conflict or the folks in Haiti who, when President Aristide and democracy returned, held up signs to our troops that said simply, "Thank you, America." And of course, it's clear that when Saddam Hussein reared up his head again in the Gulf, Kuwait and other countries looked to the United States. They know that the good men and women I came to Kuwait to thank are the strength behind our commitment to peace and to freedom.

We must maintain a strong defense so that we can protect our own security and our own interests and so that we can make the world safer and more prosperous for our children by advancing freedom, as we are here in the Gulf today.

To stay strong abroad, we also know America has to be strong at home. To do that, we have to take on challenges at home just as we do abroad. We have to do what we have to do to keep the American dream alive into the next century: a strong economy, a good society, advancing the values of work and family and community. In the last 21 months, we've made a good start, getting our economic house in order after years of neglect, starting the first serious assault on crime in a generation, beginning to make America work for ordinary citizens after a long time when they and their children were left to fall behind.

Just yesterday we got the new economic figures on the third quarter of this year, when our economy grew over 3½ percent. In 1994, more than half the new jobs were high-wage jobs, and there were more high-wage jobs coming into our economy than in the previous 5 years combined. We've got a lot to do, but we're making progress by putting the interests of ordinary Americans first, taking on problems too long ignored, helping individuals to compete and win. That's the path to the future.

In the elections we'll have in a little over a week, we'll face a choice between continuing to move forward on a path that's working or going back to flawed policies and easy promises that failed us in the past. I believe America will look forward toward tomorrow, not toward yesterday. I believe America won't give in to the easy path.

Just as we are setting the example by working abroad to help to advance the cause of democracy, peace, and freedom, we can set an example for ourselves by looking to the future at home. We owe that to the good men and women of our Armed Forces who are out here for our sake. The world they're helping to make peaceful expects no less of us, and I believe the American people will expect no less of themselves.

Thanks for listening.

NOTE: The address was recorded at 5 p.m. on October 28 at the Tactical Assembly Area Liberty in Kuwait for broadcast at 10:06 a.m. on October 29.

Statement on Signing Legislation To Reauthorize the Merit Systems Protection Board and the Office of Special Counsel
October 29, 1994

Today, I am signing into law H.R. 2970, a bill to reauthorize the Merit Systems Protection Board and the Office of Special Counsel and provide additional protections for Federal employee whistleblowers and other victims of prohibited personnel practices.

I have been advised that one provision in this bill (section 9), which concerns the apparent authority of an arbitrator to discipline a Federal employee who was not a party to the original action, raises serious constitutional questions.

Accordingly, I am directing the agencies to follow appropriate procedures to protect the constitutional rights of such Federal employees and to consider the need for remedial legislation.

WILLIAM J. CLINTON

The White House,
October 29, 1994.

NOTE: H.R. 2970, approved October 29, was assigned Public Law No. 103–424.

Remarks at the National Italian-American Foundation Dinner
October 29, 1994

Thank you very much. Can you hear me in the back? You can't hear, can you? Can the people with the sound turn it up a little bit? Now, can you hear in the back? I think some people can hear, but not see. So if the rest of you would accommodate them, I would appreciate it, or they would anyway. I can't see some of you. Thank you.

I want to thank Senator Leahy for his kind remarks. As a matter of fact, I want to thank Senator Leahy for being able to stand up here after the 3 days I just put him through. He did a wonderful job for our country on this trip to the Middle East, and I thank him for that.

I'm delighted to be back here for the third year in a row with Frank Guarini, Frank Stella, Art Gajarsa, with the distinguished Ambassador from the Vatican, and the distinguished Italian Ambassador. I have to say, Hillary wanted me to especially say tonight how sorry she was she couldn't come again. You know last year when she was here, she met Fabio, and he picked her up and carried her around. She wasn't the same for weeks afterward. [*Laughter*] She went to the Middle East with me. She needed a little energy boost tonight, so I came here thinking somebody with muscles would pick her up. But she's in California on our behalf. I had a great time here last year, too. Fabio lifted Hillary

up; Danny DeVito sat in my lap. [*Laughter*] At least it wasn't Dom DeLuise. [*Laughter*] We had a great—all of us had a good time here.

You know, I'm sure everyone thinks from time to time about what he or she might have liked to do with their lives, and a lot of you know I've been made fun of for some of my habits. But when I saw Nicholas Cage tonight, I told him that one of my great disappointments was that I wasn't hired as one of the Elvis impersonators to be in "Honeymoon in Las Vegas" with him. [*Laughter*] He promised me a role in his next movie. [*Laughter*]

Senator Leahy said in jest what I would say in jest, which is that it was nice to be home in the safety and security of the White House after going to the Middle East. [*Laughter*] I want you to know a couple of things about that, seriously. First of all, a gunman did open fire; nobody was hurt. The man was captured. The man was captured in part because of ordinary citizens who were standing there, who did their duty. And I hope that is an example for others around the country. I also want you to know the Secret Service did their usual magnificent job. I was upstairs listening to a football game, and the shots were sort of intermittent with the cheers—[*laughter*]—and they were up there within a minute. And I thank them for the fine work that they do every day for our country.

The last thing I'd like to say to all of you is, if we ever needed an example of why the Congress did the right thing to pass the crime bill, including the assault weapons ban, that was it today.

As you know, Senator Leahy and I just returned from the Middle East. We got home this morning about 8 o'clock. I went there for three reasons: first of all, to witness the historic peace treaty between Israel and Jordan, which the United States was privileged to help bring about; second, to try to continue to further the peace process in the Middle East. We now have the Washington Declaration between the PLO and Israel, and I was there working to see that it is fully implemented and that we do everything we can to minimize the ability of terrorists to kill the peace by killing innocent people and to try to further the prospect of peace with Syria and with Lebanon, without which we will never have a complete peace there. And finally, I went there to thank our troops in the Persian Gulf and to reiterate the intention of the United States to protect the freedom of the nations in the Persian Gulf.

I'm sure all of you shared the pride that I felt, the pride of an ordinary American citizen, over the last several weeks as we have seen from the Middle East to South Africa, from Northern Ireland to Haiti, the people of the world look to America to support them in their courageous efforts to support peace and freedom. They respect our strength. They respect our military and our economic strength. But they also respect our energy, our drive, our creativity, the power of our example, and the fact that they know the United States has good intentions for the rest of the world, that what we really want is to be more secure and more prosperous by helping other people to live up to the fullest of their capacities and by taking away all incentives for people to oppress each other, so that they can get on with the business of building better lives for themselves and their children.

Sometimes I think we'd all be better off if every American could just, once in a great while, travel beyond our borders, just to see a little more how other people see us. If you could have seen the people lining the streets in Jordan, the reaction from the Jordanian Parliament when I had the privilege of being the first Western leader ever to address the Parliament, the people in the streets in Israel, the people pour-ing out of their apartments in Damascus to see the first President in 20 years on the streets of Damascus, it just made me so proud of our country and so grateful to be the representative of 250-plus million people who are setting a standard, with all of our difficulties, that others want to strive for.

It is the standard that brought so many of you or your parents or your grandparents to these shores. It is our capacity for constant renewal and for continued efforts to institutionalize our sense of good will and our sense of challenge.

And if I could say anything else today, I would be happy for all the words to be forgotten if you could just remember this: This is a very great country. But it requires us to keep working to make it great. If you look at all the renewal that's going on in the world, the restoration of democracy in Haiti, the success of a booming democracy in South Africa, the struggles of the people, Catholic and Protestant, to lay down their centuries-old conflict in Northern Ireland—[*applause*]—I just said that to see whether Pat Leahy would clap. [*Laughter*] I'm always trying to test which side of his ethnicity is the more dominant. [*Laughter*] If you think about the Middle East, if you could have just—I know you saw it on television, but it was overwhelming to see those two little girls bringing flowers to Prime Minister Rabin and King Hussein, one the granddaughter of an Israeli, the other the granddaughter of a Jordanian killed in war fighting each other, and to think that our country had the chance to be a part of helping to make it possible for them to do what they desperately wanted to do. What we need to remember is, this renewal that is sweeping the world, energized in large measure by the impulses of the people themselves but in no small measure by the support and the encouragement of the United States, we also have to do that here at home for ourselves.

We have to say: Look, we have challenges; we're going to face them instead of complain about them. Instead of pointing the finger of blame, we're going to assume responsibilities. Sure we've got problems, but the promise of this country at the dawn of the next century, at the dawn of the new millennium, is far greater than the range of our problems, if only we will have the same sense of confidence in ourselves that others have in us. That is my message to you tonight, my fellow Americans.

I must say, there is something to be said—Frank took away all my good lines, because he mentioned most of the Italian-Americans in my administration that I was going to eulogize so they'd be nice to me tomorrow morning—[laughter]—but there is something to be said for the incredible spirit and energy and drive and adherence to old-fashioned Americanism that I see in every Italian-American in my administration, from Leon Panetta on down, because they keep the spirit of this country alive in our work every day. And you do that everywhere.

I do want to tell Ed Rensi that I had nothing to do with his being recognized tonight, in spite of my affiliation with McDonald's, which is well-known. [Laughter] You can see it in my eyes; you can see it in my waist. That's why I stand behind this wide podium, hoping your imagination will get the better of you.

This is a very important thing. We sometimes minimize the power of the spirit of the imagination. If I have learned anything since I have been President, it is that. This job and the work of this country involves a lot of very specific things: Do we have the right foreign policy, or don't we? Did we pass the family leave bill, or didn't we? Did we do this or that specific thing? But it is also a spirit. And it has to pervade people in their lives. It has to reach down deep into them in order for us to do what we can do.

This Nation has never been made great primarily by its Government. Its Government has to reflect the greatness, the energy, the direction of the people. And leadership in a democracy like ours is possible only insofar as it is connected to what is profoundly good and enduring but also open to change in America. The greatest thing about this country is, and the reason we're still around after more than 200 years, is that we have been rooted to a set of constitutional values and principles rooted in the deep, philosophical conviction that each and every one of us is a creature of God, entitled to be treated equally before the law, entitled to be challenged and given the opportunity to live up to the fullest of our God-given capacities.

That is what has kept us going. And rooted to those things, we have been free, therefore, to change over and over and over again with every age and time to meet whatever challenges we've faced. The freedom to change because we were rooted in these values and they were

enshrined in our Constitution and we were willing to fight and die for them—that is what has kept us here as the longest lasting free government in all of human history. It is a magical thing.

Now, if you look at the problems we have today, they largely grow out of a curious combination of our refusal to adapt to the challenges of today and tomorrow and our violation of the traditional values which got us where we are. And so I say, as you look toward the future, we have to do something that you may think is contradictory but is not contradictory at all: We have to do the basic things better, and we have to be better at facing our problems and turning them into a promise and being agents of change.

Consider the problems of America. For 30 years we have had increasingly difficult social problems, all starting with the breakdown of the solidity of the family—the institution which made most Italian-Americans what they are today, and the rest of us as well—then the breakdown of the sense of community and the other institutions of community and the availability of work, without which life does not have sufficient dignity. And all the things we don't like, the drugs, the gangs, the guns, the violence, the deterioration of the ability of our young people to exercise discipline and self-control, all of the bad things we don't like were created because of the vacuum which existed from the absence of the good things. Now, this did not happen overnight. It has been a generation in coming. And it will not turn around overnight.

Your Government has certain responsibilities, in the crime bill, to empower communities to hire more police and to defend themselves and to make the schools safer and to do more about violence within the families and to protect victims and all of the things we tried to do in the crime bill—in dealing with the assault weapons. But a lot of this has to be done at the grassroots level. Where communities and police work together, the crime rate goes down. There are many cities in this country where, for 3 years running now, we've have double-digit reductions in the crime rate. In every case, it was because of what people did where they live and work, not because of something that happened up here. We have empowered people to drive down crime and lift up kids, but they must do it; you must do it.

And in the end, all of these young people who are going astray have got to have somebody to look up to again. They have got to have somebody to look up to again. Did you ask yourselves what in God's name was going on in the minds of those kids that dropped the 5-year-old from the high rise in Chicago? What turns the heart of a 10-year-old to stone? Everybody in this world's going to look up to somebody. Who is it going to be? What will they stand for?

At the end of this congressional session, a bill little noticed and barely commented on, sponsored by the retiring Senator from Ohio, Howard Metzenbaum, passed the Congress, a bill to make it easier for Americans to adopt children without families across racial lines. It was just a small step. It was just a small step, but I hope and pray this is something we'll be able to get together people across racial lines, across religious lines, across political party lines. I am telling you, these little kids are going to look up to somebody or something. They're either going to watch 4 hours of television at night, with people with violent behavior providing cheap thrills, where the future is what happens in 5 minutes, not 10 years, or somebody is going to be putting a hand on them and showing them a different way.

And the Italian-American community can have a major impact on our ability to lift the children of America, to turn around a 30-year trend and push it back the other way. For all the modernization of America, if we continue to allow the brutalization of childhood for millions of our kids, we will not have what we need to have. And that is a fact.

Now, if you look at the economy, you find a different set of challenges. For 20 years, more or less—although there is some indication the trend may finally be changing this year—for 20 years, more or less, hourly wage earners have not gotten a raise. The average working family is spending more hours at work in 1994 than in 1969, 25 years ago.

Why? Well, there are lots of reasons. But most of it, I'm convinced, is the globalization of the economy, the globalization of wage rates, the fact that every job and every investment now has to be considered in terms of all the pressures all around the world and our failure to adapt to those changes.

Why is America coming back? Because the private sector is adapting. The United States

car companies, in 1994, sold more automobiles than the automobile companies of Japan for the first time since 1979 this year. We've had 9 or 10 months of manufacturing job growth for the first time in 10 years. For the first time in 9 years, the annual vote of international economists said America had the most productive economy in the world. Why? Because we were prepared to change.

And now we have to do more of that. We have to make some changes if this economy is going to work right. We have to move people who are dependent on welfare to work, through welfare reform. We have to provide people— you can clap for that. [*Applause*] We have to provide for a lifetime of education and training. The average 18-year-old will change jobs six times in a lifetime.

Sooner or later, in some way that people trust, that they don't think is too dominated by the Government, we've got to face the health care crisis. Another million Americans lost their health insurance this year, and they were in working families. They were not on welfare; they were working people.

So, you tell me what the answer is. I can tell you that this year, for the first time in 25 years, your Government reduced both defense and domestic spending, the first domestic spending reduction in 25 years, even though we increased investment in education. The only thing that increased was health care costs; they're exploding. We spend 14 percent of our income on it; nobody else spends more than 10 percent. And yet, we've got 40 million people without insurance, and the 85 percent with insurance almost all are at risk of losing it at some time in their lifetime. Now, if you didn't like what I tried to do, you tell me what we ought to do. But I'll tell you this: We have got to face this challenge. Burying our head in the sands is not an answer and not an option.

And I would like to say one other thing. So we've got the old problems where we violate our values; we have new challenges where we have to change. And we have to do both. One last thing I'd like to say is, I believe most of the problems we face today do not have an easy, partisan division, if you define it in terms of the rhetoric that has dominated our politics for the last 20 years. And I just want to say, since one of them is here today, the more we can have partnership instead of partisanship, the better this country is going to be. I want to thank good Republicans like Congresswoman Connie Morella, who is here, and Mayor Rudy Giuliani for their support of the crime bill. That's the kind of work we ought to be doing in America today.

You know, I always like to speak here because you're so enthusiastic. And I promised I wouldn't talk very long. And I know I'm a little tired, and tomorrow Hillary will watch this on film and tell me I talked too long. [*Laughter*] But I want to just say one other thing. A reasonably famous Italian, Niccolo Machiavelli—whom Leon can read without benefit of translation— [*laughter*]—said 500 years ago, "There is nothing so difficult in all of human affairs than to change the established order of things, for all people who will be discomforted by the change will immediately oppose you, and those who will be benefited will be lukewarm, because they are uncertain of the result." Based on the last 2 years, I'd say he was a pretty smart fella. [*Laughter*]

I ask you to remember that again, because the secret of our successes today are rooted once again—I say again, if you look at Haiti, if you look at the Gulf, in both cases, a part of that story is something that you hardly ever read about. Our ability to perform well in Haiti, our ability to move in the Gulf in part represented the success of American military strategy in the last 2 years, learning from the Gulf war, increasing our ability to coordinate our military efforts and to move more quickly— change, change in the service of traditional American values of freedom and democracy and prosperity and security.

If you look at why our economy is growing today, it's because we got the deficit down, we got our house in order, we began to invest in America again, and the private sector changed to become more competitive. Old-fashioned values, commitment to change, that is what you

represent. That's what your foundation's activities represent. That's what your personal stories represent.

And so I say, again, I wish every one of you could have been with us in the Middle East. I wish you could have looked into the faces of those people. I wish you could see this country as others see it. One of the reasons I think that immigrant families in the first or second generation are so often the most patriotic of Americans is that they still have a collective memory of America from the outside in, as well as from the inside out.

So I ask you to think about it. If we're going to go into the next century as the greatest country on Earth, and I am convinced our best days are still ahead of us, we must blend a ferocious devotion to the institutions of family and work and community and to the values of our Constitution and the integrity of the individual in this country, with a relentless willingness to change to do whatever it takes to develop and empower the capacities of our people to do well in an increasingly interdependent world. We must stand up for what we believe abroad, because it makes us more secure. But every day, we have to first stand up for what we believe at home. You can lead the way.

Thank you, and God bless you all.

NOTE: The President spoke at 9:25 p.m. at the Washington Hilton Hotel. In his remarks, he referred to foundation officers Frank Guarini, president, Frank Stella, chair, and Anthony J. Gajarsa, vice chair; Ambassador Agostino Cacciavillan of the Holy See; Ambassador Boris Biancheri of Italy; actor and model Fabio; actors Danny DeVito, Dom DeLuise, and Nicholas Cage; Edward Rensi, president and chief executive officer, McDonald's; and Mayor Rudolph Giuliani of New York City.

Remarks at a Rally for Democratic Candidates in Philadelphia, Pennsylvania
October 31, 1994

The President. Thank you. It is good to be home, and it's good to be back in Philadelphia. Thank you.

Let's give a big hand to the George Washington High School Band. [*Applause*] Weren't they great? Thank you. Thank you.

Senator Wofford, Lieutenant Governor Singel, Members of Congress, Mayor Rendell, City Council President Street, Democratic Chair Bob Brady, District Attorney Lynn Abraham, our State senator and nominee for Congress, Chakha Fattah, and my fellow Americans. It is wonderful to be here on behalf of these fine people.

You know, Harris Wofford doesn't always vote with me, but he always votes for you, and you ought to keep him there. I read the endorsement in your distinguished local newspaper, which said, "Harris Wofford has been America's conscience when we need it. He has the record, the heart, the vision that has done Pennsylvania proud, and he deserves reelection." I couldn't say it better than the Philadelphia Inquirer did.

And I read the endorsement of Mark Singel, which said that he has the better vision, a better program, mentioned his positions on education and welfare reform, two things I like to think I know something about, that are absolutely critical for any Governor. And it said, and I quote, "His blueprint for Pennsylvania is so much stronger, he deserves the chance to put it into action." And I hope you'll give it to him.

Just before I left for the Middle East, I challenged the American people to think hard about this election, to look at the record, to look at the future, to shine some light on a debate that had been pretty muddied up until a couple of weeks ago. Well folks, the Sun has begun to shine in this election.

Every day more Americans are beginning to know that the real issue here is, who will fight for ordinary Americans, for their future, for their families, for their jobs, their children's education, their parents' Social Security, their security? Who is going to be in on your side for tomorrow? The answer is, we are. And you need to help us win on November 8th.

This election represents a simple choice between going forward and going back. Twenty-one months ago, with the enormous help of the people of Pennsylvania and a terrific mandate from the city of Philadelphia, I moved to Washington to try to change this country, to try to make our country and our Government work for ordinary citizens, to try to get this economy going again, to try to make sure that every American was prepared to compete and win in this tough global economy.

Remember the challenges we faced when I went there? We'd had 4 years of the slowest economic growth since the Great Depression;

4 years in which Pennsylvania had lost 8,300 jobs—no gain, a loss. We were dealing with 12 years of trickle-down Reaganomics, which exploded our deficits and sent our jobs overseas, divided our people. We were dealing with 20 years of stagnant wages as people struggled just to hold on to their jobs with more and more uncertainty in a rapidly changing economy. We were dealing with 30 years of developing social problems in the family and on the streets with crime and violence and drugs and gangs. No one thought this could be turned around overnight. But I can tell you, my friends, after 21 months, we're beginning to make a difference, and we need to keep going.

Look at the record. We passed the family and medical leave law, which enables over 2 million Pennsylvania workers to be able to take some time off when there's a baby born or a sick parent. Senator Wofford voted for it; his opponent voted against it.

We passed the student loan reform law which enabled 20 million Americans, including 1.7 million in Pennsylvania, middle-class folks, to borrow money to go to college on better, more affordable terms. Senator Wofford led the fight; his opponent voted against it.

We passed the national service bill, a domestic Peace Corps, to say to the American people, look, if you'll go back to Philadelphia and you'll go to work on those streets and you'll help kids one-on-one in trouble, if you'll do something to help solve the problems of America and give some of your time to building our country from the grassroots, we'll give you some money to go to college. Senator Wofford led the fight; his opponent voted against it.

We cut income tax rates for 15 million working families, including over 500,000 families in Pennsylvania, people who work full time, have children in their homes, but have very modest wages. Why? Because we don't think anybody who works full time and has kids in the home should live in poverty. That is our policy. Senator Wofford supported it; his opponent voted against it.

We passed a budget that cuts spending by $255 billion, that cut the Federal bureaucracy by 272,000 positions. We changed the way Government buys things to make it more competitive, so you won't have to read about a system that produces those $500 hammers and $50 ashtrays anymore. Senator Wofford led the way on that.

Now, when we implemented this economic strategy last year, do you remember what they said, the other guys, the people that are opposing Harris Wofford and Mark Singel? Every one of them voted against the economic strategy. They said, "Oh, if you do this, you will ruin the economy. You will explode the deficit. You will lose jobs. America will be in terrible shape." Well, they were wrong. They have launched the most vicious attacks, often misrepresenting what was in that program, on every Member of Congress who stood up and gave America a chance to go into the future. But they were wrong.

What are they going to say? The deficit's going down 3 years in a row for the first time since Truman was President. We have a budget that is reducing the Federal Government to its smallest size since John Kennedy was President. There has been a new study, as it comes out annually, of international economists, saying that for the first time in 9 years, America has the most productive economy in the world.

You know, believe me, I know we've still got a lot to do. I read the story of the Philadelphia worker who said he was a part-timer in '92, and he wanted a full-time job. He's still got a part-time job; he doesn't know whether he should vote or not. Well, I have a message. Between '89 and January of '93, your State lost 8,300 jobs. In the last 21 months, your State has gained over 86,000 jobs. We're going in the right direction. Let's don't turn back now.

Imagine this folks, imagine if Harris Wofford were a Republican Senator running for reelection. No, don't boo. Keep in mind, we're all preaching to the saved today. You've got to go reach somebody else between now and election day. So, think of this. If Harris Wofford were a Republican Senator running for reelection, if these Members of Congress were Republican Members running for reelection, and they had voted to reduce the deficit, to shrink the size of the Federal Government, for the toughest crime bill in American history, to explode the economy after years of stagnation, the Republicans would be building statues to them and saying we were unpatriotic for opposing them. And they ought to be building statues to them anyway and reelecting them here today.

And instead, what are they doing? Now, they're trying to say no to the progress we have made. Three hundred and fifty of them went to Washington the other day and signed a Con-

tract With America. It's a trillion dollars' worth of promises.

Now, listen to this: big tax breaks, mostly for the wealthy, billions more on defense, revive Star Wars, balance the budget. Does that sound familiar to you? We've heard that before, haven't we? And you know what will happen. If they get control of the Congress and that's their program, you'll explode the deficit, ship jobs overseas again. You'll have cuts in Medicare, cuts in student loans, cuts in veterans' benefits. We will never fund that crime bill that Ed Rendell talked about.

The worst news is that the Republican contract could devastate Social Security and senior citizens. The House Budget Committee says to meet their program, the contract they signed, they'd have to cut Social Security about $2,000 a person a year and Medicare about $1,800 a person a year. That's $3,600 a year out of the most vulnerable people in this country, people who have worked hard all their lives, people who have paid their taxes, people who have paid their dues. That is wrong. That is wrong, and we must not allow it to be done.

I know. You know, you hear something like this, it's just incredible. You can hardly believe that they did it. But don't forget, President Reagan tried to do it in '81. The House leader proposed it in '86. Mr. North, the Senate candidate of the Republicans in Virginia——

Audience members. Boo-o-o!

The President. ——he just proposed making it voluntary Social Security, which means killing it. And now Senator Wofford's opponent says that he wants to raise the retirement age to 70, and I quote, "further if I could." Well, he can't do that if you don't let him.

So I say to you, say no to this radical attack on Social Security. Say no to billions more in tax breaks that explode the deficit and send our jobs overseas. It all sounds so good, their pretty promises, a trillion dollars' worth of promises. You know, it's a week from the election, folks. We'd all like to stand up and make you a trillion dollars' worth of promises. That's real money. We could all have a good time on a trillion dollars' worth of hot checks. [*Laughter*] But it would be wrong.

We need men and women in the Congress who will keep their promises to middle-class America, their promises to our future. They need people up there in Washington who understand that when you work all your life, you deserve the peace of mind that Social Security and Medicare give you because you have earned it, not a Government handout but a contract for people who say, "We've done our part," and the rest of us say, "A job well done."

So, my fellow Americans, that's it. That's your choice a week from today. This country's in better shape than it was 21 months ago. We've got more jobs, a lower deficit, a Government doing things for ordinary people in a world that is safer and more secure and more prosperous. We have a long way to go until everybody who wants a job has one, people who work hard get a raise, people who don't have health care get it, and people who have it don't lose it. We've got a lot to do, but the way to do it is to keep going forward, not to turn back.

You know, I just want to close with this thought. You know I just got back from a pretty arduous trip, and I hope I'm doing all right today. I'm still a little jet-lagged. I want to tell you something. Brave people in every part of this world are struggling and fighting for freedom, for democracy, for prosperity, for security, whether it's Israel and her Arab neighbors, the people in the Persian Gulf where our brave soldiers are, the people in Korea who want to make Korea all a nonnuclear peninsula, the people in Northern Ireland trying to bury hundreds of years of hatred, the people in South Africa trying to build their democracy, the people in Haiti welcoming home President Aristide. These people all over the world are trying to do this, and everywhere they wish to have America's support for their courage because they admire our values and they admire the strength of our system and they admire our willingness to change. They believe in us. And we need to believe in ourselves, just as much.

Folks, this country is not still here so many long years after the Founders first came here to Philadelphia because we took the easy way out, we listened to the easy promises, we let people divide us and play on our fears. We are here because we voted our hopes, because we voted for unity, because we voted for the future, because we had the courage to change, we looked to the future with hope and optimism. Others look at us that way. If we will look at ourselves that way on November 8th, you will elect Harris Wofford. You will elect Mark Singel. You will elect these Members of Congress who are here.

Thank you, and God bless you all.

NOTE: The President spoke at 12:43 p.m. in the Courtyard at City Hall. In his remarks, he referred to Lt. Gov. Mark Singel of Pennsylvania, Mayor Edward Rendell of Philadelphia, and Philadelphia City Council president John Street.

Interview With Don Lancer of KYW Radio, Philadelphia
October 31, 1994

Mr. Lancer. Good afternoon, Mr. Clinton.

The President. Hello, Don.

Mr. Lancer. Can you hear me?

The President. I can hear you fine. Can you hear me?

Mr. Lancer. Can you hear me, Mr. Clinton?

The President. Yes, I can hear you. Can you hear me?

Midterm Elections

Mr. Lancer. Yes. Good afternoon. You're in the State ostensibly to help Harris Wofford win election to a full term. He replaced John Heinz in a special election a couple of years ago, and he went to Washington on the matter of national health care, which we all know did not make it through the Congress this year. Polls have shown overall that the Democrats are not going to do that well in the election, come one week from tomorrow on the 8th. What's the reason for that? Why is it voters look so poorly on your party and its candidates right now?

The President. Well, first let me say I think the surveys all show that our prospects are looking up. But I think what happened was two things. There is a lag time between when you accomplish something in Washington and when people feel it in their own lives. There are still a lot of voters who have jobs, but they're worried about whether they'll lose them or they'll lose their health care or will they ever get a raise. It's a tough, fast-changing global economy, and a lot of people feel personally insecure. There are also a lot of people who are worried about crime and social breakdown. The other big problem is, when Congress is meeting and the Republicans are trying to kill everything, delay everything, talk everything to death, all of the focus is on conflict, process, failure. The American people don't know what's happened.

Now when the Congress has gone home for the last 2 or 3 weeks, you can sense a real movement out there. People sense that they've got a real fundamental choice here. If you look at Pennsylvania—you heard the quote there— we've had 86,000 new jobs in Pennsylvania. The economy is growing; the deficit is down. We've done things that the Congress had refused to address for years and years. We passed the family leave law to protect working people who have to take time off. We passed a law to expand Head Start, one to immunize children, one to give tax cuts for working families on modest incomes that have children in the home so they'll never be in poverty. We're making the Government work for ordinary people again. And we've expanded trade and promoted peace and security around the world. Russian missiles aren't pointing at Americans for the first time since the beginning of the nuclear age.

So when you look at that record and then you look at this Republican contract which promises to take us back to the eighties and would promise everybody a tax cut, especially for wealthy people, spend more money on defense and Star Wars, balance the budget—they'll have to cut Social Security and Medicare and do it steeply to pay for it. I just don't think the American people want that, and I don't think the people of Pennsylvania do.

Mr. Lancer. That is just my point, though. In recent polls—you keep talking about the recovery that's occurring, and I have no doubt that there is a recovery in certain parts of the country if they just bear that out. Here in the Northeast, however, there is no recovery; at least the perception is there is no recovery. There was a recent poll out by the Tarrence group that shows that only a third of Americans believe the claims of a recovery. My whole point to you, or my question to you is, why is it that this is the perception? It can't simply be because Republicans are trying to stonewall things in the Congress so there is gridlock?

The President. No, I think—well, I do believe that people have not gotten a lot of the informa-

tion; I think that is true. But I think—keep in mind what I said first. I think a lot of people may hear that there are more jobs, but they may feel that their personal situation is not more secure. That is, they may think, "Well, I'm still not going to get a raise," or "I might lose my job," or "I might lose my health benefits." Another million Americans lost their health care last year. That's why Harris Wofford and I worked so hard to protect the health care benefits of working people and to try to change the law so that they wouldn't lose their health care.

So there is a lot of personal insecurity out there. But the point I'm trying to make to the American people is that we're making them more secure—that's what the family leave law was all about, that's what these efforts to improve the health of our children are all about, that's what the crime bill is all about—that our economic policy is working. So the issue is, do you want to keep working for something that is plainly taking us in the right direction, or do you want to buy this Republican snake oil, you know, "We're going to give everybody a tax cut and balance the budget and increase everybody's spending, and we'll tell you how we're going to pay for that after the election."

Mr. Lancer. Okay, let's assume we're headed in the right direction. What we in the Northeast would like to know is, how long is it going to take us to get there?

The President. Well, your unemployment rate in Pennsylvania is above the national average, but it's a point lower than it was when I took office. You lost 8,300 jobs in the previous administration; you got 86,800 more under our administration. They had 12 years; we've had 21 months. You want to turn around and give the guys that put you in the hole in the first place 2 more years, 4 more years, 6 more years? You gave them 12 years. We've been given 21 months, and we've turned it around.

Now, just because everybody hasn't felt it, that's not a good reason to stay home or vote Republican. They had 12 years, and we were in a big hole. We also had 20 years, through both parties, of stagnant wages and less secure jobs and losing benefits. And we have had 30 years of rising crime and family breakdown. We are at least addressing all these things for the first time. And it's pretty refreshing, I think, to have a Government that has taken on the tough problems instead of running away from them and that can at least show we're making some progress. And the worst thing in the world you can do is to say, "Okay, we gave you these problems—we had 12 years of the other party's politics and economics, we've got 20 years of economic problems and 30 years of social problems—and we haven't felt anything in 21 months. So we're going to go back to the people that got us in the hole in the first place." That's not good thinking. If everybody will just relax and look at the record, they'll vote for Harris Wofford, they'll vote for Mark Singel, and they'll vote to keep this country moving in the right direction so that all of Pennsylvania can feel the results of these efforts.

Mr. Lancer. All right, sir. But there have been changes in the way that those figures are tallied. Anyway——

The President. That's right, there have been changes. If we were living under the same figures the Republicans had, the unemployment rate would have gone down over 1½ percent. That's right, you're absolutely right. The changes in the way the unemployment is tallied work against us, not for us.

Mr. Lancer. All right. We appreciate your taking time out from a very busy schedule today, Mr. Clinton. And thank you for joining us here on KYW News Radio this afternoon.

The President. Thank you.

NOTE: The interview began at 4:35 p.m. The President spoke by telephone from the David Lawrence Convention Center in Pittsburgh, PA.

Remarks at a Rally for Democratic Candidates in Pittsburgh, Pennsylvania
October 31, 1994

The President. Thank you, Senator Wofford. Thank you, ladies and gentlemen. Let me say, first of all, before we get into the speech, I want to thank the East Allegheny High School Band and the Pine-Richland High School Band. Let's give them a hand for playing for us tonight. [*Applause*]

I am proud to be here with Harris Wofford, with Congressman Coyne, with Governor Singel, with your State treasurer Cathy Baker-Knoll, with Tom Flaherty and Pete Forrester, Linda Rhodes, and the congressional nominees. I hope you will elect them. You have a chance to replace these two Members of Congress that are leaving with Mike Doyle and Bill Leavens, and I hope you will vote for them.

Audience members. Yes, we will! Yes, we will!

The President. Yes, you will.

Audience members. Yes, we will! Yes, we will!

The President. I also want to say a word about a few other people who are here tonight: the chairman of the Democratic Party, David Wilhelm, who has worked so hard for all of us. And I want to say a special thanks to some of our friends from the labor movement, without whom so many of our candidates—[*inaudible*]. I thank especially Jerry McEntee, the president of AFSCME, who is here; George Becker, the president of the Steel Workers, who is here; and Bill George—[*inaudible*]—AFL–CIO.

You know, this election has a lot of interesting choices. I heard, for example, recently that Senator Wofford's opponent criticized people who go to the Senate to fight for locks and dams.

Audience members. Boo-o-o!

The President. Anybody who criticizes that has never had to create a job or move a product to market. I think western Pennsylvania is lucky to have somebody who fights for improvements in the Mon River locks in Turtle Creek, Elizabeth, and Charleroi myself, and you ought to keep Harris Wofford if for no other reason.

I read the endorsement of Senator Wofford in the Pittsburgh Post-Gazette. And he said, contrary to the paid ads of his opponent, I want to quote: "Senator Wofford is not an advocate of mindless big Government. He understands Government can't possibly solve all the problems in a nation, that personal responsibility and accountability must be engendered and demanded. He remains committed to a mission built on service and opportunity, hope and humanity, vision and realism. Harris Wofford is a direct descendant of the enlightened public officials who gave us Social Security and Medicare, those lifesaving programs. His opponent is not." I couldn't say it better myself.

My fellow Americans, 21 months ago I went to Washington with the help of an overwhelming vote from the people of Pennsylvania, with a commitment to make Government work for ordinary Americans, to get the economy moving again, to prepare our people to compete and win in the global economy, to make the world more secure and more prosperous for Americans to live and work in. I called it putting people first. Well, you know, we still have problems. There are still people who want jobs who don't have them, people who are looking for a raise that hasn't come, people who are worried about losing their health care. There are still problems with crime in our streets and social problems in our communities. But I'll tell you something, folks, look at what we found: 4 years of the slowest job growth since the Depression, 12 years of trickle-down economics that blew up the deficit and drove our jobs overseas——

Audience members. Boo-o-o!

The President. ——20 years of stagnant wages, 30 years of social problems. And after 21 months we are clearly moving in the right direction. We are in better shape than we were before.

I read in one of the papers today, a voter saying, "Oh, I'm sort of disillusioned. I don't know if they've done anything for ordinary Americans." Well, here is what we've done for ordinary Americans. We passed the family and medical leave law. Over 2 million working Pennsylvanians with family members can now take some time off when there's a child born or a sick parent without losing their job. We passed college loans for the middle class for lower interest, longer repayment terms, so that everybody can go to college. Over 1.7 million Pennsylvanians can take advantage of that. We passed the national service program, thanks to Harris Wofford's spirited leadership. Our economic program had tax cuts for over 500,000 working families in Pennsylvania with children in the home living on modest wages, because we, the Democrats, don't believe if you work full time and you've got a kid in the house you should be in poverty. We want to reward work and parenting. We voted to expand Head Start and to immunize every child in this country under the age of 2 by 1996. And on all those issues, Wofford was yes; his opponent was no. We're making Government work for ordinary citizens, thanks to people like Harris Wofford.

We made a serious assault on crime for the first time in a generation with tougher punishment, more prison space for serious offenders, more police for our streets, and prevention programs for our kids to keep them out of trouble in the first place. Every last Republican who voted against that crime bill knows that every law enforcement organization in the United States supported it. And a bunch of them voted for it the first time; then it became election year, and they flipped and voted no. They didn't care about lowering crime. They wanted a political issue. Harris Wofford voted to lower the crime rate in Pennsylvania, and you ought to reward him for it.

And we voted to put our economic house in order: $255 billion in spending cuts, 272,000 fewer people working for the Federal Government, gave all of the money to you to fight crime in your local communities. We voted to change the rules by which we buy things; no more $500 hammers and $50 ashtrays for us now. And when we did this, what did our opponents say? They said, "If you do this, we will bankrupt the economy. The economy will go down. The deficit will go up." Well, they were wrong. Look at the results: in 21 months, 4.6 million new jobs. In Pennsylvania in the previous 4 years, you lost 8,300 jobs; in this 21 months, 86,800 jobs in the State of Pennsylvania.

Do you know that if Harris Wofford were a Republican running for reelection—now don't boo, listen, because you need to go out between now and then and talk to people who are not for him yet, who are not for Mark Singel yet, who haven't made up their mind how they're going to vote in these congressional races. And I want you to think about this. If Harris Wofford were a Republican running for reelection, and he got up and said this: "I should be reelected, my fellow Republicans, because I did what you've been begging for for years. I reduced the deficit 3 years in a row for the first time since Truman. I am giving you the smallest Federal Government since John Kennedy. I have given the toughest crime bill to the American people in a generation, and I have voted for policies that are growing this economy for a change"—if he were a Republican, they'd be building a statue to him. And they ought to build one anyway. [*Applause*] You know it. You know it.

What is their beef? Their beef is, they want in. And so what did they do? They said no to everything—no, no, no—no to middle class college loans, no to family leave, no to everything. They refused to compromise on health care. They killed lobby reform. They killed campaign finance reform. They even killed the Superfund bill to clean up toxic waste dumps.

Audience members. Boo-o-o!

The President. It was an amazing thing, folks. We had the chemical companies, the labor unions, and the Sierra Club all for the bill. It was almost spooky. They don't agree on when the Sun's coming up in the morning. But they agreed that we had to get together and clean up the toxic waste dumps in America. No one in America was against it except a few more than 40 Republican Senators. And they preferred to leave the poison in the ground so they would have a political issue, so Harris Wofford——

Audience members. Boo-o-o!

The President. ——so Harris Wofford could not come home to Pennsylvania and say he helped to clean it up. Now, that is the truth. And now they have this Contract With America.

Audience members. Boo-o-o!

The President. Hey, this is a sweet deal. I wish I could do this a week before the election. But I'd turn red; I'd get embarrassed. I couldn't do it. [*Laughter*] But it's a sweet deal. It's a trillion dollars' worth of promises: "I'm going to give everybody a tax cut and especially the wealthiest Americans; they'll get lots more. And we're going to spend more on defense; we're going to spend more on Star Wars. We're going to give everybody everything, and we're going to balance the budget." Does that sound familiar? "Well, how are you going to pay for it?" we asked. And they say, "We'll tell you after the election." [*Laughter*]

So we had the House Budget Committee look at how it would be paid for. Do you know what their promises would cost if they kept them all? They'd have to cut Social Security $2,000 for every American. They'd have to cut Medicare $1,800 for every American. And if they abandon it, they would explode the deficit and ship our jobs overseas just like they did the last time they had power. They had it their way for 12 years.

I say to you, you think they're not serious about Social Security? Their leader once proposed making it voluntary. The Senate candidate in Virginia, Ollie North, you know him?

Audience members. Boo-o-o!

The President. He says Social Security ought to be voluntary. That means we ought to kill it. That means we ought to kill it. And of course, Senator Wofford's opponent says that he would settle for raising the retirement age to 70, but it would be higher if he could make it higher.

Audience members. Boo-o-o!

The President. Folks, here's my question. I know that this country has problems. I know this State has problems. I know not everybody is free of worry. But let me ask you something—they had it 12 years. They have told us if we give it to them again, they will do it to us again just like they did for the last 12 years.

In 21 months, we have turned this thing around. We're going in the right direction. Let's don't turn back now. Let's don't turn back now.

Let me tell you, I want you to think about this, in closing, every one of you, I want you to think about what you're going to do for the next 8 days. And I want you to think about it in terms of what I have just been doing. You know, I just came home from this trip to the Middle East, and I have seen—[*applause*]—and I want you to think about this. A big part of what I said in '92 was that I would give primary attention to our problems at home because we couldn't be strong abroad unless we were strong at home, but that we could not withdraw from the world, we had to be involved in the world. We had to expand trade, and we had to make the world more secure and more free. So we've expanded trade. And I'm going to Detroit tomorrow. You know what the biggest problem in Michigan is today? Overtime. The autoworkers are working too much overtime. That is a high-class problem. We need more problems like that.

For the first time since the dawn of nuclear weapons, no Russian missiles are pointed at your children. And we, we here in the United States, have been asked to help brave people all over the world as they struggle for freedom and democracy. Whether it is in South Africa or South Korea, whether it is in the Persian Gulf, in Kuwait and Saudi Arabia, or in the Middle East, whether it is in Haiti or in Northern Ireland, we are helping.

And what I want you to know is, why do you think these people want us to help? Because they know this is a very great country. And they respect our values, our Constitution, our devotion to democracy, our appreciation of diversity, and our willingness to change energetically to meet the challenges of every age. That is what they like about the United States. To be sure, they admire our military strength, but it is the character of our young men and women in uniform that they admire even more than our power.

What I want to say to you folks is that we have to believe in ourselves the way they believe in us, not because we're perfect but because we can always do better and because we are now doing better because we are taking on the problems we ignored too long. We're taking on the tough fights, and we're moving in the right direction.

And what I want each and every one of you to do is to go out of here and say what I said to you. Find a friend or a neighbor who is undecided, who is a soft no on Wofford or a soft no on Singel or who hasn't made up their mind how they're going to vote in these Congress races. Find somebody and personally promise yourself you are going to seek them

out and you are going to say, "Look at the record. Look at the alternative. Look at the future. Don't go back, go forward. Reelect Harris Wofford. Elect Mark Singel. Elect these two Congressmen."

Thank you, and God bless you all. Thank you. [*Applause*] Thank you. Thank you.

Just remember, I love western Pennsylvania. You've been wonderful to me. But you need to send Harris Wofford back to the Senate, elect Mark Singel, and do it. You have 8 days. Talk to everybody you can. Bring it home.

Thank you. God bless you all.

NOTE: The President spoke at 6 p.m. in the South Hall at the David Lawrence Convention Center. In his remarks, he referred to Tom Forrester and Peter Flaherty, Allegheny County commissioners; Linda Rhodes, State Democratic Party chair; and William M. George, president, Pennsylvania AFL–CIO. A portion of these remarks could not be verified because the tape was incomplete.

Statement on Signing California Desert Protection Legislation
October 31, 1994

I take great pleasure in signing into law S. 21, the "California Desert Protection Act," an Act to preserve for the American people a resource of extraordinary and inestimable value.

The Act designates as wilderness approximately 7.7 million acres of Federal lands administered by the Bureau of Land Management and the National Park Service. The Act adds approximately 3 million acres to the National Park System, including magnificent lands adjacent to the Death Valley and Joshua Tree National Monuments, which are redesignated as National Parks. It also establishes the Mojave National Preserve as a new unit of the National Park System.

Few Presidents have the opportunity to preserve so valuable a piece of this Nation's heritage. I exercise this opportunity with enthusiasm and gratitude. I am enthusiastic because this is the first time since 1980 that the United States has set aside so rich and vast an area. The broad vistas, the rugged mountain ranges, and the evidence of the human past are treasures that merit protection on behalf of the American people. I am grateful because we have

successfully concluded the long struggle to conserve these lands.

I also note that the Act establishes the New Orleans Jazz National Historical Park. Jazz is among our country's most widely recognized indigenous music and art forms. The creation of this park is very timely given that next May is the 100th anniversary of the formation of the Buddy Bolden in New Orleans, an event many see as the birth of jazz in America.

Senators Dianne Feinstein, Barbara Boxer, Bennett Johnston, and George Mitchell, and Congressmen George Miller, Richard Lehman, and Bruce Vento deserve our thanks for their leadership and persistence in passing this legislation. I also want to thank Interior Secretary Bruce Babbitt and his staff for their tireless efforts on behalf of this Administration priority. This achievement is a tribute to the many citizens who worked with congressional leaders and the Administration to ensure the protection of these desert gems.

This Act is proof that the common good and the will of the people can prevail. Today, as

I sign this bill, I am pleased to contribute my part to the preservation of the California Desert for the enjoyment of generations to come.

WILLIAM J. CLINTON

The White House,
October 31, 1994.

NOTE: S. 21, approved October 31, was assigned Public Law No. 103–433.

Letter to Congressional Leaders on Continuation of the National Emergency With Respect to Iran
October 31, 1994

Dear Mr. Speaker: (Dear Mr. President:)
Section 202(d) of the National Emergencies Act (50 U.S.C. 1622(d)) provides for the automatic termination of a national emergency unless, prior to the anniversary date of its declaration, the President publishes in the *Federal Register* and transmits to the Congress a notice stating that the emergency is to continue in effect beyond the anniversary date. In accordance with this provision, I have sent the enclosed notice, stating that the Iran emergency is to continue in effect beyond November 14, 1994, to the *Federal Register* for publication. Similar notices have been sent annually to the Congress and the *Federal Register* since November 12, 1980. The most recent notice appeared in the *Federal Register* on November 2, 1993.

The crisis between the United States and Iran that began in 1979 has not been fully resolved. The international tribunal established to adjudicate claims of the United States and U.S. nationals against Iran and of the Iranian government and Iranian nationals against the United States continues to function, and normalization of commercial and diplomatic relations between the United States and Iran has not been achieved. In these circumstances, I have determined that it is necessary to maintain in force the broad authorities that are needed in the process of implementing the January 1981 agreements with Iran and in the eventual normalization of relations with that country.

Sincerely,

WILLIAM J. CLINTON

NOTE: Identical letters were sent to Thomas S. Foley, Speaker of the House of Representatives, and Albert Gore, Jr., President of the Senate. The notice is listed in Appendix D at the end of this volume.

Remarks in a Roundtable Discussion on the Direct Student Loan Program at the University of Michigan in Dearborn, Michigan
November 1, 1994

The President. Thank you very much, President Duderstadt. Ladies and gentlemen, first let me say how delighted I am to be back at this campus again. I visited here in 1992, and I'm glad to be here again.

One of the most important commitments I made to the voters in 1992, at least from my point of view, was that if I were to become President I would try to do something about the student loan program to make it easier for more people to access and for more people to go to college and stay in college. I'd been very concerned, based on my experience as a Governor, with the number of our young people who either didn't go to school or who started and then dropped out because of the high cost of the college education, because they either couldn't get the loans or they thought if they did get the loans they would never be able to pay them back. I was also, frankly, outraged by the high default rate among people who had loans and didn't pay them back. So it seemed to me that there ought to be an easier way to get the loans, to pay them back, and a better way to actually see that they were paid back.

What this program is designed to do is to lower the cost of the college loans to the students, give the students more flexible repayment terms, guarantee that if you choose to go into some line of work which doesn't have a high salary when you get out of college, that there is a limit to how much you can be required to repay as a percentage of your income but that if something happens and your circumstances improve and you want to pay the loan off quicker with lower interest rates, obviously you have that option as well. So I came here today just to learn how this program is working.

I want to say a special word of thanks to Congressman Ford who, as the chairman of the House Education Committee, spearheaded this, as well as to Congressman Dingell and Congressman Carr. We passed this program by the narrowest of margins in the Congress. There were a lot of people who didn't want us to pass it because there were a lot of people who were sort of middlemen in this operation who were making a good deal of money off the program. But this is amazing. We saved over $4 billion over a 5-year period in the cost to the taxpayers. We already know we're going to cut $2 billion in the cost to the borrowers. And we're going to be able to help more people in a better way, if it is properly implemented.

So we're here today, in large measure, to thank the University of Michigan and to thank Wayne State for joining the program next year. Michigan has probably had the strongest participation in the program of any State in the country so far. It's a real tribute to the leaders of your institutions of higher education that you're out ahead of this curve. But I think the students of America will demand to be included in this program, the more they hear about it, if it's properly implemented. So I came here today to listen and see how it's going and hear from all of you.

[At this point, two students explained that the new William D. Ford Federal Direct Loan Program was beneficial to students planning to enter lower salary professions due to its flexible repayment terms. Another student then expressed appreciation for the AmeriCorps program.]

The President. Let me interject here. For those of you who don't know, what Alex was talking about is AmeriCorps, the national service program, allows young people to earn credit against a college education at the same annual rate as the GI bill, for service to the United States here at home in community service work. So the two of these things together, he said, can have an even bigger impact in making it easier to complete your college education.

[Another student expressed support for the AmeriCorps program. A participant then stated that he came from a low income family and could not attend college without student loans. He also commented on the minimal paperwork required by the new program. James Duderstadt, president of the University of Michigan, then introduced David Adamany, president of Wayne State University, who praised the new program's outreach to communities with high numbers of poor and minority students in need of financial support to attend college and expressed appreciation for the Department of Education's work on the program.]

The President. Thank you very much. I think we should give a little credit here, as you did, to Secretary Riley and Deputy Secretary Kunin and Assistant Secretary Longanecker and all the others. They have worked very hard to get the mechanics right, the details right on this and to keep it going.

The other thing that I'd like to emphasize on the points you just made is that I have been very concerned about the number of our young students, and not-so-young students, who are having to really string out their college education because they want to do it all on a pay-as-you-go basis for this reason. It actually is not good economics for our country.

The average college graduate in the first year of work makes, as you all know, I'm sure, much more than the average high school graduate in the first year of work. What you may not know is that the gap between what they make now in 1994 is twice as great as it was in 1984. So these trends are rather dramatic, and they are not going to be reversed in the foreseeable future, which means that especially in areas which have traditionally had either high unemployment or low income, if you want to change the income mix of the people and change the nature of the economy, one of the things you simply have to do is to dramatically increase the percentage of people who have a college education. It's one of the few things you can do in a short period of time, meaning over a 5, 6 year period, to change the income distribution in a community.

And so this is a very important thing not just for individual Americans and their opportunities, this is a big deal for our country and for whether we can continue to promote equality of opportunity and a better living standard and a rising living standard among people who have absolutely no way other than an education to achieve it.

[*President Duderstadt introduced Representative William Ford, who discussed consolidation and refinancing of preexisting loans under the new program and the tremendous decrease in paperwork due to its expanded use of computers. James Renick, chancellor of the University of Michigan at Dearborn, noted that the program served more students without an increase in administrative staff. After President Duderstadt invited students to comment, a participant stated that the direct loan program should be expanded. Another participant then explained that according to the legislation, only 5 percent of all student loans could be made through this program during its first year, but that in approximately 5 years most institutions should be offering it.*]

The President. This law passed the Congress last summer—I mean, summer before last, summer of '93. And then we had to do the rules, the regulations, set the system up. So no one could have been involved in it before then. And this is the first year, and then next year we'll have up to 40 percent of the institutions in the country involved. And then, eventually, we'll be offering it to everybody within a couple of years. And if we can get this message out across the country that it's working very well, then I think some of the reluctant student loan offices and institutions around the country will be changing their position rather rapidly.

[*President Adamany explained that the Federal Government's involvement in the direct loan program would help colleges and universities collect loan repayments and improve the image of institutions that accept high numbers of students who depend on loans. A participant then explained that while many students currently make several different payments to more than*]

one financial institution, under the new program they will only be required to send one check per month to the Internal Revenue Service. Another participant thanked the President for making affordable student loans available and for giving students from all backgrounds a chance to attend institutions like Michigan State, scheduled to participate in the second year of the program.]

The President. They're coming the next time.

[*A participant discussed how the direct loan program was helping people see higher education as an investment in the future of individuals and of the Nation. Another participant added that the variety of loan repayment options would give more incentive and opportunity to people from low income families to get a college education. A participant then suggested that the benefits of the program should be better advertised to students.*]

The President. I think that's a very good suggestion. Let me say, we do have some money set aside for an advertising outreach program. And we wanted to wait to start to run the advertising until this first year—which is 5 percent of the institutions, as you've heard—until we had these programs up and going so we knew what would work, we had some of the kinks ironed out. And yet, we wanted to get people's attention up because, as you heard Bill Ford say, we're going to 40 percent next year, then 50 percent the year after, then anybody who wants to get in. So I think you will see some—if our program works the way it's supposed to, you should see some advertising about this program through the media within a matter of a couple of months.

[*Representative Ford noted that the Department of Education would have a toll-free telephone number to provide information about the program. A participant said that implementing the program gradually would help ensure its quality and disagreed with the criticism that offering more than one method of repayment could be confusing to students.*]

The President. Thank you.

Q. We should also note that you don't have to make a decision about anything until you reach repayment.

Q. That's right.

Q. And then if you make one decision, you can change it. You're not stuck for the rest of your life with what you decide the day you graduate from college. You can adjust what's happening in your life.

Q. Which is key, because I may plan to get out and do more service. But I guess I don't plan to be a poor starving graduate student forever, and I'd like the ability to adjust my finances accordingly.

[*President Duderstadt reviewed the benefits of the program and invited the President to make final comments.*]

The President. Well, I think, first of all, the students have said it all, from my point of view. I do want to thank the Members of Congress who are here, Chairman Dingell, who's been characteristically reticent but has been so important to all of us. And Chairman Ford, thank you, and I'm very glad this program is named for you; it ought to be. And Bob Carr, I thank you for your help on this education initiative. But mostly I thank the students for what they've said because they have pointed out why this program will work and why it's important.

Again I will say, I just got interested in this because I got tired of hearing young people in my own State tell me they were going to drop out of college because they couldn't afford to take out another loan or tell me that they wouldn't go until they had some money because they knew they'd never be able to repay the loan. And I think we have changed all that now.

We've also been able to change it with good management and actually lower the cost to the Government, not increase the cost to the Government. It's unheard of that we can make better loans available at lower cost to the borrowers and still lower the costs to the taxpayers and drastically simplify it.

I will say this is a part of a series of things we are doing. We have done the same thing with the Small Business Administration loans, where a small business person can now fill out an SBA application that's one page long and get an answer within 3 days, something which was unheard of before. So we're trying to do this piece by piece by piece throughout the Government.

I also appreciated what Kelly said about the fact that we were willing, and wanted, in fact, to have one year where we started out on a very modest way, because there's always the possibility there could have been some difficulty

here we had to deal with. But in the end, the important thing is the students of this country—increasingly nontraditional students, increasingly not students that are just between the ages of 18 and 21—understand that this program is out there for them. Now they have to use it.

We—I will say again—this country is dealing with about 20 years in which the average earnings of hourly wage earners has been virtually stagnant when you adjust for inflation. If we want to get earnings up in America and we want to make a big dent particularly in population groups like Native Americans that have traditionally been lower income, there is no other way to do it in the near term, apart from dramatically increasing the number of young people who—and perhaps not-so-young people—who go to and finish college. There is no other near-term way for us to turn our society around on this economically.

So what I'm really hoping will happen as a result of this direct loan program is that enrollments will continue to rise dramatically and people who do not drop out will continue to drop dramatically, so that our country becomes a more educated place and our economy will become more powerful and our society will become more equal because people will be able to compete and win in a global economy. That is the ultimate goal of this entire enterprise. And from what I've heard today, I think it's been an effort worth making.

I thank you all for being here.

Q. Mr. President, on behalf of the University of Michigan and our sister institutions, we want to express our gratitude for your meeting with us today and sharing in this discussion.

I should point out that the President and I had a brief discussion before we came in, and we've agreed that we are going to arrange a little basketball match-up the first week in April between Arkansas and Michigan out in Seattle. [*Laughter*] Of course, we've got to do a little bit to get there first.

The President. That's right.

Q. The rematch.

Q. Thank you very much for returning to Michigan.

The President. Thank you.

NOTE: The President spoke at approximately 10:40 a.m. in the student union at the University of Michigan at Dearborn.

Remarks at a Rally for Democratic Candidates in Detroit, Michigan
November 1, 1994

Thank you so much. Can you hear me in the back? Well, I'm doing the best I can. But if you'll be a little more quiet, I'll be a little louder and maybe you can hear. Can you hear now? I will do the best I can, and you do the best you can.

Mayor Archer, County Executive Ed MacNamara, Congressman Carr. Folks, Bob Carr gave a good speech, and you ought to give him a good vote on November 8th and send him to the United States Senate. And I hope you will support Howard Wolpe and Debbie Stabenow. I thank Senator Riegle, Senator Levin, Congressman Conyers, Congressman Ford, Congressman Kildee, Congressman Dingell, Congressman Bonior, and two people you ought to send to Congress, Bob Mitchell and Lynn Rivers, I thank them all for being here. I'm glad to see your secretary of state, Dick Austin. And I want to ask you to support Judge Conrad Mallett, who is not here today. I thank the Straight Gate Gospel Choir, the Murray Wright High School Band, the Mason Drummer Corps, and Jennifer Holiday—was she great, or what?

Ladies and gentlemen, we're a week before election. There have been some clouds in this election, but they're starting to clear. The Sun is coming out. The choice is becoming stark and clear and unambiguous. Do we want to go forward or turn back? Do we want to support people who vote for ordinary Americans or people who just vote for organized interest groups?

[*At this point, there was a disruption in the audience.*]

You know, 21 months ago—let them talk, let them talk. Wait, wait a minute. They couldn't get a crowd like this. They had to come to ours. We welcome them here; let them come. And we welcome a little free speech and debate. If we had more of it, we'd be doing even better in this election.

Let me ask you something, folks. When we came here 21 months ago, you elected me President to change this country and to move this country forward, to face up to 30 years of social problems, 20 years of economic stagnation, 12 years of their trickle-down economics, and 4 years of the worst job growth since the Great Depression. We said we could change that, and we've been working at it steadily, to make this Government work for ordinary people, to get this economy going again, to empower people so they can compete in this global economy, and to make this world safer and more secure.

And I tell you, folks, there are still a lot of problems in America, but we have made a very good start. This country is in better shape, and we don't need to go back now.

If you look at Michigan alone, because of the work of our administration, with the help of these Members of Congress behind us, 1½ million workers are now protected by the family and medical leave law, so they can take a little time off when a baby is born or a parent is sick; 400,000 working families with children in their home got a tax cut so they won't fall into poverty if they're working full time and raising their kids. You heard the mayor talking about the crime bill: more police, more prisons, tougher punishment, and prevention to give our children something to say yes to as well as something to say no to.

We brought down the deficit that the other party only talked about. We slashed the bureaucracy they only complained about. We cut the regulations that they gagged over but never did anything about. When we put this economic strategy forward, the Republicans said if it passed, the economy would collapse. Well, they were wrong. In 21 months we have cut the deficit 3 years in a row for the first time since Truman was President. We have shrunk the Federal Government, but we have invested more in your jobs, your future, and we have 4.6 million new jobs in America. In Michigan, we've seen a 1½ percent plus drop in the unemployment rate.

Is there more to do? You bet there is. Yes, there is. But if there's more to do, we ought to keep on doing what we've been doing for 21 months, not go back to what worked so poorly for 12 years before.

It was in the last 21 months that we expanded the Head Start program, that we passed a law to immunize all the kids in this country under the age of 2 by 1996, that we passed laws to have apprenticeship programs all over this country to help people who don't want to go to college move from school to work into good jobs, not dead-end jobs.

We passed the reform in the student loan laws to provide for lower cost, longer repayment student loans, so that every middle class student in this country and every poor kid in this country can afford to go to college and get a good education and not drop out and not turn back. In Michigan alone, 580,000 people will be eligible for better terms on their college loans because of this administration and its partners in the Congress.

And let me just say this. I noticed that Mr. Carr's opponent ran a television ad using my voice against him, saying if it hadn't been for him we wouldn't have passed the economic program. Well, that's why your unemployment rate is down; that's why your jobs are up; that's why this country is moving forward.

But I want to give you another one, and I bet you won't see this in his television ad. If it hadn't been for Bob Carr, we would never have had the votes to reform the student loan program; we wouldn't be having 20 million more Americans eligible for lower interest rates, lower costs, better repayment terms. If the other fellow had been there, it never would have happened. And that's the kind of choice we're facing in this election.

What have they done? They said no to student loan reform. They said no to the crime bill. They said no to family leave. They said no to the reduction of the deficit. They said no to economic recovery. That's what they did. They killed campaign finance reform and lobby reform and the Superfund bill to clean up the toxic waste dumps.

And now they have told us what they will do if you put them in office. They want to take us back, back to trickle-down economics; back to massive tax cuts for the wealthy. They have made you a trillion dollars' worth of promises. "Elect us," they say, "and all will be easy: tax cuts, spending increases, a balanced budget." Does it sound familiar?

Their contract on America doesn't say much about how they're going to pay for this. But they do say that if you give them power, they will cut $9 billion worth of college loans for over 3 million students. We ought to be sending more people to college, not less people. Vote for the Democrats, and keep this country moving forward.

Listen to this. This is their argument. This is their argument. They say, "Well, this is a tough election for Republicans. The Democrats took our issues away. We were always for jobs, against crime, against big Government. We were active in foreign policy. Now, the Democrats have given us 3 years of deficit reduction in a row for the first time since Truman, the smallest Federal Government since Kennedy, the toughest crime bill ever, a growing economy in a safer and more secure world. We would be saying, if we did it, that we should build a statue to the Republicans if we'd done it. But, my goodness, the Democrats did it. How are we going to run this race?"

"I know," they say. "We will deny that it happened. We will take the cynicism of the public and build on it. We will take the skepticism of the public and feed it. We will take the unbelievable reluctance of people to believe in this country again, and we will stoke it. We will divide the people. We will throw a smokescreen over the election. We will attack them for big Government and taxes, even though they cut taxes on working people and gave us less Government and moved the economy forward and made the country safer." That's what their program is. Their program, my fellow Americans, is to keep everybody shouting, keep the country in a turmoil, keep the people upset.

Let me tell you something. This country has problems. There are still too many people who are worried about losing their jobs, who haven't gotten a raise, who are afraid they'll lose their health care, who are looking for work and don't have it. But the country is in better shape than it was 21 months ago.

Don't let them sucker you. Keep going where we're going. Show up on election day. Stand up for what is right. Don't turn back. We can do better.

I just got back from an incredible trip. I saw our fine soldiers in the Persian Gulf standing up for freedom there. I saw the peace in the Middle East. I saw the faces of millions of people looking at America, looking to America for support. Let me tell you something, folks. From Northern Ireland to Haiti to the Persian Gulf to the Middle East to Korea, people say, "We like the United States. It's a country of energy, a country of freedom, a country of growth, a country of tomorrow." They are not cynical about us. I wish you could have seen the faces of our young men and women in uniform in the Persian Gulf there, in the desert, and all those soldiers from other countries looking at them. I wish you could see the faces of the Haitians holding up their little "Thank you, America" sign when President Aristide went home and democracy came back to those people. They aren't cynical about America.

Folks, 90 percent of the cynics about America are in America. They listen to people who are screaming all the time, who are shouting all the time, who are trying to divide this country all the time. Let me tell you something. This is a very great country, and its best days are ahead of it. Our best days are ahead of us.

We have challenges ahead of us. We do not need the easy promises and the failed policies of the past. We need to say, "This is America. We're getting this economy going. We're educating our people. We're making this Government work for average Americans again. This world

is going to be safer and more prosperous. We are going into the future."

Say no to the failed policies of the past. Say yes to going to the future. Say no to fear and yes to hope. Say no to the people who are always trying to denigrate everything we do to move this country forward. And say yes to Bob Carr and the other Democrats who are running for you and your future.

Thank you, and God bless you all. Thank you.

NOTE: The President spoke at 12:31 p.m. in the Cobo Hall Convention Center. In his remarks, he referred to Mayor Dennis W. Archer of Detroit; Howard Wolpe, candidate for Governor; Debbie Stabenow, candidate for Lieutenant Governor; Conrad L. Mallett, Jr., candidate for Michigan Supreme Court chief justice; and singer Jennifer Holiday.

Interview With Dominic Carter of New York 1 Television, New York City
November 1, 1994

Mr. Carter. Thank you for appearing here on New York 1, sir.

The President. Thank you. Glad to do it.

Midterm Elections

Mr. Carter. Mr. President, this has been a bitter, nasty campaign season across the country in which Republicans have made you the issue of local races in commercials linking you directly to the local Democrats. While many Democrats have held open arms to campaign with you, some have kept their distance. How do you feel that you are the direct target, your administration?

The President. Well, they've worked hard on this for a long time. The Republicans tend to be a Presidential party, and they are unfortunately now very extremist, very negative, and that's what they've tried to do. But you know, there is beginning to be a backlash.

First of all, the American people see that I am keeping the commitments I made to them in 1992. In 21 months, we have moved the country forward. We're making the Government work for ordinary Americans with things like family leave and college loans. We've reduced the debt. We've reduced the size of the Federal

Government. We've got more jobs coming into this economy. The world is safer and more prosperous than it was when I took office. People are feeling that, and I don't believe they're going to buy these Republican promises in this contract, this $1 trillion worth of hot check promises to go back to the 1980's and trickle-down economics.

I also would point out, Dominic, you know, there is beginning to be some division within the Republican ranks. People are recoiling; good Republicans are recoiling from this extremism and this negativism. That's why former First Lady Nancy Reagan hit Oliver North and, of course, Mayor Giuliani supporting Governor Cuomo—I think a very statesman-like decision—Mayor Riordan out in Los Angeles supporting Senator Feinstein, Mrs. Heinz in Pennsylvania attacking the Republican candidate for Senator up there.

There are a lot of good Republicans who do not like what has been happening in our country, and they don't like seeing the Republican Party being so negative, so bitterly partisan, and so extremist. So I think we've got a chance in the last 8 days to get a real vote for the future and not a vote for the past. And I'm very hopeful.

Mr. Carter. Mr. President, you touched upon a couple of topics that I want to get to, but just yesterday you were campaigning for Democrats in Pittsburgh, and we're told that you're headed to New York once again to campaign Thursday for Mario Cuomo.

The last time you were here, you said Mr. Cuomo is a national treasure, that he's New York's treasure. How do you explain him being in the tough battle against George Pataki?

The President. Well, I think, first of all, he has been Governor. And after you've been Governor awhile, you'll pick up your fair share of enemies if you take on the tough decisions and you deal with the tough issues.

Secondly, as we all know, Senator D'Amato and Mr. Pataki, their group, they're very good at attacking their opponents and they've done a good job of that. But I think Governor Cuomo is coming back. And I think if you look at the action that Mayor Giuliani took, he was a person who had to say, "Look, never mind all this negative back-and-forth, how are the people of my city going to live, and are they going to be better off depending on who the Governor is?" So he endorsed Governor Cuomo.

When I said Governor Cuomo was a national treasure but is New York's treasure first, I would just remind the voters of New York who wonder whether he really wants to be Governor again that I offered him a chance to have a very different career in Washington, DC, and he rejected it to stay with New York, because he wanted to have a chance to be Governor while he has a partner in the White House, someone really committed to helping improve the fortunes of the people of New York.

That was clear evidence to me that his heart was first, foremost, and forever with the people of New York, and I think that they'll be very well pleased with his performance in the next 4 years if they'll give him a chance to be Governor.

Mr. Carter. Thank you very much, Mr. President. We'll see you in New York on Thursday.

The President. Thank you.

NOTE: The interview began at 2:57 p.m. The President spoke by telephone from the Westin Hotel in Detroit, MI. A tape was not available for verification of the content of these remarks.

Interview With Ken Herrera and Jayne Bower of WWJ Radio, Detroit, Michigan
November 1, 1994

The President. Hello, Ken.

Mr. Herrera. Can you hear me all right?

The President. I can hear you fine, thanks.

President's Approval Rating

Mr. Herrera. You know, I wanted to start this out with kind of a lengthy question. As I looked at your list of accomplishments in office—and let me list a few: 4.1 million new jobs in the economy in the first 17 months of the administration; 2 consecutive years of budget reductions; new tax cuts to 90 percent of small businesses; a low inflation rate, lowest in 20 years, in fact; the signing of the student loan reform act; the passage of the crime bill, including the assault weapons ban, millions of dollars for local law enforcement; the victories that you've scored in foreign policy affairs, in Haiti,

the Persian Gulf, North Korea, the Middle East, and all that—do you ever find yourself sitting back at the White House and wondering, "What the heck do I have to do to have high approval ratings?"

The President. Well, you know, they're coming up. I think what you have to do is, the people have to know it. They have to know it, and they have to believe it. And I think that we had lots and lots of evidence that even now not all these things have been known. But as people know more and believe more, then they tend to want to support what I'm trying to do for our country and the Members of Congress who are supporting that direction as well. I think that if you look at just the things you mentioned, when I ran for President, I said that if I were elected, I'd try to make the Government work for ordinary Americans, empower people through education and training to compete in a global economy, get the economy moving again, and make the world safer and more prosperous.

On those scores, we're in better shape than we were 21 months ago. Now, there are a lot of people, to be fair, Ken, who haven't felt that. They still maybe feel insecure. They're insecure in their job, or they're afraid they'll lose their health care, or they haven't gotten a raise. But our country's moving in the right direction, and I think as more people know it, there will be more support for this direction and for these candidates. And I've just got to make sure that insofar as I can effect it, that people know about it and believe it by next Tuesday.

Youth Violence

Ms. Bower. Mr. President, this is Jayne Bower—phone ringing somewhere. Maybe we can just ignore that. I'd like to speak with you as a parent. Now, I have two small boys myself, a 3-year-old and a 2-year-old, and I'm frightened for them. My oldest celebrated his first birthday in Los Angeles as the city was burning. We're hearing about two kids in Chicago accused of dropping a third child out of a window. Now, the crime bill may be a step in the right direction, but I think I speak for a lot of parents when I ask you, how do we give our children some hope? And what's in the future for them?

The President. Well, first let me say, you gave the right answer yourself. The crime bill is a move in the right direction. And if the people in the local communities around the country use it, they can lower the crime rate and lower the rate of violence. They can do it by using the police, the punishment, the prevention, and the prisons, all four.

But in the end, what we've got to do in this country is to get back to the basics of child-rearing. And those children who are not getting the support they need at home, who are growing up in very mean neighborhoods, still have to have somebody to look up to and someone to learn from. And what's happening is, you talked about those two kids that dropped that 5-year-old out of a high-rise—what is it that makes the heart of a 10-year-old turn to stone, feel no guilt, feel no remorse? What is it that makes an 11-year-old shoot another 11-year-old for gang reasons?

We have got to have a system that Government can't provide alone, that people in every community deal with to reach out to these kids and make sure that they have somebody to look up to, someone to learn from who is a good, positive role model, and a future out there for them. I'm doing what I can as President by trying to get the economy in shape, trying to provide educational opportunities, trying to support working families on modest incomes with things like family leave and income tax cuts and other supports. But we really have got to have a grassroots sea change in America in every neighborhood in this country. People who can do it have got to be willing to step in and help these kids that aren't getting the support they need at home or that are spending too much time on the streets because they're, say, the children of single parents who have to be out working to try to support them.

And if we will do that, we can then—take the prevention programs, for example, in the crime bill—we can take the police programs in the crime bill and use them to actually build up people's lives and turn this situation around. It is in many ways the most significant challenge facing our country. We cannot expect to do well over the long run if we continue to lose massive numbers of our children to this kind of lifestyle.

Student Loan Program

Mr. Herrera. Again, we're speaking live with President Bill Clinton on WWJ. Mr. President, following along those same lines, last August you signed the student loan reform act. In fact, you talked about it a little bit earlier today, authorizing the implementation of what's known as the William D. Ford Federal Direct Loan Program. How does this differ from previous efforts to make sure that all those who want a higher education can, in fact, get a higher education in this country?

The President. Well, what this student loan bill does is to enable people to borrow money to go to college at lower cost, either lower fees or lower interest rates or both. And then it allows them four different options about how to repay the money. For example, if someone gets out of school, and they decide to become a teacher, then the teacher—let's say the teacher starts and he or she has a low wage in salary in the early years, you can pay back the loan as a percentage of your income. Then let's suppose at some point in the future you get a higher paying job, and you want to pay the loan off quicker so your interest payments would be lower, you can convert to a different system and repay it in that way.

So the two different things here are, number one, it's a lower cost loan; number two, the repayment terms are much better. Now, in addition to that, we have taken huge amounts of the bureaucracy and paperwork out of this, and we have strengthened the ability of the Government to collect the loan when it's due by involving the IRS and other Federal agencies in the process. This was a dramatic change. And we also cut out a lot of the middle men in the process so that we saved $4 billion in Government money over 5 years and saved the borrowers $2 billion over 5 years. It is a great program.

And today I was at the University of Michigan Dearborn campus. A lot of the students were talking there about how this was going to be better for them and their lives and their classmates. You'll get more people coming to college. You'll have fewer dropouts. And you'll have a higher repayment of the loans when they get out. It's very exciting. It's one of the best things we've done long-term for the United States since I've been President.

Midterm Elections

Ms. Bower. Mr. President, we heard you urging people to get out and vote next Tuesday when you were at Cobo Center this afternoon. Does that low voter turnout—of course it concerns you, but what can be done to change that, and more importantly to change the image of politicians?

The President. Well, if you looked at the '92 campaign, you see what can be done. If you have a vigorous debate on the issues and if you have a real hopeful campaign, if you're trying to build up not tear down, then people come out and vote. If these campaigns are totally dominated by the negative, not the positive, and by people trying to tear down, not build up, then a lot of voters just stay home. They

turn it off. And then the election tends to go to the person with the most extremist support, which is why a lot of these extreme Republicans have worked so hard on their negative campaigns and to raise so much money. They want to drive down voter turnout, diminish confidence in the political process, and give the election to the extremist element in their own party. That's their whole goal.

But I have to tell you, I think in the last couple of weeks, Americans are getting more realistic and more hopeful about their country again. They see that we're improving the economy, that we're making this Government work for ordinary people. We've got a smaller Government and a smaller deficit but a more active approach to facing the problems of this country. They see other people in other parts of the world, from the Middle East and the Persian Gulf, to Korea, to Haiti, to Northern Ireland, looking to us for energy and support. And I think they're feeling better about themselves and their country. And if that happens, we'll have a higher voter turnout.

Ms. Bower. We know you're getting ready to leave Detroit now for Ohio, Mr. President. We'd like to thank you very much for joining us this afternoon.

The President. Thank you, I've enjoyed it.

Ms. Bower. Thank you, President Clinton.

The President. And I remember the interview I did back during the campaign when your station was supposed to be interviewing my wife, and she was asleep on the bus, so I took the interview.

Ms. Bower. We got you instead.

The President. So, I finally got one in my own right today. I appreciate that.

Mr. Herrera. Thank you, Mr. President.

The President. Thanks.

NOTE: The interview began at 3:08 p.m. The President spoke by telephone from the Westin Hotel in Detroit, MI.

Interview With Bruce Newbury of WPRO Radio, Providence, Rhode Island
November 1, 1994

Mr. Newbury. Mr. President, how are you?

The President. I'm fine, Bruce. How are you?

Mr. Newbury. Nice to speak to you this afternoon.

The President. Nice to speak to you.

Midterm Elections

Mr. Newbury. And we're looking forward to having your visit with us tomorrow in Rhode Island. Now, you'll be here for a Democratic rally among some other things, and I think it's safe to say that 7 days before the election, any appearance by the President is a political event. But what kind of a message does it send for the President of the United States to appear on behalf of campaigning politicians this late in the game in their home district? I mean could this be construed as pulling out all of the stops?

The President. I hope it is, because that's what I'm trying to do. You know, the people of Rhode Island have been very good to me, and you've got some races up there that I'm very interested in and have been asked to come and support Representative Kennedy and our candidate for Governor and the others on the Democratic ticket, so I'm looking forward to being there.

And after all, our administration has had a good record in Rhode Island. In the last 21 months, we've seen over 10,000 new jobs come into the State, and in the previous 4 years, you lost almost 10,000 jobs. We've been able to give tax cuts to 38,000 working families and almost 4,800 small businesses, and we've passed the Family and Medical Leave Act. We've got middle class student loans available at lower costs than before. We're moving this country forward. We're getting things going again in the right direction in America, and I want to be able to take that message to Rhode Island, and I'd like to have some support from people in Rhode Island in the Congress for continuing to do that.

Mr. Newbury. The Republican contract is going to be a topic of discussion when you arrive here tomorrow.

The President. It should be.

Mr. Newbury. Is it, as the New York Times did today, is there going to be a point-by-point Democratic response to the Republican contract?

The President. Well, the New York Times gave a point-by-point response to it today?

Mr. Newbury. It's in a graph form, a chart form here in the——

The President. That's great. I haven't seen it, but let me say what we've attempted to do is to show what it would take to pay for the Republican contract. I mean, in typical Repub-

lican fashion, just like they did in the eighties, they made all these wild promises and never said how they'd pay for it.

Now, they've promised big tax cuts, big increases in defense spending and Star Wars and a balanced budget. And the House Budget Committee did an analysis and said that if they did that, that the only way you could keep that promise is to cut Social Security about 2,000 bucks a year and to cut Medicare about 1,800 bucks a year, because that's what's in the rest of the budget. And if they say they're not going to do it, then what they're saying is they're not going to keep their promise. Instead, they're going to give a tax cut to the wealthy, explode the deficit, start shipping our jobs overseas, and put us right back in the same hole we were in when they had office the last time.

So they cannot have it both ways. They can't go out here and give the American people a trillion dollars' worth of promises and say, "I'll tell you how I'm going to pay for this after the election." That's what they're trying to do. It's a scam. It's a bunch of easy promises. Our approach is to challenge the American people, to say, "Okay, we're going to give you the educational opportunities you need, we're going to make this Government work for ordinary people to support families again; as with family leave and immunizations for little kids, and we're going to get the economy going again. And now you've got to make the most of your lives." We're not going to give you a bunch of promises that can't be kept, that will only put this country back in the hole again.

I think when the American people understand both what we have done and what they're offering, that we're going to be in much better shape.

Health Care Reform

Mr. Newbury. Of course, the State of Rhode Island has been very much involved in the health care reform proposals with Senator Chafee and of course, Ira Magaziner. Now, when health care comes back on the table in the spring, what input can we expect from these gentlemen?

The President. Well, I hope they'll both be very much involved. I will say this: If we had more Republicans who were willing to support Senator Chafee, we'd have a health care bill today, because he was willing to deal with us in good faith, and he really wanted to get a resolution of this. But as you probably know, they all abandoned him and his plan, his original plan, because, unfortunately, the congressional leadership of the Republicans has been so bitterly partisan that they would rather defeat a bill than have the Democrats involved in helping get health care, even if the Republicans got half the credit.

They tried to do the same thing to the crime bill. The leadership tried to beat the crime bill. But again, Senator Chafee and a few others said they would not be involved in that kind of bitter partisanship, and they did what was right for America.

So I'm very hopeful that we can get a different and more bipartisan approach to crime. It depends in part on how these elections come out. You know, we've got Mayor Giuliani, the Republican mayor of New York, endorsed Governor Cuomo; the Republican mayor of Los Angeles endorsed Senator Feinstein; Nancy Reagan, our former First Lady, has attacked Oliver North in Virginia; and Mrs. Heinz, the wife of the former Republican Senator from Pennsylvania, has attacked the Republican Senate nominee in Pennsylvania. A lot of these mainstream Republicans are horrified by the destructive, extremist wing that has taken over the Republican Party, either interested in ideological politics or just power-grabbing; they don't like it. So there's a lot of good Republicans in this country that want to see us work together to solve problems, and I'm going to do my best to work with them after this election is over.

White House Security

Mr. Newbury. I want to get to the security issue with the White House. Of course, you're on the road, and it's probably a wise course with what's going on back home there. But let me ask you this. [*Laughter*] Until——

The President. That's great.

Mr. Newbury. I got a laugh out of the President; it's not a bad day. Until the Secret Service comes back to you with their findings, have you given thought to moving your family out of the White House? In all seriousness.

The President. Oh, no, no. You know, the thing with the airplane was a fluke. First of all, none of us were there. If we had been there, I think under the security procedures it would have been handled differently. But there was a guy that just came in under the radar and was obviously trying to do something to

draw attention to himself, not trying to hurt us.

In terms of the shooting incident, we have shootings in the streets of America every day. And what I hope the American people got out of that shooting incident was that the people in the Congress who voted for the crime bill and the assault weapons were right; you don't need people to be able to walk around on the streets of America and pull out a gun where you can fire off 20 or 30 bullets in one magazine before you know it.

But the Secret Service does a good job protecting the President. We will be prudent; we will be safe. But I'm not going to go into a hole and hide in a Democratic country where people are free to move around. You just have to keep doing that and take all the precautions you can. But I feel good about the job they do, and so I'm going to keep being out here among the people and take whatever precautions seem appropriate.

Chelsea Clinton

Mr. Newbury. Very good. I want to just ask you another quick question about Rhode Island. Is Chelsea coming back to Rhode Island next summer to take sailing lessons again?

The President. I don't know. She sure does want to. She loved that. She had the most wonderful time up there. She loved the school, she loved the people she met. She loved sailing. When I got back from the Middle East, I showed her a model of a boat that I brought from the Middle East that one of the leaders gave me, and she understood all about how it was constructed and how it all worked. So I will say the people who taught her last summer in Rhode Island did a good job.

Mr. Newbury. Well, all right. Well, she's more than welcome to come back, and we're looking forward to your visit tomorrow. Well, not everybody, the people that have to drive 95 aren't too choked up about it.

The President. Yes, I apologize in advance. I'm trying not to inconvenience them too much.

Mr. Newbury. I hear you, and it's been a pleasure to talk with you this afternoon. Thank you very much for giving us your time.

The President. Are you driving your Chevrolet Impala?

Mr. Newbury. As a matter of fact, I left it home today because it's raining, and it's got the original wipers on it. And those are valuable in themselves so I don't want to use them. But I know you're a car buff.

The President. I love old cars; '64 was a good year for the Impala.

Mr. Newbury. It sure was. This is a beauty. It's been in a garage for about 15 years. It's got the 230 in it, the six, but it's got some of the bells and whistles, and it's just a beautiful car. I'm tickled to death with it. I was going to drive it today, but I said, wait a minute, he's just going to be on the phone; he's not going to see it. But I'll send you a picture.

The President. Thanks, man.

Mr. Newbury. All right, sir. Hey, nice to talk to you. You take good care.

The President. All right. Bye-bye.

Mr. Newbury. And have a safe trip.

The President. Thank you.

NOTE: The interview began at 3:19 p.m. The President spoke by telephone from the Westin Hotel in Detroit, MI.

Interview With Thera Martin Connelly of WDAS Radio, Philadelphia, Pennsylvania
November 1, 1994

Ms. Connelly. Hello, Mr. President.

The President. Hello.

Midterm Elections

Ms. Connelly. It is our delight and honor to have this opportunity to interview you, sir. And we were particularly pleased to see you in Philadelphia yesterday campaigning for the Democrats. As we look at this election year, general election day, November the 8th, certainly there's a lot of shopping for votes across the Nation and here in Pennsylvania. What would you say to our listening audience to encourage them to participate on election day?

The President. I'd say first of all, you have a lot at stake in this election. The issue is whether we're going to continue to go forward to build the economy and to make the Government work for ordinary citizens or whether we're going to go back to the approach that the Republicans gave us in the 1980's where they cut taxes for the wealthy, increased defense spending, and promised to balance the budget, giving us the possibility of either big cuts in Social Security and Medicare or a big increase in the deficit and the loss of jobs.

I saw an article in one of the newspapers about a gentleman from Philadelphia who said he didn't know if he would vote because he voted for me in 1992; he had a part-time job; he wanted a full-time job, and he hadn't found a full-time job yet. I sympathize with that gentleman. But what I want to say to him and

to all your listeners is that in the 4 years before I took office, Pennsylvania lost 8,300 jobs, no job gain, a loss. In the 21 months since I've been here, Pennsylvania's gained 86,000 jobs and we're working on building more. And we're working on bringing new investments to the inner cities, which have been too long ignored.

I know there are a lot of people who still feel uncertain about their own economic situation, who are worried about crime and violence and the breakdown of their communities. But we are facing these issues. We are dealing with the problems with the crime bill, with the family leave law, with immunizing kids and expanding Head Start and providing college loans at more affordable rates and building the job base of the country. And we don't need to turn back.

So I would urge the people who are listening to me to get out there and vote, because we need to keep going in this direction. After all, the other approach was tried for 12 years without very good results. We've just had 21 months, and the country's in better shape than it was when I took office. We need to keep going. That's my message.

Ms. Connelly. Suddenly we have seen defections, if you will, where Republicans have come over and endorsed Democrats for upcoming general elections. In New York, it was the mayor of New York, Giuliani, coming out in support of Cuomo. And here in Pennsylvania, former U.S. Senator John Heinz's wife, Teresa Heinz, says that she could not see a Santorum in the

U.S. Senate. Do you see more Americans perhaps who are Republicans, on the books, jumping over to the Democratic side on election day?

The President. Well, I hope so. You know, I think a lot of Republican leaders out in the country who are not part of the congressional leadership, they always wanted to work in a bipartisan fashion. And they wanted to debate Democrats in a civilized way that would build up our country, not tear it down. And I think Teresa Heinz—well, I read her speech. She'd been very upset by some of the things that Mr. Santorum has said that have been irresponsible, divisive, negative, and inaccurate. And it took a lot of courage for her to say what she did. Mayor Giuliani in New York, just by the same token, was trying to be supportive of his people, and being a citizen first and a Republican second, when he endorsed Governor Cuomo.

The same thing happened with the mayor of Los Angeles endorsing the Democratic Senator; Mrs. Reagan, our former First Lady, attacking Oliver North in Virginia. There are a lot of good Republicans who are upset by this extremism and negativism and sort of power grab mentality that has taken over the congressional Republican Party. They do not like it, and they want to stand against it.

And the people of Philadelphia and Pennsylvania are going to have a chance to stand against it by reelecting Senator Wofford and voting in these other elections on Tuesday. And I certainly hope they'll do so.

Ms. Connelly. We're talking with President Clinton, and we've only got another minute or two with him. I understand that your schedule is very busy, sir. In closing, I wanted to get some thoughts from you, if you would, some food for thought that you could send out to our listening audience, why they should go Democrat as opposed to Republican, because there's been a lot of legislation blocked by Republicans.

The President. You should vote for the Democrats instead of the Republicans because of what we have done, because of what they stopped us from doing, and because of what they propose to do.

What have we done? We've made the Government work for ordinary citizens. We passed the family leave law so people can take some time off when their babies are sick without losing their jobs. We're going to immunize all children in the country under 2 by 1996. We expanded Head Start. We expanded college loans. You should vote for the Democrats because we've got the economy coming back. There's a lower deficit, a smaller Federal Government, and more job growth. You should vote for the Democrats because the world is more peaceful and prosperous, and that's good for Americans. We've got more trade. We've got a more peaceful world from Haiti to Northern Ireland to the Middle East. You should vote for the Democrats because we've taken the time to develop some special incentives to get investment into our inner cities to create jobs there, empowerment zones and community development banks and other things.

You should vote for the Democrats because of what we tried to do with political reform, campaign finance reform, and lobby reform. What we tried to do to clean up toxic waste dumps was stopped by Republican delaying tactics. And if you reward them, they'll just do it again.

You should vote for the Democrats because this Republican contract is a way to take us back to the trickle-down Reaganomics of the eighties: give the rich a tax cut, spend more on defense, promise to balance the budget. You're either going to have them cutting Social Security and Medicare or exploding the deficit and sending jobs overseas. There's no other alternative.

And we offer a path to the future. They want to take us back. So I hope the people in Philadelphia will vote for the future on Tuesday.

Ms. Connelly. Mr. President, I can never thank you enough for this opportunity and this honor to chat with you for a few moments. And I'm sure our listeners here at WDAS AM and FM appreciate it as well.

God bless you, sir.

The President. Thank you. Goodbye.

NOTE: The interview was recorded at 4:52 p.m. for broadcast and release at 6 p.m. The President spoke by telephone from the Westin Hotel in Detroit, MI.

Remarks at a Rally for Democratic Candidates in Cleveland, Ohio
November 1, 1994

The President. Thank you. I've had a good time tonight, haven't you?

Audience members. Yes!

The President. Mr. Stephenson, you play that horn a lot better than I do, but I love listening to you. You were great, and I thank you; You were great, and thank you, sir. And I thank the Cleveland School of the Arts for that wonderful rendition of "Lift Every Voice and Sing." Weren't they magnificent? They were great; we thank you. When I'm not as hoarse as I am tonight, I can sing that song—[*laughter*]—even the second verse.

Reverend McMickle, I'm honored to be in your beautiful church tonight; honored to be here with so many distinguished pastors, upstairs and down, and so many other concerned citizens. I'm glad to be here with the mayor, who sounded a little like a preacher tonight. [*Laughter*] When I heard Mike up here talking, it reminded me of what my grandmother said to me the first time she heard me give a speech. When it was over, she came up to me—my grandmother was about 5′ 2″, weighed about 180 pounds. She was one tough cookie. [*Laughter*] You've all had grandmothers like that. So I gave this speech and I was pouring my heart out, and she looked at me and she said, "Bill, I believe you could have been a preacher if you'd been a little better boy." [*Laughter*]

You've made a fine mayor and a good friend; I thank you, Mike White. Mr. Pinkney, I thank you for your work on this event tonight and for your service to our community. And my good friend Lou Stokes, what a fine man he is and what a great leader he is. I'm not sure, I think this is my third visit to Congressman Stokes' congressional district, maybe my fourth, but however many it is, it's however many he told me I was going to make. When I am summoned, I am here. [*Laughter*]

I want to say a special word of thanks, too, for the presence of some other people here: First, your wonderful Senator and my stout friend and a great leader for this whole country, Senator John Glenn, I appreciate his being here today. My friend and State chairman, your attorney general, Lee Fisher, I want you to reelect

him on Tuesday. Lee Fisher is a good, good attorney general.

And I want to say something about a couple of other folks who are here. Barbara Sykes, stand up, stand up. I'm going to use Barbara's story as a little illustration about the difference between us and them. Barbara Sykes is from my home State. She's from Arkansas. And she was my political director here in Ohio. And a lot of you know Ohio made me the nominee of the Democratic Party and made me the President of the United States; I got my 276 electoral votes from when Ohio was declared. So now she's running for State treasurer. And not in Cleveland where it would hurt him but down south, in the typical way these Republicans are—they say one thing one place and another, another, and hope they don't get caught—[*laughter*]—there's a big newspaper article today about how her opponent is running a picture down south, where I'm not supposed to be popular in the State, of her having her picture turn into me and turn back into her.

Now, I don't know what her relationship with me has to do with her fitness to be State treasurer or not, but since he raised it—[*laughter*]—since he raised it, I hope all the Ohio press gets this straight. Her opponent says, "She was Bill Clinton's political director, and she's from Arkansas," like it's some sort of podunk place, right? What has that got to do with being State treasurer? "I, on the other hand," he says in his ad, "I was the chief aide to Jack Kemp at HUD"—[*laughter*]—"and therefore I ought to be the State treasurer because I'm better at counting money."

Well, let me tell you something. I like Mr. Kemp; as those Republicans go, he's got some good ideas. But he's had some zingers, too. Jack Kemp was one of the guys that told President Reagan that you could increase spending and cut taxes and balance a budget at the same—[*laughter*]—right? He didn't go to the Cleveland public schools, or anyplace else. He forgot about arithmetic. [*Laughter*]

And we went all through the 1980's with their money counters. We quadrupled the debt of the Federal Government. We sent our jobs overseas. We put our economy in a ditch with their economic theory. That was trickle-down economics. Now he wants to count your money? I'd bet on her any day of the week. [*Laughter*]

I'm glad to see your distinguished and very handsome candidate for Lieutenant Governor there. And I'm glad to see some other people here. Congressman Sawyer is here. He's come all the way from Akron with some of his folks. He is a great leader in the Congress. I hope and pray he will be reelected on Tuesday.

Congressman Fingerhut met me at the airport. He may not be here, but since he's from around here, in some of the Cleveland meetings here I want to talk about him. You've seen those ads they're running against him? Oh, it's the awfulest thing you ever saw. [*Laughter*] He's one of—why would they be spending so much money to beat a first-term Democrat who is as independent as can be? I'll tell you why. Fingerhut's great passion in life is to clean up the influence of the lobbyists in Washington. He wants to pass this lobby reform bill and require them to report all the money they spend. He's got this crazy idea that you ought to know how much the organized interests in Washington spend to keep from having your interests furthered down there. So they are going bananas. And they're trying to beat Fingerhut, and they're saying all these terrible things about him. But I want to tell you something. When you see those ads, the reason they're trying to beat him is, if he comes back, he will pass the lobby reform bill that the Republicans killed this time because we ran out of time. That's what they're trying to do.

Now, this is kind of like this treasurer's deal I was telling you about. A few weeks ago when the Republicans were already counting all their victories on Tuesday, convinced they were going to win, they beat the lobby reform package, and they beat campaign finance reform at the end of the last congressional session. This was on a Saturday. On a Monday, the House Republican leader meets with the lobbyists in Washington, and he tells them—this was reported, big front-page story in the Washington Post—"Now, we took care of you. You better take care of us. And you'd better not give any money to those Democrats because we're keeping score."

The next day, it's in the paper that he met with a bunch of Republican political operatives and said, "Our goal in life is to convince people that the President is the enemy of normal Americans. We're going to make it unsafe for him to go anywhere except to talk to black voters between now and the election." That's what he said. Let me tell you something, folks. This whole country would be better off if every person in public life felt as comfortable in this church tonight as I do.

So if you can do anything for that young man, Eric Fingerhut, you ought to. He voted to get this country moving in the right direction. But the real reason they're out to get him in your neighboring district is they don't want that lobby reform to pass, and he will bust a gut to pass it if he gets reelected.

Now, Mr. Hyatt here, who's been my friend a long time—I've known him longer than nearly anybody in this church—he wants to be a Senator. And his opponent, oh, he's said all kind of terrible things about him. But let me ask you something: If you had a chance to vote for a guy who had built a business giving people legal services who had to have it and couldn't afford to pay big money for it; creating a lot of jobs for people; who'd been terrifically successful and then said, "Because I'm successful, I need to give something back to my State and my country, and I want to go up there and fight for ordinary Americans, not for organized interests. And I'm prepared to pay my fair share of taxes, and I'm prepared to do my part. I want to move this country forward," and the fellow running against him had been one of the people who brought you the trickle-down Reaganomics that nearly bankrupted this country, wouldn't you vote for Joel Hyatt? I think you ought to, and I hope you will.

Let me remind you of something else, too. The man that's running against Joel Hyatt 2 years ago was running against John Glenn when I was running for President. And I was coming to Ohio all the time, following this election very closely. Now, you may not agree with every vote Senator Glenn ever cast. He and I have a disagreement once in a while. But one thing nobody will ever question is that John Glenn is one of the most distinguished, patriotic Americans in the 20th century. Nobody could question that. I'm going to come back to this in a minute. But in 1992, the same man who wants to beat Joel Hyatt today ran against John Glenn and, because he had a lot of money to put ads on television, thought he could get away with actually questioning Senator Glenn's patriotism. I have just this to say to him: When you go fly all those planes full of bullet holes and you get in a spaceship and go up by yourself in space, then you question John Glenn. Otherwise, be quiet and do something else. Do something else.

This is an amazing year, you know; I mean, it's a strange year. And I was glad to hear the pastor quoting the Scripture. There's a lot of things we need to think about. You can go back in the Scripture, and you can find times like this when things seemed sometimes upside down. But I can tell you this: We're a week out from this election, and the clouds are beginning to clear, and people are beginning to see what this election is all about. The election is about whether we're going to keep going forward, or whether we're going to turn around and do what got us in the trouble we got in in the first place. That's really what the election is about.

You know, 21 months ago I became President, thanks to you. [*Applause*] Thank you. And I had a program that I thought would help take our country into the 21st century, to rebuild the American dream by putting the American people first. I had some very specific commitments I made. I said, "If you will vote for me, here's what I want to do: I want to make Government work for ordinary Americans again, to do more with less. I want to empower you and then challenge you to do what it takes to compete in this fast-changing, global society. I want to get this economy back on its feet again. I want this world to be a more prosperous and a safer place for Americans to operate in. And we can do that if we'll take the challenge." Well, 21 months later we haven't solved all the problems in this country, but we're in a lot better shape today in America than we were 21 months ago.

If you look at it, we're making Government work for just working people with families and jobs. That's what the family and medical leave law was all about. It protects 2 million people in Ohio who might need to take a little time off from work because there's a baby born or a parent sick, without losing their job. That's what our economic plan was all about when we lowered taxes for 500,000 working families in Ohio who are working full-time with children in the house who should not be in poverty. We ought not to tax people in poverty. We ought to lift them up if they're working and doing their best to raise their children.

That's what we were doing when we passed the Brady bill and the crime bill with more police, more prisons, more punishment, but more prevention, too, to give our kids something to say yes to and a chance to avoid a life of crime and trouble and misery and instead make something of themselves so they can lift their voices and sing. That's what that crime bill was all about.

And we have begun to empower people more. We've started a program to help every State set up apprenticeship programs for people who don't go to college but want to be in good jobs, not dead-end jobs. We provided a dramatic increase in lower cost college loans so that everybody can afford to borrow the money to go to college. And they'll have easier terms to pay it back, so they can always afford to pay it back. It is a big deal, and we need to celebrate it and use it. One million students in Ohio alone are now eligible for lower cost, better repayment college loans. That is something that can change the future of the State as well as of the people involved. That is making the Government work for ordinary people. That is empowering people. That's not giving people anything except the tools to make something of their own lives.

And we said we'd get the economy going again. And so I gave the Congress a long-range economic plan: expand trade, invest more in education and technology and defense conversion, and bring the deficit down. And when the Congress voted on our deficit reduction program the Republicans said, "Oh, my goodness, if this plan passes, the sky will fall. The economy will collapse. You ought to do it the way we did. Tell everybody what they want to hear, and let the debt go crazy, and let the economy run off the track. But at least you won't make anybody mad." I said, "Our job is to take responsibility. Better to make a few people mad and straighten things out and get us on the right road." And that's what we did.

So what has happened since our opponents said the sky would fall? Well, the unemployment rate in Ohio fell 1½ percent. And now 4.6 million new jobs have come into our economy. And in the last 3 months the economy expanded at a healthy rate of about 3.4 percent with no inflation—1.6 percent inflation. In other words, the economy is coming back. We were right, and they were wrong.

And who could fail to be pleased that for the first time since we had nuclear weapons in two countries there are no longer any Russian missiles pointed at our children tonight? There are the elements in place of an agreement that will keep North Korea from becoming a nuclear power. We've been on the side of peace and freedom everyplace from the Persian Gulf to the Middle East to Northern Ireland to southern Africa to Haiti. This world is for Americans a more prosperous and a safer place than it was 2 years ago.

Do we have problems yet? You bet we do. There are still people in Cleveland that want a job that don't have one. There are still people in Cleveland that haven't gotten a raise in years. There are still people in Cleveland worried about losing their health insurance or afraid they'll lose their job and won't be able to get another one. Yes, there are problems. What is the answer to the problems? The answer is keep on doing what works. Don't turn around and go back and do what didn't work. That's what the answer is. And that's why you need to vote on election day and make sure all your friends do.

Our Republican friends, they're an interesting lot in Congress. They want to kill things and then blame us for not having them pass. They tried to kill the crime bill. They attacked the crime bill for its prevention programs, even though they had cosponsored a bunch of them. They thought they wouldn't get caught. And they delayed, as I said, they killed the lobbying bill, the campaign finance reform bill.

They killed the Superfund legislation. A lot of you don't know what that is, maybe, but that was the bill to clean up the toxic waste dumps of the country. That's a big problem, you know? Everybody was for the bill. We had the chemical companies and the labor unions and the Sierra Club, the environmental groups. There wasn't anybody against that bill except enough Republican Senators to delay it to death. Why did they want to delay it? Because they didn't want Lou Stokes to be able to come home and be able to say, "I helped to clean up poison waste dumps." They said, leave the poison in the ground and try to put some poison in the political atmosphere. I say it's time to take the poison out of the ground and out of the political atmosphere and start building this country again and doing what's right for the people of America for a change.

Now, our Republican friends say if they get to go to Congress, they've got the answer to all of our problems, their Contract With America. I called it a contract on America, and it upset Mr. Hoke. Come to find out, I wasn't sure they knew what was in it, he and his AA. They asked me all those questions in Cleveland last week. [*Laughter*] I'll tell you what's in it. It's a sweet deal. They come to you and—I come to you with challenges; I tell you there are things you're going to have to do. I can pass the crime bill; you've got to fix crime in your neighborhood. You've got to take this and use it, use the police, use the prevention programs, use these things, and you do it. I passed the college loan bill; I'll tell you, you've still got to go to college. [*Laughter*] I can't do it for you.

What do they say? They say, "Oh, we're going to give everybody a tax cut." They don't tell you almost all of it goes to very wealthy people. "We'll give everybody a tax cut, and we're going to increase defense, and we're going to increase Star Wars. We're going to bring that back, and we're going to balance the budget." Sounds great; how are you going to pay for it? "We'll tell you that after the election." [*Laughter*]

That was the theory, by the way, of the fellow that wants to be the treasurer: "We're going to cut taxes, raise spending, and balance the budget." I wouldn't let anybody count my money that had that idea. [*Laughter*] And that was their idea; so they want to do it all over again. Now, I'm going to tell you what's going to happen. If you raise this spending and you cut all these taxes and you balance the budget, the only way to do it is to cut Social Security and cut Medicare, and that's wrong. And we're not going to let them do that; that's not right.

And if they don't mean it, if they're going to run and hide—boy, they're running for cover on that now; we pointed out what the math was—if they don't mean it, the only other alternative is to explode the deficit and drive the economy in the ditch and send our jobs overseas just like they were before. And I say we have to tell them we have been there, we have tried that. We don't want to cut Social Security and Medicare and college loans and veterans benefits, and we do not want to explode the deficit and put the economy in the ditch. No thank you very much. We'll keep going forward. We do not want to go back.

I got to thinking about this, folks. It's frustrating for them. They ran against the Government for years, you know; the Republicans said how much they hated the Government. Now we have reduced the size of the Federal Government. They ran against the deficit, even though they gave it to us. We have reduced it. They said they were for a strong economy. We got more jobs. They said they were interested in foreign policy. Our country is safer and more secure. So how are they getting away with having a close election? Why is Joel Hyatt in a close election? Why isn't Tom Sawyer and why isn't Eric Fingerhut and why isn't Lee Fisher—why aren't they being elected overwhelmingly? Because the American people have been told for so long that things are so bad, and they've been told they ought to be cynical and skeptical and nothing good ever comes out of Washington. Can anything good come out of Washington? That's in the Bible somewhere, too, right? [*Laughter*] And they remind me now of another Biblical verse because they're often straining at a gnat so they can swallow a camel. [*Laughter*]

So what is their theory? Their theory is, just deny that we did these things. Shoot, if a Republican President had reduced the deficit, reduced the size of the Federal Government, passed a tough crime bill, and promoted economic growth, they'd be saying it's unpatriotic to criticize the man. [*Laughter*] You know they would. I can hear it now in all their talk shows: "How dare they criticize our President. He reduced the deficit. He reduced the size of the Government. He grew the economy, and he got tough on crime." What do they do? They just deny that it happened. And they hope that you have been so conditioned for so long to hear only bad things, and that you hear the way people scream at each other in communication today, that it will just miss you.

They want to turn other voters, and they want you to stay home. They want you not to know what has happened. They want you not to understand what is at stake. They want you to let them go right back to the 1980's when the country was in trouble but the people they were trying to help, the organized and powerful interest groups, did just fine, never mind what happened to America. They were wrong. Let's tell them no, we're going forward to tomorrow, not backward to yesterday. Our kids depend on it, our country depends on it, and we're going to do it.

Proverbs says, "A happy heart doeth good like medicine, but a broken spirit dryeth the bones." When you are raising children, what's one of the first things you try to teach your kids when they're old enough to understand? Don't ever make a decision when you're mad. "If you're mad, count 10 before you say something." How many times have we all been told that when we were children?

We can win on Tuesday if we know what the record is, if we know what the alternative is, if we know what the future holds, and if we believe in ourselves, and if we go out and talk to our friends and neighbors and say, "Listen here, don't make a decision when you're mad. Take a deep breath. Let's have a cup of coffee. Let's go drink a Coke. Let's talk about our kids and our future and what is at stake and why we cannot walk away."

I just came back from the Middle East. I was honored to represent all of you for our country's role in helping to make peace between Israel and Jordan. And then I got to go to the desert of the Persian Gulf and see our young men and women in uniform, who stood up for freedom there and rolled back Saddam Hussein. I have seen the faces of Haitians saying "Thank you, America" when our troops took President Aristide home and reestablished democracy. I have received the President of South Africa, Nelson Mandela, thanking us for America's role in helping make sure his elections were fair and free. I have been so pleased to have our country asked to help the Catholics and the Protestants in Northern Ireland, who have been fighting for hundreds of years, finally make peace, one with another. And here's what I want to tell you. The rest of the world thinks we're a pretty good country. And we are.

I was the first American President to go to Syria in 20 years, in Damascus, the oldest continuously occupied large city in the world, rich with the texture of Biblical history. And I watched those people pouring out to their apartment windows, standing in the street, looking not at me but at America.

When I spoke to the Jordanian Parliament and I said that in our country we respect all religions—"I don't believe we've got a fight in America with Moslems, with the religion of Islam. We're against terrorism wherever it occurs, on our streets, or in your country. But millions of our people answer the Moslem call to prayer; we respect Islam."

When I woke up in Jerusalem, looking over the Holy City at sunrise, and then I saw the faces of the people in Israel looking to America, our power, our strength, our example, our ability to change, our fidelity to our ideals, I am telling you, there are no cynics about this country beyond our borders. And there should be no cynics about this country within our borders. We are going in the right direction. We are a great country. We can solve our problems.

But we have to stand up to the forces that would divide us. We have to stand up to the forces that would take us back. And we've got to stand up for ourselves. No matter what I do, I cannot take you to the polling place on Tuesday. You've got to go there yourselves. You are the bosses in this country, and I am your hired public servant. You are in control. And on Tuesday, you will be in control. And you will be in control whether you vote or don't. Because if you don't vote, that's a decision, too.

Now, I'm telling you folks, all these people that are trying to divide us by race, by region, by religion; all these people that are trying to throw a big blanket over what we've done the

last 21 months and hope nobody notices it until it's too late; all these people who are pushing us to political extremes to grab power—we have to stand up, and we have to say, "We tried that, and it got us in a lot of trouble. And we just started 21 months ago in a new direction. And if it's all the same to you, we'll keep going forward with our face toward the Sun, with the wind at our back. We will not turn back. No, no, we're going forward, every one of us, and we're going to do it together."

God bless you. We can do it. I need your help. They need your help. Let's do it. Thank you.

NOTE: The President spoke at 6:38 p.m. at the Antioch Baptist Church. In his remarks, he referred to saxophonist Sam Stephenson; Rev. Marvin McMickle, pastor, Antioch Baptist church; Peter Jones, candidate for Ohio Lieutenant Governor; and insurance executive Arnold Pinkney, coordinator for the school levy bond issue.

Interview with Ed Gordon of Black Entertainment Television
November 2, 1994

Midterm Elections

Mr. Gordon. Hello everyone, I'm Ed Gordon. Welcome to the Roosevelt Room in the White House. Today, a group of African-Americans from across the country will meet face-to-face with President Bill Clinton. They will be discussing the President's domestic policy agenda as it concerns the black community.

Mr. President, thanks for coming in. First, I get my crack at you, before we turn it over to these folks. Let me ask you, with less than now a week away from the elections, you've been on the stump for the last week and a half and will leave us today and continue—and I suspect right down to the last days.

One of the things that we are hearing, as I travel across the country and we get calls into Black Entertainment Television, is a concern of African-Americans that perhaps, particularly with what's on the line, Democrats haven't been reaching out to blacks as they hoped. What would your thought be on that?

The President. Well, I can't speak about what the local candidates are doing, because it may

differ from State to State. But I can say for sure that nationally we have continued to do that. The Democratic Party has had a massive outreach program. Reverend Jackson is traveling all around the country now, going to rallies every day, in a way that we have coordinated between my schedule, the Vice President, and his. We're all trying to hit the right places.

And we've got a real story to tell about what we've done here in the last 2 years, and about what's at stake in this election. And the Republican candidates are far—on balance, tend to be far more extreme right-wingers than they have been in the past, tend to be people who say that anything the Government does is evil and bad. And there's a lot on the line in this election.

We have made—this country is in better shape than it was 21 months ago. It's economically in better shape. We are moving here to try to address some of the concerns that working families have that especially impact the African-American community in America. So, I'm hoping that in the last 7 days we will really get a lot of energy out there and the voter turnout will go up, because I think this election—so many of these elections are so close, they are going to be determined by which side turns out. That's really what's going to turn it, who shows up to vote.

In 1992 we had an astronomical turnout. Every time I would go to a State, I look at the voting records from '92 and I see that there are whole States or congressional districts where President Bush, for example, in winning the election in 1988, with 54 percent of the vote, got exactly the same vote in 1992 in that congressional district, didn't lose any votes. But there were so many more votes—for me, for Mr. Perot—the American people got involved.

And then for 2 years, you know, they get told every night on the sort of mainstream media, and then by a lot of the kind of attack radio folk, how bad things are up here, and people get their enthusiasm dampened. But there's a lot going on here; there's a lot going on that relates to people out in the heartland. And that's got to be our message this last week.

Mr. Gordon. Let's see if I can pick up on something that you suggested. Even Reverend Jackson has said, though, that he doesn't feel that he's being utilized to his full potential in terms of getting upwards to, I think it is now, 8 million unregistered black voters. And the fact is, in '92 you did get a whole lot of votes, particularly from the African-American community. And there is a question as to whether or not this country, certainly as you suggested, the Republican Party, and even now a thought of the Democratic Party—and I know you've been fighting this for a long time—moving to the right. And blacks are the only group that are staying to the left and staying, if we can put the tag on it, liberal.

The President. I basically don't agree, though, with that formulation of it. First of all, let me say that in this year, most of the money we raised we gave to the candidates for the first time. Next year, I think we'll have to go back and do a lot more voter registration. Mayor Archer, in Detroit—I was with him yesterday. They have registered 50,000 more people in Detroit. They have sent out 50,000 absentee ballots; they've already gotten 30,000 back. So, a lot of our leaders at the grassroots level, the mayors especially, are working hard on this. Next year, I think we'll have to do more.

But what I think we've got to do is, the Democrats need to stay with our base voters. They need to stay with African-Americans; they need to stay with Hispanics; they need to stay with the blue-collar white voters; they need to stay with the small business people—the kind of people that have always been for us. And we need to do it.

And we can still appeal to the undecided voters, to the people who voted for Perot, because there is a way to invest more in our children, in our economy, in our inner cities, and still cut the size of Government, be tough on crime, and have a strong foreign policy. And what we've got to do is to get that message out and then try to get people to have enough faith in us to keep going in this direction until it affects their lives.

One of the reasons that the sitting President's party almost always loses seats in Congress at midterm—if you look in the whole 20th century, there has only been one election, Franklin Roosevelt in 1934, when the sitting President's party did not lose seats in at least one house of Congress—only one. Why? Because people are full of hope at the election and then at midterm, even if the President has accomplished a great deal, they may not have felt it in their own lives.

Mr. Gordon. But you sit with the possibility of losing, at this point, both Houses. You also—you mentioned Detroit——

The President. Let me just say this. If we had the average losses, just since World War II—just the average losses—we would come close to that. So, we're trying to beat the average, even though the Democrats have a lot more seats up than the Republicans do in the Senate. That's just bad luck of the draw. Every year a third of the seats come up, and you have no way of knowing whether there are going to be more Democratic or more Republican.

Mr. Gordon. Even with that math—new math, if you will—you're still going to face an uphill battle. You mentioned Detroit and the gains that you have and Dennis Archer bringing in new voters. But you face a big hill in Michigan. It looks like you're not going to regain—if polls are to believe—the Governor's seat, and there are close races all around. When you look at that and you understand that there is not really the zeal that you've seen from the African-American community before, what do you put that to? What do you account that to?

The President. Well, first of all, if you look at Michigan, the Governor is running for his second term in a good economy. So, most Governors running for their second term in a good economy get reelected. I think if you look at it, there has been for the last 2 years an overwhelming——

Mr. Gordon. A good economy across the State—let me interrupt you——

The President. Across the Nation—it's across the Nation, but it's also in the State.

Mr. Gordon. In the State. But Detroit is still suffering though——

The President. Absolutely.

Mr. Gordon. Though the car companies have made a comeback, Detroit is still suffering.

The President. It is. But as Mayor Archer always tells people, we need to keep doing what's working. We've got 88,000 more jobs in Michigan than we had when I took office, and in the previous 4 years Michigan lost 8,300. So that's the message I've been trying to hammer home in Michigan and the message that I hope will carry Bob Carr to the Senate seat there. And it really is a function of how many people vote in Detroit.

But if you look at it, I mean, African-Americans watch the same news at night that ordinary Americans do. If there is an overwhelming bias in what they see—based on conflict, failure, process, politics, and negativism, as opposed to just giving people the facts about what's going on—then you can't expect people to vote on what they don't know.

The truth is, as *Time* magazine said last week—they put a chart up, and they said, since World War II there have only been three times, three 2-year periods, when the Congress has given the President more than 80 percent of what the President asked for: President Eisenhower's first 2 years, President Johnson's first 2 years, and this last 2 years. In other words, no other President since World War II, except Eisenhower and Johnson, has had more than 80 percent of the initiative approved 2 years in a row by Congress.

The voters don't know that because that's not the message they get. A lot of people don't know about the family and medical leave law, about tax cuts for 15 million working Americans on low incomes with children, about immunizing all the kids in this country under the age of 2 by 1996, about the expansion in the Head Start program, about the empowerment zones for inner cities, about a lot of this stuff. So, what I've got to do in the last week here is get out and talk about what's been done and try to rev people up.

Mr. Gordon. I want to do that. But one of the reasons that they perhaps don't know—and I agree and even your critics are suggesting that maybe you have not been given the praise you deserve for some things that you've brought to the table. But many of those bills and acts don't come in immediately, and it takes time to disseminate that money. And some of them are going to be disseminated by a totally different House and Senate, at this point, which could indeed determine where those monies go.

The President. But you know—all right—let's talk about that. The President is not the only person in this world who has responsibilities.

Mr. Gordon. Oh, absolutely.

The President. Ultimate responsibility in the United States resides with the citizens. And you know, you've got all these extreme Republicans out there, promising the Moon, telling everybody they're going to take them back to the eighties, of trickle-down Reaganomics and promising tax cuts and spending increases and balanced budgets, all this ridiculous stuff. At some point, the American people have to assume the responsibility of the future of their country. They are ultimately responsible for how they vote and whether they vote. And you know, if they're not getting the straight shot from the media, they have to figure out how else to get their information. And I have to do that.

The media comes and goes in trends. They tend to be more negative when Congress is in session and less negative when they're not, even when they're not trying to be, just because it's more interesting to cover the fights, the conflicts, the processes than some success.

So somebody needs to say to the voters in this next week—that's what I'm trying to do—look, you are the bosses, and you decide, and the outcome is yours.

[At this point, BET took a commercial break.]

Administration Accomplishments

Mr. Gordon. Continuing our discussion with President Bill Clinton about issues that concern and are germane to the African-American community, one of the things that you said before we went to break was the idea that the public needs to know who to vote for and what's going to be done for them. One of the things that we continue to read, and as I travel the country I talk to people from Los Angeles to New York, that it really doesn't matter if a Democrat is in the White House or a Republican is in the White House nowadays, particularly for African-Americans, because—and I know you bristle at this—but some have joked you've been the best Republican President for the last 20 years.

The President. Well, they're wrong. They're wrong. It matters that we've got more than twice as many African-Americans in the Cabinet and in high Government positions than any President in history. It matters that, in 2 years, I appointed more than twice as many African-Americans to the Federal bench, who will be making decisions in court case after court case after court case, for decades. I appointed more than twice as many African-Americans to the bench than Presidents Reagan, Carter, and Bush combined. That makes a difference.

It matters whether we enforce the Voting Rights Act. It matters whether we enforce the antidiscrimination provisions. It matters whether we pass family and medical leave for working people so they can have some time off without getting fired when their babies are born or their parents are dead, or sick. And the past President vetoed it twice. I got it through the Congress, and I signed it. These things matter.

It matters whether you've got 4.6 million new jobs or you're losing jobs. It matters that in 1994 we've got more high-wage jobs coming into this economy than in the previous 5 years combined. And that's what I'm telling you.

The citizens of this country get sucker-punched over and over and over again by people who make money peddling cynicism. And if they fall for it, they cannot blame the President or the Congress. The people are the bosses in this country, and it's time they stopped blaming everybody else for what they don't know and going out there and finding out what are the facts, what are the differences, and voting on it. They cannot blame other people when they make statements like that which are foolish.

Now, I think the Republicans ought to think I'm a good Republican President. Why? Because we're taking the Federal Government to its smallest size since Kennedy; we're reducing the deficit for 3 years in a row for the first time since Truman; we passed a tough crime bill that was also smart; and we've got a strong economy and a strong foreign policy. If I were a Republican, they would be building a statue to me and urging everybody to vote for my Members of Congress, instead of what they're doing. But because we live in an age where if you can buy your way onto the airwaves, you can say anything, you don't have to be held accountable, they are making a race out of this.

Mr. Gordon. Let me try this. Because every time——

The President. But for you to say it doesn't make any difference is just wrong.

Mr. Gordon. I didn't say this, and every time I say that and put it on the table, I wonder if I'm going to get my invitation to the Christmas party. [*Laughter*]

The President. No, but I gave you the facts.

Mr. Gordon. Let me try this. When you see this zeal, that obviously this upsets you——

The President. Well, it's just false.

Mr. Gordon. ——a lot of African-Americans are looking at what is coming up with the Supreme Court. We're looking at race-based solution cases that they're finding with the construction companies. We saw the University of Maryland was struck down for black scholarships recently with the Federal Appeals Court and whether or not that's going to send a signal across the Nation.

The President. We stood up for minority-based scholarships.

Mr. Gordon. But people want——

The President. It matters who's the President. Some do, some don't.

Mr. Gordon. Well, let's look at that. Did you stand up—the question would be, did you stand up loud enough?

The President. Well, all I know is, no President in history—ever—has had anything that approaches the record I do on empowering African-Americans and involving them in doing things.

Mr. Gordon. Are you concerned with what you see, when you see these things falling by the wayside?

The President. Sure. But let me ask you something. Let's look at this, and let's go back to whether it makes a difference or not. People have got to make up their mind—another thing they have to make up their mind about is how much difference in what timeframe can any person make in the White House.

The social problems that are afflicting a lot of our communities—the breakdown of the families, the communities, the loss of jobs, the rise of crime and violence—this stuff has been developing for 30 years. The Republicans have been in office 20 of the last 26 years, and for the last 12 years. I have been here 21 months. We are moving in the right direction. That's my argument. And I think it's a pretty compelling argument.

Mr. Gordon. You knew coming in, though, that you were going to have to run a quick race and people weren't going to sit and give you the time that perhaps you needed.

The President. No, I knew coming in that people who fight for change in this country always wind up getting in trouble, because the people who are against you fight you like crazy and the people that are for you are always tentative until they feel the results. So when you're trying to fight for change, you've got to be willing to be unpopular to be responsible.

Racial Issues

Mr. Gordon. Should African-Americans be concerned with what they see? If you look at headlines, you look at the book "The Bell Curve" and what's being said, I mean, you look at—the USA Today today suggested that there are all of these undertones of racial code words being used with the elections. It seems to me that just as a moral leadership issue, should you step up and suggest to this country, we've got to start dealing with race and get it out on the table? We don't like to talk about it.

The President. Well, I think we should. I think that I should all the time. Last night I was in Cleveland, and I was standing in an African-American church, Antioch Baptist Church, and I talked about what the Republican House leader, Mr. Gingrich, said. He said they wanted to make me look like the enemy of normal Americans, and the only safe place I could speak was to a black audience in America. And I said that this country would be a lot better off if every public official felt as comfortable in that church as I did.

Every time I give a speech, I talk about the strength of our diversity, that one of the best things about what we did in Haiti was that America is the only country that could have gone to Haiti and produced a couple of hundred Haitian-American soldiers that could be down there speaking Creole to the people of Haiti as we prepared the way for President Aristide to come back.

I think a lot of people, a lot of white voters, have been alienated by the problems in their own life and the inability of the Government to make a difference in their own life. And so, extreme rightwing forces are telling them it's all because the Government tried too hard to help the minorities. They're wrong; the minorities are not helped very much either.

And what I've got to tell the majority population in this country is that our diversity is a source of strength. We're either going forward together or we're going to fall behind together. And this whole business that we should be divided by race is crazy. It helps the Republicans in election years, but it's a lousy way to run the country.

Mr. Gordon. Address the criticism for me, as you move toward election time—because it doesn't just speak to you as a person, it speaks to politicians in general—that the fact that you feel comfortable in a black church is all well and good, yet some of the rhetoric that you may give speaks to some of the same code words that they're concerned about: reform welfare as we know it. Many people suggest that the crime bill was all well and good, but it wasn't remedy-based.

The President. I believe, first of all—let me answer both those things.

Mr. Gordon. Please do.

The President. First of all, I believe almost 90 percent of the people in the African-American community are dissatisfied with the welfare system. I believe nearly every welfare recipient, white or black—and there's still more white people on welfare than black people in America—is dissatisfied.

Mr. Gordon. In sheer numbers.

The President. Yes. I think they're dissatisfied with the welfare system. My proposal to change welfare as we know it is not punitive, it's positive. It gives people a chance to move to independence, and it removes all the disincentives to move to independence.

Mr. Gordon. But you understand what I'm saying by the code word——

The President. It may be——

Mr. Gordon. ——that there's a black face on welfare in this country.

The President. But to me the issue is, there ought to be—I think opportunity ought to have a black face, a brown face, a yellow face, as well as a white face. That's the way I look at this welfare issue.

On the crime bill, if you'll remember—all the big battles on the crime bill were on the prevention programs, on the positive programs, where the Democrats stuck up for them and the Republicans attacked them viciously and for pure political benefit. Some of those prevention programs had been sponsored and put into the bill by Republican Members of Congress. And then as soon as we got close to the election, they turned like a dog in the night on that bill and started talking about how it was just a pork bill and just a giveaway and how midnight basketball was terrible. They did that. It was the Democrats that stood for the prevention programs, for giving our kids something to say yes to, for some remedy-based solutions, to use your phrase, in that crime bill—again showing that it makes a big difference who is in and who is not. That crime bill gives communities the tools to make a difference in young people's lives, if they will use it.

Social Security

[*Following a commercial break, Mr. Gordon introduced a senior citizen from Miami, FL, who asked about Social Security.*]

The President. Social Security is not going to be cut, and the cost-of-living increase will go through. The problem is that the Republicans say if they get control of Congress, they're going to give a big tax increase to wealthy people, small tax increase to other working people, increase defense spending, and balance the budget. The only way they can do that is to cut everything else 20 percent across the board, including Social Security. It would be a disaster—the $2,000 cut in Social Security, $1,800 cut in Medicare, on average, for every citizen in America. If they say they won't do that, then what they're telling us is they're going to do right what they did in the 1980's—they're going to explode the deficit, send our jobs overseas, and put our economy in the ditch.

So what we've been pointing out is, you can't go to the voters and make all these wild promises, just promise people anything, promise we're going to cut taxes, increase spending, and balance the budget. The only way to do that is to cut Social Security. So what I've been saying is that it's—a good reason to vote for the Democrats in this election is that we know that we have to keep Social Security sound, we have to keep it healthy, but the truth is that

Social Security costs, as a percentage of our national income, are the same today as they were 20 years ago. Our problem with the Federal deficit is the exploding cost of health care, not Social Security. And it's a mistake to take it out of Social Security and scare a lot of the elderly people in the country, just to make promises to other voters.

Discrimination

[*Mr. Gordon introduced a business executive from Detroit, MI, who questioned the Nation's progress, citing the example of an African-American executive who was denied membership in a Michigan country club that purportedly had tax exempt status as a not-for-profit organization.*]

The President. I don't approve of that. If they discriminated against him based on his race, I don't approve of it, and I don't think they ought to get tax exemptions. I guess they've probably got no—they must have gotten some local tax exemptions. I don't imagine they get Federal tax exemptions. If they do, we could certainly look into it. It doesn't sound right to me.

Mr. Gordon. Let me piggy-back off that. That's one case across the country. We know that there are more and more cases that are coming to light in terms of discrimination and the problem with race in this country. What can you do from the Federal level, from your bully pulpit to help eradicate the problems that many Africans are starting to see more overtly today?

The President. Well, first of all, I think we have to talk about them more. We cannot let it become fashionable to discriminate. What I'd like to say—and I think one of the things that African-American business and professional people I think ought to do, is to challenge other Americans, to tell them to their face what's on their mind, to engage people.

You know, I think you've got a lot of people—a lot of white people still have no black friends. It's a great loss in this country, I mean, we live—Los Angeles County has people from 150-plus different racial and ethnic groups—it is a travesty. When people discriminate against other people based on the color of their skin or their religion, it's basically because they're ignorant, afraid and under a misapprehension of the facts. If whites and blacks talked together more often, spent more time together, they would be surprised to find out how much they have in common.

And I think that the President has a responsibility to constantly speak out against this, and I try to do it; perhaps I should do it more. But I also think that people should be confronted when they have these attitudes. There's no place—the kind of thing that you just told me about—it's 1994; there's no excuse for that in this country.

Mr. Gordon. Let me go to Eric Moore, who is from Los Angeles, a police officer. Can we get you today to pledge that you will speak out publicly more against the racial problems that are happening in this country?

The President. Oh, absolutely. You know, keep in mind—if you look at what Henry Cisneros did in Vidor, Texas, with that housing project, what we did in the Denny's case where the people were discriminated against there, the law enforcement officials at Denny's, we have taken a strong stand. But I think a lot of it is, people need to say this. And when I see these polls, like you mentioned this poll today where 51 percent of white citizens in America allegedly say there's too much effort to give special consideration to black Americans—I would challenge every single one of those people to seek out a hard-working African-American and have a personal conversation with them about it. I think there is still too little honest dialog in this country.

Opportunities for Youth

[*Mr. Moore asked about presenting alternatives to dealing drugs for troubled youth.*]

The President. First, I think that you have to tell them the truth, which is that if you don't sell dope, you won't make as much money in the short run. But if you'll stay in school, obey the law, get an education, the chances are better than 9 in 10 that you'll get a decent job and you'll have a chance to have a good life.

I think what happens is, so many of these kids are living in neighborhoods where they don't see people like them who have regular jobs, who put in 40-hour weeks, who raise children, who take care of them, that they cannot imagine that if they paid the price of time, if they stayed in school 12 years—and then they went to college for 4 years, that they would be rewarded. But I think you've also got to tell them the truth. If you're 16 years old, you

can make a lot more money selling dope than you can in school, but you're going to wind up dead earlier; you're going to have a miserable life, and it's not going to work out.

Let me just make one other comment. You know more about this than I do because of the way you live your life. And I think that one answer is for more people like you to be out there. See, I've been telling everybody that this 100,000 police in the crime bill, the 20 percent increase in police on the street, the main benefit of this will be in preventing crime in the first place. Because if we put more people like you in uniform out there in the neighborhoods, who understand what the roots of this problem are, they will be better role models, and they will reduce crime by reaching children. That's what I believe.

But yes, you know, I can't tell a kid—if you're a runner at the age of 10 you're going to make more money than if you're in the 5th grade. But your life is going to be better over the long run if you do the right thing. And I think what I need to do is to try to make sure—this is one of the reasons I, by the way, trying to bring in these empowerment zones and community development banks in the inner cities—is so that people in these neighborhoods, these kids, can see people going to work every day and can image how their life could be different.

Employment and Welfare Reform

[*Mr. Gordon introduced a New York community activist who expressed concern about employment opportunities for welfare recipients and youth. Mr. Gordon then commented that many young people with college degrees could not find jobs.*]

The President. That's right. But there are far fewer of them now than there were 21 months ago. There are more jobs now than there were then. That's an objective fact.

Let me just say this. One of the things that I have challenged the Congress about is that you cannot cut someone off, you can't tell somebody they've got to go to work unless there is work for them to do. And we are trying all kinds of experiments now. I just approved, for example, what's called a waiver—and for our audience, let me—a Federal waiver means that we let you out of certain Federal rules to see if you can find a better way to solve a problem. I approved a waiver for Oregon where they are able to give the welfare checks of people who wish to go to work—they're saying, "I want to go to work"—they can give the welfare checks to the employers as a wage supplement to encourage employers to expand hiring. Now, the employers can't lay anybody off. They can't put people out of work. But if they're willing to expand hiring, we'll supplement their wage.

And I think what Oregon will find, if they can do it fairly, is that most people on welfare want to go to work. You know that; you live in the community. And I don't think we can have a welfare reform program which cut people off of welfare unless there is a job for them to go to if they have little children, because you don't want these kids suffering.

Education

[*Mr. Gordon introduced a Memphis, TN, student who questioned administration funding priorities and requested more money for historically and predominantly black colleges and universities.*]

The President. We are trying—what this administration has tried to do is, while we've reduced overall spending, we've tried to actually invest more money in education, starting with expanding the Head Start program.

I was in Michigan yesterday to talk about what we've done with college loans, and we had a lot of minority students there, talking about—because Michigan is in the forefront of implementing our college loan reform plan. Under our new plan, young people all across America can borrow money to go to college at lower cost than ever before, and now they can pay it back as a percentage of their income, so they need never worry about their ability to pay it back. So if you decide to be a police officer instead of a stockbroker, your repayment schedule is a function of your income and your ability to pay. So I think you will see the problem of minorities not going to or not staying in college—I think you'll see that begin to turn around.

Now, in the crime bill, one of the things we did which I am proud of is we made church groups and community groups eligible to get that prevention money so that they can go out and do the right things. There's not a lot of Federal rules and regulations.

We also made, in our national service program, community groups eligible to get young people to work in national service. We pay

them, and then—we pay most of the costs—and then we pay them a college scholarship; we give them whatever they'd get doing the GI bill. So we're trying to do some things that specifically give more opportunity to young people out there.

Minority Business

[*Following a commercial break, Mr. Gordon introduced Dr. Emma Chappel, founder and president, United Bank of Philadelphia, who suggested that the administration perform equity audits to evaluate Federal departments and agencies on how much business was given to the African-American community.*]

The President. I will look into that. You know, in September——

Q. By the way, both Governor candidates in Pennsylvania have already committed to doing this. They like the idea.

The President. It's an interesting idea. In September I issued another Executive order to all my agencies on these issues, because I was afraid that a lot of these departments were not implementing the laws that were on the books, that have been on the books through Republican and Democratic Presidents alike. And I think you're right. I will look into this, and I'll get back to you on it.

Q. And it takes an Executive order. Thank you very much.

Education

[*Mr. Gordon introduced a Richmond, VA, public school teacher who asked about programs to assist students at risk.*]

The President. First of all, I just signed a few weeks ago, a couple of weeks ago, the elementary and secondary education act, which changed rather dramatically the way we give Federal money to school districts. And there are a lot of things that it did, but it did three things that may relate to your concerns.

First, the bill now says that in seeking to serve educationally disadvantaged kids, that the teachers and the principals at the local school can decide how best to serve them. They don't have to be served by Federal rules and regulations. They don't have to be separated out in a class. You can decide what the best way is to do it.

Secondly, there is a special emphasis in this bill on the whole idea of the involvement of parents in education and what has to be done to help the parents do a better job with the students, which I think is important.

The third thing it does is to encourage local schools—not the Federal Government, local schools—to decide what basic values of citizenship they want to teach the children, to articulate them, to write them down, and then to teach them, instead of feeling that they can't do that, that they can't build character in their students.

But I'd be curious to know—and maybe we don't have time on this program—but I'd be curious to know what things you think we could do to help the parents do a better job who would like to do a better job and aren't sure that they, themselves, know enough to do what they ought to be doing.

Mr. Gordon. If I can step in, perhaps we can get someone in your education office that Sheila can speak with, and we'll do that before you leave.

The President. I think that's a good idea.

Antidrug Efforts

[*Mr. Gordon introduced a Cleveland, OH, pastor who asked about efforts to stop drug importers.*]

The President. We just had a very large sting operation in the last couple of weeks that our Federal authorities pulled off and that I'm very proud of. We are working hard now to try to stop these drugs at the source. Lee Brown is spending a lot of his time going to countries where these drugs—where they start, where they start growing the coca, where they start raising the opium that becomes heroin. And we believe that we have to place a much greater emphasis on trying to get the drugs at the source, get the people that are bringing them into the country. And we spent a lot of time with Louis Freeh, our FBI Director, working on international cooperation against organized crime, working on money-laundering, working on tracing this money.

The way to get these big guys is to follow the money, because you never see the drugs until you see them on the street. I mean, once in a while, you'll see we'll break in a warehouse or something but—and we work on that, we do that. And it's good when we can do it, but we're really working hard now on international cooperation, going to the source and tracing the

money. And I think that you will be able to demonstrate to the people in your community, after we've had time to really pursue this strategy, that we have been at least as tough on those folks as we have on the folks in the street.

Q. [*Inaudible*]—share with that. The other thing is that those people——

Mr. Gordon. Very quickly, Pastor.

Q. ——yes—usually have the money to buy the kind of lawyers that they need to get off. And something needs to be done to stop that as well, because the individuals who end up getting arrested, they get court-appointed lawyers.

Mr. Gordon. Let's go to Christopher Coleman now, who is a law student at Howard University and from Los Angeles, California.

The President. Good for you.

Democratic Party

[*Mr. Coleman, 1992 Clinton-Gore college campaign manager in DC, asked how to keep young voters in the Democratic Party.*]

The President. I think you have to say, first of all, that the Republicans, give them their due, they are great talkers and they're great at playing on people's fears and reservations and anxieties and cynicism. They're good at it. It's how they stayed in all these years they held the Presidency, by convincing people that Democrats were alien to their values and their interests. But we're doers. We've begun to make the Government work for ordinary people. We've begun to do something to empower people through education. We've begun to make the economy work again with more jobs, and we've begun to make the world a safer place and a more prosperous place for Americans to work in. And we're trying to do it in ways that keep all the American people together across racial and regional and income, religious lines, that we basically are working to get the 21st century to be an American century, that all young people will have the best years this country ever had. They are working to prey on people's fears and anxieties and to tell them that everything their Government does is bad and wrong. And that's just not true. I think that's what you have to say.

If you really think about—well, let me close with this: You look at what the United States has done in Haiti, how we helped South Africa conduct an election, how we stood up to Saddam Hussein recently in the Persian Gulf, how we've helped to get peace in the Middle East. Other people in the world look to us for support, from Northern Ireland to southern Africa, because they think this is a great country.

There is no room for the sort of cynicism that we sometimes feel about our own country. We've got a lot of serious problems; we just need to get about the business of solving them and doing it together. And we can best do that within a party that is committed to opportunity for everybody and challenging everybody to be responsible instead of just telling them what they want to hear. That's the way to get to the future.

The Economy

Mr. Gordon. Let me see if I can do this as we close, because the words that became so famous during your run were "It's the economy, stupid." Let me see if I can move back— and I saw Mr. Panetta at the door, so I don't know if I'm in trouble at this point or not, but let me go on and move to it.

I've got a study here, or a poll, that the University of Chicago took most recently. And it says here, 75 percent of the blacks that they polled feel that the American legal system, economic system, and American society in general has not been and is not fair to them, which may indeed speak to the problems that Republicans and Democrats are getting, or having to get African Americans to the polls.

Most of it is an economic question for everyone in this country, outside of the racial problems that minorities have. What do you say— we talked about midnight basketball, we talked about some other preventative measures that you'd put in. But there are a lot of people out there who say, "I just cannot make it on what I'm being paid."

The President. That's something we haven't talked about yet, but I'm convinced that one of the reasons that people are not feeling really optimistic, even though the economy—the statistics show the economy is booming, is that a lot of people personally haven't felt it. That is, they may have a job, but they think they're never going to get a raise, they could lose their job; they're afraid they're losing their health care; they feel personally insecure because there are so many changes going on in this country. One of the things that's going to take us a few years to work through is how to make sure

that you get investment to areas where there isn't any investment, mostly inner cities and rural areas, and how do you give people a sense of security—even if they don't get to keep the same job they got, they'll get another one.

Mr. Gordon. How do you convince me that I get it when I'm still waiting on 40 acres and a mule? Even if the panacea comes through for you.

The President. That is a worldwide phenomenon. The global economy is changing so fast that people are going to have to redefine their security. That's why all these young people that are getting a good education, they'll always have a job, but that may be a different job than the one they used to have.

My big task is, first of all, to get as many jobs as I can back in the country; secondly, to get more good-paying jobs, not low-paying jobs; and thirdly, then, to get that investment into the inner cities and the isolated rural areas where the spirit of enterprise has not gone. And that's why you've got a lot of the problems that this police officer faces, that there aren't people working, bringing home a paycheck, and helping to build the kind of future that they need.

But I've been working at it for 21 months; we're better off than we were 21 months ago. I just haven't solved all of the problems yet. [*Laughter*]

Mr. Gordon. They're telling me from the booth—and I don't know how I'm going to do this—they want to know if any of you have another question. I know one of you do, so let me see if I can do this.

Why don't you very, very quickly—go ahead. You had your hand up first.

Employment

[*A participant asked if the President would consider another economic stimulus package to address employment for youth.*]

The President. What I think we need to do is to focus more on—what I hope we can do in the welfare reform bill is to focus more on how we can get jobs to young people. What I hope we can do more with the empowerment zone legislation—we just talked about that.

We're going to have to think about what are we going to do in 1995 to get more private sector jobs into places where they don't exist now. What difference does it make to you that the unemployment rate is 2.8 percent in Nebraska? It's important to me; I'm the President of all the American people; I'm proud we've got it down so low in Nebraska. But if it's 15 percent in your neighborhood, and if it's 50 percent among young people who aren't in school and do want to be at work, then those numbers mean nothing to you. So this country has never solved that problem, but we are trying some new and different approaches. And I'm convinced now that a lot of people in both parties and across racial lines understand that we've got to put work back into our young people's lives.

Cooperation With Congress

Mr. Gordon. How willing are you to go toe-to-toe with Bob Dole and the other Republicans who inevitably are going to fight some of those programs you're putting forth?

The President. Well, all I've been doing for 2 years is going toe-to-toe with them. [*Laughter*] The real question ought to be asked of them. They ought to be asked, "Aren't you willing to stop going toe-to-toe and start working in partnership with the President, and stop worrying about short-term political gains and start worrying about America?"

Mr. Gordon. Are you concerned that it's going to continue the partisan fighting that we've seen over the course of the years?

The President. The Republicans in this Congress were the most partisan by a nonpartisan analysis—they were more partisan this year and last year than ever before since people have been studying this, since World War II. I hope that they'll be better next time.

Q. Mr. President, you've got a lot of successes. What can you do to get your message out even more?

Mr. Gordon. With about 40 seconds to go, let's let him answer that.

The President. Well, one reason I do programs like this is to get the information out. Most Americans do not know, unless they've been personally affected by the college loan program, the family leave program, the immunization program. We just have to work harder to get those messages out. And next year, I'm going to devote an enormous amount of time to doing it.

Mr. Gordon. Well, Mr. President, we're to the point where just about rubber meets the road. We will see next week what happens.

The President. Thanks.

Mr. Gordon. We appreciate you joining us, as always.

The President. Good to see you.

NOTE: The interview began at 10:15 a.m. in the East Room at the White House.

Remarks to Senior Citizens in Pawtucket, Rhode Island
November 2, 1994

Thank you very much. Congressman Kennedy—has a nice ring to it, don't you think? [*Laughter*] We'll take pictures later, okay? And I'll go over here, and we'll shake hands and take pictures, have a big time.

Let me say how delighted I am to be here. I was told in my briefing this morning that I am the first President of the United States to visit Pawtucket since Andrew Jackson. And that's not all that inappropriate. I probably care more about average Americans than any President since Andrew Jackson.

I want you to know, Mr. Mayor, how delighted I am to be here in your wonderful city. I am delighted to be here in the Portuguese Social Club. And for the members of the na-

tional press traveling with us, we have over a million Portuguese-Americans, and most of them live in Rhode Island, in Massachusetts, and in California. And I'm glad to be here in this community and in this club today.

I'm glad to be here with Patrick Kennedy. You know, he's got a shade of Irish luck. [*Laughter*] Wouldn't you love to be running for Congress against a person named Vigilante? [*Laughter*] I mean, especially in this election year with these issues. I'm glad to be here with Myrth York and with your senatorial candidate, Linda Kushner—I hope you will support them all—and my good friend Jack Reed, who has been a terrific Congressman for the State of Rhode Island.

I'm glad to be here with Senator Claiborne Pell, who just took a trip with me to the Middle East, a historic trip for the United States and for the world. And I know you must be so proud of his leadership not only in foreign affairs but also in education and in so many other areas here at home. And I thank you, sir.

Again, Mr. Mayor, let me say how glad I am to be here. I thank you for the key to the city. I already see a lot of hearts that are unlocked—[*laughter*]—and I intend to use it. I've got a little tape on my foot here—[*laughter*]—you all don't have to worry about me, I'll stick; I don't need the tape. [*Laughter*]

Twenty-one months ago, with the help of the State of Rhode Island, the people of the United States sent me to Washington to try to change the direction of this country, to get the economy going again, to empower our people to compete in a tough global economy, to get the Government to work for ordinary citizens again, to try to help make the world more peaceful and more prosperous for Americans to live and flourish in. Well, 21 months later, jobs are up; the deficit is down; we have more educational opportunities; we've taken a serious assault against crime; the tax system is fairer; we've increased trade and reduced the nuclear threat. For the first time since the dawn of the nuclear age, no Russian missiles are pointing at your children or your grandchildren. America has become recognized as the world's defender of peace and freedom and democracy. In short, we've still got a lot of problems, folks, but this country is in better shape than it was 21 months ago. And the issue is whether we're going to keep going forward.

Just remember the challenges we face: 30 years, 30 years of deepening social problems with more and more children being born into difficult family circumstances and more and more violence and gangs and drugs building up; 20 years in which most of our wage earners have worked harder every year without getting wages that even kept them up with inflation; 12 years of a very different economic policy, trickle-down economics, that really believed you could give tax cuts to the wealthy, increase spending, explode the deficit, and somehow stagger your way to prosperity. In the last 4 years before I became President, this State alone lost about 30,000 jobs.

Well, we're trying to change all that. We've tried to reward the values of work and family and strengthen our communities. Instead of making easy promises to the American people, I've tried to have disciplined commitments and challenge the American people.

We passed the family and medical leave law after 7 years, which guarantees 164,000 working families in Rhode Island if they have to take a little time off for a baby to be born or to take care of a sick parent, they won't lose their jobs now.

Thanks in no small measure to Senator Pell and to Congressman Reed, we made 20 million students and former students eligible for lower cost college loans and better repayments, including 117,000 right here in Rhode Island.

You heard Mr. Kennedy say that we provided a fairer tax system. We did ask 1.2 percent, the wealthiest of our people, to pay higher income taxes. We put all their money into paying down the deficit, along with $255 billion in spending cuts. But we gave 15 million working families, including 38,000 right here in Rhode Island, a tax cut because they work 40 hours a week, they have children in the home, and we don't believe people who are working full-time and raising kids should live in poverty in this country because of the tax system.

We did pass the Brady bill and the crime bill. And I'm proud to say I wore here a watch I got on the day I signed the crime bill from the Rhode Island Police Chiefs Association. I wore it not only because a Rhode Island chief gave it to me but to highlight the fact that even though our Republican opponents in the Congress tried to kill the crime bill after having supported it, and alleged that it was full of wasted money, even though they sponsored a lot of the programs in it, every major law enforcement organization in the United States supported the crime bill, and we gave it to the American people to make our streets safer.

Now, when we did these things, our opponents in the Republican Party—and every one of them voted against the deficit reduction package; every one of them voted against middle class college loans—they said the world would come to an end; they said the economy would go to pieces; they said we were doing a terrible thing trying to pay our bills. [*Laughter*] They said it was just awful.

Well, guess what? In the last 4 years before I showed up, your economy lost 32,800 jobs. In our first 20 months, Rhode Island gained over 10,000 jobs. This deficit is $100 billion lower this year than it would have been if we'd left their budgets in place. We are giving the future back to our children and building an economy that can compete in the 21st century. It is the right thing to do.

Believe me, I know that we have more to do. I know there are still people who don't have work, and others who have work who are afraid they'll lose their jobs or never get a raise or lose their health care. I know there are senior citizens in this country every single month who are not quite poor enough to be on Medicaid but have a hard time getting along on Medicare and Social Security, who choose every month between food and medicine. I know that. But the question before you, my fellow Americans, is if you want to make progress, are you going to go with the folks that have moved forward on jobs, forward on bringing down the deficit, forward on making the tax system fairer, forward on expanding Head Start to our kids—forward, forward, forward at home and abroad—or are you going to go with the crowd that got a program to take us back to what got us into trouble in the 1980's? That is the choice in this election.

Our opponents said no to our economic program, no to deficit reduction, no to the middle class college loans. They said overwhelmingly— almost all of them said no to the crime bill, no to family leave, no to the Brady bill. They said no. I offered a health care bill that would have reduced the deficit over the next 10 years and provided for medicine, prescription medicine, supports for elderly people who aren't poor enough to be on Medicaid, and would have begun to phase in a long-term care program in addition to nursing homes so that people who wanted to live at home or in boarding homes could have some support. And they all said no.

Once there were 24 of them who said, "We'll be for universal coverage. We at least want everybody to have health insurance." And when the time came for the floor debate in the Senate, we had gone from 24 Republicans to zero. The more we moved toward them, the more they ran out the back door on health care. Why? Because they believed that the cynicism and the skepticism and the negative feelings of the American people would be so great that they could be irresponsible on every issue. They could say no to health care. They could say no to campaign finance reform. They could say no to lobbying reform. They could even say

no to cleaning up the toxic waste dumps in this country. They could say no to it all, and they could punish us for what they didn't do. But you know what? You're smarter than that. And you're going to send them a message on election day.

Now, I watched your faces when Jack Reed and Patrick Kennedy talked to you about this Republican contract. And I can tell some of you find it hard to believe that anybody, even the most conservative Republican, would propose a plan that would cut Social Security benefits. After all, Social Security is a solemn contract. It's worked well for 60 years. The percentage of our national income going to Social Security today is almost exactly what it was 20 years ago. Social Security is not causing the Federal deficit. It's hard to believe, but it's true.

It's true. They have one Senate candidate saying Social Security ought to be voluntary, which means bankrupt the system. They have another saying that he wishes the retirement age were above 70, above 70. They have a House leader who once basically called for dismantling the system just a couple of years ago.

Now, I want you to see—this is the contract they signed. This is what they promised: They promised to give everybody a tax cut but most of it going to the wealthiest Americans; to increase defense, increase Star Wars; to balance the budget in 5 years. That costs a trillion dollars. That's real money, even in Rhode Island— [*laughter*]—a trillion dollars. Every one of us could have a pretty good time on a trillion dollars.

I wish—it's election season—I'd like to help elect this candidate for the Senate and this candidate for Governor and these fine candidates for Congress. I wish I could come here and promise to write you a trillion dollars' worth of hot checks. [*Laughter*] But I can't do it with a straight face; I just don't have it—I'm not shameless enough to do it. But they're better than we are at this; they can say anything. [*Laughter*]

So they made a trillion dollars worth of promises. Now, here's how you keep those promises. The only way you can give a tax cut to the wealthy, increase defense, bring back Star Wars, and balance the budget in 5 years is to cut everything else in the Government 20 percent. That's $2,000 a Social Security recipient a year. Now, that's it; that is the only way you can do it. Then if you say, "Oh, no, no, I never said I'd touch Social Security," you have to cut Medicare 30 percent and everything else. You really think they're going to cut the Agriculture Department, the Veterans Department, all this stuff 30 percent? That's what they have to do. They have to shut down the rest of the Government, close Yellowstone Park.

Now, if they're not serious, if they just want to do what they did in the eighties—spend the money and load all the debt onto our children and grandchildren and wreck the economy—then what they will do is explode the deficit, start shipping our jobs overseas, and put this economy back in the ditch again, just when Rhode Island is beginning to come out. There are no other alternatives, not if they intend to keep the signed contract. The third alternative is, it was just a bunch of cheap political promises to con people into voting at election time.

So I say to you, my fellow Americans, we are better than that. We are better than that. We are moving into the 21st century. We have just been voted for the first time in 9 years by the annual review of international economists the most productive economy in the world. For the first time in 10 years, we've had 9 months of manufacturing job growth in a row. For the first time in 15 years, American automakers have sold more cars around the world than Japanese automakers. We are coming back. Let's don't mess it up now. Let's don't go back.

You know, it makes a difference whether you vote and for whom you vote on election day. It is important to reward people that are moving forward and to tell people that want to take you back with beguiling promises, "We have heard this before." The senior citizens of this country—people who have seen a great World War, people who can remember, many of you, the Depression, people who have seen our country at its best and its worst, motivated by our hopes and our courage, in the grip of our fears, hopeful, fearful—you know that we ought to do the right thing.

If we're moving forward on jobs, forward on bringing the deficit down, forward on giving us Government that's smaller but does more for ordinary citizens, forward in bringing peace and prosperity, increasing trade and reduced nuclear threats to the world, we ought not to go backward. Every voter in this country on Tuesday is just like somebody that has a remote control on a movie about America. They can push for-

ward, fast forward, or reverse. Do not push reverse. You will regret it, and so will America.

You know, I just want to close with this, folks. I keep seeing how people are beat down and discouraged and they're so pessimistic because they hear all these bad things all the time. Let me tell you something, just look at what we've seen in the last few weeks. Look at what we've seen in the last few weeks about how other people look at us.

We had the President of Russia coming here to see me, a democratic country working with us on reducing the nuclear threat. We had the President of South Africa coming here to the United States to thank us for helping to conduct their free election. We have been asked to participate in helping to bring to an end the centuries-old conflict between the Catholics and the Protestants in Northern Ireland. We have been involved in restoring to Haiti the democratically elected government of President Aristide. And we were the only country in the world, by the way, that could have done that and actually had Haitian-American soldiers down there speaking Creole to the natives because America is a country for everybody. We are a country of all peoples, all ethnic groups, all backgrounds.

I went to see our young men and women in uniform in the Persian Gulf who so quickly turned back the tide of Saddam Hussein's recent aggressive move. I was there at the signing of the peace treaty between Jordan and Israel. Let me tell you something: Other people around the world, they are not cynical about America. They admire the strength, the values, the energy of this country, our capacity to grow. They know we have the strongest military in the world, but they also know we're the world's strongest peacemaker, the world's strongest economy, and the world's strongest example. That is what we owe to our children and our grandchildren. The best days of this country are before us, but they will not be before us if we divide the old against the young, if we walk away from our responsibilities to our children or to our parents and grandparents, and if we walk away from our responsibility to ourselves.

So I say to you, we're moving forward. You be thinking on Tuesday: "I am in control. I have a remote control on America's movie. I'm going to go into the polling place, and I'm going to push forward; maybe I'll even push fast forward. But I certainly won't push reverse."

Thank you, and God bless you all.

NOTE: The President spoke at 2:33 p.m. at the Portuguese Social Club. In his remarks, he referred to congressional candidate Patrick Kennedy, Mayor Robert E. Metivier of Pawtucket, and gubernatorial candidate Myrth York.

Interview With Diane Stern of WBZ Radio, Boston, Massachusetts
November 2, 1994

Ms. Stern. The President joins me live on WBZ News Radio. And welcome, Mr. President. If we could get right to the questions, we'd appreciate it.

The President. Great. It's nice to hear your voice.

White House Attack

Ms. Stern. The man who allegedly shot at the White House was in court today, as you know. He may soon be indicted on charges that he tried to kill you. I'd like to know, how do you talk to your daughter about that?

The President. Well, I think my daughter is well aware of the requirements of the office and that a lot of it involves the Secret Service. But I have to tell you, I think they do a good job. I was not in any danger, and I think this matter is being handled in the appropriate way.

Moral Guidance for Youth

Ms. Stern. We're talking live to President Clinton on WBZ News Radio 1030. Mr. President, as a parent, I'm concerned about what seems to be a moral decline in this country. Do you share those concerns?

The President. Of course I do. I'm especially concerned that so many of our young children are being raised, in effect, in a vacuum where they're so vulnerable to gangs and guns and violence and drugs and where they don't have enough people to look up to and enough people to follow. And they're not being taught right from wrong on a daily basis. I think we have to work on all those things.

One of the things that I've tried hard to do as President is to emphasize the importance of parents and churches and community groups taking responsibility for these children again. And one of the things that I liked about our crime bill was that we enabled church groups and others to apply for assistance to reach out to more of these young people. You know, every child is going to have somebody that he or she looks up to. It needs to be the right person; it needs to be somebody who has a sustained and caring relationship with the child over a long period of time. It ought to be the parents, but if it can't be, it has to be someone else. That's the only way to turn this around.

Midterm Elections

Ms. Stern. Mr. President, if we could get on to the campaign trail, campaign '94, as you know, you're not welcomed by some Democrats campaigning for election this year. Personally, how does that make you feel?

The President. Well, most elections are decided on the merits within each State. You know, when I was a Governor, I never had the President come and campaign for me, even when the President was a member of my own party and was popular, because I thought that the voters were discriminating about that. But I do think there are some national elements to this election. And particularly in a lot of these races for Congress and Senate, I'm pleased to go where I've been asked to go—I've been asked to go more places than I can—to try to say what the stakes are in this election. And they are national.

You know, the fact is that in the last 21 months, while we haven't solved all the problems in the country and while a lot of ordinary Americans still have difficulties, the country is in better shape than it was. We've got more jobs. The deficit is coming down. We're doing more for families and children. And educational opportunities have been increased. The tax system is fair. The nuclear threat is less. There's more trade in the world. There's more peace, more democracy in the world. We're moving in the right direction at home and abroad. And the voters need to go forward, not back to the easy promises of the eighties.

You know, I knew when I took this job, if I really tried to change things I'd have to shake some things up; I wouldn't always be popular.

I wouldn't always be popular everywhere in the country and certainly not when people didn't know what had been done. So my job is simply to go out in this last week and tell people what's been done, what the stakes are, what the challenges are ahead and let them make up their own minds.

Ms. Stern. President Clinton—we're talking live with the President on WBZ News Radio— what is your take on last week's endorsement of Mario Cuomo by New York GOP Mayor Rudolph Giuliani, and could you see yourself ever going out on a limb like that, backing a Republican?

The President. Well, I think he did it as an act of statesmanship. I think that Mayor Giuliani saw himself as an American first, a representative of the people of New York, and then a Republican. And he thought that Governor Cuomo would be better for the people of New York City than the policies advocated by Mr. Pataki and his sponsor, Senator D'Amato. I really respect what he did. I think it had to do with what was best for ordinary New Yorkers. I think that's the reason that the mayor of Los Angeles endorsed a Democratic Senator, Senator Feinstein. I think you're seeing a lot of that around the country today as people get worried about the extreme nature of a lot of the Republican campaigns and how divorced they are from the real concerns of ordinary Americans. So obviously I liked it, but I also believe it was an act of statesmanship.

Q. Could you envision yourself ever backing a Republican, especially considering the remarks today to Black Entertainment Television calling them far rightwingers, extreme?

The President. I didn't say they all were. I didn't say they all were. I said their congressional leadership had advocated principles that were extreme rightwing, and they have. Oh sure, under the right circumstances, if I were President and we had the equivalent of Oliver North running in the Democratic Party against a responsible Republican alternative, I believe I would do just what President Reagan and Mrs. Reagan have done in Virginia. I certainly do believe that.

President's Priorities

Ms. Stern. I know we're running short on time, but Newsweek magazine, you may have seen, gathered a focus group of voters who,

rather than being angry with your administration, say they are disappointed. Now, how might you change your agenda the next 2 years, based on what you have and have not accomplished so far?

The President. Well, I'm going to try to do what we haven't done yet. I'm going to try to get the Congress to pass welfare reform. I'm going to take another run at health care. We've got to find a way to protect the health insurance of people; a million more Americans lost it last year. I'm going to take another run at campaign finance reform and at lobbying reform and at some of the environmental measures that we need so badly.

But the most important thing I've got to do is to figure out a way to communicate with the American people better. I mean, all the evidence is that the American people basically do not know, for example, that the last 2 years our administration was only the third one since World War II in which Congress approved more than 80 percent of the measures that I recommended, that it included family and medical leave for working families and tax credits for working families with children who are just above the poverty line and immunization of all children under 2 by 1996 and an expansion of Head Start and a big expansion of more affordable college loans for middle class families; that if they did know these things they would have a totally different attitude. So, I really liked the Newsweek poll—focus group—because it showed what I think, which is that the American people, I think, if they knew what I had done and if they knew what we have achieved and if they knew where we were going, I think they'd feel better.

I have to do a better job of finding a way to communicate directly with people in an atmosphere which is overwhelmingly dominated by controversy, conflict, failure, combative communication, and just talk straight to the folks. I've given a lot of thought to it; it's a great challenge. But in a democracy, even if you do something, if people don't know it, it doesn't quite register until they begin personally to benefit.

Ms. Stern. Mr. President, the campaign trail is beckoning, I'm sure. And thank you for joining us on WBZ News Radio here in Boston.

The President. Thank you. I enjoyed it.

Ms. Stern. Let's do it again.

The President. Goodbye.

Note: The interview began at 4:42 p.m. The President spoke by telephone from the Rhode Island Convention Center in Providence, RI.

Interview With WDIA Radio, Memphis, Tennessee
November 2, 1994

Q. WDIA here in Memphis, Tennessee. We have President Bill Clinton live and on the radio with you.

Good afternoon, Mr. President.

The President. Good afternoon. How are you?

Q. I'm just fine, thank you.

Q. W.C. Brown is joining me here, and we're glad that you're joining us here by phone in Memphis. And we have a few questions we'd like to ask you, but first we'd like to give you an opportunity to make a statement.

Midterm Elections

The President. Well, first, it's good to be talking with you and to have a chance to visit with you so close to this election. The message I want to get out is that with all of our challenges in America, we're in better shape than we were 21 months ago. We're rebuilding the economy. We have more jobs; we have a lower unemployment rate; we've got more high-wage jobs coming into the economy. We're doing things for ordinary American families: the Family and Medical Leave Act, tax breaks for 15 million working families to keep them out of poverty, immunization for our children, more Head Start. We're doing things to support education: expanded college loans and apprenticeship programs for young people who don't go on to college. We've supported African-American educational programs especially strongly, and we'll continue to do that. We've supported the kinds of things that will move this country forward. We've taken steps to help communities deal with the crime problem, not just with more police and the Brady bill, the assault weapons ban but also with prevention programs for our communities so that we can help our young people live a more positive life. So we're moving in the right direction.

The Republicans offer a contract that would take us back to the trickle-down Reaganomics era of the 1980's where we explode the deficit, move our jobs overseas, and have the risk of big cuts in programs that are important to all Americans, like Medicare and Social Security. We need to keep going forward; we don't want to go back. In order to do that, in a place like Tennessee where there are so many important elections—two Senate races, all the Congress races, a big Governor's race—it's important that people go out and vote next Tuesday.

Anticrime Legislation

Q. That's very true, Mr. President. The crime bill is an issue that we talk here on the talk show programs and in the news all the time about. A lot of people are concerned about the amount of money that's earmarked for the Midsouth area, the Memphis Midsouth area, as well as whether or not the crime bill is really going to be something that can be effective here in the Midsouth or whether it's just another Band-Aid. What would you say to that?

The President. I think it depends upon what the people at the local community do with it.

Q. Okay.

The President. It is the best crime bill, in my judgment, that has been passed at least in my lifetime. It gives the local communities the ability to increase their police forces by about 20 percent over the course of the next 5 years. It gives local communities the ability to put more serious offenders behind bars. It gives local communities the ability to have prevention programs, education programs, recreation programs, alternatives to imprisonment for young people to give them a better chance at a better future. But all of this depends on what local people do. The President, the Congress, we can't fight crime on the streets; all we can do is give you the tools to make the most of it. But if your churches, your community groups, your community police forces, if they make the most of this, it will lower crime and reduce violence.

White House Attacks

Q. Thank you, Mr. President. Also, there have been two attacks on the White House itself recently.

Q. You would bring that up.

Q. I would have to bring that up. I haven't heard in the media you respond to those attacks on the White House per se. How would you respond to that? Would you say that that is, as Rush Limbaugh, a friend of yours—[*laughter*]—would say, is that the American people being expressive through those people who have enough nerve to go out and do something about it? Or are these just idle terrorist acts that are being done by people who have lost it, shall we say?

The President. The first incident I think was not even an attack. I think it was a stunt that went awry. I think the man was plainly just trying to land his plane there. The second incident, we'll have to see when all the facts get in. But I believe the Secret Service do a good job protecting me and our family, and I feel great confidence in that. I just get up every morning and do my job. I think that every President knows there's always some chance that somebody will be out there thinking about something like that; but it doesn't bother me much. I don't think about it; I just try to work with the Secret Service. I think they do a good job, and I just go on with my job.

Income Taxes

Q. Mr. President, this is W.C. Brown. Would you talk just a little bit about tax breaks? We hear that tax breaks are contained in a bill that will help to benefit the poor.

The President. Yes, our budget contained tax cuts for 15 million families. And in Tennessee, there were almost 20 times as many people who got an income tax cut as who got an income tax rate increase. Three hundred and eighty-four thousand working families in Tennessee, including a lot of them in your listening area, got a tax cut because they work full time, they have children in the home, but their incomes are still modest. We wanted to make absolutely sure that people that work full-time with kids in the house would not be in poverty. So we expanded a program called the earned-income tax credit, which not only reduces taxes but can get people a refund on their taxes if their in-comes are modest enough. It was the most significant thing done in the last 20 years to make the Tax Code fairer to working people. I'm very proud of it and I think it's not very much understood, but it's very, very important to emphasize. Senator Sasser, Congressman Cooper, Congressman Ford, in your area, these people stood up for the interest of working people, and now they are being pilloried in Tennessee in this election and accused of raising taxes on average Americans when in fact they cut taxes on almost 20 times as many Tennesseans as had their tax rates raised. And they ought to be supported for it, not criticized for it.

NCAA Basketball

Q. Mr. President, on a lighter note. We here in the Midsouth area are also big fans of your favorite team, the Arkansas Razorbacks——

The President. Boy, they're good, aren't they?

Q. ——the NCAA championship team. And of course, we know you're good friends with Nolan Richardson. What would you have to say about the team this year, their chances in repeating? And we have a game coming up in Memphis at the Pyramid pretty soon. Would you be thinking about visiting Memphis and probably supporting your team?

The President. Well, I'm looking at all the basketball schedules, seeing if I can make any of these games. Of course, they lost 2 of their 12 men on the team, but all the first 5 are coming back. They had a good recruiting year. He's a great coach; they're great kids. I think they've got a good chance to repeat. But it's very, very difficult to repeat. There's a lot of talent out there, and when you get to the end of the NCAA's, one game and you're out. So it's going to be tough, but they're a great team. They've got a great chance, and obviously I'm pulling for them.

Q. Well, thank you very much. And when you're in Tennessee, certainly we'd like to invite you to WDIA and be a part, because this is Clinton country.

The President. Thank you.

NOTE: The interview began at 4:51 p.m. The President spoke by telephone from the Rhode Island Convention Center in Providence, RI, to interviewers W.C. Brown, J. Michael Davis, and Leon Gray.

Interview With John Crane and Ann Nyberg of WTNH Television, New Haven, Connecticut
November 2, 1994

Ms. Nyberg. Mr. President, thank you for being with us tonight.

The President. Thank you.

Mr. Crane. Thank you.

Foreign Policy

Ms. Nyberg. You have just returned from an unprecedented preelection whirlwind Middle Eastern trip in the name of peace. Following the trip, polls shows your popularity up. Skeptics would say the trip was planned to boost not only popularity but know-how in the area of foreign policy. Your comments, sir.

The President. Well, we worked for 2 years, very hard, on peace in the Middle East. I had no control over the timing of the Israel-Jordan peace treaty. Obviously, they made their own decision about when to sign. They asked me to come and witness it, because of the role the United States and our administration played in that. When I was there, I went to visit our troops in the Persian Gulf. I sent them there to counter Saddam Hussein's latest aggression. Clearly, I had no control over that. There was no politics in this trip. The American people know it.

But the benefits that are coming in foreign policy, the nuclear agreement with North Korea, the work in the Middle East, the success in Haiti, they are the result of 2 years of hard work that happened to coalesce at this time. There was no politics in that, and there shouldn't be.

Midterm Elections

Mr. Crane. Mr. President, here in Connecticut and across the country, Republicans are trying to make you the symbol of all that's wrong with Government. The pictures of you appear in many GOP television ads. Do you think this midterm election is really a referendum on you?

The President. No, but I think that it is the culmination of 2 years of irresponsible conduct on their part, where they did their best to derail the Government, to put the brakes on everything, to oppose deficit reduction, to oppose our plans for economic recovery, to oppose our plans for things like family and medical leave and the crime bill. As a party, they did their

best to wreck everything and then to blame us. But the American people are beginning to see through it.

After all, let me put it to you this way. If I were a Republican President and I had followed policies which reduced the deficit, shrunk the Federal Government to its smallest size since President Kennedy was in office, increased the economic prosperity of the country, reduced the nuclear threat, expanded trade, and passed the toughest crime bill in a generation, they would be running me for sainthood. But because I'm a Democrat, they're engaged in a great disinformation campaign. And they've signed this contract to take this country back to the trickle-down economics of the eighties, a decade which, I might add, was pretty rough on the State of Connecticut, along toward the end, with all the exploding deficits and other problems. So, I believe the American people will see through that. I've got a lot of faith in the people of this country to be positive, to be forward looking. And my job is simply to get out and give them the facts, and then they'll make the decision.

Child Support

Ms. Nyberg. President Clinton, we want to go to the viewers now. As you can imagine, we asked them to give us questions for you; we were having a chance to talk to the President.

The first question is from Andrea Wilson of Norwalk. Andrea wants to know, Mr. President, what you're going to do to make deadbeat moms and dads accountable and responsible for supporting their children.

The President. I sent in the springtime a welfare reform bill to Congress which, among other things, has a much tougher mechanism of child support enforcement. I think we have to have more automatic requirements, more wage withholding, more respect for these child support orders across State lines. It has simply got to be easy to get the child support payments out there. We've got billions and billions of dollars of unpaid child support. And if we had it paid by people who can afford to pay it, the welfare problem would be much smaller, and it would be a lot easier for people who are struggling to raise their children in dignity, to do it.

Job Creation

Mr. Crane. Now for our second viewer question, Mr. President. It comes from a woman named Eva Nay, who wants to know why, if you made jobs one of your administration's top priorities, there are still layoffs and little in the way of job creation in Connecticut?

The President. Well, let me see. I've got some figures right here; I'll check it. The national economy, since I became President, has produced 4.6 million new jobs. Now, the Government didn't do all that; most of these jobs are in the private sector. But we created the environment in which the jobs could be created by bringing the deficit down, by expanding trade, by investing more in new technologies. Not every American who wants a job has one, and of course, there's nothing the National Government can do to stop some companies from laying off. What our job is is to create more jobs than are lost, and we're doing that.

But just a moment, let me check here. In Connecticut——

Mr. Crane. Take your time.

The President. Well, I'm looking here.

The unemployment rate in Connecticut has dropped more than one percentage point. We've had several hundred new jobs added since I became President. In the previous 4 years— listen to this—Connecticut lost 150,000 new jobs. So, we've got job gain now, where we had job loss before. We need to create more jobs. We have to keep working on it. The first thing I had to do was to try to stop the job loss. And I think we have done that. We're moving forward.

Ms. Nyberg. And our viewers will be happy to hear that.

President Clinton, thank you very much for taking time out of your busy schedule in Providence, Rhode Island, to be with us tonight.

The President. Nice to do it. Thank you.

NOTE: The interview began at 5:02 p.m. The President spoke by satellite from the Rhode Island Convention Center in Providence, RI.

Interview With Janet Peckinpaugh of WFSB Television, Hartford, Connecticut
November 2, 1994

Ms. Peckinpaugh. Mr. President, good evening. Thanks for joining us tonight.

The President. Good evening, Janet.

White House Attack

Ms. Peckinpaugh. The first thing I want to ask you is, how can you feel so secure about your security right now? Does this have you shaken up at all?

The President. No, not at all. In fact, when the incident occurred, within a matter of seconds a Secret Service agent was upstairs at the White House there with me. They have worked very hard to increase their ability to protect the President every year. And they get better at it every year. I have a high level of confidence in them.

This incident could have happened at any time, I suppose. I regret it, but I don't think the American people should worry about it. We

live in a democracy. People can move around freely. The one thing I do hope people will draw from this incident is that the congressional Members who were brave enough to vote for the crime bill, to stand up to the brutal pressure the NRA put on them and the threats they leveled against them, to try to get these assault weapons off the street were right. That man had a modified assault weapon with a magazine with at least 20 bullets. And I think it's a good thing that we're trying to move against that.

But in a free society where people have free movement and where there are lots of guns, this kind of thing can occur. I can't stop being President. This is a democracy. We have to get out here and—all of us—and be with one another and talk to one another. So I'm just going about my job and doing it with a very high level of confidence in the people whose job it is to protect the President.

Ms. Peckinpaugh. President Clinton, hearing that from you makes us feel a lot better. Thanks for telling us that.

The President. Thank you.

Midterm Elections

Ms. Peckinpaugh. We asked our viewers to call into us, to write into us, to E-mail us with their questions for you tonight, so I'd like to take some time and talk about some of their questions. Linda Parker from Hartford wants to know how you feel about colleagues who have distanced themselves from you lately. We have an example right here in Connecticut: Congressman Sam Gejdenson and Jim Maloney, who is running for Gary Franks' seat, did not show up when you appeared here a couple of weeks ago. How do you feel when your colleagues do this?

The President. Well, first of all, I can say for Sam Gejdenson that's just not an accurate characterization. I went to his district at his invitation and campaigned for him at a time when nationally I wasn't in nearly as good a shape in the polls as I am now, so I just think that's a bum rap. And Mr. Maloney, my wife has been to Connecticut campaigning for him. I took no offense at that.

I think that it was a very successful trip to Connecticut. Afterward, surveys show that the support rose for Mr. Curry, our candidate for Governor up there. And I feel very good about the State of Connecticut and the relationship I've had with the Democrats.

I also think, however, that every Member of Congress and every Senator should seek to run, to some extent, a campaign that is tied not to the President but to their constituents. What I like to hear a Member say is, "When I voted with the President, I didn't do it for him, I did it for you." That's the proper message.

Social Security

Ms. Peckinpaugh. Okay. Quickly, Mr. President, what about this very controversial Social

Security issue? John Francis from Stratford wants to know your thinking on that.

The President. Well, here's what happened, and I think it's very important for the voters to listen to this. The Republicans put out this contract, and they said, "If you'll give us control of the Congress, we will take you back to what we did in the 1980's, trickle-down Reaganomics. We'll give massive tax cuts, mostly to upper income people." That must be appealing in Connecticut; you have a lot of upper income people. "We'll give massive tax cuts. We'll increase defense; we'll increase Star Wars. And we'll balance the budget in 5 years."

That costs a trillion dollars. The only way to do that is to cut everything, including Social Security, across the board 20 percent. That's $2,000 a Social Security recipient. You say, we don't want to do that. Then you have to cut everything else in the Government across the board 30 percent. That bankrupts Medicare. If you don't do that, you're right back to where they were before, massive deficits, shipping jobs overseas. Connecticut lost 150,000 jobs in the last 4 years because of that kind of economic policy.

We need to invest and grow with discipline. We don't need a lot of easy promises. We need to embrace the challenges of the global economy, invest, and grow. That's my approach.

This Social Security threat is very real. If they carry through on their promises, they cannot keep their promise to cut the taxes and increase the spending and balance the budget without going after it.

Ms. Peckinpaugh. President Clinton, thanks for answering our viewer questions.

The President. Thank you.

Ms. Peckinpaugh. And thanks so much for taking the time to be with us.

The President. Thank you.

NOTE: The interview began at 5:13 p.m. The President spoke by satellite from the Rhode Island Convention Center in Providence, RI.

Interview With John Bachman and Laurie Groves of WHO Television, Des Moines, Iowa
November 2, 1994

Mr. Bachman. Mr. President, thank you very much for joining us.

The President. Thank you.

Agricultural Policy

Mr. Bachman. When you were last here, you were at the midst of the floods of '93. You saw Iowa's flooded farm fields. And this year, by contrast, farmers have record crops. But that in turn, as you know, has depressed prices, and the farm recovery is in jeopardy. What can be done, Mr. President?

The President. Well, when I get to Iowa tomorrow, I want to discuss that in greater detail. I have tried to be a good President for the farmers of this country. And our Agriculture Department, our Agriculture Secretary has done a very good job not only in the flood but afterward. I'm sure you know that there was an announcement today that the Agriculture Department will give export enhancements to seven states of the former Soviet Union to try to increase the export of livestock, particularly the pork exports to those countries. And we supported ethanol production; we still do. And we're doing a number of other things that I believe will really help the farm economy in Iowa. And I'll have some more to say about it tomorrow when I get there.

Ms. Groves. Well, I hate to push my luck with that in mind, Mr. President, but I would like to ask you about the export enhancement program, the EEP. Now, I know Iowa Secretary Dale Cochran has expressed his interest in getting some changes there, at least, that will combat some of the glut in the pork market. Would you like to give us a hint on perhaps what you think you could do to help Iowa pork producers in overseas trade?

The President. Well, we're looking at that, as well. And again, I will have more to say about all that when I get there tomorrow.

Secretary of Agriculture

Mr. Bachman. Let me give you one more opportunity, Mr. President: Have you named, or have you decided in your own mind, at least, a new Ag Secretary? And is Ruth Harkin still on your short list?

The President. No, I haven't made a decision. She has been unbelievably good where she is. And she would be good in any position, I think, in the Government, including that one. She's a very able person. She's really done more with the Overseas Private Investment Corporation than anybody has in a long time. And I think any American businessperson that's worked with us in trade and expansion would tell you that the Export-Import Bank, Ruth Harkin's agency, the Overseas Private Investment Corporation, and the Commerce Department under Secretary Brown, along with the Agriculture Department, have done more for American business than any administration has in a long time.

Mr. Bachman. Is Ruth Harkin still interested in the post? Has she given you any indication that she'd like it?

The President. No, I've gone out of my way not to talk to anybody about this right now because I'm not ready to deal with it. Secretary Espy will be there until the end of the year. He has done a superb job for the farmers of this country, and I think virtually every agricultural commissioner in every State in the country agrees with that.

Midterm Elections

Ms. Groves. President Clinton, unemployment is the lowest now it's been nationwide in years, you know this, and the economy is strong. And yet your approval rating is under 50 percent here in Iowa. Now, with that in mind, how do you think that your visit tomorrow will influence Iowa's undecided voters?

The President. Well, what we have to do is get the record out there. All the opinion surveys show that there's literally almost no awareness among the voters of what this administration has accomplished but that it's changed rather dramatically in the last 10 days to 2 weeks as Congress has gone home and people have been able to focus on the fact that there are more jobs, a lower deficit, a smaller Federal Government, less regulation, more help for ordinary working families: the family and medical leave law; the Brady bill; the crime bill; immunizations for all the kids in the country under 2; middle class college loans; apprenticeships for people who aren't going to college; an expansion of Head Start.

It's been a very long time since there has been such a productive relationship. But the people don't know it because this has been a contentious 2 years. The Republicans have been more partisan than any party has against a President of the opposing party since World War II. There's no precedent for it. And I've taken on a lot of tough issues, a lot of special interest groups. I've tried to change the direction of this country. And when you do that, you have to be willing to make enemies and you have to be willing to see your approval ratings go down in the short run as people are, at least, confused by all the conflict which is engendered. Plus, everybody knows that the nature of the way Americans get their information today is more contentious, more divisive, more adversarial than ever before.

So I've been given an opportunity now in the last week or 10 days of this campaign to get out and talk to the American people and make my case. The people of Iowa are fairminded people. And I was there when you needed me and so was everybody in my administration, in a hurry, in the flood. And we stayed, and we've seen this through. I have been a

good President for the farmers of this country and good for the Iowa economy and good for the ordinary working people of this country. And when the record comes out, the people will make the right decision.

Plus, the Republicans are offering us an unbelievable journey into the past that got us in so much trouble. I mean, they want to go back to trickle-down economics. They're making a trillion dollars' worth of promises: big tax cuts for the wealthy, more defense expenditures, a balanced budget. The only way to do it is to have a 20 percent across-the-board cut in Social Security, Medicare, and everything else. And if they don't intend to do it, they're going to explode the deficit and put our economy in deep trouble once again.

Mr. Bachman. Mr. President, I know you'll be saying more of that tomorrow right here in Des Moines. Thank you very much for joining us.

The President. Thank you.

Mr. Bachman. And have a safe trip.

The President. Thanks.

NOTE: The interview began at 5:50 p.m. The President spoke by satellite from the Rhode Island Convention Center in Providence, RI.

Interview With Van Harden, Bonnie Lucas, and Bob Quinn of WHO Radio, Des Moines, Iowa
November 2, 1994

1993 Midwest Flood

Mr. Harden. Well, we're very fortunate to have a very special guest on the phone with us here today, here on "Van and Bonnie in the Morning," President Bill Clinton. Mr. President, welcome to WHO Radio.

The President. Thanks, it's nice to be back with you. I was there once before, remember?

Mr. Harden. Yes, I was just going to say, the last time we talked we—well, you were here filling up sand bags, helping us with water jugs, and all that.

The President. Yes, we had a lot of water the last time I was there. I'll never forget that.

Mr. Harden. Times are a lot better now, we're happy to report. And we want to thank you, too, for especially the moral support you lended us during that time because, as you found out, it was not very good back then.

The President. It was difficult but, you know, I was honored to be able to do it, and I'm proud of the response that we had from the Federal Emergency Management Agency and Secretary Espy and all the others. We worked very hard with the people of Iowa on that flood, and I was honored to do it.

Mr. Harden. Well, you got a chance to see from the airplane a lot of the agricultural—our crops and things that were going on. And we have Bob Quinn, our farm director, here that would like to ask you a few questions in that regard.

The President. Hello, Bob.

Ethanol

Mr. Quinn. Mr. President, when we talked in April of '93, the first time we met in New York City, we talked about your support of ethanol and the clean air bill. Well, the clean air bill, as you well know, has kind of stalled out; it's blocked in court. What's your stance on ethanol? Still supporting ethanol?

The President. I'm still strongly for it. As you know, we stayed with our commitment, and we went forward with the ethanol policy, which was strongly supported by the farmers in the Middle West. And we've been sued in court; I think we'll win that lawsuit. I think that it is within the policy discretion of our Government to support ethanol. I think it's good for agriculture, good for the environment, and I still have the same position.

Farm Bill

Mr. Quinn. You know, we're talking about the farm bill right now, and we've heard some talk over the weekend from the Republican side that there may be some cutting of farm programs. Now, in your farm bill plan, do you hope to reduce spending or cut farm programs at all?

The President. Well, I think we need to make a distinction between what the two alternatives are here, because they are dramatic.

We've already figured into the budget and all the farm groups have supported the fact that the subsidy programs themselves will be somewhat less costly in the years ahead because of the trade agreements and especially the GATT agreement. But the reason for that is that we've got agreement from our competitors, especially in Europe, to cut their subsidies. And our products are so much more competitive, we're going to sell more on the markets around the world, and that's going to increase farm income. That's a good thing and, I think everyone would admit, an appropriate thing to do.

What they're talking about is something very different from that. They have made all these promises. They've promised to cut taxes—mostly for the rich, but they just want to throw tax cuts around; they've promised to spend more

on defense and on Star Wars; and they promised to balance the budget in 5 years.

Now, the House Budget Committee did an analysis and basically says if they do that, they'll just have to cut everything across the board: $2,000 a Social Security recipient a year, cut Medicare, cut farm programs, cut veterans programs. If they back out of cutting Social Security, then they have to cut everything else 30 percent across the board. If they back out of that, we're right back into the trickle-down economics of the eighties, where we explode the deficit and put the economy in the ditch. So, they're in a pickle. They've made a bunch of promises that the only way they can keep their promises is to devastate the farm programs.

We've got a chance to be very creative and flexible in the '95 farm bill and do some things that help farmers without being imprudent with our tax dollars. You know, we can't do what they want; we cannot. And that's why I'm telling all the people in the farm belt, you know, you just don't need to send people to Congress that are addicted to this rather way-out contract notion that you can promise people the Moon and there are no consequences to it. It's not the way to run a country. We need to run our country with discipline and look towards the future.

Talk Radio

Mr. Harden. Mr. President, the last time you were here, you graciously did a talk show for us on WHO. We were mostly talking about the flood. But when you were done, I said, "Well, you do a pretty good talk show," and you said, well, you might like to host a show like that someday. And I just was curious as to when you think you might be available?

The President. Well, I hope it won't be quite—[*laughter*]—let me say this, I hope it'll be longer before I'm available than some talk show hosts hope it will be. [*Laughter*] But I'd like to do it because I think that radio is in some ways more intimate than television even. And I think that talk shows can be very, very helpful in furthering the national dialog. But I think that it's important that they really be conversations and not screaming matches and not just a form of attack journalism. Because when you do that, nobody learns anything, and people are liable to have their heads full of facts that aren't accurate. So, I think it's like any other weapon: The more powerful it is, the more potential you have for good, the more potential you have for harm.

White House Communications

Ms. Lucas. We want to know, Mr. President, do you really have a red telephone in your office? And if so, who calls you on it?

The President. [*Laughter*] No, it's not red, but I do have two sets of phones. I have my normal set of phones, and then I have a set of phones that have absolutely secure lines that are not subject to anybody tapping or intervening on. And I use it on occasions for secure conversations, normally with foreign leaders who have something very sensitive they want to discuss with me and they're worried that they don't want anybody in their country or our country to know about it. It's not red, but it is secure.

Mr. Harden. Mr. President, thank you so much for taking the time with us, and we'll see you tomorrow here in Iowa.

The President. Can't wait.

Mr. Harden. Okay.

The President. Thanks.

NOTE: The interview was recorded at 6:05 p.m. on November 2 for broadcast at 8 a.m. on November 3. The President spoke by telephone from the Rhode Island Convention Center in Providence, RI.

Statement on Signing the International Antitrust Enforcement Assistance Act of 1994
November 2, 1994

I am pleased today to sign into law H.R. 4781, the "International Antitrust Enforcement Assistance Act of 1994." This important Administration initiative will help the antitrust enforcement agencies, the Department of Justice, and the Federal Trade Commission (FTC), to protect American consumers and businesses from price-fixing and other anticompetitive conduct by international businesses operating in our markets.

This Act will allow the Attorney General and the FTC to enter into agreements with foreign antitrust agencies. Under these agreements, the foreign agencies will, on a reciprocal basis, provide investigative information in their possession and obtain antitrust evidence on our agencies' behalf from persons and businesses within their jurisdiction. The Act includes appropriate safeguards to ensure that any confidential U.S. business information supplied to foreign antitrust authorities under those agreements will not be improperly used or disclosed.

This Act reflects the United States' commitment and resolve to ensure that American consumers and businesses reap the benefits of free and fair trade in our markets, including lower prices. It will also ensure that consumers and businesses will not become victims of anticompetitive market abuses. This legislation will help us in enforcing our antitrust laws against foreign and international firms who participate in our markets to the same extent as they are enforced against U.S. firms. Until now, U.S. antitrust enforcement agencies have often found vital evidence to be out of reach abroad.

At the initiative of Attorney General Reno and Assistant Attorney General Bingaman, this bill was introduced by a bipartisan coalition in both Houses of Congress and quickly won public and business support. I want to commend the bill's sponsors, particularly Chairman Metzenbaum and Senator Thurmond in the Senate, and Chairman Brooks and Representative Fish in the House, as well as the congressional leadership, for introducing and bringing this legislation to my desk so quickly.

I look forward with American consumers and businesses to the strengthened antitrust enforcement that should result from this Act. I am certain that we will achieve the cooperation of our trading partners as we seek to negotiate these agreements on a reciprocal basis.

WILLIAM J. CLINTON

The White House,
November 2, 1994.

NOTE: H.R. 4781, approved November 2, was assigned Public Law No. 103–438.

Statement on Signing Veterans Benefits Legislation
November 2, 1994

Today I am pleased to sign into law H.R. 5244, the "Veterans' Benefits Improvements Act of 1994" and H.R. 3313, the "Veterans Health Programs Extension Act of 1994." These bills address important areas of concern for our Nation's veterans.

The primary purpose of H.R. 5244, the "Veterans' Benefits Improvements Act of 1994," is to authorize compensation to Persian Gulf War veterans suffering from disabilities resulting from undiagnosed illnesses possibly incurred during service in the Persian Gulf theater of operations.

Some of our Persian Gulf War veterans are suffering from illnesses that cannot be diagnosed based upon current available scientific and medical data. The lack of a diagnosis at this point, however, should not stop us from providing an expeditious and compassionate response to these veterans' needs. Our Nation is keenly aware of its responsibility to the brave men and women who so capably served our country during the Persian Gulf conflict. This legislation is designed to address their needs.

The Act authorizes the Secretary of Veterans Affairs to compensate Persian Gulf War veterans who suffer chronic disabilities from undiagnosed illnesses that became manifest during or within a specified time after their service in the Gulf region. It also requires the Secretary of Veterans Affairs to develop and implement a uniform and comprehensive medical evaluation protocol for veterans of the Persian Gulf conflict suffering from unexplained illnesses. I am pleased to say that this protocol has already been established. VA medical centers and facilities are currently providing appropriate medical assessment, diagnoses, and treatment to Persian Gulf War veterans.

This Act will help to further our investigation into the adverse health consequences that may be associated with service in the Persian Gulf, including potential risks to the family members of our veterans, by requiring the VA to evaluate the health status of spouses and children of Persian Gulf War veterans. It also requires the VA to implement an outreach program for Persian Gulf War veterans, including a newsletter and a toll-free telephone number to provide information concerning available benefits.

The "Veterans Health Programs Extension Act of 1994," H.R. 3313, will extend the VA's authority to operate a number of veterans programs and activities. Significantly, this Act will extend the VA's authority to provide Persian Gulf War veterans with hospital, nursing home, and outpatient medical care for disabilities possibly incurred from exposure to toxic substances or environmental hazards during service in the Persian Gulf. It also extends the VA's authority to provide Vietnam veterans with hospital and nursing home care for disabilities, which may have resulted from exposure to dioxin. The Act also extends the VA's authority to provide priority health care services for disabilities possibly related to exposure to ionizing radiation during nuclear testing or during certain service in Japan following World War II. Finally, the Act also authorizes appropriations of $379.4 million for major medical facility construction and repair projects and 15.8 million for major medical facility leases for the VA.

Because of the important benefits that this legislation will provide to our Nation's veterans and their families, I am very gratified to sign these two bills into law.

WILLIAM J. CLINTON

The White House,
November 2, 1994.

NOTE: H.R. 5244, approved November 2, was assigned Public Law No. 103–446, and H.R. 3313, approved November 2, was assigned Public Law No. 103–452.

Remarks at a Rally for Democratic Candidates in Providence, Rhode Island
November 2, 1994

Thank you very much. Thank you for this wonderful welcome, and thank you for being about twice as large a crowd as we thought we'd have and for being so good-humored about us losing the sound. I want to thank, first of all, the bands from Cranston East and Cranston West High School. Let's give them a hand. [*Applause*] You know, folks, when I ran for President, my slogan was "Don't stop thinking about tomorrow." And there are a couple of people here with signs that say that today. But one of them is right down here with a group of people who are tomorrow, from the Maryville Elementary School. Welcome; glad to see you. I am delighted to be here today with my good friend Senator Claiborne Pell who just came back with me on our mission of peace to the Middle East. And I thank him for his leadership for Rhode Island and for America.

I am delighted to be here and to be introduced by Myrth York. And I want you to help her win this election next week. I read in the papers that she is an underdog. Well, I was an underdog—wait a minute, that's not a bad thing. I was an underdog when I started running for President. Nobody but my mother thought I could win. And then I was underdog two more times. I got up; I went down; I got up; I went down. The only election that matters is the one that the voters in Rhode Island are going to have next Tuesday.

The thing that impresses me about Myrth York is that she understands that the first job of Governor is to prepare the State for tomorrow's economy, to have Rhode Island moving strongly into the future—[*applause*]—commends her, and I want you to elect her on Tuesday.

I also want to say a few words about the others who are here. Linda Kushner sponsored and supported the Rhode Island family and medical leave act. I believe in that sort of policy. We need more of that in the Congress, not less. I want to say a special word of support for my friend, representative, soon to be Congressman, Patrick Kennedy. He has done in the legislature here what we need more of in Congress. He's been willing to stand up to vested interests and to stand up for the people of Rhode Island. I want you to help him be elected

to the Congress on Tuesday. And you're going to do it, aren't you? Now I just want to say a simple but heartfelt thank you to Jack Reed. Jack Reed was there for us on the crime bill, on the Brady bill, on the family and medical leave bill, on helping to provide more affordable, easier to repay college loans to a whole new generation of American students. Jack Reed was there, and you ought to be there for him. I also want to thank all these other fine Democrats for being here with me, your State chair, Guy DeFault, who has such a good voice he could almost speak without the microphone. Your Lieutenant Governor, Bob Weygand, Jim Langevin, Sara Quinn, and Richard James. I want you to stand with all of them on Tuesday.

I love Rhode Island. I love to come here. Today I was told that today I was the first President since Andrew Jackson to go to Pawtucket. And I said, that was good because Andy Jackson and I cared as much about ordinary Americans as anybody who ever had our jobs. I was then told I was the first President in anybody's memory to come to Rhode Island twice in the same year. I'd love to come here every month. I love it here. I mean, look around. This is America, the Italians, the Irish, the French, the Portuguese, the African-Americans, the Haitian-Americans, the Hispanics. You name it; you got it. America's future here in Rhode Island, people working hard.

My fellow Americans, 21 months ago, with the help of the voters in Rhode Island, the American people hired me to be the President on a commitment to change the direction of the country, to get the economy going again, to empower ordinary Americans to compete in this economy, to make Government work for ordinary people again and not just organized interests, to make the world a more prosperous and a safer place for Americans to live and for these children to grow up.

We had this slogan, "Don't stop thinking about tomorrow," because we had always believed that. And yet we had been through years in which people only did what was easiest today, in which we had leaders who talked tough but acted soft and did not tell us the truth and did not challenge us to do what we have to do in order to get this country into the 21st century, so that these children will have a great future and so that our best days are before us. That was my commitment 21 months ago. And I have to tell you, this country still has great challenges, but we are in better shape today than we were 21 months ago.

We have more jobs, a lower deficit, a smaller Federal Government, less regulation. We've corrected abuses like the $500 hammers and the $50 ash trays. We are giving you a Government that gives you your money's worth. We have done things for ordinary people. The tax system is fairer; 15 million working families, including thousands and thousands in this State, got their taxes reduced because they worked full-time, they have children in the home, they're just barely above the poverty line. And we do not believe, in our administration, that people who work hard and are trying to be good family people should be pushed into poverty by the tax system. We have done more on that than anybody has in 20 years.

The family and medical leave law protects families so that if there is a baby born or a sick parent, you can take some time off to deal with your family problems without losing your job. That's an important thing that we have done.

We're going to immunize all the children in this country under the age of 2 by 1996. We are expanding Head Start. We are establishing apprenticeship programs for young people who get out of high school, who don't go on to college but do want good jobs with growing wages and a better future. And we have dramatically, and I mean dramatically, changed the college loan program so that young people can borrow money to go to college at a lower cost and better repayment terms.

And the world is changing. The world is changing. There is more trade but a lower threat of nuclear problems. We continue to work with the Russians. We have made an agreement with the North Koreans not to become a nuclear state. We are expanding trade and job opportunities all around the world. We are promoting peace in a peaceful but strong manner from Haiti to Northern Ireland to the Middle East to the Persian Gulf.

This country is moving. We are moving. And the message must be to the voters of Rhode Island and America in the next week, we are moving in the right direction. In 21 months,

a good start has been made. Have 30 years of social problems been corrected? Have 20 years of economic stagnation been totally reversed? Have 12 years of trickle-down economics been totally overcome? No. But in 21 months we've made an awfully good beginning. Let's keep going.

I thought to myself over and over and over again, what could have possessed our opponents to come out with this contract on America? What could have possessed the opponents of Congressman Reed and Representative Kennedy to sign it? It is a trillion dollars' worth of promises. Oh, it sounds so good. Here we are on the eve of the election, and one more time, they're like the Pied Piper of Hamelin. You remember what happened to the people that followed him? [*Laughter*] "We'll give you a tax cut. We'll increase defense. We'll increase Star Wars. We'll balance the budget. And we'll tell you all about how we'll do it after the election."

So we're telling you how they have to do it before the election, and they're all upset about it. They wish we wouldn't tell you. But when you promise people a trillion dollars and you act like it's free, it sounds like a good time. But it's not free. To keep their promises, they would have to cut everything else that you depend upon by 20 percent across the board: Social Security $2,000 a person a year, Medicare, veterans programs, programs for farmers in the Heartland of America, everything. If they say they don't want to cut Social Security, then they have to cut everything else 30 percent across the board, devastating the Medicare program of this country. It is wrong. And if it is just a cheap election year promise, it is even more wrong, because that means they are going to explode the deficit, ship our jobs overseas again, and compromise the future of these children who are here. We have to say no to this. We're doing fine. We're going forward. We're not going to turn back.

It was bad enough when they were just saying no. When they tried to say no to the crime bill, no to deficit reduction, no to the college loans, no to family leave, no to the Brady bill, bad enough when they killed campaign finance reform, lobby reform, environmental legislation. Shoot, this crime bill, every law enforcement group in America was for it. I've got this watch on today that I got from the Rhode Island Police Chiefs Association when I signed the crime bill. But they were against it for political reasons, because they didn't want the Democrats to be perceived as being tough on crime. Never mind what really counted was not who got credit for the crime bill but whether the murder rate was going down, whether the rape rate and the violence rate was going down, whether we were saving more kids before they become criminals, whether elderly people felt safer in their homes and kids felt safer in their schools. That's all that matters.

If they would work with us, everybody could have credit. There's more than enough credit to go around. You ought to be in the driver's seat in this country, not a bunch of politicians in Washington trying to cause failure to make you mad, to hope you'll do the wrong thing. And that's their program. You've got to do the right thing. You've got to turn the lights on in America. You've got to say we're going in the right direction.

Let me say this. You know, I ought to quit, but I'm having a good time. I was asked the other day, and I got to thinking about it—somebody said the other day, said, "Did any job you ever had prepare you for being President?" And I said, well, I was a Governor a long time, but it really wasn't the same. For one reason, you can stay in touch with the people better. It was much more difficult for folks to get in the way of me and my constituents when I was the Governor of a small State. So I thought of all the other jobs I've had. And the one that my job is most like now is one I never made a penny doing, was when I worked with civic clubs on car washes—[*laughter*]—because I liked to clean the windows off. That's what we've got to do in America today. You know,

if you drive your car and there's a lot of stuff on the windshield, you can think it's dark outside when the Sun's shining. You could think there are obstacles there when the way is clear. And then there could be a huge obstacle out there and you wouldn't be able to see it, and you'd run smack-dab into it. That's what they've done. They've put a lot of dirt on America's windshield. We've got to clean it off between now and Tuesday. Will you help? Will you do your part? Will you go forward?

Folks, this is an election between hope and fear, between unity and disunity but, more than anything else, between going forward and turning back. As I told the people over in Pawtucket at the Portuguese Social Club today, think about it like this: Every one of you is in the driver's seat. And on election day, just imagine that you have a remote control in your hand and what's in the movie screen or television screen is a movie about America's future. And you've got the remote control in your hand. You can push forward, you can push fast forward, or you can push reverse. Push forward, go on and push fast forward if you want to, but say no to reverse, no, we're going forward. We're doing better; we're going to do better still. We're going forward, forward, forward!

Thank you, and God bless you all.

NOTE: The President spoke at 6:56 p.m. at the Rhode Island Convention Center. In his remarks, he referred to James Langevin, candidate for secretary of state; Sara Quinn, candidate for attorney general; and Richard James, candidate for general treasurer. A tape was not available for verification of the content of these remarks.

Teleconference Remarks at the State University of New York in Albany, New York
November 3, 1994

The President. Thank you very much. Governor Cuomo, President Swygert, Senator and Mrs. Moynihan, mayors, and ladies and gentlemen, and students: Let me say that I am very excited to be here today with Governor Cuomo and very excited to be a part of this meeting.

I'm anxious to get on with the show and to see the students that are in other places

throughout New York. But I want to try to set the stage for the importance of this event today by speaking just for a few minutes about what this means, what we're about to see, what it means for the future of all the students here, for the future of the economy of New York and that of the United States, and for how we will all live in the 21st century.

Governors, like Governor Cuomo—and I used to be one; sometimes I think it's the best job I ever had—[*laughter*]—but Governors have spent, for the last 15 years, increasing amounts of time of education. Why? Because we know that it's the only route to a guaranteed success in life economically; because we know it changes people inside, gives people a greater sense of their own capacity. The ability to develop the internal material that God has given all of us is what makes people want to look to the future and want to make the most of their own lives.

Increasingly, education has become a concern for the National Government, not because we do education—the magic of education occurs in the classroom—but because the power of the United States to lead the world economically is inextricably tied to our capacity to see that all of our children get a good education and then that people seek education for a lifetime. So we have worked hard the last 2 years to do things like expand the Head Start program to make sure that our young people are ready to learn, to have school-to-work opportunities for apprenticeships so that young people who. don't go to college can at least get good jobs and have higher level skills, to increase access to college through more affordable college loans for all students. Next year, 110 New York institutions of higher education and 160,000 New York students will be eligible for lower interest, longer repayments on their college loans. So it will be easier for young people to go to college.

But the essence of what we're trying to do is to blend two things that may seem inconsistent, a commitment to educational excellence for all students, including kids who come from poor and difficult backgrounds. One of the things we have tried to reverse in the last 2 years—and the Congress has helped—is the idea that if you come from a tough background you're really not expected to learn as much. All the whole apparatus of Federal law was directed basically toward that assumption. We don't believe that anymore, and it is unacceptable. We believe all of our children can learn, and they should be expected to learn. And high expectations in the classroom has a lot to do with how people do.

The second thing we've tried to do to go with high expectations nationally is to emphasize grassroots reform—to know that all schools, all communities, all students are different—and individualized learning, different classrooms, different schools. It's important for us not to say at the national or at the State level, "Here is the model of how you must do it," but instead to say, "Here are the standards you ought to achieve. You figure out how to do it."

The link between a national commitment to excellence and a commitment to grassroots reform and a lot of individual efforts, in large measure, is technology. We are seeing a technological revolution in this country and, indeed, all over the world. Along with that, we're seeing a revolution in the way people learn, with kind of multimedia things like we'll use today. And more and more teachers are not just talking heads, doing what I'm doing, imparting information to you, but people who help students learn, who facilitate their ability to learn through technology. So what that means is that for the Governor and for me, we have to do what we can to make sure that the technology is there for every student in every classroom in the State of New York and in the United States to hook into as much information and as much learning as possible.

New York has an information superhighway project that is connecting 6,000 schools and 7,000 libraries to businesses and other units. This is amazing. We're going to be able to do this all over the country and all over the world. That's what the information superhighway is, people sitting in Albany, New York, communicating with people in Rio de Janeiro or in Pakistan or in China or Russia or somewhere else, sharing information, learning together, growing together. It is amazing what is possible—so that we will be able to say to all of our young people, no matter where they live, "Here's a very high bar of learning. You have to clear it if you want to do well in life. And you can figure out how to do it at the local level, but the whole world will be at your fingertips." That is the commitment that Governor Cuomo has tried to push and that I have tried to push.

The last thing I want to say is that, in order for all this to work, the students have to want to do it and have to believe in it. The young people have to have a hunger to learn and an understanding that you can't drop out of school, you have to stay in, and it is the ticket to a fascinating, exciting life.

The best days of this country are ahead of us if we make the most of this information explosion and put it with what is inside the heads of all of our children.

And therefore, before I get done, if I could just compliment Governor Cuomo on one thing that is an obsession with me. The State of New York in the last 10 years has lowered its school dropout rate by almost 50 percent. And if everybody in the country had done that, our educational system would be in much better shape. That is an extraordinary achievement and a great credit to the State of New York. And I thank you for that.

So having said that, now we've got some students who are in other communities throughout the State, and I think we're ready to hear from them. Can we start?

[*At this point, teachers and students at various locations in the State described and demonstrated the ways they each used electronic technologies such as Internet, CD/ROM, and E-mail. A student then responded to a question from Governor Cuomo.*]

The President. Can we go back to Buffalo? I wanted to ask Marquis a question. You know, it's one thing to be able to work one of these computers and quite another to know how to go after the information. How hard was it for you to figure out where the sources of information were, how you would go about researching this paper? How did you learn what to look for in the computer?

Q. Well, I learned this information with the help of my computer research teacher. And I was able to use this information to go into the Internet and research various things because Internet has different kinds of information which they draw from all parts of the world. And so it's like a really big encyclopedia where I was able to find the research I needed and the graphics and things like that.

The President. Could you explain to us—one of the things that was said was that maybe now students other places could look at your research and find out what you found out about the volcano. How do you log that in? How do they go about finding that?

Q. Well, if they are able to get into the Internet, then they can go through and search through under the headlines of volcanoes, like I did, and then—I've already set up the information that they needed. They would just have

to be able to find it, and then they'll have access to information that I had.

Q. Maybe I could help Marquis out a little bit with this. Since we have developed the Worldwide Web server at our site, we'll be able to post his presentation there. So the student would simply go in and, if they were using a MacIntosh, they could just click on something that said "View a presentation on a volcano, prepared by Marquis Wilford."

The President. Marquis, what's the most surprising thing you've found out about volcanoes in your research?

Q. Well, the most surprising thing that I was able to find out is that they were able to send a robot down in to view the pictures inside the thing. I didn't know that that technology was available. And now that I've found it out, I know that we all have access to see things like that. Because the heat of the volcano and stuff, I didn't know that technology would be able to do that much.

The President. I didn't either, until you told me today. Thank you very much. Let's give him a hand. Wasn't he great? [*Applause*]

[*Patrick Swygert, president, State University of New York-Albany, thanked the President and invited him to make closing comments.*]

The President. I just want to say one thing in closing. These different examples show us what is possible. We cannot rest until every school and every student has access to the kind of technology we've celebrated and learned about today. That has got to be our goal.

This is sort of a revolution in the nature, actually, of the job that the Governor and the Senator and I do. By trying to extend the availability of this sort of technology, our primary job is not to do something for somebody else but to make it possible for other people to do things for themselves. It's the ultimate example of what is now called empowerment, and it is very exciting, very rewarding. And we've got to keep at it until every student can do what Marquis did for us today.

Thank you very much.

NOTE: The President spoke at 10:43 a.m. in the Campus Center Building at the State University of New York.

Remarks at a Rally for Democratic Candidates in Albany
November 3, 1994

Thank you. Thank you so much, Governor Cuomo. I'm too hoarse to shout over you—[*laughter*]—but I'm very happy to be here.

Thank you, Governor Cuomo, Senator Moynihan, Congressman McNulty, Comptroller McCall, to the mayor here, Mayor Jennings, and the other mayors and labor leaders and students and citizens and Americans who are here. This is a great day for New York.

I'm like Mario. I don't have a speech either—[*laughter*]—except what's in my heart. I came here to ask you to vote for Carl McCall, to ask you to send Senator Moynihan back with a record margin, send them a message back, and most of all, to ask you to make Mario Cuomo the real "comeback kid" of New York State.

This election is shaping up to be one of those classic American elections that gets replayed every so often in our history: a race between hope and fear; a race between tomorrow and yesterday; a race between people who appeal to what is best in us and those who tell us that everything is just terrible and we ought to lash out; a race between those of us who challenge the American people to do better, who try to empower them to make the most of their own lives and those who offer them cheap and easy promises of a time which never was and never will be. That is what we are facing in these closing days.

I want to tell you something, folks. I understand why a lot of Americans are frustrated today. You know, there are a lot of people out there who haven't gotten a raise or are worried about losing their health care or think that their future is uncertain. But I'll tell you something, after 21 months this country's in better shape than it was when we took office.

With all of our difficulties, we know one direction, forward. We are moving forward in jobs, 4.6 million new jobs. New York lost a half a million jobs in the 4 years before I took office. New York has gained over 110,000 jobs in just 21 months. We're going forward, not backward.

We are going forward in doing things for working families: the family and medical leave law, tax cuts for millions of working families to keep them out of poverty if they have chil-

dren and they're working 40 hours a week; immunizations for all the kids in this country under the age of 2 by 1996; more Head Start. That is forward. Let's don't go backward.

Our Republican friends, they always said big Government was the enemy and the deficit was terrible. But when they had power, they exploded the deficit and increased the Government. We have reduced the deficit. We have shrunk the Federal Government. We have given the money back to New York, to Albany, to Rochester, to the communities to fight crime and make our streets safer. That is the record. We're moving forward.

We are moving forward. The economy is coming back. The Government is working for ordinary Americans. This world is a place where there is more trade and less nuclear threat, a place where America has been a force for freedom and peace and democracy. From the Persian Gulf to the Middle East, to Haiti, to South Africa, to Northern Ireland, we are moving forward, forward, forward.

New York is moving forward. Mario Cuomo and I just came from a demonstration of educational technology where we saw children doing marvelous things in the classrooms of this State, interconnecting with their computers to sources all over the world. Do you know, the State of New York in the last 10 years has cut its school dropout rate by about 50 percent. That would be the envy of every State in the United States. We're moving forward. We're moving forward.

In education, we're moving forward. We know that people need a lifetime of learning. We're establishing apprenticeship networks all over this country for young people who don't go to college. And we're making college more affordable with lower interest loans and better repayment terms so that every young American can afford to get a college education. Forward, we're moving forward.

What do our adversaries do in this election? What do Governor Cuomo's adversaries do? They don't have other programs. They don't have a vision for the future. They just say things are bad. What do our adversaries do? Ask Senator Moynihan. Well, they kill things when they can. They killed health care reform. They killed campaign finance reform. They killed lobby reform. They even killed a bill to clean up the toxic waste dumps of America. Nobody was against it, but they killed it anyway because they didn't want Pat Moynihan to be able to come back to New York and run for reelection to the Senate by saying that he helped to take the poison out of the ground. So they left the poison in the ground so they could poison the political atmosphere. Tell them no thank you, we're going forward, forward, forward.

There are problems in this country, real things to be worried about, deeply troubling developments in our culture: the rise of crime and drugs and gangs. And we know all that. But they have been coming for 30 years. There are economic problems: stagnant wages for working people, people losing their health insurance. That has been happening for nearly 20 years. And we had 12 years of trickle-down economics. We have only had 21 months, folks, but we're in better shape. Let's keep going forward, not go backward.

What is the argument? The argument against this administration, this chairman of the Senate Finance Committee, this distinguished Governor is really you ought to be mad and go in and vote your anger. And what do they promise? They said, "Give us power in the Congress, and we'll make you a trillion dollars' worth of promises. All Bill Clinton does is nag you. All he does is tell you you've got to get a better education, you've got to be more productive, you've got to be more competitive. We'll make you a promise: Vote for us. We'll cut taxes. We'll raise spending. We'll balance the budget. Presto, no pain."

What does it cost? "A trillion dollars." How are you going to pay for it? "We'll tell you after the election." [*Laughter*] Unbelievable!

And so their promises mean, my fellow Americans, only one of two things for the people of New York. Either they will keep their promise, as Senator Moynihan has said, and they will destroy Social Security, Medicare, our ability to fund the crime bill, and other things to help New York. They will destroy the education bill I just signed which helps the cities and the local community schools to revolutionize education, by keeping their promise. Or they will abandon their promise, and they will explode the deficit, start sending jobs overseas again, and put the economy in the ditch. That is back-

ward. No, thank you, we're going forward next Tuesday. Forward, that's the direction we know.

Yes, there is frustration in the electorate. But you know, the first thing you try to teach your children as a parent once they really begin to be aware of the world is not to make an important decision when you're mad. "If you're mad, count 10 before you talk." How many times were we raised with that? What the Republicans want you to do is go in and vote before you count to two. [*Laughter*]

Well, folks, I want to ask every one of you in this enthusiastic crowd to leave this place and promise yourself that between now and Tuesday you're going to find three or four or five of your neighbors and friends who haven't made up their mind in these races, who aren't sure how they're going to vote in the Governor's race. Tell them to take a deep breath; sit down and have a cup of coffee with them and talk about moving forward.

On election day, imagine that every American has in his or her home a movie of America on the television and the remote control in your hand, and you get to push the button. You can push forward; you can even push fast forward if you want to—[*laughter*]—or you can push reverse. No; forward, always forward. That's what this country has done. That's what this country needs. You just think about it.

Let me tell you, I've just come back from this wonderful trip to the Middle East. I have looked into the eyes of millions of people who are not Americans. In all those countries I visited, I saw people looking at our fine young men and women in uniform in the Persian Gulf. I saw the Jordanians and the Israelis looking at the American President—not me, they saw America. And you know what? The people outside this country are not cynical about America. They think we're the strongest military power, the strongest force for peace, the strongest force for economic progress, the strongest force for opportunity. They are not cynical. They are not cynical.

And if on election morning the people of New York wake up and they're not cynical and they see ourselves as others see us and they see the potential of this State and the potential of this country, they will send Mario Cuomo back to the Governor's mansion in Albany.

Now, you—you must be his voice. You must be the voice for these candidates who stand for what is best in us, who stand for hope over

fear, who stand for tomorrow over yesterday—
you, every one of you. Don't miss a chance.
Don't miss a lick. Don't leave a stone unturned.
Go out there now between now and Tuesday
and say: Look at me, I represent America, hope,
and tomorrow. Help me go forward.

God bless you all.

NOTE: The President spoke at 11:55 a.m. in the
Physical Education Building at the State University of New York. In his remarks, he referred to
Mayor Gerald D. Jennings of Albany and H. Carl
McCall, New York State comptroller.

Remarks to the Community in Des Moines, Iowa
November 3, 1994

Thank you. First of all, I'd like to thank you
for giving me a drier welcome than I had the
last time I came to Iowa.

I want to thank the Dowling High School
Band, thank you very much. I thank my good
friend Senator Tom Harkin for that wonderful
speech and for being a constant source of leadership and courage and support in the United
States Senate. I don't know what I would have
done without Tom Harkin in the last 2 years.
And since I'm in Iowa, I also want to say that
Ruth Harkin is the best Director of the Overseas Private Investment Corporation and has
made more American jobs in that position than
anybody who ever held it before she took it.

I am delighted to be here with all the fine
leaders of the Democratic Party and with your
candidates for Congress: Glen Winekauf, Sheila
McGuire, Elaine Baxter, my old friend Dave
Nagle—the second time is the charm for Elaine
and Dave; I know it will be—with Neal Smith,
whom I admire more than I can say, and I
want to say a little more about him later and
about this race he is in; and with Bonnie Campbell, who ought to be the next Governor of
the State of Iowa.

Ladies and gentlemen, this election all over
America represents a choice, a choice between
hope and fear, between the mainstream and the
mean stream, between whether we're going to
be together or we're going to be divided, between whether we're going forward or we're
going to go back. I think I know the answer
to that. You want to keep going forward!

Twenty-one months ago, with the help of the
good people of Iowa, I moved to Washington
to assume the Presidency. Now, since that time,
I have kept my commitment to try to put the
American people first, to make the Government
work for ordinary people, to bring the economy
back, to empower Americans so that everybody
could assume the responsibility of living up to
the fullest of their capacities, to give you a world
that is more peaceful and more prosperous for
Americans to work in. And while I know we've
still got problems, we've still got folks who are
worried about their jobs and worried they won't
get a raise, people who still are worried about
losing their health care—yes, there are still
problems.

But I ask you to consider this: We went to
Washington to deal with 30 years of accumulated social problems, with 20 years of stagnant
wages and losing benefits for working people,
with 12 years of the consequences of trickledown economics, with 4 years of the slowest
job growth since the Great Depression. And
folks, after 21 months we've still got a good
ways to go, but this country is in better shape
than it was 21 months ago.

We've taken a stand to try to help ordinary
working people. You heard Bonnie mention the
family and medical leave law; let me tell you
what that means in Iowa. It means that 446,000
more Iowa working people can take a little time
off if there's a baby born or a sick parent, without losing their jobs. That makes a difference
here in Iowa. It means that in Iowa, 358,000
people will be eligible for lower costs on their
college loans because of our reform of the college loan program. It means in Iowa that
118,640 working families got income tax reductions because they're working full-time, they
have children in their homes, and we don't believe that anybody who does that should be in
poverty. The tax system should lift them out
of poverty, not put them in. For all their attacks
on us, 13 times as many people in Iowa got

an income tax cut as an income tax rate increase. That is the record of our administration with our supporters in Congress moving this country forward. I think we should keep doing it.

It means after years of bickering delay, we passed the Brady bill and the crime bill. And I can tell you that Iowa—Iowa—is the first State in the United States where the United States Attorney has brought an action under our "three strikes and you're out" law. If you commit three serious offenses, threatening or taking the lives of others, you should not be eligible for parole. And the first action under a law I signed 2 months ago has been taken in Iowa.

The other guys, they always told you how bad the Federal Government was. But when they were in charge, the Government got bigger. They always told you that they hated the deficit, but they quadrupled the national debt. Since we've been in office, we have reduced the Federal deficit, we have shrunk the Federal Government, and we have taken all the savings from the reduction in Federal bureaucracy and given it to local communities in Iowa and all across the United States to fight crime, to make our streets safer, to give our kids a better future. I think it's been a good bargain.

When I proposed and the Congress adopted our economic program, the other fellows said the sky would fall. They said the world would come to an end if the President's economic program was passed. Well, folks, they were wrong. They were wrong. You look at the results. In this country in the last 21 months, our economy has produced 4.6 million new jobs. For the first time in a long time—and this is very important for Iowa—more than half the new jobs created in 1994 in America played above the national average in wages and income. We had more high-wage jobs this year than in the past 5 years combined. We're moving in the right direction. We don't need to turn back now.

I told you if you would send me to Washington, I would be a President who would remember the farmers in rural America; would remember what it's like to live in the small towns, in the country crossroads, the places that Presidents don't visit and that people don't often take notice of. Well, in 21 months, in agriculture, I think we have plainly kept our commitments. We've increased loan rates. We've reformed the Nation's crop insurance system. We've given more crop disaster assistance payments; they've been based on quality, not just quantity. We've reduced the paperwork in the farm program. We've changed the farm income reporting system to more accurately reflect the real income of the average American farmer. We brought farmers into the policymaking process at the Department of Agriculture. We've reorganized. We've reduced spending. We've taken a $3.6 billion cut in the farm bureaucracy without doing what the Republicans say they want to do, which is to gut the farm programs. This is the friend-of-the-farmer administration, and you ought to support it and keep going forward.

And I want to say something especially about Tom Harkin and particularly about Neal Smith. When it came to ethanol, the Republicans said one thing but did another. I'd come out here in the middle of the farm country in Iowa and Illinois and the Dakotas, particularly in places that cared about ethanol. And people would say, "Well, we're farmers. We usually vote Republican." And I said, "Well, if you'll vote for me, I won't just talk about ethanol. I'll go to Washington and try to do something about it."

Well, during the last administration, they cultivated all the farmers, but they danced around the ethanol issue like a kid around a maypole. [*Laughter*] They'd tippy-toe here, and then they'd go back to Washington and they'd tippy-toe there. I couldn't figure out why, until I got to Washington and all the establishment in Washington tried to get me to tippy-toe, too. And I said, "Folks, I haven't been here long enough to learn this Washington tippy-toe. I told them in Iowa I was for ethanol, and I'm going to be for ethanol."

I want you to understand how tough it was. Tom Harkin, Neal Smith led the fight in the Congress to approve the promotion of ethanol. The vote was close. In the United States Senate, it came down to a tie vote, and Al Gore broke the tie in favor of ethanol. We did it to make ourselves more independent of foreign oil. We did it to promote the cleanness of our environment. We did it to create new jobs for farm families. But if it had not been for Neal Smith— I want you to think about this Tuesday—if it had not been for Neal Smith, we would not have been able to do it. And he ought to be sent back to Congress to keep fighting for you.

We are trying to help farmers all over America. We resolved the wheat dispute with Canada. For the first time—it's a big deal where I come from—for the first time ever, we opened the Japanese market to American rice and the Chinese market to American apples. Twice this year, including yesterday, something you care about, when hog prices were at their lowest mark in decades, we approved additional sales to Russia and other states of the former Soviet Union through the Export Enhancement Program. We are helping the farmers of America.

Tom and Neal and a lot of other people have been talking to me about the record corn harvest. You know how it is when you're farming: You're either flooded or you're glutted. You escaped the flood. Now you've got more corn than you know what to do with. It's depressed feed grain prices by 10 to 15 percent below the average. Today I am glad to announce that we will open the Farmer Owned Reserve for 1994 feed grains. We will provide no-cost extension of the USDA loans due next July. We'll enable the farmers to store that grain, rather than sell it when prices are too low. You clap for me, but you ought to thank Tom Harkin and Neal Smith, the chief architect of the Farmer Owned Reserve.

When I flew over Iowa last year, when I sat down and I walked through and I saw the flooded fields and the flooded cities, it made an indelible impression on me that I will never forget. I'm proud of the work that our agencies did here last year: James Lee Witt and the Emergency Management Agency, Secretary Espy, Secretary Cisneros, all the others in our administration. Well, this year, more farmers are hurting from crop losses in Texas, in the Dakotas, in Kansas, in Georgia, all across the Southeast. Today we're authorizing further disaster payments for them, just under a billion dollars from the emergency funds we set aside. And you remember what Tom Harkin said, the only reason we can do this is because you had a Democratic President working with our friends in Congress who restored the cuts made in the disaster assistance program by the previous Republican administration.

And for those who say, "Well, that's what the Democrats do, they just spend money"— no, no, no. It was the Democrats: We reduced the deficit; we reduced defense and domestic spending this year for the first time in 25 years. We did that. But because of discipline, because of a commitment to root out waste, because we changed our buying practices so there wouldn't be any more $500 hammers and $50

ashtrays, we increased our investment in disaster assistance, in Head Start, in immunizing all the kids in this country under the age of 2 by 1996, in college loans. We increased our investment in the things that count in this country. Now, what we need to do, if you really want to keep going in this direction, is to give me partners. Send these people to Congress. I need help, folks.

The other guys, what did they do? They voted no every chance they got. Every one of them voted against our program to revolutionize the college loan program, to provide for more affordable college loans. And it saved money. It saved the Treasury $4 billion. It saved borrowers $2 billion. They voted against it because the organized interests were against it. Every one of them voted against our economic program to reduce the debt and give 118,000 families in this State a tax cut because they were just above the poverty line, because they didn't like it that we asked one percent of our people to pay higher tax rates because they could afford it to reduce the deficit, every one of them.

And there are so many things that a President does, that a Congress does that have their impact in the States. You know, I had the privilege of serving my State as Governor for quite a long while. On the tough days in Washington, I think that was the best job I ever had. [*Laughter*] And I can tell you that so much that I hope to do for our economy still can't be felt unless you have a Governor with an economic strategy for high-wage jobs, to help small businesses, to bring economic opportunity to the rural areas and the places where it has been lost in the last 10 years. Bonnie Campbell will do that. I want you to help her get elected.

This crime bill we passed, it is a very important piece of legislation. It has more punishment. It has more prisons. It has more police. It also has opportunities for prevention to keep kids out of trouble. But the work of fighting crime is done at the State level; it is done at the community level. We need partners out here in the country. You have the tools now to lower the crime rate to make your children safer, to make your future safer.

The leadership of the other party tried to kill the crime bill, but we stopped them and we passed it. But now you need a Governor who understands what it takes to lower the rate of crime, reduce violence, and give our kids a better future. Bonnie Campbell proved as attorney general she does that, she knows that. Give her a chance to serve.

Now listen when I tell you what the stakes are in Congress, and why it is so important that you return Neal Smith and elect these other candidates for Congress. Last Sunday on "Meet the Press," the Republicans' top strategist in Washington, Bill Kristol, said he wanted to end farm subsidies, and as soon as the election is over, the Republican Senator from Kansas, their leader, would take the lead in doing just that. He said that; I didn't. Now, Mr. Kristol, you've probably never heard of him, but he's the fellow that tells them what to think up in Washington. [*Laughter*]

He told them, for example, to stop cooperating with us on health care. I pleaded with them. I said, "You don't like my ideas. I'll try yours. Let's cooperate on health care." Another million Americans in working families lost their health insurance last year. Farmers in this State and throughout this country pay astronomical rates for their health insurance. It isn't right. It isn't fair. I had a plan so that farmers and small business people could buy health insurance at the same rates that those of us in the Federal Government and people that work for big corporations do. And they refused to cooperate because Mr. Kristol told them it was bad politics. He said—he released his memo. Folks in Washington, one thing I'll say about them, they're not humble. They'll tell you right what they're up to. [*Laughter*]

He released this memo, and the memo said, "You folks cannot cooperate with this President on health care because if this country solves the health care problem, the middle class will go back to voting for the Democrats. So at all costs, never mind the consequences, kill health care." That's what they said in the crime debate. They intimidated their Members of Congress. They said, "Whatever you do, don't vote for this crime bill. Our job is not to reduce crime. Our job is to beat the Democrats." You don't have to take my word for it. You remember what Congressman Grandy said. He said that he was ordered not to cooperate on health care.

So now they've got this plan on farm subsidies, and they say, "We're just practicing election-year scare tactics." Well, you look at their contract, the contract that Neal Smith's opponent signed and that some of these other folks' opponents signed and that they'll all be ordered to vote for, over 300 of them. Here's what the contract says—now, pay attention. The contract says, "Vote for the Republicans, put us in charge in Washington, and here is what we will do: We'll give everybody a tax cut, but mostly people in upper income groups; they'll get 70 percent of it. We will increase defense; we will bring back Star Wars; and we will balance the budget." Well, how much does that cost? "A trillion dollars." How are you going to pay for it? "We'll tell you after the election." [*Laughter*]

I'll tell you how you're going to pay for it. We had a study done. The House Budget Committee did a study. A trillion dollars, there's only one way to pay for it. You've got to cut everything else 20 percent across the board, Social Security, Medicare, farm programs, veterans benefits, college loans—20 percent, $2,000 a Social Security recipient a year. And boy, they squealed like a pig under a gate when we said that. If you take out Social Security, you know what you have to do? Cut everything else 30 percent across the board.

And if they're not serious, then what does that mean? If they're not serious, it means just what Tom Harkin said. We're going right back to where we were in the eighties. We're going to explode the deficit again. We're going to bury our kids in a mountain of debt. We're going to ship our jobs overseas, and people will be shipping out of Iowa all over again. No, thank you, we tried that. We want to go forward. We know better than that.

Now, I read coming in here—they always try to prepare me, and I read Congressman Smith's opponent, when Neal pointed this out that he'd signed this contract and he pointed out what the consequences were, he just went nuts and ran a television ad saying it was a lie. Well, it's not a lie. It's the truth. I know he is a plastic surgeon, but there are some things you cannot make pretty, and this contract is one of them. This contract will perform reverse plastic surgery on America. And we don't want it, and you don't want it. And you need to send Neal Smith back to Congress so he can fight it.

You don't have to take my word for it. Look what Mr. Grandy said about it. He said it's the crassest kind of politics. "How may times," I quote, "how many times does the elixir salesman show up with a hair tonic before people figure out this stuff doesn't work?" Do not be suckered.

Senator Warren Rudman, the former Republican Senator from New Hampshire, very prominent in deficit-reduction efforts in the Congress before he retired, a really old-fashioned Republican who believed in working with Democrats and sticking up for what he believed in, said the other day, "I guess you'd have to give the Democrats the credit for reducing the deficit and managing the economy. All the Republicans were against it." That's what the Republicans are saying, the mainstream, old-fashioned Republicans who are also mortified by what is going on today.

Folks, we've got to stand up against this. We are going forward in jobs. We are going forward in reducing the deficit. We are going forward in helping families with things like family leave and immunizations and expanded Head Start and the tax breaks for working people. We are going forward with welfare reform. We are going forward with the crime bill. We are going forward to make this world a better place. We have reduced the nuclear threat. For the first time since nuclear weapons were developed, there are no missiles pointed at the children of Iowa and the United States. And North Korea has committed itself to be checked and not to become a nuclear state.

And we are expanding the trade opportunities through NAFTA, through GATT, through the trip I'm about to take to the Far East after the election. We are breaking down barriers to American products and American services. We are standing up for peace and democracy from South Africa to South Korea, to the Persian Gulf, to the Middle East, to Haiti to Northern Ireland—everywhere. This country is leading a movement inside and outside the world to a more prosperous and a more peaceful level. And we are challenging the American people to make the most of their own capacities and to assume responsibility for their lives.

So you have a choice. Will you be for the progress that we are making, or will you go back? Will you be for the hope that we are promoting, or for the fear that they are pandering to? Will you be for what is best in us, or will you be for their easy promises and their cynicism? You know, these elections are going to be determined, in large measure, by the state of mind people are in when they go to the polls next Tuesday. We're out here telling people, "This is a great country, we can do better. We are doing better. But we've dealt with 30

years of social problems, 20 years of economic problems, 12 years of trickle-down economics. And in 21 months, we're moving things in the right direction." [*Applause*] Thank you. They're saying, "We've still got problems. Be mad. Vote against them. Vote for us. Look at our promises."

Those of us who are parents in the audience today, we know that one of the first things we have to teach our children when they get old enough to understand it is not to make important decisions when they're mad, isn't it? How many times, those of you who are like me and can still remember your childhood, just barely, did your mama or daddy say to you, "When you're mad, count 10 before you say anything"? Their theory is, count one and vote no. [*Laughter*] That's what their theory is. They don't want you to think. They don't want you to feel. They want you to lash out. We have to say no, we're better than that.

I just came home from this unbelievable opportunity I had to represent you and our country in the Middle East; to witness the signing of the peace agreement between Israel and Jordan because of the role the United States played in making that peace; to see our young men and women in uniform in the deserts of Kuwait; to look into the faces of millions and millions and millions of people from six other countries who saw in me and in them the promise of America. And let me tell you something, folks, outside this country, people are not cynical about this country. They know America is a very great nation, leading the world to a better future.

And so I ask you, I ask you to think about that. Out here today, we're all preaching to the saved. But tomorrow there will be other voters you can talk to, you can talk to for Bonnie Campbell, you can talk to for Neal Smith, you can talk to for these other fine people running for Congress. They need you, and the stakes are high, and America needs them. We are moving forward, we have always been a country moving forward. We are taking on problems that the other guys ignored for years and years and years. And yes, sometimes it's messy, and sometimes it's hard, and challenges are not as easy to hear as easy promises. But you know this is a challenging time. And I'm telling you, the best days of this country are still before us if we take up these challenges. Stick with these people. Go forward. Vote for hope. Vote for tomorrow.

Thank you, and God bless you all.

NOTE: The President spoke at 3:20 p.m. at the Des Moines International Airport.

Statement on the Flood and Fire Disaster in Durunka, Egypt
November 3, 1994

I am deeply saddened to learn of the disaster in the Egyptian town of Durunka, as well as storm damage in other parts of the country. Mrs. Clinton and I join all Americans in extending our condolences to the families of the victims of this tragedy.

We are grateful for the warm welcome offered to us by the Egyptian people during our recent visit. I have instructed the U.S. Agency for International Development to offer cooperation and assistance to Egyptian relief operations. The people of Egypt can be sure that their American friends will stand by them in coping with the aftermath of this terrible event.

Interview With Mike Siegel of KVI Radio, Seattle, Washington
November 3, 1994

Mr. Siegel. Very good to talk to you today. You sound a little hoarse.

The President. I'm a little hoarse, but I'm feeling great.

Role of Government

Q. All right. Let's go right to it then. One thing that crosses my mind is something that you were in fact one of the creators of, back in the mid-eighties, the Democratic Leadership Council, and talked a great deal about bringing the party back to a centrist kind of position. And now we see today that there is—according to the New York Times today, a two-to-one margin of the people in this country believe Government should be less involved in solving national problems, which would be consistent with what the Democratic Leadership Council said, as you were one of those who were the inspiration to create it. And then there are those who now criticize what you have done because of the health care and the crime bill and the environmental proposals and the very large budget proposals that you've made. Are you creating big Government again, in contradiction to what you wanted to do with the Democratic Leadership Council?

The President. Absolutely not. The people wouldn't feel that way if they were given the facts. This year, for the first time in 25 years, the Congress adopted a budget that I recommended that reduced both defense and domestic spending—this year, for the first time in 25 years. The only thing that increased this year was health care costs because we refused to act, Medicare and Medicaid. We reduced domestic spending. We reduced defense spending. We have reduced the size of the Federal Government. There are 70,000 fewer people working for the Government than there were on the day I was elected. There will be a reduction of 270,000 people in the life of my budgets.

And the crime bill was a bill that empowered local governments. I don't understand where people get off saying that's the National Government interfering in crime. What we did with the crime bill was to reduce the size of the Federal Government by 270,000 and give it to local communities to hire police, to build prisons, to have the resources in the courts for tougher punishment and alternatives to imprisonment for first offenders, and to have prevention programs. That's what we did with the money. So the crime bill is evidence of reducing the size of the Federal Government to empower people at the local level to reduce the crime rate.

If you look at the initiatives we have taken, basically all the major initiatives we have taken are designed to empower individuals to assume greater responsibility for themselves: the Family and Medical Leave Act, the expansion of Head Start, the apprenticeship programs for young people who don't go to college, the better repayment terms for college loans. Basically, I have implemented, chapter and verse, the agenda of the Democratic Leadership Council.

Now what is the problem? There are three problems. One is that Republicans tried to kill all the major initiatives that we passed. They were against deficit reduction, against the middle class college loans, against the crime bill, against everything. And they characterized it as big Government and taxes because they had to find some way to cover up their opposition.

And secondly, on the health care debate, I was not for a big Government health care plan. My plan provided private health insurance for small business people and self-employed people on the same terms that those of us who work for Government and big companies got it. It wasn't presented to the American people that way because the special interest groups who were going to lose money in it spent $200 million or more to tell the American people something different. And one of the things that we have learned in this information age is if you have enough money, you can just buy your message, and it's very hard for people to know whether it's accurate or not.

But if you look at where we are today compared to where we were when I took office, we've got more jobs, we've got a lower deficit. We've got more high-wage jobs. We've got a smaller Federal Government. We've taken a serious approach to crime. We've done things to help working families, to expand education, to have more trade and a smaller threat to our national security abroad. The country is in better shape than it was 21 months ago. We're moving in the right direction.

The Economy

Mr. Siegel. Let me give you a couple of other quick questions because your time is short; your office is telling us that. In the poll that came out in the Times, CBS-New York Times poll, 27 percent of the people believe the country is going in the right direction, and 56 percent disapprove of your handling of the economy. There's something in the perception of the American people that says we're not doing the right thing. You're the CEO of the country; why do the people feel that way?

The President. Well, I have very little control from time to time over how they feel. What is the information they get? What are the facts? I deal in the facts. The facts are, job growth is very fast in the first 2 years of my administration, after the worst job growth since the Depression, under the Bush administration. The fact is that the deficit went up under the previous administrations until they quadrupled the debt. We're bringing it down. The fact is we're getting more high-wage jobs into the country. If the American people don't know it, they obviously can't act on it.

Now, what are the problems the American people have? We have 20 years of accumulated insecurity in our work force, people not getting a wage increase, people losing their health insurance, people changing jobs rapidly. I can't stop them from having to change jobs rapidly, so I'm trying to institute a system of lifetime education and training.

I tried to make sure that working people wouldn't lose their health insurance. The Republicans and the special interest groups stopped me. But I tried to deal with that. But by every objective measure, the economy is in better shape and the country is in better shape.

I would also have to say, as you well know and as studies have documented, the way people get their information today in America is overwhelmingly skewed to negative information, to conflict, to failure, to negativism. And that's just a matter of fact. I am doing my best to shed some light on this, to get the truth out to the American people. But every day, they're told bad things, bad things, bad things. The truth is very different.

When I travel abroad on behalf of our country, world leaders ask me, what is going on in the United States? How could people possibly be pessimistic when our economy is so much stronger than theirs, when we are doing so much better, when we are doing so much better than we were? The answer is, the people don't know. I am doing my very best to cut through the fog and shine some daylight and tell the truth. It's a daunting challenge, but I'm doing the best I can.

Mr. Siegel. Mr. President, I don't mean to interrupt you, I want to keep you, but your office is telling us you have to go. I'm going to be in DC November 14th for that week, broadcasting this program. I hope we can get more time to talk during that week.

The President. Well, I hope we can. And I'm looking forward to being there on Sunday. I'm going to do a rally there on Sunday at 12:30 at the Pikes Peak——

Mr. Siegel. Pike Place Market, yes. You'll have a lot of people out here then.

The President. I hope they will. And I'm going to be putting this message out there. You can't blame the people for this; they can only act on what they know. But if they had—it's a very strange situation. We have never had an election in which the information the people had was so at variance with the facts. And if they have the facts, they're going to vote to keep on going the way we are.

It's an amazing thing where the 1980's and trickle-down economics and explosion of the debt and shipping our jobs overseas—that's what got us in the trouble we're in.

Look at Washington State. Since I've been President, we're selling Washington apples in

Asia for the first time. We're selling these Boeing airplanes around the world and doing everything we can to keep those jobs at Boeing. The economy has done much, much better.

And you started with this DLC thing. I have absolutely kept the commitments I made in the DLC credo, to move this country to the center and push it forward. The people just need to have the evidence and the facts; then they need to feel it.

Mr. Siegel. Well, Mr. President, I thank you again. I'm sorry we don't have more time, but I hope we will get time during that week I'm in DC in November.

The President. Yes, well, check in with us. I'd love to do the interview.

Mr. Siegel. Thank you very much. Good to talk to you, and have a good week if you would.

The President. Goodbye.

NOTE: The interview began at 5:25 p.m. The President spoke by telephone from the Hotel Savery in Des Moines, IA.

Remarks at a Reception for Democratic Candidates in Des Moines
November 3, 1994

Thank you. Boy, I like being here. I like this. When I got off the airplane today and I thanked the people at the airport rally for giving me a drier reception than I had the last time—[*laughter*]—I began to think about all the times I've been to Iowa and how every time I come away with a renewed energy, a renewed connection to the people of this country, a renewed sense of energy that I can make a difference because of the feelings, the spirit, the character of the people I sense here. And I just want to thank you for that.

I was listening to Tom give his sermon up here, and I was thinking, you know, Harkin just has no strong feelings about anything. [*Laughter*] You never know how he stands, doesn't have any energy for the task at hand. [*Laughter*] I'll tell you what, if the rest of us had half as much energy and conviction as he did, this country would have about half as many problems as it has. I want every one of you to know that he has been—in ways that have been

public like the fight on ethanol, in ways that haven't been so public like the fight to get more money into health research, more money into projects to look into women's health, more money into the general development of our educational emphasis in all areas of research—he has made a critical difference not only for the people of Iowa but for the people of the United States. I don't know what I would have done without him in the last 2 years.

Let me also tell you, I am honored to be here with Bonnie Campbell for many, many reasons. The first is, we do have an affinity for the same kinds of issues, and I understand what it takes to be a Governor. I had the privilege of being elected several times to be Governor of my State. I loved that job. On the really tough days in Washington, I sometimes think it's the best job I ever had. [*Laughter*] One nice thing about it was that it was a lot harder for people to separate me from my constituents and to sort of turn my positions upside down than it is when you're President, you're in Washington, and you're a long way from the 255 million or so folks you represent.

But it's a wonderful job. A Governor has to embody the hopes and the spirit and set the course for a State. The economic policies a Governor follows make a difference. The United States can shape the economy of any State and region, but how well it really does depends in part on the decisions that are made State by State. She has a strategy that I think is a very good and sensible one to build more high-wage jobs here, to deal with the problems of rural areas that have been left behind even in times of economic recovery. She cares about things that will help families and help people raise their kids. She's right, I'm doing my best to stiffen child support enforcement. I'm doing my best to radically change the welfare system in this country. I'm doing my best to have the criminal justice system deal with crime in the streets but also crimes against women and children where they live; I think that's important.

To be a really great Governor, you have to have a strong sense of partnership as well as leadership. You have to be a leader and a partner. Your people, first and foremost, have to feel connected to you. They have to feel that you carry their hopes and their dreams and their best values, that you're both strong and compassionate. Then you have to be able to work with people in the legislature who often disagree with you in a spirit of good humor and good will and continuing confidence that at least you have the right motivations. And it helps if you have a partner in the White House and if you really are working together to take responsibility instead of to place blame. And for all those reasons, I think she would be an absolutely superb Governor for this State.

You know, I was just asked today about—I did a little set of television interviews before I came out here, and one of the people asked me, said, "Well, how do you explain this voter alienation? They say it's as deep as it's been in 15 years when the economy was spinning out of control, and now the economy is doing well." And I said, "Well, one thing is a lot of people still have a lot of personal problems. Even though the economy is picking up and we passed the crime bill, a lot of people still feel personally insecure in this economy and personally insecure on their streets, so they haven't felt the impact of the work we've done.

But for another, it is just in fashion to be as negative as possible today." Isn't it? We're just bathed with negative information. It blows away the positive. Very often in our communications, in the way we get our information, we hear it in attack form where people are screaming at each other and down on each other instead of talking to one another about their differences and our common problems. And in election times, as a matter of survival, even the most positive of candidates have to defend themselves from the most negative of ads.

But what I want to say to you today is that we need more responsibility in this country both from our leaders and from our citizens because cynicism is, more than anything else, a state of mind. Most of you probably will remember that, well, it's been almost a year ago now that my mother passed away. And I miss her, I think, most of all in election seasons because this is the first campaign season I've been involved in in a long time where she hasn't been there.

My mother was widowed three times, including once before I was born, and she had a lot of tough problems in her life. And honest to goodness, if I behaved the way some of these people in public life do today—[laughter]—doing nothing but spreading cynicism, being negative, pointing the finger of blame—and she were around, she would whip me, as old as I am. [Laughter] I never saw the like of it, all these people in positions of power and responsibility, and all they want to do is blame somebody else for their problems.

This is a great country. You heard Tom Harkin talking about what the United States has done just recently to restore democracy in Haiti, to work for peace in Northern Ireland after hundreds of years of the Catholics and Protestants fighting each other, to stand up against aggression in the Persian Gulf, to help to make peace between Israel and Jordan, to facilitate the peace between Israel and the PLO, to work to finish the job in the Middle East, to work to diffuse the nuclear threat in North Korea. And for the first time since the dawn of the nuclear age, there are no Russian missiles pointed at the children of Iowa. This is a great country.

And while we have reduced the nuclear threat, we have expanded trade opportunities through NAFTA, through the GATT agreement. When the election is over I have to go all the way to Indonesia, dead tired, to try to meet with the leaders of the Asian countries. You know why I'm going over there? Because it's the fastest growing part of the world economically and because I want them to buy more American products. And it's important to our future.

This country, for all of our problems, is in better shape than it was 21 months ago when I took office. Every conceivable thing—[*applause*]. And I've already told you, there are a lot of problems. The Bible says there will be problems even until the end of time. The issue is are we doing our part to go in the right direction, to make progress, to move forward. That is the test.

We are moving forward on the economy. The unemployment rate has dropped across the country. We've got 4.6 million new jobs. We have more high-wage jobs this year than in the previous 5 years combined. Our economy has been rated in the annual vote of international economists as the most productive in the world for the first time in 9 years. And for the first time in 15 years, American auto companies have sold more cars worldwide than Japanese companies.

We are moving forward. We're moving forward on the deficit. Our opponents cursed the deficit and exploded it. We have said, "Why don't we quit whining about it and do something about it?" Our opponents cursed the Government and put all their political appointments in all the jobs they could get in before I took office. They talked bad about the Government, but they were there when the checks were written. [*Laughter*] We, the Democrats, have reduced the size of the Federal Government by 70,000. We have reduced Federal regulation, saving billions of dollars for people. And we have taken the money that we got from the savings and given it to you to fight crime in the streets of Iowa and every other State in the United States.

They said they were for family values. We said, we appreciate that, but our Government follows policies that hurt families. We passed the family and medical leave law, which my opponent vetoed at least once, maybe twice, I can't remember. We passed the bill to immunize all kids under the age of 2 by 1996. We expanded Head Start. We gave tax cuts to 15 million working families with children in the home, because we don't think people who work full-time and have kids at home should live in

poverty. The tax system should lift them out, not put them down.

And yes, I tried to solve the health care problem in America, and I'm proud of it. The day after Senator Mitchell said we couldn't pass a health care bill this year, the newspapers were once again filled with the stories: More Americans are losing their health insurance. Middle class people are having to pay more for less health care. The costs of health care are running through the roof. The Government deficit will start going up again in a couple of years even if we cut everything else because health care costs are exploding. America spends 40 percent more than any other country and can't figure out how to keep working people secure. This is the fact.

What I tried to do was to give you a private system that would let farmers and small business people buy health insurance on the same terms that people like Tom Harkin and I can get it from the Federal Government or people that work for big companies can get it. That's what I tried to do.

And by the time the interest groups that are making a killing out of the present system got through spending a couple of hundred million dollars, they had me giving a big Government program and a thousand-page bill that gave people a headache and convinced them they were going to lose what they got. It wasn't true, but they did a good job of it. So we have to find another way to come back and convince the American people we are not going to have the Government take over health care, but we do think every American who goes to work should know they're not going to lose their health care; they can keep what they've got. They ought to be able to buy it at a fair price, and if they don't have it, they ought to be able to get it.

We had a million people in working families, not people on welfare, people in working families lose their health insurance. This is the only country in the whole world with an advanced economy where the percentage of people working with children in their homes with health insurance has gone down for 10 years in a row now, the only one. I say we can do better than that, and we ought to. But even there we are making progress. Never before in the history of the country has a bill to do that even gotten to the floor of both Houses of Congress.

So you have to say, "Well, people are cynical." "Well, they're frustrated." "Well, they get a lot of negative information." "Well, they still have problems." All that is true. People will always have problems. I say, what is the issue?

We're moving forward on jobs, forward on the deficit, forward on reducing the Government and giving the money back to you to fight crime, forward on crime, forward on issues that help working families. The world is more peaceful. It is more prosperous. We are moving in the right direction. We do not need to turn back. We need to stay with the people and the course that is moving this country forward. That is what we are doing.

We are going to decide next Tuesday whether we're going to keep going forward or turn back, whether we're going to vote for hope over fear, whether we're going to vote for responsibility over blame. I have challenged the American people to do what is best, which means not only having the Government do something for you but having people do something for themselves. Nearly everything I have done simply empowers people to take more responsibility for themselves. That's about all the Government can do these days. And that's what we ought to be doing. I don't know anybody who wants a handout, unless they are flat on their back and can't do for themselves. That's what we're trying to do. We're trying to empower the American people to make the most of their own lives.

The other side has come out with a contract. They talk so tough, and they cuss the Government, but what does their contract do? It's nothing but a big Government giveaway. They want to give a tax cut, most of it to real rich people, but they'll give the rest of you a pittance. They want to just get you to vote, too. They figure if you're cynical enough, you'll say, "Oh, well, rich people always get more. I'll get a dollar and a half." [*Laughter*] So they promised everybody a tax cut, promised defense increases, promised to bring up Star Wars and balance the budget in 5 years. That's their deal. That is the tough, strong, responsible Republican Party platform. [*Laughter*] And we say, "Well, okay, how are you going to pay for it?" "We'll tell you after the election, but meanwhile, we're going to blame you for the problems we created in the 12 years before you showed up." [*Laughter*] That's their deal. That's their deal.

I'll tell you how this contract is going to go down if they gain in the Congress. There are only two options if they get their way. If they slash taxes with the deficit like it is, give 70 percent of the benefits to the wealthiest Americans, have a big increase in defense, big increase in Star Wars, and commit to balance the budget, there are only two options.

First of all, if they're telling the truth, the only way they can do it is to cut everything 20 percent across the board. That's $2,000 per person for everybody in Iowa on Social Security a year. If they say, "Oh, we never said we'd cut Social Security," then they have to cut everything else in the Government 30 percent. That's a 30 percent cut in Medicare for every elderly person. That's a 30 percent cut in all the farm programs, regardless of what happens to the farmers. That's a 30 percent cut in veterans benefits. That's a 30 percent cut in middle class college loans. The other possibility is that they were kidding. [*Laughter*] Right? Now if they were kidding, what you get is exploding the deficit, putting a terrible burden on our children, shipping our jobs overseas again, running people out of Iowa, running the economy in the ditch, putting us right back where we were in the 1980's with trickle-down economics. Those are the options.

Why are they making any headway at all? Because when people are cynical and mad, they don't always think straight. And I don't mean this to insult the American people. I'm just telling you, the people of this country—this is a great country—they almost always do the right thing. But it is very important for you not to let people vote just their cynicism and their anger.

What is the test of our administration? Have we done everything right? No. If you make as many decisions as I do, you take on as many fights as I do, you'll make a mistake now and then. Have we won every fight? No. But do you know what the objective surveys show? That for the third time only since World War II, we've had 2 years in which a Congress supported a President in more than 80 percent of the initiatives the President asked the Congress to pass—for the third time only since World War II.

And people say, "Well, it doesn't make a difference." Don't tell me it doesn't make a difference. It does make a difference whether you put the deficit down or up. It does make a difference whether we're taking a serious approach to crime. It does make a difference whether your policies expand trade and create jobs for America. It does make a difference whether people can take a little time off when their babies are born or their parents are sick. It does make a difference whether kids in this country are immunized at the same rate other children are in other countries. It does make a difference whether poor children get to go to Head Start or not. It does make a difference. It matters. It matters. It matters.

So I go back to the cynicism issue. Mrs. Roosevelt said once that you could spend your whole life battling all the demons in the dark, or you could just walk across the room and flip on the light switch. [*Laughter*] What you folks need to do for Bonnie Campbell, for Neal Smith, for Dave Nagle, for all these other candidates, is to walk across the room and flip on the light switch in Iowa between now and Tuesday. That's what you need to do.

I'm telling you, if my mother were here, that's what she'd say. She'd say, "You're the President. You don't have to blame anybody else. You're taking responsibility. Get out there and tell people what you've done." I have reached out my hand to these Republicans; I have asked them to work with us, but what have they done? They have constantly said no. They have constantly said no. I think the Republican leader is here today. And I don't know if anybody asked him about the comments of Mr. Kristol, that he was going to call for eliminating the farm support programs as soon as the election was over. That's the way they do it. [*Laughter*]

But that's what he said. And Mr. Kristol is the same fellow that told them that they shouldn't cooperate with us on health care. And then he proudly released the memo and said, "You can't cooperate with the Democrats on health care. If you do and you solve the health care crisis, the middle class will support the Democrats again. If you leave it like it is, we'll be able to upset the middle class, and we'll keep them voting for us by telling them the Democrats don't share their values. They're aliens." [*Laughter*] And then he was so proud of it, they released it. They're not even ashamed of it. I'd feel better if they were a little ashamed of it. He's the same fellow that says they're going to gut the farm prices. Well, he did what they told him to—they did what he told them to do on health care.

You ask Tom Harkin. At the end of the last session of the Congress, they killed campaign finance reform; they killed lobbying reform; they killed the Superfund legislation to clean up toxic waste dumps. That was amazing. Wasn't anybody in America against it—[*laughter*]—except slightly more than 40 Republican Senators and the House leadership. We had the chemical companies, the labor unions, and the Sierra Club for it. You couldn't get them to agree on when the Sun's coming up tomorrow—[*laughter*]—but they wanted us to do this. But they would have rather left the poison in the ground than let Tom Harkin and Neal Smith come home and say, "We helped to clean it up."

Now, folks, we have a fundamental choice here: whether we're going to vote for people to assume responsibility and roll up their sleeves and do what Americans have always done or people that sit around and point the finger, whether we're going to vote for hope over fear, whether we're going to keep going forward or turn back.

I want you to imagine on a Tuesday every American is sitting at home looking at their television, and the movie on the television is the story of America. And on election day every American's got the remote control in his or her hand. You can push forward; you can push fast forward if you want to—[*laughter*]—or you can push reverse. Now, that's what it is.

And when Tom Harkin asks you to go out between now and election day and call your friends on the phone, I think you ought to go out and find people who haven't made up their mind in this Governor's race and these other races and have a cup of coffee with them, and sit down and say, "Listen, I understand you're mad, you're cynical, and you're upset." The first thing you try to teach your kids as soon as they're old enough to understand it is never to make a decision when you're mad. How many parents, how many times have you said to your child, "If you're really mad, count 10 before you say or do anything"? How many times have every one of us made a mistake in this room because we said or did something before we got to 4? [*Laughter*] What the Republicans want is for you to get to one and go out in a snit and vote for them. And what you can do as a friend and a neighbor is to say, "Look, you've got the remote control in your hand. Push forward! Vote for Bonnie Campbell. Vote for your children. Vote for hope. Vote for tomorrow."

This is a great country. If we only saw ourselves as others see us, we would know that.

This is a very great country. Thank you, and God bless you all.

NOTE: The President spoke at 7 p.m. at the Hotel Savery.

Remarks on Employment Statistics and an Exchange With Reporters in Duluth, Minnesota
November 4, 1994

The President. Good morning, everyone. I have always thought the best social policy was a good job. And with our national economic strategy that was adopted last year by Congress, we have been creating millions of those jobs.

Today we can see that in the report that the Nation's unemployment rate has fallen to 5.8 percent, its lowest level in 4 years. And while we still have more work to do to make this economy, work for all Americans, it's clear that progress has been made. While we have been shrinking the Government and reducing the deficit, America has been growing the economy. More than 5 million new jobs have been created in the last 21 months, more jobs in high-wage industries this year alone than in the previous 5 years combined.

Had we listened to the doubters, this progress never would have been made. Those who opposed our economic plan argued that growth would stall, that jobs would be lost, that the deficit would go up. They were plain wrong. We have delivered what the American people have long wanted: lower deficits, $100 billion lower than predicted; strong growth, nearly 4 percent a year since I assumed office; and with the new revision, over 5 million jobs, 5 times as many per month as were created in the previous administration.

Of course the real heroes in all this are the American people, the workers and their firms who have made America the most competitive economy in the world, the heroes in the auto industries whose facilities are filled today with more workers than they've had since 1979. And for the first time since 1979, American automobile companies have outsold their Japanese competitors all around the world. The heroes are the people who are working full-time, even though they live on modest wages.

This improving employment picture is, in short, a credit to the hard work and the responsibility and the productivity of working Americans, as well as to the partnership that our Government has established with the private sector. We have to continue with this economic policy that puts people first. It is working.

Republican Contract With America

Q. Mr. President, Haley Barbour says you're telling a big, bald-faced lie when you say the Republicans intend to cut Social Security benefits, sir. Are you playing fair? Are you telling the truth?

The President. Well, why don't you ask Mr. Barbour what his position is? They want to have it all ways. They're out here now running ads criticizing this economic plan, which has plainly played a role in this terrific recovery we have. They're playing to the worst instincts of the American people.

With their contract, what have they tried to do? They have made one trillion dollars' worth of promises. Now, you don't have to take my word for it; look at the study done by the House Budget Committee. Mr. Barbour has the following options if they intend to keep their promise—huge tax cuts, spending increases, balance the budget—the following are his options: You can cut everything 20 percent across the board, which is a $2,000-a-person-a-year Social Security cut. If you say, "Well, I don't want to cut Social Security," then you cut everything else 30 percent across the board, including Medicare. You devastate Medicare, veterans benefits, the agriculture programs, and much of the other good things done by the National Government.

Of course, there's always the possibility that Haley Barbour's right, they're just going to deliver the goodies and forget about paying for them, in which case you go right back to the 1980's, exploding deficits, shipping our jobs overseas, putting our economy in the ditch. This economy is growing. We are moving in the right direction because we have played on America's strengths. I'm interested in making this country strong; they're interested in talking tough and acting weak. And their weakness made this economy weak. They were weak when they were in office. They were weak; they let this deficit get out of control. They stopped investing in our future. They didn't expand trade as they should have. They behaved in a weak fashion. They talked tough; they played to the fears of the American people. They are very, very good at it. But they did not build America's strength. I'm interested in this country being strong at home with good jobs, strong families, safe streets, and strong abroad. And that is what this election ought to be about.

Midterm Elections

Q. Mr. President, in these final days before the election, you're focusing in on Minnesota and Michigan, California, Washington State. But you're avoiding a lot of other States where there are some very close contests, Oklahoma, Tennessee, Texas, Florida. Why aren't you going to those States instead of coming to these States twice?

The President. First of all, I'm going where I think I can do the most good. Secondly, in Tennessee, the Vice President, who is from Tennessee, has been there and is going back and is spending a lot of time. We're practicing division of labor. I've been to Florida; I've done, I think, all the good I can do there. I also think, in the Federal races, I can have more impact than in the State races. So I'm doing the best I can with the limited time we have. I have a vigorous schedule. We're going back to Michigan. We're going to try to make one or two other States, too, before the end. But I'm doing what I think is most important.

Secondly, I believe that thanks to you, all of you, that wherever I go the most important thing is to get the message out, get the message to the American people that we have made a good beginning in these last 21 months, that we are dealing with problems that accumulated for years before I took office, that I don't pretend that we have solved all the problems. I

know there are still things to do, but we ought to keep going forward, not turn back. That message goes across America no matter where I am.

Death of Michael and Alexander Smith

Q. Mr. President, the Nation has been stunned by the news of the deaths of these two children in South Carolina. Do you have any reflections on that this morning?

The President. Well, I think like every American, especially every parent, I have followed this gripping incident, and it's been a heartbreaking thing. I think today what I would like to do is to say a word of encouragement to the people of Union, the people of the community, beginning with the sheriff and all the law enforcement officials, all the children who prayed, all the people who worked to try to recover those children.

It is very important that they not, in any way, feel that their efforts are diminished. The American people looked on them with enormous admiration, the way they pulled together across racial and other lines, the way they tried to find those children, the way they worked to get to an answer, the way they prayed for the safety of the children. I just don't want them to believe that somehow what the mother did in any way diminishes the quality, the character, the courage of what they did.

And so my thoughts and prayers are with them today. And I would hope the American people would feel that way as well. I think we were all moved and deeply impressed by how that community responded, and this awful turn of events cannot undermine that.

NOTE: The President spoke at 9:15 a.m. at the Holiday Inn. In his remarks, he referred to Haley Barbour, Republican National Committee chairman, and Susan Smith, who was charged with murder in the drowning of her children after originally claiming they had been abducted by a carjacker on October 25.

Interview With Cheryl Jennings of KGO Television, San Francisco, California
November 4, 1994

Midterm Elections

Ms. Jennings. Mr. President, you are coming to California just before the November elections. Why are you choosing this State in particular?

The President. Well, I, first of all, try to come often to California. As you know, I've done a lot of work to try to bring back the California economy, to try to help deal with the immigration problems, to try to help deal with the problems of defense conversion. And I feel that I have a big stake out there in the success of California because the success of California determines, in some measure, the success of America.

And there are important races there, Senator Feinstein's race, Kathleen Brown's race for Governor. Many of our Members of Congress are in tough races for reelection. And I want to do what I can to be as supportive of those who have supported the approach we've taken. We're moving America in the right direction. In 21 months we've gone a considerable way toward reversing the problems that brought us the economic difficulties of the last 12 years. And I want the voters of California to give us a chance to keep on moving into the future.

Defense Conversion

Ms. Jennings. Two issues you brought up: military conversion, the defense issue, of course, and immigration. Let's start with military conversion. You're coming to an area in Alameda County first that's very heavily hit by that. What can you tell those folks? What can you offer them?

The President. Well, I think most of the people there know that we have worked very hard, first of all, to invest significant sums of money in trying to help the places where bases have closed, in trying to put out new technology projects for the companies who have lost defense contracts. In the case of Alameda, we're doing what we can to move the port facilities over to the local community so they can be developed for commercial purposes.

Midterm Elections

Ms. Jennings. You also talked—I heard you earlier on the radio today—about cutbacks, Social Security, for example, veterans benefits. And of course, since there are so many military bases in California, a lot of veterans are saying, "Hey, the Government lied to me. I made a contract to serve my country, and now they're not going to support me or pay for my benefits for the rest of my life."

The President. Well, we are; the Democrats are. But the Republicans are running for Congress, trying to get control of the Senate and the House, based on a commitment to a contract which says they're going to give huge tax cuts to the wealthiest Americans; they're going to increase defense spending and bring back Star Wars; they're going to balance the budget in 5 years. That costs $1 trillion. The only way they can keep that promise is to cut Government spending across the board, 20 percent cut in Social Security, veterans benefits, Medicare, everything. If they take Social Security out, then they have to cut everything else 30 percent, Medicare, veterans benefits, all those things. There is no other way they can keep that promise.

If they're kidding, if they have no intention of keeping the promise and they're just going to do the easy things, the tax cuts, the spending increases, then we're looking at an explosion in Government debt, shipping our jobs overseas, putting our economy in deep trouble, just as it was when I took office.

So I hope that the American people, and particularly the people in California and those retired military folks, will see this contract for what it is, a bogus set of promises. I hope they'll reject it and vote for the people who are committed to continuing to move this country forward and to honoring our commitments to our veterans and to the Social Security recipients.

Immigration

Ms. Jennings. Mr. President, before I lose you on the satellite, what about Proposition 187? That is the anti-illegal immigration issue.

The President. Yes, I'm familiar with it. I have two things to say about it. First of all, I sympathize with the people of California. They have a problem. The Federal Government should do more to help to stop illegal immigration and to help California bear the cost of the illegal immigrants who are there. But secondly, I don't think Proposition 187 is the way to do it. It seems to be clearly unconstitutional. And if put into effect, its primary impact would be on children: keeping children out of health clinics, which could cause public health problems in the general population; kicking children out of schools, which could turn teachers into police officers and put kids on the street where they could get in trouble and cause trouble for others, rather than in school. We already have too many kids on the street in this country.

So I think what we ought to do is to keep working on what we're doing, stiffening the Bor-

der Patrol, stiffening the sanctions on employers who knowingly hire illegal immigrants, stiffening our ability to get illegal immigrants out of the work force, increasing our ability to deport people who have committed crimes who are illegal immigrants. And then the Federal Government simply must continue to do more to help California and other States deal with the corrections, the health, and the education costs of illegal immigration. I am committed to doing that. I don't think 187 is the way to do it.

Ms. Jennings. All right. Mr. President, thank you so much for giving us some of your time this morning.

The President. Thank you, Cheryl.

NOTE: The interview began at 9:59 a.m. The President spoke by telephone from the Holiday Inn in Duluth, MN.

Interview With Luis Eschegoyan of KDTV, San Francisco
November 4, 1994

The President. Hello, Luis, can you hear me?

Mr. Eschegoyan. Yes, Mr. President. Good afternoon.

The President. Good afternoon.

Immigration

Mr. Eschegoyan. Thank you, Mr. President, for giving us the opportunity to talk to you. What is your impression of Proposition 187, included in the California ballot?

The President. I'm opposed to it. I do believe that the Federal Government has an obligation to do more to try to help California deal with the problems of illegal immigration. And I have worked hard on that, along with Senator Feinstein and Senator Boxer. We've almost doubled the border guards in southern California; we have increased our sending the illegal immigrants who have been convicted of crimes back home. We've given money to California for the very first time to deal with the costs of imprisonment.

I've tried to get much more money for education and health care costs of immigration to California. But 187 operates primarily against children. It says, kick the children out of the health clinics. That could cause health problems

for the general population. It says, kick the children out of the schools, which means teachers are turned into police officers. It means that the kids can be on the street causing problems for themselves and for others. We've already got too many children on the street.

So I believe we have to do more. I'm working hard. I found a big immigration mess when I became President 21 months ago. But this is not the answer, in my opinion, and I hope the voters will turn out and vote and reject 187. It's a way of dividing our people, it's clearly unconstitutional, and it's looking for easy answers to a tough problem. After all, some of the people that are for 187 are part of the problem. When Governor Wilson was Senator Wilson, he responded to the powerful forces in California that wanted more illegal immigrants in California to do work. He sponsored legislation to make it more difficult to remove illegal immigrants from the workplace by going easier on the employers. Now he, all of a sudden, has turned 180 degrees on this issue. But this is a complicated issue without a simple solution. I'm committed to working with you to find a solution. I don't think 187 is the answer.

I hope that our listeners, our viewers, will turn out and vote on Tuesday and vote against 187, and I hope they'll come to the Kaiser Center in Oakland tomorrow where I'm going to have a rally at 2 o'clock.

Mr. Eschegoyan. Mr. President, if 187 is approved, do you think it will affect the NAFTA treaty with Mexico?

The President. I don't know that it will affect NAFTA, but it will certainly affect our relations with Mexico. You know, in the long run, the best way to reduce illegal immigration is for more people in Mexico and these other countries to have good jobs in their own countries, to trade with us, to sell to us and buy from us, and live in stable societies.

California has benefited more from NAFTA than any other State, with the possible exception of Texas. It has brought us increased numbers of new jobs and new opportunities. And as it raises incomes in Mexico, clearly, illegal immigration will slow because there will be more job opportunities at home. People like to stay with their families and where they grew up, if they can make a living.

Mr. Eschegoyan. Thank you, Mr. President, to talk to us here at KDTV, Channel 14, in San Francisco.

The President. Thank you. Thank you very much.

NOTE: The President spoke at 10:25 a.m. by telephone from the Holiday Inn in Duluth, MN.

Interview With Jim Dunbar of KGO Radio, San Francisco, California
November 4, 1994

Mr. Dunbar. Good morning, Mr. President.
The President. How are you?

Health Care Reform

Mr. Dunbar. I'm Jim Dunbar, and I'm just fine. And it's a privilege having the opportunity to talk to you. I've got a couple of questions that I hope you haven't heard thus far this morning.

Yesterday it was announced that the First Lady was stepping aside as the administration's main point person on health care reform. Sir, is this a concession on your part that maybe she was just a little too visible in her efforts to get the health care package through Congress?

The President. No. I don't think that's right at all. What happened, I think—keep in mind, we took this health care debate further than it had ever been taken in American history. For 60 years, Presidents have tried to solve the health care problem, to secure the health insurance of people who had it, and to cover—help people who didn't and to bring costs in line. And for 60 years, they failed because of the power of the organized health care interests. This is the first time we ever got a bill to both Houses of the Congress. We could have passed the bill this year if the Republicans had been willing to work with us in a bipartisan manner.

But they abandoned their commitment to health care reform and decided to play politics with it instead.

Mr. Dunbar. Are you going to let it rest for awhile, or are you going to go right back at it?

The President. No, we're going to try to—what I have to do now is to figure out how we can go at it in a way that will make our plan less vulnerable to the $200 million or so that was spent to characterize it as a big Government plan that reduces choices for people who have health insurance. The truth is, our plan lets you keep what you have. It relies on private insurance, not the Government, and it protects people from losing their insurance. It covers people who don't. And then it gives small business people and farmers and individual people the opportunity to buy health care on the same basis as people who are in big businesses or Government. That's what we need to do.

And I just need to go back at it in a way that is less vulnerable to the interest groups attacking it. But let me say, it's come out just since we stopped our health care efforts, because we couldn't pass it through Congress, another million Americans in working families lost their health insurance last year. We are the only advanced country in the world, the only one, where people under the age of 65 are losing ground in health care coverage, where every year a lot of folks are paying more and more for less coverage, every year more and more people are losing their coverage. And we're also spending more for health care by far than anybody else. The money is going primarily to people in the middle, to clerical costs and insurance companies and what the doctors and hospitals and the others have to spend to keep up with the mindless paperwork of the way we finance the health care system.

So we can't walk away from it. It's killing the budget. It's bad for the economy. It's hurting working people. We're going to have to face up to it. I just have to find a way to do it that makes it less vulnerable to the insurance company attack that it's a big Government plan.

Midterm Elections

Mr. Dunbar. Mr. President, I only have 5 minutes here, and I do have a couple more questions. You hear a charge in California—we know you're heading here and going to be here over the weekend, and we're glad to have you—but you hear a charge that Michael Huffington is buying his way into the Senate. But I point out that Dianne Feinstein, Senator Feinstein, has spent about $15 million in her efforts to keep that seat. And both would argue that they're doing it because the other fellow is. Is there some way we could put a cap on that so that being elected to Congress doesn't come down to the guy with the most money?

The President. Well, I certainly think we should. But to be fair, Senator Feinstein's had to raise a lot of money because Mr. Huffington said he'd spend however much of his personal fortune he had to to buy the seat. And the really terrifying thing is that since people are awash in information these negative ads have an incredibly disproportionate influence over what they should. And people have no way of knowing whether the information's even true or not. So it's a terrible, terrible thing.

I tried to pass a campaign finance reform bill through Congress, and the Republican Senators killed it at the end of the last legislative session. We could have had campaign finance reform, but they had the power to filibuster it, delay it, and kill it. And they did.

The Supreme Court has said that we cannot legally stop a wealthy person from spending all the money that he or she wants on a campaign.

So the only way to discourage a wealthy person from doing that is to put limits on spending and then say if you go over these limits, we're going to set aside a fund, and your opponent gets a dollar for every dollar you spend over it. That would remove the incentive to do that and encourage people to be more efficient and to spend more time answering questions and being more positive.

I mean, these campaigns have just turned into nothing more than multimillion dollar negative-ad slugfests, and they don't have—very often they don't have a lot to do with what is going to happen the day after the election. I mean, I think the best case for Feinstein, for example, is that as far as I know, she is the only Senator in my lifetime who in only 2 years in the Senate, her first 2 years in the Senate, has sponsored three major legislative initiatives, the assault weapons ban, the requirement that there be a zero tolerance for kids having guns in schools, and the California desert bill, the biggest wilderness preserve in the history of the country. I know of no Senator in my lifetime who's done that. Now that, it seems to me, ought to be an argument for giving her a 6-year term. She did something in 2 years nobody else has ever done, and she ought to get 6 to keep on helping California.

So to me—I would like to see these races be more positive, talk about what ideas people have to build the future and help people and empower people to take responsibility for their lives. That seems to me to be what we ought to be talking about.

Mr. Dunbar. Mr. President, unfortunately our time is up. We started our egg timer here 5 minutes ago, and it just went "bing." And I agreed with your folks to let you go.

You are welcome any time you've got a little time to devote to answering questions. You're welcome any time on KGO. Thanks so much.

The President. I'd love to do that. I'll be at the Kaiser Center in Oakland tomorrow at 2, and I hope some of your listeners will come out and see me.

Mr. Dunbar. We sure will. Thank you very much, sir.

The President. Thank you.

NOTE: The interview began at 10:35 a.m. The President spoke by telephone from the Holiday Inn in Duluth, MN.

Interview With Ken Minyard and Roger Barkley of KABC Radio, Los Angeles, California
November 4, 1994

Q. And now, ladies and gentlemen, the President of the United States of America, President Bill Clinton. We wanted to make—you're probably very happy today, Mr. President, given the unemployment figures, and we thought bringing you on in this style would be appropriate.

The President. Well, thank you very much.

Q. You recognize that music, of course?

The President. I do. That's what I played on "Arsenio."

Q. That's right. That's right.

The President. Now, I'm supposed to say, "Great show," aren't I?

Q. Oh, yes. Let's start from the beginning. Ladies and gentlemen, the President of the United States.

The President. Great show, Ken and Barkley.

Q. Oh, thank you very much.

The President. I've got my lines down.

Q. You did it fine.

The President. You play my music, and I do your lines. It's great.

Q. Yes, thank you very much. Mr. President, it's a pleasure certainly for us to be able to visit with you here. We were actually broadcasting this program from your Inauguration on the morning of January 20, 1991. We were in the big scaffolding thing that was set up alongside the Capitol building where all the photographers and other broadcasters were. And you waved at us, I think. That was a very nice thing.

The President. 1993. Yes, that was great.

The Presidency

Q. '93. Yes, '93. Excuse me, '91. 1993. Now, would you say as you look back on it, nearly 2 years after that day, that you maybe went into the office somewhat naive about the reality of being President of the United States?

The President. What do you mean by that?

Q. Well, that the magnificence of that moment and the anticipation of the 4 years to follow and, perhaps, 8, how tough it was going to be. And then suddenly the reality sets in that you're dealing with Haiti and the Middle East and all the things that have——

The President. I think to some—I think I underestimated a couple of things. First of all,

the difficulty of having to manage both a domestic and a foreign policy at the same time when both needed so much change, because we need to be strong at home and strong abroad and fighting for good jobs and strong families and safe streets at home and fighting for greater security and freedom and democracy abroad, that's something I underestimated.

The other thing I underestimated was the extreme partisanship of the Republican congressional leadership which we now know from studies is the worst it's been since World War II. No President ever had to deal with that.

Now, notwithstanding that, after the Congress went home, we learned that this was only the third time since World War II when the Congress supported the President more than 80 percent of the time. And so we were able to have a historic reduction in the deficit and to provide a dramatic increase in college loans for middle class people and pass the family leave law and the Brady bill and a dramatic crime bill and immunize the kids in the country who are under 2 by 1996. We did a lot of profoundly important things, but it was an extremely partisan and negative environment.

I also underestimated the extent to which the communications in the country would continue to be so combative and negative. And I think that somehow unduly sours the American people when the truth is that, for all of our difficulties, this country's in better shape than it was 21 months ago. We're growing jobs at 5 times the rate of the previous 4 years. We've got over 5 million new jobs in 21 months. I mean, we're moving in the right direction.

President's Popularity

Q. With those accomplishments and a slew of good economic indicators, it's got to—you've got to wonder, I would think, to say, "This is— we should be in great shape here; my popularity should be at an all-time high, and it's not."

Although, by the way, I should point out to you that Orange County Register this morning opens this way in a story: "Who's the most popular politician these days in California? President Clinton." You emerged on top of all the politicians. Pete Wilson, Governor Wilson, came in second.

Q. In a poll in Orange County?

Q. In Orange County Register and other media outlets.

The President. Well, you know, for one thing, I think if you look at the time in which we live, the combative time in which we live and the frustrations people are going through, it's hard for any incumbent politician to be popular.

Secondly, I have taken on a lot of tough issues in a very short period of time. And when you go through fights and you take on a lot of strong interest groups—and we had to take on tough interest groups to pass the economic plan, to pass the college loan plan, to pass the Brady bill, to pass the assault weapons ban, to try to deal with the health care issue—when you do these things, there is—it's also, while you're doing it, it can be very unsettling to people because all the news they get is about the combat, the conflict, the things that are going on.

So I knew when I started this course that I had to keep my eye on what America would look like in the 21st century. And I had to be willing to have some ups and downs in popularity to try to solve the long-term problems of the country.

I just want the American people to know that I have—every day I get up and go to work and do the best I can trying to increase their strength for the future, to give them good jobs and safe streets and strong families and to make us stronger in the world. And I think we are getting stronger. We're moving in the right direction. And that's my job.

And I tell everybody at the White House, it's not our job to worry about our popularity, to worry about what the American people think of us every day. But we have to think of the American people every day. And in the end,

I think the approval ratings will come out okay. But I've just got to get up here and try to solve these problems. They're not easy; they're not simple.

And the only thing that I regret is that I have not been more successful in trying to dissipate some of this kind of cynical and negative atmosphere in which we operate today because the truth is, this is a very great country with enormous capacity to deal with our problems. We are making progress; we are moving forward. And we need to fight the temptation to be full of self doubt. You know, it just doesn't belong in this country.

Q. What we'd, of course, like to talk to the President of the United States about—I know you're on a short schedule, and you're going to be coming out to California. The big issue we wanted to discuss is——

The President. Yes, I'll be there today. I'm going to have a rally late this afternoon at City Hall.

Q. That's right. Tonight, for Dianne Feinstein, right?

The President. Yes.

Q. But we also wanted to sometime tackle the issue of Don Imus versus Ken and Barkley, but we'll do that another time.

The President. Well, you guys are doing pretty well, I think.

Q. Yes, we are. We would hope, indeed, that we'd have an opportunity to talk to you again. Thank you, President Bill Clinton on the Ken and Barkley Company.

The President. Thank you.

NOTE: The interview began at 10:44 a.m. The President spoke by telephone from the Holiday Inn in Duluth, MN. An interviewer referred to radio personality Don Imus.

Interview With John Watson of WILM Radio, Wilmington, Delaware
November 4, 1994

Mr. Watson. Good morning, Mr. President, how are you?

The President. I'm fine. How are you?

Mr. Watson. Thanks for being with us. You've been very busy these days; not much time for

the saxophone, I guess, which happens to be my favorite instrument, by the way.

The President. Oh, thank you. I love it myself. I'm not playing too much. I did get a chance to play a couple of weeks ago with a group that was in the White House, but I don't play enough. My lip is getting weak; I've got to practice.

Midterm Elections

Mr. Watson. Well, your message seems to be getting pretty strong, seems to be playing pretty well with the American people. I see where your personal approval rating is up quite a bit, and Democrats in general seem to be a bit more secure for reelection.

The President. Well, I hope so, not for partisan reasons but because I think it's good for the country. You know, I came in with a commitment to try to make this country stronger, with more jobs and stronger families and safer streets and to make us stronger abroad.

And we've still got some problems in this country, but we're plainly moving in the right direction. If you just take Delaware, for example, there have been 5 times as many new jobs coming to Delaware in 20 months of our Presidency as during the previous 4 years. And we were able to pass the family and medical leave law, which protected 147,000 families in Delaware, if a worker needs to take a little time off when there's a baby born or a parent sick. We've reorganized the student loan program to provide more affordable college loans to more middle class students. It made almost 42,000 students and former students in Delaware eligible for lower costs on their loans. So we're making progress. We passed the crime bill, thanks to Joe Biden's unbelievable leadership. And I have to say, that was an example of bipartisanship. You had Congressman Castle there coming in at the end and trying to help us to get through the crime bill. It's going to make a difference. It's going to empower local communities to reduce crime and violence.

So we're moving in the right direction. We're moving forward. And I don't want to see the country go backward in this election, even though there are a lot of people who are upset.

Mr. Watson. [*Inaudible*]—I suppose you'll be here to campaign for Attorney General Charles Oberly, trying to unseat Republican Senator Bill Roth. But Oberly is seen as something of an independent Democrat. Is that going to be a problem?

The President. No, I like Oberly. I think—he's an exciting character to me. You know, the Democrats are not like the Republicans; we don't mind a little independence in our party.

I think it's good for people to exercise independent judgment.

I've just come from Iowa where a retiring Congressman, Republican Congressman Fred Grandy, was complaining about how the Republicans didn't want any independence and that—he pointed out how they were ordered not to work with me on health care. So I think Oberly has the kind of characteristics and character and ability and energy that would be very good at this time.

Mr. Watson. Sir, what is your game plan, just in case the Republicans are successful, as they think they'll be, and win control of the House? Could this work in your favor at all?

The President. Well, I don't know. Some people think it could work politically for me personally, but I'm not interested in that. I'm interested in moving our country forward. And the thing that bothers me is that the Republicans have committed to a program which would take us right back to the 1980's and what got us in trouble in the first place. I mean, their contract says that if they win control of the House and the Senate, they're going to—they want to promise huge tax increases, almost all of it to wealthy individuals. They want to have an increase in defense again, and they want to bring back Star Wars. They promise to balance the budget. Now, one of two things—that costs a trillion dollars. So if the Republicans get a hold of the Congress, one of two things is going to happen. They're going to do what they say, which means they'll have to cut everything in the Federal Government besides defense and Star Wars by 20 percent, including Social Security——

Mr. Watson. We're almost out of time——

The President. All right, well, listen—but that's $2,000 a person. And on Social Security that's a lot. If they don't do that, they're going to explode the deficit, start shipping our jobs overseas again, like they did in the eighties, and we'll be in big trouble.

So I hope the American people will take a look at people like Oberly. He's an aggressive, independent, progressive person, the kind of person I think that can bring new ideas, new energy, and keep this country going forward, which is what I think we need to do.

Mr. Watson. One final question, Mr. President. You're just about out of time, but you mentioned Congressman Castle is helping you.

So how do you see the Republican Castle versus Democrat Carrie DeSantis?

The President. Well, I mentioned that Castle helped on the crime bill because I think it's important for me not to be as partisan as they have been, and I want to give him credit for that.

But the reason that I'm supporting the Democrats in these races is that even Mike Castle voted against our economic plan. And our economic program for America is working. Just look at Delaware. You've had 5 times the job growth since our administration has been there as you did in the previous 4 years, that is, in 20 months, 5 times as many jobs in the previous 4 years. The economic approach we have taken, bring the deficit down, invest in education and training, expand trade, invest in new technologies, these things will grow the American economy. And the figures that came out today show that we have now had 5 times as many high-wage jobs coming into this economy in this year than in the previous 5 years.

Mr. Watson. There are many more things that we could talk about, Mr. President, but you're out of time. And I appreciate very much you calling in. Thank you very much.

The President. Thank you very much.

NOTE: The interview began at 10:51 a.m. The President spoke by telephone from the Holiday Inn in Duluth, MN.

Remarks at a Rally for Democratic Candidates in Duluth, Minnesota
November 4, 1994

Thank you very much. Thank you, Ann. Thank you for that wonderful introduction. Thank you for that good speech. If she hadn't made a case for her candidacy before, she certainly did in those remarks. I want to thank all of you at UMD for making me so welcome, the students here. I want to thank the band for providing our music; thank you. I want to thank the children in the Kids Voting Project who are going to take their parents to the election. When my daughter was very young, I began taking her with me to vote. Now kids are taking their parents to vote. We're going to get up to 100 percent voting if that keeps going. I thank you.

I am honored to be here today. I'm glad to be here with Senator Wellstone. I was listening to him speak, you know, and I was thinking to myself, it's too bad Paul has no energy, no enthusiasm; you never know where he stands. If he could just loosen up a little bit, how much more—[*laughter*]—I'll tell you what, he's a great inspiration to all of us. He keeps everybody in a good humor and always thinking about positive things, and that's pretty tough in Washington. When all the arrows start flying and people try to be negative, Paul Wellstone will always get up in the morning and try to make something good happen for the people of Minnesota and this country.

I am delighted to be here with all these Democrats behind me and especially with our Democratic gubernatorial nominee, John Marty. Thank you for coming, John, thank you. I appreciate many things about the welcome I've been given by Mayor Doty, but especially I appreciate his taking me to run today. We went out and ran 3 miles around the overlook today, so I saw all of Duluth. And I appreciate that; it's a beautiful city.

I want to take a point of personal privilege to say that I'm glad to welcome here Ann Wynia's primary opponent, my longtime friend Tom Foley, to thank him for supporting Ann in this race and for helping us to win this race.

And I want to thank Congressman Jim Oberstar for so many things. He is a wonderful leader. You know—yeah, you can clap for that. [*Applause*] He was one of the very few Members of the United States Congress who always supported our policy of restoring democracy and President Aristide to Haiti because he understood what was at stake. And it did my heart a lot of good to hear you cheering for him a few moments ago, to think what a great country America is, that here we are in the Iron Range in northern Minnesota where people care about what happens to people as far away as Haiti. And I thank you for that.

Finally, let me thank you, Chancellor Ianni, and everyone here at this fine school—there you are. We appreciate your making this fine facility available for a little old-fashioned enthusiasm right before this election.

You know, all of you know that I came here to ask you to vote in record numbers and with great enthusiasm for Ann Wynia for the United States Senate. I want to talk to you about why, why I feel that and why I think it's so important. You all know that she's had a distinguished career in the legislature, that unlike a lot of people in politics today, she is more of a doer than a talker. We've got a lot of talkers in Washington; we need a few more doers up there. In Washington you can almost tell people between those who point their fingers and try to blame others and those who open their arms and try to assume responsibility. We've got enough blamers in Washington. We need some more people who will take responsibility for the future of this country to get it going again and face our challenges again.

You don't have to take my word for it or hers. You can look at the work she's done to provide health care for 35,000 children in Minnesota who did not have it or her work in welfare reform or for education, many other areas. But I want to talk to you today about what's going on in our country and what we have to do about it. Ann said that this is a choice between going forward and going back, and she's clearly right about that.

You know, 21 months ago I moved to Washington, with the help of the votes of the State of Minnesota, to become the President. And I set about the work of trying to change this country, trying to rebuild America, trying to bring the American people together across all the lines that had divided us, trying to make us strong.

What does it take to make a country strong at home and strong abroad? It takes strong families, good jobs, a good education system, safe streets. It takes a sense of security abroad and growing trade, democracy, freedom, and peace so that Americans can work in a world that is coming together, not coming apart. My friends, you know, we've got a lot of problems in this country, but the truth is we're in better shape than we were 21 months ago when our administration took office.

There is this vast attack today on the idea of Government, and all the surveys show that our adversaries are making gains basically because they're trying to make people cynical and negative, to convince them that Government is the cause of all of our problems, that it is inherently bad, and that it doesn't matter how outrageous they are, what ridiculous things they say, you ought to vote for them anyway because they'll bring the Government down. Now, that's the essential core of their message. They win if the American people give up hope and believe the Government is bad. Well, I'm here to tell you that the Government is neither good nor bad. It is a tool that reflects you. You control it. You're the bosses. It is yours. The question is, what should it do? How much should it cost? How should it be done? Those are the questions.

Now, if strong families make America strong, I happen to think that the Government did the right thing when we came in and reversed the position of the previous administration to adopt the family leave law which protects 845,000 Minnesota families. I think we did the right thing to lower the income taxes of 155,000 Minnesota families who are working full-time, have children in their homes, but are hovering just about the poverty line. No one should be driven into welfare by the tax system. It should lift people out of welfare to reward work and family. I believe when our administration asked the Congress to approve a plan to immunize all the children in this country under the age of 2 by 1996, that strengthens families. When we expanded Head Start, it strengthens families. That's what we ought to do, and it's a good thing to do.

I believe that we have—and all the education groups agree with us, by the way—we've done more in the last 2 years to help Americans improve education than any Federal administration has done in the last 30 years. Why? Not because people are educated by the Federal Government, not because we are dictating more but because we have changed the nature of the relationship of the National Government to the education process. And I want to mention three things, in addition to Head Start.

Number one, with two major education bills, we have said to our public schools, there should be national standards of excellence that our children should achieve. We believe that all children can achieve them, and we are tired of having Federal rules and regulations that segregate poor kids in separate classes and separate tracks and tell them that by the time they're 6 or 7 or 8 years old, "We already know you're not going to make it because you come from poor backgrounds." We reject that. We reject that; it's wrong. So what we have offered is higher standards but less Federal rules and regulations, fewer requirements, and more emphasis on grassroots reform, the kind of thing that has been pioneered in the State of Minnesota, where so many of the interesting reforms in public education have started in the last 10 years. We are trying to take that all across America.

The second thing we've done is to say that education must be a lifetime process. We need apprenticeship programs for young people who don't come to college but want to be in good jobs.

And we have to make it possible for every single American citizen who is willing to do so to go to college, stay in college, and pay off their college loans at an affordable rate. Already 419,000 people in the State of Minnesota are eligible for lower cost college loans or better repayment terms, and we're going to keep going until all the students in America are eligible for the changes we have made in the college loan program. No one should ever stay out of college because of the cost of a college education. No one should, no one.

We have given you the chance to make our streets safer by passing that crime bill. Why? Because 100,000 police may not mean much, but 10 or 20 more in Duluth could mean a lot. Because we have adopted a balanced approach, tougher punishment, more prisons where they're needed, more police to prevent crime, and prevention programs to give our young people something to say yes to as well as something to say no to in this country. That is what we are doing.

And most important of all, we know that the best social program is a good job. And look at what has happened. In the State of Minnesota and in the United States—we just got the latest unemployment figures today—we now know that the unemployment rate in this country is 5.8 percent, the lowest it's been in 4 years. It's much lower in Minnesota. We now know that over 5 million new jobs have come into this country in the last 21 months and that in 1994 we have had more high-wage jobs come into our economy than in the previous 5 years put

together. We are moving in the right direction. We don't need to turn back on this.

Just in this area, look at what has happened with the Erie Mining Company coming out of the LTV bankruptcy. Look at what's happened—yeah, you can clap for that; that's good. [*Applause*] I heard Jim Oberstar mention the National Steel Company. You know the steel industry is booming in America today, partly because the auto industry is booming in America today. For the first time since 1979, American automobile companies will sell more autos around the world than our Japanese competitors. We are back, and we're doing well.

I was in Michigan the other day meeting with the autoworkers. You know what the number one complaint there is now? They're working too much overtime, and they want more people to be hired. Now, folks, that is what I would call a high-class problem. [*Laughter*] And we need more like that.

Now, this is the record: strong at home, making efforts for stronger families, better education, safer streets, good jobs. This is the record.

Ann Wynia's opponent joined the Republican chorus in unanimously voting against our economic program to reduce the deficit. They said, all of them, that if my program passed, the economy would go down and the deficit would explode. Her opponent said, and I quote, "The Clinton budget would have ominous implications for the American economy, American jobs, and the American people." I'll tell you what, he was wrong about that. And he would have ominous implications for the American economy if his ideas were adopted by the United States Congress.

You know, you look at what's happened here. It's the economic equivalent of something you know a lot about, a hat trick. We've got unemployment going down, jobs being created, the deficit going down to its lowest level in a very long time, $100 billion lower than predicted, 3 years of deficit reduction in a row for the first time since President Truman was in office.

Our Republican opponents say they are against Government and vote for them. Don't pay any attention to what they say, because they hate Government anyway; it doesn't matter what you do. [*Laughter*] That's what they say. But when they were in office, the Federal Government got bigger. Since we have been in office, working together, we have reduced the size of the Federal Government. We are taking it down to its smallest size since President Kennedy was in office, and we're giving all the money back to you and your local community to make the streets safer. That's what we're doing, and that's our proposal.

So you have a clear choice here: someone who supports policies that have made us strong, and someone who said no, no—no to deficit reduction; no to the tax cuts for the working people on modest incomes; no to the other programs, the immunizations for children; no to middle class college loan expansion—no, no, no. He even said no to the national service legislation which is giving children and young people all across America the chance to earn some money to go to college by working for a year or two in their communities at the grassroots level to solve the problems of America. How could anybody be against that?

Instead, they offer this contract. Now, you heard Jim Oberstar talking about the contract. I've been watching the faces of the people at our rallies when our congressional candidates talk about the Republican contract, and they go blank. They can hardly believe it. And that's really what the Republicans are hoping. They're hoping that you'll hear the sweet parts and when we tell you the bad parts you won't believe it.

Here's what they promise. They say, "We're going to give big tax cuts. We'll give you a tax cut. Most of it will go to the top 2 percent— 70 percent of it—but we'll give the rest of you a buck and a half or so—*[laughter]*—everybody gets a tax cut. And then we're going to increase defense, and we're going to bring back Star Wars. And then we're going to balance the budget." *[Laughter]* And how much does that cost? A trillion dollars. That's still real money in Duluth, isn't it? A trillion dollars. *[Laughter]* That's right. We could have a good time tonight on a trillion bucks. We could go all weekend long on a trillion bucks. A trillion dollars. So you say, "How are you going to pay for this?" They say, "We'll tell you after the election."

Well, let me tell you something, folks. Here are the options. If they mean what they say, that they're going to have these tax cuts, raise defense as much as they say, bring back Star Wars, and balance the budget, there are only the following options: Number one, they can cut everything else in Government 20 percent across the board, including Social Security,

which is 2,000 bucks a Social Security recipient a year. Number two, they can say what they're going to say, "Oh, how dare him; we didn't say we'd cut Social Security." They didn't say they wouldn't, either. *[Laughter]*

So, let's say they don't do that; then what do they have to do? They have to cut everything else 30 percent across the board, a 30 percent cut in Medicare for the elderly, veterans benefits, and student loans. And then there's the other possibility, which is that they're kidding; they don't mean it. *[Laughter]* Now, what does that mean? That's also pretty scary. What that means is, we're going to explode the deficit, ship our jobs overseas again, just like we did in the years of trickle-down economics, and put this economy right back in the ditch.

Now, you have the choice. When we talk about going forward, look at what is happening. We are moving forward on jobs. We are moving forward by reducing the deficit. We are moving forward in reducing the size of the Government. We are moving forward in Head Start, forward in providing immunization to our kids, forward in so many areas. We are working for stronger families, safer streets, better education, good jobs. We are moving forward. And we need to keep moving forward.

Let me close—I want you to think about this. We're also moving forward overseas. No Russian missiles are pointed at the children of Minnesota and the United States for the first time since the dawn of the nuclear age. North Korea has agreed to be a nonnuclear state. Trade is expanding at a record rate. We are standing up for peace and freedom and democracy from Northern Ireland to South Africa, in the Persian Gulf and in the Middle East and in Haiti. We are moving in the right direction. We are getting stronger. And it's a better world for our kids to grow up in.

What is the real enemy in this election? Cynicism, negativism, lashing out. And I want to just finish with this. As a parent, one of the first things you learn to teach your children is what your parents taught you: Never make a decision when you're mad. How many times did my mother tell me when I was a child, "Bill, count to 10 before you say anything"? And how many times did I get to 2, say something, and wind up regretting it? *[Laughter]* That's what our adversaries want you to do. They want you to count to one, go vote mad, cynical, Government's bad, nothing can happen, forget about the facts, forget about the record, forget about the direction of the country.

You, you can change what is likely to happen if they win in cynicism to what is certain to happen if we win with optimism. You, you, you can say, "We're in the mainstream in Minnesota, and they want to create a mean stream for America and we reject it. We reject it." You can say that.

You look at this. This institution where we are is a monument to hope. It is a monument to hope. Everybody who comes here comes here because they believe that they will have a better life, not only a better life economically but a better life personally in terms of the values, the understanding, the depth, the quality of life that will come if you live up to the fullest of

your God-given potential. When you strip away all the details and all the rhetoric, that is what we are trying to do. We are trying to create an America in which every young person can look forward to living up to the fullest of their potential, in which the best days of this country are before us.

We need Ann Wynia in the Senate to do that. Will you send her there Tuesday? Will you help us? Will you do it? [*Applause*]

Thank you, and God bless you all. Thank you.

NOTE: The President spoke at 12:30 p.m. in the Romano Gymnasium at the University of Minnesota. In his remarks, he referred to Mayor Gary Doty of Duluth and Lawrence A. Ianni, chancellor, University of Minnesota, Duluth.

Remarks at the Los Alamitos Naval Air Station in Los Alamitos, California
November 4, 1994

Thank you very much. First I want to thank Julia. You know, I was looking at her make that talk and thinking a couple of things. One is, she's the sort of person that makes this country great. And the second thing is, as long as we've got people like her and people like you, we're going to be all right, and don't you let anybody tell you any different. I am delighted to be here with Bob Hood. You already heard him talk about the trip that he made to China with the Secretary of Commerce, Ron Brown. I'm delighted to be here with Congresswoman Harman, Senator Boxer, and of course with Senator Feinstein. I appreciate the comments that Senator Feinstein made on behalf of all of us about the importance of this agreement.

This agreement was signed just a couple of hours ago by John McDonnell, your chairman, and Li Lanqing, the Vice Premier of China, with whom I met yesterday at the White House. It is a part of our ongoing efforts to expand trade in ways that maintain high-wage jobs in the United States, increase jobs in the United States, and help other countries to grow so that they can buy more and more of our products and provide better lives for their people as well. I am delighted by the fact that these jobs will be preserved in California and that others in Connecticut and other States will benefit.

It would not have been possible, notwithstanding the trip to China by Secretary Brown and by Bob Hood, but for the work of the McDonnell Douglas employees and the continued commitment of all of you to become more and more competitive, more and more productive, more and more successful.

I want to take just a minute—we've already celebrated, and I want us to celebrate, but I want you to understand from my point of view how this fits into America's future and to your future. Twenty-one months ago when I went to Washington to try to turn this economy around and rebuild our country, the unemployment rate here in California was 9.4 percent. You had suffered because of the national recession, but you had also suffered because with only 12 percent of America's population, you had 21 percent of our defense sector, and you had taken a disproportionate hit, about 40 percent of the impact of the base closures to date, as Senator Feinstein had said.

It was obvious to me that we had to do something to turn this situation around. And we began the implementation of a comprehensive, long-term economic strategy that was very different from what had been pursued in previous years. First we decided we needed to reduce the deficit of the United States, to free up more money to invest in the private sector to create jobs in the private sector and to drive interest rates down. Then we decided we had to remove controls on American exports, especially of high-tech products which are disproportionately produced in California. Then we decided we had to increase our number of trade agreements, like NAFTA and the GATT world trade agreement, to open up new markets. We decided we needed to make a special effort to invest in new technologies and to invest in defense conversion, which obviously had a big impact here. Now, in California that meant that one-third of all the funds we've invested to try to help defense contractors move from defense to domestic production or to commercial production for the United States and the world, one-third of all that money was spent in investments here in California. We also decided that we needed a clear, sharp view about what kind of defense posture we needed to take ourselves into the 21st century with the strongest military in the world.

I want to mention just a word about the C-17 contract because it's been mentioned by others. We had to fight like crazy to preserve the C-17. And I hope we won't ever have to fight like that again, because the C-17 is important not to your jobs, your jobs are incidental to the fact that it's important to the national security of the United States of America.

And I just want to mention one thing. I think all Americans were filled with pride when they saw the comprehensive United States operation that brought President Aristide back and democracy back to Haiti with no casualties. I think they were filled with pride when they saw the lightning-like response of the United States to Saddam Hussein's aggression in the Persian Gulf. Others were amazed that we moved as quickly as we did. Why is that? Because we learned after the Gulf war, in which the United States took 4½ months to position our soldiers, our airmen, our marines, our naval personnel, and all of our equipment, that we had to move more quickly. And one of the things we have to have is much more enhanced airlift and sealift capacity. That is what the C-17 means. That is what we are developing.

So if you like what you saw in Haiti, if you like what you saw in the Persian Gulf, then continue to support the C-17, not only because of the jobs in California but because of the

job it allows the finest military in the entire world to do for the United States of America.

We have a long way to go in California. But the unemployment rate has dropped, as Senator Boxer said, from 9.4 percent to 7.7 percent. The unemployment rate in America is at a 4-year low. Jobs are growing at 5 times the rate they did in the previous 4 years. The United States has just been voted at the annual panel of international economists as the most productive economy in the world for the first time in 9 years. For the first time in 15 years, America's autoworkers will make and sell more cars around the world than their Japanese competitors. We are moving in the right direction.

Here in California, in addition to the C-17 and this contract, I want to point out again the work that's being done in defense conversion. We are turning Norton Air Force Base over to the community. The Presidio has been turned into a national park. Up in northern California, the Alameda Naval Station will be turned over to the Port of Oakland. We are moving on a massive attempt to revive the capacity of Americans to build ships, which is benefiting the shipbuilding industry in San Diego that I'm sure all of you are familiar with.

These are the kinds of things we need to continue to push ahead with. And there are high-technology investments, from the physics experiment at Stanford to the work that's just been contracted at Livermore Labs, to the continuing effort of our administration to promote the space station, something that also benefits the workers of California, that will take us into the 21st century with a defense that is smaller but still adequate to our responsibilities in the world and with a job base that is preserved.

If you look around this crowd today, you will see everything that is best about America. What makes a country strong? Abroad, it's strong security, more trade, standing up for freedom and peace. At home, it's strong families. It's strong education systems. it's safe streets. It's good jobs. That is the true strength of America. That is what we are here to celebrate today.

And I want to tell you that the economic strategy that we have pursued that is making a difference in this country would simply not have been possible without the support of your Congresswoman, Jane Harman, and your Senators, Dianne Feinstein and Barbara Boxer. It is a partnership. And the partnership we have with the private sector is in many ways, as I'm sure Bob Hood will tell you, virtually unprecedented. Abroad, we are working hard without relief, and we will continue to work until we have this economy turned around again and until every Julia Clayton in the United States can not only be a great-grandmother but can also look forward to an American economy for her great-grandchildren that will be the envy of the world.

Thank you, and God bless you all.

NOTE: The President spoke at 3:45 p.m. In his remarks, he referred to Julia Clayton, McDonnell Douglas employee, and Bob Hood, president, Douglas Aircraft, and to an amended agreement providing for U.S. assembly of 20 McDonnell Douglas aircraft to be purchased by China and originally to be assembled in China.

Remarks at a Rally for Democratic Candidates in Los Angeles, California
November 4, 1994

Thank you very much. Senator Feinstein, Senator Boxer, Kathleen Brown, distinguished Members of Congress and candidates on our State Democratic ticket, to all of you who are here, thank you for making me feel, as always, so very welcome in Los Angeles and California. I want to say a special word of thanks to the gospel group, Charity, that entertained us so well. They were great. Thank you. I want to thank Marlee Matlin for her fine comments before; thank you for being here with us. Again let me say, there are very few States who could boast a slate of candidates for State office and for the Congress as outstanding as those who have already been introduced here tonight. But I just want you to know, I am proud to be here with all these nominees of my party and your party that you will elect on Tuesday. I thank them, and I thank you.

I want to talk tonight just for a minute about what's really at stake in this election. And I want you to think about why—I was looking at Dianne Feinstein tonight, and I was thinking, I have been following public life in America for a long time now. I never lived in Washington as an elected official until 21 months ago, but I've kind of kept up, like most of you. In my lifetime, there has never been, ever, not one time, a United States Senator who, in his or her first 2 years in office, sponsored three major legislative initiatives that will change the life of America for the better, the assault weapons ban, the zero tolerance for guns in schools, and the largest wilderness bill in the history of the United States, the California desert bill. Now, how could we not give her a 6-year renewal? We have to do it.

What is the argument of her opponent? It is the argument they're all making, really. It is that Government is inherently bad, it's inherently irrelevant, it doesn't make any difference: "Who cares what I say or do; it doesn't make any difference." You look at these children behind me and the children in this crowd; it does make a difference to their future, and Dianne Feinstein will make a difference. He said, "What difference does it make if we pass any laws in Washington; they've been up there passing laws for 200 years." He's the first person ever to seek the United States Senate to run not only against Washington, he's now running against George Washington. [*Laughter*]

Folks, I don't know about you, but I think what Abraham Lincoln did in the Emancipation Proclamation and the 13th, 14th, and 15th amendments made a pretty big difference in the life of this country. I don't know about you, but I think when we had one in four Americans out of work and President Roosevelt came in and lifted us up out of the dumps and got us going forward, it made a difference in this country. It's not a partisan thing. When President Eisenhower signed the bill for the Interstate Highway System or President Nixon signed the bill for the Environmental Protection Agency, it made a difference in this country. This guy is the only person who thinks that none of this matters. You have to say no to people who say it doesn't matter, yes to Dianne Feinstein. It does matter. California matters. She matters. Reelect her on Tuesday.

Look at—consider the candidacy of Kathleen Brown. I don't want to be presumptuous, but I know something about being a Governor; I used to be one. And on the tough days in Washington, I think it's the best job I ever had. [*Laughter*] It is a joy. But it is only a joy if every day you get up and you try to build. The Governor's office is not a place for blamers; it's a place for builders. It's a place for people who take responsibility and bring out the best in us and bring us together and move forward.

When I think of what you have been through in this State, with the recession, with the defense cutbacks—the unemployment rate in California when I took office was 9.4 percent. I have done everything I could do to bring it down to 7.7 percent, to get those 400,000 jobs, to get this State going again. But I need a partner here, someone who wants to work for California, not point the finger of blame.

You know, I want to say two things about your slogan here. The one is, I want to talk about 187. But the first thing I want to do— I've got plenty to say about that, but the first thing I want to do is to ask you this: You're going to vote on 187, and I hope to goodness you're going to beat 187. But after the election somebody is going to be Governor with 4 years of hard work to do. Will you have a job? Will your schools get better? Will your streets get safer? Will your air get cleaner? Will your State move forward? That is the question.

We don't know what the incumbent wants to do, but we know Kathleen Brown has a plan, a good plan, that will make California a better place, a building place. How did California become the symbol of America's future? By building, not by blaming; by bringing together, not by tearing apart. Why does California have a chance to lead our country into the 21st century? Because of our diversity, not in spite of it, because our diversity opens the world to us.

Now let me say this to people who disagree with us on 187. Let me say this: It is true that the State of California has borne an unfair burden in the cost of illegal immigration. That is true. And it is true that in tough times, that burden is hard to bear. But what I want to tell you is, from the day I became President, because I had served with Governors in California, in Florida, in Texas and other States, I started to do something about it. I worked with Senator Feinstein; I worked with Senator Boxer; I worked with your congressional delegation. I tried to work with your Governor. I didn't think it was a partisan issue. We have almost doubled the border guards in San Diego. We have provided funds for the first time for the cost of incarceration. When I have been reducing the Government deficit, we have increased by one-third the amount of money coming to California to deal with the cost of illegal immigration. We haven't been laying down, folks, we've been answering the call to do something about it.

Do we need to do more? Yes, we do. But this is not the answer. Look at 187; what does it say? It says that the adults of this country and the authorities are not able to keep illegal immigrants out of California, so we will punish their children. That's what it says. It says, close the health clinics to them, even if it creates a public health problem for everybody else. It says, turn the teachers into police officers and kick the kids out on the street. Let me ask the children here, don't you think we've got enough kids on the street already? We need more kids in school, making this State a better place.

Folks, the whole immigration system was a mess when I took office 21 months ago. I am trying to fix it. It is better than it was; it will get better still. Now, a lot of the people who are pointing the finger of blame at this election, who are trying to make you mad, you angry, you lash out, you vote for this, they helped to create the problem. When the Governor was a Senator, he voted for a bill to make it easier for illegal immigrants to be in California, because powerful interests wanted them to work for low wages. You know it as well as I do. And then, when he became the Governor, and a President of his party was in Washington, his friend, his ally, he never raised a peep about this to put any heat on him, and they did nothing. Then when Senator Feinstein and Senator Boxer and President Clinton showed up, we did not say this about the Governor. We said nothing bad. We opened our hands. We said, "Let's roll up our sleeves; let's take responsibility; let's face this problem in a way that brings California together, not drives California apart." And that is what I have tried to do. Get me a partner in the Governor's office who will do the same thing.

Let me say again—let me say again, folks. Why are they doing well? Because they say "If we can just make the American people"—this is nationally and in California—"if we can make people mad enough, they will vote without thinking. If we can make them cynical enough, the Democrats will stay home. And if we can make them believe that Government is bad, that it always makes things worse, then we win all the way around because when the economy gets better, we can say, well, that happened in spite of the President and the Congress. If things get better, we'll say Government had nothing to do with it. If it gets worse, we'll blame Government. And we can say any kind of outrageous thing we want to appeal to extremists and mean elements in our country, and we can still get elected." That is their strategy.

Well, let me ask you something. I don't know about you, but I think it mattered when you had that earthquake and we produced $11.5 billion in record time. I think it mattered when we fixed I-5 and all the other roads in record time, something never before done in the United States of America. Do you know, today we reopened the last earthquake-damaged freeway, the Route 14 connector on I-5? I think that matters, and I think you think it matters.

I think it matters that 4.9 million families in California are protected by the family leave bill, so they can take a little time off when a child is born or a parent sick without losing a job. I think it matters. I think it matters when 2.1 million families in this State get an income tax cut so they can raise their children and work and not be in poverty. I think that matters.

After all you've been through with the cost of higher education going through the roof, I think it matters that our student loan reform makes 1.6 million Californians eligible for lower cost college loans. And when we put hundreds of millions of dollars into defense conversion and give a third of it to people out here struggling to get off of the terrible recession you've been through, that matters. When we invest in scientific research at your laboratories and create jobs, it matters. When we revitalize the shipbuilding industry in San Diego, it matters. When we do these things, it matters.

When we do things that build the future, it counts. That's why today we had this wonderful news that unemployment is at a 4-year low, that over 5 million new jobs have now been created. That matters. That makes a difference.

Folks, you have to decide what sort of future you want. I want a strong America. And what makes us strong? What makes us strong is strength abroad and strength at home. We cannot be strong abroad, even though we have the strongest military, unless we have strong families and strong education system and safe streets and good jobs. That is the strength we are bringing to America, and we need to keep right on doing it. We don't need to turn back now.

And this whole thing comes down to the state of mind of the people of California on election day, because if people are cynical and angry, they either won't vote or they will vote against their own interests. You know, as a parent, one of the first things I tried to do, like most parents, as soon as my child was old enough to understand it, was to say, "Never, never make an important decision when you are mad. When you are mad, count to 10 before you say something." And every time I only got to 2, I wound up in a lot of trouble. [*Laughter*]

Now that is exactly what the Republicans are trying to get you to do in this election. You look at the Wilson ads; you look at the Huffington ads; you listen to them. What they want you to do is not to take time to count to 10, not to remember that this State is the hope of America, not to remember what we can do when we're at our best. They want you to lash out, or they want you to give up. They want you to stay home or come out and vote for not the future but the past. That is what is going on in this election. If you say, "No thank you, we are going forward in jobs, forward in bringing our deficit down, forward in investing in our future, forward in education, forward in building strong families," we will win. We will win because you will win. You will win. We'll win.

Now, I just want you to think about this. I know you think I'm beating a dead horse, but I've been all over this country and I know what I'm talking about. We will win if people think and feel their best and look at the record and look at the positions. And if that happens, Dianne Feinstein will be reelected. It is unbelievable that anybody with her record should even have a close race. You need to send her back there with an enormous, enormous ovation of support. And Kathleen Brown will be elected because she represents the future, not the past, for California.

Folks, I have done everything I know to do to be a good partner to the people of California. I have done everything I know to do. I have tried to take this immigration issue on. I've tried to bring this economy back. I've tried to help you with defense conversion. I've tried to help you build your high-tech base. I've tried to help you sell your products all over the world. I have tried to do things that no President has ever done. The farmers in the valley are selling California rice to Japan for the first time under this administration. And we did not do any of that by going to work in a cynical, negative frame of mind, saying that we're never going to make anything good happen.

My fellow Americans, your Government is neither good nor bad, inherently. It is our tool. It is a reflection of us. Whether it is good or bad, what it does, how much it costs, how well we do it is a function of what we believe and where we are going. Let's go into the future.

Let's don't go back. Let's don't go back. Let's don't go back.

Every one of you, promise yourselves you're going to ask somebody to vote for Dianne Feinstein, vote for Kathleen Brown, vote no on 187. Go see your neighbors, and turn it around. Go forward! Yes to the future!

Thank you, and God bless you all.

NOTE: The President spoke at 6:01 p.m. at City Hall. In his remarks, he referred to actress Marlee Matlin.

Remarks to the National Association of Realtors in Anaheim, California
November 5, 1994

Thank you very much, Bob Elrod, for those kind remarks. Gil Woods, Secretary Cisneros, I'm delighted to have you with me here today, and I thank you for your outstanding work in the area of housing, for all the things you are doing to make our country a better place. I'd also like to thank the United States Marine Corps Band from El Toro who played before I came. I thank them.

I am delighted to be here with all of you, including, I understand, hundreds of you from 36 nations, including some newly emerging economies, who have traveled here for this convention.

I was kind of looking forward to coming here today. You know, Saturday is traditionally moving day in America, and families think about moving toward new homes. For me, it was just another opportunity to move out of Washington and come see you. [*Laughter*]

This has been an interesting 2 years for me. There have been some great times and some not-so-great times, some that were exhilarating and some that were nearly bizarre. Some days I feel like the boy who told his mother that he really didn't feel like going to school, and his mother said, "But Son, you have to go to school. I raised you to do the right thing." He said, "But it's not fun for me at school anymore, Mother. I mean, the students don't like me. The teachers don't like me. The coaches groan when I walk by. Even the custodial workers don't like me." She said, "Son, you have got

to go to school. You're intelligent; you're healthy. You don't have a good excuse. Besides, you're 45 years old, and you're the principal." [*Laughter*] So I try to show up, regardless. And I'm glad to show up here today.

Today I want to talk with you about the dream of homeownership and the larger American dream of which it is a part and what we can do together to keep the economic renewal that began 21 months ago going. I ran for President of this great land of ours because I felt that for too long our National Government had neglected issues that are fundamental to our national strength, our security, and our future: good jobs, strong families, better schools, safe streets, and a world more full of security, trade, freedom, and peace.

In this country, when I took office, we had already been grappling for 30 years with profound social problems that have disturbed every person in this great hall today, affecting the breakdown of our families, our communities, the rise of crime and drugs and gangs and guns.

We have lived, and certainly you have lived, with about 20 years of economic stagnation for many ordinary Americans who are the bulk, the heart and soul of the home-buying public, people who work year in and year out for wages that have barely kept up and often have not kept up with inflation. And we have had—we had had 12 years of a policy which became loosely known as trickle-down economics, with which I deeply disagreed and with which you as an association at least disagreed with specific parts of, as I heard in my introduction, the things that we reversed from the '86 tax act.

When I became President, we put together an economic strategy that was comprehensive in approach, long-term in vision, but quite basic: reduce the deficit; change the way Government works, make it smaller with less regulation, more efficiency, a greater emphasis on partnership, and increase the impact of the things that you should do; ease the credit crunch; help small business; invest more in the security of our families and the skills of our people; invest in new technologies and defense conversions; increase trade.

We have pursued this strategy with discipline and persistence and success. The deficit includes a spending cut of $255 billion. This year alone, it is $100 billion less than it was projected to be when I took office. We are looking at 3 years of deficit reduction in a row for the first time since Harry Truman was the President of the United States.

In changing the way Government works in this country, we have adopted now two budgets covering 6 years, which will reduce the size of the Federal Government by 272,000, to its smallest size since John Kennedy was the President of the United States. Already there are 70,000 fewer workers working for the Federal Government than there were on the day I was inaugurated President.

We have deregulated banking, deregulated trucking. We have gone a long way to deregulate Federal rules and regulations on States, giving 20 States permission to try their own ideas to move people from welfare to work, giving 9 States permission to try their own ideas to find ways to increase the number of working people who have health insurance in this country.

We are working hard to change the way our Federal Government relates to our schools with very strong national standards of excellence in education but deregulating the way the schools meet those standards, instead emphasizing local reforms, grassroots initiatives, all kinds of changes initiated by people at the local level to help achieve the kind of learning that we simply have to have if our people are going to compete and win in the 21st century.

And inasmuch as I am here in Orange County, I have to say a special word of thanks to a member of my administration who happens to be an Orange County Republican. Roger

Johnson, who runs the General Services Administration, has helped to spearhead our reinventing Government initiative to make sure that we not only downsize the Government, that we also make the Government work better. If you ask the people in California, for example, we rebuilt all the highways out here that were damaged by the earthquake in about half the time that people said we could do it if we worked flat out. We did it not by Government mandate but by simply saying we would pay you more if you finished quicker. [*Laughter*] A novel idea, long discarded by the Government, revised for the California earthquake rebuilding effort.

We finally adopted a bill to change the way the Government buys $200 billion worth of goods and services with your tax money every year. And in so doing, by stripping away rules and regulations, we are saving $50 on every single Federal Government purchase, under $2,500, a year. No more $500 hammers. No more $50 ashtrays. We have opened the markets to the kind of competitive pressures all of you observe.

This year, even though we reduced defense and domestic discretionary spending for the first time in 25 years, we are investing more in Head Start, in more affordable loans for middle class students, in national service to allow young people to earn money for their college education by serving their communities at the grassroots level, in apprenticeship programs for people who don't go to college but do want good training and good jobs for the future.

And we are taking all the money that we are saving by reducing the Federal bureaucracy by 272,000 and putting it into financing the crime bill, giving the money right back to grassroots communities to hire police officers, to institute the prevention and the punishment programs that I believe can lower crime and violence in this country if people at the community level will spend the money in the proper way. We took the money from the Washington bureaucracy and gave it to every community represented by every person in real estate in this entire hall. I think it was a good switch. It will make our country safer.

We have also increased our investment in new technologies and defense conversions to help communities that have been hurt by base closings or by their big industries losing defense contracts. And we have dramatically expanded trade with NAFTA, with the GATT world trade agreement. As soon as the election is over, literally a couple of days after that, I have to go all the way to Indonesia for the second annual meeting of the leaders of the Asian-Pacific economic group. It's a leadership organization that I really got to meet for the first time as leaders in Seattle last year. Why am I doing this? Not because I want to take another trip 2 days after the election but because Asia is the fastest growing part of the world economy and the United States needs to be in those markets. It's high-wage jobs for us. We have to continue to push that approach.

Let me say that just this year, our exports to Mexico since we adopted NAFTA are up by 18 or 19 percent, 3 times the overall growth in our trade. Auto exports to Mexico are up 500 percent. I just came back from Michigan, where the biggest complaint is the amount of overtime the autoworkers are having to work. That, folks, is a high-class problem.

Now, this is the strategy of which you were a part when your organization supported our efforts last year. What I want you to know is it is working. Just yesterday we learned that unemployment in the United States had dropped to 5.8 percent, a 4-year low, and that unemployment in California had dropped to a 3-year low at 7.7 percent.

For those of you who aren't from here, let me tell you what happened to California. They not only went through the national recession, but California, with 12 percent of the population, had 21 percent of defense expenditures and suffered the impact of 40 percent of the base closings. So they're lagging a little behind the national recovery, but they are coming, too. They had a substantial drop in unemployment last month; now they're at a 3-year low.

Overall, the economy of our country has produced more than 5 million new jobs in the last 21 months, 91 percent of them in the private sector. In this year, the best news may be that about half the new jobs are high-wage jobs, that more high-wage jobs have come into the American economy in 1994 than in the previous 5 years combined. That's good news for homeownership. It's good news for the American middle class. It may mean that after a very long period of time, we are turning around average wage levels by changing the job mix in America.

I mentioned the auto industry to you; there are more people working in the auto industry now than in any year since 1979, even though they are much more productive and it takes far fewer workers to produce a car than it did in 1979. For the first time since 1979, automakers in the United States have produced worldwide and sold more cars worldwide than their Japanese competitors, for the first time in 15 years. And in the annual vote that occurs every year of international economists, for the first time in 9 years the United States was voted the most productive economy in the world. We are moving in the right direction.

I have to say, as has already been noted, that we have focused intensely on the real estate industry as a part of all of this, because you are one-fifth of our gross domestic product, because we need a healthy real estate sector. And in the economic program last year, when you asked for passive losses to be restored for real estate professionals, when you asked for FHA limits that moved with the markets, when you asked for mortgage revenue bonds to be extended permanently, when you asked for a secondary market for commercial real estate loans, you got those things in our economic program because they were good for the United States and for our economy.

Housing starts are up 30 percent since January of '93. And after declining by 664,000 the previous 4 years, construction jobs have increased by 436,000 since those changes were made and since we have begun to move this economy forward in the last 21 months. And I thank you for your contribution to the economic progress of the United States.

I want to talk now about where we go. But I have to say, just for a moment, if you will indulge me, since I know I have a good bipartisan crowd here—there may be more, indeed, Republicans then Democrats in this audience—this is a rather curious election season. I mean, after all, if I were a Republican President who said to you, "Look, we've reduced the deficit, reduced the size of Government, gotten the economy going again, adopted the toughest crime bill in history, promoted peace, and reduced the nuclear threat and increased trade all around the word," the Republicans would say it would be unpatriotic to campaign against the people who voted for those policies in their races for Congress. I think that's right.

And yet, we are living in a time of such cynicism that a lot of these races all around the country are being dominated by people who say, "Vote for me because I know that the Government is inherently bad, that everything they do is wrong, that anything they do will make the problem worse, that if anything good happens in this country while Mr. Clinton is in office, it's either in spite of him or unrelated to the fact that, like the principal, he shows up for work every day." [*Laughter*]

Now imagine this—suppose your office worked that way. And some guy comes in, and he says, "Hire me to work in your real estate office because the real estate industry is inherently sick, and you couldn't do anything right if you wanted to. And if you hire me, I'll sit in the office all day, and I won't try to sell a house." [*Laughter*] If half the people who came to work in your place every day said, "I'm showing up for work, but really we're going in the wrong direction, and we can't make anything good happen, and that glass is half empty," you would all be broke. And we are seriously entertaining giving our votes to people who tell us these things.

Folks, the Government is neither inherently good or bad. It is our tool. It is the instrument that reflects us. It is what we make of it. It can do wrong; it can do right. It can be good; it can be bad.

My view has been that we have tended to see Government in too much black or white terms. We'd look to Government as a savior when we're in trouble, and the rest of the time we say that we ought to junk it. It's either our savior, or we want it on the sidelines. The truth is, in my opinion, as we move toward the 21st century, Government should be seen as an instrument that seeks to create opportunity in the private sector. It seeks to empower people and then challenges people to assume both individual and community responsibility, because that's where most of the action is in America today. The Government cannot do as many things directly, and should not try; but without a sensible, aggressive, focused Government, working in partnership and challenging people to assume responsibility for their own lives, this country cannot live up to its potential.

Many of the things that we do actually matter. The family and medical leave law made a difference in the lives of millions of Americans who wanted to be successful parents and workers, who wanted to be able to take a little time off when they had a baby born or a sick parent without losing their jobs.

Our expansion of Head Start made a difference. That program works. A lot of kids are going to wind up being good students and good citizens now who might have taken a different path in life. Those things make a difference.

The changes we made in the real estate laws, reversing the mistakes that were made in 1986, made a difference to you. It makes a difference whether we do the right thing or the wrong thing.

So the only thing I ask you to do, without regard to your party or your philosophy, is to remember what we did here has made a difference. As they say back in Arkansas, where I come from, if you find a turtle on a fencepost, chances are it didn't get there by accident. [*Laughter*] And I think you ought to think about that.

And what we need in this country so much is to get away from this whole kind of negative-dominated way of talking, where we scream at each other instead of visit with each other. Believe me, I don't have all the answers. And if you try to do as many things as I've tried to do, you'll make a mistake or two, and I acknowledge that. But what we need in this country is people in public life who do what you expect when you're trying to get to sell real estate: You've got to show up every day with a positive attitude and a willingness to look at the facts and a willingness to learn and a determination to make progress. That's what we need. We need to discuss these things with one another.

These social problems we've got in this country, I say again, have been developing for 30 years, but they are of profound importance. We can fix the economy and if we lose millions of our kids, like those kids that dropped that 5-year-old out of that high rise in Chicago, well, it's going to be hard for America to be what it ought to be.

And these economic problems are of profound complexity. When people work harder and they get more productive and they make the economy grow with no inflation, then the first thing they're told is, "The economy is growing with no inflation, but we might have inflation, so we're going to raise interest rates so you won't get an increase in your income." These are frustrating, complex problems. On the other hand, we don't want inflation. You look at these countries that are gripped with inflation. It will kill your economy. These are complicated problems. But what we need in America today is a country that should be full of optimism and hope and a conviction that we can all make a difference.

When I came back from the Middle East, I was so impressed by that. I looked at the faces of our young men and women in uniform in the Persian Gulf who moved so quickly against Saddam Hussein's aggression. I looked at the people who were there at the peace signing between Jordan and Israel and how grateful they were for the role of the United States in that peace. And I thought to myself, around the world, nobody is cynical about the United States; they know this is a very great country. All I ask you to do is to bring your differences into the framework that this is a very great country, moving in the right direction, leading the world. And we can solve our problems but only if we speak with one another and listen to one another and stop just throwing these verbal bombs across the fences that divide us and turn us into cynical and negative people. We're not going to get anywhere doing that. [*Applause*] Thank you.

I'd like to take the remainder of my time to talk a little about what you came here to discuss, and that is homeownership and whether as partners we can do anything to increase it. If you think about it, the idea of having your own home is the ultimate expression of optimism. Homes are for families. They make for a more secure environment for our children. They create pride and self-esteem. They are the extension of our personality, our hopes, our dreams. For most of us, they're the main harbor of all of our collected memories. They are the most important investment in financial security that most Americans ever make. And most people who own homes care more about their own communities and have a bigger stake in solving the kind of problems that we've been here talking about today.

You know, I was thinking this morning as I flew over here, I have very vivid memories of every home I ever lived in, even when I was just 3 or 4 years old. And I bet all of you do, too. I can hardly remember anything about my very early childhood, but I remember the feel, the look, the atmosphere of the first home I ever lived in. I think we all agree that more Americans should own their own homes,

for reasons that are economic and tangible and reasons that are emotional and intangible but go to the heart of what it means to harbor, to nourish, to expand the American dream.

A national survey recently found that most people won't start saving for a home until they believe that they can actually buy a home. And I want to say to the American people, and especially to young families, if that's what you think, you ought to start saving now, because I am determined to see that you have the opportunity and together we can make that opportunity for the young families of our country.

I am committed to a new and unprecedented partnership between industry leaders and community leaders and Government to recommit our Nation to the idea of homeownership and to create more homeowners than ever before. I heard the kind introduction—well, of course the home mortgage deduction helps millions of ordinary citizens to achieve the dream of homeownership. Of course it does. But I believe we can do even more.

As the economy recovers, we know that we're going to make progress anyway. There are 1.5 million more homeowners in America today then there were 22 months ago. Housing starts are up and sales and profits are up. Here in California, where, as I said, the economy has been in difficulty, the pace of home sales for the first 9 months of this year is the highest in 5 years.

But still we face serious problems. Troubling changes occurred in the housing sector after 1980. After 46 years of steady growth, homeownership expansion began to head downward. Inflation, recession, stagnant incomes, the failure to enforce laws prohibiting discrimination in housing and lending, high costs and a reduced role for FHA perhaps all played a role. But by 1992, the national rate of homeownership had slipped dramatically. Homeownership for young families fell from 44.5 percent in 1980 to 37.6 percent by 1992. In 1980, more than 70 percent of our children lived in homes owned by families. In 1991, that had fallen to less than 63 percent. By 1990, 2 million young American families who would have become homeowners if the upward trend had continued, did not have the chance to own their own home. We have got to turn this around. We have to move this measure or our national prosperity forward as well. And I am convinced that we can do it.

Therefore, today, I am directing HUD Secretary Cisneros to develop, in cooperation with the most significant members of the housing industry and government at all levels, a plan to boost homeownership to an all-time high in the United States before the century is out.

This initiative will draw heavily on the expertise of those of you in real estate, financing, and building. Representatives of State and local governments and nonprofit community-based groups will join in. Participants from our administration will include the Assistant to the President for Economic Policy, the Assistant to the President for Domestic Policy, the Secretary of Agriculture, the Secretary of Veterans Affairs. I want them to write and send me, within 6 months, a detailed strategy that recommits America to homeownership, that will add millions of new homeowners by the end of this century.

I can assure you—just don't forget, the end of this century is just a couple of years away— I can assure you that this is not a report that will sit on a shelf. It is one that will be implemented. And let me be clear, this is not a Government program. I have asked for the involvement of realtors, homebuilders, mortgage bankers, Fannie Mae, Freddie Mac, insurers, the Habitat for Humanity, bankers groups, nonprofits, 40 other groups already on board to do their part. This is an initiative based on cooperation, not a Government program.

We can achieve the results we seek for America's homeowners if we take seriously the lessons I mentioned earlier about the way we reinvent and change the role of Government, not what Government can provide but what Government can help make it possible for you to provide. Specifically, I've asked the Secretary to focus, in the beginning, on at least three areas. First, I directed this group to find ways to cut the costs and the regulations involved in buying a home. I want it to be simpler, less costly.

Second, I want to target new markets, underserved populations, tear down the barriers of discrimination wherever they are found. Let me just make this point—[*applause.*] Thank you. Look at our trade policy. What are we trying to do? We tore down barriers to trade with Mexico because we knew they'd buy more of our products. We would buy more of theirs; they would buy more of ours. It would change the job mix in America for more high-wage jobs. The biggest untapped market in America for

many of us are the millions and millions and millions of people that the economy of the 1980's left behind, people who live in our cities, people who live in our isolated rural areas, people with productive capacities who, if they can become consumers, can explode the American economic growth rate well into the next century. That is what this is all about, and we should all focus on it.

Third, I want to develop new strategies for educating those who haven't considered becoming homeowners because they don't have an adequate comfort level or enough information to act. And believe it or not, at least our research indicates it's a much bigger problem than I would have thought when we began to look into it. Let me go through these issues briefly one at a time.

A modest starter home today costs about $94,000 in many parts of the country, even more here in California. With only a 5 percent down payment and closing costs, that's about $9,000 up front. Half the young families in this country make about $25,000 a year. Well, it's hard to save $9,000 when you're raising children on less than $25,000 a year. Many families are paying more in rent than it would cost them to own a home and to build equity, but they can't come up with the front-end money. We have to do better.

Secretary Cisneros has taught me the term "lifer." As an old attorney general, I thought that had to do with the criminal justice system. But today, more and more, it refers to people who are renters for life, middle class Americans who have no hope of becoming homeowners. We can do better than that, and we will.

We have to do a better job of reaching the underserved, of eradicating discriminatory practices that prevent minority families from finding, financing, or buying the home of their choice. It's wrong for anybody with a solid work history to be denied a home. And as so often is the case in the United States, if we do the right thing, it will be good business. It will be more money for all Americans and a greater rate of economic growth.

The third and final element of the plan will involve improving our efforts at education and outreach. According to one national survey, fewer than half of all American adults know what they need to know to navigate the real estate market successfully. Surely with all the communications technology available today, we can do better than that in America. Every day you counsel, you educate, you elevate the comfort levels of potential homeowners. We need your help in learning how to do this better for people throughout the United States.

If we do these three things—and perhaps this group, which will include representatives of your industry, will come up with others—we can widen the circle of home ownership beyond anything we have ever seen. And in so doing, we can slowly begin to restore the confidence of battered middle class American families who fear that even in times of economic recovery, their own family security will not be enhanced. That is the key to restoring the American dream, having working people believe that they can live in the turbulent, fast-changing times of the 21st century and still come out winners if they work hard, become lifetime learners, play by the rules, and raise their kids well. And finding a way for these people to own their own homes is a critical part of restoring the sense of American security and the reality of the American dream. I want you to help me do that.

My fellow Americans, through Presidents and administrations of both parties, the American people have been committed across party lines to the idea of homeownership. We have shown through things like the FHA and the GI bill

that we can work in partnership to empower people who will take responsibility for their own lives. I am trying to do that now in many, many other areas of our national life. We are trying, all of us, to face problems we have ignored too long. We are trying to deal with the challenges and seize the opportunities that await us.

I just want to say this last thing in closing: I am convinced that the best days of this country are ahead of us, if we will only seize these challenges, seize these opportunities, and maintain the attitude that all of you inculcate into everybody who works with you every day. I am telling you this is still the strongest country in the world, the greatest peacemaker in the world, the most powerful economy in the world. The only thing that can get in our way is our failure to believe in ourselves and our unwillingness to work together to face the challenges before us. If we can get rid of that, there is no limit to America's future.

Thank you, and God bless you all.

NOTE: The President spoke at 9:40 a.m. at the Anaheim Convention Center. In his remarks, he referred to Bob Elrod, president, and Gil Woods, president-elect, National Association of Realtors.

The President's Radio Address
November 5, 1994

Good morning. I'm speaking to you today from Los Angeles. In many ways, California is the cutting edge for a nation always on the move, always seeking new challenges. And I want to talk to you today about those challenges, about the choice we face between continuing to go forward on the path to a better future or going back to policies that failed America in the past.

Just yesterday, Friday, we learned that the economy is continuing to move forward. The Labor Department reported that the unemployment rate has fallen to 5.8 percent, its lowest level in 4 years. In the 21 months since I took office, over 5 million jobs have come into our economy, and the jobs are getting better. In

1994, more high-wage jobs came into our economy than in the previous 5 years combined.

Our strategy is beginning to work: reduce the deficit; increase investment in education, training, and defense conversion; increase trade. We passed an economic plan that is cutting spending by $255 billion and cutting the Federal bureaucracy by 272,000 positions. We slashed regulations and saved billions. We're also investing in new technology and defense conversion. We're expanding trade dramatically. In Mexico alone this year, the sales of American automobiles increased 500 percent.

We're also increasing our investments in education and training, even as we reduce overall spending. This will help our people to compete and win in the tough global economy: increasing

Head Start; apprenticeships for young people who don't go to college but do want good jobs; a dramatic increase in affordable college loans, making 20 million Americans eligible for lower cost loans on better repayment terms; and national service, the opportunity for people to serve their communities in solving problems person to person and earn money for their college education.

To rebuild America, we have to keep working for good jobs and better education. But to be strong, we also need strong families and safe streets. That's why we've worked hard for the family and medical leave law that's protecting millions and millions of American workers who don't lose their jobs now if they take a little time off when a child is born or a parent is sick; why we're immunizing 2 million American children under the age of 2 by 1996; why we've provided tax decreases, tax cuts, to 15 million working families with children because they work full time with children in the home and they're hovering above the poverty line. We want to lift them out of poverty, not put them in. We're working to make our streets safer with the Brady bill and the crime bill. Already extra police are appearing on streets and cities all across America.

Of course, we've got a long way to go until everybody in this country who wants a job has one, until people who work hard and deserve a raise get that raise, until people who have coverage don't lose their health care insurance. But America is clearly moving forward. The new economic statistics are real. There really are more than 5 million jobs in the last 21 months and more than 5 times as many per month are coming into our economy as was the case in the previous administration.

As I traveled our country this last week, I met some of the men and women who are the real heroes of this economic recovery and whose futures will be shaped by the results of the election this Tuesday, in Michigan, where our auto industry is roaring back with more workers than they've had since 1979 and where for the first time in 15 years American auto companies are outselling their Japanese competitors all around the world. At State universities in Michigan and New York, I met young people who are preparing for a high-skill, high-tech, high-wage future. I've also met older workers who are learning new skills for new careers.

Recently I received a letter from Antonio Dodero of Cerritos, California, who lost his job in the aerospace industry 2 years ago. He enrolled in a retraining program our administration has worked to expand, and he wrote just to thank me because that training helped him find new work as an air conditioning and heating technician. Mr. Dodero, thank you for having the courage to learn those new skills and to face the future with confidence.

Despite the progress we're making and the fact that the direction we're pursuing is clearly correct, there are forces in this country who are not looking forward, who don't want to invest in people like Mr. Dodero and those college students. Instead of building the future, they're making a trillion dollars' worth of easy promises: big tax breaks, mostly for the wealthy; big increases in spending for defense and Star Wars; and a promise to balance the budget.

A trillion dollars in promises? How will they be paid for? There are just two alternatives: It would require a 20 percent cut across the board in every other part of Government. That's cuts in Social Security, Medicare, student loans, assistance to farmers, veterans benefits, the crime bill, the things that make us stronger, smarter, more secure. If you take out Social Security, it would require a 30 percent cut in Medicare and student loans and all those other things. Of course, there's always the possibility they're kidding, that they're just going to give us the goodies without the cuts. What does that mean? An explosion in the deficit, sending our jobs overseas, putting our economy in the same deep trouble we had in the years of the eighties.

This is not the time for America to turn away from the future, to turn back to the easy promises of the past. We're helping brave people all around the world move toward their own freedom and democracy, their own peace and prosperity, whether it's Israel and her Arab neighbors; the people in the Persian Gulf or Haiti, where our brave soldiers are serving; the people in Korea who are building a nonnuclear peninsula; the people in Northern Ireland trying to bury hundreds of years of hate; or people in South Africa trying to build their democracy. Their hearts and minds are open to our ideas. Their markets are opening up to our goods and services. They admire our values, our strength, our willingness to change. They believe in our country.

And at this hopeful and historic moment, when America and the world are moving forward to the future, we must believe in our country, too. Why would we ever want to turn back to policies that failed us? When we can be strong, why would we ever want to be weak? The future of our children and our country are at stake.

With all of my heart and soul, I believe America will continue to make the choice to keep moving forward, to be strong, to seize the future.

Thanks for listening.

NOTE: The address was recorded at approximately 8:05 p.m. on November 4 at the Beverly Hilton Hotel in Los Angeles, CA, for broadcast at 10:06 a.m. on November 5.

Interview With Cynthia Louie and Fred Wayne of KCBS Radio, San Francisco, California
November 5, 1994

Midterm Elections

Ms. Louie. Mr. President, thank you very much for your time, and welcome to KCBS.

The President. Thanks, Cynthia. It's nice to hear your voice.

Ms. Louie. There is a new poll out today from Newsweek, and I'm sorry to give you this bad news, but there is a new poll out today from Newsweek showing that your approval rating has dropped to 40 percent. And these polls seem to come out fairly frequently with results up and down. Why do you suppose you're down now, and do you pay much attention to these surveys?

The President. No, because, first of all, the polls are directly related to how much people know about the record of the administration. And all the surveys show that about—over 60 percent of the American people approve of the work of this administration if they know the facts. The frustrating thing is, and the frustrating thing in all these elections, is that people have so little way of getting the facts.

If you look at this California election, it's a classic example. I mean, look at the Senate race. Dianne Feinstein has done things in the United States Senate in only 2 years that no Senator in our lifetime has ever accomplished: the assault weapons ban, a law requiring no tolerance for gun ownership—possession for children in school, the California desert bill. And she's being opposed by Michael Huffington, who never even lived in California until 1991, who bought a race in the Congress with his fortune and then, when he ran for the Senate, lost his own congressional district in the Republican primary and still looks like he has a chance to win because he can spend money to put things on the television that aren't true.

This is a very negative, confused, difficult time. And the truth is, in a lot of these polls it depends on what information the voters have and how you ask the question. The only things that really count are these elections, but it's getting harder and harder and harder for voters to make good decisions if all they get is a constant barrage of negative information and they never get the facts.

The truth is, we've got a 4-year low in unemployment; jobs are growing 5 times as fast under our administration as they did under the Bush administration. We're doing things for working people like the family leave law, immunizing all of our children under 2, expanding Head Start, lower cost college loans. We're moving this country in the right direction. And we are leading the world in moving toward peace and freedom and democracy.

If people think about the record and understand the direction, they give us a lot of support. But you can't blame people for not voting on what they don't know.

Immigration

Mr. Wayne. Mr. President, let's get on to the subject of illegal immigration. We of course know that you are on record against Proposition 187 in this State. That whole issue is causing so many ill feelings; there's anger on both sides. What can you tell us about the threat that California could lose Federal funding if that initiative passes, one, and as a second part, what commitment can you make to our listeners about what the Federal Government might be able to do to help with the problem of illegal immigration?

The President. Well, first of all, let's try to— let me try to talk some sense about this issue. The people of California do have a problem with illegal immigration, which is more severe when the economy is in trouble. But since I became President, I have been trying to help you solve it. I mean, from the day I got in office I knew I had a mess in immigration on my hands, and I started trying to fix it 21 months ago.

What have we done? We have almost doubled the border guards in San Diego, along the border down there. We have almost doubled the number of illegal aliens who have been convicted of crimes we're sending back out of the country. We're giving money to California for the first time to help deal with the cost of imprisonment. I've asked Congress to appropriate literally hundreds of millions of dollars to help you deal with the cost of education and health care. We have increased funding to California to deal with immigration by one-third, even though we are reducing Federal spending overall for the first time in 25 years. So we are moving to deal with this problem. We are also looking at ways that we can be tougher on incentives for employers not to hire illegal aliens and how we can keep up with the records.

So I think the people of California should want more done. I think the Federal Government should do more. I have been in the forefront of doing that, working with Senator Feinstein, Senator Boxer, and others.

I simply don't agree that 187 is the right way to go because, first of all, nearly everybody thinks it's unconstitutional. Secondly, it will be directed primarily against children. If you kick children out of the health clinics, you may run the risk of causing health problems for the general California population. If you say kids have got to be kicked out of school, you turn the teachers into police officers and you say, "We're going to put more kids on the street." Well, we've got too many kids on the street in America and California today already. It's liable to raise the crime rate and cause all kinds of problems.

So my view is that 187 is not the right way to do this, and it could cause California a lot of problems. You know, California is coming back economically. You've got the lowest unemployment rate in 3 years here. I have worked as hard as I know how to get investment back into California, to sell California high-tech products around the world, to sell California agricultural products around the world. We're even selling California rice in Japan for the first time. The strength of California is in its diversity. So the issue is how can we enforce the immigration laws and still build on our diversity. And I don't think 187 is the way to go.

Ms. Louie. Mr. President, we have so many more questions for you. Unfortunately, your people are telling us that you are out of time, your time is limited, and you have to go. So thank you very much for joining us today on KCBS.

The President. Thank you. I'm on my way up to the Kaiser Center in Oakland at 2:30, and I hope I see some people up there, too. Thanks.

Mr. Wayne. Mr. President, you'll see us there. Thank you very much.

The President. Great.

NOTE: The interview began at 12:45 p.m. The President spoke by telephone from the Anaheim Convention Center in Anaheim, CA.

Remarks at a Rally for Democratic Candidates in Oakland, California
November 5, 1994

Thank you very much. It's nice to be back in Oakland. Thank you. Thank you. Senator Boxer, thank you for your leadership in the Senate, for your energy, your enthusiasm, your passion, your friendship. California is richly blessed to have Barbara Boxer and Dianne Feinstein in the United States Senate. Congressman Stark; Congresswoman Woolsey; Mayor Harris; a special word of thanks to my friend, the chairman of the House Arms Services Committee, your Congressman, Ron Dellums. I wish every one of you who live in Ron Dellums' district had the opportunity to travel to Washington to watch him in action, to see the way he balances the best of politics: the way he passionately sticks up for what he believes in and still runs his committee in a fair way, the way he is unfailingly decent and fair to people who disagree with him, people who are in other parties, people who are on diametrically opposed sides of the issue. That is the best of American politics. We ought to get back to it, to treating each other with respect, to building up this country.

Folks, before I get into my speech and give you a lot of chance to cheer again—*[laughter]*—I'm going to ask you to do something that normally we wouldn't do at a Democratic rally. And I want you to be very quiet and listen to me for a minute, because this is important.

One of the worst things that's going on in our country today is this incredible meanness of spirit that is being promoted among people who differ with each other. And I want us to set that aside just for a moment while I make this announcement. A few moments ago today, President Reagan announced that he was suffering from Alzheimer's disease. And when he said that, it touched my heart in a particular way, because I went to visit him after I was elected President and he talked to me for a long time. It was a fascinating conversation, but once in the middle of the conversation he said, "You know, I forgot what I was talking about, and it really makes me mad." You know, we've disagreed on a lot of things over the years, all of us have, with Mr. Reagan. But he always fought with a sense of optimism and spirit. And in the days since he left the White House, I have to say that he's been willing to put partisanship aside to stand up for our country. He helped me on the trade agreement with Mexico. He stood up for the assault weapons ban, for the Brady bill. He and his wife stood up against Oliver North in Virginia. They were capable of putting aside partisanship. And so, having nothing to do with any of those issues, I want every one of you in this room now to give Ronald Reagan a hand and wish him well and Godspeed as he deals with this illness. *[Applause]*

Ladies and gentlemen, I come here with all these fine nominees of the Democratic Party, with my good friend Insurance Commissioner Garamendi, with Lieutenant Governor McCarthy, with so many others who are here, to ask you to think about your future. I come here on behalf of Dianne Feinstein and Kathleen Brown. I can put in a couple of sentences why I hope they will both win on Tuesday.

First, let me tell you about Senator Feinstein. I've been watching the scene in Washington for a long time, although I never worked there before 21 months ago. In 21 months, only 21 months, Dianne Feinstein has, as a freshman Senator, sponsored the biggest wilderness bill in American history, the California desert bill, which I signed last week; sponsored a bill that requires every school in the country getting Federal aid to have a zero tolerance for handguns, which will do more to get guns out of our schools and make our kids safe than anything else; and taken on the powerful NRA, which is trying to get revenge on every single person that had the courage to vote for the assault weapons ban. No one has done anything like that in my lifetime in that short a period of time.

Now, if 21 months with that kind of results doesn't get you a 6-year contract, I don't know what could commend the voters—or Dianne Feinstein. I don't know what else you could do.

What is the campaign against her? A hundred percent negative ads by someone who says, "I moved to California in '91. I bought myself a Congress seat. Eight months later I started running for the Senate. When I ran for the Senate, I lost my own congressional district in the Republican primary, but that doesn't matter. I'm just running against the other person. You don't have to know anything about me."

Are you going to vote for somebody who produced for you or somebody who is playing to your fears? Vote for somebody who worked for you, who will work for you in the future, who cares about you; not someone who cares about the job, someone who cares about what the job can do for you.

And with Kathleen Brown, it's a simple choice, really, isn't it? You have a builder and a blamer. You know, very often blamers make you feel better. Sometimes when we're frustrated and we're down and we want to get angry and we want to lash out, a blamer makes us feel better. They give us somebody to be mad at. And they want you to vote mad this time, folks. They do want you to vote mad.

Now, as a parent, the older I get the more I realize the wisdom of my mother who raised me. As soon as your children get old enough to understand, the first thing you try to tell them is never, never make a decision when you're mad. How many of us were told on our mother's and father's knee, "When you're mad, count to 10 before you say anything"? How many times did we find ourselves so upset we were incapable of taking our parents' advice, and so we started talking at about 2 instead of 10? And every single time we did it, we regretted it. And if you do it this time, you will regret it. Don't regret it. Vote for a builder, not a blamer. Vote for Kathleen Brown. Give California a better future.

You know, you have a simple choice on Tuesday. If you vote your anger, your fears, your frustrations, you will be voting for a crowd that is committed to take us back to what they did before, to the trickle-down economics of the 1980's, to the neglect of our most profound problems. Or you can vote to keep going forward.

Sure, we've still got problems. But let me ask you this: 21 months ago, when California and the rest of this country sent me to Washington, you did with a commitment to rebuild this country, to make Government work for ordinary people, to bring the economy back, to try to make a more peaceful and prosperous world for us to live and work in and for our children to bring the 21st century in with. And even though we've still got problems, folks, this country is in better shape than it was 21 months ago. Yesterday unemployment figures came out, a 3-year low in California, a 4-year low in the United States. We're going in the right direction. Let's don't turn back now.

I have been dedicated to making this country strong. What makes a country strong? Strong families, strong communities, strong schools, safe streets, good jobs, a strong foreign policy that makes us more secure, more prosperous, and promotes peace and freedom. We're making progress on all fronts. We're getting stronger. Let's don't give in to our weaknesses. Let's stand up for our strengths.

And we are getting stronger together. In the Government and the country of my dreams, there is room for all of us. We reach across all lines. Everybody's got a seat at the table of America. This is the most diverse and still the most excellent commitment that this administration has made, more than any other. We have people from all walks of life, from all backgrounds, of all colors in the administration, moving America forward together, and we ought to keep doing it just that way.

You know, when I took office, we were dealing with 30 years of accumulated social problems. You know it as well as I do. We see it today in the violence, the gangs, the guns. We see it sometimes in heartbreaking pictures, like those 10-year-old boys that dropped that 5-year-old to his death at the highrise in Chicago. But they did not happen overnight. They have been building on us for 30 years.

We were dealing with 20 years of accumulated economic problems for ordinary Americans: the stagnation of wages, the frequent loss of jobs, the constant threat of losing your health insurance, your retirement, and other benefits. This has been building up for 20 years.

For 12 years, the American people attempted to address it with an entirely different theory of politics and economics. We called it trickle-down for short, but the basic idea was you could increase spending in some areas, cut taxes, especially for the wealthy, sit on the sidelines, and let nature take its course. Well, it didn't work. In the last 4 years before I took office, we had the slowest job growth since the Great Depression. And we were not doing what it took to compete and win in the 21st century, to make it an American century, to guarantee the American dream for all these children that are up here in this audience today.

That is the fact that we face. And I took office saying, look, folks, there had been a big debate about the role of Government. I don't think Government is inherently good or bad; it is a reflection of us. The question is, what should it do, and what should we do? In my judgment, the obligation of our Government is to create opportunity, to empower people to take advantage of it, and then to insist that you, as individuals and communities, assume the responsibility to take yourselves together into the future and to live up to the fullest of your God-given capacities.

Now, our opponents believe—and I must say, this year our opponents in the other party represent a more extremist point of view, on the whole, than in any time in my experience. They say that Government is inherently bad, that anything it touched it makes worse. I don't know how they explain Social Security or Medicare; I don't how they explain the student loan program; I don't know how they explain a lot of things. But they say, "Anything the Government does is worse. Therefore, if anything good happens while Mr. Clinton is President, it happened by accident or in spite of what he did." And they say, "Since we're not going to do anything anyway, it doesn't matter how outrageous our comments are, because we're probably kidding; we won't do anything."

Now, in a cynical time, this has appealed because people say, "It doesn't make a difference." Well, folks, where I come from, they say if you find a turtle on a fencepost, it didn't get there by accident. So you tell me, you tell me if we have made America stronger for strong families. I believe it made a difference when 4.9 million Californians were protected by the family and medical leave law so they could get a little time off when a sick baby or a sick parent was there. And I think it made a difference when 2.1 million California families got income tax cuts because they were working hard with kids in the house and they had modest wages and we didn't want them in poverty.

I think it made a difference when we immunized all the kids in this country under the age of 2 by 1996—that will make a difference to the future of our families. I think it made a difference when we said people who are dealing with AIDS are part of our family and we quadrupled housing funds, we doubled research, we fully funded the Ryan White Act. I think that made a difference and made us stronger.

I think it made a difference when we expanded Head Start and when we changed the way we give money to the local school districts to take all these Federal rules and regulations off and said, "We now think all kids can learn without regard to their color or their income; go ahead and teach them all and have high expectations for all of them and let them all rise up. We're not going to segregate them anymore and tell them they can't learn because they're poor."

I think it will make a difference as we set up national systems of apprenticeships for young people who don't go to college but do want to be in good jobs. I think it will make a difference when we qualify 20 million Americans for lower cost college loans so that everybody can afford to go to college and stay there.

Here in the bay area, I think you know it makes a difference that our national service program is making it possible, over the next 3 years, for 100,000 young Americans to serve their country, to solve community problems, and earn the money to go to college. I think that makes a difference.

I think our streets will be safer because of the Brady bill and the crime bill, because of the police, the punishment, the prisons, the prevention, and the assault weapons ban. I think it will make a difference, and I think you do, too.

I think it makes a difference that we reduced our deficit and increased our investment in new technologies and defense conversion. I think it makes a difference that we reduced the size of the Government and gave all the money to people to fight crime in their neighborhoods. I think it makes a difference. And you know something? It did. It did. This economy has produced 5 million jobs in the last 21 months. This year, we had more high-wage jobs coming into America than in the previous 5 years combined.

I think it makes a difference that you had an administration that said we're not going to sit by and watch California just die because of the base closings. So we're going to give the Alameda Naval Station to the Port of Oakland so they can build it up and create jobs and go forward. And we're going to invest—we're going to make the Presidio a national park. We're going to invest in laboratories like Stanford and Livermore. We're going to create the high-wage jobs of the future. We're going to rebuild shipbuilding. We're going to keep the airline industry afloat. We're going to do things that help California and help America. We're going to sell our computers from California all over the world. That has made a difference. Don't tell me that we're not stronger and it doesn't make a difference. It does make a difference.

I hear them; they say it doesn't make a difference. I think it makes a difference that for the first time since the dawn of the nuclear age, there are no Russian nuclear missiles pointed at these children here. That makes a difference. I think it makes a difference that North Korea says they won't be a nuclear power. I think it makes a difference that we're expanding trade to Mexico and building friendship instead of enmity. I think it makes a difference that we have democracy and freedom in Haiti again. I think it makes a difference. I think it makes a difference that our young men and women in uniform went to the Gulf with lightning speed to stand up to Saddam Hussein. And it makes a difference that the United States is involved in peace in the Middle East and in Northern Ireland and in helping South Africa to make its elections and its democracy a success. It does make a difference. They are wrong when they say the Government is inherently bad and it doesn't make a difference.

So what is it that they want? Well, for America, they want their contract. Their contract is— oh, listen, it sounds good. Here we are just a few days before the election; it's like music to your ears. It says, "The Government is really bad, so we will give everybody a tax cut, but almost all of it will go to people in the upper 2 percent of incomes. But we'll give the rest of you a couple of bucks so you don't boo so loud. And then we will have a big increase in defense, and we will bring back Star Wars. And we will balance the budget."

So we said to them when they said this was their contract, "Well, what does this cost?" "A trillion dollars." Now, folks, even in big old California, a trillion dollars is real money. [*Laughter*] I could take every one of you out on the town tonight for a trillion dollars and have money left over. We could have a good time on a trillion dollars. "Well, how are you going to pay for this trillion dollars?" we asked. They said, "We'll tell you after the election." [*Laughter*] That sounds familiar: "We're going to raise spending, cut taxes, balance the budget; we'll tell you later."

Now, here's the facts, folks. I've been fooling with these budgets for 2 years. I have given you 3 years of deficit reduction for the first time since Truman; I know something about these budgets. I know something about these budgets. And here's what is going to happen. If they win the Congress, here is what happens.

In order to keep their promises to balance the budget, cut taxes, increase spending, they have to cut everything else 20 percent across the board: Social Security, college loans, Medicare, you name it, the farmers in the valley, everybody—anybody that gets any help, 20 percent cut. That's $2,000 per Social Security recipient a year. And then they say, "Well, oh, no, no, no, we didn't say we would cut Social Security." They didn't say they wouldn't do it, either.

Okay, if you take Social Security off, then you have to cut everything else 30 percent, a 30 percent cut in college aid, in Medicare, in everything else. It will eviscerate some of the things that keep this country going.

Now, there's always the chance that they're kidding. That's what happened last time; they were kidding. So they'll just give you the goodies, and they won't pay for it. Then what will happen? The deficit will go up; we'll start shipping our jobs overseas again; we'll put the economy in the ditch again. Tell them, "No thank you on your contract. We want a strong America, not a weak America. We want to be strong, not weak."

And in California, what is their program? Their sole program is, "I don't have any program for the future; I want you to give me a contract for the next several years based on a vote you're going to take, so I don't have to do anything. I want you to vote for 187 and vote for me because I'm for it," they say, "and give me a 4-year contract. And I'm not going to tell you what I'm going to do. I just want you to be mad, vote for 187, and give me a paycheck for 4 years."

Now, what is wrong with 187? Let me ask you to think about this. First of all, it is not wrong for you to want to reduce illegal immigration. And it is not wrong for you to say it is a national responsibility, not just a State responsibility. And Senator Boxer and Senator Feinstein and I, we tried to work with the Governor, without regard to party, to deal with this issue. We have nearly doubled the border guards in San Diego. We have nearly doubled the number of people convicted of crimes we have sent back home. We have given money for the very first time to pay for the costs of imprisonment. When we are shrinking the Federal budget, we have given a one-third increase to the State of California in the money we're giving you to deal with the costs of immigration. We should do more. But folks, we have done a lot, and the crowd before us didn't hit a lick at it. We have really tried to help.

Now, we need to do more, and we will. But 187 puts the cart before the horse. In fact, it puts the cart way out there so the horse can't find it. [*Laughter*] One-eighty-seven says, "Let's be real mad and take it out on the kids. Let's don't let any of these kids go to the health clinic." But they might get sick, and then they might make everybody else sick that lives around them. "Oh, we'll worry about that later. We're mad now." One-eighty-seven says every teacher has got to be a police officer: "Go check all these kids, and if you find a kid who's in an undocumented family, just put them out on the street." And we say, "But we've already got enough kids on the street. We need the kids on the street to come back and go to school, not the other way around." But they say, "No, no, no, we'll worry about that later. We're mad now. We want you to be mad now and worry about that later."

So, that's what's going on. They've got a contract that says, "Here's a trillion dollars' worth of promises; take this sweet thing now, worry about the details later. Here's this 187; be mad now, worry about the details later." Folks, if you want to build, not blame, you've got to worry about the details now. You've got to care about the kids now. You've got to think about the future now. Let's build, not blame. Let's do the right thing. Let's vote for Kathleen Brown and Dianne Feinstein and against 187. We can do it. We can do it.

You know, I want you to think about this. You heard what Kathleen said when she closed her speech about turning the lights on in California. This whole deal, all across America and certainly here, this whole election—these elections are so close in so many States, this whole thing will come down to the spirit that is welling up inside the voters of this country on election day. This whole thing will come down to that.

Do you know what an election is like? It's like everybody has equal power. And you might imagine that you wake up on election morning and you're looking at the television, and the movie on the television is the story of America. And you've got this remote control in your hand. You can push "forward," you can push "fast-forward," you can just leave it fixed, or you can push "reverse." What they hope is that you'll stay home and then a bunch of folks will push "reverse." What I hope is you'll say, "This is my movie; I'm pushing 'forward.' This is my movie; I'm pushing 'forward.'"

My fellow Americans, this election is something that is outside the normal course of American history. In the depths of the Depression, when one in four Americans was out of work, our great President, Franklin Roosevelt, told the American people, "The only thing we have to fear is fear itself." These people who our oppo-

nents say—our opponents say in this election, "Well, even though the Democrats are facing our problems and we're making progress, we want you to vote your fears and give us power."

Look at what the Republican Presidents, the great ones in the past, said. Teddy Roosevelt said the credit belongs to the person in the arena, the person who is trying to deal with the problems of the day. These folks say in this Senate race—this says, "Punish the people in the arena. Put me in, and I won't try at all." That's the complaint.

You look at what that greatest of all Republicans, perhaps our greatest President, Abraham Lincoln, said: "With malice toward none; with charity for all . . . let us move on to finish the work we are in." These folks say, "We're going to have malice toward anybody who gets in our way and tries to stop us from finishing the work we're in, and keep everybody in a turmoil from now til kingdom come so we can be in office." President Lincoln said that we had to be driven by the better angels of our nature. They say, "If we can keep people in a foul mood, we'll be home on election day." President Lincoln said our Government was of, by, and for the people. They say, "If we can just keep people mad enough, they'll stay away from the polls, or they'll vote for us. We'll go back to Government of, by, and for the organized interests and the favored few."

Folks, that is the choice here. It is a deep and profound thing. It goes way beyond all the details. This cynicism, this negativism, this country never got anywhere on this. These kids are here today because, for more than 200 years, every time we had a pivotal choice to make, we voted for the future. Every time people tried to get us to go back, every time people tried to divide us, every time people tried to get us to vote our fears, every time people tried to get us to be angry, we said no, this is America. This is the greatest country in human history. We are one nation under God, together, going forward. You do that, and we'll be home Tuesday night.

Thank you, and God bless you all.

NOTE: The President spoke at 4:28 p.m. at the Harry J. Kaiser Convention Center. In his remarks, he referred to Mayor Elihu Harris of Oakland, CA.

Remarks at a Rally for Democratic Candidates in Seattle, Washington
November 6, 1994

Thank you. You know, it is great to be back in Seattle, and it is great to be here at this spot where we had this many people in 1992. And I hope we have the same results. Governor Lowry, Senator Murray, distinguished Members of Congress and candidates for Congress, and Mayor Rice, Gary Locke, ladies and gentlemen, I am honored to be here, honored to be here on behalf of our candidates, the forces of change, and especially on behalf of Ron Sims for the United States Senate.

You know, a couple of years ago when you sent me to Washington, I went there to promote change in this country, to lift up the hopes of the American people. I went there to be a builder, not a blamer; to be a uniter, not a divider. I didn't much like the gridlock I had seen, and I wanted to break it.

We knew that the obstacles to change were great, that we had profound social problems that had been developing over 30 years, resulting in too many of our children living in an atmosphere of crime and violence, without the strong family and community support they needed. We knew we had difficult economic problems that had developed over 20 years, where too many people worked hard and were never sure they could keep their job or would ever get a raise, or were always afraid that they might lose their health insurance or their retirement. We knew that for 12 years the other party had controlled the Presidency, and for 20 of the last 24 years, and they had built an enormous apparatus for their trickle-down economics and their politics of division. And we knew that for 4 years we'd had the slowest job growth since the Great Depression.

Well, folks, America's still got some problems. There are still people who need work who don't have it. There are still people who deserve a raise who haven't gotten it. A million Americans, working families—working families—lost their health insurance last year. There are still some problems. But I can tell you one thing, this country is in better shape than it was 21 months ago when we began. We're in better shape because jobs are up. The deficit is down. We've got a smaller Government doing more for ordinary citizens. And this world is more secure, more peaceful, and more democratic for the American people to live and flourish in.

I asked you to help me become President because I wanted to see our country strong again. I had heard enough tough talk accompanied by weak action. I wanted to see real strength. What is the real strength of our country? Strong families, strong schools, good jobs, safe streets, national security meaning peace and prosperity growing around the world. On all those fronts, we are stronger today because we did not just talk tough, we did the right things to make this country move forward.

When our economic program was before the Congress and every single Republican voted against it, striving as hard as they could for gridlock, they all said, "If this passes, we'll have recession; if this passes, the deficit will go up; if this happens, big Government will swallow us up and crush our economy." Well, what are they going to say today? The Government is smaller; the deficit is way down; the economy is up. They were wrong. Vote for Ron Sims to help keep making it right.

If people in politics were judged the way people at work are judged and the way students in school are judged, every single Democrat in this congressional delegation would be elected again resoundingly on Tuesday because the people of Washington are in better shape. The unemployment rate is down, the economy is growing because of the courage of the people here on this platform and their colleagues throughout the State of Washington. You ought to elect them and send Harriet Spanel to join them.

You know, this is sort of an interesting election, my fellow Americans. They wanted so badly, our adversaries, to say we had failed. And then when we didn't fail, when the economy began to grow, when the policies began to work, when the airplane contracts and the sales of Washington apples began to be announced, they didn't know what to do. They wanted to say all these things that they didn't get to say. So what did they then do? They said, "Well, Government is still the problem. And if anything good happened, it was in spite of that Bill Clinton in Washington and the Democrats. They didn't have anything to do with it." You know, folks, where I come from we say if you're walking down a road and you find a turtle on a fencepost, chances are it didn't get there by accident. [*Laughter*]

They want you to just keep on being cynical. They want you to keep on being negative. They want you to keep on supporting gridlock, even though you don't. They have tried all over this country to bury us in a mountain of negativism, hoping that Americans will not see the Sun shining through.

They talk tough on crime and vote against the crime bill. They talk against the deficit, and they vote against reducing it. They talk for education, and they vote against more affordable college loans. They say they're pro-family, and then they vote against policies designed to help families, like immunizing children and lowering the taxes of low-income working people so they can raise their kids out of poverty. In short, they talk tough, but they do things that make America weaker. We make America stronger. Let's vote for strength on Tuesday.

You know, they say—I don't know how you figure it—they want you to vote for them on the promise that they will return us to the policies that got us in the fix we were in when you voted for me in the first place. They have two lines of attack. They say, "The Democrats are the party of Government, and it's bad. So if anything good happens, they didn't have anything to do with it. But put us in, and we will implement our commitments. We will cut taxes, increase defense, bring back Star Wars, and balance the budget."

And we say, well—you think about this; it's an issue in every one of these House races and this Senate race—they say, "Give us power, and we will give you goodies." And we say to them, as you might say to your child, we say, "Well, how are you going to pay for this?" And they say, "We'll tell you after the election." [*Laughter*] I say it's Sunday afternoon, and it's pretty, we're all dressed up; tell us right now. We want to know. Tell us right now.

You know, how much do their promises cost? One trillion dollars. Look at this vast sea of people. I could take every last one of you out here tonight, and we could have a good time on a trillion dollars. The problem is, it's a trillion dollars. So I'll tell you what the facts are, folks, about their promises. There are only two options: Either they're serious, or they're kidding. [*Laughter*]

Now, if they're serious, here's what happens. To pay for a trillion dollars' worth of promises, you have to cut everything else in the Government 20 percent: $2,000 a Social Security recipient a year, 20 percent off the Medicare of the older people in this audience, 20 percent off the student loans of the kids we want to go to college, 20 percent off the Head Start when we're trying to fully fund Head Start.

Now, they say, "Oh, oh, but we didn't say we'd cut Social Security." They didn't say they wouldn't. [*Laughter*] So we say, well, okay, let's take Social Security off. Then you have to cut everything else 30 percent. You can just destroy Medicare and the college loan program and the Head Start program.

Now, there's the other possibility, which is that they could be just like they were the last time they were in control: They could be kidding, they could be kidding. [*Laughter*] But if they're kidding, you know what happens? We explode the deficit; we start shipping jobs instead of Washington products overseas; we put this economy back in the same ditch it was in the last time they gave us trickle-down economics. So let us say, "No thank you. We want a strong America. We want strong families, strong education systems, good jobs, safe streets, and a strong country. We're going to vote for Ron Sims and these agents of change here."

Folks, when the Seattle Post-Intelligencer endorsed Ron Sims—listen to this—they praised, and I quote, "his practical idealism, his political wisdom, his humanitarian instincts." That's another way of saying he's a real person. Believe me, we could use a few more of them in the Congress.

One of the reasons that your Senator is so successful is she comes across as a real person in the Congress. Patty Murray comes across as somebody who's raised a family, understands the problems of ordinary Americans, and is determined to work with people to get things done. We have too much gridlock there, too much partisan politics there. We need a person with a head and a heart who has lived the very message he preaches. We don't need any more people who talk tough and make us weak. We need people who are strong inside, who will make us strong and take us into the future. That's why we need Ron Sims. We need to say no to the negativism in Washington and yes to Ron Sims.

You know, I want to ask you to think about the atmosphere that they have tried to create in this election and measure it against our greatest national leaders of both parties. Franklin Roosevelt said, when one in four Americans was out of work, "The only thing we have to fear is fear itself." This crowd says, "Please vote your fears and give us power." Right? Teddy Roosevelt, a great Republican President, said the credit belongs to the person in the arena who is trying. These people say, "Punish the people who try; Government's bad." Abraham Lincoln said, "With malice toward none; with charity for all." He said, "Let us listen to the better angels of our nature." Sounds like he'd be a Democrat if he were around today, doesn't it? [*Applause*]

Folks, you've got a big chance on Tuesday to do something for yourselves, your children, and your future. You can say no to gridlock, no to cynicism, no to talking tough and acting weak. You can say yes to hope, yes to cooperation, yes to a builder, not a blamer. You can say yes to being strong. You can say, "We in Washington State are sending a message to Washington, DC: America is going forward, not turning back." Ron Sims, the Democratic Congressmen, help us to keep changing this country and moving forward.

God bless you all, and thank you.

NOTE: The President spoke at 1:30 p.m. at the Pike Place Market. in his remarks, he referred to Mayor Norman Rice of Seattle and Gary Locke, county executive, King County.

Interview With Larry King in Seattle, Washington
November 6, 1994

Mr. King. Welcome to a special Sunday night edition of "Larry King Live." Our special guest is the President of the United States. A beautiful day here in Seattle; it rained earlier this morning, but there's no city like this. You seemed revved up here today.

The President. It's a wonderful city. They've been very good to me. But it's just an exciting place. It's a real future-oriented place with a lot of different kinds of folks. They get together. They work together. It's a real upbeat, positive city.

Midterm Elections

Mr. King. Do you like campaigning again?
The President. I do.
Mr. King. It seemed like you were just campaigning.
The President. I know.
Mr. King. Do you like this?
The President. I do like it. In large measure I like it because it's one of the few times I get to really go out and put out our record, my message. And I also just like to see the American people. You know, I like to see them excited and energized again.
Mr. King. I remember when you were running. We were in Ocala, and you said to me, "God, I love this."

The President. It was wonderful. Remember that we were in that rodeo arena? Remember that?
Mr. King. Where Elvis Presley once sang.
The President. Yes, that's right.
Mr. King. You were revved up, and you seem the same way now. It would seem that after this time you've been President for 2 years that it's old hat by now.
The President. But these are the people I work for. And perhaps the most frustrating part of being President is how hard it is to stay in touch with them, to stay connected to them, for them to really know what you do on a daily basis. And so to be able to come back out here with someone like Ron Sims, whom I admire so much, that represents what's best in this country, that's cutting against all this cynicism and negativism that is blanketing the airwaves, it's really just a great thing to do.

Negativism in Politics

Mr. King. What do you make of that? We'll start there. And there's lots of bases we're going to cover, of these—lots of radio talk shows, other areas of negativism, that's more than just criticism. It's anger. What do you make of it?
The President. Well, it's almost like an institutionalized approach to life, you know, that every-

thing is given the most negative possible spin, information is presented in attack mode. The American people hate it, but they react to it.

Mr. King. But portions of them listen to it.

The President. Portions of them listen to it, of course. And even if they listen for entertainment, the surveys show in these elections that they react to it, which is, of course, why the politicians do it.

Mr. King. So what does it mean to you when you see it, hear it, about you, about people you like, about anyone?

The President. Well, it—what I think is it's not very good for America. It's not good for our people. It makes it harder for people to take a deep breath and face their problems and seize their opportunities and move forward.

I mean, this is a very, very great country. And as I have a chance, for example, to go to the Middle East to participate in that peace signing, other leaders are bewildered at the negative attitudes in America. They say, "Gosh, you know, your economy is coming back; your deficit's going down; things are happening in your country. You're leading the way to peace around the world. Why would the American people be in a negative frame of mind?" And I always say, well, first of all, a lot of Americans have personal insecurity in their lives. I mean, let's face it, there's some reality out there. There are a lot of people who are afraid they're going to lose their jobs. They haven't gotten a raise in a long time. They may lose their health care or their retirement. They're living in a neighborhood where they feel personally insecure. They see things like these children killing children. It violates their sense of——

Mr. King. So they have a right to that feeling?

The President. Well, no, there's some insecurity there. In other words, the picture is not all positive. But I think the direction is positive, and the future is more positive than negative. But I think the other thing is, the overwhelming way that most Americans get their information tends to be both negative and combative and assaultive, almost. And what I tried to do in the Presidential campaign in '92 with all those town meetings, starting way back in '91, where I listened to people and they talked to me, with insisting on three debates and having one debate with the public there asking questions of the candidates for President, with the bus tours we did was all designed to get people

involved, let them vent their frustrations, and then focus on what we were going to do.

And that's very important. And that's the thing that has been missing too much in this election. And of course, the Republicans like that because if people are mad, then they think the Democrats don't vote and the extremists on the right in their party do vote, they get a big advantage and it helps them get into power. But it doesn't do anything to help America solve their problems.

Mr. King. How do you deal with it personally, I mean, the carping, the anger, the up and down in the polls, personally?

The President. Well, on the up and down in the polls, I basically try to ignore it.

Mr. King. Ignore it?

The President. Not because—I care what people think about the issues, but I knew when I started this job that while everybody said they wanted us to change, if it were easy to do it, someone else would have done it. So to get the deficit down, we had to make some tough decisions.

If you're going to make college loans more affordable to Americans within the budgetary constraints we had, we had to make some tough decisions, take on some interest groups. If you want to pass the Brady bill and the crime bill, you've got to make some tough decisions. The NRA got real mad at us, and now they're trying to take it out on every candidate in the country that stood up for safer streets.

So anybody who ever fights for change is going to have to be willing to risk going down in the polls some. What bothers me more is the general atmosphere where people tend to believe the worst about people in public life, rather than the best, and tend to have a negative view, generally. Because the truth is that this country is in better shape than it was 21 months ago. Unemployment is down. Jobs are up. The deficit's down. The Government is smaller, but it's doing more for ordinary working people. The streets are going to be safer because of the crime bill. And we're a lot closer toward having a safer, more democratic, more free world. The Russian missiles aren't pointing at us. The North Korean nuclear agreement means they won't present a threat to us in terms of nuclear weapons, if we go through with that. We have the progress in Haiti and in the Persian Gulf and the Middle East and Northern Ireland. We are moving in the right direction at home and abroad. We have a lot of problems, but we're moving in the right direction.

And for people to be kept in a constant turmoil all the time, where they don't listen to one another, they don't talk to one another, they just are bombarded by these negative ads on television, I think is not good for our democracy. And it is, frankly, not realistic. If you could see the way other people look at us, they know this is a very great country. And we should feel that way, too.

Mr. King. When there's extreme negativism, do you condemn it on both sides?

The President. Sure.

Mr. King. When Democrats do it and Republicans do it?

The President. Absolutely. Particularly if it is unrelated to the work of the job, you know. But let's be realistic, now. This whole thing started from the get-go with the determination of the congressional leadership in the Republican Party not to work with us on the economic program.

Mr. King. Deliberate?

The President. Oh, absolutely. They were very forthright about it: "You're not going to get any votes out of us no matter how you change this program." That's how it started.

[*At this point, the stations took a commercial break.*]

Death of Smith Children in Union, SC

The President. [*Inaudible*]—were abducted. And there was this little town in South Carolina where there apparently had been maybe some division or something in the past, but they were all coming together. You saw those gripping pictures of the schoolchildren praying. You saw blacks and whites going out together to look for the kids. People really were trying to do their best to do a good and noble thing.

And then they found out that the mother had done it. And unlike previous cases—we've had some other cases, horrible cases, where parents kill their children. But this was—it stood in such stark contrast to those people praying, working, desperately trying to find those children. I think they had a sense of betrayal, of outrage, of bewilderment, of pain. And I think the experience that the people in the community felt riveted all across our country, indeed, across the world. I think every parent was just sickened by it.

Racial Issues

Mr. King. The fact that—and remember the case in Boston with the call to 911—that she drew the picture of a black man tells us what about racism in America?

The President. I think it tells us that we have at least some assumptions about race that still color our thinking, our talking, sometimes our voting. The people in that community, without regard to race, were out there looking for those boys. And most African-Americans in this country get up every day and go to work, work their hearts out, pay their taxes, raise their kids, obey the law. And while the crime rate is higher among African-Americans, they're also more likely to be victims of crime. And it's all really—it's a complicated thing, but it's plainly related to the combined impact of the breakdown of family and community and the loss of economic opportunity working together.

I saw a poll in the Wall Street Journal the other day, a fascinating poll, which said that both African-Americans and white Americans agreed that this breakdown of social order in the family, the community, the rise of crime, violence, drugs and gangs and guns was the biggest problem in our country. They agreed with that. They all supported welfare reform—I mean, not all, 85 percent of both races. But there was a huge difference in attitude between blacks and the whites about what caused it, where the whites were more likely to say it's just all personal misconduct, and the blacks were more likely to say it was the breakdown of economic order and opportunity that holds families together and gives people——

Mr. King. The classic American clash.

The President. Yes. And the truth is, in my judgment, they're both right, and they're both wrong. That is, you need a combined approach to it. We have to rebuild these communities. It's hard to have an orderly society without work. It's hard to have a coherent family without work. It's hard for parents to have all the self-respect they want if they know they'll never have a chance to go to work.

But on the other hand, we simply cannot tolerate the behavior that has become all too commonplace. I mean, what is it that turns the heart of a 10-year-old to stone in Chicago and makes it possible for them to let go of a 5-year-old boy? These are big, deep questions. And again I say, the thing that is so wrong about so much of the political dialog in this election or political ads, is there's no dialog. There's no honest talk. People aren't reaching out across racial lines and trying to figure out how to affirm what is best in this country, how to support the lives and the futures of these kids.

Mr. King. Are you saying they're playing to the worst in us, the racist in us?

The President. I think they're playing to the— they're playing to the lowest common denominator, to the fear, to the division, to the anxiety. I believe that it's better to play to the best in us, to address fear, to address anxiety, to admit it, to say it's legitimate, say, okay, what are you going to do about it?

Midterm Elections

Mr. King. Is this the ugliest off-year elections, politically, advertising-wise, you've seen?

The President. Well, certainly the most expensive and probably the most negative certainly in a very long time. And it's very troubling. You know, I tried to get this campaign finance bill passed. And it was delayed to death at the end of the session by our opponents, like a lot of other bills were. But we don't need that. We need to reform the campaign finance system.

In every one of these races of major importance, there ought to be two or three debates. There ought to be town hall meetings. There ought to be things that involve people, that let them express their anger and frustration and then say, "Okay, now, what are you going to do about it?" Because what we run the risk of doing in this election—which is why I've been out here working like crazy since I got home from the Middle East—is we run the risk of seeing people vote for candidates whose platforms and positions they absolutely disagree with just because they say, "I'm out; put me in. I'm mad, too."

Mr. King. "Throw the rascals out."

The President. "Government's bad; put me in." Yes.

O.J. Simpson Trial

Mr. King. I haven't seen you quoted on it, and every American has talked about it and they all want to know what their President thinks. You were an attorney general in your State, a prosecutor, so it's a twofold question: Can there

be a fair trial in the O.J. Simpson case? And two, should television cameras be allowed?

The President. Well, the answer to the first question is, I think there can be a fair trial, but it is much more difficult to empanel a jury that has no opinion.

Mr. King. There's never been anything like this.

The President. No, there has never been anything like it. Secondly, I'm not so troubled about the trial itself being televised. What bothers me is that all the previous proceedings have been televised, all the preliminary things, all the back-and-forth arguments. And I know there are arguments pro and con. But on balance, I think it would have been better if they hadn't been, because I think it would have been easier to empanel a jury that had no fixed views, no— at least predisposition to believe it. Now, what these folks have to say and what they had to convince the judge of was that whatever they had heard in the past, they could put aside and be fair.

But I just think all of us, we can't help being affected by the things we know. And the wrenching pretrial publicity I think is more damaging than whatever publicity might have come in the trial itself.

Mr. King. Are you impressed with Judge Ito?

The President. Very much.

Mr. King. And the prosecution and defense?

The President. They all strike me as competent and committed. And the judge strikes me as someone who has been firm and fair. He's trying very hard, and he has an enormously difficult task.

Mr. King. Is this the kind of case, when you were prosecuting, you would have liked to prosecute or not like to prosecute?

The President. Well, of course, any—I think most prosecutors would, at a kind of a personal, professional level, welcome the chance to be in a big case like this. But it's a very sad case. It's the sort of thing that brings great pain to a country.

Mr. King. No winners.

The President. No. I mean, there are—people are dead. The feelings that we all had about O.J. Simpson and everything—it's a very sad case. So it's not something I can say I would relish doing because the whole thing is enormously tragic.

[*The stations took a commercial break.*]

Midterm Elections

Mr. King. Beautiful downtown Seattle on a beautiful Sunday afternoon in the American-Pacific Northwest with President Bill Clinton, 2 days away from the election. Friday night on this program, Bob Dole said that on Tuesday night, when the Republicans take the Senate—if they take the Senate and the House, the first person he calls will be you. He will ask to meet with you Wednesday morning. Win or lose, whatever happens, they're ready to cooperate. Comment.

The President. I don't think they're going to win the House and the Senate. But whatever happens, I hope he'll call me Tuesday night, and I hope he'll be willing to cooperate.

Mr. King. Hope, but don't think?

The President. Well, I don't know yet. All I can tell you is that we had bipartisan support for that crime bill, and it turned into naked politics. And the Republicans that did stick with us were lacerated by their leadership.

I hope they don't really, seriously believe that we can go back and do what they did in the eighties and have all these massive tax cuts for upper income people and pay for big defense increases and bring back Star Wars and balance the budget in 5 years and not tell anybody how to do it. There is no way to do it without massive, massive cuts in Social Security, Medicare, college loans. If you take Social Security off, you have to cut everything else in the budget 30 percent.

So all I'm saying is, I want to cooperate. I always wanted to cooperate. My door has always been open. I tried to cooperate in the health care debate. When we started the health care debate——

Mr. King. They said you didn't. They said it was secretive.

The President. No, that's not true. We met with them in advance. We even offered to work with them on drafting a bill. We were told, "No, you go ahead and put your bill in; then we'll put our bill in and then we'll work." They announced an approach where more than half the Republican Senators supported universal coverage. The bill never came. By the time it came to talk about the bill, there were zero Senators from the Republican Party on that.

So—and by the way, then they released the memo of their strategist, Bill Kristol, who wasn't even ashamed to release the memo and say,

"You must not cooperate on health care because if the middle class ever gets security about health care, they'll probably support the Democrats again. Whereas, if we keep them all torn up and upset and angry, we can either keep them home or get them to vote for us."

So I want—let me just say this—I want more than anything to have a bipartisan effort. I want more than anything to move this country forward, not see it go back. But I have not obstructed that bipartisan effort. My door has been open. I have wanted to work together. And I have seen a level of intense obstructionism that I never thought I'd ever see.

So what the American people have to say is—first of all, I think we're going to do better than everybody thinks because jobs are up, unemployment is down, the deficit is down, the Government is smaller, all these things are different from the way it was before. We are doing things for ordinary Americans like middle class college loans, national service, tax cuts for low-income working people, the Family and Medical Leave Act. When people know this, I think we're going to do much better than the experts think, because I think people want to keep going forward, they don't want to go back.

But whatever happens, I hope we talk. I have always wanted to talk; I have always been willing to meet. And I hope we work together.

Mr. King. Worse-case scenario—they take the House. Could you work with Newt Gingrich?

The President. I can work with anybody who will work with me. But I do not believe the American people really want us to go back——

Mr. King. I meant worst-case scenario for you. I'm not taking a stand. For you, worst-case scenario.

The President. I can work—the American people are the bosses of this country. They run this country. They decide who's in the Congress, and they decide who's President.

Mr. King. You work for them.

The President. I work for them. And so does the Congress. So we will do what we are told to do by the American people. They are the bosses. But I will say again, I have worked very hard to get this economy going, to bring the deficit down, to get investment back in education and training, to pass that crime bill—and now we have to implement it so we make our streets safer—to make our country stronger. What I think is going to happen is the American people are going to think about, in the next couple of days, do we want to keep going forward, or do we really want to go back to trickledown economics? Do we want to go back to exploding the deficit, shipping the jobs overseas, causing the country trouble, or do we want to keep working forward?

A lot of Republicans did work with me. But without exception, when they work with me on anything tough—except for the trade bill, except for NAFTA, and except for some education legislation, in a lot of these other areas they were subject to withering, withering pressure and attack from the leaders of their own party. So I want to work with them, however these elections come out. I think we'll probably see the Democrats keep control of the Senate and the House because we are changing things for the better, and the American people now are seeing what the record is.

Mr. King. But you'll take that call, and you'll meet with whoever it is you have to meet with?

The President. Absolutely. That's right. You bet I would. I would have always taken it. I want it to be that way. When I ran for President, I ran as a former Governor—I was a Governor. I never shut the Republicans out of my office. I always thought my job was to work with anybody the people elected. That's the right thing to do.

[*The stations took a commercial break.*]

Mr. King. Sunday evening in Seattle with the President of the United States, Bill Clinton. A lot of bases to touch, and later we'll get some predictions on some individual races that the President is very aware of.

A couple of other things in the news. Johnny Apple today in the New York Times says that the administration is starting to take on a Truman-esque approach already: They're the bad guys. And that's the way Harry Truman won in '48, by knocking the no-good, do-nothing Congress. Are we adopting that mode?

The President. No. For one thing, I don't believe we're going to lose the Congress if the American people know what has been done.

Mr. King. So you'll have no Congress to knock in '96.

The President. There is—well, whether the Democrats or the Republicans are in the majority, a minority can frustrate the will of the majority just with the filibuster in the Senate, if for nothing else, which killed the campaign finance reform, lobby reform, environmental reform, and a number of other things last year.

My instinct is to get something done. But this Congress that we just finished was only the third one since World War II that cooperated with the President in over 80 percent of the President's initiatives in both years. That only happened three times since World War II, once for President Eisenhower, once for President Johnson, and then this one.

Mr. King. So there's no Truman plan.

The President. No. I'll say again, it depends on who the American people send to Congress and what their attitude is. I will work with anybody who will work with me to move the country forward. When I ran for President in '92, I said I thought the Democratic Party had to change. We had to do something about getting the economy going again, bringing the deficit down, shrinking the Government, being tougher on crime, all things the Republicans had previously said they were for, although the deficit went up, the economy was in trouble, and they just talked about crime for 6 years.

All right, now we have reduced the deficit, reduced the size of the Government, passed a good crime bill, which now will have to be implemented at the grassroots level. Even as we speak, we've got police officers being hired all over the country because of this crime bill.

What are we going to do? My door is open. My hand is outstretched. I am a builder, not a blamer. I'm not like that.

Mr. King. This ain't going to be a Truman "give 'em hell, Bill" campaign?

The President. It depends on what they do. It depends on what they do. If they want to work with me, then we will work together. I do believe that we're going to—that the people who gum up the works need to be held more accountable.

Mr. King. You're optimistic.

The President. I am optimistic.

Administration Accomplishments

Mr. King. Reports in recent books of disorganization in the Presidency, 2 years of unwieldiness, I'm sure you've heard about this, if you haven't read the books. Comment?

The President. Well, my comment is, if we were all that disorganized, how do we have the third most successful record in success with Congress, one of only three with over 80 percent of our initiatives passing, including major advances in bringing the deficit down, education reform, trade expansion, crime, and a number of other things, first of all? Secondly, we've done pretty well in foreign policy: no Russian missiles pointed at the United States, North Korea, Haiti, Northern Ireland, the Persian Gulf, the Middle East.

Mr. King. Are you saying we're looking at the process, not the result?

The President. But I'm saying the process is more open than perhaps in previous administrations because we are going through a period of historic change. And when—for example, when I tried to get my economic program together, after I was elected, but before I took office, we all agreed we had to bring the deficit down; we still had to invest more in education and defense conversion and new technologies. And we had to do things that would expand the economy. We wanted to help low-income working families. And we wanted some other incentives to spur economic growth that cost money, some tax incentives. But there were all kinds of differences on the details.

So we got a lot of people in from different points of view, and we talked it through. And it was a lively process. Now some people wanted to have the image that somebody brings a President a little one-page memo with two options, and you just check off and say that's the way it is, and it's all neat. This is a complicated world with a lot of variables.

Mr. King. Is yours too open?

The President. I don't think so. It may be unsettling to people that we have honest debates in the White House. But you know, when I think about some of the major mistakes that my predecessors have made, I think the absence of honest debate may have caused some of that.

So, can we get the process better? Can we get better organized? I think so. I think that the White House today is much better organized than it was 30 days after I took office. I think it's more orderly; it's running more smoothly, decisions are made in a more disciplined fashion. I think a lot of people have learned to do their jobs better and better and better.

But again, I say the—a lot of the best companies I know of in America have very lively, open discussions on important issues. They take real time on important issues because then that shapes what the future is. And so far, I say, if you judge us on our results, we're making pretty good decisions.

Health Care Reform

Mr. King. Critics have said now that you fired your wife from health care. I haven't seen you comment. What caused this change, and who's running the health care battle?

The President. Oh, I didn't do that.

Mr. King. She has not been fired?

The President. No. But she was never hired. She was a volunteer.

Mr. King. I know, but critics are saying—what happened in that change?

The President. For one thing, there's no process to manage now. She never did—she never signed on to, agreed to, or was willing to manage the congressional process. What she did——

Mr. King. She took the ball, though.

The President. She took the ball, but what she did was to put hundreds and hundreds of people together to go out and consult all the Members of Congress, to run a 2-day seminar on health care for Republicans and Democrats in Congress, and to try to get the work product up and then be the spokesperson. Now whatever we wind up doing on health care, she will be still speaking out on that and doing a number of other things.

Mr. King. Then what was the announcement?

The President. But the—what we were saying is that she wouldn't have primary responsibility for actually deciding what move next to make in Congress and lobbying that. That's not a good thing for the First Lady to have to do and not anything she signed on to do the first time around.

Mr. King. Did she dislike doing it?

The President. No, I think she liked it, but she didn't want to be in a position where that's all she would do. And that's the only issue she could be involved in, and she didn't want to be in a position where—she got caught up——

Mr. King. She became the focus.

The President. It's where she got caught up in the process of—the lobbying of the Congress process. She wants to be a spokesperson for health care, for solving a problem, not the person who has to manage the process in Congress. And I don't think she should be.

Mr. King. So we will be hearing a lot from Hillary in the next 2 years.

The President. Yes, she—you know, she's invested a lot in this. She's done a wonderful job. And she's—what we think about the health care deal is that, first of all, keep in mind how long it takes to get things done in Washington. Family leave took 7 years. The Brady bill took 7 years. The crime bill took 6 years. Banking reform took 7 years. I mean, we've gotten things done that took years that other people couldn't do. But it was probably unrealistic to think you could get health care reform in a year and a half, given the fact that it's bigger than all those other things.

[The stations took a commercial break.]

California Senatorial Campaign

Mr. King. [*Inaudible*]—on this beautiful Sunday in Seattle—[*laughter*]—a little off-the-cuff joke there, folks, best left unsaid—with the President of the United States, Bill Clinton. By the way, this is the President's seventh appearance, all together, running and as President, on this program. It's always great to have him with us. We're touching a lot of bases. Now some election bases. Going to win the Senate in California?

The President. I think Senator Feinstein will win. If there was a ever a case for campaign finance reform, it's this. The Republican candidate moves to California in '91 from Texas, essentially buys a Congress race, announces 8 months later for the Senate, loses his own congressional district in the Republican Senate campaign but spends, it looks like, $35 million or something, some enormous amount of money, just to run negative ads against Feinstein.

She, by contrast, in only 2 years, passes the assault weapons ban, a law that requires zero tolerance for handgun possessions in schools by students, and the biggest protection act, natural protection act in history, the California desert bill.

Mr. King. It's his money, though.

The President. It's his money, but it shows you why we need some sort of campaign finance reform. No Senator in my lifetime has gotten as much done in as short a period of time as Dianne Feinstein. And those three things may not be popular everywhere, but they are supported by a majority of the people of California.

Washington Congressional Campaign

Mr. King. Three hundred miles from here, over the hills in Spokane—Mr. Foley, Speaker of the House—what's going to happen there?

The President. Well, you know, he was way behind. He's fought himself back to where he's even, some say a little ahead. I think the people

of every—every time there's a Speaker who comes from a rural district, there's always the problem of the people in the district thinking that the Speaker is more interested in the national job than the grassroots job.

All I can say is that of all the leaders of Congress I've ever known in both Houses and in both parties, Tom Foley is the one who speaks most often about his constituency and is most in contact with what he thinks they're thinking about. He's the one who talks to me all the time. It's amazing. And I think that if— my feeling is that the people have seen him back there working, defending his positions, defending his record, defending his service for the district. If it's just a question of who can do more for the people in that district to build their economic future and to meet their needs, I don't think there's much question. I think he wins in a walk, but it's a tough race.

Ross Perot and 1996 Presidential Campaign

Mr. King. Our old friend Ross Perot's entrance into the race, endorsing some Republicans, some Democrats, independents and calling for basically a Republican victory.

The President. Well, it's curious to me because if you look at what I've done as compared with what Ross Perot advocated, I disagree with him on GATT and on NAFTA, but so does the Republican congressional leadership. So both sides disagree with him on trade. So what else was his campaign about? It was about reducing the deficit, reducing regulation and the size of Government, and getting political reform, campaign finance reform, lobby reform, line-item veto. Okay.

We reduced the deficit without any Republican votes. We reduced the size of Government without any Republican support. We've deregulated in banking and trucking. We've deregulated a lot of the Federal rules on welfare reform, giving 20 States the right to move people from welfare to work. We've done things that he said he was for.

I supported and most Democrats supported, most Democrats supported, campaign finance reform, lobby reform, a bill to make Congress live under the same laws it imposes on private business. These are things we did. Their leadership opposed it. So what we are doing and where we stand and what we want to do in the future is much more consistent with what

Ross Perot said he wanted to do if he were President.

Mr. King. Then what do you make of this?

The President. I don't know. I'll leave that to you to make of it. All I can tell you is, we have really faithfully pursued the reform agenda that he and I shared in common when we both ran for President. So the truth is, he'd come a lot nearer getting what he said he wanted done in '92 in fact done in '95 if we kept the Democrats in the Congress who are committed to change.

Mr. King. Do you expect him to run again?

The President. I don't have any idea.

Mr. King. Do you expect Democrats to oppose you?

The President. I don't have any idea.

Mr. King. Do you have a Republican favorite you'd like to run against?

The President. No, I'm going to leave that up to them. I'll say this, sooner or later, we'll have a debate and a discussion in this country about what, in fact, has been done and what has not been done.

Mr. King. And it will have to be one person.

The President. We'll have to get over being mad and being negative and talk about what we're going to do to build this country. We cannot for long afford to give in to the blamers instead of the builders. I mean, this is a country—you look—we've got a lot of challenges we have to work through to get this country into the 21st century as the strongest country in the world, with the American dream alive and well.

Right now, we are strongest militarily. We're strongest again economically, according to the annual vote of international economists, for the first time in 9 years. We're outselling all other auto companies, Americans are, for the first time in 15 years. We are moving in the right direction.

At some point, people who tempt our anger and our frustration but promise to reverse the progress we have made and put us back in the economic trouble we were in just a couple of years ago, are going to have to be held accountable. That's what this election ought to be about. And if it is, the Democrats who represent hope, the future, and the progress that's been made in the last 21 months ought to have a chance. Why should we give up the progress of the last 21 months and not give me a chance to finish and go back to what failed us for 12 years?

Mr. King. But can we also say, therefore, can I trace in what you said in the beginning that if you do run for reelection, you will debate your opponent or opponents?

The President. Yes.

Mr. King. There will be no backing off debates.

The President. No, not once, but several times.

[The stations took a commercial break.]

President's Legal Defense Fund

Mr. King. We're back with President Bill Clinton, touching a lot of bases. The legal defense fund, are there any second thoughts about that, or was it necessary or—do you have second thoughts?

The President. No. I think with a strict limit on contributions, there's no possibility of any conflict of interest there. And, you know, I have the lowest net worth, I guess, of any person to be President in a very long time. And all these things are—like the Whitewater thing, it's—these things come up. If we're going to——

Mr. King. They have been embarrassing, though.

The President. If we're going to make Presidents a subject for the first time in history—this has never been done to anybody before—to things like special counsels looking into things that happened long before the President became President, that were fully aired in the Presidential campaign—I don't think Presidents should make money being President, but I don't think they should be bankrupt when they leave because of legal fees. Nor do I think that Presidents should expect lawyers to work for nothing.

So, once again, we're in a situation here where—do you really want to say that unless you're fabulously wealthy you shouldn't be able to be President? You shouldn't be able to run for an office because you can't buy enough negative television ads to trash your opponent? I think what we did was appropriate, legal, proper, and restrained.

Former President Ronald Reagan

Mr. King. A couple of other things. Ronald Reagan's announcement, and I know you commented that you'd——

The President. I did.

Mr. King. ——spoken to him awhile back and that he, in the middle of a sentence, got angry that he had forgotten what he had been talking about.

The President. Yes, he just said once, he said, "I forgot." He said, "I lost my memory on that, and it really makes me mad."

Mr. King. Did you then think that this might have been Alzheimer's, a common thing to think in people over 80? Did you think it?

The President. I didn't know. I don't know that I know the difference between the manifestations of Alzheimer's for someone who's 80 and just not remembering things as well. But he and I have always had a very cordial personal relationship. When I was a Governor, I supported and worked with the White House when we got the first big welfare reform legislation through back in '88. And even though we've had our differences, I always liked the fact that he was positive about America, that he was an upbeat person, that he—at moments he was capable of going beyond partisanship, as he has since he's left office. You know, he supported NAFTA and the Brady bill and the crime bill with the assault weapons ban in it, because, I think, of the experience he had with Jim Brady and the terrible scars it left on everyone.

So I just—I wanted to say that. I was probably in the most Democratic congressional district in America yesterday. And when I asked them, they all just applauded and they gave him a big cheer.

Mr. King. Do you think it will help focus emphasis on Alzheimer's? Do you think he was right to do it, to make the announcement?

The President. First of all, I think he was very right to do it. I think it was a brave thing to do. And he sat down and wrote the letter himself——

Mr. King. I know.

The President. ——in his own words. And it was vintage Ronald Reagan. I think it will help to focus attention on Alzheimer's. I personally appreciated it, because I lost both an uncle and an aunt to Alzheimer's. And so I think it's one more thing that the American people have to be appreciative to him about.

[*The stations took a commercial break.*]

Secretary of State Warren Christopher

Mr. King. We're back with Bill Clinton. Our remaining moments, some other quick bases to cover—Senator Dole the other night said he likes Warren Christopher, thinks he's done a great job. Is Warren Christopher staying at State?

The President. He's done a good job, and as far as I'm concerned, he's the Secretary of State.

Press Secretary Dee Dee Myers

Mr. King. Dee Dee Myers is sitting here, looks very strong, very active.

The President. She looks pretty good, doesn't she?

Mr. King. There was rumors that she was going to be leaving that post, and she seemed to have strengthened it. Is she here?

The President. She's doing a good job.

Mr. King. Will she be here through the next 2 years?

The President. She hasn't told me yet.

Mr. King. Do you want her to stay?

The President. She looks pretty good.

Mr. King. Yes, she does. Do you want her to stay?

The President. She's doing a good job, and she's going to stay as long as we decide she's going to stay, she and I together.

Mr. King. First time the whole night you've been a little——

The President. I've been a little evasive on all personnel questions.

Mr. King. You don't want to discuss personnel?

The President. I think Presidents should always be slightly evasive on personnel questions unless there's some great policy issue involved.

Heavyweight Boxing Champion

Mr. King. George Foreman. Comment.

The President. George Foreman I like, because I identify with him. He's not as young as he used to be, not as fast as he used to be, not as thin as he used to be. He's still got a terrific punch. I'd like to think that there are a lot of us who could identify with that.

And he doesn't quit. You know what he said yesterday? He said he was really grateful to America for giving him the chance to fight. That's the way I feel. I'm grateful to America for giving me the chance to fight.

Mr. King. So you felt an association with him. You're only a little older than he is.

The President. Yes, I know.

Mr. King. You have the same kind of midriff, and he eats like you, fast foods.

The President. He does. I don't really eat fast foods anymore. That's a big myth.

Mr. King. Well, you don't?

The President. No. It's part of Dee Dee's counseling to me. [*Laughter*] She won't let me do it—no, we don't do that much anymore.

Midterm Elections

Mr. King. We're under a minute. Virginia, Senate.

The President. Senator Robb's doing well there.

Mr. King. Cuomo in New York.

The President. He's come back; he's been heroic.

Mr. King. Senate in—governorship, Texas.

The President. Well, I haven't been there, but Ann Richards is supported in her job by over 60 percent of the people. So if they support the work she's done for Texas, you would think they would renew her contract.

Mr. King. Were you asked to go there at all?

The President. No.

Mr. King. And——

The President. Oh, I was at the beginning. I was asked to go, actually, to El Paso, but we couldn't do it.

Mr. King. We're out of time. Thanks.

The President. Thank you. You've been great.

Mr. King. Are you predicting victory in the Senate and the House? You will retain control of both?

The President. I think we're moving in the right direction, and I think we'll have them both on Wednesday morning when we wake up, because I think the American people want to keep going forward, not going back.

NOTE: The interview was recorded at 3:30 p.m. at the Columbia DuBrin Realty Advisors Building for broadcast at 9 p.m.

Remarks at the Minnesota Victory Rally in Minneapolis, Minnesota
November 7, 1994

Thank you very much. Thank you, Madam President. Thank you, Pam Pearson. Sounds good, doesn't it, Madam President? Out of my own past I feel compelled to say someone ought to thank the band for being here to play with us today. Thank you for dressing up. Thank you, Senator Wellstone. Poor Senator Wellstone has no energy, no conviction. [*Laughter*] He's a walking fireplug for Minnesota. There are many public officials here. I don't want to introduce them all, but I would be remiss if I did not thank Congressman Martin Sabo, Congressman Bruce Vento, and the distinguished retiring Congressman from Minnesota, someone who knows the difference between talk and action on the deficit, the economy, and a lot of other things, Congressman Tim Penny. Thank you all for being here.

Most of what needs to be said about this race has already been said here today. But I want you to focus on what you could do between now and tomorrow to talk to other people—there's a high rate of undecided in all these surveys—to make sure that Ann Wynia wins. And I have given a great deal of thought to

this. This really is a contest between whether we will continue going into a future that is full of opportunity and challenge or go back to the easy answers of the past. It really is, as the First Lady said, a contest between the doers and the talkers, or the builders and the blamers.

You know, for all of our problems—and we do have profound problems, 30 years of accumulated social problems, 20 years of basically stagnant wages and working people being at greater and greater risk of losing their health care or not getting a raise or having to change jobs—for all of these problems, we had 12 years of their side's approach. They had 12 whole years of trickle-down economics. We've had 21 months, and this country is in better shape than it was 21 months ago. Jobs are up. The deficit is down. The Federal Government is smaller, but it's providing more opportunity for working families, for education, for family leave and in so many other ways. The country is getting stronger. I want America to be strong. What makes a country strong? Strong families, strong education systems, safe streets, good jobs, a strong foreign policy that promotes peace and prosperity for Americans in the world. On all these counts, this country is in better shape than it was 21 months ago.

Just last week we got the news that we had now over 5 million new jobs coming into this economy. The Minnesota unemployment rate has dropped about 1½ percent. We're at a 4-year low in unemployment in the United States as a whole. For the first time in 15 years, American auto companies are number one in the world in all of their sales. For the first time in 9 years, we've been voted again, finally, after 9 years, the most productive economy in the world. Why would we want to give the Congress to people who want to take us back to what almost wrecked us in the 1980's? Say no to them; say yes to our people.

There is always a little lag time between things that you do being done and things that you do being felt by voters. I understand that. And there are real frustrations and anxieties that the American people feel about their future that go way beyond normal politics. But what is the argument of our opponents, of Ann Wynia's opponent, of the Republican majority leader? They had a very clever strategy from the beginning; they have pursued it with a vengeance. Their strategy was, "The electorate is frustrated about the mess in Washington; let's keep them frustrated." Their strategy was, "Let's stop whatever we can. We can kill health care reform, lobby reform, campaign finance reform, important environmental legislation. And when we can't stop something, let's at least deny that it happened or deny that it did any good." So they say, "If anything good happened in the last 21 months, it was either in spite of or irrelevant to the work the rest of us did in Washington."

Well, you know folks, where I come from, we say, if you're walking down a road and you find a turtle on a fencepost, chances are it didn't get there by accident. Now, you think about that. [*Laughter*] Here is what—when we were voting last year and Tim Penny was working his heart out last year on a plan to reduce the Federal deficit after the debt had exploded, had quadrupled in the 1980's, threatening the future of our children, taking up all the money that needed to be invested in the private sector to create jobs, keeping interest rates high even in a recession, and the future of the country was on the line, the two people who are on the other side of town speaking today, here's what they said. The minority leader, Mr. Dole from

Kansas, said, this is not real deficit reduction. And Ann Wynia's opponent said that this economic plan has ominous implications for the American economy and the American jobs. That's what they said.

Now they want to hold us accountable for all the messes that we inherited from them. At least we can hold them accountable for the decisions they've taken in the last 21 months. They were wrong. They were wrong on the deficit; they were wrong on the economy; they were wrong on the future of this country. Surely, even in this age of 30-second ads and negative sound bites and lobbing verbal bombs across the wall, surely someone, somewhere today will ask them, "Weren't you wrong about the deficit? Weren't you wrong about the economy? Why should we give you our future? You were wrong; all you did was try to stop progress for the last 21 months, and you were wrong." Somebody ought to say that to them and say, let's keep going forward.

They say the American people are so cynical, it is irrelevant what I do anymore, because everything the Government does makes no difference to you and can't make your life better. Well, I don't know about you, but I think it makes a difference that 845,000 families in Minnesota are now protected by the family leave law so they can be good workers and good parents when their children are sick or born. And I think it made a difference that 155,000 families in Minnesota had their income tax rates cut because they worked for modest wages. And we don't think people who work full-time and raise children should be in poverty, we think they should be rewarded for what they do.

I think it's making a difference that we're going to immunize all the kids in this country under the age of 2, so we'll have more little kids that look like these do in the future, without regard to their race, their income, or where they live. I think that matters. I think it matters that we're making 20 million Americans, including over 400,000 people right here in Minnesota, eligible for lower cost, more affordable college loans, so that every person in the country who wants to go to college can go.

Now someone ought to say today, if you have a clear choice between someone who supports those policies and someone who opposes those policies, shouldn't we vote for the person who is for building the ability of the people of Minnesota to compete and win, to make the most of their God-given abilities? I think the answer is yes.

Make no mistake about it, my fellow Americans, what they say is, "There is gridlock in Washington, you're frustrated with Washington; give us control." Well, if they had had control, there would have been no family leave law, no student loan reform, no immunization of all the kids under 2, no expansion of Head Start, no deficit reduction, no economic expansion. That is what they would have done if they had been in control. Look at how they voted: no Brady bill, no crime bill. That is how they voted.

So I say, think, folks. Look at the record. Hold them as accountable as they seek to hold us. I would gladly take a simple even standard: Hold me accountable, hold them accountable for what we said and what we did. If that happens, Ann Wynia is going to the United States Senate tomorrow.

You know, one of their greatest Presidents was Theodore Roosevelt. He was a great fellow. I would have been sorely tempted to vote for him if I'd been around. [*Laughter*] And one of the things I liked about Roosevelt was Teddy Roosevelt said the credit belonged to the person who is in the arena who is trying. These folks say, "Punish the people who have tried and reward the people who sit on the sidelines and whine and bellyache and complain and point the finger and run for cover every time it's time to take responsibility for the future." Vote for the party of Teddy Roosevelt; that's now us and Ann Wynia. That's right.

Their greatest President was Abraham Lincoln. He is all of our President. Do you hear his words in their campaigns? Remember what Abraham Lincoln said? "With malice toward none." Can you imagine him saying that today? "With charity for all, . . . let us press on in the work we are in," driven by "the better angels of our nature," because this is a "Government of, by, and for the people." They do not use those words. They seek to use malice and cynicism, our least charitable impulses, the lowest common denominator. That is not the Minnesota way.

I got really tickled—it would be laughable if it didn't work from time to time, that now Ann Wynia's opponent, who voted no on all those things I just said, is trying to convince the senior citizens of this State at the last minute that she is their enemy. [*Laughter*] Ann Wynia is a friend of children, a friend of working families, a friend of the elderly.

Her opponent wants to go to Washington to implement what they said they would do, cut taxes, increase spending, and balance the budget. Does that sound familiar? [*Laughter*] Folks, let me tell you something, and this is the last thing I want to say. I wasn't going to bring this up, but I heard that he was attacking her for being the enemy of senior citizens. If you promise to increase defense, bring back Star Wars, give the wealthy a tax cut, and balance the budget, there are only two possibilities. One is you're serious, and the other is you're kidding. [*Laughter*] And when I finish, don't take my word for it; go ask Mr. Penny, he's the budget expert, and he's not running. But we fool with these budgets. If they are serious in doing what they say, here are their options. You've got to cut everything else in the Government 20 percent across the board, including Social Security and Medicare. That is the enemy of seniors. That's $2,000 a person, Social Security.

If you say, "Oh, no, we won't cut Social Security," because they'll always say—they'll probably say that here today: "We didn't say we'd cut Social Security." They didn't say they wouldn't. [*Laughter*] Then you have to cut everything else 30 percent across the board. That devastates the student loan program. That devastates the Head Start program. That devastates the crime bill and putting police on our streets, ask the mayors. In other words, they are the enemy of the solemn contract we had with the elderly people of this country. Unless, of course, they're kidding. [*Laughter*]

Now, the last time they had power they were kidding. [*Laughter*] So what did they do? They talked so tough; they say, "We are strong; we are tough." But they acted so weak. And so what happened? They exploded the deficit. They sent our jobs overseas. They put our economy in the drink.

Let us say: Sorry, we've been there; we tried that; we didn't like it. We like the unemployment rate going down, the deficit going down, jobs going up, more investment in education, a better future for our kids. We like Ann Wynia. We like hope, not fear. We like the future, not the past. Lift her up. Let's go on. Let's win on Tuesday. We can do it.

Thank you, and God bless you all.

NOTE: The President spoke at 9:25 a.m. at North Hennepin Community College. In his remarks, he referred to Katherine Sloan, president of the college, and Pam Pearson, former student of Democratic candidate Ann Wynia at the college.

Remarks at a Rally for Democratic Candidates in Flint, Michigan
November 7, 1994

Thank you. I'm glad to be back in Flint, glad to be back in Michigan, glad to be here for Bob Carr.

Ladies and gentlemen, Hillary and I are delighted to be here today with all of you. I want to begin by thanking the nominees who are here behind me, the wonderful members of the labor movement, the educators who are here, and others who are doing their best to see that Michigan makes a good decision for the future tomorrow. I also want to say a special word of thanks out of my own history to the Davison High School Band over here for playing for us. Thank you very much. You know, the chancellor at this distinguished institution, Dr. Charlie Nelms—we've got another band up there? What? Northern High School up here. Give them a hand. [*Applause*]

Folks, the chancellor of this fine institution, Dr. Charlie Nelms, grew up in my home State. And he just got back from his college reunion. I won't tell you which one. [*Laughter*] He was one of 11 children. And I say this not to embarrass him but to tell you that right before we came out here he said, "I want you to know something, Mr. President. If it hadn't been for people believing in me, giving me a chance, and providing programs like these college loans that get so many students into this institution, I wouldn't be here today. I want to stick with the people who believe in education, who believe in ordinary citizens, who believe in the future of this country."

I want to thank Mayor Woodrow Stanley for being my friend and my supporter and your great leader. They used to call me the Comeback Kid. You ought to call Flint the comeback city under Woodrow Stanley. And the thing I like about Woodrow Stanley—I want to say more about this in a minute, because it goes to your choice in this election—is that he is a builder, not a blamer. I want to thank your Senators, Senator Carl Levin and Senator Don Riegle—we wish you well in your retirement, and we thank you for representing Flint, Michigan, and the United States. I want to welcome the Democratic nominees for Governor and Lieutenant Governor, Howard Wolpe and Debbie Stabenow, and ask you to help them tomorrow and support them.

I just have to say this: The unemployment figures came out last week, and we had a 4-year low in unemployment. And the Governor here always says, "Well, the Michigan economy is getting better." That's true, but did you ever notice that it didn't get very much better when the Republicans had the White House and the economic policy? And even though I think an enormous amount of credit goes to the automobile industry for their incredible efforts at partnership, labor and management, bringing us back to number one in automobiles in the entire world, the rest of the States are doing pretty well, too. We're going up or down together; that is my message.

I want you to help these people and especially I want you to help Bob Carr because if nothing else you know, if you look at this fine institution of higher education, if you look at this city, if you look at this State, if you think of our country, we are going up or down together. And you only have one choice who is clearly 100 percent on your side. Bob Carr is 100 percent on your side.

I also want to echo what Hillary said about Congressman Dale Kildee. I want to say a special word of thanks to him for his leadership in the most productive congressional session for education in 30 years. We expanded Head Start. We changed the Federal law on aid to our public schools so that we will emphasize grassroots reform and get rid of this ridiculous assumption that just because kids are poor, from disadvantaged backgrounds, they can't learn—from now on, the same expectations, the same opportunity, the same achievement for children without regard to their background. And you heard him talking about the School-to-Work Opportunity Act I signed. That's a bill for young people who don't go on to college but don't want to be in dead-end jobs, who want good training and are willing to engage in a lifetime of learning. And I did sign that bill on a desk built by the students at the manufacturing technology project right here in Flint, Michigan, who will benefit from that sort of effort.

I also want to thank Congressman Jim Barcia and our candidate, Bob Mitchell, for being here. Send them back to Washington so we'll have partners for progress.

You know, folks, this has really turned out to be an amazing election in ways that are both wonderful and troubling. The American people know that there are still things that need fixing in Washington, and they know there are things that need fixing back here at home. They know that, in spite of the fact that we've got an enormous amount of job growth—over 5 million jobs in the last 21 months—in spite of the fact that we've got more high-wage jobs coming back into America this year than in the previous 5 years combined, in spite of the fact that the biggest problem in the auto industry is not no time, it's now overtime—a high-class problem—they know that there are still a lot of people who are worried about losing their jobs; a lot of people who are afraid they'll never get a raise; a lot of people who are worried about losing their health insurance, as one million people in working families did last year; a lot of people who still want work in some of our cities and isolated rural areas who don't have jobs. This country has problems. They know that we've still got too much crime and violence and too much disintegration of our families and our communities that make people feel personally insecure or at least violate their sense of values. That's all true.

Now the question is, what are we going to do about it? And what these guys say is, our opponents, they say, "Be mad about it, be frustrated about it, be cynical about it, and put us in because we are going to play on your fears, your frustrations, and your cynicism." That's their argument; their argument is, "Look, nothing good has happened, and if you find something good that happened, it did not happen because the President was there. It did not happen because he had partners in the Congress. It happened in spite of that. It was irrele-

vant to that." That's their argument; you listen to them.

Well, you know what, folks? Where I come from, people say if you find a turtle on the fencepost, it did not get there by accident. And so I say to you, don't let a frustrated electorate wind up voting for what you're against and against what you're for. That's what they want.

Look what they say they're for. They say they are for a new plan that will give a huge tax cut to the wealthy, that will bring back big increases in defense and revive Star Wars and will balance the budget. Does that sound familiar to you? They say, "Ignore what happened in the last 21 months; it doesn't matter. Ignore the jobs, the growth, the help for ordinary working Americans, the fact that the world is growing more prosperous and more peaceful. Ignore all that; take our new set of promises."

Now, I want you to think about this. There are really only two possibilities with these Republican promises: they're either serious, or they're kidding. Now listen to me. If they're serious, they have made you a trillion dollars' worth of promises: "We're going to cut taxes on the wealthy, bring back defense and Star Wars, and balance the budget." What does it cost? "A trillion dollars." When you ask them, "How will you pay for it?" they say, "We'll tell you after the election."

Do you know why? Because the only way to pay for it is to cut everything else in the budget 20 percent across the board: $2,000 a person in Social Security, cut Medicare 20 percent, cut the student loans 20 percent, cut the AIDS prevention 20 percent, cut the Head Start 20 percent. That is their program. Then they say, "Well, we didn't say we would cut Social Security." They didn't say they wouldn't. But if you take out Social Security, then our opponents in the Senate and the House have committed to a set of promises that mean 30 percent cuts across the board in all those things.

Of course, there's always the chance that they didn't mean it, they're kidding. If they're kidding, what does it mean? "We will give you the goodies without the price." And what does that mean? We're going to explode the deficit. We're going to ship our jobs overseas. We're going to put our economy back in the same mess that this same crowd, with these same policies, put it in in the trickle-down economics years of the 1980's.

Tell them no. We want Bob Carr. We want Dale Kildee. We want Jim Barcia. We want Bob Mitchell. Those are the people we want. Tell them no. Tell them no.

You know, folks, one of the most amazing things to me is this effort that they are making to take a frustrated electorate and say, "It does not matter what we say. It does not matter what we do. Anything the Government does is either irrelevant or makes it worse." Can you imagine, can you imagine entering into any other human endeavor with that attitude? Can you imagine going to school with that attitude? Can you imagine building a business with that attitude? Can you imagine going to work with that attitude? Can you imagine building a house with that attitude? Can you imagine building a family with that attitude? No! Well, why would we want to build a Congress with that attitude?

You know, folks, I don't know about you, but when I showed up in Washington I wanted to rebuild the American dream; I wanted to bring this country together; I wanted to make America strong. I don't mean I wanted to talk strong; I wanted to be strong. And to be strong you need stronger families, better schools, safer streets, more jobs, a safer and more prosperous world.

Well, I don't know about you, but I believe it made a difference when we gave 1½ million Michigan families the protection of the Family and Medical Leave Act so they could take a little time off from work and keep their jobs. And I believe it made a difference when almost 400,000 Michigan families that work full-time with kids in the house and are hovering above the poverty line got an income tax cut under our administration, so you could succeed at work and at home, being a parent and a worker. I think it made a difference. I think it made a difference when we made almost 600,000 people in Michigan eligible for lower cost and better repayment college loans, so more people could go to college and no one need ever turn away. I think that makes a difference. And I think it made a difference when we lowered the deficit and increased our investment in our future and got this economy going again. And that's why the unemployment rate in America is at a 4 year low and it's dropped 2 percent in Michigan in the last 21 months. I think that matters, and I think you think it matters.

So I think it matters that for the first time since the dawn of the nuclear age, there are no Russian missiles pointing at these children here. I think it matters that North Korea has agreed not to become a nuclear power. I think it matters that the United States is expanding trade and opportunity for high-wage jobs. I think it matters that we are making peace and helping peace come about and standing up for freedom from the Persian Gulf to Northern Ireland, to Haiti, to the Middle East. I think that matters. I think that matters. And so I ask you, my fellow Americans, why would we want to go back?

This election is, more than anything else, an election about the state of mind of our voters. If people are thinking about the issues and what's in their issues and who's on their side and what's best for our future, they will have to vote for Bob Carr over his opponent. Their great hope is that everybody wakes up tomorrow mad, the Democrats stay home, the extremists go vote—the people who want a bunch of easy promises, the people who want a lot of tough talk that will lead not to strength but to weakness for most of us—that that will prevail. My great belief is that tomorrow, whatever the weather, you're going to wake up with the Sun shining in your mind, seeing clearly, thinking about tomorrow, thinking about tomorrow.

Folks, you just think about this. You think about what really counts when you go to work, when you build a business, when you get an education, when you rear a family. It is a positive, building, unifying, compassionate idea of what you are as a person and what you can become. That is what we represent. We've still got a lot of problems in this country, folks, but this country is in better shape than it was 21 months ago. We are stronger than we were 21 months ago. We are moving forward.

Don't turn back; go forward. Elect Bob Carr and Dale Kildee and Jim Barcia and Bob Mitchell and Howard Wolpe and Debbie Stabenow. Help these people. Lift Michigan; go forward. Come on, we can do it. Thank you, and God bless you all.

NOTE: The President spoke at 1:57 p.m. at the University of Michigan.

Remarks at a Rally for Democratic Candidates in Wilmington, Delaware
November 7, 1994

Thank you very much. Thank you, Charlie Oberly. Thank you, Mayor Sills. It is great to be back in Wilmington again. I thank Carrie DeSantis and all the other Democratic candidates who are here with us.

I thank Governor Carper for his longtime friendship and his stirring defense of our record. I was thinking to myself, if I could clone Tom Carper and have that speech given in every country crossroads in America, the political future of our administration and our party would be secure. Didn't he do a fine job?

And Hillary and I both feel a special indebtedness for the friendship and the leadership of Joe Biden, without whom there would have been no crime bill this year and because of whom lives will be saved and children will grow up safer and this country will be a less violent place in the years ahead. We are in his great and abiding debt.

You know, the last time I did a rally here a couple of years ago, I had just about lost my voice. Well, I've been a little hoarse, and some things don't change, but I kind of got pumped up tonight, and my voice is coming back, and I want your voice to be heard tomorrow.

You know, the last time I came to Delaware, my first trip as President, I met with students from Sussex County who were training to enter the aerospace industry. They were working people, good young people from all different kinds of backgrounds who just wanted to get a good education so that they could compete and do well, so that they could earn a decent living, have some security, have a good marriage, raise children, and make a good life here in this wonderful State. The struggles that they faced, the opportunities that they have, the changes we all have to make—those young people from Sussex County, they are the symbol of why we do not need to turn back tomorrow, why we need to go forward, and why we need Charlie Oberly in the United States Senate.

You know, I ran for President from another small State that raises a lot of chickens—[*laughter*]—because I did not want my daughter or our children to grow up to be the first generation of Americans to do worse than their parents. I did not want our country to come apart by race, by region, by income when if we will just celebrate our diversity and learn to live and work together, there is nothing we cannot do as a nation.

And we have been hard at work at that. Now all the pundits tell us that the voters are still hungry for change. Well, we do need some changes, all right, but those changes won't come overnight. The problems of crime and violence, of family and community breakdown, of guns and gangs and drugs—those things didn't come up overnight. They've been building for 30 years. The economic problems of increasing insecurity of our working people, people working harder and not getting a raise, worried about losing their health insurance or their retirement, having to change jobs so many times—those things didn't come up overnight. They've been developing for 20 years. And 21 months ago when I took office, we'd had 12 years of trickle-down economics which was culminated by 4 years of the slowest job growth since the Great Depression. Folks, we hadn't been there long, but this country is in better shape than it was 21 months ago.

Yes, there are things we have to do. Another million Americans in working families lost their health insurance last year. I don't believe we're the only big country in the world that can't figure out how to keep people with their health insurance, give people in small businesses and self-employed people the same prices as people in big business and Government get. I don't believe we can't afford to figure out how to give it to our kids, and I don't think that we have to tolerate a situation where elderly people on Medicare choose every week between their medicine and their meals. I believe we can do better. I know we have changes to make.

I know there is still work to be done on welfare reform. Tom Carper and I have been working on it for 7 years now. I know we still need to pass political reform, campaign finance reform. There's a Senate race in California where the Republican challenger moved to the State 3 years ago, bought a congressional seat, stayed 8 months, declared for the Senate, ran, lost in his own district in his own primary, and is still in the race because he spent $30 million of his own money. We sure do need that.

We need lobby reform, and we need a law out of Congress that requires the Congress and the Federal Government to live under the same laws we impose on people in the private sector. We need a lot of things to change in this country.

The question is, how do you get that change? Tonight, folks, I want to make the case for Charlie Oberly by asking you and asking the American people in this last speech to look at what the record of the two parties has been in the last 2 years, and what the program of our parties for the years ahead is. That is how you tell how you get the change you want, not by being mad.

One of the reasons that I like Delaware is that I think you folks are a little more immune than sometimes people in bigger places are to all this negative, cynical, destructive stuff that they keep trying to put on us to take our citizenship and our good sense away from us. The kind of Democrats you elect here don't believe that Government can solve all the problems, but they don't think Government can sit on the sideline either.

Our Government is not inherently bad or inherently good. It is what we make of it. And what I think the people of Delaware want is a Government that creates opportunity so we can say, "Okay, the opportunity is there. Now you have the power to assume the responsibility to make the most of your own lives and your community." That's what I think the people want out of Government in this country and in this State.

I want a strong America. But very often, what politicians give us is strong talk and weak action. What makes a strong America? Strong families; better education; safer streets; more jobs; a more peaceful, more prosperous world. That's real strength, folks, not all that tough talk, not all those negative ads. That's real strength, something you can build a life on, raise a child on, and be proud in your old age of. That is the kind of America that I want to build.

Now, that's what we've been working for. What have they done? Our opponents have fought us every step of the way. They have had a simple, clear, unwavering strategy, and give them credit, folks, they stick to it. They don't even get embarrassed when you catch them at it. [*Laughter*] Their whole deal is,

"Fight them every step of the way. Do everything you can to derail them. And if they win anyway, then deny that it makes any difference." [*Laughter*] Say if anything, their theory is, kill it if you can, and if you can't kill it and something good happens, say, "It happened in spite of the Democrats; it happened in spite of the President. They didn't have anything to do with it." And they're good at it. They're good at it.

Well, I have this to say to the Republicans. The same kind of people that say don't count your chickens before they hatch will understand the saying that is pretty prominent where I come from. They say, if you're walking down a road and you see a turtle on a fencepost, the chances are it didn't get there by accident. [*Laughter*] You know, they say, "Well, these things don't make any difference," or they try to kill them. Well, let me ask you this—you heard what Tom Carper said—I think it makes a difference that 147,000 families right here in Delaware are protected by the family leave law, so they can take a little time off if there's a baby born or a sick parent without losing their jobs. I believe it makes a difference that 36,000 working families in the State of Delaware, working full-time, barely hovering above the poverty line, got an income tax cut under this administration, so they can succeed as parents and workers.

I think it makes a difference that we've increased child support enforcement, that we're pushing for welfare reform, that we've given 20 States the permission to slash through rules and regulations to figure out how to move folks from welfare to work in dignity that enables them to support their children and be self-respecting citizens.

I think it makes a difference that in Delaware 41,700 people are eligible for lower cost, better repayment, more affordable college loans, so that everybody can afford to go to college in this country and not drop out. I think that makes a difference.

I think it makes a difference that we expanded Head Start, that we support apprenticeship programs. I think it makes a difference that the job growth rate in Delaware is now—listen to this—14 times as fast as it was before this administration took office. I think that makes a difference.

I think it makes a difference that the crime bill passed and that Delaware will get 650 more police officers to walk the streets and prevent crime and be a good role model for our children—I think that matters—that we're going to have funds for drug education and drug courts and boot camps and things that give our kids a chance to avoid spending their lives in prison and give them a chance to spend their lives at work and in school. I think it makes a difference.

What I want you to know is—I'll say it again—Charlie Oberly mobilized the attorneys general; Joe Biden saved the crime bill in its darkest hour. Do not take my word for it; you ask Joe Biden. When you think about this tomorrow—[*laughter*]—no, no, not this. Listen to me. When we were in our darkest hour, we couldn't figure out what is going on: Why did the Republicans, when they all voted for the crime bill the first time it came up, why were they all being pressured to vote against the crime bill? They said, "Oh, it had so much money in it." On an annual basis it had slightly less money in it than it did the first time they voted for it. They said, "These prevention programs are no good." We found that a whole bunch of them had been sponsored by Republicans. You've got to give them credit. They have no shame. They're not embarrassed about this. [*Laughter*] They're not—I'll tell you what, you ask Senator Biden. It's because their leader told them that their job was not to lower the rate of crime, their job was to defeat the Democrats, never mind the rate of crime.

Joe Biden said, "No, thank you, I'd rather have America safe. I'm interested in the children, not in the politics of this." And I thank, I thank Charlie Oberly and Joe Biden for what they did on the crime bill. I also want to say about Charlie Butler—don't you forget this—he's running to be the top law enforcement officer in your State against someone who opposed the crime bill. Vote for somebody who wants to keep you safe. Vote for Charlie Butler.

Let me say this: I think it makes a difference that we have a more peaceful and prosperous world, that there's more trade, that there are no Russian missiles pointed at these children for the first time since the dawn of the nuclear age, that we are a force for peace and freedom in the Persian Gulf, in the Middle East, in Northern Ireland, in Haiti. I think that makes a difference. It makes us all better and stronger.

So don't let them say it doesn't make a difference what we have done. If it had been up to them, as a group, if they were in charge—

and that's what they're asking you tomorrow—they say, "Every vote for every Republican Senator, every vote for every Republican Congressman is a vote to put us in charge, to put Mr. Dole and Mr. Gingrich in charge." Let me tell you something, folks, if they had been in charge—listen now—if they had been in charge, no family leave law, no Brady bill, no crime bill, no deficit reduction, no middle class college loans, no tax cuts for working people, no economic recovery. I think that's one issue we can say no to, thank you very much, no.

It kind of tickles me. We're giving them 3 years of deficit reduction for the first time since Truman. When we get done, we'll have the smallest Federal Government since Kennedy. We've got the toughest crime bill in history and an economic recovery. A self-respecting mainstream Republican would support that. But they have no shame. Let's take credit for it for them and take care of it for them and keep this country going forward.

Now, so people say, "Well, that's okay, but I still don't feel so good." So look at the future. I told you what our future is. Our future is, implement the crime bill, keep the recovery going, keep a steady hand on the spending, implement welfare reform, go back until we solve the health care problem, implement political reform and environmental legislation.

What is their future? Their future is, "I got a promise to make you. I got a contract to make with you. We're going to cut taxes, especially for the wealthiest 2 percent. We're going to increase spending on defense and Star Wars, and we're going to balance the budget." Well, how much does it cost? "A trillion dollars." And how are you going to pay for it? "We'll tell you after the election." [*Laughter*] Oh, they have no shame. [*Laughter*] "We'll tell you after"—so I will tell you how they have to pay for it. We've made a study of it. Since we reduced the deficit and they didn't, we know something about that.

Here's how you have to pay for it. There are only two possibilities, folks, with this promise of theirs: Either they mean it, or they're kidding. Now, if they mean it, they have to cut everything in this Government 20 percent: $2,000 a year in Social Security, 20 percent on Medicare, 20 percent on Head Start, 20 percent on college loans. If they say, "Well, we never said we'd cut Social Security," we say, "Well, you never said you wouldn't." But let's say they don't. Then they have to cut everything 30 percent: Medicare, college loans, Head Start, break the Government down, break the support of the middle class down.

Then there's always the chance that they were kidding. That's what they did to us in the eighties. They gave us the goodies and didn't pay the bill. What does that mean? Explode the deficit, send our jobs overseas, and put this economy in the ditch. We tried it that way. We've been there. No, thank you. We'll go forward, we don't want to go back. We don't want to go back.

My fellow Americans, our children deserve better than that. They deserve vigorous, cooperative, positive leadership. They do not deserve to be caught up in this whirlwind of negative, cynical stuff. Our kids deserve better.

And let me ask you this: All the papers and the pundits say, "Well, people are so mad they're just going to vote against who's in, and they're going to vote against the Democrats because the Democrats have both Houses of the Congress, even though the Republicans through the filibuster have frustrated most of the progress. They're just going to vote no because they're mad."

You know, we ought to be ashamed of ourselves if we just vote no because we're mad. Those of us who are parents know that the first thing we try to teach our kids, as quick as they're old enough to understand it, is what we've been taught by our parents: Never make a decision when you're mad. Count to 10. How many times did my mama say, "Count to 10"? And how many times did I get to 2 or 3 and say it anyway and live to regret it? [*Laughter*] That's what will happen to America unless we wake up with the sunshine and a clear head and vote for Charlie Oberly and vote for progress in this country, and vote to keep going forward.

Listen to what these folks say. They say we've got people out there running saying, "We promise to do nothing except give you the goodies. And everything about Government is bad, but we want to go draw a Government check for 6 years." That's what they're saying. You would not hire somebody to build a house, do a job, start a business, you certainly wouldn't make a marriage with somebody that had that kind

of attitude. But they want you to send a whole boatload of folks to Congress on that kind of negativism. Tell them no. Tell them no.

You know, we ought to keep going forward. We shouldn't give in to our fears. Franklin Roosevelt said, "The only thing we have to fear is fear itself." They say, "Vote your fears." Look at the Republican Presidents you all admire: Teddy Roosevelt, "The credit belongs to the person who is in the arena who is trying." They say, "Punish the people who've tried, and give it to us. We just pointed the finger of blame; we wouldn't take any responsibility for anything. We made you mad because we gummed up the works. Now reward us because you're mad." Teddy Roosevelt must be shaking his head in shame at them tonight.

What about their greatest Republican President, Abraham Lincoln. He said, "With malice toward none," not how much malice can you stir up in the electorate to turn people off. He said, "with charity for all," not how much meanness and division can you stir up to keep some folks home and other folks mad. He said we should govern by "the better angels of our nature," not the lowest common denominator of our darkest fear. That's what he said.

Folks, tomorrow, this election is going to be decided throughout this country by whether people wake up and act in the voting booth the way they want to act as parents, as workers, as business people, in their clubs, in their churches, in every other area of their lives. We know it is wrong to be negative, it is right to be positive; it is wrong to blame, it is right to build; it is wrong to be guided by fear, it is right to be animated by hope. We know we ought to be fighting for the future.

If the American people wake up in that frame of mind tomorrow, you will send Charlie Oberly to the Senate in Delaware; we will keep moving toward the future throughout this country. We will do it for our children because it is right. You can do it here. We need you.

Thank you, and God bless you all. Thank you.

NOTE: The President spoke at 6:07 p.m. in Rodney Square. In his remarks, he referred to Mayor James Sills of Wilmington and congressional candidate Carrie DeSantis.

Letter to Congressional Leaders Transmitting a Report on Cyprus
November 7, 1994

Dear Mr. Speaker: (*Dear Mr. Chairman:*)

In accordance with Public Law 95–384 (22 U.S.C. 2373(c)), I am submitting to you this report on progress toward a negotiated settlement of the Cyprus question. The previous report covered progress through July 31, 1994. The current report covers the period August 1, 1994, through September 30, 1994.

During this time frame U.S. Ambassador Richard Boucher met regularly with the leaders of the two communities. He is working closely with the United Nations in an effort to bring Mr. Clerides and Mr. Denktash together for face-to-face meetings. I am very concerned with the lack of progress during this period and believe direct meetings between the two leaders are crucial to avoid an impasse.

James Williams was appointed on October 21 as U.S. Special Coordinator for Cyprus. He will travel shortly to Athens, Ankara, and Nicosia to consult with the parties.

Sincerely,

WILLIAM J. CLINTON

NOTE: Identical letters were sent to Thomas S. Foley, Speaker of the House of Representatives, and Claiborne Pell, chairman, Senate Committee on Foreign Relations.

Interview With John Gambling of WOR Radio, New York City
November 8, 1994

Midterm Elections

Mr. Gambling. Mr. President, good morning.

The President. Good morning. Good morning, John.

Mr. Gambling. Important day for you, the Democrats, Republicans, and independents. It's election day, and you know, they give frequent flyer miles on Air Force One, you're going to get a free trip to anywhere. You have been busy.

The President. Well, it's been a busy week. But you know, I had to take that very important trip to the Middle East, and when I came back, a lot of our candidates asked me to get out there and campaign, including Governor Cuomo, so I tried to do all I could to make the best argument for why we're moving our country in the right direction and we don't want to go back to the policies that failed us before in the eighties. So this morning I'm just taking a last opportunity to encourage the American people to go out and vote, to make their voices heard today. The stakes in this election are quite high, as they always are in any midterm election, but especially in this one. So I hope the people within the sound of my voice will exercise their citizenship today and get out there and vote.

Mr. Gambling. Interesting contrast for you; maybe you can talk about it for just a second, between the events of the Middle East and our political system and the fact that the peace treaty signing—coming so close to our election.

The President. Well, of course, we've been working on that very hard for a couple of years. It's just a coincidence that it came as close as it did to our election. But I would hope that it would remind the American people of the great potential of this country and the greatness of this country. And I hope it would keep our people in a positive frame of mind. One of the unfortunate aspects of so much of modern campaigning is that the negative tends to outweigh the positive, and the negative television ads, the whole business about the tone and tenor of our elections. This is actually quite a great country with a great past and an even greater future if the people who are going to be affected by it will invest in it and vote for it and vote for people who will build the country, not just place blame, vote for people who will keep moving us into the future.

That's really the lesson of the Middle East, that people want the United States involved in the peacemaking and the problem solving of the world, whether in the Middle East or in

Haiti or Northern Ireland, just to name three, because they think we have a good system and that we are a good people. And sometimes I think we forget it, and we need to remember it. This is election day. We can go out, be heard, and make a difference.

Mr. Gambling. As a man that has spent his entire life in politics, how do you define politics? Is it program or is it more the essence and the basics of hope, security, fulfillment?

The President. Well, I think the programs matter, but I also think the principles matter. I think giving voice to people's hopes to getting people together, giving energy to other people is very important. So much of what we do down here in Washington basically is an effort to empower people to take responsibility for their own lives. There aren't so many things that the Government does directly. I mean, we pay for medical care for the elderly through Medicare. We finance the Social Security system. We run a wonderful National Park System. We do a number of other things directly, but a lot of what we do is to empower people: the student loan program, the Head Start program, the crime bill which enables the city of New York to hire more police officers and have programs for kids to keep them out of trouble.

All these things basically give people in their individual, family, or community lives the ability to take responsibility for themselves. So part of it's programs, but a lot of it is setting the right tone and the right direction, looking to the future all the time. This country is always at its best when it's coming together and moving to the future.

Mr. Gambling. I hear a frustration in your voice about the mood of the country, the cynicism, the negative advertising that's taking place on all sides in the past weeks.

The President. Well, I don't know that I'm frustrated. I think it has too much sway over our national life, but I think our communications in general with one another are too negative these days. We ought to be having more honest conversations with one another and doing less verbal bomb-throwing. I think the American people are frustrated by it, and that's why I hope that there will be a good turnout today for candidates like Mario Cuomo who have essentially been a positive force throughout their public careers. Because it's just so easy to give in to the kind of pounding-attack communications that tend to dominate not just the elections

but often the daily communication of our public life. And it's not a very good way to run a railroad or a country, and we're better than that. And whatever happens today in these elections, I'm going to be determined over the next few years to try to lift our country out of that.

Mr. Gambling. President Bill Clinton on the "Rambling With Gambling" phone this morning. Along those lines, if, as predicted by some, the Republicans gain control of the Senate, will your agenda for the next couple of years have to change?

The President. No, but I will have to have more responsible bipartisan efforts on all parts. I will make my effort, and we'll see others make theirs, I hope.

On the other hand, if the American people turn out in equal numbers, if the Democrats turn out as well as the Republicans do at the polls today, I don't think that'll happen. It's really, in so much measure, a question of who cares enough to go and vote and whether the spirits of a lot of normally Democratic voters are dampened by the negative atmosphere of the moment.

You know, the country's economy is coming back, we're tackling our problems like crime, we're facing things long ignored, and this is a time to keep going forward.

Mr. Gambling. Where do you vote today? Do you vote in Arkansas by——

The President. Yes. I voted absentee in Arkansas. I voted for my Governor, and I called him last night and told him I did. [*Laughter*]

President's Security

Mr. Gambling. Well, that's good. The security question, the events of the last couple of weeks—I understand—and I'm not looking for specifics here but just generalities—I understand your routine has changed a little bit.

The President. Well, we've asked the Secret Service to take a look at all the procedures and everything, as they periodically do. Every year, I think for quite a long while now, Secret Service has increased its ability to protect the President, and I think they are continuing to do it. I have a lot of confidence in them, and the trick is to permit them to do that without having the President completely cut off from the public at large, because this is a great, free society, and one of the problems the President always has is trying to avoid losing touch.

Mr. Gambling. Exactly. Probably the most difficult thing, you've got to keep in touch with the folks. I want to thank you very much, Mr. President, for choosing us this morning to talk about politics on election day, 1994. Thank you very much.

The President. Thanks again. I want to urge all your listeners to go on and vote today. Thank you.

NOTE: The interview began at 7:12 a.m. The President spoke by telephone from the Oval Office at the White House.

Interview With Paul W. Smith of WWDB Radio, Philadelphia, Pennsylvania
November 8, 1994

Mr. Smith. What a pleasure, indeed, it is to welcome back to the program, in an exclusive Philadelphia interview, live from the White House, ladies and gentlemen, the President of the United States.

Mr. President, good morning to you. Happy election day.

The President. Thank you, Paul W. It's nice to hear your voice again.

Midterm Elections

Mr. Smith. Well, it's nice to have you back. It indicates to me how important you feel the voters of Pennsylvania and New Jersey are and Delaware are in this election year, because you have been all over the place. I recall several weeks ago, the Washington press corps alleging that there weren't a lot of people who wanted the President to come out and campaign for them. But as Dee Dee Myers pointed out then, and as you certainly have seemed to prove over the last several days, you couldn't possibly get to all the places where people wanted you. You and Mrs. Clinton have been all over the country campaigning.

The President. Well, we have, and the Vice President and Mrs. Gore have also been out there a lot. Leon Panetta's been out there a lot, and our Cabinet has.

But we have been confronted with quite a challenge just in the generally negative tone of the atmosphere that has concerned me some about the turnout. You know, I had to take a few days to go to the Middle East on what was a truly historic mission for our country and for the cause of peace in the world. And when I was there and when I was coming back, I was struck by how strongly and how positively the rest of the world looks at the United States, at our system, at the strength of our economic recovery, at the fact that we seem to be facing problems that we ignored for a long time. And they are often asking me questions—world leaders in other places—about how this negative feeling creeps over our people and why it has such a hold at election time.

So I wanted to do these election morning interviews more than anything else just to encourage our citizens to get out and vote, to make their voices heard, not to sit this election out simply because they feel negatively about perhaps some of the ads or some of the tone of the campaign. Because our country is facing our problems, we're moving into the future, and we need the American people to be engaged in this process. And we need all kinds of people to be engaged in the process, just ordinary mainstream Americans showing up to vote and to try to have their interests and their values advanced in this election.

Mr. Smith. Why do you think, Mr. President, this has appeared to be the sleaziest, dirtiest, worst campaign yet? And if, in fact, it works for some candidates, one wonders just how bad it will get the next time around.

The President. Well, of course, that's the whole point I'm trying to make. I'm afraid it's been that way because this is a place where the people rule, and a lot of the polling data indicates that sometimes these negative campaigns work, that when people get down on the political system and down on politicians, they're a little more prone to believe the worst as opposed to the best.

And actually, if you look at the history of this country, the rich and strong and long history, we have often had our difficulties in the political system. And we've had a scoundrel or two in the history of America, but most of our public officials have been honest and straight-forward people. And most of the time the differences have been over what direction we should take. And when we get into voting about who is the worst, as opposed to what do these people believe and what are they going to do, I think that puts us at some risk of making bad decisions.

And that's what I've been trying to do traveling around the country since I've come back from the Middle East, is to say to the American people, you know, whatever you do, let's look at this in a forward-looking way. How are we going to go forward? How are we going to work together and move this country forward? We don't want to go back, and we don't want to be divided, and we don't want to think less of ourselves as a result of this election, because we have a very great country. And others who maybe sometimes see us more clearly than we even see ourselves know that for all of our problems, we're facing them, we're moving forward, and we have enormous potential. Our best days are still ahead of us. And every election is an obligation of those of us who are citizens to kind of keep this ball moving forward.

Mr. Smith. Mr. Clinton—Mr. President, you have extended, kind of in advance, an olive branch saying that you will work with everyone and that you can, your administration can work with everyone. How do you feel this election morning in terms of the chances that there will be more Republicans? Republicans have not held majorities in both Houses of Congress simultaneously since 1954. There is a very good chance you're going to have many more Republicans there on the Hill than we've had in a number of years. Do you sense this morning that that will be the case, or would you rather wait until the polls close?

The President. I think it depends entirely on the turnout, really. I think they have some things going for them: the fact that in every

election in the 20th century but one the party opposite the President has made gains in at least one House at midterm, and I think all elections but three they made gains in both Houses; the fact that we've had for most of the last 30 years a divided Government—some people are used to that—that is, the President in one party, the Congress of another.

I think there are some things working against that: the fact that we have been able to accomplish quite a bit that, in the atmosphere in which we were operating in, almost no one knew until about 3 weeks ago—we finally being able to get a little bit of information out about how much the President and the Congress accomplished working together. And I think we have to just keep working on that and keep going forward.

Mr. Smith. Mr. President, thank you for being with us. We do appreciate it again——

The President. Thank you.

Mr. Smith. ——and it's quite an honor to have the President of the United States twice in one week.

The President. Well, it's great to hear your voice. And of course, you know I think the world of Senator Wofford; I hope he'll be re-elected today. And I hope that your listeners in these other States will go out and vote, and I hope their voices will be heard. And I hope they will do it in a good spirit, believing in our country, believing in our future. This is not the time for negativism. This is a time to be upbeat but aggressive in tackling our problems and seizing our opportunities.

And I thank you for talking to me today.

Mr. Smith. By the way, President Clinton, thank you for the kind words about President Reagan's revelation over the weekend. It was most appreciated around the country, I think.

The President. Thank you.

NOTE: The interview began at 7:21 a.m. The President spoke by telephone from the Oval Office at the White House.

Interview With Joe Templeton of ABC Radio
November 8, 1994

Midterm Elections

Mr. Templeton. Good morning, Mr. President. After 8 days on the campaign trail, how do you see this midterm election shaping up?

The President. Well, Joe, I don't know. You know, I must say, there are a lot of these races that are very, very tight. And the thing I want to say to the American people today is that it's important for us not to go to the polls in a negative frame of mind. There's been a little too much negativism, some places a lot too much, in this election.

This is a very great country. I just got back from the Middle East peace signing. I am, again, captured by the idea that others know what a great country we have, that we have the capacity to seize our opportunities and to face our problems. We're trying to do that here; we just need to keep going forward. And we need to get out there, all of us, and vote today but to do it with a belief in our country, a belief in our future, a belief in our possibilities to make life better.

Mr. Templeton. Now, if Republicans win the House and Senate, and many pollsters are saying that's a very good possibility, what does this do to your prestige in the rest of the term?

The President. Well, I don't know. That'll be up to the American people to decide. But for most of the last 40 years, we've had divided Government. We've had the Congress in one hand and the Presidency in the other. The American people have kind of gotten used to that. So I don't know that it will make a great deal of difference in that sense.

I hope that the Democrats who have taken courageous decisions to bring the deficit down and to get the economy going again and to try to improve education and make the streets safer, who have taken the tough decisions, will be rewarded for their courage and not punished for it. Because you know, we always say we want people to be brave, to ignore the polls of the moment, and to take the tough decisions that will get us into the future. I think it's important when those folks come up for election that we reward them for that and not punish them for it because of the barrage of negativism that seems to characterize so many of our campaigns.

So again, I would just urge all the people who are listening to us to vote but also to do it in a positive frame of mind. Our country is moving forward economically, we are addressing the crime problem, we're addressing some of these terrible social problems that we've ignored for too long, and we're taking up issues that have to be taken up. They don't have simple and easy answers, and I think it's important that we don't give in to simplistic and essentially negative messages about them. We are a great country; we can do what we have to do, and we ought to try to do it together across party lines.

Mr. Templeton. Now, you have been out there stumping for the Democrats for 8 days or so. Do you feel you've really made any headway?

The President. Well, you know, you never know. When I was a Governor, I was never sure that the President did any help or damage to anybody in my home State. And I never thought, really, people would listen to me in terms of telling them for whom to vote.

What I tried to do was to clarify the issues. I tried to put the record of our administration that the candidates I campaigned for supported; I tried to clarify the stakes and say from my point of view what our position toward the future was, what their position was. I did the best I could to do that.

I think people are capable of making up their minds on their own about candidates. Every race is different; every State is different. But I hope I was able, at least, to focus the attention of the public in a more positive way on the choices before us.

Mr. Templeton. Well, now they're talking about 70 million voters or so turning out today. I wonder if you voted?

The President. Oh, yes, I did. I voted early. I voted absentee back home in Arkansas.

Q. Thank you, Mr. President, for being with us this morning.

NOTE: The interview began at 7:29 a.m. The President spoke by telephone from the Oval Office at the White House.

Remarks at a Reception Honoring White House Volunteers
November 8, 1994

Thank you so very much. Thank you. It is great to be with all of you. It's especially great to be with you on election day. I hope all of you have had a chance to go to the polls, and if you haven't, I hope you'll go before they close tonight. This is a fitting time for the event honoring the White House volunteers because as people all around our country go out and exercise their right to vote, they're exercising their full right and their full responsibility as an American, just as all of you do through your service in the White House.

At these midterm elections, it is critical that people understand that there are clear choices between going forward and going back, between a Government that works for ordinary families and one that works for organized interests, between a Government that does something about our great national problems like crime and one that just tries to talk them to death.

It is very important in this election season that the American people not vote in anger or cynicism. You know, these last 8 days I've had the opportunity to go out and make our case to the American people have been bracketed by two events that ought to deny that: first, the opportunity I had to represent you in the Middle East, seeing our young men and women in uniform in the Gulf, going to the signing of the peace treaty. I looked into the eyes of millions of people. I saw how they viewed our country. They know this is a great country. They know we have a strong defense, a strong economy, and we are now also number one in making peace around the world. They think this is a good country, and so should we.

And now, at the end of this season, I look at you and I think of the hours you have worked, how you have made even more sacrifices this year than last. I do not know how the American people could say anybody, just because we've got some difficult problems and some unresolved challenges, which we have always had and we always will have, that there is something inherently wrong with America's Government. If they could see you, they would know that we are a good people with a good Government, working hard to help the American

people realize their dreams and to respond to their hopes and their needs.

I just want to say, for the benefit of all of you and, of course, our friends who are covering this event, I wish I could thank all of you by name, but I don't want to keep you here all day and into the night. [*Laughter*] I do want to say that I think I should represent—name a few representative people we are fortunate to call White House volunteers.

Jeffery Cohelan, a former Member of the House of Representatives, and his wife, Evelyn, are loyal volunteers in Hillary's correspondence office. We thank you for continuing to serve the United States.

Jenny Lou Dodson lives in Charlotte, North Carolina. She works for an airline, and she flies to Washington every Wednesday to work in the White House Personnel Office. Let's give her a hand.

Al Carpenter worked at the White House from 1947 to 1950. Now he's volunteering his time to take calls on the comment line. He used to work on the Presidential yacht; for the voters who haven't voted, we don't have one anymore. [*Laughter*] He traveled to Key West and the Caribbean with President Truman. Now he travels to the White House to talk to people over the phone all over the United States.

Eddymarie McCoy worked on Capitol Hill and has been part of several campaigns, like the one that's culminating today. Now she's sharing her experience with the Office of Legislative Affairs.

Some of you have been through several administrations. Evelyn and Ward Russell first volunteered at the White House in 1953. We also have dedicated volunteers from many universities and local colleges like Georgetown, American, George Washington, Howard, and George Mason. We thank you all. We have members of the Shiloh Baptist Church here. We have students from Stone Ridge School of the Sacred Heart. And last but not least, we have the hardworking, ever-faithful residents of the U.S. Soldiers and Servicemen's Home. We thank all of you for being here.

If it weren't for you, we literally couldn't do the job we were sent here to do. But with your help, we can not only continue to make progress for our country, continue to keep moving forward with confidence into the future but we can do it in a way that responds to the hopes and the dreams and the real problems of the thousands and thousands and thousands of Americans who write this White House, who call us and ask for help, who send a gesture of their concern, a gesture of their friendship, a gesture of their hope to this White House. All of them deserve to be recognized. All of them deserve to be heard. All of them deserve to be treated with courtesy, with respect, and with dignity.

You have permitted the United States and this administration to do that. We could not do it without you. And I only hope America knows that the White House, like so much of America, runs not on requirements but on the volunteer spirit that is represented in this great audience today.

Thank you all, and God bless you. Thank you.

NOTE: The President spoke at 3:25 p.m. on the South Lawn at the White House.

Letter Accepting the Resignation of David R. Gergen as Special Adviser to the President and Secretary of State
November 8, 1994

Dear David:

As you indicated, when I asked you to concentrate on foreign-policy last June, we agreed on a six-month assignment. Foreknowledge, however, does not lessen the regret with which I accept your resignation as Special Adviser to the President and Secretary of State, effective December 31, 1994.

You have made a remarkable contribution to our Administration over the last eighteen months. Your wise counsel helped us dramatically improve public understanding of our economic plan, and its resulting passage restored fiscal responsibility to our government while helping to create an economic climate that has produced millions of new jobs.

Your life's example sent a powerful signal about the value of bipartisanship, and commitment to public service over partisan gain. That example, and your unflagging determination to build coalitions across the partisan divide, helped us to achieve many non-partisan victories, including passage of NAFTA, the Brady Bill, National Service, and Goals 2000.

And finally, your insightful analysis and thoughtful recommendations about America's relationships with the rest of the world have helped us to ensure that democracy flourishes and peace extends around the globe—in the former republics of the Soviet Union, in the Middle East, in Haiti, and elsewhere.

When you joined our Administration last year, you reaffirmed your allegiance to the noblest aims of public service in America: to work long and hard for the people that hired us, in order to ensure that each of them has a chance to live the American Dream, and to guarantee that the greatest nation in history stands forever tall.

That is exactly what you have done. Thank you for your dedication, for your counsel, and for your friendship. I hope that I have reserved the right to call on each in the years to come.

Sincerely,

BILL CLINTON

NOTE: The Office of the Press Secretary also made available Mr. Gergen's letter of resignation.

The President's News Conference
November 9, 1994

The President. Good afternoon.

Ladies and gentlemen, last night and again this morning I spoke with both Republicans and Democrats to congratulate those who won and console those who lost their elections. I also called the leaders of the next Congress, Senator Dole and Congressman Gingrich, to tell them after this hard-fought campaign that we are ready to work together to serve all the American people in a nonpartisan manner.

The American people sent us here to rebuild the American dream, to change the way Washington does business, to make our country work for ordinary citizens again. We've made a good start by cutting the deficit, by reducing the size of the Federal Government, by reinventing much of our Government to do more with less. We have increased our investment in education and expanded trade, and our economy has created more than 5 million jobs. We've also made a serious start in the fight against the terrible plague of crime and violence in this country. I remain committed to completing the work we have done.

Still, in the course of this work, there has been too much politics-as-usual in Washington, too much partisan conflict, too little reform of Congress and the political process. And though we have made progress, not enough people have felt more prosperous and more secure or believe we were meeting their desires for fundamental change in the role of Government in their lives.

With the Democrats in control of both the White House and the Congress, we were held accountable yesterday. And I accept my share of the responsibility in the result of the elections.

When the Republican Party assumes leadership in the House and in the Senate, they will also have a larger responsibility for acting in the best interest of the American people. I reach out to them today, and I ask them to join me in the center of the public debate where the best ideas for the next generation of American progress must come.

Democrats and Republicans have often joined together when it was clearly in the national interest. For example, they have often chosen to put international affairs above politics. I urge them to do so again by passing the GATT agreement this year. Our prosperity depends upon it, and there can be no compromise when the national interest and the livelihood of American households are at stake.

Last night the voters not only voted for sweeping changes, they demanded that a more equally divided Congress work more closely together with the President for the interest of all the American people. So I hope that we can do that on GATT and that by doing so, we will pave the way for further cooperation on welfare reform and on health care reform, on a continued investment in our people's educational opportunities and the continued strength of our economy.

We must also take more steps to restore the people's faith in our political institutions and agree that, further, in the best tradition of our own foreign policy, that politics will continue to stop at the water's edge.

To those who believe we must keep moving forward, I want to say again, I will do everything in my power to reach out to the leaders and the Members of this new Congress. It must be possible to make it a more effective, more functioning institution. It must be possible for us to give our people a Government that is smaller, that is more effective, that reflects both our interests and our values.

But to those who would use this election to turn us back, let me say this: I will do all in my power to keep anyone from jeopardizing this economic recovery by taking us back to the policies that failed us before. I will still work for those things that make America strong: strong families, better education, safer streets, more high-paying jobs, a more prosperous and peaceful world. There is too much at stake for our children and our future to do anything else.

Well, a lot has changed since yesterday. But what hasn't changed is the reason I was sent here and the reason the Members of the Congress will be sent here, to restore the American dream and to make this country work, this Government work, this city work for the interest of ordinary Americans again. That is what the American people expect of us.

Last night they said they were not satisfied with the progress we had made. They said the Democrats had been in control of the White House and the Congress. They said they were going to make a change, and they did make a change. But they still want the same goal. I pledge today to work with all the Members of the Congress, and especially the new Republican leadership, to achieve that goal. If they will work with me, and they have pledged to do so today, then we can make great progress for this country. We should be optimistic, and we should work to make that optimism real.

Terry [Terence Hunt, Associated Press].

Midterm Elections

Q. Yesterday not a single Republican incumbent lost in any race for Governor, House, or Senate while the Democratic Party, your party, suffered its worst losses for decades. Do you view this as a repudiation of you, or is there another common denominator in this election that we're missing?

The President. Well, I think that I have some responsibility for it. I'm the President. I am the leader of the efforts that we have made in the last 2 years. And to whatever extent that we didn't do what the people wanted us to do or they were not aware of what we had done, I must certainly bear my share of responsibility, and I accept that.

You know, a lot of us haven't had a lot of sleep, and we're going to need a few days to digest all these results. There will be a lot of you doing exit surveys, asking the American people what they meant and said. But what I think they said is, they still don't like what they see when they watch us working here. They still haven't felt the positive results of things that have been done here that they agree with when they hear about them, but they don't feel them. They're still not sure that we understand what they expect the role of Government to be.

I think they want a smaller Government that gives them better value for their dollar, that reflects both their interest and their values, that is not a burden to them but that empowers them. That's what I have tried to do, but I don't think they believe we're there yet, by a long shot. They want us to do more.

I went back today and read my announcement speech for President, and I said in that speech that the job of Government was to create opportunity and then to expect citizens to assume

the responsibility to make the most of that opportunity. I think that's about where the American people are. They don't think we've done that yet.

And the only thing I think they knew to do yesterday was to try to make a change in the people who were in control and who had been. I regret that some of the people who lost are people who made this a lot better country and who will always, when the history books are written, get the credit they deserve, in hindsight, for helping to make the American people more secure.

I don't believe the American people were saying, "We're sorry the deficit has been reduced; we're sorry the size of Government has been reduced; and we're sorry you've taken a tough stand on crime; we're sorry you're expanding trade." I don't believe that. I don't think they were disagreeing with a lot of the specifics. I do think they still just don't like it when they watch what we do up here, and they haven't felt the positive impact of what has been done. And since I'm the President, I have to take some responsibility for that.

Q. Would you have survived if you had been on the ballot yesterday?

The President. Well, some Democrats did. I like to think I would have because I believe that I would have been a ferocious defender of what we have done, and I hope that I could have characterized what the choices were. But I don't know that, and neither does anybody else.

I think it's important to say that yesterday's election, like every election, was fundamentally about the American people. And they looked at us, and they said, "We want some more changes, and we're going to try this and see if this works." There is a lot of evidence—I've read it in a lot of your reporting—that the American people believe, a majority of them, and have believed for decades now that divided Government may work better than united Government. As you know, I disagree with that— why I did my best to make it work the other way—but they didn't agree, and they're in charge. We all work for them, every one of us. And their will, their voice was heard. We got the message. And now we have to think about it, analyze it, rest up, and move on.

But this country is facing its problems. And what I think they told us was, "Look, 2 years ago we made one change; now we made another change. We want you to keep on moving this country forward, and we want you to accelerate the pace of change," in the areas that I mentioned.

I do not believe they voted for reversals of economic policy or the positions on crime. I don't think they voted for a reversal of the Brady bill or the military assault weapons ban. I don't believe that. But I do think they sent us a message, and I tried to hear it. And we're going to work together and do the best we can.

Republican Agenda

Q. What do you think this does for your expected bid for reelection, and how will you deal with the contract for America if there are proposed cuts in Social Security, Medicare, veterans benefits, the whole 9 yards?

The President. Well, first of all, we've got plenty of time to worry about the next election. The American people are sick of the one they just had, and they want to get away from politics for a while. I think we should think about the people, their interests. I think we should say, "What message were they sending us, and what are we going to do about it, and how can we pull this country together?" How can the Democrats and the Republicans in the Congress and the White House and the Republican leadership work together in a nonpartisan way to push this country forward?

Now, on the contract, as I said specifically in Cleveland and elsewhere, there are some things in that contract that I like. I hope the Congress will give me the line-item veto and do it quickly. If they do, we'll bring this deficit down even more quickly. I hope that we will have aggressive efforts to work together on welfare reform. I hope we will be able to still reduce several areas of Federal spending and continue this whole reinventing Government effort to do more with less.

The issue in the contract is what it has always been. I do not believe that we can afford to go back to the days of exploding deficits, which I believe would lead to a weaker economy, to lost jobs, and to a more difficult future for ourselves and for our children. So the question there is, how will all of this be paid for?

I do not believe, now many Republicans in the campaign said they do not believe that we should cut Social Security or Medicare. So if we can't cut Social Security or Medicare, if we must maintain the world's strongest defense,

which I think the Republican leadership and I are strongly in agreement on, then what else are we going to do? And that will be a challenge. But you know, give them a chance. They've got to enjoy their victory today. Give them a day or so to enjoy their victory, and don't push them too far in the future. They will come to grips with that, I'm sure.

Q. Do you really think you are going to be able to compromise with them on that?

The President. Well, I'm not going to compromise on my convictions, what makes America strong. We are stronger today, but we have more strength to get. We have to have—I'll say again what I think makes our country strong: strong families, better education, safer streets, more high-paying jobs, a Government that reflects their values and the interest of the American people, and work to make a world that's more prosperous and more peaceful. Those are the principles on which I do not intend to compromise.

But I want to work with them. Look, let me just give you one example. I have always wanted to make The Tax Code more fair. The Tax Code is more fair today than it was when I took office. We did cut income tax rates for families with incomes of up to $27,000. They want to go further than that. I would like to go further than that. The question is, how far can we go; can we focus on working families with children; how are we going to pay for it? We have to answer now the details. And in large measure, that is a question that can only be answered by some sort of partnership and by getting their views. And again, I say: Let's give them a day or two to enjoy their victory, and then they'll have an opportunity to work forward.

Tax Cut

Q. Mr. President, following up on that, would you support a tax cut such as they propose in their Contract With America, of $500 for every family under $200,000 income, if you don't think it's paid for? Or, would you veto it? Would you get into that kind of confrontational mode with them on something specific?

The President. Well, first of all, let me say they have to have a chance to look at the budget now. When you're in opposition, you can be an advocate entirely, and you can put out ideas you think are good.

I hope we can find some way to continue to improve the fairness of the Tax Code and to help middle class working Americans. When I was trying to reduce the deficit in 1993 and make the Tax Code fairer, we had to stop at $27,000 in income for families with children, working families with children, in our tax relief. I think perhaps we can go further. But I don't want to get into a lot of details today. I'd just say that if we do this, we need to pay for it. We don't need to explode the deficit again. We do not need to weaken the economic recovery again. We need to be responsible with our budget and with our future. I still believe that the American people want us to do that.

Yes, Bill [Bill Plante, CBS News].

Welfare and Health Care Reform

Q. Mr. President, you talked a moment ago about the role of Government. And Government's intervention seems to be what a lot of the voters ruled out, voted against. Are you willing to scale back your expectations in areas like health care and welfare reform, or are you going to go in with plans that look like the ones you had this past year and wait for them to compromise, or will you go to them with something less than you had asked before?

The President. Well, first of all, let me say, if you look at the welfare reform issue—let's take that first. I sent them a bill last March that is quite similar to one that several Republicans themselves have proposed. I don't think anybody would characterize it as a Government intervention bill. It's a bill designed to move people from welfare to work after a certain set time, to have tougher child support enforcement, to provide education and training and support for people who go into the workplace so they can know their children are all right. I think there is over 80 percent support in this country among Americans of both parties, among people of all races and backgrounds for doing something like this. So I think we will get an agreement.

On the health care issue, I will concede that by the time the folks who were characterizing our program had finished with it—and one of your publications said that they thought about $300 million had been spent in lobbying against the health care reform—it looked like a Government program designed to solve the problem by restricting the choices of the American people and injecting the Government more into health care. That is not what I want to do. And I will concede this: I have got to find

a way to reassure the American people that if they like what they've got, they can keep it.

But let me say, I remain committed to solving the health care problem. Last year another million Americans, almost all of them in working families, lost their health insurance. We have more and more people—I talk to them all the time when I go out in the country—small business people and others who have health insurance that is so limited because their copays and deductibles are so high that all they've really got insurance against is losing their home if they get sick. So I remain committed to finding a way to keep Americans from losing their health insurance if they change jobs or if someone in their family gets sick; to controlling the cost increases in health care by market mechanisms; to providing ways for people in small businesses and self-employed people to buy health insurance at the same rates that those of us in Government or big employers, working for big employers, can do it.

This is still a problem. And let me say, as the Republicans leaders know—they've been here working on this budget—we reduced both defense and domestic spending this year for the first time in 25 years. The only thing that went up this year was the cost of Medicare and Medicaid. So this problem will not go away, and I expect to work with the Congress to address it.

Mike [Michael Duffy, Time].

Entitlement Programs

Q. You seem to have backed yourself into a corner on the budget. You say that Medicaid and Medicare cuts will go to fund health reform. Will your next budget outline what you will do to keep the budget deficit going down, particularly if you won't cut Social Security?

The President. Well, I will work with the Republican leadership on that. I will be interested to see what their ideas are. I believe furthermore—as you know, the Kerrey commission has been looking at the whole entitlement question and the long-term implications for our country. I have said, on the Medicare savings, that I thought Medicare savings should be used to help deal with the health care problem because Medicare is paid for entirely by a payroll tax, the purpose of which is to deal with health care. So that's what I have said.

Now, Social Security I think should be dealt with on its own terms. As you know, several years into the future, it is projected that we will once again have a Social Security problem. Ten years ago, a bipartisan commission met and worked out the problems and dealt with that in ways that have, in essence, solved the Social Security problem well into the next century. But we must always be vigilant about that.

The point I want to make about Social Security, though, is that as a percentage of our national income, Social Security is about the same it was 20 years ago, 22 years ago. The Social Security tax has, in fact, produced a surplus for some years now. So it doesn't seem to me to be the right thing to do to try to restrict benefits to recipients overall when the Social Security tax has more than paid its own way all these years.

Now, as you know, in the last session of Congress, we did ask the most well-off—about 12 or 13 percent—of Social Security recipients to pay taxes on a higher percentage of their income, more like private retirees. But I do not believe we should be in the business of cutting Social Security to pay for a tax cut in some other area. I think that would be an error.

Brit [Brit Hume, ABC News].

Midterm Elections

Q. Mr. President, did you mean to say here, sir, that the message the voters sent yesterday was basically an extension of the demand for change they made when you were elected in '92, and that you've been going in the right direction but perhaps need to go farther and faster with the sense of the same agenda?

The President. Well, I think they were saying two things to me—or maybe three. They were saying—maybe 300. [*Laughter*]

I think they were saying, "Look, we just don't like what we see when we watch Washington, and you haven't done much about that." You know, we haven't changed the lobbying reform laws. Congress is still not required to live under the same laws that it imposes on private employers. There's still no line-item veto. There's still not campaign finance reform. "We don't like it when we look at it. It's too partisan, too interest group oriented; things don't get done, too many people up there playing politics. Democrats are in charge; we're holding you accountable. And we hope you hear this, Mr. President." I think they said that.

The second thing I think they said is, "Look, you may have done all these things, although we haven't heard much of it, and we're not sure we believe it. But even if the deficit is down, the Government is smaller, more is being invested in education, the crime bill passed, and the economy is growing, we still feel insecure. We don't feel that our incomes are going up, that our jobs are more stable, that our neighborhoods are safer, that the fabric of American life is growing more civilized and more law-abiding."

Then I think the third thing they were saying—and this maybe gets to the point of your question—is, "There are things we expect Government to do, but we don't think Government can solve all the problems. And we don't want the Democrats telling us from Washington that they know what is right about everything. We want the Government to be smaller. We want it to be more efficient. We want it to create opportunity, to empower us. And we want it to demand responsibility of people who aren't behaving responsibly. In short, we want it to reflect our interests and our values." And I think what they were saying is that the Republicans did a good job of defining us as the party of Government, and that's not a good place to be. I think that was a clear message that they were sending in the election.

Q. Those are all things, sir, that you have said. Are you essentially saying that the electorate yesterday was agreeing with you?

The President. I think they were agreeing with me, but they don't think we produced them. In other words—let me say it in another way. I'm saying that I agree with much of what the electorate said yesterday. Now, there were segments of that majority the Republicans put together obviously that I do not agree with and on matters of conviction I can't say I agreed with. I don't agree that we should repeal either the assault weapons ban or the Brady bill. The NRA would like to do that. I don't think we should. I don't agree that the answer to the abortion problem is to criminalize abortion again. That was a big part of that vote. So I'm still pro-choice, not because I'm pro-abortion; I'm not. But I still believe that it's a mistake to criminalize that. So I don't agree with all that.

But I think that the swing voters, the people that first of all voted for Bill Clinton and Ross Perot in '92 against the incumbent President and then voted for the Republicans for Congress against the incumbent Democrats—and in the challenging races and out in the country—were making a statement about what they think about Government. They still believe that Government is more often the problem than the solution. They don't want any party to be the party of Government. They don't want the presumption to be that people in Washington know what's best. They do want the Government to protect their interest, promote their values, I think, and to empower them. And then they want people held accountable.

So I'm saying that, to that extent, that message—I got it. I accept responsibility for not delivering. To whatever extent it's my fault that we haven't delivered back to the American people what they want on that, I have to accept that responsibility.

But you know, I've worked hard, the Vice President has worked hard on this whole business of downsizing the Government, deregulating several areas of our national life. We have not done as much as we are going to have to do to satisfy the voters, but we also have to recognize that this Government has a responsibility to protect and promote certain fundamental interests that I think the people really also want protected and promoted.

But they sent us a clear message. I got it, and I'm going to try to redouble my efforts to get there. I think that the Republican congressional leadership will at least have the chance to work with us. I'm going to do my dead-level best to do that, and to be less partisan. Most Americans are not strongly partisan, and they don't want us to be.

Downsizing Government

Q. Mr. President, if one of the signal messages of yesterday is that Americans want smaller Government, how much smaller do they want it, and what can you do to shrink it?

The President. Well, we're shrinking it already. One thing we can do——

Q. What can you do that you haven't done, that you haven't done already, to shrink it?

The President. Well, I think it's important, though—let me put the record out. All we have to do is to stay with the present 6-year plan, and we will reduce the size of Government by 272,000. We have already passed major laws to deregulate banking and interstate trucking. We have already given 20 States total freedom from Federal regulations to pursue their welfare reform experiments and about 9 States freedom

to pursue their health care experiments. And the education bill cuts a lot of Federal strings that are tied to the States to improve the performance of children in the schools.

So what I think we have to do is to look at every single Government department, every single Government program, and especially the nature of Government regulation and ask ourselves: Is there a better way to do this? Is this something where the American people will think we're more of a burden than a help? Is there a way to give more flexibility to people at the State and local level and in private life to achieve the same goal?

We're going to have to continue, in other words, to review everything that this Government does. And I think that there are more things that can be done. I'm going to propose them. I encourage the Republicans in Congress to propose them and the Democrats in Congress to propose them. I think that this is—we're in the middle of a revolution here in the way organizations work in America, in the world, and the Government is still behind the eight ball. And we're going to have to keep pushing until people believe that they have a Government that works for them, that they have confidence in, and that they think gives them good value for their dollar, and that doesn't overreach where they think it shouldn't overreach.

Wolf [Wolf Blitzer, Cable News Network].

Whitewater Investigation

Q. Mr. President, you know, the Republicans are taking over the Senate now and the House, so they'll be in charge of all of the committees. Are you especially concerned that Senator Alfonse D'Amato, if he becomes chairman of the Senate Banking Committee, and Representative Jim Leach, if he becomes chairman of the House Banking Committee, will now intensify their Whitewater investigations?

The President. No. I have said I would cooperate with the Congress, and I will continue to cooperate with the Congress, as I have. I think that they will have, obviously, other responsibilities as well now, and I think that they will just fulfill those responsibilities as they see fit. I'll do my best to fulfill my responsibilities.

One more.

Midterm Elections

Q. Mr. President, the recurring refrain in the preelection interviews was that this was the nastiest campaign in modern times. Do you agree with that? If you do agree, what do you think caused that, and what do you think can be done about it?

The President. Well, I think it is—the causes are many and complex, partly because of the real feelings people have about where they are in their own lives and what they saw here in Washington and how it was presented to them for a good long period of time, partly because of the enormous expenditure of funds for negative ads of all kinds. And I think campaign finance reform would help some. But let me say that there were pockets in this country, there were elections in this country where people won by being more positive and less negative, but they could only do it if the voters felt that they were part of a process.

If you ask me for one of the mistakes that I think that I have made since I've been here, I have spent so much time trying to pass bills through Congress that I haven't spent as much time as I was able to spend when I was running for President making sure that the people understood, were in on, and felt a part of the process by which we make decisions. And I believe that, again I will say, as much as the specific decisions that were made, it was the alienation people feel from the Government and the process.

Let me just give you another example. If you look at North Dakota, where Senator Conrad and Congressman Pomeroy were elected in a State where I lost by a large margin in 1992, and yet they supported these programs, these initiatives, and the economic plan, I asked myself: Did that happen in part because it's a small enough State where people can talk together, they can work together, they are less easily moved by the negative ads? What can I do to use modern technology better, to work with the Republicans in Congress and the Democrats to involve the American people in this as we go along? What responsibility is there? In other words, the President can work 60, 70 hours a week and lose his voice several times and pass a bunch of bills, and if people don't feel that they're a part of it, then so what if I'm signing another piece of paper up here.

If you look at—Governor Romer in Colorado has some very interesting thoughts about this and has worked very hard on this. But I think this is something that I'm going to have to really ask others about and get some advice about,

because one of the things I prided the 1992 campaign on—and I give credit to the other candidates as well—but for all of the attacks and the criticisms in '92, the fact that there were some negative ads back and forth, the truth is we had a big turnout based largely on hope. We had three debates, one of which people were involved in, ordinary citizens. We had countless town meetings, two of the candidates did. We had other things that constantly made the American people feel that they had some say up here. And I think that—to go back to Brit's question—I think that part of it is they think that we get up here and we just get up every day and, even if we're working hard, we just are going this way, when they may want to go this way. And it just doesn't mean anything to them. They worry then about having a Government that is more of a burden than a support. And it's something we have to find a way to crack. It's not a simple issue.

I'll take one more. Go ahead.

Democratic Party's Future

Q. Do you feel at all that this election has pushed you politically to the right? And would you have any message for the Democrats in Congress, like Senator Shelby, who are considering or might be considering switching to the Republican Party?

The President. I think he did switch.

Q. Yes, I know, but if there are Democrats in the House who are considering switching.

The President. Oh, I see what you mean. Well, first of all, let me say that if we can have a bipartisan coalition, then we can be both nonpolitical and more centrist. I ran for President saying that we should not be governed— we should not be governed by either Republicans or Democrats who are pushed too far in either direction, that most of the good ideas are ideas that take us into the future, not push us left or right.

There were times when our inability to have cooperation in the Congress dictated a solution that came primarily out of the Democrats. When we got cooperation, when we were able to work together—to give you two examples—on NAFTA and on the crime bill I ultimately signed, we had a bill I think that resonated pretty well with the American people. So I feel good about that. I want to have a bipartisan cooperation.

A lot of the things they have advocated I have advocated, like the line-item veto, the lobby reform, the congressional reform, further reductions in unnecessary spending and regulation. I do not believe that we should give up on our efforts to make the economy stronger, the streets safer, our people better educated, our families more supported in the work of parenting and work. But I think there's a lot we can work together on that will be consistent with my convictions, consistent with what I have always believed, consistent with what I've always worked for. And when we can do that, we ought to do that.

I always felt, in the last 2 years, that we could work together, consistent with our convictions, more than we were working together because of politics. When we can't work together because our convictions are different, I will stand on my convictions.

Yes, go ahead.

Q. Even before you ran for President, you had an idea of where the Democratic Party had to go to reclaim the center and become a majority again. Now that your party is a minority in Congress and in the statehouses, what do Democrats have to do to avoid becoming a permanent minority party?

The President. I think we have to, first of all, as I said, take a little nap, take a little sleep, take a little rest, let the Republicans enjoy their victories, and analyze why they won, and ask ourselves to what extent do we also believe some of the things the voters believe.

You know, sometimes in life—let me just say this—sometimes in life, you have to be in the minority because you just cannot, in good conscience, go along with what's popular. Sometimes that happens. I really regret the loss of some of these fine young progressive Members of Congress who clearly are in the mainstream of their views to the people back home, because they could not defend themselves against either the efforts of certain groups on votes like the crime bill or because they couldn't find a way to convince the majority of their constituents that when they voted for that economic plan it would bring the deficit down, it was a sacrifice worth making, it will make the country stronger. I regret that.

But those people did what was right for their country and for the future. And if they hadn't done it, we wouldn't be where we are today economically, and we would be in a terrible fix with regard to the deficit. And we wouldn't have the middle class college loan program. We wouldn't have a lot of things. So I regret that.

But I think we have to analyze the results of the elections, hear what the voters were saying, and go back to them and say: We believe that the Government is not inherently bad. We agree that the Government needs to be smaller and more efficient. We believe it needs to reflect our values as well as our interests. And we believe that we have more to offer in that regard, and here is what it is and here is what the distinctions are.

That, I think, was the work that we have been trying to do for 10 years. I believe that a lot of these things that we saw yesterday were the culmination of many years of trends, as well as a dissatisfaction with the last 2 years. And I think that we have an opportunity now to go back and capture the imagination of the American people with good ideas consistent with Democratic values.

I've got to go. Thank you.

NOTE: The President's 78th news conference began at 3:33 p.m. in the East Room at the White House.

Remarks at the Edmund A. Walsh School of Foreign Service at Georgetown University
November 10, 1994

Thank you very much, Father O'Donovan, for your introduction and for our wonderful trip to the Middle East. Thank you, Dean Krogh, for your comments and for your outstanding leadership. To the Members of Congress, the Cabinet, and the administration who are here, members of the faculty, the diplomatic corps, the students, and a special word of hello and thanks to many of my former classmates who are here. It's nice for us to be here with no obligation to take notes. [*Laughter*]

I want to thank Robert Wagner for endowing this series of lectures, and also Ron Lignelli and the Georgetown Phantoms for keeping you all entertained. It is wonderful to be back in this magnificent hall. And I am particularly honored to be here to give this first, inaugural lecture.

In the fall of 1964, with about 200 other freshmen in the School of Foreign Service, I was enrolled in Carroll Quigley's Western civilization course. All of us—that was 30 years ago; it's kind of spooky now to think about it. [*Laughter*] All of us who were there then—and there were a bunch of us here who were there then—we can remember things from those lectures. At the end of the series he did a lecture on Plato, and he always had this appropriately beat-up copy of the "Republic" which he ripped into at the end of the lecture and threw across the room and said, "Plato was a fascist." [*Laughter*]

Even then I was a decent politician, and I remember the best grade I made on any of his tests was the question about Plato and the myth of the cave, and I only wrote one page in the little test book and three other lines. And he said, "If you can explain it in this short a duration, you obviously understand it"—[*laughter*]—"98." Hooray! I might add, it was the only 98 I received in the entire year. [*Laughter*]

Carroll Quigley's ideas were expressed well, both in the very terse prose of his book on civilizations and the high drama of his lectures. He left a lasting impression, I think, on every one of us who ever entered his class. And as you have already heard Father O'Donovan say, he drummed into us that Western civilization was the greatest of all, and America was the best expression of Western civilization because of its commitment to future preference, the belief that the future could be better than the present and that we have an obligation to make it so. It is interesting that we would come here today at a time when, frankly, a lot of our fellow Americans, in the face of ample evidence to support Carroll Quigley's dictum, are not sure they believe it anymore.

Three years ago, here in this hall as a candidate for President, I had an opportunity on three different occasions to speak about those lessons of Professor Quigley's and how I thought they applied to the present moment. And I expressed the belief then that, working together, we could shape the future and meet the challenges of a rapidly changing world at home and abroad at the end of the cold war, but that we could only do it by leaving behind the old political debates and the divisions and forging a new dynamic center of American politics, not a compromise but a move forward based on the ideas of opportunity, responsibility, and community.

I argued 3 years ago that the main job of Government is not to solve all our problems. In this day and age, it simply can't do that. But it's also not to sit on the sidelines and shout and preach at people because that's not enough. Instead, I believed then and I believe today that the primary obligation of Government is to empower citizens to make the most of their own lives and then to insist on responsible behavior in turn.

Finally, I urged that we should see ourselves not as isolated individuals but as members of interdependent communities, locally, nationally, and of course, globally, communities in which we have to work together if we're going to make the most of our opportunities and deal with our problems.

After I was elected President, I was well aware going into the office that it would be very difficult to translate these ideas into specific policies, then to get them enacted into law, and to keep the country with me during a process which would take time and patience, which would inevitably be contentious, and which would require a delicate balance between a determination to stand on principle and a willingness to have principled compromise.

Why is this? First of all, the problems we face are absolutely immense. The social problems of crime and violence, rooted in the breakdown of families and communities, have been building in this country for 30 years at least. And they plainly require for their reversal much more than specific governmental actions. Indeed, no matter what we do, millions of Americans are going to have to decide to change their ways, to put the interest of their families, their communities, and their own personal development ahead of momentary selfish impulses.

The economic problems we face—the stagnation of American incomes, the declining rate of security in jobs and health care and retirement—these things have been building for 20 years. And they, too, plainly require for their reversal more than simply specific governmental policy changes, although these are imperative.

The pressures of the global economy are relentless and dynamic. And Government can help to deal with them, but it cannot reverse them. The fact that workers must be willing to upgrade their education and their skills throughout a lifetime is absolute. Government can help to create opportunities to do that, but workers must take advantage of them and cannot deny the facts of economic life.

We also know that in this time, particularly as we are going through a period of change, people feel uncertainty because they don't have a new framework within which to view the world after the cold war that is neat and understandable and that has a definable enemy. And here at home, people feel genuine insecurities that are personal to them, an uncertainty about their personal future.

We see it all the time. Yesterday there were several stories about people saying, "Well, yeah, there has been a recovery, but I don't think it's going to last." There is this feeling that we're waiting for the other shoe to drop. A lot of people feel that even as they walk home every day. I never will forget the man in New York who told me during the campaign—he was working in a hotel—that he had come here from another country; he was proud to be an immigrant. He was doing well economically. But his son wasn't free. And I asked him what he meant, and he said, "Because my son can't walk across the street and play in the park unless I go with him. My son can't even walk two blocks to school unless I go with him." He said, "My son has read up on all the candidates. He says I should vote for you. If I do, I want you to do one simple thing: Make my son free." In this atmosphere, people are easily unsettled.

Finally, there is the immutable fact that in every age and time, real change is difficult. Most everybody is for change in general but then against it in particular. Machiavelli said over 400 years ago, "It must be considered that there is nothing more difficult to carry out, nor more doubtful of success, nor dangerous to handle than to initiate a new order of things." He turned out to be pretty smart. [*Laughter*]

In spite of all these difficulties, until Tuesday I thought we'd made a pretty good beginning. [*Laughter*]

The voters clearly all along had wanted smaller, more effective, less intrusive Government that reflects both our values and our interests, governmental action that brings stability into their lives and doesn't create too many problems because most folks think they've got enough problems already. But they plainly want us also to be strong and secure and to lead them into the next century in a country that is strong and secure, with the American dream alive.

The reason I thought we'd done pretty well is that in the last 22 months, we brought the deficit down more than at any time in history in a comparable period, and next year we'll have 3 years of deficit reduction in a row for the first time since Mr. Truman was President. We've reduced the Federal work force by 70,000 already and put it on a path to shrink to its smallest size since Mr. Kennedy was President. More than 5 million new jobs have come into our economy, and this year for the first time in a good, long while, a lot of them are high-wage jobs. We have more high-wage jobs coming into the American economy this year than in the last 5 years combined.

We have deregulated significant parts of our economy, and we've freed States from regulation so that they can pursue their own paths to reform welfare and health care and education.

We passed a very strong crime bill with tough penalties and funds for prison and police and with prevention programs that have enjoyed the support of members of both parties and all law enforcement agencies. We've supported working families with the family leave law, with childhood immunizations, with expanded Head Start and more affordable college loans and income tax cuts for 15 million working families with incomes of up to $27,000.

We've expanded trade dramatically in these last 2 years, opened new markets, relaxed a lot of our controls on our own products so they can be sold overseas in the aftermath of the cold war. We have kept the world's strongest, most mobile, most flexible defense. We've worked for peace and freedom from the Persian Gulf and the Middle East to Northern Ireland and southern Africa and of course in Haiti. And for the first time since the dawn of the nuclear age, there are no Russian missiles pointed at the people of the United States.

Most of these measures required the support of members of my party in Congress, especially in the especially polarized environment in which we have been operating. In an ordinary time, that record would have generated support for Congress men and women who made it, and a desire to have more people to have that kind of record continue. Even though some of the decisions were tough, and change is always controversial, and there is always a lag time between when change occurs and when it is felt, nonetheless, in an ordinary time, even though tough decisions were required, especially in the area of deficit reduction and crime where things had gotten so out of hand for so long, the people who made that record would have been supported.

But this is no ordinary time. And on Tuesday the voters reflected their frustration with the pace of change and the messy and often, to them, almost revolting process by which it was made; their frustration that some things were not done which ought to have been done, particularly in the area of political reform. And they clearly said that we have to do more to limit Government's reach into their lives and to make more efficient the Government they pay for.

They also thought that, frankly, we sent them some mixed signals, especially in the area of the economic program, the crime bill with the very controversial assault weapons ban, and the health care program, where after over $200 million by the best estimates had been spent by people who were organized against it, a remarkable feat of reverse plastic surgery was performed.

Well, anyway, the reasons for this vote will be analyzed by experts who are more objective than I am for a long time. But you don't have to be as bright as a tree full of owls to say that it was a smashing victory for the Republicans, for their strategy, their tactics, and their message that Government is no longer the problem—that was their message in the eighties—now Government is the enemy.

Well, I think it's also clear that I bear some responsibilities for policies and political decisions that hurt our candidates. I do believe that we were moving in the right direction, and I think we have to continue to try to address the problems of this country. But I also regret particularly the loss of those who were trying to take the country in the direction that the voters said they wanted: the people who voted to reduce the deficit, to reduce Government, to deregulate large areas of our economy; people who voted

to break partisan gridlock. I regret that in this swirl, this national sea change, that people who actually were building the blocks of the future that the American people in every survey say they want were lost to the Congress. And I hope they will have a chance to serve again.

Regardless, the American people have now entrusted their fate and their future to a Republican-led Congress and a Democratic President. I have heard them, and I will continue to listen closely to them. With all my strength I will work to pursue the new Democrat agenda I outlined here at Georgetown in 1991. And I hope the Republicans will move beyond the rancor of the campaign rhetoric to be new Republicans as well.

After all, the American people told us to make America work for them. They want to be the subject of this debate—not the Republicans, not the Democrats, not the President, not the Congress—they want to be the subject of this debate. They want us to rebuild the American dream, to stop playing politics now and start pulling together.

I know we can do it. There is clear evidence in what has already happened in the last couple of years. In this last Congress, there were bipartisan majorities who stood up for education reform, for the new trade agreements, for national service, for a tough crime bill, for many other efforts to move our country forward.

Now the American people want us to move ahead to help solve the problems that still block our progress as a people. I am ready to share responsibility with the Republican Party when it assumes leadership in the Congress. I ask them only to join me in the center of public debate, the place where the best ideas for the next generation must arise. I ask them to join me in moving forward to keep America strong. Already there are areas where clearly we can work together: welfare reform, congressional reform, the line-item veto, continuing efforts to reduce and reinvent Government. And I must say, their term limits proposal is looking better to me every day. [*Laughter*]

I hope we'll be working together on lobby reform, campaign finance reform, continued advances in education and training, and health care reform that leads us to real solutions. Above all, we must not do anything to jeopardize this country's economic recovery.

All of us who do the people's business must be ready to work, as Professor Quigley said over and over again, to make the future better than the present. That commitment is not only important at home, it is terribly important when it comes to our crucial role in the world. From the beginning of this administration, we have chosen to engage fully in this rapidly changing world, and the results are known to the people the world over, from Haiti to North Korea, from Northern Ireland to the Middle East. We have remained firm in our commitments to build greater security, to spread democracy, and to usher in a new age of prosperity and open markets all across the world.

Today I want to talk with you about the third of those goals, our strategy in the global economy, and three crucial events that are coming up in rapid succession in the next couple of weeks that will help to broaden and bolster our progress.

When I came to this hall as a candidate for President in 1991, I said something that I'm still having trouble getting everybody in the country to focus on, that we had to tear down the wall in our thinking between domestic and foreign policy and forge a new economic policy, rooted in our own security interests, that would serve ordinary Americans by launching a new era of global growth. I argued then that all our efforts to lead the world would fail if we weren't strong at home, but that if we withdrew from the emerging global economy, our workers and our families would inevitably be hurt. And from the day I took office, we have acted on those beliefs.

Our economic strategy embraces change and prosperity, growth and security. We are pursuing this strategy because it promotes peace and prosperity around the world, but also because it is clearly in the interests of our working people and their families. It's good for American families. It produces high-wage jobs. It's a strategy that enables the United States to keep leading the fight to open markets worldwide, a strategy to promote free trade and the growth that undergirds democracies and helps to assure peace, a strategy to help every American family, every American worker, every American farmer benefit from the worldwide growth and the prosperity it will yield. The center, the heart of our economic policy must be an unbreakable link between what we do to open the global marketplace and what we do to empower American workers to deal with that marketplace.

Understandably, at the end of the cold war when the nuclear threat is receding, when we have so many pressing problems here at home and when people are clearly worried about their own personal circumstances, and when the Government itself faces serious financial constraints because of years and years and years of piling up massive deficits, there are those on both the traditional left and traditional right in our country who would like us to withdraw more from the world, politically, strategically, economically, to stay more within our own borders.

We have not; and we need only look around the world, to Kuwait, to the former Soviet Union, to the Middle East, to the Korean Peninsula, to NATO and its Partnership For Peace, to Haiti to see how important it is for America to continue the role of engagement in the world.

Long before the cold war was over, a new global economy was emerging, an economy which started 20 years ago to put great pressures on the wages and benefits of our working people, to put great pressure on many of our companies to compete and win, to make internal changes in order to survive and prosper.

Now, this has helped to prompt a serious question about what our country should want and about whether Government should act or should retreat in this area of our national life. I think what we have to want is a strong America, a strong America in terms of national security and national defense, but also in terms of stronger families, better education, higher paying jobs, and safer streets. Strong at home, strong abroad; two sides of the same coin.

The United States has never been in a stronger economic position to meet both these challenges to compete and win in the world. We have the world's most productive work force, an economy that is gaining strength every day, an economy that just since I became President has created now over 5 million new jobs. And as I said, there are more high-wage jobs this year than there have been in the previous 5 years. And this gives us some hope that finally we have begun to move to counteract this 20-year trend of stagnant wages, a trend which unbelievably last year—at a time when we had rapid growth, millions of new jobs, and no inflation—still led to a slight drop in the average income of American workers.

Our Government is working as a partner with the private sector on this strategy. We are reemerging as the world's largest producer of automobiles, for the first time in 15 years. We've regained our position as the globe's top seller of semiconductors. We're creating the industries of tomorrow, from biotechnology to express delivery. We've opened markets with our Japanese partners in products from cellular telephones to rice. We've sold power plants to India, fiber optic systems to Indonesia. Our businesses are proving that they can meet and beat the global competition if only given a chance to do so.

But we know that we cannot meet the challenges of competition unless we help all Americans also adjust to the changes we're all facing. For too many of our people, trade still appears to be a gale-force wind, just another threat ready to blow away the prospects of a stable job at a good wage, just another problem adding to the already unstable, uncertain condition of their lives.

I believe that if we continue to work together on this trade issue—Democrats, Republicans, and independents—as Americans, we can agree on ways to help all our people make their way in the new economy. We must help workers whose jobs are threatened by changing the workplace, by doing what we have to do to help them deal with imports or shifting winds. They'll have to retool. They'll have to reengage. But we can do that.

In the recovery which is occurring now, the economy has created more high-wage jobs. It is growing steadily. But as I said, our workers' wages, millions of them, are still caught in that period of stagnation. And last year more than a million Americans lost their health insurance. Almost all of them were in working families. This is not a problem that will go away. We are the only nation with an advanced economy, the only one, where in the last 10 years the percentage of our people with health care coverage under 65 has declined. So it is easy to understand why many Americans still aren't feeling the impact of growth. It's also easy to understand why many Americans are frustrated by what it takes to sustain that growth.

On Tuesday morning, I had an interesting conversation with a radio talk show host in Detroit who said to me, "Mr. President, I'm not one of those cynics." He said, "I see these jobs coming into our economy. The biggest problem we've got now in the auto industry is people complaining about overtime." But he said, "I want to ask you something. Is it absolutely necessary for the Fed to raise interest rates every time we announce more jobs? I don't mind helping other people to get jobs, but I don't see why my income should go down just because we're hiring new people." And he said, "If you've got a variable mortgage, or you're about to go buy a car, that's what happens. We get punished. The economy adds jobs; my income goes down. I don't get it. If there were inflation, I would understand." These are interesting questions, but this is the way the American people are thinking about this complex global society in which we live.

So our ultimate goal has to be to both spur the growth and provide the skills and create the package of high-wage jobs that will reverse the trend and increase the ability of our people to feel secure in the face of all this change, to see the changes that are going on as our friend and not our enemy. Of course, I believe very strongly that the only way we can do it is to keep breaking down barriers and keep expanding our exports. Every billion dollars in exports creates about 16,000 jobs in America, and on average, those jobs pay much better than other jobs in our work force.

Look at NAFTA, our trade agreement with Mexico and Canada that provided our greatest moment of bipartisan cooperation in the last Congress. Thanks to NAFTA, new exports to Mexico and Canada have helped our businesses create as many as 100,000 jobs. In the 6 months after the treaty's adoption, exports from the United States to Mexico increased by nearly 20 percent, about 3 times the rate of our overall export growth in this time of economic expansion. And the future looks brighter still and will be even brighter as the growth rate in Mexico picks up.

But NAFTA and the debate that led up to its passage also reminds us of the changing nature of the economy. In a time when capital and factories and entire industries are completely mobile, our competitive edge and the ultimate source of our wealth must be our own people's knowledge and skill and their ability to continue to learn throughout a lifetime. At the dawn of this century, this new century, and indeed this new millennium, the livelihoods of one-half our people will depend upon their ability to engage in what we now call lifetime learning. As never before, we are what we know; we earn based on what we learn.

Again I say, this should not be a partisan issue. We should continue our vigorous program to give our children and our workers the world's finest education and training and retraining. In less than 2 years, with bipartisan support in Congress, we've already expanded Head Start, established the first-ever national standards for our schools, put our Nation on the right road by saying, "Here are the national standards; we'll help you measure how you're doing. But you get to decide, with fewer Federal strings, not more, how to meet those standards."

We've created a national network of youth apprenticeship programs to help high school students who want to go on into the workplace, don't go to college, but do want good jobs to continue to increase their educational attainment, again with bipartisan support. We reformed the student loan program to give millions and millions of Americans lower cost and better repayment options so that no one should ever refrain from going to college because they're afraid to borrow the money because they're afraid they'll never pay it back.

Now, our next big challenge in the coming Congress is to replace the unemployment system with reemployment, helping workers who are laid off, most of whom now will never be called back to their jobs, but who do need new training to develop new skills and find new jobs. The present unemployment system is geared to yesterday's economy. It is premised on the idea that you will be called back to your old job and you will be given a living standard that is far below what you're earning in the workplace just to get you by until you're called back. Most people are not called back in America anymore, and it is time to fundamentally change that system. It would be better for workers, but it would plainly be better for employers as well because they would not be paying for an unemployment system that does not achieve the objectives that it was originally designed to achieve.

This will help our workers because, as I say, nobody, nobody can promise to remove the uncertainty from modern international economic life. They will face uncertainty whether we act or not. What we wish our people to do is to look at the future with more confidence, more optimism. And if together we help them to get the tools they need to be ready for whatever the future holds, they will be able to do that.

In the coming weeks, we have the opportunity to continue pursuing our economic strategy and to put in place three more crucial building blocks for American success in the 21st century. Next week, as part of our strategy to develop regional initiatives that put the United States at the center of emerging and dynamic regions, I'll be in Indonesia to meet with leaders of the Asia-Pacific Economic Cooperation forum. I'll be following that up with meeting with 33 democratically elected leaders of our hemisphere at next month's Summit of the Americas down in Miami. And in the midst of these meetings, as Congress reconvenes, we'll be engaged in an historic effort to pass GATT, the largest, most comprehensive trade agreement ever.

In this century there have been a handful of congressional votes that have demonstrated what kind of country we are and what kind of people we're going to be. The vote on the League of Nations after the First World War was one. And when the United States failed to engage, we paid a terrible price and so did the rest of the world in economic stagnation, isolation, and eventually another world war.

After the second war, Congress faced a vote on the Marshall plan. At that time, we rose to the challenge and put aside our partisan differences and helped to launch 50 years of peace and prosperity, not only with the Marshall plan but with other institutions that rebuilt our former enemies and constructed the framework of security which enabled us ultimately to prevail in the cold war.

Now once again we face such a test. The United States has been leading the world in pushing for the adoption of GATT. And now we've got to follow through and lead once again. We should not delay GATT. That will jeopardize our leadership and our prosperity. Negotiations among scores of nations have produced an agreement that will produce the biggest tax cut in history and in the long run help tie together a global economy and usher in a new era of prosperity. It is the key link to free trade, more open societies, and economic growth all around this world.

For the United States it means both free and fair trade. For 40 years our markets have been more open than those of other major economies. These rules are not right for 1994. GATT will require all nations to finally do what we have already done, cut tariffs, eliminate nontariff barriers, protect copyrights and patents. It will create hundreds of thousands of new jobs here in United States, good-paying jobs, and it will level the playing field for our companies, our workers, our farmers. It will make our exports more competitive, exactly when our ability to send more American products and services overseas is expanding.

For 8 years, Presidents of both parties, from President Reagan to President Bush to our administration, have worked hard to complete this agreement. We were able to do it. GATT has enjoyed the kind of broad bipartisan support in Congress that NAFTA did. And it's supported by a wide range of business and consumer and farm groups. I invite the leaders and the members of both parties once again to put aside our partisan differences and do what's right for all Americans. And I'm confident that Congress will ratify the GATT this month.

While we work to pass GATT, I'll also be looking ahead to continuing to cement our relations with two of the fastest growing regions in the world, Asia and Latin America. For decades, our sights have been set on traditional economic relationships, the large, mature economies of Europe and Japan. These nations will remain close allies, key competitors, and critical markets for us. But the new century demands a new strategy, and it is clear that the young, vigorous economies of Asia and the Western Hemisphere offer enormous untapped potential for our people to prosper.

Consider this: Asia's dynamic economies account now for 4 out of every 10 dollars of world trade. Almost one-third of our own exports go now to the Pacific Rim. Markets in Asia have already created more than 2 million American jobs. And over the next 6 years, the Asian members of APEC plan to invest $1.1 trillion in infrastructure, enough to rebuild 15 Santa Monica freeways every day.

Yet, despite these opportunities, the presence of stiff economic competition and the end of the cold war have left some Asians to wonder whether we're ready to withdraw from the region. Nothing could be further from the truth. That's why, after visiting six countries in 3 days in the Middle East, and coming home for 8 days of this campaign, and trying to stand here without missing a beat on my speech—[*laughter*]—I am going to Indonesia to say, we remain engaged.

We must say to the world, we will maintain and strengthen our bilateral security relationships with Japan, with South Korea, with Australia, with the Philippines, with Thailand and others, including that forward presence of our troops to deter conflict. We will encourage stronger regional security structures, and we will continue our active work to implement the agreement for a nonnuclear Korean Peninsula.

We are also committed to expand our economic ties across the Pacific. And as I said, in spite of all the events of the last few days and the fact that I'm a little bit jet-lagged from the first round, I think it's important for the United States to be in Jakarta. When we met in Seattle a year ago it was at my invitation, because I wanted the leaders of the 14 Asian economies to come together for the first time, to invigorate APEC, to embrace a vision of a new Asia-Pacific community with no artificial dividing line down the middle of the Pacific.

Next week we'll move from a common vision to a common direction. We'll work to set concrete goals to open the way for doing business in Asia, taking down tariff walls, eliminating nontariff barriers, simplifying procedures and standards to smooth the flow of goods. I hope and I expect we'll set a target date for achieving free and open trade among all the Asia-Pacific economies.

APEC is fundamentally an economic institution, so our meetings will focus on those questions. But there will be private meetings, and during them, I will also raise some other questions. I'll raise our concerns about many other issues, including the progress of human rights and democracy in the region.

These things require patience and persistence, but we must not give up on our commitment to the values in which we believe, even as we pursue our own economic interests. Over the long run, we have learned in America that justice and progress go hand-in-hand, and it will also be true for our interests in the world.

Even though there may be no sudden breakthroughs, we must continue to be persistent. As in the past, I will be doing everything I can to be frank in terms of our differences as well as our potential partnerships with the Chinese, with the Indonesians, and with others.

I don't think we have to choose between increasing trade and fostering human rights and open societies. Experience shows us over and over again that commerce can promote cooperation, that more prosperity helps to open societies to the world, and that the more societies are open the more they understand that maximizing freedom and prosperity can go hand-in-hand. The rule of law, accountable government, the free flow of ideas, all these things encourage economic development and political maturity and freedom.

The advance of human rights and democratic values also requires strong government-to-government contacts. So I'll continue to promote without apology those rights and values in Asia and around the world. We have a long history of friendly relations with Indonesia, with other countries, but we are engaged in a range of bilateral and global issues with the Indonesians, with the Chinese, and with others. We recognize and we respect the differences among cultures. Like all Americans, I struggle with our own society's ongoing tensions and inequities and very difficult social problems. But I don't believe the search for human dignity is peculiar to the American culture. Everywhere people aspire to be treated with dignity, to give voice to their opinions, to have a say in choosing their leaders. At a time when we are strong enough to inspire people around the world, we have to keep pressing on for freedom.

In Asia and elsewhere, we have good reason for hope, we have good reason for progress because free markets and democracy are on the move. The new global community is taking place all around the world, enshrouding the values of tolerance and liberty and civil society. I guess I really do believe that history is on our side and we have to keep trying to push it along.

If we're looking for further confirmation of these trends, of course, we can find them in abundance in our own hemisphere. One month from now, leaders from South and Central America, the Caribbean, and North America will be in Miami at our invitation to discuss the future of our hemisphere and to celebrate the spread of freedom and democracy. Think of it: 33 leaders, including President Aristide of Haiti, will attend the Summit of the Americas, the first such hemispheric gathering in almost three decades; all democratically elected leaders.

There, we'll be able to work to strengthen the roots of those democracies through sustainable development; we'll be able to take crucial steps to increase trade, to maintain growth in the region, to lay concrete plans to open markets, to expand trade. We'll have a partnership for prosperity that stretches from Canada to the tip of South America. It means more jobs and higher income. It also means more peace, more freedom, and more security.

As with GATT and APEC, the Summit of the Americas will move us toward a future of greater prosperity. It will tie us to new partners. And if we follow through, historians will look back at these events and see that our generation reached across the oceans and the borders to cement relationships with nations that will rank among the economic and political powers of the 21st century. We will have demonstrated that the American people have learned the lessons of the past, have learned the lessons of the present, and are ready for all the challenges that lie ahead.

Thirty years ago in this hall, Carroll Quigley told the class of freshmen that I was a part of that our greatness rested on the extraordinarily American belief that we could make the future better than the past. Many Americans today don't believe it, but the evidence is there; the future is there. We have to have the courage to act on that belief, to seize that future, and to keep our people optimistic, outward-looking, and strong. If we are strong in our convictions, the reality is that our future will be strong as well.

Thank you all, and God bless you.

NOTE: The President spoke at 11:36 a.m. in Gaston Hall at Georgetown University. In his remarks, he referred to Rev. Leo J. O'Donovan, S.P.J., president, Georgetown University; Peter F. Krogh, dean, School of Foreign Service; and alumnus Robert Wagner.

Remarks on the Appointment of Patsy Fleming as National AIDS Policy Director and an Exchange With Reporters
November 10, 1994

The President. Thank you very much, Secretary Shalala, ladies and gentlemen. In the last 13 years, AIDS has claimed the lives of more than a quarter million of our fellow citizens.

Today, it is the leading cause of death among all Americans between the ages of 25 and 44.

For nearly every American now, the face of AIDS is no longer the face of a stranger but the face of a friend. Now more than ever, we must redouble our efforts for effective treatments, for a vaccine, for a cure.

I have committed this administration to working hard to stop the spread of HIV and to finding a cure for AIDS. In the last 2 years, as Secretary Shalala said, we've increased the Federal resources directed at AIDS by 30 percent. We've increased funding for AIDS-related research by 25 percent, funding for the Ryan White Care Act by 82 percent, bringing services to thousands of Americans who are in desperate need of medical and social services. We've reorganized the Office of AIDS Research at NIH. And we've done this at a time when, this year, for the first time in 25 years, there was an actual reduction in Federal domestic, as well as, defense spending. We've stepped up our efforts to develop and improve new AIDS drugs. We're working hard to find an effective vaccine. We've put forth a very frank HIV prevention campaign aimed at young adults.

And soon we'll announce the creation of a new advisory council made up of experts from the community to advise our administration on the important steps that must still be taken in this fight. We're making progress, but we have to keep pressing forward. Defeating this epidemic demands a disciplined and passionate approach.

That's why I'm so pleased to announce the appointment of Patsy Fleming to serve as the AIDS Policy Director here at the White House. For more than a decade, she has been an important voice in our national response to HIV and AIDS. She helped to shape our new AIDS education message and push for aggressive AIDS drug development. She put together an immediate response to research results that could help to stem the rate of infection from infants born to HIV positive women.

In her short tenure as the interim AIDS Policy Coordinator, her tremendous performance convinced me that she is the best person for the job. And I'm glad she decided to accept my request that she stay on. She'll head a newly structured AIDS Policy Office. She'll have direct access to me, to members of the Cabinet. She'll play an important role in developing our budget and our policy proposals.

I ask her to provide me with a detailed report on the rapid increase of AIDS among adolescents and to examine the efforts we are now making to reverse these terribly troubling trends. As we continue our struggle against this disease, I'm pleased to have her at my side.

And as I ask her to come up and make remarks, I'd just like to remind all of you that—and all the people who are watching this day—that this is a disease with a human face. And my human face today is—I would like to dedicate this announcement to my dear friend Elizabeth Glaser.

Thank you.

Do you want the box back? Where's the box?

Ms. Fleming. I'm a little shorter than you are.

Secretary Shalala. It's my box. [*Laughter*]

The President. This is a step up. [*Laughter*]

[*At this point, Ms. Fleming thanked the President and outlined her agenda as Director of the Office of National AIDS Policy.*]

Representative Newt Gingrich

Q. Mr. President, can you respond to Newt Gingrich calling you a "countercultural McGovern-nik"? [*Laughter*]

The President. I'm a middle-age man who's worked very hard in his life—[*laughter*]—to be a mainstream American. And I think I've done a reasonable job of it.

Q. Do you think this will make it harder to work with him if he keeps coming out with statements like that, sir?

The President. Oh, the American people can draw their own conclusions. I can only control my own words and my own deeds. My hand is open to them—[*inaudible*].

Office of National AIDS Policy

Q. Sir, a question on AIDS. AIDS activists and gay groups have demanded you pick a prominent, high-profile czar and also asked for a seat at the Cabinet table. Why did you choose this route and what about the seat at the Cabinet table?

The President. Because I think that—I made a decision that—the most important thing we could have is a good advocate, is a person I knew, had great confidence in, and had real access to the White House and a real chance to influence me and my decisions.

I think it was the right decision. And a very large number of people who are interested in

AIDS recommended it to me even before I told them I was thinking about it. So I think that the people who are here can answer the question better than me.

Thank you.

NOTE. The President spoke at 1:55 p.m. in the Roosevelt Room at the White House.

Remarks on the Asian-Pacific Trip
November 11, 1994

The President. Good morning. I want to speak with you for just a few moments before I leave on this trip to the Philippines and Indonesia. From the beginning of our administration, we have worked to build greater security for America, to spread prosperity and democracy around the globe, and to usher in a new age of open markets. We are tearing down the old walls which have existed for so long between domestic and foreign policy in our country, forging a strong recovery here at home by expanding opportunities for Americans around the world.

We are pursuing this strategy because it is clearly in the best interest of our people, and it offers the best opportunity for them to acquire the kind of security for their families that so many millions of Americans are still struggling to achieve. The ultimate goal is to produce a strong America, a strong America in terms of national security and national defense but also in terms of stronger families, better education, more high-wage jobs, and safer streets. Strong at home and strong abroad: two sides of the same coin.

The United States is in a better economic position than any other nation in the world today to compete and win in the global economy. Our work force is the most productive in the world. Our economy has produced 5 million jobs and more in the last 22 months. And finally, this year, high-wage jobs are coming back into this economy, more new high-wage jobs this year than in the previous 5 years combined.

But it is not enough. Too many Americans, millions and millions of them, still find the present and the future uncertain and unsettling: stagnant wages, benefits at risk, an uncertainty in the future about their jobs. We simply must turn insecurity about our future into confidence. The American people do best when they are confident, outward looking, and working together.

This strategy must include breaking down trade barriers, opening markets, and increasing our exports because export-related jobs pay significantly more on the average than those which are not related to exports.

In the coming weeks, we will have the opportunity to put into place three crucial building blocks of this strategy by working with Congress to pass the GATT agreement, by strengthening our ties to the dynamic economies of the Asian-Pacific region, and by continuing to forge a partnership for peace and prosperity here in our own hemisphere. For decades, we have concentrated our international economic efforts on the mature and strong economies of Europe and Japan. They will remain our close allies, our key competitors, our critical markets.

But the new century demands a new strategy, and that is where this trip fits into the picture. Last year in Seattle, I brought together 14 leaders of the economies of the Asian-Pacific cooperation council. They met for the first time, and there we arrived at a common vision of a new and more open Asian-Pacific community. Next week in Jakarta, I hope the leaders will embrace a common direction toward that vision, setting a goal for free and open trade among all our countries and agreeing on a process to get there.

In my visit to the Philippines and my meetings in Jakarta, I will also stress our continuing commitment to promote security and democracy throughout Asia and the Pacific region. We'll discuss how to strengthen important bilateral relationships, create stronger regional security structures, how to rapidly and effectively implement the agreement for a nonnuclear Korean Peninsula. No problem is more important to the United States and its allies than stopping the proliferation of nuclear materials and weapons in general and specifically ending North Korea's nuclear program. I will also use these meetings to talk about the advance of human rights, worker rights, and democratic values. We must continue to pursue this path with patience, persistence, and determination.

Two other crucial events will follow this trip to Asia: the Summit of the Americas in Miami, with 33 other democratically elected leaders in the Caribbean and Latin America, and the congressional vote on GATT. GATT is the largest and most advantageous trade agreement in our history. The congressional vote will be a defining decision for our economy and our working people well into the next century. I believe both parties will come together to vote for open markets, free and fair trade, and most importantly, more high- wage jobs for the American people.

This week the American people told us, all of us here in Washington, to work together, to put politics aside to create a stronger, a more secure America. This trip to Asia and the other events of the next 6 weeks give us a unique opportunity to join hands and do just that. By reaching across oceans and borders, we can help to build peace and prosperity around the world and more security and prosperity for our own people here at home.

Thank you very much.

Q. Mr. President, how would you describe the prospects for GATT to the Asian leaders?

The President. Good.

NOTE: The President spoke at 10:25 a.m. in the Rose Garden at the White House.

Remarks at a Veterans Day Ceremony in Arlington, Virginia
November 11, 1994

Thank you very much. Thank you. Commander Sioss, distinguished leaders of our veterans organizations, Secretary Brown, Secretary Perry, General Shalikashvili, officials of the Veterans Administration, to our men and women in uniform and their families, our veterans, my fellow Americans, I am proud to share this Veterans Day with you in this magnificent place of rest and reverence.

Today we honor all those who gave their lives and all those who have risked their lives so that our Nation might remain free. And we honor, of course, all those who at this very moment are standing watch for freedom and security, from our bases across the United States to our mission around the world. To each and every American who has worn the uniform of the United States Armed Forces, we say simply, from the bottom of our hearts, thank you.

Over the past few months at home and abroad, I have had the privilege of saying that thank-you in person to men and women who are keeping our Nation's commitment. Today we say a special word of thanks to our troops who are helping the Haitian people turn from fear and repression to hope and democracy and a special word of thanks to our troops in the Persian Gulf who are insuring that Iraq does

not again threaten its neighbors or the stability of the vital Gulf region. All over the world our military is providing that kind of support to freedom and proving that when America makes a promise, we will keep it.

A few hours from now I leave for the Far East, where we will celebrate the keeping of another historic promise, General MacArthur's vow to return to the Philippines to help its people restore their freedom. In the 50 years since, we have forged remarkable partnerships for peace and prosperity in Asia, but we know that these blessings are the fruit of our veterans' sacrifice 50 years ago. And we know they endure to the present day because of the vigilance of thousands of Americans who are still in uniform and still there to help maintain the security, the peace, and the freedom in Asia.

This morning I was honored to start the day with veterans of that Pacific campaign and, I might add, a remarkable, jaunty group of parachuters who jumped into Normandy in 1944 and then jumped in again in 1994. There they are back there. To all of them and to all of you here assembled who have worn our Nation's uniform, you must know that America will never forget the service you have rendered.

And America will never forget those who did not return from our battlefields. Today we renew the commitment of this administration to obtain the fullest possible accounting for their fate.

For all of you who have helped America live up to its promises, your Nation has a special obligation to keep its commitments to you. That means, in the beginning, making sure that our military remains the best equipped, the best trained, and the best prepared in the world. We are keeping that commitment.

I'd like to say two things about that this morning. The first is that the success of the operations in Haiti and in the Gulf are due in no small measure to the advances which have been made just in the last couple of years in preparation, in pre-positioning, in mobility, in training—fresh evidence that we can never again afford to erode the confidence, the strength, and the ever-growing capacity of our military.

The second point that I'd like to make is that maintaining the best trained and prepared military in the world also has its very high human price. And every year, men and now women we may not know as battlefield heroes give their lives so that we can continue to do the kind of training that makes it less necessary for us to have to fight in battle. And I ask especially that we remember them, for their training and their sacrifice and their lives helped to make us so strong that we did not have to fight again in the Gulf and that we were able to enter Haiti without military incident. We thank them as well for their sacrifices, and their families.

I'd like to say a personal word of thanks to Secretary Brown, to Secretary Perry, to General Shalikashvili, and the other military leaders, without whom I could not carry out my duties and from whom I draw strength, wisdom, and advice to try to make the right decisions to keep our commitments to all of you.

Our obligation also includes, as Commander Sioss said and as Secretary Brown said, continuing the service this country owes our veterans after your service in uniform ends. That is why

it has given me particular pleasure in recent weeks to address concerns that are important to thousands upon thousands of our veterans. I was pleased to sign into law a bill that authorizes compensation to Gulf war veterans suffering from undiagnosed illnesses possibly incurred during their service there. Sometimes even the most sophisticated tools don't enable us to diagnose certain illnesses. The lack of a diagnosis must not stop us from responding both quickly and compassionately to veterans' needs. Now it will not.

At the same time, we've required the VA to evaluate the health of the families of Gulf war veterans. We know that the spouses and children of our troops may not wear the uniform, but they, too, bear the burden of defending our Nation. And today we say thank you to the children and the spouses and the families as well.

Finally, we extended the VA's authority to provide care to veterans of the Gulf war, Vietnam, and World War II for disabilities they may have incurred through exposure to toxic substances. We set aside nearly $400 million for the VA to build, lease, and repair major medical facilities around this country.

I know these actions—indeed, no actions can ever fully repay the service and the sacrifice of those of you who are here and those who never returned whom you represent. There are no words equal to the task of expressing just what your devotion and your sacrifice have meant to our Nation. But let me say at least we have this beautiful day God has given us which belongs entirely to you, to your commitment to our freedom, our prosperity, and our security. A grateful nation thanks you with this day and with all our hearts for what you have done and what you continue to do.

God bless you all, and God bless America.

NOTE: The President spoke at 11:35 a.m. at Arlington National Cemetery. In his remarks, he referred to Donald A. Sioss, national commander, Disabled American Veterans.

Remarks to the Military Community at Elmendorf Air Force Base in Anchorage, Alaska
November 11, 1994

Thank you very much, General Boese, General Cox, General Case, General Needham. On this Veterans Day, I would be remiss if I did not say a special word of thanks to General Needham for his work in trying to recover the information we need about our POW's and MIA's in Vietnam. I thank you, sir, for your work there. Governor Hickel, Senator Stevens, Mayor Mystrom, former Governor Sheffield, ladies and gentlemen, I'm glad to be here in Alaska. I've been trying for 2 years to get here to Alaska. At times I find the President is Commander in Chief of the Armed Forces but not of his own schedule. [*Laughter*]

Twenty-five years ago, before I met her, my wife came to Alaska and worked for a summer. So you can say to me, welcome to Alaska, but for Hillary, it's welcome back to Alaska. I've heard so much about it I always felt that I had imagined it, seen it all in my mind. Those of you who, like me, have been married for a while, we've told each other the same stories so many times I feel that I could tell you what it was like when I worked in Alaska 25 years ago. [*Laughter*] But I'm glad to be here to see the real thing.

I've also heard a lot about Alaska from another group, the veterans of the 208th Coastal Artillery, a National Guard unit from my home State of Arkansas that defended Dutch Harbor in the Aleutians during World War II. One of my best friends and one of my former chiefs of staff lost his brother in that brave struggle. And I just want you to know that I know you're a long way from the rest of our country territorially, but we're proud to be here in the United States and proud of the contribution that Alaska has made to the United States of America.

I am especially pleased to be here on Veterans Day because, as all of you know, Alaska is veteran country, the State with the highest concentration of both current armed forces personnel and former servicemen and women in the entire State of the Union.

I began this morning at Arlington National Cemetery, and that's what this little pin is. This is the pin the National Cemetery did for Veterans Day this year, honoring all those who served. It was a beautiful day there—a little warmer. [*Laughter*] The sun was shining; there were still a few autumn leaves on the trees. And the great amphitheater at Arlington is being closed for—it's being repaired. Many of you have seen that amphitheater there. So instead, we celebrated Veterans Day at the foot of the long steps up to the Tomb of the Unknown Soldier. And it was so incredibly moving, walking up those long flight of stairs to put the wreath down and then turning around and looking just as far as you could see down a sweeping, beautiful hillside with American veterans, their families, their supporters standing in the midst of the magnificent graves of Arlington Cemetery.

I'm on my way to Manila now to honor other soldiers, those who fought in the Pacific Theater during the Second World War—to recall those who left home and family for places they never heard of, places they could barely imagine, for dangers they certainly could not have imagined. To those of you here who defended us in that war, whether in the islands of the Far East or here in Alaska with distinguished units like the Eskimo Scouts, on this Veterans Day, I salute you, and on behalf of all the American people, I thank you.

We also honor and remember all those who, in war and peace, have given so much to America so that we could remain free and strong. To all the veterans of our Armed Forces, your country will never forget the extraordinary service you have performed. We owe you the safety of our shores and the liberty we enjoy. We have a special obligation to all of you who are veterans. Even when your service in uniform ends, the country's service must continue.

In recent weeks I signed into law two bills that addressed the concerns of thousands of veterans. The Veterans Health Program Act of 1994 extends the Veterans Administration's authority to provide hospital, outpatient, and nursing home care to veterans of the Gulf war, Vietnam, and World War II to any exposure they may have had from toxic substances. The act also provides about $400 million—[*applause*]—thank you, thank you. The act also provides nearly

$400 million for the VA to build, lease, and repair medical facilities around our country. The Veterans Benefit Improvement Act of 1994 authorizes compensation to Gulf war veterans suffering from undiagnosed illnesses from Operation Desert Storm. No one who wears our uniforms, no member of their families should have to suffer because of difficulty in diagnosing a particular illness. Thanks to this act, we will be able to respond quickly and compassionately to veterans' needs plainly related to what they have done in the service of our country.

Today we also must pay tribute to those of you who at this very moment are standing watch for freedom, demonstrating skill and professionalism here in Alaska and around the world. I know that personnel from Elmendorf and Fort Richardson are now deployed in support of the operation in Haiti, where our troops have helped a nation turn from fear, oppression, and intimidation back to democracy and hope. And I thank you for that. I thank you also for your service in humanitarian missions, from Rwanda to Papua New Guinea. You have shown that we stand by our ideals. Thank you. [*Applause*] Somebody back there sounds like he wants to go back. [*Laughter*] Thank you.

Here at the Alaskan Command, your strength and preparedness has helped America to keep its security commitments in Asia as well. Alaska Command plays a vital role in maintaining security on the Korean Peninsula, where I have visited our troops and where we have just concluded an agreement with North Korea to make sure that that nation becomes a nonnuclear state and does not contribute to the proliferation of weapons of mass destruction.

And finally, I thank you for the support of our troops in the Persian Gulf, where we moved with amazing speed and strength to make sure that Iraq poses no threat to its neighbors or to the stability of the vital Gulf region. I thank you for your contribution in that.

This kind of decisive action tells the world that when America makes a commitment, we keep that commitment. And I want you to know that we all understand it is your strength, your ability, your preparedness, and your devotion to duty that makes it possible for me as President to make and keep commitments on behalf of the United States. We are all in your debt on this Veterans Day for that, and on every day. And because of that, it is imperative that you remain the best equipped, best trained, best prepared fighting force in the world, and we will see that you do so.

You know, here in Alaska, the home of Senator Ted Stevens and Senator Frank Murkowski and Congressman Don Young, I want to say that in light of the elections last Tuesday giving a majority of the Congress to the Republican Party, I want to pledge again to work with them on issues of concern to the State of Alaska and to work with them, more importantly, as well as all others of both parties, in a nonpartisan way on behalf of problems of this country, which are in many cases new, different, challenging, unlike anything we have faced before, and unable to be put into clean and neat partisan categories. Let us now join together to move this country forward in the best American spirit.

All over our country today, we have a unique situation, as far as I know, in the history of America. We are in the midst of an economic recovery that is the envy of the world, and yet still, a majority of ordinary Americans, the people who keep this country going, who get up every day and work hard to try to build their families and raise their kids to do the right thing and have a good life, a majority of those people feel personal insecurities, insecurities that are economic, insecurities that are social. They're worried about the crime in our streets or the stability of their jobs or the security of their health care benefits.

Interestingly enough, when I went to Europe to celebrate D-Day, I met on two separate occasions with very large numbers of American service personnel who were celebrating the end of the cold war with the D-Day celebration and with the other celebrations because they knew that we were able to reduce our force in Europe somewhat. But over and over and over again these fine people who had worn our uniform said, "Well, if I go home, Mr. President, will I be able to find a job? If I find a job, Mr. President, will it be a job with health benefits with my kids, or without them? Because as long as I'm in the military, I have that."

This is a significant new development in the history of our country where, because of the radical changes in the global economy and because of social problems we've been dealing with in our Nation for 30 years now, you have a majority of ordinary Americans feeling uncertainty in the midst of developments which appear to be very, very hopeful.

Well, I can tell you that both are true. The events are hopeful, the trends are good, but the reasons for insecurity and uncertainty are real. We have to continue to work together to reduce the size of our Government where it is too big, to make sure that you get better value for the dollar, to make sure that people at the State and local level, where folks are in touch with the grassroots realities, have more freedoms to pursue reforms in their schools, in their welfare systems, in their health care systems. We have to do what we can also, together, to keep this economic recovery going so that we not only get more jobs, we get higher paying jobs and greater stability and security and support for those jobs.

Finally this year, after a very long time, we are beginning to see high-wage jobs come back into the American economy, more this year than in the previous 5 years combined. But folks, make no mistake about it, you here on America's frontier know that we are in a global economy, know that we have to fight and struggle for every single opportunity we have, and know that we have to be as competitive, as efficient, and as dominant where we can, economically as we are militarily. Your strength must be mirrored in the strength of every American business, every American community, and every American family. If we can equal your performance economically, we will do just fine well into the 21st century for our children and our grandchildren.

Believe it or not, I know you'd never know it from the press, but we've actually worked together some before in the last 2 years. I thank—for example, I would like to thank Senator Stevens and Senator Murkowski for supporting the Family and Medical Leave Act, which made it possible for 66,000 people here in Alaska to take a little time off when a baby was born or a parent was sick without losing their job.

And so I say to you, we've got a lot of work to do as a country. In the military, you've done a brilliant job of setting up a continuous, continuous education and training program. Why are we doing so well? Because the military is always changing but still rooted to its traditional values. That is what America must do.

One of the little-known facts about the success of our operation in Haiti and the success of our operation in the Gulf recently is that both of them reflected lessons learned in the last 2 years to increase our mobility by land, by air, by sea; to pre-position materials; to train people to do new and different skills; to have the services working together as never before. The Haitian operation was the most integrated, jointly planned, jointly executed operation in American history. That is what we have to do in our private lives as well, always learning, always growing, always moving forward.

That is a new challenge for America. It does not have a partisan label on it. It is very important; the national interest is at stake. We've always done what it took for the national defense. We have always understood that national security required us to be strong around the world. But we know ultimately that the security of America is in our strong families, our strong communities, our education systems, our ability to generate good jobs, and our ability to keep our streets safe and our laws sacred—strong at home and strong abroad.

On this Veterans Day, I want to say that one of my most prized possessions as President are the coins that I get whenever I visit any base, any unit. I now must have 100 on a big table in the Oval Office. Anybody that comes in to see the President of the United States sees a big, flat table covered with military coins from all over the world and all over the United States, a constant reminder of the service that you have rendered to our country. And I ask you to think about that on this Veterans Day. Being strong abroad and being strong at home are two sides of the coin we should have for America and we should leave to our children.

God bless you all, and God bless America. Thank you.

NOTE: The President spoke at 4:15 p.m. in Hangar 1. In his remarks, he referred to Lt. Gen. Lawrence E. Boese, commander, Alaskan Command; Maj. Gen. Hugh L. Cox III, adjutant general, Alaska National Guard; Brig. Gen. Thomas R. Case, commander, 3d Wing; Maj. Gen. Thomas H. Needham, USA, commander, U.S. Armed Forces, Alaska; Gov. Walter J. Hickel of Alaska; and Mayor Rick Mystrom of Anchorage. A tape was not available for verification of the content of these remarks.

Remarks at the Anchorage Museum of Art and History
November 11, 1994

Well, let me just say, as I said out at the base, I've been trying for 2 years to get to Alaska, and I finally made it today. And I thank the Governor, the Senator, and the mayor for coming out to meet Hillary and me. I also want to say that this is my first trip to Alaska—now I can say that in the last couple of years I've been to every State in America—and I hope I'll be coming back. But it's not Hillary's first trip to Alaska; she is coming back. She worked here 25 years ago when she was about 6 and violated the child labor law. [*Laughter*]

So I thought I would just ask her to come up here and say a word, because it's been—this has been a very meaningful trip to her. I was trying to get a little sleep, and when we started—we finally got into the airspace of Alaska, she was beating on me, saying, "Wake up, wake up, look at this, look at this." [*Laughter*] So I heard the story again for the 500th time—[*laughter*]—which I love; now I can tell it as well.

So please come up and say a word.

[*At this point, Hillary Clinton briefly described her first visit to Alaska and her job there cleaning fish.*]

The President. You know, it really is good preparation for Washington. You do need the hip boots and the raincoat, but you have to trade the spoon in for a shovel. [*Laughter*]

Let me say, what we'd like to do now is just to say hello to everyone. I do want to say again how very proud I am to be here. Let me just make one comment specific, if I might, to Alaska. When I was coming down—I've been so excited about this trip. One of the things that is most fascinating about this country is how incredibly different and diverse it is, from one coast to the other and all places in between, and yet how there are certain ties that bind us together.

About a week ago, or maybe a little—[*inaudible*]—a week ago now, I was in Pawtucket, Rhode Island. It's about as far away from here as you can get and still be in America. And I was the first President since Andrew Jackson to go there, which is appropriate. [*Laughter*] But I was in the Portuguese Social Club. America has over one million Portuguese-Americans.

Most of them live in Rhode Island and Massachusetts, although there is also a big contingent in California. And I was thinking then, you know, I said, gosh, here I am with Portuguese in Rhode Island, and I'm about to go to Alaska.

And if you think about it, that is the great promise of this country. There is no other nation in the world so well positioned to move into the next century, in which the world gets smaller and smaller, because we already have everybody here. And if we can figure out how to deal with the honest differences we have, in ways that permit us to build unity out of our differences, there will be no stopping this country.

It is astonishing—every place I go in the world, I meet somebody with a relative in the United States. Every place I go, people think they can relate to us, in no small measure because we have welcomed others from all over the world, of different faiths, to our shores. And we still have stood up for our constant values, freedom and democracy.

The most amazing part of the trip I took to the Middle East, when Hillary and I went over there for the signing, that didn't—I don't think it made a lot of impression here at home, and it had the biggest impact, I think, there—the opportunity I had to stand in the Jordanian Parliament and tell those folks that we had millions of Americans that answered the Muslim call to prayer every day and that we respected Islam. We knew there was nothing in their religion that would divide us, that would promote terrorism, that would be destructive of our values, and that the things that we opposed that we saw—the terrorism there in the Middle East is something that we oppose anywhere, anyplace, coming from any group of people. And it was stunning. They had never really thought about it before, that America was a place that all who share our values and obey our laws can call home.

It's our meal ticket to the future, and we have to nourish it. That means that whoever is the President, whoever is in charge of the National Government, even though there won't be always easy answers or perfect answers to these problems, we have to be sensitive to the fact that Alaska is different from Rhode Island,

Colorado is different from Florida. The problems are different; the challenges are different; the opportunities are different.

I'm glad to have a chance to be here. And I hope we have a lot of opportunities to work together.

Thank you very much.

NOTE: The President spoke at 5:50 p.m. A tape was not available for verification of the content of these remarks.

Statement on the Death of Pedro Zamora
November 11, 1994

Hillary and I are deeply saddened by the news of the death of Pedro Zamora.

In his short life, Pedro educated and enlightened our Nation. He taught all of us that AIDS is a disease with a human face and one that affects every American, indeed every citizen, of the world. And he taught people living with AIDS how to fight for their rights and live with dignity.

Pedro was particularly instrumental in reaching out to his own generation, where AIDS is striking hard. Through his work with MTV, he taught young people that "The Real World" includes AIDS and that each of us has the responsibility to protect ourselves and our loved ones.

Today, one in four new HIV infections is among people under the age of 20. For Pedro, and for all Americans infected and affected by HIV, we must intensify our efforts to reduce the rate of HIV infection, provide treatment to those living with AIDS, and ultimately find a cure for AIDS.

Our hearts are with Pedro's family in this difficult time. In the months ahead, let us rededicate ourselves to continuing Pedro's brave fight.

The President's Radio Address
November 12, 1994

I'm speaking to you from Anchorage, Alaska, at the end of the first leg of my trip to Asia. The next stop is the Philippines, where I'll take part in a ceremony especially appropriate just a couple of days after Veterans Day. There I'll have the privilege of helping to honor the sacrifices made by those who fought in the Pacific during World War II to preserve our freedom and democracy.

In the 50 years since, America has helped to build a world of peace and prosperity. But we know that these blessings are the fruit of our veterans' brave fights. That's why yesterday, on Veterans Day, we honored and remembered all who, in war and peace, have given so much so that America would remain free. We have a special obligation to make sure that our Nation never forgets their work and that we do everything we can to keep our country strong in the face of our challenges at home and abroad.

We also have an obligation to honor those who are standing watch for freedom and security now, from our bases across America to our outposts around the world.

Over the last few months, at home and abroad, I've had the privilege of saying thank you in person to our men and women in uniform, those who are keeping our Nation's commitments. Our troops in Haiti are helping the Haitian people turn from fear and repression to hope and democracy. In the Persian Gulf, they're ensuring that Iraq does not again threaten its neighbors or the stability of the vital Gulf region. All over the world, our military is proving that when America makes a promise, we'll keep it.

The results are clear. The threat of nuclear war is receding. For the first time since the dawn of the nuclear age, no Russian missiles are pointed at Americans. North Korea has recently agreed to become a nonnuclear state and to remove that threat of proliferation of weapons of mass destruction. Peace and freedom are on the march, with American support and involvement in the Middle East, in the Gulf, in Haiti, and also in Northern Ireland and South Africa where we've been asked to be involved.

Our national security plainly depends on our strong military and on a strong foreign policy. But our strength is more than military around the world. It also depends upon strength in a global economy. The future of every nation is really a global future. It means jobs and incomes in the United States. And expanded trade has always been a goal of mine and this administration because, whether we like it or not, we are in a global economy that we can't run from and trade-related jobs pay so much more on the average than jobs not related to trade.

That's where the rest of this trip to Asia fits in. Next week in Jakarta, Indonesia, I'll meet with the 14 leaders of the Asian-Pacific Economic Cooperation forum, called APEC. We'll continue the work we began last year when I called the group together for the first time in Seattle. We've already forged a common vision of a more open community. When we meet in Jakarta, I hope we'll embrace a common direction, setting a goal for free and open trade among all our economies.

Then when I return from the trip, we'll face another crucial test about our future in this global economy. Congress will reconvene soon to vote on ratifying GATT, the largest, most comprehensive trade agreement ever. GATT will require all nations to finally do what we've already done, to cut tariffs and other barriers and open up trade to our products and our services. It will level the export playing field for American companies and American workers all around the world and, in so doing, will create hundreds of thousands of new high-paying jobs right here at home.

It will make our exports more competitive exactly when we have recovered our ability to sell more American products and services. This year, America's economy, for the first time in 9 years, has been voted the most productive in the world by the annual review of international economists. And for the first time since 1979, American automobile makers are selling more cars all around the world than their Japanese competitors.

The congressional vote on the GATT will be a defining decision for America as we head into the next century. And I believe that members of both parties will put aside partisanship to do what's right for our country and our future.

I also hope that both parties will take other opportunities to join together when the national interest is at stake, and we're moving into a future which has no easy partisan label tied to the past. Our common goal must be to produce a strong America, strong in terms of national commitments abroad. On this Veterans Day weekend, we know that a strong America means to be strong abroad. But surely, we also know that it means being strong at home, that our strength comes at bottom from strong families, strong communities, better education, higher paying jobs, safer streets. Strong at home, strong abroad: two sides of the same coin.

We have to keep going because a majority of hardworking Americans still feel uncertain about their economic future and their personal and family security, even though we're in the midst of a significant economic recovery. We've got to keep going to bring our deficit down and keep shrinking the size of the Government, to increase trade and increase education and training, to keep these jobs going up and to get more high-wage jobs. We've got over 5 million new jobs in the last 22 months. And for the first time, this year, we have some high-wage jobs coming back into this economy, more than in the previous 5 years combined.

So let's make our goal to be number one militarily, number one economically, and number one in the strength of our families and our communities. Strong at home, strong abroad: That's an America that builds on the opportunities others have sacrificed so much to give us. And it takes responsibility to keep those opportunities alive for our children.

Thank you, and God bless America.

NOTE: The address was recorded at 5:45 p.m. on November 11 at the Anchorage Museum of Art and History in Anchorage, AK, for broadcast at 10:06 a.m. on November 12.

Remarks at the American Cemetery in Manila, Philippines
November 13, 1994

President and Mrs. Ramos, Secretary Christopher, Ambassador Negroponte, Mr. Perrine, Mr. De Ocampo, Colonel Barth; Mr. Quashan, thank you for that wonderful introduction; distinguished members of the Philippine Government, distinguished members of the diplomatic corps, especially to the young students and to the Peace Corps volunteers that are here, and most especially to the Philippine and American veterans here in attendance: Hillary and I are deeply honored to be with you today. I was told this morning that I am the first sitting President since President Eisenhower to visit this hallowed site, and it is a profound honor for me and for our entire party.

We gather to honor and to remember. In this place, only a few miles from the ocean named for peacefulness, we always remember the fury of war, the 17,206 American and Philippine men and women who are buried here, arrayed in the long arcs I saw this morning as if still deployed in our defense, the 36,281 more whose names are engraved on these magnificent marble walls. Nowhere else outside the United States are so many American heroes honored and interred.

Some of their brethren, heroes from American units and Filipino units, thankfully are still here with us today. Time has diminished none of our pride in them. They are among the finest people our nations have ever produced. Their presence here reminds us of the meaning of courage and determination. Their example will inspire us for ages to come. On behalf of a grateful nation and an increasingly free world, I thank them, and I ask all the Philippine and American veterans of World War II who are here to stand and receive the thanks of all of us. [*Applause*]

We can hardly imagine today the perils that met these young men in the full bloom of their lives. They left families and loved ones and home to go to places they never heard of to confront dangers they never imagined. They had to liberate territory bit by bit, enduring constant fear of ambush in island jungles. At sea they stayed on course in the face of a new terror, the suicide dive bomber. On American carriers, our pilots took off never knowing if they would find their ships again. This ordeal engulfed the Philippines, our oldest friend in Asia, a nation that has done so much to enrich the United States.

On the same day that Pearl Harbor was bombed, the American garrison in the Philippines was attacked. Troops under General MacArthur dug in for battle not far from here on the Bataan Peninsula and on Corregidor. Our joint forces in Bataan resisted for 4 months. Then, low on ammunition, weakened by hunger, reduced by sickness, they could fight no more. Their nightmare was just beginning. A death march to prison camps and a horrifying internment claimed the lives of about 25,000 Filipinos and Americans. Corregidor became the last bastion.

Just before coming here, I had the honor of touring the island with the President and with a group of our veterans, including a man named Bill Martin who is with us here today. His road in the war was long, from Bataan to Corregidor to a prison camp in Manchuria. Today marks the first time Bill Martin has been on the rock since he was captured there 50 years ago, the first time he has seen this place where so many of his friends and comrades lie at rest. Welcome back, Bill Martin, and thank you.

I saw on Corregidor the remains of many evidences of Americans and Filipinos sharing the familiar diversions of everyday life, the fields where the games were played, the remnants of three movie theaters. But the most important thing they shared was a ferocious love of freedom. When a shell fragment cut the halyard on the embattled garrison's flagpole, it was a Philippine civilian named Panorio Punongbayan who braved the shelling with two Americans to catch the flag before it touched the ground and, under fire, to retie the line and raise the flag again. Their commander, General Wainwright, said what they had done was not only courageous but helped the battered rock's morale beyond any words.

A month after Bataan fell, time ran out for Corregidor, as the sky over the island turned to lead with 16,000 shells a day. Relief was impossible; freedom's last foothold seemed lost.

Soon—we forget this now—Japanese forces controlled land and water stretching from Alaska's Aleutian Islands to Wake Island near Hawaii. From New Guinea, they menaced Australia. With our fleet devastated at Pearl Harbor and Hitler ruling Europe from the English Channel to the Russian heartland, free people everywhere stood in fear.

In this, one of our Nation's darkest hours, our troops and our leaders might have given up, but their spirits never failed. An enlisted man who survived the fighting and hunger, the death march, and 3 years in prisoner of war camps gave voice to that spirit and to its ultimate source. Almost incapable of walking when he was liberated, he was still unbowed and said, "When a man allows God to sustain him, he can go through hell if he has to. That's what I did. Yes, sir, I refused to die." That man, Corporal Ishmael Cox, is still unbowed and refusing today, living in Missouri.

After the occupation, tens of thousands of Filipinos and a handful of Americans fought the most valiant guerrilla effort in the Pacific theater. Meanwhile, American forces, with Australians and New Zealanders, began the agonizing crawl, island by island, back across the Pacific. They fought their way through the Solomons, the Admiralty Islands, Palau; their battles at Midway, Guadalcanal, and Iwo Jima are now legends.

Driven by General MacArthur's determination that our friends in the Philippines should not have their freedom delayed, Americans put to shore at Leyte in 1944, with an invasion force larger than that of the opening phase of Normandy. In the surrounding gulf, more than 800 United States ships stretched across the horizon and there fought and won the largest naval battle of all time. General MacArthur did return, and so would freedom. Countless horrors still lay in the way, including the butchery of house-to-house fighting in Manila. The savagery turned the Pearl of the Orient into another Warsaw. But the tide turned once and for all.

When he returned to Corregidor, General MacArthur saw the now-famous old flagpole still standing, and he ordered, "Hoist the colors to the peak, and let no enemy ever haul them down."

These heroes, those who rest here and those still among us, gave everything so that all of us might be free. Here in the Philippines, one million people, one in every 17, gave their lives.

But the spirit of Bataan and Corregidor did not die. The defense of democracy, the determination to spread freedom, the refusal to bow before aggression are principles at the core of our identities as nations today.

Those who were once our foes, Japan, Germany, and Italy, are now our friends because they, too, now embrace these ideals. These same principles saw us through the long ordeal of the cold war, and today, they unite us with our allies, including our friends here in the Philippines, who stand with us in the constant march of freedom and democracy.

It is fitting that we commemorate these heroes today not only because of the common cause that joined our peoples 50 years ago but because the great wave of democracy that has swept the world in our time began here in the Philippines. Eight years ago, when President Ramos and others stood up bravely, they, too, showed the defiant courage of Bataan. So did the crowds that filled the streets here when people power blossomed and Corazon Aquino led the Philippines into a new era. What happened here, all of you in the Philippines should know, strengthened the magical current of democracy that was then sweeping all around the world. It encouraged events in countries like Poland, Czechoslovakia, Hungary, and Russia.

We mark now the fifth anniversary of the fall of the Berlin Wall just this past week. A new generation of democracy has come into the world in South Africa, South America, much of Asia, parts of the Middle East. What you did here encouraged the spirit of freedom for the world, just as surely as your defiant courage in World War II buoyed the forces of freedom then. We thanked you then; we thank you now.

Like those we honor today, we must still stand against aggression and cede to no country the right to dominate its neighbors, its region, or its hemisphere. The United States looks to the Pacific not as an ocean that separates us from Asia but as a body of water that unites us with Asia. To fulfill the vision of those who fought here, we must, and we will, remain engaged with the Philippines and elsewhere. We will make the most of peace and partnership and, as President Ramos said, the opportunities for prosperity. But if threats arrive, we will confront them as well.

On the Korean Peninsula, there has been such a threat in the possible proliferation of weapons of mass destruction. The agreement we reached with North Korea to freeze and then to dismantle North Korea's ability to build nuclear weapons was achieved in concert with South Korea and Japan. But it furthered the cause of security in the Philippines and, indeed, throughout all of Asia.

Our final responsibility is to remember what those young people did here a half a century ago and to remember that it is undying. Today, when I got out with Hillary at the cemetery, the first grave I visited was that of a soldier from my home State. He came from a town where I have spent many happy days, a town like so many little towns that dot our wonderful country and form the backbone of America. Private First Class William Thomas, on April 22d, 1945, was not quite 23 years old when his unit entered the Zambales Mountains, 85 miles from here. They were assigned to help clear the enemy from Luzon. He was a long way from his hometown of Wynne, Arkansas, that day.

The enemy was well dug in when his company attacked along a ridge, and he was hit by an explosion that blew off both his legs below the knees. But he refused medical help and instead continued firing until a bullet knocked out his gun. Still he kept on fighting, throwing his grenades. His heroism allowed his unit to capture that position. The price of his unit's victory was William Thomas' life. For his valor, he received the Medal of Honor, America's highest military honor, one of 28 recipients so remembered here.

William Thomas, for your sacrifice and for that of all others here laid to rest, your Nation remembers you and is forever grateful. And you serve us still, as do all the names and graves of those here commemorated serve us still, for nothing, nothing protects us and our freedom like the vigilance of memory.

Thank you.

NOTE: The President spoke at approximately 1:30 p.m. In his remarks, he referred to John D. Negroponte, U.S. Ambassador to the Philippines; World War II veterans Paul Parrine, who gave the invocation, and William H. Quashan; Col. Emmanuel De Ocampo, president, Veterans Federation of the Philippines; and Col. Wayne M. Barth, USA, Director, Joint Military Assistance Group.

Remarks at a State Luncheon in Manila
November 13, 1994

President and Mrs. Ramos, former President Macapagal, former President Aquino, distinguished members of the Philippine Government, members of the business community here, members of the diplomatic corps, my fellow Americans who are here: Let me begin by thanking President Ramos and Mrs. Ramos for making Hillary and me and all of our delegation here feel so very welcome on our all too brief but very enjoyable and very important visit to the Philippines.

One hundred thousand Americans call the Philippines home, and now about 1½ million Filipinos call the United States home. Indeed, I was trying to count up all the Philippine-Americans I brought with me on this trip, and I lost count. But we have people here from the Agency for International Development; we have three of my Navy stewards; my personal physician, Dr. Connie Mariano; and of course, the executive with the Export-Import Bank, a long-time friend of yours, Mr. President, Maria Louisa Haley. We're all glad to be here, but those with roots here in the Philippines are the happiest of all to be home. You have made us all feel at home, and we thank you for that.

We have worked together in many ways over a long period of time. President Ramos just described the 50th observation of our partnership in the Second World War. I have heard a very moving account of the events of last October from Secretary of Defense Perry and General Shalikashvili. General Ramos' Philippine soldiers also fought side by side with Americans in Korea and in Vietnam. And you were there, sir, in both conflicts. We thank you for that individually and for your country.

During the cold war, the United States led an effort to stand against the tyranny of communism. You were our partner then. In the last several years, you have led the world in the sweeping resurgence of democracy, beginning

8 years ago when you and others exposed yourselves to considerable risks to stand up for freedom here in your own country, following through with the remarkable people power movement of President Aquino, where people held flowers in the face of tanks and captured the imagination of the entire world.

And now, sir, under your leadership we see the Philippines moving forward, respecting the dignity, the rights of all people and aggressively pursuing a modern economic program designed to bring prosperity to all the tens of millions of people who call these wonderful islands their home.

You know, President Ramos is a fitting leader for this time. We know in America that in 1946—he doesn't look that old—[*laughter*]—but in 1946, he won the only Filipino scholarship to the United States Military Academy. I met several others of you who graduated from West Point here today, and all of you know that when one graduates from West Point, he—and now she—becomes a member of the Long Gray Line, linked forever with all of those who went before and all of those who will come after.

Well, Mr. President, you symbolize the link between our two nations, which is equally as strong and will always exist. We are linked by our history; we are linked by the populations that we share, the Americans here, the Filipinos there. But most of all, we are linked by our shared values, our devotion to freedom, to democracy, to prosperity, and to peace.

And for that common devotion, I ask all of you to stand and join me in a toast to President and Mrs. Ramos, to all the people of the Philippines, to their health, to their prosperity, and to their eternal partnership with the United States.

NOTE: The President spoke at approximately 3:40 p.m. in the Ceremonial Room at the Malacanang Palace. In his remarks, he referred to President Fidel Ramos of the Philippines and his wife, Amelita; and former Philippine Presidents Diosdado Macapagal and Corazon Aquino.

The President's News Conference With President Fidel Ramos of the Philippines in Manila
November 13, 1994

President Ramos. Thank you, Mr. Secretary. Good evening, ladies and gentlemen. Today President Clinton and I took concrete steps towards enhancing Philippine-American relations. During our bilateral meeting, I expressed my sincere appreciation to President Clinton for the substantial participation of the United States Armed Forces in the commemoration of the 50th anniversary of the Leyte landing, 3 weeks ago.

Our meeting this afternoon enabled us to discuss a wide range of issues with direct import on our bilateral relations and the peace and stability of the Pacific. I acknowledged our debt of gratitude to America's commitment, to America's strength, and to America's keeping faith with her ideals and values in such areas as Haiti, the Persian Gulf, and the Korean Peninsula.

We both agreed to build our partnership on the basis of mutual respect and mutual benefit, reinforced by our common commitment to democracy and the rule of law. President Clinton and I recognize the value of enhancing the security and stability of the Asia-Pacific region and reiterated our commitment to the peaceful resolution of conflicts. We agreed that only under such conditions can the full economic growth and prosperity of the Asia-Pacific region be realized.

I assured President Clinton that the Philippines will continue to support the peacekeeping initiatives of the United States and the United Nations, as we have recently manifested in a dispatch to Haiti of an initial contingent of 50 international police monitors, or IPM, from this country. And I also congratulated him for the United States role in the series of breakthrough agreements for peace and development in the Middle East and in the Korean Peninsula, which has lifted our hopes for its eventual denuclearization.

I have been assured, in turn, by President Clinton that they will encourage a higher level of investments by Americans. I also acknowledged his government's support for our bid to attain newly industrializing country, or NIC, status by the turn of the century. We further agreed to find ways and means to improve our two-way trade. The United States continues to be our number one trading partner, and we believe that we can greatly expand our trade by the further lowering of trade barriers.

To accelerate trade liberalization, President Clinton and I agreed on the urgency of the ratification of the Uruguay round of the General Agreement on Tariffs and Trade by member countries. I assured him of the Philippines' commitment to trade liberalization and investment facilitation, which must be accompanied by conditions of national stability and political will.

We also agreed that the Asia-Pacific Economic Cooperation, or APEC, leaders summit in Indonesia will be a landmark forum that will shape the future course of the economy of the entire Asia-Pacific area and, indeed, of the world.

And we both affirmed the value of the Philippines-U.S. Mutual Defense Treaty, or the MDT, and its contribution to regional security and stability. We agreed that our joint exercises, which are planned by the Mutual Defense Board, should be continued to ensure the interoperability of military units.

I appreciate President Clinton's effort to help resolve the longstanding issue of the claims of Filipino veterans of World War II with the United States Government. Even as I acknowledged the concern of leading members of the U.S. Congress for the restoration of Filipino veterans' rights. I welcome these assurances that the United States will work hand-in-hand with the Philippine Government in helping to promote the welfare of Amerasians in the Philippines.

President Clinton and I renewed our commitment to the protection of the environment and the preservation of the world ecological balance.

And lastly, I reiterated my appreciation for the warm welcome, hospitality extended by President Clinton and the American people during my visit to the United States last year. We look forward to moving Philippines-United States partnership to a higher and more mutually beneficial level in the years to come.

Thank you very much. *Salamat.*

President Clinton. Thank you very much. First, let me thank President Ramos for the warm welcome that the United States delegation has received here in the Philippines.

We had a very good bilateral discussion in which the President expressed the Philippine position and the interest of the Filipino people very articulately to me on a very large number of issues.

I would like to point out in general that over the last 50 years, the relationship between the United States and the Philippines has changed, has grown, has matured, but we are still very much bound together in ways that I think are positive. There are, after all, 100,000 Americans and more who make their home here permanently, and in the United States there are about 1½ million Americans of Philippine ancestry.

We admire your democracy, and we have especially admired all the things which have been done in the last 8 years. We have an important security relationship. You heard the President talk about the joint exercises. I also was able to inform President Ramos that the United States will be able to supply the Philippine Armed Forces with two C–130's soon and that we will continue to discuss the possibility of shared equipment to build up the strength and the security of the Philippine Armed Forces.

We talked about regional security in general, and I want to again thank publicly President Ramos for the support that he has given to the agreement we have reached in cooperation with the South Koreans and the Japanese with North Korea, in which North Korea has agreed to become a nonnuclear state and to remove that threat of the proliferation of weapons of mass destruction. I also thanked President Ramos for the participation of the Philippines in our remarkable international coalition in Haiti.

Finally, we discussed our economic relationships. Most of what should be said has already been said by President Ramos, but let me say that I was deeply impressed when the President came to the United States and told me that his new policy was trade, not aid. That's a welcome message.

The United States purchased $5 billion in products from the Philippines last year. We are the largest investor here. We like being the largest purchaser and the largest investor. This morning, the Secretary of State hosted a breakfast which I attended for leading American business interests here, and I pledged to the President I would do what I could to increase the interest of the American business community in investment in the Philippines.

We both support GATT and hope that both of our legislative bodies will ratify it shortly. I am going home when I leave the APEC conference to achieve that objective, and I hope we do. I believe we will. And we are going to APEC with a view toward continuing to break down the barriers to trade and investment.

The United States will and must remain engaged in the Pacific region for security reasons and for economic reasons. One-third of our exports, supporting some 2 million American jobs, already go to the Asian-Pacific region. This is a very important thing for us. And the fact that we have the sort of relationship we do and that both of us are now going to Indonesia to try to deepen the idea that we should be working together across the vast Pacific to support the prosperity and future of our respective peoples is a very important one indeed.

So for all those reasons, I consider this to be a successful trip. And again, I thank the President for his kind hospitality and for his frank and open and straightforward way of stating the position of the Philippine Government and the Philippine people.

Thank you.

Philippine-U.S. Military Cooperation

Q. Good evening, sirs. My question is for President Ramos. Earlier today you applauded America's intention to remain engaged in the Asia-Pacific region. There has been much talk lately of U.S. plans for pre-positioning war material within the territories of strategically located countries such as the Philippines. Even now, reports indicate Manila and Washington are looking at a proposed agreement allowing U.S. warships to resupply and to refuel in the Philippines. Given these developments, in what direction do you want Philippine-American military cooperation to change or to evolve into during your term, or just how active a military presence do you want America to have both in the Philippines and within ASEAN's territory in the future?

President Ramos. Thank you.

First of all, we should distinguish between the floating depot issue and the lesser issue of servicing, which includes rewatering, refueling, and minor repairs and also rest and recreation. The servicing aspect is already being done, and example of this would be the visits last year of a British—of an American ship, plus other ships from other countries. We're doing this for

them. And the most recent example is the visit here in Manila and later on in the Subic area of the ships that went on to participate in the Leyte landings.

In regard to the so-called floating depots, we really have not seen any official proposal in regard to that kind of an arrangement. And we will, however, be happy to consider this at the level of the working officials, meaning at the level of the mutual defense board. But by no means is that a policy right now of the Philippine Government.

Now, as far as directions that I would like to see the security relationship between the Philippines and the U.S. is concerned, I think I said that on many occasions during the course of this day—I said we would like to be closely related with the U.S. under our U.S.-Philippine Mutual Defense Treaty which has been in force since 1951. And under this arrangement, we're able to have combined and joint exercises to test the interoperability of our military units.

The Philippines derives a great deal of benefit from this kind of an exchange because we get to know what are the new technologies in military science. And also, under the treaty, there is a regular mechanism for consultation among our highest military officials, represented on the part of the U.S. by the commander in chief of the Pacific, no less, and our chief of staff of the armed forces.

So we feel that this is a very important relationship, and the approach must be based on our commitments under the Philippine-U.S. Mutual Defense Treaty.

Thank you.

Cooperation With Republican Leaders

Q. I'd like to ask President Clinton—sir, a lot of world leaders are wondering about the meaning of Tuesday's elections. As you go into APEC and talk with these other world leaders, what will you tell them about the Republican takeover of Congress and what that means about the strength of your administration and the direction of U.S. foreign policy?

President Clinton. First, I would say that I don't expect it to have any impact on our foreign policy. The Republican House and Senate leaders—and I spoke, as you know, before I came—they expressed their support for this trip and for our policy generally. The foreign policies that I have pursued, particularly the mission that I'm on now with regard to APEC, have enjoyed broad bipartisan support among centrists in both parties. And insofar as they have drawn opposition, they have drawn some opposition again from both parties, particularly in the trade area.

But I believe that the position of the United States is certainly just as strong as it ever has been. Beyond that, we do not have a parliamentary system. The power vested by the Constitution in the President to represent the United States in foreign affairs, particularly in areas of this kind, is quite clear.

But the most important thing is, I'm convinced that what I'm doing is in the interest of all the American people without regard to party and is supported by leaders of both parties in the United States Congress.

I hope you wear that tie at home sometime when we are having a dark day. [*Laughter*]

Toxic Waste Cleanup

Q. Good evening. President Clinton, in a hearing at the Philippine Senate a few days ago, a group of scientists, citing Pentagon reports, identified more than 40 sites in Clark and Subic believed to be contaminated with hazardous wastes. Your Government has offered financial assistance and technical support for surveys to check if there are environmental damages in both former U.S. military bases. Is your Government willing to accept moral as well as financial responsibility for cleaning up the bases in case these surveys prove that there are toxic wastes in Clark and Subic?

President Clinton. First of all, I'd like to point out that when the United States left Subic Bay, we spent about $6 million on cleanup, and we left 5,000 acres of virgin tropical forest, which was an enormous environmental resource for the Philippines. We have, since that time, worked very hard to cooperate with the authorities here about what the condition of Subic Bay is and each area of the bay. It's a vast area, as you know. We will continue to do that and to exchange information and to work on it.

We have no reason to believe at this time that there is a big problem that we left untended, first of all. We clearly are not mandated under any treaty obligations to do more, but we are concerned. We want Subic Bay to be a vast economic resource for the Philippines in a way that preserves the environmental heritage of the area.

We were very pleased and supportive of the agreement signed, I believe just today, and witnessed by the Secretary of State, between Federal Express and the authorities there to develop the area in a responsible way.

So we're excited by this; we want it to be a very good thing for you. We have spent some money there, we have given some important environmental resources, and we are continuing to work on it. But in the absence of the evidence of some serious problem that we left untended. I don't think I can commit at this moment to further expenditures. But I can tell you we are continuing to work with the Philippine Government on this, and we will continue to do so.

President Ramos. May I just add by way of confirmation, ladies and gentlemen, that I brought up the issue during our one-on-one talk with President Clinton, and he readily agreed that at the level of the technical people and the working people, principally in the departments of foreign affairs, environment, and natural resources, as well as the base authorities, that we put all our expertise together about the subject, because we have studies on our side, there are records on the part of the U.S. Government which have not yet been thoroughly collated, so that we will get to the truth of the matter. And while it may not be just toxic waste, we may really be talking here about pollutants which could have been sourced from many other places in addition to the naval forces in Subic. But anyway, we will get a good effort going together. Thank you.

President Clinton. If I could add just one more sentence. President Ramos did bring this up, and we talked about it in some detail. What I would like to say is, on a matter like this, I think it is very important not to let the general policy pronouncements or the rhetoric outrun the facts we have on the case. So we decided we should focus on finding the facts now, and when we find them, deal then with the facts as they are.

Cooperation With Republican Leaders

Q. Mr. President, Newt Gingrich, who is likely to be the next Speaker of the House, said the other day that he thought on the many things where he believes he represents the vast majority of America there will be no compromise. Cooperation, he said, yes; but compromise, no. Given this, do you expect to be able to work with Republicans, and can you move far enough toward the center to work with them and still not alienate the core constituency of your own party and perhaps invite a challenger for renomination?

President Clinton. Well, first of all, I think that any rational analysis of our position would say that's where we have been. It was not the opposition party, it was the Democrats that reduced the size of the Federal Government and reduced the Federal deficit for the first time in a very long time, the Democrats that passed a crime bill that had the toughest punishments of any crime bill in American history. So I think we will be in the center.

There are several specific things that they have advocated that I have long agreed with. To mention just two, I ran on the line-item veto, and I ran on welfare reform. And I presented a welfare reform bill to the Congress last spring, so I think there will be other areas in which we can work together. I am still looking for ways—the Vice President and I have had at least three different discussions, two before and once since the election, about how we can carry forward our downsizing the Federal Government with the reinventing Government initiative. So I think there will be many areas in which we can work together.

Will there be some areas of disagreement? Of course there will. What is my standard? My standard is, does it make America stronger or weaker to do this? As I said, does it weaken our posture abroad in terms of national defense and economic strength? Does it weaken our posture at home in terms of building stronger families, better schools, more high-wage jobs, and safer streets? That is my standard. Insofar as I can work with them, I will do my best to do it.

But my job as President is to make America strong and make the working people of the country who voice their frustrations, their anxieties, their uncertainties, more secure and make sure their children's future is better. That will be what guides me, not the politics of the matter but what makes America strong.

Democratic Governments in Asia

Q. My first question is for President Clinton. The second question will be for President Ramos. President Clinton, some political analysts read your Manila visit as a statement of support to democracy in view of the authoritarian governments of other Eastern countries. Do they read you right? If so, what global and, in particular, American interest is served by a democratic government in Asia?

And for President Ramos, are you satisfied with the support you are getting from friends like the United States on the path of democracy that you have taken?

President Clinton. I want to make sure—my hearing is not the best; I want to make sure that I heard the question right. You asked me what American interests were served by the advance of democracy in Asia. Is that right?

Q. Why you chose the Philippines, chose to visit the Philippines of all the other countries.

President Clinton. I chose to come to the Philippines partly because of the stunning success and resurgence of democracy here in the last 8 years. I chose to come here because I thought I ought to be here during this period when we are celebrating the 50th anniversary of the return to freedom of the Philippines. And I came here, frankly, because of the relationship I enjoy with your President and my immense admiration for him and for what he is trying to do not only in preserving democracy and enhancing individual rights but in modernizing the Philippine economy and trying to give the people here the kind of prosperity that they deserve for their hard work, which is legendary the world over. So those are the three reasons that I came here.

Do I believe that democracy in general advances the cause and the interest of the United States? Yes, I do. Democracies are highly unlikely to go to war with each other. They are more likely to keep their word to each other. They are more likely to see their future greatness in terms of developing the human potential of their people rather than building walls around their country, either economic walls or military walls.

No democracies are perfect. All democracies have their ups and downs. But on balance, the world has been much better served by the march of democracy. And the United States is more secure when there are more democracies. Our national defense interests are threatened less; our economic interests are enhanced more. So that is why I intend to continue to push this throughout the world.

President Ramos. I may just make two points very clear. First of all, we are trying to achieve economic and social reform in this country under a democratic framework. While this may be a little more time consuming and may require a little more patience than other systems, we feel we are on the right track. And we are now seeing the initial fruits of that devotion to the rule of laws, to people power, and to the overall democratic system.

Secondly, I think no one can ignore the fact that over the last 20 years, there are now more democracies functioning in Asia-Pacific, our region, than there were two decades ago. And so, to me, this is the right track. And the Philippines is following precisely that way to its political, social, economic, and cultural development.

Human Rights

Q. Mr. President, it's clear that security and trade will be among the issues discussed at the APEC conference, but there is some speculation at this point that perhaps human rights will not come up. Specifically, do you intend on discussing human rights with China and Indonesia?

President Clinton. Absolutely. Let me make a distinction here between the APEC conference itself, the purpose of which by the very name of the group is economic cooperation, and the bilateral meetings that I will have with the leaders of the individual countries. And in both

the cases that you mentioned, human rights has been discussed in every meeting I've had and will be discussed in these meetings. It's an important interest of the United States. We are engaging these countries in many, many areas, across a broad range of areas. And human rights is too important, particularly now, to pass by us. So it will be a point of discussion in those bilateral meetings.

Press Secretary Myers. That concludes the press conference. Thank you very much.

President Clinton. Thank you.

President Ramos. Thank you. Ladies and gentlemen, permit me to make a small presentation to President Clinton, since he stayed for such a short while and could not play golf in our Malacanang Golf Club.

[At this point, President Clinton was presented with a hat.]

President Clinton. You owe me a golf game. Thank you.

NOTE: The President's 79th news conference began at 6:20 p.m. in Kalayaan Hall at Malacanang Palace.

The President's News Conference in Jakarta, Indonesia
November 14, 1994

The President. Good afternoon. I'm very glad to be here in Indonesia for this APEC meeting. As I said before I left the United States, I am here because this opportunity for me to meet with leaders throughout this region can lead to more economic opportunities for Americans and a reduced threat of nuclear proliferation.

Today I had the opportunity to meet with President Jiang Zemin of China, Prime Minister Murayama of Japan, Prime Minister Keating of Australia, and President Kim of South Korea. The most important topic of our conversations was the situation on the Korean Peninsula. All the leaders indicated their strong support for the agreement we reached with North Korea to freeze and then to dismantle its ability to build nuclear weapons. All agreed on the importance of resuming the dialog between North and South Korea. This agreement marks an his-

toric step to freeze and, ultimately, to end the greatest security threat in this region.

Prime Minister Murayama of Japan and South Korean President Kim agreed that we must maintain our close cooperation as we begin to implement the agreement. And the three of us plan to meet briefly again later this evening to follow up on our earlier conversations.

In all my meetings today I made it clear that the fundamental interests of the United States in the Pacific remain unchanged. And each of the leaders welcomed the assurance that the United States will continue to exercise active leadership in the region.

In each of the meetings today there was also strong agreement that the early ratification of GATT would be absolutely essential to maintaining a climate that promotes global economic growth and expanding trade. I told each of the leaders that I would do everything I could to pass the GATT, that Congress would come back soon, and that I thought it would pass. It was clear to me that the rest of the world is looking to the United States for leadership on this issue. It's also clear to me, I will say again, that it is very much in our interest to pass GATT because it means more high-wage jobs for Americans.

Finally, in each of the meetings we discussed the APEC leaders meeting which begins tonight. I expressed my strong support for the efforts of President Soeharto to build on the common vision of the Asian-Pacific community that we set forth at Seattle last year in the first of these leaders meetings.

This week's discussions I believe will allow us to take a critical step forward toward free and open trade throughout the region. After all, this is very important to the United States. Already one-third of our exports go to the Asia-Pacific region; already 2 million American jobs are tied to this region. This is the fastest growing part of the world. So it is very important that we proceed first with GATT and second with APEC so that we can continue the economic recovery at home and continue to provide increasing opportunities for our people.

All these meetings today reinforced my belief that the United States is strong in the Asian-Pacific region, that we are getting stronger in this region, and that in so doing we are strengthening Americans economically and in terms of our security. In short, we are moving in the right direction. This is a good investment. We need to make the most of it.

Terry [Terence Hunt, United Press International].

North Korea

Q. Mr. President, APEC—as an economic organization—what kind of statement of support or commitment are you seeking from APEC about implementing the nuclear agreement with North Korea? Are you hoping that all the leaders have something to say on this?

The President. I think that the leaders who are most concerned with it may have something to say. I don't know that the organization itself will.

President Kim and I obviously have worked most heavily on it. And Prime Minister Murayama has been terribly interested in it. But we had a long discussion today between President Jiang Zemin and myself about it, and it

will become a topic of conversation elsewhere, as well. Prime Minister Keating was very intent on being supportive of the agreement.

I don't know that there will be an APEC statement, because it's an economic group. But I have not yet talked to anyone who does not believe it's an important first step forward and that it ought to be implemented.

East Timor

Q. Mr. President, as you know, some students have taken over or have occupied the parking lot in the U.S. Embassy here and are calling for the release of one of the leaders of the Timor human rights movement. They've asked to meet with you, sir. Has there been any contact between your entourage and these students? And how do you feel about their demands?

The President. Well, first, the whole issue of East Timor has been of a concern to the United States at least since I've been President. I talked about it in the campaign of 1992, and we have raised it in our conversations with Indonesian leaders. We will continue to do so. The contacts they've had, insofar as I know them, have occurred in an appropriate way through our Embassy there. But this is an issue which is a part of our dialog with the Indonesians, and it should be.

Cooperation With Republican Leaders

Q. Mr. President, Congressman Gingrich is known to feel that he was never properly or publicly thanked for his help on NAFTA. He has, however, said that he's committed to helping to get the GATT legislation passed. First, have you discussed that issue, the GATT legislation, with him? And do you feel that you have anything else to say to him about his participation in NAFTA?

The President. Well, I don't know about that. When NAFTA passed, I tried to be profuse in my thanks to the Republicans as well as the Democrats. Congressman Gingrich, Mr. Kolbe, Mr. Dreier, and others were critical in the success of NAFTA, and they are critical to the success of the GATT. I was encouraged by my conversations with both Congressman Gingrich and Senator Dole about GATT, and I look forward to working with them.

Rita [Rita Braver, CBS News].

Q. While you're here having the summit with the Asian-Pacific leaders, I wondered if you'd given any thought to when you return to Washington having sort of a summit with the incoming Republican leaders, some kind of series of face-to-face meetings where you'd work on a mutual agenda, and whether at this point you've fixed on any kind of strategy toward working with them?

The President. Well, my strategy will be to have an open door and to have a lot of contact. And I certainly intend to meet with them. I said before I left in my conversations with Senator Dole and Congressman Gingrich that I looked forward to having a chance to meet with them when I come back. I left, frankly, as you know, shortly after the elections, so there wasn't a great deal of opportunity to think through all the details. And I asked them to work with Mr. Panetta about that, and I presume they are doing so.

Yes, sir.

North Korea

Q. Mr. President, do you feel that—[*inaudible*]—what President Jiang Zemin said in reaction to the agreement on North Korea nuclear issue? And also, do you expect a firm commitment from Prime Minister Murayama and President Kim when you meet with them later this evening?

The President. Well, they all said that they strongly supported the agreement and that they thought it was very important that we continue to work it through. They understood that the implementation of the agreement would not be without difficulty and it would require a lot of efforts on several fronts.

They all also agreed that we ought to see a resumption of the North-South dialog, that these two countries have some things to resolve between themselves that the rest of us simply cannot do for them. A lot of these things they're going to have to talk through themselves. But I was very encouraged by what President Jiang said and what Prime Minister Murayama said and what President Kim said about the agreement. They were all very forthright and strong in their support of it.

Wolf [Wolf Blitzer, Cable News Network].

Human Rights

Q. Mr. President, some of your critics back home are suggesting you're giving too much importance to trade and economic issues with China, with Indonesia, other members of APEC and not enough to human rights. Specifically,

this morning in your meeting with the Chinese leader, you didn't forcefully address these human rights issues, presumably as forcefully as many human rights groups would like. And at this time that you're here in Indonesia, Amnesty International is suggesting that human rights abuses here in Indonesia are getting worse. How do you respond to these critics?

The President. That the United States, perhaps more than any other country in the world, consistently and regularly raises human rights issues. There was a discussion of human rights issues in the meeting with President Jiang Zemin this morning in which a number of specific things were raised and in which we made it absolutely clear that in order for the United States' relationship with China to fully flower, there had to be progress on all fronts.

So I think it was quite clear. And as I said, I have met with President Soeharto before; I have met with these other leaders before. Wherever there is a clear human rights problem, I have tried to address it and will continue to do so and use whatever influence we can in a positive way.

United Nations and Foreign Aid

Q. Senator Helms is talking about cuts in foreign aid and cuts for U.N. funding, saying that a lot of our money in years past has gone down what he called "foreign ratholes." Does this bode well for your relationship with him, and does it undercut your position at meetings like this one?

The President. Well, let me say, first of all, I think that all Americans would agree that not every dollar that was spent by the United Nations in the past was spent as efficiently as possible. We have been very active since Ambassador Albright has been at the United Nations in pushing for U.N. reforms to increase the efficiency of the organization and to increase the impact of the dollars and other currencies that are spent there. And we have made some progress in improving the efficiency of the United Nations. I am proud of the work that Madeleine Albright and others have done in supporting that.

Now, having said that, it still seems to me that we are far better off working where we can with other nations of the world and trying to make our fair contribution as long as we know our dollars are going to be well spent.

If I might just point out, one of the things that we're looking forward to as we go through the various phases of our mission in Haiti is turning over our mission to a United Nations operation to complete the overall mission in Haiti of training the police force, the armed forces, and being there until the next elections are conducted. That's an area in our own backyard where the presence of the United Nations and the willingness of other nations to participate and to contribute is of economic benefit to us.

So I think we have to be—I agree with anyone, including Senator Helms, who wants the United Nations to be efficiently run and to say we have to continue to work at it. But I do not agree that it is a mistake for us to support peacekeeping. I think it is a good thing, a good allocation of our resources if properly done. And I would hope to be able to persuade a majority of both parties in the Congress, and in the Senate especially where there's so much foreign affairs interest, that that is the right course.

Human Rights Demonstrations

Q. Mr. President, the protesters at the Embassy are demonstrating in the best nonviolent American tradition. And we're all going to move on, but they're going to still be here and have to face the justice system. Are you going to send any signal to the Indonesian Government this week that we're worried about how they'll be treated after we're all gone?

The President. We've already done that. We've already said that we had no problem with these young people coming and expressing their views in our Embassy grounds, that we talked with them, we worked with them. And we have been assured that there will be no retribution against them for exercising their political expression and bringing their concerns to us. We have been assured of that, and I feel comfortable that the commitment we received will be honored.

APEC Summit

Q. Mr. President, in terms of the goals of this economic summit, I understand that you're hoping that a timetable of action aimed at liberalizing trade comes out of this meeting. That may not seem like a giant political payoff for people back home, and I'm wondering, how do you explain what the benefits of this meeting are to Americans who are wondering why you came to Jakarta?

The President. Well, first of all, let's wait and see what happens. But I would like to make two comments about it. I told the American people when I sought this office that it was necessary for the President to look to the long-term economic interests of the country as well as to the short-term economic interests of the country, that we were moving into a global economy in which we had to make long-term commitments and expect others to make them if we wanted Americans to have good jobs and stable incomes and brighter futures.

We don't yet know—I don't want to jump the gun on what the agreement will be, but I think most Americans would like it very much to know that at some date certain that every market in this part of the world, the fastest growing part of the world with already some of the most powerful economies in the world, would be as open to our products as our markets are to theirs. I think Americans would like that.

And I would ask that the Americans who want immediate results to remember that after 2 years of hard work, we have the economy going in the right direction. We need to provide more stability and higher wages in it and more security, ability to afford health care and things of that kind. And we have seen some significant advances in foreign policy in the Middle East, in Northern Ireland, in Haiti, with the missile agreement with China, with the nuclear agreement with North Korea. These things take time, but you do get the payoff if you invest the time.

This is a remarkable thing, the fact that these 15 leaders are meeting for the second time in 2 years and talking about ripping down the barriers that divide us so that all of our people can be more prosperous in the future.

I did not want, when I became President, I did not want to see this world polarized by trading blocs which would take the place of the nuclear blocs of the cold war. I wanted to see regions cooperate within themselves but also reach out beyond their borders. That's what I have worked for in Europe, in Latin America, in Africa, and certainly in Asia. It is the fastest growing part of the world. The American people cannot be as prosperous as they need to be unless we succeed here in Asia.

Thank you.

Bosnia

Q. Mr. President, we haven't heard you on Bosnia. Do you care to say something about that?

The President. Well, I can say that I've obviously been very concerned about the events of the last few days in Bihac. We have tabled a— we have put forth a proposal to our allies there and to the members of the Contact Group. And we are hoping to see the situation stabilize.

Q. What about the embargo, the criticism that you——

The President. We have been criticized by some of our allies, but I think they need to understand the situation. The United States Congress had a heavy majority in favor of unilateral lifting of the arms embargo. Instead of that, we got a bill through the Congress which said that we should pursue a multilateral lift of the arms embargo through the United Nations if the Contact Group proposal was not adopted but that we would stop spending American tax dollars to enforce the embargo directly.

Now we know that the Bosnian Government itself, which enjoys such wide support in the Congress in both parties, has asked us not to lift the arms embargo for a period of 6 months while they continue to work to try to sell the Contact Group proposal.

We have worked very hard in the last few days—I want to compliment the Secretary of State and the Secretary of Defense and others in our administration, including the United Nations Ambassador and the National Security Adviser—we've all worked hard to try to explain to our allies exactly what we have done and what we have not done. We are not violating the arms embargo. We are observing the international arms embargo. We will continue to do it. But the arrangement which we have adopted on enforcement is the product of intense negotiations in the United States Congress, which Senator Nunn and others helped us to work out to avoid what I believe would have been a very serious mistake, which would have been a unilateral vote by the Congress to lift the arms embargo.

Thank you.

Q. Mr. President, can you take one question from Indonesian press?

The President. Yes, I think I owe you one. I was looking for someone to raise their hand. Go ahead, I'll give you one.

Military Sales and the APEC Summit

Q. Mr. President, does the relationship between the civilian and the military in a developing country affect U.S. military sales to the country?

The President. Well, there are many things that affect United States military sales to a country. And so I guess the answer to that would be, it depends on the facts; it would depend on the specifics of a case. But we have been quite careful in what we do with our military equipment and sales, and we will continue to do that.

You didn't ask this question, but I do think I should say again—I want to hammer this home for the Indonesian press, if not for the American press—this is a remarkable thing that is being done here in Indonesia and quite remarkable that President Soeharto is trying to spearhead a clear and specific commitment on the part of all these nations in the fastest growing part of the world to tear down their trade barriers. It is a very significant thing.

So far as I know, there is no precedent for it. I had hoped such a thing would occur when I convened the leaders in Seattle last year, but I knew that this was something that would have to bubble up from the grass-roots, from the people in the fast-growing economies of Asia. And this is a remarkable meeting that, in history, will be looked back on as a very important part of what the world looks like well into the 21st century.

Thank you.

Q. Any jet lag?

The President. Just a tad. I think I'm still somewhere between Jordan and Jerusalem. [*Laughter*]

NOTE: The President's 80th news conference began at 4:37 p.m. at the U.S. Ambassador's residence. In his remarks, he referred to Prime Minister Tomiichi Murayama of Japan; Prime Minister Paul Keating of Australia; President Kim Yongsam of South Korea; and President Soeharto of Indonesia.

Letter to Congressional Leaders on the Proliferation of Weapons of Mass Destruction
November 14, 1994

Dear Mr. Speaker: (Dear Mr. President:)

Pursuant to section 204(b) of the International Emergency Economic Powers Act (50 U.S.C. 1703(b)) and section 201 of the National Emergencies Act (50 U.S.C. 1631), I hereby report to the Congress that I have exercised my statutory authority to declare a national emergency and to issue an Executive order that consolidates the functions of two existing Executive orders, eliminates provisions that have been superseded by legislation, and expands certain existing authorizations in order to enhance our ability to respond to the threat of weapons of mass destruction-related proliferation activities around the world.

The new Executive order consolidates the functions of Executive Order No. 12735 of November 16, 1990, that declared a national emergency with respect to the proliferation of chemical and biological weapons, and Executive Order No. 12930 of September 29, 1994, that declared a national emergency with respect to nuclear, biological, and chemical weapons and of the means of delivering such weapons. This new order includes all of the authorities in Executive Order No. 12930 and, with the exception discussed below, continues the authorities previously in Executive Order No. 12735.

The new order eliminates certain redundant authorities and other authorities that will be rendered unnecessary in the wake of congressional or multilateral action. The order eliminates obsolete provisions relating to the negotiation of a global convention relating to chemical weapons (CW) because the Chemical Weapons Convention has already been negotiated, signed, and is now in the ratification process. The order also eliminates an obsolete requirement to develop a list of items for CW-related controls. Such a list and the controls in question have already been implemented.

Finally, the new order provides additional authorization to further important nonproliferation goals that are not present in existing legislation or the other Executive orders. First, the order expands previous provisions on the imposition of export controls by referring to weapons of mass destruction and missiles rather than to

chemical and biological weapons. Second, the order provides for the imposition of sanctions on foreign persons for proliferation activity contributing to chemical and biological weapons programs in any country. Existing sanctions legislation is limited, absent Presidential action, to activity that contributes to chemical and biological weapons programs in the countries on the terrorist list. This provision closes a loophole in the existing sanctions legislation and comports with the global requirement of the Chemical Weapons Convention not to assist CW programs anywhere in the world.

I have authorized these actions in view of the danger posed to the national security, foreign policy, and economy of the United States by the continuing proliferation of weapons of mass destruction and their means of delivery.

The Secretary of State, the Secretary of the Treasury, and the Secretary of Commerce are authorized to take such actions and to issue any regulations necessary to implement these requirements. These actions shall be implemented in accordance with procedures established under Executive Order No. 12851 of June 11, 1993. I am enclosing a copy of the Executive order that I have issued exercising these authorities.

My Administration continues to believe that the harmonized proliferation sanctions legislation it included as part of the proposed new Export Administration Act represents the best means of maximizing the effectiveness of sanctions as a tool of U.S. nonproliferation policy while minimizing adverse economic impacts on U.S. exporters. Until such harmonized sanctions legislation is enacted, however, I believe that it is appropriate as an interim measure to take the steps described above to consolidate and streamline the restrictions of the former nonproliferation Executive orders.

Sincerely,

WILLIAM J. CLINTON

NOTE: Identical letters were sent to Thomas S. Foley, Speaker of the House of Representatives, and Albert Gore, Jr., President of the Senate. The Executive order is listed in Appendix D at the end of this volume.

The President's News Conference in Jakarta
November 15, 1994

The President. Good evening—or good morning, to the people who are watching this back in America. At our meeting in Bogor today, the Asian-Pacific leaders pledged to achieve free and fair trade and investment between our nations by the year 2020, with the industrialized countries reaching this goal by 2010. This agreement is good news for the countries of this region and especially good news for the United States and our workers. I want to thank President Soeharto for hosting this meeting and for his leadership in crafting the agreement.

When the United States brought the APEC leaders together in Seattle for the very first time last year, we agreed on a common vision of a united, open trading system. At this year's meeting, we have committed to make that vision real through free and fair trade and to do it by a date certain. We'll meet again next year in Osaka. Meanwhile, we'll develop a detailed action agenda, a blueprint, for achieving our goal of free and fair trade, which I hope and believe will be approved when we meet in Osaka.

APEC is primarily an economic organization, and today's talks focused on those issues. While I believe stronger trade ties also will lead to more open societies, I remain committed to pursuing our human rights agenda, as I did in my individual meetings with the leaders this week. This is an agenda we must be willing to pursue with both patience and determination, and we will.

From the beginning of this administration, we have worked to create high-wage jobs and a high-growth economy for the 21st century by expanding our ability to trade with and do business with other nations. The Asia-Pacific region is key to the success of this strategy because it's the fastest growing region in the world, with rapidly expanding middle classes who are potential American customers. Already a third of our exports go to these nations, with 2 million American jobs tied to them. And we know that export-related jobs on average pay much higher than regular jobs in America.

These free and fair trade agreements will benefit Americans for a simple reason: Our Nation already has the most open markets on Earth. By opening other markets, our products and services become more competitive, and more sales abroad create more high-wage jobs at home.

Under this agreement, individual APEC nations will have to tear down trade barriers to reap trade benefits. And no country will get more in benefits than it gives; no free riders. Today's agreement will lower barriers even further than the historic GATT world trade agreement.

Let me just give you one example. Even after the GATT world trade agreement takes effect, tariffs on American automobiles in Malaysia, Thailand, Indonesia, and the Philippines will still be between 30 and 60 percent, lower than they are today but very high. By contrast, our tariffs on automobiles are 2.5 percent.

The market in just these four countries alone in 6 years will be as great as the total market in Canada and Mexico combined. This APEC agreement will knock down Asian tariffs even further, and American autos will, therefore, be more affordable. That means for an autoworker in Detroit or Toledo more secure jobs and factories with more workers, factories that are growing, not shrinking.

I'm proud of the leadership of the United States in creating a post-cold-war world that is both safer and more prosperous, a better place for Americans to live and work in. Trade agreements like NAFTA, the GATT agreement, and now the Bogor Declaration, along with the Summit of the Americas next month, are important in their own way just as are the agreements we've made with the Russians and Ukraine on nuclear missiles, the North Korean nuclear agreement, and the agreement on missile deployments with China. I'm convinced this declaration will prove to be of historic importance.

Americans may hear about this declaration and think, well, 2010 is a long time to wait for any benefits. That is—let me emphasize—the completion date for the process. The benefits will begin for America as soon as we begin to implement the blueprint, which we will develop in this coming year.

But first things first. Our first meeting in Seattle last year created the conditions that helped make it possible to get agreement among the nations of the world on the GATT world trade agreement. Without the meeting in Seattle, we might well not have had a GATT agreement.

Now, when we return to Washington, our first order of business must be for Congress to pass the GATT. Every leader I spoke with here, every leader I spoke with here asked me about United States leadership on GATT and on world trade issues generally. America's opportunities and our responsibilities demand a spirit of bipartisanship, especially when it comes to keeping our country strong abroad.

That cooperation was demonstrated in the historic NAFTA victory and in the encouragement I received from the Republican leaders before I left for this trip. Now, I call upon the Congress, members of both parties, to use this momentum from this trip to pass the GATT. The economic recovery going on in our country and taking hold in the world depends upon the passage of GATT and our continued leadership.

At the end of the Second World War, the United States had a bipartisan effort to create an enduring partnership with our allies that helped keep the peace and helped spawn an era of global prosperity, that created enormous opportunities for the American people.

Now, at the end of the cold war, we are building a new framework for peace and prosperity that will take us into the future. It is imperative that the United States lead as we move toward this new century. That is our great opportunity, and that is the best way we can help all Americans toward a more prosperous future.

East Timor

Q. Mr. President, as you know, nearly two decades ago, the Portuguese withdrew from East Timor, and the Indonesian military moved in. Sir, do you feel East Timor deserves self-rule, and tomorrow when you meet with President Soeharto, will you ask him to withdraw his troops and allow East Timor to pursue democratic elections?

The President. The position of the United States and the position that I have held since 1991, since long before I held this office, is that the people of East Timor should have more say over their own local affairs. I have already spoken with President Soeharto about this in the past in our personal meetings, and it will come up again in our discussion tomorrow.

Interest Rates

Q. Mr. President, back on economics, the Federal Reserve raised interest rates five times this year, and they're expected to do so again today. Many critics think that the Fed has gone too far and that another boost will push the country into a recession. I know that you always say that the Fed is an independent agency, but I wonder if, now that it's gone this far, if you have something to say?

The President. Well, of course, the pressure that it's under is because of world trading and currencies. I would just like to point out that the United States has produced over 5 million jobs in 22 months. We have the lowest inflation in 29 years. We have more high-wage jobs this year than in the previous 5 years.

So yes, it is important to keep the proper balance, to keep our currency stable, and to keep going and growing. But we are having investment-led growth based on highly productive workers with no inflation. So I just would say the important thing is to make every judgment based on what it takes to keep economic growth going in the United States. And I am very proud of what we have done, and I think we have to continue to pursue this course. I'm going to do what I can control.

I have noticed, however, that almost anything I say about this may be misinterpreted, not just here but primarily around the world. So I'm not going to comment on it, except to say the United States has an economic growth pattern that is the envy of advanced nations in the world. We're growing at a healthy rate. We have literally the lowest inflation in 29 years. And finally, we're creating some high-wage jobs after years and years and years of stagnant wages for American working people.

So I'm going to do everything I can to keep that recovery going. And I believe that the members of the Fed will do their best to keep the recovery going. That's what I would urge them to do and to make the best judgment they can.

Cooperation With Republican Leaders

Q. Mr. President, while you've been here, the Republicans are preparing for the transition over in the House and the Senate. As you've been monitoring their comments, what is your sense: Is there going to be a big fight, or is there going to be an opportunity for some consensus, some cooperation? And when will you invite the new Republican leadership to the White House for a sort of mini-summit that's been talked about?

The President. I believe that Mr. Panetta is meeting with them today, as we all agreed before I left. And I look forward to meeting with them as soon as I can, as convenient with all of our schedules, when I get back.

And as I said, I am willing to cooperate. There are areas in which I believe we can cooperate. I have mentioned several: the line-item veto, the welfare reform, continued reductions in the Federal Government, and continuation of our whole reinventing Government initiative so that we can do more with less. On the middle class tax cut, I believe the first thing we had to do was to get control of the deficit and to do as much as we could on that. We got as far as 15 million families in 1993. We got up to $27,000 in income. I would like very much to go further, but we mustn't explode the deficit. We've got to pay for it.

So there are all these areas where I think we can work together and where I am certainly willing to. And that's the spirit in which I will go home.

The Presidency

Q. You mentioned a few moments ago that this was a historic agreement—[*inaudible*]—here today. I'm wondering, in light of this meeting and the other meetings you've had overseas previously to this, if it's not perhaps beginning to seem to you that perhaps foreign affairs and foreign trade is really the essence of the modern Presidency, more so than domestic and especially in light of what you're looking ahead to in the next few years.

The President. Well, first of all, I think that the Presidency is certainly more than making laws. And the Congress has to pass laws. And I've always thought that.

But let me emphasize to you that I do not believe that I could be here doing what I am doing today if we hadn't taken vigorous action to bring the deficit down and if we hadn't passed the NAFTA agreement in Congress and if we hadn't also already taken strong steps to try to protect and promote the interests of ordinary Americans, including the family leave law, the crime bill, and things that address our problems at home.

I see these things as two sides of the same coin. I don't believe we can be strong in the world, I don't believe we can secure the future for our working people unless we have good policies at home and good policies abroad. I think that strong families and good education systems and better paying jobs and safe streets and expanding trade and being free from the threat of nuclear war, I think these are two sides of the same coin. So, to me, I have to do them both.

I will say this, there have been more opportunities and more responsibilities in this particular year than even I could have foreseen when I ran for President even last year. A lot of the work that we have been doing came to fruition this year, particularly in the Middle East peace talks, in the Partnership For Peace and what we are doing in Europe, and of course in Asia in expanding economic activities.

I think that more and more the job of the modern President will involve relating with the rest of the world because we are in an interdependent world. Whether we like it or not, money and management and technology are mobile, and the world is interdependent. And we have to make sure Americans do well in that kind of world. And we have the—the President has a special responsibility there.

Yes?

School Prayer

Q. President Clinton, one of the other things the Republicans talked about yesterday in your press conference was the idea that they would propose a constitutional amendment to restore prayer to public schools. Is that something that you would support? Do you think the country needs that?

The President. Well, what I think the country needs and what I think the schools need is a sense that there are certain basic values of citizenship, including valuing the right of people to have and express their faith, which can be advocated without crossing the line of the separation of church and state and without in any way undermining the fabric of our society. Indeed, the schools, perhaps today more than ever before, need to be the instrument by which we transfer important values of citizenship.

One of the things that was in the elementary and secondary education act that I signed, that passed with strong bipartisan support but was little noticed, was the advocacy of basically the teaching of civic values in the schools.

Now, on the school prayer thing, I can only tell you what my personal opinion is about that. I have always supported voluntary prayer in the schools. I have always thought that the question was, when does voluntary prayer really become coercive to people who have different religious views from those that are in the majority in any particular classroom? So that, for example, I personally did not believe that it was coercive to have a prayer at an outdoor sporting event or at a graduation event because I don't believe that is coercive to people who don't participate in it. So I think there is room for that.

Obviously, I want to reserve judgment. I want to see the specifics. But I think this whole values debate will go forward and will intensify in the next year. And again, I would say, this ought to be something that unites the American people, not something that divides us. This ought not to be a partisan debate. The American people do not want us to be partisan, but they do want us to proceed in a way that is consistent with their values and that communicates those values to our children.

So let's just—I'll be glad to discuss it with them. I want to see what the details are. I certainly wouldn't rule it out. It depends on what it says.

Cooperation With Republican Leaders

Q. Mr. President, have you had time to reflect on the elections results, specifically, what happened? And while we've been here, Congressman Gingrich, among his quotes, "This is time to be open to dramatic, bold changes." That's what you ran on, and I'm wondering if you'll take any new attitude with you to Washington after some time off.

The President. Well, first of all, we gave the American people a lot of changes. And the changes we gave them required tough decisions. And if we now are going to have a partnership for further bold changes, nothing could make me happier. But we reduced the deficit more than any time in history. We did it for 3 years in a row for the first time since President Truman. We have reduced the Federal Government by 70,000. We're taking it down to its smallest size since President Kennedy. We have deregulated major parts of the American economy. We have given States the ability to get out from under Federal rules to promote welfare reform,

health care reform, education reform. We are making dramatic changes.

I would like to have a bipartisan partnership to go further. There are some things we didn't get done last time that I would like to see done. We ought to be able to have a bipartisan welfare reform bill. I ask only that the same spirit exists there that I exhibited when I was a Democratic Governor in 1988, I reached out my hand in partnership to the Reagan administration and to the Republicans and Democrats in Congress.

There are a lot of things we can do together, and I've already mentioned several of them. So I'm very hopeful. And we do need a lot more changes, and we can do them together if we are determined to put America first and not put partisanship first.

Q. Mr. President, as you look to the next 2 years of your term and the changed political realities of Washington, is there some previous President that you look to as a sort of model on how you're going to proceed?

The President. I don't think so. I don't think that there's an exact historical analogy. I think there are some obvious similarities, but they all break down.

I have read, since I've been President, even though I had read widely about our Presidents before I took office, I've read a number of biographies, histories of the administrations of many Presidents. I have seen times when the usual pattern between a President and Congress was, in fact, more contentious than the one we had the last 2 years. Even though the American people seem to perceive it as very contentious, the truth is that it was, as you know, only the third Congress since World War II when a Congress adopted more than 80 percent of the measures a President recommended. So I think we'll just have to see.

What I need to be guided by is not the past but a devotion to America's future, to making America stronger, to making the future of working people stronger, to the kinds of things that I have worked for. And I will do my best to do that with the facts as they develop. And I'm looking forward to it.

Foreign Policy

Q. Mr. President, in mentioning the special responsibility of a President in foreign affairs, do you see any limits on your own personal ability to continue being a personal diplomat, and do you intend to continue the growing pace of travel?

The President. Well, as I said, I think that we have had a series of unusual opportunities and responsibilities this year: getting the Partnership For Peace off; getting the nuclear agreement between Russia and Ukraine, which led to no Russian missiles being pointed at the United States for the first time since the dawn of the nuclear age; pursuing the Middle East peace in my meeting with President Asad in Geneva and then the 3 days I spent in the Middle East. And then, of course, we had the 50th anniversary of World War II. So these things—there were some unusual things which required a great deal of time this year.

I think every President from now on, for the foreseeable future, will be required to participate in the building of an architecture which promotes peace and prosperity and security for the American people and is increasingly involved in the rest of the world. But I expect that the lion's share of my work will continue to be done at home, and I will continue to do it. I don't think anyone could say I had a less than ambitious domestic agenda this year and didn't pursue it with great vigor. So I think you will just have to—we'll have to do both from now on. Yes.

Asian-Pacific Trade Agreement

Q. Mr. President, the report reaching us is that China and South Korea do not have to meet the free trade objective until 2020. Does this give these countries an unfair advantage in your opinion, and what will you do to address it?

The President. First of all, whether China and South Korea have to meet this objective by 2020 or 2010 depends upon their own rate of growth. That is, there was no definition today of industrialized countries that excluded them in 2010. Indeed, I think most of the people who were in that room today thought that, given South Korea's growth, they might well meet that and, in fact, might be expected to meet it before 2010 and that the Chinese could meet it, depending on whether they're able to sustain a certain level of growth.

Secondly, let me emphasize that while the agreement provides for two different times for the parties to be willing and able to get rid of all their trade barriers, we assume an equivalence of treatment among all the countries so

that even if, let's say, China or some other country, Thailand—any country, you name it—doesn't have to go down all the way until 2020, their relationship with the other countries involved, including the advanced countries, will be dictated still by an equivalency. There will be no unilateral give-ups; there will be a negotiated downward movement in the barriers among all parties.

So I think this is very good. This simply recognizes that under the best of circumstances, some nations may be so far away in economic disparities, they may not be able to get there by 2020. There is nothing in those two times that disadvantages, let's say, Japan or Canada, not to mention the United States.

Q. Mr. President, given the tough fight that you had over NAFTA and the nervousness over GATT, how can you convince Americans they will benefit from free trade with Asia, especially when there is such a big gap with some countries on workers' wages and rights?

The President. I would say—I would make two arguments. First of all, look at the fight we had over NAFTA, and look at the results. We had a 500 percent increase in automobile exports to Mexico in one year. Our exports to Mexico increased by 19 percent, about almost 3 times what our overall exports went up since NAFTA passed. NAFTA has been a job winner for the United States, and basically the jobs we're gaining in are upper income jobs. So if NAFTA is the test, it should make us want more of these things.

The second point I'd like to make is that when we started APEC—keep in mind the atmosphere that was existing in Seattle last year. When we started APEC, what was the worry? The worry was that the world would be developing into three huge trade blocs: the European Union; the United States, Canada, Mexico, Central, South America, and the Caribbean; and Asia, and that Asia was the fastest growing region in the world, that trade among the Asian nations was going up but people were afraid we would be shut out of that market.

So if everything we do has some equivalency to it, that is, if there is no unilateral give-up by the United States, what we are doing in this agreement is opening the fastest growing market in the world. Look at—just take this country we're in, Indonesia. They are growing at a phenomenal rate and have been for quite some time now. Their capacity to purchase, to engage, to trade, and for themselves to compete and win in the global economy is increasing every day.

So what I would say is, we could never walk away from the Asian market; we should be walking toward it on terms that are fair. And that's what I think we're doing.

Yes.

Foreign Policy

Q. Mr. President, how can you prevent the Republicans from blocking foreign policy initiatives you might want to pass, such as the operations—the administration seems increasingly comfortable in multilateral operations such as Haiti, potential U.S. involvement in a future Bosnia peace enforcement operation, potential U.S. commitment to peacekeeping in the Golan. How are you going to prevent the Republicans from blocking you in that area?

The President. Well, historically, the Republicans have favored a strong American foreign policy and a robust one. And most of what I have been able to do as President has enjoyed bipartisan support. And when the—some of the things that have not enjoyed Republican support have also generated significant Democratic support. I had bipartisan opposition to some of the things I have sought to do in foreign policy.

I believe that with careful and honest and open consultations, that in critical matters to our national security, we will be able to put the interest of the United States first. That is certainly the challenge that we must all face.

The Congress and the President have had tensions between them on foreign policy for a very long time now when both parties were in different positions. I don't expect that to go away. And we are creating a new world in which there are new questions to be asked and answered. There's been controversy over foreign policy directions in the last 2 years. I don't expect that to go away. But I do think on the really pivotal matters we'll be able to achieve the kind of bipartisan or perhaps even a nonpartisan consensus to do what's right for the country. That will be my goal.

Yes.

Asian-Pacific Trade Agreement

Q. Mr. President, this may be historic, but a lot of this is often nonbinding—the APEC accord. And a year ago, this forum was boycotted by one member. What gives you any confidence that this kind of deal will not fall apart at some point in the future? And what should the U.S. do to try to avoid that?

The President. I would say there are two things that give me confidence that it will not fall apart. One is that it is in the interest of the Asian countries because they have decided that they want expanded trade in an open world trading system, not in closed trading blocs. The second is the constant reaffirmation of commitment to this by the Asian leaders themselves.

Finally, I would say we have some historic evidence that should give us some encouragement. On a smaller scale, look at the ASEAN agreement, the regional trade agreement where they promised that they would break down trade barriers among themselves. And it was all voluntary, but they met and they worked on it and they laid out a platform. And they just recently shortened by 5 years the time deadline they imposed on themselves for taking all the barriers away.

So if you look at the experience of their conduct, if you look at the conviction by which they express this commitment, and if you look at it, in very cold terms, their own self-interest in wanting to do more in the rest of the world, I think all those things should be very encouraging in terms of having you think that it's more likely than not that it will occur.

Foreign Policy

Q. Mr. President, your administration is in the process of changing its policy or developing its policy on expanding NATO and strengthening CSCE. Will you be going to the CSCE summit in Budapest? And when you look at your foreign travel, your past foreign travel, in recent weeks you've gone to the Middle East; you've spent several days here; you're going to be hosting the Summit of the Americas; you have an ambitious foreign agenda next year. Are you becoming, in essence, a foreign policy President?

The President. Well, let me answer both questions. First of all, I plan to make a very—a brief but I think quite critical trip to the CSCE. I decided to do it after having communications with both Chancellor Kohl and President Yeltsin and looking at what is at stake there in terms of the future of European security. After all, the United States played a strong leadership role in the Partnership For Peace and encouraging the growth of the European Union and European security arrangements.

What I have sought to do is to create a stronger Europe that was more independent but also more closely allied with us and one that at least created the possibility that there would not be another dividing line in Europe just moved a few hundred miles east. We have a big stake in that. So I will go quickly and come back quickly, but I think I should go.

Secondly, on the question of foreign policy versus domestic, let me say, if you look at what happened, in the last 2 years, we had only the third Congress in the history of—since World War II which gave a President more than 80 percent of his domestic initiatives as well as the foreign policy initiatives, including sweeping education reform, the family leave law, the Brady bill, the crime bill, and a number of other very important issues.

So I have no intention of withdrawing from the domestic field. But we had an unusual number of responsibilities this year, an unusual number of opportunities. And Americans are both more prosperous and more secure because of these efforts, and they will be more so in the future. So if I were to give up one in favor of the other, I would be doing a disservice to the American people. I have to try to pursue both courses.

It's been somewhat more busy on the foreign front than I could have anticipated in the last few months because of the unusual developments.

Asian-Pacific Trade Agreement and GATT

Q. Mr. President, it looks like you've made some concessions on letting them come in in 2020 and 2010. China also wants to join GATT and some other world trade organizations. If they want to join and be held to a lesser standard than the major industrial nations—China's the third largest economy in the world. What is your position on letting China into these world trade organizations? Will you give them a break on this, or will you insist that they be held to the same standard as the industrial nations?

The President. Let me answer the first question. First of all, I will say again, whether a country is an industrialized country or a developing country as of 2010 is a question of fact that cannot be answered now. There are some we can be pretty sure will be still industrializing, still developing; some we can be certain will be developed; others we're not sure. There was

no concession given because there must be equivalency in the reduction of trade barriers, a fairness on both sides. But as a practical matter, it will take developing countries longer to get down to zero, even if they have great incentives to do so in dealing with other countries.

Now, on the GATT. To be a founding member of GATT, whether you are a developing country or an industrialized country, without regard to your status, you must agree to observe three or four basic commitments in terms of the way you handle your financial exchanges, in terms of the transparency of your trade laws, in terms of your whole approach to the international economy. There are four basic commitments that all 123—I think the number is—people who have agreed to be founding members of GATT have agreed to do.

So the United States position is that China ought to be in GATT, ought to be a founding member of GATT. They're a very big country; they ought to be a part of this. It's in our interest to do it because it will open more Chinese markets to American products. But every country that has agreed to be a founding member, even the poorest countries, even the smallest countries, have agreed to these four basic criteria. And we believe that anyone who goes in as a founding member should do the same.

Q. Mr. President, you mentioned GATT as your top priority when you get back from this trip. How troubling is it to you that Senator Dole is clearly not on board on this, and how are you going to address the problems—the sort of populist conservative criticisms of WTO as somehow eliminating sovereignty?

The President. Well, it's not just the populist conservatives, there are also some populist liberals who aren't sure about it.

Just before I left, when I called on Senator Dole and we had our conversation, he said that he thought that we could work it out, that we could have some language which would make it clear that our sovereignty was intact, that would not violate the GATT agreement. And I believe that, so I think that's what we'll do. I think he's trying in good faith to get that done based on his representation to me, and we certainly are. And that is our objective.

That's an understandable concern when people first hear about this. You know, they want to be reassured that we're not giving up the ability to run our own affairs. So we're working on it, and I think we'll resolve it.

The Economy

Q. Mr. President, you've mentioned here several times your achievements and your record with Congress and the things you've gotten done. But as you know, one of the big problems you face politically is that the American people don't believe their lives have changed as a result of the things that have been done.

Now, here you have another long-term agreement; it's going to take place over the next generation. And while it may be very beneficial to the country, how are you going to convince Americans that this is going to affect their lives, and how are you going to do it within the next 2 years before you have to face the voters?

The President. Well, I think there were two issues there. One is, as you know, there were a lot of Americans who did not know a lot of the things that had been done. And it is my job to do my best to make sure people know that. Then there is the inevitable fact that there is a time lag between when you pass any law or take any executive action and it can be manifest in the lives of Americans.

You know, one of the problems with the nature of the economy today, from the point of view of the average American working family, is that even if more jobs are coming into the economy, people may not feel more personal job security; even if the economy is growing with low inflation, people may not get a raise. Most Americans, wage earners, particularly hourly earners, have not had an increase in real income, that is, above inflation, in quite some time now.

These are conditions that I am working hard to remedy. There are only two or three ways to remedy them. You have to change the job mix and get more high-wage jobs, you have to increase the skill level of the work force so people can take those jobs, and you have to get enterprise and investment into isolated areas, that is, pockets of the inner cities, pockets of the rural areas which have been left behind. These things may require long-term solutions.

It is my job to do what is best for the American people in the future. I'll do my best to get credit for it, but the most important thing is that I do the right thing. And you know, if I can find a way to get credit for it, I'll be very happy. But the most important thing is that I do the right thing. And I think that as time goes on—most Americans say, if you

ask them, "Do you want us to have a long-term vision, do you want us to have a long-term strategy, do you want us to look at that?" they'll say yes. And then they hear things on a daily basis that are so contentious and so conflicting and so kind of clouding of the atmosphere that it's hard to think about that.

My job is to try to keep lifting the sights of the country above that and keep looking at the long run. The credit will have to either come or not, but that's not as important as trying to do the right thing.

I think I ought to take a question or two from the Indonesian press; I'm sorry.

Q. Mr. President——

The President. Go ahead, and then I'll take this lady first and then you, sir. Go ahead.

APEC and Media Coverage

Q. Mr. President—[*inaudible*]

The President. That the media is?

Q. [*Inaudible*]—media is so completely dominated by the first world?

The President. First of all, if I might—her question was sort of related to your question. Your question is, how do we know that this is going to happen, implying that maybe these folks aren't serious. Her question, in a way, is the same question from a different point of view. If there is no institutionalized mechanism, how do we know that it will go on when those of us who are here aren't here anymore?

And I have to tell you that I think the critical question is, will the leaders themselves continue to meet personally every year, even when it is inconvenient for them to do so? Like now, you know—[*laughter*]—will they continue to do that? Will they continue to meet, even when it is inconvenient for them to do so? And secondly, will they make some specific, concrete progress every time they meet?

So, for example, I feel very good about this; this is potentially, I think, a very historic declaration. But next year, if we don't adopt the blueprint, I'd say that's not a good sign. If we do adopt a blueprint, that is a very good sign. So that is my test.

Now, let me say, on the question of the media being, if you will, dominated by the first world, I think you should be encouraged that, for example, in many of our major news outlets, there is enormous attention given now, much more than previously, not just to—to foreign policy concerns that affect the developing world and not just the largest powers that dominated the cold war debate, number one. Number two, there are now more specific outlets, particularly CNN, for example, that has a whole separate channel dealing with global affairs which gives more and more attention to the developing world. I'll get in a lot of trouble with all of the other networks now. [*Laughter*]

But I think—look at all these people here from all the American outlets. I can't speak for BBC or the French television network or the German network, but every major American media outlet, just about, sent someone to Indonesia, which was, as you know, originally the leader of the nonaligned movement in the United Nations. Every person who is here now has a little different understanding of the problems and the promise of this country, the other countries here represented at APEC.

I think you have to be a little patient with us, too. We are learning more about the rest of the world beyond our borders and beyond our previous habits of encounter. And I think the more we do that, the more you will see a broader coverage of world affairs right across the board.

Educational Exchanges, Politics, and Economics

Q. I watch you every day on CNN, Mr. President, but now you are real. Thank you very much for being here.

Let me introduce myself, chief editor of the Economic and Business Review of Indonesia. I have two questions, Mr. President. First of all, do you agree with me that education, in fact, has been the best investment of the United States in Indonesia, because you have so many economists and people in high position and in key, strategic positions who graduated from the United States? I, myself, am a product of George Washington University; it so happens I'm chairman of the U.S. alumni association.

Somehow, the U.S. effort in this, United States effort in encouraging and developing education, in terms of providing scholarships for Indonesians to the United States, has been less today than some years back. In fact, education for the armed forces has been curtailed. What is your view on this, Mr. President?

The second question is, while liberalization and globalization seems to have been the trademark of APEC, you know yourself that economies do not determine history. Often politics determine history. How do you harmonize this globalization trend with international politics, Mr. President? Thank you very much.

The President. Well, first let me say, I definitely agree that the investment the United States has made in times past in international educational exchanges and bringing people to our country to attend our universities and our colleges and sending our young people abroad to attend school in other countries has been a very, very important thing.

It is true that there has been some reduction in Federal support for such programs, which I very much regret, but it is a function of the fact that we quadrupled the national debt of America from 1981 to 1993, that in a 12-year period we exploded our debt, our Government deficit was high, and we started having to cut back on a lot of investments, including things that we wanted to do.

I will say that most of our major universities now, particularly a lot of our State universities, are investing much more of their money and their effort in trying to recruit students from around the world and to promote these sort of educational exchanges. And what I would need to do before I could make a final judgment is to see what the total effort is in our country. But we should be doing more of it. So I feel very strongly about that.

Now, what was the second question you asked? Yes, yes, the economy and politics. Let me just say about that, I believe that the business of politics is, not completely but in large measure, to give the maximum opportunity for the positive economic forces in the world to succeed within each country or within each— in my case, within each of our States within our country. That is not the whole business, but that is a major part of the business. So a lot of what we try to do in the United States is to think about the good things that are happening in our country and in the world and what we can do to accelerate them and then to think about the problems, the roadblocks, the obstacles, and what we can do to eliminate them so that we try to harmonize those things.

Very often when politics can mess up economics, it's because it becomes obsessed with some other goal which is destructive of the human spirit. Politics should be more than economics—I talked about human rights here today—but it should be very heedful of making those good things happen through the economic system.

I'll take this lady's question, the last one.

WTO and President's Visit to Istiqlal

Q. Thank you, Mr. President. Who will the United States support for the job of Secretary General of the WTO, Salinas, Ruggiero, or Kim?

And my other question, while Indonesians are very proud that a Christian—my Christian uncle built the Istiqlal Mosque, I find it difficult to explain to my readers why the President of the United States took his time to visit that mosque. Thank you, Mr. President.

The President. Let me answer the second question first. I went to the mosque because, first of all, I wanted to see it—it's a massive and impressive and important structure; secondly, because Indonesia is a predominantly Muslim country that has a very vibrant Catholic, Protestant, Hindu, and Buddhist heritage and active religions today in all those areas. And the Minister of Religious Affairs here made available some time for me to go to the mosque, to talk with him about what was going on there, and to explain to me personally how these various religions had come into this country and how they operated today within the country together, without undermining or conflicting one with the other.

Finally, I have tried to do a lot as I have traveled the world—and I did this when I was in Jordan, speaking to the Jordanian Parliament—to say to the American people and to the West generally that even though we have had problems with terrorism coming out of the Middle East, it is not inherently related to Islam, not to the religion, not to the culture. And the tradition of Islam in Indonesia, I think, makes that point very graphically. It's something our people in America need to know; it's something people in the West, throughout the West, need to know.

With regard to the World Trade Organization, I will have an announcement about that in the next couple of days. You won't have to wait long.

Thank you very much.

NOTE: The President's 81st news conference began at 7:10 p.m. at the Jakarta Hilton. In his remarks, he referred to Tarmizi Taher, Minister of Religious Affairs of Indonesia. A reporter referred to Mexican President Carlos Salinas, former Italian Trade Minister Renato Ruggiero, and South Korean Minister of Trade, Industry and Energy Kim Chol-su as candidates for Secretary General, World Trade Organization.

APEC Economic Leaders' Declaration of Common Resolve, Bogor, Indonesia
November 15, 1994

1. We, the economic leaders of APEC, came together in Bogor, Indonesia today to chart the future course of our economic cooperation which will enhance the prospects of an accelerated, balanced and equitable economic growth not only in the Asia Pacific region but throughout the world as well.

2. A year ago on Blake Island in Seattle, USA, we recognized that our diverse economies are becoming more interdependent and are moving toward a community of Asia Pacific economies. We have issued a vision statement in which we pledged:
—to find cooperative solutions to the challenges of our rapidly changing regional and global economy;
—to support an expanding world economy and an open multilateral trading system;
—to continue to reduce barriers to trade and investment to enable goods, services and capital to flow freely among our economies;
—to ensure that our people share the benefits of economic growth, improve education and training, link our economies through advances in telecommunication and transportation, and use our resources sustainably.

3. We set our vision for the community of Asia Pacific economies based on a recognition of the growing interdependence of our economically diverse region, which comprises developed, newly industrializing and developing economies. The Asia Pacific industrialized economies will provide opportunities for developing economies

to increase further their economic growth and their level of development. At the same time developing economies will strive to maintain high growth rates with the aim of attaining the level of prosperity now enjoyed by the newly industrializing economies. The approach will be coherent and comprehensive, embracing the three pillars of sustainable growth, equitable development and national stability. The narrowing gap in the stages of development among the Asia Pacific economies will benefit all members and promote the attainment of Asia Pacific economic progress as a whole.

4. As we approach the twenty-first century, APEC needs to reinforce economic cooperation in the Asia Pacific region on the basis of equal partnership, shared responsibility, mutual respect, common interest, and common benefit, with the objective of APEC leading the way in:

—strengthening the open multilateral trading system;

—enhancing trade and investment liberalization in Asia Pacific; and

—intensifying Asia Pacific development cooperation.

5. As the foundation of our market-driven economic growth has been the open multilateral trading system, it is fitting that APEC builds on the momentum generated by the outcome of the Uruguay Round of Multilateral Trade Negotiations and takes the lead in strengthening the open multilateral trading system.

We are pleased to note the significant contribution APEC made in bringing about a successful conclusion of the Uruguay Round. We agree to carry out our Uruguay Round commitments fully and without delay and call on all participants in the Uruguay Round to do the same.

To strengthen the open multilateral trading system we decide to accelerate the implementation of our Uruguay Round commitments and to undertake work aimed at deepening and broadening the out come of the Uruguay Round. We also agree to commit ourselves to our continuing process of unilateral trade and investment liberalization. As evidence of our commitment to the open multilateral trading system we further agree to a standstill under which we will endeavour to refrain from using measures which would have the effect of increasing levels of protection.

We call for the successful launching of the World Trade Organization (WTO). Full and active participation in and support of the WTO by all APEC economies is key to our ability to lead the way in strengthening the multilateral trading system. We call on all non-APEC members of the WTO to work together with APEC economies toward further multilateral liberalization.

6. With respect to our objective of enhancing trade and investment in Asia Pacific, we agree to adopt the long-term goal of free and open trade and investment in Asia Pacific. This goal will be pursued promptly by further reducing barriers to trade and investment and by promoting the free flow of goods, services and capital among our economies. We will achieve this goal in a GATT-consistent manner and believe our actions will be a powerful impetus for further liberalization at the multilateral level to which we remain fully committed.

We further agree to announce our commitment to complete the achievement of our goal of free and open trade and investment in Asia Pacific no later than the year 2020. The pace of implementation will take into account the differing levels of economic development among APEC economies, with the industrialized economies achieving the goal of free and open trade and investment no later than the year 2010 and developing economies no later than the year 2020.

We wish to emphasize our strong opposition to the creation of an inward-looking trading bloc that would divert from the pursuit of global free trade. We are determined to pursue free and open trade and investment in Asia Pacific in a manner that will encourage and strengthen trade and investment liberalization in the world as a whole. Thus, the out come of trade and investment liberalization in Asia Pacific will not only be the actual reduction of barriers among APEC economies but also between APEC economies and non-APEC economies. In this respect we will give particular attention to our trade with non-APEC developing countries to ensure that they will also benefit from our trade and investment liberalisation, in conformity with GATT/WTO provisions.

7. To complement and support this substantial process of liberalisation, we decide to expand and accelerate APEC's trade and investment facilitation programs. This will promote further the flow of goods, services and capital among

APEC economies by eliminating administrative and other impediments to trade and investment.

We emphasize the importance of trade facilitation because trade liberalization efforts alone are insufficient to generate trade expansion. Efforts at facilitating trade are important if the benefits of trade are to be truly enjoyed by both business and consumers. Trade facilitation has also a pertinent role in furthering our goal of achieving the fullest liberalization within the global context.

In particular we ask our ministers and officials to submit proposals on APEC arrangements on customs, standards, investment principles and administrative barriers to market access.

To facilitate regional investment flows and to strengthen APEC's dialogue on economic policy issues, we agree to continue the valuable consultations on economic growth strategies, regional capital flows and other macro-economic issues.

8. Our objective to intensify development cooperation among the community of Asia Pacific economies will enable us to develop more effectively the human and natural resources of the Asia Pacific region so as to attain sustainable growth and equitable development of APEC economies, while reducing economic disparities among them, and improving the economic and social well-being of our peoples. Such efforts will also facilitate the growth of trade and investment in the Asia Pacific region.

Cooperative programs in this area cover expanded human resource development (such as education and training and especially improving management and technical skills), the development of APEC study centres, cooperation in science and technology (including technology transfer), measures aimed at promoting small and medium scale enterprises and steps to improve economic infrastructure, such as energy, transportation, information, telecommunications and tourism. Effective cooperation will also be developed on environmental issues, with the aim of contributing to sustainable development.

Economic growth and development of the Asia Pacific region has mainly been market-driven, based on the growing interlinkages between our business sectors in the region to support Asia Pacific economic cooperation. Recognizing the role of the business sector in economic development, we agree to integrate the business sector in our programs and to create an ongoing mechanism for that purpose.

9. In order to facilitate and accelerate our cooperation, we agree that APEC economies that are ready to initiate and implement a cooperative arrangement may proceed to do so while those that are not yet ready to participate may join at a later date.

Trade and other economic disputes among APEC economies have negative implications for the implementation of agreed cooperative arrangements as well as for the spirit of cooperation. To assist in resolving such disputes and in avoiding its recurrence, we agree to examine the possibility of a voluntary consultative dispute mediation service, to supplement the WTO dispute settlement mechanism, which should continue to be the primary channel for resolving disputes.

10. Our goal is an ambitious one. But we are determined to demonstrate APEC's leadership in fostering further global trade and investment liberalization. Our goal entails a multiple year effort. We will start our concerted liberalization process from the very date of this statement.

We direct our ministers and officials to immediately begin preparing detailed proposals for implementing our present decisions. The proposals are to be submitted soon to the APEC economic leaders for their consideration and subsequent decisions. Such proposals should also address all impediments to achieving our goal. We ask ministers and officials to give serious consideration in their deliberations to the important recommendations contained in the reports of the Eminent Persons Group and the Pacific Business Forum.

11. We express our appreciation for the important and thoughtful recommendations contained in the reports of the Eminent Persons Groups and the Pacific Business Forum. The reports will be used as valuable points of reference in formulating policies in the cooperative framework of the community of Asia Pacific economies. We agree to ask the two groups to continue with their activities to provide the APEC economic leaders with assessments of the progress of APEC and further recommendations for stepping up our cooperation.

We also ask the Eminent Persons Group and the Pacific Business Forum to review the interrelationships between APEC and the existing sub-regional arrangements (AFTA, ANZERTA and NAFTA) and to examine possible options to prevent obstacles to each other and to pro- mote consistency in their relations.

NOTE: The joint statement was made available by the Office of the Press Secretary but was not is- sued as a White House press release.

Nomination for Commissioner of the Social Security Administration
November 15, 1994

The President today announced his intention to nominate Shirley S. Chater, Ph.D., the cur- rent Commissioner of Social Security, to head the Social Security Administration when it be- comes an independent agency next year.

"In the year since she was sworn in as the current Commissioner, Dr. Chater has taken de- cisive steps to improve service to Americans with disabilities, to streamline the agency and make it more efficient, and to enact high cus-

tomer service standards for the more than 49 million Americans who receive Social Security or Supplemental Security Income benefits," the President said. "I can think of no better person to protect and maintain the administration's commitment to Social Security."

NOTE: A biography of the nominee was made available by the Office of the Press Secretary.

Remarks to the International Business Community in Jakarta
November 16, 1994

Thank you very much, Secretary Brown, for the introduction and for your tireless work on behalf of American businesses and American workers. Thank you, Mr. McNabb, for your tes- timonial, and congratulations. I want to come back to northern California and see you after you've doubled your work force. Congressman Mineta, it's great to see you here. Ambassador and Mrs. Barry, distinguished ministers of the Indonesian Government, and the mayor of Ja- karta, and all of our fine hosts from Indonesia who have made this such a wonderful visit for me and for the First Lady and the entire Amer- ican delegation. This is my second trip to Asia as President, and as I was watching Secretary Brown give his remarks, I thought if I keep coming back here I might become as well- known in Asia as Secretary Brown is. [*Laughter*]

I want to thank all of you here from the American private sector who are in the audience for your presence but more importantly for your commitment to keep our Nation engaged eco- nomically across the world.

Keeping America on the front lines of eco- nomic opportunity has been my first priority since I took office. We are pursuing a strategy

to promote aggressive growth in the short run and in the long run. We began by putting our house in order. Our deficit was exploding; the public debt in America had quadrupled between 1981 and 1993. Now we're looking at a reduc- tion in the deficit for the third year in a row for the first time since President Truman was President. Federal spending is the lowest it's been in more than a decade. We cut domestic and defense spending last year for the first time in 25 years. And the Federal work force is shrinking to its lowest level since President Ken- nedy was in office.

The second thing we are doing is working hard to expand trade and investment. That's what NAFTA was all about. That's what the GATT agreement is all about, what the Summit of the Americas, soon to be held in Miami, and obviously this wonderful APEC meeting are all about.

The third thing we're working to do is to develop a system of lifelong learning for our people, from expanding preschool programs like Head Start to providing more affordable college education to our people, to changing the whole unemployment system in America to a continuous retraining system for people who must find new jobs in a rapidly changing global economy.

Lastly, we're trying to change the way our Government works. Secretary Brown talked about it a little bit. There was, I think, a perception among American businesses when we took office that both parties, historically, were wrong in their approach to business, looking to the future, not to the past; that the Democratic Party sometimes tended to see the relationship between business and Government as adversarial and the Republican Party sometimes seemed to be philosophically committed to being inactive on the theory that anything the Government did with the private sector would probably make things worse.

In a world in which all economics is global as well as local, clearly the important thing is partnership, efficiency, and good judgment. We have deregulated our banking and interstate trucking industries. We have changed our whole way of purchasing things in the Government. We have invested more in defense conversion and new technologies, in partnerships with the private sector. We have deregulated our relationships with our own local governments, permitting States to pursue their own reforms in health care and education and, most importantly, in changing our welfare system.

But perhaps over the long run the most significant thing we have done is to reorganize the way we relate to the private sector, requiring all of our departments to work together and to look outward in partnership. The key to making this strategy work is erasing the dividing line between domestic and foreign economics, between, therefore, domestic and foreign policy.

So far, I think, we're off to a pretty good start. Now the figures for the first 22 months are in. We have over 5 million new jobs in our economy. Our industrial capacity is operating at its highest level in 14 years, with our lowest rate of inflation in 29 years. And after years and years in which we weren't seeing any increased income among our working people, this year we have more high-wage jobs coming into the American economy than in the previous 5 years combined. [*Applause*] Now, that's worth clapping for.

But the success of this ultimately rests on what our private sector does, on the productivity of our workers, the skill of our management, our continuing commitment to investment, to technologies, to enterprise, and to outreach.

That's why we have pursued from the beginning a vigorous export strategy, a strategy rooted in tearing down trade barriers that deny our people the opportunity to compete and in actively promoting the sales of American goods and services in other nations.

We have especially tried to target, thanks in large measure to Secretary Brown, not just our traditional markets but the big emerging markets, the markets of the 21st century, places like China and Indonesia, Mexico and Brazil. In a departure from the behavior of previous administrations of both parties, we have unashamedly been an active partner in helping our business enterprises to win contracts abroad.

I know that many of you in this audience have already benefited from the coordinated and vigorous efforts of the Commerce, State, Treasury Departments, the Export-Import Bank, the Overseas Private Investment Corporation, the Trade and Development Agency. One of the things I most enjoy now when I go abroad is I always try to take a little time to meet with American business people operating in other countries. And repeatedly they tell me that, for the first time ever, they see an American State Department interested in economic advancement as well as diplomatic progress. All these things are important.

I have to say to all of you that the most important thing we have to do this year is to go home and get the Congress to pass the GATT agreement. When the APEC leaders met in Seattle last year for the first time, and President Soeharto came there along with leaders from 14 other countries, one of the things we did at APEC was to let the rest of the world know that we weren't going to sit around while they decided whether we were going to have a GATT agreement. And so it wasn't very long before we got a GATT agreement. But now that the leaders have agreed on it, the legislative bodies of all these nations must adopt it. And the world is looking to the United States for leadership here, as well they should.

We've had opposition to GATT in our Congress from members of both parties. But we've also had strong bipartisan support. So I say that I am going home to seek to capitalize on that bipartisan support, to ask the Democrats to support GATT and to invite the new Republican leaders in Congress to ratify one of their great predecessors Senator Vandenberg's admonition that partisanship should stop at the water's edge.

That used to apply to national security defined in military terms. Today, it applies to national security defined in economic terms. We must pass the GATT, and we should do it right away.

For five decades after the Second World War, our presence in Asia was intended to help guarantee security and to allow prosperity to take root. In meetings this week I reaffirmed the United States commitment to strengthen our important bilateral security relationships, to bolster regional alliances in security, and to rapidly implement the very important agreement we have reached with North Korea for that nation to become a nonnuclear nation. All these things will make this region more secure and, therefore, enable more prosperity to take root.

I have tried to make it clear to all the leaders of Asia that the United States will honor its commitments to Asian security. But it's also a fact, and a healthy one, that the balance of our relationship with Asia has tilted more and more toward trade. As a result of the efforts of the Asian people, the Asian economies are clearly the most dynamic and rapidly growing on Earth. Already they account for one-quarter of the world's output. Over the next 5 years, the growth rate in Asia is projected to be over 50 percent higher than the growth rate in the mature economies of the G–7 countries.

This means expanding markets to those who have the most attractive products and services. Increasingly, we like to believe those products and services are American. One-third of our exports already go to Asia, supporting more than 2 million American jobs. Over the next decade, we estimate that if we are vigorous and effective, Asia could add more than 1.8 million jobs to the American economy, jobs that pay on average 13 percent above non-export-related jobs. That is a very important thing for us and an important thing for every American to think about. These facts compel us to remain ever more committed to deeper and deeper and deeper economic, political, and security engagement in Asia.

For decades, we concentrated our economic efforts on Europe and, of course, on Japan. These nations will remain our close allies, our key competitors, our critical trading partners. But this new century we're about to enter compels a new strategy. Indonesia, Thailand, China, India, among others, must be a big part of that strategy.

The importance of Asia to our future is what has animated the intense interest of the United States in the APEC meetings. APEC, for me and for our country, is a long-term commitment. A year ago, as I said, 14 of the APEC leaders met for the first time in the United States in Seattle. We wanted to say to our trading partners and friends in Asia that the United States wants to remain engaged. We want the Pacific Ocean to unite us, not to divide us. We want to see the world growing in an open trading system, not breaking up into various trading blocs opposed to one another. We sought to give this incredibly diverse Asian-Pacific region a common identity rooted in a common purpose, committed to free trade and investment.

This week at the summit, thanks in large measure to the leadership of President Soeharto, we began to transform that vision into a reality. We established concrete goals to reduce barriers to trade and investment throughout this region by a date certain. And we are now committed, next year in our meeting in Osaka, to come up with a practical, day-to-day blueprint for achieving that goal, to simplify customs procedures, harmonize standards, identify other bottlenecks, lower tariff and nontariff barriers.

This commitment to achieve free trade and investment in the Asian-Pacific region by 2020 may sound like a long time to most people, and in our country, most of our teenagers think tomorrow is a long time away. But the truth is that, number one, it's not so far away, and number two, that is the end date. We will begin reducing barriers to trade and investment as soon as all of the parties to APEC agree on a blueprint and agree to implement it. I am profoundly encouraged by this prospect.

Yesterday I got an interesting question from the American press which I might have gotten from American business people, who say, well—they said, "Mr. President, this is not a mandatory agreement. How do you know it will be carried through?" Good question. I said I believe it will happen for two reasons. Number one, it is in the interests of all the countries involved to do it. And number two, I have seen it work in this region. ASEAN, after all, committed to reduce barriers to trade by a date certain, and the commitment was so strong that the leaders reduced the date certain by 5 years. They moved the calendar closer. That can happen here as well. I hope it will. It will be good for all the nations involved if it does.

Our industries and businesses have proved that they can compete in this region and with Asian companies as long as they are allowed to do so in a fair way. We have regained our position throughout the world as the leading seller of semiconductors. This year, for the first time in 15 years, American automobile manufacturers have outsold their Japanese competitors in the world markets. We have done things that I think are very important for the future in the changes we've made to become more competitive in computers and in telecommunications. According to a recent survey that's conducted every year by the world economic forum in Geneva, the United States was voted for the first time in 9 years the world's most competitive economy. That's thanks in no small measure to a lot of you and a lot of American workers back home and some pretty wrenching and difficult and painful changes we had to undertake.

In the 6 months from March to August of this year, our companies won 34 major contracts in Asia, from turbine generators in China to waste incinerator technology in Taiwan. These contracts alone will generate $5.3 billion in U.S. exports, supporting 85,000 jobs back home. And this week alone, as you know, American companies signed contracts in the Philippines, Malaysia, here in Indonesia for everything from fiber-optic phone networks to environmentally friendly geothermal plants.

Secretary Brown was just at the signing ceremony. As he said, we had projects worth over $40 billion. I know that there is increasing wealth in Indonesia and throughout Asia, but where I come from, $40 billion is still real money, and we're grateful for the business. Of course, as the American President, the most important thing to me is that these contracts will support jobs, thousands of them, back home from every place from Germantown, Maryland, to Oakland, California; from Evandale, Ohio, to Plantation, Florida.

For all these successes, if we're going to keep going, we have to recognize that there are still some barriers—let me just cite two examples— and that's why this APEC agreement is so important. By the year 2000, the market for automobiles in Indonesia, Malaysia, Thailand, and the Philippines will be equal to—I believe will exceed—today's market in Canada and Mexico combined, combined. Now, even after GATT takes effect, tariffs in these nations on U.S. cars are between 30 and 60 percent, as opposed to a 2.5 percent tariff already in existence in the United States. That makes it harder to sell a Ford in Bangkok than it is to sell a Honda in Los Angeles.

Let me give you another example. The Asian APEC countries plan to invest more than $1 trillion in infrastructure projects over the next 6 years. For those of you here from California who know that our busiest highways are in southern California, that's like rebuilding 15 Santa Monica freeways every single day. Here again, tariffs imposed even after GATT include 25 percent levies on hydraulic turbines, up to 15 percent tolls on steel. These are things that the American companies are eager to take down so that we can take part in the emerging adventure of Asia.

The bottom line is that if we're going to have freer trade, it must be fairer. The APEC leaders have made their commitment to this goal. It is very, very exciting.

Let me also say that I'm very often asked by our press, and sometimes by the global press as I travel around the world, whether or not our pursuit of economic engagement undermines our commitment to human rights throughout the world. And I have said many times, I will say again, I think it supports our commitment to human rights throughout the world. In every private meeting I have with leaders, not only in this region but around the world, we talk about human rights issues and the other values, the things that make up the quality of life in any nation, things that are important to Americans from all walks of life.

We do not seek to impose our vision of the world on others. Indeed, we continue to struggle with our own inequities and our own shortcomings. We recognize that in a world and in a region of such diverse and disparate cultures, where nations are at different stages of development, no single model for organizing society is possible or even desirable. And we respect the tremendous efforts being made throughout this region to meet the basic needs of people in all these countries.

At the same time, we remain convinced that strengthening the ties of trade among nations can help to break down chains of repression, that as societies become more open economically, they also become more open politically. It becomes in no one's interest to depress the legitimate aspirations and energies, the hopes, the dreams, and the voices of the many people who make up all of our nations. Commerce does tend to open more closed societies. Throughout this region, we will see as markets expand, as information flows, as contacts across borders and among people multiply, the roots of open societies will grow and strengthen and contribute to stability, not instability. More nations will learn that the freer and more educated people are, the more they are able to be creative and to change with the fast-changing winds of the global economy. Japan, Taiwan, and South Korea have all demonstrated this to an admirable degree.

We in the United States also believe, however, that some basic rights are universal, that everywhere people aspire to be treated with dignity, to give voice to their opinions, to have a say in choosing their leaders. We permit it on a regular basis in the United States, even when we don't like the results. [*Laughter*] And these aspirations are part of human nature. We see it in the stunning life story of President Kim of South Korea or the courageous dissidents like Wei-Jing Sheng in China or Aung San Suu Kyi. We see it in the lives of these people.

Our Nation has sacrificed many of our sons and daughters for the cause of freedom around the world in this century. So we are moved and we will continue to be moved by the struggle for basic rights. But I will say again, even though we will continue to promote human rights with conviction and without apology, we reject the notion that increasing economic ties in trade and partnerships undermine our human rights agenda. We believe they advance together and that they must.

At a time when our Nation is strong, in a time when our inspiration has permeated across the world and people from South Africa to Northern Ireland have asked us to help them in their struggle for democracy and freedom, we cannot turn away from that cause, and we will not. But your work and your progress and your success is also central to that cause.

We live in amazing times. It was only 5 years ago this month that the Berlin Wall fell, an amazing thing. Look what has happened to the world in the last 5 years. For the first time since the dawn of the nuclear age, no Russian missiles are pointed at the children of the United States. For the first time since the end of World War II, there are no Russian soldiers in Eastern or Central Europe. And even though we have differences with our friends in Russia from time to time, we are working in genuine partnership across a whole range of areas that once would have been unthinkable.

After hundreds of years of fighting, the Catholics and Protestants in Northern Ireland are working hard to resolve their differences. We do see now the prospect that the nuclear threat will fade from the Korean Peninsula. We see a new determination for freedom in the Persian Gulf, which we are proud to support, and the historic, almost breathtaking, recently unimaginable prospect of peace in the Middle East, the home of the three great monotheistic religions of the world, including Islam, which is followed by the vast majority of the people in this fine country.

This is a remarkable time. And I am convinced that the increasing freedom of economic activity, rooted in your commitment to invest, your commitment to risk, your commitment to think and imagine and visualize what you might do and to mobilize human resources in this cause, is an absolutely pivotal part of continuing the march of freedom.

So I ask you as we leave this remarkable meeting to recommit yourselves to fulfilling the human potential of your enterprise and all those whom you touch. For when the history of this era is written, it will be written in those terms. These changes, at bottom, are good because we are permitting, sometimes slowly, often rapidly, more and more and more and more people to fulfill the potential that has lain within them.

Thank you, and bless you all.

NOTE: The President spoke at 3:05 p.m. at the Jakarta Convention Center. In his remarks, he referred to Thomas McNabb, president, Aquatics Unlimited; U.S. Ambassador to Indonesia Robert L. Barry and his wife, Peggy; and Gov. Surjadi Soedirja of Jakarta.

Remarks to the Military Community at Hickam Air Force Base in Honolulu, Hawaii
November 16, 1994

Thank you so much. It's good to be home. Thank you. Admiral Macke, General Kealoha, Senator Akaka, Congresswoman Mink, Congressman Abercrombie, Governor and Mrs. Waihee, to Governor-elect Cayetano, and Lieutenant Governor-elect Hirono, and Mayor Harris. Hillary and I and our distinguished Secretary of Commerce, Ron Brown, we're all very glad to be here with all of you.

I want to say a special word of thanks and appreciation to the service members and the spouses, the families of the Army, the Navy, the Air Force, the Marine Corps, the Coast Guard, all of you stationed here in Hawaii. And I'd like to say a special word of thanks to the Marine Corps Band for making me feel so very at home when I got off the airplane. Thank you.

I'm glad to be back at Hickam. I want all of you to know that while you're a long way from the mainland, you're never far from the hearts of every American who understands what you're doing here to keep our country safe and strong. I thank all of you for that.

As you know, I have just returned from a trip to Asia, a trip that began on Veterans Day at Arlington National Cemetery, where on behalf of the American people I was able to express our gratitude for those who paid the ultimate sacrifice to keep our Nation free. I then stopped at our airbase in Alaska. It was rather different than here. [*Laughter*] It was about 23 degrees. The snow was already knee-deep and coming down, but it was very warm. And the men and women there in uniform are also doing a very important job for America. And I went to Manila in the Philippines to honor those who fought in World War II.

It has been an immensely rewarding time for me to serve as the President and Commander in Chief. Just a few days ago I was in the Persian Gulf with our forces there who got there so quickly and stopped the aggression of Saddam Hussein before it ever got started, thanks to the United States.

So to all of you here and all of your counterparts around the world, I say the world knows that the skills of our fighting men and women have never been higher. Your capacity to carry out our missions has never been greater. Your commitment to liberty has never been stronger. The world is more peaceful and secure because of you. And the most important thing I came here to say tonight is thank you.

You know, the world is changing profoundly. There are still threats out there, and they are significant, threats of proliferation of weapons of mass destruction, threats of terrorism, the growing international drug trade, and the rise of international organized crime in the wake of communism's fall.

But if you really look around the world, you'd have to say that security, peace, and freedom are on the march, that all these children here today holding their American flags will in all probability grow up in a world where they will have less fear than their parents and their grandparents faced because of you.

If you look at what's happened from the Persian Gulf and the Middle East to north Africa and Northern Ireland and South Africa to Haiti, if you look at the fact that with North Korea we just concluded an agreement to make certain that that nation becomes a nonnuclear nation, not selling nuclear materials to others, if you look at the agreement we reached with China to stop the proliferation of missiles, and if you look at the fact that in Russia for the first time since nuclear weapons came on the face of the Earth, there are no Russian missiles pointed at American children, you'd have to say we're on the move.

Our forces in the Pacific are at this moment undertaking critical missions from Haiti to the Sinai, from joint exercises with Japan to your role in deterring Iraq. I appreciate all of that. I know well that the success of our diplomatic efforts depends in large measure on our military strength. It is imperative that you remain the best fighting force in the world. And we are determined to do everything we can to make sure that that is exactly what happens.

Let me say, too, that all of you know, even though your role as workers might be in our national defense, that the world of America at home is changing, too, in ways that are both good and troubling. We've had problems in our system that are profound: 60 percent of American wage earners are earning the same or less today that they were earning 15 years ago when you adjust for inflation. We know that this has been especially hard on working men with limited educations. We know that our country still has rates of crime, violence, and family and community breakdown that are too high and unacceptable. We know that a lot of people have a deep sense that our Government, except for you, in which they have confidence, only works for organized special interests and is too often unable to protect the interests or the values of the ordinary Americans. The deep concern and frustration of our people about these conditions led to the changes they voted for in both 1992 and in 1994.

But just because the Congress changed hands, I think I can say for these Members of Congress here behind me, we don't think the message of the American people is, "We want more gridlock. We want an enhanced role for organized interests over ordinary citizens, which is what always happens when we have gridlock." I think what the American people said is, "You've got to keep working together until you change this enough to make it right, until you turn the difficult trends around, until America is going in the right direction at home as well as abroad." And I can tell you that I am committed to doing that.

If you look at what makes a strong country, it's a lot of what makes a strong military: strong families, good schools, safe streets, good-paying jobs, the kind of things that allows people to live up to the fullest of their God-given potential.

We've made a beginning on that, and we've got to keep going. We've got more jobs, a smaller deficit, a smaller National Government doing more for the American people than we had 2 years ago, thanks to Senator Akaka and Senator Inouye, Congressman Abercrombie and Congresswoman Mink, and a lot of other people who helped.

We've taken some stands for strong families. The family and medical leave law will help about 200,000 people in this State to keep their jobs if they have to take a little time off when there's a baby born or a sick parent. That's something good the Government did to stand up for strong families, and we ought to be proud of that.

They worked for better education when we reorganized the student loan law so that now all over America middle class working families can have their children borrow money to go to college at lower interest rates and better repayment terms so that no one need ever walk away from a college education because of the cost again.

And even though there was great controversy about it in the election, I know that we will be able to make our streets safer because we passed the Brady bill and the crime bill and we're putting more police officers on the street and in getting military assault weapons off the street. You should have them, not people walking up and down the streets of our cities.

And we now have in this economy over the last 22 months more than 5 million new jobs. Our industries are operating at the highest capacity in 14 years. We have the lowest inflation in 29 years. And finally—slowly, slowly—we are beginning to see trends which may indicate that people will begin to get wage increases again. This year, there have been more high-wage jobs come into the American economy than in the last 5 years combined. We have to build on these changes, not tear them down. There is still a lot of change that needs to be done to reward people who get up every day, care for their families, obey the law, do the best they can to be good citizens. We have to keep that momentum going.

You know, let me just say one other thing in Hawaii. A lot of the problems we face today are because of big, sweeping trends in the world. A lot of the reasons a lot of Americans have trouble getting pay increases is because of the pressure of the global economy and competition from people who work for wages that Americans couldn't live on. That's been developing for 20 years now. We have to make a choice, whether we're going to embrace these changes and make them work for us or try to run away from them. One thing I want to say in Hawaii, that is on the frontier of America militarily and economically, is that you know that global change can be our friend. The reason I went to Asia is because whether we like it or not, the Asian economies are going to be a big part of the world's future. They are the fastest growing economies in the world. A third of our exports already go to Asia, supporting 2 million American jobs today.

Now, we have to decide. I believe as strongly as I can say that just as your military strength permits America to have diplomatic strength, so that national security is both military and diplomatic, national security is also being strong at home as well as being strong abroad. And there is no longer a clear dividing line between what is foreign policy and what is domestic policy, not when everybody's job depends on whether we can compete in a global economy.

If we educate our people well, that's good foreign policy. If we raise our kids well, that's strong national security. And if we can sell more American products abroad, then that means better jobs at home. That's good domestic policy. If we do not accept any other lesson in this calendar year, let us say there is no easy dividing line between our role in the world and our role at home. We must be strong at home and strong abroad. They are two sides of the same coin.

And so, let me say that I went to Indonesia, a long way from America, because I thought it was good for Americans, because we made an agreement in Indonesia that we would by a date certain take down all the barriers to trade and investment in all the countries of the Asian-Pacific region that were there. And that is a big deal, because we already have the most open markets in the world. So if others lower their markets, it means more sales for Americans, more jobs, and higher incomes.

The United States this year at the world economic forum in Switzerland was voted the most productive economy in the world for the very first time in 9 long years, 9 years. We are coming back. We need a fair chance to sell America's products and services around the world, just as we can promote America's ideals and values around the world. And that's what this trip was all about. That's what my work is all about.

And without regard to our party, let us agree, there's no easy line between our role in the world and our role at home. We can't be strong abroad if we're not strong at home. We'll never be strong at home if we withdraw from our responsibilities around the world. What really makes us strong is strong families, good education, safe streets, good jobs, and national security. You, as much as any group in America today, embody all those, and all Americans are in your gratitude.

Thank you, and God bless you all.

NOTE: The President spoke at 7:05 p.m. In his remarks, he referred to Adm. Richard C. Macke, USN, commander in chief, U.S. Pacific Command; Brig. Gen. Dwight M. Kealoha, USAF, base commander; Gov. John Waihee of Hawaii and his wife, Lynne; Governor-elect Benjamin Cayetano; Lieutenant Governor-elect Mazie Hirono; and Mayor Jeremy Harris of Honolulu.

Remarks at the Children's Discovery Center Benefit and Tribute to Governor John Waihee in Honolulu
November 18, 1994

Thank you very much. Governor Waihee, Lynne, Governor-elect Cayetano, Lieutenant Governor-elect Hirono, Senator Akaka, Congressman Abercrombie, Congresswoman Mink, Mayor Harris, Admiral Macke, ladies and gentlemen: I wanted very much to be here tonight, but I was worried when I heard that John was going to be canonized; I thought maybe he was desperately ill or something. [*Laughter*] Then I realized that you really did just want to do something nice for him and for Lynne and that you were going to do it in a wonderful cause.

This Children's Discovery Center, to me, is a symbol of what is best in our public life: people working in partnership, people working in a positive way, trying to light the flame of an imagination in each child's life and eyes. It is so very different from so much of what dominates our public discussion today, but it is so very like what I will always think of when I think of John Waihee.

He didn't tell you that a couple of years ago when the Democratic Governors had a meeting in Washington and we talked about my running for President, that he—it's true that he thought that I would be elected. It's also true that he and my mother were the only people in America who believed that at the time. [*Laughter*] And he gave me a—I don't know if he remembers this—he gave me a scarf and a cap to take to New Hampshire because it was so cold up there. Now I may just wear it all the time in Washington. [*Laughter*]

Once I remember John and I were talking about his ancestry and how he was the first native Hawaiian to be elected Governor, and he was talking to me about King Kamehameha, the enduring power of spirits. We were on a golf course at the time; that's where we usually are when we talk about such important matters. [*Laughter*] And he said, "It's a very powerful thing, and you need to understand this." So I was listening to him, and I teed off, and I hit the ball a very long way. But unfortunately, at the end of the rough, which was—we were on the Big Island—it was into the lava—[*laughter*]—and my ball disappeared into the lava. He never breaks a—so help me, this is true—he never missed a beat. He kept talking, he went up, he hit his ball exactly, I mean, exactly in the same place I hit mine, and it bounced into the middle of the fairway. [*Laughter*] Well, after nearly 2 years in this job, I no longer need John's ancestors to keep me humble. [*Laughter*] But I often remember it, anyway.

Let me say, if I might, just one other thing, in all seriousness. This country of ours is a very great place. But like all democracies, we sometimes go through wrenching changes that we don't fully understand. And while we're going through them, sometimes we have enormous national debates, even debates within each home in the country, about exactly what we ought to do about the various challenges that we face.

We are going through several big changes at once now as a people. And to me, it is very interesting to see how people deal with it in different places, in different ways. As a nation, we're plainly going through the end of the cold war period and trying to construct a new world of peace and prosperity and freedom. And we're making quite a bit of progress at it, by the way, from the Middle East to the Persian Gulf to Northern Ireland to South Africa to Haiti. For the first time ever, no Russian missiles are pointed at American children, since the dawn of the nuclear age. We're moving in the right direction. But no one can say what they said in the cold war, "Here's the cold war, and

there's the enemy; organize your life accordingly."

We're going through real changes in the economy. The average 18-year-old will now change jobs five or six times in a lifetime. Many of these changes will be glorious and wonderful and fascinating. A lady came up to me tonight when I got here and gave me a little CD for me to take home to my daughter, showing—it was a CD about Hawaii, and it was sort of a contribution to the information superhighway that will sometime, not in the very distant future, link all the schoolchildren in American with libraries and other resources all over the world.

But it's also true that there are a lot of problems with this global economy, and our workers are often increasingly insecure, working for years without a wage increase, working longer, worrying in other States, unfortunately, about whether they're going to lose their health care benefits. And so these things are difficult to deal with.

Everybody knows that in America, even though we're in some ways the most old-fashioned country in the world, we have significant problems with breakdowns in our communities and the rise of crime and violence. What we have to ask ourselves, I submit to you, is how we are going to deal with these things as a people. What you have done here—I wish I could have seen the whole film, but I know John Waihee, and I've gotten to know the people of Hawaii. And what impresses me is that when you have a challenge, you try to figure out what to do about it so that people will have a better life and so that people will win, everybody will win; they'll be able to live in a more robust and rich and fulfilling way.

That is what we must do as a nation. We don't need to become divided so that we have some winners and some losers. We don't need to demonize our own Government. It is, after all, the instrument of our own will; it's either good or bad or somewhere in the middle, depending on what we expect it to do and whether it does it. What we really need to do is just simply to face our challenges.

What you have done here in health care is basically what we ought to do everywhere. And I continue to be surprised and somewhat disappointed that Hawaii has done this and improved the business climate, lowered the cost of health care, increased the health of its citizens, but the people who profit greatly from the other sort of health system that the other 49 States have were able to spend a couple of hundred million dollars to convince the American people that when I said we ought to do what Hawaii did, I wanted the Government to take over the health care system. I'm trying to keep the Government from taking over the health care system, but I would like for people who work hard, pay their taxes, obey the law, and raise their kids the best they can not to lose their health care every year. That's what I would like, and I think that's a worthy goal.

You know, another million Americans and working families lost their health insurance last year. We're the only advanced country in the world where there's a smaller percentage of families under the age of 65 without health care today—or with health care today, a smaller percentage with health care today than there were 10 years ago. Why? Because we haven't done in America what Hawaii did or something else to solve the problem.

Well, tonight is a night for John and Lynne and the Children's Discovery project, but what I want to say to you is that this is an example of what America must do. In this period of transition and change, we have to fall back on what has always made us great. And what has always made us great is not moaning or being negative or being divisive or running down people who are different from what we are. What's

always made us great is coming together, facing our problems, joining together, and figuring out some practical, hard-headed way to solve problems so that our children would be better off than we are. That is what has made us great, and that is the only thing that will make us great from now on into the future.

And so, I would like to say that all of you probably have a better feel for the enduring legacy of this Governor and his fine wife and their administration that I do in the details. But we worked together closely for 8 years, and I know him very well. And the thing that I want you to know is that I have probably spent more unguarded moments with him than most of you have. And I can tell you that about as much as anybody I've ever known, he is in private the way you see him in public. His values are what he says they are when he speaks. And he gets up every day trying to figure out how he can make something good happen in this State. And I think that this country needs more people like that. If we all got up every day trying to make something good happen, like John Waihee, our future would be assured.

And that, sir, is your legacy. I thank you.

God bless you. God bless all of you, and good luck. Thank you.

NOTE: The President spoke at 7:20 p.m. at the Hilton Hawaiian Village.

Letter to Congressional Leaders Reporting on the National Emergency With Respect to Iran
November 18, 1994

Dear Mr. Speaker: (*Dear Mr. President:*)

I hereby report to the Congress on developments since the last Presidential report on May 14, 1994, concerning the national emergency with respect to Iran that was declared in Executive Order No. 12170 of November 14, 1979, and matters relating to Executive Order No. 12613 of October 29, 1987. This report is submitted pursuant to section 204(c) of the International Emergency Economic Powers Act, 50 U.S.C. 1703(c), and section 505(c) of the International Security and Development Cooperation Act of 1985, 22 U.S.C. 2349aa–9(c). This report

covers events through October 18, 1994. My last report, dated May 14, 1994, covered events through March 31, 1994.

1. There have been no amendments to the Iranian Transactions Regulations, 31 CFR Part 560, or to the Iranian Assets Control Regulations, 31 CFR Part 535, since the last report.

2. The Office of Foreign Assets Control (FAC) of the Department of the Treasury continues to process applications for import licenses under the Iranian Transactions Regulations. However, a substantial majority of such applica-

tions are determined to be ineligible for licensing and, consequently, are denied.

During the reporting period, the U.S. Customs Service has continued to effect numerous seizures of Iranian-origin merchandise, primarily carpets, for violation of the import prohibitions of the Iranian Transactions Regulations. The FAC and Customs Service investigations of these violations have resulted in forfeiture actions and the imposition of civil monetary penalties. Additional forfeiture and civil penalty actions are under review.

3. The Iran-United States Claims Tribunal (the "Tribunal"), established at The Hague pursuant to the Algiers Accords, continues to make progress in arbitrating the claims before it. Since my last report, the Tribunal has rendered 6 awards, bringing the total number to 557. Of this total, 373 have been awards in favor of American claimants. Two hundred twenty-five of these were awards on agreed terms, authorizing and approving payment of settlements negotiated by the parties, and 150 were decisions adjudicated on the merits. The Tribunal has issued 38 decisions dismissing claims on the merits and 85 decisions dismissing claims for jurisdictional reasons. Of the 59 remaining awards, 3 approved the withdrawal of cases and 56 were in favor of Iranian claimants. As of October 18, 1994, the Federal Reserve Bank of New York reported that the value of awards to successful American claimants from the Security Account held by the NV Settlement Bank stood at $2,353,030,872.61.

The Security Account has fallen below the required balance of $500 million almost 50 times. Until October 1992, Iran periodically replenished the account, as required by the Algiers Accords. This was accomplished first by transfers from the separate account held by the NV Settlement Bank in which interest on the Security Account is deposited. The aggregate amount transferred from the Interest Account to the Security Account was $874,472,986.47. Iran then replenished the account with the proceeds from the sale of Iranian-origin oil imported into the United States, pursuant to transactions licensed on a case-by-case basis by FAC. Iran has not, however, replenished the account since the last oil sale deposit on October 8, 1992, although the balance fell below $500 million on November 5, 1992. As of October 18, 1994, the total amount in the Security Account was

$203,349,297.01 and the total amount in the Interest Account was $20,160,414.78.

The United States continues to pursue Case A/28, filed last year, to require Iran to meet its financial obligations under the Algiers Accords to replenish the Security Account.

4. Since my last report, the Tribunal has issued two significant awards in favor of U.S. citizens who are dual nationals, for their respective shares of corporations expropriated by Iran. The Tribunal awarded members of the Khosrowshahi family $2,484,746.31 plus interest. The Tribunal awarded members of the Ebrahimi family $5,265,697.00 plus interest.

5. The Department of State continues to present United States Government claims against Iran, in coordination with concerned government agencies, and to respond to claims brought against the United States by Iran. In July 1994, the United States filed a new case, Number A/29, seeking to compel Iran to make its payments for Tribunal expenses in a timely manner. Over the past 2 years, Iran has failed repeatedly to make its payments for extended periods of time, until pressed by the United States in Cases A/28 and A/29.

The United States also recently filed its Rejoinders in, respectively, Case A/15 (I:D and I:H), a claim brought by Iran for the return of certain amounts held in U.S. banks, and Case A/27, a claim brought by Iran for the alleged failure of the United States to enforce a Tribunal award in its favor against a U.S. national.

In August, the United States filed a Production Request in Case B/1, a case in which Iran alleges the United States is liable for termination costs and the nondelivery of goods and services under contracts through the Foreign Military Sales (FMS) program. The United States is seeking the return of FMS documents that remained in U.S. military offices in Iran after the Revolution.

6. United States arbitrator Howard Holtzmann, one of the original members of the Tribunal, resigned July 31, 1994, after 13 years of service. To replace him, the United States appointed Charles T. Duncan, who assumed his duties on August 1, 1994. Until his appointment, Mr. Duncan was Senior Counsel to the law firm of Reid & Priest.

7. As anticipated by the May 13, 1990, agreement settling the claims of U.S. nationals against Iran for less than $250,000, the Foreign Claims Settlement Commission (FCSC) has continued

its review of 3,112 claims. As of October 18, 1994, the FCSC has issued decisions in 3,066 claims, for total awards of more than $68 million. The FCSC expects to complete its adjudication of the remaining claims this year.

8. The situation reviewed above continues to implicate important diplomatic, financial, and legal interests of the United States and its nationals and presents an unusual challenge to the national security and foreign policy of the United States. The Iranian Assets Control Regulations issued pursuant to Executive Order No. 12170 continue to play an important role in structuring our relationship with Iran and in enabling the United States to implement properly the Algiers Accords. Similarly, the Iranian Transactions Regulations issued pursuant to Executive Order No. 12613 continue to advance important objectives in combatting international terrorism. I shall continue to exercise the powers at my disposal to deal with these problems and will continue to report periodically to the Congress on significant developments.

Sincerely,

WILLIAM J. CLINTON

NOTE: Identical letters were sent to Thomas S. Foley, Speaker of the House of Representatives, and Albert Gore, Jr., President of the Senate.

Remarks Following Discussions With Prime Minister Yitzhak Rabin of Israel and an Exchange With Reporters
November 21, 1994

Bosnia

The President. I would like to make a brief comment and then give the Prime Minister a chance to make a comment.

First of all, with regard to the NATO attack this morning on the airfield, it was a strong and entirely appropriate response. That airfield had been used to conduct air attacks against the Bihac region, and it was the right thing to do. The situation in Bihac remains quite serious. We'll just have to see how it next develops. But I strongly support the NATO action today.

Middle East Peace Process

With regard to the meeting that we have just had, let me say that it was, as always, a good meeting. We remain committed to achieving a comprehensive peace in the Middle East. I have reaffirmed my support for the current aid level to Israel as well as for certain security assistance, including the Arrow missile program in the years ahead, so that we can continue to support the security conditions that, in my judgment, are the precondition for Israel being able to make a just peace with all her neighbors in the Middle East.

Mr. Prime Minister, would you like to——

Prime Minister Rabin. In the last 2 years, the Middle East has seen dramatic change in the interrelationships between the Arab coun-

tries and the Arab peoples and Israel. As you remember, in September '93, here on the lawns of the White House, we signed the Declaration of Principle between us and the PLO representing the Palestinians. We started to tackle the longest and the most complicated conflict in all the conflicts of the Arab-Israeli conflict. Since then, we have implemented the first phase. There are problems, but we are continuing this, the process of reconciliation and solving the Palestinian-Israeli conflict.

President Clinton visited the area when we signed the peace treaty with Jordan, the second peace treaty ever to be signed between Israel and an Arab country and the first one after the convening of the Madrid peace conference.

We are committed to continue the negotiating with the Palestinians, with Syria, and Lebanon, with the purpose to achieve comprehensive peace. I'm sure that without the United States involvement, support, under the leadership of President Clinton to Secretary Christopher, it would be much more difficult, if at all, to achieve this progress in the peace process that we all witnessed and so many people did not believe that it would be possible to be done.

Therefore, in our discussions, the President said what has been agreed, and we'll continue to adhere to our responsibility to achieve comprehensive peace. There will be obstacles; there will be difficulties. But I believe, with the support, involvement of the United States, we will achieve comprehensive peace.

Q. Do you have any possibility of Syria in '95, of a peace agreement, Mr. Prime Minister?

Prime Minister Rabin. In accordance to the Bible, all the prophets came from the Middle East. I would not advise anyone to become a prophet what will happen in the Middle East today. We will try our best.

Senator Jesse Helms

Q. Mr. President, do you think that Jesse Helms owes you an apology?

The President. Tomorrow I'm going to have a more extensive opportunity to meet with the press; I'll be glad to answer all those questions. I'd rather just answer questions today on these two matters we've discussed.

Bosnia

Q. [*Inaudible*]—is NATO on crisis? Are the European allies and the Americans pulling in opposite directions? Do you intend to assert your leadership to try to get the allies to be more in accord with the American policy on using NATO force? Despite today's attack, Europeans have refused to enforce exclusion zones.

The President. Well, let me say that you know what our position has been all along, and I think today's action is a good step in the right direction. We are moving forward. I will have a chance to meet with many of our allies in Budapest in the next few days, and we'll continue to work on it. But this was a step in the right direction.

Senator Jesse Helms

Q. Are you talking to Helms about the Israeli aid and Arab aid, and are you talking also about NATO?

The President. We're having extensive consultations and will continue to with the congressional leadership. But as I said, I'd rather talk about these matters today, and I'll answer some other questions tomorrow.

Q. Mr. President, on these matters——

Q. Senator Helms' office says——

Middle East Peace Process

Q. [*Inaudible*]—to the Middle East leaders like the Prime Minister when the incoming head of the Foreign Relations Committee calls this process a fraud?

The President. I don't think—well, the Prime Minister has already said the process is not a fraud; it's been quite successful. It's been the most successful process since Israel became a nation. And we'll just keep working at it to try to make it work better.

Q. Can you clarify your position on the constitutional amendment——

Q. Senator Helms also opposes troops on the Golan Heights——

The President. I think it's—on the Golan issue, let me say, generally, we shouldn't get in the way of the parties making peace themselves. And I don't think I should say or do anything on that that would undermine the possibility of the parties reaching a peace. I think that ought to be the position that all Americans take. Now, the Prime Minister can comment on this better than I, but you know there have been American troops in the Sinai for quite a long time without incident. And I don't think any American would begrudge the investment we've made in the historic peace that grew out of Camp David.

Prime Minister Rabin. Do you know that there are today a thousand Americans, about a thousand Americans, that served for 15½ years in the Sinai as part of the multinational force in which there are participation of military civilians from Austria, New Zealand, Colombia, Canada, and this force is in existence since we signed the peace treaty with Egypt, on the demand of Israel?

All of the Americans there, as the others—and there is one fighting infantry battalion, American uniformed soldiers, in the Sinai. Their role is not to defend Israel. Their role is to monitor the military annex of the peace treaty, the peace treaty between Egypt and Israel. And it serves effectively. No American was hurt there by any terror activities, because it is an area controlled by the Egyptian armed forces. We work in cooperation. We have all the machinery of cooperation.

No doubt, on the Golan Heights, for 19 years, we had no one act of terror toward the lines between Syria and Israel. The Golan Heights today is the safest from terror because the Syrians keep their commitment under the disengagement agreement of 1974.

Q. Mr. President, the Prime Minister is describing a monitoring force. Is that how you anticipate Americans being used, as monitors, or is it—which is something entirely different?

The President. First of all, there has been no discussion—he described to you what came out of Camp David. There has been no discussion among the parties of a role for American forces yet. That would—let's let the people who have to make this agreement make it. And then, if we're asked by the parties themselves to become involved at some point in the future, I will come to the American people, I will come to the Congress, and I will make the case at that time based on an agreement that they would reach. There has been no agreement of any kind about this. We're jumping the gun here on this part of it.

Senator Jesse Helms

Q. Are you going to see Helms yourself, Mr. Prime Minister? Are you going to see Mr. Helms, Senator Helms?

The Prime Minister. He's not in town.

[*At this point, one group of reporters left the room, and another group entered.*]

Aid to Israel

Q. Mr. President, with a new Republican Congress, what will happen to the foreign aid and to the American troops in the Golan Heights?

The President. Well, first of all, with regard to the foreign aid, I have just pledged to the Prime Minister that I will support next year continuing the aid to Israel at its present level, in addition to some new security initiatives with regard to the Arrow missiles, supercomputers, and a couple of other things. So we are going to have a very robust security relationship with Israel, and I believe the aid levels will be maintained. We have enjoyed in this country, historically, a bipartisan level of support for Israel.

Now, with regard to the Golan, I can only tell you that we in the United States must await an agreement of peace between Israel and Syria. If a peace agreement is reached regarding the Golan in which we were asked to participate, obviously that is something that I would consider.

We have been in the Sinai, as a result of the agreement between Egypt and Israel, for quite a long time now without incident. I am very proud of the role the United States has been asked to play there as a monitor, not as a defender of Israel's security but as a monitor. But that has not been discussed now; we are a good ways from that. And that is something

for Israel and for Syria to resolve between themselves before the United States can be involved in that.

Aid to Palestinians

Q. Mr. President, can you shape foreign policy with Jesse Helms in Congress, and can you speed up foreign aid to Arafat, who seems to be on the brink of civil war?

The President. I do think we should speed it up. There will be a meeting next week, a donors' meeting in Brussels, and we're going to try to move about $125 million out in a hurry. I do believe that the donors must work to get the assistance out quickly to enable the people in the areas to receive and to feel some benefits of the peace. I think that's critically important.

Middle East Peace Process

Q. Mr. President, do you see any chance of resuming the talks here in Washington between Israel and Syria in full scale of delegations and military——

The President. I have no comment about that except to tell you that we will continue to do everything we can to reach a peace agreement and to facilitate the peace between the parties.

Q. Mr. President, in view of the Republican victory in the election to the Congress, do you intend to change the foreign policy of the United States vis-a-vis the Middle East, or do you feel that this policy enjoys a bipartisan support in the American Congress or in the American public?

The President. No, I have no intention of changing it; it's working. My policy in the Middle East is to support the peace process, to support a comprehensive peace, to stand behind Israel in its security, to increase the feeling that peace is possible, and then to make the benefits of peace apparent to all the parties who sign on to it. So that policy has worked very well for 2 years, and I intend to continue it.

Q. Mr. President, what do you think of what happened in the Gaza Strip in the last few days?

The President. Well, I think we have to work hard to stand up against terror and to try to bring the benefits of peace to the people who support the peace. And that is a difficult situation; we know that it is. But our policy will remain clear and steadfast there. We'll continue to support the peace process.

Q. Don't you think that the way that President Asad treated you, it was an insult from your point of view?

The President. I wouldn't characterize it in that way. I would say that if you look at the way my press conference and my comments about terrorism were played in the Syrian media, I don't think you can say it in that way. I do think that we have to keep working to build more trust and confidence between the two countries. And I have urged President Asad to do that, to do whatever can be done to reach out to the people as well as to the Government of Israel to make it clear that Syria does genuinely wish a peace.

I am convinced that the President of Syria wants to make peace with Israel, but I think that my opinion is not nearly as important as not only the opinion of the leaders of Israel but the people of Israel. Israel is a very great democracy, and the people need to feel in their bones that peace and security are both possible. And I am going to keep working to that end.

Q. Mr. President, yesterday the Palestinian Minister said that unless sponsors speeded up aid to the territories very soon it might be too late. Do you share that bleak assessment, and what role do you think the violence in Gaza— I'm sorry—what do you think the connection was between the violence in Gaza and the fact that the economic situation is hurting?

The President. I don't think you can draw a direct connection, but I do believe that when you bring peace to a place, you need to work hard to make sure that the benefits of peace become apparent to people who are the targets of the enemies of peace. And the poor in Gaza are clearly the targets of the enemies of peace. So we have to work harder and more aggressively, all of us who support the peace process, to try to make the benefits more apparent.

We all knew that this would be difficult. The Prime Minister knew it would be difficult. There had never been, in effect, a national Palestinian Government there, if you will. There are difficulties. But I think the responsibility is on all of us who wish to see benefits of peace to keep pushing it. That's what the donors conference is about. And I think there is a sense of urgency among those who understand that the money, the investment need to go out.

Discussions With Prime Minister Rabin

Q. Mr. Prime Minister, what did you achieve in your meeting today with President Clinton?

Prime Minister Rabin. I'll say a few words in English, and with your permission, President, I will pass to Hebrew.

First, I thanked the President for his involvement in sending the Secretary of State to the region, because in the last 2 years, we have achieved, to my humble opinion, dramatic changes in the Arab-Israeli conflict.

We started to tackle the longest, the most complicated complex of conflict, the Israeli-Palestinians. I knew that there would be ups and downs, there would be enemies of the achievement of a solution to the Israeli-Palestinian problem. But I believe that regardless to what happened in Gaza, we are on the right track.

We signed the peace treaty with Jordan, the country that has got the longest border with Israel, and it goes mostly the implementation of the peace treaty. We are still in process, not easy ones, with negotiations with Syria and Lebanon. This all happened in the last less than 2 years.

I told the President that I, the Government of Israel, the people of Israel, thank him for his guidance, for his involvement, for his readiness, as he once wrote to me, and has kept his commitment that when Israel takes risks for peace, the United States would try its best to minimize these risks.

And the support that we got from the President, from the administration, the Secretary of State, and what you were told by the President that for the next fiscal year the President will keep the same level of assistance to Israel, will recommend to the Congress to keep the same level, with the additions that the President mentioned, all this means backing Israel in its effort and assisting wherever it is needed, wherever it is possible by the United States to advance towards comprehensive peace. There are problems, but I'm proud of what has been achieved towards peace in the last 2 years.

And now I shall be brief, with your permission.

[*At this point, Prime Minister Rabin spoke in Hebrew, and a translation was not provided.*]

Islamic Extremists

Q. Mr. President, one more question. The Prime Minister mentioned the danger of the

Islamic extremists. Do you intend, as the President of the most powerful country, to build a coalition against the Islamic extremists and the danger?

The President. First, let me say that I agree that it's a danger, and we are monitoring it very closely. We keep up with it, and we're going to do whatever is appropriate.

NOTE: The President spoke at 12:38 p.m. in the Oval Office at the White House. A reporter referred to Palestinian spokesman Nabil Shaath. A tape was not available for verification of the content of these remarks.

Message on the Observance of Hanukkah, 1994
November 21, 1994

Warm greetings to all who are celebrating Hanukkah.

Arriving this year in advance of winter, the Festival of Lights casts a warm glow that can see us through the cold months ahead. Hanukkah fills our hearts with the story of a people's deep and enduring faith. Families around the world tell of a faith that guided the Maccabees to victory and that preserved a day's worth of oil for eight days. By the rich light of the menorah, people everywhere celebrate a faith that has sustained the Jewish people for millennia.

Today, this same powerful belief that light may prevail over darkness continues to illuminate a path toward a brighter future. We have seen Israel join hands with its old adversaries, brought together by the desire to give all children a world finally free from violence. The partnerships taking root in the Middle East have not come easily, and the challenges that remain are great. This year, let the menorah lights shine as a harbinger of a day filled with light—light of a land graced with prosperity, of nations blessed by peace. Let us look forward to a time when the whole world is united in believing that tomorrow can be better if we have the faith to make it so.

Hillary and I extend best wishes to all for a joyous Hanukkah and a wonderful holiday season.

WILLIAM J. CLINTON

NOTE: This message was released by the Office of the Press Secretary on November 21.

Remarks Welcoming President Leonid Kuchma of Ukraine
November 22, 1994

Mr. President, Mrs. Kuchma, members of the Ukrainian delegation, representatives of the Ukrainian-American community, distinguished guests: It is indeed an honor to welcome to Washington the leader of one of the world's youngest democracies and oldest nations. To have you here with us today, Mr. President, is to be reminded that we live in an era of wonders, a time when peoples long denied hope are having age-old dreams fulfilled, a time when the unstoppable power of men and women who wish to be free has been demonstrated anew.

The rebirth of Ukraine as an independent state after centuries of rule by others is one of the most inspiring developments of our time. For ages Ukraine was divided by competing empires, then subjugated to czars and commissars. Despite efforts to create an independent Ukraine, dictators, terrible famines, and relentless oppression all combined to deny your people the right to shape their own fate. Despite these ordeals, the Ukrainian people have endured, preserving hope and their identity and contributing greatly to the glories of European civilization. Now, finally, Ukraine has reclaimed its independence and its place as a pivotal state in the new Europe.

We congratulate you, Mr. President, and all Ukrainians on your remarkable achievements in the almost 3 years since regaining your freedom. You held a historic referendum and began the hard work of reform and building democratic institutions. Above all, Ukrainians are weathering the immense difficulties of political and economic transition. In the face of continuous hardship, you have shown patience, bravery, and the ability to overcome all obstacles, an ability your young athletes, like Oksana Baiul, showed so spectacularly in the Olympic competition.

We honor you, Mr. President, in our Nation's Capital as the man who is leading a Ukrainian renaissance. Your boldness in the face of daunting problems reminds us of one of our greatest leaders, Franklin Roosevelt, who provided leadership in a time of great hardship in the United States. Like him, you inherited a nation in the throes of economic depression. And like him, you have lighted the darkness and created hope.

You have blazed a path ahead on the two most critical issues for the future, economic reform and nuclear weapons. Thanks to your leadership, Ukraine is making the hard choices that will ensure the prosperity Ukrainians deserve. And thanks to your vision and that of the Ukrainian Parliament, you are removing the threat of nuclear weapons and laying the groundwork for an era of peace with your neighbors. I salute the courage you have shown.

America will stand with you to support your independence, your territorial integrity, and your reforms. We are bound together by a dedication to peace and a devotion to freedom. The flame of that commitment to freedom was kept burning during the cold war by nearly a million Ukrainian-Americans, some of whom are with us here today, who never forgot Ukraine and who are today contributing to its reawakening. Now that your country is again free, all Americans are determined that the flame of Ukrainian freedom will burn ever brighter. We will stand with you.

Seventy-seven years ago today, Mr. President, on November 22d, 1917, another generation of Ukrainian leaders declared the independence of Ukraine. It was a tragedy that civil war and bolshevism doomed that new state while it was still in its infancy.

Today we are pleased and honored to welcome you, the leader of a Ukraine that is conquering the challenges of independence, poised to fulfill its hopes, a nation that will grow into one of the great nations of Europe. And we say, *Vitayemo.* Welcome.

NOTE: The President spoke at 11:08 a.m. on the South Lawn at the White House.

The President's News Conference With President Kuchma of Ukraine
November 22, 1994

President Clinton. Good afternoon. President Kuchma and I had an excellent set of meetings today, and I have very much enjoyed getting to know him. The work we have done follows on the successful meetings in Kiev between President Kuchma and Vice President Gore. It has strengthened the friendship between our two nations that was already on a very firm basis.

Since his election just 5 months ago, President Kuchma has bravely and squarely confronted the two greatest challenges facing Ukraine, economic reform and the nuclear question. He has taken hard, practical steps required to secure a more peaceful and prosperous future for his people. I applaud his leadership and the leadership of the Ukrainian Parliament in acceding last week to the Non-Proliferation Treaty.

Ukraine's move is a major step toward ensuring that nuclear missiles never again will be targeted at the children of our nations. I told President Kuchma that the United States will continue to work with Ukraine to dismantle completely its nuclear arsenal. Three hundred and fifty million dollars of our total $900 million, 2-year aid package is targeted toward that goal, and there could be no better use of the funds.

In addition, Ukraine's decision will permit the United States, Russia, and the United Kingdom to extend formal security assurances to Ukraine. It will allow the START I Treaty to be brought into force, enabling the process of nuclear weapons reductions to move forward. It will permit us to strengthen our military relations with Ukraine. It will open up Ukraine to a new range of business and technological opportunities. In addition, we pledge to help defray some of the costs for participation by Ukraine in the Partnership For Peace.

On economic issues, the President and I discussed the far-reaching reforms he has initiated. These reforms put Ukraine on the right path toward a future of increasing prosperity and economic integration with the Western market economies.

At this moment in our history, we have an extraordinary opportunity to improve the lives of all of our people by working more closely together and trading together more. Ukraine's reform program can speed this development, and I have pledged to support it to the fullest of our ability to do so. In 1994 and '95, our economic assistance of $550 million, including balance-of-payment support, will be speedily delivered to help to stabilize the economy. Our new U.S.-Ukraine enterprise fund will soon start making loans to new small businesses. We'll continue our work together in aerospace and high tech.

As Ukraine's economy continues to improve, the opportunities for both our countries will multiply. The IMF and the World Bank are also working hard to make sure these reforms bear fruit, and Russia and Turkmenistan have given badly needed help. I'll continue to press our G–7 partners, especially the European Union and Japan, to do more to contribute to this effort.

President Kuchma and I discussed other issues, including the nuclear power complex at Chernobyl. The G–7 nations and Ukraine have a common interest in agreeing on a plan to improve the safety and the efficiency in the Ukrainian energy sector and in closing down the Chernobyl plants.

We've worked hard today. And the agreements we've reached promise to help deliver concrete results: increased security, increased prosperity for Ukrainians and Americans. Our relations continue to grow stronger as they have since Ukrainian independence just 3 years ago. Our friendship will grow because our futures are intertwined.

I'd now like to turn the microphone over to President Kuchma for his remarks, and then we'll answer your questions, beginning with an American journalist, alternating with Ukrainian journalists.

Mr. President.

President Kuchma. Thank you very much, Mr. President, ladies and gentlemen. President Clinton and I have just signed very important documents, the Charter of Ukrainian-American Partnership, Friendship, and Cooperation and also the Agreement on Cooperation on Space Research for Peaceful Purposes. We also signed several bilateral accords on the ministerial level.

Thus, by joint effort, both countries have made another concrete step toward solidifying the legal basis of relations between the United States and Ukraine and enriching the relationship of democratic partnership with practical content.

The signing of these documents has become possible due to a constructive and purposeful effort of politicians, diplomats and experts in both countries. It is noteworthy that the charter signed today removed the last barriers which to an extent held back the development of Ukrainian-American relations in a very first and extremely important stage of their formation. We can now say that we have not simply signed several bilateral documents but opened the way to a full-fledged cooperation in the political economic, humanitarian, and other areas in the interests of both nations. That was the main purpose of my state visit to the United States.

The current Ukrainian-American summit, the talks we had today, which can be characterized with a spirit of a constructive, businesslike, and mutual interest in reaching practical results. And I'm very thankful to the President of the United States, Bill Clinton, and Vice President Al Gore. Thus, we are the participants and witnesses of a process where our relations are being formed step by step and cooperation is being enriched, such a perspective, to our extent, in the development of relations and in the interest of both nations.

Ahead of us lies practical work to realize the reached, signed accords. Without such implementation, we will not be able to move ahead to a stronger bilateral cooperation. I would like to assure you, Mr. President, that Ukraine will fulfill its pledges and is ready for a further active cooperation.

Senator Jesse Helms

Q. Mr. President, I'd like to ask you about some recent comments by Senator Jesse Helms.

Last week he said that you weren't fit to be Commander in Chief, and then yesterday he said that you better have a bodyguard if you ever come to North Carolina. But I wonder what's your reaction to his remarks and if you feel comfortable with him being chairman of the Foreign Relations Committee that's going to oversee your foreign policy?

President Clinton. I think the remarks were unwise and inappropriate. The President oversees the foreign policy of the United States. And the Republicans will decide in whom they will repose their trust and confidence; that's a decision for them to make, not for me.

NATO Membership

Q. President Clinton, first of all, for you a question. Will American policy change in Budapest in December towards expansion of NATO to the Eastern Europe? And would you mention Ukraine as a NATO member without Russia? And President Kuchma, would you imagine Ukraine being a member of NATO, not now but in a couple of years?

President Clinton. First, let me say that I believe we will have discussions in Budapest about how we might go about expanding NATO but not about when and which particular countries would be let in; I think that is premature. Secondly, as I have said all along, I am working hard for the prospect of an integrated Europe. I have encouraged it economically; I have encouraged it politically; I have encouraged it in terms of security. Therefore, I would not say or do anything that would exclude the possibility of Ukrainian membership. That would be up to Ukraine, and it will be up to all of us, working together, to try to determine what is the best way to promote the security of what I hope and believe can be a united Europe, something that has never before occurred, I might add, in the whole history of nation states on the European Continent. We have an historic opportunity, and we ought to do everything we can to seize it.

President Kuchma. I would like to make my comment. I would like to say that I do agree with President Clinton. The security on the European Continent is a very important issue, and it shouldn't be solved by the revolutionary way but rather by the evolutionary method. It is not important who enters where, but it is very important that we do not have a new Berlin Wall in Europe.

Republican Leaders

Q. Mr. President, since the election returns, the Republicans have played hardball, and they have threatened legislative reprisals against your agenda and also have tried to force tradeoffs on GATT. What are you going to do about it?

President Clinton. Well, first, let me answer the GATT question. I am encouraged by the progress that we have made in working with Senator Dole on the substantive issues surrounding GATT. And I appreciate the very constructive attitude that has prevailed there. I disagree that there should be some deal cut regarding capital gains; I don't think that's the right thing to do. This is an important agreement on its own merits. Everyone concedes it will lead to hundreds of thousands of jobs.

In the wake of the election, let me say that one of the things that has been discovered again is something that I began talking about several years ago, long before I ever thought of running for President, and that is the declining wages of many of our working people. It's not surprising that a lot of people aren't a lot happier, even when we add millions of jobs, if all of the people who were working in the first place think they're never going to get a raise and don't think their jobs are more secure.

Many Americans think that trade causes that. That was one of the fights over NAFTA, if you'll remember. My argument is that we have an open trading system here, so we already get whatever downside there is to trade. We know when we create jobs related to trade, they pay on average 13 percent higher than average jobs. So my argument for the GATT is that it will raise incomes of American workers. And I think that is our most urgent economic job, not just to create jobs and to keep low inflation and high investment but also to pursue whatever strategies are available to us to raise incomes. So I think we should pursue the GATT vigorously. I think it's in the interest of the American working people. I hope it will prevail.

As to these other issues, again I will say there are a lot of areas where we can work together with the Republicans. We can finish the battle that this administration began with the last Congress to change what I would call yesterday's Government. We have begun the downsizing of the Government; we have begun the deregulation that we need to do. We know there is much more that can be done.

We still have an enormous amount to do in the area of political reform that surely we can agree on: the line-item veto, campaign finance reform, lobby reform, applying the laws to Congress that they apply to the private sector, the Kempthorne-Glenn bill on mandates, which I strongly endorsed and worked on, which was caught up in all the delays in the last session, to reduce mandates on State governments, giving the States and localities more flexibility in many areas, a lot of the things we can work on.

I do not believe the American people want the next Congress to repeal the things which benefited ordinary Americans. I don't think they want to repeal family leave or the Brady bill or the assault weapons ban or any of those substantive achievements, and I will resist that.

Q. Are you surprised at the vengeful attitude?

President Clinton. Well, let me say, you characterize it in that way. I can only tell you that my job is to stand up for the interests of ordinary Americans; that's what I will do. I will do my very best to work with them, where we can work together. There are opportunities in the area of governmental reform where their contract and their agenda overlaps with mine. I will do my best to resist exploding the Government deficit, sinking the economic recovery, or repealing the gains that working people made in the last session of Congress.

Ukraine-U.S. Relations

Q. Mr. President, you said that you have made another step in the development of relations. What would be the realization of that step? How do you visualize it? And is there long-term perspective in the nuclear disarmament, that the United States can help Ukraine?

President Kuchma. I'm very glad that you are asking about the future, but I would like the current agreements between Ukraine and the United States be realized, first of all. Then we will think about the future in long perspective. Currently, we have agreed on some things which provide very longstanding perspective for—[inaudible].

President Clinton. If I could just answer that question briefly, it is a measure of the importance that we attach to Ukraine and to its impact on the entire future of Europe well into the next century that in this 2-year period, a very difficult budget situation in America where we are trying to bring our deficit down and where we are cutting overall spending, Ukraine is the fourth largest recipient of American foreign assistance in the entire world because we think it is so important to complete the work of denuclearization, but also because we think your long-term economic development, your commitment to democracy and to an open economy is so important that we want to be there over the long run.

So, I agree with the President. We have to do what we are already agreeing to do. But there will be much more in the years ahead. As your country continues to grow and flourish, there will be much more.

Federal Budget and Prayer in Schools

Q. Mr. President, there seems to be still some confusion over your position on the constitutional amendment involving prayer in public schools. And today there's some confusion resulting from Secretary Reich's comments, a proposal that he floated that $111 billion could be cut in subsidies for big corporations, as part of your new budget, over 5 years. Your Commerce Secretary says he doesn't know anything about that. What exactly is your position on that proposal and on prayer in public schools?

President Clinton. Let me answer the second question first, because I think we can dispose of it rather quickly. I have not reviewed the specifics of Secretary Reich's proposal. As I understand it, he was speaking to the Democratic Leadership Council group today, and they have what they call a cut and invest theory which calls for a complex of further budget cuts, phasing out various tax subsidies and then using that money to finance the middle class tax cut as well as further investments in education. Conceptually, it's an attractive idea. I have to have time to review the details in the context of our budget. I have made absolutely no decision about any of the specifics in Secretary Reich's proposal.

Now, with regard to the school prayer amendment, let me make a few general comments, first of all. I want to make it absolutely clear that this is not a political issue with me; it never has been, and it never will be. Secondly, I have a very long record on this issue. I have been coming to grips with it for at least a decade.

The comments I made in Indonesia, I'm afraid—and those of you who were there with me know we had been on a rather rigorous trip schedule for the last few weeks—may have been overread. I made a generalized commitment after the election in the press conference that I had, and also to all of our people, that we would read and review or listen to any proposals the Republicans might have before condemning them. We ought to at least listen, and we ought to look for ways to work together.

My position on the prayer issue is, I have always supported a moment of silence. When I was a Governor, I supported the moment of silence legislation. I do not believe that we should have a constitutional amendment to carve out and legalize teacher- or student-led prayer in the classroom. I think that that is inherently coercive in a nation with the amount of religious diversity we have in this country. I think that would be an error.

As I understand it, that is what is being proposed by the Republican Congressman from Oklahoma, and I would be opposed to that. I don't believe that—I think the very nature of the circumstances mean that, for large numbers of our children, it could not be truly voluntary, and I would oppose it.

NOTE: The President's 82d news conference began at 4:56 p.m. in Room 450 of the Old Executive Office Building. President Kuchma spoke in Ukrainian, and his remarks were translated by an interpreter.

Joint Summit Statement by the Presidents of the United States and Ukraine
November 22, 1994

On the occasion of his State visit to the United States on November 21–23, 1994, Leonid D. Kuchma, President of Ukraine, met with William J. Clinton, President of the United States, to open a qualitatively new stage in the growing U.S.-Ukrainian partnership aimed at furthering bilateral and multilateral cooperation on a broad range of issues between the two countries.

The Presidents renewed their shared commitment to broaden the bilateral democratic partnership into which the two countries have entered. President Clinton underscored the importance the United States attaches to the independence, sovereignty and territorial integrity of Ukraine. In this context, President Clinton assured President Kuchma that the United States will continue to give high priority to supporting Ukraine in its efforts to achieve genuine economic independence, its transition to a market economy and its integration into the global economic system.

Bilateral Relations

In keeping with their commitment to strengthen bilateral relations, President Clinton and President Kuchma signed the Charter of American-Ukrainian Partnership, Friendship and Cooperation. The Presidents praised the Charter as the framework for developing closer relations over the coming years. President Clinton noted in particular Ukraine's valuable contribution to this new framework by its momentous decision to accede to the Nuclear Non-Proliferation Treaty, which is an historic step forward on the road toward strengthening the international nuclear weapons nonproliferation regime and global security and stability.

The Presidents inaugurated this new framework of bilateral relations by signing an Agreement on Cooperation in the Exploration and Use of Outer Space for Peaceful Purposes and agreed to work closely to explore additional bilateral cooperative space-related opportunities in the future. They noted that this process had begun with a U.S.-Ukraine discussion of Ukraine's interest in the commercial launch market.

Both Presidents expressed their determination to broaden bilateral cooperation in a range of new areas. During the visit, the two governments brought into force a bilateral customs cooperation agreement and announced their intention to conclude negotiations on a bilateral civil aviation agreement. The Presidents recognized the threat that organized crime and corruption pose for reform and expanded business activity in Ukraine, and they agreed to cooperate in combating crime and promoting the rule of law as an essential safeguard of social stability and civil and human rights. The Presidents will encourage exchanges among Ukrainians and Americans in the fields of science, technology and education. The Presidents, noting the valuable role of culture in bringing nations closer together, voiced support for wide-ranging cultural contacts between the United States and Ukraine. Both Presidents also recognized the importance of health care for the well-being of their people, and President Clinton announced that the United States would provide Ukraine hospital equipment, medical supplies and assistance with health programs.

The Presidents intend to maintain frequent high-level bilateral contacts to assure timely and effective implementation of activities. President Kuchma invited President Clinton to make an official return visit to Ukraine at the earliest convenient opportunity. President Clinton accepted this invitation with pleasure.

Economic Cooperation

The Presidents agreed that market-oriented economic reform provides the surest path to Ukraine's economic revival and its integration into the world economy. President Clinton reaffirmed full U.S. support for the reform policies recently adopted by President Kuchma's government and its conclusion of an IMF Systemic Transformation Facility program. President Kuchma outlined plans for accelerating the process of economic reform. These plans include intensifying structural reform efforts to encourage competition through enhanced macroeconomic stabilization and increased privatization. President Clinton commended President Kuchma for his leadership on economic reform and encouraged him to work toward early completion of negotiations with the IMF on a standby program. He stressed the importance of Ukraine's reform measures and the United States' readiness to support Ukraine in their implementation.

President Clinton announced that the United States would provide $200 million in new assistance to Ukraine in Fiscal Year 1995. Of this amount, $103 million will finance technical and economic assistance activities. The remaining $97 million will provide balance of payments support, consisting of $72 million in an energy sector grant and $25 million in USDA

concessional food credits, as provided in agreements signed by the two Governments during the State visit. When combined with $3 million of pharmaceuticals and other commodities from Fiscal Year 1994, the United States will provide $100 million in balance of payments support in the next few months to reinforce Ukraine's IMF program.

This United States economic support is in recognition of Ukraine's major initiative to launch a comprehensive economic reform program. This support is in addition to the $350 million in economic assistance committed to Ukraine in March 1994, the major part of which will take effect once reforms have begun. The Presidents reviewed the progress made in the implementation of economic assistance programs for Ukraine and agreed to work together to accelerate delivery and ensure the full disbursement of all current and previous commitments, as well as the effectiveness of these programs.

President Kuchma expressed appreciation for United States leadership in mobilizing international support for Ukraine, particularly the prompt United States response to the Ukrainian request for balance of payments support. Looking to the future, President Clinton reaffirmed United States commitments made at the Washington donor session and the Winnipeg G–7 conference in October and his intention to continue the United States' leading role in encouraging international support for Ukrainian reform.

The Presidents recognized the important contribution the private sector can make to Ukraine's economic prosperity through expanded trade and investment. President Clinton welcomed Ukraine's ratification of the bilateral investment treaty and noted that the Western NIS Enterprise Fund has now opened its offices in Kiev. President Kuchma expressed the hope that the U.S. Senate would ratify the treaty at an early date. The leaders emphasized the importance of privatization if expanded cooperation between American enterprises and an emerging private sector in Ukraine is to begin in earnest.

On November 21 President Kuchma and members of his government participated in an OPIC-sponsored business conference which reviewed investment opportunities in Ukraine. Both Presidents agreed that there was enormous potential for private sector cooperation in developing key sectors of the Ukrainian economy. They specified, in particular, agriculture and food processing; pharmaceuticals and medical equipment; energy, including fossil and environmentally sound and safe nuclear power; aerospace, consistent with international obligations; civil aviation; telecommunications; environment and defense conversion.

The two leaders noted that the first session of the Joint U.S.-Ukrainian Commission on Trade and Investment is meeting during the State visit to discuss ways of promoting business cooperation and removing barriers to expanded trade and increased investment in Ukraine. The Commission is discussing the tax, legal and regulatory changes that Ukraine will need to adopt to support private business activity. President Clinton recognized the special circumstances facing economies in transition, such as Ukraine's, which seek to expand export markets, and offered to consult with the U.S. Congress on appropriate ways of reflecting this in U.S. trade legislation. The Presidents noted that expanded trade will be critical to the success of Ukrainian economic reform and agreed to make the expansion of trade and investment a priority in their economic cooperation efforts.

The Presidents also agreed to work toward expanding economic cooperation within a multilateral framework and to promote Ukraine's integration into the global economy. President Clinton reaffirmed the United States' support for Ukraine's accession to the GATT/WTO, and noted that the United States is providing assistance to the Ukrainian government to support this process. The United States is also chairing the working group in Geneva overseeing Ukraine's accession.

The Presidents noted that the resolution of Ukraine's energy problems would have an important and positive impact on Ukraine's economic recovery. President Kuchma welcomed the United States' decision to provide part of its special balance of payments assistance in the form of an energy sector grant. Both leaders reviewed the progress that has been made in implementing cooperative programs aimed at the restructuring and reforming of Ukraine's energy sector and improving nuclear reactor safety. President Kuchma informed President Clinton of the recent agreement Ukraine reached with IAEA on the application of IAEA safeguards to all nuclear materials, except those for nuclear propulsion, utilized in Ukraine.

The Presidents agreed to continue to work together for the full implementation of the G-7 Naples Action Plan, and recognized that this will require G-7 cooperation and assistance. President Clinton drew attention to the significant resource commitments made at Naples, Corfu and Winnipeg and to the importance of receiving early assurances that the Chornobyl reactors would be shut down in accordance with the G-7 Action Plan. President Kuchma assured President Clinton that Ukraine takes seriously the international community's concerns about the continued operation of the Chornobyl nuclear power plant. He expressed Ukraine's readiness to work with the G-7 nations in the implementation of the Naples Action Plan, noting that its successful implementation is connected with a series of measures, including preparing the closure of the nuclear reactors, minimizing the social impact on the plant's personnel, and ensuring that sufficient economically-priced electricity is available to meet Ukraine's domestic needs. He also stressed the importance that Ukraine places on improving the stability of the shelter installed over the damaged reactor. Both Presidents agreed on the need for further close work in the G-7/Ukraine Task Force to ensure the future closure of Chornobyl, as envisioned in the G-7 Action Plan, as an integral part of a comprehensive solution to Ukraine's energy problems.

Defense and Security

The Presidents expressed satisfaction with the accomplishments and pace of implementation of the January 14 Trilateral Statement signed by the Presidents of the United States, Ukraine, and the Russian Federation. In addition, they renewed their commitment to international efforts to reduce sharply the threat and proliferation of nuclear weapons.

President Clinton congratulated Ukraine on its decision to accede to the Treaty on the Non-Proliferation of Nuclear Weapons and the historic renunciation of nuclear weapons which it represents and reaffirmed the U.S. commitment to provide security assurances to Ukraine in connection with its accession to the NPT by signing a Memorandum on Security Assurances on the margins of the Budapest CSCE Summit.

The Presidents look forward to early entry into force of the START-I treaty and agreed that the Lisbon Protocol Signatories should exchange instruments of ratification on the margins of the Budapest CSCE Summit. Both Presidents reiterated their views that the START-

I treaty would not only serve the mutual interests of both countries, but also would serve to strengthen global peace and stability.

Both Presidents agreed to work closely to ensure the timely implementation of Nunn-Lugar programs intended to facilitate the dismantlement of strategic offensive arms and the security of nuclear weapons, achieve our joint non-proliferation objectives, and help in the conversion of Ukraine's defense industries. The Presidents agreed on the importance of identifying as soon as possible programs of assistance under the Nunn-Lugar program, using the $75 million allocated to Ukraine out of Fiscal Year 1995 Nunn-Lugar funds. Both acknowledged the progress that had been made to date, noting in particular the utility of U.S. deactivation assistance, procurement of missile fuel storage tanks and the imminent completion of a U.S.-Ukraine communications link. The Presidents also recognized the significant contribution of the fourteen Western countries and the European Union in providing $234 million of dismantlement and related assistance for Ukraine.

The Presidents discussed the evolving European security structure. They agreed that this process should be managed in a manner that strengthens the stability and security of all nations of Europe. As a tangible example of Ukraine's overall importance in European security and the U.S. commitment to expanded Ukrainian cooperation with NATO, President Clinton announced that the United States would make funds available to Ukraine under the Warsaw Initiative to support Ukrainian participation in the Partnership for Peace. The funds will contribute to Ukraine's ability to promote the objectives of the Partnership.

The two leaders announced that the two countries had agreed to move forward with a $600,000 International Military Training and Education Program to assist in the professional development of Ukraine's armed forces. The Presidents also pledged to continue to expand military and defense contact programs designed to assist Ukraine in the restructuring of its defense establishment which is now under civilian

leadership for the first time. In addition, the sides announced that Ukraine will host a U.S.-Ukraine combined peacekeeping training exercise late next spring. In the area of defense industry conversion, President Clinton informed President Kuchma that the United States would continue to provide assistance to U.S.-Ukraine joint ventures and would seek new partners for the important work of defense conversion.

The Presidents noted the importance of proceeding with defense industry conversion priorities and the need to expand opportunities for trade and investment in high technology industries. They also underscored the importance of the bilateral U.S.-Ukraine Memorandum of Understanding on the Transfer of Missile Equipment and Technology signed last May 13. The Presidents also recognized the importance of broader international cooperation in ensuring reliable control over exports of sensitive materials and technology. President Clinton expressed the hope that Ukraine would become a member of the MTCR at an early date and reiterated that the U.S. would support Ukraine in achieving this goal. They agreed to work together toward Ukraine's full participation in a successor regime to COCOM. President Clinton was pleased to note that a Science and Technology Center, funded by the United States and other donors, will soon begin operations in Ukraine and that this would assist Ukraine in redirecting the work of former defense scientists and engineers to civilian purposes.

Diplomatic Endeavors

Consistent with the new stage of bilateral relations, the Presidents also underscored the importance of ensuring that the diplomatic missions of both countries be fully capable of conducting their operations without hindrance. With this in mind, the Presidents announced the exchange of diplomatic notes to lift employment restrictions on diplomatic personnel and their families. President Clinton also used this occasion to welcome Ukraine's newly appointed Ambassador to the United States, Yuriy Shcherbak, to Washington, D.C.

Joint Statement on Future Aerospace Cooperation Between the United States and Ukraine
November 22, 1994

President Clinton and President Kuchma underscored the important role that cooperation in civil and commercial aerospace activities can play in furthering scientific, technical and economic ties between the United States and Ukraine. As a first significant step in this cooperation, the two Presidents signed an agreement on cooperation in the exploration and use of outer space for peaceful purposes that will expand joint efforts in space communications, space technology, life and microgravity sciences applications, remote sensing and earth sciences, space sciences and telecommunications.

The two Presidents agreed that future joint activities should be explored. Both Presidents recognized that the Ukrainian aerospace industry can make a valuable contribution to Ukraine's economic reform and development as it undertakes the transition to a market economy. They resolved to work together to open prospects for Ukrainian access to international aerospace markets. Noting that a preliminary dialogue addressing the potential for commercial space opportunities between the United States and Ukraine had already begun, they agreed to hold further talks on commercial launches and the scope of these activities, in accordance with market principles, with the principles contained in international arrangements for integrating economies in transition into the international space launch market, and consistent with current obligations of the two countries.

President Clinton and President Kuchma also directed the National Aeronautics and Space Administration and the Ukrainian National Space Agency to identify potential experiments and payloads which could qualify for flight on the Space Shuttle and also to create an opportunity for a Ukrainian Payload Specialist to fly on the Space Shuttle. Both agencies will jointly report their recommendations for such a mission by March 31, 1995.

Remarks at the State Dinner for President Leonid Kuchma of Ukraine
November 22, 1994

Ladies and gentlemen, President Kuchma, Mrs. Kuchma, members of the Ukrainian delegation, diplomatic corps, Ukrainian-Americans, and distinguished guests, tonight we meet to celebrate a new friendship between our two nations and a new freedom for the people of the Ukraine. We also celebrate our peoples' devotion to the shared values that produce peace and prosperity. In a time when it is tempting to take the easy way out, Ukraine has set for itself the highest goals.

Mr. President, people around the world admire you for your wisdom in leading your country toward a nonnuclear future, a move now heralded around the world. And we applaud your courage on embarking on the difficult path of economic reform, a path that holds the promise of turning the vast resources of your country into real prosperity. As you strive to build a peaceful and prosperous Ukraine, we will stand by you and work with you.

The Slavic root of the name Ukraine means "borderland," but the independent Ukraine of today is at the very heart of Europe. It occupies a central place in our world. Our freedom and your freedom are bound together. We share the same desire to build a safer and better world for our children.

Mr. President, you are renowned as the man who ran Pivdenmash, the largest aerospace plant in the world. Just as you brought that vast operation to the pinnacle of technical excellence, we know you will be able to bring the hard work of reform down to earth and that you will deploy all your engineering skill to the construction of a new democratic nation. I might also add that a democratic Ukraine supports the idea of a democratic Russia, which is best for Russia, Ukraine, and the United States.

Let me close with a story. More than a century ago in the winter of 1858, the great Ukrainian national poet Taras Shevchenko had just returned to St. Petersburg from internal exile in the Russian Far East. There he met the acclaimed American black actor Ira Aldridge, who was in the city performing Shakespeare. The son of Ukrainian serfs and the son of American slaves became fast friends. Theirs was a friendship born of shared ideals, above all the dream of freedom for all peoples. It was that dream that led Shevchenko to condemn despotism with the line, "Freedom knows no dying." Ira Al-

dridge was so impressed by his friend Shevchenko that it was said of him that forever after he carried Ukraine in his heart.

The steadfast devotion to freedom that brought Shevchenko and Aldridge together has also brought us together tonight. So I ask all of you to join me in a toast to President and Mrs. Kuchma, to the growing friendship of our peoples, and the bright future of a prosperous and free Ukraine.

NOTE: The President spoke at 8:28 p.m. in the State Dining Room at the White House.

Letter to Congressional Leaders on Bosnia-Herzegovina
November 22, 1994

Dear Mr. Speaker: (Dear Mr. President:)

I last reported to the Congress on August 22, 1994, on our support for the United Nations and North Atlantic Treaty Organization's (NATO) efforts to achieve peace and security in Bosnia-Herzegovina. I am informing you today of recent developments in these efforts, including the use of U.S. combat aircraft on November 21, 1994, to attack airfields and related facilities in Serb-held Croatian territory used by Serb forces to launch air strikes against the town of Bihac in Bosnia-Herzegovina.

Since the adoption of United Nations Security Council Resolution (UNSCR) 713 on September 25, 1991, the United Nations has actively sought solutions to the humanitarian and ethnic crisis in the former Yugoslavia. Under UNSCRs 824 (May 6, 1993) and 836 (June 4, 1993) certain portions of Bosnia-Herzegovina have been established as safe areas, including the town of Bihac. Member states, acting nationally or through regional organizations, have been authorized to use all necessary measures, through the use of air power, in and around the safe areas, to support the United Nations Protection Forces (UNPROFOR) in the performance of its mandate.

The air strikes conducted on November 21, 1994, were in response to Serb air strikes launched November 18 and 19, 1994, from Udbina airfield in the Krajina region of Croatia against the town of Bihac and other areas of northwest Bosnia. The United Nations has in-

formed us that the Serbs dropped napalm and cluster munitions during their attack on November 18 in Bihac, placing approximately 1,200 UNPROFOR troops deployed in Bihac in jeopardy. We are further informed that the Serb attack on November 19 was against the town of Cazin, about 10 miles north of Bihac, causing between 9 and 15 civilian casualties.

In response to the Serb attacks, the United Nations Security Council unanimously adopted UNSCR 958 on November 19, 1994, expressly deciding that the authorizations in previous resolutions also applied in the Republic of Croatia. Meeting the same day, the North Atlantic Council agreed to respond positively to UNSCR 958 and authorized the Commander in Chief, NATO Allied Forces Southern Europe (CINCSOUTH), in accordance with existing procedures, to conduct air strikes in response to attacks on or that threaten the U.N. safe areas in Bosnia-Herzegovina launched from U.N. protected areas of Croatia.

The NATO strikes launched on November 21, 1994, included 39 aircraft from the Netherlands, France, United Kingdom, NATO, and the United States. The aircraft struck targets at Udbina airfield, including runways, taxiways, radars, and air defenses located at the airfield. No aircraft were lost or damaged in conducting the attacks. Initial battle damage assessments indicate that runways and taxiways were cratered and that an air defense radar was destroyed.

I authorized these actions in conjunction with our NATO allies in order to carry out the U.N. and NATO decisions of November 19 and to answer UNPROFOR's request for assistance. As I have indicated in the past, our efforts in the former Yugoslavia are intended to assist the parties to reach a negotiated settlement to the conflict. I have directed the participation by U.S. Armed Forces in this effort pursuant to my constitutional authority to conduct the foreign relations of the United States and as Commander in Chief and Chief Executive.

I am providing this report as part of my efforts to keep the Congress fully informed, consistent with the War Powers Resolution. I am grateful for the continuing support that the Congress has provided, and I look forward to continued cooperation with you in this endeavor. I shall communicate with you further regarding our efforts for peace and stability in the former Yugoslavia.

Sincerely,

WILLIAM J. CLINTON

NOTE: Identical letters were sent to Thomas S. Foley, Speaker of the House of Representatives, and Albert Gore, Jr., President of the Senate. This letter was released by the Office of the Press Secretary on November 23.

Remarks and an Exchange With Reporters at the Thanksgiving Turkey Presentation Ceremony
November 23, 1994

The President. Well, good morning.

Audience members. Good morning!

The President. It's nice to see all of you here. I want to especially welcome the fifth graders from Murch Elementary School. I'm glad you're here and hope you're having a good time. And I'm glad the Sun is shining down at least on some of you. I want to thank Larry Fanella, the chairman of the National Turkey Federation, and say a special word of thanks to Robert Strickler and to Shawn Arbogast, the 10-year-old boy who raised this year's turkey in Dayton, Virginia. Let's give him a hand. [*Applause*]

Tomorrow we'll all celebrate Thanksgiving. It's an opportunity and a responsibility for all of us to give thanks for our many blessings in this life, to appreciate the good things we have in this country, and to think about those who still live among our ranks who don't have the things that many of us take for granted. In a few hours, Hillary and I will visit So Others Might Eat, a local soup kitchen, to help prepare Thanksgiving dinner for some of Washington's less fortunate families. I think that this is an important time for all of us to think about the larger American community of which we are a part.

The very presence of these children from schools and the different walks of life and backgrounds from which they come reminds us that this has always been a country of great diversity, and the great strength of America is that we offer an opportunity for all different kinds of people to live up to the fullest of their God-given capacities. We can only do that if we're committed to creating a stronger and better American community every day. That is the commitment of our administration. That is the commitment of the public education movement in this country. That is the commitment of everybody devoted to the idea that every child can learn and that we can all do better if we work together.

So I would like to leave you with that thought on this Thanksgiving. And now I want to accept the turkey, and a lot of you know this already, but this will be the second official Presidential pardon of my administration. I granted one to a turkey last year. Unlike the 45 million American turkeys who will make the supreme sacrifice this Thanksgiving for the rest of us, this turkey will retire to Kidwell Farms, a replica of the 1930's working farm in Frying Pan Park in northern Virginia. So I'm glad I can make at least one turkey happy this year. [*Laughter*]

Thank you very much.

Are we going to let the kids come up and see the turkey?

Q. Mr. President, what do you have to be thankful for this year?

The President. A lot, but let me just—I'll mention two things. One is there's more than 5 million Americans more who have jobs, and who therefore can afford to have Thanksgiving, this Thanksgiving than there were two Thanksgivings ago, right after I was elected. And I'm very thankful for that. And I'm very thankful for the opportunity that my family and I have been given to get up here every day and work on the problems and the opportunities of this country. Those are the two things that I feel very grateful for.

Q. When are you going to Camp David?

The President. When am I going? Tonight when Chelsea gets home from her activities. We're going up late tonight.

NOTE: The President spoke at 10:10 a.m. in the Rose Garden at the White House. In his remarks, he referred to Robert Strickler, assistant to the general manager, Rocco Turkeys, Inc.

Remarks on the General Agreement on Tariffs and Trade
November 23, 1994

Good morning. Today we have moved one step closer toward gaining broad bipartisan support for GATT. I'm pleased to announce that an understanding has been reached with Senator Dole to reaffirm our United States sovereignty and to make sure that the reaffirmation will be protected in the GATT process. That means that the WTO will be accountable and fair and will meet our expectations.

The Uruguay round is the largest, most comprehensive trade agreement in world history. It creates hundreds of thousands of high-paying American jobs. It slashes tariffs on manufactured and agricultural goods. It protects intellectual property. It's the largest international tax cut in history. Most importantly, this agreement requires all trading nations to play by the same rules. And since the United States has the most productive and competitive economy in the world, that is good news for our workers and our future.

For the past 50 years, our country has led the world to create a more open and a more prosperous trading economy. A bipartisan vote in support of the Uruguay round next week will ensure that we will lead the world for decades to come.

I want to express my deep thanks to Senator Dole, to Senator Packwood, Senator Moynihan, who are here, and ask them to speak. I thank Ambassador Kantor for his heroic work in this endeavor and the Secretary of the Treasury, Secretary of State for what they have done. The Secretary of State and the Secretary of the Treasury and I are going to have to excuse ourselves to go meet with the Mexican President-elect, President Zedillo.

I also want to make a brief announcement today. As part of our ongoing nonproliferation efforts, Kazakhstan has delivered into our security nuclear materials capable of making some 20 nuclear weapons. That means that one more threat of nuclear terrorism and proliferation has been removed from the world. Today—this is a good day—we are making progress toward making our people more secure and more prosperous.

Again, let me say how excited I am about the prospect of the GATT round passing the Congress and to express my appreciation to Senator Dole for the very constructive working relationship that we have had. I'd like now to excuse the Secretary of State and Secretary of Treasury and ask the others who are here to make some comments, beginning with Senator Dole.

Thank you.

NOTE: The President spoke at 12:07 p.m. in the Rose Garden at the White House.

The President's Radio Address
November 26, 1994

Good morning, and a happy Thanksgiving weekend to all of you. To the millions of Americans who have traveled to be with loved ones during this special time of year, I wish you a safe and peaceful journey home. We Americans have a lot to be thankful for this Thanksgiving.

On behalf of all of our citizens, I want to begin by thanking our brave service men and women who are so many miles from home this Thanksgiving, serving our country with honor overseas, in every corner of the world and especially those who are working at restoring democracy in Haiti and keeping the peace in the Persian Gulf.

This is the first Thanksgiving since the dawn of the nuclear age when parents can tuck their children into bed at night knowing that no Russian missiles are pointed at the children of the United States. The third largest nuclear power, Ukraine, has just agreed to eliminate all of its nuclear weapons, and they're being dismantled with our assistance. Just this week, the United States removed a major nuclear stockpile, enough for 20 nuclear devices from the former Soviet republic of Kazakhstan. And finally, we have concluded an agreement with North Korea to freeze and dismantle that country's ability to build nuclear weapons.

Over the past year, we've also been privileged to see the American dreams of freedom, democracy, and peace advanced with our support in the Middle East, in Northern Ireland, in South Africa, in Haiti, and Eastern and Central Europe, full of people who are making courageous efforts to escape the shackles of the past and realize their own dreams for tomorrow.

For America to remain strong, however, around the world, we know we have to be strong at home. Therefore, we must keep striving to keep our Government working again for ordinary Americans, to improve our economy, to give our people the chance to build a more prosperous and secure future in the 21st century.

We're in the process of great changes, but we have more to do. We have 5 million more jobs than we had 22 months ago, but still too many people who never get a pay raise and who are losing their health benefits. We have

more loans for middle class college students. But still there are too many who need more education all throughout their lives, including working people. We have a tough new crime bill, but there's a lot to do to make our streets safer.

We've done things for working families like the family leave law and tax cuts for 15 million families who live on modest incomes. But there's still too much family breakup. There are too many children born where there were never families in the first place. There's a lot to be done here.

We're making great changes in our Government. It's smaller, it's more effective, but there is still more to be done before we liberate our National Government from the stranglehold of special interests.

We must be thankful, with all of our challenges, for what's right with America. And we have to remember that the real strength of our country is still in the work of our citizens. They're the ones who keep our country strong, who keep us together, who keep us moving forward. They're what America is all about, people who take responsibility to improve their own lives and to make a difference in the lives of others.

I'm committed to make your Government work for ordinary Americans again. Nobody wants Government on our backs, but we do need a strong, if limited, Government by our side. Everything we do in Washington should be as relevant and responsive to your lives as the work of those just around you.

Consider the Americans who are fighting crime. Just last month, several strangers in New York City came to the rescue of a man who was being mugged and stabbed as he tried to use a bank teller machine. These brave heroes helped the victim to safety and then held the assailant down until police could come to make an arrest. Our new crime bill puts 100,000 more police on the streets and takes military assault weapons off the streets, but we still need citizens like this to make our streets safe.

Remember the Americans who are doing so much to help others. Every day thousands of members of our new domestic Peace Corps,

AmeriCorps, are working to make our people smarter, safer, and healthier. Out in rural Kansas, Nanci Ridge has been trained by AmeriCorps to give emergency medical assistance. Now every day she helps police or fire departments or teaches school kids safety. But she spent Thanksgiving fielding emergencies at the local county hospital, giving some of the regular staff the holiday off and keeping the country protected. That's what AmeriCorps is about; that's what America's about.

And finally, let's think about the Americans who are doing so much to help our children live up to their God-given potential. Five years ago in Buffalo, New York, Lloyd Hargrave helped start a parent resource center to get parents more involved in the education of their children. Today, the center offers nightly tutoring programs to help parents do a better job at helping their children learn. And the center lends computers to families that otherwise wouldn't have them in their homes.

Working with children in that way is one of the most important things any of us can do to keep our country strong. Our Government can help, and we are. We're expanding Head Start, promoting programs in our schools like character education. But in the end, children need to know that adults care about them, that they're part of a loving family, a caring community. They need to be told by someone that they're the most important person in the world.

So this holiday season as we count our blessings and face our challenges, let us commit ourselves to giving our children a future they can be thankful for every Thanksgiving for a long, long time.

I hope you enjoy this holiday weekend, and thank you for listening.

NOTE: The address was recorded at 10:29 a.m. on November 25 in the Laurel Lodge at Camp David, MD, for broadcast at 10:06 a.m. on November 26.

Remarks on the General Agreement on Tariffs and Trade
November 28, 1994

Thank you very much, Mr. Vice President. Jim Miller and Jim Baker, thank you for your moving and compelling remarks. Mr. Speaker, Leader Michel, Members of the Congress, members of the Cabinet, and to all of you who have come here from previous administrations and from different walks of life, proving that this GATT agreement not only tears down trade barriers, it also bulldozes differences of party, philosophy, and ideology: I thank you all for being here.

We have certainly demonstrated today that there is no partisan pride of ownership in the GATT agreement. It is not a Republican agreement or a Democratic one. It is an American agreement, designed to benefit all the American people in every region of our country from every walk of life.

Jim Baker spoke so eloquently about how this represents yet another historic choice for the United States in the 20th century. When we walked away from our leadership and engagement responsibilities, as we did after the First World War, the world has paid a terrible price.

When we have attempted to lead, as we did after the Second World War, it has not only helped the world, it has helped the people of the United States. We saw the greatest expansion of the middle class in our country and prosperity for working families in our country in the years after we tried to put together a system that would preserve peace and security and promote prosperity after World War II.

We have done as much as we could here at home to try to deal with the difficult and daunting economic challenges we face, to bring the deficit down, to shrink the size of the Government, to simultaneously increase our investment in education and technology and defense conversion. But we know that without the capacity to expand trade and to generate more economic opportunities we will, first of all, not be able to fulfill our global responsibilities and, secondly, not be able to fulfill our responsibilities to the American people.

I'd like to address a third argument, if I might, just from my heart. It's been raised against this agreement and raised against

NAFTA. Jim Miller adequately disposed of the arguments that this is a budget buster and that this somehow impinges on our sovereignty. That isn't true. And he did a very compelling job of that. But let me say there is another big argument against this trade agreement that no one has advanced today but that is underlying all of this. And I saw it in an article the other day written by a columnist generally sympathetic to me. He said, "There he goes again with one of his crazy, self-defeating economic ideas, pushing this GATT agreement, which is one more prescription for the demise of the lower wage working people in America, which is the reason the Democratic Party's in the trouble it's in today, doing things like this that just kill working people."

That is a wrong argument. But that is really the undercurrent against this GATT. The idea is that since we live in a global economy and there are people other places who can work for wages we can't live on, if we open our markets to them, they will displace our workers and they will aggravate the most troubling trend in modern American life, which is that the wages of non-college-educated male workers in the United States have declined by 12 percent after you take account of inflation in the last 10 years.

Now, that has great superficial appeal. Why is it wrong? It's wrong because, number one, if we don't do anything, we'll have some displacement from foreign competition. But if we move and lead, we will open other markets to our products. And our Nation has gone through a wrenching period over the last several years of improving its productivity, its ability to compete. We can now sell and compete anywhere.

When we did NAFTA, they made the same argument. What's happened? A hundred thousand new jobs this year. What's happened? A 500 percent increase in exports of American automobiles to Mexico. What's the biggest complaint in Detroit now? The autoworkers have too much overtime they have to do. If you think about where we were 10 years ago, that's what, at home, we call a high-class problem. [*Laughter*]

Now, that is the problem we face in America. And the resentments of people who keep working harder and falling further behind and feel like they've played by the rules and they've gotten the shaft, they will play themselves out, these resentments, in election after election

after election in different and unpredictable ways, just like they did in 1992 and 1994. But our responsibility is to do what is right for those people over the long run. That is our responsibility. And the only way to do that is to open other markets to American products and services, even as we open our markets to them.

Yes, we have to improve the level of lifetime training and education for the American work force. Yes, we have to deal with some of the serious, particular problems of the American economy. But in the end, the private sector in this country and the working people of this country will do their jobs if they have half a shot at the high-growth areas of the world. And what are the highest growth areas of the world? Not the wealthy advanced economies but Latin America, Asia, and other places.

GATT, along with NAFTA and what we're trying to do with the Asian-Pacific countries and what we're going to try to do at the Summit of the Americas, this keeps America leading the world in ways that permits us to do both things we have to do at the end of the cold war, to continue to be engaged, to continue to lead, to work toward a more peaceful and secure and prosperous world, and at the same time to deal with the terrible, nagging difficulties that so many millions of American families face today.

There is no other way to deal with this. There is no easy way out. There is no slogan that makes the problem go away. This will help to solve the underlying anxiety that millions and millions of Americans face and, I might add, millions of Europeans and millions of Japanese and others in advanced economies all around the world, and at the same time make the world a better place and the future more secure for our children.

And we have to do it now. We can't wait until next year. We don't want to litter it up like a Christmas tree and run the risk of losing it. Every time I talked to a world leader in the last 6 months, they have asked me the same thing: When is the United States going to act on GATT? The rest of the world is looking at us.

So we have a golden opportunity here to add $1,700 in income to the average family's income in this country over the next few years, to create hundreds of thousands of high-wage jobs, to have the biggest global tax cut in history, and to fulfill our two responsibilities, our responsibility to lead and remain engaged in the world and our responsibility to try to help the people here at home to get ahead. We need to get on with it and do it now.

Thank you very much.

NOTE: The President spoke at 11:38 a.m. in the East Room at the White House. In his remarks, he referred to former Office of Management and Budget Director James C. Miller III and former Secretary of State James A. Baker III.

Statement on House of Representatives Action on the General Agreement on Tariffs and Trade
November 29, 1994

Tonight the United States House of Representatives cast an historic vote for American workers, farmers, and families. This overwhelming bipartisan vote in support of the GATT legislation demonstrates our confidence in America's ability to compete and win in the global economy.

Passage of the Uruguay round will provide enormous benefits for the United States: hundreds of thousands of new U.S. jobs, $100–$200 billion per year in increased GDP, and a $744 billion global tax cut.

This vote demonstrates to the American people that Democrats and Republicans can work together in the national interest. The Uruguay round agreement is the product of 8 years of work by three administrations—Republican and Democratic. A strong majority of each party cast votes in favor of the agreement.

The eyes of the world are now on the United States Senate. I call on the Senate to pass GATT with the same strong, bipartisan support as it received in the House of Representatives.

Statement on the Student Loan Program
November 30, 1994

Today the Department of Education announced that its new direct lending program has reached the congressionally mandated benchmark of 40 percent in new loan volume for the next academic year. A total of 1,495 schools will participate in this new program. The program will provide $8 billion in loans to two million students in the next school year.

The American people want a Federal Government that works better, costs less, and expands opportunities for all Americans. The new direct lending program is an important example of reinventing Government to better meet the people's needs.

It will reduce complexity and costs for millions of student borrowers. And the option to repay loans as a percentage of income over time will reduce burdens on young families and make it easier for young people to serve their communities and their country.

The new direct lending program is good news for taxpayers as well. Financial analysts in a recent Morgan Stanley newsletter have already described this new program as a "budgetary winner" that will "lower Government spending and reduce the deficit." Over the long term, we expect to save taxpayers $4.3 billion once this program is fully up and running. Direct lending represents the most innovative student financial aid program since the creation of the Pell grant program in 1973, more than 20 years ago.

Government can work better, cost less, and direct lending proves it.

Letter to Congressional Leaders on Locality-Based Comparability Payments
November 30, 1994

Dear Mr. Speaker: (Dear Mr. President:)

In accordance with section 5304(d)(3) of title 5, United States Code, I hereby report to the Congress on the implementation of locality-based comparability payments for General Schedule employees for calendar year 1995.

I have directed the President's Pay Agent to put into effect the locality-based comparability payments shown on the enclosed table, effective in January 1995. The report of the President's Pay Agent, which includes the information required by section 5304(d)(3) regarding comparability payments for 1995 and 1996, is also enclosed.

Sincerely,

WILLIAM J. CLINTON

NOTE: Identical letters were sent to Thomas S. Foley, Speaker of the House of Representatives, and Albert Gore, Jr., President of the Senate. This letter was released by the Office of the Press Secretary on December 1. The related memorandum is listed in Appendix D at the end of this volume.

Remarks Announcing the Appointment of George Mitchell as Special Adviser for Economic Initiatives in Ireland
December 1, 1994

Good morning. Ladies and gentlemen, today is the last day of this session of Congress. And therefore, it's the last day that all of us in America have the privilege of having George Mitchell as the Senate majority leader. I will personally miss him very much, his wise counsel, his support, his strong leadership for the American people.

I know that his colleagues on both sides of the aisle and the American people will also miss his leadership and the thoughtfulness and the courage that have distinguished him throughout his long career. My regret about his retirement is tempered, at least in some measure, by the fact that as one chapter in his life of extraordinary public service closes, another is opening. Today Senator Mitchell has agreed to work on an issue of central importance to me and to our country as Special Adviser to the President and the Secretary of State for Economic Initiatives in Ireland.

We stand on the verge of a new and peaceful era in Northern Ireland. For over 3 months, the historic cease-fires between the IRA and the loyalist parliamentary groups have held. I welcome today's invitation by Downing Street to Sinn Fein to begin an exploratory dialog by December 7th. A just and lasting settlement that respects the rights and traditions of the two communities in Northern Ireland is, after so many years of bloodshed, finally within reach. But at this hopeful and historic moment, it's essential to create more economic opportunity in a region whose prospects have been so blighted by bloodshed. There must be a peace dividend in Ireland for the peace to succeed. Peace and prosperity depend upon one another.

One of the most important ways that we here in the United States can ensure that peace takes root is to promote trade and investment in the areas of Ireland that have suffered the most from violence. That's why last month we announced our economic initiatives for Ireland. They're a response to the call of all the parties in the region for the development that will help them to lift themselves out of the cycle of conflict and despair. As we have in the past, the United States stands ready to help those who are taking risks for peace. To do that, we'll work in close cooperation with the private sector here in the United States and with Britain, Ireland, and other concerned parties in Europe and elsewhere.

Ultimately, of course, the success of the peace process will depend most on those who have been most affected, on whether they believe it will give them a better future. That's why our initiatives to help revitalize the economy are so important and why I wanted someone of great talent, great stature, and great wisdom to lead in that effort here in the United States. No one fills that bill like George Mitchell. He will oversee the White House Conference on Trade and Investment in Ireland which will be held in April of next year in Philadelphia. I've asked him to ensure implementation of all the initiatives we announced last month, to explore additional opportunities for helping peace and prosperity grow in Ireland. He'll consult with the International Fund for Ireland, with the Congress, and with others to strengthen the Fund's programs. He'll also begin a dialog with the European Union, its individual member nations, and other nations to promote economic development in all these areas.

I believe in the weeks and months ahead, the people of Ireland will come to respect and admire George Mitchell just as much as all of us here in the United States have.

George, I am delighted today to be able to say thank you, again, for public service, and not just farewell.

NOTE: The President spoke at 10:27 a.m. in the Oval Office at the White House.

Remarks on Defense Readiness and an Exchange With Reporters
December 1, 1994

The President. Good afternoon. Secretary Perry, General Shalikashvili, members of the Joint Chiefs of Staff, I have pledged that throughout the life of this administration, our military will remain the best trained, the best equipped, the best prepared fighting force on Earth. I'm happy to be here today with Secretary Perry and with the Joint Chiefs to reinforce that commitment and to announce a new initiative to ensure military readiness and to give our military and their families the support they deserve.

During our first year in office, we undertook a fundamental review from the bottom up of our Nation's defense capacity and our strategy. Building on the efforts of the previous administration and bipartisan support in the Congress, we continue to restructure our Nation's military forces to meet the challenges to American leadership in the post-cold-war era. I directed that our Armed Forces be ready to face two major regional conflicts occurring almost simultaneously. Since then, I have repeatedly resisted calls to cut our forces further, to cut our budget below the levels recommended in that bottom-up review, and I have drawn the line against further defense cuts.

During these past 2 years, our military has time and again demonstrated its readiness and its war-fighting and peacekeeping capabilities. From Korea to Macedonia to Rwanda and Haiti, we have placed great burdens on our men and women in uniform, and they have responded magnificently. They have demonstrated a truly outstanding ability to deploy quickly, provide security, and to help ensure stability.

When our forces deployed with extraordinary speed and efficiency to the Persian Gulf in October, Saddam Hussein got the message. We decisively deterred the Iraqi threat to the region's security. And when our armed services, cooperating in an unprecedented fashion, stood ready to back up our diplomatic efforts in Haiti, we helped set the stage for restoration of democracy in that nation.

Whether our forces are engaged in combat, acting as peacekeepers, or delivering humanitarian assistance, we must continue to review their requirements, provide adequate funding, and keep our military edge. Secretary Perry and I have repeatedly stated that our number one commitment is to the readiness and well-being of our men and women in uniform.

I'm announcing today a five-part initiative to ensure that our Armed Forces receive the resources and the support they need to continue their high standard of performance. First, I intend to ask Congress to add an additional $25 billion to our planned defense budgets over the next 6 years. Second, I will seek the full pay raise allowed by law for our uniformed military through the turn of the century. Third, I will fully support other quality-of-life initiatives which were outlined by Secretary Perry last month. We will spend what is required to ensure that our military live in adequate housing and are provided the necessary child care and receive the support they and their families need to serve our Nation. Fourth, I will ask the Congress to provide for real growth in the defense budget during the last 2 years of our next 6-year plan to help ensure that the American military enters the 21st century with the most modern equipment available. And finally, we will send to Congress with our budget next year an emergency supplemental funding for the current fiscal year to reimburse the military for its unanticipated expenditures with the operations in the Gulf, the Adriatic, Haiti, and elsewhere and to protect us from dipping into important readiness funding. These funds will enable us to maintain the readiness and training we will need to accomplish our missions in the coming year.

I urge Congress to quickly approve this supplemental request so that we do not face the kind of problems we confronted this fall when Congress delayed its approval of the last supplemental funding request.

These actions I'm announcing today reinforce our administration's commitment and my personal commitment to maintaining the highest training standards for our military, to preparing them to depart on missions around the world at a moment's notice. They will ensure that our men and women in uniform can be assured that their families are getting the kind of support they need and deserve. We ask much of our military, and we owe much to them in return.

Our Armed Forces are the backbone of our national security strategy. They stand behind our efforts to maintain peace and security all around the world. I call on the new Congress to give these initiatives their full support.

Thank you very much.

Bosnia

Q. Mr. President, are you ready to send U.S. ground troops to Bosnia to help in any evacuation of U.N. peacekeepers if that is necessary?

The President. There has been no discussion of that, and the U.N. peacekeepers have not decided to leave Bosnia.

Thank you.

Defense Readiness

Q. Mr. President, some critics might argue that your action today is a passive admission that defense has been cut too much.

The President. That's not right. What we have done—I'll remind you, we started out, when I became President—when I became President I said, we have a commitment to maintain readiness and the quality of life for our troops; we have a commitment to be able to meet our strategic mission, which is principally to be able to conduct two regional conflicts nearly simultaneously. We have reviewed that; we have managed that. In the last 2 years, we have also had significant costs for other things, as you know. And our military has performed very well in Haiti, in the Gulf, in dealing with the migration problems in Cuba, in Haiti, and in many, many other areas. We've also stepped up a lot of our operations in the Adriatic and in the area around Bosnia.

So we have had a lot of unanticipated costs. And what we've tried to do is to look at this and then decide what it would take to maintain our readiness in the short term and in the long run. The short-term problems can be readily remedied by the emergency supplemental that I've asked for and by the budgetary changes that I am making. The long-term problems will require the adoption of this five-point plan.

We are moving into the future with a very aggressive strategy. It is consistent with the commitments I made when I came here. And we have seen the military, frankly, have to deal with an amazing number and variety of unanticipated challenges. They have done so with great skill, but now they need the support that I think we ought to give them.

And in this era when we are definitely going to continue to reduce the size of the budget, we are going to continue to cut Government, we are going to give the American people a leaner Government, I still believe the people of this country expect us to do right by our men and women in uniform and to maintain our readiness and preparedness and to plan for the future. And that's what this budget does. That's my job; that's the Secretary of Defense's job; that's the Joint Chiefs' job, and we're here doing it today.

Thank you.

NOTE: The President spoke at 12:54 p.m. in the Rose Garden at the White House.

Letter to Congressional Leaders on Seismic Safety of Existing Federally Owned or Leased Buildings
December 1, 1994

Dear Mr. Speaker: (Dear Mr. President:)

Under Public Law 101–614 the President is to adopt, no later than December 1, 1994, "standards for assessing and enhancing the seismic safety of existing buildings constructed for or leased by the Federal Government which were designed and constructed without adequate seismic design and construction standards." The statute gave the task of developing the standards to the Interagency Committee on Seismic Safety in Construction (ICSSC), which is chaired by the National Institute of Standards and Technology.

The ICSSC developed a set of "Standards of Seismic Safety for Existing Federally Owned or Leased Buildings and Commentary" (Standards), and recommends that Federal departments and agencies adopt these Standards.

The intent of the Standards is to identify common minimum evaluation and mitigation measures for all Federal departments and agencies, and to allow all Federal entities to have an agency-conceived and controlled seismic safety program for their existing owned or leased buildings. I have signed an Executive order adopting

these Standards. A copy of that order is attached.

The Executive order adopts the Standards as the minimum level of seismic safety for federally owned and leased buildings. It requires seismic evaluation and, if necessary, rehabilitation under certain conditions identified in the Standards. The order directs all Federal departments and agencies to develop an inventory of their owned and leased buildings within 4 years of signing, and to estimate the cost of mitigating unacceptable seismic risks in their buildings.

Adoption of these Standards provides the critical first step for determining how these Standards can be applied to buildings that receive Federal financial assistance or are regulated by a Federal agency.

Sincerely,

WILLIAM J. CLINTON

NOTE: Identical letters were sent to Thomas S. Foley, Speaker of the House of Representatives, and Albert Gore, Jr., President of the Senate. The Executive order is listed in Appendix D at the end of this volume.

Letter to Congressional Leaders Reporting on Sanctions Against the Federal Republic of Yugoslavia (Serbia and Montenegro)
December 1, 1994

Dear Mr. Speaker: (Dear Mr. President:)

On May 30, 1992, in Executive Order No. 12808, the President declared a national emergency to deal with the threat to the national security, foreign policy, and economy of the United States arising from actions and policies of the Governments of Serbia and Montenegro, acting under the name of the Socialist Federal Republic of Yugoslavia or the Federal Republic

of Yugoslavia, in their involvement in and support for groups attempting to seize territory in Croatia and the Republic of Bosnia and Herzegovina by force and violence utilizing, in part, the forces of the so-called Yugoslav National Army (57 *FR* 23299, June 2, 1992). The present report is submitted pursuant to 50 U.S.C. 1641(c) and 1703(c). It discusses Administration actions and expenses directly related to the exercise of powers and authorities conferred by the declaration of a national emergency in Executive Order No. 12808 and to expanded sanctions against the Federal Republic of Yugoslavia (Serbia and Montenegro) (the "FRY (S/M)") contained in Executive Order No. 12810 of June 5, 1992 (57 *FR* 24347, June 9, 1992), Executive Order No. 12831 of January 15, 1993 (58 *FR* 5253, January 21, 1993), and Executive Order No. 12846 of April 26, 1993 (58 *FR* 25771, April 27, 1993).

1. Executive Order No. 12808 blocked all property and interests in property of the Governments of Serbia and Montenegro, or held in the name of the former Government of the Socialist Federal Republic of Yugoslavia or the Government of the Federal Republic of Yugoslavia, then or thereafter located in the United States or within the possession or control of United States persons, including their overseas branches.

Subsequently, Executive Order No. 12810 expanded U.S. actions to implement in the United States the United Nations sanctions against the FRY (S/M) adopted in United Nations Security Council Resolution (UNSCR) 757 of May 30, 1992. In addition to reaffirming the blocking of FRY (S/M) Government property, this order prohibited transactions with respect to the FRY (S/M) involving imports, exports, dealing in FRY-origin property, air and sea transportation, contract performance, funds transfers, activity promoting importation or exportation or dealings in property, and official sports, scientific, technical, or other cultural representation of, or sponsorship by, the FRY (S/M) in the United States.

Executive Order No. 12810 exempted from trade restrictions (1) transshipments through the FRY (S/M), and (2) activities related to the United Nations Protection Force (UNPROFOR), the Conference on Yugoslavia, or the European Community Monitor Mission.

On January 15, 1993, President Bush issued Executive Order No. 12831 to implement new sanctions contained in UNSCR 787 of November 16, 1992. The order revoked the exemption for transshipments through the FRY (S/M) contained in Executive Order No. 12810, prohibited transactions within the United States or by a United States person relating to FRY (S/M) vessels and vessels in which a majority or controlling interest is held by a person or entity in, or operating from, the FRY (S/M), and stated

that all such vessels shall be considered as vessels of the FRY (S/M), regardless of the flag under which they sail.

On April 26, 1993, I issued Executive Order No. 12846 to implement in the United States the sanctions adopted in UNSCR Resolution 820 of April 17, 1993. That resolution called on the Bosnian Serbs to accept the Vance-Owen peace plan for the Republic of Bosnia and Herzegovina and, if they failed to do so by April 26, called on member states to take additional measures to tighten the embargo against the FRY (S/M) and Serbian-controlled areas of the Republic of Bosnia and Herzegovina and the United Nations Protected Areas of Croatia. Effective April 26, 1993, the order blocked all property and interests in property of commercial, industrial, or public utility undertakings or entities organized or located in the FRY (S/M), including property and interests in property of entities (wherever organized or located) owned or controlled by such undertakings or entities, that are or thereafter come within the possession or control of United States persons.

On October 25, 1994, in view of UNSCR 942 of September 23, 1994, I issued Executive Order No. 12934 in order to take additional steps with respect to the crisis in the former Yugoslavia. (59 *FR* 54117, October 27, 1994.) Executive Order No. 12934 expands the scope of the national emergency declared in Executive Order No. 12808 to address the unusual and extraordinary threat to the national security, foreign policy, and economy of the United States posed by the actions and policies of the Bosnian Serb forces and the authorities in the territory that they control, including their refusal to accept the proposed territorial settlement of the conflict in the Republic of Bosnia and Herzegovina.

The Executive order blocks all property and interests in property that are in the United States, that hereafter come within the United States, or that are or hereafter come within the possession or control of United States persons (including their overseas branches) of: (1) the Bosnian Serb military and paramilitary forces and the authorities in areas of the Republic of Bosnia and Herzegovina under the control of those forces; (2) any entity, including any commercial, industrial, or public utility undertaking, organized or located in those areas of the Republic of Bosnia and Herzegovina under the control of Bosnian Serb forces; (3) any entity, wherever organized or located, which is owned or controlled directly or indirectly by any person in, or resident in, those areas of the Republic of Bosnia and Herzegovina under the control of Bosnian Serb forces; and (4) any person acting for or on behalf of any person within the scope of the above definitions.

The Executive order also prohibits the provision or exportation of services to those areas of the Republic of Bosnia and Herzegovina under the control of Bosnian Serb forces, or to any person for the purpose of any business carried on in those areas, either from the United States or by a United States person. The order also prohibits the entry of any U.S.-flagged vessel, other than a U.S. naval vessel, into the riverine ports of those areas of the Republic of Bosnia and Herzegovina under the control of Bosnian Serb forces. Finally, any transaction by any United States person that evades or avoids, or has the purpose of evading or avoiding, or attempts to violate any of the prohibitions set forth in the order is prohibited. Executive Order No. 12934 became effective at 11:59 p.m., e.d.t. on October 25, 1994. A copy of the Executive order is attached for reference.

2. The declaration of the national emergency on May 30, 1992, was made pursuant to the authority vested in the President by the Constitution and laws of the United States, including the International Emergency Economic Powers Act (50 U.S.C. 1701 *et seq.*), the National Emergencies Act (50 U.S.C. 1601 *et seq.*), and section 301 of title 3 of the United States Code. The emergency declaration was reported to the Congress on May 30, 1992, pursuant to section 204(b) of the International Emergency Economic Powers Act (50 U.S.C. 1703(b)). The additional sanctions set forth in subsequent Executive orders were imposed pursuant to the authority vested in the President by the Constitution and laws of the United States, including the statutes cited above, section 1114 of the Federal Aviation Act (49 U.S.C. App. 1514), and section 5 of the United Nations Participation Act (22 U.S.C. 287c).

3. There have been no amendments to the Federal Republic of Yugoslavia (Serbia and Montenegro) Sanctions Regulations (the "Regulations"), 31 C.F.R. Part 585, since the last report. Treasury's blocking authority as applied to FRY (S/M) subsidiaries and vessels in the United States has been challenged in court. A case involving a blocked subsidiary, *IPT Company,*

Inc. v. United States Department of the Treasury, No. 92 CIV 5542 (S.D.N.Y.), is pending a decision by the court on the Government's motion for a summary judgment.

4. Over the past 6 months, the Departments of State and Treasury have worked closely with European Union (the "EU") member states and other U.N. member nations to coordinate implementation of the U.N. sanctions against the FRY (S/M). This has included visits by assessment teams formed under the auspices of the United States, the EU, and the Conference for Security and Cooperation in Europe (the "CSCE") to states bordering on Serbia and Montenegro; deployment of CSCE sanctions assistance missions (SAMs) to Albania, Bulgaria, Croatia, the former Yugoslav Republic of Macedonia, Hungary, Romania, and Ukraine to assist in monitoring land and Danube River traffic; bilateral contacts between the United States and other countries for the purpose of tightening financial and trade restrictions on the FRY (S/M); and ongoing multilateral meetings by financial sanctions enforcement authorities from various countries to coordinate enforcement efforts and to exchange technical information.

5. In accordance with licensing policy and the Regulations, the Department of the Treasury's Office of Foreign Assets Control (FAC) has exercised its authority to license certain specific transactions with respect to the FRY (S/M) that are consistent with the Security Council sanctions. During the reporting period, FAC has issued 144 specific licenses regarding transactions pertaining to the FRY (S/M) or assets it owns or controls, bringing the total as of October 25, 1994, to 821. Specific licenses have been issued (1) for payment to U.S. or third-country secured creditors, under certain narrowly defined circumstances, for pre-embargo import and export transactions; (2) for legal representation or advice to the Government of the FRY (S/M) or FRY (S/M)-controlled entities; (3) for the liquidation or protection of tangible assets of subsidiaries of FRY (S/M)-controlled firms located in the United States; (4) for limited FRY (S/M) diplomatic representation in Washington and New York; (5) for patent, trademark and copyright protection, and maintenance transactions in the FRY (S/M) not involving payment to the FRY (S/M) Government; (6) for certain communications, news media, and travel-related transactions; (7) for the payment of crews' wages, vessel maintenance, and emergency sup-

plies for FRY (S/M)-controlled ships blocked in the United States; (8) for the removal from the FRY (S/M), or protection within the FRY (S/M), of certain property owned and controlled by U.S. entities; (9) to assist the United Nations in its relief operations and the activities of the UNPROFOR; and (10) for payment from funds outside the United States where a third country has licensed the transaction in accordance with U.N. sanctions. Pursuant to U.S. regulations implementing UNSCR 757, specific licenses have also been issued to authorize exportation of food, medicine, and supplies intended for humanitarian purposes in the FRY (S/M).

During the past 6 months, FAC has continued to oversee the liquidation of tangible assets of the 15 U.S. subsidiaries of entities organized in the FRY (S/M). Subsequent to the issuance of Executive Order No. 12846, all operating licenses issued for these U.S.-located Serbian or Montenegrin subsidiaries or joint ventures were revoked, and the net proceeds of the liquidation of their assets placed in blocked accounts.

Bank regulators again worked closely with FAC with regard to two Serbian banking institutions in New York that were not permitted to conduct normal business after June 1, 1992. The banks had been issued licenses to maintain a limited staff for audit purposes while full-time bank examiners were posted in their offices to ensure that banking records were appropriately safeguarded. Subsequent to the issuance of Executive Order No. 12846, all licenses previously issued were revoked. In order to reduce the drain on blocked assets caused by continuing to rent commercial space, FAC has arranged to have the blocked personalty, files, and records moved to secure storage. The personalty will be liquidated and the net proceeds placed in blocked accounts.

A similar liquidation involved the motor vessel Bor, a Montenegrin-owned, Maltese-flagged vessel, blocked in Norfolk on September 15, 1992. The owners of the vessel requested that it be sold in order to provide funds for the support of another of their Maltese-flagged vessels, the M/V Bar, blocked in the port of New Orleans. The FAC submitted this request to the U.N. Sanctions Committee, which approved sale of the Bor on March 11, 1994.

Through a contractor, FAC auctioned the vessel on June 24, 1994, for $1.35 million. Prior to authorizing the sale, FAC determined that the purchaser of the vessel was neither organized or located in a country subject to U.N. or U.S. economic sanctions, nor owned or controlled by entities that are organized or located in a country subject to economic sanctions, nor owned or controlled by, or acting or purporting to act directly or indirectly on behalf of, the government or *de facto* regime of a country subject to economic sanctions.

The proceeds of sale were deposited into a blocked, interest-bearing account in a U.S. financial institution, after certain payments were made related to the costs of maintaining the vessel in blocked status and the costs of sale. During the 2 years that the Bor was blocked, vendors continued to provide provisions and fuel to the vessel despite deferred payment due to lack of funds. U.N. Security Council Sanctions Committee approval of the sale also provided for Treasury reimbursement of auction and other expenses from the proceeds of the sale.

The previous and new owners of the vessel concluded the transaction on July 28, 1994, and the vessel was unblocked and removed from the Treasury's list of blocked entities. Arrangements were made for payment of wages to the crew and their travel to their port of embarkation.

During the past 6 months, U.S. financial institutions have continued to block funds transfers in which there is an interest of the Government of the FRY (S/M) or an entity or undertaking located in or controlled from the FRY (S/M) and to stop prohibited transfers to persons in the FRY (S/M). Such interdicted transfers have accounted for $91.5 million since the issuance of Executive Order No. 12808, including some $7.3 million during the past 6 months.

To ensure compliance with the terms of the licenses that have been issued under the program, stringent reporting requirements are imposed. More than 292 submissions have been reviewed since the last report and more than 193 compliance cases are currently open.

6. Since the issuance of Executive Order No. 12810, FAC has worked closely with the U.S. Customs Service to ensure both that prohibited imports and exports (including those in which the Government of the FRY (S/M) has an interest) are identified and interdicted, and that permitted imports and exports move to their intended destination without undue delay. Violations and suspected violations of the embargo are being investigated and appropriate enforcement actions are being taken. There are currently 59 cases under active investigation. Since

the last report, FAC has collected 31 civil penalties totaling more than $141,000. Of these, 24 were paid by U.S. financial institutions for violative funds transfers involving the Government of the FRY (S/M), persons in the FRY (S/M), or entitles located or organized in or controlled from the FRY (S/M). Five U.S. companies, one organization, and one law firm have also paid penalties related to exports or unlicensed payments to the Government of the FRY (S/M) or persons in the FRY (S/M) for trademark registrations.

As previously reported, FAC has issued a series of General Notices announcing the names of entities and individuals determined by the Department of the Treasury to be Blocked Entities or Specially Designated Nationals (SDNs) of the FRY (S/M). On May 4, 1994, Treasury announced the identification of three companies registered in Cyprus as FRY (S/M) owned or controlled. Additionally, on September 15, 1994, FAC announced that two firms previously named as SDNs of the FRY (S/M), had changed their corporate names. The FAC published those name changes. These additions and amendments bring the current total of Blocked Entities and SDNs of the FRY (S/M) to 853. All prohibitions in the Regulations pertaining to the Government of the FRY (S/M) apply to the entities and individuals identified. United States persons on notice of the status of such blocked persons are prohibited from entering into transactions with them, or transactions in which they have an interest, unless otherwise exempted or authorized pursuant to the Regulations. Copies of these announcements are attached to this report.

7. The expenses incurred by the Federal Government in the 6-month period from May 30 through November 29, 1994, that are directly attributable to the authorities conferred by the declaration of a national emergency with respect to the FRY (S/M) are estimated at about $4 million, most of which represent wage and salary costs of Federal personnel. Personnel costs were largely centered in the Department of the Treasury (particularly in FAC and its Chief Counsel's Office, and the U.S. Customs Service), the Department of State, the National Security Council, the U.S. Coast Guard, and the Department of Commerce.

8. The actions and policies of the Government of the FRY (S/M), in its involvement in and support for groups attempting to seize and hold territory in Croatia and the Republic of Bosnia and Herzegovina by force and violence, the actions and policies of the Bosnian Serb military and paramilitary forces, and the authorities in the areas of Bosnia and Herzegovina under the control of those forces, continue to pose an unusual and extraordinary threat to the national security, foreign policy, and economy of the United States. The United States remains committed to a multilateral resolution of the conflict through implementation of the United Nations Security Council mandate.

I shall continue to exercise the powers at my disposal to apply economic sanctions against the FRY (S/M) as long as these measures are appropriate, and will continue to report periodically to the Congress on significant developments pursuant to 50 U.S.C. 1703(c).

Sincerely,

WILLIAM J. CLINTON

NOTE: Identical letters were sent to Thomas S. Foley, Speaker of the House of Representatives, and Albert Gore, Jr., President of the Senate.

Remarks on Senate Action on the General Agreement on Tariffs and Trade
December 1, 1994

The President. Thank you very much. Let me begin by expressing my thanks to all those who are here and to some who are not, beginning with Senator Mitchell and Senator Dole. I thank them for their strong leadership in the remarkable vote in the Senate tonight. I also want to thank Senator Packwood, who is here, and Senator Moynihan, who is not, for their fine work. I thank Speaker Foley and Congressman Gibbons, Congressman Matsui. I'd also like to say a special word of thanks to Leader Michel and to Congressman Gingrich, who worked so hard on this. I thank Ambassador Kantor and Secretary Bentsen and Mr. Panetta, Mr. Rubin, and all of the others in the administration who worked so terribly hard to see this victory for America tonight, a bipartisan victory that really, really gives our country the boost we need to keep moving forward toward the 21st century to create more high-wage jobs for the American people.

Many things have been said about the GATT in the last few days, and some of them not altogether favorable in some quarters. [*Laughter*] But I was especially struck by what Senator Barbara Mikulski said during this debate. She said, and I quote, "I'm associated with the protectionist wing of the Democratic Party, but I'm going to go for GATT because I'm absolutely convinced that the old ways are not working, that the world is changing, that a new economy is about to be born."

She is absolutely right, and the American people know it. According to a new survey, for the first time ever, a majority of our fellow countrymen and women see trade as an opportunity, not a threat. For middle class Americans who work hard and play by the rules, more trade and fair trade means more and better high-wage jobs for themselves and for their children. It will help us to build good lives and to restore not only jobs but rising wages in America.

Just like the historic vote on NAFTA a year ago, this vote for GATT shows once again that our country is moving in the right direction, reaching out to the rest of the world, and looking at the best interest of our own people. We're also going to be doing that again next week at the Summit of the Americas, pushing for open markets here and around the world but especially in our hemisphere.

Let me close by saying that this vote was really a vote about the two greatest challenges we face, our role in the world and what we're doing for our own people. We said loud and clear that America will continue to lead the world to a more prosperous and secure place after the cold war. We also said loud and clear we're going to do what it takes to get our incomes growing and our jobs going in the right direction.

I urge everyone here to continue to work to keep our country optimistic and hopeful and outward-looking, brave as we march into the future. Let's make the GATT vote the first vote of a new era of cooperation. America's best days are still ahead of us.

I'd like now to ask Senator Mitchell to come up and make some remarks and thank him again and Senator Dole for their great cooperation and the stunning parity and depth of support among both Republicans and Democrats in the Senate tonight.

[*At this point, Senator George Mitchell made brief remarks.*]

The President. Before I introduce Senator Dole, I want to make two other brief acknowledgements. First of all, I apologize for my failure to introduce Congressman David Dreier, who did so much on the Republican side to help us pass this. Thank you very much. He and Congressman Kolbe were pivotal to our success in NAFTA last year, and I thank him for his leadership on GATT.

The second thing I'd like to do is to say how much I think we all should express our appreciation to the teams who started work on GATT under Presidents Reagan and Bush, and I would like to thank them for their support of this agreement, as well as President Carter and President Ford, who was making phone calls right up until the vote today; I thank him especially for his efforts.

And now I'd like to ask Senator Dole to come up here and explain to us how it really was democracy in action and everybody's free will that produced exactly 76 percent of the votes from both parties for this. [*Laughter*]

[*At this point, Senator Bob Dole made brief remarks.*]

The President. That's great. Thank you. Thank you.

I'd like to give the last word to Speaker Foley. Certainly, his last vote as the Speaker was one of the most momentous of his illustrious career. We are very grateful for his leadership on so many things, but especially for his leadership on GATT.

NOTE: The President spoke at 7:54 p.m. at the South Portico at the White House.

Teleconference Remarks With the National League of Cities
December 2, 1994

The President. Thank you very much, Carolyn Long Banks, and thank you all for that very warm welcome. I wish you the best in your new job, Carolyn, as league president. I want to say to all of you, I wish I could be there in Minneapolis with my many friends in the National League of Cities.

I'd like to say a special word of hello to two of your members of the board of directors whom I have known for a very long time, from my home State, Sharon Priest, the city director of Little Rock, and Martin Gipson, alderman in North Little Rock. I'd also like to say a special word of thanks to your outgoing president, Sharpe James, who's been a good friend of mine. And because of his leadership and the leadership of other league members, we now have the toughest and smartest crime bill in our history. I thank you for that, Sharpe, and I thank all of you.

I have long admired the work of the National League of Cities. As a Governor, I worked with many of you on many tough issues. And as President, I'm committed to doing all I can to face those issues with you in a genuine spirit of partnership. To do that, I believe, as many of you do, that while Government cannot be society's savior, neither can it sit on the sidelines.

Our job, yours and mine, is to create opportunity, to remove barriers to that opportunity, to give our people the tools they need to make the most of their lives. When it comes to our cities, we've developed a public-private partnership designed to provide opportunity where it's most needed. We've encouraged businesses to take root and grow in neglected communities. With the Community Development and Regulatory Improvement Act, we're steering billions of dollars in private investment to the places people need it the most. And very soon, we'll announce the winners of our empowerment zones and enterprise communities. We're helping Americans to rebuild the American dream for themselves. The most important thing we can do, what we've been working to do since the beginning of our administration, is to create high-quality, high-wage jobs, jobs that enable our people to build good lives for themselves.

In recent days, we've had a string of indicators that show just how strong this recovery has been. This morning we have the latest job figures that show strong success in building good jobs for Americans. Unemployment is down to 5.6 percent, the lowest it's been in 4½ years. Since I became President, our economy has produced 5.2 million new jobs. So far this year, there have been more new jobs created in high-wage industries than in the previous 5 years combined. Manufacturing jobs are up for 11 consecutive months for the first time in more than a decade. And more construction jobs have been created this year alone than in the previous 9 years combined.

Our strategy of opening up foreign markets to our goods and services has certainly contributed to this success. In just a year, NAFTA has created an estimated 100,000 new jobs. And yesterday, with strong bipartisan support, we took an historic step and passed the GATT world trade agreement, which will create hundreds of thousands of good jobs here in America.

Despite these successes, you and I both know there are too many hard-working Americans who are still deeply anxious about their economic futures and their families. I understand that. For 20 years, stagnant wages and a declining rate of job security have taken a terrible toll. As our workers face these terrible changes and these exciting challenges of the global economy, they are rightly worried about how they and their children will adjust. We know that male workers without a college education have actually seen a decline in their earnings over the last 10 years. And we know that most working families are actually working more; they have less leisure time. We also know that this is the only advanced country in the world where working people are actually losing ground in terms of their health coverage. A million Americans in working families lost health insurance last year alone. That's why, even as we open up trade and create jobs, we've got to work hard to help Americans adjust to these changes so that they can win in the global economy.

The most important thing we can do is to help our people to learn the skills they need to compete and win in the years to come. That's the idea behind the education and training programs we've worked so hard for in the 103d Congress: a big expansion of Head Start; the Goals 2000 program with its high national standards; the elementary and secondary education reform act, with its grassroots reforms; more computers for our schools; things like charter schools, more public school choice, better education for poor children; character education in our schools. That's what's behind our determination to give more affordable loans for millions and millions of middle class students to go to college. It's behind the national service act, AmeriCorps, which allows tens of thousands of our young people to earn money for their college education by serving their communities at the grassroots level. And it's what's behind our apprenticeship programs for people who don't go to college but do want to have good jobs and good skills.

The strength of all these programs is that they're rooted in the idea that individual citizens and communities can decide how best to build their own futures. Now for you, nothing in our agenda may be more important than our efforts to fight crime. The crime bill we passed is the crime bill many of you helped to write. It's a model for how we must continue to reinvent our Government to meet the needs of our people and to move power out of Washington back to the grassroots. We're moving quickly to put 100,000 more police on the street and to institute our prevention and our punishment programs. And we're paying for it by reducing the Federal work force by 272,000 positions to its smallest level since President Kennedy. Already, there are more than 70,000 fewer people working for the Federal Government than there were on the day I was inaugurated President. And every dollar we save is going back to you, going back to grassroots communities who know best how to fight crime in the streets. That's a good deal. It will work for America.

We've made a good beginning on crime, a good beginning on the economy. But to do more, I hope we can continue the spirit of cooperation with the new Congress that we've seen on GATT this week. I hope we can find common ground on your concerns about unfunded Federal mandates which I have long opposed; the Glenn-Kempthorne legislation would restrict these mandates. And we're working closely with the lawmakers to make this bill

a priority early, early in the next session of Congress.

We should also continue to cooperate on health care reform. The American people still want it, and they still need it. We have to find a way to provide working families with that help. We can't continue to be the only advanced country in the world where more and more working people are losing their health insurance every year and where the cost of health care is going up at 3 times the rate of inflation. And for small businesses, health insurance premiums this year went up at almost 5 times the rate of inflation. When the health of the American people and working families suffer, the health of our economy suffers. All of you know that more and more of our Federal budget is going to health care. Medicare, Medicaid, they're the fastest increasing areas of the Federal budget. We've held everything else constant or reduced it. So we need to find ways that, step by step, we can in a bipartisan spirit make progress on this.

We also have to find ways to cooperate on welfare reform. We have to build a strong bridge from dependency to work for millions of Americans. We have to attack problems that feed dependency, including the runaway problem of teen pregnancies. I've been working on this welfare reform issue for more than a decade now. I know that the people on welfare overwhelmingly want to get off. We have got a system that was designed for another age, as so many governmental systems are, and we need to change it dramatically to make it rooted in independence and responsibility, not to subsidize dependence. Every American wants this, and we're going to do it and do it together.

On these and many, many other issues, I hope and believe we can cooperate with the new Congress. But cooperation for me cannot mean abandoning principle, abandoning the hard work we have already accomplished together in our fight to restore our economy, our fight against crime, our fight to give this country back to hard-working people who play by the rules. I will oppose any efforts to take us back on those issues. We've worked too hard to build an economic recovery and a job strategy and to reduce this deficit that 12 years of irresponsible explosive spending left us. And I will fight efforts that jeopardize the strategy to create jobs, fight efforts that will explode the deficit, fight efforts that will put new burdens on the backs of our children.

The assault weapons ban that you helped to win stands between the citizens you and I must protect and the gangs and thugs that would terrorize them. I will do all in my power to keep the next Congress from doing anything that will jeopardize the safety of our people.

And I truly hope the new Congress understands how important these things are to the American people and to their elected representatives at the grassroots level. We've made a good beginning to build together, and we have to get on with the job. It's no secret that the landscape in Washington shifted dramatically last month. But what must not shift is my commitment and your commitment to continue to work for what will actually help hard-working, middle class Americans restore the hope that they can keep the American dream alive and that will provide opportunities and insist on responsibilities for others to move into that great middle class.

What must not change is our conviction that we work best when we work together as partners and when we all share responsibility. Diversity of government is the great genius of the American system. From the smallest of our communities to the biggest of our cities to the statehouses and to the Halls of Congress and the White House, no part of our effort can be isolated. That's why we must keep talking with one another and listening to one another and working together.

If we work at all our levels, we can help take America in the direction it must move. We can help our people find the best path on to the bright new century that awaits us. We can give the American people a smaller Government, a more entrepreneurial Government, a more flexible Government that reflects their values and promotes their interests, if we do it together.

Thank you very much. Thank you.

[At this point, the moderator introduced the participants.]

Q. Mr. President, I'm Lucy Allen, mayor of Lewisburg, North Carolina, where the red carpet will always be out should you choose to visit.

The President. Thank you. You know, I've always felt especially safe in North Carolina. *[Laughter]*

[Mayor Allen asked about changing the Federal Government's pattern of preempting local authority.]

The President. I'd like to suggest three things. First of all, we need to pass a sensible unfunded mandate bill. We need to get on with that area.

Secondly, we need to continue the work we are doing here in Washington to try to increase our capacity to give more flexibility to State and local governments to take their own initiatives in areas of national interest where the circumstances are different from locality to locality.

Let me just give you an example. Our administration has given 20 States the waiver authority to create their own welfare reform programs, in 9 States the authority to create their own health care reform programs. We're examining things that we can do to accelerate that process and to help local governments, cities as well as States, in that process. I think that the American people know there are great national purposes we must pursue but that they differ in their facts from place to place.

And the third thing I think we have to do is to set up a much better system of consultation with local government before Congress enacts laws or the Federal executive branch enacts regulations that can affect you. And let me just give you one example. You mentioned one, so I'll use the one and try to show the example that I mean. In the telecommunications legislation that was proposed last year but not quite passed, there would have been some restriction on the ability of local government to confine access to local cable channels. It was not an intended intrusion on the right of local government but rather the desire to build a true information superhighway with very few barriers to access all across America. There may be an argument for not doing that. And one of the things I hope we can do is to get together with administration officials and interested people in Congress and representatives of local government early, early next year so that we can hear your concern about that. And I feel the same way about land use, zoning issues, and other things.

I don't believe we ought to be out here passing laws or adopting regulations until there has been a real effort to resolve differences at the local level. Because if there is one thing that's clear from this election and from the mounting frustrations of mayors and Governors and county officials all across America over the last 10 to 15 years, it is that people want most decisions that affect their lives made by that level of government as close to them as possible. If it can be done by something outside the government, that's what they want. But if it's a governmental decision, they'd like it made as close to them as possible. So our job is to help see that that is accomplished.

On the other hand, this telecommunications issue is a great national enterprise. Creating the information superhighway will create jobs and opportunity for Americans; it will allow poor children in little isolated rural places access to information that was formerly the province of the wealthiest people in the most well-funded school districts in America. This can do a great thing for our country, but we have to do it, as I said, in partnership. And I'll do my best to do that with you.

Thank you very much.

Q. Thank you, Mr. President.

[A participant asked about proposed middle class tax cuts and their impact on local economies.]

The President. Well, there are a lot of tax cut proposals around, as you know, in the Congress. And the Republican contract calls for several hundred billion in tax cuts. I can't remember the exact figure. There's already been a bill introduced to cut income taxes 20 percent across the board.

The first thing I want to say is that I think we need more tax fairness in the Federal Tax Code, we need to give hard-working middle class people a dividend from the end of the cold war and the dramatic downsizing of the Federal Government that is going on. They haven't really received it yet. And I think that's very, very important.

I also think, however, that most hard-working Americans have a vested interest in seeing us keep this deficit under control. In a couple of years, interest payments on the debt will be greater than the defense budget because of the explosion of debt that grew up between 1981 and 1993, when the Federal deficit, national debt, was quadrupled. We cannot continue on

that track. I'm trying to turn it around in the other way. I don't think people ought to be spending over 20 percent of their income tax payments every year just paying interest on the debt that was piled up in that period.

So while I favor a middle class tax cut and I don't rule out working with the Republican Congress on some of their ideas, my standard will be: Will it help increase incomes for the middle class, will it promote jobs and growth, and can we pay for it? That will be my standard. If we do it in that way, I think that the municipalities will be all right, except that we're going to have to cut a lot of spending up here. And especially, I would urge our friends in the National League of Cities who are in the Republican Party, to make sure that the Congress understands what the consequences are of all these budgetary decisions.

I can't predict what will happen. All I can tell you is, I want better tax fairness, I want to do something that increases middle class incomes, I want a dividend from the end of the cold war and the downsizing of the Federal Government.

We made a beginning last year, by the way, when we cut taxes on 15 million working families, with 50 million people in them, with incomes of up to $27,000. But we have to do more. I think there's a way to do it in ways that will actually help the economic climate of our cities, by putting more money into the pockets of your citizens, if we do it with real discipline and care. But again, as you implied in your question, there are consequences to all these decisions, especially if we're going to be disciplined and pay for them. So I would say that the National League of Cities ought to ask to be a partner with Congress in the decisions about how the taxes are going to be cut and what the implications for the cities are. I hope you will ask for that partnership, and our door will always be open to you.

Thank you.

NOTE: The President spoke at 10:36 a.m. by satellite from Room 459 of the Old Executive Office Building to the meeting in Minneapolis, MN.

Statement on Federal Funding of Research on Human Embryos
December 2, 1994

The Director of the National Institutes of Health has received a report regarding Federal funding of research on human embryos. The subject raises profound ethical and moral questions as well as issues concerning the appropriate allocation of Federal funds. I appreciate the work of the committees that have considered this complex issue, and I understand that advances in in vitro fertilization research and other areas could derive from such work. However, I do not believe that Federal funds should be used to support the creation of human embryos for research purposes, and I have directed that NIH not allocate any resources for such research. In order to ensure that advice on complex bioethical issues that affect our society can continue to be developed, we are planning to move forward with the establishment of a National Bioethics Advisory Commission over the next year.

The President's Radio Address
December 3, 1994

Good morning. December and the holiday season it ushers in is a wonderful time of year. The pace slows and moods brighten as the holiday spirit lifts us up and brings us closer together. We have a chance to visit with family and friends, to celebrate, to reminisce, to think about the year ahead as well as the year we've just finished. We have the chance to reflect on our accomplishments as individuals and as a nation.

In the last 2 years, our administration has made a good start. We've worked hard to downsize the Government and reduce the deficit and to create jobs and opportunities and to help middle class Americans take advantage of both. Unemployment is at a 4-year low. We're having the most rapid economic growth in 7 years. Things are moving in the right direction. But despite this progress, we know Americans have a lot of problems that we still have to work on up here in Washington, including stagnant incomes and crime and other difficult social challenges.

But I think all of us know that nothing we can do will truly restore the American dream unless individual Americans exercise more personal responsibility for their own lives. That's why we must continue our work here to reform welfare and to help educate more Americans with better education and training to face the challenges of a global economy in the future. The most important thing any of us can do is to take that personal responsibility for our communities, our families, and ourselves.

During the holiday season it's particularly important for all of us to take responsibility to keep our highways safe. Some 18,000 people will die this year in alcohol-related auto crashes, about one every 30 minutes. Well over a million people will be injured, one person every 26 seconds. These terrible incidents happen so frequently and are so pervasive that more than 40 percent of all Americans will be involved in an alcohol-related crash at some time in their lives. Because of the determined work of private organizations, like Mothers Against Drunk Driving, the number of alcohol-related traffic deaths has dropped about 30 percent in the last 10 years, but it's very clear that we've got a long, long way to go.

Nothing is as terrible as collisions that occur when an adult under the influence gets behind the steering wheel with a child in the car. For any adult to recklessly endanger the life of a child in this way is beyond disgraceful; it's an atrocity. The crime bill I signed in September makes it clear that we won't tolerate this kind of behavior. It puts tough, new penalties on the books for people who drive drunk with children in the car and makes it easier for States to prosecute anybody who drives under the influence of drugs or alcohol.

But no matter how many laws we put on the books, no matter how many hours dedicated volunteers put into public education campaigns, these terrible deaths will only be prevented if each and every one of us takes the responsibility to do something about it ourselves. The sad truth is these crashes are caused by people who know better but drink and drive anyway, hurting themselves and often hurting others. And don't fool yourself, if you let a friend drive while under the influence of drugs or alcohol, you're their accomplice as much as if you were behind the wheel yourself.

Preventing these disasters is simple. Stay away from drugs completely. They're illegal, and they're dangerous, and they're liable to kill you in or out of a car. If you're going to drink, be responsible. Do it in moderation and choose a designated driver who doesn't drink at all. And if you see a friend about to get behind the wheel when you know it isn't a good idea, take the keys away. It may not be easy at the moment, but it will be the greatest favor you may ever do for him or her.

Right after this radio address, I'm going to sign an order making this National Drunk and Drugged Driving Prevention Month. December is a good month for that, not only because of the increased celebrating that goes with the holiday season but because the holiday season helps to bring out the best in all of us. It makes us think a little more about each other. It reminds us of the obligations we all share to improve our communities, to keep them safe and sound for our children and our grandchildren.

In that spirit, the best gift you can give anyone this year is a simple promise to yourself: If you're going to drink, don't get behind the wheel; if you see a friend about to, don't let him. Make it a New Year's resolution. Start to observe it today, and keep it for the rest of your life.

Thanks for listening.

NOTE: The President spoke at 10:06 a.m. from the Oval Office at the White House. The National Drunk and Drugged Driving Prevention Month proclamation is listed in Appendix D at the end of this volume.

Statement on the Death of Elizabeth Glaser
December 3, 1994

Hillary and I are deeply saddened at Elizabeth Glaser's passing. She was our friend and an inspiration to us as she was to millions of others. Our prayers are with Paul and Jake, her parents, and her brother.

Elizabeth confronted the challenge of AIDS in her own life and lost her beloved daughter to AIDS at a time when our Government and our country were too indifferent to this illness and the people who had it.

She refused to let that indifference stand, fighting bravely for more investment in AIDS research and better treatment and care, especially for children with AIDS. She enlisted Americans from both parties and all walks of life in her cause, and she awakened America to AIDS.

I will never forget what she said about her daughter in her address to the Democratic Convention:

"She taught me to love when all I wanted to do was hate. She taught me to help others when all I wanted to do was help myself. She taught me to be brave when all I felt was fear. My daughter and I loved each other with simplicity. America, we can do the same."

We will all miss Elizabeth Glaser. We need more like her. We must honor her memory by finishing the work to which she gave everything she had.

Remarks to the Conference on Security and Cooperation in Europe in Budapest, Hungary
December 5, 1994

Thank you, President Klestil, President Goncz. I am delighted to be here in this great city in Central Europe at this historic meeting.

The United States is committed to building a united, free, and secure Europe. We believe that goal requires a determined effort to continue to reduce the nuclear threat; a strong NATO, adapting to new challenges; a strong CSCE, working, among other things, to lead efforts to head off future Bosnias; and a strong effort at cooperating with the United Nations and an effort by all the nations of Europe to work together in harmony on common problems and opportunities.

In the 20th century, conflict and distrust have ruled Europe. The steps we are taking today will help to ensure that in the 21st century, peace and prosperity reign.

The forces that tore Europe apart have been defeated. But neither peace nor democracy's triumph is assured. The end of the cold war presents us with the opportunity to fulfill the promise of democracy and freedom. And it is our responsibility, working together, to seize it, to build a new security framework for the era ahead. We must not allow the Iron Curtain to be replaced by a veil of indifference. We must not consign new democracies to a gray zone.

Instead, we seek to increase the security of all, to erase the old lines without drawing arbitrary new ones, to bolster emerging democracies, and to integrate the nations of Europe into a continent where democracy and free markets know no borders but where every nation's borders are secure.

We are making progress on the issues that matter for the future. Today, here, five of this organization's member states, Belarus, Kazakhstan, Russia, Ukraine, and the United States, will bring the START I treaty into force and reduce the nuclear threat that has hung over our heads for nearly a half century. START I will eliminate strategic bombers and missile launchers that carried over 9,000 warheads. And it opens the door to prompt ratification of START II, which will retire another 5,000 warheads. These actions will cut the arsenals of the United States and the former Soviet Union

more than 60 percent from their cold war peak. The world will be a safer place as a result.

But even as we celebrate this landmark gain for peace, the terrible conflict in Bosnia rages not 300 miles from this city. After 3 years of conflict, the combatants remain locked in a terrible war no one can win. Now each faces the same choice: They can perpetuate the military standoff, or they can stop spilling blood and start making peace.

The Government of Bosnia-Herzegovina has made the right choice by accepting the international peace plan and agreeing to recent calls for a cease-fire. So I say again to the Bosnian Serbs: End the aggression; agree to the cease-fire and renewed negotiations on the basis of the Contact Group plan. Settle your differences at the negotiating table, not the battlefield.

We mustn't let our frustration over that war cause us to give up our efforts to end it. And the United States will not do so. If we have learned anything from the agony of Bosnia, it is clearly that we must act on its lessons. In other parts of Europe, ethnic disputes and forces of hatred and despair, demagogs who would take advantage of them threaten to reverse the new wave of freedom that has swept the Continent.

So as we strive to end the war in Bosnia, we must work to prevent future Bosnias. And we must build the structures that will help newly free nations to complete their transformation successfully to free market democracies and preserve their own freedom. We know this is not something that will happen overnight. But over time, NATO, the CSCE, other European and transatlantic institutions, working in close cooperation with the United Nations, can support and extend the democracy, stability, and prosperity that Western Europe and North America have enjoyed for 50 years. That is the future we are working to build.

NATO remains the bedrock of security in Europe, but its role is changing as the Continent changes. Last January NATO opened the door to new members and launched the Partnership For Peace. Since then, 23 nations have joined that partnership to train together, conduct joint military exercises, and forge closer political links.

Last week we took further steps to prepare for expansion by starting work on the requirements for membership. New members will join country by country, gradually and openly. Each must be committed to democracy and free markets and be able to contribute to Europe's security. NATO will not automatically exclude any nation from joining. At the same time, no country outside will be allowed to veto expansion.

As NATO does expand, so will security for all European states, for it is not an aggressive but a defensive organization. NATO's new members, old members, and nonmembers alike will be more secure. As NATO continues its mission, other institutions can and should share the security burden and take on special responsibilities. A strong and vibrant Conference on Security and Cooperation in Europe is vital.

For more than a decade, the CSCE was the focal point for courageous men and women who, at great personal risk, confronted tyranny to win the human rights set out in the Helsinki accords. Now, the CSCE can help to build a new and integrated continent. It has unique tools for this task. The CSCE is the only regional forum to which nearly every nation in Europe and North America belongs. It has pioneered ways to peacefully resolve conflicts, from shuttle diplomacy to longstanding missions in tense areas. Now that freedom has been won in Europe, the CSCE can play an expanding role in making sure it is never lost again.

Indeed, its proposed new name, the Organization for Security and Cooperation in Europe, symbolizes the new and important mission we believe it must undertake. The CSCE should be our first flexible line of defense against ethnic and regional conflicts. Its rules can guard against the assertion of hegemony or spheres of influence. It can help nations come together to build prosperity. And it can promote Europe's integration piece by piece.

By focusing on human rights, conflict prevention, dispute resolution, the CSCE can help prevent future Bosnias. We are taking important steps at this meeting for that crucial goal by strengthening the High Commissioner for National Minorities, establishing a code of conduct to provide for democratic civilian control of the military, reinforcing principles to halt the proliferation of weapons of mass destruction, and preparing to send CSCE monitors and peacekeepers to potential trouble spots outside Bosnia. These actions will not make triumphant headlines, but they may help to prevent tragic ones.

The principles adopted in Rome made clear that any peacekeeping mission must aim for a freely negotiated settlement by the parties themselves, not a solution imposed from the outside. And they hold that no country can use a regional conflict, however threatening, to strengthen its security at the expense of others.

I am very encouraged that with the support and involvement of the Russian Federation, we are on the verge of an agreement that the CSCE will lead a multinational peacekeeping force in Nagorno-Karabakh. The United States appreciates the willingness of many nations to contribute troops and materiel for this mission. The continuing tragedy in Nagorno-Karabakh demands that we redouble our efforts to promote a lasting cease-fire and a fair settlement. The United States strongly supports this effort and calls upon all CSCE members to contribute toward it.

The CSCE also has an important role to play in promoting economic growth while protecting Europe's resources and environment. We should strengthen its efforts to increase regional and cross-border cooperation. Such efforts can bring people together to build new highways, bridges, and communication networks, the infrastructure of democracy.

Since 1975, when the countries of Europe expressed the desire to form a community founded on common values and founded the CSCE, more progress has occurred than even dreamers might have hoped. We know that change is possible. We know that former enemies can reconcile. We know that eloquent intentions about democracy and human rights can promote peace when transformed from words into actions.

Now, almost 20 years later, our challenge is to help the freedoms we secured spread and endure. The task will require energy and strength. Old regimes have crumbled, but new legacies and mistrust remain. Nations have been liberated, but ethnic hatred threatens peace and tolerance. Democracy and free markets are emerging, but change everywhere is causing fear and insecurity.

Three times before in this century, our nations have summoned the strength to defeat history's dark forces. They have left us still with a great responsibility and an extraordinary opportunity. Our mission now is to build a new world for our children, a world more democratic, more prosperous, and more secure. The CSCE has a vital role to play.

Thank you very much, Mr. Chairman.

NOTE: The President spoke at 9:58 a.m. in Patria Hall at the Budapest Convention Center. In his remarks, he referred to President Thomas Klestil of Austria and President Arpad Goncz of Hungary. A tape was not available for verification of the content of these remarks.

Remarks at the Denuclearization Agreements Signing Ceremony in Budapest
December 5, 1994

President Yeltsin, President Kuchma, President Lukashenko, President Nazarbayev, Prime Minister Major. Today we herald the arrival of a new and safer era. We have witnessed many signatures. Together they amount to one great stride to reduce the nuclear threat to ourselves and to our children. The path to this moment has been long and hard. More than a decade has passed since the first negotiations on the START I treaty. But perseverance, courage, and common sense have triumphed.

Skeptics once claimed that the nuclear threat would actually grow after the Soviet Union dissolved. But because of the wisdom and statesmanship of the leaders who join me here, the skeptics have been proven wrong.

Ukraine's accession to the Non-Proliferation Treaty completes a bold move away from the nuclear precipice. Ukraine has joined Belarus and Kazakhstan in ridding itself of the terrible weapons each inherited when the Soviet Union dissolved. Presidents Lukashenko, Nazarbayev, and Kuchma have done a very great service for their own people, their neighbors, and indeed all the peoples of the world.

And there is no greater service that the rest of us could do for our nations, our neighbors, and the peoples of the world than to follow the advice already advanced here by President Yeltsin and Prime Minister Major and agree to the indefinite extension of NPT in 1995.

Creating security in the post-cold-war era requires that we unite, not divide. The pledges on security assurances that Prime Minister Major, President Yeltsin, and I have given these three nations move us further in that direction. They underscore our independence, our commitment to the independence, the sovereignty, and the territorial integrity of these states.

And today we have also reached a milestone in fulfilling the promise of this new era by putting the START I treaty into force, the first treaty that requires nuclear powers to actually reduce their strategic arsenals. It creates the most far-reaching verification system ever agreed upon and will eliminate over 9,000 warheads from our arsenals. It lays the foundations for even deeper arms reductions.

President Yeltsin and I have vowed already to work to put the START treaty into force at our next summit in 1995. That will cut our arsenals by another 5,000 warheads. Together these treaties will leave the United States and the former Soviet Union with only a third of the warheads they possessed at the height of the cold war. They will help us to lead the future to a direction we have all dreamed of, one in which the nuclear threat that has hung over heads for almost a half century now is dramatically reduced.

On this historic afternoon, we have shown that today's community of free nations can and will create a safer globe than did the divided world of yesterday. Together we have helped to beat back the threat of nuclear war and lighted the way to a more peaceful day when the shadow of that destruction is finally vanquished from the Earth.

I thank you all. Thank you.

NOTE: The President spoke at 11:41 a.m. in Patria Hall at the Budapest Convention Center, at a signing ceremony in which the parties to the START I treaty exchanged documents of ratification formally bringing START I into force. In his remarks, he referred to President Boris Yeltsin of Russia,

President Leonid Kuchma of Ukraine, President Aleksandr Lukashenko of Belarus, President Nursultan Nazarbayev of Kazakhstan, and Prime Minister John Major of the United Kingdom.

Remarks to the American Community in Budapest
December 5, 1994

Thank you, Ambassador Blinken and Mrs. Blinken, ladies and gentlemen, and boys and girls, and people associated with the American Embassy, with our CSCE delegation, to the Peace Corps volunteers, the American-Hungarian Chamber of Commerce members who are here.

I am delighted to be here on this all-too-brief trip. I'd like to point out some of the people who came with me: Our Ambassador to the United Nations, Madeleine Albright, is here; and from the United States Congress, Senator Dennis DeConcini from Arizona, Congressman Steny Hoyer from Maryland, and Congressman and Mrs. Tom Lantos from Hungary—and California.

This is a very important trip for the United States because I came here to reaffirm our Nation's commitment to a secure and united Europe. As the Ambassador said, we put the START I nuclear reduction treaty into effect today, and Ukraine has joined Belarus and Kazakhstan in acceding to the Non-Proliferation Treaty. We strengthened the CSCE to help to prevent ethnic and regional conflicts. So as a result of what has happened today, this world is a safer place.

The START I treaty alone will permit us to reduce the nuclear arsenals of the United States and the former Soviet Union countries by 9,000 nuclear warheads, to destroy delivery systems with the best verification systems ever. It will permit us to now start work on START II, which will cut our arsenals by another 5,000 warheads. This means that when we finish this work, we will have reduced the nuclear arsenals of the world by more than two-thirds over their cold war height. That's good news for the children in this audience and for the rest of us as well.

One of the things that we have got to do now is to keep working until we achieve next year an indefinite extension of the Non-Proliferation Treaty, so that we can continue to keep down the risks of the development of nuclear weapons, especially in an era in which the biggest problem may be the proliferation of weapons of mass destruction to heretofore unusual and unconventional hands.

I'd like to say a brief word about this CSCE meeting. The United States believes the CSCE has a vital role to play in promoting democracy and diminishing conflict throughout Europe. We believe it can help nations work together to bring democracy and prosperity to their peoples and to continue our effort of promoting European unity.

Our host, Hungary, like its democratic neighbors, is making steady and strong progress toward full integration into Europe. I believe it can and will complete its transformation to a free market. I believe its commitment to playing an important, responsible role in the new Europe is good news for all of us.

Last January, almost a year ago, I went to Brussels and then on to Prague and on to Russia to begin the work of building a new and united Europe. In the nearly one year since, I have come back to this continent three times to work toward that goal.

From our initiatives to open and to expand NATO, to reducing the threat of nuclear weapons, to making trade more free and fair, to building up institutions like the CSCE, to working toward preventing conflicts before they get out of hand, through all these efforts, this European Continent is becoming more secure, more prosperous, and more united.

Yes, there are problems, and there always will be as long as human beings populate the globe. But we are clearly moving in the right direction, and that is good for the United States.

As I close, let me say a special word of thanks to the American missions in Hungary and to the CSCE staff. I didn't want to leave Budapest without having a chance just to tell you how much we appreciate your service, your sacrifice at a time of very great challenge. I also thank the Peace Corps volunteers for their important contributions. They represent the best of our country around the world. I'm very proud of all of you. I thank you for the warm welcome today. I wish I had longer to stay, but this is a wonderful way to end the trip.

Thank you very much.

NOTE: The President spoke at 2:45 p.m. at Hangar LRI–1 at Ferihegi Airport. In his remarks, he referred to Donald M. Blinken, U.S. Ambassador to Hungary, and his wife, Vera; and Annette Lantos, wife of Representative Tom Lantos.

Memorandum on Educational Excellence for Hispanic Americans
December 5, 1994

Memorandum for the Heads of Executive Departments and Agencies

Subject: Executive Order No. 12900— Educational Excellence for Hispanic Americans

Recognizing the importance of the educational needs of our Nation's Hispanic community, I signed Executive Order No. 12900 on February 22nd of this year. The Executive order took a strong, interagency, approach to identifying and correcting the shortcomings of our educational system in serving Hispanic youth. The Executive order created the President's Advisory Commission on Educational Excellence for Hispanic Americans ("Commission"), which advises the President and the Secretary of Education on these issues. Further, the Executive order established the White House Initiative on Educational Excellence for Hispanic Americans ("White House Initiative"), which is housed in the Department of Education. Additionally, the Executive order states, in part, that:

> [E]ach Executive department and each [agency designated by the Secretary of Education] shall prepare a plan for, and shall document, both that agency's effort to increase Hispanic American participation in Federal education programs where Hispanic Americans currently are underserved, and that agency's effort to improve educational outcomes for Hispanic Americans participating in Federal education programs. ° ° ° ° Each agency's plan shall provide appropriate measurable objectives for proposed actions aimed at increasing Hispanic American participation in Federal education programs where Hispanic Americans currently are underserved.

Given the current status of Hispanics in education and the need to prepare all of our youth for productive employment and lifelong learning, we must make the education of Hispanic youth and adults a high priority in order to achieve the goals set for us by title I of the Goals 2000: Educate America Act ("Goals 2000"). This will require that each of you, as stewards of your agencies, take a more active role in ensuring that the education-related programs of your agency serve Hispanics equitably, both qualitatively and quantitatively.

Consistent with this purpose and with Executive Order No. 12900, I am directing that you identify as soon as possible a senior official who will act as liaison to the Commission and the White House Initiative to assist in this interagency initiative. The official should be at the Deputy Secretary level. Additionally, a second official in the agency—if possible, a Hispanic senior official—should be designated to serve as a co-liaison, who will be responsible for carrying out requests from the Commission. These two officials will work closely with the Executive Director of the White House Initiative.

I know that you will cooperate fully with both the Commission and the White House Initiative. I also ask that to the extent practicable you honor any requests for appropriate information, including available data relating to the eligibility for, and participation by, Hispanic Americans in Federal education programs and the progress of Hispanic Americans in relation to the National Education Goals, as set forth in the Goals 2000 Act.

WILLIAM J. CLINTON

Remarks on the Resignation of Lloyd Bentsen and the Nomination of Robert Rubin To Be Secretary of the Treasury
December 6, 1994

The President. Good morning, everyone. Today, with deep regret, I accept the resignation of the senior member of our economic team, Secretary of the Treasury Lloyd Bentsen.

I first began to think about asking Lloyd Bentsen to join our administration and to be a part of our economic efforts to restore economic opportunity in America, to restore the fortunes of the middle class, to give poor Americans a chance to work their way into the middle class when we talked on a bus going through Texas in 1992. I had known and respected him for many years, but we'd never really had a long and detailed discussion about what was happening in America, about the number of people who were working hard and still falling behind, about the growing inequality in our country among hard-working people. He made a profound impression on me that day and in all the days since. And I thank him for his outstanding service for a job very, very well done.

Lloyd Bentsen likes to say that you can serve your fellow men and women in many ways, as a healer, a teacher, a preacher, but you can never touch as many lives as in public service. He has given more than half a century of his life to public service, as a pilot in the Army Air Corps in World War II flying combat missions over Europe, as a county judge, as a Congressman, as a businessman, a United States Senator and distinguished chairman of the Senate Finance Committee, a contender for President, our party's nominee for Vice President, and finally as a very outstanding Secretary of the Treasury. He has served in every capacity with dignity and distinction. By any stead, he ranks as one of the outstanding economic policymakers in this country since World War II.

As Secretary of the Treasury, his work has touched nearly every field of accomplishment of this administration: making our economy work again for ordinary Americans, restoring discipline to our budget, helping private enterprise create new jobs, expanding trade, passing the Interstate Banking Act which saved billions in regulatory costs, ensuring greater tax fairness in our Tax Code through giving a tax break to 15 million hard-working American parents. And he's also made the Treasury Department a full partner in our fight against crime and drugs.

The results are there for all to see: the biggest deficit reduction in history, the biggest expansion of trade in a generation, over 5 million new jobs in this economy on this Christmas than there were two Christmases ago, and this year more high-wage jobs into this economy than in the previous 5 years combined. The earned-income tax credit has given 50 million Americans who live in hard-working families with modest incomes more money in their pocket and a greater chance to have a fair deal in America.

Beyond all this, however, I also have to say that I have valued Secretary Bentsen's good counsel and his unfailing good spirits. He represents the best tradition of American public service and of Americans working together for the common good. He fights hard for what he believes in. He treats his adversaries with respect, something all would do well to follow. And at the end of the day, he has worked hard to find common ground for the common good.

If you know very much about Lloyd Bentsen you know that the word "retire" sounds like an oxymoron in his vocabulary. He's not saying farewell to active life. He is going home to Texas, to the private sector that he loves and knows is the heart and soul of our economy. He wants to spend more time with B.A. and with his family, including his three children and his seven grandchildren, whom the latest was born just last month.

He has promised me that he would come back here on a regular basis to be part of a seasoned kitchen cabinet to try to help steer this administration through the challenges and seize the opportunities of the next 2 years. And I appreciate that very, very much. But I want you to know, Mr. Secretary, I loved having you here every day, and I'm really going to miss you.

Thank you.

[At this point, Secretary Bentsen made brief remarks.]

The President. Well, as Secretary Bentsen implied, I have now taken both his and Bob Rubin's advice on who should be the Secretary of the Treasury. Before joining our administration, Bob built a brilliant career at Goldman, Sachs and Company where he manifested a concern for the well-being of all Americans, including those who live in our great cities who yearn for more opportunity than they have.

He has helped our administration to do something that had never been done before, to have an economic team that really works together as a team, with talent and with discipline and with a common vision. Forty-seven years ago, President Truman created the National Security Council so that officials in foreign policy and defense could work together. With Bob Rubin's leadership, we have created a National Economic Council so that our economic policymakers can work together for the good of the American people. He's the consummate honest broker who brings economic wisdom, common sense, and common decency to every one of our challenges.

To borrow a famous phrase from the Treasury Secretary, I know Lloyd Bentsen. Lloyd Bentsen is a friend of mine. And Bob Rubin will be a worthy successor to Lloyd Bentsen.

[*At this point, Secretary-designate Rubin made brief remarks.*]

The President. Thank you very much. Let me just say that during the period of time between Secretary Bentsen's leaving and when Bob is finally confirmed as Secretary of the Treasury, Frank Newman will be our Acting Secretary of the Treasury. He has been a distinguished member of Lloyd Bentsen's team. He put together a very distinguished career in banking before joining the Treasury Department as Under Secretary for Domestic Finance, and I thank him for his willingness to serve.

In closing, let me also just say a special word of thanks to the families of these two people, to Judy Rubin, to B.A. Bentsen, and to their families for the extraordinary sacrifice that public service entails today. This is in many ways a sad farewell, but it is also a celebration, a celebration of the success of the leadership of Lloyd Bentsen, the success of the idea of a national economic partnership and a team, and the success of our continued commitment to move forward with Bob Rubin's leadership until we finish our job, until we have really opened up the doors of opportunity to the American middle class, to those who are working hard and deserve it and deserve a better future.

Thank you all, and good-bye.

NOTE: The President spoke at 11:17 a.m. in the Rose Garden at the White House.

Teleconference Remarks on the Business Enterprise Trust Awards
December 6, 1994

Thank you, Diane. I'm sorry I can't be with you in New York today, and I'm glad at least we have a one-way superhighway. Maybe by the time the Vice President leaves today, he will explain how it can be a two-way superhighway by next year.

Before the presentations of this year's awards, I want to say a few words about the importance of the work you're doing. I wanted just to be able to come in this way to you, even though the Vice President was good enough to come up there and express our full thoughts about this. But I wanted to say a few things, because I think it's very important that people be recognized who understand that there is no necessary conflict between doing well and doing good and

between what is in one's short-term personal interest and what is in the long-term best interest of a company or a community or a country.

I want to thank Jim Burke, the chairman of the Business Enterprise Trust, and my longtime friend Norman Lear for leading this vital initiative. I hope that this idea that is behind the awards that are going out will somehow find its way into the mind and into the heart of decisionmakers all across America.

I also want to congratulate the five honorees today: Mario Antoci, the chairman and CEO of Savings Bank of California; Barbara Roberts, president of FPG International; Howard Schultz, the CEO of Starbuck's Coffee; the Fel-Pro Corporation; and the Xerox Corporation. This gathering represents a remarkable groundswell of leadership within the American business community, people who are leading this country into the 21st century with integrity and with vision. The private sector always has been the engine of wealth creation and job creation in our country. But now it must also help us to lead the way and share in the partnership of getting all of us to take responsibility for ourselves, our families, our communities, and our countries.

As companies regain their prosperity in this growing economy, business leaders with the future in mind know we have to share the fruits of the recovery with the employees, the workers, the backbone of our success. Ultimately, the stability of our work force and our society depends upon the faith of people that if they work hard, they'll get ahead, and they'll be treated fairly. That's what's really at issue here. You may have your differing interpretations about the results of the elections in 1994 or even those in 1992. But one thing is abundantly clear: The most alienated people in our society are people who are working harder than they were 10 years ago for lower wages, who feel insecure, who feel that they're just a cog in a machine—that if they lose their job, no one will really care; if they lose their health benefits and their children can't go to the doctor, no one will really care; if they can never send their children to college, no one will really care.

All of you know that investing in your workers is the most important investment you can make. You're being honored today because you've treated people not like cost centers to be cut but wealth centers to be strengthened because they, too—your workers—face the competitive pressures of the global economy. That's a job that you and I must share and a job we have to get all other Americans to share. We have

got to restore the faith of hardworking people that they can be in and be successful in the middle class. We've got to be able to send a shining signal to poor Americans that if they work hard, they can work their way into the middle class. We've got to give people a sense that all of us know we're all in this together. And we have to do it together. I commit myself to doing that with you in the years to come.

Joe Wilson, the pioneering founder of Xerox, recognized the need for this kind of visionary leadership when he said, "Our society needs business people who can articulate lofty goals and demonstrate high dedication to those goals while they profit from the services they offer." Those words are very fitting today. The companies being honored have proven that you can have strong values and a strong bottom line. I've had personal experience with some of them, and I thank them.

This is a time for all Americans and all leaders to be bold. We can be confident, we can have the kind of enthusiasm and vision you exhibit every day because of the successes that we are seeing in the American economy. But we have got to keep working until all Americans feel that they are a part of this success.

I applaud you for your efforts in that regard. And I am grateful, very grateful, to the Business Enterprise Trust for leading this profoundly significant effort.

Thank you very much.

NOTE: The President spoke at 12:57 p.m. by satellite from Room 459 of the Old Executive Office Building to the Business Enterprise Trust meeting in New York City. In his remarks, he referred to journalist Diane Sawyer and television producer Norman Lear.

Statement on the Department of Agriculture Reorganization
December 6, 1994

Today Secretary Espy announced that the Department of Agriculture is closing over 1,200 field offices across the country. I commend Secretary Espy for his leadership and outstanding efforts to make Government function better and more productively.

By creating one-stop-shopping field centers that consolidate a multitude of services under one roof, we are showing a true commitment to streamline Government and to make it work better and cost less.

When fully implemented, the changes will save about 2.5 million hours annually of farmers' time by slashing the paperwork burden and reducing other bureaucratic requirements. This streamlining, coupled with the overall reorganization of the Department, will save taxpayers $3.6 billion over 5 years and serve rural Americans with the common sense they deserve. The effort to restructure the USDA has been implemented with bipartisan support and is an example of how Democrats and Republicans can work together.

I am proud of the USDA reorganization because it shows that with a lot of hard work, Government can be changed to do a much better job with fewer dollars. We are making a USDA that makes sense for the customer and the taxpayer. Secretary Espy should be commended for implementing these changes in a sensible and businesslike way.

Statement on Webster L. Hubbell
December 6, 1994

Webb Hubbell is an old friend, and Hillary and I were saddened by today's events. We should also remember that Webb is a man who has given much to his family, his community, and his country. The matter is in the hands of the court, and I don't think it would be appropriate to say anything more at this time.

NOTE: Former Associate Attorney General Webster L. Hubbell pleaded guilty to mail fraud and tax evasion charges on December 6.

Appointments for the President's Export Council
December 6, 1994

The President today announced his intention to appoint 25 members to the President's Export Council, including C. Michael Armstrong as Chair and Elizabeth J. Coleman as Vice-Chair of the Council.

"I am proud to announce the appointment of such a talented and experienced group of individuals to the Export Council," the President said. "I look forward to their recommendations as we move ahead to reduce the barriers of trade, open worldwide markets to our goods and services, and create jobs for American workers."

NOTE: Appointments of the following members were announced: J. Joseph Adorjan; C. Michael Armstrong; John J. Barry; Carol Bartz; George Becker; Edgar Bronfman, Jr.; Dean Buntrock; John F. Carlson; Elizabeth J. Coleman; Susan Corrales-Diaz; Lawrence Ellison; Ellen R. Gordon; Steven J. Green; Ray R. Irani; Michael H. Jordan; Thomas Labrecque; Leslie McCraw; John F. McDonnell; John Jay Moores; Dennis J. Picard; Safi Qureshy; Frank Savage; Kathryn Turner; Thomas Urban; and C.J. Wang.

Remarks at the Democratic Leadership Council Gala
December 6, 1994

The President. Thank you very much. Thank you, Congressman McCurdy. Thank you. Thank you. Thank you, Congressman McCurdy. Hillary and I are delighted to be here. I was so glad when Michael Steinhardt and Al From and Will Marshall came up on the stage. I thought we were occupying the right wing all by ourselves here tonight. [*Laughter*] I want to—it'll get funnier as you think about it. [*Laughter*] I want to thank everybody on this stage, my wonderful and longtime friend Lindy Boggs, who had me in her home in the Presidential campaign and who has been such great inspiration to us. And I thank Senator Lieberman and Senator Breaux for whatever they said they were doing, their kosher-Cajun partnership. [*Laughter*] They have been wonderful.

I thank Dave McCurdy for the courageous battle that he waged in Oklahoma against some forces that I want to talk about more in a moment and for going to New Hampshire for me and for being the embodiment of what the DLC is all about. He is very young. I have lost two elections; I will make a prediction about which I know quite a bit: He will be back.

I want to thank my friend of many years, Senator Chuck Robb, for waging what may have been the most courageous campaign in America. Twenty million dollars and all they could throw at him later, he's still standing and well and proud, and we're proud of him. I want to thank Al From and Will Marshall and Michael Steinhardt for believing in the DLC and the PPI, for believing in the power of ideas in public life.

You know, I was trying to think of what I ought to say here tonight. I've gotten all these good and bad and in-the-middle reports about all these deliberations here. They gave me some remarks at the office. I didn't like them, so I wrote some down; so no one is to blame for what I say but me. But the problem is I'm hurtling into middle age, and I can no longer read my own writing from this distance. [*Laughter*] But I'm going to do the best I can.

Audience member. Do you want my glasses?

The President. I've heard all these—no, I brought my glasses, but I'm too vain to wear them while I talk. [*Laughter*]

I got to thinking about, you know, how I could describe this election, and was it one of these situations where, well, they just didn't know what we'd done; they didn't recognize what we'd done—the Democrats. There's some of that.

It reminded me of the story of the fellow that ran a cleaners in New York City for 40 years. And his wife passed away, and his children were all grown and educated, so he just cashed in. He had a million dollars. He went out and had a hair transplant, joined a spa and lost 30 pounds, married a lady 40 years younger than he was, and went to Florida on his honeymoon, where a storm came up when he was walking on the beach, lightning struck him dead, and he was taken to heaven immediately. And he looked in the face of God, and he said, "I don't want to be blasphemous, but how could you do this to me? I mean, for 40 years I was faithful to my family. I educated all my children. I worked 6 days a week. I paid every nickel I ever owed in taxes. Finally, I have a chance to have a little fun. How could you do this to me?" And God said, "Oh, Jake, I'm sorry, I didn't recognize you." [*Laughter*]

So maybe, you know, there was a little bit of that in this election. Then I thought, well, maybe what we did was good, but they just didn't appreciate it. And I thought about the story of the elderly couple rocking on the porch. And they were way up in their seventies, and they'd been married over 50 years. The husband was a man of few words, and he looked at his wife and he said, "Sarah, you know, before we run out of time, there are some things I have never said to you in our married life together, and I'd feel remiss if I didn't. We got married, and I didn't have a nickel to my name. And we worked hard. But the Great Depression came along, and as soon as I built my business, it broke me, and I was absolutely devastated. But you never flinched, and you never left me. You were so wonderful." And she said, "Yeah, that's right." He said, "Then I had to go to World War II, and I got that terrible wound. It took me a year to recuperate, but you were there by my side every step of the way." And she said, "Yeah." He said, "Then, finally in 1952, we finally saved up enough money to move in our own home. We weren't there 6 weeks before a tornado came along and blew it down. We didn't have any insurance or anything. It took us another 10 years to get a house, but you stayed with me all the way through." She said, "Yeah, I sure did." He said, "Well, before it's too late, I want to say one thing to you. Sarah, you're bad luck." [*Laughter*]

Well, there was also some real things. I want to talk about them. But since one of their leaders was quoting Roosevelt the other day, I ought to say, I think we're a lot more like Lincoln than they are like Roosevelt. And it reminded me of when Lincoln sustained a defeat, he said that it hurt too much to laugh and he was too old to cry, but it was a slip and not a fall. And what I want to talk to you tonight about is what's really going on in this country, not about the Democrats and the Republicans and who loses and who wins, but who loses and who wins out in America.

In 1992, late '91 really, I got into the race for President basically because I was convinced deep down inside that there was something amiss in this country, that we were in danger of losing the American dream, that more people were working harder for less, that people who were poor but wanted to work themselves into the middle class weren't able to do so, that we were coming apart when we ought to be coming together, and that the political system had reached the point where it was almost incapable of dealing with fundamental problems. I ran out of a conviction that as a citizen I ought to try to do something about it. I ran because my experience as a Governor made me believe that you really could roll up your sleeves and reach across party lines and other lines and solve real problems that real people have. I ran because the DLC made me believe that ideas could matter in national politics just like they do in other forms of public endeavor.

And when I started this campaign, nobody but my mother gave me much chance to win. But you know, what I was afraid of was that I would win and people wouldn't understand how hard it would be to really change, not only to change things on their merits but to deal with the culture of Washington and to communicate through the fog and the blizzard to folks out in the country and also to have communication be two-way, never to lose touch with people, never to sever that mystic cord that has to exist between a President and a Government and the people.

I knew that there were many dangers. One is, just taking on tough issues is taking on tough issues. If they were easy issues, somebody else would have done them because a poll would say it was popular to do. The second is if you try to do a lot of things in a short time, you're going to make some mistakes. And I've made my fair share, and I accept that. The third is that it is easy to be misunderstood in a difficult time when you're a long way from where people live. Ask Mr. McCurdy and Senator Robb. It's even easy to be demonized when you're a long way from where people live so that the very people you try hardest to help are those who turn away.

That's the thing I regret about this election more than anything else. All the people who are working harder for lower wages and less security then they were 10 years ago, they're the people I ran to help. All the people who are trying to follow the rules and are sick and tired of people benefiting who don't, who take advantage of the system whether they're rich or poor or somewhere in between, those are the folks that the Democratic Party ought to be championing and the ones who ultimately will benefit if we stay on the right course.

Well, we did a lot of things that they didn't like very much, especially after it got explained to them, as we say at home. I think I was right when I opposed discrimination and intolerance, but a lot of folks thought I was just more concerned about minorities than the problems for the majority.

I believe we were right when we stood up to the NRA and said we ought to take these military assault weapons off the street. But a long way from the battlegrounds of the inner cities, a lot of folks out in the country said, "My Lord, I'm paying too much in taxes, I can't hold my job, and now they're coming after my gun. Why won't they just let me alone?"

I believe we were right when we fought to bring this terrible deficit down. Let me tell you something, folks. The budget would be in balance this year, were it not for interest payments on the debt accumulated when they had control and they ran this country into the ditch. And before you listen to the siren's songs that will be offered in the next year, you just remember this: Next time you make out your Federal income tax check, 28 percent of it is going to pay interest on the debt accumulated in the last 12 years before we took over. So I think we were right to do that.

And yes, I think we were right to try to find a way to stop health care costs from going up at 3 times the rate of inflation, to stop people from losing their health care or having it explode if they have a kid sick or if they change jobs, to try to find an affordable way for small business people and self-employed people to buy private health insurance. But by the time it got to the American people, in both cases, it was characterized as the Democrats are the party of Government and taxes. And they don't have a lot of trust or faith in Government because they're working harder for less, less money. Males in this country without a college degree are making 12 percent less than they were making 10 years ago working a longer work week. We are the only country in the world with an advanced economy where the percentage of people with health insurance under 65 is lower today than it was 10 years ago.

That's why these numbers don't mean a lot. That's why the story I told you about John and Martha don't mean a lot. That may be a good story. Sometimes you're not happy even if somebody does something good, if you don't like the result. There are still people out there just killing themselves, thinking, "I'm doing everything I can. I'm working a longer work week. I can't afford a vacation anymore. I'm paying more for health care. I may lose my job tomorrow. My kid could get shot on the way to school. And all my money is going to people who misbehave." Now, that's what a lot of people think. And they're the very people that I've been up here killing myself for 2 years trying to help and the people they've been trying to help. Can we get them back? You bet we can. But they have to know we heard the lesson in the election. They have to know we got the message. But we cannot tell them we will always agree. We cannot tell them we will always agree. And we cannot tell them, even if the cost is very great.

Sometimes people make decisions when they are very, very angry, and sometimes those decisions are good. Sometimes they're not so good. One of the first lessons I was ever given at my mama's knee was, "Count to 10, Bill, before you say something." I still don't do it all the time, and every time I don't, I'm sorry. [*Laughter*] Every time I don't, I'm sorry.

There is no prescription for a perfect world in a difficult time of change where every election works out and everybody is happy. But we've got to let these folks know that we heard them, because they're the very people that I ran for President to help. Now, all my life, ever since I was a little boy, I have seen people like that mistreated, disadvantaged, and then I have seen them inflamed with anger and enraged and taken advantage of. So I'm telling you, forget about us. We owe it to them to let them know we heard and we're fighting for them and we're going to deliver.

I've got three things that I want to say. I think we've got to reaffirm our convictions with clarity. We've got to say what we did and be proud of it. And we've got to engage the Repub-

licans in a spirit of genuine partnership and say, "You have some new ideas. We do, too. Let's have a contest of ideas. But stop all this demonization and get on with the business of helping America to build this country."

Sometime in the next 2 or 3 days, if you want to know how to state our principles with clarity, go back and read the New Orleans Declaration, 5 years ago. It's just as good as it gets:

We believe the promise of America is equal opportunity, not equal outcomes. The Democratic Party's fundamental mission is to expand opportunity, not Government. America must remain energetically engaged in the world, not retreat from it. The United States must maintain a strong and capable defense. The right way to rebuild America's economic security is to invest in our people and to expand trade, not to restrict it. We believe in preventing crime and punishing criminals, not explaining away their behavior. The purpose of social welfare is to bring the poor into the economic mainstream, not to maintain them in dependence. Government should respect individual liberty and stay out of our private lives and personal decisions. We believe in the moral and cultural values most Americans share, individual responsibility, tolerance, work, faith, and family. We believe American citizenship entails responsibilities as well as rights. And we mean to ask our citizens to give something back to their communities and their country.

I believe that, and if you do, we've got a great future.

Now, this is what I want to say to you: You have to decide what your mission is in this new world, because the truth is we are already making a difference in the new Democratic Party. In the last 2 years, despite the atmosphere of contentiousness and all the difficulty, more of the DLC agenda was enacted into law and will make a difference in the lives of the American people than almost any political movement in any similar time period in the history of the United States. And you ought to be proud of that.

You should not ask for a medal and we shouldn't ask for a medal because wages are still stagnant and the future is still too uncertain for too many millions of Americans, because the country is still coming apart at the seams in many places because of family breakdown and crime, and because Government is still too much of a burden on a lot of people. But you sure ought to be proud of the start that has been made.

And if you don't tell it, nobody else will. So stand up and say, "Here is what we have done. We're going to build on it. We're going to go forward. We heard the message in the election, but let's don't tear down what has been done that's good for the people who control the future of this country."

You go back and read, go back and read what the DLC specifically advocated. Principles are fine, but sooner or later you've got to do something, too. It really does matter, you know. One of the great political thinkers who is here in this audience tonight, whom I will not embarrass, said to me, "You know, one of the problems, Mr. President, is you've been trying to do something." And he told me, he mentioned another political leader, and he said, "You know, his popularity is very great in this country because he has talked a lot, but he hasn't tried to do anything, so he hasn't upset anybody very much."

We have tried to do things. You should be proud of that. It was not easy to bring the deficit down 3 years in a row for the first time since Truman. The DLC said we ought to do it, and we did it. It was not easy.

It was not easy to figure out how to do that and provide tax reductions—the first step in the middle-class tax relief—to 15 million working families with 40 million Americans in it, people who work hard, have children at the house, are on modest wages. We don't want them to go into welfare. We want them to be out. We don't want to tax anyone into poverty. That's what the earned-income tax credit was. That was a DLC idea. We did it. It provided more tax fairness than at any time in 20 years, and you should be proud of it. It changed people's lives.

They talk about less Government. There are 70,000 fewer people working for the Federal Government today than there were on the day I was inaugurated. We are reducing the size of the Federal Government by more than a quarter of a million. If not one other thing is done, because of what the Members of Congress here present have already voted for, we will have the smallest Federal Government since John Kennedy was President at the end of this budget cycle. That is what we have already done. The Republicans want to do more? Come on, let's do it. Let's have a partnership. Let's have a contest. Let's have at it. We're not

through reducing Government, but don't deny the fact that we have started it. We led the way. They didn't begin it; we did. Ask them to join us. Let's go forward.

And a dramatic thing happened that Mr. McCurdy mentioned a minute ago: The Democratic Party moved away markedly from protectionism, into GATT, into NAFTA, into reaching out to the Asian countries, into this Summit of the Americas with all the countries in our region that are democracies. We did that. It was a fundamental break with the past, and it is opening up new vistas of opportunity. And we did it for one simple reason. All the pressures we have to keep wages down and to displace low-wage workers from trade are there no matter what we do. But because we demanded access to markets and a fairer deal for American workers and for American companies, we're going to create new high-wage jobs for America. That was the DLC position. We have done it: more trade advancement than at any time in a generation. You ought to be proud of it, and you ought to stand up there and defend it and talk about it.

And what are the results? Over 5 million new jobs, more construction jobs this year than the last 9 years combined, 11 months of manufacturing job growth rate for the first time in a decade. Those are the results.

And finally, we're beginning to see some high-wage job growth, more high-wage jobs this year than the previous 5 years combined. What is the challenge? How to get incomes up and how to help people when they change jobs not be riven with insecurity. That is the challenge.

So, how are we going to do that? The first thing we've got to do is to provide a system of lifetime education and training. You want to reverse income inequality in this country? There is an education premium, and we had better give it to every American who's willing to take it. That is the only way to do it.

Look at the education agenda, the best year for education in 30 years: expanded Head Start; national standards with grassroots reforms, like charter schools and character education programs, advocated by the DLC; apprenticeship programs for young people who don't go to college. I had 13 CEO's of the biggest companies in this country today into the White House to talk to me about how we could get all the companies in the country to participate in our school-to-work program; how we can get 2 million more young people, getting out of high school and not going on to college, getting decent jobs. And the middle class college loan program that we had to face down enormous vested interests to pass, making millions of young people eligible for lower interest college loans and able to pay it back as a percentage of their income so that nobody need walk away from college. That was all DLC advocacy. We did it. The American people should know it, and you should be proud of it.

The family leave law, immunizing all the kids in this country under 2, tougher child support enforcement, the welfare reform bill that's been in the Congress since last March, these things are good for America. This administration has also tried to give power back to the States, something the GLC has always been for. Twenty States, 20, have already received permission to cut through Federal rules and regulations to have their own welfare reform proposals; 9 States, health care reform proposals. These are things you have advocated that we've already done.

The Republicans say they want to give more power back to the States, more power back to the cities. Tell them to come on. Let's contest their ideas. Let's do it. Let's do it together. But don't you walk away from the fact that we started it, and we intend to finish it, and we want them to go with us.

And we still have to implement that crime bill, folks. A hundred thousand police means that cities will get an average—and small towns and rural areas—of 20 percent more police. We know if they're deployed properly, that it will lower the crime rate. Community policing, a DLC idea; we've been advocating it for years. And we believe in the prevention programs; read our record. They don't. We're right. The police are on our side. Let's fight to save those prevention programs. Let's get those police in place. Let's have the tougher punishment. If they have more ideas on crime, let's have at it. But let's not stop implementing the crime bill until we lower the crime rate and make streets safe for American families and their children again. And don't forget that we passed it.

Finally, let me say that I want you to see national service as the embodiment of what we want to do. It has been attacked by some who are coming into this new Congress. It is not a Government program. It's a corporation with Republicans and Democrats on the board. It is not a bureaucracy. It's totally grassroots oriented. It is designed to promote the concept of service in America and to reward it with educational credits. There are already more people in national service solving the problems of America at the grassroots level than there were in the Peace Corps in its largest year. There are 20,000 this year. Year after next, if by cutting and investing we can get the money, we will have 100,000. So let us say, that's where we are. That's where the new Democratic Party is. That's where the DLC is. Let's ask the Republicans to support national service, not to tear it up, to go forward to build this country and make it what it ought to be.

The best thing you could do is what you have done, put out 10 new ideas as a counterpoint to the Republican contract. That is the best thing you can do. Let's stand on them. Let's fight for those ideas.

Next week and the week after, I'll be announcing some more of my new ideas. Let's do this with vision. Let's do it with conviction. Let's make the effort it takes. Let's put country over party and challenge the Republicans to do the same. Let's say we do not want to roll back the gains that the DLC fought so hard for. They're not liberal or conservative. They brought our party together. They'll bring our country together. And the more the American people know about it, the better they will like it. The answer is not to reverse what we have done but to build on it. The answer is to reach out to the middle class and say, "We know why you're angry. We know why you're frustrated. We got the message of the election. We're not going back on our principles, but we're coming right at you because we are hired to help you build a better future for yourselves. That is our only purpose." If we do these things, their predictions of our demise will be entirely premature.

But I ask you now, once again, to think about what your responsibility is. We always talk about what other people's responsibilities are. What's your responsibility? It's to join me in the arena, not in the peanut gallery, in the arena, and fight and roll up your sleeves and be willing to make a mistake now and then and be willing to put your shoulder to the wheel, be willing to engage, be willing to struggle, be willing to debate, and enjoy this.

The American people are going through a great period of change. But let me tell you something, folks, this is a very great country. We can stand this conflict. This can be good for us. It can be good for our party, but more importantly, it can be good for the American people. Never forget that it is no accident that it was the United States that was asked to be involved in putting an end to all this conflict that's gone on for centuries in Northern Ireland, the United States that was asked to stand up to aggression in the Gulf or work on peace in the Middle East or restore democracy to Haiti. We are committed to the rest of the world, but we should see ourselves sometimes a little more the way they see us. This is a very great country.

The responsibility we have is not to win elections, it is to fight for the people about whom elections are fought. If we fight for them and their children, then the elections will take care of themselves. And if they don't, we'll still be doing what's right. That's my commitment, and it ought to be yours.

Thank you, and God bless you.

NOTE: The President spoke at 8:26 p.m. in the Green Room at the Sheraton Washington Hotel. In his remarks, he referred to Michael Steinhardt, chairman, and Will Marshall, president, Progressive Policy Institute; Al From, president, Democratic Leadership Council; and former Representative Lindy Boggs.

Teleconference Remarks to the Pearl Harbor Survivors Association
December 7, 1994

The President. Nice to hear your voice. Are you having a good meeting?

Lee Goldfarb. It's great, sir, and we're in the middle of it. And everybody is gung ho, waiting to do the right thing.

The President. Well, good for you. I thank you for the invitation to come down and address the banquet this evening. And I'm sorry I couldn't come, and I'm very grateful to have this brief chance to speak with you.

Let me begin by saying, on this very special day, that I and all Americans can never forget the services rendered and the sacrifices made by the members of your association. I cherish the occasions that I've had to meet with you and with other members of veterans service organizations, and especially the times that have meant the most to me are the times that we've gathered to honor your efforts in wartime. I look forward to participating in the World War II 50th anniversary commemorations next year.

It was a real honor for me, also, I want to say, to sign the National Pearl Harbor Remembrance Day proclamation. I can't believe that it took us 53 years to issue the first one, but I'm very glad that we're doing it now.

One other point I wanted to make is that I really appreciate the fact that you, Lee, have sensitized me and the rest of Americans to the fact that we must always recognize the contributions not only of the naval personnel but of the non-Navy, non-Pearl Harbor people who often are slighted. And I'm glad that your association includes veterans who were stationed throughout the island of Oahu, and not just at Pearl Harbor.

All of you who survived Pearl Harbor, as I'm sure you must know, are a terrific inspiration to all Americans and a constant reminder that we must remain ever vigilant, that we must never again be unprepared. Just a few days ago, the Secretary of Defense and General Shalikashvili and I made a recommendation to beef up the defense budget in critical areas over the next 5 years to make sure that we maintain the strongest defense in the world. And that is one of the lessons we have learned from your service and your sacrifice.

Today, let me say again, I join with all the American people in giving thanks to those who served at Pearl Harbor on December 7th, 1941, and to all the other veterans of World War II for the priceless liberty you have helped us to secure. I thank you for your service in wartime, and I thank you for your continued citizenship and service to our country.

Thank you very much.

NOTE: The President spoke at 9:52 a.m. by telephone from the Oval Office at the White House to the association meeting in Tampa, FL. Lee Goldfarb was president of the association.

Remarks on Lighting the National Christmas Tree
December 7, 1994

Thank you, John Betchkal, Mrs. Betchkal, Reverend León. I want to thank especially our wonderful entertainers tonight: Willard Scott, who would make anybody believe in Santa Claus; Trisha Yearwood, it's wonderful to see you again; Richard Leech, you are terrific. If I had a voice like you, I would have stayed out of politics. [*Laughter*] And I want to say a special word of thanks and congratulations to the magnificent Aretha Franklin who was recently honored at the Kennedy Center Honors. We are glad to see all of you here tonight. Thank you. We congratulate the Cathedral Choir of Men and Boys for the wonderful job that they did.

Let me say that Hillary and Chelsea and I are delighted to be back here for our second Pageant of Peace. I don't know how many of you were here last year, but it was a lot colder. And I still feel in the Christmas spirit and more comfortable doing so. I'm glad to be here tonight, and I appreciate this wonderful weather.

This year, we have a lot to be grateful for. This is the first Christmas since the beginning of the cold war when our parents can tuck all of their children into bed on Christmas Eve knowing that there are no Russian missiles with nuclear warheads pointed at them.

In holy Bethlehem and throughout the Middle East, ancient enemies are taking giant steps toward peace and reconciliation. Peace is making progress in Northern Ireland, in South Africa, in Haiti, and Eastern and Central Europe, where people are making courageous steps to escape the shackles that have bound them.

Here at home, I appreciate what Willard Scott said about prosperity coming back. And we do have the strongest economy we've had in many years, but let us never forget that many of our people are living in poverty and others are working hard in insecurity, and that as we celebrate the birth of Jesus Christ, the Prince of Peace, let us not forget His lesson that one day we will be asked whether we lived out His love in ways that treated all of our brothers and sisters as we would have treated Him, even the least of them. He taught us all to seek peace and to treat all people with love.

In this holiday season as we gather our families and often go back to the places where we grew up, this is a time to rededicate ourselves to the things which matter most, to our responsibilities, to our families, our communities, and our country.

With all of our challenges in this holiday season, we can take great comfort in knowing that when we come together and seek God's help, we can meet any challenge. At this holiday season also, my fellow Americans, let us extend our special gratitude and prayers for the men and women of our Armed Forces who protect the peace and stand sentry for our freedom. Many of them are very, very far from their families and friends; they must be close to our hearts.

Finally let me say, this wonderful evergreen Christmas tree, the "Tannenbaum" about which Aretha Franklin sang, is a symbol of the enduring values of our lives. As we light it, let it rekindle in our hearts faith and hope and love for one another.

And now I wish God's blessings on you all at this special season, and I'd like to ask Hillary and Chelsea to join me as we light the Christmas tree.

NOTE: The President spoke at 5:53 p.m. on the Ellipse. In his remarks, he referred to John J. Betchkal, chairman, Pageant of Peace, and his wife, Kathleen; Rev. Luis León, pastor, St. John's Episcopal Church; and entertainers Willard Scott, Trisha Yearwood, Richard Leech, and Aretha Franklin.

Remarks on Signing the Uruguay Round Agreements Act
December 8, 1994

Thank you very much, Mr. Vice President. As usual, you did a generous and magnificent job of recognizing the contributions of all these people who made this day possible. You did, however, leave one very important person out. If you hadn't gone on television in that national debate on NAFTA and refuted the theory of the giant sucking sound—[*laughter*]—I'm not sure we would be here today. And we thank you for that.

I thank the Members of Congress who are here and those who are not who have been acknowledged. I thank the members of our administration. I am so proud of all of them. I want to say a special word of thanks to Secretary Espy for helping us resolve these terribly difficult agricultural issues, without which we would not have been able to get this agreement. I thank Mickey Kantor and Rufus Yerxa and John Schmidt and John Emerson, all the people who worked on our team. I thank the business community, a bipartisan group, a remarkably diverse group, for standing up and being counted and working hard on this and our other trade initiatives.

I thank the Vice President for what he said about trade. In the last 2 years we've not only had NAFTA and GATT, but we have done our outreach to Asia through the Asian-Pacific Economic Cooperation group. We've had two meetings of the leaders of the APEC countries now. We have reached a new agreement with Japan which I believe is a very good one, and we continue our efforts there. And this evening I am leaving for the Summit of the Americas in Miami, which Mr. McLarty and others have done so much work on to make a success.

Two days ago when I regrettably accepted his resignation, Secretary Bentsen said that history would show that the economic future of our children and grandchildren will be more secure because of the politically difficult decisions taken in the last 2 years. I appreciate his saying that. He had a lot to do with them, and he's earned a well-deserved rest.

But I want to emphasize again how important I think this trade issue is and why I think it's important for the people who are not on the program today, the people who are working in our factories and working in our offices and trying to raise their children and having a difficult time.

When this administration and our economic team took office, we were rightly concerned about economic problems gripping every advanced country in the globe and certainly affecting the United States, the problems of low growth, high unemployment, stagnant incomes, declining benefits for working people, increasing insecurity. It seemed to me then and it seems to me now that we had to have a serious, disciplined strategy to reverse these trends; that if we continue to see increasing inequality and loss of opportunity, not among the working and the nonworking but among people who are all working full-time and longer workweeks today than they were working 20 years ago, that it is going to be very difficult for us to preserve the essence of what America is, the whole core of the American dream that people here who work hard and obey the law and play by the rules are going to be given a chance to do better, going to be given a chance to build a better world for their children.

There were those, 2 years ago, and certainly there were those even in this debate on GATT, who believe the only way we can do that is to try to create a world that used to be. I wonder sometimes about that world that used to be. I remember what Will Rogers used to say: "Don't tell me about the good old days. I lived through them. They never was." [*Laughter*] Well, that's somewhat true, but it is also true that for the last 10 or 15 years we have been struggling with longer workweeks, declining security, increasing inequality, and a lot of people who literally have worked harder for less.

Some say the answer is to try to just hunker down within our borders. That is clearly not an option. No country can escape the global economy, and the greatest, largest, most powerful country in the world cannot escape the global economy. We must lead it in a direction that is consistent with our values, consistent with our interests, consistent with what is necessary to keep the American dream alive. That's really what GATT is all about.

We've worked hard here, these folks and a lot of our friends from the Congress—and a lot of you in this room have helped us—to try to bring the deficit down, to try to reduce what I call yesterday's Government, to try to reduce destructive regulation and unleash the forces of creativity and enterprise, to try to increase investment in the education and training of our work force and in the technologies of the future. But no matter what we do, unless we can expand the markets for America's products and services, we will ultimately fail in our economic mission.

Yes, it is true that one of the reasons for stagnant wages in the United States is intense competition in our own markets and in other markets from people who work for wages our folks couldn't live on. That will happen if there is never another trade agreement in the history of the United States. The reason NAFTA was important, the reason GATT's important, the reason our outreach in Asia is important, the reason this Summit of the Americas is phenomenally important, and why I wanted to be in this building today with the fine Secretary General we're very proud to see in this leadership position, is because America cannot and will not succeed and we will never restore stability to the lives of the working people of our country until we have more folks buying what we sell, until the work of our people is rewarded more. And that can only happen if we have a fair and increasingly open world trading system that allows the free market to work and rewards the most productive people in the world.

There are not many of them here today, maybe, but the real victors in GATT are the autoworkers, the accountants, the engineers, the farmers, the communications workers, the people who will now have a chance to be more rewarded for their labors. Ultimately, that is what the purpose of any country is about. So I am very, very happy to be here.

All of you know what's in this agreement. Let's never forget what's behind it, and let's never forget, too, that this is ultimately a victory for a couple of simple ideas, that people ought to be able to relate more and more and more every year now to people beyond their borders, to work in harmony. The end of the cold war imposes more than relief. It gives us a respon-

sibility to finally take advantage of the interconnections that exist in the world today. It's a victory for the idea that America can lead in the 21st century, that we need not fear competition, that we want our neighbors to do better than they have been doing, and when they do better, we will do better—old-fashioned, simple ideas.

We must never run away from the world. We must go into the 21st century convinced that the only way to preserve the American dream is to be involved with the rest of the world, to be willing to compete, to be determined to win, to be serious about overcoming our problems, but to realize that the only way you can ever do it is to see the opportunities that are plainly there.

I want to thank every Republican and every Democrat here. I thank my predecessors for the work they did on this treaty. I thank, especially, Presidents Carter, Ford, and Bush for their lobbying here for the votes we needed at the last minute. But most of all, I am very pleased to see in recent days evidence in public opinion surveys that for the first time in history, the American people see trade as more of an opportunity than a threat. That is, of course, the ultimately critical factor, because we all serve at the sufferance of the people. They have to believe in themselves and their future and in an open world. And I think that all of you who fought these battles, and especially this last debate on GATT, played a major role in persuading the American people that the future is bright, that our best days are ahead, and that we are going forward with confidence. That ultimately may be the most important significance of the bill I am now proud to sign.

Thank you very much.

NOTE: The President spoke at 9:30 a.m. at the Organization of American States Building. In his remarks, he referred to Cesar Juairia, Secretary General, Organization of American States. H.R. 5110, approved December 8, was assigned Public Law No. 103–465. The proclamation of December 23 implementing the Uruguay Round Agreements and the related memorandum of December 23 on acceptance of the World Trade Organization Agreement are listed in Appendix D at the end of this volume.

Statement on the White House Initiative on Welfare Reform
December 8, 1994

Today, after meeting with a group of Governors from both parties, I am announcing that the White House will convene a national bipartisan working session on welfare reform next month.

Welfare reform is a top priority for my administration, for the Governors, for the new Congress, and above all, for the American people. Americans have asked their elected officials to put aside politics as usual and begin earnest work to solve our Nation's problems, and welfare reform is at the very top of our agenda.

I have called for this session as a first step in an honest dialog about our country's broken welfare system and what we must do to fix it. Washington doesn't have all the answers, and Government doesn't, either. Every one of us in this country has to begin taking individual responsibility for turning this country around.

I have worked on this issue for my whole career in public life. When I was a Governor,

I worked closely with President Reagan and Senator Moynihan to develop the bipartisan consensus that led to passage of important legislation to strengthen families and move people from welfare to work.

I believe we must end welfare as we know it, because the current welfare system is a bad deal for the taxpayers who pay the bills and for the families who are trapped on it. The American people deserve a Government that honors their values and spends their money judiciously and a country that rewards people who work hard and play by the rules.

People want their leaders to stop the partisan bickering, come together, and roll up their sleeves and get to work. This meeting will be the beginning of a new day, not just for the welfare system but for how our Government works.

Remarks to Summit of the Americas Volunteers in Miami, Florida
December 8, 1994

The President. Thank you. Thank you. Well, ladies and gentlemen, the first thing I want to say is a hearty thank-you for letting the "he-coon" stay in the tree in Tallahassee for 4 more years.

I am delighted to be here and Hillary is delighted to be here with Lawton and Rhea, with Buddy and Anne, and with Bob and Adele Graham and so many of our friends here in Florida.

You know, I was trying to remember just exactly how I got talked into having this summit in Miami, and it——

Audience member. The weather!

The President. Yeah—[*laughter*]—when I got out of the airplane tonight I remembered why I was smart enough to want to come here in December. Actually, I have very vivid memories of this sort of one-two punch that I got not all that long ago. We decided to have this summit after NAFTA was successfully concluded, and it wasn't long before I started hearing from

all my friends from Florida. And it wasn't long before Lawton and Buddy said that they had to see me about a matter of dire importance—[*laughter*]—reminding me not once but 500 times of all the things they had done for me—[*laughter*]—and for Al Gore and for our administration. And then when they got through, I got a call from Bob Graham, who reminded me about how many years we sat together in the Governors Conference when he taught me how to be a Governor. [*Laughter*] And by the time they got through with me, I couldn't see anyplace else on the map. [*Laughter*]

I want to thank you all for the magnificent job you have done. The leaders have all been recognized, and I thank all of them all over again. I thank our team who's worked so hard on this, the Secretary of the Treasury and our Trade Ambassador, Secretary Bentsen and Ambassador Kantor. I want to say a special word of thanks to Mack McLarty who coordinated this for the White House; he did so much work.

I appreciate the way you cheered for Janet Reno. I don't know if you all know this—I didn't know it myself, or I'd forgotten it until I picked up the Miami Herald this morning, but I now have three Cabinet members from Dade County. They say we've got to get away from any sort of quotas—that's what the Republicans are telling us—and so I just "over-quota-ed" Dade County. [*Laughter*] Janet Reno and Carol Browner, and there's a wonderful article in the Miami Herald today about the Secretary of Treasury-designate, Bob Rubin, who grew up here and went to high school. And so we are delighted to be here.

Let me just say one serious word to all of you, those of you who have worked so hard for months and months and months, this is basically a celebration, a chance for us to say thank you. It was urged on me by some quarters that the appropriate thing to do, if we were going to have leaders from all over the hemisphere here, was to have this meeting in Washington. And I said, the last time I checked, most Americans were somewhere else—[*laughter*]—and that when deciding where we ought to have this, that Miami was the place that was most representative of our whole hemisphere in the United States.

I hope that you can fully grasp the significance of what we are here doing. Every country in the world today, at the end of the cold war and the emergence of an exploding global economy with all sorts of opportunities but profound problems, every country is fighting a battle within itself between hope and fear, between reaching out and drawing back, between believing in the best of its potential and giving in to the worst, or at least walking away from the challenge.

This morning at the magnificent headquarters of the Organization of American States, the Vice President and I went there to the auditorium, and I signed the legislation adopting the GATT world trade treaty. In the last 2 years, our administration has relentlessly pursued an economic strategy designed to make sure Americans could compete and win and be rewarded for their work in the 21st century, not by withdrawing from the world and hunkering down but

by reaching out to the world and embracing it. We have reduced our deficit. We have increased our investment in education and training. We have focused on the needs of every region of our country. We worked hard here, for example, to try to help rebuild after the things that happened to Homestead and the rest of south Florida in the hurricane.

But we know, we know no matter what else we do, unless we have people around the world who buy our products and services, people who will join with us in combating the problems of the world from environmental problems to terrorism to organized crime to the drug problems, unless we have people who will be our partners in democracy and freedom, we can never be fully what we ought to be. That is the significance of this summit.

It builds on what happened with NAFTA. It builds on this GATT agreement. It builds on our efforts to reach out to the world. This is the largest summit of world leaders ever hosted here, 34 democratically elected leaders from this entire hemisphere joining hands together, not because we agree on everything but because we agree on the important things and because we believe in the promise of freedom; we believe in the promise of democracy; we believe in the promise of open, free trade; we believe in the promise of the human potential of the people of the United States and every other country here.

And so we come here representing people from the tip of Alaska to the tip of Argentina, to plan and to build and to dream for all of you and for your children. Because we believe in the promise of America, we are elated that others have embraced the challenge and the promise of freedom and democracy and free enterprise. I know you wish us well, and if this meeting turns out to have the profound historic significance that it should, I hope for the rest of your life you will remember how hard you worked on it and be justly proud.

Thank you, and God bless you all.

NOTE: The President spoke at 10:15 p.m. at the Sheraton Bal Harbour. In his remarks, he referred to Gov. Lawton Chiles of Florida and his wife, Rhea; Lt. Gov. Buddy MacKay and his wife, Anne; and Senator Bob Graham and his wife, Adele.

Remarks on Goals of the Summit of the Americas in Miami
December 9, 1994

Thank you very much, Mr. Vice President. Thank you, ladies and gentlemen, for that warm welcome. Hillary and I and Vice President and Mrs. Gore are delighted to be here.

We thank Governor Chiles and Mrs. Chiles, the Lieutenant Governor and Mrs. MacKay, the members of the Florida congressional delegation, Senator Graham, Senator Mack, the distinguished Members of Congress who have come from all over the United States to be here. I want to say a special word of thanks to Dante Fascell, the honorary cochair of this summit and a great man. I thank the mayors of Miami Beach and Miami, all the people who are involved in the metro Dade government, all the people who have worked so hard on this summit.

You know, when we first announced the plans to hold the Summit of the Americas here in Miami, it seemed that it was a natural choice. This city, after all, has been variously described as the hub, the melting pot, the gateway, the crossroads of the Americas. But in the end we chose Miami because of the commitment of the people who live and work here to make this summit a success, led as the Vice President said by the Governor and the Lieutenant Governor.

I won't dwell on all the subtle and not-so-subtle details of our many conversations about this. But let me say that they persuaded me that this was the reverse of that wonderful line in the movie "Field of Dreams," where they said to us, "If you come, we will build it." And you have, and I thank you.

Your efforts have been extraordinary, and we are grateful for them. I have just been amazed at the energy that has come out of this community and this State over the last several months, the kind of energy that's supposed to be generated only by the Florida Sun. You promised that the citizens of Miami would do it right, and it's clear that you have delivered. I think I can say for all of those who have come from around America to be here, we knew we would need to be warm in December, and now we are, in more ways than one. And we thank you very, very much.

History has given the people of the Americas a dazzling opportunity to build a community of nations committed to the values of liberty and the promise of prosperity. Now, over the next 3 days, the 34 democratically elected leaders of our hemisphere will gather to begin to seize this opportunity.

I convened this Summit of the Americas with three clear goals in mind: First, to open new markets and create a free trade area throughout our hemisphere; second, to strengthen this remarkable movement to democracy; and third, to bring together our nations to improve the quality of life for all of our people. If we're successful, the summit will lead to more jobs, opportunity, and prosperity for our children and for generations to come. We will have launched a new partnership for prosperity.

Today we gather in Miami to mark a quiet revolution and to launch a new era, for here in the Americas, as all of us know, nation after nation has freed itself from dictatorship and debt and embraced democracy and development. When historians look back on our times, they will marvel at the speed with which democracy has swept across the entire Americas. Consider this: At the time of the last hemispheric summit in 1967, 10 countries suffered under authoritarian rule, and there were fewer here. But today, 34 of the hemisphere's leaders have won their posts through ballots, not bullets.

This weekend we will welcome leaders like President Aristide of Haiti. We have all seen his commitment to reconciliation and the rule of law and how it is now moving his people from fear to freedom. And I hope I can take a moment of pride to salute the brave American men and women in uniform and their partners from around the world who helped to restore that democracy and freedom to Haiti. We are very proud of them. [*Applause*]

Here at the Summit of the Americas, the people of the United States will meet a whole new generation of leaders, a generation no longer subject to the dictates of military juntas who stifle liberties and loot their nation, a generation that has proved in Central America that bloody regional conflicts can be peacefully concluded through negotiation and reform and reconciliation, a generation which has pledged to support democracy collectively wherever it is imperiled in this hemisphere. That's a commitment no other region in the world has made.

These leaders are here in Miami because they have tapped what Simón Bolivar, the Liberator of Latin America, called "the most sacred spring," "the will of the people." Today, just a day before the anniversary of the adoption of the Universal Declaration of Human Rights, we honor them, all of them. And we must also honor the brave men and women who dedicated themselves to the cause of freedom and liberty and who today lie all across this hemisphere in unmarked graves. This summit is also a tribute to their astonishing sacrifice. And it is their triumph as well.

Only one nation in our hemisphere is not represented here. It's the only one where democracy is still denied. We support the Cuban people's desire for peaceful, democratic change, and we hope that the next time we have one of these summits and the people of all the Western Hemisphere send their leaders here, a leader of a democratic Cuba will take its place at the table of nations. [*Applause*] Thank you.

The wave of political freedom that has swept across the Americas has also been matched by unprecedented economic reform. In these times of very great stress, farsighted leaders in nation after nation have adopted sound policies to tame inflation, to restore economic growth. They've cut tariffs, stabilized currencies, opened their economies to foreign investment. They have worked together to shrink mountains of debt. They've privatized; they've decentralized.

Argentina has cut its central government by 60 percent in 4 years. Bolivia has given back to local communities more responsibility for health, for education, for agriculture. Brazil has slashed its inflation rate. The so-called lost decade in Latin America is a fading memory. These reforms are working wonders. Investment is growing. The middle class is again on the rise. The Western Hemisphere now boasts the second fastest growing economies in the world. And if current trends continue, within just a decade our hemisphere will be the biggest market in the world, more than 850 million consumers buying $3 trillion worth of goods and services. These are remarkable, hopeful times.

Here in the United States, we, too, have developed a comprehensive economic strategy to reap the rewards of this moment. We had a lot of work to do just to put our economic house in order. We've made deep cuts in our deficit, in Federal spending, in the size of the Federal Government. For the first time since Harry Truman was President, this year we will have 3 years of reduction in our deficit in a row. We are already taking our Federal Government down to its smallest size since John Kennedy was President. We have made major steps toward deregulation in banking and trucking and deregulating the States in the areas of welfare, health, and education. And we have just begun to move in this direction.

Our country has produced over 5 million new jobs in the last 22 months. We've got the lowest unemployment rate in 4 years and have been voted by the annual panel of international economists as the world's most productive economy for the first time in 9 years. But the thing that gives me the most hope, after all the years—nearly two decades—in America of American families working longer workweeks for stagnant wages and more fragile benefits, is that this year more high-wage jobs have come into our economy than in the previous 5 years combined. We hope that we are seeing the beginning of the end of a 20-year trend in stagnant wages, and the beginning of the restoration of the American dream by reaching out to the world and into our hearts.

Still, we know that millions of Americans have not felt this economic recovery. Millions of Americans are still working harder for less and feeling very uncertain, even as they read all the good statistics in the newspaper. We have a lot of work to do. But the truth is that the United States has never been in a stronger economic position to compete and win in the world.

We're also taking bold steps to open new markets and to make the global economy work for our people. For 40 years, our markets have been more open than those of any other nations. We led the restoration of economic hope and opportunity after the Second World War. But now that competition is everywhere and productivity is growing and the lessons of management, technology, and investment are readily apparent to hardworking people all across the world, we cannot allow that to continue. We simply must be able to export more of our goods and our services if we are going to create more high-wage jobs.

Just a year ago yesterday, I signed into law NAFTA, the North American Free Trade Agreement. You can clap for that. [*Applause*] When Congress voted for NAFTA, that event committed the United States to continuing leadership and engagement in the post-cold-war world. It marked a new era in world trade relations for America, and it gave birth to this summit, which could not have occurred if that hadn't happened.

In the first 9 months of this year, our exports to Mexico jumped 22 percent. Increased exports to Mexico and Canada have helped us to create more than 100,000 new jobs in America in this year alone. Auto exports to Mexico are up 500 percent. And I might say, Mexican exports to the United States are also up. It's been a good deal for us, a good deal for them. There has been no "giant sucking sound," except for American goods going across the border.

Last month in Indonesia, we agreed with 17 other Asian-Pacific nations, including Mexico and Chile, two countries represented here, to achieve free trade in the Asian-Pacific region by the year 2020. The tariffs will begin to fall and give us new access to new markets in the fastest growing economies of the world far before then.

And just yesterday I signed into law the bill implementing the General Agreement on Tariffs and Trade, the largest agreement ever for free and fair trade. And GATT, like NAFTA before it, passed because we had strong bipartisan support in Congress. That is a pattern that must prevail as we continue to pursue open markets and prosperity in this hemisphere and around the world. And I strongly urge all the nations in our hemisphere who have not yet done so to follow what America has done and implement this agreement now. It is an important thing for our future growth.

Finally, let me emphasize that our economic strategy seeks to prepare our own people to fill the high-wage jobs of the future. For too many people, as I said earlier, these times are ones of great uncertainty. Pressures of the global economy have held down wages and increased job turnover for people who are not in a position to take advantage of the developments now occurring.

We owe it to those Americans to provide the kind of lifetime education and training that will give them a chance to win in this economy as well. And we must ensure that basic labor standards are preserved and promoted so that freer trade means better working conditions for all. After all, in America, our people, our workers, are the most important asset we have. And that is true in every other nation as well. That's

why democracy and free trade go hand-in-hand. More free trade is worthwhile only if its benefits actually change the lives of real people for the better.

But as I have said over the last 2 years, that does not mean that we can repeal the laws of change, repeal the sweeping changes taking place in the global economy. If we do nothing to reach out to other countries than to expand trade, if we had walked away from NAFTA, if we had walked away from GATT, if we don't reach out here and throughout the world, the United States will still continue to suffer the burdens of trade, for we can't walk away. But if we reach out, as we are with NAFTA, with GATT, with the Summit of the Americas, if we act wisely, then we can make this new world work for us. Trade can be a benefit to our people. When we have the opportunity to sell American products and services around the world, we know we can compete, and we know that means new jobs and a rising standard of living, the core of the American dream.

I will say again, we must in the United States not only create jobs but raise incomes. And we can only do that if we train people for higher wage jobs and if we create those jobs. One of the only ways we can create those jobs is to expand trade, especially in this hemisphere. So that's why every American worker in every part of the United States should be glad we are all here today at the Summit of the Americas.

Now, I hope I've established why that is my primary goal for this summit. We have a real opportunity here to build on the momentum of NAFTA and GATT. That's what this new partnership of prosperity is all about, creating a free trade area that stretches from Alaska to Argentina. Let no one underestimate the significance of this—[applause]—someday I'll learn to coordinate my speech lines and the applause. [Laughter]

Let me tell you, though—think about it— from Alaska to Argentina. People have talked about free trade in this hemisphere for years. It's been talked about and talked about. The difference is, here in Miami we have the chance to act, and we're going to take it.

Let me try to describe in graphic terms what this means. Latin America is already the fastest growing region in the world for American exports. Of every dollar Latin Americans spend on exports, 44 cents buy goods made in the

U.S.A. Despite trade barriers that are, on average, 4 times higher than ours, Florida alone sold almost $9 billion worth of goods in the Americas in last year alone. And by the year 2005, if current trends continue, our country will sell more to Latin America than to Western Europe or Japan. That's why we're here. That's an investment worth making. Creating a free trade area would be good news throughout the Americas. Here in the United States, our exports to Latin America could literally double by the year 2005. That would create over one million new jobs.

Exports also create good-paying jobs. On average, export-related jobs pay 17 percent more than average wages in America. They're the kind of jobs that guarantee the families that we are concerned about a fair shot at the American dream. And that is why we must succeed here.

But trade is not the only goal of this meeting; there are two others. The second goal of our summit must be to preserve and strengthen our community of democracies. Continued economic prosperity clearly depends upon keeping the democracies alive and stronger. And we can only do that if we address the dangers to democracy that face all nations.

Many of the dangers we face—consider them: international crime, narcotics trafficking, terrorism, environmental degradation—these things can only be overcome if we act in harmony. So in the days ahead we will discuss ways to seize the assets of money launderers, to explore new ways like those developed in Chile to prevent corruption from corroding our democracies, to move forward on all of these fronts.

We must also keep our democracies healthy and open. Our hemisphere has come too far and the cost has been too great to return to the days of repression and dictatorship. So at the summit we will discuss how the Organization of American States can help to reconcile political disputes and ensure that democratic constitutions actually live and breathe.

Here in the United States we know that democracy is hard work. We've been at it over 200 years, and we know we still have to defend it every day. We have to continually review how well our governments perform and even whether they should be doing some things at all. Our own efforts to cut the size and cost and improve the performance of Government, led by the Vice President and his reinventing Government team, demonstrates the immense importance and the

great rewards of this undertaking. And we, too, have only just begun.

The third goal of the summit is to bring our nations together to pursue sustainable development. That is far more than a buzzword. Our democracies and our prosperity will be short-lived if we do not figure out how to deal with the things that enable us to grow and come together and maintain our quality of life over the long run. Improving the basic health and education of our peoples is a key part of that sustainable development strategy.

Consider our common efforts to eradicate polio, banished from our hemisphere since 1991. That shows you what cooperation can bring. So at this summit we will discuss ways that we can combat poverty, combat disease, increase health care, increase education, remove threats from millions and millions of our fellow citizens.

Our summit agenda also calls for important talks aimed at making our environmental and trade policies mutually supportive. Threats to our environment respect no border and ultimately can undermine our economies. We must discuss initiatives that will make progress. We're going to talk about things like banning lead from gasoline in every country, conserving nature's diversities, spreading innovative environmental technologies. We will be doing the kinds of things that will permit us to sustain the remarkable trends of the last few years.

At the summit, in support of expanding trade and democracy and sustainable development, we will consider more than 20 initiatives, all told, to plot a course for the future. And I am convinced that we will succeed as long as we recognize that the bonds that unite us are stronger than the forces that divide us.

Once the United States and our neighbors were clearly divided by seemingly unbridgeable cultural and economic gulfs. But today, super-highways, satellite dishes, and enlightened self-interest draw us together as never before. Our economies are increasingly interwoven. And Latin American and Caribbean contributions to American culture, in great novels, fine foods, spirited music, free television networks, and many other ways, grow every day. By the year 2020, the United States of America may well boast a Spanish-speaking population second only in size to Mexico's. The connections between north and south in the Americas are, in short, a source of great energy. We have to strengthen these bonds. We've got to make them work for the benefit of all of our people.

On this very day, 170 years ago, the foot soldiers of Bolivar's army won the Battle of Aya- cucho, the last battle for liberation between the people of the New World and colonial Spain. With that triumph, Peru proclaimed its inde- pendence, and a new era began in our hemi- sphere. It was an era that Bolivar hoped would produce greater unity among the pan-American states. Well, his dream was not realized in his lifetime, and generation after generation has struggled without success to make it real.

In our own century, President Roosevelt's Good Neighbor Policy, as Vice President Gore said, sought to unite the hemisphere by urging mutual respect among all and recognizing even then, long ago, the importance of our inter- dependence. Three decades later, President Kennedy's Alliance for Progress inspired the peoples of the Americas with its vision of social justice and economic growth.

Today, we can build on those foundations and do what could not be done in former times.

We can create a partnership for prosperity where freedom and trade and economic oppor- tunity become the common property of the peo- ple of the Americas. Just imagine it: a hemi- sphere where disputes among and within nations are peacefully and honorably resolved, where cultures and nations are universally and mutually respected, where no person's rights are denied and labor is not abused, where ideas and trade flow freely across borders, where work is re- warded and families and communities are strong. Just imagine it.

My fellow Americans, this is a magic moment. Let us seize it.

Thank you very much.

NOTE: The President spoke at 12:30 p.m. at the Jackie Gleason Theater for the Performing Arts. In his remarks, he referred to Gov. Lawton Chiles of Florida and his wife, Rhea; Lt. Gov. Buddy MacKay and his wife, Anne; Mayor Seymour Gelber of Miami Beach; and Mayor Steve Clark of Miami.

Remarks at a Reception for Heads of State at the Summit of the Americas in Miami
December 9, 1994

Let's give all our distinguished guests a hand here. [*Applause*] To our distinguished heads of state, Vice President and Mrs. Gore, Members of the Congress and the Cabinet, Governor and Mrs. Chiles, Lieutenant Governor and Mrs. MacKay, Mayor Clark, to the distinguished lead- ers from the business community and non- governmental organizations that work so won- derfully together, to the co-chairs and others from the host committee who have done such a wonderful job of putting together this extraor- dinary event, and to all of our distinguished guests from other lands, let me say a hearty welcome to this remarkable summit.

Let me begin by thanking the wonderful city of Miami for rising so magnificently to the chal- lenge of hosting the Summit of the Americas. If we leaders can match the dedication of the citizens of Miami and south Florida to the work of this week, we will truly bring our people and our hemisphere closer together.

The end of the cold war has given all of us a great opportunity to build bridges where, for 50 years, only barriers stood. We in the United States have worked hard to seize this moment for peace and prosperity, from the Middle East to Northern Ireland to southern Africa to Haiti. And through our commitment to expanded trade through NAFTA and the GATT agreement, we are doing our best to demonstrate our willingness to reach out to the rest of the world to promote the peace and prosperity we all want.

But here in our own hemisphere we are espe- cially privileged, all of us, to live at a moment of great opportunity. And with that opportunity comes a heavy obligation upon all of us who occupy positions of leadership in this hemi- sphere. It is in the spirit of that opportunity and that obligation that I proudly welcome the 33 democratically elected leaders of the Ameri- cas to the United States and to Miami.

This week we have come together to build a better world and a better future for our children. Students of the Americas will recognize this as an old dream. In the 1820's, at the dawn of freedom for the new Latin American republics, Simón Bolivar dreamed the Americas could be the greatest region on Earth, I quote, "not so much by virtue of her area and wealth, but by her freedom and her glory." Now, some 170 years later, Bolivar's dream for the Americas is becoming a reality. The people represented here are free, we are friends, and we are committed to creating the best century in our history. We can become true partners for prosperity, and we can begin this week.

Our goals for the summit are clear: We want to extend free trade from Alaska to Argentina, we want to strengthen our democracies, and we want to improve the quality of life for all our people. It is clear that these goals are bound together. If we grow more prosperous through trade, we will strengthen our democracies and our friendship. If we confront our common problems, the common threats to democracy, in a spirit of genuine partnership, we will increase our chances at prosperity. And if together we can confront our common challenges in the environment, in health, and education to provide for long-term sustainable development, both our prosperity and our freedom will be secure.

A partnership for prosperity, stronger democracies, improving our people's quality of life, these are the opportunities that lie before us. So, my fellow citizens of the Americas, let us make the most of them.

Thank you very much.

NOTE: The President spoke at 8 p.m. at the Biltmore Hotel Country Club.

Statement on the Resignation of Joycelyn Elders as Surgeon General
December 9, 1994

Dr. Joycelyn Elders is a physician of outstanding ability, energy, and commitment. As a pediatrician, she dedicated her life to improving the health of children. As Surgeon General, she worked tirelessly to reduce teen pregnancy and AIDS and to improve the health of all Americans, especially our children.

Dr. Elders' public statements reflecting differences with administration policy and my own convictions have made it necessary for her to tender her resignation.

Those statements in no way diminish her devotion to her work and the enormous positive impact she has had on the problems she tackled and the people she served.

I will always be grateful for her service.

The President's Radio Address
December 10, 1994

Good morning. Earlier this week, I signed the GATT agreement, the most far-reaching international trade pact in our history. And this weekend in Miami, we in the United States are hosting the Summit of the Americas, where the leaders of 34 countries have gathered to promote trade in our own hemisphere.

This Summit of the Americas and GATT and everything we've done to expand international trade is really about opening up foreign markets to America's goods and services, so that we can create high-wage jobs and new opportunities for our people here at home.

But despite all the progress we've made— despite the fact that we have over 5 million new jobs in the last 22 months, the biggest expansion of trade in history, we've had more new construction jobs this year than in the last 9 years combined, and we've had a year of manufacturing job growth for the first time in a decade—in spite of all that, millions of hard-working people are still out there killing themselves, working longer hours for lower pay, paying more for health care or losing their health coverage, than ever before. More and more Americans, even in this recovery, are worried that they could lose their job or their benefits at any time. There's less disposable income for most working Americans than there was just a decade ago. Many people can't even image being able to afford a vacation anymore, let alone send their children to college. And I'm talking about hard-working Americans who play by the rules; they're tired of watching their earnings benefit people who don't.

There's no greater gap between mainstream American values and modern Government than we find in the welfare system. The welfare system was set up for all the right reasons: to help people who had fallen on hard times temporarily, to give them a hand up for a little while so they can put their lives back in order and move on. And it still works that way for an awful lot of people. But for millions and millions of people, the system is broken badly, and it undermines the very values, work, family and responsibility, that people need to put themselves back on track.

The people who are stuck on welfare permanently will be the first to tell you that if we're going to fix it, we have to return to those values, and we have to put them front and center. People who have worked their way off of welfare, after being afraid they'd be on it forever, will be the strongest in saying we've got to put work, family, and responsibility back into the system.

We have to change welfare so that it drives people toward the freedom of work, not the confines of dependence. Work is still the best social program ever invented. Work gives hope and structure and meaning to people's lives. And we won't have ended welfare as we know it until its central focus is to move people off welfare and into a job so that they can support themselves and their families.

We have to change welfare so that it strengthens families, and not weaken them. There is no substitute, none, for the loving devotion and equally loving discipline of caring parents. Governments don't raise children, parents do. There's some people out there who argue that we should let some sort of big, new institution take parents' place, that we should even take children away from parents as we cut them off

welfare, even if they're doing a good job as parents, and put the children in orphanages. Well, those people are dead wrong. We need less governmental interference in family life, not more.

We have to change the welfare system so that it demands the same responsibility already shouldered by millions and millions of Americans who already get up every day and go to work and struggle to make ends meet and raise their children. Anyone who can work should do so. Anyone who brings a child into this world ought to take responsibility for that child. And no one—no one—should get pregnant or father a child who isn't prepared to raise the child, love the child, and take financial and personal responsibility for the child's future.

That's why welfare reform must include a national campaign against teen pregnancy and the toughest possible enforcement of our child support laws, along with the requirement that people on welfare will have to get off of it and go to work after a specified period of time. It also means that if you're going to require that, there has to be a job there for them and support for people who are working to raise their children in the proper way.

I've worked on this welfare reform issue for 14 years, since I first became Governor of my State. I've worked with other Governors, with Members of Congress from both parties, but most importantly with people on welfare and people who've worked their way off of it. I know that most people out there on welfare don't like it a bit, would give anything to get off, and really want to be good, hard-working citizens and successful parents.

There are a lot of ideas out there for reforming welfare. Some are really good, and some are just political attention-getters. Since I became President, I've worked hard on this. I've already introduced welfare reform legislation in the last session of Congress. We've also given 20 States relief from cumbersome Federal bureaucracy rules so that they can pursue welfare reform on their own. We've done that for more States than the previous two administrations combined.

There's still some disagreement about what we ought to do, but everybody agrees that the system is badly broken and needs to be fixed. It's a bad deal for the taxpayers who pay the bills, and it's a worse deal for the families who are permanently stuck on it.

Two days ago, after meeting with Governors from both the Democratic and Republican Parties, I announced that we're going to host a national bipartisan working session on welfare reform at the White House in January. I call for this session as a first step in an honest and forthright discussion about America's welfare system and how to fix it. It's not going to be easy, but our responsibility to the American people is to put aside partisan differences and to turn our full attention to the problems at hand.

The American people deserve a Government that honors their values and spends their money wisely and a country that rewards people who work hard and play by the rules. Working together, that's what we can give them.

Thanks for listening.

NOTE: The address was recorded at 6:19 p.m. on December 8 in the Oval Office at the White House for broadcast at 10:06 a.m. on December 10.

Remarks Following the First Session of the Summit of the Americas in Miami
December 10, 1994

Good morning. We have just completed the first working session of our summit on trade and economic integration. We are off to an excellent start. The 34 democratically elected leaders of our hemisphere have agreed to establish a free trade area of the Americas. This historic step will produce real opportunities for more jobs and solid, lasting prosperity for our peoples.

The agreement is specific and concrete. We have set the year 2005 as our deadline for negotiating a free trade area, and we have agreed that there will be real progress before the end of the century. The agreement will cover a comprehensive list of areas, from tariffs on goods to services to agricultural and intellectual property. We have set a highly detailed timetable that will include regular meetings of our ministers for trade. Talks will begin next month.

In less than a decade, if current trends continue, this hemisphere will be the world's largest market, more than 850 million consumers buying $13 trillion worth of goods and services. When our work is done, the free trade area of the Americas will stretch from Alaska to Argentina. It is the key building block in our creation of a partnership for prosperity. It will build upon the many bilateral and multilateral agreements already existing between our nations.

We want to replace the many conflicting and different trade and other regulatory agreements with one that is consistent, while making sure to assist smaller economies in transition. We will

ask the Organization of American States and the Inter-American Development Bank to assist in this transition and integration. And we have pledged that our free trade area of the Americas will not raise new barriers to nations outside our region and will be fully consistent with the rules of the World Trade Organization. We have reaffirmed our commitment to make our individual trade and environmental policies mutually supportive and to further secure the observance and promotion of workers' rights.

Let me emphasize, none of us—none of us—underestimates the hard work ahead. But from the leaders of our hemisphere's largest economies to the smallest, we believe the rewards will be great and very much worth the effort. We believe the agreement we have made today to launch the free trade area of the Americas will produce more jobs, higher incomes, and greater opportunities for all of our people.

From here we're going to a working lunch, where we'll discuss issues affecting sustainable development. Our final session this afternoon will focus on the steps we will take to strengthen our democracies. I can think of no more appropriate way to end this day, the anniversary of the adoption of the Universal Declaration on Human Rights.

Thank you very much.

NOTE: The President spoke at 11:30 a.m. in the Gardens at Vizcaya.

Remarks on Signing the CONCAUSA Agreement in Miami
December 10, 1994

Thank you very much, Mr. Vice President. To my colleagues, the leaders of the Central American nations, I am very pleased to join you today in signing the Conjunto Centroamericano-USA or, in shorthand, CONCAUSA. The United States is proud to become a partner in your alliance to promote sustainable economic growth. This declaration is the product of farsighted leadership by the nations of Central America.

A little over a year ago, when I hosted many of you at the White House, you proposed to establish an alliance for sustainable development. Just 9 months later you made good on your pledge. This alliance is a remarkable sign of the powerful transformation you have achieved in Central America. You have demonstrated strength and energy in bringing your people together to resolve conflicts peacefully and turning your attention to creating new economic opportunity in your nations.

As the Vice President said, this alliance is already demonstrating that democracy, economic growth, and concern for the environment are complementary goals. Now, through CONCAUSA, all our nations will cooperate on a wide range of concrete programs. These include supporting protected areas from northern Guatemala to eastern Panama, phasing out the use of lead in gasoline, and strengthening environmental laws and enforcement.

We will also work to harmonize environmental rules to facilitate trade and investment. And I am committed to seeking prompt congressional passage of the interim trade program.

Your Excellencies, the United States is proud to join your partnership to promote sustainable development. This is a new day of cooperation between the United States and Central America, and we urge other nations to follow our lead. So many of the challenges we face know no borders, and we must unite to meet them.

Now I'd like to invite to the microphone the Secretary of the Central American nations, President Figueres.

NOTE: The President spoke at approximately 5 p.m. on the East Terrace at Vizcaya. In his remarks, he referred to President Jose Maria Figueres of Costa Rica.

Remarks at the Concert of the Americas in Miami
December 10, 1994

Thank you. Thank you, Michael, my fellow leaders of the Americas and their families, and to all of our distinguished guests tonight. I know you all join me in a heartfelt thanks to David Salzman and to our friend Quincy Jones and all the wonderful entertainers from all over our hemisphere who made us so wonderfully happy tonight.

We are gathered tonight as a family of nations, each with cultures that are unique and yet familiar to all of us. The arts help us to appreciate and to gain a deeper understanding of our hemispheric heritages, as well as the ideas, the voices, the images that we share as members of the larger American family.

We all know that art strengthens the bonds among us. Our nations grow ever closer as we delve into the souls of our culture through our artists: the soaring voice of a Placido Domingo, the rich performances of the wonderful, late Raul Julia, the magical words of Nobel Prize winner Derrick Wolcott, and the many artists who are performing for us tonight.

The poet Pablo Neruda, on receiving the Nobel Prize for literature, spoke of moving toward the splendid city. He reminded us that as we build a better world, the two guiding stars of our journey are struggle and hope. "Do not forget," he said, "on the way to the splendid city, there should be no such thing as a lone struggle and no such thing as a solitary hope."

Neighbor with neighbor, we have gathered here tonight in that spirit, to share our gifts, to contemplate our common destiny, to celebrate not only who we are but the joyous possibilities of what this splendid community of democracies can yet become.

Thank you very much.

NOTE: The President spoke at 9:43 p.m. at the James L. Knight Center. In his remarks, he referred to actor Michael Douglas, television producer David Salzman, and musician Quincy Jones, who served as master of ceremonies.

Remarks at the Final Session of the Summit of the Americas in Miami
December 11, 1994

The President. Your Excellencies, distinguished guests, ladies and gentlemen, let me begin by thanking the members of the host committee and the people of the city of Miami and the State of Florida.

I am very, very pleased that we made the decision to come to Miami. I thank Governor Chiles and Lieutenant Governor MacKay and all those who made the case that we should be here. Our hosts have done a tremendous job of hosting this historic event. At this extraordinary moment of opportunity and responsibility, they have made our work easier and, especially last evening, much more enjoyable.

The Summit of the Americas has more than fulfilled our expectations. Future generations will look back on the Miami summit as a moment when the course of history in the Americas changed for the better. We worked hard to arrive at this point. Yesterday, we achieved agreement on the many issues before us. Our talks were lively, open, and wide-ranging. They were filled with the spirit of democracy and mutual respect and a deep determination to increase the jobs and incomes of our people, improve the quality of their lives, and protect their freedoms.

Meanwhile, the First Lady's summit on children, all of our spouses working together, looking toward the future of our children in this hemisphere, in many ways captured what the spirit of this meeting is all about, for all of our efforts will fall more to the benefit of our children than to our generation.

Now I would like to ask the representatives of each of the major geographical regions of the Americas, the Caribbean, North America, Central America, and South America, to report on the agreements we have forged. In addition, we will hear from the leaders of two dynamic and vital institutions that are serving our hemisphere and that will loom large in our plans for the future, the Inter-American Development Bank and the Organization of American States. Then President Aristide of Haiti, who embodies our hemisphere's determination to uphold the sovereign rule of the people, will speak.

Let us begin the plenary.

[*At this point, the final plenary session of the summit proceeded.*]

The President. First let me thank all those who have spoken before. I thank the Prime Minister and the Presidents, distinguished President of the Inter-American Development Bank, Secretary General of the Organization of American States. I thank especially President Aristide for his moving remarks. And I thank all of you here present who have supported the multinational effort to restore democracy to Haiti.

We come here to begin a new era, an era of real promise. When Vice President Gore and I asked the American people to give us a chance to serve, we relied upon two phrases that we said over and over again. One was "Put people first." The other was "Don't stop thinking about tomorrow." In this meeting, for these days, we have put our people first, and we have thought about tomorrow.

We are bound together by geography, by history, by culture, but most important, now by shared values: a ferocious devotion to freedom, democracy, social justice; a determination to improve the lives of all our people; and a determination to preserve the natural world we have inherited and that we must pass on.

We have tried to give life to these values at this summit by agreeing to create a free trade area throughout our hemisphere, to bring together our nations to improve the quality of life for our people, and to strengthen and make permanent the march of democracy. These achievements have been given concrete expres-

2173

sion by our commitment to negotiate with specific steps a free trade agreement for a free trade area of the Americas by 2005.

This is more than words; this is a commitment to deeds. Free trade in our hemisphere has been talked about for years, but because of this process we've launched this weekend, it will now become a reality. Free trade will yield dramatic benefits in terms of growth and jobs and higher incomes. It will permit us to pursue economic opportunities and at the same time to reaffirm our commitment to promote the rights and interests of our workers so that all our people have the chance to benefit from free trade.

I couldn't help thinking, when President Figueres was talking about the gross national product measuring everything but what is most important to us, that that is true but that unless we attend to the health of our economy, the things that are most important to us are more difficult to achieve.

If you think about how many millions of people in this hemisphere, including in our country, are working harder today than they were just a few years ago for lower incomes, if you think about how many millions of people have less security in the face of the bewildering changes in the world we live in, what it means is they have less time for their families, for raising their children, less time for leisure, less time for citizenship, less time for learning in a calm and open atmosphere what the major issues of the day are. And there is not so much room in their spirit for the clear head and the generosity it takes to be an effective citizen in a strong democracy.

So that all these things we care about, that we want for our people, require us to do our best to make sure that they can be victors in this great cauldron of change that is bringing on the next century.

We also vowed to do our best to make our governments work better; to protect our democracies by making sure we could do the job we're supposed to do well, and that we stop doing things we shouldn't be doing; to protecting human rights; to fighting illicit drugs and international crime; to rooting out corruption. And we agreed to pursue vigorously sustainable development.

In a way, sustainable development is an unfortunate phrase because it has so little poetry about it. But the meaning is very profound. It means to me that we must pursue short-term goals, consistent with our enduring values. It means we must pursue individual opportunity, consistent with our responsibility to our larger communities. It means we must share in the Earth's bounty without breaking our bonds with Mother Nature. It means we must take for ourselves in ways that leave more for our children. It means we must expand the circle of those who are able to live up to their God-given capacities, the women, the indigenous people, the minorities, the poor children of this hemisphere.

For all these commitments, I thank you, all of you who have come here representing all these nations. The agenda we have embraced is ambitious and worthy. We have actually committed ourselves to 23 separate and specific initiatives and more than 100 action steps protecting the diversity of plant and animal species, phasing out lead in gasoline, reducing infant mortality, improving education and health care. Our goal is to create a whole new architecture for the relationship of the nations and the peoples of the Americas to ensure that *dichos* become *hechos*, that words are turned into deeds.

So as we come to the end of this historic Summit of the Americas, as we proclaim the dawn of this new partnership, as we say we have done this to put our people first and we have kept our eye on tomorrow, let us remember that the road ahead will be full of challenges and difficulties and that beyond all of the specifics of what we have done, perhaps most enduring is the friendship, the spirit of trust that has been built here. There is truly a spirit of Miami.

And in future years when the difficulties mount up, when it is difficult to sustain the hope about which President Aristide spoke so beautifully, may future leaders remember the spirit of Miami. *O espirito de Miami. L'esprit de Miami. El espiritu de Miami.* The spirit of Miami.

Thank you all, and God bless you.

Now we will sign the declaration—if they will bring it to us.

NOTE: The President spoke at 10:14 a.m. at the James L. Knight Center. In his remarks, he referred to Enrique Iglesias, President, Inter-American Development Bank, and Cesar Juairia, Secretary General, Organization of American States.

Remarks Welcoming Chile to the North American Free Trade Agreement Partnership in Miami
December 11, 1994

Mr. Prime Minister, President Zedillo, President Frei: I would like to begin my remarks by expressing my appreciation on behalf of the United States to the leaders and the people of Mexico and Canada for being such good partners in NAFTA this last year. This has been a very, very good deal for the United States of America.

Beginning with our agreement with Canada, and with our completion of the NAFTA agreement, we have seen a substantial increase in trade and an increase in jobs, good-paying jobs, for the American people. In the last year alone, we estimate that 100,000 jobs have been added to the American economy because of increased trade opportunities flowing directly out of NAFTA. We have a 500 percent increase in exports of automobile products to Mexico alone in the last year because of NAFTA. So while I think this is good for the world and good for our region, I want to begin by saying a special thank you, because this agreement and the good faith that has been followed in adhering to it has been good for the working families of the United States.

The second thing I would like to do is to say how very proud I am that we are welcoming Chile to the NAFTA partnership. This is a country, like our three countries, that has benefited from disciplined and responsible economic leadership. Chile has high economic growth, low inflation, has virtually extinguished its foreign debt, and has done so while manifesting the commitment to the labor and environmental standards and to the welfare of the people of Chile that are embedded in our commitments in NAFTA. So Chile is an ideal partner.

I think you could see from the comments of the Prime Minister of Canada and the President of Mexico, we are actually quite proud to be entering this partnership.

I think, furthermore, that this agreement we announce today will be further proof of our intentions, our serious intentions, to complete the free trade agreement for all the Americas by 2005. That is what we agreed to do in this summit. And this should be evidence that we intend to accelerate the process; we intend to keep working.

And let me say again, on behalf of the United States, NAFTA is a good deal for us; it will be a better deal with Chile in it. And we are honored, honored to be in partnership with a country that shares our values and that has demonstrated that it can succeed by doing the right things and doing them well in a free society.

Thank you very much.

NOTE: The President spoke at 12:50 p.m. at the James L. Knight Center. In his remarks, he referred to Prime Minister Jean Chrétien of Canada, President Ernesto Zedillo of Mexico, and President Eduardo Frei of Chile.

The President's News Conference in Miami
December 11, 1994

The President. Good afternoon. Ladies and gentlemen, this Summit of the Americas we just concluded represents a watershed in the history of our hemisphere. I want to begin by thanking again the people of Miami and the people of Florida for working so hard to make this a stunning success and for treating these deliberations with such great respect. I would say a special word of appreciation to the people who dem-onstrated in the Orange Bowl in such large numbers but in a way that spoke up for their deepest convictions for freedom and democracy for Cuba, in a way that was supportive of the other deliberations of this summit.

From my point of view, the mission of this summit was accomplished, first, in our specific commitment to a free trade agreement of the Americas by 2005, which, going with NAFTA, with Chile's coming into the NAFTA partnership, with the recent success of the GATT world trade agreement, puts us on the right road. And for the Americans here in the audience, I would just like to ask you to consider that just in the last 2 weeks the United States has concluded agreements to push for regional free trade in the two fastest growing areas of the world, first at Bogor in Indonesia with the Asian-Pacific economies and now here with the free trade agreement at the Summit of the Americas. These things, along with the implementation of GATT and the expansion of the NAFTA arrangement, will set the agenda for world trade for years to come in ways that benefit ordinary American families, that generate more high-wage jobs in this country and more opportunity in the countries of our trading partners.

Secondly, we reaffirmed our commitment to continuing to work together to strengthen our democracies and to promote sustainable development, to promote education and health care and labor standards and the environment, to fight drugs and international crime and corruption, in other words, to push not only for economic growth, for improvements in the quality of life. This spirit of Miami was embodied in 23 very specific declarations and a specific work program that will begin immediately. That makes it quite a bit different than most summit declarations of the past.

And finally and perhaps equally important, we saw here in the interlocking networks of people that began to meet and work together both in preparation for this summit and then here—not just the world leaders but others who were here in huge numbers from these various countries—the beginning of the kind of working relationship that will be absolutely essential to bring this hemisphere together in an atmosphere of trust and a true spirit of partnership. So from my point of view, this has been a very successful summit, indeed. I am pleased. I am deeply indebted to the leaders of the other countries, as well as to the people who did all the work to make it a success on our side.

Helen [Helen Thomas, United Press International], I'm sorry about your accident last night, but you look just fine.

Taxes

Q. The water was fine. [*Laughter*]

Mr. President, there are strong indications that you read the election results, and as a result of them, you plan to give a middle class tax cut, and you're going to cut the programs from the poor. And my question is, are you going to promote or support a middle class tax cut, and are you going to cut programs for the people who are the most vulnerable and less able to defend themselves?

The President. Well, first of all, before the election, long before the election, I announced on more than one occasion, as did others who are in our administration, that we wanted to complete the work of being fairer in our Tax Code by providing a middle class tax cut that would go with what we did with the earned-income tax credit in 1993, which, I would remind you, gave 15 million American families with 40 million Americans in it—that's a significant number of people in a country of 254 million—an income tax cut. Already we have done that. I want to build on that. I want to fulfill the commitment of our campaign and my commitment to tax fairness and to give the working people of this country, many of whom have had declining incomes or stagnant incomes for a long time, some benefit from the end of the cold war and the downsizing of the Federal Government, which is well underway. So I am working to do that. I am working to do that, however, in the context of not a lot of irresponsible promises but the real discipline of the real world. That is, I do not want to see this deficit start going up again.

That is my objective. I think we can achieve that objective without hurting—not only without hurting poor people who are poor through no fault of their own but while creating an environment in which the poor will be encouraged and empowered to work their way into the middle class.

Keep in mind—I think sometimes we lose sight of this—I believe—you know, people read the elections any way they want; I think the important thing is to do what we think is right. But there are two components to restoring the American dream today. One is rooted in the fact that working Americans without college degrees have stagnant wages or declining wages for a long period of time. We want them to have more security in their jobs. We want them to be rewarded for their work. We want them to stop losing their health benefits. The second is that the percentage of people living in poverty, including working people in poverty, is going up. A big part of the American dream has always been the opportunity that poor people had to work their way into the middle class.

So I don't believe that we should be pitting the middle class against the poor who themselves are willing to embrace the values of work and family and community. And I don't think that we have to do that.

So I think when you see our budget, our proposals, our cuts, they will be perceived by the American people as fair, fair to both the middle class and to the poor in this country who are willing to work hard to make themselves independent or who through no fault of their own are poor.

Q. So the answer is yes on a middle class tax cut?

The President. No, the answer is—the answer is what we have said for months and months and months: I intend to propose one as long as I can pay for it, without—that's the answer. But I do not believe that what we need in this country is a war of the middle class against the poor, because most poor people believe in family, work, and community. Most poor people would gladly work themselves into the middle class. And a lot of people living in poverty today live in families where people work.

What I think—if you want to know what I think the people believe on this, it's what I believe, what I think most Americans believe, which is that no one should get a check for irresponsible conduct, that Government funds should not be used to reward irresponsibility. But if people are temporarily poor through no fault of their own, if they're doing their best to improve their lot in life, if they are responsible parents and trying to do the best they can, I don't think the American people want us to put a lot of folks in the street or take a lot of kids away from loving parents and put them in state-run orphanages or do any of that stuff.

I think that we can show discipline in welfare reform and discipline in a lot of these other programs and still not be anti-poor. What we ought to want is for the middle class to be rewarded and for the poor to be empowered to work their way into the middle class and rewarded for that.

Federal Government Downsizing

Q. Mr. President, also on an economic issue, back in Washington your deputies are working on budget proposals that might include the elimination of a Cabinet department such as Energy or HUD. Do you concur with the idea that a Cabinet agency might have to be abolished? And if so, what are your thoughts on where their functions would go and why they should be eliminated?

The President. Well, I don't think we should—I think that's starting at the end rather than at the beginning. So let me try to answer the question.

It has been apparent for more than a year that the exploding cost of health care, which I was unable to persuade the Congress to act on, will cause the deficit to start to go up again next year, unless we take further steps.

The American people should know something I don't think they do know now, which is that this budget the Congress just adopted—the first budget adopted with all agencies on time in, like, 17 years—reduced both domestic and defense spending for the first time since 1969; domestic spending was reduced. What did not go down was interest on the debt, Medicare, and Medicaid.

So what we have to do is to continue to reduce spending. If we want to have a middle class tax cut, if we want to invest more in the education and training of our work force, if we want to train people to move from welfare to work, we have to find the money to do that. So we're going to have to continue to cut back on Government.

Our people have been looking for, well, 6 months or more now, at what our options are. And what I instructed them to do was to basically ask a certain set of questions: Does this program, or would the elimination of this program, advance the interest of working people's jobs and incomes, of the desire to have poor people work their way into the middle class, of our desire to have safer streets and stronger families and stronger communities, of our need to be strong in the world, promoting peace and prosperity? Those are the criteria.

And I said, "Let's measure all this, everything the Federal Government's doing, and let's take a fresh look at it. And don't rule anything out, but don't make a lot of decisions until you analyze these things rigorously, because it's obvious that we're going to have to continue to reduce the size of the Federal Government, to give more authority back to States and localities, to consider whether we need to be doing some things at all."

But I think it's important to see this as a continuous process. In the last 2 years we deregulated banking, intrastate trucking; we deregulated much of what the Federal Government was doing with the States in education, in welfare and health. So I think we have to keep doing it. And I wouldn't rule anything out.

But the questions you asked me about any particular department are all the questions that would have to be asked and answered. If you ask me a purely political question, do I think it's necessary to do that for show, the answer is no, I don't think it's necessary to do that for show. Do I think it is terribly important that we continue the work of reinventing Government, which the Vice President has spearheaded, that we continue to downsize the Government? Yes, I do.

Keep in mind, among other things, we are already obligated to reduce the size of the Federal Government by 272,000, and we have already reduced it by 70,000, but not more.

Now, what I would like to do is to alternate from here on in between journalists from other countries and American journalists. So, the gentleman over here. I'll do my best.

Customs Inspections

Q. It is really not easy for us to interview the President of the United States, so I beg you a followup, please. My first question is when we can really expect a change from the approach of the United States? You have told me in the past that you would like to be the best President since John Kennedy, and certainly many changes have been done to Latin America. But for all of us Colombian citizens, it's very difficult to pass through an airport in the United States. When will we see and expect a change?

The President. What I said was I wanted the people in Latin America to perceive the United States as a good friend of Latin America, as they did when Kennedy was President. I do believe that. And I don't know what you're referring to. I mean, we—you mean because they question you at the airports?

Q. [*Inaudible*]—Colombians that are honest people. Not all Colombians are—[*inaudible*].

The President. I agree with that. But we also—when people come into our borders, many honest people are tested and questioned, and their effects are examined. That's the nature of our system here. If you think that it's disproportionately prejudicial to Colombians, I will

look into that. No one has ever raised that question with me before. But that's what border inspections are all about. You have to inspect the honest and the dishonest; otherwise you would never—no one knows who is or isn't in the beginning. That's why you have inspections.

Russia

Q. Mr. President, while you've been here, the Russians have moved into Chechnya. And I'm wondering if you have any comment on that and if you have had a chance to discuss that with President Yeltsin, or if you plan to.

The President. Well, we haven't had direct discussions; President Yeltsin and I have not. But we have had some discussions with our contacts in Russia, and they with us. The first thing I want to say is, obviously, it's something we're monitoring closely; we're concerned about it. It is an internal Russian affair, and we hope that order can be restored with a minimum amount of bloodshed and violence. And that's what we have counseled and encouraged.

Cuba

Q. [*Inaudible*]—Cuban-American. You have said in the past that you feel our pain. Do the other 33 heads of state feel that pain? And if so, why wasn't it mentioned here today? Why does it seem to be so difficult to present a united front against the last remaining tyranny in this hemisphere?

The President. In our private meetings yesterday, a substantial number of the heads of state spoke up on behalf of democracy in Cuba and the need for changes, political changes there. And as you know, President Menem and one or two others did publicly when they were here, as well.

I think the differences, frankly, are over what the best way to achieve that objective is. Most of these countries don't agree with the United States policy—not because they don't agree with our objective; I didn't find much sympathy with the political structure in Cuba among these leaders. There was a great deal of feeling that it is urgent to restore democracy to Cuba, and it was very widespread. The differences were over whether or not the approach we have taken is the correct one. And I think because they couldn't agree on what to do about it, they decided not to say what they feel about it. But I don't think you should underestimate the depth of feeling throughout Latin America that every country should be free.

Russia

Q. In the past couple of weeks, Russia has taken a number of actions that raise questions about its reliability as a strategic partner, specifically the failure to sign on to the Partnership For Peace, the U.N. veto on Bosnia, and then blocking a statement on Bosnia at the CSCE summit. Do these things cause you to question or have second thoughts about your policy of trying to work for a close relationship with Moscow?

The President. No. And I'd like to say why. They don't, because Russia is still a democracy. Russia is still pursuing economic reform, which is critical to the kind of political stability that will lead to responsible partnership. Russia followed through in its efforts on the Non-Proliferation Treaty, and we now can see START I entering into force. There are no Russian missiles pointed at the United States for the first time since the dawn of the nuclear age. And maybe more to the point here, Russia also kept its commitment to withdraw its troops from the Baltic States that, as you know, I worked very hard on with President Yeltsin.

When we first met, President Yeltsin and I did, back in the spring of 1993, I said then, and I will reiterate now, there will always be some areas of difference between us; there will be some times of greater or lesser difficulty. But I think that our continuing engagement with the Russians, our involvement with them, our working with them is quite important. We have some differences about Bosnia, as you know. But we have some differences with our close allies in Western Europe over Bosnia, as well.

I was disappointed, frankly, that the agreement about Russia's relationship with NATO and the Partnership For Peace was not signed, because Russia has participated in the Partnership For Peace. We have done military exercises in Russia as well as in Poland, and we had done our best to prepare the groundwork in cooperation. So I am disappointed about that. And obviously, I felt that the exchange of statements that we had in Budapest reflected some modification of what the United States thought the Russian position was.

But these things are to be expected in the relationships of great nations that have a lot of irons in the fire. And we'll have to—I'll watch

them; I'll work on them; I'll do whatever is necessary to protect our interests. But I think, on balance, our policy has been the right one, and I think there have been far more pluses than minuses to it. Consider what the alternative might have produced. I don't think it would have produced nearly as much as has been produced in the last 2 years.

Cuba

Q. [*Inaudible*]—in order to bring democracy to Haiti. Will you be doing the same on Cuba?

The President. But what we did—we had a lot of support from other countries. And we have a lot of support from other countries to bring democracy to Cuba, but no agreement on what the policy should be. Our policy toward Cuba is embodied in the Cuba Democracy Act, which calls for an embargo and then permits calibrated steps toward normalizing economic and other activities in response to things which might happen in Cuba.

Most other countries believe that time is on our side, that if you look at what has happened in Russia and the former Soviet Union and Eastern Europe, that a more aggressive engagement would produce democracy more quickly. So that is the difficulty. We have a policy difference. You could see it in the recent U.N. vote.

I think what we need to do—and that goes back to the question that the lady in front of you asked—what we need to do is to try to persuade our friends, to say, "Look, even if you disagree with the specifics of American policy, you ought to keep speaking out publicly about this because you will change the environment." And changing the environment is an important thing. I think President Menem made an important contribution to that when he was here.

Surgeon General Joycelyn Elders

Q. Your Surgeon General, Joycelyn Elders, was forced to resign this past week over remarks she had made last weekend at an AIDS conference in which she appeared to be suggesting alternatives to dangerous forms of out-of-wedlock sex. She apparently was forced to resign because you didn't agree with those comments. I was wondering, what exactly is it that you didn't agree with, or what do you think was wrong about the way she made the statement? And how do you answer those critics who say that her firing was essentially bowing to pressures from Republicans who just last week,

Newt Gingrich, for example, asked for her resignation?

The President. Well, first of all, if I wanted to do it for political reasons, it would have been done before the election, not afterward.

Secondly, I think you ought to go back and read my statement. My statement makes it clear that I held her in the highest esteem. She is a person of great energy and conviction, and she's devoted her life to child health and reducing teen pregnancy and fighting AIDS. But there have been a number of things where we just have different positions, and I think that at some point the President is entitled to have people in certain positions who agree with him and who don't depart from the policy positions and the personal convictions that a President has. I think that that is a legitimate thing. It's not political; it's what is necessary for a government to have coherence and integrity and direction.

But I still admire her; I still like her. But we just have a whole series of differences which I thought made this an appropriate decision.

Argentina

Q. Did Argentina ask the United States to mediate between England and Argentina for the Malvinas Islands? And if that happened, what would be the U.S. position?

The President. Well, I'm in enough trouble already without answering that. [*Laughter*] No, let me answer. No one—President Menem has never asked me to do that, and I have found it quite useful in life not to answer hypothetical questions.

Q. A summit question?

The President. A summit question, one summit question? Sure.

Cooperation of Summit Participants

Q. Your aides are speaking now of—discussing your influence, your leadership in the summit, and it appears that the American positions did prevail across the board. I wonder, given the new partnership in this hemisphere, what you can tell us other countries brought to this summit and why we were not swayed in issues like Cuba and others?

The President. Well, first, there was a difference of opinion among them over Cuba, too, so it wasn't as if it was 34 to 1. The question of whether our embargo is the right policy was one of only many questions there. We had some

good discussions about Cuba individually and in our smaller groups.

But let me also say that when we say the American positions essentially prevailed in critical areas, like in the free trade area, I think it's important to note that Mr. McLarty and Mr. Altman and a lot of others did an enormous amount of background work. I don't know how many times Mack McLarty went to various countries involved in this, and our trade people, Mickey Kantor and others. There was a lot of background work done to try to get a feel for what these other countries' concerns were, what their legitimate concerns were, so that there was really a shaping of the ultimate position coming up to the summit which reflected many of their concerns.

And I think you could hear some of their concerns, for example, in the statement of the representative of the Caribbean today. You know, if you listen to what he said, they have some very fixed views there, and they wanted to know that we were going to try to push for legislation in the Congress to make sure they wouldn't be disadvantaged by NAFTA. We said we would. That's an important thing they got out of the summit. Although I intended to do that all along, the fact that they made that case here at the summit, were able to do it when there was a very strong bipartisan delegation of Congress here, I thought was quite important.

To give you another example, a lot of the countries in South America are willing to, I think, work very hard to try to stamp out drug trafficking. But they wanted to know that we were willing to renew our efforts to reduce consumption in America, to reduce the demand for drugs in America, and to help them to consider alternative ways to move the farmers away from coca production. And a lot of that is implicit in the summit. They liked that. They wanted to know that it wasn't just the American position that they had to do more but that we would listen, that we would be willing to do more. And those are just two examples.

So there were many areas when—I mean, I appreciate the fact that people who work for me want me to—want to give us credit for things; that's their job. But you have to give these people an enormous amount of credit, these other leaders, because they gave huge amounts of time to this process before we ever showed up here. And they would say things like, "Okay, this is what you want to do in this area, and we will go along with that, but this is our concern." So we would work along to get their concerns worked out.

So I think that if the United States deserves any credit here, it is in the process by which we found common ground, by moving into the future in ways that took account of the legitimate concerns of all these other countries.

And if I could just give you one example in closing—I haven't seen it much noted in the last couple of days, but this summit represented a remarkable partnership between the United States and Brazil, two countries that have in the past been at odds over trade and other issues and at least have not had the kind of closeness of relationship that the two largest

countries in this hemisphere ought to have had. And I am especially grateful to President Franco and to the Brazilians generally for the work they did to help us keep this together.

So I would give a lot of credit to the other guys. I think they deserve it, and I hope they get it.

Thank you very much.

NOTE: The President's 83d news conference began at 1:15 p.m. at the James L. Knight Center. In his remarks, he referred to President Carlos Menem of Argentina; Summit of the Americas Coordinator Thomas F. (Mack) McLarty; Summit of the Americas Deputy Coordinator Roger Altman; Prime Minister Owen Arthur of Barbados; and President Itamar Franco of Brazil.

Statement Congratulating the Nobel Peace Prize Recipients
December 11, 1994

On behalf of the American people I wish to extend congratulations to Prime Minister Yitzhak Rabin, Chairman Yasser Arafat, and Foreign Minister Shimon Peres on being selected as the Nobel Peace Prize laureates for 1994.

It was with great pride that we welcomed these leaders to the White House on September 13 last year to sign the historic Israel-Palestinian Declaration of Principles. It is fitting that this achievement be recognized by award of the Nobel Peace Prize and that the presentation

take place in Norway, the country which contributed so much to making it possible.

There is still much work to be done by all who support and share with this year's Nobel laureates the goal of a just, comprehensive, and lasting peace in the Middle East. The ceremony in the Oslo City Hall not only marks a great achievement, it encourages all of us to redouble our efforts to realize the promise of peace for all the people of the Middle East.

Message on the Observance of Christmas
December 15, 1994

Warm greetings to Americans everywhere during this joyous Christmas season.

The timeless story of a baby born in a manger amid humble surroundings is the fulfillment of a promise, an affirmation of faith. Jesus' birth demonstrates the infinite love of God. We celebrate the gift of His life, and Christmas softens our hearts and rekindles in us a sincere desire to reach out to others in peace and friendship.

As we rejoice in the miracle of Christmas, we reflect on the Holy Family and draw

strength from their example of faith. We are reminded that the bonds between parent and child, between husband and wife, and between neighbor and stranger are opportunities to answer Jesus' call to love one another, and we are reminded that one day we will be asked whether we lived out His love in ways that treated all of our brothers and sisters—even the least of them—as we would have treated Him.

In holy Bethlehem and throughout the Middle East, ancient enemies are putting aside their differences and coming together in goodwill. Recognizing that there is still much work to be done, let us build on this success and nurture love and caring in our world, in our neighborhoods, and in our homes. With this commitment, we can all share in the fulfillment of the Christmas promise.

Hillary joins me in wishing you joy and peace this Christmas.

BILL CLINTON

Statement on the California Bay Delta Agreement
December 15, 1994

When I campaigned for President, I said many times that environmental protection and economic growth can go hand in hand.

Today's historic Bay Delta agreement demonstrates that this goal can be achieved. It resolves one of the most contentious and important public policy issues affecting the State of California. It puts an end to a bitter conflict that has persisted for decades.

This is a solution that serves all the people of California. It means farmers will have a reliable supply of water to grow their crops; that commercial and sport fishermen will have reliable supplies of fish; that cities in California will have consistent, predictable supplies of water at reasonable rates; and that those who love the outdoors will find places throughout northern California with fish, birds, and clean, fresh water.

Under the leadership of Secretary Babbitt and Administrator Browner, the Federal Government aggressively faced up to its responsibilities, took a process that had previously failed, and made it work. We made certain all the Federal agencies worked together, not at cross purposes; we challenged our scientists to create new ways of using water more efficiently; and we invited all stakeholders to take responsibility for a comprehensive solution.

The result is an innovative plan that protects both water quality and water supplies; that enhances environmental and economic progress; and that provides the certainty necessary for water users to plan well into the future. It demonstrates that, with strong leadership and a cooperative spirit, environmental laws can be properly and productively enforced.

This historic agreement is good for economic growth, good for the environment, and good for California and the Nation.

Address to the Nation on the Middle Class Bill of Rights
December 15, 1994

Good evening. My fellow Americans, ours is a great country with a lot to be proud of. But at this holiday season, everybody knows that all is not well with America, that millions of Americans are hurting, frustrated, disappointed, even angry. In this time of enormous change, our challenge is both political and personal. It involves Government, all right, but it goes way beyond Government, to the very core of what matters most to us. The question is, what are we going to do about it?

Let's start with the economic situation. I ran for President to restore the American dream and to prepare the American people to compete and win in the new American economy. For too long, too many Americans have worked longer for stagnant wages and less security. For 2 years, we pursued an economic strategy that has helped to produce over 5 million new jobs. But even though the economic statistics are moving up, most of our living standards aren't. It's almost as if some Americans are being punished for their productivity in this new economy. We've got to change that. More jobs aren't enough. We have to raise incomes.

Fifty years ago an American President proposed the GI bill of rights to help returning veterans from World War II go to college, buy a home, and raise their children. That built this country. Tonight I propose a middle class bill of rights.

There are four central ideas in this bill of rights: First, college tuition should be tax deductible. Just as we make mortgage interest tax deductible because we want people to own their own homes, we should make college tuition deductible because we want people to go to college. Specifically, I propose that all tuition for college, community college, graduate school, professional school, vocational education, or worker retraining after high school be fully deductible, phased up to $10,000 a year for families making up to $120,000 a year. Education, after all, has a bigger impact on earnings and job security than ever before. So let's invest the fruits of today's recovery into tomorrow's opportunity.

Second, bringing up a child is a tough job in this economy. So we should help middle class families raise their children. We made a good start last year by passing the family leave law, making college loans more affordable, and by giving 15 million American families with incomes of $25,000 a year or less an average tax cut of more than $1,000 a year. Now I want to cut taxes for each child under 13, phased up to $500 per child. This tax cut would be available to any family whose income is less than $75,000.

Third, we should help middle income people save money by allowing every American family earning under $100,000 to put $2,000 a year tax-free in an IRA, an individual retirement account. But I want you to be able to use the money to live on, not just retire on. You'll be able to withdraw from this fund, tax-free, money for education, medical expenses, the purchase of a first home, the care of an elderly parent.

Fourth, since every American needs the skills necessary to prosper in the new economy—and most of you will change jobs from time to time—we should take the billions of dollars the Government now spends on dozens of different training programs and give it directly to you, to pay for training if you lose your job or want a better one.

We can pay for this middle class bill of rights by continuing to reduce Government spending, including subsidies to powerful interests based more on influence than need. We can sell off entire operations the Government no longer needs to run and turn dozens of programs over to States and communities that know best how to solve their own problems.

My plan will save billions of dollars from the Energy Department, cut down the Transportation Department, and shrink 60 programs into 4 at the Department of Housing and Urban Development. Our reinventing Government initiative, led by Vice President Gore, already has helped to shrink bureaucracy and free up money to pay down the deficit and invest in our people. Already, we've passed budgets to reduce the Federal Government to its smallest size in 30 years and to cut the deficit by $700 billion. That's over $10,000 for every American family. In the next few days, we'll unveil more of our proposals. And I've instructed the Vice President to review every single Government department program for further reductions.

We've worked hard to get control of this deficit after the Government debt increased 4 times over in the 12 years before I took office. That's a big burden on you. About 5 percent of your income tax goes to pay for welfare and foreign aid, but 28 percent of it goes to pay for interest on the debt run up between 1981 and the day I was inaugurated President. I challenge the new Congress to work with me to enact a middle class bill of rights without adding to the deficit and without any new cuts in Social Security or Medicare.

I know some people just want to cut the Government blindly, and I know that's popular now. But I won't do it. I want a leaner, not a meaner Government, that's back on the side of hard-working Americans, a new Government for the new economy—creative, flexible, high quality, low cost, service oriented—just like our most innovative private companies.

I'll work with the new Republican majority and my fellow Democrats in Congress to build a new American economy and to restore the American dream. It won't be easy. Believe you me, the special interests have not gone into hiding just because there was an election in November. As a matter of fact, they're up here stronger than ever. And that's why, more than ever, we need lobby reform, campaign finance reform, and reform to make Congress live by the laws it puts on other people.

Together, we can pass welfare reform and health care reform that work. I'll say more about what I'll do to work with the new Congress in the State of the Union Address in January.

But here's what I won't do: I won't support ideas that sound good but aren't paid for, ideas that weaken the progress we've made in the previous 2 years for working families, ideas that hurt poor people who are doing their dead-level best to raise their kids and work their way into the middle class, ideas that undermine our fight against crime or for a clean environment or for better schools or for the strength and well-being of our Armed Forces and foreign policy. In other words, we must be straight with the American people about the real consequences of all budgetary decisions.

My test will be: Does an idea expand middle class incomes and opportunities? Does it promote values like family, work, responsibility, and community? Does it contribute to strengthening the new economy? If it does, I'll be for it, no matter who proposes it. And I hope Congress will treat my ideas the same way. Let's worry about making progress, not taking credit.

But our work in Washington won't be enough. And that's where you come in. This all starts with you. Oh, we can cut taxes and expand opportunities, but governments can't raise your children, go to school for you, give your employees who have earned it a raise, or solve problems in your neighborhood that require your personal commitment. In short, government can't exercise your citizenship. It works the other way around.

The problems of this new world are complicated, and we've all got a lot to learn. That means citizens have to listen as well as talk. We need less hot rhetoric and more open conversation, less malice and more charity. We need to put aside the politics of personal destruction and demonization that have dominated too much of our debate. Most of us are good people trying to do better. And if we all treated each other that way, we would do better. We have got to be a community again.

Yes, some people do take advantage of the rest of us by breaking the law, abusing the welfare system, and flaunting our immigration laws. That's wrong, and I'm working to stop it. But the truth is that most people in this country,

without regard to their race, their religion, their income, their position on divisive issues, most Americans get up every day, go to work, obey the law, pay their taxes, and raise their kids the best they can. And most of us share the same real challenges in this new economy. We'll do a lot better job of meeting those challenges if we work together and find unity and strength in our diversity.

We do have more in common, more uniting us than dividing us. And if we start acting like it, we can face the future with confidence. I still believe deeply that there is nothing wrong with America that can't be fixed by what's right with America. This is not about politics as usual. As I've said for years, it's not about moving left or right but moving forward, not about Government being bad or good but about what kind of Government will best enable us to fulfill our God-given potential. And it's not about the next election, either. That's in your hands.

Meanwhile, I'm going to do what I think is right. My rule for the next 2 years will be: Country first and politics-as-usual dead last. I hope the new Congress will follow the same rule. And I hope you will, too.

This country works best when it works together. For decades after World War II, we gave more and more Americans a chance to live out their dreams. I know; I'm blessed to be one of them. I was born to a widowed mother at a time when my State's income was barely half the national average; the first person in my family to finish college, thanks to money my parents couldn't really afford—scholarships, loans, and a half a dozen jobs. It breaks my heart to see people with their own dreams for themselves and their children shattered. And I'm going to do all I can to turn it around. But I need your help. We can do it.

With all of our problems, this is still the greatest country in the world, standing not at the twilight but at the dawn of our greatest days. We still have a lot to be thankful for. Let's all remember that.

Happy holidays, and God bless America.

NOTE: The President spoke at 9 p.m. from the Oval Office at the White House.

The President's Radio Address
December 17, 1994

The President. Good morning. Today I'm speaking from the Northern Virginia Community College in Annandale, Virginia, where I'm joined by 50 students and the Secretary of Education, Dick Riley, who will speak with you in a moment.

In this holiday season, families come together to reflect on the past year and plan for the year ahead. It's a time to be with our children and think about their futures. For students near the end of high school, it's a time to think about continuing their education after graduation.

Our people face greater challenges than ever to get ahead. For too long, too many Americans have worked harder for less. I ran for President to change that, to help ordinary people compete and win in the new American economy, to restore the American dream for middle class families.

For 2 years, we've pursued an economic strategy that has helped to produce over 5 million new jobs. But this growth has not produced higher incomes for most Americans, especially those without more than a high school education, at the very time it's more important than ever to get a good education after high school and then to keep learning throughout adult life.

It's more expensive than ever before. In the decade before I took office, the cost of college tripled. Too many people are being priced out of a fair shot at high-quality education. If we can't change that, we're at risk of losing our great American middle class and of becoming a two-tiered society with a few successful people at the top and everyone else struggling below.

Fifty years ago, an American President proposed the GI bill of rights. It helped World War II veterans go to college, buy a home, raise their children; it built this country. Last Thursday night, I proposed a middle class bill of rights, four new ideas to help middle class Americans get ahead. Here's how it will work.

The first proposal is especially important to people at this community college. If your family makes less than $120,000, the tuition you pay for college, community college, graduate school, professional school, vocational education, or worker training will be fully deductible from your taxable income, phased up to $10,000 a year. Nothing like this has ever been done before.

Second, if your family makes $75,000 a year or less, you'll receive a tax cut phased up to $500 for every child under the age of 13.

Third, if your family makes less than $100,000 a year, you'll be able to put $2,000 a year, tax-free, into an individual retirement account, but you'll also be able to withdraw the money, tax-free, for education, a first home, or the care of an elderly parent.

Finally, the middle class bill of rights will take the billions of dollars that Government spends on job training and make that money directly available to American workers so that you can spend it as you decide, when you need to learn new skills to get a new job or a better job.

Of course, we have to pay for all this. On Thursday night I proposed dramatic reductions in three more Cabinet departments. And Monday morning Vice President Gore and I will outline these cuts in more detail. But today I want to ask Secretary Riley to talk about why education is a top priority in the middle class bill of rights.

Secretary Riley.

[*At this point, Secretary Riley made brief remarks.*]

The President. Thank you, Secretary Riley.

My fellow Americans, this middle class bill of rights will further the agenda of this administration and, more importantly, our common mission as Americans: to expand middle class incomes and opportunities; to promote the values of work and family, responsibility and community; and to help Americans compete and win in the new American economy of the future.

With all the challenges we face today, ours is still the greatest country in the world. Let's keep it that way for our children and for future generations. I thank Secretary Riley for joining me and wish you all a very happy holiday season.

Thanks for listening.

NOTE: The President spoke at 10:06 a.m. from the Richard J. Ernst Community Cultural Center at Northern Virginia Community College in Annandale, VA.

Statement on the Helicopter Tragedy in North Korea
December 18, 1994

We have been informed by the Government of the Democratic Republic of North Korea, through Congressman Bill Richardson who is in Pyongyang, that one of the pilots of the U.S. Army helicopter that strayed into North Korean airspace on December 16, Chief Warrant Officer David Hilemon of Clarksville, TN, was killed in the downing of the helicopter. North Korean officials have told Congressman Richardson that the other crewman, Chief Warrant Officer Bobby Hall of Brooksville, FL, is alive and reportedly uninjured. Our thoughts and prayers are with the families of both of these dedicated aviators.

Congressman Richardson, who has been in continuing contact with Secretary of State War-ren Christopher during this period, has at my instructions told the North Korean Government that we want prompt access to Chief Warrant Officer Hall and his return to a U.S. facility along with the remains of Chief Warrant Officer Hilemon. We are using all available channels to press for an early resolution of this matter.

This tragic loss of life was unnecessary. Our primary concern now is the welfare of Chief Warrant Officer Hall and his return along with the body of Chief Warrant Officer Hilemon. Congressman Richardson, who has worked tirelessly to resolve this matter over the past 2 days, is staying in North Korea for now and will remain in constant contact with North Korean officials on our behalf.

Remarks on the Middle Class Bill of Rights and North Korea
December 19, 1994

The President. Last week, I outlined my proposal for a middle class bill of rights to help the American people restore the American dream. The GI bill after World War II gave a generation of Americans a chance to build their own lives and their own dreams. Now we can help a new generation of hardworking people get the right education and skills, raise their children, and keep their families strong so that they can get ahead in the new American economy.

I want to take just a moment to remind you of the four features in that bill of rights. First, for a family making less than $120,000, the tuition they pay for postsecondary education, training, and retraining would be fully deductible from a taxable income, phased up to $10,000 a year; second, for a family with an income of $75,000 a year or less, a tax cut phased up to $500 a year for every child under the age of 13; third, for families with incomes under $100,000 a year, the ability to put away $2,000 tax-free into an IRA and then withdraw that money tax-free for costs of education, health care, first-time home, or the care of an elderly parent. Finally, we will make billions of dollars available that the Government normally spends itself, through separate job-training programs, directly to workers who can decide on how best to use the money to learn new skills.

There's only one reason we can afford to do this at this time. We have worked very hard to cut Government spending and to bring the deficit under control. The Government debt increased by 4 times during the 12 years before I took office. I want to remind you what that burden means. It means that this April when people make out their checks to the Government, 28 cents of every dollar of Federal income tax will be necessary to pay interest on the debt accumulated between 1981 and the day I was inaugurated. It is our responsibility to turn that around, and we have been working to fulfill it. We have already passed budgets that cut the deficit by $700 billion, eliminate 100 Government programs, and cut over 300 others.

A major part of this endeavor has been the reinventing Government initiative led by the Vice President. I have worked hard to reduce and to redirect governments for many years, since my early days as Governor of my State, when we were one of the first States in the country to adopt a statewide total quality management program, which resulted in cutting regulation and paperwork, eliminating agencies and departments and programs that were unnecessary. Now we are cutting things that can be cut. We propose to stop doing things that Government doesn't do very well and that don't need to be done by Government. And we believe we should increase our efforts where Government can make a real, positive difference in the lives of ordinary Americans. We have to change yesterday's Government and make it work for the America of today and tomorrow.

In the last 2 years, we have made a good beginning. We have begun to shrink the Federal Government's bureaucracy to its smallest size in 30 years. The work force of the Federal Government is already almost 100,000 below where it was on the day we were inaugurated. We are on the way to a reduction of 272,000 positions, cuts that are freeing up money to invest in our people. For example, every dollar that goes to fund the crime bill, which is a direct transfer of investment to our local communities at the grassroots level, comes from the cuts we are making.

Later today at the Justice Department, I will announce new efforts under the crime bill to finish our commitment of putting 100,000 more police officers on the street and stop the crime that punishes so many American families.

We have to continue to meet our responsibilities to the next generation. We must pay, therefore, for the middle class bill of rights with new reductions in Government spending, dollar for dollar, spending cuts to pay for tax cuts, with no new cuts in Medicare and Social Security. I call on Congress to meet that same responsibility in their deliberations.

Our administration has just completed a review in which we have identified $24 billion in cuts in bureaucracy, redtape, and outmoded programs to help to do this. And we are committed to continuing the freeze on discretionary spending, which will save another $52 billion in the next 5-year budget cycle.

We will do even more to shrink yesterday's Government. I have called on the Vice President to review every single Government program and department for further possible reductions. He's also going to review the Federal regulatory process, and we have spent a good deal of time on that already, so that we can get better results for the public with less interference in their lives.

Vice President Gore is here to discuss the details of our next round of proposals in reinventing Government, along with Director Alice Rivlin and the heads or representatives of five agencies in which we are proposing reductions now, including Secretary Cisneros, Secretary Peña, Deputy Secretary White, General Services Administration Director Roger Johnson, and Office of Personnel Management Director Jim King. I want to thank them and our entire economic team for their hard work in the last few weeks.

I also want to say a special word of thanks to people who often get overlooked in this, and that is the employees of the United States Government. The work they have done in the last 2 years to help us to reduce the size of the Federal work force by 100,000 already, to implement plans to take it down to a total of 272,000, and even more with the announcements we are making today, that work is truly exemplary. It would be envied by many of our biggest corporations in this country. They have rolled up their sleeves; they have been creative; they have found ways for us to save taxpayer money and redirect that into the middle class bill of rights and to investing in our future.

This has been—I want to emphasize—a very disciplined, well-organized process. We have not let rhetoric and recklessness dominate it. This has been about reality. And again, as we go into the New Year, that ought to be our motto, as I said the other night: Country first, politics-as-usual dead last; focus on reality, not rhetoric and not recklessness.

It is not enough to cut Government just for the sake of cutting it. Government is not inherently good or bad. In a new time, with a new economy, with new demands on ordinary American families, we need a leaner but not a meaner Government. We need to put Government back on the side of hardworking Americans. That means I will oppose certain cuts if they undermine our economic recovery, undermine middle class living standards, undermine our attempts to support poor people who are doing their best to raise their children and want to work their way into the middle class, undermine our attempts to improve education, protect our environment, and move us into the future with a high-wage, high-growth economy.

As I said last Thursday night, what we really need is a new American Government for this new American economy in the 21st century, one that is creative and flexible, that's a high-quality, low-cost producer of services that the American people need and that can best be provided at the national level. The best thing we can do in this process is to follow the model that smart companies have done, which is to develop a good plan, put good people in charge, and pursue the goal with vigor.

I am confident that I chose the right person to lead the reinventing Government effort. I want to thank the Vice President and all of his team. They have done wonderful work. And I'd like now to turn the podium over to Vice President Gore.

[*At this point, the Vice President outlined the reinventing Government plan and introduced the agency officials who presented the new proposals.*]

North Korea

Q. Can we ask the President a question?

The President. Let me just—let me make a brief statement. I want to say just two things about the North Korean situation. First of all, I called the families of the two soldiers involved today to express my concern, and in the case of the gentleman who was killed, my condolences, to the family. And I told them what I can tell you. I've worked on this all weekend. I'm going to keep working on it, and we're working on an early resolution of it. We're doing the very best we can. I don't have any details to tell you now.

As you know, I think, Congressman Richardson is in North Korea, and he is working with us and also doing a very fine job. I have nothing else to say at this time, except it's a high priority, we're working on it, and we're going to do our best to resolve it.

NOTE: The President spoke at 12:13 p.m. in Room 450 of the Old Executive Office Building.

Remarks Announcing the Appointment of Joseph Brann as Director of Community Oriented Policing Services
December 19, 1994

Thank you very much, Chief Brann, for your remarks and your commitment. We're delighted to have you and your fine family here and on board. Chief Sanders, thank you for your remarks and for your work. To General Reno and to Director and former Chief Brown, and the Deputy Attorney General, the Associate Attorney General, to the Members of Congress who are here, and the mayors, and other leaders of people who will benefit from this work that is being done. This is a very happy day for the people of the United States.

I ran for President because I wanted to restore the American dream and bring this country together as we move into the 21st century. And there were three sort of slogans that, from time to time, I used to try to capture what I thought we ought to be about. One was "putting people first," restore the values of middle class America. The other was, "Don't stop thinking about tomorrow," which basically means we're hurtling into the future at a rapid rate, and we better prepare for it. The third was the idea that we needed a covenant in this country, not just a deal but a covenant, a solemn agreement that we would attempt in the Government to provide more opportunity, but that the citizens of America would assume more personal responsibility for themselves, their families, and then in the process we would build the American community again.

We can't do any of that if the people of this country feel afraid on their streets, in their homes, and in their schools. And we are taking a stand against that. But we're also doing it in a way that reinforces our commitment to thinking about the future and the need for people to assume more personal responsibility, all of us.

When I had the honor of addressing the Nation last Thursday night, and I was able to outline the middle class bill of rights, which will be at the center of our agenda when the Congress comes back, to give people the opportunity to invest in their children's education, in the raising of their children, in savings so that the money will be there if it's needed for health care or caring for a parent or preparing for future education, I said that we were going to do that not by increasing the Government deficit or raising taxes but by reducing the size of Government, by paying for it.

The deficit of this country quadrupled in the 12 years before I became President, and I want you to think about this when you make out your income tax check in April: 28 cents of every dollar you pay to us next April will go to pay for the interest run up on the debt accumulated between 1981 and January of 1993.

So today the Vice President and I announced some dramatic changes in reductions in the Federal Government, cutting yesterday's Government so we could invest in tomorrow's community empowerment through the middle class bill of rights. But the first example of doing that is what we're here to celebrate today, the crime bill. Cut and invest.

We did not raise the deficit a penny to pay for the crime bill. We did not raise taxes a penny to pay for the crime bill. The Congress supported a reduction in the Federal Government to its smallest size in 30 years so that we could put these 100,000 police on the street. That is an example of what the Government should be doing to exercise its responsibility to give people at the community level and law enforcement and the local leaders the power they need to move forward.

And I'd like to say that I'm very proud of everything that was in that crime bill. I'm proud of the 100,000 police. I'm proud of the punishment and the prevention. I believe in "three strikes and you're out," and I believe in trying to keep kids from making the first strike. And I think most law enforcement people do as well. And I believe that those of you who live and work in our communities, know best what your problems are and can best solve them.

One of the things that I learned as a Governor for a dozen years is that we really do

need national leadership in many areas, but when it comes to deciding exactly how to solve problems, and how to seize opportunities, there's very little I can do in Washington, DC, that will solve the problems that Chief Sanders deals with in San Diego, except to give him the tools to do the job. That is the ultimate decision that the Congress made in the crime bill.

I want to say a special word of thanks to Chief Brann for agreeing to come all the way across the country to the most regularly condemned city in America, Washington, DC, to do this job. He was selected in part because he believed in community policing. And you heard that today.

One of the new ideas that I came across as I traveled the country was this whole idea of community policing, not just as a device for patrolling the streets but as the chief said, as a philosophy of law enforcement. And it makes so much sense. You've already heard that we have now put about 10,000 of our 100,000 police officers in process to be on the street. And we're going to keep going until it's all done.

Today we have over 600 jurisdictions in our country who are going to get police officers: over 300 in Chicago, almost 50 in San Diego—that's not why the chief came here to brag on this, though; he really believes in it—almost 100 in Detroit, nearly 80 in Baltimore, over 150 in Philadelphia.

Not long ago, I received a letter jointly signed by the mayor and the police chief of Odessa, Texas. That was one of the first cities to receive community policing money from the crime bill. They told me that since they began to institute aggressive community policing, serious crimes have dropped 43 percent, fewer murders, fewer rapes, fewer robberies, fewer assaults. I say this to make this point: One of the things that I saw happening out in America when this crime bill was being debated in Congress is that the American people one day would wake up and they would cheer the Congress for trying to deal with crime. And then someone would raise a question about this effort or that effort or the other effort, and their cynicism would rise up because they said, "Oh, the crime rate has been going up for 30 years, and it's terrible, and it's never going to get any better, and nobody can do anything about it."

That is wrong. The crime rate can go down, just as it came up. And we are committed to taking it down. Ultimately, the purpose of the crime bill is to give people at the grassroots the power to lower the crime rate, not to hire more police, to have fewer crimes. That is the purpose of what we are doing. And it can happen. It happened in Odessa, Texas. It's happened in a lot of big cities around this country. It can happen all over America.

I know that Members of this new Congress have some ideas about fighting crime. I welcome those ideas. I ask them only to remember that we should do what was done in the last Congress: listen to the people in law enforcement; listen to the people in community organizations; listen to the people at the grassroots level who know how to catch criminals, but who also know how to prevent crime and lower the crime rate. If we listen to people at the grassroots level and enlist ourselves as your supporters, then we can continue to make progress on crime. But I also have to say that I don't think we should turn back on the progress we have made. We shouldn't give up on this community policing program. We ought to keep going until there are 100,000 more police on the street. And I'm going to do my dead-level best to make sure we don't turn back.

I'm going to come up with plenty of budget cuts. But we shouldn't cut the money that Lee Brown and people all over America need for drug prevention, drug education, drug treatment, things to lower the problem of drugs so we can lower the crime rate in that way. We shouldn't do that.

And even though we did not have a majority in both parties for the Brady bill, and we certainly didn't have a majority in both parties for the assault weapons ban last time, I think we ought to leave them right where they are. We

ought to stay with it, and go forward and implement it.

I think all of you know that there's one thing the skeptics said during the crime bill debate that was right. It wasn't an argument to vote against the crime bill, but it was true. We can pass all these laws and come up with all this money and all these prohibitions, but if we don't implement it right at the grassroots level, the crime rate won't go down. That is true. We could have 50 crime bills and a million police officers, and if the American people don't join in the fight, the crime rate won't go down.

So the last thing that I'd like to say is that if community policing is more than a deployment of police officers, and is really a philosophy of law enforcement, it is two words: police and community. That means that neighbors have to help neighbors, parents have to raise kids, that schools have to do things they didn't used to have to do. But if we do this together, then this community policing can be the banner of a safer America. And if we can lower the crime rate again, and make people feel safer on their streets, in their homes, and in their schools, we will begin to see this country coming together as a community again, we will begin to see people believing in our country again, we will begin to see people willing to make sacrifices for the common good again.

For all that all of you have done to that end, I thank you very much.

NOTE: The President spoke at 2:28 p.m. in the Great Hall at the Justice Department. In his remarks, he referred to Police Chief Jerry Sanders of San Diego, CA. Police Chief Brann of Hayward, CA, will administer the Department of Justice police hiring program.

Remarks on Presenting Medals for Service in Operation Uphold Democracy
December 20, 1994

Secretary Perry, Admiral Owens, members of the Joint Chiefs; to General Shelton and Mrs. Shelton, members of the Shelton family; to the representatives of each of our military services who served in Haiti and their families; all the

other distinguished guests here, welcome to the Rose Garden.

We gather today to honor General Shelton and members of our Armed Forces for their service to our Nation in Operation Uphold Democracy. All those who have served and all those who still serve in Haiti have served with extraordinary skill, courage, and dedication.

For 3 years, the United States and other countries throughout the world tried everything short of force to remove Haiti's illegal military regime and to restore its democratically elected government. It wasn't until the regime's leaders knew our armed forces were on the way that they agreed to step down peacefully.

Think for a moment where we would be today had we not acted and had General Shelton and the other members of our Armed Forces not performed their mission so admirably. The military regime would still be in power in Haiti, terrorizing the people there. Tens of thousands of refugees would continue to pose a threat to our region's stability. The march of democracy in the Americas would have suffered a severe setback. And the commitments of the United States in the international community would have proved empty.

Instead, we kept our word. President Aristide, Haiti's freely elected leader, has returned to office. The parliament is functioning. A sense of security and hope has replaced the climate of fear. The private sector is beginning the job of getting back on its feet. The rebuilding process has begun. And clearly our region is more stable and secure.

At the Summit of the Americas last week when we had 34 democratically elected leaders from our hemisphere, I think no one would dispute the fact that the emotional highlight of the weekend was President Aristide's speech in three languages, expressing his gratitude to those who supported freedom and democracy in Haiti.

General Shelton, your careful planning and your ability to adapt to a fast-changing situation were at the heart of our success in Haiti. The strong personal leadership, the steady hand, and the real determination that you, personally, conveyed to the military leaders of Haiti in the first days, from the first moment of your action there were, I know, absolutely critical to the success of this operation and to its peacefulness.

First, we asked you to prepare an innovative, integrated invasion force, drawing on the special capabilities of each of our services. Then, when the regime agreed at the 11th hour to leave, you had to switch gears immediately, and to ready our troops for a soft entry into Haiti.

On the ground, you have done a magnificent job of laying a secure foundation for the future. This has allowed 800 international police monitors from all around the world to work with an interim police force that is gaining the respect of the Haitian people. As a result, we've been able to draw down our own forces from 20,000 to about 6,000 at Christmas time. This number will soon decrease further as we transfer our mission in Haiti to the United Nations.

Through your efforts, General, Haiti today is democratic and free and much more secure. The Haitian people themselves, of course, must meet the difficult challenges ahead. It will take time for rebuilding and progress, but now at least all Haitians have a chance to work for a better future for themselves and their children.

The hand-painted signs we see in Haiti today say it all: Thank you, America. Today America says: Thank you, General. And thanks to the men and women of our military who served so well in Haiti.

In a few moments I will be honored to award General Shelton the Army Distinguished Service Medal. But first I want to recognize the exceptional concern the General has also shown for the men and women under his command. I know that their safety and their well-being were always his first priority. And for that our Nation is also grateful to General Shelton.

General, you requested that enlisted members from all our military branches join you today to receive the Armed Forces Expeditionary Medal on behalf of their respective services. The soldiers who stand before us are the finest of America's finest. Each also will be awarded an individual commendation for meritorious service in Haiti.

I'd like to recognize them now: from the Coast Guard, Radioman 1st Class Charles Brown; from the Air Force, Staff Sergeant John McCormick; from the Navy, Senior Chief Operations Specialist Samuel Wood; from the Marine Corps, Sergeant Paul Panici; from the Army, Staff Sergeant Morris Jones; and from the Special Forces, Sergeant 1st Class Shannon Davis. Each of you has helped to prove once again that our military is the best prepared, the best equipped, the best trained, the most devoted and highly motivated military in the entire world.

It is now my privilege to present all of you and General Shelton with your awards. Let our history recall that you answered the call of duty, you did your job, you advanced America's mission. Freedom and democracy are better as a result. Haiti's long night of fear has given way to a new day of hope.

NOTE: The President spoke at 2:47 p.m. in the Rose Garden at the White House. In his remarks, he referred to Adm. William A. Owens, USN, Vice Chairman of the Joint Chiefs of Staff; Lt. Gen. Henry H. Shelton, USA, commander of U.S. forces in Haiti; and General Shelton's wife, Lee.

Letter to Congressional Leaders Transmitting the Report on International Exchange Programs
December 20, 1994

Dear Mr. Speaker: (*Dear Mr. Chairman:*)

As required by section 229(a) of the Foreign Relations Authorization Act, Fiscal Years 1994 and 1995 (Public Law 103–236), I am submitting the enclosed final part of my report on the extent to which federally funded international exchange programs share similar objectives.

As I observed in my letter of July 28, 1994, United States Government educational, cultural, scientific, and professional exchange programs enhance communication and understanding between the United States and other societies. These programs are among our more effective tools for achieving long and intermediate range objectives of U.S. foreign policy.

The initial findings of the United States Information Agency (USIA) review of government-wide exchange programs concerned activities with foreign language and area studies dimensions. This analysis focuses on exchanges related to the encouragement of democratic processes abroad.

Strengthening democratic development and the intellectual foundations of democracy through the exchange of people and practical information is a vital complement to economic assistance to countries seeking to build democratic institutions and entrepreneurial cultures.

Programs that share similar objectives related to support of democratic development abroad are sponsored primarily by the Department of State, the Department of Commerce, the Department of Defense, the Department of Justice, the Department of Labor, the Inter-American Foundation, the National Endowment for Democracy, the Peace Corps, the U.S. Agency for International Development, the U.S. Institute of Peace, the Woodrow Wilson International Center for Scholars, and USIA. These programs are described in the enclosure to this letter.

As always, my Administration will continue to work closely with the Congress to realize our shared goals of improving efficiency and reducing costs.

Sincerely,

WILLIAM J. CLINTON

NOTE: Identical letters were sent to Thomas S. Foley, Speaker of the House of Representatives, and Claiborne Pell, chairman of the Senate Committee on Foreign Relations.

Teleconference on Empowerment Zones and Enterprise Communities
December 21, 1994

The President. Hello, can you all hear me? Governor Jones?

Gov. Brereton Jones. Yes, sir.

The President. Mayor Harris?

Mayor Elihu Harris. Yes.

The President. Mayor Campbell?

Mayor Bill Campbell. Yes, sir.

The President. Mayor Daley?

Mayor Richard M. Daley. Here.

The President. Mayor Cleveland—Cleaver. Mayor Cleaver?

Mayor Emanuel Cleaver II. Here.

The President. Mayor Steineger?

Mayor Joe Steineger. Here.

The President. Mayor Schmoke?

Mayor Kurt Schmoke. Yes, sir.

The President. Mayor Menino?

Mayor Thomas Menino. Here.

The President. Mayor Archer?

Mayor Dennis W. Archer. Here, Mr. President.

The President. Mayor Rendell?

Mayor Edward Rendell. Here.

The President. Mayor Webster?

Mayor Arnold Webster. Here, President.

The President. Mayor Rendell, that's the weakest "here" I ever heard out of you. Are you sure you're there? [*Laughter*]

Mayor Rendell. You don't want us to tell you what's happening here. You don't want to get into it. [*Laughter*]

The President. Mayor Giuliani?

Mayor Rudolph Giuliani. Hello, Mr. President.

The President. Is Congressman Rangel there with you?

Mayor Giuliani. Yes, he is.

Representative Charles B. Rangel. Hello, Mr. President.

The President. Watch him close——

Mayor Giuliani. Former Mayor Dinkins is here, also.

The President. Oh, great. It's good to hear your voice, Mayor.

David Dinkins. Thank you.

The President. Mayor White?

Mayor Michael R. White. I'm right here, Mr. President.

The President. Mayor Lanier?

Mayor Bob Lanier. Here, Mr. President.

The President. Jerry Rickett from Kentucky?

Jerry Rickett. Here, Mr. President.

The President. Willis Brumfield——

Willis Brumfield. Yes, sir, Mr. President.

The President. ——from Leflore County? Humberto Rodriguez?

Humberto Rodriguez. Good afternoon, Mr. President. Kika de la Garza's here.

The President. It's great to hear all of you. And I want to congratulate you for being selected as empowerment zones and supplemental zones and enhanced enterprise communities. As I'm sure you know, we had 500 applications from people all across America who wanted to be a part of this program, and yours were the

best. I hope you're all very, very proud of what you have done.

I want to thank the Vice President and Secretary Cisneros and the others in our administration who worked on setting up the genuinely competitive process to honestly review all of these applications. And I want to thank you for your participation, as well as all the others.

I know the Vice President wants to say a few words, but let me say that when I ran for President in 1992, I advocated setting up these empowerment zone ideas. I advocated seeing if we could have a partnership between the National Government, grassroots communities, and the private sector to get investment going in places where too many people have been left behind. And I believe that we can do it. We are not only making this announcement today, I want you to know we're going to stay with you all through this process. We're going to work hard with you. And we're going to make sure that all of us do our part to have a success.

[*At this point, the Vice President congratulated the winners and praised the efforts of Secretary Cisneros and Secretary Espy.*]

The President. I wanted to say just a word about a couple of things that were done. If I might—I wish I had time to talk about all these projects—but I wanted to say a special word of appreciation for Detroit getting more than $2 billion in private sector commitments to help revitalize the city, including a commitment by the auto companies to train and hire residents of empowerment zones, as well as local banks investing over a billion dollars in home-ownership and small businesses in the zones. That made a big difference because, after all, we've got to know that the private sector is going to carry the bulk of the load. And Mayor Archer, I want to congratulate you on that.

Mayor Archer. Thank you very much, Mr. President.

The President. And I also wanted to say something about the mid-delta project in Mississippi. You know, that's very near my home State and where I grew up. And I know a lot about the conflicts that have existed too long in the communities there. And I thought the spirit of cooperation that was manifested in the black and the white communities really made a big difference to me and to all of us when we reviewed this application. If you can keep that going, we're going to change a lot of people's preconceptions about what it's like in the Deep South, and we're also going to give a lot of people jobs and opportunities who don't have it. I want to congratulate you, Willis Brumfield, and all the people who worked with you on this application.

Mr. Brumfield. Thank you, Mr. President, and we are committed to see this on through to success.

The President. I know you'll do it.

I wanted to say, too, just a word about the joint projects, the one that won the empowerment zone and the other—that's Philadelphia and Camden and the other one in Kansas City, Missouri, and Kansas. We believe that regional cooperation is very, very important. And I want to congratulate the mayors of Philadelphia and Camden, here on the phone, I know, for showing the potential for regional cooperation across State lines. And I also want to congratulate Mayor Cleaver of Kansas City for what he did. I thank you for what you did——

[Mayor Cleaver of Kansas City, MO, said that he and Mayor Steineger of Kansas City, KS, intended to make the program work across State lines. Philadelphia Mayor Rendell said that Philadelphia, PA, and Camden, NJ, would also take a regional approach. Mayor Steineger then thanked the President for his initiative.]

The President. Thank you, Mayor Steineger.

I wanted to say a couple of more words. Chicago had over 200 organizations participating in the application. I've always thought that Chicago had the advantage of still having an enormous strength in its grassroots communities, but when I saw that 200 organizations had participated in the application process, that certainly is evidence of it. And it's a real tribute to Mayor Daley, to the leadership that you and others are providing out there.

Mayor Daley. Mr. President, I want to thank the community organizations, our fine elected officials—Senator Braun is here—former Congressman Dan Rostenkowski, who fought for this—elected officials providing not only jobs but economic opportunities for the people within the empowerment zones.

The President. I'm glad Dan Rostenkowski's there with you. And there's no telling how many times he talked to everybody about that application and reminded us that you had a couple hundred groups working on it. I hear him laughing in the background. I just want him to know

that, even though I'm getting older, I haven't lost my memory. *[Laughter]*

[The Vice President praised Baltimore's efforts to connect empowerment zone residents with major private employers, and Baltimore Mayor Schmoke thanked the Maryland congressional delegation for its hard work. The Vice President then praised New York's cooperative efforts among various levels of government, and New York Mayor Giuliani, Representative Rangel, and former Mayor Dinkins commended them also.]

The President. Well, let me just say a word of special appreciation to Charlie Rangel for one thing he did. When we were—when I brought this empowerment zone idea to the Congress, Charlie strongly urged that we not only have tax incentives but that we have some Federal investment to encourage some State and local investment and to show that the Government would be a partner with the private sector. And I think he was right about that. And I thank him for it. And I think we've got a stronger program today as a result of it.

I also want to say to Mayor Schmoke, I liked hearing—I could hear the smile in your voice. When I saw you a couple of days ago, you looked like an expectant father with worry in your eyes, and I couldn't say a word to you. So I hope you will forgive me, but—*[laughter]*.

Mayor Schmoke. I hope that I didn't look like I was pleading too much. *[Laughter]*

The President. It's never pleasant to see a grown man cry, but you did a graceful job of it.

Mayor Schmoke. I really do appreciate it. Everybody in the city does.

The President. I want to say a special word before we get off this telephone call about Atlanta, because—*[applause]*——

Mayor Steineger. *[Inaudible]*—could have had a crowd here in Kansas City.

The President. Well, I'd have done it earlier if I'd known you were all on the phone. *[Laughter]*

The thing I want to emphasize about Atlanta is the integration of the social services and the public safety and the physical development of the community to make what they call urban villages, and to do it in a way that coordinates what's being done with the Olympic games. I think that is so important that a city instead of trying to just emphasize everything that's going well and hiding all of its problems is going to try to use the run-up to the Olympics to actually solve its problems and show that effort in a positive way. And, Mayor Campbell, you deserve a lot of credit for that. That's a very impressive thing to do.

[*Atlanta Mayor Campbell thanked the President and Vice President and commended Gov. Zell Miller of Georgia on his efforts in education. Philadelphia Mayor Rendell thanked Senator Bradley for encouraging the two-State effort and thanked the Vice President. Cleveland Mayor White then promised a cooperative effort in his area to make the program work and thanked Representatives Stokes and Fingerhut.*]

Mayor Menino. Tom Menino from Boston. How are you?

The President. Mayor Menino?

Mayor Menino. How are you doing?

The President. Fine. How are you?

[*Mayor Menino thanked the President for his commitment to the cities and Senator Edward M. Kennedy for his efforts. Senator Kennedy thanked the Massachusetts congressional delegation and Mayor Menino. Houston Mayor Lanier thanked the President and assured him that program would work in Houston.*]

The President. Let me just say one thing. Mayor Lanier, I really think all of America is in your debt in proving that the crime rate can be reduced in a breathtaking fashion in a relatively short time. And if you can do as much with this assistance as you've done in reducing the crime rate, then we can all come to Houston and learn some things.

And I want to say to Mayor Menino, I've had the honor to be in Boston several times since you've been mayor, and it's wonderful to be in a place with that kind of energy and that kind of togetherness. And you deserve a lot of credit for it. We're looking forward to working with you.

Mayor Harris, were you on the line?

[*Oakland Mayor Harris thanked the President for his initiative and expressed hope that the Congress would be supportive.*]

The President. Thank you very much. I hope Congress will support us, too. We believe in this, and we're going to keep pushing it.

Mayor Harris. [*Inaudible*]—he's been very forthright in his commitment to the administra-

tion and certainly forthright in his advocacy on behalf of our city. And we hope that you'll extend, as we will, our gratitude for his help.

The President. Let me say right before we sign off, I want to give our friends in Kentucky, Governor Jones and Jerry Rickett, and Mr. Rodriguez and our friends in South Texas the opportunity to say anything they want to say before we sign off.

[*Mr. Rickett and Mr. Rodriguez, representatives of rural empowerment zones, expressed their appreciation.*]

The President. Let me just say a brief word to you, sir, and to all of you in these rural districts. I also want to emphasize very strongly how hard Secretary Mike Espy worked on these projects. He and I worked for years before I ever dreamed of running for President on the problems of rural economic development in the Mississippi Delta, which is still the poorest part of our country. And then when I had the chance to go to south Texas and a chance to go to eastern Kentucky in the campaign and to see what people were dealing with and what they were working with, it was obvious to me that we needed to try a different approach. And so I want to thank again Secretary Cisneros and Secretary Espy for the work they did and the long effort that all of us have made in the area of rural development, which is too often forgotten. We're really pulling for all of you.

And let me say to those of you in south Texas, you couldn't be better represented than you have been by Kika de la Garza. He talked to me so often about this project. And he cared so deeply about it. And he does deserve a lot of the credit for your success today.

[*Mayor Archer and a group of participants in Detroit wished everyone a Merry Christmas. Governor Jones of Kentucky then expressed his appreciation to the President.*]

The President. I thank you all. And I also want to send our congratulations to Los Angeles, which could not be on the telephone call today, but we're very proud of them and looking forward to working with them and all the other communities. I really believe that you all are going to do something special and different and really meaningful.

And I wish you a Merry Christmas. I want to give the Vice President a chance to say a couple of words, and we're going to sign off.

The Vice President. Congratulations again. Have a great holiday season, and Happy New Year. You've gotten a jump on a happy new year. Let's make the best of it.

The President. God bless you, folks.

NOTE: The teleconference began at 1:25 p.m. The President spoke from the Oval Office at the White House.

Remarks on Empowerment Zones and Enterprise Communities
December 21, 1994

Thank you very much. I want to thank the Vice President for his strong leadership in the Community Enterprise Board, Secretary Espy, Secretary Cisneros, Secretary Shalala, Attorney General Reno, the other members of the Cabinet and the administration who are here. And I congratulate all the communities who have won here today.

This is an especially happy day for me because this announcement completes a commitment that was rooted in the campaign I waged for President but far more in my personal history as a public servant. There are many people here in this room to whom I owe a great deal of gratitude. But I want to say a special word of thanks to all those who worked with me for years and years and years, before I ever thought of even running for President, on the complex job of developing poor and distressed areas.

Secretary Espy and I were partners a long time before we ever thought he'd ever be the Agriculture Secretary or I would be the President. I thank my friend, Bob Nash, from Arkansas for the work he's done in rural development. Henry Cisneros and I were having the conversations that we celebrate today for years before we were ever in the positions that we now hold. And there are others here, too numerous to mention, who were an inspiration to me because of what they did at the community level. But I'd like to mention in particular the outstanding work done by Andrew Cuomo, before he came to work at HUD, in New York and dealing with the problems of housing and homelessness.

I say this because I came to this job with the absolute conviction that most problems in America had been solved by somebody somewhere and that we would never solve any of our most fundamental problems unless we did it at the community level. And if you look at the work that we have done in this administration, the work that Attorney General has done in law enforcement; getting people together at the community level; what is embodied in the crime bill, community strength, taking money by reducing the size of the Federal Government and giving it back to the community; if you look at the work that we have done in human services with giving 21 States permission to pursue welfare reform and get through Federal rules and regulations, nine States permission to pursue the work of health care reform; if you look at the work we have done in education and training and the way the Federal laws have been rewritten to push more decisionmaking, more power down to the grassroots level, it is clear that to me, we have got to rely on the energy and the capacity of people to work at the community level where, frankly, they work in a far less partisan atmosphere than we have worked in Washington, where people deal with human problems in a human way and reach across the divisions of party and income and race and background to try to get something done. That is what I came to Washington to do.

If you look at any number of other areas, you will see that. If you look at the fact that we've been able to solve some of the long-standing environmental problems; if you look at some of the things that are being done by Director Brown in the drug control area; just over and over and over again, what we want to do is to empower people at the community level to make the most of their own lives by solving their problems, and have the Federal Government be a support to them for a change and not a burden.

That is what this is all about. And if I could construct a model of how it would all work in the end, it would be what national service does today, what the AmeriCorps program does.

It is a totally nonbureaucratic, nonpolitical, grassroots, creative, entrepreneurial way of solving human problems. That is what we ought to be about. And for all of you that worked on this program, for all of you that had anything to do with my personal history before I came to this job, I thank you for the contribution that you have made because this is a very important departure from the way the National Government has operated for years and years and years. And it is critical to the work that we must do here to restore a sense of opportunity and a sense of responsibility to this country and to rebuild the middle class.

If you look at the announcement that I made last week advocating a middle class bill of rights, looking forward to the next session of Congress, it furthers the goal of personal empowerment, recommending first of all, that people ought to be able to deduct the cost of post-high school education for themselves and their kids and have a tax break for raising their children. It advocates that we should let everybody save more money in an IRA, but also take it out for something other than retirement if they need to take care of themselves for education or first-time homebuying or health care or the care of a parent, building on the capacity of people to solve their own problems. But the most important thing we can do is to do it in a way that helps communities to grow, that helps families to grow, that helps individuals to prosper.

You know, we spent a lot of time in the last 2 years trying to clean up some of the problems we found here and fix things so that we could do things like what we celebrate today. We had to bring the deficit down in order to do that. We made a downpayment on middle class tax fairness by giving an income tax cut to working families with incomes under $25,000 of an average of $1,000 a year this year. That's something I'm very proud of because it shows that we're going in the right direction.

But because we've got the deficit down, we can move on to have these empowerment zones. We can move on now to do the kinds of things that are in the middle class bill of rights. And we should continue to work on it, always with the idea that at the end of the day the actions of government should empower people and communities to take more responsibility for their own lives and their own successes. That's what the family leave law was all about. That's what expanding Head Start was all about. That's what

changing the whole student loan law was all about, so more people could borrow money at lower interest rates to finance their college education. And that's what, as I said earlier, national service was all about, and it is certainly what the middle class bill of rights is all about.

I want to say, also, that we have to do this in a way that is responsible not only for today but for tomorrow as well. Too many times, because of the heat of this election or this election or the one just ahead, politicians have told people the easy answers without telling them the hard ones as well. And I want to say, I am especially proud of the fact that we have paid for these empowerment initiatives through reducing the size of the Federal Government, through getting rid of a lot of yesterday's Government so we would have more of tomorrow's opportunity.

This week, as you know, the Vice President and I announced another round of reinventing Government, of reductions that some of the Cabinet members here present took in their own operations to generate another $24 billion to pay for the middle class bill of rights. We will continue to do more of that.

Because we have been responsible and disciplined, the overall health of the economy is sound. We have produced more than 5.2 million new jobs in this country in the last 2 years, and we will continue to do that if we can keep overall economic conditions favorable. What we now have to do is to bring the benefits of those overall things to ordinary Americans. The middle class bill of rights will do it by having more tax fairness, focusing on education, focusing on growth.

All the community initiatives will do it, whether it's in the crime bill or the education bill or in the initiatives at HUD, or in national service. And this empowerment zone program will do it by saying to the American people, the Government's going to be a help to you, not a burden. Just imagine this, Chicago got 200 separate organizations to roll up their sleeves and work and agree on a project. You're lucky in Washington if you can get two people to agree to do that. [*Laughter*]

But out there where people live, where they're not worried about what's in today's headlines but what their children's lives are going to be like tomorrow, they can do it if we help them. Just imagine in Detroit, a city that was given up for dead 10 years ago, the private sector committed $2 billion to this endeavor. All we had to do was to put up the $100 million and the prospect of the tax benefits. How did it happen? Because of the energy generated at the local level just because the Federal Government said we want to help you decide your own future for a change. And I tell you, as you probably heard on the telephone call, I've been in the hills and hollows of Kentucky. I have walked up and down the poorest communities in America in the Mississippi Delta. I have been all over south Texas. I know those places. And they have good, smart people, too. And their children deserve a future, too. And all we did was to give them a chance to figure out how they can make a better future for themselves.

Now, that's what this administration is all about. That's what public life is all about out there on the main streets of America. And what we ought to do at this Christmas season is make a new year's resolution that next year with the middle class bill of rights, with more responsibility, with more empowerment, with more opportunity, that's what we're going to make public life like in Washington for a change.

Thank you, and God bless you all.

NOTE: The President spoke at 2:17 p.m. in Room 450 of the Old Executive Office Building.

Statement on the Death of Dean Rusk
December 21, 1994

Today we mourn the passing of Dean Rusk, who served our Nation with dignity and with strength as Secretary of State under Presidents Kennedy and Johnson. Dean Rusk belonged to that great generation of Americans who helped guide our Nation and its allies through the dangerous years of the cold war. The world has changed immeasurably since he served at the side of Presidents, but the principles he helped forge—steadfast American promotion of freedom and opposition to tyranny—are as vital as ever.

Dean Rusk's decency, and his loyalty to the Presidents whom he served and to those who served under him, remains a source of inspiration. When he concluded his 8 years as Secretary of State—the second longest tenure of any American who served in that position— President Johnson awarded him the Presidential Medal of Freedom, and he said, "The man who has served me most intelligently, faithfully, and nobly is Dean Rusk."

We will always treasure Dean Rusk's contribution to the United States. And we will honor his memory by always striving to emulate his example.

Statement on the Pacific Northwest Forest Plan
December 21, 1994

Today a U.S. District Court upheld the Northwest Forest Plan. This decision allows us to continue to move forward in pursuit of my commitment to the people and the environment of the Pacific Northwest and northern California.

For years, gridlock over the management of public forest lands created an uncertain future for the people of the region. It was a problem my administration inherited, and one that we made a priority to solve.

Just 7 months after the announcement of the forest plan, much has already been done. Unemployment for the entire region is at its lowest level in years, millions of dollars have been distributed to more than 100 communities for economic revitalization, and work is underway to analyze and restore damaged watersheds and protect millions of acres of old-growth habitat.

The plan approved today will provide for a sustainable level of timber harvesting, while protecting the environment.

In the true spirit of reinventing Government, the plan is a model of interagency cooperation with seven different Federal agencies working together, sharing information, and making joint decisions. It is the common sense way to do business and will prevent us from falling back to the days of gridlock. We are moving forward at last, and my administration and I remain committed to the people, to the economy, and to the environment of the Pacific Northwest and northern California.

Exchange With Reporters at Press Secretary Dee Dee Myers' Final Press Briefing
December 22, 1994

The President. I thought I should come in and get you out of hot water, since that's what you've been doing for me for years. [*Laughter*]

What I want to know is, why didn't our Hearts games make this list?

Press Secretary Myers. That's the things I will not miss.

The President. Oh. [*Laughter*]

Press Secretary Myers. Because that would be on my top 10 list of things I will miss.

Q. Do you have a list, Mr. President?

The President. Well——

Q. Favorite questions?

The President. Favorite questions? No, I—Dee Dee is my best Hearts partner. That's a trauma I'm trying to deal with here at Christmas time.

No, I have nothing to say about this business work. I just wanted to come in here and say in front of all of you how very grateful I am for everything Dee Dee has done for me since long before I became President, starting in our campaign. I reminded her of the first trip we took together was on a little bitty airplane, and I fell asleep, which was some sort of omen about how helpful I would be in answering difficult questions. And we've had a wonderful professional relationship. We've had a good personal friendship. I think she is one of the best people I have ever had the privilege of working with. And I'm really going to miss her. And I'm especially going to miss the card games. And Air Force One food is not all that bad. [*Laughter*]

Q. Who is going to replace her?

The President. No one is going to replace her.

And I want you all to—I'm going to cut you some slack. We don't have to talk anything serious today. This is Christmas season. And I wish you all a very merry Christmas. I hope you have a wonderful holiday. I hope you get some rest. And consistent with this entirely fiscally and otherwise responsible moment in our history, within those limits, I hope you have a little fun at Christmastime. [*Laughter*] And I hope you come back full of energy and bright-eyed and everything, because it's going to be a very interesting year next year. [*Laughter*] And I am really looking forward to it, more every day. [*Laughter*]

Q. Are you going to spend some more time with us in these kinds of informal Q&A sessions?

The President. Yes. [*Laughter*] Sure.

Q. Do you have an attitude about the Gingrich book?

Q. When you came in, we were just asking Dee Dee about that.

The President. You know, I made $36,000 a year for 12 years and was glad of it. I don't even know how to think in these terms. [*Laughter*]

Thank you very much. Merry Christmas.

NOTE: The President spoke at approximately 12:30 p.m. in the Briefing Room at the White House.

Nomination for Ambassador to Israel
December 22, 1994

The President today announced his intention to nominate Martin Indyk as Ambassador to Israel.

"I am proud to nominate Martin to this vital post," the President said. "I am confident his extensive background and experience in the region as well as his commitment to furthering the peace process and the role he has played as my adviser on these issues will serve to promote American interests in the Middle East."

NOTE: A biography of the nominee was made available by the Office of the Press Secretary.

Letter to Congressional Leaders on Continuation of the National Emergency With Respect to Libya
December 22, 1994

Dear Mr. Speaker: *(Dear Mr. President:)*

Section 202(d) of the National Emergencies Act (50 U.S.C. 1622(d)) provides for the automatic termination of a national emergency unless, prior to the anniversary date of its declaration, the President publishes in the *Federal Register* and transmits to the Congress a notice stating that the emergency is to continue in effect beyond the anniversary date. In accordance with this provision, I have sent the enclosed notice, stating that the Libyan emergency is to continue in effect beyond January 7, 1995, to the *Federal Register* for publication.

The crisis between the United States and Libya that led to the declaration on January 7, 1986, of a national emergency has not been resolved. The Government of Libya refuses to comply with United National Security Council Resolutions 731, 748, and 883 calling upon it to demonstrate, by concrete actions, its renunci-ation of terrorism. Such Libyan actions and policies pose a continuing unusual and extraordinary threat to the national security and vital foreign policy interests of the United States. For these reasons, the national emergency declared on January 7, 1986, and the measures adopted on January 7 and January 8, 1986, to deal with that emergency, must continue in effect beyond January 7, 1995.

Sincerely,

WILLIAM J. CLINTON

NOTE: Identical letters were sent to Thomas S. Foley, Speaker of the House of Representatives, and Albert Gore, Jr., President of the Senate. This letter was released by the Office of the Press Secretary on December 23. The notice of December 22 is listed in Appendix D at the end of this volume.

Letter to Congressional Leaders Reporting on Peacekeeping Operations in the Former Yugoslav Republic of Macedonia
December 22, 1994

Dear Mr. Speaker: *(Dear Mr. President:)*

I am providing you my fourth report on the continuing deployment of a U.S. Army peacekeeping contingent as part of the United Nations Protection Force (UNPROFOR) in the Former Yugoslav Republic of Macedonia (FYROM), consistent with the War Powers Resolution.

As you know, U.N. Security Council Resolution 795 established the UNPROFOR Macedonia mission as part of an effort to prevent the Balkan conflict from spreading and to contribute stability in the region. This mission was initially composed of a Nordic battalion, which deployed in early 1993. In July 1993, I directed that a U.S. Army contingent be deployed to FYROM in order to augment the UNPROFOR Macedonia mission, a deployment welcomed by the U.N. Security Council in its Resolution 842. In April of this year, the United Nations requested that we increase the U.S. contingent in order to replace elements of the Nordic battalion, which was being redeployed to Bosnia-Herzegovina. In response to this request, we augmented the U.S. contingent with the deployment of an additional U.S. Army reinforced company.

Through observation and monitoring operations along the FYROM border with Serbia, UNPROFOR Macedonia continues to be effective in preventing a spillover of the conflict. This mission has been carried out safely with no hostilities encountered and no U.S. casualties since the operation began. The mission has the support of both the FYROM Government and its people. Our forces will remain fully prepared not only to fulfill their peacekeeping mission,

but to defend themselves if necessary. The units currently comprising the U.S. contingent will soon be replaced by approximately 500 soldiers from 3rd Battalion, 5th Cavalry Regiment, 1st Armored Division, Kirchgons, Germany.

The U.S. contribution to the UNPROFOR Macedonia peacekeeping effort is part of our larger continuing commitment toward resolving the extremely difficult situation in the former Yugoslavia. I have continued the deployment of U.S. Armed Forces for these purposes pursuant to my constitutional authority to conduct foreign relations and as Commander in Chief.

I remain grateful for the continuing support the Congress has provided, and I look forward to continued cooperation with you in this endeavor.

Sincerely,

WILLIAM J. CLINTON

NOTE: Identical letters were sent to Thomas S. Foley, Speaker of the House of Representatives, and Robert C. Byrd, President pro tempore of the Senate. This letter was released by the Office of the Press Secretary on December 23.

Statement on the Observance of Kwanzaa
December 23, 1994

Warm greetings to everyone who is observing the festival of Kwanzaa.

A vibrant and energizing celebration, Kwanzaa offers millions an opportunity to embrace the rich cultural traditions of the African heritage. The seven principles of Kwanzaa, unity, self-determination, collective work and responsibility, cooperative economics, purpose, creativity, and faith, serve as vital tools in building hope and opportunity in our communities and throughout our country, and I am pleased that so many

of my fellow Americans are celebrating this year. All of you can be proud of your efforts to infuse the holiday season with diversity and new purpose.

Hillary joins me in wishing all of you a wonderful celebration and a Happy New Year.

NOTE: An identical message on the observance of Kwanzaa, December 26–January 1, was also made available by the White House.

Statement on Disaster Assistance for Florida and Georgia
December 23, 1994

I am designating Federal emergency assistance today to help those communities in Florida and Georgia damaged by the recent severe

weather. The people of both Franklin County, Florida, and Macon, Georgia, have worked hard to help those directly affected by the storm.

As you continue with the cleanup, I hope this Federal assistance will aid in the economic recovery of both communities.

NOTE: This statement was included in a statement by the Press Secretary announcing emergency funding to help Florida and Georgia recover from damage caused by Tropical Storm Alberto.

Appointment for the National Bankruptcy Review Commission
December 23, 1994

The President today announced his intention to appoint Representative Michael Synar as Chair, and Jay Alix and Babette A. Ceccotti to be members of the National Bankruptcy Review Commission.

"I am pleased to name Mike Synar to the Bankruptcy Review Commission. Over the years, we have worked closely together, and I have a great deal of respect and admiration for him and the work he has accomplished during his 15 years in the Congress. As he has shown us in the past, he will serve the American people with efficiency and integrity," said the President.

NOTE: Biographies of the appointees were made available by the Office of the Press Secretary.

The President's Radio Address
December 24, 1994

Good morning; Merry Christmas; Season's Greetings. All across our country, families are gathering to share this joyous time and to give thanks for the good things in our lives.

This holiday season, one of the greatest blessings of all is that our Nation is at peace, freedom is on the march, and the world is a safer place than it was a year ago. I'm proud of our efforts to turn conflict into cooperation, to transform fear into security, to replace hatred with hope. In a world that is ever more bound together, those efforts have been good for millions of people around the globe, and very good for America.

Perhaps most important of all, for the first time since the dawn of the nuclear age, for the first time in nearly half a century, parents can put their children to bed at this Christmas season knowing that nuclear weapons from the former Soviet Union are no longer pointed at those children. Just this month, we signed the START I agreement with Russia that guarantees the elimination of thousands of missiles from the former Soviet arsenal and clears the way for further reduction. And Belarus, Kazakhstan, and Ukraine, three republics of the former So-

viet Union, are now fulfilling their commitments to give up every one of the weapons they inherited after the collapse of the Soviet Union. Finally, in North Korea, our firm diplomacy secured an agreement that requires that country first to freeze and then to dismantle its nuclear program, all under international inspections.

On a separate note, let me say that our thoughts, Hillary's and mine, and I know all of America's, are with the family of Chief Warrant Officer Hilemon, who was killed last week in a tragic incident in North Korea. We are pleased that his remains have been returned to his family, and we are hopeful that his crewmate, Chief Warrant Officer Hall, will soon be back with his family.

Our steady diplomacy has helped to achieve real progress on many fronts. But when necessary, our troops have also proved themselves ready to defend our national interests, to back up our commitments, and to promote peace and security. For 3 years, a brutal military regime terrorized the Haitian people and caused instability in our hemisphere. It wasn't until the regime knew our troops were on their way that finally they agreed to step down peacefully and to return power to the democratically elected government. Now, under President Aristide, Haiti is free, democratic, and more secure. Its people have a chance to rebuild their nation. Our hemisphere is more democratic and more stable, and that's good for America.

When Iraq again threatened the stability of the Persian Gulf, I ordered our troops, ships, and planes to the region to stop a would-be aggressor in his tracks. In this vital part of the world, too, we have protected the peace.

I know all Americans share my pride in the brave men and women of our Armed Forces who are standing watch for freedom and security today and in this holiday season in Haiti and the Persian Gulf and, indeed, all around the world. I wish all our troops could come home for the holidays, but those who aren't are doing important work for our Nation. And as you gather in your homes this week, I hope you'll join me in a prayer for their well-being and the health and happiness of their families.

All around the world, our efforts to build peace have contributed to progress in solving what once seemed to be unsolvable problems. In South Africa, the long night of apartheid has given way to a new day of freedom. In Ireland, after centuries of struggle, a lasting set-tlement between Catholics and Protestants is finally within reach. And in the Holy Land, so close to the hearts of many of us at this time of year, Israelis and Arabs are turning the page on the past and embracing a future of peace.

Of course, there are still too many people, from Bosnia to the refugee camps outside Rwanda, who are plagued by violence and cruelty and hatred. And we must continue our efforts to help them find peace. But we should remember how many people around the world are moving toward freedom and how fortunate we are here in America to have been able to help them to move toward freedom. To them, America is a beacon of hope. They admire our values and our strength. They see in us a nation that has been graced by peace and prosperity. They look to us for leadership and for eternal renewed energy and progress.

For Hillary and for myself, I want to wish you and your loved ones a safe and happy holiday.

God bless you all, and God bless America.

NOTE: The address was recorded at 1:40 p.m. on December 22 in the Map Room at the White House for broadcast at 10:06 a.m. on December 24.

Christmas Greeting to the Nation
December 24, 1994

The President. On this special day, we send our best wishes to you and your family, and especially to the families of our service men and women who are so many miles away from home this Christmas, doing America's work overseas, keeping the peace in the Persian Gulf, and bringing freedom and democracy to Haiti. We salute them as they make the world a safer place for all of us, for our children and for future generations.

Hillary Clinton. And we thank all of you who are giving your time today serving others, the police and fire and medical staffs on duty and all the mothers and fathers, friends and volunteers who are caring for loved ones and neigh-bors nearby. Thank you all for spreading good will and for showing what the true spirit of Christmas is all about.

The President. As 1994 comes to a close, we wish everyone the joy and peace of this blessed season and good health and happiness throughout the coming year. Enjoy the holiday.

Hillary Clinton. And have a Merry Christmas.

The President. And a Happy New Year.

NOTE: The greeting was videotaped at 1:30 p.m. on December 16 in the Diplomatic Reception Room at the White House for broadcast on December 24. A tape was not available for verification of the content of these remarks.

Remarks Announcing the Nomination of Dan Glickman To Be Secretary of Agriculture and an Exchange With Reporters
December 28, 1994

The President. Good morning. I am very pleased that Dan Glickman has accepted my offer to become the next Secretary of Agriculture. He comes to the Cabinet after a distinguished 18-year career representing Wichita and south central Kansas in the House of Representatives. During that period, he rose to prominence on the House Agriculture Committee and became a leading spokesman for American agriculture and a key architect of the last four farm bills. His knowledge, experience, his understanding of the needs of the American farmer make him exactly the right person to be Secretary of Agriculture in 1995 when we will be writing the next farm bill.

I've told Dan that I expect him to continue being a vocal advocate of the interest of American agriculture and to carry on the groundbreaking work done by Secretary Mike Espy during the last 2 years. I am very proud of the work that our administration, under the leadership of Secretary Espy, has done for America's farmers and ranchers and for America's taxpayers.

Mike Espy has been tireless in his efforts to expand trading opportunities. I can tell you as a citizen of the largest rice-growing State in America, I never thought I would live to see the day when American rice would be available in Japanese markets. But thanks to Mike Espy, it is.

The reorganization that he has put into effect at the United States Department of Agriculture is the most sweeping in 50 years. And in many ways, it's the prototype of the plans we have to streamline the entire Federal Government to make it work better for the American people.

Mike Espy has been a partner of ours in developing the empowerment zones for distressed rural areas where we try to solve our most fundamental economic problems by creating partnerships at the grassroots level to help people help themselves. When livelihoods and lives were threatened by the awful floods and natural disasters in the Midwest and elsewhere, Secretary Espy managed our agriculture relief efforts with speed, compassion, and confidence. He did a superb job. In the area of crop insur-

ance, in the area of food safety, in so many other areas Secretary Espy and his administration were friends of the American farmers.

I am confident that Congressman Glickman will not only carry on the innovations begun by Secretary Espy but break new ground in our efforts to increase farm exports and bridge the differences between rural and urban Members of Congress.

I can say one thing that has pleased me greatly over the last year or so, and that is to travel around America and have farmers come up to me and say that they now consider the Department of Agriculture a friend and not a problem in their efforts to produce food for the United States and for the world. It will be our goal to continue that as we work so hard to balance the concerns of farmers and ranchers, consumers, environmentalists, and others.

I know Dan Glickman will meet this challenge. He has always been more interested in solving problems for people than scoring political points. The many awards and the recognition he has received from farm groups, from environmental groups, from consumers testify to his fairness and to his ability. I picked him for this job because the Department of Agriculture and rural America more than ever need a leader who is experienced, aggressive, and innovative. I know he will be an advocate and a spokesman for making sure that American agriculture enters the 21st century on a prosperous and solid foundation. Our agricultural system is the envy of the world, and it must remain so.

I also chose Dan Glickman for his common sense and his good humor. He says he always wears a sunflower on his lapel to remind him of where he's from, the values of the heartland that make him what he is. I hope and expect he will keep wearing that sunflower and keep us in a sunny disposition.

Mr. Glickman.

[At this point, Representative Glickman made brief remarks.]

North Korea

Q. Mr. President, what do you hear about the talks in North Korea? And would you hold up that January 21st oil shipment if Airman Hall is not released?

The President. Well, let me say first of all that we have made it clear to the North Koreans that we want the prompt release of Airman Hall and that there is no reason for his detention. He was on a routine training mission; that's all. They made an error, which we have acknowledged, and drifted into North Korean airspace.

We now have an administration official in North Korea, as you know, and talks are ongoing. And I think it would be premature for me to say anything else at this time. Let's give our people there a chance to do their work and see what happens.

Q. Are we asking for an apology, and isn't there a split in the North Korean Government between the military and the——

The President. I think it would be better for us to say nothing until my representative there has a chance to do his work. And we are in constant contact with him; he's working hard. We want Airman Hall released. There is no reason to detain him. It was a routine training mission. Anything else would be premature at this time.

Thank you.

NOTE: The President spoke at 10:14 a.m. in the Rose Garden at the White House.

Letter to Congressional Leaders Transmitting a Report on Cyprus
December 28, 1994

Dear Mr. Speaker: (Dear Mr. Chairman:)

In accordance with Public Law 95–384 (22 U.S.C. 2373(c)), I am submitting to you this report on progress toward a negotiated settlement of the Cyprus question. The previous report covered progress through September 30, 1994. The current report covers October 1, 1994 through November 30, 1994.

During this period, senior U.S. officials met frequently with President Clerides and other officials of the Republic of Cyprus. In late October, Greek-Cypriot leader Clerides and Turkish-Cypriot leader Denktash had five face-to-face meetings in Nicosia under the auspices of the United Nations. No concrete agreements were reached, but all the main issues involved in a settlement were addressed. Mr. Clerides has stated his willingness to continue discussions if a substantive basis for negotiations is established

within the framework of U.N. resolutions and the high-level agreements of 1977 and 1979.

In addition, Mr. Denktash wrote to U.N. Secretary General Boutros-Ghali on November 21 reaffirming his commitment to a bizonal, bicommunal federation. He has also stated his willingness to enter immediate negotiations with Mr. Clerides. We hope that these statements will facilitate efforts to develop a basis for immediate talks between the two leaders on an early implementation of the U.N.-proposed package of confidence-building measures and on an overall solution.

Sincerely,

WILLIAM J. CLINTON

NOTE: Identical letters were sent to Thomas S. Foley, Speaker of the House of Representatives, and Claiborne Pell, chairman of the Senate Committee on Foreign Relations.

Statement on the Resignation of R. James Woolsey as Director of Central Intelligence
December 28, 1994

Jim Woolsey has been a staunch advocate of maintaining an intelligence capability that is sec-

ond to none. He has taken initiatives to streamline and improve costly collection systems, improve the quality of both analysis and intelligence, and correct security and management lapses in the critical area of counterintelligence. Jim Woolsey deserves the gratitude of all Americans for his service to our country. He has my deep appreciation.

Intelligence is a vital element of our Nation's power and influence. The men and women of U.S. intelligence must know how grateful I am for their dedicated and often unheralded service.

I remain committed to ensuring that they have the support, resources, and leadership needed to continue their outstanding service to their country.

NOTE: This statement was included in a White House statement announcing that the President had accepted the resignation of R. James Woolsey as Director of Central Intelligence at the CIA.

Statement on Grants to Projects Aiding the Homeless
December 29, 1994

It is imperative that we not turn our backs on the Nation's homeless. The number of homeless families and young people suffering from abuse and neglect continues to rise. It is my hope that these grants will help those who need our help the most. I am also pleased that AmeriCorps members will be engaged in the

struggle to end homelessness. This is an example of national service at its best.

NOTE: This statement was included in a White House statement announcing the award of grants to projects aiding the homeless.

Letter to Congressional Leaders on Trade With Russia
December 29, 1994

Dear Mr. Speaker: (*Dear Mr. President:*)
On September 21, 1994, I determined and reported to the Congress that the Russian Federation is in full compliance with the freedom of emigration criteria of section 402 and 409 of the Trade Act of 1974. This action allowed for the continuation of most-favored-nation (MFN) status for Russia and certain other activities without the requirement of a waiver.

As required by law, I am submitting an updated report to the Congress concerning the

emigration laws and policies of the Russian Federation. You will find that the report indicates continued Russian compliance with U.S. and international standards in the area of emigration.
Sincerely,

WILLIAM J. CLINTON

NOTE: Identical letters were sent to Thomas S. Foley, Speaker of the House of Representatives, and Albert Gore, Jr., President of the Senate.

Remarks on the Release of Bobby Hall by North Korea and an Exchange With Reporters
December 29, 1994

The President. Good evening. I have just spoken with Army Chief Warrant Officer Bobby Hall. He's crossed the Demilitarized Zone to

freedom. He's safe. His medical condition is currently being evaluated. But we had a good visit, and he said he was feeling well.

Chief Warrant Officer Hall was held for too long after his helicopter strayed off course on a routine training mission. But we are very glad that he has been released and is now in freedom.

Earlier this evening, I called his wife, Donna, to tell her that he would be released and how pleased we all were. I know that all Americans join me in sharing the Halls' happiness that they and their loved ones will now be able to be together and celebrate New Year's, reunited as a family.

At the same time, I know I can speak for all Americans in saying that we, once again, send our deep condolences to the family of Chief Warrant Office David Hilemon, who died in the same incident. So as we welcome the release of Chief Warrant Officer Hall we must also remember the supreme sacrifice and the service made by his comrade in arms.

We wish all the families our best. We thank them all for their service and their devotion of our country. We wish them Godspeed in the new year.

Thank you very much.

Q. Mr. President, can you tell us, sir, what the United States may have given up in this deal? And the fact that the agreement signed talks about future contacts with the North, was that a concession to the North, and does that cut out South Korea?

The President. No. And the briefings will make that clear. The terms of the agreement are clear from their own words. And we were faithful to all of our commitments to our allies and to our commitments to our own policy.

And I want to thank the team that worked very hard on this. They did a very good job. They performed with dedication, with great discipline, and I'm very pleased by the way it was handled.

Thank you.

NOTE: The President spoke at 10:50 p.m. in the Briefing Room at the White House.

Statement on the Attacks on Women's Clinics in Boston, Massachusetts
December 30, 1994

I strongly condemn the meaningless violence which abruptly ended the lives of two women and wounded five others in Massachusetts today.

Violence has no place in America. No matter where we stand on the issue of abortion, all Americans must stand together in condemning this tragic and brutal act. Nine years ago, President Reagan, a staunch foe of abortion, called for "a complete rejection of violence as a means of settling this issue." We would do well to heed those words today.

We must protect the safety and freedom of all our citizens. I am strongly committed to ending this form of domestic terrorism. I have called for a thorough investigation into this attack, and Attorney General Reno and FBI Director Freeh have already begun that task. I urge local officials to work closely with the Federal law enforcement community.

Hillary and I extend our deepest sympathy to the friends and families of those who were murdered. I speak for all Americans in expressing my hope for a full and complete recovery for those who were wounded.

The President's Radio Address
December 31, 1994

Good morning. The celebration of the New Year is an occasion for optimism and hope; it's full of dreams for the years ahead. At the same time, it's important that we take last year's lessons with us into the future, which is exactly why we make New Year's resolutions. They're an avowal to work even harder in the coming year to be the best we can be.

New Year's is also a very good time to think about what we want for America, as well as for our own families in the year ahead, and about what each of us can do to make our great Nation the best that it can be.

My New Year's resolution to all of you is simple: I'm going to keep doing the work we have begun to help Americans compete and win in the new global economy and to restore the American dream for middle class families.

First and foremost, we should do nothing to jeopardize the economic recovery we have helped to create over the last 2 years. Our deficit reduction plan has already cut our deficit by $700 billion. That's over $10,000 of debt for every American family. The economic strategy we have pursued, reducing the deficit, expanding trade, investing in the education and training of our people in the technologies of the future, this strategy has helped to produce over 5 million new jobs in the last 2 years and, in 1994, more high-wage jobs than in the previous 5 years combined.

We're cutting the Federal bureaucracy by over 272,000 people to its smallest size in 30 years. And with these cuts in Government, we've used the savings to invest in the American people, to expand Head Start, to make college loans more affordable to 20 million Americans, and already giving a tax cut to over 15 million working families with incomes under $27,000 a year.

But last year made it very clear that all the good statistics in the world don't necessarily mean more money in the pockets of working Americans or more security and peace of mind for them. Most Americans haven't had a pay increase in this recovery. Most Americans are working longer work weeks than they were 10 years ago. Over a million Americans in working families lost their health insurance in 1994. And as other costs go up, disposable income and job security go down. So the average American is simply not receiving enough benefit from this robust economic recovery. And we have to keep working until we change that.

Two weeks ago, I proposed a middle class bill of rights, four new ideas to help middle class Americans build a future that lives up to their dreams.

First, to help Americans get the skills and education they need to get and keep high-paying jobs, I proposed that college tuition, community college costs, costs for graduate school, professional school, vocational education, or worker training be fully deductible from your taxable income, phased up to $10,000 a year if your family makes less than $120,000 a year. Second, to better support working families raising children, if your family makes $75,000 a year or less, I propose a tax cut phased up to $500 for every child under 13. Third, if your family makes less than $100,000 a year, I propose allowing you to put $2,000 a year tax-free into an individual retirement account, but also to enable you to withdraw the money tax-free for education, for buying a first home, for paying for health care expenses, or for the care of an elderly parent. Finally, I want to take the billions of dollars that Government now spends on job-training programs of all kinds and make that money directly available to working Americans, to spend as you decide when you need to learn new skills to get a new job or a better job.

As we do this, we must not go back to the irresponsible practices of the past, back to trickle-down economics and exploding the deficit. Every single penny of the middle class bill of rights that I propose is paid for by dramatic cuts in the Government, which I have proposed. An important part of my New Year's resolution is this: I won't allow anyone to destroy the progress we have made in reducing the deficit.

On this New Year's Eve, I want to welcome the new Congress. I ask them to put aside partisan differences, as I pledge to do, and join me in a New Year's resolution to do everything we can to help Americans prosper; to reduce yesterday's Government but help Government stay on the side of American families; to give the middle class tax relief but to do it responsibly, without exploding the deficit; to keep investing in education and job training; and to make our tax relief targeted toward the future, toward raising children, educating and training people, toward the things which make America great.

I want to close by asking all of you to join me as well. Nothing we do here will succeed unless each of you takes a personal responsibility first to develop your own capacity and those of your family members and then to rekindle a sense of community and common purpose in America. We are not enemies in this country. We are all in this together. We are going up or down together. With all of our diversity and differences, unless we work together, we can never make America the best it can be. So let's all make a New Year's resolution to face the future challenges together so that we can realize together the opportunities that lie ahead.

Tomorrow, as you visit with your friends and your family, I hope you'll talk about the ideas in the middle class bill of rights. In the coming weeks, when you're back at work or when you're on the phone with friends, I hope you'll talk about the future and about the future you want for your families and your country. And I hope you'll do a lot of listening to each other and arguing with each other, but don't forget for a moment that we have more in common than what divides us. This is the great source of our abiding strength.

Hillary and I wish you and your family a very happy New Year. Please be careful tonight, and thanks for listening.

NOTE: The address was recorded at 10:55 a.m. on December 28 in the Roosevelt Room at the White House for broadcast at 10:06 a.m. on December 31.

Statement on the Cessation of Hostilities in Bosnia
December 31, 1994

I welcome the agreement of the parties for a 4-month cessation of hostilities in Bosnia.

We hope it will be respected fully and pave the way for a negotiated settlement that brings peace to all the long-suffering people of Bosnia.

We applaud the flexibility that the parties have shown and commend the United Nations and former President Carter for their efforts.

We will be working with our Contact Group partners, the United Nations, and the parties in a renewed effort to seize this opportunity for peace.

Appendix A—Digest of Other White House Announcements

The following list includes the President's public schedule and other items of general interest announced by the Office of the Press Secretary and not included elsewhere in this book.

August 1

In the morning, the President traveled to Jersey City, NJ, where he met with families from the State to discuss their problems with the health care system. In the late afternoon, he returned to Washington, DC.

August 2

In the evening, the President and Hillary Clinton attended a Democratic National Committee fundraiser at a private residence in Oxon Hill, MD.

The President declared major disasters in Oregon and Washington following severe damage to the ocean salmon fishing industries caused by the El Niño weather pattern and recent drought.

The White House announced that the President has invited President Leonid Kuchma of Ukraine to Washington, DC, for an official working visit on November 29.

The President announced his intention to appoint Dolores Kohl as a member of the White House Commission on Presidential Scholars.

The President announced his intention to nominate the following individuals to the National Science Board:

Eve L. Menger;
Claudia Mitchell-Kernan;
Diana S. Natalicio;
Robert M. Solow;
Warren M. Washington; and
John A. White.

The President announced his intention to appoint the following individuals to the National Advisory Council on Indian Education:

Joseph Abeyta;
Agnes Cavis;
Rosemary Ackley Christensen;
Mark Maryboy;
Aleta Paisano-Suazo;
Janine Pease Windy Boy;
Scott Ratliff; and
Sherry Red Owl.

August 3

The President announced his intention to appoint Barbara Blum, LaDonna Harris, Loren Kieve, and Catherine Baker Stetson to the Institute of American Indian and Alaska Native Culture and Arts Development Board of Trustees.

The President announced his intention to appoint Kit Dobelle as a member of the White House Commission on Presidential Scholars.

August 4

The President announced his intention to nominate Herschelle Challenor to the National Security Education Board.

The President announced his intention to nominate Sheldon C. (Shay) Bilchik as Administrator of the Office of Juvenile Justice and Delinquency Prevention at the Department of Justice.

August 5

In the afternoon, the President and Hillary and Chelsea Clinton went to Camp David, MD.

The President announced his intention to nominate Kenneth Spencer Yalowitz as Ambassador to Belarus.

The President announced his intention to appoint Joseph M. Aragon, Stephen R. Colgate, and Kenneth Young as members of the Board of Directors of Federal Prison Industries.

August 6

In the afternoon, the President traveled from Camp David, MD, to Detroit, MI, where he attended the "Michigan Salutes the President" dinner. He returned to Camp David in the evening.

August 8

In the morning, the President and Hillary and Chelsea Clinton returned to Washington, DC. Later in the morning, the President met with the Law Enforcement Steering Committee.

The President announced his intention to nominate Vincent Sorrentino to be a member of the Advisory Board of the Saint Lawrence Seaway Development Corporation at the Department of Transportation.

August 9

In the morning, the President met with business leaders to discuss health care reform.

The President announced his intention to appoint Jorge Perez to the National Council on the Arts.

The White House announced that the President has directed that the Deputy Secretary of Defense and the Director of Central Intelligence conduct an immediate inquiry into the National Reconnaissance Office headquarters construction project and that the project be declassified.

August 10

The President announced his intention to nominate Frederick Pang to be Assistant Secretary of Defense for Force Management.

The President announced his intention to appoint John C. Phillips as a member of the Korean War Veterans Memorial Advisory Board.

The President announced his intention to appoint the following individuals to the President's Board of Advisors on Historically Black Colleges and Universities:

Lloyd (Vic) Hackley;
Lucille Ish;
Robert Albright;
Oswald P. Bronson;
Ramona Hoage Edelin;
Sebetha Jenkins;
Arthur E. Johnson;
Adib Akmal Shakir;
Dolores Spikes;
Arthur E. Thomas;
Valora Washington;
Bernard C. Watson; and
Barbara D. Wills-Duncan.

August 11

In an afternoon ceremony at the White House, the President received diplomatic credentials from Ambassadors Erstein Mallet Edwards of Saint Kitts and Nevis, Ekwow Spio-Garbrah of Ghana, Roberto Flores Bermudez of Honduras, Sonia Picado of Costa Rica, Snezhana Botusharova of Bulgaria, Pedro Echeverria of Venezuela, Tuleutai Suleymenov of Kazakhstan, John Biehl of Chile, and Yuliy Vorontsov of Russia.

Later in the afternoon, the President met with President Meles Zenawi, head of the transnational government of Ethiopia.

The President announced his intention to nominate Bruce Morrison as Chair of the Federal Housing Finance Board.

The President announced his intention to nominate J. Clifford Hudson as a member and Chair of the Board of Directors of the Securities Investor Protection Corporation.

The President announced his intention to nominate Patricia Hill Williams as a member of the Inter-American Foundation Board of Governors.

The President announced his intention to appoint Kristine Norosz as a member of the International Pacific Halibut Commission.

The President announced his intention to appoint Billie Maxine Glory and A. Michael Neimeyer to the National Advisory Council on Indian Education.

August 12

In the morning, following a breakfast with Cabinet members, the President traveled to Minneapolis, MN.

In the evening, the President returned to Andrews Air Force Base, MD, where he was joined by Hillary and Chelsea Clinton. They then went to Camp David, MD.

The President named Jodie R. Torkelson as Deputy Assistant to the President for Management and Administration, effective September 1.

The President announced his intention to nominate Lori Esposito Murray to be Assistant Director for the Multilateral Affairs Bureau, U.S. Arms Control and Disarmament Agency.

August 14

In the morning, the President and Hillary and Chelsea Clinton traveled from Camp David, MD, to Temple Hills, MD, where they attended services at the Full Gospel A.M.E. Zion Church. The President and Hillary Clinton returned to Camp David, MD, in the afternoon.

August 15

In the morning, the President and Hillary Clinton returned to the White House from Camp David.

The President announced his intention to appoint Alan Krueger as Chief Economist at the Department of Labor.

The President announced his intention to appoint Gary Rodrigues and Lucy Williams to the Advisory Council on Unemployment Compensation.

The President announced his intention to appoint the following individuals to be members of the National Commission for Employment Policy:

Clayola Brown;
Warren Frelund;
Frank Garrison;
Edward Shumaker; and
Arthur White.

August 16

In the evening, the President met with Republican Members of Congress to discuss anticrime legislation. Later, the President had a telephone conversation with President Kim Yong-sam of South Korea.

August 17

In the afternoon, the President met with Dr. C. Everett Koop, former Surgeon General of the Public Health Service. Following the meeting, the President had lunch with the Vice President.

August 22

The White House announced the President will attend the summit of the Asia-Pacific Economic Cooperation forum in Indonesia, November 14–16. The President also has accepted the invitations of President Fidel Ramos of the Philippines for a state visit in Manila on November 13 and of President Soeharto of Indonesia for a state visit in Jakarta on November 16.

August 24

The White House announced that President Nelson Mandela of South Africa has accepted the President's invitation to make a state visit to Washington, DC, October 4–6.

The President announced his intention to nominate Yerker Andersson, Audrey McCrimon, Debra Robinson, and Irving Zola as members of the National Council on Disability.

The President announced his intention to nominate Rhea L. Graham to be Director of the U.S. Bureau of Mines at the Department of the Interior.

The President announced his intention to nominate Alfred H. Moses to be Ambassador to Romania.

August 26

In the evening, the President and Hillary and Chelsea Clinton traveled to Martha's Vineyard, MA, for a vacation.

The President announced his intention to nominate Peter Jon de Vos to be Ambassador to Costa Rica.

The White House announced that the President has nominated Gen. Ronald R. Fogelman, USAF, to be Chief of Staff of the Air Force.

The White House announced that the President has asked a delegation of Americans, headed by C. Payne Lucas, president of Africare, to travel on his behalf to Burundi, Rwanda, and eastern Zaire, August 27–31. The delegation will urge resolution of the political crisis in Burundi and review relief efforts for Rwandan refugees.

August 29

The President announced his intention to appoint Anita Arnold to be a member of the Board of Trustees of the John F. Kennedy Center for the Performing Arts.

September 2

The President announced his intention to appoint R. Keith Higginson as a member of the Western Water Policy Review Advisory Commission.

September 5

In the morning, the President traveled from Martha's Vineyard, MA, to Bath, ME, where he toured the U.S.S. *Laboon* under construction at the Bath Iron Works Corp. In the afternoon, he returned to Martha's Vineyard.

September 6

The President announced his intention to nominate George J. Opfer to be Inspector General for the Federal Emergency Management Agency.

The President announced his intention to nominate Jacquelyn L. Williams-Bridgers to be Inspector General for the Department of State.

The President announced his intention to appoint Jeffrey H. Smulyan as Head of the U.S. Delegation to the International Telecommunications Union Plenipotentiary Conference in Kyoto, Japan, September 19–October 15.

September 7

In the afternoon, the President and Hillary Clinton returned from a vacation on Martha's Vineyard, MA, to Washington, DC, where they stayed at Blair House, their residence until completion of remodeling of the Residence at the White House.

The President announced his intention to appoint Ralph B. Everett, Burnett Joiner, Earl S. Richardson, and Myer L. Titus to the President's Board of Advisors on Historically Black Colleges and Universities.

September 8

The President announced his intention to nominate Debbie Branson as Vice Chair and public member of the Board of Directors of the Securities Investor Protection Corporation.

September 9

In the morning, the President traveled to New Orleans, LA, where he attended the Democratic National Committee Business Leadership Forum luncheon and met with the executive board of the National Conference of Black Mayors. In the afternoon, he returned to Washington, DC.

The President announced his intention to nominate Norwood J. Jackson, Jr., as Inspector General for the Federal Deposit Insurance Corporation.

The President announced his intention to nominate James (Bum) Atkins as Chair and member and Scott Lukins as a member of the Federal Retirement Thrift Investment Board.

The President announced his intention to nominate Martha Farnsworth Riche of Maryland as Director of the Bureau of the Census, Department of Commerce.

The President announced his intention to appoint John Roth to be a member of the U.S. Holocaust Memorial Council.

September 10

In the late afternoon, the President and Hillary Clinton hosted a reception honoring the PBS television series "Baseball" on the South Lawn. In the evening, they went to Camp David, MD.

September 11

In the morning, the President and Hillary Clinton traveled to Aberdeen, MD. In the afternoon, they returned to Camp David.

September 12

In the morning, the President and Hillary Clinton returned to the White House.

The President announced his intention to nominate Charles E. Redman to be Ambassador to Germany and Marc Grossman to be Ambassador to Turkey.

September 13

In the evening, the President attended the Professional Golfers Association President's Cup Dinner at the White House.

The President declared a major disaster in the State of Alaska following severe storms and flooding which began August 8.

The President declared a major disaster in the State of California and ordered Federal aid to supplement State and local recovery efforts in the area struck by the continuing effects of the warm water currents known as El Niño on the 1994 Coho salmon fishing season, May 1–October 31.

The President announced his intention to nominate Clifford O'Hara, Albert Nahmad, and Vince Ryan to the Board of the Panama Canal Commission.

The President announced his intention to appoint Frank Annunzio to serve as Chairman and John Pierce, Thomas K. Thomas, and Agnes Vaghi as members of the Board of Trustees of the Christopher Columbus Fellowship Foundation.

The President announced his intention to appoint Thomas A. Farrington, Kassie Freeman, and William (Sonny) Walker to the President's Board of Advisors on Historically Black Colleges and Universities.

The President announced his intention to nominate the following individuals to be members of the National Museum Services Board:

Kinshasha Holman Conwill, Chair;
Townsend Wolfe;
Robert G. Breunig;
Nancy Marsiglia;
Arthur Rosenblatt;
Ayse Manyas Kenmore; and
Ruth Tamura.

September 14

The President announced his intention to nominate Bernard Rostker to be Assistant Secretary of the Navy for Manpower and Reserve Affairs.

The President announced his intention to appoint Jean L. Hennessey as a member of the Board of Trustees of the Woodrow Wilson International Center for Scholars.

September 15

The President announced his intention to appoint Betty Bolden as Chair of the Federal Service Impasses Panel.

September 16

The President announced his intention to nominate Susan Hayase as a member of the Civil Liberties Public Education Fund Board of Directors.

The President announced his intention to nominate Howard Terry Rasco, Christine Warnke, Mary Ellen R. Fise, and Steve M. Hays as members of the Board of Directors of the National Institute for Building Sciences.

The White House announced that the President requested that former President Jimmy Carter, chairman of the Senate Armed Services Committee Sam Nunn, and former Chairman of the Joint Chiefs of

Staff Colin Powell travel to Haiti to meet with the de facto regime.

September 17

In the morning, the President attended meetings at the Pentagon.

September 19

The President announced his intention to appoint Dolly M. Gee and Edward F. Hartfield to the Federal Service Impasses Panel.

The President announced his intention to nominate Isadore (Irv) Rosenthal as the fifth member of the Chemical Safety and Hazard Investigation Board.

September 20

In the afternoon, the President met with Organization of American States Secretary General Cesar Gaviria.

The President announced his intention to nominate J. Timothy O'Neill as a member of the Federal Housing Finance Board.

The President announced that Freeman J. Dyson and Liane B. Russell are winners of the Enrico Fermi Award.

September 21

In the morning, the President attended a breakfast fundraiser for Pennsylvania gubernatorial candidate Mark Singel at the Hay-Adams Hotel.

The President announced his intention to nominate Vonya B. McCann for the rank of Ambassador during her tenure of service as the Deputy Assistant Secretary for International Communications and Information Policy for the Department of State.

The President announced his intention to appoint Frederick Humphries to the President's Board of Advisors on Historically Black Colleges and Universities.

The President announced his intention to appoint William A. Gollick and Warren J. Seyler as members of the National Advisory Council on Indian Education.

September 22

In the morning, the President met with Foreign Minister and Deputy Prime Minister Yohei Kono of Japan. In the afternoon, he met with Prime Minister Eddie Fenech Adami of Malta.

The President announced his intention to nominate Robert Clarke Brown as a member of the Metropolitan Washington Airports Authority.

The President announced his intention to nominate William J. Hybl and Walter R. Roberts to be members of the U.S. Advisory Commission on Public Diplomacy.

The President announced his intention to appoint Barbara Handman as a member of the Franklin Delano Roosevelt Memorial Commission.

The President announced his intention to appoint Frances Ann Ulmer and Gerald W. Pavletich to the North Pacific Anadromous Fish Commission.

The President announced his intention to appoint the following individuals as members of the Enterprise for the Americas Board:
  Lawrence Harrington;
  Douglas X. Patino;
  Linda A. Randolph;
  John C. Sawhill; and
  Diane Walton Wood.

September 23

In the afternoon, the President traveled to Chicago, IL, where he attended a Democratic Senatorial Campaign Committee reception.

The President announced his intention to nominate Juliet Garcia and David J. Cortiella as members of the President's Advisory Commission on Educational Excellence for Hispanic Americans.

The President announced his intention to appoint Rosalyn Queen to the Board of Trustees of the Christopher Columbus Fellowship Foundation.

The President announced his intention to reappoint I. King Jordan as Vice Chair of the President's Committee on Employment of People With Disabilities.

The President announced his intention to appoint John H. Catlin to the Architectural and Transportation Barriers Compliance Board.

The President announced his intention to appoint Richard Nathan to the Advisory Commission on Intergovernmental Relations.

The President announced his intention to appoint William F. Woo to the President's Commission on White House Fellowships.

The President announced his intention to nominate James E. Hall to be Chair of the National Transportation Safety Board.

The President announced his intention to nominate Virgil Speakman and Jerome F. Kever to serve as members of the Railroad Retirement Board.

The President announced his intention to appoint Brig. Gen. Eugene S. Witherspoon as Chair and a member of the Red River Compact Commission.

September 24

In the morning, the President traveled from Chicago, IL, to Minneapolis, MN. In the afternoon, he traveled to Kansas City, MO, and in the evening, to New York City.

September 25

In the afternoon, the President had meetings with United Nations Secretary-General Boutros Boutros-Ghali and President Alija Izetbegovic of Bosnia at the Waldorf-Astoria Hotel. Following the meetings, he hosted a reception for African heads of state who attended the General Assembly.

September 26

In the afternoon, the President met with President Franjo Tudjman of Croatia at the United Nations Building. Later in the afternoon, the President returned to the Waldorf-Astoria Hotel where he had

meetings with President Heydar Aliyev of Azerbaijan, President Ion Iliescu of Romania, and President Carlos Salinas of Mexico.

In the evening, the President returned to Washington, DC.

The President announced his intention to nominate Dennis M. Duffy as Assistant Secretary for Policy and Planning for the Department of Veterans Affairs.

The White House announced that the President has invited Crown Prince Hassan of Jordan and Foreign Minister Shimon Peres of Israel to a trilateral meeting at the White House on October 3.

September 28

In the evening, the President and Hillary Clinton attended a dinner hosted by President Boris Yeltsin of Russia and Naina Yeltsin at the new Russian Embassy.

The President announced his intention to nominate Martin Neil Baily as a member of the White House Council of Economic Advisers.

September 29

In the afternoon, the President met with Deputy Prime Minister and Foreign Minister Richard Spring of Ireland.

The President announced his intention to nominate Kenneth B. Hipp to the National Mediation Board.

The President announced his intention to appoint William B. Gould IV to the Council of the Administrative Conference of the United States.

The President announced his intention to appoint the following individuals to the World War II Memorial Advisory Board:
  Rear Adm. Ming E. Chang, USN (Ret.);
  Melissa Durbin;
  Miguel Encinias;
  Helen Fagin;
  William Ferguson, Sr.;
  Jess Hay;
  Jon Mangis;
  Bill Mauldin;
  Sarah McClendon;
  Maj. Gen. Robert Moorhead;
  Bill Murphy; and
  Peter Wheeler.

September 30

In the morning, the President attended the Supreme Court investiture ceremony of Associate Justice Stephen Breyer.

The President announced his intention to nominate Steven L. Zinter, Joseph E. Stevens, Jr., and E. Gordon Gee to the Board of Trustees of the Harry S Truman Scholarship Foundation.

The President announced his intention to appoint the following individuals to serve on the Committee for Purchase From People Who Are Blind or Severely Disabled:
  Hugh L. Brennan;
  Carol Dortch;

Ira L. Kemp;
Robert M. Moore;
Steven B. Schwalb; and
Suzanne B. Seiden.

October 3

In the afternoon, the President met with Vice Premier Qian Qichen of China.

October 4

The President announced his intention to nominate J. Michael Nussman as a Commissioner (Recreational Fishing Representative) of the International Commission for the Conservation of Atlantic Tunas.

The President announced his intention to nominate Robert Sussman, Shirley A. Jackson, and Dan Berkovitz to the Nuclear Regulatory Commission.

The President announced his intention to appoint Ray Owen and Robert Jones as U.S. Commissioners to the North Atlantic Salmon Conservation Organization.

October 5

In the morning, the President attended the Senate prayer breakfast on Capitol Hill.

In the afternoon, the President and Hillary Clinton attended an AmeriCorps reception in the Roosevelt Room.

The President announced his intention to appoint Robert G. Valentine as a member of the Utah Reclamation Mitigation and Conservation Commission.

The President announced the following three additional appointments to the Federal Advisory Committee on Greenhouse Gas Emissions From Personal Motor Vehicles: Patrick Dougherty, Sonia Hamel, and George Giek.

The President announced his intention to appoint Kenneth L. Salazar as Chair of the Rio Grande Compact Commission.

The President announced his intention to nominate the following individuals to the Advisory Committee on Trade Policy and Negotiations:
Robert Allen;
Edwin L. Artzt;
Owen Bieber;
Robert J. Eaton;
George M.C. Fisher;
Kathryn S. Fuller;
George Harris;
Jerry Junkins;
Rhoda Karpatkin;
J. Bruce Llewellyn;
Jack Valenti;
Linda J. Wachner; and
Andrew Young.

October 6

In the morning, the President traveled to Norfolk, VA. Following his arrival, he went to the U.S. Atlantic Command Headquarters where he was given a briefing by Adm. Paul D. Miller, commander in chief of the U.S. Atlantic Command, and military officials on the situation in Haiti. He then participated in a video teleconference with military commanders in Haiti. In the afternoon, he returned to Washington, DC.

In the late afternoon, the President met with Prime Minister Chuan Likphai of Thailand.

The President declared a major disaster in the Republic of the Marshall Islands and ordered Federal aid to supplement the Republic's recovery efforts in the area struck by high tides.

The President announced that he has nominated Robert Pitofsky as Chair of the Federal Trade Commission.

The President announced his intention to appoint Gov. William J. Sheffield as Chair and member of the Federal Salary Council.

The President announced his intention to appoint Gov. George A. Sinner as Chair and a member of the White House Commission on Presidential Scholars.

October 8

In the morning, the President and Hillary Clinton went to Camp David, MD.

October 9

In the afternoon, the President returned to Washington, DC.

October 11

In the morning, the President traveled to Dearborn, MI, where he toured the Ford Mustang plant.

In the afternoon, the President traveled to Detroit, MI, where he met with United Auto Workers union leaders at the Westin Renaissance Hotel. He then went to the Detroit Free Press Building where he met with the members of the newspaper's editorial board. He returned to Washington, DC, in the evening.

The President announced the nomination of Charles (Lindy) Marinaccio as a member of the Board of Directors of the Securities Investor Protection Corporation.

The President announced his intention to appoint Mufi Hannemann as Representative to the South Pacific Commission.

October 12

In the afternoon, the President met with Prime Minister Anibal Cavaco Silva of Portugal. Following the meeting, the President and Hillary Clinton hosted a reception on the State Floor for members of the Portuguese-American community.

The President announced his intention to nominate Howard W. Cannon, William Quinn, and Lynda Hare Scribante as members of the Board of Trustees for the Barry Goldwater Scholarship and Excellence in Education Foundation.

October 13

In the evening, the President attended a fundraiser for Representative Bob Carr at the Hay-Adams Hotel.

The President announced his intention to appoint Ygnacio Garza, Peter Silva, and Lynda Taylor as members of the Board of Directors of the Border Environment Cooperation Commission.

October 14

In the evening, the President and Hillary Clinton hosted a dinner at the White House honoring arts and humanities awards recipients.

The President announced that he has appointed the following four members to the Commission of Fine Arts: J. Carter Brown (reappointment), Rex Ball, Carolyn Brody, and Eden Rafshoon.

The President announced his intention to appoint Linda Walker Bynoe and Barry Gordon to the Board of Governors for the United Service Organizations, Inc.

October 15

In the morning, the President and Hillary Clinton traveled to Stratford, CT.

In the afternoon, they traveled to Miami, FL, where they attended a fundraiser for senatorial candidate Hugh Rodham.

October 16

In the early morning, the President returned to Washington, DC.

October 17

In the morning, aboard Air Force One en route to Albuquerque, NM, the President had telephone conversations with King Hussein of Jordan and Prime Minister Yitzhak Rabin of Israel to congratulate them on the Israel-Jordan peace treaty and with Chancellor Helmut Kohl of Germany to offer congratulations on his victory in the German election.

In the afternoon, the President met with Latino leaders at the Albuquerque Convention Center. Following the meeting, he returned to Washington, DC.

The White House announced that the President has accepted the invitation of King Hussein of Jordan and Prime Minister Yitzhak Rabin of Israel to participate in the signing ceremony for the Israel-Jordan peace treaty on October 26.

October 18

In the evening, the President and Hillary Clinton attended the Democratic National Committee Jewish Leadership Forum dinner at the Corcoran Gallery of Art.

The President announced his intention to appoint Jewell Jackson McCabe to be a member of the U.S. Holocaust Memorial Council.

The President announced his intention to appoint Robert H. McKinney to be a member of the Board of Directors of the Credit Standards Advisory Committee.

October 19

In the afternoon, the President traveled to New York City where he attended a congressional fundraiser. In the evening, he traveled to Boston, MA.

The President declared a major disaster in the State of Georgia and ordered Federal aid to supplement State and local recovery efforts in the area struck by severe weather, heavy rains, flooding, high winds, and tornadoes on October 1 and continuing.

The President announced the appointment of George F. Dixon to the Federal Advisory Committee on Greenhouse Gas Emissions From Personal Motor Vehicles.

The President announced his intention to appoint Lori L. Zande as a member of the Architectural and Transportation Barriers Compliance Board.

October 20

In the afternoon, the President returned to Washington, DC.

The President announced his intention to appoint Steven Pennoyer as U.S. Commissioner of the North Pacific Anadromous Fish Commission and as U.S. Commissioner of the International Pacific Halibut Commission.

October 21

In the morning, the President and Hillary Clinton attended a fundraising breakfast for Florida senatorial candidate Hugh Rodham at the International Brotherhood of Electrical Workers building.

October 22

In the morning, the President traveled to San Francisco, CA. In the evening, he traveled to Seattle, WA.

The President announced his intention to appoint Eamon Mahony, Jr., as the Federal Commissioner and Fred D. Helms as the Alternate Federal Commissioner of the Arkansas River Compact Commission.

October 23

In the morning, the President attended services at University Presbyterian Church in Seattle.

In the afternoon, the President traveled to Cleveland, OH.

October 24

In the afternoon, the President attended a reception for Ohio Attorney General Lee Fisher at the Ritz-Carlton Hotel. He then traveled to Akron, OH, where he toured the Inventure Place construction site.

In the evening, the President returned to Washington, DC.

October 25

In the morning, the President and Hillary Clinton traveled to Cairo, Egypt.

The President announced his intention to appoint Robert Robles, Barbara J. Sabol, and Kaye Theimer as members of the Commission on Child and Family Welfare.

The President announced his intention to appoint Barbara H. Britten, M. Austin Forman, James T. McCarthy, and Michael F. Tillman to be U.S. Commissioners of the Inter-American Tropical Tuna Commission.

October 26

Following their arrival in Cairo in the very early morning, the President and Hillary Clinton were met by President Hosni Mubarak of Egypt and Mrs. Mubarak and then participated in a wreath-laying ceremony at the Tomb of the Unknown Soldier and the Tomb of Anwar Sadat. They then rested at El-Qubbah Palace.

Later in the morning, the President met with President Mubarak in the President's Library at the palace. The two Presidents then met with Palestine Liberation Organization Chairman Yasser Arafat. In the late morning, the President and Hillary Clinton traveled to Aqaba, Jordan.

In the afternoon, the President attended a trilateral luncheon at the Aqaba Royal Palace. He and Hillary Clinton then traveled to Amman, Jordan.

In the evening, the President and Hillary Clinton attended a welcoming ceremony at the Parliament. Later in the evening, they attended a dinner hosted by King Hussein and Queen Noor of Jordan at the Nadwa Palace.

The President announced his appointment of Dudley R. Herschbach as Chairman and Cathleen S. Morawetz, Susan Graham, and William J. Wilson as members of the President's Committee for the National Medal of Science.

October 27

In the morning, the President traveled to Damascus, Syria, where he met with President Hafiz al-Asad at the Presidential Palace.

In the afternoon, the President traveled to Tel Aviv, Israel, where he was joined by Hillary Clinton.

In the evening, the President met with Prime Minister Yitzhak Rabin at the King David Hotel. He and Hillary Clinton then went to the Knesset where they participated in a wreath-laying ceremony at the Eternal Flame.

The President announced his intention to nominate William Martin as a member (NOAA Representative) of the International Commission for the Conservation of Atlantic Tunas.

October 28

In the morning, the President had a breakfast meeting with President Ezer Weizman of Israel at his residence.

Later in the morning, the President traveled to Kuwait. Following an arrival ceremony, he met with U.S. and coalition troops, viewed military equipment, and attended a briefing with coalition commanders at Tactical Assembly Area Liberty.

In the evening, the President met with Amir Jabir Sabah of Kuwait at Bayan Palace in Kuwait City. Following the meeting, the President traveled to King Khalid Military City, Saudi Arabia, where he met with King Fahd.

October 29

In the morning, the President returned to Washington, DC, from King Khalid Military City, Saudi Arabia.

October 30

In the evening, the President and Hillary Clinton attended the Ford's Theatre Gala at Ford's Theatre.

October 31

In the morning, in an Oval Office ceremony, the President signed California desert protection legislation. He then traveled to Philadelphia, PA, where he attended a reception for Senator Harris Wofford at City Hall.

In the afternoon, the President traveled to Pittsburgh, PA, where he attended another reception for Senator Harris Wofford at the David Lawrence Convention Center.

In the evening, after returning to Washington, DC, the President attended a fundraiser for Senator Charles Robb at the Senator's residence in McLean, VA.

November 1

In the morning, the President traveled to Detroit, MI, where he attended a luncheon for Representative Bob Carr at the Westin Hotel.

In the afternoon, the President traveled to Cleveland, OH. Following his return to Washington, DC, in the evening, he attended a fundraiser for Democratic senatorial candidates Thomas H. Andrews and Charles Oberly at the Hay Adams Hotel.

November 2

In the afternoon, the President traveled to Providence, RI. In the evening, he attended the Rhode Island Democratic Coordinated Campaign fundraising dinner at the Rhode Island Convention Center and then returned to Washington, DC.

November 3

In the morning, the President traveled to Albany, NY, and, in the afternoon, to Des Moines, IA. In the evening, he traveled to Duluth, MN.

The President announced his intention to appoint Alfred Lloyd Goldson as a member of the National Cancer Advisory Board.

The President announced his intention to appoint Waldemar Rojas to the President's Advisory Commission on Educational Excellence for Hispanic Americans.

The White House announced that the President has invited President Leonid Kuchma of Ukraine to make a state visit to the United States, November 21–23.

The White House announced that the President has made available $1 billion in emergency funding for payments for 1994 crops damaged by disasters, including severe freezing conditions, particularly in Mississippi; flooding in the southeast resulting from Tropical Storm Alberto; and recent flooding in east Texas.

November 4

In the afternoon, the President traveled to Los Alamitos, CA, and later to Los Angeles, CA.

November 5

In the morning, the President traveled from Los Angeles to Anaheim, and in the afternoon, he traveled to San Francisco, CA.

November 6

In the late morning, the President traveled to Seattle, WA. In the afternoon, he traveled to Minneapolis, MN.

November 7

In the morning, the President and Hillary Clinton traveled to Flint, MI, and in the afternoon, they traveled to Wilmington, DE. They returned to Washington, DC, in the evening.

The President announced his intention to appoint Richard St. Germaine as a member of the National Advisory Council on Indian Education.

The President announced his intention to nominate Johnnie Carson to be U.S. Ambassador to Zimbabwe.

November 10

The President announced his intention to appoint David H. Swinton, Adele Simmons, Bobby Charles Simpson, and Chang-Lin Tien to the National Commission for Employment Policy.

November 11

In the morning, the President and Hillary Clinton traveled to Anchorage, AK. In the evening, they traveled to Manila, Philippines.

November 12

In the evening, the President and Hillary Clinton arrived in Manila.

November 13

In the morning, following an arrival ceremony at the Malacanang Palace, the President and Hillary Clinton participated in a wreath-laying ceremony at the Rizal Monument. Later in the morning, they toured Corregidor Island, and in the afternoon, they toured Malacanang Palace.

In the evening, the President and Hillary Clinton traveled to Jakarta, Indonesia.

November 14

In the morning, the President met with President Jiang Zemin of China in the Summit Room at the Jakarta Convention Center. Following the meeting, the President visited the Istiqlal Mosque. He then went to the U.S. Ambassador's residence where he met with Prime Minister Tomiichi Murayama of Japan.

In the afternoon, the President had a working lunch with Prime Minister Paul Keating of Australia at the U.S. Ambassador's residence. He then met with President Kim Yong-sam of South Korea.

In the evening, the President attended an APEC leaders dinner at the Jakarta Convention Center. Following the dinner, he met with President Kim of South Korea and Prime Minister Murayama of Japan.

The President announced his intention to appoint Bonnie Prouty Castrey and Mary Jacksteit to the Federal Service Impasses Panel.

The President announced his intention to appoint Benjamin F. Montoya and Richard H. Truly as members of the Board of Visitors of the U.S. Naval Academy.

November 15

In the morning, the President went to Bogor, Indonesia, where he attended meetings with APEC leaders at the Istana Bogor.

Following a luncheon in the afternoon, the President continued his meetings with APEC leaders at the Istana Bogor.

November 16

In the morning, the President met with President Soeharto of Indonesia at the Istana Merdeka and then participated in a wreath-laying ceremony at the Kalibata National Heroes Cemetery.

In the afternoon, the President met with a group of American business people at the Jakarta Convention Center.

In the evening, the President and Hillary Clinton attended a state dinner hosted by President Soeharto at the Istana Negara. Following the dinner, they traveled to Oahu, HI.

November 17

The President announced his intention to appoint Stanley M. Fisher to the Federal Service Impasses Panel.

November 19

In the evening, the President and Hillary Clinton departed from Honolulu, HI, for Washington, DC.

November 20

In the early morning, the President and Hillary Clinton arrived in Washington, DC.

November 21

The President announced his intention to nominate Robert Talcott Francis II as a member of the National Transportation Safety Board.

The President announced his intention to appoint James Lents to the Board of Directors of the Mickey Leland National Urban Air Toxics Research Center.

The President announced his intention to appoint Morton Bahr as a member of the National Commission for Employment Policy.

November 23

In the afternoon, the President had a working lunch with President-elect Ernesto Zedillo of Mexico. Later in the afternoon, the President and Hillary Clinton helped to serve a Thanksgiving meal to the homeless at So Others Might Eat.

In the evening, the President and Hillary and Chelsea Clinton went to Camp David, MD, for the Thanksgiving holiday.

November 27

In the afternoon, the President and Hillary and Chelsea Clinton returned to the White House from Camp David, MD.

November 28

The President declared a major disaster in the State of Florida following severe tornadoes and flooding from Tropical Storm Gordon, which began on November 14, and ordered the Federal Emergency Management Agency to assist State and local recovery efforts.

November 29

The President announced his intention to appoint Margaret Walls as a member of the Federal Advisory Committee on Greenhouse Gas Emissions From Personal Motor Vehicles.

The President announced his intention to nominate Sanford D. Greenberg as a member of the National Science Board.

The President announced his intention to nominate Thomas H. Moore to the Consumer Product Safety Commission.

November 30

The President announced his intention to nominate Terrence B. Adamson to the Board of Directors of the State Justice Institute.

December 1

In the morning, the President met with six young Americans living with HIV/AIDS to discuss the ongoing effort to confront the AIDS epidemic.

In the afternoon, the President met with Senator Bob Dole and Representative Newt Gingrich, majority leaders of the incoming 104th Congress.

December 2

The President announced his intention to nominate Eleanor Hill as Inspector General of the Department of Defense.

The President announced his intention to nominate Joan Challinor to be a member of the National Commission on Libraries and Information Science.

The President announced his intention to nominate Tony Scallon, Sheila Smith, and Mindy Turbov to be members of the Board of Directors of the National Consumer Cooperative Bank.

The President announced his intention to appoint Tom Daly as Chair and Eleanor Chang as a member of the Board of Directors of the Credit Standards Advisory Committee.

December 4

In the afternoon, the President and Hillary Clinton hosted a reception for the Kennedy Center Honors recipients.

In the early evening, the President traveled to Budapest, Hungary, to attend the Conference on Security and Cooperation in Europe.

December 5

In the morning, the President arrived in Budapest.

In the afternoon, following a meeting with President Arpad Goncz and Prime Minister Gyula Horn of Hungary, the President returned to Washington, DC.

In the evening, the President and Hillary Clinton hosted a congressional reception in the Diplomatic Reception Room at the White House.

December 6

In the late morning, the President met with the School to Work National Employer Leadership Council.

The President announced his intention to nominate Eugene Branstool to be Chairman of the Federal Agricultural Mortgage Corporation.

December 7

The President announced his intention to appoint Milton Irvin and Judith A. Scott to be members of the Advisory Committee on the Pension Benefit Guaranty Corporation.

The President announced his intention to appoint JoAnn Jones as a member of the National Advisory Council on Indian Education.

The President announced his intention to nominate Lilliam Rangel Pollo to be a member of the National Council on Disability.

December 8

The President announced his intention to nominate John L. Bryant, Jr., and Phillip Frost to be members of the National Museum Services Board.

The President announced his intention to nominate Albert J. Dwoskin to be a member of the Board of Directors of the Securities Investor Protection Corporation.

In the evening, the President and Hillary Clinton traveled to Miami, FL, to attend the Summit of the Americas.

December 9

The President announced his intention to appoint Michael Lewan as Chair and Maura Temes as a member of the Commission for the Preservation of America's Heritage Abroad.

The President announced his intention to appoint Harry Robinson to be a member of the Commission of Fine Arts.

The President announced his intention to appoint David Gardner to be a member of the President's Committee on the Arts and the Humanities.

December 10

In the morning, the President attended a working lunch with Summit of the Americas leaders at Vizcaya in Miami, FL.

In the evening, the President and Hillary Clinton cruised aboard the yacht *The Virginian* to Fishers Island, FL, where they hosted a summit dinner at the Vanderbilt Mansion.

December 11

In the afternoon, the President and Hillary Clinton returned to Washington, DC.

In the evening, the President and Hillary and Chelsea Clinton attended the "Christmas in Washington" performance at the National Building Museum.

December 12

The President announced his intention to nominate Cutberto Garza, Shiriki K. Kumanyika, Kailash Mathur, and Suzanne P. Murphy to the National Nutrition Monitoring Advisory Council.

The President announced his intention to appoint Prudence Rice and Eugene Thaw to be members of the Cultural Property Advisory Committee.

The White House announced that the President has invited President Zhelyu Zhelev of Bulgaria to meet with him in Washington, DC, on February 13, 1995.

December 15

The President announced the appointment of Ginger Ehn Lew to the Council of the Administrative Conference of the United States.

The President announced his intention to appoint Paul Hae Park to the Board of Trustees of the Woodrow Wilson International Center for Scholars.

December 19

The President announced his intention to appoint Mayor Bruce Todd of Austin, TX, and Mayor Victor Ashe of Knoxville, TN, as members of the Advisory Commission on Intergovernmental Relations.

The President announced his intention to appoint Frank Pearl, Ronald Perelman, Jay Stein, and Thomas Wheeler to the Board of Trustees of the John F. Kennedy Center for the Performing Arts, Smithsonian Institution.

December 20

The President announced his intention to appoint Noel Hankin to the President's Board of Advisors on Historically Black Colleges and Universities.

The President announced his intention to appoint Richard K. Fox and Ellen Hume to the Commission on Protecting and Reducing Government Secrecy.

The President announced his intention to appoint Gilbert Carrillo to the Federal Service Impasses Panel.

December 22

In the afternoon, the President hosted a Christmas celebration for children in the State Dining Room.

The President announced his intention to nominate Ray L. Caldwell for the rank of Ambassador during his tenure of service as Deputy Assistant Secretary of State for Burdensharing.

The President announced his intention to nominate Bismarck Myrick as Ambassador to Lesotho.

December 23

The President appointed John C. Truesdale to be a member of the National Labor Relations Board. Mr. Truesdale will serve as a recess appointee and will temporarily fill the vacancy in the seat previously held by Dennis M. Devaney, whose term expired December 16, 1994. Mr. Truesdale's term will expire upon the confirmation of a successor.

December 29

The White House announced that Prime Minister Jean-Luc Dehaene of Belgium has accepted the President's invitation to pay an official working visit to Washington on February 15, 1995.

The White House announced that Prime Minister Wim Kok of The Netherlands has accepted the President's invitation to pay an official working visit to Washington on February 28, 1995.

December 30

In the morning, the President and Hillary and Chelsea Clinton went to Camp David, MD.

The President announced his intention to nominate William L. Wilson as a member of the Advisory Board of the Saint Lawrence Seaway Development Corporation.

.

Appendix B—Nominations Submitted to the Senate

The following list does not include promotions of members of the Uniformed Services, nominations to the Service Academies, or nominations of Foreign Service officers.

Submitted August 5

Robert N. Chatigny,
of Connecticut, to be U.S. District Judge for the District of Connecticut, vice Warren W. Eginton, retired.

Judith D. McConnell,
of California, to be U.S. District Judge for the Southern District of California (new position).

Submitted August 8

Kenneth Spencer Yalowitz,
of Virginia, a career member of the Senior Foreign Service, class of Minister-Counselor, to be Ambassador Extraordinary and Plenipotentiary of the United States of America to the Republic of Belarus.

Sheldon C. Bilchik,
of Maryland, to be Administrator of the Office of Juvenile Justice and Delinquency Prevention, vice Robert W. Sweet, Jr., resigned.

Luise S. Jordan,
of Maryland, to be Inspector General, Corporation for National and Community Service (new position).

Andrea N. Brown,
of Michigan, to be a member of the Board of Directors of the Corporation for National and Community Service for a term of one year (new position).

Thomas Ehrlich,
of California, to be a member of the Board of Directors of the Corporation for National and Community Service for a term of 3 years (new position).

Christopher C. Gallagher, Sr.,
of New Hampshire, to be a member of the Board of Directors of the Corporation for National and Community Service for a term of 4 years (new position).

Reatha Clark King,
of Minnesota, to be a member of the Board of Directors of the Corporation for National and Community Service for a term of 5 years (new position).

Carol W. Kinsley,
of Massachusetts, to be a member of the Board of Directors of the Corporation for National and Community Service for a term of 5 years (new position).

Leslie Lenkowsky,
of Indiana, to be a member of the Board of Directors of the Corporation for National and Community Service for a term of 4 years (new position).

Marlee Matlin,
of California, to be a member of the Board of Directors of the Corporation for National and Community Service for a term of 2 years (new position).

Arthur J. Naparstek,
of Ohio, to be a member of the Board of Directors of the Corporation for National and Community Service for a term of 4 years (new position).

John Rother,
of Maryland, to be a member of the Board of Directors of the Corporation for National and Community Service for a term of 2 years (new position).

Walter H. Shorenstein,
of California, to be a member of the Board of Directors of the Corporation for National and Community Service for a term of 3 years (new position).

Submitted August 9

Henry J. Cauthen,
of South Carolina, to be a member of the Board of Directors of the Corporation for Public Broadcasting for a term expiring January 31, 2000 (reappointment).

Frank Henry Cruz,
of California, to be a member of the Board of Directors of the Corporation for Public Broadcasting for a term expiring January 31, 2000, vice Lloyd Kaiser, term expired.

Submitted August 10

Thomas R. Carper,
of Delaware, to be a member of the Amtrak Board of Directors for a term of 4 years, vice Tommy G. Thompson, term expired.

Robert L. Gallucci,
of Virginia, a career member of the Senior Executive Service, to be Ambassador at Large.

Eddie J. Jordan, Jr.,
of Louisiana, to be U.S. Attorney for the Eastern District of Louisiana for the term of 4 years, vice Harry A. Rosenberg, resigned.

Submitted August 12

Robert J. Cindrich,
of Pennsylvania, to be U.S. District Judge for the Western District of Pennsylvania, vice Gustave Diamond, retired.

David A. Katz,
of Ohio, to be U.S. District Judge for the Northern District of Ohio, vice Alvin I. Krenzler, retired.

Sean J. McLaughlin,
of Pennsylvania, to be U.S. District Judge for the Western District of Pennsylvania, vice Glenn E. Mencer, retired.

Robert Edward Service,
of California, a career member of the Senior Foreign Service, class of Minister-Counselor, to be Ambassador Extraordinary and Plenipotentiary of the United States of America to the Republic of Paraguay.

Submitted August 15

Kenneth Burton,
of Virginia, to be a member of the Board of Trustees of the Morris K. Udall Scholarship and Excellence in National Environmental Policy Foundation for a term of 2 years (new position).

D. Michael Rappoport,
of Arizona, to be a member of the Board of Trustees of the Morris K. Udall Scholarship and Excellence in National Environmental Policy Foundation for a term of 2 years (new position).

Submitted August 16

Jorge M. Perez,
of Florida, to be a member of the National Council on the Arts for a term expiring September 3, 1998, vice Nina Brock, term expired.

Joseph Francis Baca,
of New Mexico, to be a member of the Board of Directors of the State Justice Institute for a term expiring September 17, 1995, vice James Duke Cameron, term expired.

Robert Nelson Baldwin,
of Virginia, to be a member of the Board of Directors of the State Justice Institute for a term expiring September 17, 1995, vice Carl F. Bianchi, term expired.

Jennifer Chandler Hauge,
of New Jersey, to be a member of the Board of Directors of the State Justice Institute for a term

expiring September 17, 1995, vice Sandra A. O'Connor, term expired.

Florence K. Murray,
of Rhode Island, to be a member of the Board of Directors of the State Justice Institute for a term expiring September 17, 1995, vice Malcolm M. Lucas, term expired.

Elaine F. Bucklo,
of Illinois, to be U.S. District Judge for the Northern District of Illinois, vice John A. Nordberg, retired.

David H. Coar,
of Illinois, to be U.S. District Judge for the Northern District of Illinois, vice Ilana Diamond Rovner, elevated.

Robert W. Gettleman,
of Illinois, to be U.S. District Judge for the Northern District of Illinois, vice John F. Grady, retired.

Paul E. Riley,
of Illinois, to be U.S. District Judge for the Southern District of Illinois (new position).

Submitted August 22

Martin Jay Dickman,
of Illinois, to be Inspector General, Railroad Retirement Board, vice William J. Doyle III.

Celeste Pinto McLain,
of California, to be a member of the Amtrak Board of Directors for the remainder of the term expiring March 20, 1995, vice Carl W. Vogt.

Celeste Pinto McLain,
of California, to be a member of the Amtrak Board of Directors for a term of 4 years (reappointment).

Frederick F.Y. Pang,
of Hawaii, to be an Assistant Secretary of Defense, vice Chas. W. Freeman.

Submitted August 23

Gil Coronado,
of Texas, to be Director of Selective Service, vice Robert William Gambino, resigned.

Marc Lincoln Marks,
of Pennsylvania, to be a member of the Federal Mine Safety and Health Review Commission for a term of 6 years expiring August 30, 2000, vice L. Clair Nelson, deceased.

Submitted August 25

Clifford B. O'Hara,
of Connecticut, to be a member of the Board of Directors of the Panama Canal Commission, vice William Carl.

Reginald B. Madsen,
of Oregon, to be U.S. Marshal for the District of
Oregon for the term of 4 years, vice Kernan H.
Bagley, resigned.

Eve L. Menger,
of New York, to be a member of the National Science
Board, National Science Foundation, for a term expiring May 10, 2000, vice Arden L. Bement, Jr., term
expired.

Alfred H. Moses,
of Virginia, to be Ambassador Extraordinary and Plenipotentiary of the United States of America to Romania.

Robert M. Solow,
of Massachusetts, to be a member of the National
Science Board, National Science Foundation, for a
term expiring May 10, 2000, vice Peter H. Raven,
term expired.

Anne Jeanette Udall,
of North Carolina, to be a member of the Board
of Trustees of the Morris K. Udall Scholarship and
Excellence in National Environmental Policy Foundation for a term of 4 years (new position).

Richard Thomas White,
of Michigan, to be a member of the Foreign Claims
Settlement Commission of the United States for the
term expiring September 30, 1996, vice Frank H.
Conway, term expired.

Timothy M. Barnicle,
of Maryland, to be an Assistant Secretary of Labor,
vice John D. Donahue.

James A. Beaty, Jr.,
of North Carolina, to be U.S. District Judge for the
Middle District of North Carolina, vice Richard C.
Ervin, retired.

David Briones,
of Texas, to be U.S. District Judge for the Western
District of Texas, vice Lucius Desha Bunton III, retired.

Peter Jon de Vos,
of Florida, a career member of the Senior Foreign
Service, class of Minister-Counselor, to be Ambassador
Extraordinary and Plenipotentiary of the United States
of America to the Republic of Costa Rica.

John A. Gannon,
of Ohio, to be a member of the National Council
on Disability for a term expiring September 17, 1995
(reappointment).

Helen W. Gillmor,
of Hawaii, to be U.S. District Judge for the District
of Hawaii (new position).

Okla Jones II,
of Louisiana, to be U.S. District Judge for the Eastern
District of Louisiana, vice Frederick J. R. Heebe, retired.

Bruce A. Morrison,
of Connecticut, to be a Director of the Federal Housing Finance Board for a term expiring February 27,
2000, vice William C. Perkins, resigned.

Fred I. Parker,
of Vermont, to be U.S. Circuit Judge for the Second
Circuit, vice James L. Oakes, retired.

Joe Bradley Pigott,
of Mississippi, to be U.S. Attorney for the Southern
District of Mississippi, vice George L. Phillips.

G. Thomas Porteous, Jr.,
of Louisiana, to be U.S. District Judge for the Eastern
District of Louisiana, vice Robert F. Collins, resigned.

John R. Tait,
of Idaho, to be U.S. District Judge for the District
of Idaho, vice Harold L. Ryan, retired.

Vincent J. Sorrentino,
of New York, to be a member of the Advisory Board
of the Saint Lawrence Seaway Development Corporation, vice Leo C. McKenna.

Submitted September 12

Marc Grossman,
of Virginia, a career member of the Senior Foreign
Service, class of Counselor, to be Ambassador Extraordinary and Plenipotentiary of the United States of
America to the Republic of Turkey.

Gabriel Guerra-Mondragon,
of the District of Columbia, to be Ambassador Extraordinary and Plenipotentiary of the United States
of America to the Republic of Chile.

Charles E. Redman,
of Florida, a career member of the Senior Foreign
Service, class of Minister-Counselor, to be Ambassador
Extraordinary and Plenipotentiary of the United States
of America to the Federal Republic of Germany.

Frank N. Newman,
of California, to be Deputy Secretary of the Treasury,
vice Roger Altman, resigned.

Edward. S. Knight,
of Texas, to be General Counsel for the Department
of the Treasury, vice Jean E. Hanson, resigned.

Devra Lee Davis,
of the District of Columbia, to be a member of the
Chemical Safety and Hazard Investigation Board for
a term of 5 years (new position).

Gerald V. Poje,
of Virginia, to be a member of the Chemical Safety and Hazard Investigation Board for a term of 5 years (new position).

Cecil James Banks,
of New Jersey, to be a member of the Board of Directors of the African Development Foundation for a term expiring November 13, 1995, vice T. M. Alexander, Sr., resigned.

Marciene S. Mattleman,
of Pennsylvania, to be a member of the National Institute for Literacy Advisory Board for the remainder of the term expiring October 12, 1995, vice Jim Edgar, resigned.

Lynne C. Waihee,
of Hawaii, to be a member of the National Institute for Literacy Advisory Board for a term of 3 years (new position).

Submitted September 13

Thomas E. McNamara,
of the District of Columbia, a career member of the Senior Foreign Service, class of Minister-Counselor, to be an Assistant Secretary of State, vice Robert L. Gallucci.

Jerome Gary Cooper,
of Alabama, to be Ambassador Extraordinary and Plenipotentiary of the United States of America to Jamaica.

Geraldine A. Ferraro,
of New York, for the rank of Ambassador during her tenure of service as the Representative of the United States of America on the Human Rights Commission of the Economic and Social Council of the United Nations.

Martha F. Riche,
of Maryland, to be Director of the Census, vice Barbara Everitt Bryant, resigned.

Ruth Y. Tamura,
of Hawaii, to be a member of the National Museum Services Board for a term expiring December 6, 1996, vice James H. Duff, term expired.

Patricia Hill Williams,
of New York, to be a member of the Board of Directors of the Inter-American Foundation for a term expiring September 20, 2000, vice James R. Whelan, term expired.

Submitted September 14

Karen Nelson Moore,
of Ohio, to be U.S. Circuit Judge for the Sixth Circuit, vice Robert B. Krupansky, retired.

Roslyn Moore-Silver,
of Arizona, to be U.S. District Judge for the District of Arizona, vice Earl H. Carroll, retired.

Maxine M. Chesney,
of California, to be U.S. District Judge for the Northern District of California, vice John P. Vukasin, Jr., deceased.

James Robertson,
of Maryland, to be U.S. District Judge for the District of Columbia, vice George H. Revercomb, deceased.

Thomas B. Russell,
of Kentucky, to be U.S. District Judge for the Western District of Kentucky, vice Edward H. Johnstone, retired.

Sidney H. Stein,
of New York, to be U.S. District Judge for the Southern District of New York, vice Pierre N. Leval, elevated.

Alvin W. Thompson,
of Connecticut, to be U.S. District Judge for the District of Connecticut, vice Ellen Bree Burns, retired.

William H. Walls,
of New Jersey, to be U.S. District Judge for the District of New Jersey, vice Harold A. Ackerman, retired.

Hazel Rollins O'Leary,
of Minnesota, to be Representative of the United States of America to the 38th Session of the General Conference of the International Atomic Energy Agency.

Ivan Selin,
of the District of Columbia, to be Alternate Representative of the United States of America to the 38th Session of the General Conference of the International Atomic Energy Agency.

Nelson F. Sievering, Jr.,
of Maryland, to be Alternate Representative of the United States of America to the 38th Session of the General Conference of the International Atomic Energy Agency.

John B. Ritch III,
of the District of Columbia, to be Alternate Representative of the United States of America to the 38th Session of the General Conference of the International Atomic Energy Agency.

William Hybl,
of Colorado, to be a member of the United States Advisory Commission on Public Diplomacy for a term expiring July 1, 1997 (reappointment).

Albert H. Nahmad,
of Florida, to be a member of the Board of Directors of the Panama Canal Commission, vice Robert R. McMillian.

Vincent Reed Ryan, Jr.,
of Texas, to be a member of the Board of Directors of the Panama Canal Commission, vice Walter J. Shea.

Peggy Goldwater-Clay,
of California, to be a member of the Board of Trustees of the Barry Goldwater Scholarship and Excellence in Education Foundation for a term expiring June 5, 2000, vice Barry M. Goldwater, Jr., term expired.

Niranjan Shamalbhai Shah,
of Illinois, to be a member of the Board of Trustees of the Barry Goldwater Scholarship and Excellence in Education Foundation for a term expiring August 11, 1998, vice Timothy W. Tong, term expired.

Robert F. Drinan,
of Massachusetts, to be a member of the Board of Directors of the Civil Liberties Public Education Fund for a term of 3 years (new position).

Cherry T. Kinoshita,
of Washington, to be a member of the Board of Directors of the Civil Liberties Public Education Fund for a term of 2 years (new position).

Elsa H. Kudo,
of Hawaii, to be a member of the Board of Directors of the Civil Liberties Public Education Fund for a term of 2 years (new position).

Yeiichi Kuwayama,
of the District of Columbia, to be a member of the Board of Directors of the Civil Liberties Public Education Fund for a term of 3 years (new position).

Don T. Nakanishi,
of California, to be a member of the Board of Directors of the Civil Liberties Public Education Fund for a term of 2 years (new position).

Michael R. Ramon,
of California, to be U.S. Marshal for the Central District of California, vice Craig L. Meacham, resigned.

Submitted September 16

Alice M. Rivlin,
of the District of Columbia, to be Director of the Office of Management and Budget, vice Leon E. Panetta.

Submitted September 19

Sandra L. Lynch,
of Massachusetts, to be U.S. Circuit Judge for the First Circuit, vice Stephen G. Breyer, elevated.

Charles R. Wilson,
of Florida, to be U.S. Attorney for the Middle District of Florida for the term of 4 years, vice Larry Herbert Colleton, resigned.

Robert G. Breunig,
of Arizona, to be a member of the National Museum Services Board for a term expiring December 6, 1998 (reappointment).

Kinshasha Holman Conwill,
of New York, to be a member of the National Museum Services Board for a term expiring December 6, 1997, vice Willard L. Boyd, term expired.

Ayse Manyas Kenmore,
of Florida, to be a member of the National Museum Services Board for the remainder of the term expiring December 6, 1995, vice Daphne Wood Murray, resigned.

Nancy Marsiglia,
of Louisiana, to be a member of the National Museum Services Board for a term expiring December 6, 1998, vice George S. Rosborough, Jr., term expired.

Arthur Rosenblatt,
of New York, to be a member of the National Museum Services Board for a term expiring December 6, 1997, vice Richard J. Schwartz, term expired.

Townsend Wolfe,
of Arkansas, to be a member of the National Museum Services Board for a term expiring December 6, 1995, vice Rosemary G. McMillan, term expired.

H. Terry Rasco,
of Arkansas, to be a member of the Board of Directors of the National Institute of Building Sciences for a term expiring September 7, 1997, vice Arnold L. Steinberg, term expired.

Christine M. Warnke,
of the District of Columbia, to be a member of the Board of Directors of the National Institute of Building Sciences for a term expiring September 7, 1995, vice Louis L. Guy, Jr., resigned.

Audrey L. McCrimon,
of Illinois, to be a member of the National Council on Disability for a term expiring September 17, 1997, vice Robert S. Mueller, term expired.

Susan Hayase,
of California, to be a member of the Board of Directors of the Civil Liberties Public Education fund for a term of 3 years (new position).

James Clifford Hudson,
of Oklahoma, to be a Director of the Securities Investor Protection Corporation for a term expiring December 31, 1994, vice James G. Stearns, term expired.

James Clifford Hudson,
of Oklahoma, to be a Director of the Securities Investor Protection Corporation for a term expiring December 31, 1997 (reappointment).

Submitted September 20

Kathleen M. O'Malley,
of Ohio, to be U.S. District Judge for the Northern District of Ohio, vice John W. Potter, retired.

Rhea Lydia Graham,
of New Mexico, to be Director of the U.S. Bureau of Mines, vice T.S. Ary, resigned.

Submitted September 22

Barbara Blum,
of the District of Columbia, to be a member of the Board of Trustees of the Institute of American Indian and Alaska Native Culture and Arts Development for the remainder of the term expiring May 19, 1996, vice Wiley T. Buchanan, resigned.

LaDonna Harris,
of New Mexico, to be a member of the Board of Trustees of the Institute of American Indian and Alaska Native Culture and Arts Development for a term expiring May 19, 2000, vice Gail Bird, term expired.

Loren Kieve,
of New Mexico, to be a member of the Board of Trustees of the Institute of American Indian and Alaska Native Culture and Arts Development for the remainder of the term expiring May 19, 1996, vice William Stewart Johnson, resigned.

Catherine Baker Stetson,
of New Mexico, to be a member of the Board of Trustees of the Institute of American Indian and Alaska Native Culture and Arts Development for a term expiring May 19, 2000, vice James D. Santini, term expired.

Walter R. Roberts,
of the District of Columbia, to be a member of the U.S. Advisory Commission on Public Diplomacy for a term expiring April 6, 1997 (reappointment).

Sven E. Holmes,
of Oklahoma, to be U.S. District Judge for the Northern District of Oklahoma, vice James Oliver Ellison.

Vicki Miles-LaGrange,
of Oklahoma, to be U.S. District Judge for the Western District of Oklahoma, vice Lee Roy West.

John D. Snodgrass,
of Alabama, to be U.S. District Judge for the Northern District of Alabama, vice E.B. Haltom, Jr., retired.

Mary Ellen R. Fise,
of the District of Columbia, to be a member of the Board of Directors of the National Institute of Building Sciences for a term expiring September 7, 1996, vice Virginia Stanley Douglas, term expired.

George J. Opfer,
of Virginia, to be Inspector General, Federal Emergency Management Agency, vice Russell Flynn Miller.

Bernard Daniel Rostker,
of Virginia, to be an Assistant Secretary of the Navy, vice Frederick F.Y. Pang.

Submitted September 26

Madeleine Korbel Albright,
of the District of Columbia, to be a Representative of the United States of America to the 49th Session of the General Assembly of the United Nations.

Edward William Gnehm, Jr.,
of Georgia, to be a Representative of the United States of America to the 49th Session of the General Assembly of the United Nations.

David Elias Birenbaum,
of the District of Columbia, to be an Alternate Representative of the United States of America to the 49th Session of the General Assembly of the United Nations.

Karl Frederick Inderfurth,
of North Carolina, to be an Alternate Representative of the United States of America to the 49th Session of the General Assembly of the United Nations.

Victor Marrero,
of New York, to be an Alternate Representative of the United States of America to the 49th Session of the General Assembly of the United Nations.

Patrick J. Leahy,
of Vermont, to be a Representative of the United States of America to the 49th Session of the General Assembly of the United Nations.

Frank H. Murkowski,
of Alaska, to be a Representative of the United States of America to the 49th Session of the General Assembly of the United Nations.

Steven Scott Alm,
of Hawaii, to be U.S. Attorney for the District of Hawaii for a term of 4 years, vice Daniel A. Bent, resigned.

Calton Windley Bland,
of North Carolina, to be U.S. Marshal for the Eastern District of North Carolina for a term of 4 years, vice William I. Berryhill, Jr.

Michael D. Carrington,
of Indiana, to be U.S. Marshal for the Northern District of Indiana for a term of 4 years, vice J. Jerome Perkins.

Robert Bradford English,
of Missouri, to be U.S. Marshal for the Western District of Missouri for a term of 4 years, vice Larry J. Joiner.

James E. Hall,
of Tennessee, to be Chairman of the National Transportation Safety Board for a term of 2 years, vice Carl W. Vogt, term expired.

John R. Murphy,
of Alaska, to be U.S. Marshal for the District of Alaska for a term of 4 years, vice John A. McKay.

Lori Esposito Murray,
of Connecticut, to be an Assistant Director of the U.S. Arms Control and Disarmament Agency, vice Michael Lorne Moodie, resigned.

J. Timothy O'Neill,
of Virginia, to be a Director of the Federal Housing Finance Board for the remainder of the term expiring February 27, 1997, vice Marilyn R. Seymann, resigned.

John Edward Rouille,
of Vermont, to be U.S. Marshal for the District of Vermont for the term of 4 years, vice Christian J. Hansen.

Herbert M. Rutherford III,
of the District of Columbia, to be U.S. Marshal for the District of Columbia for the term of 4 years (reappointment).

Submitted September 28

Richard P. Conaboy,
of Pennsylvania, to be a member of the U.S. Sentencing Commission for a term expiring October 31, 1999, vice William H. Wilkins, Jr., term expired.

Richard P. Conaboy,
of Pennsylvania, to be Chairman of the U.S. Sentencing Commission, vice William W. Wilkins, Jr.

Deanell Reece Tacha,
of Kansas, to be a member of the U.S. Sentencing Commission for a term expiring October 31, 1997, vice George E. MacKinnon, term expired.

Wayne Anthony Budd,
of Massachusetts, to be a member of the U.S. Sentencing Commission for a term expiring October 31, 1999, vice Ilene H. Nagel, resigned.

Michael Goldsmith,
of Utah, to be a member of the U.S. Sentencing Commission for a term expiring October 31, 1997, vice Helen G. Corrothers, term expired.

Philip C. Wilcox, Jr.,
of Maryland, a career member of the Senior Foreign Service, class of Minister-Counselor, for the rank of Ambassador during his tenure of service as Coordinator for Counter Terrorism.

Submitted September 30

James H. Atkins,
of Arkansas, to be a member of the Federal Retirement Thrift Investment Board for a term expiring September 25, 1996, vice Roger W. Mehle, resigned.

Jay C. Ehle,
of Ohio, to be a member of the Advisory Board of the Saint Lawrence Seaway Development Corporation, vice Conrad Fredin.

Steve M. Hays,
of Tennessee, to be a member of the Board of Directors of the National Institute of Building Sciences for a term expiring September 7, 1997, vice Dianne E. Ingels, term expired.

Charles Hummel,
of Delaware, to be a member of the National Museum Services Board for a term expiring December 6, 1994, vice Marilyn Logsdon Mennello, term expired.

Charles Hummel,
of Delaware, to be a member of the National Museum Services Board for a term expiring December 6, 1999 (reappointment).

Scott B. Lukins,
of Washington, to be a member of the Federal Retirement Thrift Investment Board for a term expiring October 11, 1995, vice John David Davenport, term expired.

Submitted October 3

Frederic James Hansen,
of Oregon, to be Deputy Administrator of the Environmental Protection Agency, vice Robert M. Sussman, resigned.

Christine A. Varney,
of the District of Columbia, to be a Federal Trade Commissioner for the unexpired term of 7 years from September 26, 1989, vice Dennis A. Yao, resigned.

Submitted October 5

David Folsom,
of Texas, to be U.S. District Judge for the Eastern District of Texas, vice Sam B. Hall, Jr., deceased.

Thadd Heartfield,
of Texas, to be U.S. District Judge for the Eastern District of Texas, vice Robert M. Parker, elevated.

Lacy H. Thornburg,
of North Carolina, to be U.S. District Judge for the Western District of North Carolina, vice Robert D. Potter, retired.

Submitted October 7

Charles T. Manatt,
of the District of Columbia, to be a member of the Board of Directors of the Communications Satellite Corporation until the date of the annual meeting of the Corporation in 1997, vice Rudy Boschwitz.

Appendix C—Checklist of White House Press Releases

The following list contains releases of the Office of the Press Secretary which are not included in this book.

Released August 2

Transcript of a press briefing by Press Secretary Dee Dee Myers

Statement by Press Secretary Dee Dee Myers on the upcoming visit of President Leonid Kuchma of Ukraine on November 29

Released August 3

Transcript of a press briefing by Press Secretary Dee Dee Myers

Transcript of remarks by Chief of Staff Leon Panetta on health care reform

Transcript of remarks by Health Care Express participant John Cox

Released August 4

Transcript of a press briefing by Press Secretary Dee Dee Myers

Statement by Press Secretary Dee Dee Myers on support from economists for prompt ratification of the GATT agreement

Transcript of a press briefing on the anniversary of the passage of the economic program by Assistant to the President for Economic Policy Bob Rubin, Office of Management and Budget Director-designate Alice Rivlin, Chair of the Council of Economic Advisers Laura D'Andrea Tyson, Secretary of Labor Bob Reich, Secretary of Commerce Ron Brown, Small Business Administrator Erskine Bowles, Deputy Secretary of the Treasury Roger Altman, and U.S. Trade Ambassador Mickey Kantor

Transcript of remarks by Secretary of Health and Human Services Donna Shalala, Secretary of Commerce Ron Brown, and Secretary of Labor Robert Reich on health care reform

Released August 5

Transcript of a press briefing by Press Secretary Dee Dee Myers

Statement by Special Counsel to the President Lloyd Cutler on appointment of a new independent counsel

Released August 8

Transcript of a press briefing by Press Secretary Dee Dee Myers

Transcript of a press briefing on universal health care by Health and Human Services Secretary Donna Shalala, Interior Secretary Bruce Babbitt, Education Secretary Richard Riley, Housing and Urban Development Secretary Henry Cisneros, and Deputy Assistant Secretary of Health and Human Services Ken Thorpe

Announcement of Presidential Medal of Freedom recipients and text of the citations

Released August 9

Transcript of a press briefing by Press Secretary Dee Dee Myers

Transcript of an interview with the First Lady by health care reporters

Joint Statement on Relations Between the United States of America and the Republic of Armenia

Statement by Press Secretary Dee Dee Myers announcing the President's planned meeting with President Meles Zenawi, head of the transnational government of Ethiopia, on August 11

Statement by Press Secretary Dee Dee Myers on the inquiry into the construction costs of the National Reconnaissance Office in Chantilly, VA

Announcement of nomination for a U.S. Attorney for the Eastern District of Louisiana

Released August 10

Transcript of a press briefing by Press Secretary Dee Dee Myers

Transcript of a press briefing by Gov. John Waihee of Hawaii and Small Business Administrator Erskine Bowles on health care in the State of Hawaii

Released August 11

Announcement of policy forbidding Presidential appointees from accepting travel services or accommodations from any company regulated by or doing business with the appointee's agency

Released August 12

Statement by Press Secretary Dee Dee Myers on delivery by the State Department, Defense Department, Central Intelligence Agency, and National Security Council of 3,723 unclassified and declassified documents on U.S. policy toward El Salvador to the House Foreign Affairs Committee and the Senate Foreign Relations Committee

Transcript of remarks by the Vice President at the swearing-in ceremony for Supreme Court Justice Stephen G. Breyer

Letter to the Congress from Chief of Staff Leon Panetta on congressional action on the crime bill

Released August 15

Transcript of a press briefing by Press Secretary Dee Dee Myers

Transcript of remarks by Dewey Stokes, Steven Sposato, Janice Payne, and Marc Klaas on the crime bill

Released August 16

Transcript of a press briefing by Press Secretary Dee Dee Myers

Text of editorials on the crime bill from 10 newspapers around the country

Statement by Chief of Staff Leon Panetta on the President's meeting with 11 Republican Members of the Congress who supported the crime bill

Statement by African-American religious leaders supporting the crime bill

Announcement of the President's signing of H.R. 868, the Telemarketing and Consumer Fraud and Abuse Prevention Act

Released August 17

Transcript of a press briefing by Press Secretary Dee Dee Myers

Statement by Special Counsel to the President Lloyd Cutler announcing that the White House will make available to the public documents generated or received by the health care working group in 1993

Released August 18

Transcript of a press briefing by Press Secretary Dee Dee Myers

Transcript of a press briefing by Health and Human Services Secretary Donna Shalala, Secretary of Commerce Ron Brown, and Labor Secretary Robert Reich on health care legislation

Released August 19

Statement by Press Secretary Dee Dee Myers on Cuban refugees

Statement by Press Secretary Dee Dee Myers on Counselor to the President Thomas F. (Mack) McLarty's trip to Saudi Arabia

Transcript of a press briefing by Attorney General Janet Reno on Cuban refugees

Released August 22

Transcript of a press briefing by Press Secretary Dee Dee Myers

Statement by Press Secretary Dee Dee Myers on the upcoming summit of the Asia-Pacific Economic Cooperation forum in Indonesia, November 14–15

Released August 23

Transcript of a press briefing by Press Secretary Dee Dee Myers

Statement by Press Secretary Dee Dee Myers announcing that a delegation of senior officials will visit Florida to consult on Cuban migrants

Released August 24

Transcript of a press briefing by Press Secretary Dee Dee Myers

Transcript of a press briefing on Cuban refugees by Secretary of Defense William Perry, Attorney General Janet Reno, Under Secretary of State for Political Affairs Peter Tarnoff, and Immigration and Naturalization Service Commissioner Doris Meissner

Statement by Chief of Staff Leon Panetta on confirmation by the Congressional Budget Office of 3 years of deficit reduction

Statement by Press Secretary Dee Dee Myers on the Presidential election in Mexico

Statement by Press Secretary Dee Dee Myers on the upcoming state visit of South African President Nelson Mandela, October 6–8

Announcement of nomination for U.S. Marshal for the District of Oregon

Announcement of nomination for a Commissioner of the Foreign Claims Settlement Commission

Released August 25

Transcript of a press briefing by Under Secretary of State for Political Affairs Peter Tarnoff on Cuban refugees

Announcement of nomination for Assistant Secretary for Policy and Budget at the Labor Department

Released August 26

Transcript of a press briefing by Press Secretary Dee Dee Myers

Statement by Press Secretary Dee Dee Myers announcing the President's nomination of Gen. Ronald R. Fogelman, USAF, to be Chief of Staff of the Air Force

Statement by Press Secretary Dee Dee Myers announcing the delegation to travel to Burundi, Rwanda, and eastern Zaire on August 27

Statement by Press Secretary Dee Dee Myers on emergency funds for the Small Business Administration's Disaster Loan Program for fiscal year 1994

Announcement of nomination for U.S. Attorney for the Southern District of Mississippi

Released August 29

Transcript of a press briefing by Press Secretary Dee Dee Myers

Statement by Press Secretary Dee Dee Myers announcing the establishment of Presidential Emergency Board No. 225

Released August 31

Transcript of a press briefing by Press Secretary Dee Dee Myers

Statement by Press Secretary Dee Dee Myers announcing a revised pay schedule for Federal white-collar employees

Statement by Press Secretary Dee Dee Myers on the President's letter to the Chairman and members of Presidential Emergency Board No. 225

Released September 2

Transcript of a press briefing by Foreign Minister Richard Spring of Ireland

Transcript of a press briefing by Labor Secretary Robert Reich and Council of Economic Advisers Chair Laura D'Andrea Tyson on the economy

Statement by Council of Economic Advisers Chair Laura D'Andrea Tyson on the economy

Released September 7

Statement by Deputy Chief of Staff Harold Ickes on the release of health care working group documents

Released September 8

Transcript of a press briefing by Press Secretary Dee Dee Myers

Transcript of a press briefing by Corporation for National and Community Service President Eli Segal on AmeriCorps

Released September 9

Statement by Press Secretary Dee Dee Myers on the Cuba-U.S. agreement on migration

Announcement of nomination for two members of the National Institute for Literacy Advisory Board

Released September 12

Statement by Press Secretary Dee Dee Myers announcing release of $16.2 million in appropriations to address needs arising from Tropical Storm Alberto, the January earthquake in California, mudslides in Kentucky, and Midwest floods of 1993

Transcript of a press briefing by Under Secretary of the Treasury Ron Noble and Special Agent Carl Meyer, U.S. Secret Service, on the aircraft crash at the White House

Released September 13

Transcript of a press briefing by Press Secretary Dee Dee Myers

Statement by Press Secretary Dee Dee Myers announcing that the President will address the Nation on Haiti on September 15

Released September 14

Transcript of a press briefing by Press Secretary Dee Dee Myers

Announcement of nomination for U.S. Marshal for the Central District of California

Announcement of nomination for a member of the Civil Liberties Public Education Fund Board of Directors

Announcement of nomination for two members of the Board of Trustees of the Barry Goldwater Scholarship and Excellence in Education Foundation

Announcement of nomination for two U.S. Tax Court judges

Released September 15

Transcript of a press briefing by Press Secretary Dee Dee Myers

Released September 16

Statement by Press Secretary Dee Dee Myers announcing the White House meeting of representatives of countries participating in the multinational force in Haiti

Transcript of a press briefing by United Nations Ambassador Madeleine K. Albright, Prime Minister Eugenia Charles of Dominica, and Prime Minister Lester Bird of Antigua on Haiti

Transcript of a press briefing by Deputy Assistant to the President for National Security Affairs Sandy Berger and Special Envoy to Haiti William Gray on Haiti

Statement by Press Secretary Dee Dee Myers announcing that the President will make available appropriations of $188 million for the Forest Service for fighting fires in the National Forests

Released September 17

Transcript of a press briefing by Press Secretary Dee Dee Myers

Released September 18

Transcript of a press briefing by Secretary of State Warren Christopher, Secretary of Defense William

Perry, and Chairman of the Joint Chiefs of Staff John M. Shalikashvili on Haiti

Released September 19

Statement by Press Secretary Dee Dee Myers announcing the White House Counsel's memorandum on compliance with the Federal grand jury subpoena requesting documents relating to Harry Thomason or Darnell Martens

Announcement of memorandum to the Secretary of Housing and Urban Development on the Federal Plan To Break the Cycle of Homelessness

Released September 20

Transcript of a press briefing by Joint Chiefs of Staff Chairman John M. Shalikashvili on Haiti

Announcement of the President's letter to congressional leaders on Haiti

Statement by Press Secretary Dee Dee Myers on the President's meeting with Organization of American States Secretary General Cesar Gaviria

Statement by Press Secretary Dee Dee Myers on the Vice President's meeting with John Hume, leader of the Social Democratic and Labor Party of Northern Ireland

Statement by Press Secretary Dee Dee Myers on the meeting of National Security Adviser Anthony Lake, Director of Operations for the Joint Chiefs of Staff Lt. Gen. John Sheehan, USA, Deputy Special Adviser for Haiti Jon Plebani, and Director of National Security Affairs Lawrence Rossin with President Jean-Bertand Aristide of Haiti

Released September 21

Statement by Press Secretary Dee Dee Myers on the meeting of National Security Adviser Anthony Lake and Vice President Albert Gore with a delegation of Ulster Unionist Party leaders from Northern Ireland on September 22

Released September 22

Statement by Press Secretary Dee Dee Myers on the President's meeting with Deputy Prime Minister Yohei Kono of Japan

Statement by Press Secretary Dee Dee Myers on the Comprehensive Test Ban Treaty negotiations

Statement by Press Secretary Dee Dee Myers on the meeting of Vice President Albert Gore and National Security Adviser Anthony Lake with a delegation of Ulster Unionist Party leaders from Northern Ireland

Released September 23

Statement by Press Secretary Dee Dee Myers on the President's meeting with Prime Minister Eddie Fenech Adami of Malta

Transcript of a press briefing by Treasury Secretary Lloyd Bentsen and Under Secretary of the Treasury for Domestic Finance Frank Newman on the Riegle Community Development and Regulatory Improvement Act of 1994

Transcript of a press briefing by Chief of Staff Leon Panetta on restructuring the White House staff

Announcement by Chief of Staff Leon Panetta on restructuring the White House staff

Announcement of nomination for U.S. Marshal for the District of Vermont

Announcement of nomination for U.S. Marshal for the Eastern District of North Carolina

Announcement of nomination for U.S. Marshal for the Northern District of Indiana

Released September 25

Transcript of remarks by Gov. Mario Cuomo of New York at the Bethel A.M.E. Church in New York City

Fact sheet on U.S. assistance to the Bosnian Muslim-Croat Federation

Transcript of a press briefing by U.N. Ambassador Madeleine K. Albright on the President's visit to New York City

Released September 26

Transcript of a press briefing by U.N. Ambassador Madeleine K. Albright on the 49th Session of the U.N. General Assembly

Fact sheet on U.S. policy on a landmine control regime initiative

Statement by Press Secretary Dee Dee Myers on the President's invitation to Crown Prince Hassan of Jordan and Foreign Minister Shimon Peres of Israel to meet with him at the White House on October 3

List of suspended U.S. unilateral sanctions on Haiti and a statement by President Jean-Bertrand Aristide of Haiti

Released September 27

Statement by Press Secretary Dee Dee Myers on the Presidential decision directive establishing a Security Policy Board to assure more cost-effective and efficient U.S. security policies, practices, and procedures

Statement by Press Secretary Dee Dee Myers and fact sheets on Russia-U.S. commercial agreements on trade and investment

Transcript of a press briefing by Secretary of State Warren Christopher on the President's discussions with President Boris Yeltsin of Russia

Transcript of a press briefing by U.S. Trade Representative Mickey Kantor on the General Agreement on Tariffs and Trade

Released September 28

White House statement extending President Clinton's and Russian President Boris Yeltsin's condolences on behalf of the American and Russian people to the families of the victims of the ferry disaster in the Baltic Sea

Joint U.S.-Russian statement in support of the Timan Pechora Project

Agreement between the Government of the United States of America and the Government of the Russian Federation on Cooperation and Mutual Assistance in Customs Matters

Announcement on the U.S.-Russian agreement on mutual customs assistance

Fact sheet on the Partnership for Economic Progress: Joint Statement on Principles and Objectives for the Development of Trade, Economic Cooperation, and Investment

Announcement on the crime assistance package for the Russian Federation

Released September 29

Transcript of a press briefing by Press Secretary Dee Dee Myers

Statement by Press Secretary Dee Dee Myers on the President's meeting with Foreign Minister Richard Spring of Ireland

Released September 30

Transcript of a press briefing by Press Secretary Dee Dee Myers

Released October 3

Joint communique by President William J. Clinton, Crown Prince Hassan of Jordan, and Foreign Minister Shimon Peres of Israel

White House statement on the President's decision to lift the ban on contacts between U.S. officials and Sinn Fein party members in Northern Ireland and text of a letter from National Security Adviser Anthony Lake to Sinn Fein leader Gerry Adams

Statement by Press Secretary Dee Dee Myers on the President's meeting with Vice Premier Qian Qichen of China

Released October 4

Transcript of a press briefing by Press Secretary Dee Dee Myers

White House statement on the August 31 letter to the President from 11-year-old Niya Powell

Released October 5

Statement by Press Secretary Dee Dee Myers on the President's discussions with President Nelson Mandela of South Africa

Fact sheet on U.S.-South African cooperation

Released October 6

Statement by Press Secretary Dee Dee Myers on the President's discussions with Prime Minister Chuan Likphai of Thailand

White House statement on the Southern Africa Development Fund

Released October 7

Statement by Press Secretary Dee Dee Myers on the underground nuclear test conducted by China at the Lop Nur test site

Announcement of legislation signed by the President

Statement by Assistant to the President Robert Rubin on the delay of SEC funding passage

Announcement of nomination for the Board of Directors of the Communications Satellite Corporation

Released October 10

Announcement of legislation signed by the President

Released October 11

Statement by Press Secretary Dee Dee Myers announcing the release of the White House Counsel's report on Agriculture Secretary Mike Espy

Released October 12

Transcript of a press briefing by Press Secretary Dee Dee Myers

Statement by Press Secretary Dee Dee Myers on the President's meeting with Prime Minister Anibal Cavaco Silva of Portugal

Released October 13

Transcript of a press briefing by Press Secretary Dee Dee Myers

Statement by Press Secretary Dee Dee Myers on the President's request that Congress repeal certain provisions of the Treasury, Postal Service and General Government Appropriations Act, 1995, and the Department of Defense Appropriations Act, 1995, concerning staffing levels and use of personnel resources

Statement by Press Secretary Dee Dee Myers on the abduction of Israeli Corporal Nahshon Waxman

Released October 14

Statement by Press Secretary Dee Dee Myers announcing the White House conference on trade and investment prospects for U.S. firms with Central and Eastern Europe

Statement by Press Secretary Dee Dee Myers announcing a series of humanitarian steps relating to Cubans in safe havens in Guantanamo and Panama

Statement by Press Secretary Dee Dee Myers announcing the report and recommendations of Presidential Emergency Board No. 225

Transcript of a press briefing by Special Adviser to the President William Gray III and Deputy National Security Adviser Sandy Berger on Haiti

Transcript of a press briefing on the baseball strike by Labor Secretary Robert Reich, mediator William Usery, baseball players representative Donald Fehr, and commissioner of baseball Bud Selig

Fact sheet on lifting of Haiti sanctions

Announcement and list of the Presidential delegation to Haiti

Released October 15

Statement by Press Secretary Dee Dee Myers on the President's telephone conversation with Prime Minister Rabin of Israel on the death of Nahshon Waxman

Released October 17

Statement by Press Secretary Dee Dee Myers on the President's telephone conversation with King Hussein of Jordan and Prime Minister Rabin of Israel on the Israel-Jordan peace treaty

Statement by Press Secretary Dee Dee Myers on the President's telephone conversation with Chancellor Kohl of Germany offering congratulations on the German election

Statement by Press Secretary Dee Dee Myers on the President's acceptance of the invitation to participate in the signing ceremony for the Israel-Jordan peace treaty

Announcement of legislation signed by the President

White House statement announcing the signing of the proclamation to establish tariff-rate quotas on certain wheat

Released October 18

Transcript of a press briefing by Press Secretary Dee Dee Myers

Transcript of a press briefing by Ambassador Robert Gallucci on the nuclear agreement with North Korea

Announcement of legislation signed by the President

Statement by Press Secretary Dee Dee Myers on the President's Report on Immigration

Released October 19

Statement by Press Secretary Dee Dee Myers announcing that Counsel to the President Abner Mikva received a subpoena from the Independent Counsel investigating Secretary of Agriculture Mike Espy

Announcement of legislation signed by the President

Released October 21

Transcript of a press briefing by Deputy Secretary of Education Madeleine Kunin and Deputy Assistant to the President for Economic Policy Gene Sperling on the individual education account program

Announcement of legislation signed by the President

Released October 22

Statement by Chief of Staff Leon Panetta on the President's opposition to Social Security and Medicare cuts

Transcript of remarks by Senator Dianne Feinstein at Carlmont High School, Belmont, CA

Released October 24

Transcript of a press briefing by Anne Edwards on trip logistics for the Middle East

Statement by Press Secretary Dee Dee Myers announcing legislation signed by the President

Released October 25

Announcement of legislation signed by the President

Released October 26

Transcript of an exchange with reporters by Palestine Liberation Organization Chairman Yasser Arafat in Cairo, Egypt

Released October 27

Transcript of an interview with Chief of Staff Leon Panetta

Transcript of a press briefing by Secretary of State Warren Christopher on the President's meeting with President Hafiz al-Asad of Syria

Transcript of a press briefing by Treasury Secretary Lloyd Bentsen and former Social Security Commissioner Robert Ball on the economy

Released October 28

Statement by Press Secretary Dee Dee Myers on the President's signing of the Executive order changing the definition of "Field Duty" to ensure parity among deployed troops

Transcript of a press briefing by the Vice President on the economy

Transcript of a press briefing by CENTCOM Commander Gen. Binford J.H. Peay III, USA, and National Security Adviser Anthony Lake on U.S. military operations in Kuwait

Released October 29

Transcript of a press briefing by Chief of Staff Leon Panetta and U.S. Secret Service Assistant Director for Protective Operations Richard Griffin on the shots fired at the White House

Released October 30

Transcript of a press briefing by Press Secretary Dee Dee Myers, Under Secretary of the Treasury for Law Enforcement Ron Noble, and U.S. Secret Service Assistant Director for Protective Operations Richard Griffin on the shots fired at the White House

Released October 31

Transcript of a press briefing by Treasury Secretary Lloyd Bentsen on the review of White House security

Released November 1

Statement by Press Secretary Dee Dee Myers announcing legislation signed by the President

White House statement on supporting peace in Northern Ireland

Statement by Press Secretary Dee Dee Myers announcing that National Security Adviser Anthony Lake will visit Haiti, November 2–3

Released November 3

Transcript of a press briefing by Labor Secretary Robert Reich and Assistant to the President for Economic Policy Robert E. Rubin on employment statistics

Fact sheet on Haiti

Released November 8

Statement by Press Secretary Dee Dee Myers announcing David Gergen's letter of resignation and the President's letter of acceptance

Transcript of a press briefing by Brig. Gen. Harold W. Nelson on the President's visit to the Far East

Released November 10

Statement by Press Secretary Dee Dee Myers on the Executive order on declassification of selected records within the National Archives of the United States

Transcript of a press briefing by National AIDS Policy Director Patsy Fleming

Released November 11

Transcript of a press briefing by Secretary of State Warren Christopher and Chinese Foreign Minister Qian Qichen on their discussions at the APEC ministerial meeting

Transcript of press briefing by Deputy Secretary of State for Public Affairs Michael McCurry, Assistant Secretary of State for East Asian and Pacific Affairs Winston Lord, and U.S. Ambassador to the People's Republic of China J. Stapleton Roy on Secretary of State Christopher's activities at the APEC ministerial meeting

Released November 13

Transcript of remarks by the First Lady at a breakfast with Philippine NGO representatives in Manila

Released November 16

Background material on U.S.-Indonesian commercial transactions

Released November 17

Statement by Press Secretary Dee Dee Myers on Ukraine's vote to accede to the Nuclear Non-Proliferation Treaty

Released November 19

Transcript of a radio address by the Vice President

Released November 21

Statement by Press Secretary Dee Dee Myers on National Security Adviser Anthony Lake's meeting with Jennifer Harbury on the disappearance of her Guatemalan husband, Efrain Bamaca

Released November 22

Statement by Press Secretary Dee Dee Myers on elections in Mozambique

A Charter for American-Ukrainian Partnership, Friendship, and Cooperation

Joint statement by the United States and Ukraine on expansion of trade and investment

Joint statement by the United States and Ukraine on encouraging academic and professional exchanges and contacts

Joint statement by the United States and Ukraine on cooperation in promoting the rule of law and combating crime

Statement by Press Secretary Dee Dee Myers on U.S.-Ukraine defense and military relations

Statement by Press Secretary Dee Dee Myers on U.S.-Ukraine trade and investment

Statement by Press Secretary Dee Dee Myers on the action plan for Chernobyl shutdown and energy sector reform

Summary of the U.S.-Ukraine bilateral charter

Summary of discussion of the energy sector

Fact sheet on the Western NIS Enterprise Fund

Fact sheet on the bilateral civil space agreement

Fact sheet on U.S. bilateral assistance to Ukraine

Fact sheet on Nunn-Lugar assistance to Ukraine

Announcement of nomination for a U.S. Marshal for the District of Maryland

Released November 23

Statement by Press Secretary Dee Dee Myers on the President's meeting with President-elect Ernesto Zedillo of Mexico

Joint statement by the United States and Kazakhstan on the transfer of uranium

Statement by Press Secretary Dee Dee Myers on the Kazakhstan-U.S. announcement of transfer of vulnerable nuclear materials to safe storage

Fact sheet on transfer of nuclear materials from Kazakhstan

Released November 29

Transcript of a press briefing by Press Secretary Dee Dee Myers

Text of a letter to the President dated November 23 from former Presidents Gerald R. Ford, Jimmy Carter, and George Bush supporting the General Agreement on Tariffs and Trade

Released November 30

Transcript of a press briefing by Press Secretary Dee Dee Myers

Statement by Press Secretary Dee Dee Myers on National Security Adviser Anthony Lake's invitation to Sinn Fein leader Gerry Adams for a meeting on December 5

Released December 1

Statement by Press Secretary Dee Dee Myers on the appointment of Senator George Mitchell as Special Adviser for Economic Initiatives in Ireland

Transcript of a press briefing by Deputy Secretary of Defense John Deutch on the defense readiness initiative

Fact sheet on defense spending and military readiness

Released December 2

Transcript of a press briefing by Assistant to the President for Economic Policy Robert E. Rubin and Council of Economic Advisers Chair Laura D'Andrea Tyson on the economy

Statement by Press Secretary Dee Dee Myers on the President's support of Carlos Salinas' candidacy to lead the new World Trade Organization

Released December 4

Transcript of an exchange with reporters by Secretary of State Warren Christopher and Hungarian Foreign Minister Laszlo Kovacs in Budapest, Hungary

Released December 5

Transcript of an interview of Chief of Staff Leon Panetta by network and radio pool reporters

Released December 6

Statement by Press Secretary Dee Dee Myers on National Security Adviser Anthony Lake's meeting with Sinn Fein leader Gerry Adams

Released December 7

Transcript of a press briefing by Press Secretary Dee Dee Myers

Transcript of a press briefing on the Summit of the Americas by Deputy National Security Adviser Sandy Berger, Treasury Secretary Lloyd Bentsen, Commerce Secretary Ron Brown, U.S. Trade Representative Mickey Kantor, and Under Secretary of State for Economic Affairs Joan Spero

Released December 8

Transcript of a press briefing by the Vice President on the Summit of the Americas

Released December 9

Transcript of a press briefing on the Summit of the Americas by Summit of the Americas Coordinator Thomas F. (Mack) McLarty, Deputy National Security Adviser Sandy Berger, U.S. Trade Representative Mickey Kantor, Secretary of Labor Robert Reich, Secretary of Commerce Ron Brown, and Under Secretary of State for Economic Affairs Joan Spero

Transcript of a press briefing by Chief of Staff Leon Panetta on the resignation of Surgeon General Joycelyn Elders

Released December 10

Transcript of a press briefing by Secretary of State Warren Christopher in Miami, FL, on the Summit of the Americas

Transcript of remarks by Secretary of State Warren Christopher and Foreign Minister Jose Gurria of Mexico in Miami, FL

Transcript of remarks by Secretary of State Warren Christopher and Foreign Minister Guido Di Tella of Argentina in Miami, FL

Transcript of a press briefing by U.S. Trade Representative Mickey Kantor in Miami, FL on the plan of action and declaration for creating a free trade area

Transcript of a press briefing by Environmental Protection Agency Administrator Carol Browner and Director of the White House Office of Environmental Policy Kathleen McGinty in Miami, FL, on sustainable development and a partnership for pollution prevention

Summary of the Summit of the Americas trade initiative

Released December 11

Joint statement by the leaders of Canada, Chile, Mexico, and the United States on preparations for Chile's accession to NAFTA

Released December 12

Transcript of a press briefing by Press Secretary Dee Dee Myers

Statement by Press Secretary Dee Dee Myers on the upcoming visit of President Zhelyu Zhelev of Bulgaria

Statement by Press Secretary Dee Dee Myers announcing the President will address the Nation on December 15

Statement by Press Secretary Dee Dee Myers announcing that National Security Adviser Anthony Lake will lead a delegation of senior administration officials and Africa experts that will travel to eight African countries, December 12–22

Released December 14

Statement by Press Secretary Dee Dee Myers on contacts between former President Jimmy Carter and Bosnian Serb leader Radovan Karadzic

Statement by Press Secretary Dee Dee Myers announcing a letter from Sally Katzen, Administrator of OMB's Office of Information and Regulatory Affairs, to Representative Newt Gingrich

Statement by Press Secretary Dee Dee Myers announcing the initiative to revitalize the Haitian economy

Released December 15

Transcript of a press briefing by Press Secretary Dee Dee Myers

Released December 16

Transcript of a press briefing on the middle class bill of rights by Labor Secretary Bob Reich, Treasury Secretary Lloyd Bentsen, Education Secretary Richard Riley, and Chief of Staff Leon Panetta

Released December 17

Statement by Press Secretary Dee Dee Myers announcing the Defense Department statement on the helicopter downed in North Korea

Released December 20

Statement by Press Secretary Dee Dee Myers on the presentation of medals for service in Operation Uphold Democracy

Released December 21

Transcript of a press briefing by Assistant Secretary of Housing and Urban Development Andrew Cuomo and Deputy Secretary of Agriculture Bob Nash on empowerment zones and enterprise communities

Released December 22

Transcript of a press briefing by Press Secretary Dee Dee Myers

Released December 23

Statement by Press Secretary Dee Dee Myers on Libya

Released December 27

Announcement of nomination for a U.S. Marshal for the Southern District of New York

Released December 28

Announcement of nomination for a U.S. Attorney for the Southern District of Alabama

Released December 29

Announcement on grants to aid the homeless

Appendix D—Presidential Documents Published in the Federal Register

This appendix lists Presidential documents released by the Office of the Press Secretary and published in the Federal Register. The texts of the documents are printed in the Federal Register (F.R.) at the citations listed below. The documents are also printed in title 3 of the Code of Federal Regulations and in the Weekly Compilation of Presidential Documents.

PROCLAMATIONS

PROCLAMATIONS—Continued

EXECUTIVE ORDERS

EXECUTIVE ORDERS—Continued

OTHER PRESIDENTIAL DOCUMENTS

Subject Index

ABC Radio—2042

Abortion. *See* Health and medical care

Acquired immune deficiency syndrome (AIDS). *See* Health and medical care

Administrative Conference of the U.S.—2215, 2221

Advisory. *See* other part of subject

Aeronautics and Space Administration, National—1654, 2121

Africa Prize for Leadership for the Sustainable End of Hunger—1706

African-Americans
See also specific subject; Civil rights
World War II veterans—1564

Agency. *See* other part of subject

Agricultural Mortgage Corporation, Federal—2220

Agriculture
Apple exports—1494
Crop insurance system—1741
Disaster assistance—1673, 1973, 2219
Ethanol production—1961, 1972
Farming, legislation—1961
Grain storage—1973
International government subsidies—1961
Livestock exports to former Soviet Union—1959

Agriculture, Department of
Budget—1673
Commodity Credit Corporation—1673
Food and Nutrition Service—1673
Food Stamp Program—1673
Forest Service—1674
Loans, extension—1973
Reorganization—1738, 1741, 2151
Secretary—1681, 1700, 1723, 1738, 1741, 1959, 2006, 2151, 2195, 2204
Special Supplemental Food Program for Women, Infants and Children (WIC)—1673

AID. *See* Development Cooperation Agency, U.S. International

AIDS. *See* Health and medical care

AIDS Policy, Office of National—1414, 2060

Air Force, Department of the
See also Armed Forces, U.S.
Chief of Staff—2213

Airline industry. *See* Aviation industry

Airline Industry, National Commission to Ensure a Strong Competitive—1474, 1493

Alabama, flooding—1673

Alaska
President's visit—2065, 2068, 2069
Storms and flooding—2214

All-American Cities Award—1520

Ambassadors. *See* specific country; State, Department of

American. *See* other part of subject

America's Heritage Abroad, Commission for the Preservation of—2221

AmeriCorps—1492, 1532, 1535, 1536, 1813, 1833, 1835, 1920, 2206, 2216

Angola
Economic sanctions—1583
National Union for the Total Independence of Angola (UNITA)—1474, 1583
U.S. national emergency—1474, 1583

APEC. *See* Asia-Pacific Economic Cooperation forum

Appeals, U.S. Court of—1505, 1555, 1580

Architectural and Transportation Barriers Compliance Board—2215, 2217

Arctic region, environmental protection—1654

Argentina, President—1630, 2178-2180

Arkansas, airbase investigation—1719

Arkansas River Compact Commission—2217

Armed Forces, U.S.
See also specific military department; Defense and national security; Defense, Department of
Civilian reemployment rights—1746
Commander in chief, Atlantic Command—1538, 1594, 2216
Commander in chief, European Command—1406
Deployment in Haiti, participants—1594, 2190
Environmental cleanup at military bases—2077
Expeditionary Medal—2191
International role. *See* specific country or region
Military installations in foreign countries, cost-sharing arrangements—1705
National Guard—1746
Pay—2130
POW's/MIA's—1636
Reserves—1557, 1558, 1746
Supreme Allied Commander, Atlantic—1538, 1562

Armenia
Economic assistance—1454
Nagorno-Karabakh region—1453, 1648, 2145
President—1453

Arms and munitions
See also Defense and national security; Nuclear weapons
Arms control negotiations and agreements—1629, 1660, 2084
Chemical and biological weapons—1437, 1660, 1666, 1887, 2084
Export controls—1484, 2084
Land mines—1629
Missile systems and technology—1660
Nonproliferation—1485, 1666, 2084

Arms Control and Disarmament Agency, U.S.—2212

Army, Department of
See also Armed Forces, U.S.
Corps of Engineers—1506

Name Index

Document Categories List